FOR REFERENCE

The Papacy
An Encyclopedia

Published with the assistance of the Centre national du livre in France
and the Goodbooks Foundation

The Papacy
An Encyclopedia

VOLUME 1

Abbreviator–Furnishings

Philippe Levillain, *Université de Paris X*
GENERAL EDITOR

Routledge

New York   London

Published in 2002 by
Routledge
29 West 35th Street
New York, NY 10001

Published in Great Britain by
Routledge
11 New Fetter Lane
London EC4P 4EE

Editorial Staff:
Kevin Ohe, *Senior Editor*
Laura Kathleen Smid, *Project Editor*
Daniel Yacavone, *Senior Editorial Assistant*
Tenessa Gemelke, *Editorial Assistant*
Cynthia Crippen, *Indexer*
Richard Steins, *Development Manager*
Sylvia K. Miller, *Publishing Director, Reference*

Originally published as *Dictionnaire historique de la papauté*,
© Librairie Arthème Fayard, 1994

10   9   8   7   6   5   4   3   2   1

Library of Congress Cataloging-in-Publication Data

Dictionnaire historique de la papauté. English
     The papacy: an encyclopedia / Philippe Levillain, general editor; John W. O'Malley, English language edition editor.
      p. cm.
     Includes bibliographical references and index.
     ISBN 0-415-92228-3 (set)
     ISBN 0-415-92229-1 (volume 1)
     ISBN 0-415-92230-5 (volume 2)
     ISBN 0-415-93752-3 (volume 3)
     1. Papacy—Dictionaries. I. Levillain, Philippe, 1940– II. O'Malley, John W. III Title.

BX955.2 .D53 2002
282'.092'2—dc21
[B]

2001041859

Printed on acid-free, 250-year-life paper
Manufactured in the United States of America

Contents

Entries A to Z

ENTRIES

ENTRIES

ENTRIES

Preface and Acknowledgments

The Papacy: An Encyclopedia is a translation of the French *Dictionnaire historique de la papauté,* published in 1994 by Librairie Arthème Fayard. This A to Z encyclopedia covers all of the popes (and antipopes), as well as topics related to the papacy such as encyclicals, religious orders, and the arts. A comprehensive index, end-references, and internal cross-references (in small capital letters) will aid the reader in navigating this three-volume reference work. Bibliographies are provided with almost all entries, maps are included in the entries "Papal States" and "Vatican City State," and appendices are provided in volume three that list all the popes chronologically, all the martyred popes, and all the popes who are saints. *The Papacy* is intended for use in academic libraries, seminaries, religious institutes, and public libraries, and we trust that it will prove a valuable source for scholars, students, religious leaders, and interested general readers.

The majority of the text in *The Papacy* is direct translation of the French edition; however, some changes, additions, and updates were necessary in order to make this edition appropriate for an English-speaking audience and to account for developments that have occurred in the seven years between publication of the two editions. We have tried to include the most current information available, particularly in articles dealing with Pope John Paul II and his travels, communications, and beatifications. The bibliographies from the French edition have been augmented to include significant recent and English-language sources (many thanks to Elizabeth Russell). In addition, a few articles—the article on Americanism, for example—were commissioned specifically for this edition.

Although each article appears with the signature of its original contributor, it should be noted that most of these contributors wrote in French and were not involved in the translation of their work into English. The translation of the *Dictionnaire historique de la papauté* was a challenge in that it required not simply a literal translation, but, at times, a translation of complex concepts and technical terms into their English equivalents. For this reason, a qualified team of translators and scholars was called upon. Translations were done by professional translators, supervised by Routledge; each translated article was reviewed by at least one, in many cases two, subject-matter experts in ecclesiology, church history, or canon law.

Making this important work of scholarship available to the English-speaking world for the first time has been an honor for the Routledge Reference editorial team. We extend our sincere gratitude to all those who assisted in the translation, review, copyediting, proofreading, and indexing of these volumes—a labor of almost four years' duration. Translators, reviewers, and other advisors are credited in a list facing the title page. In particular, we are extremely grateful to John W. O'Malley, S.J., whose expertise in the topic of this encyclopedia was indispensable in preparing this edition, and who gave freely and cheerfully of his time and effort from the start of the translation through the arrival of the last page proof. We also wish to thank the French Ministry of Culture for its generous assistance in the publication of this translation.

Introduction to the French Edition

The idea of compiling a historical dictionary of the papacy and not simply a biographical dictionary of the popes stemmed from the close observation of "little facts," Stendhal's cherished *petits faits*. May those we are providing as examples guide the reader in the use of a collective work that is meant to be both scholarly and accessible.

In 1978, the papacy was at the center of three events that drew the attention of the public at large: the death (6 August) and funeral (12 August) of Paul VI; the election (26 August) and funeral (28 September) of John Paul I; and the election (16 October) of John Paul II. In less than two and a half months, the Church had three popes. At the time of Paul VI's death, the papacy was undergoing a crisis within the Church, reputedly caused by the Vatican II Council (1962–5). Some believed that the Council had been conducted too hastily; others believed that the papacy should never have convened a council in the first place. The debate not only concerned Catholics and the Church hierarchy, but also caused anxiety among various countries affected by the two-thousand-year-old institution—an institution singularly visible, especially in Europe, no matter how much ground it might have lost since the middle of the 19th century—that seemed capable of offering to the world a message for the future in the *aggiornamento* proposed by John XXIII (1958–63). Thus, the first little fact we noticed: the idea that these successive elections might be shaking the papacy did not cross the minds of commentators. On 16 October 1978, St. Peter's Square in Rome was filled with a crowd on the lookout for a signal—white for a positive vote, black for the opposite—that was to rise from the unsightly chimney located on the roof of the Sistine Chapel. The world's television cameras were aimed at the Loggia delle Benedizioni where the name of John Paul I's successor was to be announced, along with the papal name he had selected. The façade and dome of St. Peter's were flooded with artificial light from the projectors. It felt that night as if the most symbolic monument in the history of the papacy had just been rediscovered on the bottom of the ocean floor by dazzled and breathless divers. The suspense of this feverish expectation about the new pope went beyond that produced by any monarchy, past or present.

The pope is a monarch elected by a restricted college, and he reigns for life. This adherence to the system for electing a sovereign pontiff was given more visibility in 1978 than in previous decades due to the media-generated curiosity about an institution with such a unique mode of functioning. The papacy had gone through periods during which the conclaves became interminable. Antagonisms had bred antipopes, and states had intervened in the designation of a pope through their veto power. On 16 October 1978, these historical moments seemed very remote. The media did not even discuss them during those troubled months. It was clear that the shaken Church would have a new pope.

From St. Peter to John Paul I, how many popes had occupied the papal throne? Scholarly works, which do not agree with the list provided by the *Annuario pontificio*, hesitate over the exact number: 260? 264? 269? Who was the person about to proclaim the name and patronymic of the elected pope and under what authority? This person was rumored to be Cardinal Felici, famed as the exacting and skillful secretary of the Vatican II Council. But what was not mentioned was the fact that this function was explicitly the responsibility of the first of the cardinal deacons, who was indeed Cardinal Felici. In addition, no one had pointed out that it was a matter of custom to elevate the secretary of a council to cardinal, and that Paul VI had done just that as of the first consistory convened after Vatican

II (27 June 1967). Seeing and knowing are two different things. The same goes for using terms appropriate to a given institution. At the beginning of the conclaves in 1978, it was often said that they had opened (much like a session of a civil assembly), since they were just beginning to meet. In fact, the conclaves of 1978 were held locked (conclave = *cum clave*) by the prefect of the pontifical house (a title dating from 1967) in the presence of the marshal of the conclave, a responsibility assumed by a member of the Roman nobility.

Another little fact was also observed during the same period: many cardinals called to Rome during that hot summer complained about the inhumane conditions they had to endure. They suffered from the total isolation, imposed by an archaic method of preserving the secrecy of the proceedings, and from Spartan living conditions. Some favored conducting the papal election of 1978 in a way that would not require the Sacred College to be sequestered. Secrecy, they maintained, would be guaranteed through collective discipline. In October 1978, in more pleasant weather, the same cardinals found themselves very glad to have kept to a medieval rule that had allowed them to choose the cardinal-bishop of Cracow, the representative of a silenced Church, severely persecuted in the past but now under the control of a communist state with a more realistic attitude toward the Church. Had the conclave not been conducted according to traditional rules established in the Middle Ages, could it not have been said that Cardinal Wojtyla (to whom the conclave was becoming more and more favorable) or someone close to him had made contact with the *attaché* of the secretary general of the Polish communist party, Edward Gierek, to inform him of his chances? How was he able to negotiate the conditions for the election of St. Peter's successor to be both glorious for Poland and embarrassing for a State controlled by the Red Army? Even if he had not done so, what suspicions might not have weighed on this pontificate, which was soon to be confronted with a militant form of Catholicism taking advantage of the designation of a Slavic pope representing spiritual authority on an international scale?

Here is another fact. This one is not about losing the significance behind appearances or questioning ancient rules in the name of present realities. In 1978, it was repeatedly stated that John Paul II was the first non-Italian pope since Adrian VI (of Utrecht, 1522–3) and that his election had interrupted a long sequence begun by Clement VII (1523–34). However, this observation relies on viewing the papacy in terms of the unification of Italy, which led the kingdom of Piedmont-Sardinia to overtake Rome on 20 September 1870. From Clement VII to John Paul I, the papacy was Italic, not Italian. In other words, episcopals or archiepiscopal heads governing local churches on the Italic peninsula held the papacy. The contemporary notion of "nationality" is not applicable to the history of the papacy. Of course, it is true that the geographical area of the Italic peninsula provided 203 popes, or 69% of St. Peter's successors. Nonetheless, there were also ten popes from the ancient Greek world and eight from the Near East. The *Annuario pontificio,* which establishes the official list of sovereign pontiffs since St. Peter, designates Telesphorus (125–36) and Hyginus (134–40) as Greeks, Anicetus (155–66) as a Syrian, Victor I (189–99) and St. Gelasius I (492–96) as Africans, and Dionysius (259–68) as "of unknown origin." In the early days of the Church, it was the clergy and the Roman people who elected the Bishop of Rome, whose primacy as the vicar of Christ, established on St. Peter's seat, was long debated. A little known tradition from these times has survived to this day. Cardinals are still titulars of one of the churches in Rome (or in the suburbs or the Roman countryside). In other words, they are "pastors" of a diocesan parish where they occasionally perform liturgical functions and are much appreciated by the faithful.

Their crests are displayed on the façades of these local churches, and many of them are buried there. The archbishop of Cracow in 1978 was the titular of the Church of St. Cesareo on the Palatine. There was a time, however—between the 14th and 19th centuries—when the title of cardinal was bestowed even upon persons who were not ordained, a concession to the administrative needs of the Roman Curia. It was also the case with Cardinal Antonelli, Secretary of State for Pius IX (1846–78). Yet practice shifted toward a return to tradition, and John XXIII established the rule that all cardinals had to be bishops. The cardinals who elect the pope are all titulars of a church from the diocese of Rome or a suburban Roman diocese. Nevertheless, nothing obliges them to designate one of their own as the successor to St. Peter. They could even choose a layman, on condition that once designated he be immediately ordained a priest and invested as a bishop, that is, as bishop of Rome, and therefore a sovereign pontiff. A great secular theologian could very well be called one day to the seat of Rome. For this to happen, however, some kind of alchemy would have to take place between the needs of the Church and the way they are perceived by the Sacred College. The rule followed since the end of the 13th century, according to which the pope is a cardinal, is therefore merely a tradition. That of the strict independence of the conclave, much commented on in 1978, comes, on the other hand, from a new freedom recently acquired by the papacy. Up until the election of Pius X, many great powers had secular representatives at the conclave and could exercise their (exclusive) right to veto the conclave's choice. The Austro-Hungarian Empire used this veto in 1903 to prevent the designation of Cardinal Rampolla, Leo XIII's secretary of state, supported by Republican France, and favored instead the election of the patriarch of Venice, Cardinal Sarto.

The institution of the papacy has grown like a tree in the midst of the world; that is, its lower branches have been pruned and foliage has sprouted around the trunk of its vocation implanted in Roman soil. It has extended its authority gradually, first by modeling itself on the administrative structures of the Roman Empire within which the bishops, as successors to the apostles, founded local churches. The maps distributed by Mussolini on the present via dei Fori Imperiali provide a symbolic reading of this battle between ancient and Christian Rome, between the Roman Empire and the Catholic Church. Read while walking toward the Coliseum, they describe the gradual extension of the Rome of Romulus to the Empire of Constantine in the 4th century. Read in the opposite direction, they show the progressive retreat of the Western Roman Empire, toward Rome under pressure by the Barbarians. Byzantium became the axis of an eastern Christendom with a hegemonic vocation. As the bedrock of Christendom's resistance in the West, Rome experienced, throughout history, various tribulations, its status as capital of Christendom lowered to that of diocese of a disputed territory. Rome was threatened many times: in 452, by Attila's hordes, in 1527 by the mercenaries of the constable of Bourbon, an ally of Charles V; in 1870, it was overtaken by the Piedmontese army. Its primacy was contested in 1054 by Byzantium and in 1534 by Henry VIII of England, thereby diffracting its principle of universality, establishing an Eastern Church against the Latin Church, a Church in which the monarch established himself as supreme head against the papacy.

The reason for these confrontations is always the same: the move from the *"pusillus grex"* (small flock) constituted by the successors of the apostles, responsible for spreading the good news (Gospel) throughout the Mediterranean, to the thousands of bishops today forming the teaching Church under pontifical authority. The papacy has constantly been driven to exclude rather than to negotiate. It has based its development on Peter's vocation as Vicar of Christ rather than on interpretations of Christianity outside of its teaching.

After Attila's siege against Rome, Leo the Great (440–61) established the juridical bases of a Roman government for the Catholic Church. While the Roman Empire was falling into the hands of authoritarian Christian dynasties in the East, the successors of Leo the Great, aware of Rome's fragility in the West, allied themselves with the new masters of Western and Central Europe. Stephen II (752–57) consecrated King Pepin. Leo III (795–816) crowned Charlemagne emperor on Christmas Day in the year 800. The Carolingian Empire granted the papacy a territory, which it committed itself to protecting. The pontifical states were thus established and continued to grow, transforming the pope into a temporal, elected monarch to whose designation no power could remain indifferent, even after the integration of Rome into Italy in 1870.

The tight interconnection between the temporal nature of the papacy and its spiritual mission led to its inclusion in the society of nation-states and armed it with a weapon much feared by these same nation-states, namely the double affiliation of the princes' subjects as both nationals and Christians. To a certain extent, the same problem occurred in the 20th century, with regard to Communist party militants who had to offer allegiance to Moscow until 1989. The comparison is not gratuitous. Just as at the beginning clerics from throughout the world occupied the seat of Rome, thereby making it into an "international" institution, it also had nations assume responsibility for the hopes of men and women in a way that went far beyond the interests of temporal kingdoms. The Church presented itself as the image of the kingdom promised by Christ, who in the edifying life he had lived in Palestine, a Roman province, had conferred upon Jerusalem a heavenly destiny that Rome had the task of fulfilling. The Church therefore spread its language throughout civil societies. Its governmental administration, practices, and commandments established it as a competitive and imperious society. Peter's successors, such as Gregory VII (1073–85), fought to liberate the Church from the control that princes meant to exert over it, and affirm a supremacy over souls and individuals, clerics or otherwise, based solely on its nature as a spiritual institution. The popes created laws (Gregory VII's *Dictatus papae*, compiled in the middle of the 12th century) and a faithful administration. They brought religious orders under their own jurisdiction, thus making them exempt, or not subject to the authority of local bishops, which proved to be of benefit to both the Church and the orders (especially to the Dominicans and the Jesuits). Popes also influenced the spirit of the Crusades and imposed the force of the priesthood against the pretensions of empires and monarchies (against Germanic Holy Roman Empire under Gregory VII, for example, or against Philip the Fair at the beginning of the 14th century).

This temporal power was buttressed by an extraordinary conviction that nothing could shake. It would resist persecutions, exile, or internal struggles for the occupation of St. Peter's throne. In the 14th century (Avignon), it nevertheless had to confront the discrepancy between its opulent appearance and the spirit it claimed to embody. A centralized institution, living off oppressive fiscal measures with spectacular displays of luxury, the papacy was criticized both for its unevangelical worldliness and an excessively strict theology served by an administration that ruled over bodies and souls through excommunication and the Inquisition. The confrontation between tradition and the expansion of humanism at the end of the 15th century was terrible indeed. From Erasmus to Henry VIII, including Luther and Calvin, a shock wave ran through Christian Europe, the equivalent at the time of the upheaval in Eastern Europe at the end of the 1980s. Thanks to its very situation as an elective monarchy and, despite appearances, its reputation for incarnating Peter's mission of service, the papacy countered the spirit of the reformation with triumphant tenacity. Paul III (1534–49), born into a noble family from Latium (the Farnese), was the embodiment of all the sins of a Roman Curia where careers were made through nepotism and intrigue. Made Cardinal at the age of seventeen, father of children born out of wedlock, Paul III was the pope who had to call a council (the Council of Trent) to respond to the demands for reform. Once again, the papacy used a delicate weapon in a new situation: a meeting of all the bishops, all of them from the apostolic college. This collegiality had many times placed the papacy in a difficult position. During the 12th and 13th centuries, and above all, the 15th century, the council tended to define itself as a decision-making organization, reducing the pontifical function to a role similar to that of a secretary-general of the United Nations. However, the Council of Trent, watched over by European monarchies, controlled by papal legates, influenced by the Jesuits, defenders of Roman authority, clearly decided once again in favor of St. Peter's Rome and against another Rome dreamt of by Luther. On 7 October 1571, in the Gulf of Lepanto, Christianity triumphed over the Ottoman Turks in a naval battle of 170,000 forces, half of them galley slaves, some of whom were commanded by Marcantonio Colonna, captain of the papal galleys.

Once the Reformation had been dealt with, the papacy had to face other confrontations. The world order which it had to face from now on was no longer the same. The papacy had to deal with the debate over its perpetuation in a world where its very existence constituted a challenge no longer taken up by war but by diplomacy. From the 17th to the end of the 18th century, the papacy was treated as a power whose illustrious past impressed monarchs. Moreover, it was able to make numerous concessions because it had the ingenuity to establish itself in Rome as a modern power.

It took the audacity of Nicholas V (1447–55) to envision substituting the basilica built during the era of the emperor Constantine on the presumed site of St. Peter's tomb with another building *più moderno*. Nicholas' project of replacing a sacred monument of Christianity worn away by time meant that Rome was adapting to a new frame of reference, different from that provided by the great civilization originally nourished by a she-wolf, in which citizens' rights for Christians were established by the Edict of Milan in 313. At a time when the Church exerted such authority, a new space was needed in Rome (the *Urbs*) to channel the crowds enthralled by the ceremonies for the jubilee (instituted by Boniface VIII in 1300) and the pilgrimages to the tombs of Peter and Paul. This radical project remained dormant for fifty years, until Julius II (1502–13), taken with the splendor of this apostolic manifesto at the very moment it was beginning to be contested, entrusted Bramante and Sangallo with reconstructing the basilica *di nuovo*. They were to build over the 4th century edifice according to contemporary architectural and artistic canons. It took more than one hundred years to do so. The enterprise progressed—fourteen popes from Paul III to Paul V (1605–21) encouraged it—while the papacy was building up the Counter-Reformation through the Council of Trent and taking part in the Battle of Lepanto. The construction of St. Peter's Basilica in Rome proclaimed the realism of the theology of the Church. The enduring strength of the papacy was more than ever anchored around the dome rising above a territory with monopolistic ambitions, a basilica in the apostolic tradition and the center of Catholicism. St. Peter's Basilica in Rome had an emotional function expressed through the Baroque, the art of rising curves, and also served as a break with a past no longer comprehensible. The age of the masses came to reinforce the cult of the martyrs.

It was in the 16th century that the break between the tradition of the Church and the manifestation of its temporal existence occurred. From now on the centralization of the papacy would be ensured by the mysterious operations of a bureaucracy comparable to other state bureaucracies but having the advantage of centuries of experience. Longevity was turning into an incredible immortality. It was this improbable longevity that the French Revolution and the First Empire attacked in the name of a civil order that could no longer tolerate this Messianic one.

The building and embellishment of St. Peter's Basilica over time had as its main function the reconstruction of a past no longer accessible to most pilgrims and contested by the Reformation's advocates. The Basilica defined a post-Tridentine Catholicism that allied discipline with the marvelous. The complexity of the place mirrored the complexity of an institution in full control of the clockwork of its initial vocation—striking the hours of salvation. The presumed seat of St. Peter was set in a monument that represents apostles and doctors of the faith as marble giants. Over the seat, the Holy Spirit opens its dove's wings in a stained-glass window flooded with the unique light of the Roman skies. Facing the seat of St. Peter, at the intersection of the nave and the transept, the papal altar, set off by Bernini's baldachin, was erected right above St. Peter's tomb. St. Peter's keys were placed at the entrance wall of the nave. They echo St. Peter's vocation as it is inscribed, in a bas-relief from the original Constantinian basilica, under the Loggia delle Benedizioni from which the sovereign pontiff appears to the crowds assembled on the square designed by Bernini. From the 13th century, St. Peter's Basilica was to Rome what the Centre Pompidou is today to Paris: a promotion of a certain aesthetic; a heightening of the power through which the mysteries of creation were to be apprehended. Finally, St. Peter's originated with the urban renewal of Rome, that was begun by Sixtus IV (1471–84), and meant to connect the Vatican with the city's centers of economic activity on the opposite bank of the Tiber (a project similar in intent to the development of the Champ de Mars in Paris).

The 17th and 18th centuries were the calmest in the history of the papacy. It was agreed that the sovereign pontiff was a monarch. He had an army that no longer participated in European conflicts. He acted, instead, through diplomatic channels. His preferences were known. Ambassadors were established in Rome to protect his interests and keep him informed. The papacy had the best information network imaginable at its disposal through its legates, its nuncios and clergy. Beginning with Clement XI (1700–21), the papacy embarked on an austerity campaign while maintaining the courtly splendor for which it was known. The apostolic see, which had been the object of bloody rivalries between the great feudal powers of the Italic peninsula in the Middle Ages, passed into the hands of an Italic nobility whose sons were admitted in the Curia. Rome was indeed Roman, and the pope headed a triple jurisdiction: civil, state, and theological. The French Revolution destroyed this *état de grâce* by calling for the right of all peoples to self-determination. The uniting of Avignon and of the *comtat* Venaissin with France through a plebiscite in 1790 smashed the mosaic of territories assembled in the age of medieval fiefdoms. The splendor of modern citizenship was set against the obsolescence of the Papal States. Once again, the papacy had to suffer persecutions, deportations, and exiles, as in Byzantine times or during the struggle between the clergy and the Empire. The Revolution and the First Empire lowered the status of the sovereign pontiff. Napoleon's coronation by Pius VII at Nôtre Dame was intended to solemnly proclaim that the pope had become the chaplain of a civil authority that accepted the Church so as better to rule over Christendom. This was the opposite of Charlemagne's consecration memorialized in the *porphyry disk* placed at the entrance of St. Peter's Basilica in Rome: an allegiance by rather than to the papacy. It was at most a marriage of convenience. Settled in a city hemmed in by the encroaching countryside and eroded by time, the papacy had to face internal rebellions prompted by liberal aspirations, as well as deal with the constant intervention of the European superpowers who would take on the task of defending it but with their own territorial and ideological agendas. The Rome Pius VII found in May of 1814 bore little resemblance to the one from which he had been dragged away. His successors, Leo XII (1825–29) and Gregory XVI (1831–46), after the ephemeral reign of Pius VIII (1829–30), attempted a reform of the papal administration, but it was hampered by the scrutiny of civil societies. Multiple projects for Italian unification resulted in the idea of a sort of moral presidency of the pope over the peninsula—a kind of neo-Guelfism, and an impossible alliance between a liberal parliamentarian Italy, and a papacy that would have become, throughout its States, a civil and spiritual model—a society in which the freedom of conscience would have gone along with the obligations of the faith. Pius IX (1846–78) paid dearly for the Augustinian ambiguity of an ideal State, that is, of a city of God on Italian land harking back to an imperial territory (the Roman Empire). The Papal States, devoured by the nations of Europe in a dramatic battle on the Italic peninsula, fell into the hands of the House of Savoy, which at the time was to Italy what Prussia was to the whole group of Germanic territories. On 20 September 1870, without any significant battles, Rome became the capital of Italy, and Pius IX closed himself off in the Vatican. Victor Emmanuel II turned the Quirinal palace into a royal residence where, as it turned out, he would only spend a few nights.

Here we come back to our first point. The papacy as a Roman entity and as a monarchy was no more, as the whole world acknowledged, yet it managed to survive without the Papal States. The papacy relied on one tradition and one tradition alone: the vocation of St. Peter, buried in Rome, a tradition made visible by the palaces in which the papacy had imprisoned itself and by a basilica that the Law of Guarantees (enacted by the Italian parliament in May 1871) gladly conceded to it. Yet sequestering the pope in the Vatican only served to create even more rumors and gossip about the mystery connected to a power that had in fact become quite extraordinary. *The Secrets of the Vatican, Secret Vatican, the Cellars of the Vatican*—all kinds of titles proliferated in popular, "confessional" literature or fiction feeding a public hungry for stories about labyrinths, occult events, and wondrous tales connected to a strange destiny. This was a way of explaining the survival of the papacy.

In 1807, Germaine de Staïl's heroine, Corinne, has a different vision of this survival. In approaching St. Peter's, her first thought is to represent this building as it would be when it in turn became a ruin, an object of admiration for centuries to come. She imagines these now erect columns, half lying on the ground, this portico broken, and this vault open to the sky. Finally, dawn breaks and from the top of St. Peter's, Corinne contemplates the city of Rome thrown into the middle of the uncultivated countryside like an oasis in the Libyan desert. Devastation surrounds the city, but this multitude of bell towers, cupolas, and obelisks dominating it, with St. Peter's still towering above them, give the city its wholly marvelous kind of beauty. The response to this is inscribed in capital letters over one meter high on the drum of the basilica of St. Peter's: "*Tu es Petrus, et super hanc petram aedificabo ecclesiam meam. Et tibi dabo claves regni caelorum.*" Invisible to most mortals, the papacy multiplied its dogmatic interventions through encyclical letters, the most famous of which was about workers' conditions, the *Rerum novarum*, published by Leo XIII (1878–1903) on 15 May 1891.

The papacy was called upon to act as a mediator in international conflicts, such as the affair of the Carolina Islands pitting Germany against Spain. Through the influence of resolute, and devoted Christians, it continued to reign over a world veering toward atheism. It attempted to prevent World War I by countering it with the ideal of an international order, which could not prevail given the sacrifices made in 1917. In the period between the wars, it successively condemned fascism (1932), and both Nazism and communism (1937). In February of 1929, the Lateran agreements gave the pope a new legal framework and a new status in international law by creating the State of the City of the Vatican on forty-four hectares of land protected by Italy. The papal administration continued to proceed by bulls, briefs, letters, and consistorial allocutions. The pope wore a tiara, was transported in the *sedia gestatoria* surrounded by *flabella*, and was the head of a government consisting of a secretary of state, other officers, dicasteries, and tribunals. The Vatican had special stores reserved for its citizens: the *annone*. It issued its own stamps and minted its own money. Visitors flocked to its museums. The pope received visitors either in a public or private audience, *bacciamano*, or a state visit, a private or collective event. In short, one witnessed history unfolding during a strange episode in an already exotic story.

It fell to John XXIII to reconcile the modern manifesto of St. Peter's Basilica and the imprescriptible mission of the one holy Catholic Church by calling the twenty-first (XXI) ecumenical council at the Vatican in the nave of St. Peter's (1962–65). What Vatican II did was to offer a uniquely mindful image of the Catholic Church that the modern world could grasp.

Ever since the age of the masses, each new pontificate has seemed at odds with the preceding one. From Leo XIII (1878) to John Paul II (1978), eight popes have reigned in a hundred years. The average reign has been twelve and a half years. But this crude calculation hides a more complex reality. Pius X died in August of 1914, after attempting in vain to prevent World War I. Pius XI reigned from 1922 to 1939, and his successor was chosen on the eve of World War II. The election of Cardinal Roncalli in 1958 was a true surprise. Supposedly a transition pope, he convened a council, that turned out to be earth shattering. Paul VI made it clear as of 1974 that he would leave to his successor, hopefully in the near future, the task of implementing the decisions of Vatican II. John Paul I, as it happened, was pope for only 33 days, having been most likely overwhelmed by the enormity of the task before him. The Queen of England, crowned in 1952, has met five popes, and Franco four. The agreement with Spain first considered in 1938 was not signed until 1953. The dialogue with the Anglican Church was marked by numerous advances and numerous setbacks.

The vaunted break with the preceding pontificate comes from the fact that the newly elected successor is neither a royal heir nor a democratic candidate. The new pope confronts a history controlled by an administration—the Curia—that is the repository of a tradition all the popes have been faced with, each one more so than his predecessor, since its role has been strengthened by those very predecessors. The very strong pendulum swing between the papal power supported by the Curia and the episcopal power demanded by public opinion reached a climax with Vatican II, recalling the conciliarism of years past. Paul VI had to re-center Catholicism's pendulum by making Rome its axis and by getting the council to establish that the term "Catholic" has a double meaning. "Catholic" means universal, and therefore centrifugal, but is also centripetal because it is in a tight, apostolic relationship with the papacy. Paul VI's trips contributed to this definition. John Paul II is today fulfilling the missionary and collegial spirit of these journeys. If the pope is now a much-discussed spiritual sovereign, we can attribute this to the needs of the public at large. Confused about the world's ultimate meaning, it seeks out the papacy as a means of freeing itself through the mystery of a salvation that no longer exists on a political level but on a moral one. Individual morality is marked by a tradition of compassion and pardon, the heart of the Catholic Church's mission, where the papacy responds with a collective morality in reference to a manifestly Christian theology, through action and contemplation. The papacy is therefore at a crossroads between meaning and appearance.

It was tempting to address the history of the papacy in a chronological manner, period by period: Christian Antiquity, Middle Ages, Modern Era, and Contemporary Era. This type of history would encompass a political, economic, and social chronology of an institution that, from its origin, offered another history that was not always evident or accepted. The confrontation between a secular history and a sacred history led us to create this multiple-entry dictionary. This dictionary thus has at its core the prosopography of the popes and antipopes (and even pope Joan) as well as an overview—widening, as it were, in concentric circles—of the pontifical administration at significant moments when the papacy was confronted by a history that involved it directly (Lepanto), excluded it (the schisms), or worked against it (the unification of Italy). In short, this is an exhaustive dictionary on the popes, the nature of the papacy, and its evolution in history. Ultimately, this dictionary will be completed by the responses to the questions it has raised, and to whatever has been omitted from its pages. For the moment though, its usefulness lies in the indispensable ability to date, name, and recognize people, places, concepts, and events.

Philippe Levillain

Abbreviations

AAS: Acta Apostolicae Sedis.
ACO: Ed. Schwartz, *Acta conciliorum oecumenicorum.*
ADSS: Actes et documents relatifs à la Seconde Guerre mondiale.
AESC: Annales. Économies, sociétés, civilization.
AG: Analecta gregoriana.
AHP: Archivum historiae pontificiae.
ASR: Archivio delle Società romana di storia patria.
BEFAR: Bibliothèque des Écoles françaises d'Athènes et de Rome.
BIHR: Bulletin de l'Institut historique belge de Rome.
*CC: Corpus christianorum, collectus a monachis O.S.B. abbatiae S. Petri in Steen-
       brugge.*
CC, SL: Corpus christianorum, series latina.
CEFR: Collection de l'École française de Rome.
CSEL: Corpus scriptorum ecclesiasticorum latinorum.
DACL: Dictionnaire d'archéologie chrétienne et de liturgie.
DBF: Dictionnaire de biographie française.
DBI: Dizionario biografico degli Italiani.
DDC: Dictionnaire de droit canonique.
DHGE: Dictionnaire d'histoire et de géographie ecclésiastiques.
DIP: Dizionario degli istituti di perfezione.
DS: Dictionnaire de spiritualité ascétique et mystique. Doctrine et histoire.
DTC: Dictionnaire de théologie catholique.
EC: Enciclopedia cattolica.
EHR: English Historical Review.
Fliche-Martin: A. Fliche and V. Martin, *Histoire de l'Église depuis les origines
       jusqu'à nos jours.*
ICUR: Inscriptiones christianae Urbis Romae saec. VII antiquiores.
JEH: Journal of Ecclesiastical History.
JE: P. Jaffé and P. Ewald.
JK: P. Jaffé and F. Kaltenbrunner.
JL: P. Jaffé and S. Löwenfeld.
JRS: Journal of Roman Studies.
JW: P. Jaffé and G. Wattenbach, *Regesta pontificum Romanorum ab condita Ecclesia
       ad annum post Christum natum MCXCVIII.*
LexMA: Lexikon des Mittelalters.
LP: L. Duchesne, *Liber pontificalis*, text, introduction, and commentary.
LTK: Lexikon für theologie und Kirche.
MAH: Mélanges de'archéologie et d'histoire. See *MEFRM.*
Mansi: J. D. Mansi, *Sacrosancta concilia...*
MEFRA: Mélanges de l'École française de Rome, Antiquité.
MEFRM: Mélanges de l'École française de Rome. Moyen Âge et Temps modernes.
MGH: Monumenta Germaniae historica.
MIÖG: Mitteilungen des Instituts für Österreich. Geschichtsforschung.
MHP: Miscellanea historiae pontificiale.
NCE: New Catholic Encyclopedia.
Pastor: L. von Pastor, *The History of the Popes from the Close of the Middle Ages*,
       40 vols., London, 1891–1953.
PL: J. P. Migne, *Patrologiae cursus completus. Series latina.*
Potth: A. Potthast, *Regesta pontificum Romanorum inde ab. a. 1198 ad a. 1304.*
QFIAB: Quellen und Forschungen aus italienischen Archiven und Bibliotheken.

RB: Revue bénédictine.

RDC: Revue de droit canonique.

RHE: Revue d'histoire ecclésiastique.

RHEF: Revue d'histoire de l'Église de France.

RSCI: Rivista di storia della Chiesa in Italia.

SAB: Sitzungsberichte der Deutschen Akademie der Wissenschaften zu Berlin. Philosophisch-historische Klasse.

SC: Sources chrétiennes.

Schneider: *Die Epitaphien der Päpste und andere Stradtrömische Inschriften des Mittelalters,* Rome, 1933–.

Silva Tarouca: C. Silva Tarouca, *Epistularum Romanorum pontificum ad vicarios per Illyricum ... collectio Thessalonicensis.*

Watterich: J. B. Watterich, *Pontificum Romanorum ...vitae.*

ZKG: Zeitschrift für Kirchengeschichte.

ZRGKA: Zeitschrift für Rechtsgeschichte, Kanonist Abteilung.

ZSSR: Zeitschrift der Savigny-Stifung für Rechtsgeschichte

Contributors

Marc Agostino, *University of Bordeaux–III*

Giuseppe Alberigo, *University of Bologna*

R. P. Paul Amargier, O.P.

R. P. Robert Amiet, *Catholic Faculty of Lyon*

Jean Andreau, *l'École des Hautes Études en Sciences Sociales*

Pierre Arizzoli-Clémentel, *Musée de l'Union des Arts Décoratifs*

Pascal Arnaud, *University of Bordeaux–III*

Michel Balard, *University of Paris–I*

Michel Banniard, *University of Toulouse–II*

Bernard Barbiche, *l'École Nationale des Chartes*

Marie-Francoise Baslez, *University of Orleans*

Richard Bavoillot-Laussade, *Rome*

R. P. Guy Bedouelle, O.P., *University of Fribourg*

Jean Bérenger, *University of Paris–IV*

Philippe Bernard, *University of Paris–IV*

Jacques Biarne, *Université du Maine*

Jean-Noël Biraben, *l'Institut Nationale des Études Démographiques*

R. P. Pierre Blet, S.J., *Gregorian University*

Uta Renate Blumenthal, *Catholic University of America*

Laurence Bobis, *Bibliothèque Nationale*

Thérèse Boespflug, *l'Ecole Française de Rome*

Agostino Borromeo, *University of Rome, La Sapienza*

François Bougard, *University of Paris–X*

Alain Boureau, *l'École des Hautes Études en Sciences Sociales*

Pascale Bourgain, *l'École Nationale des Chartes*

Jean Boutier, *l'École des Hautes Études en Sciences Sociales*

Marie-Paule Boutry, *University of Viterbo*

Philippe Boutry, *University of Paris–XII*

Henri Bresc, *University of Paris–X*

Catherine Brice, *l'Ecole Française de Rome*

Ghislain Brunel, *Archives Nationales*

Jean-Pierre Brunterc'h, *Archives Nationales*

Msgr. Charles Burns, *Vatican Archives*

Marina Caffiero, *University of Camerino*

Cristina Carbonetti, *University of Rome, La Sapienza*

Francine Cardman, *Weston Jesuit School of Theology*

Hélène Carrère d'Encausse, *l'Institut d'Etudes Politiques de Paris*

Jean-Michel Carrié, *l'École des Hautes Études en Sciences Sociales*

Jean-Luc Chabot, *University of Grenoble–II*

Gérald Chaix, *Mission Française en Alemagne*

Olivier Chaline, *l'École Normale Supérieure*

Sylvie Chambadal, *l'École du Louvre*

André Chastagnol, *University of Aix-Marseille–III*

Raymond Chevallier, *University of Tours*

Michel Christol, *University of Paris–I*

Ivan Cloulas, *Archives Nationales*

Philippe Contamine, *University of Paris–IV*

R. P. Jean Coste, *l'Ecole Française de Rome*

Herbert E. J. Cowdrey, *St. Edmund Hall, Oxford*

Francine Culdaut, *Catholic Institute of Paris*

Michael F. Cusato, O.F.M., *The Franciscan Institute, St. Bonaventure University*

Ségolène de Dainville-Barbiche, *Archives Nationales*

Jacques Dalarun, *l'Ecole Française de Rome*

Claudio De Dominicis, *Vatican Archives*

Dominique Delmaire, *University of Charles-de-Gaulle Lille–III*

Jean-Marie Delmaire, *University of Charles-de-Gaulle Lille–III*

Frédéric Delmeulle, *Bibliothèque Nationale de France*

Jean Delumeau, *Collège de France*

Jeanne Demarolle, *Metz University*

Alain Demurger, *University of Paris–I*

Georg Denzler, *University of Bamberg*

Janine Desmulliez, *University of Charles-de-Gaulle Lille–III*

Jean-Luc Desnier, *Mission à l'Hotel de la Monnaie*

Marie-Christine Devedeux, *Université Jean Monnet Saint-Etienne*

R. P. Henry Donneaud, O.P., *Toulouse*

Alain Ducellier, *University of Toulouse–Le Mirail*

Jean-Dominique Durand, *University of Lyon–III*

Jean Durliat, *University of Toulouse–Le Mirail*

R. P. André Duval, O.P., *Bibliothèque du Sauchoir*

Msgr. Louis Duval-Arnould, *Vatican Library*

R. P. Marc Dykmans, S.J.

Liliane Ennabli, *Centre National de la Recherche Scientifique, Tunisia*

Anna Esposito, *La University of Rome, La Sapienza*

Agnès Ètienne-Magnien, *Archives Nationales*

Abbé Jean-Michel Fabre

S.E.R Msgr. Edmond Farhat, *Apostolic Pronunzio in Algeria*

Janice Farnham, *Weston Jesuit School of Theology*

Jean Favier, *Bibliothèque Nationale de France*

Robert Favreau, *Centre d'Etudes Supérieures de la Civilisation Médiévale de Poitiers*

Msgr. Alonso Justo Fernandez, *Spanish Center of Ecclesiastical Studies, Rome*

Luigi Fiorani, *Vatican Library*

Robert Folz, *University of Dijon, emeritus*

Raymonde Foreville, *University of Caen, emeritus*

Marina Formica, *University of Perugia*

François Fossier, *University of Lyon–II*

Christiane Fraisse-Coué, *Centre National de la Recherche Scientifique, Paris*

Thomas Frenz, *University of Passau*

Jean Gaudemet, *University of Paris–II*

Nancy Gauthier, *University of Tours*

Anne-Cécile Germe-Tizon, *Centre des Archives, d'Outre-Mer, Aix-en-Provence*

Gérard Giordanengo, *l'École Nationale des Chartes*

Paul Grendler, *University of Toronto, emeritus*

Jean-Claude Grenier, *University of Montpellier–III*

Jacques Grès-Gayer, *Catholic University of America*

Pierre Grimal, *Institut de France*

Rolf Grosse, *l'Institut Historique Allemand, Paris*

Maurilio Guasco, *University of Turin*

Bernard Guillemain, *University of Bordeaux–III*

Jean Guyon, *Centre Camille-Jullian, Aix-en-Provence*

Olivier Guyotjeannin, *l'École Nationale des Chartes*

Anne-Marie Hayez, *Centre National de la Recherche Scientifique, Paris*

Michel Hayez, *Vaucluse Archives*

Klaus Herbers, *University of Tübingen*

Peter Herde, *University of Würzburg*

Bernd-Ulrich Hergemöller, *University of Münster*

Klaus-Jürgen Herrmann, *Schwäbisch Gmünd Archives*

Bernard Heyberger, *University of Mulhouse*

Yves-Marie Hilaire, *University of Charles-de-Gaulle Lille–III*

Abbé Bruno Horaist, *l'École du Louvre*

Étienne Hubert, *Centre National de la Recherche Scientifique, Paris*

François Jankowiak, *University of Versailles–Saint-Quentin at Yvelines*

Philippe Jansen, *University of Bordeaux–III*

Pierre Jugie, *Conservateur de l'Inventaire Général de Bourgogne*

David Kertzer, *Brown University*

Hans-Henning Körtum, *University of Tübingen*

Nöelle de La Blanchardière, *Bibliotheque de l'Ecole Français de Rome*

William J. La Due, *Tucson, Arizona*

Régis Ladous, *University of Lyon–III*

Aldo Landi, *University of Florence*

Msgr. Bernard de Lanversin, *Auditor of the Rota, Vatican City*

Madeleine Laurain-Portemer, *Centre National de la Recherche Scientifique, Paris*

Bruno Laurioux, *University of Paris–I*

Henri Lavagne, *l'École Practique des Hautes Études*

Marcel Le Glay, *University of Paris–I*

Jean-Loup Lemaitre, *l'École Practique des Hautes Études*

Nicole Lemaitre, *University of Paris–I*

Pierre-Yves Le Pogam, *Musée National du Moyen Âge*

Msgr. Dominique Le Tourneau, *University of Navarre*

Henriette Levillian, *University of Caen*

Philippe Levillian, *University of Paris–X*

John E. Lynch, C.S.P., *Catholic University of America*

Jean Lionnet, *Centre de Musique Baroque de Versailles*

Roger-Charles Logoz, *University of Lausanne*

Dietrich Lohrmann, *Historical Institute of Hochschule d'Aix-la-Chapelle*

Jean-Pierre Machelon, *University of Paris–V*

Monique Maillard-Luypaert, *Belgian Historical Institute of Rome*

Jean-Claude Maire-Vigueur, *University of Florence*

Federico Marazzi, *University of Turin*

Francesco Margiotta Broglio, *Cesare Alfieri Institute, Florence*

Jean-Marie Martin, *Centre National de la Recherche Scientifique, Paris*

Jean-Pierre Martin, *University of Paris–IV*

R. P. Giacomo Martina, S.J., *Gregorian University*

Rossana Martorelli, *University of Cagliari*

Christopher R. Matthews, *Weston Jesuit School of Theology*

Christian Michel, *University of Paris–X*

Olivier Michel, *Centre National de la Recherche Scientifique, Paris*

Hélène Millet, *Centre National de la Recherche Scientifique, Paris*

Michel Mollat, *Institut de France*

François Monfrin, *University of Paris–IV*

Elisa Mongiano, *l'Archivio di Stato of Turin*

Christine de Montclos, *Centre d'Etudes et des Recherches Internationales*

Roberto Morozzo Della Rocca, *University of Rome–III*

Jacques Nobécourt, *Roman Correspondent for* Le Monde

Joël-Benoît d'Onorio, *European Institute of Church-State Relations*

Claude Orrieux, *University of Caen*

James O'Toole, *Boston College*

Marcel Pacaut, *University of Lyon–II; International Commission on Comparative Ecclesiastical History*

Élisabeth Paoli, *Centre National de la Recherche Scientifique, Paris*

Agostino Paravicini Bagliani, *University of Lausanne*

Michel Parisse, *University of Paris–I*

Michel Pastoureau, *l'École Practique des Hautes Études*

Gilles Pécout, *Ecole Normale Superieure*

Marco Pellegrini

Philippe Pergola, *Pontifical Institute of Christian Archeology*

Michel Perrin, *University of Arras*

Paola Piacentini Scaccia, *Italian Encyclopedia Institute*

Jean-Charles Picard, *University of Paris–X*

Charles Pietri, *l'Ecole Française de Rome*

Luce Pietri, *University of Paris–IV*

Émile Poulat, *l'École Practique des Hautes Études*

Claude Prud'homme, *University of Lyon–III*

R. P. Paulius Rabikauskas, S.J., *Gregorian University*

Odile Redon, *University of Paris–VIII*

Wolfgang Reinhard, *Historiches Seminar, Universität Freiburg*

Christian Renoux, *l'Ecole Française de Rome*

Andrea Riccardi, *University of Rome–III*

Jean Richard, *Institut de France*

Pierre Riché, *University of Paris–X*

Mario Rosa, *Scuola Normale Superiore, Pisa*

Wipertus Rudt de Collenburg, *Rome*

Giuseppe Ruggieri, *Institute of Religious Sciences, Bologna*

Elizabeth W. Russell, *Harvard University*

Msgr. Patrick Saint-Roch, *Pontifical Institute of Christian Archeology*

Jean-Marie Salamito, *University of Strasbourg*

Jean-Marie Sansterre, *Free University of Bruxelles*

Gilles Sauron, *University of Dijon*

Bernhard Schimmelpfennig, *University of Augsburg*

Tilmann Schmidt, *University of Tübingen*

Karl Schnith, *University of Munich*

Georg Schwaiger, *University of Munich*

Ghislaine de Senneville

Pierre-André Sigal, *University of Montpellier–III*

Bruno Simon, *University of Saint-Étienne*

Silvano Sirboni, *Interdiocesian Seminar of Alessandria, Italy*

Marc Smith, *Archives Nationales, Paris*

Micheline Soenen, *General Archives of the Belgian Kingdom, Bruxelles*

Claire Sotinel, *l'Ecole Française de Rome*

Kenneth Stow, *University of Haifa*

Nicholas Terpstra, *University of Toronto*

Pierre Toubert, *Collège de France*

Jean Tulard, *University of Paris–IV*

François-Charles Uginet, *l'Ecole Française de Rome*

Marc Venard, *University of Paris–X*

Marco Venditelli

Jacques Verger, *École Normale Superieure*

Jean-Pierre Viallet, *University of Grenoble–III*

Giovanni Maria Vian, *La University of Rome, La Sapienza*

R. P. Marie-Humbert Vicaire, O.P., *l'Albertinum de Fribourg*

Catherine Vincent, *University of Paris–I*

Robert-Jean Vinson, *Architect DPLG*

Catherine Virvoulet, *l'Ecole Française de Rome*

Cinzia Vismara, *University of Sassari*

Jean-Louis Voisin, *University of Dijon*

Ernst Voltmer, *University of Treves*

Ludwig Vones, *University of Cologne*

Brigitte Waché, *University of Saint-Étienne*

Michael Walsh, *Heythrop College, University of London*

Harald Zimmerman, *University of Tübingen*

The Papacy
An Encyclopedia

A

ABBREVIATOR. An abbreviator was responsible for drafting, in an abridged version, the minutes (*nota* or *minuta*) of a document before it was recopied in final form, either by himself or by someone else. The PAPAL CHANCERY had abbreviators beginning in the the 13th century. They were the private assistants of notaries. Toward the end of the century, the vice-chancellor asked some of them to assist in the final verification of documents that were ready to be issued. In the 14th century, besides the *abbreviatores notariorum*, there were *abbreviatores litterarum apostolicarum*, who were employed to draft minutes for the *litterae gratiosae*. BENEDICT XII (1334–42) set the number at twenty-four. Some reviewed assembled documents *prima visio*, while others assisted the vice-chancellor in the decisive *iudicatura* of specific papers. In the 15th century, there were three categories of abbreviators: *abbreviatores de parco majori* or *majoris praesidentiae*; *abbreviatores de parco minori* or *minoris praesidentiae*; and *abbreviatores de prima visione*. CALIXTUS III (1455–58) fixed the number of *abbreviatores de parco majori* at twelve. In 1463, PIUS II assembled the abbreviators into a college of seventy members, which was dissolved the following year by its successor, PAUL II. SIXTUS IV reconstituted it and fixed the number at seventy-two. The PAPAL BULL *Divina aeterni* (11 January 1479) became the constitutional charter of the college (ed. M. Tangl, *Die päpstlichen Kanzleiordnungen*, Innsbruck, 1894, 195–205). It determined the college's organization, its management of funds, and its power to create its own statutes and rules. Later on, only the *abbreviatores de parco majori* retained their previous positions, and even their activity within the Chancery was gradually reduced. The abbreviators *de prima visione* were no longer mentioned as of the 16th century. The number of abbreviators *de parco minori* was greatly diminished, and they had almost disappeared by the 19th century. Finally, PIUS X eliminated the position of abbreviator in 1908 and transferred the abbreviators' responsibilities to the college of PROTONOTARIES *de numero participantium*. The *abbreviator de curia* is cited as of 1478. He was responsible for preparing minutes of particular interest and those concerning the APOSTOLIC CAMERA. This office was also eliminated by Pius X in his reform of the ROMAN CURIA.

Paulius Rabikauskas

Bibliography

Ciampini, G. *De abbreviatorum de parco majori . . . munere, dignitate, praerogativis et privilegiis*, Rome, 1691.

Del Rè, N. "Abbreviatore," *EC*, 1 (1948), 40–41.

Fournier, E. "Abréviateurs," *DDC*, 1 (1935), 98–106.

Frenz, F. "Die Gründung des Abbreviatorenkollegs durch Pius II und Sixtus IV," *Miscellanea in onore di Mons. Martino Giusti*, I, Vatican, 1978, 297–329.

Rabikauskas, P. "Abbreviatori della Cancelleria pontifica nella prima metà del secolo XIV," *Annali della Scuola speciale per archivisti e bibliotecari dell'Università di Roma*, 12 (1971), II, 153–65.

Schwarz, B. "Abbreviature officium est assistere vice-cancellario in expeditione litterarum apostolicarum. Zur Entwicklung des Abbreviatorenamtes vom grossen Schisma bis zur Gründung des Vakabilistenkollegs der Abbreviatoren durch Pius II," *Römische Kurie. Kirchliche Finanzen. Vatikanisches Archiv*, II (*MHP*, 46), Rome, 1979, 789–823; "Die Abbreviatoren unter Eugen IV." *QFIAB*, 60 (1980), 200–74.

ABDICATIONS, PAPAL. See **Resignations, Papal**.

ACADEMIES, PONTIFICAL. Like many other institutions created by the Holy See, the pontifical academies, of which there are presently five, are built on foundations that go back to the Renaissance and attest to the close connections between faith, theology, the liturgy, art, and science. The individual history of each institute is discussed in a brief entry in the ANNUARIO PONTIFICIO. It is clear that the above-mentioned connections varied in significance during different periods of Church history. The academies are labeled "pontifical" because they depend on the pope, even though he does not actually preside over any of them. Highly placed dignitaries, such as the SECRETARY OF STATE, or figures named by the sovereign pontiff serve as their presidents. The pope designates academy members directly in certain cases (e.g., the Pontifical Academy of Sciences); in others, he delegates this task. In some cases, members of one academy, especially Academies of Theology associated with the academies within an elite, are also members of other academies, which consolidates the influence group of specialists close to the Holy See.

The two most active academies are the Pontifical Institute of Christian Archaeology and the Pontifical Academy of Sciences. The former, presided over by the Secretary of State, gathers together specialists in Christian archaeology (mostly from Rome), who are responsibile for maintaining an active network of scholarly exchanges in the field. The latter is composed of seventy secular members who are named for life, as well as official members (director of the Observatory of Castel Gandolfo, prefects of the LIBRARY and the VATICAN ARCHIVES), and honorary members. Their goal it is to recruit world-renowned specialists in mathematics and the experimental sciences, mostly from European and American universities. All members are recruited based on their scientific qualifications alone and are not required to be Catholic. The Academy of Sciences holds a plenary session every two years, followed by a study week in which twenty-five invited guests participate. On these occassions the pope adresses the Academy in the presence of the SACRED COLLEGE. In addition to an honorary tribute, the Pope also delivers a commentary on the relationship between the sciences and the Church. Pope PIUS XII's speeches to the Academy remain famous. It was also before the Academy of Sciences that JOHN PAUL II rehabilitated Galileo in November 1979. Every two years, the Academy awards a young scholar with a medal of honor, a tradition instituted by PIUS XI.

Some academies are more active and dynamic than others. The pope has the power to found new academies at any time. John Paul II has manifested a particular interest in scholarly societies as places of research and intellectual exchange where ideological conflicts can be transcended. This interest is reflected in the prominent role currently played by the Academy of Sciences, and by certain projects under development, such as the Academy of Social Sciences.

List of the Pontifical Academies. There are currently five Pontifical Academies. All are intellectual networks serving the papacy and the Catholic world rather than research centers in the strict sense of the term:

1. In spite of its title, the *Ecclesiastical Pontifical Academy*, founded by CLEMENT XI in 1701 and mainly intended to train young clerics in diplomatic relations, does not really belong in this category since its main function is teaching.

2. The *Roman Pontifical Academy of Archaeology*, created in the 15th century under the sponsorship of Pomponio Leto, has been dissolved and reconstituted several times. Its present format can be attributed to PIUS VII and GREGORY XVI. First and foremost a model for the other academies, its function consists mainly of distributing prizes for scholarly works.

3. The *Accademia dei Lincei* was founded in 1603 by Prince Federigo Cesi and takes its name from the emblem of the lynx, symbolizing the keenness of the human spirit confronted with questions raised by mysterious nature. After various vicissitudes, it was renamed the Pontifical Academy of Sciences (*motu proprio* of Pius XI *In multis solaciis* of 27 October 1936) and was housed with its eighty members in the Corsini Palace.

4. The *Roman Theological Pontifical Academy*, founded in 1695 under the patronage of Cardinal Imperiali and annexed into the academy of the nobles by Clement XI (1707), underwent a thorough restructuring during the contemporary period. Pius XII approved new statutes for it and assigned it the mission of covering the totality of Catholic theology. On a narrower scale, LEO XII decided (on 15 October 1879) to create the *Academy of St. Thomas Aquinas*, based on his belief that a renewal of Thomist thought and scholarship would help prepare the Church to face the modern era. In 1934, it absorbed the former *Academy of Catholic Religion*, founded in 1801, and has since gained an international reputation through its research efforts.

5. The last academy created was the *International Academy of Mary* (1946). The vocation of its founder Father Carlo Barlic was to spread devotion to the Virgin from the seat of the Antonianum and to dedicate scientific and speculative studies to her. The "pontifical" designation, accorded to it by JOHN XXIII (1959), was approved by PAUL VI in 1964 at the same time as its statutes.

Philippe Levellain

Bibliography

Annuario pontificio per l'anno 1992, Vatican City.
Richard, P. "Académies romaines et pontificales," *DHGE*, I, 250–252.

ACTS OF PETER. The Acts of Peter is one of the so-called five major apocryphal acts of the apostles, along with those of Andrew, Paul, John, and Thomas. In his discussion of writings bearing the name of Peter, EUSE-BIUS offers our first direct evidence of "the Acts bearing his name," identifying it as unorthodox (*Hist. eccl.* 3.3.1–2). Origen's mention of Peter's request to be crucified head downward in his *Commentary on Genesis*, mediated by Eusebius (*Hist. eccl.* 3.1.2–3), may reflect his knowledge of the *Acts of Peter*. Although the *Acts of Paul*, known to Tertullian by A.D. 200, has been thought by some to be indebted to the *Acts of Peter* in various sections, this is disputed. In any case, it is probably reasonable to date the *Acts of Peter* sometime in the later part of the second century. The place of composition is unknown, but Asia Minor is a likely candidate. The condemnation of the apocryphal acts already visible in Eusebius and quite clear in the writings of Augustine resulted in their widespread suppression (e.g., they are proscribed in the *Decretum Gelasianum*). Nevertheless, the *Acts of Peter* continued to be read in various Christian circles, and portions of it were incorporated into later works.

Except for P. Oxy. 849 (= *Acts of Peter* 25–26), the Greek original of the *Acts of Peter* survives only in the account of Peter's martyrdom, which also circulated as an independent text. Thus, most of the content of the *Acts of Peter* is known today from a single 6th–7th century Latin codex from Vercelli (Codex Vercellensis 158), whose translation of a Greek exemplar can be dated to the 4th or 5th century. Comparison of the Latin text with the surviving Greek witnesses indicates that the Latin translation is generally reliable. Nevertheless, various signs of editorial activity have been identified that suggest that the Latin version may already involve an adaptation of the original *Acts of Peter*. Other versions (e.g., Coptic, Syriac, Armenian, Arabic, and Ethiopic) of the *Acts of Peter*, principally the martyrdom, attest its wide circulation.

Following the Vercelli manuscript, the *Acts of Peter* opens with a brief account of Paul's activity in Rome and his departure for Spain (chapters 1–3). Next Simon Magus arrives in Rome claiming to be the "great power of God" (see Acts 8:10) and leading the church astray (4). Peter receives a vision about "Simon whom you expelled from Judea" (see Acts 8:18–24) and sets sail from Caesarea for Rome (5–6). Upon his arrival the crowds repent and beg Peter to overthrow Simon, who is lodging with a certain senator Marcellus (7–8). Peter goes to the house but the doorkeeper refuses to announce him. So Peter sends a large dog granted the power of human speech to summon Simon (9). Marcellus witnesses this miracle and repents (10–11). After cursing Simon the dog returns to Peter and predicts a great contest between Peter and Simon (12). Many people believe after Peter throws a smoked fish into a pond and it becomes alive and swims (13). Marcellus throws Simon out of his house (14). Peter has a seven-month old infant rebuke Simon with the voice of a man (15). Jesus appears to Peter and encourages him for the upcoming contest (16). Peter recounts

his past dealings with Simon in Judea (17–18). Next he goes to Marcellus's house, where he engages in healing, teaching, and prayer. He is strengthened by a vision of Marcellus (19–22). The great contest between Simon and Peter takes place in the Roman forum. Peter raises a series of three men from the dead. He challenges Simon to raise the last, a senator's son, and when after great efforts he fails, Peter raises him (23–29). Peter continues to preach and heal (30–31). Simon astonishes the crowd by flying, but at Peter's prayer he falls to earth and later dies (32). Peter remains in Rome and prominent women convert to a life of purity and leave their husbands' beds. In the ensuing social upheaval the prefect is urged to do away with Peter (33–34). Peter sets out to leave Rome in disguise but encounters the Lord entering the city and asks where he is going (*Quo vadis?*). The Lord answers, "I am coming to Rome to be crucified." Peter comes to himself and returns to meet his fate (35). He is arrested and is crucified head downward (36–37). After a long speech on the mystery of the symbolism of his upside-down crucifixion, he gives up his spirit. Marcellus sees to his burial and Peter appears to him (38–40). Nero is enraged at Peter's death, since he had wished to continue punishing him. But he is warned in a vision to leave the Christians in peace, which he does out of fear (41).

According to the Stichometry of Nicephorus, the *Acts of Peter* consisted of 2,750 lines, which means that the extant version has suffered a loss of about one-third of the original. One fragment from the lost first part of the *Acts of Peter* appears to be preserved in Berlin Coptic papyrus 8502. In this section, Peter is asked why he does not heal his beautiful but paralyzed daughter. He does so but then immediately returns her to her infirmity. He explains that her condition is profitable for her insofar as it came about miraculously to prevent her sexual violation after an abduction. Augustine (*Contra Adimantum* 17) refers to this story together with a similar narrative that likely derives from the *Acts of Peter* about a gardener's only daughter who dies when Peter is asked to pray for her. In this second account, which is found in the pseudo-Titus epistle, when the gardener begs Peter to raise his daughter, he does so. But several days later a man appears and seduces her and they run off never to be seen again.

As is the case with other examples of its genre, the *Acts of Peter* represents a type of pious popular literature intended to edify and instruct as well as to entertain. It supplemented the canonical Acts by filling in the void between the disappearance of Peter from the biblical account and the tradition of his martyrdom at Rome (see *1 Clement* 5). Its focus on miracles and ascetical teachings, wedded to the plot of Peter's struggles against Simon the heretic, portrayed the victory of God over the devil by means of dramatic narrative rather than theological proposition. Although its adoption by heretical groups ensured its condemnation by the church, it survived in a variety of literary adaptations and a number of its memorable images (e.g., Simon's fall from the sky, Peter's upside-down crucifixion) that found new life in Christian art over the succeeding centuries.

Christopher R. Matthews

Bibliography

Bremmer, J. N., ed. *The Apocryphal Acts of Peter: Magic, Miracles and Gnosticism.* Studies on the Apocryphal Acts of the Apostles 3. Leuven, 1998.

Poupon, G. "Les 'Actes de Pierre' et leur remaniement." Pp. 4363–83 in W. Haase, ed. *Aufstieg und Niedergang der römischen Welt: Geschichte und Kultur Roms im Spiegel der neueren Forschung.* Part 2, *Principat,* 25.6. New York, 1988.

"AD LIMINA" VISITS. The ad limina visit that every diocesan bishop must make to Rome has a threefold aim: (1) to venerate the tombs of the holy apostles Peter and Paul; (2) to meet Peter's successor, the bishop of Rome, and to have contact with the dicasteries of the Roman Curia; and (3) to present a report on the state of his diocese. The regulations call for the presentation of this report every five years, except if the year planned for the visit coincides with the first or second year of the bishop's appointment as head of the diocese.

In the case of a legitimate hindrance, the diocesan bishop's place may be taken by his coadjutor or, failing that, by his auxiliary or another priest residing in his diocese. The apostolic vicar may fulfill the obligation through a proxy, even if he resides in Rome. The prefect and the apostolic administrator are not bound by it. On the other hand, ordinaries for the armed forces (John Paul II, apostolic constitution *Spirituali militum curae,* 21 April 1986) are bound by it, as are the other prelates for whom a similar obligation has been prescribed.

The custom of making a pilgrimage to Rome to pray at the tombs of the apostles Peter and Paul is an ancient one. The ad limina visit has been in existence since the 5th century. Leo the Great called for the presence of three Sicilian bishops at the provincial council held in Rome each year, in the autumn. Gregory the Great made it obligatory for these same Sicilian bishops to come to Rome every three years, later changing that to every five years. At the Roman synod of 743, Pope ZACHARIAS gave the Italian bishops a similar obligation. The early popes took advantage of these visits to hold their synods.

By the 11th and 12th centuries, the duty had become an annual one. Based on PASCHAL II's testimony, the archbishops of the Latin Church who were the farthest from Rome carried out this yearly obligation, at least by proxy (Decret. Greg. IX, 1. I, tit. VI, *de electione et electi*

potestate, c. 4 in fine). GREGORY IX had included an oath in his Decretals that was demanded of the Italian bishops (cap. 4, X, *de iureiur.* II, 24) committing them to go to Rome each year, in person or by proxy. However, a special apostolic indult often exonerated them. ALEXANDER IV abolished all these exonerations (constitution *Importuna,* 3 August 1257).

The frequency of these visits made it highly inconvenient for the bishops to fulfill their residential obligations in their dioceses, and the visits seemed to fall into disuse. SIXTUS V reformed the institution (apostolic constitution *Romanus Pontifex,* 20 December 1585) and extended the obligation to all bishops, who had to promise faithfully to carry out the visit. He divided the bishops into four groups, all bound to come to Rome, respectively, every three, four, five, or ten years. Nonobservance of this rule entailed suspension ipso facto from spiritual and temporal administration of the diocese, and even suspension *ab ingressu ecclesiae* until the absolution of the bishop by the Holy See. This is the first time that the obligation of periodical journeys to Rome, including giving the pope an account of the situation in the dioceses, was imposed on the Latin episcopate as a whole. The visits were under the jurisdiction of the Congregation of the Council created by SIXTUS V (apostolic constitution *Immensa aeterni Dei,* 22 January 1588). The dioceses in the mission territories—except for the Hispano-American dioceses—were incorporated for this purpose in the Congregation de Propaganda Fide, created 22 June 1622.

In 1725 BENEDICT XIII established the points that the bishops should cover in their reports. BENEDICT XIV confirmed the existing discipline and extended it to the prelates nullius, whose territories were separate from a diocese (constitution *Quod sancta,* 23 November 1740). The First Vatican Council proposed modifying the discipline but was prohibited from doing so because of the interruption of its work.

Under PIUS X, the Consistorial Congregation was entrusted with overseeing the ad limina visits (apostolic constitution *Sapienti consilio,* 29 June 1908). On 31 December 1909 it reorganized the matter of the visits (decree *De relationibus diaecesanis et visitatione SS. Liminum*) and drew up a questionnaire consisting of 150 points (*Ordo servandus in relatione de statu ecclesiarum*). The frequency of visits was fixed at five years, beginning with 1 January 1911. The Congregation of Propaganda governed, independently, the method of the presentation of the reports of the ordinaries depending on that congregation (encyclical letter, Easter, 1922). The Code of Canon Law of 1917 covered this question in canons 340–2. The Consistorial Congregation devised a new formula for the report (4 November 1918). The obligation of the ad limina visit was extended to the chaplains of the armed forces (Consistorial Congregation, decree *Ad Sacra Limina,* 28 February 1959).

The Congregation for the Bishops (which replaced Consistorial) decided to issue new norms that better conformed to the then-present situation and that were more explanatory than constraining (decree *Ad Romanam Ecclesiam*, 29 June 1975); the five-year frequency began 1 January 1976. The bishops were divided as follows: first year, Italy, Spain, Malta, North Africa, West and East Africa; second year, other countries in Europe and Africa; third year, North America, Central America, the Caribbean, Oceania; fourth year, South America (except Brazil), South and Central East Asia; fifth year, Brazil, rest of Asia.

Pope PAUL VI introduced change by organizing collective visits on the part of the episcopates or apostolic regions instead of individual visits. In autumn 1972 the work of the bishops' synod prevented the Roman pontiff from individually receiving the Spanish bishops then paying their ad limina visit. He collectively received a group of six of the bishops, who came from different ecclesiastical provinces. A similar meeting was held with two groups of Canadian bishops, one from the civil province of Alberta on 31 October 1974, the other from the pastoral region of Montreal on 14 December following. After the decree *Ad Romanam Ecclesiam* came into force, Paul VI retained the system of collective audiences. He justified it by the supradiocesan character of certain situations which needed to be dealt with on a community basis.

With JOHN PAUL II, even if the bishops came to Rome according to apostolic region, each one was received individually by the pope.

Bishops whose dioceses are under the jurisdiction of the Congregation for the Eastern Churches or the Congregation for the Evangelization of the Peoples (or of both at the same time) must reply to a supplementary questionnaire. The Secretariat of State prepared a new questionnaire in 1975, which was published in 1982: *Formula relationis quinquennalis*.

These various questionnaires must be sent to the territorially appropriate congregation (of Bishops, for the Eastern Churches, for the Evangelization of the Peoples), which then forwards elements of interest to the different dicasteries of the Roman Curia.

The 1983 Code of Canon Law outlines the general framework in c. 399–400. The institution was revised by John Paul II, within the context of the reorganization of the Roman Curia (apostolic constitution *Pastor bonus*, 28 June 1988, articles 28–32), and by the Congregation for the Bishops (*Direttorio per le visite "ad limina,"* 29 June 1988). The ad limina visit strengthens the bonds of hierarchical communion and provides evidence of the Catholicity of the Church and the unity of the college of bishops. The new general regulations of the Roman Curia, which came into force 7 June 1992, provided additional details on the preparation of the quinquennial episcopal visits (art. 124 to 126).

Dominique Le Tourneau

Bibliography

Boudinhon, A. "La visite 'ad limina' et le rapport sur l'état du diocèse," in *Le Canoniste contemporain* 33 (1910), 219–36.

Cárcel Orti, V. "Legislación vigente sobre la visita 'ad limina,' El decreto 'Ad Romanam Ecclesiam' de 1975," *Questioni canoniche* 23, Milan, 1984, 99–136; *Historia, Derecho y Diplomática de la visita 'ad limina,'* Valencia, 1989.

Congregation for the Bishops, "Directoire pour la visite 'ad limina,'" *L'Osservatore Romano en langue française*, 26 July 1988, 6–10.

de Echeverría, L. "La visita 'ad limina,'" *Revista Española de Derecho Canónica*, 32 (1976), 361–78.

Ghirlanda, G. "La visita 'ad limina,'" *La Civiltà Cattolica*, 3341, 1989, 359–72; "Rapporti Santa Sede-Vescovi: la visita 'ad limina Apostolorum,'" *La Curia Romana nella Cost. Ap. Pastor bonus* (ed. P. A. Bonnet and C. Gullo), Vatican City, 1990, 123–49.

Martin, V. "Pape," *DTC* XI, Paris, 1932, 1909–15.

ADALBERT. See **[Albert]**.

ADEODATUS I. *In Latin called Deusdedit (b. Rome ?, d. Rome, 8 November 618). Made pope on 19 October 615. Inhumed at St. Peter's in Rome. Saint (inscribed into Roman martyrology by Baronius).*

This cleric, son of a cleric, returned to Sabinian's policies aimed at giving back to the secular clergy certain functions often transferred to the monks by Gregory the Great (GREGORY I). The son of the subdeacon Stephen (known mainly through a note in the LIBER PONTIFICALIS and for his epitaph), he must have had to work his way up the hierarchical ladder, since he was elected pope after having been a priest for forty years. Apparently too aged to truly wield power, he witnessed the first manifestations of independence in Italy as a mere spectator. It was deemed necessary to wait for the visit of Eleutherius, the exarch of Ravenna, to have Adeodatus consecrated as pope. He imposed a daily mass (*secunda missa*) on the Roman clergy, the only group over which he had disciplinary authority. He also decided that upon his death the Roman clergy would receive a year's wages as a bonus, which until then the law had allowed only after the election of a successor. The earthquake and epidemic that shook Rome before his death did not seem to have particularly moved him. This is why the population did not truly mourn his passing. It was not until HONORIUS I, became pope (625–38) that an epitaph was engraved on Adeodatus's tombstone.

Jean Durliat

Bibliography

JW, 1, 222.
LP, 1, 319–320; 2, 698–759.
Arnaldi, G. "Adeodato," *DBI*, 1 (1960), 271–2.
Schneider, *ICUR*, 19, 4160.

ADEODATUS II. *(d. Rome, 17 June 676). Elected pope on 11 April 672. Inhumed at St. Peter's in Rome.*

Adeodatus II was the first in a long line of aged transitional popes who implemented the policies defined by the Roman clergy and nobility without significantly influencing their course. He was a Roman, son of a certain Jovinianus, and a monk since his youth in the community of San Erasmo on the Calian Hill. He was representative of the opinions held by the Roman ruling class. During his pontificate, he carried out measures favorable to his city and his clergy. The *LIBER PONTIFICALIS* notes that he was very gentle and particularly mindful of foreigners, that is, pilgrims who by flocking to the city were in a new way making it feel like a capital again. To better consolidate his local authority, or due to pressure from his entourage, he raised the salaries of the entire clergy. This reveals an increasing autonomy in the management of public finances allocated to church needs. Roman particularism was getting stronger. Moreover, the *Liber pontificalis* was giving renewed attention to the construction of churches and monasteries. For example, the pope transferred revenues from various domains to his monastery at San Erasmo.

Like most Romans, Adeodatus was moved by reading the *Hypomnesticum*, in which a Greek monk ca. 668 recounts the suffering imposed on MARTIN I and *Maximus the Confessor*. Roman patriotism was ignited by this document, and the pope, whose election was quickly confirmed by the exarch of Ravenna, refused the synodical letters of the new patriarch of Constantinople, Constantine (675–7), who had remained faithful to his monothelitic views. Thus Rome participated fully in the political-religious life of the Empire, while becoming increasingly autonomous. A remark in the *Liber pontificalis* illustrates this state of affairs. The Arabs, having attacked Sicily in 673, seized a great many spoils, including a bronze statue Constantine II had stolen from Rome. Imperial greed was benefiting the worst enemies of the Empire!

In the West, the pope maintained close relations with England. He confirmed the exemption of St. Peter's Monastery in Canterbury from episcopal jurisdiction. Yet the date of the letter is based on the years of the imperial reign. In another letter Adeodatus supposedly announced to all the bishops of Gaul the privileges he would have given St. Martin of Tours. This is a false document since no pope at the time could have directly addressed the entire clergy of a given kingdom.

Jean Durliat

Bibliography

JW, 1, 237.
LP, 1, 346–7.
PL, 87, 1139–44; 129, 681–90.
Bertolini, O. *Roma di fronte a Bisanzio e ai Longobardi*, Bologna, 1971, 364–5.

ADMINISTRATION OF THE PATRIMONY OF THE HOLY SEE. See **Administrative Offices, Roman; Finances, Papal**.

ADMINISTRATION, PAPAL. The papal administration is similar in many ways to the public administration of a state. Yet there is one basic difference: this is a form of service and not a profession. The authority (of any of its members) does not depend on the importance of the function he performs within the administration, but on the magnitude of the service rendered to the Church and to the person of the sovereign pontiff. The notion of "career" is juridically unknown. Advancement is not a right that can be claimed at any point. *The General Regulation of the Roman Curia (RGCR)* of 1968 expressly states that promotions are granted when posts are vacated, but that objective abilities take precedence over seniority. In the distant past, it was possible to make a career for oneself in the Curia. Yet, even if some young priests had illusions about the prospect of a Vatican career, they were eventually disabused. There are enough examples of positions that became dead-ends or that their holders abandoned along with the attendant traditional honors to prove that the pontifical functionary is solely a servant of the Holy See and the Church, and not of his ambitions or of Mammon. As a result, the pope freely decides who is to be nominated, and each pontificate is familiar with the "pope's men," whose assignments, when analyzed by experienced people, especially at the beginning of the pontificate, provide an idea of the pope's overall policy or of a specific intention. In this regard, pontifical administration shows that the Curia is an instrument in the service of the sovereign pontiff and has maintained many of the characteristics of a court adapted to the principles of universal government.

Since 1968, papal functionaries, formerly separated into three categories, are divided into four: superior prelates, major officers, minor officers, and subordinate personnel. Cardinals who head dicasteries are not part of this categorization scheme. There are two classes of superior prelates: the first has thirteen members and consists exclusively of bishops, except for the secretary of the prefecture of Economic Affairs. The prefect of the PAPAL HOUSEHOLD, although a bishop, belongs to the second class, which comprises five people, including the dean of Rota, whose class is not mentioned, but who is not a bishop. There are also two classes of major officers: the first includes all the closest collaborators of the superior prelates of the first class, some of whom have been delegated power to provide signatures in certain areas. The second includes those who are in charge of a particular service and who ensure the liaison between this service and the dicastery.

The hierarchy of the minor officers is more complex. It includes four grades, each of which is divided into two classes:

— The *Minutanti* or their equivalents are included in the first grade. These include, for example, editors, research assistants, and COURT NOTARIES attached to the Papal Household. Their work is divided according to both territory and field, and therefore implies much specializations.

— In the second grade are the *Adetti* or their equivalents: archivists, administrative attachés, and statistical data processors.

— In the third grade, there are personnel responsible for questions of etiquette, shipping clerks, distributors, etc.

— The subordinate level is divided into three grades: office clerks; orderlies, messengers, and or ushers; and auxiliary personnel. Their duties range from processing the mail to guarding the facilities.

The General Regulations of the Roman Curia establishes a hierarchy that allows certain exceptions. These include the Apostolic Signature, the ROTA Romana, also the Prefecture of Economic Affairs, and the Administration of Patrimony. There are also the Palatine administrations that are administered autonomously: the Fabric of the basilica of St. Peter; the Vatican Library and Vatican Archives; the Printing Office and Vatican Bookstore; and the newspaper *Osservatore Romano*. On the other hand, the Curia regulations do apply to the Secretary of State and diplomatic corps.

Access to a position in the pontifical administration is subject to rigorous requirements. The Regulations say nothing about higher prelates and, a fortiori, about the cardinal-deacons heads of dicasteries who are selected at the pope's discretion. Neither do the Regulations say anything about the representatives of the Holy See and the auditors of the Rota Romana all of whom are pre-selected on the basis their training and degrees in academic and administrative subjects. The Regulations specifically concern the papal functionaries who are major officers and those underneath them in the hierarchy. These are selected from different countries based on criteria of competency and pastoral experience. If the merits of competing candidates are equal, the recommendation of the episcopal conferences is a deciding factor. This means that in certain countries a collective procedure predetermines the number of candidates that serve the Holy See. Yet, this system allows for the recommendation of candidates, a principle that in earlier times was strongly contested.

The recruitment of minor officers proceeds according to strict criteria. The candidate must be between 24 and 35 years old and in good physical condition, free of military duties or legal encumbrances. His religious moral, and civic standing must be attested to by a bishop or a parish priest if he is a layperson, or, if he is a priest, he must have been granted the *"Nihil obstat"* from the bishop of the diocese where he was ordained. Certain specific diplomas are also required and, if necessary, competitive examinations. The competition, which was mandatory under Pope Pius X's reform of the Curia in 1908, is now optional. The Regulations limit themselves to providing details about the required diplomas. Candidates must hold a doctorate in theology or canon law, or an equivalent university degree. They must know Latin and two modern languages, including Italian. The Adetti must have a doctorate or an archivist's diploma from the Vatican School of Archives whenever possible, as well as a degree in accounting or a technical diploma, according to the functions they will exercise. The Scrittori must have a diploma in secretarial skills, typing, or stenography. Subordinate-level personnel must have a certificate of studies. The competitive examination has been replaced by a probation period of one or two years for minor officers and subordinate personnel. At the end of this period, a nomination is made. Whereas the higher prelates and major officers are designated by the pope, the minor officers are designated by the Cardinal prefect following the consent of the administration of Patrimony and the pope's approval. This approval is not necessary for the admission of subordinate personnel. In the case of a vacancy a promotion will take place based on the sole criterion of "objective capacity" and from a given class and grade to those immediately above. It is possible to transfer from one dicaster to another with the consent of the prefect cardinals concerned.

Papal functionaries can take advantage of leaves of absence for illness or family reasons. They can resign by writing to the prefect cardinal. The age of retirement is set at the age of 74 years for higher prelates, 70 for major and minor officers, and 65 for subordinate personnel. They receive a monthly salary based on a biannual system (increased by 2 percent every two years since 1980) and on a sliding scale calculated according to the cost of living index for the city of Rome. A policy dating from 2 April 1985 divides the salaries of the personnel employed by the Administration of Patrimony into ten levels based on an index ranging from 100 to 161 and corresponding to a sum ranging from 1,056,000 to 1,700,000 lira, calculated on the basis of thirteen monthly payments. The increase set by the application of the biennial regime was between 24,700 and 39,767 lira. Lay employees receive family allowances and merit based scholarships for those of their children who qualify for a university education. Papal functionaries also receive a pension at retirement, calculated according to Italian law. These benefits include a direct pension (80 percent of the last salary earned) plus a severance payment (equal to the last gross annual salary multiplied by the number of years of service). For those who have not served a sufficient number of years, there is a retirement benefit representing the last gross annual salary increased by one-twelfth for each year of service, and completed by a severance payment equal to 51 percent of the last gross salary multiplied by the number of years of service. There is also a pension for the family of a deceased functionary and a special pension for employees of the Holy See who become disabled while in service.

Papal functionaries also benefit from many social services, especially public health services, for which they are automatically eligible. In addition, there are economic advantages, such as a tax exemption for practically all consumer goods as well as material benefits, such as housing for certain functionaries. In exchange, they are required to adhere to certain obligations, whose breach leads to sanctions.

The papal administration had a bad reputation in the nineteenth century. It was said that Pope Pius IX is said to have made the following remark to a doctor who was complaining about his rebellious son, a lazy student who only cared about hunting: "I see. So, you think he'd be a good candidate for our administration." Since the reform of the Roman Curia in 1908, the administration has been constantly improving. However, there are fewer and fewer candidates who wish serve the Holy See as minor officers and subordinate personnel.

Philippe Levillain

Bibliography

Bachelet, V. "L'organisation administrative du Saint-Siège et de la Cité du Vatican," *Revue internationale des sciences administratives*, 2, 1955.

Cardia, C. *Il governo della Chiesa*, Bologna, 1984.

Del Rè, N. *La Curia romana. Lineamenti storico-giuridici*, 23, Rome, 1970.

Delgado, G. *La Curia romana. El gobierno central de la Iglesia*, Pamplona, 1973.

Domestici-Met, M. J. "La Cité du Vatican," *L'Aministration des grandes villes dans le monde*, Paris, 1986.

D'Onorio, J. B. "L'administration pontificale," *Annuaire européen d'administration publique*, Paris, 1982.

D'Onorio. J. B. *Le Pape et le gouvernement de l'Eglise*, Paris, 1992.

Martin, V. *Les Cardinaux et la Curie. Tribunaux et offices. La vacance du Siège apostolique*, Paris, 1931.

ADMINISTRATIVE OFFICES, ROMAN. The DICASTERIES of the Roman CURIA, which have an administrative role with decision-making powers, are known as its offices (*officia*). The curial reform of 1967 listed six, of which only three remained under that heading in the reform of 1988: the APOSTOLIC CAMERA, the Administration of the Patrimony of the Apostolic See, and the Prefecture for the Economic Affairs of the Holy See. To these, however, should be added two other papal institutions that are called offices although they are not dicasteries: the Office for the Liturgical Celebrations of the Supreme Pontiff and the Central Labor Office.

Apostolic Camera. Together with the old Apostolic CHANCERY, this is one of the most ancient agencies of papal government, dating from the 11th century, when BENEDICT VIII entrusted it with the administration of the movable and immovable properties of the Holy See (constitution *Quoties illa a Nobis*, 1017). Before that time, it existed in the embryonic form of an office called a *palatium* or *fiscus*, recalling the Latin period when the emperor's treasury, and then, by extension, the place where it was kept, was known by the term *camera*. Later, the term would be applied to the administrative and financial services of the Church, whence is derived the title of their administrator, who, at the end of the 11th century, succeeded to the archdeacon of the Roman Church: *camerarius* (though the name first appears in an official document only in 1159), that is, the camerlengo, a person of high rank, usually a bishop or archbishop, or even a cardinal. He was treasurer to the pope and kept his accounts in the *Liber censuum Ecclesiae romanae*, begun by cardinal Cencio Savelli (the future HONORIUS III), who was camerlengo from 1188 to 1198. The Apostolic Camera would become the most important organ of the Curia, providing the financing of the papal COURT and of the whole curial staff. Its powers extended to the temporal affairs of the PAPAL STATES. In the 14th century, its duties were expanded by URBAN V (constitution *Apostolatus officium*, 1363) and URBAN VI (constitution *Apostolicae camerae*, 1379) to cover all judicial matters relating to the administrative and financial rights and interests of Rome and the Papal States. GREGORY X had decided that the powers of the camerlengo of the Holy Roman Church would remain intact when the papal throne was left vacant (constitution *Ubi periculum*, 1274), an arrangement that has been confirmed by all his successors up to the present.

To assist him in his task, the camerlengo had two principal collaborators: the vice-camerlengo and the auditor general. The first had universal civil juridical authority and was aided by one lieutenant responsible for civil affairs and several others responsible for criminal affairs. From the 15th century, the vice-camerlengo usually combined his function with that of the governor of Rome, with increased responsibilities in the area of criminal investigations and public safety (constitution *Etsi pro cunctarum*, 1587, and *In sublimi beati*, 1587). The auditor general of cases of the Apostolic Camera headed the tribunal established within that institution to hear all cases concerning offenses of a fiscal or financial nature, regardless of the nobiliary or ecclesiastical rank of the parties (cardinals, patriarchs, and ambassadors were included), following the dispositons of INNOCENT VIII (constitution *Apprime ad devotionis*, 1485). As it reached the saturation point, this jurisdiction, known by its initials simply as the tribunal of the A.C. (*Auditor Camerae*), was coupled with the tribunal of the "A.C. met" (*Auditor Camerae semet*) which, as the Latin name indicates, was presided over by the auditor general himself, though in reality he was replaced by his deputy, the two of them constituting, as it were, one and the same legal person. Sentences tried in this first court could be appealed before the camerlengo himself, and then, from the second third of the 15th century, before the plenary chamber, which would sit as often as three times a week. This tribunal was not abolished until 1847 when PIUS IX combined it with the tribunal of the government of the Papal States and put the auditor general in charge of the ministry of Justice. The treasurer general of the Apostolic Camera also was a person of prominence: with his vice-treasurer he was given a sizable corps of collectors and under-collectors who supervised itinerant tax collectors throughout the Catholic world. In the mid-18th century, the treasurer general was even, at one time, superintendent of pontifical customs, administrator of CASTEL SANT'ANGELO, and general commissioner of the sea. Under ALEXANDER VI, the 12 clerks of the chamber (*clerici Camerae*) were made governors of several cities in the Papal States (constitution *Etsi ex pastoralis*, 1502), and under LEO X they carried out yearly inspections of all the lands of the States (constitution *Licet felicis*, 1517). Over the years they came to preside over streets, banks, prisons, customs and COINS, supplies, etc. Other prominent positions in the Apostolic Camera were those of procurator and counsel of the treasury, the counsel of the poor, and, in the 17th century, the general commissioner of the Apostolic Camera for the defense of the fiscal administration.

The cardinal camerlengo also had authority over the pontifical mint (*Zeeca*), and in addition took up the post of chancellor of the Pontifical University of La Sapienza. His annual salary, amounting to some 12,000 to 14,000 crowns in the 17th and 18th centuries, reflected the importance of his functions. The office occupied by the institution, in the vast Montecitorio Palace (now the Italian Chamber of Deputies), was an unmistakable sign of its eminent place in the pontifical bureaucracy.

The 19th century brought a profound change in the functions of the Apostolic Camera. First, PIUS VII in 1816 and 1817, and then LEO XII in 1824 and 1828, reduced its powers; then GREGORY XVI in 1834 limited its judiciary tasks to fiscal affairs. Later, the dicastery saw its internal services broken up into numerous ministries. In 1847, Pius IX made the camerlengo minister of commerce, industry, agriculture, and fine arts, all at once; he made the vice-camerlengo, minister of police; the auditor general, minister of grace and justice (all three henceforth shed their judiciary duties); and a clerk of the chamber, minister of the armies. In the following year, however, these temporal responsibilities were handed over to laymen. The fall of Rome in 1870 marked the decline of the Apostolic Camera. Its clerks were reclassified by LEO XIII into a college of prelates attached to the Congregation of the Council and set up for the examination of the quinquennial reports of diocesan bishops under the name of congregation *super statu Ecclesiarum*. PIUS X retained the Apostolic Camera, but under his papacy its powers were considerably weakened, being confined to the period when the papal see was vacant (apostolic constitution *Sapienti consilio*, 1908), a development that would be confirmed by PAUL VI (apostolic constitution *Regimini Ecclesiae universae*, 1967) and later by JOHN PAUL II (apostolic constitution *Pastor bonus*, 1988). The latter, renewing tradition, has stressed the economic responsibilities of this dicastery by recalling that, during the *sede vacante*, the cardinal camerlengo of the Holy Roman Church has "the right and the duty" to require all the administrations of the Holy See to produce a report on their patrimonial and financial situation, and to arrange for the Prefecture for the Economic Affairs of the Holy see to communicate to him the statement of expenses for the preceding year and the provisional budget for the next. This explains the presence, along with the vice-camerlengo and that of the auditor general, of a prelate who still bears the title of general treasurer of the Apostolic Camera. Once they have been studied, the documents are submitted to the college of cardinals.

The college of cardinals, not the Apostolic Camera, is charged with the temporary government of the Church upon the death of the pope, according to the prescriptions of the apostolic constitution of John Paul II *Universi dominici gregis* of 1996. That is why, when this circumstance arises, the camerlengo is aided in his task by three other cardinals, called "assistants" (representing the three orders of cardinal bishops, priests, and deacons); above all, he must obtain the express approval of the college of cardinals in important affairs and at least its a priori agreement even in secondary matters. His function is thus at once personal and collegial. His authority is symbolized by the golden ferula, received from the pope upon his nomination; this little baton of authority is carried only during the interregnum and only in the solemn processions in which the cardinals wear their liturgical vestments.

The cardinal camerlengo has canonical authority to verify the death of the pope, of which he must furnish a written report. In olden times, ritual demanded that he tap three times with a small silver mallet on the deceased pope's forehead, calling him by his Christian name, and then make the official proclamation: *Papa vere mortuus est!* Next, the camerlengo announces the pope's death to the cardinal vicar of Rome, who immediately communicates the news to the general population. Then the camerlengo breaks the pontifical seal (*anulus Piscatoris*) and takes possession of the three palaces, of the Vatican, of St. John Lateran, and of Castel Gandolfo, which he hands over to the prelates of the Apostolic Camera for safekeeping. Together with the college of cardinals, he organizes the funeral ceremony, and with the cardinal dean, he sees to preparations for the CONCLAVE. Sometimes powers are delegated to the camerlengo *sede plena*, as they were by John Paul II during his first two notable travels in Mexico and Poland during the first half of 1979.

The cardinal camerlengo of the Holy Roman Church: Cencio Savelli (Honorius III, 1188–98), Ottavio Conti (1198–1213), Stefano da Ceccano (1213–1227), Guglielmo di San Lorenzo (?–?), Tommaso de Ocra (1294–8), Teodorico Ranieri (1298–1305), Arnaldo (Frangier) de Cantalupo (1305–7), Bertrand de Bordis (1307–11), Arnauld d'Aux (1311–19), Guasbert de la Val (1319–47), Stefano Aldebrandi Cambaruti (1347–60), Arnaud Aubert (1361–71), Pierre Gros (1371–83), François de Conzif (1383–1431), Francesco Condulmaro (1432–9), Ludovico Scarampi (1440–65), Latino Orsini (1471–7), Guillaume d'Estouteville (1477–83), Raffaele Riario (1483–1521), Innocenzo Cibo (1521), Francesco Armellini de' Medici (1521–8), Agostino Spinola (1528–37), Guido Ascanio Sforza (1537–64), Vitellozzo Vitelli (1564–8), Michele Bonelli (1568–70), Luigi Cornaro (1570–84), Filippo Guastavillani (1584–87), Enrico Caetani (1587–99), Pietro Aldobrandini (1599–1621), Ludovico Ludovisi (1621–3), Ippolito Aldobrandini (1623–38), Antonio Barberini Jr. (1638–71), [pro-camerlengos: Federico Sforza (1645–6) and Lorenzo Raggi (1650–3)], Paluzzo Altieri (1671–98), Giambattista Spinola (1698–1719), Annibale Albani (1719–47), Silvio Valenti Gonzaga (1747–56), Girolamo Colonna (1756–63), Carlo Rezzonico (1763–99), Romualdo Braschi Onesti (1800–2), Bartolemeo Pacca (1814–24), Pier Francesco Galleffi (1824–37), Giacomo Giustiniani (1837–1843), Tommaso Riario Sforza (1843–57), Ludovico Altieri (1857–67), Filippo de Angelis (1867–77), Gioacchino Pecci (Leo XIII, 1877–8), Camillo di Pietro (1878–84), Domenico Consolini (1884), Luigi Oreglia di Santo Stefano (1885–1913), Francesco Salesio Della Volpe (1914–16), Pietro Gasparri (1916–34), Eugenio Pacelli (Pius XII, 1935–39), Lorenzo Lauri (1939–41), Benedetto Aloisi Masella (1958–69), Jean Villot (1969–79), Paolo Bertoli (1979–85), Sebastiano Baggio (1985–93), Eduardo Martínez Somalo (1993–).

Administration of the Patrimony of the Apostolic See. On 15 May 1878, Leo XIII created a consultative commission of cardinals to manage the pontifical patrimony. But the following 9 August he decided to replace it with a more efficient body, the Administration of the Property of the Holy See, directed by Cardinal Lorenzo Nina, who took up the position of secretary of state on the same day. In 1880, however, the pope abolished this office and entrusted the responsibility for movable assets to the Prefect of the Sacred Apostolic Palaces and that for real estate to the Office of the Obole. In 1882, another cardinals' commission, presided over by the secretary of state, was appointed in charge of the assets of the Holy See and Peter's Pence, an annual offering of the Catholic faithful to provide for the needs of the central government of the Church. After Cardinal Merry Del Val, secretary of state to Pius X, had stabilized the Vatican finances, PIUS XI expanded the responsibilities of the Administration of Property to cover the budgets of the dicasteries, except for the Holy Office and the Propagation of the Faith (motu proprio *Provida cura*, 1926). The conclusion of the LATERAN PACTS of 1929 led to the creation of the Special Administration of the Holy See; its task was to manage the 1.75 million lire (in cash and treasury bonds) paid out by Italy as compensation for the pillages of 1870.

In 1967, PAUL VI combined the Administration of Property and the Special Administration into one office, the Administration of the Patrimony of the Apostolic See, which was put under the control of the new Prefecture for the Economic Affairs of the Holy See.

This office, which was headed by the cardinal secretary of state until 1979, consists of two sections. The Ordinary Section is responsible for remunerating the papal staff and keeps the accounts of all the dicasteries (except the Congregation for the Evangelization of Peoples, which is still financially autonomous). The Extraordinary Section took over the duties of the former Special Administration for the Management of Italian Indemnities of 1929; consisting of a dozen offices (secretariat and treasury, accounting, real estate, personnel, verification, cashier, archives, information center, technical and legal offices), it also serves as a central bank.

Since 1979, the Holy See has published a detailed annual budget which, beginning in 1984, has made a distinction between the profit accounts of the Vatican State (deriving mainly from tourists and pilgrims through the sale of POSTAGE STAMPS, MEDALLIONS, and MUSEUM entry tickets) and the largely debit accounts of the Roman Curia and the other institutions connected to it. This chronic deficit comes from the remuneration of 2,300 active employees and 900 retired personnel, the cost of the VATICAN RADIO, which is constantly being modernized, the Vatican periodicals and printing press, the costs of the production and distribution of an ever-growing number of documents arising from extensive preliminary consultations and the financing of numerous meetings (dicastery meetings, sessions of the SYNOD OF BISHOPS, the consistories of cardinals, etc.); the maintenance of the hundred-odd existing NUNCIATURES and the opening of new ones in Eastern Europe; the payment of Italian payroll tax; aid to Third World dioceses, and so on. To that should be added a portion of the expenses arising from the pope's pastoral travels, which make up part of the mission of the modern papacy. The deficit (U.S. $4 billion in 1992) has been met chiefly by Peter's Pence (U.S. $60 million in 1992) plus the contributions of dioceses, religious institutes, and foundations, but the reserve funds have had to be dipped into and part of the profits of Vatican City go to replenish the apostolic FINANCES.

A Council of Cardinals was set up by John Paul II for the study of Organizational and Economic Questions of the Apostolic See (letter *Comperta habentes*, 1981); all its fifteen members are diocesan cardinals, who come from all over the world and meet twice a year with the secretary of state to examine economic problems. The trend is toward diocesan monetary contributions, on the ground of ecclesial solidarity with the Apostolic See, which, in the spirit of ca. 1271, is the servant of the universal Church. The same holds true for the religious and secular institutes. This resolve was strengthened in April 1991, when the presidents of all the bishops' conferences held a meeting in Rome. It will be noted, however, that the budget of the Holy See is lower than that of certain large German or American dioceses and represents half of that of international organizations such as UNESCO or the Food and Agriculture Organization (FAO). Moreover, its artistic patrimony is no more convertible into cash than that of any other state.

Lastly, it may be useful to note that the Institute for the Works of Religion—which created quite a stir in the 1980s—is responsible only for the private capital entrusted to it by some twelve thousand depositors (citizens of the Vatican, Curia staff, religious institutions, charitable associations, etc.). It does not, therefore, manage the holdings of the Holy See. Created in 1887 under the name Administration of the Works of Religion, in 1942 it was granted juridical personality (corporate status) which allowed it to escape the control of the Italian fascist state. In this way, the Institute ensured safety and stability in the circulation of funds for spiritual or charitable purposes, without their being burdened with the usual taxes and rates so that they could reach the beneficiaries without any loss of value. In order to avoid fresh political-financial slipups, John Paul II has given the Institute a more rigid structure: under the control of a cardinal's commission of vigilance it has been headed since 1989 by a supervisory council of five members of the LAITY chosen from among leading international financial experts and assisted by three auditors.

The presidents of the Administration of the Patrimony of the Apostolic See: Amleto Giovanni Cicognani (1967–69), Jean Villot (1969–79), Giuseppe Caprio (1979–81), Agostino Casaroli (1981–84), Agnello Rossi (1984–89), Rosalio José Castillo Lara (1989–95), Lorenzo Antonetti (1995–8), Agostino Cassigvillan (1998–).

Prefecture for the Economic Affairs of the Holy See. Founded in 1967, during Paul VI's reform of the Roman Curia (constitution *Regimini Ecclesiae universae*), this office takes its inspiration simultaneously from the French Court of Accounts (*Cour des Comptes*), the Ministry of the Budget, and Ministry of Financial Inspection and ensures the economic control of all pontifical institutions. To this end, the prefecture examines their patrimonial and economic reports, budgets, and balance sheets, and inspects their accounts; it also gives advice on investments and supervises their growth. It presents the general balance sheet and budget of the Holy See to the supreme pontiff for his approval. Its competency extends to all pontifical property and agencies, whether in Rome or outside Rome (the Roman Curia, the nunciatures and apostolic delegations, Vicariate of Rome, the pontifical universities, the pontifical sanctuaries in Italy, etc.). Only the Institute for the Works of Religion is outside its jurisdiction, since it manages only private capital. The Prefecture works closely with the Council of Cardinals for the Study of Organizational and Economic Questions of the Apostolic See and has at its disposal a body of economic consultors and auditors.

Presidents: Angelo Dell'Acqua (1967–8), Egidio Vagnozzi (1968–80), Guiseppe Caprio (1981–1990), Edmund C. Szoka (1990–7), Sergio Sebastiani (1997).

Office for the Liturgical Celebrations of the Supreme Pontiff. This new office was created in 1988 (apostolic constitution *Pastor bonus*) when it was split from the PREFECTURE OF THE PAPAL HOUSEHOLD, of which it had been an integral but autonomous part since 1968. It has inherited the liturgical duties of the former Ceremonial Congregation the origins of which go so far back that it can hardly be dated with any accuracy. There is general agreement that it originated during the pontificate of SIXTUS V, though a *magister caeremoniarum apostolicarum* had been in existence long before that. The congregation's powers were threefold: liturgical, covering matters of worship; secular, covering the ceremonial of the papal court; and legal, concerned with settling the many conflicts of precedence between ecclesiastical and civil dignitaries. This last area has furnished a wealth of jurisprudence on pontifical protocol, in particular from the 19th century, for example on the honorary title of Assistant to the Throne, which was disputed by the Orsini and Colonna princes, or the dress of Benedictine cardinals suggested by Cardinal Pitra. In his reforms of 1908, Pius X stripped the congregation of its legal duties, leaving it confined to two areas: the sacred celebrations of the Roman pontiff or cardinals outside the papal liturgies, and the civil ceremonies of the papal court with chiefs of state and ambassadors. Accordingly, the Ceremonial Congregation directed the ritual of the dispatching of the pontifical ablegates and members of the NOBLE GUARD who brought the new cardinals, respectively, their birettas and red skullcaps. By law, the Congregation was presided over by the cardinal dean of the SACRED COLLEGE, who was its *praefectus natus* by virtue of his age and experience in curial traditions; the secretary who had the rank of apostolic PROTONOTARY *ad instar*, was invariably the prefect of pontifical ceremonies. Today, the new Office for the Liturgical Celebrations of the supreme Pontiff is headed by the master of pontifical ceremonies, assisted by several pontifical masters of ceremonies appointed by the secretary of state. The Office must plan the conduct of sacred ceremonies that take place in the presence of the pope or his representative. In 1991, it was also given responsibility for the apostolic sacristy, commonly known as the "Sistine treasure," where the TIARAS, vases, and sacred ornaments of past centuries are kept.

Labor Office of the Apostolic See. An office in charge of relations with the personnel of the Holy See was first instituted on 9 May 1971, with the function of receiving and investigating complaints put forward by pontifical employees. But its ineffectuality led John Paul II to replace it with the Labor Office of the Apostolic See, which was created on 1 January 1989 (its definitive statutes were approved on 30 September 1994, *motu proprio Le sollicitudine*). Granted a wider sphere of activity, it is now entrusted with guaranteeing the economic and social rights and responsibilities of the agents of the Holy See (clergy and laity) according to the principles of the Church's SOCIAL TEACHING. Its duties cover the whole working community of the Holy See, that is, not only the Roman Curia but also the Vatican State, Vatican Radio, and all other sectors or bodies, whether in Rome or outside Rome, directly administered by the Apostolic See. The Office is presided over by a cardinal appointed by the pope and assisted by a vice-president who is an archbishop and by two lay assessors, specialists in labor law and in personnel management, who are chosen from outside the PAPAL ADMINISTRATION. A lay general director is responsible for managing the Office together with a representative council of eighteen persons: the president; the vice-president; the two assessors; an expert appointed by the Secretariat of State; one representative each of the Government of the Vatican City State, the Congregation for the Evangelization of Peoples, the Administration of the Patrimony of the Apostolic See, the Vatican Printing Press and Publishing House, Vatican Radio, and the Fab-

ric of St. Peter's; and seven staff delegates (one for clerics, one for male religious, one for female religious, four for laypersons). A College of Conciliation and Arbitration, composed of six members, is empowered to make the final decision in the labor disputes brought before it. But the primary task of the Office is a positive one: the making use of all that concerns the status of the clergy and laity employed by the Holy See, the application of the general and particular rules governing each administrative sector, the coordination of the training and management of personnel, the improvement of their economic and social conditions, and so on.

Finally, there is the Central Statistical Office of the Church, founded by Paul VI in 1967. This annex to the SECRETARIATE OF STATE exists for the purpose of gathering and coordinating all the statistical data of universal Catholicism. It is also responsible for bringing out the *Annuario Pontifico*, a kind of administrative directory which originated in 1716 and whose 2,500-odd pages list, and give a brief biography of, all the cardinals, patriarchs, archbishops, and bishops; provide the most important figures on the dioceses and other ecclesiastical circumscriptions; describe the composition of all the agencies of the Apostolic See as well as the diplomatic legations; and list the heads of all Institutes of Consecrated Life and Societies of Apostolic Life of pontifical right; it also lists the pontifical academic institutions and so on. The Central Statistical Office also published the *Annuarium statisticum Ecclesiae*.

Joël-Benoît d'Onorio

Bibliography

Annuario pontifico per l'anno 2000, 1337–43, 1349–50, 1352, 1393–4.

Del Rè, N. *La Curia romana—Lineament storico-giuridici*, 4th ed., Rome, 1998.

d'Onorio, J. B. *Le Pape et le gouvernement de l'Église*, Paris, 1992.

Fabre, P. *Étude sur le "Liber censuum" de l'Église de Rome*, Paris, 1892.

Salerno, F. "Gli Uffici," *La Curia romana nella Const. ap. Pastor bonus*, Vatican City, 1990.

Thierry, J. J. *Les Finances du Vatican*, Paris, 1978.

ADRIAN I. See **Hadrian I**.

ADRIAN II. See **Hadrian II**.

ADRIAN III. See **Hadrian III**.

ADRIAN IV. See **Hadrian IV**.

AFRICA AND THE PAPACY. At the beginning of the 3rd century, in the western part of the empire, the papacy faced only one truly organized province: Africa. The higher authority was the bishop of CARTHAGE, primate of Africa, who called the COUNCILS. Each province had its own council called by the primate of the province, who was generally the oldest of the bishops. In Africa, the PRIMACY of Rome as the see of PETER (Matt. 16:18–19) was recognized; its authority, deriving from tradition, was not denied, but its direct jurisdiction was not supported. Africa maintained its own customs, while seeking harmony with Rome, just as St. Cyprian (bishop of Carthage, 248–58) had done with Pope CORNELIUS (251–4) in the matter of the reintegration of the *lapsi*. Frequent clashes took place among the personalities involved, as can be seen, for example, around the question of the rebaptism of heretics: the heavy-handed behavior of Pope STEPHEN ended in the excommunication of St. Cyprian. Peace was reestablished upon the accession of SIXTUS II (August 257), who renewed relations with the Church of Africa. The African custom of rebaptism was abandoned only in July 314 at the council of Arles, when Africa sought the support of the tradition represented by the papacy against the Donatist HERESY. It was on the occasion of the condemnation of Pelagianism that, on 1 May 418, the council of Carthage forbade appeals to the pope on pain of forfeiting communion with the Churches of Africa. There followed shortly thereafter, the affair of Apiarius, a priest of Sicca Veneria (El Kef), who had been excommunicated by his bishop. Though his status was only that of a priest, he appealed to Pope ZOSIMUS, who at the time favored an intervention in African affairs, Aurelius of Carthage having, in sovereign fashion, laid down the law in the question of Pelagianism. The affair was brought to a conclusion on 25 May 419 by the council of Carthage, in the presence of the pope's envoys; a synodal letter addressed to the pope reaffirmed the autonomy of the African Church. It was on this occasion that the *Codex canonum ecclesiae africanae* was assembled. At the end of 425 and the beginning of 426, Apiarius, once again excommunicated for serious offenses, made a new appeal to the pope; this entailed a new judgment before the council of Carthage, always in the presence of the papal LEGATE Faustinus. Apiarius having confessed his offenses, the matter was settled and the papal claims to local control were denounced. The appeal of bishops to Rome became an issue during the affair of Antony of Fussala, whose people had rejected him on account of his abuses. The settling of the Pelagian question and these assorted legal matters had not been successes for the policy of the papacy in Africa. Relations with Rome, interrupted during the Vandal conquest, were reestablished only in 446 with Leo I (440–61). He expressed, in a letter, a concern in the face of marked irregularities in Caesarean Mauretania in the election of bishops, along with an in-

tention to affirm his authority over the bishops concerned and in everything having to do with the organization of the Church. The Byzantine reconquest in 533 led Africa into the struggle against Justinian's condemnation of the Three Chapters (543). The African bishops mobilized to excommunicate the pope when he finally gave in to the emperor in February 554. Justinian's successor, Justin II, reestablished peace. From 591 to 596, GREGORY the Great, in his letters to African correspondents, seemed to fear a recrudescence of Donatism, against which he would even ask for the assistance of the civil authorities. His contacts allowed him to assess quickly the real importance of the so-called renewal of Donatism. He became the recourse for the Numidian bishops and the support of Dominic of Carthage. These developments once again cut Africa off from Rome. During a council in 649, four bishops, among them Victor of Carthage, expressed their communion with the pope, but were unable to send representatives to Rome. The correspondence between the popes and the primates of Carthage sheds some light on the end of Christianity in Africa; one of the last pieces of evidence, from 1076, is a letter from Prince Al-Nasir to Pope GREGORY VII asking him to consecrate a bishop for Sétif.

Liliane Ennabli

Bibliography

Conciliae Africae (A.345–A. 525), CC, s.l., CXLIX, Turnholt, 1974.

Gaudemet, J. *L'Église dans l'Empire romain* (IVe-Ve siècle), Paris, 1958, 408–51.

Lancel, S. "Africa," §B, *Augustinus Lexikon*, 1, one solidus two (1986), 205–16.

Lepelley, C. "Saint Léon le Grand et l'Eglise maurétanienne, primauté romaine et autonomie africaine au Ve siècle," *Les Cahiers de Tunisie* (1967), 189–204.

Pietri, C. Roma Christiana (2 vols.), Rome, 1976, 1151–1275.

Schnidler, A. "Afrika" I, TRE, 1 (1977), 640–700.
Prosopographie chrétienne du Bas-Empire, 1, Prosopographie de l'Afrique chrétienne (305–533), Paris, 1982.

AGAPITUS I. *(b. Rome, ?, d. Constantinople, 23 April 536). Crowned on 13 May 535. Buried at St. Peter's in Rome. Saint.*

Agapitus belonged to a Roman family of consequence that had already given the Church Pope FELIX III; his father, the priest Gordianus, of the title of SS. Giovanni e Paolo, attended the Roman COUNCILS of 487–99 and was killed in 502 during the riots against Pope SYMMACHUS. Agapitus was archdeacon of the Roman church when he was elected to succeed Pope JOHN II (died 8 May 533). From the time of his accession, he showed himself anxious for appeasement: he saw to it that the ANATHEMA BONIFACE II had exacted of the Roman priests against his rival Dioscorus was burned.

Agapitus owned a library of patristic works in Greek and Latin the dedicatory inscription of which has been preserved. In 535, with the praetorian prefect Cassiodorus, he formed the project of founding a School of Scripture studies at Rome, but the war in Italy forced him to abandon the idea. He affirmed the authority of the Apostolic See, with regard to both the local Churches and the imperial power. In Gaul, his letter of 18 July 535 revealed to Bishop Caesarius of Arles his decision to have the matter of Bishop Contumeliosus of Riez reconsidered *ab ovo*: the case was to be entrusted to new judges, and in the interim, Bishop Contumeliosus was authorized to regain his church, but without the power of exercising episcopal authority within it. At the same time, he forbade Caesarius, who had asked his permission to sell ecclesiastical goods to pay for the maintenance of the poor, to alienate any Church property; he recommended that Caesarius scrupulously observe the canons and included with his letter documentation in support of his decisions.

From Africa, recently freed from the Vandals, Agapitus I received a delegation sent by the African bishops with a letter (addressed to his predecessor JOHN II) concerning the problems posed by the Arians and by the African clerics who were going to Italy; on 9 September 535, he responded with a letter in which, after having congratulated the Church of Africa on its fidelity to the Apostolic See, he forbade any reintegration of the reconciled Arian clerics into the Catholic hierarchy, and prohibited African clerics from making their way to Italy without the necessary authorization. At the same time, he invited Bishop Reparatus of Carthage, who had congratulated him on his election, to acquaint all the metropolitans with Rome's decisions.

Soon after his accession, Agapitus I also intervened to reaffirm ecclesiastical discipline and the rights of the HOLY SEE against the encroachments of the Church of Constantinople on Illyricum. In a letter of 15 October 535 to Justinian, concerned, on the eve of the reconquest of Italy, about having the Arian clergy reintegrated into the Catholic hierarchy, Agapitus I made a very firm refusal based on the canons; and he accepted the imperial proposal to have the Roman LEGATES settle the matter—already mentioned by Pope BONIFACE II—of Bishop Stephen of Larissa, who had been deposed by Patriarch Epiphanius of Constantinople, and of Bishop Achilles, who had been ordained in his place, though he underlined that this constituted an attack on the privileges of the Holy See on the part of the Church of Constantinople. He likewise informed Justinian that the issue of the prerogatives of *Justiniana Prima*, defined by the emperor without consulting Rome, would also have to be examined by the pontifical legates. In fact, he sent five legates to the East, but soon afterward he had to travel to Constantinople himself, charged by the Ostrogothic king Theoda-

had with asking Justinian to halt his preparations to conquer Italy. Moreover, the pope received complaints, especially from the monasteries of Constantinople and Jerusalem, against Anthimus, the new patriarch of the imperial capital (consecrated in June 535), who he was denounced for having quit the see of Trebizond for that of Constantinople and accused of collusion with the Monophysites in the protection of Empress Theodora. In order to pay for his voyage, Agapitus had to borrow from Gothic financiers and even sell sacred vessels.

When he arrived in Constantinople before March 536, he was honorably received; but he failed in his diplomatic mission, since Justinian refused to stop his preparations for conquest. As far as Anthimus was concerned, the pope was intransigent. Despite pressure and threats, he refused to enter into communion with him unless Anthimus subscribed to the orthodox faith and returned to the see of Trebizond; Anthimus refused, and the pope—whom the emperor, about to go to war in Italy, thought it necessary to deal with carefully—prevailed. Anthimus surrendered the pallium, and on 13 March 536, Agapitus I (the first of the Roman pontiffs to do so) consecrated the new patriarch of Constantinople, the priest Menas; Menas subscribed to a profession of faith in accordance with Chalcedonian orthodoxy. On 16 March, Agapitus received an identical profession of faith from the emperor: for the first time, an emperor officially recognized the *Tu es Petrus* and proclaimed that the Apostolic See was custodian of the Catholic faith. Agapitus I also wrote to Patriarch Peter of Jerusalem to announce the removal from office of Anthimus, and asked for a written statement of his adherence. But Justinian, no doubt anxious to show a token favor to the Monophysites, who continued to develop their propaganda openly in Constantinople, asked Agapitus I to accept the profession of faith he had submitted to John II and that had been approved by him, containing the Theopaschite formula ("One of the Trinity suffered in the flesh"). On 18 March 536, the pope in his turn was obliged to accept this profession of faith, while emphasizing that it was not proper for laymen to intervene in matters of faith. He thus continued the excommunication against the Acoemete monks and declared imperial Christology conformable with the dogmas of the Apostolic See. Monks and bishops continued to lodge complaints against Anthimus, asking the pope to complete what he had begun by requiring an orthodox profession of faith from him, or else to name a new bishop to Trebizond. He was also asked to intervene against the partisans of Anthimus, some of whom had already been condemned by the Apostolic See, and the demand was made that he have the writings of Severus of Antioch against the *Tome* of Pope LEO and against the council of Chalcedon burned. It is possible that the pope and the emperor planned the calling of a council; but the pope, who had designated as *apocrisarius* the deacon Pelagius (the future Pelagius I), fell seriously ill, and he died on 22 April 536. After a solemn funeral in Constantinople, his body was interred in Rome on 17 September 536.

Agapitus I—temporarily—reestablished the authority of the Apostolic See over the imperial authority and succeeded, for a time, in restoring Chalcedonian orthodoxy: the council held from 2 June to 6 June 536 in Constantinople under the presidency of Menas, with the participation of the Roman legates, confirmed the sentence Agapitus I had pronounced against Anthimus along with those pronounced by Pope Hormisdas against certain leading Monophysites.

Christiane Fraisse-Coué

Bibliography

LP, I, 287–9.

Agapitus, *Epitulae, Coll. Auel*, 85–8, *CSEL*, 35, 1, 328–38.

Batiffol, L. "L'empereur Justinien et le Siège apostolique," *Cathedra Petri*, Paris, 1938, 280–6.

Coll. Auel, 91, ibid., 342–7.

Duchesne, L. *Vigile et Pélage*, extract from "Etude sur l'histoire de l'Eglise romaine au milieu du VIe siècle," *Revue des questions historiques*, 34 (1884), 10–12.

Epistula 6–7, *Coll. Arelatensis*, 55–7.

Liberatus, *Breviarum causae Nestorianorum et Eutychianorum*, 21, *ACO*, II, 5, 135–6.

Magi, M. *La sede romana nella corrispondenza degli imperatori e patriarchi Bisantini* (VIe–VIIe s.), Rome, 1972, 118–92; *Bibliothèque de RHE*, 57.

AGAPITUS II. *(b. Rome, ?, d. Rome, early December 955). Consecrated pope on 10 May 946. Buried at St. John Lateran.*

Of Roman birth, he was elected pope, like his predecessors (LEO VII, STEPHEN VIII, and MARINUS II), in accordance with the wishes of Alberic II of Spoleto (d. 954), who reigned supreme over Rome. With Alberic II, he favored monastic reform; though dependent on Alberic, he managed to impose his authority, especially north of the Alps. In his reforming measures he supported Abbot Odo of Cluny, who was active in Rome beginning in 936. Around 950, he entrusted the abbey of St. PAUL'S OUTSIDE THE WALLS to Andrew of Gorze, sent upon his request by Abbot Agenold. The importance of his intervention in the dispute over the archdiocese of Reims is worth recalling. The dispute must be situated in the context of the internal conflicts in the kingdom of France, between the Carolingian monarchy and its adversaries, Hugh the Great and Herbert II of Vermandois. Hugh, the son of Herbert II, and Artaud, a monk of St. Remy, had long contested the see of the archdiocese of Reims. In 946, King Louis IV managed to restore the archiepiscopal see to Artaud, who had already been driven from it once. Hugh, fortified by the support of Hugh the

Great, the father of Hugh Capet, refused to give up his demands. For that reason, Agapitus II sent Archbishop Robert of Trier as pontifical LEGATE to settle the matter. The negotiations ended in favor of Artaud during the SYNODS of Verdun (November 947) and Mouzon (January 948). In the meantime, the DEACON of Reims, Sigebaut, had traveled to Rome and, with the help of a letter supposedly written by the suffragan bishops of Reims, obtained from the pope a promise to demand the reinstatement of Hugh in his see. In order to bring about a definitive decision, Agapitus sent Bishop Marinus of Bomarzo as his legate. It was the first time a pontifical legate had been present at a synod in the Germanic kingdom since Hohenaltheim in 916; the synod of Ingelheim, over which he presided and which the kings Louis IV and Otto the Great attended, decided in June 948 to confer the archiepiscopal title on Artaud. A few months later, during a synod at Trier, likewise held under the presidency of the legate Marinus, Hugh the Great was excommunicated. The following year in Rome, Agapitus confirmed these decisions during a synod. After having established contact with Agapitus II—the legation of Marinus had greatly contributed to this—Otto I, king of Germania, once he had become sovereign of Italy, in 951 began negotiations for the imperial crown. But Agapitus, undoubtedly under pressure from Alberic, opposed these plans. On the other hand, the pope showed a more favorable disposition in the matter of the ecclesiastical reorganization of the northern and eastern borders of the Germanic kingdom: In January 948, he confirmed the rights of the Church of Hamburg-Bremen and placed under its authority the newly conquered territories of the Danish, the Norwegians and the Swedes, as well as all the other Nordic territories. In 955, he agreed to allow the king to create dioceses as he saw fit, but Otto's plan to make Magdeburg an archdiocese ran up against stubborn resistance on the part of Archbishop William of Mainz, whom Agapitus had recently named *vicarius* and *missus* in Gaul and Germania. At the end of August 954, while Agapitus was still alive, Alberic had the Roman NOBILITY swear to elect his son Octavian pope as soon as the pontifical seat became vacant. Agapitus died at the beginning of December in 955.

Rolf Grosse

Bibliography

LP, 2, 245.

Arnaldi, G. "Agapet II," *DBI*, 1 (1960), 367–8.

Kirsch, J. P. "Agapet II," *DHGE*, 1 (1912), 890–2.

Schwaiger, R. "Agapet II," *LexMA*, 1 (1977–80), 202.

Wolter, H. *Die Synoden im Reichsgebiet und in Reichsitalien von 916 bis 1056*, Paderborn-Munich-Vienna-Zurich, 1988, 42ff.

Zimmermann, H. *Das dunkle Jahrhundert*, Graz-Vienna-Cologne, 1971.

Zimmermann, H. *Papstregesten*, 72–98; *Papsturkunden*, 1, 191–249.

AGATHO. *(b. Sicily, ?, d. Rome, 10 January 681). Consecrated pope on 27 June 678. Buried at St. Peter's in Rome. Saint (ancient cult, in the West and in the East).*

This brief pontificate has claimed attention above all because Agatho signed the acts of the council *in Trullo* —the hall in the imperial palace in Constantinople—that marked the end of the monothelite HERESY. However, the sources throw even greater light on the institution of the papacy and show its position in the Christian world as a whole.

A monk of Eastern origin who came to Rome from Sicily, Agatho was perfectly assimilated into Roman life. His knowledge of Greek and his theological training facilitated the discussions with the patriarch of Constantinople and the emperor. In Rome itself, his position grew stronger over time. The pomp of the ceremonies, a copy of the Constantinopolitan protocol, surpassed everything done in the courts of the West and impressed the Romans as well as the foreign pilgrims. The whole ritual, which developed in a completely autonomous fashion, established itself slowly. The papal ADMINISTRATION too established its own rules and expanded its services. The management of the papal domains was slipping away from imperial control. Agatho even obtained the abolition of the payment due to the Constantinopolitan administration on the occasion of his consecration. His consecration remained subject to the confirmation of the emperor, but this was a strictly formal procedure. Strong in his autonomy, the pope for a time assumed the office of treasurer (*arcarius*) of the Church, expanded the privileges of the clergy, and set aside a considerable sum of money (30 pounds of gold) to be distributed after his death to the clergy and certain churches.

Too influential in his city for anyone to attack him as long as the LOMBARDS remained well disposed—and they had just signed a peace treaty with the emperor—the pope increased his influence in the West. Roman authority was accepted once and for all by the archbishop of RAVENNA, Theodore (677–91); his successors were to be consecrated by the pope, who would bestow the pallium on them. The whole of the Italian clergy felt solidarity with the pope. In England, the very active Theodore, archbishop of Canterbury, refused the nomination of the monk Wilfrid as bishop of York. He appealed the royal decision to the pope. Agatho confirmed the decision, no doubt because he could not do otherwise, but the king of Northumbria allowed the archbishop to leave for Rome. In addition, the pope was able to send John, priest and head of the choir at St. Peter's, on a mission to teach Roman chant to the English, and also to draw up a report on the situation of the Churches in the isle. Finally, some direct contacts between the pope and the bishops are worthy of notice: to Edictus, bishop of Vienne, he sent an account of his dealings with the emperor and requested that he have it read by all the bishops of Gaul; after the Roman COUNCIL of 680, he informed all the bishops that the decisions of the Apostolic See were to be accepted as decisions confirmed by St. Peter.

This gradual reinforcement of the papal position in the West accounts for the skill with which Agatho negotiated the abandonment of monothelitism, desired by Constantine IV as a way of bringing about religious, and therefore political, peace in the eastern part of the empire, as well as of reestablishing good relations with the pope, a governing component of his diplomacy in Italy and in the West. Agatho welcomed the proposal sent to Donus but received only after the death of the latter (12 August 678). He required only the holding of preparatory councils in all the Churches of his patriarchate. The record of those presided over by Theodore of Canterbury in Hatfield (17 September 680) and by Mansuerus of Milan has been preserved. However, the latter, who was head of the Lombard Church, sent the acts of the council, which were otherwise in conformity with the wishes of the pope, directly to the emperor. Simultaneously, the pope assembled a large council of 125 Italian bishops on 27 March 680. In his desire to gather the greatest possible number of supporters in his patriarchate and show the emperor that he was in a position of strength he sent the emperor two letters apologizing for his delay and cleverly insisting on the extent of his constituency and on the obligations of prelates, which left them little time for these questions of dogma. In the meantime, Constantine IV had replaced the monothelite patriarch Theodore with a certain George (November 579) and sent a second invitation to the pope in which he promised not to exercise control in his position as emperor and even to accept the condemnation of his predecessors.

In these conditions, the council of reconciliation could be held. The Roman delegation arrived on 10 September 680; the sessions of the sixth ecumenical council—which is also the council of Constantinople III—began on 7 November and lasted until 16 September 681. The emperor had issued the convocations, set the agenda, and handled all the material arrangements, as was customary. After the council fathers had defined the orthodox position, he promulgated their decision in the form of an edict and set forth the civil punishments that all offenders would incur. The council adopted the Roman positions on the essential matter: there were two wills in the one person of Jesus Christ. The council showed itself conciliatory in its presentation: Pope HONORIUS I was condemned as a monothelite and MARTIN I for high treason; no explicit reference was made to the Lateran council. Agatho died while the council was still going on, but the bishops, like the emperor, recognized that the reconciliation was indeed the fruit of his labor.

Jean Durliat

Bibliography

Arnaldi, G. "Agatone," *DBI*, 1 (1960), 373–6.
Bede, *HE*, 4, 18; 5, 19.

Bertolini, O. *Roma di fronte a Bisanzio e ai Longobardi*, Bologna, 1971, 377–83.

[ALBERT] (ADALBERT). *Antipope (February 1101).*

After the capture and the condemnation of the ANTIPOPE THEODERIC, and almost immediately after his death in 1101, his partisans elected as his successor the cardinal bishop Albert of Silva Candida (Sta Rufina). Named and consecrated bishop around 1084, probably by CLEMENT III (Guilbert of Ravenna), he was among the principal CARDINALS of the ANTIPOPE. Immediately after his election, disturbancs broke out in Rome. Albert took refuge in the house of one of his partisans near the basilica of S. Marcello. Facing a rough struggle, his protector John, son of Ocdolinde, allowed himself to be corrupted and handed Albert over to PASCHAL II. Albert was subjected to the public humiliation of being led to Paschal II at the Lateran and condemned to spend the rest of his days in detention in the monastery of S. Lorenzo of Aversa (north of Naples, in territory ruled by the Normans). We know nothing else about him.

Georg Schwaiger

Bibliography

Mollat, G. "Albert," *DHGE*, 1 (1912), 1435–6.
Servatius, C. *Paschalis II*, Stuttgart, 1979, 69–72, 339–40.
Tellenbach, G. *Die westliche Kirche vom 10 bis zum frühen 12. Jahrhundert*, Göttingen, 1988, 201–8.

ALEXANDER I. *(b. Rome ?–d. Rome, 115 or 118). Elected pope in 105 or 108. Saint.*

Most of Peter's early successors are only names to us today. This is true of Alexander I, who, according to Evaristus (see Irénée, *Contre les hérésies*, III, 3, 3), was the head of the Roman Church from 105 or 108 to 115 or 118 (see Eusebius, *Histoire ecclésiastique*, IV, 1; *Chronique*, ed. Helm, 195). All of the texts bearing the name Alexander I are apocryphal.

Jean-Marie Salamito

Bibliography

LP, 1, 127.
Testini, P. *Archeologia cristiana*, 2nd ed., Bari, 1980, 249–50 and bibliography, 806.

ALEXANDER II. *Anselm of Baggio (b. Milan, ca. 1010–1015–d. Rome, 21 April 1073). Elected pope in Rome on 30 September 1061; consecrated at St. Peter in Chains on 30 September–1 October 1061. Buried at St. John Lateran.)*

Son of Arderico of Baggio, of high *Capitanale* aristocracy, Anselm was the first Milanese to occupy the seat of St. Peter. From his early youth, he was a member of the Ambrosian Church and received his training at the cathedral school of Milan. He maintained close ties with Lanfranc of Bec, the "father of scholastics," originally from Pavia, but did not attend his school in Normandy, as is often contended. Likewise, Anselm never belonged to the German Palatine Church. On the other hand, he did in fact owe his diocese in Lucca to Henry III, who was still alive at the time (d. 1056), and to Godfrey of Bouillon of Lorraine-Tuscany, who was present during his nomination. The diocese was granted to Anselm in 1056 at Spire, and he kept it even after he was elected pope. In Lucca, he advocated reform of the clergy by encouraging communal life (*vita communis*) and the veneration of the saints. He also undertook the reconstruction of St. Martin's Cathedral and took care of the reorganization and exploitation of episcopal land. In close contact with the Roman Church reform group, he was sent on several missions as a legate. He went with Hildebrand, later GREGORY VII, on a mission to the court of Empress Agnes, and accompanied Pierre Damian to Milan to calm the struggle opposing Archbishop Gui and the popular revolutionary movement "Pataria," of which Alexander II has been falsely designated as the founder. In addition, he went on his own on a mission to the Germanic court.

Conflicts with the imperial government had cast a shadow over the end of NICHOLAS II's pontificate. So, after Nicholas's death, someone well known and well respected in the German court, someone capable of settling the conflict—in other words, someone like Anselm of Lucca—appeared to the Roman archdeacon Hildebrand and his entourage to be the ideal successor to St. Peter's throne. Nevertheless, contrary to the decree of 1059 on pontifical elections, the German court's assent was not requested. In Rome, the opposition movements made Alexander II's coronation impossible to hold in ST. PETER's basilica. Thus, at nightfall, the new pope was crowned in another church dedicated to St. Peter, St. Peter in Chains. Representatives of the aristocratic Roman faction went to the court of the young Henry IV, to whom they gave the insignias patrice of the Romans, and along with a few Lombard bishops, they "asked" for a pope according to their wishes. Now, the bishop, Cadalus of Parma, the antipope elected in Basel on 28 October 1061, who had taken the name HONORIUS II, received insufficient support from the groups who had contributed to his proclamation when he had to impose his authority. As for Alexander II, he had the support of the Normans in southern Italy, as well as that of Godfrey of Lorraine-Tuscany and his wife Beatrice, who offered him their protection in Lucca until the issue of the schism had dissipated.

At the instigation of Peter Damian, Archbishop Anno II of Cologne, chancellor of the Empire, convened the Council of Mantua in 1064 to end the schism. Alexander II swore to his innocence and managed to dispel the accusations of simony that had been made against him. On the other side, Cadalus refused to participate because he had not been given the presidency of the synod, which finally fell to Alexander, recognized as the legitimate pope by the episcopate of the Empire.

The archdeacon Hildebrand was certainly the dominant personality in this pontificate, a fact of which his contemporaries were quite aware. Peter Damian, in one of his spirited epigrams, designated him the "lord of his highness the pope" (*plus domino papae quam domno pareo papae*). Alexander II's personality only became manifest on rare occasions. He reorganized religious life, following in the steps of Nicholas II. During his first Lateran synod in 1063, he reiterated the validity of the reform canons promulgated by his predecessor. Furthermore, discussions about bishops accused of simony, lust, or other infractions to religious discipline in general, constituted a recurrent theme in his synods. The main objective of the Lateran synods, held regularly in the spring, was to arbitrate conflicts arising in the French dioceses or disciplinary cases submitted by the Italian and German churches. Among the disputes opposing bishops and monasteries were Nantes and Déols, Mâcon and the Abbot of Cluny, Nîmes and St. Gilles, Paris and St. Denis, Amiens and the Abbot of Corbie. There were also bishops who were suspended or deposed, such as the bishops of Saintes, Amiens, and Orléans. Thus, the pontifical synods, with participants from all nations, constituted the supreme decision-making authority unanimously recognized within the Western Church. A new fact, the alliance between the papacy and the Normans of southern Italy, allowed measures of coercion and sanctions to be exacted against the bishops of this region, until then allied with BYZANTIUM, when they did not concur with the ideals of the reform. As a result, the archbishop of Trani was deposed in 1063. In 1067, during the pontifical synods of Siponte, Melfi, and Salerno, other bishops were called upon to come and defend themselves, and they were replaced with partisans of the Roman Church. Thanks to Abbot Didier of Monte Cassino (later VICTOR III), the Roman Church was able to extend its influence and ecclesiastical hierarchy to the south of the peninsula. Pontifical LEGATES were sent to France and, for the first time, to Spain as well. Among these was Cardinal Hugo Candidus, who played an ambiguous role between the parties. As for Spain, Alexander II's pontificate stands out for having succeeded in winning over the Mozarabic Church to the ROMAN LITURGY. In 1068, King Sanchez I, Ramirez of Aragon, went to the tombs of the apostles and entrusted his kingdom to the pope. The future of the idea of the CRUSADES was greatly advanced by the granting of the first INDULGENCE in 1063 to crusaders, especially the French participants in the "reconquest" of Spain. Thus, military virtues involved in a just war led for the defense and diffusion of the Christian faith and obedience to Rome were encouraged, utilized, and rewarded by the papacy. With the same intentions, the *vexillum sancti Petri* (St. Peter's flag) was bestowed upon military commanders in Spain and Campania; upon Erlembaldo, chief of the Pataria and "the first knightly saint in the history of the world" (C. Erdmann); and finally, in 1066, upon Duke William of Normandy when he departed for the conquest of England. It is difficult to say whether the flag was only a symbol of holy war or whether it also signified royal investiture and the constitution of a feudal tie. The oath that archbishop Guibert of Ravena had to swear to the pope in 1073—which then served as a model for all the oaths required of bishops, abbots, and functionaries of the CURIA by future popes—undeniably assumed feudal language. This proves the degree to which the feudal spirit had pervaded the Curia.

As opposed to the preceding pontificates characterized by their brevity and political fragility, Alexander II's reign was relatively long and allowed him to consolidate the reforms of his papacy. As he had done in Lucca, Alexander also attempted in the Lateran to win over a group of clerics to the cause of reform. During his regular visits to Lucca, he employed *scriniaires* from Lucca and also brought them to Rome. During this time of peace, he began to put the affairs of the Sacrum Palatium in order. A register for the letters was kept again, something that had been impossible during troubled times. However, the register must have disappeared in the 13th century with other collections in the VATICAN ARCHIVES. Today, the only traces of Alexander's register are in the records of people who used it.

Rome's relations with the German court remained strained, and some clergymen were called to Rome to respond to accusations of simony or relations with excommunicated persons. Among these were Anno of Cologne, upon whom penance was imposed. Peter Damian put an end to Henry IV's plans to separate from his wife Bertha of Turin by threatening that the future imperial coronation might be refused. The latent conflict became more pronounced upon the death of Archbishop Gui of Milan (1071). The king wanted to impose his candidate Godfrey on the Milanese, yet the Patarins, with the approval of a papal legate, elected the Milanese cleric Atto. Atto had to escape to Rome, where he was recognized archbishop by Alexander II. When Henry IV did not heed the pope's warnings inciting him to change his position in the Milanese schism, Alexander excommunicated five of the king's counselors during his last synod, held during Lent in 1073. This event was probably instigated by Empress Agnes, who had returned to Italy intent on dedicating herself to religious reform, faithful to her religious convictions and under the spiritual guidance of Peter Damian (d. 1072). She also wanted to distance her son from the influence of counselors she disliked. Alexander II died a short time later, and his successor Gregory VII had the task of dealing with the problem of investitures.

It would be false to define Alexander II's pontificate as a preliminary phase in the battle over investitures. On the contrary, the exigencies of reform were imposed gradually in a calm atmosphere. Alexander II did not favor radical ideas, which, in the disputes opposing an episcopate attached to tradition, communities of clerks and monks imbued with a new kind of piety and popular movements were a source of conflict. Faithful to his original training, he was more on the side of his episcopal brothers. For this pope devoted to reforming the Church, a sense of balance when faced with extremist demands and opinions best guaranteed the reformist ideal.

Tilmann Schmidt

Bibliography

Calderoni Masetti, A. R. "Anselmo da Baggio e la cattedrale di Lucca," *Annali della Scuola Normale Superiore di Pisa*, ser. III, 7 (1977), 91–116.

Keller, H. *Adelsherrschaft und städtische Gesellschaft in Oberitalien*, Tübingen, 1979 (*Bibliothek des Deutschen Historischen Instituts in Rom*, 52).

Schmale, F. J. "Synoden Papst Alexanders II" (1061–73): Anzahl, Termine, Entscheidungen," *Annuarium historiae conciliorum*, 11 (1979), 307–38.

Schmidt, T. *Alexander II. (1061–1073) und die römische Reformgruppe seiner Zeit*, Stuttgart, 1977 (*Päpste und Papsttum*, 11).

Schwaiger, G. "Alexander II," *LexMA*, 1 (1977–80), 371–2.

Schwarzmaier, H. "Alexander II," *Theologische Realenzyklopädie*, 2 (1978), 235–7.

Siegwart, J. "Die Pataria des 11. Jahrhunderts und der hl. Nikolaus von Patara," *Zeitschrift für schweizerische Kirchengeschichte*, 71 (1977), 30–92.

Violante, C. "Alessandro II," *DBI*, 2 (1960), 176–83.

ALEXANDER III. *Orlando (Roland) Bandinelli (b. Siena, ca. 1005–d. 30 August 1181). Elected pope 7 September 1159; consecrated in Nympha on 20 September 1159. Buried at St. John Lateran (Francesco Borromini monument commissioned by Alexander VII).*

An important pope of the medieval period, Alexander III's pontificate was part of a major series of popes that began with GREGORY VII and ended with INNOCENT III. His reign corresponded to the first phase of the battle between the priesthood and the Empire. During this period, the Church worked on developing legislation to reinforce its centralization.

Orlando Bandinelli was born into an affluent family in Siena. Entering the priesthood, he undertook serious theological studies, which gave him a profound knowledge of the masters of his time, Hugo of St. Victor and Peter Abelard. Bandinelli studied CANON LAW attentively, and his professor at the School of Bologna was no doubt the celebrated Gratian, author of the *DECRETUM*. Around 1140, Bandinelli taught law at Bologna before becoming canon of the cathedral church of Pisa and professor of the episcopal school of the city. There he wrote two works: a treatise on theology, *Sentences*, and a commentary on the *Decretum, Summa*, which ranked him among the top intellectuals of the day. The second work immediately made him more famous than the first.

Apparently, it was Bandinelli's celebrity that led to his being called into the service of Pope EUGENIUS III at the end of 1148. Eugenius III made him CARDINAL deacon of Sts. Cosmas and Damian in 1150, cardinal priest of St. Mark's in 1151, and finally on 16 May 1153, CHANCELLOR of the Roman Church, the highest office of the CURIA. Bandinelli continued to occupy this post during the pontificates of ANASTASIUS IV (1154) and HADRIAN IV (1154–1159). During Hadrian's tenure, Bandinelli became one of the most respected advisers within the SACRED COLLEGE and a leader of the anti-German, pro-Sicilian party.

The German-Sicilian division was due to upheavals occurring in the Italian territories. When Frederick I Barbarossa ascended to the German throne, giving him the right to the imperial crown (1152), he proclaimed his intention of reviving the "splendor" of the Empire. In other words, he planned to take control again of the German episcopate by interpreting the clauses of the CONCORDAT OF WORMS (1122) to his advantage and to reinstate his authority over the kingdom of Italy, indeed, over the entire peninsula. Despite his uneasiness with the arrangement, Eugenius III had chosen to collaborate. Frederick I and the pope agreed to the treaty of Constance (1153), which allowed the prince to be crowned emperor in June 1155. The agreement did not, however, provide the Holy See with the assistance expected, and the imperial power began to bear down heavily on Lombardy and the neighboring countries. In this situation of fear, Hadrian IV, having been forced to deal with the king of Sicily, William I (1156), and to finally settle the problems that had long troubled the papacy's relations with him, formed a group of cardinals ready oppose Germanic enterprises and to find support for this effort in the southern kingdom. Chancellor Bandinelli was the head of this group. In October 1157, sent as a legate to Frederick, who was then staying in Besançon, Bandinelli provoked a volatile incident with another legate by asking from whom the monarch held the Empire if it was not from the pope. In the following months, he worked on strengthening ties with William I and close relations with Milan and other anti-imperial cities. He thus proved himself to be a courageous and clear-sighted man of action, because imperial control over Italy would have led to the end of the Roman Church's freedom of action.

After the death of Hadrian IV on 1 September 1159, the cardinals met at St. Peter's on 7 September. The city was in a state of unrest created by the agents of Frederick I Barbarossa in an attempt to put pressure on the cardinals. In such an atmosphere, the election was dramatic indeed. Bandinelli received the most votes (24, according to his supporters, obtained after several rounds of voting). Cardinal Octavian of Monticelli, chief of the pro-German clan, received only a few votes (perhaps 8 or 9 in the beginning and 3 at the end). A few days later, Bandinelli was consecrated at Ninfa, taking the name Alexander III. His adversary did the same on 4 October and took the name VICTOR IV (V). This double election and the schism within Christianity that resulted from it dominated the history of the pontificate. In fact, almost right away the emperor convened a council under his own authority that met in Pavia in February 1160. This council was comprised mostly of German bishops and some Italian prelates, and its final act proclaimed Victor's legitimacy and condemned Alexander. In March, Alexander, who had already excommunicated Victor, responded by pronouncing the same sentence against Frederick I, thereby releasing his subjects from the obligation to keep their oath of loyalty. Moreover, a large part of Christendom recognized Alexander's authority: as of 1160, Sicily, the Iberic kingdoms, France, and England, and in 1161, the kingdom of Jerusalem. This happened despite the efforts of the German sovereign, who attempted to ward off the movement and even tried in September 1162 to intimidate Louis VII at the meeting of St. John de Losne. Nevertheless, he was unable to get the king to change his position. As for Victor IV, he benefited from the support of imperial countries or other countries under their influence (Denmark, Hungary). In the kingdom of Burgundy (Comté, Savoy, Dauphiné, Provence), many of the bishops leaned toward Alexander III, as did some Italian prelates, who went along with local powers (as in Milan and Genoa). The archbishop of Salzburg was noncommittal.

Even though Alexander III had the support of the Byzantine emperor and the Cistercian order, which was the most dynamic of congregations, his situation was not perfect. On the contrary, in the face of the emperor's politics of might, he barely had the means to resist, and he could not even manage to hold his position in Italy. In the spring of 1162, he fled to France and settled in Sens, where he worked to build a vast alliance against the Empire, but was unable to translate it into positive action. Realizing that the real fight would unfold in the peninsula and that he had to be present to lead it, Alexander decided to return to Rome. There he was able to establish himself in April 1165, thanks to some of its inhabitants being well disposed toward him. Frederick I, who had previously succeeded in imposing himself in northern Italy through violence (Milan was taken, besieged, and razed to the ground), reacted very strongly and resolved to achieve a definitive victory. At the end of May 1165, at the diet of Wurzburg, he obliged the German bishops to swear an oath never to ally themselves with Alexander. Taking the oath himself, he swore that prelates who pledged obedience to PASCHAL III—the antipope who succeeded Victor IV—would never be deprived of their dignity. At the end

of 1166, Frederick I led his army into the peninsula and marched on Rome, which he took in 1167. Alexander III was forced to flee, and Frederick installed Paschal there, who crowned him for the second time.

However, a terrible epidemic spread throughout Frederick's troops, transforming one of the most brilliant political and military operations of the century into a disaster. Beaten by destiny, the emperor returned to Germany and saw Italy slip through his hands in a few weeks. The northern cities rose up against him at the initiative of Cremona, a city that had previously been favorable to Frederick. On 1 December 1167, the "Cremonese union" joined the anti-imperial group that had united (since March 1164) Verona, Vicenza, and Padua to Venice. Together they formed the Lombard League. Its leaders developed a program that constituted the foundation of the GUELPH movement. The pope seized the opportunity to reestablish an active Italian politics, especially because he was still supported by both Sicily and Byzantium. By 1166, he had named an energetic man, Galdin, as archbishop of Milan, where the inhabitants had been driven away by force. At the news of the Lombard uprising, Galdin grouped together citizens of the destroyed city and stirred up the ardor of the rebels. They built the metropolis back up from its ruins creating the new city of Alessandria in 1168 as a symbol of their alliance. Frederick I had been detained in Germany for several months and only came back in 1174. He besieged Alessandria, but was forced to leave by a federal army. He then attempted to negotiate with the Lombard League to isolate Alexander, but the Lombards refused to separate the peace of Italy from that of the Church. Hostilities reignited, and the emperor was beaten at Legnano on 20 May 1176. Discussions followed that lasted many months. The pontiff finally agreed to negotiate the return to unity and the end of the schism independently from settling the problems of the peninsula. He thus showed that even if he could be accused of cynicism, his will was not to implicate the Church in political and territorial matters. The preliminary talks were concluded in Anagni (October–November 1176), and the emperor went to Venice to prostrate himself before the pope on 24 July 1177. On 1 August, Frederick ended the conflict with a treaty in which the fundamental clause was the recognition of Alexander as the pope; in return, Frederick's excommunication was rescinded, and he received absolution. It was also agreed that most of the Alexandrine prelates driven from their seats by the Imperials would be reinstated, a few schismatic bishops would be pardoned, and the fate of most of the rest of them would be decided by Alexander. Likewise, it was understood that the Empire would return the territories that it had improperly held, although these were not specifically defined, and the problem was left to a joint commission to resolve. At the same time, the pope acted as an intermediary between Frederick and Sicily and the Lombards to obtain a suspension of the hostilities; a 15-year truce was signed with William II, and a 6-year truce with the Lombard League.

During some of this time, another problem had greatly preoccupied the Roman Church, although it was not directly involved: the serious conflict between Henry II of England (one of the Plantagenets) and the archbishop of Canterbury Thomas Becket. The king, in an attempt to better control the clergy, had in January 1164 promulgated a series of measures known as the Constitutions of Clarendon, presenting them as a recasting of the ancient customs of the kingdom. This legislation was no doubt motivated by a desire to maintain the peace, but it contained articles that were nevertheless contrary to the traditional freedoms of the Church (e.g., the royal prerogative for designating bishops, the restriction of the judiciary privilege of the clergy, hindrances to appeals in the court of Rome, and the limitation of the right of clerics to leave the kingdom). Nevertheless, the sovereign had persisted because he believed he could count on the archbishop he had promoted to support him in these efforts. However, Henry was deeply disappointed and surprised when Becket refused to give his approval and openly opposed Henry's decisions. Becket was then called before the king's court. In October 1164, he escaped to France and continued his struggle from there, excommunicating the bishops who remained loyal to the king and multiplying his protests.

Alexander III, who was called to intervene, condemned the offensive articles of the Constitutions of Clarendon. At the same time, he tried to avoid aggravating the situation. It was necessary that he remain prudent because he realized Henry II might become an ally of Frederick through sheer frustration. He also did not completely share Thomas Becket's views on the relations between the two powers, and he no doubt felt closer to those English prelates who constituted a third, more moderate party. Alexander therefore sent legates to gather information and to find a means of bringing about a reconciliation. He was able to succeed with the assistance of Louis VII of France, and in 1170 Henry II accepted the return of the archbishop to his seat and abandoned pursuing him. A short time later, Becket was assassinated by four knights who believed they were rendering a service to their sovereign. Disturbed by Becket's murder, the pope condemned his killers and imposed a personal interdict on the monarch. Henry was forced to submit. The affair ended with his absolution in Avranches on 21 May 1172. An agreement was reached, called the concordat, in which Henry rescinded the rules of Clarendon and agreed to do penance.

These two conflicts—one in which the pope played a major role and the other in which he was more in the background—and his generally cordial relations with Louis VII and other princes, illustrate both Alexander III's original thinking on the relationship between spiritual and political power, and the evolution of the theocracy since Gregory VII. For both popes, the spiritual dominated the temporal, due to its nature and finality, and because of the pope's special mission as Peter's successor, he can intervene in the actions of temporal powers when these call into question either his freedom or matters of faith. Alexander believed that the spiritual domain could be considerably enlarged to encompass related matters. He considered the freedom of Italy as a spiritual cause, because it guaranteed the Holy See's freedom and therefore that of the universal Church. He felt entitled to forbid cities that battled for Italy to abandon their commitments under pain of excommunication (see the papal bull *Non est dubium*). On the other hand, contrary to extremist Gregorians, he believed that the Church should not use its spiritual authority to exact political sanctions in the defense of the same principles. He excommunicated Frederick I; he did not depose him, as Gregory VII had done to Henry IV. Alexander believed that as pope he should not get involved in areas God had given to emperors and kings, except for spiritual reasons and with spiritual weapons. His doctrine relied on the distinction between political and religious offices and on their necessary cooperation, a view first expressed around A.D. 500 during the pontificate of GELASIUS I. It does not completely eliminate the pope's ability to act in the political domain. Thus, for example, Alexander conferred a royal title upon Prince Henry of Portugal because no other power in the world had the authority to do so.

Alexander III's doctrine emphasized the notion of *auctoritas*—that is, exercise of full sovereignty only when there is an undeniable necessity and other powers have only a *potestas*. This doctrine, inspired no doubt by certain commentators on Gratian who deeply influenced the canonists of the time (e.g., Simon de Bisignano, Uguccio, INNOCENT III), indicates that Alexander III paid close attention to the ecclesiastical and religious sectors. His work in this area is ultimately more significant for the general history of the Church than is his involvement in the conflict with the Empire. He was continually concerned with the progress made by heretical beliefs, particularly among the Cathars in the Languedoc region of France. He sent several legations, the most celebrated of which was led in 1178 by Cardinal Peter of St. Chrysogonus. On his own initiative or that of his entourage, an attempt was made to distinguish those who deeply desired spiritual renewal and who thus did not fear criticizing the clergy from those who deliberately spread falsehoods. Valdo, who came to Rome in 1179, was authorized to preach penance. Likewise, Alexander III never lost sight of the dangerous situation in the kingdom of Jerusalem and the neighboring Frankish principalities. He was quick to ask the West to organize a Crusade as soon as the conflict with Frederick I had been settled.

In these two actions, which for Alexander were inherently connected to his mission, he presented himself as the sole leader of the Church, although he led with the assistance of the cardinals, who assembled in consistory in order to make important decisions and render major judgments, and who were also called upon individually. As for the Curia, it dealt with a progressively greater number of matters, and the chancellery played an eminent role in these. Among other things, the chancery issued responses to bishops' questions when the law was not clear or the matter ambiguous. These responses, or DECRETALS, immediately became the rule for the universal Church. With 470 decretals, Alexander III was clearly one of the main legislators of the medieval Church (after Innocent III who had close to 600). Alexander is especially recognized for establishing that the Roman pontiff is undeniably the unique source of law. The rules he pronounced were meant to clarify procedures of judiciary appeal from one ecclesiastical court to another; to redefine exemption; to reaffirm the election of bishops by cathedral chapters; to determine in a precise manner the means of intervention for secular powers; and to entrust only the ordinaries with the institution of the parish priests (*cura animarum*). All of these rules reinforced pontifical authority by introducing it into all functions of the clergy and into society in general. The same is true of the legislation promulgated by several decretals on the subject of marriage. The decisions made during the Third Lateran Council, called by the pope in March 1179, are a kind of summary of his accomplishments. The purpose of this council was to solemnly declare the end of the schism; to rally or sanction the Victorian bishops; to demonstrate the unity of the Church around Alexander III; and to have his decisions made public and be recorded. The council's decisions reiterated the rules previously proposed in the decretals (e.g., on episcopal status and election of bishops, the right of patronage over parishes, the religious orders and the EXEMPTION, the appeals). Others reiterated prescriptions from previous councils (e.g., against tournaments for the truce of God, the protection of the weak). In particular, Alexander III had a solemn condemnation of heresies approved and made public. In addition, he showed his concern for developing education by reiterating one of his decretals with a canon obliging each bishop to maintain a school where students could take courses without charge and could obtain, if intellectually worthy, the *licentia docendi*. This measure was destined to considerably encourage schooling and the birth of UNIVERSITIES. Finally, aimed at avoiding contested elections such as those of 1159 and 1130, Alexander III's most celebrated contribution was a constitution defining new rules for pontifical elections. Peter's successors were to be chosen from then on by all the cardinals in assembly, and for a canonically valid decision, a two-thirds majority vote would be required. This system lasted until PIUS XII, who changed

the required majority to two-thirds plus one vote. On the other hand, the council did not deal with the Crusade, which was Alexander III's main concern until his death two and a half years later, on 30 August 1181.

Marcel Pacaut

Bibliography

JW, 2, 145–418, 721–5, 761–6.

LP, 2, 397–446.

PL, 200, 69–1320.

Brezzi, P. "Alessandro III," *DBI*, 2, (1960), 183–9.

Ellis, G. M. , trans., *Bosso's Life of Alexander III*, Totowa. N.J., 1973.

Fliche-Martin, IX, 9.

Löwenfeld, S. *Epistolae pontificum romanorum ineditae*, Leipzig, 1885, reprint, Graz, 1959, 149–209.

Miscellanea Rolando Bandinelli-Papa Alessandro III, ed. F. Liotta, Rome, 1986.

Pacaut, M. *Alexandre III: recherche sur la conception du pouvoir pontifical dans sa pensée et dans son oeuvre*, Paris, 1956.

Pacaut, M. *La Théocratie*, Paris, 1989.

Schwaiger, G. "Alexander III," *LexMA*, 1 (1977–80), 372–3.

Somerville, R., *Pope Alexander III and the Council of Tours (1163)*, Berkely, Calif., 1977.

Watterich, 2, 377–649.

Weigand, R. "Magister Rolandus und Papst Alexander III," *Archiv für katholisches Kirchenrecht*, 149 (1980), 3–44.

ALEXANDER IV. *Rinaldo da Ienne (b. Ienne, near Anagni, ca. 1185–d. Viterbo, 25 May 1261). Elected pope on 16 December 1254 in Naples, consecrated on 20 December. Buried at San Lorenzo in Viterbo.*

Alexander IV's inaction in face of political difficulties, his abuse of spiritual punishments, and his consenting to alienate some States from the Church gave his pontificate a negative image.

Rinaldo da Ienne belonged to the family of the counts of Ienne, feudal lords of the monastery of Subiaco since the end of the 11th century. Under INNOCENT IV, Rinaldo II, then cardinal of Ostia, became the owner of the fief, and after his death, he left it to his nephews, Rinaldo III Rosso and Giovanni di Gavignano, as stipulated in his father Philip II's will.

From a young age, Rinaldo da Ienne was part of the cathedral chapter of Anagni, where he is first mentioned in 1209. The title *magister* accompanying his subscription seems to indicate that he had had educational training in theology or canon law. As of 1219, Rinaldo appears in papal documentation, first as the subdeacon and chaplain of Pope HONORIUS III and then as chaplain of Cardinal Ugolino of Ostia, the future GREGORY IX, to whom his family was related and whom he accompanied in his legation to Lombardy in 1221.

It seems that Rinaldo was a *cameriere* before being promoted to cardinal on 23 September 1227 at the deaconry of St. Eustache at the beginning of Gregory IX's pontificate. In 1231, he was named to the seat of Ostia and Velletri, thus following in the footsteps of his protector. He nevertheless continued to serve as deacon of St. Eustache until his consecration in 1235. During the second part of Gregory's pontificate, Rinaldo da Ienne dedicated himself to judiciary activities that kept him more often than not at the CURIA. In addition, several missions led him, outside Rome, to Anagni in 1231 and to Perusa and Viterbo. In 1237, he was given the task of reconciling Lombardy, the march of Treviso, and the Veneto with Frederick II and of insuring the protection of Milan. The negotiations of June 1240, though hardly satisfactory after the defeat suffered by the Church at Cortenuova, nevertheless provided an occasion for Rinaldo da Ienne to forge a friendship with the emperor.

Although the nature of the relationship between Rinaldo and INNOCENT IV is not known, it is clear that the cardinal did not accompany the pope to the Council of Lyon in 1245, although the pope had asked him to do so. In the pope's absence, Rinaldo's activities in Campania linked him to Cardinals Riccardo Annibaldi and Stefano Conti. Yet his main interests were the "minors," especially the Franciscans and Poor Clares, for whom he was the protector.

Eleven days after the death of Innocent IV in Naples on 7 December 1254, Rinaldo was elected pope by the CONCLAVE; he selected the name Alexander, perhaps in memory of Alexander III, to whom his family owed the fief of Ienne. The urgent problem posed by the succession of Frederick II and the activity of his son Manfred, who aspired to succeed him, added to the existing difficulties in Italy: turbulence in Rome, expansion of the Lombard domains, and partisan struggles in the context of localities.

Immediately after his election, the new pope rejected Conradin's tutelage. Conradin was the legitimate grandson of Frederick II, and had been entrusted to the Holy See by his father, Conradin. Instead, Alexander confirmed the candidacy of Edmund of England on 9 April 1255. He sent Cardinal Ottaviano Ubaldini as his legate to Manfred, but otherwise refused to recognize him.

Given the increasing discontentment in Rome against Brancaleone degi Andaló, the sole senator since 1252, the pope went to stay at the Lateran in November 1255. There he attempted in vain to name a senator more favorable to his cause. Only after the death of Brancaleone did the pope obtain a return to the double senatorial mandate given to the nobility in 1258. Thus, he managed to block the attempts made by the three candidates to the throne of Sicily (Alphonse of Castilla, Richard of Cornouailles, and Manfred) to directly intervene in the Roman situation.

The same year, Manfred, who became regent during the reign of Conradin, began to spread false rumors about the death of his ward and had himself crowned in Palermo on 11 August 1258, openly defying the pope's rights of suzerainty. This was the beginning of a series of direct interventions in Tuscany, Lombardy, and the PAPAL STATE.

In Tuscany, the reconciliation between Pisa and the Holy See in 1257 was not enough to compensate for the threat posed by the alliance between Siena and Manfred. The numerous diplomatic maneuvers of each commune did not take into consideration the overall political situation, nor did it prevent Siena from renewing hostilities against Montalcino, long an object of rivalry with Florence. All the forces hostile to the GHIBELLINES were destroyed with Florence by Manfred and his army in the Battle of Montaperti on 4 September 1260.

In Lombardy, the pope's legate Philip Fontana, archbishop of Ravenna, after having retaken the GUELPH cities of Padua and Vicenza from Ezzelino da Romano, attempted to woo Uberto Pallavicini onto the side of the Church. Instead, he was taken prisoner by Ezzelino in the Battle of Soncino in 1258. Ezzelino's death in 1259 was followed by general relief, but no initiative was undertaken to encourage the partisans Azzo d'Este and the Count of San Bonifacio, who remained attached to the Church. Pallavicini then established a domain around Brescia, stronger than the one he had held in 1254–1257. In a letter Alexander IV wrote on 13 December 1259 to Henry de Suse, his new legate, the pope advised him against intervening in a regrouping of forces and left him free to decide whether to pursue actions in Lombardy. Ultimately, there was no one to represent the papacy in northern Italy at the end of Alexander's pontificate, and as a result, these lands were delivered into the hands of Pallavicini and, through him, to the king of Sicily.

Within a few months, Perceval Doria, Manfred's vicar, spread his authority to The Marches. In addition to this retreat of pontifical authority, there were many concessions made to the nobility and to the communities of Viterbo and Orvieto, as well as various juridical encroachments on rights reserved for the Holy See.

The pope nevertheless made the mendicant orders his priority. The enemies of the Church were considered heretics, and their pursuit was entrusted to the INQUISITION. It was in this climate that the crusade against Ezzelino and the role of the inquisitor Rainerio Sacconi in Milan took place. The importance of the Inquisition, strengthened by the papal bull *Ad extirpenda*, explains the frequent recourse to sentences of excommunication and interdict and the general indifference with which they were received.

Alexander IV once again took the side of the mendicant masters of the University of Paris. On the occasion of the polemical debate raised by the *Liber introductorium in evangelium aeternum* written by the Franciscan Gerardo de Borgo San Donnino, William of Saint-Amour echoed the secular masters by refuting the work, first in his *Libellus de Antechristo* and then in his *Tractatus brevis de periculis novorum temporum*. The cardinals' commission, which met at Anagni in 1255, issued a declaration against San Donnino. However, a year later, the bull *Romanus pontifex* condemned the pamphlet by William of Saint-Amour, who was in turn banished from the university. The mendicant masters definitively acquired the right to teach and confer university diplomas. The pope's support of the Franciscans was once again evident when he canonized Clare, cofounder with Sts. Francis and Agnes of the order of nuns known as the Poor Clares, and drafted the first constitution of the order. Furthermore, he confirmed the foundation of a new mendicant order, the Hermits of St. Augustine, in the bull *Licet ecclesia* on 9 April 1256.

Alexander IV paid special attention to the monastery of Subiaco, granting numerous privileges and facilitating the management of its finances. During his second trip to Subiaco and Ienne in 1260, the pope wrote a new version of the internal rules of the monastery. This text is one of the most significant documents regarding monastic life. In addition, there was also an exchange of letters between two notaries of the Curia, Giordano Pirunti and Giovanni da Capua, which demonstrates an original form of literary jousting on the subject of the pontiff.

This wait-and-see attitude also influenced the Sacred College, reduced to eight cardinals by 1261. Fearing disapproval from his main advisers—Ottaviano Ubaldini, Giangaetano Orsini, John of Toledo, and Riccardo Annibaldi—and their possible withdrawal from collaborating with him, the pope created no new cardinals. The growing tension between Annibaldi and Orsini was perhaps the cause, as it clearly influenced the two following promotions. The negative burden of the partisan battles at all levels and the necessity of confronting them with the means adapted to the stakes involved appeared all the more evident.

Thérèse Boespflug

Bibliography

Andreotta, S. "La familiglia di Alessandro IV e l'abbazia di Subiaco," *Atti e memorie della Società tiburtina di storia ed arte*, 35 (1962), 63–126; 36 (1963), 5–87.

De Lubac, H. *La Postérité spirituelle de Joachim de Flore*, Paris, 1978, 80–4.

Jordan, E. *Les Origines de la domination angevine en Italie*, Paris, 1909, 94–290.

Les Registres d'Alexandre IV (1254–1261), C. Bourel de La Roncière ed., 3 vols. Paris, 1895–1950.

Manselli, R. "Alessandro IV," *DBI*, 2 (1960), 189–93.

Paravicini Bagliani, A. *Cardinali di Curia e "familiae" cardinalizie dal 1227 al 1254*, 2 vol., Padua, 1972, 41–60.

Potth, 1286–1473, 2124–9.

Sambin, P. *Un certame dettatorio tra due notai pontifici (1260). Lettere inedite di Giordano da Terracina e di Giovanni da Capua*, Rome, 1955.

ALEXANDER V. *Pietro Philarghi (b. Crete, c. 1340–d. Bologna, 3 May 1410). Elected pope 26 June 1409 following the meeting of the council of Pisa; consecrated on 7 July. Buried at S. Francesco of Bologna.*

In Crete, the orphaned Pietro Philarghi received the name Peter of Candia and learned the Greek language. The friar minor who had taken him in taught him Latin as well, and Peter himself entered the Franciscan order in 1357. The order sent him to the West to study theology. From Italy he went to England, where he earned a bachelor's degree at Oxford. For his license degree, he went to Paris. There, Blanchard, the chancellor of the university, was fleecing the students. However, according to Etienne de Conti, Peter was able to pay the eighty gold francs and take his exams thanks to a subsidy from the king of France.

Peter's commentary on the *Sentences* made him famous. There are twenty-five known manuscripts, not counting the partial copies spread throughout Europe. As a good Franciscan, Peter developed the dogma of Mary's Immaculate Conception. His works are little known today, like so much of the writing of the scholastics of that era.

One of the consequences of the Great Schism of 1378 was the exclusion of the allies of the Roman pope, Urban VI, from the University of Paris: originally supportive of debate among those of diverse opinions, the university was compelled by Charles VI's uncles to rally behind Clement VII. Like so many others, Peter of Candia left France, and by 1384, he had established himself in Pavia.

This move affected the rest of his life. His fortunes followed those of Gian Galeazzo Visconti, who quickly came to appreciate him. First bishop of Piacenza (1386) and then of Vicenza (1388), Peter was transferred to Novara (1389), where he stayed for more than a dozen years. His eloquence, knowledge of Greek, generous nature, and appreciation of the pleasures of a good table earned him a reputation in the world of letters as well as in the world of politics. In 1395, Visconti sent him to the embassy in Prague to see Emperor Wenceslas. With his humanist friend Uberto Decembrio traveling as his secretary, Peter succeeded in his mission, obtaining for Visconti the title of duke. The speech for Visconti's investiture, which Peter delivered upon his return to Milan, was a true triumph and aroused the admiration of the audience. The new duke, who had nothing but praise for Peter's services, intervened to help him obtain the archbishopric of Milan in 1402. A few months later, Visconti died, leaving Peter among the members of the regency council.

Closely linked to the court of France, Visconti's court was nevertheless still loyal to Urban, and continually threatened to defect to better cover its incursions into the PAPAL STATES. The pope at AVIGNON, BENEDICT XIII, despite suffering significantly when the French clergy withdrew its obedience to him, was making progress in Liguria. In Rome, INNOCENT VII sought an ally in Pietro Philarghi, made him cardinal in 1405, and immediately invested him with the title of legate in northern Italy. The new cardinal of Milan did not participate in the conclave of 1406 in which GREGORY XII was elected and was not involved in the events that led Gregory and his rival to be discredited by their respective cardinals. Yet as soon as his Roman colleagues gave the signal to rebel, Pietro informed them that he supported their plan to call a council to deal with the issue of the unity of the Church.

The council opened in Pisa on 25 March 1409. Pietro, who had worked assiduously during the preparations, played an active role in the trial that led to the joint condemnation of the two rival pontiffs by the council assembly on 5 June. When the unionist cardinals entered into a conclave to select a new pope, Pietro's candidacy quickly attracted the support of both parties. Elected on 26 June, Pietro was consecrated Pope Alexander V on 7 July, he was hailed as pope by the nations that had participated in the council. After the last session, the council fathers departed, leaving the new pope with the immense task of reforming the Church in order to better unify it.

In one of his first acts as pope, Alexander V ratified the council's acts, lavishly distributed dioceses, and performed other favors. The curialist Dietrich von Niem, who created an unflattering portrait of the pontiff, held these acts against him, as did those who were excluded from the pope's largesse. The secular priesthood felt slighted when Alexander promulgated bulls favorable to the Franciscans, whom he perhaps thought would be able to regenerate the Church.

A true return to order could only be achieved when the pontiff returned to Rome. But first Ladislas Durazzo, who had remained loyal to Gregory XII, had to be ousted. Alexander V entrusted this mission to Louis II of Anjou, Ladislas's rival for the kingdom of Naples, and to Cardinal Baldassare Cossa. The cardinal invested all his energy and finances in the mission. Rome fell in January 1410, but Alexander V never arrived there. Residing in Bologna, where the reconstituting of the CURIA was taking place, Alexander V fell ill and died. He was buried at the Franciscan church of the city.

Hélène Millet

See also ANGEVINS.

Bibliography

De Nyem, T. *De scismate*, Leipzig, 1890, 319–28.

Ehrle, F. *Der Sentenzenkommentar Peters von Candia, des Pisaner Papstes Alexanders V*, Münster, 1925.

Emmen, A. *Petrus de Candia OFM. De immaculata Deiparae conceptione*, Quaracchi, 1954, 235–334.

Lampen, W. "Prosae seu poemata Petri de Candia," *Archivum Franciscanum Historicum*, 23 (1930), 172–82.

Petrucci, A. "Alessandro V," *DBI*, 2 (1960), 193–6.

ALEXANDER VI. *Rodrigo Borja (Borgia in Italian), b. Jávita, Spain, ca. 1431–d. Rome, 18 August 1503. Elected pope on 11 July 1492; consecrated on 26 July. Buried in the San Andrea rotunda near St. Peter's in Rome; transferred in 1610 to the Spanish church in Rome, Sta Maria de Montserrat.*

Nephew of Pope CALLISTUS III and son of Joffrey and Isabelle Borgia (Callistus's sister), Rodrigo Borgia was invited to Rome by his uncle, the pope. Callistus then sent him to study in Bologna, where he obtained his doctorate in law on 3 July 1456. The pope also named him notary of the Holy See on 10 May 1455, and cardinal deacon of the title of San-Nicolà-in-Carcere on 20 February 1456. A few months later, on 1 May, he was promoted to vice-chancellor of the CURIA, a high office he occupied until he was elected pope. Borgia obtained many other favors from his uncle and his uncle's successors, including the Abbey of Subiaco (1471) and the dioceses of Gerona (1457–1458), Valencia (1458–1492), Carthagena (1482–1492), Majorca (1489–1492), and Erlau (1491–1492). On 30 July 1471, Borgia was designated cardinal bishop of Albano and elected dean of the SACRED COLLEGE. This accumulation of responsibilities, especially the chancellery, ensured him significant revenues. As a result, he was reputed to be the richest cardinal after Cardinal de Estouteville, and he had the lifestyle of a great Renaissance lord, although he was reknowned for his frugality.

A refined mind, an excellent jurist, an able political negotiator, and a good administrator of the Curia, Borgia was nevertheless a victim of both his sensuality and his excessive love for his children. On 11 June 1460, PIUS II severely reprimanded him for his debased morality, his love of luxury, and his cupidity. This did not, however, prevent Borgia from fathering numerous children with several women. From 1462 to 1471, the following children were born to him of an unknown mother: Pedro Luis, named Duke of Gandia and Grandee of Spain in 1485 by Ferdinand the Catholic; Girolama (d. ca. 1484); and Isabelle (d. 1519). Rosa Vannozza de Catanei (1442–1518)—who married Domenico d'Arignano, then Giorgio de Croce, and finally Carlo Canale (all members of the Curia)—gave birth to Borgia's most famous children: Cesare (1475–1507), John (1476–1497), Lucrezia (1480–1519), and Joffrey (1481–1517). Borgia also became the father, while pope, of John, duke of Camerino and Nepi (1498–1548), and Rodrigo, born in

1502 or 1503; their mother's name is unknown. In addition, Borgia had a liaison with Giulia Farnese, which continued during the first years of his pontificate but produced no offspring.

Besides the vice-chancellery, Borgia occupied numerous other positions. Callistus III had already named him legate for a year in the Ancona region (1456–1457), where he was marvelously successful. He was then commissary general of the papal armies in Italy (11 December 1457). SIXTUS IV sent him to Spain as a legate *a latere* in order to preach in favor of the Crusade of 22 December 1471. This legation successfully took place between 17 May 1471 and 25 October 1473. Later, in 1477, Borgia once again returned to Italy, still a legate, in order to crown Jeanne, queen of Naples. He played a significant role in the election of Popes PIUS II, PAUL II, and Sixtus IV. At Sixtus's death, he himself became a candidate, but following Giuliano della Rovere's advice, he rallied behind the election of INNOCENT VIII (1484). However, during this pontificate, Borgia split with Giuliano, who favored the Neapolitans' cause, to unite with Ascanio Sforza, the brother of Ludovico the Moor.

At the time the conclave opened on 6 August 1492 following Innocent's death, it was inconceivable that Giuliano della Rovere could be chosen, due to the arrogance he had demonstrated during Innocent VIII's pontificate and his friendly relations with France. On the other hand, the favorites of Milan, Ardicino della Porta and Ascanio Sforza, had a good chance of being elected. Rodrigo Borgia's Spanish origins worked against him because many cardinals opposed the idea of a foreign pope. However, in the first votes, Sforza did not succeed in being elected, and neither did della Porta. As for himself, Borgia had gathered some votes during the early ballots, but they were too few to win the election. At the end of the third vote, on the morning of 10 August, Axanio firmly supported Borgia's candidacy, and many cardinals decided to vote for him, hoping that, once elected pope, he would equitably distribute the high offices and benefices among them. Others supported him without expecting to get anything in return. Borgia was therefore unanimously elected on the night of 10–11 August. None of his contemporaries mentioned his immoral conduct or the existence of his children, which were not considered very important at the time. In fact, many popes and cardinals had children, including Innocent VIII (two sons); Pius II (two daughters); Cardinal d'Estouteville (four sons); Giuliano della Rovere (three daughters), who later became JULIUS II; and Cardinal Riario (a daughter). What played in favor of Rodrigo Borgia and motivated the choice of the most honorable cardinals was his great experience in administration and politics. This was judged to be extremely useful given the highly complex situation in the Italian states, which the king of France threatened to invade. This is why Rodrigo's election was, with few exceptions,

a welcome event, according to Sigismondo dei Conti. Immediately after his election, the new pope, following the example of Callistus III, declared that he would like to bring peace and harmony to the Italian states and affirmed that he favored an alliance with the Christian princes against the advancing Turks. His manner of governing led people to expect good administrative organization, justice, and fervent support for Church reform, along with a relentless fight against the Turks.

Very quickly, however, Alexander VI was mixed up in Italian political intrigues. In the beginning of 1493, he brought upon himself the wrath of Ferrante of Naples when Virginio Orsini, Ferrante's *condottiere*, sold Franceschetto Cibo, son of Innocent VIII, the castles of Cerveteri and Anguillara, which belonged to the Papal States. This move was accomplished with support from Pietro de' Medici and Cardinal Giuliano della Rovere, who, faced with Alexander VI's reaction, left to seek refuge in his castle in Ostia. After this episode, the pope reinforced his alliance with Milan, agreeing on 25 April 1493 to the League of San Marco uniting Venice and Milan. He also had his daughter Lucrezia marry Giovanni Sforza, nephew of Ludovico the Moor. In addition, the pope attempted to damage the alliance between Milan and the king of France, who was coveting the kingdom of Naples. The pope refused his request in August 1493 when the French ambassador, Perron de Baschi, came to solicit it explicitly. In the meantime, Alexander had reconciled with the king of Naples and the king of Aragon, Ferdinand II (Ferdinand V of Castile). Ferdinand favored the marriage of his cousin Maria Enriquez to the pope's son Cardinal John Borgia, second duke of Gandia. He also prepared the concession of the Alexandrine bulls on the New World discovered by Christopher Columbus in 1492. To perfect his relationship with the kingdom of Naples, the pope had his son Joffrey marry Sancha of Aragon (on 7 May 1494). The next day, Cardinal John Borgia, in the capacity of legate *a latere*, crowned Alfonso II as king of Naples.

Charles VIII, king of France, encouraged by Giuliano della Rovere, who had fled to France, held firm in his plan to invade Italy in order to conquer the kingdom of Naples. The invasion began in 1494. There was little resistance to the invasion, which was supported by Ludovico the Moor and the city of Florence. Alexander VI alone continued to vehemently oppose it. When he met Charles VIII on 31 December 1494 in Rome, Alexander made many concessions, but he refused to recognize him as king of Naples. The kingdom was nevertheless occupied, and Alexander VI immediately felt threatened. Given the Italian states' lack of resistance and the fact that Ferdinand of Aragon was also at war against the king of France, on 31 March 1495 Emperor Maximilian I, the city of Venice, Ludovico the Moor, and the pope founded the Holy League, ostensibly to defend Christendom against the Turks and to support the Holy See. In reality, the league was a coalition formed against Charles VIII who had turned down the pope's pleas to engage his troops in the Crusades. The Aragonese troops then penetrated into the kingdom of Naples, and in March 1497, General Gonzalve of Cordoba reconquered for the pope Giuliano della Rovere's castle in Ostia, which had been besieged by the French.

During the night of 14–15 July 1497, Alexander's son, John Borgia, who had been named captain general of the Church, was mysteriously assassinated, and his body was thrown into the Tiber River. His death deeply upset the pope, who then seemed to become serious about reforming the Church *in capite et in membris*. He named a commission of cardinals to prepare a series of reforms, but only some of them were implemented. The pope then became absorbed once again in the problem of Italy's stability. Between 1495 and 1498, a conflict had been developing with the Dominican Girolamo Savonarola, who had been preaching since the time of Sixtus IV against the abuses within the Church. As prior of St. Mark's in Florence, he had intensified his efforts, presenting himself as a chosen prophet with divine visions. He not only attacked Rome and the pope, but he also wanted to found a theocratic state in Florence. Also, without any compunction, he had supported Charles VIII's invasion, which he believed would ultimately aid Church reform. Early on, Alexander VI had approved Savonarola's apostolate, but later, having patiently tolerated his imprecations, the pope was obliged to excommunicate him in order to defend his authority and avoid a schism. Condemned to death by the secular authorities, Savonarola was hanged on 23 May 1498.

From then on, a new period began, which was characterized by the activities of Cesare Borgia. Created cardinal in 1493, he was secularized by the Sacred College on 17 August 1498. Cesare then settled in France, where Louis XII granted him the duchy of Valentinois and favored his marriage with Charlotte d'Albret, the king of Navarre's sister. Strengthened by the support of the king of France and the consent and aid of the pope, Borgia undertook military campaigns that led to the conquest of the greater part of The Romagna and The Marches. Although these regions belonged to the Church, their governors reigned as feudal lords and frequently treated Rome with arrogance. Niccolò Machiavelli, who met Borgia during the last of these campaigns, sung his praises, both for his politics and because he was a man of character. Nevertheless, over the years, countless historians have contested this appreciation.

In the meantime, Lucrezia Borgia's marriage to Giovanni Sforza was annulled on 20 December 1497. On 21 July 1498, she married Alfonso de Bisceglie, the bastard son of Alfonso II of Aragon, king of Naples. De Bisceglie was assassinated on 18 July 1500, probably at the behest of Cesare Borgia. Lucrezia married for a third time on 30 December 1501, to Alfonso d'Este, the son of the duke of Ferrara. Each of these marriages denotes the constantly fluctuating political alliances of the time.

Despite this frenetic political activity, Alexander VI conscientiously handled his papal obligations. The accusations of heresy made against him were pure slander. In fact, his zealousness for preserving the purity of the faith was demonstrated by his efficacy in repressing heretical tendencies in Bohemia, Moravia, and Lombardy. He strongly supported various religious orders, especially the Minim friars of St. Francis of Paola in 1493. He energetically defended ecclesiastical liberties before the nationalist tendencies in Holland. He was particularly devoted to St. Anne and the Virgin Mary. In this connection, in 1502 he confirmed Sixtus IV's bull on the Immaculate Conception and granted indulgences to all visitors to Mary's shrines. He regularly attended ceremonies and encouraged people to recite the Angelus. He was extraordinarily popular with pilgrims from all over the world, and he further demonstrated his piety by celebrating the jubilee year 1500.

Alexander VI's solid support of the Crusades, affirmed at the beginning of his pontificate, was especially apparent in 1500 after the successive Turk victories in 1498 and 1499. On 11 March 1500, he addressed the ambassadors of all the kingdoms of Europe—France, Spain, England, Naples, Venice, Savoy, and Florence—and urged them to unite against their common enemy. On 1 June of the same year, he published the bull of the Crusade, sending legates to the different countries along with preachers of the indulgence. Nevertheless, only Italy and Spain responded favorably to the pope's request. Their ships joined forces under the command of Gonzalve of Cordoba and were victorious in some battles at the end of 1500 and the beginning of 1501. However, when Venice signed a treaty with the Turks in 1502, the successes of the Christian armies were reduced to nil. The Alexandrine bulls, published at the request of the Catholic kings after the voyage to America by Christopher Columbus, are particularly significant. The bull *Inter caetera*, promulgated on 3–4 May 1493, was especially important, because it granted the kings all the territories they would discover in the West. The pope encouraged them to send missionaries with perfect morals, doctrine, and experience to convert the native peoples to the Christian faith. The pope himself nominated Friar Bernard Boyl for the American territories. In the second bull, a clause mentioned a "line of demarcation" between Spain and Portugal. The Alexandrine bulls were of enormous significance, as they are at the heart of the immense task of the evangelization of the New World. They also indicate the prestige enjoyed by the papacy, despite the setbacks it was suffering at the time.

Alexander VI was a noted patron of the arts. His favorite painter was Pinturicchio, who decorated the papal apartments with admirable frescoes. One of these is a most faithful portrait of the pontiff, and another the different stages of the Castel Sant'Angelo, which was restored by the architect Antonio da Sangallo. Alexander also had Sangallo build the splendid caisson ceiling at the basilica of St. Mary Major, gold-leafed with the first gold brought from America. In addition, he had the University of Sapienza in Rome built (1497–1499), and on the occasion of the holy year of 1500, he opened a direct road between Sant'Angelo and the Vatican, called first the Alexandrine Way and then Borgo Nuovo.

In August 1503, the pope fell ill and died. Although the illness is likely to have been malaria, there is also speculation that the pope died of a poison intended for a cardinal who had been his dinner host.

Alexander VI had some serious faults, due to his sensual nature and his practice of nepotism. His enemies, mainly Julius II and then historians and writers of the 17th through 19th centuries, made all sorts of accusations against him, creating the "legend of the Borgias." Those seeking to make an evenhanded judgment of him would do well to avoid following both his unconditional defenders and those detractors who accuse him of countless crimes and depravities.

Alonso Justo Fernandez

Bibliography

Battlori, M. *Alejandro VI y la casa real de Aragon*, Madrid, 1958.

Battlori, M. *Dicc. de Hist. ecles. de España*, I, Madrid, 1972, 36–9, 274–6.

Bellonci, M. *Lucrezia Borgia*, Milan, 1939.

Burckard, J. *Liber notarum*, ed. E. Celani, 2 vol., Città di Castello, 1906.

Pastor, L. 5 and 6.

Picotti, G. B. "Nuovi studi e documenti intorno a papa Alessandro VI," *RSCI*, 5 (1951), 169–262; "Ancora sul Borgia," *ibid.* 8 (1954), 313–65.

Picotti, G. B. *Diz. biografico degli italiani*, II, Rome, 1960, 196–205.

Schuller-Piroli, S. *Die Borgia Päpste, Kalixt III. und Alexander VI.*, Vienne, 1979; *Die Borgia-Dynatie. Legende und Geschichte*, Munich, 1982.

Soranzo, G. *Il tempo di Alessandro VI papa e di fra Girolamo Savonarola*, Milan, 1960.

Soranzo, G. *Studi intorno a papa A. VI (Borgia)*, Milan, 1950.

ALEXANDER VII. *Fabio Chigi (b. Siena, 13 February 1599–d. Rome, 22 May 1667). Elected pope on 7 April 1655; crowned on 18 April. Buried at St. Peter's in Rome.*

Alexander VII is one of the most significant figures in the history of the papacy and the Catholic Church toward the middle of the 17th century, because of the political, diplomatic, religious, and disciplinary problems he had to face, both before and after he became pope. Born into an aristocratic family from Siena, Fabio Chigi was a descendant of the "magnificent" Agostino, Raphael's protector. His literary and artistic tastes were refined in his hometown. In 1626, he went to Rome where he began a career in the CURIA. He was then referendary of the Two Signatures (1629); vice-legate in Ferrara until 1634; bishop of Nardò in the kingdom of Naples (1635) (although he never resided there); inquisitor; and apostolic delegate to Malta.

By 1639, Chigi held the prestigious position of nuncio in Cologne, where he remained until 1651. This was a period of essential training for him, especially after he was named papal representative to the Congress of Münster for the peace of Westphalia. During these difficult diplomatic negotiations, he was torn between the different sides. On one hand, he had instructions from Rome demanding an uncompromising defense of Catholic interests—interests that were defined by the politics of the popes from URBAN VIII to INNOCENT X. On the other hand, he had to deal with the imperial, "political" Catholics who leaned toward greater concessions to Protestant and French demands. He could do nothing more than to witness, powerless, the stipulation of the "infamous" peace of Münster, as he defined it. In the eyes of the Roman CURIA, this peace resulted in a religious schism, the principle of territorial churches, and the spoliation of the ecclesiastical property.

It is important to note that, thanks to his personal qualities, Chigi's position in with the Roman Curia and the European powers did not suffer much. The one exception to this was the French hostility, expressed several times then and later on by Jules Mazarin, which manifested itself in a nonofficial EXCLUSION made against Chigi and later rescinded, during the conclave that finally elected him pope. In any case, Fabio Chigi must have appeared to the Curia not only as a zealous executor of directives from the pontiff and the secretary of state, but also as the essential safeguard of Roman positions. In fact, following the suggestion of Cardinal Spada, one of the most influential of the prelates who had adopted an extremely rigid position on the Jansenist question, Innocent X named Chigi in 1651 to succeed Cardinal G. G. Panciroli as secretary of state.

After twelve years away from the Curia, Chigi would once again have to confront the problem of Cornelius Jansen's *Augustinus*. When in 1642-3 he had dealt with the issue as nuncio in Cologne, Chigi had endorsed his nephew A. Bichi, the *internuncio* from Brussels, for the publication of the bull *In eminenti*, the first condemnation of the work of Jansen, the bishop of Ypres. Chigi had made formal corrections in the document concerning the dating that had provoked doubts regarding the document's authenticity. These doubts were widely exploited then by the Jansenist polemic. Within a special new cardinals' congregation for Jansenism (1651–53), Chigi, who had in the interim been named cardinal and bishop of Imola, had a lot of weight, as did F. Albizzi, who had drafted *In eminenti*. In these discussions, far from expressing a doctrinal orientation foreign to his training, he imposed a strict discipline which was increasingly needed in theological debates. The participation of Cardinal Chigi, along with Albizzi, was a decisive factor during the preparation of the definitive text of the new bull, *Cum occasione* (1653), which condemned five propositions cited from the works of Jansen. It was also decisive in convincing the hesitant Innocent X to promulgate it in the name of the authority of the Holy See and the infallible judgment of the pontiff in controversies of faith. Thus, a period of internal conflict within the Catholic Church began. It would have incalculable consequences during Chigi's pontificate and for a century and a half afterward.

Elected pope after the death of Innocent X in 1655, Chigi chose the name Alexander VII in memory of the third pontiff, who bore this name. Once again, he confronted the problem of Jansenism, which became more of a burning issue after *Cum occasione*, from Holland to Gallican and parliamentary France. Antoine Arnauld had proposed making a distinction between questions of law and questions of fact. In this famous proposition, he denied the presence of the five condemned propositions in the work by Jansen, and on the question of fact, he advanced the theory of "respectful silence." This meant that there could be a purely disciplinary obedience of the Holy See's condemnation. Alexander VII reacted and, prompted by Albizzi, promulgated a new bull, *Ad Sanctum Beati Petri Sedem* (1656). In it, he explained and confirmed the preceding constitution. Accepted by the assembly of the French clergy, it was not recorded by the parlements. *Ad Sanctum* thus aggravated the polemics and displaced the debate from the Jansenist issue to the more vast problem of the extension of the INFALLIBILITY of the Church and the pope to questions of fact.

An extremely serious crisis in French ecclesiastical and religious circles resulted. The crisis was significantly aggravated by the publication of Alexander VII's bull *Regiminis Apostolici* (1655) and the obligation to sign a form accepting the condemnations. The latter led to resistance in France from Jansenist groups, including the famous group of religious women, Port-Royal. In any case, Alexander VII's will to impose rigid discipline was not only applicable to the Jansenist disagreement. With interventions aimed at maintaining a difficult balance, he attempted to moderate conflicting tendencies, which in terms of theology and morality and in the area of the missions, had in the interim matured in Catholicism since the COUNCIL OF TRENT.

Although a diplomatic man of the Curia and a methodical organizer faithful to the idea of a strong Roman Church, Alexander VII seems to have lacked a true sense of centralization. Instead of the nepotism that had constituted political influence under the popes Borghesi and Barberini, Alexander made decisions based on discussions and councils. Thus, there was new activity in the Roman congregations: the State was entrusted to Giulio Rospigliosi (who became CLEMENT IX); the Immunity, directed by the Cardinal *datarius* Corrado; the Abundance, controlled by the expert Cardinal Sacchetti; and the Index (Alexander VII had asked for an updating of the list of forbidden books in 1664). Alexander VII was influenced by those close to him, trusted advisers such as Albizzi and especially the Jesuit P. Sforza Pallavicino, to whom he granted the red hat, as well as the pious and learned Cistercian Bona. Bona greatly influenced the ascetic spirit of Alexander VII and, along with Pallavicino, steered him toward certain key religious choices. Faced with the excesses of Probabilism in moral theology, denounced in particular by Pascal in his *Lettres provinciales*, and in a climate of heightened rigor favored by Jansenists and Augustinians, on Pallavicino's advice, Alexander VII rejected the idea of making a blanket condemnation of Probabilism. Two separate decrees from the Holy See (1665 and 1666) were written it seems by Bona and the future Cardinal Casanate. These were aimed at attacking two groups of laxist propositions and were thus a prelude to a more extensive condemnation of other laxist propositions under INNOCENT XI. It was a matter of basic decisions for developing the moral Catholic theology during the 17th century and afterward.

These interventions by Alexander VII had clear repercussions in Europe and were curiously balanced by greater flexibility in matters concerning the missions elsewhere. After the political failure of the papacy in Europe with the treaty of Westphalia, great prospects of conquest were opening up to the missions, which would see great development under Alexander VII. In 1656, a papal decree authorized the "Chinese rites" (homage to Confucius and the cult of ancestors). Tolerated by Jesuit missionaries, such practices had been condemned ten years earlier by Innocent X. Now, however, Chinese Christians could practice such rites, as long as they expressed only their civil and political beliefs and were in no way religious. Later, accompanied by special instructions from the Congregation for the Propagation of the Faith (1659), three apostolic vicariates were created in territories between India and China. These aimed at breaking up the Portuguese monopoly in this area, established by the ancient right of the crown's patronage.

Alexander VII's interest in the universal Church did not distract him from the problems posed by the Papal States and ways of governing. The pontiff was deeply concerned with the rationalization of the Curia's services, whose poor and abusive functioning he had been able to see directly under Innocent X. The Chancellery was reorganized (1655), and the precise standards for ordination were established (1659). Alexander modernized these functions, paving the way for the suppression of the venality of positions, later realized by INNOCENT XII in 1694. However, the results were less tangible in the financial area, despite Alexander VII's efforts to reduce the public debt. After the Thirty Years' War and the expensive politics of the Barberinis, this debt had climbed way out of sight. Significant actions, such as the reduction of the interest of the "*luoghi di Monte*" (titles of public debt) and commercial investments were not enough to solve the chronic financial problem. The small sums saved were quickly used by the administration, to pay for new buildings and for art projects. Alexander VII's support for the arts gave the truest image of the pontificate for, besides his taste for discipline and organization, he had a highly refined aesthetic sense. If he was faithful to a "pious humanism," inspired by his reading of St. Francis de Sales, he was also a fine Latin poet in his youth and, in his mature years, was the heir to late Renaissance and baroque culture. In fact, his sensibility was expressed by his patronage of the arts, especially architecture, urbanism, scholarship, and books. He worked in close collaboration with Bernini and had him build the colonnade in St. Peter's Square, finish the *scala regia* at the Vatican, build a part of the secret Vatican Archives, enlarge the Quirinal Palace, rearrange the piazzas of the Pantheon and the Minerva, and open up the Corso. Alexander VII was also involved in supporting the Roman university, Sapienza, to which he bequeathed his rich, personal library, and the Vatican Library, for which he guaranteed the acquisition of the magnificent collection of manuscripts of the dukes of Urbino. Alexander VII's patronage thus gradually progressed from architectural marvels to cultural institutions. These interests coincided with the Roman climate of the long visit of Christina of Sweden in the Catholic capital and with the presence of scholars and learned individuals such as Allacci, Holstenius, Kircher, Ughelli, and Pallavicino.

Nonetheless, Alexander's greatest failure, which darkened the last years of his reign, was the conflict with France. As mentioned, the roots of this conflict date from the Peace of Westphalia. During Mazarin's last years as minister and at the beginning of the reign of Louis XIV, certain decisions made by the pope aggravated the situation. In the beginning of the 1660s, Alexander VII had adopted policies favorable to the Empire, which was then fighting against the Turks in the Balkans. He thus opposed French ambitions in Germany and the attempts to weaken the Hapsburgs and, consequently, maintain Ottoman pressure on the eastern borders. The pope's Corsican guard insulted the ambassador of France in Rome (1662) and caused Alexander VII a string of serious political and diplomatic humiliations, ending with an arduous reconciliation in 1664. This confrontation with the young

French sovereign was another result of the papacy's weakness following the Peace of Westphalia and the changes in the balance of power in Europe. It was also the most visible sign of a political crisis that had worsened, due to Jansenism, especially during Alexander VII's pontificate. This crisis, having become institutional and religious, concerned the entire Catholic Church. Alexander VII was able to face it, but its repercussions nevertheless highlight the contradictory nature of the Chigi papacy, enlightened and often positive, but still marked by shadows and deep and long-lasting fractures.

Mario Rosa

Bibliography

Albert, M. *Nuntius Fabio Chigi und die Anfänge des Jansenismus (1639–1651)*, Rome-Fribourg-Vienna, 1988.

d'Apprieu, R. "Le pape Alexandre VII et l' "Introduction à la vie dévote," *Revue savoisienne*, 102 (1962), 50–4.

Bernstock, J. E. "Bernini's Tomb of Alexander VII," *Saggi e memorie di storia dell'arte*, 16 (1988), 167–90, 363–73.

Borg, V. *Fabio Chigi Apostolic Delegate in Malta (1634–1639). An edition of his official correspondence*, Vatican, 1967.

Ceyssens, L. *La Fin de la première période du jansénisme. Sources des années 1654–1660*, I–II, Bruxelles-Rome, 1963–5 (*Inst. hist. belge de Rome*, 1963–5); "Le "fait" dans la condamnation de Jansénius et dans le serment antijanséniste," *RHE*, 69 (1974), 697–734.

Incisa Della Rocchetta, G. "Gli appunti autobiografici d'Alessandro VII nell'Archivio Chigi," *Mélanges Tisserant*, Vatican City, 1964, VI, 439–57.

Krautheimer, R., and Jones, R. B. S. "The Diary of Alexander VII: Notes on Art, Artists and Buildings," *Römische Jahrbuch für Kunstgeschichte*, 15 (1975), 199–233.

Krautheimer, R. *The Rome of Alexander VII, 1655–1667*, Princeton, N.J., 1985.

Marcocchi, M. *Colonialismo, cristianesimo e culture extreuropee. L'istruzione di Propaganda Fide ai vicari apostolici dell'Asia orientale 1659*, Milan, 1981.

Morello, G. "Documenti beniniani nella Biblioteca Apostolica Vaticana. Bernini e i lavori a S. Pietro nel "Diario" di Alessandro VII," *Bernini in Vaticano*, s.l. 1981, 311–40.

Repgen, K. "Die Finanzen des Nuntius Fabio Chigi. Ein Beitrag zur Sozialgeschichte der römischen Führungsgruppe im 17. Jahrhundert," *Geschichte, Wirtschaft, Gesellschaft, Festschrift für Clemens Bauer*, Berlin, 1974, 229–80.

Rietbergen, P. "A Vision Come True: Pope Alexander VII, Gianlorenzo Bernini and the Colonnades of St.

Peter's," *Mededelingen van het Nederlands Instituut te Rome*, 44–5 (1983), 111–63.

Rietbergen, P. "Papal Patronage and Propaganda: Pope Alexander VII (1655–1667), the Biblioteca Alessandrina and the Sapienza Complex," *Mededelingen*, op. cit., 47 (1987), 157–77.

Rosa, M. "Alessandro VII," *DBI*, 3 (1960), 204–15.

Springhetti, E., S.I., "Alexander VII P.M. poeta latinus," *AHP*, I (1963), 265–94.

Wright, A. D. *The Early Modern Papacy: From the Council of Trent to the French Revolution, 1564–1789,* London, 2000.

ALEXANDER VIII. *Pietro Ottoboni (b. Venice, 22 April 1610, d. Rome, 1 February 1691). Elected Pope on 6 October 1689. Buried at St. Peter's in Rome.*

The pontificate of Alexander VIII, which lasted approximately a year and a half, was too short to allow any real involvement on his part in the most important matters bearing on the life of the Church and the Christian world. Nevertheless, it was a significant transitional period between the rigorism of INNOCENT XI and the conciliatory spirit of INNOCENT XII, for whom he opened the way to the rapprochement with France.

Ottoboni belonged to a Venetian family of the recent nobility. After his studies in Padua, where he obtained a license in law, he took advantage of his good relationship with URBAN VIII and of the support of Venetian friends long resident in Rome to move to the capital. He was rapidly named referendary of the two Signaturas, then governor of Terni (1638), Rieti (1640), and Città di Castello (1641). In 1643, he became AUDITOR of the Rota. His excellent knowledge of the administrative world, his capacity for hard work, and a legal background were rewarded by his being elevated to the cardinalate on 19 February 1652. Though he seemed destined from then on for a niche in the Roman CURIA, he was named bishop of Brescia on 7 December 1654. He remained for ten years in this Lombard diocese, on which he left the mark of his abilities and his legalistic cast of mind. The latter was especially manifest in the rigor with which he attempted to redress certain forms of non-orthodox religious experience. In the Val Camonica, a mountainous region where Ghibelline and anti-Roman feeling was strong, a group of quietists had taken it upon themselves to proselytize. Cardinal Ottoboni began by issuing warnings and then moved on to repressive measures with the help of the Inquisition of Brescia and Venice. Upon his return to Rome, he renewed old friendships, principally with Cardinals Azzolino and Chigi. CLEMENT X named him datary, and Innocent XI chose him as secretary of the HOLY OFFICE. He thereupon became one of the principal figures in the Curia, within which he devoted himself once again to quietism. He condemned Fr. Romiti and his disciples from Matelica (Macerata), placed the works of Cardinal Petrucci on the INDEX, and scrutinized the slightest actions and stirrings of the adherents of these teachings, especially in Rome and the PAPAL STATES. He was later called upon to deal with the issue of the REGALE. To Innocent XI, he suggested firm opposition to the extension of royal right over all the churches in France.

Upon the death of Innocent XI, the CONCLAVE, which opened on 23 August 1689, was blocked by the opposing interests of the cardinals who were partisans of France, of the Holy Roman Empire, and of the *zelanti* of the Curia. The debates were prolonged, and it was only after careful study of the reports sent from Rome by the duke of Chaulnes and Cardinal de Bouillon that Louis XIV decided to advise the French cardinals to vote for the Venetian cardinal, who was firmly supported by the curialists, such as Chigi and other *zelanti*. In the end, even the cardinals who were partisans of the empire voted for him. On 6 October, Cardinal Ottoboni became pope under the name ALEXANDER VIII. The jurisdictional conflict between the HOLY SEE and Louis XIV, which had reached a point of rupture with Innocent XI (in the suspension of diplomatic relations), was naturally the most urgent matter to occupy the new pope. Though he conceded nothing in terms of principle, his legalistic cast of mind nevertheless was able to find compromises allowing the negotiations to be resumed. Once the first difficulties had been overcome, the situation was opened up thanks to reciprocal concessions. The king restored Avignon and the Comtat Venaissin to the Church. The pope made a cardinal of the bishop of Beauvais, Forbin-Janson (July 1690), who had signed the four articles of Gallican liberty and was for that reason very close to the sovereign. Not everything was resolved, however, and the pontiff continued to be wary of the claims of Louis XIV. In fact, the king continued to demand that bishops designated by him for vacant dioceses be recognized, and the Pope continued to protest against the non-abrogation of the Gallican articles. On his deathbed, Alexander VIII was still writing the BRIEF *Inter multiplices* against the extension of the royal perogatives and against the legitimacy of the assembly of the clergy of 1682. Yet the resumption of the discussions and the will to renew the dialogue (Pastor speaks, with some exaggeration, of an extreme complacency on the part of the pope with regard to the king) were elements that facilitated a solution of the conflict when his successor, Innocent XII, had to concern himself with the matter.

If his involvement with France was intense, that with the Holy Roman Empire was less so. He gave some limited assistance to Leopold I in the latter's war against the TURKS (in accord with Venice, at the time rather anxious over Vienna's great success in the East). He raised none of the emperor's candidates to the cardinate, and pursued a policy clearly favorable to Louis XIV. Moreover, the Most Christian King was seeking to strengthen his image as defender of Catholicism after the alliance between the empire and Protestant England. During the long war that bloodied Europe, this was to be one of the themes most readily invoked by Louis XIV in order to attract the good-will of the pope and the Catholic sovereigns.

In the religious realm, Alexander VIII was responsible for the censuring of two laxist propositions (24 August 1690), for the condemnation of thirty-one of Jansen's ninety-six propositions incriminated by Innocent XI, and for other affirmations on the sacraments and the cult of the Virgin Mary. He ordered the Oratorian Matteo Petrucci, whose works had been placed on the Index for quietism in 1688, to leave Rome for good and return to Iesi, the seat of his diocese (a moderate measure by contemporary standards). In sum, these were interventions that brought to a conclusion courses of action embarked upon by his predecessors.

Alexander VIII can hardly be said to have had the time to concern himself with the Papal States. Nevertheless, he became very popular among the Romans for having lowered taxes, for having brought a measure of liberalization into the grain trade, and for having restored to the city a relatively relaxed and happier atmosphere, something that had almost disappeared under the pontificate of the austere Innocent XI. But another difference from his predecessor was clear in his manifest NEPOTISM. His family soon left Venice for Rome, where they obtained well-paying positions, and his nephews and great-nephews were made cardinals. These were signs of an inauspicious weakness that cast a shadow over his brief pontificate. These elements, added to his taste for culture and works of art, suggest that without doubt certain characteristics typical of the humanist pontiffs of the Renaissance were revived in him.

Luigi Fiorani

Bibliography

Bischoffshausen, S. V. *Papst Alexander VIII. und der Wiener Hof (1689–1691)*. Stuttgart-Vienna, 1900.

De Bojani, F. *Innocent XI, sa correspondance avec ses nonces*, Rome, 1910–12, II, 467–79, III, I, passim.

Dubruel, M. "Le pape Alexandre VIII et les affaires de France," *Revue d'histoire ecclésiastique*, 15 (1914), 282–302, 495–514.

Gerin, G. "Alexander VIII et Louis XIV," *Revue des questions historiques*, 22 (1877), 135–210.

Guerrini, P. "Quietisti e pelagini in valle Camonica ed a Brescia," *Brixia sacra*, III (1912), 30–48.

Michaud, E. *La Politique de compromis avec Rome. Le pape Alexandre VIII et le duc de Chaulnes*, Bern, 1888.

Pastor, 32.

Petrocchi, M. *Il quietismo italiano del Seicento*, Rome, 1948, passim.

Petrucci, A. *DBI*, 2, 215–19.

Recueil des instructions données aux ambassadeurs et ministres de France . . . , Rome, by G. Hanotanx II, Paris, 1911, passim.

Richard, P. *DHGE*, II, 244–51.

Scarabelli, G. "In margine all'elezione al sommo pontificato del card. P. Ottoboni già vescovo di Brescia," *Brescia sacra*, 10 (1975), 135–7.

Schiavo, A. "La definitiva sepoltura di Alessandro VIII," Strenna dei romanisti, 45 (1984), 508–15.

Wright, A. D. *The Early Modern Papacy: From the Council of Trent to the French Revolution, 1564–1789*, London, 2000.

ALEXANDRIA. Alexandria and Rome were two centers of early Christianity that, within the framework of the original autonomy of the episcopal sees, during the first three centuries after Constantine, created two highly individualized traditions. The founding of Constantinople and the growing intervention of the emperors in problems of doctrine gave to the sees of PETER and "of MARK" repeated opportunities to forge a solidarity in the service of orthodoxy, from the middle of the 3rd to the middle of the 5th century. Was this relationship somewhat embellished by Roman tradition, which drew from it historical justifications in support of the PRIMACY the see of Peter? Interrupted but implicit during the interval between the periods when they were active, relations between Rome and Alexandria were gradually mediated by Constantinople, whose political authority was coupled after the COUNCIL of Chalcedon (451) with a spiritual authority closely subjected to the former. This date represents even more of a major turning point, in that then Egypt embarked in a lasting way upon paths outside orthodoxy. Thus was broken the solidarity that for two centuries had united the Roman and Alexandrian "popes," at the same time that the influence of the two Apostolic Sees was about to evolve in opposite directions, toward ascendancy for Rome, and decline for Alexandria.

In the modern era, the description of this relationship is often adapted to the apologetic positions of Roman universalism, in a way that distorts the historical perspective. Michel Le Quien, in the introduction to the Egyptian chapters of his *Patrologia orientalis* (1740), established an image of Alexandria as a patriarchate subordinated to Rome by virtue of historical legitimacy: Mark would have been destined to create the Church of Egypt *magistri sui Petri nutu, iussuque Christi*, Peter directing toward Egypt the investiture by the Holy Spirit descended upon Mark at Pentecost. This is the transmutation into a historical event of a doctrinal construction progressively developed by Rome and to which the names of JULIUS I, of DAMASUS, and of Leo the Great

(Leo I) are closely linked. The reconstruction thus proposed, of the apostolic preaching in general, and of the life of Peter in particular, is more cautiously received today by historians of the Church.

The Alexandrians were no better able to be precise in their account of Mark and his relations with Peter, but the fact that they never developed a local version in response to the Roman version of the historical facts seems to indicate that they felt hardly threatened by that version in their claim for autonomy. By at the end of the 6th century, Roman teaching on this matter had received what from then on would be its final form, which Gregory the Great (Gregory I) set forth to his Alexandrian colleague Eulogius (*Letters*, VII, 40): "Although there were a number of apostles, nevertheless, by reason of this primacy, only the see of the Prince of the Apostles has affirmed his authority, which belongs to Rome alone to extend over three places" (these were understood to be Alexandria, Antioch, and Rome). What follows completes the line of reasoning: if the legitimacy of the three apostolic sees goes back to Peter, the bishops who are successors of the apostles represent a kind of spiritual triumvirate within which preeminence legitimately belongs to the one holding the Roman see. This theory was based on Holy Scripture (Matt. 16:18) and could find justification in Eusebius of Caesarea, who was also the first to mention Mark as the founder of the Alexandrian Church; but it is clear that Rome had a vested interest in it as canceling out the moral benefit enjoyed by the Church of Alexandria on account of its supposedly earlier creation. On the other hand, a strict chronological view would have favored the apostolic see of Antioch, founded by Peter before he set out on his mission in the West: it was therefore better for Alexandria to recognize, within the limits that distance helped to impose, the primacy of Rome rather than of another Eastern see.

It should also be recognized that at the time Gregory used such language, it was no longer the power of the Alexandrian see that could have lessened its practical significance, but the existence of a patriarchate of Constantinople with ecumenical pretensions, negating the Roman interpretation of the MAGISTERIUM of Peter and of its transmission. Two centuries earlier, this way of speaking was just starting to be developed and would have done little to impress an all-powerful, independent, and rich Alexandrian Church, whose bishop had absolute authority over more than a hundred bishops and an army of monks. Alexandria then was dealing with Rome on a footing of equality. It was making full use of the privilege of jurisdiction, granted to it in 325 by canon 6 of the council of Nicaea, in order to have its voice heard loud and strong throughout the East. Its spiritual prestige extended to the West, where it continued, while christianizing it, a certain tradition of Egyptophilia, and Athanasius, the author of the *Life of Anthony*, was able to make known some of the ideals and realities of Egyptian MONASTICISM in a direct way during his Roman exile. Later on, Rome would prefer to this Egyptian eremitic monasticism the Cappadocian cenobitic monasticism (Basil) or the Syrian monasticism spread in the West by Jerome, even though he was the translator of Pachomius. This moral authority of Alexandria, fortified by the vitality of its theological school, to which so many illustrious names were linked, found itself put to the service of orthodoxy in a struggle that led it naturally to an understanding with Rome, not through acceptance of Rome's universalist plan, but with a view to a kind of geographical sharing in the leadership of the Christian world. Successively, Arianism and Nestorianism gave the two apostolic sees an opportunity to affirm their identical views in the matter of trinitarian, and then Christological, theology, and to manifest their solidarity in questions of dogma against the pretensions of the emperors and to set forth the *Credo*. Both had previously struggled with such problems, during the last third of the 3rd century, at the time of the Sabellian teaching (which tended to make no distinction between the Father and the Son), which, forty years after its condemnation in Rome by Calistus, had become influential in Cyrenaica, where the faithful had asked for doctrinal clarification first from Dionysius of Alexandria, a genuine Origenist, and then from DIONYSIUS of Rome (in 257). This first debate facilitated maturation over time in that, having held positions that were palpably different and in truth somewhat heterodox, and that in the 240s had deepened the disagreement between Origen and Pope Fabian, Rome and Alexandria brought their positions closer together, the former by nuancing its monarchianism (the affirmation of the oneness of the divine person) and the latter by softening its subordinationism (the doctrine professing the subordination of the Son to the Father). This agreement, however, was more apparent than real, and the *Apology* of Dionysius of Alexandria, meant to prove his fundamental agreement with Dionysius of Rome, cannot cancel out the Arianism already put forward in other contexts in his *Letter* of 257 to SIXTUS II. The conditions were nevertheless created for the temporary formation, given the right circumstances, of what Henri-Irénée Marrou has called the "Rome-Alexandria axis." As soon as Arius began his intrigues in Palestine following his condemnation by an Egyptian council, Alexander, pope of Alexandria, began a rich correspondence with Bishop Silvester (this term respects the terminology then in force, the use of the papal title in the West being later than in the East). In the same way, during the entire preparatory phase for Nicaea, he made sure through his correspondence with Rome that they held common views. From 325 to 381, in order to defend the Nicaean definition of consubstantiality (*homoousios*) against Arianism, Alexandria and Rome conducted a parallel combat that sometimes united them more directly.

Thus, when Athanasius, whose personality dominated the Alexandrian 4th century, was deposed in 335 by an episcopal tribunal meeting at Tyre, and then reestablished in 337 by Constantine II, emperor of the West, and the Eastern anti-Nicaea party addressed itself to Julius, the bishop of Rome, they did so not to solicit his arbitration, as Socrates and Sozomen would have us believe anachronistically, but rather to obtain his support. For his part, Athanasius first sought the support of an Egyptian council; but he took advantage of the Roman proposal for a synod at the time when his expulsion from Alexandria prompted him to return to Rome, the place of refuge for persecuted Eastern Nicaeans.

It was therefore in Rome, indifferent to the first conflicts between Athanasius and the imperial power, and cautious in its justification of such an unusual legal procedure, that the sentence of Tyre was reexamined and invalidated in 340 in the voluntary absence of the accusers. A product of circumstances, this intervention of the see of Peter in the affairs of Egypt, a double repudiation of the CHURCHES OF THE ORIENT and of the imperial power, should not be overestimated: it remains an isolated episode that inaugurated no sustained practice, and when the council of Sardica treated the more theological aspects of the "case of Athanasius," it no longer bore a Roman mark. When Liberius, thirteen years later, sought to reexamine the SYNOD of 340, still apropos of Athanasius, it was a complete failure. But the harmony was dealt an even more serious blow when Liberius, after having attempted to defend Athanasius against the emperor, and having paid for his resistance with exile, obtained his return to Rome (358) in exchange for the retraction of the sentences pronounced by Julius. The accord failed again in its attempt to harmonize the computation of the date of Easter, and did not even envisage harmonizing the ritual. It is therefore above all the alliance of the two popes in 339–40 that left the most lasting mark on the Alexandrian memory, and even more on the Roman annals. As though astonished at his own boldness, Julius developed a legitimation of his jurisdiction (*Epistula ad Orientales*) in which the theory unites with and surpasses this spontaneous affirmation of Roman primacy, carrying the seed of future eccelesiological developments. His successors did not forget this.

The 370s were a time when a new orthodoxy was being developed in the East, to the definition of which the great Cappadocians (Basil of Caesarea, Gregory of Nazianzus, Gregory of Nyssa) made the essential contribution, and from which Alexandria originally sought to divert Damasus, by presenting it to him as a disguised form of Arianism. Forty years after Athanasius, Peter II, exiled by Valens, chose Rome to prepare and stand surety for his return to Alexandria, and then added his voice to that of Damasus in order to condemn Apollinarism (in 377 and 378 respectively) and lead the council of Antioch

(379), which established the revised orthodoxy. Timothy and Damasus together opposed the episcopal designations of Theodosius (Gregory of Nazianzus, Nectarius, Flavian): under an emperor who was a champion of orthodoxy, it was no longer doctrinal disagreement that set these battle in motion, but the political rivalry between the ecclesiastical power and the imperial power, in the face of which Rome and Alexandria defended their spiritual independence, with all the temporal extensions they saw implied by it. On the other hand, Theodosius wanted to break up the ecclesial organization and integrate it within the imperial structure, by modeling it on the civil DIOCESES and by balancing the spiritual primacy of Rome and the Alexandrian imperialism with an elevation of the episcopal see that was more directly at the beck and call of the political power: that of the Eastern capital. Initiated at the council of Constantinople (381), this project was finally realized in 451.

With the condemnation of Nestorius by the council of Ephesus (431), sought and obtained by Cyril, and already pronounced by the time Celestine's LEGATES arrived, Alexandrian power reached its zenith. Its pretensions knew no limits under DIOSCORUS, the maladroit successor to Cyril: he swayed the council of Ephesus II (449) toward an Apollinarist pronunciamiento, and had the patriarch of Constantinople, Flavian, deposed. Leo the Great defended the latter with calculated inefficacy, even though the Alexandrian had already sought to have the adopted TWELVE ANATHEMAS of Cyril, the language the Roman formulations of which, inspired by Ambrose, would be judged heretical. Dioscorus fought on two fronts: ecclesiological and political against Constantinople, and theological against Antioch. Leo's calculations were no less complex, his carping demand that the primacy of Rome be recognized interfering with his theological positions. Two years later (451), the council of Chalcedon delivered a decisive blow to Alexandria's ambitions. Two interpretations are possible of this council convoked "to put an end to the disputes and define the true faith:" For Grillmeier, the council opposed Leo's formulations to Dioscorus because Leo's *Tome* offered the best response possible to the problems of the Incarnation (but might this not be taking too literally the diplomatic politeness of Emperor Marcian, his flattery of Leo, whose public approbation was indispensable, and who he knew was drawing back on account of canon 28 regarding the patriarchates?). According to W. H. C. Frend, the council welcomed in Leo the only authority judged to be compatible with the positions of Cyril, who was recognized as the major reference, in such a way that Dioscorus could be disqualified with respect to his own roots. Antioch would in a way have shielded itself behind Rome in order to settle its accounts with Alexandria, while maintaining in essence the formula of union ("one person, two natures") which Theodosius II's desire for pacification had obtained from Cyril and the Antiochenes in 438, without the participation of Rome (despite what SIXTUS III said of it after the fact). Dioscorus's audacity rebounding against him, the true winners would have been Constantinople and the emperor. At Chalcedon, Alexandria lost as much in the dogmatic realm as in the realm of spiritual and moral authority, which it had to share henceforth with three other Eastern "patriarchates" (a term made official only at this time), at the head of which was Constantinople, accordingly to be considered the equal of the apostolic sees. Leo had every reason to be concerned likewise about this rise in power of the Eastern Rome, to which the council had granted a complete jurisdictional equality, without reaffirming by means of the Petrine argument the preeminence of the Roman see. However, Dioscorus burned his bridges with Rome, in demanding Leo's excommunication, thus depriving him of the traditional alliance with Alexandria to counterbalance Constantinople's authority.

Once Dioscorus had left the scene, Pope Leo no longer agreed to the projected discussion of the faith that Leo, the new emperor, wanted to open between partisans and adversaries of Chalcedon. It was surprising that the traditional understanding between the two metropolises on the Christological definitions had been able to fall apart so brutally and irreparably. In fact, this agreement had rested for some time on more than one misunderstanding. We can note that Cyril, whose memory was associated with Leo's definitions by the council fathers of Chalcedon, was likewise claimed by the Monophysites as the founder of their theology. In fact, the slide from orthodoxy toward Apollinarism, the first step on the path to monophysitism, was accomplished from the time of Cyril, who was misled by the apocryphal writings attributed by the HERESY to Athanasius. Yet would Cyril have been unaware of the hoax if he had not himself had a leaning toward the Egyptian sensibility, which privileged the divine element in Christ, considered alone capable of saving the human soul from the terrors and threats of the world, and which admitted the two natures on a strictly intellectual and abstract level, while denying their real existence? We can note also that Apollinaris himself had originally been a faithful disciple of Athanasius.

Liberatus reported that in 482, when the formula of reconciliation (*Henoticon*) proposed a basis for an understanding theoretically acceptable to everyone (in truth, it granted much more to the Monophysites than to the Chalcedonians), Peter Mongos acknowledged in a letter to Pope SIMPLICIUS "that fundamentally he approved the council of Chalcedon, but that before his people he was bound to pretend and to anathemize it." Without judging the sincerity of intention on the part of the patriarch, we can recall that his analysis recognized both the disproportion between the causes and the consequences of the rupturing of the Catholic world, and the power of factors having nothing to do with doctrine but very much linked to the affirmation of a national culture. The Alexandrians still proclaimed, in a document sent to Pope ANASTASIUS II (496–8), the "*adfinitas, ac veluti cognatio*" (a relationship by alliance and, as it were, a blood relationship) linking the two apostolic sees. The unity of thought with Rome lives on at this point like a great shipwrecked dream in which still can be read, shining through, the nostalgia for the Alexandrian project to share with its apostolic sister the hegemony over the Christian world.

After the long parenthesis of the Acacian SCHISM (484–519), Rome was reintroduced on the Eastern scene by Justin and Justinian. Justinian's vacillating religious policy offered to Rome a fluctuating and contradictory framework for action. The monophysite triumph of 535, establishing Theodosius in Alexandria under Theodora's protection, was followed beginning in the next year by the Chalcedonian *reconquista* of Alexandria and the delta under the aegis of Pope AGAPITUS and then of his APOCRISARIUS at Constantinople, the future Pope PELAGIUS; they designated the first two patriarchs sent to hold the orthodox bridgehead in Egypt. But as soon as these Western projects were realized, Justinian reversed himself and turned toward Eastern problems, to which he sacrificed the Roman dogmatic positions. The COUNCIL of Constantinople of 553, proposing a union based on Origenist doctrines and furthered by the condemnation of the Three Chapters, sanctioned a de facto rupture between East and West: we can note that on this occasion the Alexandrian Apollinaris was more Roman than Vigilius, a shaky moment indeed. More durable, the maintenance of orthodoxy in Alexandria created possibilities there for an understanding with Rome that would be made the most of in the last quarter of the 6th century, by PELAGIUS II and then GREGORY the Great, under the patriarchate of Eulogius. The rest of Egypt was left to be towed along behind Antioch, yet was indifferent to all external overtures and, for that reason, was either fought against or spared by the imperial power.

The historian desirous of understanding the mechanisms of this absurd and tragic misunderstanding returns again and again to Chalcedon and its consequences. It has been observed that Alexandrian theology was most often defined by contradiction vis-à-vis Constantinople, to the point where it risked contradicting itself—which, to tell the truth, did not much disturb it—and we have difficulty avoiding the brilliant formula of J. Maspero, for whom "monophysitism was not a heresy, but only a schismatic intention." It is still necessary to seek to understand, before depreciating it, the ancient Egyptian spirituality's taking of its historical revenge through Christianity. From the beginning an object of fascination/repulsion for the Greeks, this cultural fount, at the moment of its gushing to the surface, found itself rejected out of hand by Christian Hellenism, which had lastingly persuaded us of its supposedly intellectual vulgarity. A retrospective view, warped by the imbalance of later evolutions, then came to add anachronism to incomprehension.

At the time, the affirmation of this difference in an ancient world ideally pursuing a project of unification—no matter here that in practice it was belied—entailed contradictory consequences for Christianity in the land of Egypt. Cyril had deeply unified the Alexandrian and Egyptian sensibilities, until then separated. On the other hand, this was also the prelude to a provincialization of the Alexandrian see that would be accentuated in the 6th century with the atomization of Egyptian monophysitism and its theoretical impoverishment. Perhaps paying the price of its past arrogance, Alexandria, under Justinian, was no longer the spiritual head of a united province that once might have appeared to the West as a model for the christianization of a regional society, but rather a spiritual center lacerated by its divisions. Carrying this cutting off to its most extreme consequences, the religious inconstancy of the imperial power crossing from orthodoxy to monophysitism, aggravated by its authoritarianism, led that power to a kind of symmetrical failure. Breaking the moral cohesion of the *Romanitas*, Constantinople turned Rome toward the barbarian kingdoms, and detached from it an Egypt that would abandon it all the more easily at the time of the Islamic expansion.

Jean-Michel Carrié

Bibliography

Dvornik, F. *Byzance et la primauté romaine*, Paris, 1964.

Frend, W. H. C. *The Rise of Christianity*, London, 1984.

Frend, W. H. C. *The Rise of the Monophysite Movement*, 2nd rev. ed., Cambridge, 1979.

Grillmeier, H., and Bacht, H., eds., *Das Konzil von Chalkedon: Geschichte und Gegenwart*, 3 vols., Wurzburg, 1951–54, 2nd ed. 1959 (especially 1, 345–87: P. Galtier, "Saint Cyrille d'Alexandrie et saint Léon le Grand à Chalcédoine").

Grillmeier, H. *Jesus der Christus am Glauben der kirche*, 2 vols., Freiburg-Basel-Vienna, 1982; Fr. trans. of vol. 2, *Le Christ dans la tradition chrétienne, II, 1. Le concile de Chalcédoine (451). Réception et oppositoin (451–513)*, Paris, 1990.

Griggs, C. W. *Early Egyptian Christianity from its Origins to 451 C. E.*, Leiden, 1990.

Hardy, E. R. *Christian Egypt: Church and People; Christianity and Nationalism in the Patriarchate of Alexandria*, New York-London, 1952.

Joannou, P. *Die Ostkirche und die Cathedra Petri*, Stuttgart, 1972.

Kannengiesser, C. *Athanase d'Alexandrie évêque et écrivain. Une lecture des "Traités contre les ariens,"* Paris, 1983.

Kannengieser, C., ed., *Politique et théologie chez Athanase d'Alexandrie (Actes du Colloque de Chan-* *tilly, 1973)*, Paris, 1974 (especially 93–126: C. Pietri, "La question d'Athanase vue de Rome" [338–60]).

Maspero, J. *Histoire des patriarches d'Alexandrie depuis la mort de l'empereur Anastase jusqu' à la réconciliation des Églises jacobites (518–616)*, Paris, 1923.

Nouvelle Histoire de l'Église, 1: Des origines à Grégoire le Grand, Paris, 1963.

Pearson, B. A., and Goehring, J. E., eds., *The Roots of Egyptian Christianity*, Philadelphia, 1986.

Pietri, C. *Roma christiana*, 2 vols., Rome, 1978.

Stein, E. *Histoire du Bas-Empire*, 2 vols. in 3, Paris, 1949 and 1959; 2nd ed., Amsterdam, 1968.

ALLOCUTION BY THE POPE TO THE ROMAN ROTA.

Since PIUS XII, the Roman pontiffs have frequently addressed the prelate auditors of the Rota (37 times in 52 years), to place before them current subjects or to apprise them of issues regarding the administration of justice in the Church. Listed below are the ideas central to these papal interventions with, in parentheses, indications of the dates on which they were given.

Pius XII: The right to marry, nullification of marriages and dissolution of the bond (3 October 1941); qualities of moral certainty (based upon objective motives) that the judge must have to pronounce a sentence (1 October 1942); the sole purpose in the examination of matrimonial cases (2 October 1944); essential differences between ecclesiastical and civil judicial procedures (2 October 1945); defense of the faith and freedom of conversions (6 October 1946); essential differences between the finality of ecclesiastical society and that of civil society (19 October 1947); the objective rules of law according to Christian principles (13 November 1949).

John XXIII: The history of the Rota, tribunal of the Christian family (19 October 1959); the threatening of the sanctity of marriage (25 October 1960); the indissolubility of marriage (13 December 1961).

Paul VI: The preparation for marriage (16 December 1963); the deepest respect for justice in ecclesiastical tribunals (11 January 1965); the pastoral function of the ecclesiastical judge. Legalism (25 January 1966); justice as the foundation of social life (23 January 1967); the service that the Rota renders the Church and the Roman pontiff (12 February 1968); authority in the Church. Juridism (27 January 1969); the judiciary's power in the Church and objections against it (29 January 1970); the exercise of authority in the Church (28 January 1971); the necessity and revision of canon law (28 January 1972); the pastoral nature of law in the Church and canonical equity (8 February 1973); the sacred character of the judge's role (31 January 1974); protection of the intangible values and pastoral solicitude in judiciary activity. The motu proprio *Causas matrimoniales* (30 January 1975); juridical reality and love in marriage (9 February 1976); the conditions for a canonical procedure in the service of the salvation of souls (28 January 1978).

John Paul II: The Church, rampart of personal rights (17 February 1979); the process for nullifying marriage (4 February 1980); safeguarding the values of marriage (24 January 1981); recognizing the value of marriage (28 January 1982); juridical instances in ecclesiastical communion (26 February 1983); using the new Code of Canon Law in Church practice (26 January 1984); serving justice and truth (30 January 1986); the difficult search for psychological causes for nullifying marriage (5 February 1987); the defender of the bond preserving the Christian vision of marriage (25 January 1988); the guarantee and regulation of the right for defense (26 January 1989); the pastoral dimension of canon law (18 January 1990); the evangelical doctrine on marriage (28 January 1991); the immutability of divine law, stability of canon law, and the dignity of man (23 January 1992); canon law and the annulment of marriage (29 January 1993); the splendor in justice and law (28 January 1994); right of trial defense (10 February 1995); judges cannot bend the objective norm or interpret divine law in an arbitrary way (22 January 1996); rediscovering law as interpersonal reality (27 January 1997); on an instrument of wise jurisprudence (17 January 1998); true marriage requires a reciprocal gift of exclusive, indissoluble, and fruitful love commitment (21 January 1999); the current divorce mentality in relation to the doctrine of the indissolubility of ratified and consummated marriage, and the limits of the Roman pontiff's power over such marriage (21 January 2000); God himself is the author of marriage (February, 2001).

Dominique Le Tourneau

Bibliography

The originals of these texts in Italian may be found in the corresponding number of the *Acta Apostolicae Sedis*. A French translation, partial for the older speeches listed, is in *La Documentation catholique* (except the interventions from 1941, 1942, 1944, 1975, and 1978).

Bersini, F. *I discorsi del Papa alla Rota*, Vatican City, 1986.

Le Tourneau, D. "Discursos del Papa Juan Pablo II a la Rota Romana y comentario" (Text of the Speeches from 1978 to 1988, with analytic table and commentary), *Ius Canonicum XXVIII* (1988), 541–618.

ALLOCUTION, CONSISTORIAL. The primacy of the supreme pontiff, a principle gradually formulated over the course of history, traditionally has been given important practical application on the occasion of the allocutions delivered by the pope during the opening and then the closing of the meetings of the CARDINALS in CONSISTORY. These oral interventions, a privilege of governmental power, are not explicitly called for by the CODE OF CANON LAW of 1983; but nevertheless have real legal impact; the pontifical allocution constitutes the official inaugural act of the session and generally establishes the agenda by defining its priorities. In similar fashion, allocution closes the session by drawing up a summary of proceedings, and often cites various prospects or intentions for their being extended throughout the life of the Church. The consistorial allocution is not meant to be normative. It is, above all, a means of announcing broad orientations to the Catholic world at large.

Philippe Levillain

See also PRIMACY, PAPAL.

ALMONER, APOSTOLIC. The institution of an apostolic chaplaincy goes back to GREGORY X (1272–6). Without attributing to it a special hierarchical rank, he transformed the responsibility of handling direct assistance from the pope, in the form either of cash or of provisions for the poor, priests, and laymen, independently of aid provided for special works that had developed within the charitable tradition proper to the DIOCESES. Gregory X defined the features of the apostolic chaplaincy as follows: "*Pauperum amantissimus, primus omnium in apostolico palatio piarum in illos largitionum praesidem constitui.*" ("Being most fond of the poor, I was the first of all living in the papal palace to place someone in charge of aimsgiving to the poor.") Tolemeo da Lucca, bishop of Torcello, was the first to hold this position. Over the centuries, the role grew, particularly enhanced by ALEXANDER V's bull of 1409.

In the scope of reforms undertaken in the Curia beginning in 1967 (apostolic constitution *Regimini Ecclesiae universae*) and then in 1988 (apostolic constitution *Pastor bonus*), the status of the apostolic chaplaincy oscillated. On one hand, in May 1968 it became the pope's personal assistance service, and its director continued to be called the pope's chaplain. On the other hand, with its former title, it was included as a recognized member of the papal FAMILY in 1988. From this point on, the apostolic chaplain's rank has been on the same level as that of an archbishop, and he holds a seat in official audiences. He can also delegate the pope's blessings. His role is an essentially symbolic one, since the personal funds of the pope available to him allow him to draw only a modest salary.

Philippe Levillain

Bibliography

Annuario pontificio per l'anno 1993, Vatican City, 1993.
d'Onorio, J. B. *Le Pape et le gouvernement de l'Eglise*, Paris, 1992, 309 and 385.

ALTAR, PAPAL. The papal altar is the altar in a patriarchal BASILICA on which the sovereign pontiff alone can officiate, except in the case of specially granted written authorization in a BRIEF. The title and privilege attached to a papal altar are related to the cult of martyrs near tombs where their remains are housed. By the 4th century, freedom of religion offered the chance to build churches where the altars were placed directly above martyrs' tombs. Before that time, the Mass was celebrated on tombs as often as possible. Christian Antiquity attached great importance to the intercession of martyrs for the expiation of sins. The altar built above a tomb took the name "altar of confession" or "confessional" in memory of the martyrs who had confessed their faith in that place.

St. Peter's altar of confession was built above his tomb in various stages, from the original building erected by ANICETUS I (155–66), according to the *LIBER PONTIFICALIS* up through the consecration of the present basilica by URBAN VIII in 1626. The first altar around Saint Peter's tomb, built during the reign of Constantine, was a cube-shaped marble casket more than two meters high, completely surrounding the tomb. Mass was celebrated in front of it. Later, Gregory the Great (GREGORY I) undertook renovation work to raise the level of the apse, installing a semicircular crypt and building an altar on the upper part of Constantine's monument. Thus, the first confessional appeared as an architectural complex that allowed the liturgy to be linked to the proximity of the tomb. It was approached by a fenestrelle situated inside the papal altar, the opening through which recovered objects were taken down below and kept as relics. CALLISTUS II (1119–24) had new marble laid to renovate Gregory the Great's altar, which is still partially visible inside the crypt. The present altar was built above Callistus II's altar during the reign of CLEMENT VII (1592–1605), whose name is engraved on it. The present confessional is on a level with Constantine's basilica. Bernini's baldachin (canopy) topping the three altars expresses a vertical relationship between the rock of St. Peter and the domed cupola, in which is written in letters 1.4 meter high *Tu es Petrus et super hanc petram aedificabo Ecclesiam meam* ("Thou art Peter, and on this rock I shall build ny Church").

Philippe Levillain

Bibliography

Guarducci, M. *Die Petrustradition im Vatikan im Lichte der Geschichte und Archäologie*, Rome, 1963.
Kirschbaum, E. *Die Gräber der Apostel fürsten*, Lucerne, 1959.

ALUM OF TOLFA / TOLFA ALUM. "Today, I bring you victory against the TURKS. Each year, they extort more than 300,000 ducats from Christians for the alum we need to dye fabrics. [. . .] I have discovered seven mountains so rich in alum that we can furnish seven worlds. [. . .] You can prepare the CRUSADE against the Turks, the mines will give you the necessary finances." It was in these terms that the humanist Pope PIUS II Piccolomini reported in his *Commentaries* the announcement by Giovanni de Castro, an Italian merchant and financier, of the discovery, probably in May 1462, of a deposit of alum in the mountains of Tolfa, a volcanic region to the northeast of Civitavecchia. Alum is a mineral—a double aluminum sulfate—used in the textile industry to allow colors to set during the dyeing of fabrics. The conquest of Constantinople by the Turks had thrown into disarray the provisions of alum to Europe which had long depended on the mines in Phocaea and Mytilene, exploited by the Genoese, it had encouraged the search for new mines, discovered in Tuscany, near Volterra, around 1458, and then in Mazarrón, near Cartagena, in Castille, in May 1462. The exploitation of the Tolfa mines, at the latest in November 1462, belongs to this set of circumstances but from the beginning took on another dimension.

The pope attempted, in effect, to make this "alum of the crusades"—the profits from its exploitation were placed in the till of the crusades—the subject of a monopoly throughout the Christian world. Pius II, as of 1463, forbade Christian merchants to buy Turkish alum, and his successor, PAUL II, in 1465, established the Tolfa alum as the sole source of the supply to the Christian world, a measure reiterated by JULIUS II in 1506. The papacy, despite a prolonged effort, did not succeed in imposing the monopoly. In the end, it almost did so in the Italian peninsula when the competing mines of Agnano, in the kingdom of Naples, and of Volterra, in Tuscany, closed, during the second half of the 16th century. The true competitors were first of all Spanish alum, throughout the 16th century, and then, during the 17th century, the mines in Liège, the German lands, England, and Sweden, which closed off Central Europe, the Baltic, and the British Isles, as of 1667, to Roman alum; in the meantime, Turkish alum continued to be imported, though in modest quantities, especially through the ports of Venice and Marseille.

With over seven hundred workers in the 1560s, the Tolfa mine had a labor force twice the size of that in the

Castilian mines and was ranked first among the European mining enterprises of the period. In the 15th century, the APOSTOLIC CAMERA separated production, which long remained in the hands of those who had discovered the mine, and sales, which were handled by large companies of merchant bankers, among whom were the Medici, the Pazzi, and the Rucellai. As of 1500, production and sales were consolidated by the Camera into a single company paying an annual leasing fee. The banker Agostino Chigi and his associates from Siena were succeeded first by the Genoese, in the years 1531–78, and then by the Florentines, who were in control almost continuously until 1660. Contracts, beginning in the mid-16th century, were signed for periods of twelve years.

The level of production remained very high throughout the 16th century. Exports reached their highest levels during the Genoese period, and the summit was attained during the Sauli lease (1553–65), when an average of close to 2,079 tons/1,890 metric tons were exported yearly. Constant exceeding of the expectations in the leasing contract made clear the dynamism of the enterprise. But, beginning in the 1620's, stocks began to accumulate in the warehouses of Civitavecchia, the pontifical port from which the alum was exported, and gradually the contracts lowered the theoretical levels of production. Competition was not the only source of the difficulties. In the 18th century, the plants and equipment were already run down and the veins were exhausted. Despite a genuine investment effort, production declined. Ceded to the Tourn of Allumiere, and then to Monte di Pietà of Rome, the mines were finally sold in 1873 to the Société financière de Paris, which was unable to remedy the situation and closed them a few years later.

Tolfa alum (in tons/metric tons, average yearly)

	Production	Exports
1462-99	1513/1375	1186/1078
1500-49	1540/1400	1513/1375
1550-99	+2031/1846	2031/1846
1600-49	1723/1566	1670/1518
1650-99	1214/1104	1223/1112
1700-49	859/781	937/843
1750-99	626/569	–
1802-03	517/470	–

(statistics based on J. Delumeau, pp. 124–7)

Jean Boutier

Bibliography

Delumeau, *L'Alun de Rome I, XVe–XIXe siècle*, Paris, 1962.

Heers, M. L. "Les Génois et le commerce de l'alun à la fin du Moyen âge," *Revue d'histoire économique et sociale*, 32 (1954), 30–53.

AMBASSADORS. See **Diplomatic Corps Accredited to the Holy See**.

AMERICANISM. Americanism was a controversy at the end of the 19th century, concluded by the papal encyclical *Testem Benevolentiae*, 22 January 1899, in which LEO XIII condemned several theological propositions that had been labeled "Americanism." At issue was the nature of the Church in the United States, its relation to civil government and society, and whether it served as a model that might be emulated in other countries. Few laypeople were touched by the dispute, which was largely confined to the internal politics of the hierarchy. Still, it had measurable effects on the Church in America until the time of the VATICAN II COUNCIL (1962–65).

Historical Context. By the 1890s, two long historical trends, one in Europe and the other in America, were coming to a climax, and these provided the background for Americanism. In Europe, the reassertion of papal power that had begun with the accession of PIUS IX in 1846 was nearing completion. The pope's temporal power had dissolved with the final collapse of the PAPAL STATES in 1870, but the pontiff's spiritual and administrative supremacy within the Church had never been greater. After the dogma of the IMMACULATE CONCEPTION was defined in 1854 and papal infallibility was endorsed by the FIRST VATICAN COUNCIL (1869–70), Pius controlled the doctrine and discipline of the Church as few of his predecessors had. The concurrent expansion of the Vatican's administrative bureaucracy was extending the papacy's practical reach into the life of the Church around the world. Greater scrutiny was given to the appointment of bishops, for example, and the hierarchy everywhere was increasingly dependent on the central administration and responsive to its demands. All this placed a greater value on uniformity, with local and national variations less likely to be tolerated.

At the same time, the Church in the United States had achieved unprecedented success. Since the establishment of its hierarchy a century before, the American Church had grown into a far-reaching and impressive institution. There were almost ninety dioceses and more than six million Catholics, making them the largest single religious denomination in the country. These numbers had been swelled by successive waves of immigrants, and the marshaling of resources to meet their religious, educational, and social service demands had been remarkably effective. Though anti-Catholic nativism achieved periodic ascendancy, American Catholics flourished, entering fully into the world of politics and achieving rapid social and economic advancement. Amid this success, however, Catholic bishops frequently differed over the problem of how their flocks could be both fully Catholic and fully American. Moreover, the Church had grown from a small, uncertain missionary operation into a powerful institution, the leadership of which was worth contending for.

Two distinct factions emerged, each eager to extend its influence. Though contemporaries often characterized them as "liberals" and "conservatives," these imprecise terms are unsatisfactory; later, they would sometimes be identified as "Americanists" (those who favored a greater degree of distinctiveness in the American Church) and "ultramontanes" (those who, like their European counterparts, looked "over the mountains" to Rome as the universal standard for all things Catholic). The former were led by John Ireland of St. Paul, and included James Gibbons of Baltimore and John Lancaster Spalding of Peoria. They were joined by John Keane, rector of the Catholic University of America in Washington, D.C., and Denis O'Connell, rector of the American College in Rome, who acted as their agent at the Vatican. The opposing group was led by Michael Corrigan of New York and Bernard McQuaid of Rochester. They made common cause with several Midwestern bishops, especially those of German extraction, including Sebastian Messmer of Milwaukee; they also enjoyed the support of the editors of the *American Ecclesiastical Review* and Rome's *Civilta cattolica*.

Polarization of the Hierarchy in the United States. Several issues provided occasions for maneuvering by the contending factions. First, the two groups took differing stands on "the school question." At the Third Plenary Council of Baltimore (1884), the American hierarchy had established the principle that there should be a desk in a Catholic school for every Catholic child, but in many places this ideal was honored largely in the breach. Gibbons and others considered public school education good for Catholics, since it helped integrate them into the American mainstream. John Ireland had even experimented with overt cooperation with local public schools in his diocese, agreeing to let public authorities lease parochial schools; these schools were attended by all students, regardless of creed or affiliation, with religious instruction for Catholic pupils confined to after-school hours. This plan brought sharp denunciation from other bishops and only reluctant acceptance from Rome. At the same time, the fledgling Catholic University of America, opened in 1889, created additional controversy. Appointment of faculty and administrative officers proved contentious, and larger questions of educational philosophy were also divisive. The openness of its instructors to modern intellectual movements (such as evolution and psychology) was viewed with suspicion by those who wanted strict adherence to neo-Scholastic modes of thought.

More broadly, the two factions disagreed over the stance of the Church toward American culture as a whole. Ethnic tensions exacerbated this problem. Those who were labeled Americanists believed that Catholic immigrants should acculturate themselves to American society as rapidly as possible. Practically, this meant replacing their native languages with English, but there were larger, ideological issues at stake as well. The easy American acceptance of religious liberty, enshrined in the First Amendment to the Constitution, was a departure from traditional Catholic practice. This raised an important question: was the individual's freedom to choose a religion (and thus, potentially, to choose the "wrong" one) a positive good or merely a necessary evil? Ireland and others pointed to the great success Catholicism had enjoyed in the United States, while Corrigan and his allies were inclined to think that religious liberty was far from ideal and tolerable only in the interest of civil order. Separation of church and state raised the same dilemma. Corrigan and others never thought seriously of challenging the American resolution of this matter, but they remained convinced that it was not the perfect arrangement, preferring state-sanctioned Catholicism wherever possible. Ireland and his forces rejected this view, pointing to the ways in which the American Church had prospered, unencumbered by state involvement. With the emergence of the United States as a world power, especially after its successful war with Spain in 1898, Ireland and his colleagues spoke expansively about the prospect of exporting these American views abroad. Since this seemed to imply that the American Church was different from (and perhaps superior to) those in other parts of the world, these opinions attracted increasingly skeptical scrutiny from Rome.

Events of the Controversy. A series of events brought these conflicts to a head and eventually produced the papal denunciation of "Americanism." In 1892, Archbishop Francesco Satolli visited the U.S., ostensibly to accompany several rare maps from the Vatican Library that were to be displayed at the World's Columbian Exposition in Chicago, but also to study the general conditions of the American Church. Thinking him sympathetic to their program, the Ireland-O'Connell faction had initially supported making Satolli a permanent apostolic delegate to the Church in America, a position without official diplomatic standing. Satolli announced in January 1893 that he would indeed take up this title and almost immediately turned against his erstwhile supporters, first by issuing a strong statement in support of parochial schools. He also criticized the participation by Gibbons in the Parliament of Religions, an interfaith gathering of clergy at the Chicago exposition: sharing the stage with Protestant and non-Christian officials seemed to suggest that all churches had equal standing. Increasingly under the influence of Corrigan, Satolli began to report regularly to Rome on what he took to be dangerous heterodoxies.

Rejection of the Americanist position quickly gathered momentum. In 1895, Leo XIII acted on the negative reports he had been receiving by issuing a letter (*Longinqua oceani*) praising the growth of the American Church but expressly drawing the line at the notion that its example might profitably be followed elsewhere. It was "erroneous," the pope said, to conclude that America offered "the most desirable status of the church" or to believe it best that church and state be "dissevered and divorced." A year later, John Keane was summarily removed as rector of the Catholic University. A speech by Ireland, praising freedom of conscience in America, and another by O'Connell, favorably citing the work of an American priest who was an enthusiastic disciple of Darwin, brought swift denunciation from Roman sources, evidently with official sanction.

The final spark was set by the appearance in 1897 of a French edition of an earlier biography of Isaac Hecker (1819–88), founder of the Paulists. The translation had been prepared by Felix Klein, a French seminary professor who was active in progressive intellectual circles. Klein saw in Hecker an embodiment of what the church should be everywhere, a radical notion for those churchmen (especially in France) who believed church and monarchy to be inseparable and thus viewed American notions of freedom and democracy warily. When O'Connell soon afterward delivered an address entitled "A New Idea in the Life of Father Hecker," speaking openly of an "ecclesiastical Americanism," the opposition found sufficient grounds for denunciation. A full-scale investigation of the American Church was undertaken in Rome, influenced primarily by the opponents of Ireland, O'Connell, and their supporters.

That process concluded with Leo's letter, *Testem Benevolentiae*, in January 1899. The document was a curious one. It denounced "opinions which some comprise under the head of Americanism," without ever asserting that anyone actually held those opinions or that the title was at all apt. Echoing the sentiments of his predecessor in the SYLLABUS OF ERRORS of 1864, Leo rejected the notion that "the Church ought to adapt herself" to modern civilization to any significant degree. More specifically, he made it clear that the Church's teachings could not "admit modifications according to the diversity of time and place"; rather, they were always and everywhere the same. Accepting the contention of Klein's critics that Hecker had overemphasized the direct action of the Holy Spirit in the hearts of individual believers and that the Paulist had stressed "active" over "passive" religious virtues, Leo reasserted the need for authoritative "guidance" from the church. The pope acknowledged that the term "Americanism" itself was confusing—since it also denoted simple (and commendable) national patriotism—but he nonetheless repudiated those who might "conceive of and desire a church in America different from that which is in the rest of the world."

Ireland and his allies immediately denied that they held any of the condemned positions, and it is for this reason that the entire affair has sometimes been called a "phantom heresy." More recent historical work, however, suggests that Hecker, Ireland, Gibbons, and others did indeed conceive of a Church with peculiarly American characteristics. Whether these views were formally heretical is a theological rather than a historical question, but there seems little doubt that the Americanists were in fact groping toward new formulations of religious liberty and church-state relations, based on the American experience. The condemnation of their ecclesiology meant that American Catholic leaders for a generation fell back into a kind of anti-intellectual orthodoxy, always vaguely suspicious of their own culture. The Americanist approaches were generally endorsed by the Second Vatican Council, however, and by then the specific dispute was long past. Still, the controversy had been an important turning point in the developing maturity of the Church in America.

James M. O'Toole

Bibliography

Curran, R. *Michael Augustine Corrigan and the Shaping of Conservative Catholicism in America, 1878–1902*, New York, 1978.

Fogarty, G., *The Vatican and the Americanist Crisis: Denis J. O'Connell, American Agent in Rome, 1885–1903*, Rome, 1974.

Fogarty, G. *The Vatican and the American Hierarchy from 1870 to 1965*, Wilmington, Del., 1985.

Klein, F. *Americanism: A Phantom Heresy*, Atchison, Kans., 1951.

McAvoy, T. *The Great Crisis in American Catholic History, 1895–1900*, Chicago, 1957; reissued as *The Americanist Heresy in Roman Catholicism, 1895–1900*, Notre Dame, Ind., 1963.

O'Brien, D. *Isaac Hecker, American Catholic*, New York, 1992.

O'Connell, M. *John Ireland and the American Catholic Church*, St. Paul, Minn., 1988.

Reher, M. "The Church and the Kingdom of God in America: The Ecclesiology of the Americanists." Ph.D. diss.: Fordham University, 1972.

Reher, M. "Leo XIII and Americanism," *Theological Studies* 34 (1973): 679–89.

ANACLETUS I. *(d. Rome, 91?) Elected pope in 80? Saint.*

In antiquity, most authors call him Anacletus; others call him Cletus. The *Liberian Catalogue* of 354 treats him as two separate figures, Cletus and Anacletus, who follow Clement in the succession list of the first popes. This erroneous duplication can be found also in the

LIBER PONTIFICALIS, which wrongly names Cletus as a martyr and anachronistically attributes to him the establishment of a Roman presbyteral college of twenty-five members. According to the most authoritative document, a 2nd-century list passed down by Irenaeus of Lyon (*Against Heresies*, III, 3, 3), Anacletus was BISHOP OF ROME) and after Linus, who had been designated by the apostles, and before Clement. Eusebius of Caesarea *Ecclesiastical History*, III, 13 and 15; *Chronicle*, ed. Helm, p. 189) dates his pontificate between the years 80 and 91, which remains an acceptable approximation. Around 850, Pseudo-Isidorus forged three letters using the name Anacletus.

Jean-Marie Salamito

Bibliography

LP, 1, 122 and 125.
Bardy, G. "Anaclet Ier," *Catholicisme*, 1 (1948), 501, and 2 (1950), 1248.
Kirsch, J. P. "Anaclet Ier," *DHGE*, 2(1914), 1407–8.
Pietri, C. *Roma christiana*, Rome, 1976, 1, 392 and 625.

[ANACLETUS II]. *Piero Pierleoni (b. ?, d. Rome, 25 January 1138). Antipope elected on 14 February 1130.*

Cardinal Piero Pierleoni was born into a Roman family of Jewish businessmen who had converted to Catholicism. A member of the SACRED COLLEGE as CARDINAL deacon, apparently from 1112, he was made cardinal priest in 1120 by CALLISTUS II. Pierleoni achieved a certain importance among the upper clergy of Rome under the pontificate of HONORIUS II (1124–30). He was regarded as among the most noteworthy of the prelates, those intent on pursuing the Gregorian REFORM without the least compromise with the emperor and—though the sources on this point are not clear and may have been somewhat oriented by subsequent history—rather suspicious of Germanic enterprises in Italy. In any case, he was one of those who opposed the group of cardinals who also wanted to strengthen the restoration accomplished since GREGORY VII, but by fully accepting the concordat of WORMS and collaborating with the German sovereign on the condition that he not intervene in ecclesiastical matters. Moreover, owing to the influence in the city of his family, around whom an ambitious party had organized itself, he had against him the hostile faction of the Frangipani.

In February 1130, Honorius II was on the point of death, and the news caused great agitation. The cardinal CHANCELLOR Aimeric, whose influence was great and who inclined toward the Frangipani, obtained from his colleagues the establishment of a commission of eight cardinals—five with Frangipani leanings, three close to the Pierleoni—responsible for choosing the new pope and having their choice approved by the whole Sacred College. The pontiff died during the night of 13 or 14 February, and as soon as he was buried, the chancellor convened those members of the commission who were present, six cardinals in all, only one of whom represented the Pierleoni. By five votes to one, the six designated one of their own group, the cardinal deacon of St. Gregory, who had very close ties to the Frangipani. They quickly informed other cardinals of their party, who confirmed their choice, and the one they had elected took the name INNOCENT II. A few hours later, the other cardinals, who were in the majority, elected Piero Pierleoni, who became ANACLETUS II. From the canonical point of view, both elections were irregular, even if the majority of the cardinal bishops, whose responsibility it was, according to the decree of NICHOLAS II of 1059, to choose the pope and then to propose their candidate to the other cardinals, had supported Innocent II. The limited college consisting only of cardinal bishops had not officially been convened, and Aimeric's commission could not act as its substitute, especially since it had reached its decision in the absence of two of its members. The matter was accordingly one for Christendom, for the political powers, and for the bishops to decide. The Romans supported Anacletus II, and his partisans forced his adversary to leave the city and then to leave Italy. He received the obedience and support of many cities in the north and in the center of the peninsula, especially MILAN. He straightaway had the adherence of the NORMAN sovereign Roger of Sicily, who had just conquered the southern territories and who, by means of threats, had had his right recognized by Honorius II. As of the month of September 1130, Anacletus agreed to confer on him the royal title, thereby making Sicily and the lands south of the PAPAL STATES into a hereditary kingdom, in exchange for homage to the pope and the payment of an annual rent. On the other hand, owing principally to the activity of St. Bernard but also to that of some other figures (St. Norbert), Emperor Lothair, King Louis VI of France, King Henry I of England, and a good number of princes and prelates of the Iberian Peninsula recognized Innocent II. As a result of this recognition, and despite the support of several bishops, especially those of Aquitaine led by Gerard of Angoulême, support for Anacletus from the beginning was much weaker than that for his rival.

Thanks to the emperor, Innocent II was thus able to return to Rome at the end of 1132 or the beginning of 1133. But he was not able to occupy the entire city. The Pierleoni pope maintained control over certain sections and had the luck to see Lothair return to the German lands as soon as he had received the imperial crown, which allowed him to force his rival into exile once again. During the exile in Pisa, however, thanks to St. Bernard, the city of Milan and other cities took up Innocent's cause. Soon Anacletus had, besides Aquitaine and the Romans only King Roger II left to support him. And Roger himself, having undergone a new offensive in 1136–7, was forced, even though he had resolved a difficult situation, to remain on the defensive and give up all initiative. The result was that the schism died out on its own after the death of Anacletus, on 25 January 1138, and the abdication of his successor, the ANTIPOPE VICTOR IV.

Marcel Pacaut

Bibliography

JW, 1, 911–19; 2, 716.

PL, 179, 690–732.

Fliche-Martin, IX-1.

Graboïs, A. "Le schisme de 1130 et la France," *RHE*, 76 (1981), 593–612.

Manselli, R. "Anacleto II," *DBI*, 3 (1961), 17–19.

Palumbo, P. F. *Lo scisma del MCXXX*, Rome, 1942.

Schmale, F. J. *Studien zum Schisma des Jahres 1130*, Cologne-Graz, 1961.

Stroll, M. *The Jewish Pope*, Leiden-New York, 1987.

Vacandard, E. "Anaclet II," *DHGE*, 2 (1914), 1408–19.

ANASTASIUS I. (*b. Rome, ?, d. 14 or 19 December 402). Elected pope on 26 November 399. Buried in the cemetery of Pontian. Saint.*

A Roman by birth and the son of a certain Maximus, he was the thirty-seventh pope according to Prosper of Aquitaine (*Chron.*, *MGH*, *AA*. 9, 464). This chronicler places the pontificate of Anastasius between 398 and 402, but it is recognized that SIRICIUS died in 399. Anastasius seems to have been highly appreciated by his contemporaries. Our sources are Jerome, who lauds his taste for poverty (*Ep.* 130, 16) and his zeal for the true faith (*Ep.* 127, 10), and Paulinus, bishop of Nola. The latter recounts to Delphin, bishop of Bordeaux, that Anastasius, soon after his election, wrote to the bishops of Campania in order to recommend the priest of Nola to them, and Paulinus adds that, when he visited Rome on the occasion of the feasts of the apostles PETER and Paul (400), Anastasius received him with kindness (*Ep.* 20, 2, *CSEL*, 29, 144–5). Finally, Theophilus, bishop of Alexandria, speaks of his pastoral solicitude and his zeal for defending the faith. Anastasius is known to us through three letters that give us an idea of his apostolic activity. His pontificate was thrown into confusion by the controversy over Origen: alerted by Theophilus, patriarch of Antioch, at the beginning of 400 and warned against Rufinus of Aquileia, the translator of Origen, Anastasius wrote two letters in sucession, one to Simplician, bishop of MILAN (*Ep.* 2, *PL*, 20, 73), the other to Venerius, his successor (definitively attributed to Anastasius, *PLS*, 1, 791), in which he condemned Origen's teaching, (Concerning the preexistence of souls, repentance of the devil, and the mode of resurrection). Yet Anastasius

seems not to have been completely familiar with the teachings of the great doctor of ALEXANDRIA. He was primarily attempting to settle a personal quarrel. In fact, Jerome and Rufinus of Aquileia, in effect, were at loggerheads over the teachings. Rufinus, having translated the *First Principles*, was threatened by his enemies, and addressed to Anastasius his *Apologia ad Anastasium* (*PL*, 21, 623–6), in which he justifies his translation and expounds his faith in a thoroughly orthodox fashion. Reassured as to Rufinus's own thinkings, Anastasius replied to John, bishop of Jerusalem, who was uneasy over the turn events had taken: if Rufinus has translated Origen in order to recommend him, he is worthy of condemnation; if he has hoped to repudiate him, he has done well (*Ep.* 1, *PL*, 20, 68–73). We know from Jerome that Anastasius wrote a letter to the bishops of the East on Origen's teachings (*Apologia aduersus Rufinum*, *PL*, 23, 471–472), but this letter has been lost without our having any sense of its content. Anastasius, at the same time, was confronted with the Donatist problem, an African schism rooted in intolerance of the *lapsi* and the *traditores*, or those who had foundered during the persecutions and wanted to establish a Church of the just. After the synod of CARTHAGE (spring 401), Anastasius received an envoy from the African episcopate who informed him of its shortage of priests. The pope sent a letter to the African episcopate; it has not come down to us, but we know its contents thanks to Aurelius, bishop of Carthage, who read it at the synod of 13 September 401. In it, Anastasius exhorts the bishops of Africa to be vigilant against the Donatists, but this council, driven by necessity, was asking that schismatic priests who wanted to convert be admitted into the ranks of the orthodox priests. According to the *Liber pontificalis*, it was Anastasius who ordered bishops to stand and bow their heads slightly during the reading of the Gospel. He is also said to be the author of the prohibition against admitting mutilated persons into the priesthood. Anastasius had the Crescentiana basilica built in Rome, in the second region; its exact location is unknown, though the *Liber pontificalis* states that it was on the via Mamertine. Anastasius is cited in the *Martyrologium Hieronymianum* and in the Roman Martyrology.

Ghislaine de Senneville

See also HERESIES.

Bibliography

JW, I, 42.

LP, I, 218.

PL, 20, 65–76.

CSEL, 29, ed. G. de Hartel.

Gaudemet, J. *L'Eglise dans l'Empire romain*, Paris, 1958.

Jerome, *Lettres*, III, introduction, text, and commentary by J. Labourt, Paris, 1953.

Mansi, *JW*, 3, 940ff.

ANASTASIUS II. *(b. Rome, ?, d. Rome, 19 November 498). Elected on 24 November 496. Buried at St. Peter's in Rome.*

During his brief pontificate, Anastasius, effecting a clear break with the hard-line attitude of his predecessor GELASIUS, adopted a conciliatory policy with respect to the emperor in order to end the Acacian schism, which had lasted since 484. His policy received little support in Rome, however, and when he died suddenly, many priests had already withdrawn from communion with him, thereby ushering in the Laurentian schism.

Before being consecrated pope, Anastasius was deacon of the Church of Rome, as we learn from his epitaph. It is possible that he participated in the council of 495, which rehabilitated Bishop Misenus, whom FELIX III had excommunicated after the failure of his legation to Constantinople. There was, in any case, a deacon of this name among the participants, though that one may be the deacon of the same name attested in 499. Once consecrated bishop of Rome, Anastasius sent a legation, consisting of Bishop Germanus of Pesaro and Bishop Cresconius of Todi, to Constantinople, and at the same time, King Theodoric also sent an embassy, this time a senatorial one, charged with asking Emperor Anastasius to recognize Theodoric as king of Italy. The pope announced his election to the emperor—something his predecessor Gelasius had refused to do—justified the Roman policy concerning Acacius by explaining that it was legitimate to judge the actions of the deceased, reminded the emperor that he was obliged to follow the directives of the Apostolic See, and asked him to facilitate the return of the Alexandrians to the Roman communion. He was specific in stating that all the acts of the Acacian pontificate were valid and, in particular, that the priests named by Acacius and the Christians he had baptized were not affected by the excommunication. The policy of Anastasius was novel only because he took the initiative in approaching Constantinople and adopted a conciliatory tone. In the imperial city, Germanus and Cresconius many times encountered the *apocrisarii* of Alexandria. They affirmed the orthodoxy of Leo's *Tome* and refused to discuss the case of the bishops of ALEXANDRIA, Dioscorus, Timothy Aelurus, and Peter Mongo, who had been condemned by Rome, but perhaps under the influence of the senator Festus, Theodoric's ambassador, they agreed to pass on to the pope a statement justifying the attitude of the Egyptian archbishops, expressing the hope for renewed relations with Rome, but also containing a profession of faith close to the *Henoticon*. As for Festus himself, of whom we are not sure whether or not he was mandated by the pope, he multiplied the initiatives in order to hasten reconciliation: he obtained Constantinople's agreement to celebrate the feast of Peter and Paul on 29 June, as in Rome; he suggested to the archbishop of Constantinople, Macedonius—without success owing to the imperial cen-

sorship—that he write to the pope; and most important, he promised the emperor in secret to have the *Henoticon* ratified by the pope. At his end, in Rome, Anastasius pursued his conciliatory policy: in 497, he opened negotiations with the bishop of Thessalonica, Andrew, whom Gelasius had denounced as a Monophysite, but who had just publicly condemned Acacius. Anastasius entered into communion with the deacon of Thessalonia, Photinus, who hastened to proclaim in all quarters that he had gotten his reconciliation cheap.

In Rome, the pontifical policy was poorly understood: Anastasius seemed to be multiplying the concessions—when in fact he had conceded nothing of substance—and betraying his predecessors. According to the witness of the LIBER PONTIFICALIS, many priests refused communion with him, initiating a SCHISM. But all of a sudden the pope died, on 19 November 498, before the situation had a chance to develop.

The memory of Anastasius suffered from this lack of understanding, and even more from the Laurentian schism. It seems, in fact, that when they were about to elect his successor, the partisans of Lawrence claimed to have been responsible for the diplomatic successes of Festus in Constantinople, while those of SYMMACHUS chose a return to the Gelasian severity. The fragment of the Laurentian *Liber pontificalis* seems favorable to Anastasius, whereas the entry in the *Liber pontificalis* is quite hostile, attributing to him the secret plan to have Acacius rehabilitated. Senator Festus, who returned to Rome after the death of Anastasius, remained a supporter of the antipope LAWRENCE until 507. This bad reputation accounts for Anastasius having been placed in hell by Dante (among the heretics, Canto XI). In fact, there was no immediate *damnatio memoriae*, since he was buried in St. PETER'S, and his epitaph has been preserved.

Claire Sotinel

Bibliography

ICUR, n.s., 12, 9.
LP, I, 44, and 259.
Anastasius, *Epistulae*, Thiel, I, 615–37.
Bertolini, P. "Anastasio II," *DBI*, 3 (1961), 21–4.
Kirsch, J. P. "Anastase II," *DHGE*, 2 (1914), 1473–5.

ANASTASIUS III. *(b. Rome, ?, d. October 913?) Elected pope in September 911(?). Buried at St. Peter's in Rome.*

Anastasius, a native of Rome, was the son of a certain Lutianus. Since precise information is lacking, the duration of his pontificate can only be deduced. The likelihood is that he was elected at the beginning of the month of September 911 and died in October 913. The only authentic pontifical ACT passed down from this period concerns the extraordinary concession of the pallium to Bishop Ragimbert of Vercelli (904–24). The patriarch Laurence of Grado (912–25) would also have received the archbishop's pallium from him at this time, but only later acts, dating from the beginning of the 11th century, inform us of that. On the request of the king of Italy, Berengar I of Friuli (888–924), the pope also is thought to have conceded certain privileges to the bishop of Pavia, the city where the royal residence was located. These included the use of insignias and the seat on the pope's left during COUNCIL sessions. The act established for Hoger, archbishop of Bremen-Hamburg (909–915), is certainly a forgery dating from the 12th century without any authentic basis. On another front, in 913, the pope was led to put an end to a SCHISM declared in Narbonne the previous year, after the assassination of Archbishop Arnustus (896–912). In 912, the Byzantine emperor Alexander (912–13) and the patriarch Nicholas Mysticus (901–7 and 912–25)—whom he had just restored to his functions—sent him letters from Constantinople that, blaming the attitude adopted until then by Rome and Pope SERGIUS III (904–11) in the controversy over tetragamy that had been unleashed by the fourth marriage of Emperor Leo VI (886–911), announced the end of the schism provoked by these developments in the patriarchy. What the pope's reactions would have been, to Byzantium as well as to Narbonne, is not known, since he died prematurely. The epitaph that has come down to us lauds his qualities as pope.

Harald Zimmermann

Bibliography

Bertolini, P. "Anastasius III," *DBI*, 3 (1961), 24.
Clerval, A. "Anastase III," *DHGE*, 2 (1914), 1475.
Schwaiger, G. "Anastasius III," *LexMA*, (1977–80), 572.
Zimmermann, H. *Papstregesten*, 3–6.

ANASTASIUS IV. *Conrad of Subura (b. Rome, ca. 1070/1075, d. 3 December 1154). Enthroned on 12 July 1153. Buried at St. John Lateran.*

His choice of name as pope perhaps is linked to the monastery of St. Anastasius, near Rome, which his predecessor EUGENE III had directed. Conrad was probably born into a family of the Roman middle class; Subura is a quarter located between the Esquiline and the Viminal. A frequently aired opinion is that he had been a canon regular and that he had belonged as such to the monastery of St. Rufus, near Avignon, or to a religious order in northern Italy, but no source confirms this. The only visible link with St. Rufus is a confirmation of possessions granted by him as pope to the abbey.

Until his elevation by PASCHAL II to the dignity of CARDINAL priest of the title of St. Pudenziana, which took place between 1111 and 1114 (before 25 February 1114),

nothing is known of his life. In 1118, he was one of the electors of GELASIUS II; in 1125, HONORIUS II gave him responsibility for arbitrating a contentious election to the head of abbey of Farfa. In 1127, he attempted, without success, to settle the problem of succession at Monte Cassino caused by the deposition of the abbot. Created cardinal bishop of Sabina by HONORIUS II, Conrad is mentioned for the first time in this capacity on 7 May 1128. During the contentious pontifical election of 1130, he was the oldest cardinal among the partisans of INNOCENT II. He is cited in the sources as one of the principal artisans of that election. Conrad did indeed participate in the preparatory electoral commission, but was certainly not particularly active in the unfolding of the external events that led to the SCHISM. When Innocent II left for France, he named Conrad pontifical vicar in Rome; this function, which he probably exercised intermittently between 1130 and 1153, afforded him judicial as well as other powers. His vicariate is attested for 1130–7, 1139, 1147, and 1151. In general, the bishop of Sabina did not stay at the papal court except when it was located in Rome or the environs. Conrad seems not to have traveled beyond the Alps. Should the hypothesis be admitted that Conrad would have served as intermediary between the popes and the Roman SENATE, as spokesperson for the communal movement that appeared in Rome at the beginning of the 1040s? The sources contain nothing to confirm such activity. Conrad was elected pope, either in Tivoli or in Rome, shortly after the death of Eugene III. His consecration must have taken place in the Lateran basilica. Anastasius IV encountered no difficulty in establishing his RESIDENCE at the Lateran. Whereas the disorder rampant in Rome had forced his predecessor to live most of the time outside the city, Anastasius probably lived in Rome without intermission. Gerhoh of Reichersberg describes him as an infirm old man, and Otto of Freising underlines his advanced age and his long experience with the business of the Curia. He seems to have satisfied his electors, who sought a balance between the papacy and the Romans. Whereas Eugene III had built a palace close to St. Peter's, on the periphery of the city, thereby illustrating his position in relation to it, Anastasius IV allowed himself to undertake the construction of brand new palace in the heart of the city, steps from the Pantheon—of course the purpose of this building is unknown. Tradition holds that the pope had a predilection for the Lateran basilica, to which he granted important privileges. During his pontificate, it is difficult to discern a particular policy in the choice of cardinals. The designation of Gregory as cardinal bishop of Sabina was a special case. Anastasius IV was indulgent in his relations with Frederick I Barbarossa. The king had not wanted a legate responsible for arbitrating an electoral controversy in Magdeburg: Anastasius IV accepted this and then confirmed the king's candidate. Nothing in the sources indicates that the treaty of Constance between Eugene III and Barbarossa had been renewed. In the long dispute over the archdiocese of York, the pope deviated from the policy of his predecessor by reinstating William Fitzherbert in the see. In the month of November 1154, he confirmed the organizational measures taken in Norway and Sweden by Cardinal Nicholas Breakspear, the future HADRIAN IV. Sweden thereafter paid the Peter's Pence. Posterity has generally considered Anastasius IV, elevated to the throne of St. Peter at an advanced age, a pope unsuited to the taking of energetic measures. Nevertheless, it should be emphasized that in restoring peace in Rome, even though his pontificate lasted only seventeen months, he acquitted himself worthily indeed. Unlike his predecessors and his successor, he was a "pope of the Romans." Anastasius IV was buried in the Lateran basilica, in a porphyry sarcophagus that came from the mausoleum of Empress Helena.

Karl Schnith

Bibliography

JL, 2, 89–102.

LP, 2, 388.

PL, 188, 989–1088.

Classen, P. "Zur Geschichte Papst Anastasius IV," *QFIAB*, 48 (1968), 36–63.

Clerval, A. "Anastase IV," *DHGE*, 2 (1914), 1475–6.

Maleczek, W. "Das Kardinalskollegium unter Innocenz II. und Anaklet II.," *AHP*, 19 (1981), 27–78.

Manselli, R "Anastasio IV," *DBI*, 3 (1961), 24–5.

Schwaiger, G. "Anastasius IV.," *LexMA*, 1 (1977–80), 572–3.

Schmale, F. J. *Studien zum Schisma des Jahres 1130*, Graz-Cologne, 1961.

Zenker, B. *Die Mitglieder des Kardinalskollegium von 1130 bis 1159*, Wurzburg, 1964.

[ANASTASIUS BIBLIOTHECARIUS]. *(b. between 800 and 817, d. 879). Antipope from 21 to 23 September 855.*

Anastasius, a Roman, was a close relative (son or nephew) of the bishop of Orte, Arsenius. His education, characterized by the study of Greek—an unusual thing at the time—quickly made of him a figure of extremely valuable culture, especially at the CURIA. LEO IV, shortly after coming to power in 847, made him CARDINAL priest of the title of S. Marcello. Yet very soon the two men clashed, probably, it is thought, because Anastasius had quickly made it clear that he had his eye on the throne of St. Peter. In 848, Anastasius fled Rome in order to find refuge in northern Italy, in the diocese of Aquileia. During the years following, the pope repeatedly ordered him to return and to appear before a COUNCIL, but in vain. In the end, the pope condemned him, with greater and greater severity: per-

sonal excommunication (16 December 850), ANATHEMA against his supporters (May–June 853), and, finally, the loss once and for all of the dignity of the priesthood (8 December 853).

When his adversary died (17 July 855), Anastasius seized the opportunity, being assured of the support of Emperor Louis II and of his party in Rome. The embassy that had set out to notify the sovereign of the election of BENEDICT III was stopped en route, and Anastasius marched on Rome with the imperial representatives, took control of St. PETER'S and of the Lateran and deposed Benedict III whom he imprisoned (21 September 855). The adventure, however, ended abruptly: the clergy and the people joined forces against him, and two of the three consecrating bishops refused to rally to him. The goal was then to find an honorable solution to the crisis. Benedict III was freed, and then consecrated before the *missi* of Louis II on 23 September; Anastasius was admitted once again to communion and given the abbatial title of Sta Maria in Trastevere, the preliminary step in his progressive reintegration into the Church.

Having abandoned his pontifical ambitions, Anastasius was living in studious retreat in Trastevere when the conflict broke out between Rome and Photius, which allowed him to use his knowledge of Greek to put himself forward as an expert in the relations with the CHURCH OF THE ORIENT. Accordingly, he drafted several letters sent by Nicholas I to the *basileus* or the patriarch. Having become indispensable as a private secretary, he was promoted by HADRIAN II, soon after his accession, to librarian of the Holy See, and at the same time authorized to resume his priestly dignity (December 867). He was regularly consulted as a specialist, especially on the question of whether or not to authorize the use of Slavonic in the Moravian liturgy (Anastasius was favorable to it).

In the years following, he was engaged in many diplomatic missions on behalf of both the pope and the emperor. At the end of 869, he left for the East, charged by both Louis II and NICHOLAS I to lead the negotiations relative to the projected marriage between Ermengard, the daughter of Louis II, and Constantine, the son of Emperor Basil I. At that time, the final sessions of the eighth ecumenical COUNCIL of Constantinople, called in order to deal once more with the case of Photius, were being held. Without officially participating in the pontifical delegation present at the SYNOD, Anastasius evidently gave valuable assistance, if only in checking the content of the Greek texts and speaking out against the omission of formulas relative to the imperial dignity of Louis II. He then used his influence (assisted by Louis II's *missi*, who had accompanied him in the matter of the marriage) to have returned to the pontifical legates their copies of the conciliar acts, which had been removed so that the corrections he had called for would not have to be made. In the end, it was his own copy of the acts that was placed into the hands of Hadrian II in the spring of 870, the legates having been robbed of their copies by pirates during the course of the return journey.

After his return from the East, Anastasius was once again solicited for his talent in writing, this time by Louis II, who owes to him a famous letter, written at the beginning of 871, to Basil I in reply to an earlier letter. Between Charlemagne and Otto I, Louis II, in the thinking of Anastasius, crucially paved the way for the defense of Roman claims to the Western Empire in opposition to BYZANTIUM. Finally, before the end of 872, Anastasius was sent to Naples, once again mandated by the pope and the emperor, to attempt to bring back under obedience a part of the clergy that had rebelled against Bishop Athanasius, who had been exiled by Duke Sergius II. With the coming of JOHN VIII to the throne of St. Peter (14 December 872), Anastasius's activity gradually lessened. His last years were devoted above all to the translation of numerous Greek texts, a life's project he had never set aside. He had already translated the acts of the synod of Constantinople of 867–9, and to him also are owed the Latin text of the seventh ecumenical council (Nicaea, 787), of the *Tripartite Chronology* (a collection from the mid-9th century, meant to serve as preparation for an encyclopedia in the tradition of Isidore of Seville), and of numerous Lives of the saints. He also wrote the entry on Nicholas I in the LIBER PONTIFICALIS; so prolific was he that until well into the 18th century, the authorship of the whole work was attributed to him.

François Bougard

Bibliography

JW, 1, 341.

Arnaldi, G. "Anastasio Bibliotecario," *DBI*, 1, (1961), 25–37.

Berschin, W. *Medioevo greco-latino da Gerolamo a Niccolò Cusano*, Naples, 1989, 209–17.

Lapôtre, A. *De Anastasio bibliothecario sedis apostolicae*, Paris, 1885.

Leonardi, C. "Anastasio Bibliotecario e l'ottavo concilio ecumenico," *Studi medievali*, 8 (1967), 59–192.

Lohrmann, D. "Eine Arbeitshandschaft des Anastasius Bibl. und die Überlieferung der Akten des 8. Ökumenischen Konzils," *QFIAB*, 50 (1971), 420–31.

ANATHEMA. *Anathema* and *excommunication* are two terms that gradually emerged in ecclesiastical usage to describe the situation of those who, through their behavior or the doctrines they profess, place themselves outside the mystical and social body of the Church. Later a jurisdiction was established that defined anathema also as practical sanction of this state.

Anathema comes from the Greek word αναθημα, originally meaning "offering." However, the Septuagint systematically adopted the word as a translation of the Hebrew *heräm*, thus giving it a meaning close to the Latin *sacer*. Applied to a person, the term designates one who is separated from the community and left to perish in God's wrath. The word thus includes the idea of malediction. The New Testament still maintains these two meanings—that of classical Greek (e.g., Luke 21:5) and that of the Septuagint (e.g., 1 Cor. 12:3; 16:22; Rom. 9:3; Gal. 1:89, 3:13). The verb *anathematizein* has the same meaning, both in the Septuagint and in the New Testament—transcribed as such in Latin or more rarely translated as *anathemare* (Mark 14:71).

In the New Testament, an anathema is a person who is separated from God or the community. If judgment of the guilty is clearly reserved for God, the texts do not allow for precisely defining the reasons for exclusion. Nevertheless, in Judaism, there was a regulated practice of exclusion from the synagogue, mentioned in the New Testament (see John 9:22; 12:42; 16:2; 1 Cor. 5:9–11; 2 Thess. 3:14; Col. 2:5–11). This exclusion is also mentioned in the communities of Qumran. Christian excommunication, in the general sense, is the heir to this practice. As in Judaism, the change from expressing a malediction to sanctioning exclusion occurred when the Church became a social body regulated by canon law. It is important to note that exclusion from the synagogue and Christian excommunication are not the same. The synagogue does not constitute a soteriological community—one believing in salvation—like the Church, and rabbis do not have the power to exclude anyone from Judaism. In Christianity, excommunication and anathema constitute a separation from the Church as a society of believers making up the mystical body of Christ. The question of who had the power to levy the censure of anathema and excommunication soon became an issue in the young Church. It is therefore not surprising that the juridical formulation for excommunication occurred simultaneously with the development of the discipline of penance. The question of anathema and excommunication represents an important juncture in the reflection on ecclesiastical authority, and therefore the definition of Roman authority.

Anathema vs. Excommunication. Up until at least the 6th century, anathema and excommunication were not clearly distinguished, and the means and scope of involving them were not strictly defined. Toward the year 300, the sentences of the council of Elvira did nothing to establish a clear distinction between the two. Canon 52 was the first mention of anathema by a council, and thus the first indication of its disciplinary usage. The first known formulations for excommunication are 58 canons, which use various expressions referring mostly to the deprivation of the Eucharist for a specific period of time, or for life. As for the quotation of the epistle to the

Galatians (1:9), which became the canonical formula of anathema until VATICAN I—*anathema estô*—it was first mentioned in 343 in the sentences of the council of Gangres in Paphlagonia.

Anathema and excommunication were expressly distinguished by the second council of Tours in 567 (c. 25 [24]: *SC*, 354, 386–7—trans. by J. Gaudemet and B. Basdevant):

> If he stubbornly persists in his usurpation, and he refuses, after a third admonition, to relinquish the property . . . , [then] absolutely all, unanimously, must meet, with our abbots, our priests and our ministers . . . ; so that with the help of Jesus Christ, in the circle of the choir of ministers, the Psalm 108 be pronounced before the assassin of the poor who usurps Church property, and that the malediction of Judas befall him, he who as bursar spirited away the resources of the poor. May he die, not only excommunicated, but also anathema, and may he be struck down by the heavenly sword, since in his contempt for God, the Church and the pontiffs, he dared to assume such a degree of perversion.

It was nevertheless not until the 9th century, with the "Engeltrudam Canon" (Gratian, *caus*. III, q. 4, c. 12: attributed without certainty to John VIII) that the distinction between a reversible condemnation, conditional on the guilty party's amendment (excommunication), and the anticipated announcement of an eschatological judgment anathema were made explicit. Excommunication separates the individual from the *communio fidelium* (community of the faithful), whereas anathema separates *ab ipso corpore Christi* (the communion of the mystical Church).

Thus, a differentiation was established not only in terms of degree, but also in terms of punishment. For anathema, the accent was for a time on malediction. Yet afterward, this differentiation between anathema and excommunication tended to fade away. For the ancient periods, it is impossible to retrace a precise casuistics, either in terms of the type of infractions or the gravity of the faults committed. Contrary to what has sometimes been suggested, it does not seem that anathema was intended for sanctioning doctrinal errors or excommunication for punishing disciplinary faults. In most cases, at least for the Western councils from the 6th to the 7th centuries, anathema punished political crimes.

Degrees of Excommunication. The technical vocabulary of excommunication was established at a relatively late date. Before the 4th century—when the Christian neologisms *excommunicatio*, *excommunicare*, and *excommunicatus* were first used—writers and councils used various phrases to describe the separation of certain members of the community. It was not until the 5th century at the earliest that a formal distinction was made between the different degrees of exclusion, if the two fragments by Gelasius, which are the first evidence of such distinction, are retained as authentic. Fragment 49 mentions an exclusion from ecclesiastical communion (with an exclusion from the society of the faithful), whereas Fragment 37 only mentions an exclusion from Eucharistic communion (specifically, in order to sanction the frequentation of someone who is excommunicated: Thiel, 510). Previous council decisions nevertheless show that the distinction between these two sanctions—corresponding to the later distinction between major and minor excommunications—certainly goes back to the 4th century. (The previously cited canon 20 of the council of Elvira perhaps foresees an exclusion from ecclesiastical communion, not only Eucharistic communion). In any case, Pope INNOCENT I's letter to Bishop Exupery of Toulouse distinguished at the beginning of the 5th century (405) two autonomous sanctions: exclusion from ecclesiastical communion and exclusion from Eucharistic communion (*PL*, 13, 1172).

Which Authority Is Entitled to Practice Censure? As of the 2d century (in the context of the anti-Gnostic debate), the power of exclusion appeared as one of the aspects defining the power of the ordained ministries in as much as it is a consequence of the power to "bind and loose." Among the important stages in this development was Tertullian's contribution, which the Montanist dispute led to pose the question of the concrete power given by God to his servants. Afterward, there was Cyprian, for whom the question of penance and the "power of the keys" was one of the points from which the principle of episcopal authority was developed. And it was thus that the issue of excommunication was early on implicated in the discussions on the nature of Roman primacy. Yet, if Cyprian identified communion with Cornelius of Rome and communion with the Church (see, for example, *ep.* 55:1, 59:14), then it was because as *ecclesia principalis*, the Church of Peter mystically engendered the unity of the Church. Moreover, the seat of Rome did not at the time claim the exclusive power of the keys, or the jurisdictional primacy that it implied. When the bishop of Rome demanded the application of Roman decisions—for example, in the adoption of the date for Easter, or regarding the baptism of heretics—these claims relate to the application of a discipline, but do not truly define the communion with the Church as communion with Rome on a concrete level. Nevertheless, as of the end of the 4th century, Rome tended to exert decisive influence on the discipline of penance by arguing Peter's authority (i.e., Innocent I and especially LEO the Great). However, it was not until the dispute leading to the Acacian schism that the Roman pontiffs developed argumentation leading to making excommunication a pontifical prerogative. It was so in Simplicianus's letter 3, which cites the anathema of Gal. 1:8

(with an allusion to Cain's destiny) and explicitly claims the power of the keys and the principle of apostolic succession to have the Roman norm applied and ecclesiastical discipline respected. It was so too in a series of letters written by FELIX II (III). Among them, *ep.* 14, 2–3, makes communion with the bishop of Rome the criterion of communion with the universal Church (see also *ep.* 11, 4; 17, 2; 18), and especially letter 7 (Thiel), which—by basing for the first time, it seems, the affirmation of his authority on apostolic succession by citing Luke 11:23 (*Qui mecum non est, contra me est, et qui mecum non colligit, spargit*)—explicitly identifies communion with the bishop of Rome and communion with Christ. Felix II (III) thus posed the bases for an argumentation taken up later by Gelasius I (see *ep.* 27 [Thiel], 30), assuring the passage from an ecclesiological theme to the claim of universal, jurisdictional supremacy, by interposing in the delegation of God (Christ)–Peter–the Church, the pontifical vicariate concretely conceived according to a monarchist principle, to arrive at the configuration God (Christ)–Peter–pope (or the Roman Church)–bishops (or Churches).

Françoise Monfrin

Bibliography

Amaneiu, A. "Anathème," *DDC*, (1935), 512–16.

Forkman, G. *The Limits of Religious Community,* Lund, 1972.

Gaudemet, J. "Note sur les formes anciennes de l'excommunication," *Revue des sciences religieuses*, 23 (1949), 64–77.

Jombart, E. "Excommunication," *DDC*, 5 (1953), 615–17.

Michel, C. "Anathème," *DACL*, 1 (1907), 1926–40.

Vacant, A. "Anathème," *DTC*, 1 (1930), 1168–70.

ANGELS. The bishops of Rome in Christian antiquity did not get involved in angelology, a complicated science rendered suspect by Gnostic speculations even before GREGORY the Great (pope from 590 to 604). The cult of angels did appear in Rome during the 5th century (later than in the East) when the "basilica of the Angel on the via Salaria" was known to have existed, just outside Rome. The Leonine sacramentary marked its feast day on 29 September.

The scholar J. B. De Rossi believes that this church must have existed contemporaneously with the churches in Umbria dedicated to the archangel St. Michael. In the beginning of the 6th century, there was at least one other Church of St. Michael inside the walls of Rome. Pope SYMMACHUS (498–514) had this church enlarged, according to the *LIBER PONTIFICALIS*. In the beginning of the 7th century, there was a story of Hadrian's mausoleum, not yet connected to the legend of St. Michael's appearance.

The legend, spread by John Deacon in the 9th century, held that the procession, organized by Gregory in 590 to stave off the plague that was devastating the city, had seen the Archangel Michael at the summit of the mausoleum, put the sword of the plague back into its sheath. This story was connected to Gregory, the first pope to formulate a reflection on the angels. In the 34th homily on the gospel of St. Luke, the pope commented on the parable of the lost drachma, comparing the nine remaining drachmas to the nine orders of the angels who remained in God's friendship. On this occasion, he explained the difference between the angels, archangels, virtues, powers, principalities, dominations, thrones, cherubins, and seraphim, who, for him were especially distinguished by their various ministries. He explained the significance of the names Michael, Raphael, and Gabriel and showed his listeners that angels were to be models. This doctrine was essentially inspired by Ambrose and Jerome, but was also influenced by Eastern thought, especially that of Pseudo-Dionysius the Areopagite. In Gregory's other exegetical works, in particular in *Moralia in Job*, which he composed in Constantinople, his reflection on the angels is often present, but discreet, just as their cult was discreet in Rome.

Occasionally, from the 5th century on, the Roman seat was referred to as angelic. As of this period, Pope LEO was thus designated by the deacon Porphyrius during the COUNCIL of Chalcedon, and in the correspondence from the Eastern bishops. During the Acacian schism, there were announcements made to the pope that messengers were being sent to his "angelic seat." The meaning of this expression can no doubt be traced to a letter from Remi of Reims, who explained to his correspondent that bishops are angelic because they are the "angels of the Church" of whom John's Apocalypse speaks. In any case, in May 519, when a bishop of Prevalitana wrote to Pope Hormisdas regarding a "master equal to the angels in his merits," he no doubt announced the later use of the term coangelic, inspired from the Greek. This term appeared perhaps as early as the end of the 6th century, is exclusively reserved for popes as of the 8th century, and is symbolized by their white garment.

Claire Sotinel

Bibliography

Davidson, G. *A Dicionary of Angels*, New York, 1967.

De Rossi, J. B. *Bollettino di archeologia cristiana.* (1871), 146–7.

Keck, D. *Angles and Angelology in the Middle Ages*, New York, 1998.

Lewis, J. R., et al., eds. *Angels, A to Z*, New York, 1996.

Marshall, G. J. *Angels: An Indexed and Partially Annotated Bibliography of over 4300 Scholarly Books and Articles since the 7th Century*, Jefferson, N. C., 1999.

ANGELUS. This is a prayer in honor of the Incarnation and is composed of three versicles separated by an Ave Maria and ending with a collect. The term also represents the sound of the bell, indicating to the faithful the hours for this prayer—morning, midday, and evening. JOHN XXII (1316–34) recommended the recitation of the Angelus in the evening and gave INDULGENCES to those who said it. CALLISTUS III (1455–58) encouraged its recitation to halt the military successes of Sultan Muhammed II. A popular prayer that is generally part of the practice of individual piety and does not need to be recited in a particular place of worship, the Angelus has only recently become a part of the Roman activities of the sovereign pontiff.

Since JOHN XXIII's pontificate, the custom has been for the pope to give a Sunday blessing at noon from his place of residence, the Vatican, or Castel Gandolfo. The ritual prayer, giving ten years' indulgence for each recitation (morning, noon, and evening), is the occasion for an intimate encounter between the sovereign pontiff and the crowd assembled to pray with him or to us or hear him. At the stroke of noon, the pope appears on the third floor of the PAPAL APARTMENTS, at the window of his office; a curtain is hung for the occasion.

The recitation of the Angelus occurs as part of the customary ceremony during which the pope speaks extemporaneously according to the season and the occasions. This papal ceremony (the pope's words are not published) has led to various, and sometimes surprising affirmations, advice, and revelations. For example, in 1976, PAUL VI responded to personal attacks on the occasion of an Angelus. Before the ASSASSINATION ATTEMPT on his life, in 1981, JOHN PAUL II, spoke out strongly against the Soviet government's attitude toward Poland; after being shot, he talked about the event and about his health.

Since 1978 the pope has regularly spoken on the nature of his Sunday schedule, his activities, and sometimes, his plans. This is a public version of his opinions and the activities of the Holy See, intended for a wide and free audience. The pope presents himself as the bishop of Rome, the vicar of Christ, and a Roman who spends his day in the capital of Christendom. The practice is the same when the pope is in residence at Castel Gandolfo in the summer. The recitation of the Angelus and the blessing close this special meeting between the pope and these pilgrims. The rite is the same in Rome and Castel Gandolfo. In recent years, a public address system has transmitted the pope's recitation of the Angelus, which is done in Latin.

The text of the Angelus follows:
V. - Angelus Domini nuntiavit Mariae
R. - Et concepit de Spiritu sancto.
Ave Maria, gratia plena, Dominus tecum: benedicta tu in mulieribus, et benedictus fructus ventris tui, Jesus.
Sancta Maria, Mater Dei, ora pro nobis peccatoribus, nunc et in hora mortis nostrae. Amen.
V. - Ecce ancilla Domini.
R. - Fiat mihi secundum verbum tuum.
Ave Maria, gratia plena, Dominus tecum: benedicta tu in mulieribus, et benedictus fructus ventris tui, Jesus. Sancta Maria, Mater Dei, ora pro nobis peccatoribus, nunc et in hora mortis nostrae. Amen.
V. - Et Verbum caro factum est.
R. - Et habitavit in nobis.
Ave Maria, gratia plena, Dominus tecum: benedicta tu in mulieribus, et benedictus fructus ventris tui, Jesus. Sancta Maria, Mater Dei, ora pro nobis peccatoribus, nunc et in hora mortis nostrae. Amen.
V. - Ora pro nobis, sancta Dei Genitrix.
R. - Ut digni efficiamur promissionibus Christi.
Oremus. Gratiam tuam quaesumus, Domine, mentibus nostris infunde: ut qui, Angelo nuntiante, Christi Filii tui incarnationem cognovimus, per passionem ejus et crucem, ad resurrectionis gloriam perducamur. Per eumdem Christum Dominum nostrum.
R. - Amen.

Philippe Levillain

Bibliography

Thurston, H. "The Angelus," *Month*, 98 (1901), 483–99, 607–16; 99 (1902), 61–73, 518–32; 100 (1903), 89 ff.

ANGEVINS. The Angevin dynasty of Naples, implanted in the Norman and Germanic heritage of the kingdom of Sicily by the express will of the papacy, was, early on, an inconvenient instrument for papal plans and the CURIA. If the link uniting the kingdom of Sicily and the empire was effectively shattered by the French presence on the throne transferred from Palermo to Naples, the French dynasty did not take too long to renew Frederick II's hegemonic ambitions on Italian lands. Whether admitted or not, these were in competition with those of the Holy See, and the political rivalry prolonged the conflicts of the 13th century, occasionally taking on a more markedly religious, even theological, character.

The Church of the Avignon period, then the Roman papacy of the GREAT SCHISM, had to use all methods available including feudal sovereignty, orthodoxy, the threat of excommunication, foreign ambitions, rebel princes, and Great Companies to have its authority recognized by a proud lineage, torn apart by rivalries between its branches, but conscious of the strength which the state's mystique and the efficient bureaucratic tradition inherited from Roger II and Frederick II gave to the King of Sicily. The French dynasty's final defeat in southern Italy and Provence before the competing ambitions of the Valois-Provence and the Transtamare branch established in Barcelona in 1412 was largely due to a twofold harassment. On one hand there was the Holy See, which humiliated and weakened it, and on the other, the parties of Avignon cardinals who sharpened contradictions between the princes and developed strategies to acquire the kingdom intended to encircle the papal throne. After having established the Angevin domination in southern Italy between 1250 and 1266, the papacy was faced with a powerful competitor.

The Holy See had resolved, under INNOCENT IV, to make a decisive break in its southern politics, and decided to reclaim the Kingdom of Sicily, depriving the House of Souabe of it, thus detaching it from the fortunes of the empire. This was accomplished through the marriage between Constance de Hauteville, heiress to the south, and Henry VI, which avoided any return to the imperial papacy of the 10th and 11th centuries.

The choice of a Capetian prince, Charles of Anjou, brother of Louis IX, born in 1226 and master of Provence since 1246, was intended to guarantee the papal enterprise with the support of the powerful French kingdom. The Curia had long vacillated between the direct administration of the Kingdom of Sicily and awarding its oversight to a foreign prince on strict conditions (homage, rent, the renunciation of the privilege of "apostolic legation" that made the King of Sicily a permanent LEGATE on the island, renunciation of the royal right to designate bishops and regulate their relations with Rome). The prince was becoming the military arm of the Holy See in southern Italy. The Treaty of 1263 between URBAN IV and Charles limited the future ambitions of the prince. Now relegated to southern Italy and excluded from Rome and Tuscany, he was obliged to accept severe conditions including liberty of the Church, homage at each royal and papal succession, 10,000 ounces of gold in annual rent, and control of successions.

Although these measures largely reduced royal sovereignty, Charles I did not hesitate to manifest the extent of his ambitions even before his crushing victory of Benevento and the death of Manfred (1266). He obtained a senatorial seat in Rome and undertook to establish Angevin domination over the Piedmont and western Lombardy by starting in Provence and sending contingents to the GUELPHS of Tuscany. This aspiration to assume a wide Italian hegemony, consolidated by his triumph over Conradin (and his subsequent execution in 1268), expanded Charles's ambitions, prompting conquests including Tunis, the ports and islands of central Maghreb, Constantinople, and the restoration of the Latin Empire. In addition, he sought to establish vassal feudal domains for Angevin princes in Albania, Achaia (Peloponesia), and Sardinia, as well as reinstate the Kingdom of Acre. On the domestic front, these grand plans relied on the reestablishment of the administrative and fiscal order of the State of Frederick II, entrusted to the man-

agement of French and Provençal feudal lords, southern jurists imbued with the idea of majesty, and Amalfitan technical financiers.

GREGORY X and NICHOLAS III's latent concerns and hostility were to lead to a politics of equilibrium, the Holy See covertly supporting the adversaries of Charles I, Rudolf of Habsburg in Germany, Michael VIII Palaeologus in the East, and chasing Charles from the Roman Senate and imperial vicariate in Tuscany. This hidden opposition and that of Marguerite of Provence, widow of St. Louis, who was involved in intrigues to recover her counties gave confidence to the internal opposition, that of the urban knights of the Sicilian cities, divided between the moderate Guelphs and GHIBELLINES nostalgic for the empire, without weakening the king of Sicily or limiting his ambitions. All were hostile to the transfer of the capital to Naples and to the joint Franco-Provençal and Amalfitan government. At the time when, by a normal swing of the pendulum, the SACRED COLLEGE elected a French, pro-Angevin pope, MARTIN IV, the combined intrigues of Michael VIII, threatened by the crusade led by Charles, and of the daughter of Manfred of Sicily, Constance, wife of the King of Aragón, Peter I, were disturbed and accelerated by a spontaneous uprising of the population of Palermo against the Angevins. The Sicilian Vespers of 1282 placed the island under the immediate protection of the Roman Church and marked the failure of the Angevin attempt to obtain Mediterranean hegemony.

The years 1282 through 1289 were a significant digression in this first era of affirming Angevin sovereignty. The Church first put itself at the service of the French dynasty to save its own base of influence in the south of Italy. It sent the legate Gerard of Parma to support the king against the subjects who were calling for the immediate sovereignty of and management by the Church. It then deposed Peter I of Aragón, who had taken possession of the island of Sicily, and penetrated into Calabria. Finally, it organized a CRUSADE, entrusted to Charles of Valois, proclaimed King of Aragón, against Catalonia. The capture of Charles the Lame, duke of Calabria and heir to the kingdom (1284), by the Aragonese flotilla and the death of Charles I forced, from 1285 to 1289, the direct papal management of the Neapolitan kingdom. Martin IV organized the interim reign, as was the duty of the suzerain, and entrusted it to CARDINAL Gerard of Parma for the political aspects and to the Capetian prince Robert of Artois for the military. Both were "bayles established by the Holy Roman Church." This reestablishment of the effective exercise of pontifical suzerainty on what remained of the Kingdom of Sicily still held by the Angevins (Naples, Campania, Puglia, Abruzzo, the Aragónese front in Lucania and in the principality of Salerno) also included measures meant to secure the sympathy of populations after the rigid fiscal policies of Charles I. By favoring the liberty of communes and the autonomy of the feudals, this was eventually successful in weakening the Angevin dynasty, impoverished and obliged to rely on its Roman tutor. The Holy See was also rediscovering means of controlling the Angevins: The war could not be halted without its agreement to the terms of the truce or the peace, both in the name of the suzerainty and *ratione peccati*; excommunication and INTERDICT weighed heavily on the king of Aragón and his people. HONORIUS IV, then NICHOLAS IV, refused, in 1286 and 1287, to recognize the terms of the treaties concluded between Charles II, prisoner in Aragón, and the son of Peter I. The liberation of Charles II, a scrupulous prince of troubled faith, confirmed the importance given to the internal politics by the cardinal-legate. This caused a significant weakening of the Angevin State. This fact was, however, both masked by and compensated for with the insertion of Charles II in the very politics of the Curia and by the success of the matrimonial politics that gave the inheritance of the Arpadian Kingdom of Hungary to his son Charles Martel. Charles II's influence seemed to be significant at the election of CELESTINE V, which took place in the climate surrounding the millennium, nourished with apocalyptic hopes and aspirations to evangelical life in Franciscan poverty. The second son of Charles II, Louis, chose the Franciscan order in 1296, and died with a reputation for sanctity two years later. The peace with Aragón and the multiple marriages between the houses of Aragón and Mallorca reinforced among the Angevins of Naples tendencies favorable to spiritualism to the point of heterodoxy which provided the Holy See with even more leverage to control them.

The first decade of the 14th century was a decisive turning point in the establishment of the Angevin dynasty. This period included installation of the elder branch in Hungary and peace with the house of Aragón in Sicily (Caltabellotta, 1302), including various and as-

Genealogy of the Angevins

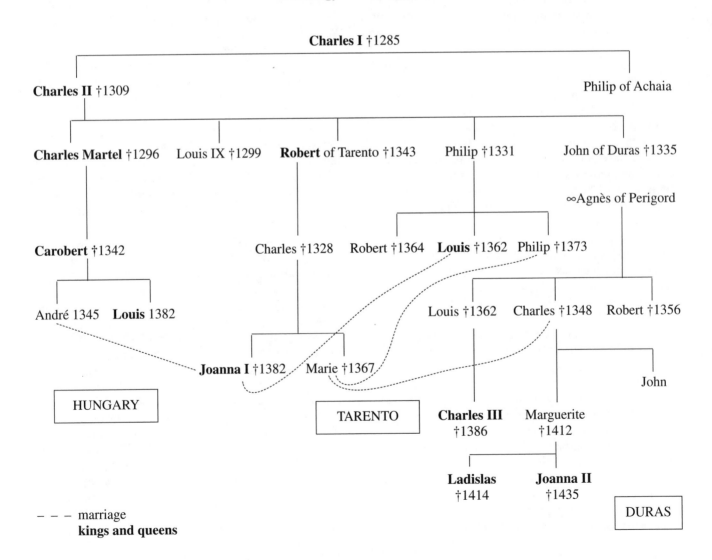

Charles I †1285

Charles II †1309   Philip of Achaia

Charles Martel †1296   Louis IX †1299   Robert of Tarento †1343   Philip †1331   John of Duras †1335

∞Agnès of Perigord

Carobert †1342   Charles †1328   Robert †1364   Louis †1362   Philip †1373

André 1345   Louis 1382   Louis †1362   Charles †1348   Robert †1356

Joanna I †1382   Marie †1367   John

HUNGARY   TARENTO   Charles III †1386   Marguerite †1412

Ladislas †1414   Joanna II †1435

DURAS

– – – marriage
kings and queens

sorted matrimonial ties, under the close surveillance of BONIFACE VIII. Boniface VIII required that the kingdom of the island of Sicily ("kingdom of Trinacria") be kept as a feudal domain, pay tribute to the Church, and return after one generation to the Angevins, who would keep the title "kings of Sicily." At the death of Charles II, his younger brother, Robert, took over Charles I's politics of expansion with vigor. He advanced in Piedmont, in Rome (as senator), and in Greece. In addition, he defended Tuscany against the imperial enterprises of Henry VII of Luxembourg, and those of Louis of Bavaria. Robert's politics were nuanced by the king and his entourage's passionate attachment to evangelical poverty and to the Franciscan spirituals, as well as by his personal and political hostility to JOHN XXII. The king of Naples, a great preacher (who delivered 289 sermons) wrote a treatise on poverty against the pontifical doctrine and denounced, in a treaty on beatific vision, the heterodoxy of John XXII's teaching. If Robert was obliged to renew the war against the Aragónese of Sicily due to the Ghibelline explosion of 1310, his politics and his will manifested his concern with removing all Church control over his inheritance. He left this inheritance to his daughter Joanna, at the price of a reconciliation with the Hungarian branch of the dynasty and of maintaining state structures. His death led to the liquidation of his political practices. Joanna I's accession to the throne at the age of seventeen, gave the Curia multiple reasons and means of action to control the Angevin kingdom. CLEMENT VI invalidated Robert's will and imposed direct government through a legate, in the name of the queen in her minority. He reinstated the ceremony of homage in forms most humiliating to royal dignity. In the chaotic history of the reign of Joanna, the Church assumed the well-being and direct management of the kingdom through its legates on several occasions (1344, 1348–49, Albornoz in 1364.)

The Church maintained close, paternal control through the threat of excommunication and interdict (for nonpayment of rent, but also for the familial crimes of the Angevin princes). It also used the threat weighing on the kingdom in the form of the Hungarian dynasty and the Great Companies, which the cardinals had available in Lombardy. Onto this official politics was grafted that of the cardinals' parties, Gui of Boulogne and Talleyrand of Perigord, allied to two princely branches, to the dukes of Duras, and to the princes of Tarento, without counting the ambitions of other cardinals desirous of carving out principalities for their nephews in the south. For Perigord and Bologna, it was a matter of obtaining power in Naples through the marriage of their nephews to Joanna or her presumptive heiresses, her sister or her nieces. Seizing power in Naples and Provence completed the strategy of encircling Avignon, which was meant to ensure them, or their nephews (Gui of Bologna, Robert of Geneva, the future Pope CLEMENT VII) the pontifical throne. The clash

of these strategies led to the dissolution of the agreement with Hungary. André of Hungary, Joanna's husband, was assassinated and the murder set off conflicts between the Duras and the Tarento families, as well as the Hungarian invasions. The incestuous marriages, lust, various kidnappings, and summary executions proliferated between the two Neapolitan branches of the dynasty, which Joanna cleverly let exhaust themselves, assured her of support. Eros, in the court of Naples, is indeed a metaphor of power, but also one of arms.

The unleashing of ambitions of the various factions of cardinals, grafted onto the long Duras-Tarento conflict, led to a double crisis in the Church and in the kingdom. The partisans of Robert of Geneva and their connections in Avignon (Pierre Ameilh, Jean de la Grange) did not hesitate before the schism. The last of the Duras, Charles de la Paix, joined URBAN VI, a former partisan of Talleyrand of Perigord. Consequently, the schism had, as its first battleground, the kingdom and Provence, torn between two obediences and two dynastic legitimacies. Charles III, who had Joanna I executed and who was the last descendant of the Angevins of Naples, was opposed by a partisan of Clement VII, Louis I, brother of Charles VI and Duke of Anjou, adopted by Joanna I.

The third period of the history of the Angevin dynasty was marked by the very rapid renewal of collaborations and conflicts between the Roman Church and Naples in the context of the schism. At the same time that the devastating invasions of the claimants of the house of Anjou-Provence destabilized the Italian South and the dangers multiplied, Aragón increased its power with the annexation of Sicily to its crown and a branch of the Castilian dynasty of Transtamare rose to power in Barcelona. Charles III quickly broke off with Urban VI, his protégé, who was demanding an immense principality in Campania for his nephew Francesco Prignano. The Roman pope was arrested in Naples but managed to escape and proclaim the confiscation of the kingdom and immediate regency, supported by an important Urbanist party. To conquer the kingdom, an army was raised, entrusted to Joanna I's last husband, Otto of Brunswick. Charles III renewed the ambitions of the first Angevins with respect to Rome and Hungary and was recognized as king in Buda, but was immediately assassinated. His son, Ladislas, benefited from a change in papal politics, still centered on Naples, of which Urban VI's successor, BONIFACE IX, and the majority of the Roman Sacred College were natives. Recognized and crowned by the Roman pope he, in turn, became involved in the politics of hegemony over Rome and the PAPAL STATES. He was the first to lead an adventurous and military politics with humanistic touches ("Caesar or nothing" was the motto on his flags). The solution to the schism in Pisa, then in Constance, limited Ladislas's means to act. Not only did he lack the support of Provence, he was also subjected to attacks from Louis II, the claimant from Valois-Provence and later from Louis III, recognized by MARTIN V, who unleashed the companies of the *condottiere* Sforza against Naples. At Ladislas's death, his sister and heiress, Joanna II, was obliged to cede everything to Martin V: the immediate evacuation of Rome and the Papal States, the liberation of her husband, Jacques de la Marche, and the constitution of a principality in Campania for the pope's brother. The reconstituted papacy, therefore, ceded nothing. Martin V demanded the payment of the rent and even appealed to Louis III of Anjou-Provence. EUGENIUS IV claimed to settle the royal succession on Joanna's death, and even have the immediate regency assumed by Cardinal *condottiere* Giovanni Vitelleschi, then turned it over to René of Anjou-Provence. These issues were, however, all but settled: The papacy managed only to revive a ghost of its former rights. The reality is that of the balance between Italy and the Transtamare of Aragón. Supported by a transnational state where bankers ensured the rapid conveyance of funds and by the Catalan flotilla, an army of mercenaries and the imperial and military ideology of the humanists, Alfonso V, "man of Providence," shook up René of Anjou and the Roman popes. His decision to support the Council of Basel and the election of FELIX V paralyzed them and allowed him to obtain an advantageous agreement. More efficient than the Angevins, he restored their state against the papacy, leading to Lorenzo Valla's devastating criticism of the DONATION OF CONSTANTINE and the Holy See's political pretensions. Collaboration mixed with competition gave room for the restored state to keep the south safe from pontifical ambitions.

Henri Bresc

Bibliography

Bresc, H., ed. *La Correspondance de Pierre Ameilh, archevêque de Naples puis d'Embrun, 1363–1369*, Paris, 1972.

Caggese, R. *Robert d'Angiò ed i suoi tempi*, 2 vol., Florence, 1922–1931.

Fodale, S. *La politica napoletana di Urbano VI*, Caltanisetta-Rome, 1973.

Fodale, S. "Carlo III d'Angiò Durazzo," *DBI*, 235–239.

Herde, P. "Carlo I d'Angiò," *DBI*, 20 (1977), 199–226.

Housely, N. *The Italian Crusaders: The Papal-Angevin Alliance and the Crusades Against Lay Powers*, Oxford U.K., 1982.

Leonard, E. G. *Les Angevins de Naples*, Paris, 1954.

Nitschke, A. "Carlo II d'Angiò," *DBI*, 227–235.

ANGLICANISM. This religious tradition issued from the reformation of the Church of England developed in the British colonies, and led to the establishment of many local Churches united in the Anglican communion under the primate of honor, the Archbishop of Canterbury. It was only in the last years of the 19th century that Rome became interested in Anglicanism as such. Until that time, the perspective of the papacy was to seek a resolution to the SCHISM through the use of canonical, political, and diplomatic measures. These interventions, which must be understood within the political and theological context of the times, formed the backdrop for the debate that would later unfold.

Henry VIII's request (1528) to annul his marriage with Catherine of Aragón was unacceptable to Rome for political reasons. CLEMENT VII did not wish to alienate Emperor Charles V, the queen's uncle. Henry VIII wanted, above all, to put pressure on Rome when, with the support of Parliament, he systematically cut off canonical ties to the papacy and assumed powers that had been refused to him. This was accomplished through the issuance of the seven bills, spread out over the years 1532 and 1534. By acting in this manner, he was risking excommunication, which was indeed pronounced against him on two occasions (1533, 1535), but was never promulgated. Clearly, the parties were waiting for a successful reconciliation between France and the Empire, which would have allowed for armed intervention on the island. The minority of Edward VI (1547–53) allowed his entourage to model the Church of England according to the spirit of the continental Reformation, in particular by authorizing the marriage of priests and in establishing a new LITURGY (*Prayer Books* and *Ordinals* from 1549 and 1552). Neither PAUL III nor JULIUS III became directly involved. This wait-and-see attitude can be explained, above all, by the king's youth and by his desire to safeguard the future. This behavior seemed justified given the succession to the throne in 1553 of Mary Tudor, who did not hide her Catholic faith. Upon her request, Julius III entrusted Cardinal Reginald Pole with restoring the ties between the Church of England and the Apostolic See. The LEGATE received all necessary authority for this task, as well as recommendations to use moderation and prudence (BULLS *Dudum cum charissima* and *Cum proximis superioribus*, 1554). He had some success in reconstituting the Catholic hierarchy, but the use of force and his insistence on papal jurisdiction contributed to definitively alienating many moderate Englishmen. The election of PAUL IV (1555) marked a toughening of pontifical politics, which became evident once Elizabeth I became queen. In response to her revival of her father's politics, the pope explicitly encouraged the revolt of English Catholics and a coalition of Catholic powers in order to allow for the investiture of a sovereign faithful to Rome. PIUS IV, who succeeded Paul IV in 1559, was more diplomatic and sought to directly negotiate with the queen. These efforts, along with the reopening of the COUNCIL OF TRENT, roused new fears of a Catholic conspiracy. Elizabeth went further with her structuring project (Elizabethan Settlement) and published a revised

Book of Common Prayer (1559) as well as the thirty-nine Articles of Religion (1563).

The acts of rebellion manifested in 1559 were especially directed against the Protestant politics of the royal council. This time, they received the direct support of Pope PIUS V who, in the bull *Regnans in excelsis* (1570), excommunicated Elizabeth and absolved her subjects from the duty of obedience. In the eyes of most English subjects, papal intervention confirmed the negative image of "popery" and its danger for national unity. Moreover, this involvement came too late to truly weaken the queen and put English Catholics in a very difficult dilemma, by opposing their loyalty to the crown and their fidelity to the faith. Despite the persecutions that followed, this attitude of reconquest was maintained by Pius V's successors. Although GREGORY XIII offered a less combative interpretation of the bull (1580), it continued to serve as justification to the many internal conspiracies and external threats that finally led to the failed invasion of the Invincible Armada (1588).

After the failure of canonical and political efforts during the 16th century, it was through diplomacy that the post-Tridentine papacy attempted to resolve the English secession during the 17th century. There were two goals: stop the weakening of Catholicism by obtaining an official status for it, and prepare for a general return to the true faith by working on the conversion of the sovereign and the nobility. These tasks were made difficult by the divisions within the English clergy brought about by the extremism of certain Catholics (the Gunpowder Plot 1605). By imposing a new oath of allegiance (1606), James I attempted to isolate the most dangerous opponents. PAUL V quickly condemned the measure. It was through the marriage of King Charles I to Henrietta of France, sister of Louis XIII (1625), that the Holy See was called to act in a more direct fashion. URBAN VIII accorded the necessary DISPENSATIONS on the condition that the laws affecting Catholics be softened and that the queen's practice of her religion be permitted. This public appearance of Catholicism was the source of much confusion, whereas Anglicanism, under the influence of Archbishop W. Laud and the Carolines divines, was more concerned with emphasizing the richness of the religious tradition before the break. The subsequent Roman emissaries, Dom Leandro of Saint Martin (1634), Gregorio Panzani (1634–37), Georges Con (1636–39), and Carlo Rosseti (1639–41) saw in this a reconciliation that could foreshadow a reestablishment of secular ties. Neither the pope nor the king shared this illusion. However, by igniting Protestant hostility, this "anglo-Catholicism" contributed to a resurgence of the persecution of Roman Catholics. The civil war that followed led to the fall of the monarchy and the established Church, to the benefit of a Calvinist republic (the Commonwealth), then to the "protectorate" run by Oliver Cromwell (1641–61). The restoration of the Anglican Church followed that of the monarchy (1661). Charles II's personal sympathies leaned toward Catholicism (he converted on his deathbed), but political prudence led him to refuse the behavior that had produced mortal consequences for his father. This was no doubt a sensible approach considering the phobia attached to "popery," illustrated by the Test Act of 1673, which obligated all those with a civil or military job to receive communion in the Church of England and to reject the doctrine of transubstantiation. There was also the panic of the Popish Plot (22 August 1678). In Rome, it was understood that England's conversion could not be accomplished by force or by court influence. It was enough to have friendly relations with the Crown, which strengthened the structure of the small Catholic community, mainly by establishing an APOSTOLIC VICAR (Philip Howard, 1672). Given these perspectives, the accession to the throne of a Catholic king, James II (1685), who converted once he became heir to the throne, was welcomed with prudence. Despite INNOCENT XI's recommendations to proceed with moderation, the king sought to introduce Catholics into public life. The Declaration of Indungences, which he published in 1687, incited strong resistance, resulting in the Glorious Revolution of 1688–89, during which he lost his throne to his daughter Mary and son-in-law William of Orange. During the first part of the 18th century, the same Roman prudence was found regarding attempts to restore the Stuart dynasty (Jacobitism), though officially it received formal support.

While supporting the efforts of British Catholics to obtain their emancipation (1778–1829), the Holy See pursued the diplomatic path in attempting to establish sovereign State relations with the United Kingdom. In this respect, the missions of Cardinal Consalvi obtained a highly satisfactory result, the international recognition received at the Congress of Vienna (1815). On the religious level, the growth of the Catholic community due to Irish immigration, but also due to numerous conversions, was creating a new situation. By underscoring the Catholic aspect of Anglican tradition, the Oxford Movement opened a dialogue with the Roman Church, which led to some striking conversions (John Henry Newman, 1845). The reestablishment of the hierarchy (1850), under the direction of Nicholas Wiseman, gave a completely different meaning to these developments. It was in response to the hopes of a corporate union that Rome, for the first time, directly undertook a theological approach to Anglicanism.

Anglican Ordinations. LEO XIII's bull *Apostolicae curae* (1896) invalidated the orders received in the Anglican Church. The meaning of this important decision has been elucidated by recent access to relevant Vatican archives. The question had been dealt with in a polemical manner in the religious controversy in England during the 17th century and revisited in France in the beginning of the 18th century. Basing itself on historical precedents and a theological analysis of liturgical books, members of the commission presided over by Cardinal M. Mazzella arrived at this conclusion, which was confirmed by the pope. Two main points came out of this analysis: a dogmatic interpretation of the canonical decisions made, during the legation of Cardinal Pole, regarding the clergy ordained during the schism, and a neo-Scholastic interpretation of the formulation of reformed rituals. This perspective had not been shared by all the members of the commission, and the dominating influence of R. Merry del Val has been noted on this subject. His influence reflected the pontificate's direction and the desire to favor individual conversions by clarifying matters once and for all. It is likely that the very evolution of Anglicanism had exerted a significant influence on the decision, and on the manner in which it was made explicit thereafter. As of 1867 it had led to the first conference of Lambeth, where the representatives of local Churches met under the presidency of the Archbishop of Canterbury.

The following Conferences (1878, 1888) developed an ecumenical program tending practically to the establishment of a non-Roman Catholicism (quadrilatery of Lambeth). There were numerous and fruitful dialogues of union established with the Churches that came out of the Reformation and with the old Catholics and the Orthodox on the following quadruple foundation: Holy Scriptures, Symbol of Nicaea, Sacraments of Baptism and the Eucharist, and Historical Episcopate. This special comprehensiveness allowed for the coexistence of divergent, if not opposite, views and went against the centralizing tendency of Catholicism and a desire for homogeneity. In addition, the Anglican Church accepted what would soon be called "modernist tendencies," already present in the Broad Church or Latitudinarian currents, interpreted as a subjectivist approach regarding the facts of faith and an almost systematic rejection of magisterial authority. It is, therefore, not surprising at all that *Casti connubii* (1930) appeared as a negative response to the position taken at the Lambeth Conference in 1930 in favor of birth control.

Rome and the Anglican Communion. Although it is essential not to minimize the content of the early 18th-century exchanges between Gallican theologians and the Archbishop of Canterbury, W. Wake, they can hardly be considered to have facilitated relations between Rome and Canterbury. By establishing an irenic correspondence with the Anglican primate, L. Ellies Du Pin (1657–1719) and P. F. Le Courrayer (1681–1776) proved their independent spirit, which was very suspect in the eyes of the papacy. In contrast, the Anglo-Roman campaign led by the Abbot F. Portal at the turn of the 19th century was much more prudent, even if the *Apostolicae curae* made it ineffective. Portal also initiated the conversations under the direction of Cardinal D. Mercier at Malines (1922–6). Although they were unofficial they contributed to making major points of disagreement emerge, not the least of which was Roman PRIMACY as defined by Vatican I. The development of the ecumenical movement and the influence exerted on it by the Anglican *via media* made a Catholic stand, going beyond the initial condemnations, inevitable. Once again, it was from France that the theoretical initiative came, particularly with the work of Father Yves Congar (*Chrétiens désunis*, 1937), whose work presented the importance of a deep understanding of the ecclesiological tradition of the Church of England for a "Catholic ecumenism." The meeting in December 1960 between Archbishop G. Fisher and Pope JOHN XXIII thus took on a historical dimension that was made concrete with the invitation of Anglican observers to the Vatican II COUNCIL. In the document on ecumenism (*Unitatis redintegratio*, 13), the special place of Anglicanism among the communities separated from the Roman see was recognized. PAUL VI confirmed this in his reception of Archbishop M. Ramsey, when a commission was established to ensure the dialogue between Anglicans and Roman Catholics (November 1966). This preparatory committee drafted a report (Malta, 1968) specifying the bases for a future dialogue. That document was entrusted to a new international commission (ARCIC) established in 1969, which first met in 1970. The fruit of these exchanges were four common declarations on eucharistic doctrine (Windsor, 1971), ministry and ordination (Canterbury, 1973), the authority in the Church (Venice, 1976), and clarifications on eucharistic doctrine, ministry, and ordination (Salisbury, 1979). A final report (Windsor, 1981) completed them, emphasizing an ecclesiology of communion (*koinonia*). The entirety of the documents was distributed to the member Churches of the Anglican communion as well as to the episcopal conferences concerned.

If the Lambeth Conference of 1988 accepted the basic tenor of these documents, the reception was less enthusiastic on the Roman side. Despite enumerating the constructive aspects of the document, the official response published on 5 December 1991, under the presidency of the Congregation for the Doctrine of the faith and of the Council for Christian Unity, underscored the main unresolved difficulties. In 1975 the report of another special commission was published regarding the theology of marriage and its applications in mixed marriages. A new commission (ARCIC-II), established during Pope JOHN PAUL II's visit to Canterbury (1982), published a common declaration on salvation and the Church and worked on a project entitled "Growth in Communion," about the ordination of women, the reconciliation of ministries, moral questions, and the posible establishment of full communion.

Jacques Grès-Gayer

See also ORDINATIONS, ANGLICAN.

Bibliography

Aveling, J. C., Loades, D. M., and McAdoo, H. R. *Rome and the Anglicans. Historical and Doctrinal Aspects of Anglican-Roman Catholic Relations*, Berlin-New York, 1982.

Congar, Y. *Chrétiens désunis. Principes d'un "oecuménisme catholique,"* Paris, 1937; *Chrétiens en dialogue. Contributions catholiques à l'oecuménisme*, Paris, 1964.

Fouilloux, E. *Les Catholiques français et l'unité chrétienne, du XIXe au XXe siècle. Itinéraires européens d'expression française*, Paris, 1982.

Hill, C., and Yarnold, E. J., eds. *Anglican and Roman Catholics: The Search for Unity*, London, 1994.

Hughes, J. J. *Absolutely Null and Utterly Void. An Account of the 1896 Papal Condemnation of Anglican Orders*, Washington, 1968.

Jalons pour l'Unité (ARCIC, 1971–1981), Paris, 1982.

Ladous, R. *Monsieur Portal et les siens (1855–1926)*, Paris, 1985.

Norman, E. *Roman Catholicism in England, from the Elizabethan Settlement to the Second Vatican Council*, Oxford, 1985.

Pawley, B. and M. *Rome and Canterbury Through Four Centuries, 1530–1973*, London-Oxford, 1974.

Rambaldi, G. "La bolla Apostolicae Curae di Leone XIII sulle ordinazioni anglicane," *Gregorianum*, 64 (1983), 631–7; 66 (1985), 53–88.

Simon, M. *L'Anglicanisme*, Paris, 1969.

Tavard, G. *A Review of Anglican Orders. The Problem and the Solution*, Collegeville, Minn.,1990.

van de Pol, W. H. *La Communion anglicane et l'oecuménisme d'après les documents officiels*, Paris 1967.

Von Gutten, A. F. "Les ordinations anglicanes. Le problème affronté par Lèon XIII," *Nova et Vetera* (1988), 1–21.

ANICETUS. *(b. Emesa (Homs) ?, d. Rome, 166). Elected in 155. Buried at St. Peter's in Rome. Saint.*

The tenth successor to Peter, his pontificate followed that of PIUS I. Celebrated on 17 April, Anicetus, according to the LIBER PONTIFICALIS was a Syrian from Emesa (Homs). There is very little extant information about his pontificate, and only Irenaeus and Eusebius of Caesaria have passed down some precise details (it is true that at this time Irenaeus could have been staying in Rome). The *Liber pontificalis* attributed to Anicetus a disciplinary prescription forbidding members of the clergy to wear their hair long. This seems unlikely for the time, but reflects the dirth of information available.

One of the few, but illuminating, certainties on the spirit of the pontificate was his attitude toward Polycarp, the bishop of Smyrna. Polycarp, who was then quite aged, came to Rome, possibly accompanied by two of his disciples, Irenaeus and Florinus. The objective of this long trip was to discuss certain points regarding ecclesiastical life, the most important of which was the discrepancy in the date for Easter. The Eastern custom did not have Easter necessarily fall on a Sunday, as opposed to Roman tradition. Anicetus and Polycarp discussed the matter, but could not agree. Anicetus did not, however, offer any condemnation but, on the contrary, allowed Polycarp to preside over the celebration of the eucharist locally as a gesture of peace. He may, however, have been influenced by the bishop's relationship with John and the other apostles, whom, according to Irenaeus, he knew personally.

It was also under his pontificate that Hegesippus, the great Syrian scholar, came to Rome and established the episcopal list there. At the same time, there were representatives of various factions within the Church, in particular the gnostic Valentin, Cerdo, and Marcion, who came to organize an independent community. Polycarp had the opportunity to meet Marcion and to salute him as "Satan's first born." At the same time, Justin was spreading his teachings throughout Rome and his disciple Tatian was getting there. We do not know what relations Anicetus had with them, or what his attitude was toward Gnosticism, then in full development. At his death, about which we know nothing, his body was deposited next to St. Peter's at the Vatican, according to tradition.

Jean-Pierre Martin

Bibliography

Bardy, G. *Catholicism. Hier, aujourd'hui, demain*, 1 (1948), 574–575.

Bareille, G. *DTC*, II, 1 (1931), 1302–1303.

Eusebius, *HE*, IV, 11, 1; 11, 7; 14, 1; 14, 5; 19, 1; 22, 2; V, 6, 4; 14; 16; 17.

Irenaeus, *Adv. haeres.*, III, 3–4; 4, 2.

Kirsch, J. P. *DHGE*, 3 (1924), 280–281.

Richard, M. "La question pascale au IIe siècle," *L'Orient syrien*, 6 (1961), 179–212.

Weltin, E. G. *NCE*, 1 (1967), 544.

ANIMALS. Animals have played a more important role in the daily lives of the popes than is often realized. The APOSTOLIC CAMERA and the secret Treasury mention them throughout the folios in the accounting registers, and they are obviously part of the immediate, familiar, and necessary environment of the popes, whether they serve to feed, clothe, or simply entertain.

Although raw materials from animals were used for fabrics and furs, parchments, leather, and waxes, the place of animals in the papal kitchens merits special mention. When one thinks of the papal court's needs in terms of food, one has only to note that it was the main expense of the Camera under BONIFACE VIII. The consumption of meat and fish is, in fact, surprisingly diversified and significant. In AVIGNON, for example, the pontifical table offered butcher's meat, hares and rabbits, poultry (chicken, but also goose, pheasant, and capons), game (mainly venison), game birds (quail, turtledoves, pigeons, cranes, starlings, partridges, etc.), and a wide variety of fresh and saltwater fish and seafood (some imported from quite a distance) including bream, mullet, conger eel, gurnard, bass, tuna, hake, squid, sturgeon, whale, dolphin, salmon, carp, tench, trout, perch, and eel.

Some of the animals that ended up on the papal tables came from parks and fish ponds belonging to the pope. The garden in the palace in Avignon housed a deer park, managed by an individual called the *custos cervorum*, where there were also goats. The park was mentioned in Rome under the pontificates of URBAN V and later PIUS II, in the Palace of Avignon throughout the 14th century, and also in the Palace of the Pont-de-Sorgues under GREGORY XI. Rabbits were bred on a more regular basis. In fact, deer and rabbits were sometimes sent over great distances: Gérald Mercadier sent rabbits from Avignon to Rome in 1369. Guillaume Périer, Urban V's gardener, accompanied five deer from Rome to Montefiascone. There was a deer park in the garden of Belvedere under the reign of PAUL VI, as well as a large farmyard. There were also wild animals roaming the area, as evidenced by reports between 1535 and 1537, of the gardener Lucerta killing ten foxes in the Belvedere and even finding himself face to face with a wolf. Game parks, farmyards, and gardens were most often the responsibility of the same warden.

In addition to their immediate uses (for meals, especially during festivities), these animal reserves had another function. The pope used live animals—especially pigs, hares, and deer, but also steer, calves, and sheep—as Christmas or Easter gifts for cardinals and various officers of the CURIA. On occasion, animals were given as gifts to high-ranking visitors such as ambassadors, princes, or foreign sovereigns.

The equine species maintained an eminent position in court life, both on the material and symbolic levels. A significant part of the papal budget was dedicated to the stables and the role played by mules, ambling mares, and palfreys in the cavalcades surrounding the pope during his public appearances, where the mule of the Holy Sacrament led the way, bearing the sacred host. The ancient association between the horse or the white mule and the notion of *imperium* and sovereignty is linked to this complex ceremony. Popes rode on elaborately harnessed white horses or in a palanquin drawn by two white mules. The emperor was required to hold the stirrup and lead the

pope's white palfrey by the bit for nine Roman steps. Each year the King of Naples offered the tribute of the ambling mare to the pope in recognition of his suzerainty, a ceremony that was part of the same symbolism. Solemnly presented by an ambassador, the animal, carrying on its saddle a silver vase with rent of 7,000 ducats in gold, would get down on its knees in the Vatican basilica the night before the feast of Sts. Peter and Paul. The Church of Bamberg had to offer the same tribute.

There is very ancient evidence of the maintenance of exotic animals to the point where these constituted veritable menageries. Besides wild animals entrusted to a special warden, the menageries were apparently managed by the gardener, who was also the warden for the game reserve. Under BONIFACIO VIII, sums were regularly allocated to master Nicholas "for the animals in Saint Peter's garden" and to Brother Montoni for taking care of a leopard. In Avignon, JOHN XXII possessed a camel (offered in 1326 by the King of Sicily), some bears, and a lion for which a small building was erected near the tower of Trouillas, next to the stables and the farmyard. Under BENEDICT XII and CLEMENT VI, there was a lioness occupying this abode that ate quarters of mutton and was entrusted to a special guard, Bertrand de Casademont. LEO X kept the lions offered to him, in symbolic homage to his name, in the arcades of the corridors linking the Vatican to CASTEL SANT'ANGELO. According to Albertini, the Belvedere, as of 1509, housed monkeys, parrots, civets, and chameleons, to which was added an elephant, offered by the king of Portugal on the occasion of Leo X's election. Unfortunately, the rhinoceros sent in 1517 by this same sovereign died at sea and arrived stuffed in Rome. All these animals served at times, to reinforce the majesty of some cortèges and no doubt constituted a popular attraction. Leo X thus exhibited his elephant in honor of his brother, and three camels belonging to him were paraded in the triumphal Fat Thursday cortège in 1520. Less peaceful uses of animals included combats staged as part of a festivity. In Florence in 1459, lions were enclosed with horses, wild boar, dogs, and a giraffe to welcome PIUS II. ALEXANDER VI, whose coat of arms included a bull, made bullfights fashionable. Bullfights were also held during the festivities of the Roman carnival in the 16th century.

It seems that birds, especially, were favorite animals of the popes: the wardrobe master was responsible for them. Several popes had parrots (BONIFACE VIII, MARTIN V, Pius II, SIXTUS IV, PAUL III) and Leo X had a nightingale. Hunts constituted another form of entertainment, an expensive pastime probably introduced in Rome by Cardinals Ludovico Scarampi and Ascanio Sforza. There is, however, evidence that the sport was already practiced by BONIFACE IX, GREGORY XII and much earlier, GREGORY IX. Yet it was especially during the pontificates of Leo X and Paul III that hunting was in its glory days. Pietro d'Aversa, guardian of the hunting grounds, was designated in 1545 as master of the hunt. He was especially responsible for the birds of prey, goshawks, hawks, gyrfalcons, falcons, tiercelets, sparrow hawks, and eagles, some imported from far away. Leo X had hawks imported from Pisa, from Candia in Crete, goshawks from Greece and Armenia, and falcons from Venice. The pack, established under the reign of Leo X at the foot of the Santo Spirito hill, was entrusted to a *canattiere*, in charge of the bloodhounds (who flushed out the wild game) and greyhounds to hunt rabbit and hares. There was also a *bracchiere* responsible for the pointers that hunted bigger game. These dogs came from breeders in Italy (the one in Mantua was reknowned), but also from Spain, England, and France. Leo X even hunted leopard on occasion. A groom would mount the animal from behind and then release it on its prey at the opportune moment.

Some traces of the affection popes had for domestic animals have come down to us and they are all the more precious because they are rare. Paul II's biographer notes his exemplary compassion for animals and his horror at their impending death, which caused him to pity the farmyard animal and tear a calf, goat, birds, and chickens from the hands of his domestics or the butchers. Parrots, small dogs, and especially cats received a great deal of attention and were cared for by Paul II's doctor, Giacomo Gottifredi. This singular attitude earned Paul II one epigram in which the grief he felt at the death of one of his cats was mocked. Paul III's favorite was a small dog. He had a collar made for the dog in 1536 decorated with eight little spherical bells made of silver. The cat that Leo XII had raised in the pleat of his cassock was famous for having been passed on to Chateaubriand in February of 1829. A sweet, little gray cat, Micetto, who had been born in the Raphael dressing rooms was familiarly called "the pope's cat" in Paris.

Cardinal Nasalli Rocca, PIUS XII's valet, recounted in his *Memoirs* the image of the pope taking his meals in silence and feeding his canaries while he was read to in his chamber. Some journalists revealed how sensitive Pius XII was to animals in general, especially when he came across a wounded goldfinch who had entered the papal apartments by chance. The bird was taken in by Sister Pasqualina and adopted by the pope who freed it as soon as it was healed. There is even mention of a concert of owls accompanying the pope's last days. Later, PAUL VI had golden peacocks raised at Castel Gandolfo, which he went to feed every evening during his constitutional around the gardens of the summer residence he enjoyed so much. It seems that as of PIUS IX, the animal is no longer a familiar figure in the daily lives of popes. The popes led relatively reclusive lives in the Vatican up until 1929, and their isolation could have led them to enjoy this

type of companionship; however, there is no evidence of this. It is, quite remarkable that no pope of the contemporary period has become attached to the canine species, perhaps because of the trouble dogs would cause in daily life. Animals are still present at the Vatican, in the city, even if they are extremely discrete. The blessing of the sheep on the day of St. Agnes (21 January), intended to start production of a special wool for the pallium, is still customary today.

Laurence Bobis

Bibliography

Delort, R. *Le Commerce des fourrures en Occident à la fin du Moyen Âge*, Rome, 2 vols., 1978.

Dorez, L. *La Cour du pape Paul III*, 2 vols., Paris, 1932.

Gebhart, E. *Etudes méridionales: la Renaissance italienne et la philosophie de l'histoire, Paris*, 1887.

Gnoli, D. "Le cacce di Leone X," *Nuova antologia*, XLIII (1893), 1–15.

Loevenbruck, P. *Les Animaux sauvages dans l'histoire*, Paris, 1955.

Loisel, G. *Histoire des ménageries, de l'Antiquité à nos jours*, Paris, 1912.

Rodocanachi, E. *Rome au temps de Jules II et Léon X*, Paris, 1912.

Traeger, J. *Der reitende Papst: ein Beitrag zur Ikonographie des Papsttums*, Munich-Zurich, 1970.

Zeppegno, L., and Bellegrande, G. *Guida ai misteri e piaceri del Vaticano*, Milan, 1974.

ANNATES. Annates are taxes collected by the papacy from an ecclesiastical benefice on the occasion of its collation by the pope. The annate (known as "first fruits") is a year of payments equal to net revenues, after the deduction of costs for management and maintenance by the beneficiary. Although first established under CLEMENT V in 1306, and put into widespread use under JOHN XXII, the tax had to be renewed under each pontificate because it was never considered to be a regular payment. Theoretically, the tax was only on benefices granted by the pope, but in practice, the generalization of reserves by the time of CLEMENT VI, made it a tax that affected the majority of benefices. The basis for the annate was that benefices were taxed one time only. For a long time the practice was irregularly administered, with the collector choosing to collect either the entire profit of the benefice, or only the net revenue, leaving the surplus to the beneficiary. When URBAN V cut taxes in half in order to recognize the economic crisis, collectors limited themselves to the new tax. The ecclesiastical beneficiaries paid a special annate for small and minor services. For the clergy, the annates are the symbol par excellence of pontifical fiscality. Polemists, during the GREAT SCHISM of the

West, and reformers during the councils of the first half of the 15th century, questioned the annates in principle and the Council of Basel eventually abolished them with the decree of 9 June 1435. However, in reality, the pope's agents continued to demand annates in various forms and with uneven success.

Jean Favier

Bibliography

Baix, F., and Uyttebrouck, A. *La Chambre apostolique et les "libri annatarum" by Martin V (1417–1431)*, Rome-Brussels, 2 vols., 1947–60 (*Analecta vaticano-belgica*, 14).

Brouette, E. *Les "libri annatarum" . . . pontificats d'Innocent VIII et d'Alexandre VI, 1484–1503*, Rome-Brussels, 1963 (*Analecta vaticano-belgica*, 24).

Costello, M. A. *De annatis Hiberniae*, I, *Ulster*, Dundalk, 1909 [the sequel, for the other archdioceses in Ireland, 15th–early 16th century appeared in supplements in issues of *Archivium hibernicum*, 2 (1913) to 28 (1966)].

Kirsch, J. P. *Die päpstlichen Annaten in Deutschland während des XIV. Jahrhunderts*, Paderborn, 1903.

Lunt, W. E. *Financial Relations of the Papacy with England, 1327–1534*, Cambridge, Mass., 1962.

Lunt, W. E. *Papal Revenues in the Middle Ages*, 2 vols., New York, 1965.

ANNONA. The annona is an institution of the PAPAL STATE that primarily handled regulating the provision of grains to the capital. Constituted due to circumstances during the 16th century, it was maintained through the end of the 18th century. It was the subject of a great deal of literature until the beginning of the 20th century because it was at the heart of the debate opposing partisans of liberalism and tenants of state interventionism. Present research, founded on the study of *avvisi* ("newspapers" of the period), on the archives of the annona service and on those of the APOSTOLIC CAMERA upon which it depended, have served to calm the debate and place the institution in the context of the economic history of Rome.

Until the 19th century, the relationship between the towns (or at least those of a certain size) and the countryside that fed them was very tenuous. Price hikes and food shortages were feared during poor harvests because they were likely to cause popular emotional upset and destabilize the existing powers. Consequently, the authorities in charge were involved with handling provisions for the cities, at least during crisis periods. In Rome, the popes of the modern period inherited a long tradition of organizing provisions, going back to the days of the Roman Empire. Furthermore, the spiritual as well as temporal nature of their power gave them moral obligations toward the population which they had always

accepted from time immemorial. As of the end of the 6th century or at the latest at the beginning of the 7th century, until the break with the Byzantine Empire in the 8th, the task of providing food for Rome was under papal control. With the agreement of the emperor in Constantinople, the pope managed the civil annona of the city of Rome, whose population at the time was between 50,000 and 90,000 people, just as other bishops did in their towns. Even at the time of the communal autonomy during the Middle Ages, although the municipal authorities were supposed to provide food to the city, the popes continued to demonstrate their care for the Roman people. In 1283 MARTIN IV personally donated 5,000 florins to the capital to purchase Sicilian wheat. In 1300 BONIFACE VIII drew up a constitution derogating the laws prohibiting exports of food outside the PATRIMONY OF SAINT PETER by conceding "*de gratia [. . .] speciali, quod deferatur ad Urbem.*" Even during the GREAT SCHISM the popes attempted, through the intermediary of the LEGATES, to organize provisions for the Italian provinces from AVIGNON. The measures taken by GREGORY XI in 1374–5, although they failed, contained a good number of controlling procedures that were used in the following century. In fact, it was in the 15th century that the beginnings of the papal annona can be placed. The first registers of the "Abundance of Rome" appeared under PAUL II and SIXTUS IV. Certainly, there still exists a municipal "college" of the annona and "*militi grascieri, commissarii dell'abbondanza,*" but we also see the functioning of the CAMERLENGO, always entrusted to a cardinal. One of his numerous duties, comparable to the ancient city prefect, was the general surveillance of provisions. To assist him with this responsibility, there was a college of clerics from the Apostolic Camera. At the time there were seven members, one of whom was especially adept at problems concerning agriculture and food provisions.

Throughout the 16th century, the services of the annona, as they would function until the end of the 18th century, gradually took over municipal institutions. There was an identical movement going on throughout Italy at the time wherein governmental administrations were replacing municipal authorities for matters concerning food provisions, which had become too difficult for them to handle. In Florence the Medici took over the direction of the Abbondanza in 1556. In Naples, as of 1550, the vice-king named a prefect of the annona. In Rome, the population and needs of the city increased significantly. In 1523 there were 55,000 inhabitants, but nearly 100,000 at the end of the century, with an annual demand estimated at approximately 345,000 hectoliters of grain in 1587, the date of the first evaluation of the annual needs of Rome, requested by SIXTUS V. At the same time, the population diminished along with the lands cultivated for wheat in the Roman countryside, that is, in the region bordered by Montalto in the north, Terracina in the south, Amelia in the east, and Ostia in the west. Numerous factors account for this situation including, as Jean Delumeau has demonstrated so well, the resurgence of banditry and the development of grazing pastures. The authorities encouraged the latter for fiscal reasons since the State perceived a "duty for the pastures." This evolution was linked to the reinforcement of large properties, but the popes never took any measures to modify the structures of property within the Papal State. These conditions explain the fragility of ensuring provisions for Rome at the time. Food shortages were frequent and often quite serious, such as those of 1555 and the following years, or the scarcity that wreaked havoc from 1590 through 1593. To combat this type of situation, the popes were led to create a real administrative service responsible for provisions, more completely eliminating the municipal functionaries. They also were prompted to enact through this service a series of measures that concerned the Roman countryside and the provinces of the neighboring Papal State of the Urbs. The following are among the multiple stages of creating annona services during the 16th century.

CLEMENT VII was the first to submit (1594) municipal magistrates responsible for provisions to a general commissioner named by the pope, thus attacking the prerogatives of conservatives that had been confirmed by JULIUS II's brief in 1512.

The food shortage of the 1550s led to the nomination, between 1550 and 1555, of three commissioners responsible for food supply and endowed with full powers. In 1556, the title and function of the prefect of the annona reappeared, and was held by the celebrated jurist Bartolomeo Camerario de Benevento. He was so unpopular due to the measures he undertook during the shortage of 1557 that he ended his days in prison. The idea of a prefect of the annona was not mentioned again until 1575. At that time, the food supply problems caused by the holy year led GREGORY XII to restore the function, definitively this time. The jurisdiction of the prefect extended throughout the Papal State, although its main function was to ensure the supply of grain to the capital. It proceeded to purchase grain when there was an insufficient supply, during the years of the last quarter of the 16th century, and to stock it in the granaries created for this purpose by GREGORY XIII near the ruins of the Diocletian baths.

The municipality of Rome maintained another role in the matter of food supplies. It fixed food prices, watched over the markets (especially the weight of bread), and issued permits for milling in case of food shortages. It was Sixtus V who, after a conflict with the municipal authorities, withdrew their prerogatives (and the pricing of wheat then became a task handled by the Apostolic Camera). In addition, all their decisions had to be approved,

from then on, by the prefect of the annona. At the same time (1588) he created a congregation *pro ubertate annonai status ecclesiastici*, a kind of ministry of food that supervised the prefect. This congregation frequently competed with the prefect and fell into disuse by the 17th century. It was replaced by special congregations whenever a particular need arose. Thus, in 1611, PAUL V instituted a consultative commission of experts *pro ubertate annonae et grasciae*. As of the end of the 16th century, the main structures of the annoniary administration were in place.

How did the annona ensure a regular supply of wheat at a stable price to the city of Rome? First of all, there was a requisition of available wheat from the Roman countryside (*le districtus Urbis*) and the so-called annoniary provinces, that is the provinces of the Patrimony and Campania, Lazio, Maritima and Sabina. In a normal year, the production from these regions was sufficient to meet Roman needs. In case of difficulties, an appeal was made to other provinces in the Papal States (to the Ancona marche, in particular) or even to imports from abroad. In order to requisition the wheat, the annona had to be inventoried, once in January, for the lands sowed with wheat, and again after the harvest for the quantities reaped. All these grains had to be transported to Rome, with the exception of the necessary quantities for domestic consumption and for sowing. In theory, exports from these provinces to foreign countries was forbidden, but the system was tempered by agreements negotiated each year by the pope when the needs of the Papal State were met.

The grant or refusal of these export authorizations is a major problem in the study of the functioning of the annona. There were liberal popes, such as LEO X at the beginning of the 16th century, who generously conceded the right to export wheat, and authoritarian popes who limited or prohibited the export of grains. Pope PIUS IV, in a letter dating from 1562, proclaimed a prohibition on exports for the entire Papal State. Gregory XIII and Sixtus V limited, as much as possible, the free circulation of grains. In fact, the pontiff's attitude was largely dependent on the circumstances, whether the years were abundant or lean. In order to break from this logic, Clement VII, in 1523, established a system for exports based on a sliding scale. In this way, the authorizations for exporting a fixed proportion of the harvest was automatically authorized as long as the price of wheat on the Roman market did not exceed a specified sum. Such procedures were enacted several times in the history of the annona (by CLEMENT VIII in 1597, ALEXANDER VIII in 1689, etc.), but the system never really established itself. It had one major defect: the producers could not foresee from one year to the next if the state of the market allowed them to export or not. They were, therefore, not encouraged to expand the lands cultivated for wheat.

The services of the annona were also responsible, at least as of the end of the 16th century, for organizing distribution in Rome. The annona oversaw stock (and fought against hoarding with a team of sworn measurers), supervised retail commerce, and controlled the prices. As for this last matter, from Paul V's perpetual tarif (1605), there was a sliding scale that established a fixed relationship between the price of grain on the market and the weight of a *pagnotta* of bread, maintained at a fixed price. For the price of grain itself, each year the annona fixed a maximum and bought grains at market prices that it resold at "political" prices. This practice, originally reserved for years when there were food shortages, became a permanent practice as of the 17th century. Henceforth, the annona provided at least a quarter of the necessary grains for consumption, in small part, directly to individuals (for example, at the Campo di Fiore market), but especially to storekeepers and bakers.

Finally, the annona also functioned as an agricultural credit institution. In 1588 Sixtus V established a fund of 200,000 écus that was originally intended to serve as loan money to farmers but was more substantially used to buy grains during the great crisis of the years 1590 through 1593. As of 1594 through 1595, Clement VIII granted loans to restore farmlands. As of 1611 Paul V established a system of regular loans to farmers, first at moderate interest, then for free, as of the middle of the 18th century, but the sums advanced, often less than 1,000 ecus, were insufficient to increase cereal production and were for emergency purposes only. The second half of the 18th century was the period in which the annona system, as we have described it, failed. As of the 1760s, the difficulties in providing food became such that the annona had to increase its activities in a spectacular way and regularly ensure most of the food supply for Rome. After 1770 the annona never handled less than half of the annual sales of grains on the Roman market. This constituted a significant change for a service that had previously contented itself with a politics of limited intervention. Perhaps this evolution can be explained by the exhaustion of the private treasuries that made recourse to public treasuries necessary, yet the pontifical annona was not financially substantial enough to assume such a role. Certainly, for the most part, provisions were distributed and the tensions on the Roman market were minimal, at least until 1785 through 1790, but this was achieved at the price of the financial ruin of the annona. Until the crisis of 1763 through 1767, the annona had a reserve of 400,000 écus available; between 1767 and 1779 its annual deficit was about 700,000 to 800,000 écus. By 1797 the deficit reached 4 million écus. Faced with the failure of the annona, PIUS VII abandoned the former system in 1800 and established the annonary deputation. This created a free market for grains, liberated pricing, and encouraged importations. In short, it was the application of the system

advocated by the liberals for more than a century that aimed at invigorating production by allowing producers to gain substantial profits through the total liberalization of the commerce of grains. Such a system did not, however, manage to reestablish prosperity in the countryside of the Papal States, for it only regulated the market without affecting the structure of farm production.

Thus, during the 16th through 18th centuries, the services of the annona were increasingly important for the food supply of Rome, despite attempts by certain pontiffs to halt this movement. Alexander VIII in 1689, and BENEDICT XIII forty years later, tried in vain to fix a maximum amount of grain that the stocks of the annona could have. In a sense, one can say that the papal annona reached some of its objectives. Until the 1760s, when the stability of prices ended, price controls were rather efficient and favorable to modest consumers. Prices fixed by the annona were more or less representative of those effectively practiced and allowed a stabilization of the rates, in particular by limiting the seasonal shifts. Nevertheless, the existence of the annona did not prevent food shortages. It did not resolve the deeper problem of the fragility of the food supply for Rome, the decadence of its countryside. On one hand, the leading personnel of the service had no interest in restoring prosperity to the country around Rome. The prefects of the annona and the commissioners in the provinces were almost all tightly connected to the *mercanti di campagna* and, as such, profited from the situation. On the other hand, and most especially, the services of the annona never weighed on anything but the market and did not affect the structures of production, which were the source of the fragility of the Roman food supply.

Jean Boutier and Catherine Virlouvet

Bibliography

Delumeau, J. *Vie économique et sociale de Rome dans la seconde moitié du XVIe siècle*, 1–2, Paris, 1959.

Durliat, J. *De la ville antique à la ville byzantine, le problème des subsistances*, Paris, 1990.

Kalsbach, A. "Annona," *Reallexikon für Antike und Christentum*, ed. T. Klauser, 1, 1950, 443–6.

Nicolaï, N. M. *Memorie, Leggi ed Osservazioni sulle campagne e sull'annona di Roma*, 3 vols., Rome, 1803.

Revel, J. "Le grain de Rome et la crise de l'annone dans la seconde moitié du XVIIIe siècle," *MEFRM*, 1972, 1, 201–81; "Les privilèges d'une capitale: l'approvisionnement de Rome à l'époque moderne," *AESC*, 1975, 563–74.

ANNUARIO PONTIFICIO. The *Annuario pontificio* (pontifical directory) is both a personnel directory and a flow chart of the various organisms of the Holy See. It is published at the beginning of the second trimester of the year following its date, and is prepared by the Central Statistical Office of the Church, which is a service of the SECRETARY OF STATE. Its first publication was the work of secular printers who, in 1716, using the title *Notizie per l'anno . . .* (News of the Year), gathered together diverse reports on events and lists of personalities in and around the papal court and church hierarchy. The periodical oscilated for a while between a chronicle and a directory, which led to various parallel publications. The Apostolic Camera in turn published an annual directory in 1851 in Italian entitled *Hierarchy of the Holy Apostolic Catholic and Roman Church in the World and According to all the Rites with Historical Notices*. As of 1860 this publication became the *Annuario pontificio*, the true ancestor of the present version. Information related to the administration of the PAPAL STATES and the list of dignitaries and functionaries in the hierarchy of the Church were attached. The preparation of this publication was entrusted to the *Giornale di Roma*. Suspended after 1870 following the taking over of Rome, the publication of the *Annuario pontificio* resumed in 1872 with the title *Catholic Hierarchy and the Papal Family for the Year with Appendice and News Concerning the Holy See*. Commissioned to a secular printer, the *Catholic Hierarchy . . .* was taken over by the Vatican typographers in 1885, 1899, and 1904 with the note, "official edition." The former title, *Annuario pontificio*, returned as of 1912 and the specification "official edition" disappeared as of 1924.

The present structure of the *Annuario pontificio*, resulting from the fusion of various publications mentioned above, was organized according to three themes: the hierarchy, the Roman CURIA, and VATICAN CITY. The list of religious institutions (orders, congregations, etc.) is attached, as well as a certain number of scientific institutions attached to the HOLY SEE (universities, colleges, academies). A few unclassifiable entities, such as the IOR (Istituto delle Opere di Religione—Institute of Religious Works), are included at the end, before a long appendix with a short description of each of the pontifical institutions. Using the *Annuario* is relatively simple because the numerous alphabetical indexes provide names of people and institutions. However, even though its consultation is irreplaceable for information about the Roman Curia, the picture it gives should be completed with knowledge of certain realities not expressly mentioned in it. The best example is perhaps that of the role of the private secretary of the pope. A key person in gaining access to the sovereign pontiff, he is the one through whom most requests for a private audience with the pope are filtered. Yet, be it Paschale Machi, PAUL VI's secretary, or Stanislas Dziwisz, JOHN PAUL II's, the private secretary figures in the *Annuario* only as a second-class employee of the Secretary of State, lost among the editorial attachés ("*minutanti*"), without any mention of the particular functions linking this official to the pope.

As a source for biographical research, the *Annuario pontificio* is hard to replace. It gives the birth date and all the essential facts concerning the ecclesiastical careers of all the cardinals and bishops. For a very long time, it has been an irreplaceable means of access to the office and home telephone numbers of the key persons in charge of the Roman Curia. Recently, a telephone book for Vatican City has been available in bookstores.

Philippe Levillain

Bibliography

Annuario pontificio per l'anno 2000, Vatican City.

ANNUARY, TELEPHONE, TELEPHONE BOOK. See **Telephone**.

ANTECHAMBER. See **Apartments, Papal**.

ANTERUS. (*?, d. 3 January 236*). *Elected pope on 21 November 235. Buried in the crypt in the cemetery of Callistus.*

When Anterus succeeded Pope PONTIAN, the Roman community was shaken by conflicts. Hippolytus and his partisans had assembled in a dissident Church, and Emperor Maximinus Thrax (235–238) had subjected Popes ZEPHYRINUS, CALLISTUS, and Pontian to persecutions. Maximus, who was the successor to Alexander Severus (assassinated by his soldiers), had arrived in the Empire during a period of increasing external difficulties threatening the Rhine and the Danube in the west and the Euphrates in the east. Hard on the wealthy, he was equally so on the Church. Eusebius of Caesarea affirms that Maximinus "due to his resentment against the house of Alexander, made up a of majority of faithful, provokes a persecution." Eusebius adds that his edict was also aimed at bishops "in charge of teaching according to the Gospel." Hippolytus and Pontian were deported to Sardinia and condemned to forced labor. The latter, isolated from the Roman community, had renounced his position and died following ill treatment (*LP*, I, 145). Anterus replaced him and was crowned on 21 November 235 (*Catalogue libérien, MGH, AA*, 9/1, 75).

The LIBER PONTIFICALIS indicates that Anterus was of Greek origin (*natione Graecus*), but the name could indicate that he was a freed slave. We know little about his pontificate, which was very brief, lasting one month and ten days, according to the *Catalogue libérien*, a month and twelve days, according to the *Liber pontificalis*. It is possible that he, too, was a victim of the persecution that took place on 3 January 236; however, a natural death is more likely in his case. His epitaph is known (*ICUR*, 4, 10558). There his simple name appears with his position as *episcopus*.

Michel Christol

Bibliography

Catalogue libérien, MGH AA, 9/1, 74–5.

LP, I, 147 = *MGH*, GPR, 1, 26.

LP, 1, 5.

Eusebius, *HE*, VI, 28.

Josi, E. *Il cimitero di Callisto*, Rome, 1933.

Keresztes, P. "The emperor Maximinus' decree of 235 A.D.. Between Septimius Severus and Decius," *Latomus*, 28 (1969), 601–18.

Lebreton J., and Zeiller, J. *De la fin du IIe siécle à la paix constantinienne*, Fliche-Martin, 2, Paris, 1943, 101–7, 119–21, 408–9.

Moreau, J. *La persécution du christianisme dans l'Empire romain*, Paris, 1956, 89–91.

Testini, P. *Archeologia cristiana*, I, Rome-Paris-Tournai-New York, 1958, 208–214.

Vogel, C. *Le Liber pontificalis* (republished, 1957), III, 74.

ANTICHRIST. The term Antichrist is the literal translation of the Greek *Antichristos*, mentioned for the first time in the Epistles of John (1, 2, 18–22; 1, 4, 3; 2, 7). It means the "adversary of Christ" (not the "precursor of Christ").

The Christian concept of the Antichrist is rooted in a Jewish eschatological tradition, and is associated with the final assault of hostile forces against the people of Israel before the new coming of Yahweh, who would triumph over his enemies in Jerusalem and begin his reign. This tradition was enriched in the 2nd century B.C.E. with a new apocalyptic current, an extension of prophetism (Book of Daniel). Historically, the realization of the divine plan for the end of time was announced through oracles, presages, and visions. The demoniacal figure that opposes God takes on many forms. It can be an adverse pagan political power, an allegorical figure (Gog and Magog, the four Beasts of Daniel, etc.), a human enemy (Antiochus IV Epiphanus, then Rome . . .), a false prophet, a religious adversary (Satan himself, his double), a spirit evoked by him (Belial, Behemoth), or a combination of these. This tradition was always present in the Jewish milieu from which Christianity emerged, and remains perceptible in intertestamentary writings (the manuscripts of the Qumrân, the Apocalypse of Eliah, *The Sibilline Oracles*, etc.), the Talmud, and the Midrashim. It seems, however, to disappear, despite a few reappearances, after A.D. 135. The Antichrist then generally takes the form of the Roman world or one of its leaders (especially Pompeii, Caligula, or Nero).

In the New Testament, there are four groups of texts concerning the Antichrist, a figure borrowed from the Old Testament and embellished. First there are the texts written by John, the only one to use the term, and perhaps its inventor. Sometimes used in the singular and sometimes in the plural, the term does not evoke a political power or a tyrant, but rather apostates, false prophets, or the Seducer (the Liar). The latter negates the Father and the Son, does not confess faith in Jesus, and rejects the Incarnation. He is already manifested in the form of human beings animated by Satan and is incarnated, therefore, more in one or several individuals than in a specific collectivity. One of John's texts echoes a passage of the Gospel of Mark (13:22) where Jesus mentions "the false Christs and false prophets who will work signs and miracles to deceive the chosen, if possible." Moreover, an enigmatic text whose attribution to Paul is far from certain (2 Thess. 2:3–10) alludes to the Antichrist. Under the name of the "Man of Iniquity" and the "Son of Perdition," this adversary of God, the Impious One par excellence, appears as an individual who will be revealed at the end of time and will persecute believers while pretending to be God. Then the Lord will make him disappear.

Finally, some authors recognize in the Beasts of John's Apocalypse (13:11–18) the symbol, incarnated in Rome, of the human power of the Antichrist. This power is manifested in both the imperial cult and in the number 666, the number of the Beast. Others feel that the Antichrist can be found in the figure of the False Prophet (20:7).

From the Old to the New Testament the Antichrist remains a marginal figure, characterized by his arrival and temporary reign, during which a complete reversal of all political, social, moral, and religious values will announce the Second Coming. The Antichrist is, therefore, directly linked to the end of time and the battle that precedes it. As for the form he takes, it varies a great deal and is manifold. He can take the shape of an individual, a collectivity, an ideology, or even a monstrous animal.

Living for a long time in expectation of the parousia, and faced with a world, which up until Constantine was generally hostile, divided by sects, and torn apart by heresies, the Christians of these centuries, especially in the east, naturally gave the Antichrist an important role. From the *Didachè* to Hippolytus's *Antichrist* (the first work dedicated to the Antichrist), the figure of the Antichrist is almost fixed, marked out by the writings of Polycarp of Smyrna, Justin, Irenaeus of Lyon, and Tertullian. It relies on the entire tradition, to which it adds circumstantial elements over the years, such as anti-Judaism. The Antichrist, from the tribe of Dan, would be crowned in the temple of Jerusalem and rely on the Jews for support. Seducer, corrupter, cheater, apostate, heretic, and false prophet, he was conceived of less and less as a false doctrine, and more and more as a character, a person acting as Satan's instrument. He is adored as God, causes strife by having peoples rise up against each other, and advances surrounded by violence, hatred, magic, and upheavals in all areas, both cosmic and human. His arrival, originally believed to be imminent, raises several questions. Is it linked to the destiny of the Roman Empire? Would he come before or after the disappearance of the Empire? Given the delay, people began to wonder as of the 3rd century, based on the second Epistle to the Thessalonians, about obstacles that would thwart his arrival: the Empire? the grace of the Holy Spirit?

The upheavals of the 4th and 5th centuries and the demise of the western Empire further increased the importance of the Antichrist. He is identified with several personalities (Emperor Julian, Nero *redivivus*, Simon Magus). People awaited, with some impatience, his arrival and the end of the world, the two events judged by St. Augustine to be unavoidable. Nevertheless, in various traditions, given the uncertainty (6,000 years?) of the time frame for his arrival, the official discourse of the Church remained discreet. It kept to the New Testament and did not commit its authority. This prudence was inaugurated by St. Augustine in a long, highly celebrated passage entirely concerned with the Antichrist (*City of God*, 20, 19). This passage followed a refutation of millenarianism, a refutation rekindled later by Bede the Venerable and by the Spaniard Beatus de Liebana. Liebana proposed an *Explanation of the Apocalypse* (between 776–80) whose iconography was recopied and transformed through the 12th century.

From then on, the intensity of the evils of the times (the capture of Jerusalem by the Persians in 614, by the Moslems in 638; famines, epidemics, political instability, social tensions, all kinds of wars, etc.) fed the belief in the coming of the Antichrist. In addition, it encouraged the interpretation of the world based on a reading of the Apocalypse. Were not the Jews allies of the Antichrist? Would they be saved at the Second Coming of Christ? Were not the Moslems, sons of Ismael, also the cohorts of the Antichrist, as suggested at the end of the 7th century by Pseudo-Methodius of Patara and Pseudo-Sebeos? The more people waited for the end of the world, the more the Antichrist was perceived concretely with more and more specific features. A simple fellow from Berry for Gregory of Tours at the end of the 6th century or mentioned in a sermon attributed to St. Eloi, the Antichrist became a familiar figure in Christianity. The fervor over the advent of the millennium was such that his image invaded Christians' daily existence. For Adson, abbot of Montier-en-Der, who wrote toward 953, in response to Queen Gerberge, a *De ortu et temporer Antichristi*, "whoever, secular, canon, or even monk, lives in an unjust way, combats the rule of his order and blasphemes what is good is an Antichrist and a servant of Satan." For this abbot, the time of the Antichrist had not yet arrived. If the year 1000 did not result in the catastrophic break and the advent of collective terrors long imagined, it was still a great inspiration for certain preachers. The abbot of Fleury-sur-Loire, Abbon, remembered that in his childhood, around 970, exasperated by hearing predictions of the coming of the Antichrist, he began to fight, he writes, "vigorously this opinion, relying on the Gospel, the Apocalypse and the Book of Daniel." One text had a profound influence over these popular beliefs. It was the oracle of the Tiburtine sibyl, *The Tiburtine*, written in the middle of the 11th century based on a Syrian original from the end of the 4th century. It took up Pseudo-Methodius' themes and enriched them with the elaboration of the episode of the king of the Romans and the Greeks who would destroy the temples of the idols, baptize the pagans, convert the Jews, and exterminate the 22 peoples of Gog and Magog before returning his kingdom to God the Father and to Jesus Christ in Jerusalem. At the end of his 12-year-long reign, the Antichrist would appear to all and would be killed by the archangel Michael on the Mount of Olives. Henceforth, through the 16th century, these two antinomical and complementary figures—the emperor of the last days, with whom each prince is often identified when rising to power, and the Antichrist—would reappear.

As of the first crusade, the figure of the Antichrist was still present. Guibert de Nogent, who attended the Council of Clermont (November 1095) and who reported on Pope URBAN II's speech, explained the desire to go to Jerusalem by the concern for "bringing back to faith the countries of the East" in order to pave the way for the coming of the Antichrist. The Antichrist would spare the Jews and the pagans, would only attack Christians, and would only be realized with the re-establishment there of the reign of the "plenitude of nations," an obligatory prerequisite for the end of time. The phrase "the apostasy must be accomplished" (2 Thess. 2:3) was taken literally. An army of pilgrims would thus set off for the east guided by a papal legate and the conquered lands would come back to the Church. New ideas were grafted onto older sentiments. Beatus de Liebana was already comparing Islam to the ten-horned beast, the Saracens to the grasshoppers, and Mohamed to the Antichrist, of whom he had become an emblematic figure.

Parallel to this Antichrist outside Christianity, there were other ideas and images of the Antichrist that continued to be present within it. With the declared heresies, the break was a clean one. Very early on, Catharism appeared as one of the forms of the Antichrist. For Hildegarde of Bingen, its expansion into the Rhine Valley (between 1160 and 1167) constituted one of the precursory signs of the end of the world. Priests and even popes were convinced that the heresies, despite their diverse appearance, were linked to one another, brought on by Satan and Antichrists, and could even have been part of an alliance with the Saracens. More ambiguous were the attitudes demonstrated by the visionaries—prophets, itinerant preachers, and messiahs—who were often associated with millennaianist movements that crystallized on them the signs of the Christ and King of the last days. Inevitably, they came to oppose the established Church, ecclesiastical powers, and the papacy, and began to consider themselves as the true Church. For them, the pope tended to incarnate the Antichrist. Likewise, some of them were considered by the Church to be precursors of the Antichrist, blasphemers of the Church of Christ. Two examples can be cited. Between 1112 and 1115, Tanchelm, a clergyman, is regarded as a messenger of the Antichrist by the Church of Utrecht because he "disregarded the pope, the bishops, the archbishops, the priests and the clergy" and "pretended that the only Church resided within himself." Nevertheless, although the bishop of Cologne condemned him, he was never declared heretical by the papacy. On the other hand, EUGENE III condemned the Briton Eon de l'Etoile during the synod of Reims in March 1148. Moreover, the emergence of strong and ambitious political powers that rose up against the papacy or competed with it to direct Christianity rekindled the figure of the Antichrist. During the quarrel over Investitures between Henry IV and GREGORY VII, the emperor is compared by the papacy to Antiochus Epiphanus, the symbol of the Antichrist. A letter from the pope to Hermann of Metz is explicit. In it, the pope recommends that he be able to repress the malicious actions of the *membra Antichristi* (those who prefer their own interests to those of God), who opposed the *membra Christi* (those who obeyed the will of God).

It is important to note that it was in German-speaking nations where the belief in the last emperor of the end of the world was the most widespread in the 12th century. This is where the *Ludus de Antichristo* was performed and played three centuries later. It is also where a theologian from the diocese of Augsburg, Gerhoh de Reichersberg, wrote *De investigatione Antichristi* and where a nun named Ava, the first female poet of the German language, composed a poem around 1120 entitled *Der Antichrist*.

Thus, there were several forms of Antichrist co-existing in the 12th century. The most simple of these belonged to the world outside Christianity: the Moslem, the Jew, and even Merlin. The two others reflect the expression of a double confrontation with the Church and with the papacy. These are religious confrontations, often associated with heresies, the millenarian fervor, and the drive to reform Christianity. In fact, these were confrontations with the powers in control, which were not only religious but also political. In both cases, each maintained that his adversary represented the Antichrist or one of his lieutenants. During each period of anxiety, these figures reemerged, preceded, or accompanied by speculations separated into two visions: one, the optimistic millenarianist version; the other, the pessimistic and eschatological version.

Joachim of Flora (ca. 1135–1202) synthesized these two traditions in his *Expositio in Apocalipsim*, composed in 1184 and submitted to CLEMENT III in 1188, in which he developed the idea that the history of the Church and humanity could be explained through the book of the Apocalypse. This history is organized into three ages corresponding to the three persons of the Trinity. The last age, that of the Spirit, was to begin in 1260. It would be announced by a period of crises marked by the coming of the Antichrist—or the Antichrists—for the Calabrese abbot believed that there were multiple Antichrists. Further, he indirectly weakened the papacy of his time by ruining the hope of realizing a perfect Christianity and by thinking that the institutions of the Church would be renewed through the spirit of charity, beginning with the Holy See itself.

In 1215 the LATERAN IV COUNCIL condemned the theses propounded by Joachim of Flora. Despite everything, a pseudo-Joachimite literature developed after his death, especially thanks to the mendicant orders. Thus, the interpretations of the spiritual Franciscan Gerard di Borgo San Donnino reinforced the conviction that the end of time and the arrival of the Antichrist were imminent (theses condemned in 1254 by INNOCENT IV). Later, those of the Franciscan from the Languedoc region, Peter John Olieu (or Olivi, 1248–98), opposed the bodily Church and the spiritual Church and juxtaposed the eschatological announcement and the establishment of a pseudo-pope, incarnation of the Antichrist (condemned in 1326 by JOHN XXII). In turn, the mendicant orders were recognized as the image of the Antichrist by Guillaume de Saint-Amour, a professor at the University of Paris, in his *De periculis novissimorum temporum*, which was condemned the year after it appeared (1255) by ALEXANDER IV.

Emperor Frederick II was also seen as the Antichrist, especially after his second excommunication in 1239 when he was considered as "more cruel than Nero, more cruel and vile than Julian the Apostate." Frederick II retorted that the pope was the "Great Dragon" and the incarnation of the Antichrist. In these accusations, the emperor was supported by a dissident Dominican, Arnold the Souab, who also considered the pope to be the Antichrist and the priests as members of the Antichrist's body. The Antichrist was also considered to be present in the Mongols who, after 1240, directly threatened Christianity and were considered part of the damned peoples, Gog and Magog. A century later, the Antichrist took on the guise of the Turk. Likewise, the spiritual Franciscans saw him in John XXII, who was the enemy of the spiritual Franciscans, was denounced by Marsilus of Padova, and was qualified as the Antichrist by the antipope NICHOLAS V. In a more general way, Thomas Aquinas envisioned the Antichrist as "the leader of all God's enemies" (*Sum. theol.*, 3a, 8, 8).

With the GREAT SCHISM, the anxieties of the 14th and 15th centuries, the critique of the hierarchical Church, the proliferation of the flagellants, and the increase in the practice of magic, led to the expansion of Satan, his devils of innumerable names, and his infernal legions. Never before had Christianity spoken so much of the Antichrist, whose representations at the time were numerous and varied. Each side accused the other of being guided by the Antichrist. In England, Wyclif, for whom the visible Church had become the body of the Antichrist, accused both URBAN VI and his adversary in Avignon of being Antichrists. He believed that the election of the popes was a diabolical invention and affirmed that the true Church was invisible. In his treatise *De Christo et adversario suo Antichristo*, he established a catalog of the virtues of Christ and opposed them to the vices of the papacy, which was viewed as the Antichrist. In Prague, the canon Matthias of Janow explained the Great Schism as the result of a subversive action led by the Antichrist for centuries. Matthias of Janow judged that the bad Christians were the disciples of the Antichrist and together were assembled in a monstrous body, the antithesis to the *corpus mysticum*. For him, the pope in Avignon, CLEMENT VII, was the Antichrist himself. As for Vincent Ferrer, he reached an audience of millions by traveling through western Europe preaching the end of the world and the coming of the Antichrist. In Florence, Savonarola (whose adversaries considered him to be the Antichrist) associated the Roman Curia and the Antichrist. In Thuringia, a sect of heretical flagellants associated their founder, Conrad Schmid, with Elijah and Enoch, called to combat the Antichrist, that is, the Church of Rome. For John Hus, who spoke out in Prague against the Antichrist and his servants, the Antichrist was an abstraction "that paved the road to evil," an institution (the hierarchical Church), and a specific person (Pope John XXII).

This flood of anxieties, predictions, and terrors related to the end of the world and the coming of the Antichrist was worrisome. "We are overwhelmed and nauseated by these prophesies announcing the coming of the Antichrist, the signs of the next Judgement, and the reform of the Church," stated Bernardino of Siena. Also, in the session of 19 December 1516, the LATERAN V COUNCIL forbade preachers from announcing precise dates for the coming of the Antichrist or the Last Judgment. The same ban was reiterated in the following year by a provincial council held in Florence and presided over by the archbishop of the city, the future Clement VII.

Whether or not the ban was respected, or whether it was more a matter of evolving mentalities and the manifestation of a new sensibility, another perception of the Antichrist gradually took hold. The obsession with the end of time was relegated to the back burner, although it nevertheless remained an important preoccupation tinged with hopes and fears during the first half of the 16th century. Luther, Thomas Müntzer, Bullinger, Melanchthon and, on the Catholic side, the Franciscan Fra Francesco di

Montepulciano, began to identify the Antichrist as a person, be he pope or Protestant, since the accusation was formulated by everyone. Luther was the first to do so in the most classic of medieval traditions. As of 1520, for Luther, the pope was the Prince of Darkness, the sworn enemy of true Christianity, and the Antichrist announced by Paul. He believed that to destroy the "three walls of Romanism" was to work for God against the Antichrist. If the latter was in power in his kingdom in Rome, it was because the end of history was near. Luther burned the papal bull *Exsurge Domine* of 15 June 1520 in which he was asked to retract. His response was to ask the pope and cardinals to do penance, commenting on the bull of the Antichrist (*Wider die Bulle des Endchrists*). He published a text with an explicit title (*De captivate babylonica ecclesiae*). Even HADRIAN VI, who took responsibility by assuming the faults of the Church (November 1522), was treated as a hypocritical tyrant, a figure of the Antichrist. In 1545 Luther wrote another pamphlet, *Against the Papacy in Rome Created by the Devil*. Nonetheless, there had always existed for him another Antichrist, just as ominous, in the form of the Turk.

Of these two aspects of the Antichrist it is mostly the first that was retained by the Protestants of the 16th and the beginning of the 17th century. Even if they anathematized one another and called each other the Antichrist, they all agreed in recognizing the pope as the Antichrist par excellence and viewing Rome as the new Babylon. Thus, in 1610, the Protestant Nicholas Vignier drafted a list of 28 Protestant authors from ten different countries all proclaiming that the Antichrist was the pope. This did not even include Vignier's immense treatise entitled *L'Antéchrist romain* (1604)! These clichés are embellished by images and groups of pamphlets illustrated by great artists (Dürer, Cranach, Holbein) who spread them and popularized them. Thus, in 1521 the *Passional Christi und Antichristi*, illustrated by Cranach, showed 13 contrasting images of good and evil, Christ of the Gospels and the Pope of Rome. The format was a success. In 1578 in Geneva, they were still publishing small illustrated works opposing the images of the life of Jesus and life in the papal court (*Antithesis Christi et Antichristi*). The identification was complete and unequivocal. In the lampoons that followed, the monster (the Antichrist) and the Great Prostitute (Rome-Babylon, whose siege in 1527 appeared to some as punishment and even as a purification) both wear the papal tiara. In his *Mystère d'iniquité, c'est-à-dire l'histoire de la papauté* (*Mystery of iniquity, that is, the history of the papacy;* 1611), Philippe Duplessis-Mornay, a diplomat and Huguenot theologian, identifies the history of the papacy with the Progress of the Antichrist and Agrippa of Aubigné in his *Tragiques*, portrays the pope as the "elder son of Satan." The accusation became so common that in 1603, the national synod of French Protestants added an article to the Confession of the Faith declaring that the pope was "the Antichrist and son of perdition." In 1631 an English Puritan stated: "He who can swear that the pope is the Antichrist and that one must eat meat on Fridays is a Protestant." By crossing the English Channel, the polemic found a second wind.

Faced with these attacks, which tended to snowball, Catholics did not remain passive. A preacher, Georges Wizel, denounced Luther's terrorizing pedagogy in 1536. He wrote: "Luther believed that by frightening souls he would more easily attract them to his new doctrine and that is why he spoke so much of the Last Judgment and the coming of the Antichrist." In 1571 the Catholic theologian Nicholas Sanders refuted the Protestant accusation in 40 demonstrations and turned it back against the Protestants. In 1576 the Jesuit Robert Bellarmine inaugurated his teaching at the Roman College with the *Controversia* (published as of 1588). In these he showed that the Antichrist, a "unique and eschatological character, could not designate the succession of popes" and underscored the Protestant authors' contradictions in their chronological prognostications about the end of time. These contradictions and fantasies were also noted by an ex-Protestant, Florimont de Raemond who, in his *Antéchrist* (1597), affirmed that the Antichrist would appear, but that he had not yet. Malvenda supported the same idea in his *De Antichristo* (1604). Thus, it appeared that the Protestants had made a mistake about the Antichrist, unless the Antichrist was the heretic himself, as claimed by the Jesuit Leonard Leys (Lessius) in his *Antichristo*, which appeared in Antwerp in 1611.

However, except in England (Winstanley, Lilburne, Cromwell), the polemic lost wind and became a marginal academic issue. Calvin, who had recognized the Antichrist in the pope, had equated Lutherans and Catholics in the following terms: "In the papacy, nothing is more widespread and over-used than the coming of the Antichrist." Bullinger had already stated that the first Beast of the Apocalypse was not the papacy, but rather the pagan Roman Empire, yet it was especially thanks to the rational exegesis of the Spanish Jesuit Luis de Alcazar that the identification between the popes' Rome and the Great Prostitute became obsolete. According to him (1614), the Apocalypse could not be reduced to a historical interpretation.

Although this did not prevent preoccupations concerning the Antichrist and the end of time from reemerging, the papacy was hardly implicated, apart from a few exceptions such as Montesquieu's *Lettres persanes*: "There is another magician stronger [than the king of France] who is as much master of his own mind as that of others. This magician is called the pope." In addition, Protestant periodicals (often of Baptist inspiration) during the Protestant crusade in the United States in the 1820s denounced papism as an anti-Christian blasphemy. The An-

tichrist also slipped into other domains. The coming of the Antichrist worried mathematicians such as John Napier. His main interest in the logarithms he invented was to facilitate calculations concerning the number of the Beast. For Napier, 1639 signaled the beginning of the disintegration of the Roman Church.

Persecuted victims and adversaries have seen the Antichrist as a man (Louis XIV, Robespierre, Alexander I of Russia, Bonaparte, Hitler, Stalin, etc.) or as a doctrine or ideology propounded by him. The Antichrist has become a literary figure (the Grand Inquisitor in Dostoyevski's *Brothers Karamazov*, the end of *Rendez-vous de Patmos* by Michel Déon, the investigator in *The Name of the Rose* by Umberto Eco) more than a subject of theological and philosophical debate (Nietzsche's *Antichrist* is an ethical attitude unique in the genre). The Antichrist was even used on an allegorical level (Péguy views Money as the Antichrist of our times), but he is no longer implicated in the papacy, and except in the minds of a few marginal characters, he has disappeared from the general consciousness.

Jean-Louis Voisin

Bibliography

Berce, Y. M. *Le Roi caché*, Paris, 1990.

Carozzi, C., and Taviani-Carozzi, H. *La Fin des temps. Terreurs et prophéties au Moyen Age*, Paris, 1982.

Delumeau, J., and Leouin, Y. *Les Malheurs du temps*, Paris, 1987.

Delumeau, J. *La Peur en Occident (14th–18th centuries)*, Paris, 1978.

Emmerson, R. K. *Antichrist in the Middle Ages: A Study of Medieval Apocalypticism, Art and Literature*, Seattle, 1981.

Ermoni, V. "Antichrist," *DTC*, II, 2 (1923), 1361–5.

Hadas-Lebel, M. *Jérusalem contre Rome*, Paris, 1990.

Hartman, S., et al. *TRE*, 3 (1978), 20–50.

Jenks, G. C. *The Origins and Early Development of the Antichrist Myth*, Beihefte 59 of *Zeitschrift für die neutestamentliche Wissenschaft und die Kunde der Urchristentums*, Berlin, 1991.

Lohmeyer, E. *RAC*, 1 (1950), 450–7.

Mayeur, J. M., and Pietri, L., ed. *Histoire du Christianisme*.

McGinn, B. *Antichrist: Two Thousand Years of Human Fascination with Evil*, San Francisco, 1994.

Norelli, E. ed. trans. *L'Anticristo* by Hippolytus, Florence, 1987.

Reeves, M., ed. *Prophetic Rome in the High Rennaissance Period*, Oxford, Eng., 1992.

Sbaffoni, F. *Testi sull'Antichristo seculi* I–II, Florence, 1992.

Wright, R. M. *Art and Antichrist in Medieval Europe*, Manchester, Eng., 1995.

ANTIOCH. Evangelized by Christians from Jerusalem dispersed by the persecution following the martyrdom of St. Stephen (Acts 11:19–20), capital of the Roman province of Syria, and then the third city of the Empire after Rome and Alexandria, Antioch was first a "memorial place" for the papacy. It was there that the disciples had, according to the Acts of the Apostles (11:26), first received the name of Christians. Antioch was the center and heart of the expansion of Hellenistic Christianity in contrast to Jerusalem, which remained the center for Christians of Jewish origin. According to legend (reported by Eusebius in *Ecclesiastical History*, III, 26, 2), Antioch's first bishop was St. Peter himself. His presence in the area is documented in 48 and 49, before having elected St. Ignatius, martyred in Rome in around 107, to this post, and then St. Theophilus in the 180s.

Canon 6 of the Council of Nicaea (325) confirmed the preeminence and privileges of the Church of Antioch, coming just after Rome and Alexandria. Long troubled by conflicts and upheavals due to the Arian crisis, it was the seat of several SYNODS including the one called "the Nicene" (341), which somewhat modified the symbol defined in Nicaea 16 years earlier. Suffering from a schismatic situation in 361 involving the two Catholic bishops, Melecea, supported in the East by St. Basil, and Paulinus, recognized by Pope DAMASUS I (366–84), Antioch did not stabilize religiously until after 415. It later experienced a new conflict with the extension of Monophysitism (in the 6th century). From the time of Paul of Samosate (bishop of the city in 260) and St. Lucian (martyr under Diocletian in 312), Antioch had housed a brilliant exegetical and theological school that was especially influential during the end of the 5th century and throughout the first half of the 6th century. Today, Antioch is the seat of the uniate Greek patriarch, in residence in Aleppo, and a uniate Syrian patriarch to whom PAUL VI (1963–78) conceded in the *communio ecclesiastica* on 20 March 1968, as well as a Maronite patriarch. All of these patriarchs are assisted by various vicariates in different locations such as in Iraq, Turkey, Kuwait, Lebanon, and Jerusalem. Antioch thus constitutes one of the most important and prestigious relay points for Catholicism in Eastern lands.

François Jankowiak

Bibliography

Dauvillier, J. *Les Temps apostoliques* (Histoire du droit et des institutions de l'Eglise en Occident, II), Paris, 1970.

Devreesse, R. *Le Patriarcat d'Antioche depuis la paix de l'Eglise jusqu'à la conquête arabe*, Paris, 1945.

Festugiere, A. J. *Antioche païenne et chrétienne*, Paris, 1959.

MacDonald, M. Y. *The Pauline Churches. A Socio-Historical Study of Institutionalization in the Pauline and Deutero-Pauline Writings*, Cambridge, 1988.

Munk, L. *Paulus und die heilsgeschichte*, Copenhagen, 1954.

Von Harnack, A. *Mission und Ausbreitung des Christentums*, 2 vols., Leipzig, 1924.

ANTIPOPE. An antipope is any person who took the name of pope and exercised, or claimed to exercise his functions, without canonical foundation. The antipope can be a pope elected in a non-canonical manner after the death or deposition of a regular pope (a problem that led to appreciation of the importance of regular elections or succession), or a competitor designated under dubious circumstances who confronts a regularly elected pope (a problem that elucidates the origin of the SCHISM). Finally, an antipope can be an intruder who usurps the current pontificate by force. The definition is simple, but its application, as can be imagined, is very difficult, especially in earlier periods when clear norms for papal elections had not yet been established.

Even the term "antipope" was not officially used until the end of the 14th century, after a long period of normalization of ecclesiastical structures and the development of CANON LAW, sharp conflicts, and the regulation of papal elections. Of course, beginning in the age of the Gregorian reform, the polemical literature in the two camps was full of insinuations and language denying any legal power to an adversary. Thus, there are examples of the refusal to use the papal title: GREGORY VII was qualified by the emperor as "Bishop (or "false monk") Hildebrand," while his supporters called his rival, the antipope CLEMENT III, simply "Gilbert of Ravenna." The descriptives used to qualify these names were numerous. Peter Damian called the same Clement III, among other niceties, "disturber of the holy Church, destroyer of the apostolic discipline, enemy of the salvation of humanity, root of evil, herald of the devil, apostle of the ANTICHRIST, arrow too often shot from Satan's bow, Assur's prick, son of Belial, son of perdition . . . new heresiarch." During antiquity and the early Middle Ages, the term most used was "intruder," which meant invader and usurper (*invasor*, *pervasor*, *usurpator*). More rarely, as as well as later on, the terms "heresiarch" and "schismatic" were used. Antonyms for "pope" included "false pope" (*falsus papa*, *adulterinus papa*), "pseudo-pope," and even the Hellenism "catopope." This is not to say that the term "antipope" was unknown. M. E. Stoller found evidence of it in 16 texts, mostly in the English language, from the 12th century. Even before its official adoption, the term came to enjoy a growing popularity, no doubt facilitated by the play on words antipope/antichrist. It seems that, by imitation, terms such as *anti-cardinalis* and *antiepiscopus* came to be used in early low medieval Latin, but were not passed down into the Romance languages.

Despite the difficulty of the task, canonists and historians attempted to establish objective criteria to judge the "antipapal" character of certain reigns. These criteria included the irregularity of the vacancy at the time of the election (forced resignation or violent deposition of a predecessor), irregularity in electoral procedures (problematic meetings, external pressures, etc.), and/or indignity or the absence of required conditions in the person elected, yet the norms varied. The sources were rare and partial. All the antipopes were convinced that they were rightfully popes. Many of them were honest, and some of them were not even contested by their contemporaries. There were highly polemical debates during the period of the REFORMATION (Protestants sometimes negating the character of the antipope given to the emperor's candidates during the Middle Ages). Later, the archbishop of Sorrento, Lodovico Agnello Anastasio, wrote the first work on the antipopes (*Istoria degli antipapi*, Naples, 2 vols., 1754), in which he recognized 26 of them, from NOVATIAN to FELIX V. Today this text is only of historical interest, mainly because it offers little explicit ideological justification for the compilation. In 1751, on the occasion of the restoration of the frescoes on the outside wall of ST. PAUL'S OUTSIDE THE WALLS, the Guardian of the Roman CATACOMBS, Giovanni Marangoni, drew up a list of popes and antipopes, which although unsatisfying, was reproduced in the *ANNUARIO PONTIFICIO* from 1913 to 1946. Nineteenth- and twentieth-century Church historians have often revisited the issue with lists varying from 25 to 40 antipopes, but Cardinal Angelo Mercati's list quickly became the official one. Reproduced at the beginning of the *Annuario pontificio* as of the 1947 edition, it includes 39 antipopes, two of whom (CLEMENT VIII, 1423, and BENEDICT XIV, 1425) are only mentioned in the notes. His notes also question the status of four other pontificates: those of LEO VIII, SILVESTER III, GREGORY VI, and CLEMENT II.

These uncertainties and variations explain the numerous inconsistencies in the ONOMASTIC of the antipopes and their numbering. Some of them are the only ones to bear their name and never received numbers: HIPPOLYTUS (217–35), NOVATIAN (251–8), URSINUS (366–7), EULALIUS (418–19), LAWRENCE (498, 501–6), DIOSCORUS (530), PHILIP (768), CHRISTOPHER (903–4), THEODERIC (1100–01), Albert/Adalbert (1101). Some other antipopes who lasted a short time never received official numbers even though there were existing namesakes. These included: PASCHAL and THEODORE (687), CONSTANTINE (767–8), JOHN (844), and ANASTASIUS BIBLIOTHECARIUS (855). More numerous as of the 11th century were those whose numbers were later reattributed, a practice leading to no small amount of confusion. To avoid this risk, it became customary to write the antipope's number in parentheses in order to distinguish between, for example, INNOCENT (III), antipope elected in 1179, and INNOCENT III,

regular pope elected in 1198. Thirteen antipopes belong in this category: GREGORY (VI), 1012; HONORIUS (II), 1061–4; CLEMENT (III), 1080–1100; GREGORY (VIII), 1118–21; CELESTINE (II), 1124; CALLISTUS (III), 1168–78; INNOCENT (III), 1179–80; NICHOLAS (V), 1328–30; CLEMENT (VII), 1378–94; BENEDICT (XIII), 1394–1423; JOHN (XXIII), 1410–15; CLEMENT (VIII), 1423–29; and BENEDICT (XIV), 1425. For four others, the numbers were never reattributed afterward: SILVESTER IV (1104–11), ANACLET II (1130–8), PASCHAL III (1164–8), and FELIX V (1439–49). One last case, similar to the preceding ones, was that of the antipope VICTOR (IV), elected in 1138, but whose name and number another antipope assumed when elected in 1159. The latter kept the name of Victor IV, which no other regular pope has ever selected. Besides the antipopes without numbers and the antipopes with reused numbers or unattributed numbers, there were a few antipopes who were considered regular popes, and whose numbers were conserved when their successors chose the homonym. This is the case for FELIX II antipope elected in 355 (although FELIX III and FELIX IV, regular popes, were sometimes numbered "II" and "III," respectively, but one speaks of Felix V, who was also an antipope). This was also the case for BONIFACE VII, antipope elected in 974; JOHN XVI, antipope elected in 997; BENEDICT X, antipope elected in 1058; and ALEXANDER V, antipope elected in 1409.

After the era of the GREAT SCHISM, the norms and practices of papal elections were more strictly applied, and there were no more antipopes. However, in the contemporary era, there is an interesting anecdote. The priest Michael Collin attempted in vain in 1951 and 1961 to proclaim himself the only legitimate pope after PIUS XII and JOHN XXIII. He called himself Clement XV.

List of the Antipopes. Each antipope has a specific entry in this text. The list below gives a summary of the reasons, more or less well grounded, for considering them antipopes. The names of the authors cited refer to titles in the bibliography. This list presents the names of the antipopes divided into three categories with distinctive characteristic: (1) official antipopes (as per the list in the *Annuario pontificio*), in Latin characters; (2) the names of those who were not officially considered antipopes, but whose status was questioned by certain historians or by the *Annuario pontificio* itself (doubts expressed in the notes), in *italics*; and (3) the names of those who were officially considered antipopes, but whose attribution as such by the *Annuario pontificio* has been contested by historians (in **bold**).

1. Saint Hippolytus, 217–35. Proclaimed himself pope to confront his adversary Callistus; the first antipope in papal history (if we do not include Natalius, proposed under Zephyrinus by the Adoptionist party) to end his

reign in prison. There he found Pope Pontian, and the schism was ended by their mutual reconciliation, soon sealed by the death of the martyrs.

2. Novatian, 251–8. He, too, originated a schism, this one directed against Pope Cornelius. Excommunicated, he was the instigator of small, schismatic communities that survived through the 5th century.

3. Felix II, 355–65. Imposed by Emperor Constantius during the exile of Pope Liberius.

4. Ursinus, 366–7. Elected by the partisans of Felix II against Pope Damasus. Dethroned after the victory of Damasus and exiled to Gaul.

5. Eulalius, 418–19. Selected by a portion of the electors against Boniface I. Dethroned by the emperor.

6. Lawrence, 498, 501–6. Selected by a portion of the electors against Symmachus, he was soon pushed away by the Ostrogoth king Theodoric. He returned to power through force from 501 to 506, the date of his definitive expulsion from Rome.

7. *Vigilius*, 537. Elected after the contested deposition of Silverius, whose death (11 November 537) returned all legitimacy to the continuation of the pontificate.

8. **Dioscorus,** 530. The repudiation of his pontificate after his death and his later rehabilitation under Agapitus II led to doubts on the part of some historians as to whether or not he should be considered an antipope. If he is not considered as such, then his competitor, the official pope Boniface II should be. This latter's legitimacy, designated by Felix IV before his death, is no longer in doubt after the early death of Dioscorus.

9. *St. Eugene*, 655, then a regular pope from 655–6. Perhaps he was an antipope at the beginning of his pontificate (A. P. Frutaz) because he was elected while his predecessor, Martin I, was still alive. It is true that Martin I, who was deported to Constantinople, did not seem to have protested the election. In any case, Eugene certainly became a regular pope at Martin I's death (September 655).

10. **Theodore,** 687. His official title as antipope is not well-founded. Rather, on two occasions, he was a losing candidate in papal elections (2 August 686 and 21 September 687). He did, however (as opposed to Paschal), respect the newly elected popes (Conon then Sergius I).

11. Paschal, 687–92. When Sergius I was elected pope (15 December 687), Paschal refused to accept defeat and sought support from the exarch of Ravena. He was locked up in a monastery, but until his death (692), he refused to recognize Sergius.

12. Constantine, 767–8. Antipope as a result of a double canonical vice: his election, which was imposed by his brother the Duke of Nepi, and his lay status. Deposed by the Lombard troops.

13. Philip, 768. Antipope for a day. A. P. Frutaz does not recognize him as an antipope, emphasizing that he was elected only under Lombard influence after the cap-ture of the antipope Constantine. Yet this "election" was limited to a declaration made by the priest Waldipert, representative of Lombard interests in Rome, before the arrival of the candidate supported by the chief notary Christopher.

14. John, 844. Antipope, quickly abandoned by his few supporters against Sergius II. As A. P. Frutaz remarks, he was elected at the same time as Sergius—the Roman nobles' candidate—at the death of Gregory IV.

15. Anastasius, 855. Despite the reservations expressed by A. P. Frutaz and A. Amanieu, he can be considered an antipope. He refused Benedict III's election and attempted to use imperial influence to counter it by having his rival imprisoned for a time. He is most of all an antipope because he was unsuccessful, the Roman clergy having refused to recognize him in spite of imperial entreaties. This did not prevent him from pursuing a brilliant ecclesiastical career.

16. Christopher, 903–4. An outright usurper, he imprisoned Pope Leo V and took his place. Deposed, he was nevertheless buried at St. Peter's.

17. *Sergius III*, 904. Considered to be a regular pope, but many historians have expressed serious reservations. He was first elected from the "antiformosian" faction (897) before resigning. He was then elected on 29 January 904 against the antipope Christopher, before having him strangled to death in the company of his predecessor Leo V.

18. *Leo VIII*, 963–4. Clearly an antipope for A. P. Frutaz, H. G. J. Beck, and A. Amanieu, for the *Annuario pontifico* he is only a hypothetical antipope. He was a layman, elected after the deposition of John XII by Otto I, an act whose legitimacy remains in doubt. Thereafter his adversary was the Roman's chosen man, Benedict V, whom he deposed with the help of the emperor.

19. Boniface VII, 974 and 984–5. Twice he imposed himself by force: once with the support of the Crescenzi, he got rid of Benedict VI (974). Pursued, he arrived in Constantinople. When he returned to Rome, he got rid of John XIV (984).

20. John XVI, 997–8. Encouraged by the Roman faction of Crescenzi against Gregory V, he was expelled by Otto II.

21. Gregory (VI), 1012. Elected by the Crescenzi against Benedict VIII. Expelled from Rome and forced to resign.

22. *Silvester III*, 1045. Definitely an antipope for A. P. Frutaz, H. G. J. Beck, and A. Amanieu, he remains a hypothetical antipope in the *Annuario pontificio*. Elected in the tumult caused by the Roman uprising against Benedict IX, who reappeared in Rome in April 1045, and whose renunciation can be considered suspect in canonical terms. Definitively deposed at the Council of Sutri in 1046, which did not prevent him from pursuing his episcopal career.

23. *Gregory VI*, 1045–6. Elected following the Roman uprising against Benedict IX.

24. *Clement II*, 1046–7. Imposed by the emperor after a series of depositions following the Roman uprising against Benedict IX.

25. *Benedict IX*, 1047–8. His status was contested by some. All agree to consider him a regular pope, in spite of his dissolute life, for the period from 1032 to 1045, until his deposition in 1046 (in 1045, he would have stepped down in favor of Gregory VI). There are, however, reservations weighing on the legitimacy of his reappearance as pope from 1047–8.

26. Benedict X, 1058–9. Elected by the Roman nobility when the clergy elected Nicholas II. Resigned in 1059.

27. Honorius (II), 1061–72. Elected with the emperor's agreement against Alexander II, then abandoned by the emperor. Remains involved in the schism until his death in 1072.

28. Clement (III), 1080–1100. Elected under imperial influence against Gregory VII.

29. Theoderic, 1100–1. Elected to succeed Clement (III).

30. Albert, 1101. Elected to succeed Theoderic. Imprisoned.

31. Silvester IV, 1105–11. Elected under imperial influence against Paschal II. Abandoned by the emperor, which forced his submission.

32. Gregory (VIII), 1118–21. Elected under imperial influence against Gelasius II. Imprisoned.

33. **Celestine (II)**, 1124. Antipope due to weakness; improperly added to the official list of antipopes. Regularly elected by a fraction of the cardinals, he was deposed by force and died before being consecrated.

34. Anacletus II, 1130–8. Elected by the Pierleoni faction against Innocent II. The election is difficult to judge. It was more a matter of a true schism than the intrusion of one pope against another. Under the influence of St. Bernard, the Church quickly recognized the legitimacy of Innocent II. Anacletus remained without great power until his death.

35. Victor (IV), 1138. Elected to succeed Anacletus II. Stepped down the following May, which gave additional value to the canonicity of Innocent II's election.

36. Victor IV, 1159–64. Elected with imperial favor against Alexander III.

37. Paschal III, 1164–8. Elected with imperial favor to succeed Victor IV.

38. Callistus (III), 1168–78. Elected with imperial favor to succeed Paschal III. Stepped down in August 1178 after having been abandoned by the emperor.

39. Innocent (III), 1179–80. Elected without imperial favor to succeed Callistus (III).

40. Nicholas (V), 1328–30. Elected by Emperor Louis of Bavaria against John XXII, in whose favor he soon resigned.

41. Clement (VII), 1378–94. Elected by a fraction of the cardinals against Urban VI. He was at the origin of the Great Schism, to which popes 42 through 46 belong.

42. Alexander V, 1409–10. Antipope due to bad luck. Elected at the Council of Pisa, which had just deposed two of his rivals, Benedict XIII (official antipope) and Gregory XII (official pope), whose place he could not occupy.

43. John (XXIII), 1410–5. Elected to succeed Alexander V as the schism continued. Deposed by the Council of Constance.

44. Clement (VIII), 1423–9. Elected by the supporters of Benedict XIII, he stepped down before Martin V.

45. Benedict (XIV), 1425–?. Elected by a cardinal who supported Benedict XIII in order to contest the already schismatic election of Clement (VIII).

46. Felix V, 1439–49. Antipope of the conciliar crisis, elected at the Council of Basel which had just deposed Eugene IV. Stepped down before Nicholas V.

Olivier Guyotjeannin

Bibliography

Amanieu, A. "Antipape," *DDC*, 1 (1935), 598–622.

Beck, H. G. J. "Antipope," *NCE*, 1 (1967), 632–3.

Frutaz, A. P. "Antipapa," *EC*, 1 (1948), 1483–9.

Mercati, A. "The New List of the Popes," *Mediaeval Studies*, 9 (1947), 71–80.

Stoller, E. "The Emergence of the Term *Antipapa* in Medieval Usage," *AHP*, 23 (1985), 43–61.

ANTIPOPISM. See **Papism; Reformation**.

APARTMENTS, PAPAL. The term "papal apartments" is used in nonofficial language to designate the rooms occupied by the pope within the so-called apostolic palace, where he resides. There are as many papal apartments as there are residences where the pope stays for the night. In Rome, two apartments are always prepared to receive the pope and his entourage: one in the palace of the Vatican and the other in the pope's villa at Castel Gandolfo.

After the 1870 siege on Rome, PIUS IX was obliged to reside permanently in the Vatican where he already occupied the 2nd floor of the palace overlooking St. Peter's Square. This is where he slept, took his meals, and gave private audiences. LEO XIII followed his example, but PIUS X preferred to set up the 3rd floor of the palace where the cell he occupied during the conclave was located. Thus, the private apartment, as such, came into existence as opposed to the stately apartment (the Italian names vary: *appartamento nobile, appartamento ponti-*

ficio) on the 2nd floor where the pope continued to receive in a private manner.

The stately apartment consists of a series of rooms around a courtyard (*cortile di Sisto V*) ending with the private library, a vast room with two windows overlooking St. Peter's Square. The pope, according to protocol, receives either in the library or in one of the other rooms. The order of these rooms was once designated by the expression "pontifical antechamber." Each had a special category of dignitary responsible for keeping and magnifying access to the pope, but this tradition was abandoned by PAUL VI in 1968. The antechamber rooms and the library had been decorated in a late 19th-century style. Over the years, improvements were limited to the replacement of worn fabrics and furniture, but Paul VI made a radical change in 1969. The red damask on the walls, including that in the library, was replaced with pastel colored velvet. The large chandeliers were replaced with fluorescent tube lighting hidden behind the curtains. The thrones, of various dimensions depending on the room, often became important masonry works. The gilded furniture was replaced with velvet upholstered fine wood pieces. The decor was completed with modern and ancient works of art. Since these transformations, the stately apartment has not undergone any significant changes.

The private apartment on the 3rd floor was sufficient for the popes' needs from Pius X to JOHN XXIII. Each pope has included something from his own past and reserved access to his close collaborators, family, and friends. PIUS XII found the apartment empty and completely redecorated it with the furniture given to him by the German episcopate when he left his nunciature in Berlin. John XXIII inherited the same from his predecessor. Paul VI had everything redecorated during the summer of 1963. The following year, he ordered a new decoration for the private chapel situated on the same floor and began to undertake the renovation of the attic roof (*soffittoni*). At this level, a 200-square-meter terrace was created (1965–6). JOHN PAUL II, who often received in his private apartment, completed the renovation of the roof and had nine guest rooms built. Since this time, access to the papal apartments is through the St. Damaso courtyard by way of the main staircase (*scala nobile*), which only serves the 1st and 2nd floors. The doors of the 3rd floor remain closed and can only be accessed by internal elevators. The stately apartment and the private apartment both open onto covered balconies (*ballatoi*) overlooking an interior courtyard (*cortile di Sisto V*) which allow one to move from one end of the apartment to the other without crossing through the rooms.

The papal palace at Castel Gandolfo—which was never seized by the Italian government but left in a state of abandonment from 1870 to 1930—was completely renovated by PIUS XI, who used it for the first time as a summer residence in 1934. The decoration of the papal apartment situated on the 1st floor of the palace was deliberately an imitation of the Vatican apartment: red damask, gilded consoles supporting crucifixes or clocks, oak thrones with coats of arms, tapestries, and well known works of art. In the same way and to the extent possible, Paul VI transformed the decor of the villa on the model of the palace in Rome. John Paul II changed nothing, but had a swimming pool built in the Villa Barberini next door. The frequency of the pope's visits to Castel Gandolfo prompted the technical services department of Vatican City to install central heating there.

Pius XI commissioned painter I. H. Rosen to decorate the pope's private chapel. In it, Rosen depicted two episodes of Polish resistance (against the Tatars and against the Bolsheviks) framing the face of the Black Madonna of Czestochowa.

Philippe Levillain and François-Charles Uginet

Bibliography

Barbier De Montault, X. "Le Vatican," *Oeuvres complètes*, II, Poitiers, 1889.

Chattard, *Nuova descrizione del Vaticano o sia del Palazzo Apostolico di S. Pietro*, Rome, 1766.

Panciroli O., Posterla, F. *Roma sacra e moderna*, Rome, 1725 (reed. Bologna, 1977).

Redig De Campos, D. *I Palazzi Vaticani*, Bologna, 1967.

Taja, A. *Descrizione del Palazzo Vaticano*, Rome, 1766.

Witcombe, C. L. C. "The Vatican Apartment of Cinzio Aldobrandini—notes and documents," *AHP*, XIX (1981), 173–189.

APOCRISARIUS. *pl. apocrisarii.* For late Classical authors, this word of Greek origin (*apocrisiarios*) was used to mean the person who was delegated to negotiate in someone else's name. In particular, this occurred when there was a significant geographical distance preventing a direct transaction. The apocrisarius was responsible for bringing the person on behalf of whom he acted the responses related to the matter at hand, which were of chief importance. Thus, the entrusted man was called either an apocrisarius or a responsal, or even a responder (since he transmitted the responses). In the medieval period, there were words of mixed etymology such as *aprocrisiatus*. These were originally civilian employees of the imperial court, of modest rank, who acted as couriers for the chancellery. Their role existed parallel to that of the military apocrisarii who were officers who had the power to judge cases implicating their subordinates.

The specifically ecclesiastical apocrisiat was inaugurated when the first episcopal envoys were sent to the metropolitans. It developed after Constantine's conversion, then became an official practice under Justinian, in connection with the imperial will of obliging bishops to remain at their residence as much as possible (law of 20 February 528, meant for the patriarch Epiphanius of Constantinople, novella of 26 March 535 dealing with ordinations). The distinction was progressively established among apocrisarii of various ranks, according to the dignity of the prelate they represented and the authority to which they were accredited. The patriarchal apocrisaries, whose first figure was the DEACON Anatole, representing the Church of ALEXANDRIA in Constantinople in 449, played the most important role until the Arab conquest. Hincmar of Reims situates the appearance of apocrisarii from the Roman pontiff in Constantinople at the beginning of the 4th century. Today, we date their existence from the middle of the 5th century and, among others, include the following as apocrisarii: the future Pope VIGILIUS (537–55), the deacon Pelagius representing St. Agapitus in 536, Pope GREGORY (590–604) from 578 to 584 at Tiberius II's court, and perhaps also MARTIN I (649–55). Later on, there were the Cistercian and Clunisian apocrisarii, monks entrusted with representing their abbot at the general chapter of the order or before imperial courts. These helped perpetuate this plurisecular institution.

François Jankowiak

Bibliography

Morin, J. *De catechumenorum expiatione*, Paris, 1703, 101–6.

Pargoire, J. "Apocrisiaire," *DHGE* (1907), 2537–55.

Wiegand, F. *Katechese und Predigt vom Anfan des IV. bis zum Ende des VI. Jahrhunderts*, Breslau, 1884.

APOLOGETIC. The New Testament (1 Pet. 3:15) exhorted Christians "always be ready to defend themselves [*pro apologian*] against anyone who would ask for a reason for the hope in you." This is the translation presented in the Jerusalem Bible. It is nevertheless necessary to review the original text because, in the original, it is clear that it is not a matter of a defense *against* someone, but rather an apology *before* or *in the presence* of someone. In fact, in the historical context, this apology took place during a trial. Christians brought before the judge had to "defend themselves" by exposing the motivation for their hope. Although disputable from a philological standpoint, the interpretation of the Jerusalem Bible is historically justified. The translator instinctively interpreted the biblical passage by relying on memory. The truth is that very often the "defense" of Christianity is made *against* others and not "softly and respectfully" as the biblical text cited recommends in the following verse.

The first Greek apologists intervened "softly and respectfully." Among them, Quadratus must be cited (between 125 and 130), Aristides of Athens (who, like Quadratus, dedicated his apology to the Emperor Hadrian), the *Letter to Diognetus* (circa 140), Justin (between 150 and 160), Tatien (between 150 and 178), Athenagorus (betwen 176 and 180), Theophilus of Antioch (end of the 2nd century), and Hermias. This respectful behavior was not the fruit of virtue. If we gloss over Hermias's sarcastic work, which is difficult to date but which could be much later; Aristides, for example, demonstrates a strong polemical spirit in denouncing the errors and vices of the barbarians, Greeks and Jews. The fact that the Christians were a minority obliged them to adopt a conciliatory attitude and search for a "common" reference point to explain the Christian difference. This common reference was especially sought in certain aspects of middle Platonism and Stoicism of the period. Thus, the Stoic doctrine of the Logos allowed apologists of the 2nd century to show that everything true and good in the pagan philosophers was due to the influence of the equation Logos = Christ.

In this sense, the theologians of ALEXANDRIA provided a decisive contribution. Clement (140/150–221?) spoke of his conviction that there was basic agreement between Christianity and the highest teachings of Greek philosophy. He composed his main works in this spirit, all of which demonstrate a remarkable literary quality: *Protrepticus*, *Paedagogus*, and *Stromateis*. Origen (185–254) wrote his *Contra Celsum* around the year 246 against a Platonist named Celsum who had written a work between 177–80 denouncing Christianity. Celsum criticized Christians for being the enemies of widely accepted values. Origen, while underscoring that faith, did not rely on philosophical reasoning, attempting to reach those who lacked faith or whose faith was weak, by establishing the plausibility of the Christian mysteries. His argumentation was complex, because he sought not only rational analogies, but also historical ones (for example, between the death of Christ and the death of Socrates). Moreover, attempting to prove that Christians did not constitute a danger for the Empire, he had to conceive of a political theology.

This attitude changed during the 4th century, after Constantine's conversion. When Eusebius of Caesaria (264?–340?) was writing, it was a conqueror who expressed himself and no longer a man claiming his right to life. His *Praeparatio evangelica* (ca. 314) introduced a meaningful category, that of "preparation." This idea had great success. All history preceding Christianity was viewed as a "preparation." Since the advent of Christianity, things have become clear. Christianity was called in to "absorb" history and not to be present "in" history. Athanasius's main apologetic texts (*Oratio contra gentes* and *Oratio de incarnatione Verbi*) are to be read from the same perspective.

After the Council of Nicaea, apologetic literature suffered a decline. This was only parenthetically interrupted with Julian the Apostate (Emperor Flavius Claudius Julianus; 361–63) who motivated authors such as Diodorus of Tarsus, Gregory of Nazianzus, and John Chrysostom to start writing against him. Yet, it is generally agreed that the most significant apologetic work from the East came from Theodoret of Cyrrhus (393–495). His *Graecarum affectionum curatio* is a work in which the Christian doctrine appears as the only one capable of giving ultimate responses to questions posed by philosophy and religion. This demonstration can be situated in a neo-Platonist context, which earned its author much appreciation from the philosophers of the Renaissance period.

The Latin apologists were generally more sensitive than the easterners to the legal and political aspects of the Christians' place within the Empire. The oldest and most celebrated of these were mostly of African origin: Tertullian (ca. 160–220), Minucius Felix (between the 2nd and 3rd centuries), Cyprian (200/210–58), Arnobius (who wrote on the occasion of Diocletian's persecution), Lactantius (Lucius Caelius Firmianus Lactantius; Caecilius; ca. 250–25) and Augustine (354–430). There is a debate regarding Minucius Felix's *Octavius* and Tertullian's *Apologeticum* as to which predates the other. In any case, the structure of the two works is not very different. Minucius Felix was mainly concerned with demonstrating the dignity of Christian morality. Tertullian, using the most highly perfected rhetoric of a great Roman lawyer, aimed at proving that Christianity could be reconciled with the good of the Empire. He did not, however, attempt a dialogue with pagan culture, given that in his eyes Christianity constituted an entirely superior form of religious practice. What he demanded was the right to exist as such, so that doctrine could be shown as it was. Besides the *Apologeticum*, other works of his to be cited are: *Ad nationes*, *De testimonio animae*, and *Ad scapulam*. Although Tertullian spoke of the *anima naturaliter christiana*, his method remained dialectical. In fact, baptism alone was necessary to become Christian. One was not born Christian, but became Christian. The apologetic discourse was constituted by concrete evidence of Christian life rather than a theoretical confrontation.

The change in Latin apologetics of the 4th century, already announced with Lactantius, was affirmed with Julius Firmicus Maternus who, between 346 and 350, presented his *De errore profanarium religionum* to Emperors Constans II and Constantine. This text exhorted the emperors to weed out the remains of paganism, if necessary, by force. It was in the same spirit that Ambrose confronted the prefect Symmachus. It was not until Augustine that a wider perspective appeared. His apologetical writings contain all the arguments later developed over the centuries: from the role of reason to the argument of the moral miracle of the Church, from the analysis of the internal dynamism of man to the reflection on the theology of history and the meaning of Christianity in humanity's development. In *City of God*, written after the capture of Rome by Alaric in 410, it is difficult to separate Augustine's apologetic intention aimed at the outside world (accusing Christianity of being responsible for the ruin of the Empire) from his preoccupation regarding his community, confronted with experiencing the inconsistency of the world. We find other traces of classical apologetics, even if this evidence is sometimes minimal, throughout the Middle Ages in both the east and the west. However, the confrontation had already transformed into something more abstract. It was often incorporated into veritable theological treatises on the relationships between faith and reason. For the east, the polemics engaged in by Barlaam in the 14th century should be mentioned in light of the relationships between reason and faith (linked to those between tradition and innovation). In addition, we can note the discussions involving George Gemist Plethon's interpretation on the subject of Plato in the 15th century. As for the West, it was the gradual introduction of Aristotle that prompted similar debates, which were generally better articulated than the discussions in the East.

In any case, the veritable heritage of classical apologetics can be found in the treatises written against the Jews and the Muslims. The confrontation with the Jews went as far back as the period of the New Testament and the times of the apostles. We can situate the following texts in this same vein: Barnaby's letter, Justin's pacifist *Dialogue with Trypho the Jew*, a text by Tertullian called *Adversus Judaeos*, which has come down to us incomplete, Cyprian's *Liber Testimoniorum*, a text called *Dialogue between Timothy and Aquila*, which is difficult to date and attribute, the Syrian Aphraates's *Demonstrationes XI–XXIII*, and the homilies by John Chrysostom. The list is not exhaustive. The anti-Jewish frame of mind was exploited for a long time, especially during medieval times. In the East, in the 8th and 9th centuries, we can cite Theodore Agukara, Anastasia the Sinaite, and according to minor, often unpublished testimony, Gennadios Scholarios (ca. 1405–72). The West offers more ample evidence of anti-Jewish apologetics. Among the principal ones, we should cite the polemic between Dagobart of Lyon and Amul, under Louis I the Pious and Charles the Bald in France. During the same time period, but in the context of the particular ambience then reigning in Spain, we can also cite the epistolary exchange between Alvarez of Córdoba and Bodo-Eléazar. In the 10th century, an anonymous author wrote *Altercatio ecclesiae contra Synagogam*. In the 11th century, we can note Fulbert de Chartres, Albert de Metz, Peter Damian, and Gilbert Crispin. Among the Jewish converts to Christianity who debated with their former religious communities, we can cite the following authors: Peter Alphonse (1062–1110), Hermann de Scheda (1107–70), Rupert of Deutz (1075–1129), Raymond Martini (1220–85), Gautier of Châtillon (1135?), Guibert of Nogent

(1053–1124), and Joachim of Flora (1132–1202). All were not capable of obtaining as wide a perspective as Abelard (1079–1142) in his *Dialogus inter philosophum, judaeum et christianum*. The main problem was interpreting the Old Testament in terms of Christ. In the Orient, except for the novels in the anonymously written *Doctrina Patrum de Incarnatione Verbi* (7th century), the confrontation with Islam mostly aimed at defending the divinity of Christ and showing the erroneous nature of Mohammed's prophesies. This approach began with John of Damascus (ca. 670–750), if he is in fact the author of the *Concertationes cum Saracenis* and the *Disceptatio Christiani et Saraceni*. We can note the summary polemics of Bartholomy of Odessa in the 9th century and the much more complex and subtle arguments of Nicetas of Byzantium. The latter greatly influenced Euthymios Zygabenos. The ex-emperor John Canacuzena, who had become a monk, composed in 1360 a voluminous apology against Mohammed. In the 15th century, there was a great deal of literature written against Islam within the crumbling Byzantine Empire. John of Brienne and Manuel II Palaeologus can be cited in this connection, and, after the fall of Constantinople, Gennadios Scholarios and George of Trebizond.

The West was later than the East in its reaction to Islam. Alvarez of Córdoba was one of the first to have direct knowledge of Islam and foresee its danger. Yet in the 11th century, Embricone of Mayence composed a *Vita Mahumeti* inspired by legendary tales. The first truly informed description in the Latin West, but still in Spain, was contained in Peter Alphonse's *Dialogi*. This previously cited work was also a refutation of Islam. Peter the Venerable (1092/1094–1156), the Abbot of Cluny, had the Koran translated into Latin for the first time and composed an apology *Contra sectam sive haeresim saracenorum*, an important text in terms of its openness in spirit and consciousness of the value of the adversary. Among the Christians, who in different ways but with an obvious apologetic intention wrote about Islam, there were: Alan of Lille (ca. 1120–1202), Olivier of Cologne (ca. 1170–1277), William of Tripoli (1220–73), Thomas Aquinas (1225–74), and Ricoldo di Montecroce (1243–74). Raymond Lulle (1235–1316) especially dedicated his life to converting Muslims. He conceived of a type of complex combinatory logic to search for the truth and allow for the recognition of Muslims and other infidels. In the 15th century, Torquemada, Nicholas of Cusa, Dionysius the Carthusian, and Savonarola can be identified, although each with a different spirit and willingness to understand.

The 16th century brought radical change. The "other" was no longer outside of Christianity, but within it. The "problem of disbelief" was thus posed. Yet the awareness of it was not yet generalized. In 1543, *De veritate fidei christianae* was published after the death of its author, the humanist Juan Luis Vives (1492–1540). Rational and liberal, this work wanted men "to be led to believe according to the only arguments whose force of persuasion does not seem to essentially depend on the authority of God's voice alone." A disciple of Montaigne published *The Three Truths* in Bordeaux in 1594. For the first time, the soon classical tripartite Catholic apologetics were formally presented. He first intended to write against the Jews and Muslims to defend the truth of Christianity on one hand, and against the Protestant Duplessis-Mornay (to defend the truth of the Catholic Church) on the other. He then proceeded to the demonstration of religious truth against atheists who have "the behavior and take on the air of Christians." This was a seed of the apologetics that would be developed against the libertines and deists in the following centuries. First of all, it was necessary to demonstrate the truth of religion (*demonstratio religiosa*) *against* the unbelievers; then the truth of Christianity (*demonstratio christiana*) *against* other religions; and finally, *against* the Protestants, the truth of Catholicism (*demonstratio catholica*). Modern apologetics was, therefore, going to be an apologetics of hostility.

The intellectual libertine movement (in France, *le libertinage*) was the great adversary of 17th century apologetics. With the doctrine of "double truth," libertines attempted to join faithfulness and the rational negation of the principal religious values, whereas they posited the acceptance of pleasure as a criterion for new moral conduct supposing a deterministic view of things. A legion of apologists including Augustinians, Thomists, and humanists took up arms against the enemy: Jean Boucher, Jean Macé, Jean Bagot, Mersenne, Yves de Paris, and others were involved.

Pascal (1623–62) had read the other apologists, from Antoine Sirmond to Jean de Silhon, and back in history, from Pierre Charron to Raymond de Sebonde, whose *Theologia naturalis* (1484) had been translated by Montaigne. The argument of the "wager" had its proponents, but Pascal added his mark of genius to this proposition. Perhaps this is why he had practically no influence on the apologetics of his contemporaries. It would be enough to cite the case of the Jansenist Pierre Nicole (1625–95) because he refined the demonstration of Christianity by using rational and Cartesian proofs. In theology, it is difficult to speak of a positive embrace of Pascalian apologetics before the first part of the 20th century. The reason is not difficult to determine. Perhaps the theologians could not accept the "profession of two opposites," this simultaneous faithfulness in different orders of the real: bodies, spirits, and charity. The scientist was not absorbed by the philosopher, and the philosopher was not absorbed by the Christian. Pascal's apologetics in fact rely on the difficult unity of the three orders.

For Catholic apologists, it was much easier to refer to Descartes who offered two precious things: a hermeneutics of certainty and the clear distinction between the soul and the body. Malebranche's thought (1638–1715) is marked by a grandiose hermeneutics of certainty, placed under the sign of internal necessity. Less abstract, yet equally reliant on the simplicity of providential certainty, is the apologetic reading of history underpinning the work of Bossuet (1627–1704). Bossuet attempted to keep his distance from the criticism directed against Descartes, although he triumphed, and even Fénelon (1651–1715) owed him something. The Benedictine François Lamy was a faithful Cartesian, and it was in the Cartesian movement that authors blended a form of anthropology and apologetics, that is, the Great Arnauld, the Cardinal Retz, and Tournemine, among others.

Spinoza's *Tractatus theologico-politicus* appeared in the same year as Pascal's *Thoughts* (1670). Spinoza's *Ethics* appeared in 1677, but was incomprehensible for the public at large. On the other hand, his *Tractatus* upended the apologetical equilibrium and established a new atmosphere. Two key points demanded new responses: the negation of a positive revelation that could no longer be reduced to a rational knowledge of God, and the approach to the Holy Scriptures as a book written by men. Without naming him, Bossuet dedicated at least four chapters of his *Discourse* to Spinoza. Daniel Huet (1632–1721), in his *Demonstratio evangelica*, gathered together many of the arguments used against him. Others included Claude Frassen (1620–1711), the Benedictine Jean Martianay (1647–1717), the Oratorian Michel Le Vassor, who was inspired by Protestants such as Grotius and Abbadie and wrote *Of Veritable Religion* (1688), and the Jesuit Ignace de Laubrussel (1663–1720), who attempted to demonstrate how libertinage was already embodied in philological criticism.

Moreover, the polemical front kept expanding. It became necessary not only to defend the Holy Scriptures, but also the teachings of the Fathers of the Church. The Jesuit Baltus fought against Van Dale and Fontenelle, the Benedictine Ceillier against Jean de Barbeyrac's introduction to the French translation of Pufendorf's work in which the Fathers were accused of gross errors in matters of morality. Many years later, the Italians Michelangelo Griffini (1762) and Liberato Fassoni (1767) were still writing against Barbeyrac, and against others in Austria and in Germany. In the meantime, deism came to continental Europe as a result of French libertinage and the Italian Renaissance, via England. Anthony Collins's *A Discourse of Free-Thinking* was first published in London in 1713 and as of the following year, still in London, it came out in French as well. John Toland, against whom well-known authors such as Bentley, Berkeley, Clark, and Butler had written, had already published his *Christianity Not Mysterious* in 1696. Pierre Bayle himself disturbed the minds of many. On one hand, he criticized Spinoza and held that the miracle was plausible; on the other, he

defended the moral dignity of the atheistic attitude, placing all in the shadow of his critical detachment. The apologetical embarrassment was great indeed. Some abandoned history, seeking refuge in the more certain traditional elements guaranteed by the Church's authority (J. Hardouin, 1646–1729). Others in France, like Houtteville (1686–1742), considered that it was only in terms of history that this challenge could be met. The era of the great apologists like Pascal, Bossuet, and Fénelon had passed. The adversaries of Catholicism were then marking the eventful dates: 1734, Voltaire's *Lettres philosophiques*; 1751, the beginning of the *Encyclopédie* directed by d'Alembert and Diderot; 1758, *De l'esprit* by Helvétius; 1762, the publication of Rousseau's *Emile* and the *Social Contract*, attacked by apologists, although apologistic in its own way; and 1764, Voltaire's *Dictionnaire philosophique*. It is very difficult to choose from the multitude of apologists of the time, all worthy of mention. Claude-François Nonnotte (1711–93) replied to Voltaire, who had accused him of historical inaccuracy; Antoine Guenée (1717–1803) attempted to uncover Voltaire's anti-Semitism and his "erudite gasconnades." In any case, Nicolas-Sylvestre Bergier (1718–90) was the greatest apologist during the 18th century in France. He wrote against Rousseau, was imitated by the Italians Antonino Valsecchi, Vincenzo Fassini, and Nicola Spedalieri in his response to the *Examen critique des apologistes de la religion chrétienne*, falsely attributed to Nicolas Fréret, but in fact a work of the Holbach-Naigeon group. He gathered within a *Dictionnaire théologique* in three volumes, articles of his that had been dispersed throughout the *Encyclopédie*, and also took a position against certain burning issues such as divorce and the source of authority in the assembly, then in the process of being formed.

Although the French were often translated and imitated in Germany and Italy, in Germany the connection between apologetics and theology was much tighter. However, we cannot affirm that there was, in fact, an exchange with the new developments in critical historical exegesis, especially on the Catholic side. In addition, Wolff's scholasticism in Germany was as influential as was Descartes's. Among a long list of names we must cite J. Simon who, in 1773, wrote *De religione contra libertinos*; E. Klüpfel (1733–1811); B. Stattler (1728–97); H. Goldhagen (1718–94), who directed an apologetic review entitled *Religions-Journal*; Alois Merz (1727–92); Beda Mayr (1742–94); and A. Janitsch, who wrote in 1792 on the relationships between natural religion and revealed religion, and received Pope Pius VI's approval. Among the Italians of the period, the following merit mention: Casto Innocente Ansaldi (1710–80), Daniele Concina (1687–1756), Tommaso Vincenzo Moniglia (1686–1767), Alfonso Muzzarelli (1749–1813), Vincenzo Fassini (1738–87), Giacinto Sigismondo Gerdil

(1718–1802), Alphonsus Liguori (1696–1787), Antonino Valsecchi (1708–91), as well as men such as C. Amaduzzi (1740–92), who, without being a theologian or an apologist, attempted in the context of what was called Enlightenment Catholicism to find an accord between philosophy and religion.

The FRENCH REVOLUTION fueled apologetics, which was confronted with a society that had dethroned religion. Minds were divided between those who attempted a kind of reconciliation, like Adrien Lamourette (1742–94) or the abbot Gregory (1750–1831), and the more numerous group of those who saw the opposition as a battle between good and evil. In papal Rome itself, the personality of Nicola Spedalieri (1740–95) constituted a problem. In 1791 Spedalieri published *De' diritti dell'uomo* (Of the Rights of Man) in which he attempted an apologetic recuperation of the problem of natural rights to conclude with a defense of the Church.

In the 19th century, apologetics experienced a crisis that was resolved by a radical transformation. At the same time, the Roman courts entered into the arena to settle the more delicate points of the confrontation, by deciding on matters of reason and faith. After the condemnations by GREGORY XVI and PIUS IX of semi-rationalism on one hand, and excessive traditionalism on the other, the VATICAN I council labored to find a balance to simultaneously ensure a role for reason while attributing a greater role to the authority of God and the Church. Throughout the century, apologetical works continued to be written in the traditional sense of the term. Great names wrote to defend the cause of the truth of the faith against the errors of the century, such as LIBERALISM, socialism, positivism, materialism, etc. Thus, Restoration France witnessed the success of the writings of Chateaubriand (1768–1848), Joseph de Maistre (1753–1821), Bonald (1754–1840), and Louis-Eugène Bautain (1796–1867). Others, such as Lamennais (1782–1860) and Lacordaire (1802–61) embarked on new paths by paying greater attention to the exigencies of the liberalism of their time. In Spain, Jaime Balmes (1810–48) and Juan Donoso Cortès (1809–53), the former with moderation and the latter with vehemence, hardened the opposition between Christianity and MODERNITY. In Italy, where Mauro Cappellari, the future Pope Gregory XVI, had written in defense of the authority of the Church and where original figures such as Gioacchino Ventura (1792–1861) appeared, the author, who no doubt merits being set apart for his theological rigor, is Giovanni Perrone (1794–1876). However, others showed the necessity for establishing very different bases for the confrontation between Christianity and modernity. Thus, in Germany, the theologian from Tübingen, Johann Sebastian Drey, attempted to establish a strictly theological basis for apologetics, in an original mediation with German idealism. Of especial note is Drey's *Die Apologetik als wissenschaftliche Nachweisung der Göttlichkeit des Christentums in seiner Erscheinung* (3 vols., Mayence, 1838, 1843, 1847).

Apologetics, therefore, begins to privilege less the act of denouncing the error of others and more that of reflecting on the foundations of faith. In this way, it adopted the attitude of a mediator in terms of the mentality of the times. The transformation of apologetics was thus announced as "fundamental theology," that is, a reflection of the foundations of faith and theology itself. A favorable attitude in relation to the thought of the times was announced by the ill-fated attempts made by Georg Hermes (1775–1831), Jacob Frohschammer (1821–93), and Anton Günther (1783–1863) in Germany and in Austria, and Rosmini in Italy. All became victims of Rome's condemnations, each for different reasons. In England, John Henry Newman explored the logic of the assent of faith, thus opening the way later for followers during the Modernist crisis and afterward, with the new reflections during the first half of the 20th century. Newman's *An Essay in Aid of a Grammar of Assent* (1870) remains a reference to this day, yet it was in France that the crisis erupted. During the last decade of the century, a great debate began on the utility of referring to historical arguments taken from the Old Testament (Brugère, d'Hulst, Mignot, Durant, Didiot, and others). Men such as Ferdinand Brunetière (1849–1906), Léon Ollé-Laprune (1839–98), Georges-Pierre Fonsegrive-Lespinasse (1852–1917) insisted on the vital, psychological, and moral aspect of keeping the faith, in order to affect modern sensibilities. In this way, the path for the work of Maurice Blondel (1861–1949) was opened. In 1893 Blondel published *L'Action*; in 1896, the *Lettre sur les exigences de la pensée contemporaine en matière d'apologétique . . . (Letter of the exigencies of contemporary thought regarding apologetics)*, and in 1904, *Histoire et dogme*. Nothing has been the same since these works appeared. In the area of apologetics and therefore, consequently, in Catholic theology in general, Blondel introduced the necessity of immanence as proper to modern man: "Modern thought, jealously vulnerable, considers the notion of *immanence* as the very condition of philosophy. In other words, if, among the reigning ideas, there is a result to which it is attached as if to certain progress, it is to a basically sound idea. This idea is that nothing can enter into man that does not come out of him and does not in some way correspond to a need for expansion. No historical fact, traditional teaching or added outside obligation has any truth that counts or is an admissible precept without in some way being autonomous and autochthonous." The history of theology in our century, in both its refusal and acceptance of the same, is marked by Blondel's contention. First throughout the modernist crisis, then in a more subdued way over the following decades, apologetics was to undergo a transformation. In fact, accepting the principal of immanence no longer meant that one was defending the transcendence of the Christian truth *against* "others," but rather that one was attempting to reconcile the absolute gratuity of grace with the exigency of immanence proper to the times. Resistance was strong. Men such as H. Gayraud, M. B. Schwalm, C. Le Bachelet, and especially J. de Tonquédec led this resistance. Others, such as Auguste and Albert Valentin (coauthors of a famous article on "Immanence" in 1915 wherein there was a famous distinction between exclusive immanence, unacceptable for a Christian, and relative immanence, which could be reconciled with the supernatural), C. Dimnet, and F. Mallet defended Blondel. L. Laberthonnière was even more radical. Other theologians followed different paths. In 1907, the year of Pope PIUS X's ENCYCLICAL against Modernism entitled *Pascendi*, A. Gardeil published *La crédibilité et l'apologétique (Credibility and apologetics)*. While recognizing the importance of moral dynamism in the adhesion of faith, he in fact remained anchored to the traditional scholastic vision of the analysis of faith. On the other hand, the thinking of the Jesuit P. Rousselot was more creative and original. He decisively contributed to a new reflection on Thomism, the formal acceptance of an immanent dynamism of the subject in the connection of faith. Theologians respectively took their places behind the Dominican Gardeil and the Jesuit Rousselot in the reconsideration of the conditions of Christian apologetics. However, the 1950s, with the announcement of the VATICAN II COUNCIL, marked the end—perhaps the definitive ending—of the great period of apologetical hostility.

Giuseppe Ruggieri

Bibliography

Arnou, R. "Platonisme des Pères," *DTC*, XII/2 (1935), 2258–2392.

Aubert, R. *Le Problème de l'acte foi*, Louvain, 1958.

Bouillard, H. "De l'apologétique à la théologie fondamentale," *Les Quatre Fleuves*, I (1973), 57–70.

Busson, H. *La Penée religieuse française de Charron à Pascal*, Paris, 1933.

Busson, H. *Le Rationalisme dans la littérature française de la Renaissance (1533–1601)*, Paris, 1971.

Chadwick, H. *Early Christianity and the Classical Tradition*, Oxford, 1966.

Cristianesimo nella storia, XI/3 (1990).

Dulles, A. *A History of Apologetics*, London, 1971.

Febvre, L. *Le Problème de l'incroyance au XVIe siècle. La religion de Rabelais*, Paris, 1957.

Momigliano, A. *Il conflitto tra paganesimo e cristianismo nel secolo IV*, Turin, 1968.

Monod, A. *De Pascal à Chateaubriand*, Geneva, 1970 (reprint of the 1916 Paris edition).

Nock, A. D. *Conversion*, Oxford, 1933.

Pottmeyer, H. J. *Der Glaube von dem Anspruch der Wissenschaft*, Freiburg im Breisgau, 1968.

Poulat, E. *Histoire, dogme et critique dans la crise moderniste*, Tournai-Paris, 1962.

Ruggieri, G. "Per una storia dell'apologia cristiana nell'epoca moderna. Note bibliografiche e metodologiche," *Cristianesimo nella storia*, 4 (1983), 33–58.

Ruggieri R. ed., *Enciclopedia di teologia fondamentale*, vol. I, Genoa, 1987, 1–400.

Werner, K. *Geschichte der apologetischen und polemischen Literatur der christlichen Theologie*, 5 vols., Osnabrück, 1966 (reprod. de l'éd. de 1861–67).

APOSTASY. The definition of apostasy was quite clear as of the first centuries of the history of the Church. This term designated the act committed by a person who, having received the sacrament of baptism, publicly, totally, and instantaneously (that is, in a single act) abandoned the Christian faith. The total character of apostasy distinguishes it from HERESY. Since St. Thomas Aquinas (*Summa Theologiae*, II a, II ae, q.XII, a.l) modern canonists and theologians have used the term apostasy in three different but related senses: (1) renunciation of the Christian faith after having embraced it (*apostasia a fide*); (2) flight from religious life after solemn profession of vows (*apostasia a religione*); (3) abandonment of one's status in major orders as deacon, priest, or bishop (*apostasia ab ordine*).

Repeated pontifical legislation, especially marked by the DECRETALS (themselves specified by the decretal *Sacerdotibus et clericis* by EUGENE III [1145–53], then by BENEDICT XIV and PIUS IX), determined the penalty incurred by the deposition, excommunication, and ANATHEMA without automatically excluding the possibility of reconciliation, and even, reintegration. Excommunication was declared *latae sententiae* and reserved for the Holy See for clerics in the major orders. PAUL IV, in his constitution *Postquam* (20 July 1558) was even able to affirm, at the height of a period of apostasy from religious life, that "every day, the offense of apostasy is committed by some religious." His successor PIUS IV found it necessary to legislate on the matter two years later with the constitution *Sedis Apostolicae* (3 April 1560). There is no known case of an apostate pontiff. LEO III was obliged by the Roman nobility to undergo an official deposition ceremony on 25 April 799, but this was due to an "ASSASSINATION ATTEMPT" which did not affect belief in Christian dogma or violate the rules of consent for evidence.

Bibliography

Amanieu, A. "Apostasie de religion," *DDC*, I (1935), 664–74.

Barbosa, B. *De officio et potestate episcopi*, Venice, 1707.

Boudinhon, A. *La Nouvelle Législation de l'Index*, Paris, 1924.

Ojetti, B. *Synopsis rerum moralium et juris pontificii*, Rome, 1912.

APOSTOLIC CAMERA. The central organization for the management of pontifical finances was established in the first years of the 14th century, when it became necessary to have differentiated administration of the various segments of the Church. This system replaced the Curia, which had become limited in numbers and effectiveness due to the itinerant nature of the papacy over the preceding half century. Under BONIFACE VIII, the strict distinction between the finances of the pope and those of the cardinals was established. The finances of the cardinals were managed by a small chamber of cardinals, which played only a secondary role since the finances of the cardinals essentially consisted of half of the cost for the COMMON SERVICES paid by bishops and abbots for their collation. This half was shared among the cardinals present at the consistory during the collation. The cardinals essentially lived off the revenue from the major and minor benefices attributed to them in administration, referred to in modern times as "commendum."

The Apostolic Camera, on the other hand, was developed to answer the need for strict management of the revenue produced from the taxation levied on the churches, which increased in the time of JOHN XXII. It also took advantage of the material stability of the pontifical administration that resulted from its establishment in AVIGNON. The Apostolic Chamber, which was still in its embryonic stage under the Chamberlains Arnaud de Canteloup (1305–7), Bertrand de Bordes (1307–11), and Arnaud d'Aux (1311–9), owes its definitive organization to the long rule of chamberlain Gasbert de Laval (1319–47). It was under his stewardship that the incompatibility between the office of chamberlain, or CAMERLENGO, and the dignity of the office of cardinal was established. De Laval's successors often preferred to hold the rank of archbishop and exercise the functions of a chamberlain, which was thought to hold greater authority and influence than that of a mere cardinal. It is to a great extent thanks to the experience of chamberlains Pierre de Cros (1371–83) and François de Conzié (1383–1432) that the Avignon papacy survived for so long the financial difficulties arising from the GREAT SCHISM OF THE WEST.

The Apostolic Camera was a management organization. The treasury, which was responsible for the collection and payment of revenue to the Curia, enjoyed real autonomy within the chamber, so much so that the treasurer, generally a bishop, was only in rare cases the assistant to the camerlengo or chamberlain. Should the head of the Camera be unavailable, the chamberlain appointed a lieutenant or deputy manager, generally from among the officers of the chamber. The appointment of the treasurer to perform this interim function was not at all automatic, but was nonetheless frequent. The power and influence of the chamberlain arose from the fact that he was the only person who knew about the overall financial situation of the HOLY SEE, and that he had the privilege of expressing the will of the pope. In other words, apart from his duty to appoint COLLECTORS, his decisions and actions were never covered by a BULL. The collectors had to be appointed apostolic NUNCIOS by the pope before they could be nominated by the chamberlain. When the chamberlain referred to the will of the pope as expressed verbally to him, no one questioned the legitimacy of his actions. In practice, everyone was aware that the chamberlain made decisions in the name of the pope. François de Conzié at one point admitted that the personal will of the pope was, in fact, a myth. He wrote that the pope's letters were written *de mandato domini nostri, ut dicitur* (on the orders of our lord, as we say). The privilege granted to the chamberlain made him an exceptional individual. Although the cardinals had the privilege of deciding on behalf of the pope during his absence, notably in instances of diplomatic legation, the chamberlain enjoyed this privilege on a continuous basis at the Curia. He was responsible for the staff as well as for the movement of funds, and he chose the clerks of the Camera, the collectors, the auditors sent to the provinces, and the dominical officers of the papal state in Italy and the Venaissin County. He supervised the work of collectors regarding taxes, and of treasurers and receivers regarding domanial finances. Both collectors and treasurers came under the same administrative organization, whereas different bodies within the financial systems of the temporal princes often governed them.

Not only did the camerlengo receive an *a posteriori* report following the audit accounts by the Apostolic Camera, he was also kept abreast of the entire process through an important correspondence with his local agents. During the great Schism of the West, this was one of the great weaknesses of the Roman papacy with respect to the Avignon papacy: the inability to reestablish control over local management of funds. In Avignon, this was achieved with the help of officers who had been in place before the schism and by the keeping of records. The chamberlain controlled the discharges and allocations, which reduced the movement of money by having the collectors and under-collectors make a large number of payments, and, if necessary, by making advance payments of local revenue. After a rendering of the accounts the chamberlain gave quittances to the finance officers. From 1385 in Avignon, the pope cancelled in advance any quittance directly granted by himself, merely reserving the right to grant general and non-justified quittances, which were intended as a grace and not as the conclusion of a management operation. Only the treasurer received an annual quittance from the pope, which was delivered only after the Apostolic Camera had audited the accounts. The chamberlain received bonds for small services and established the time limit for the payment of these bonds, which could be cashed only at the treasury. He also had the authority to restore prelates from the excommunication imposed on them for lateness or default of payment.

The chamberlain was the judge of all matters relating to pontifical finances and to the pope's claim over his beneficiaries and officers. He therefore had a body of auditors, or auditory, before which he could raise any cause he deemed necessary. He could examine the numerous complaints lodged by taxpayers against collectors and auditors. In practice the auditory was presided over by an auditor of the chamber. One can therefore see two separate courts emerging: the court of the auditors, the normal judicial instance for financial, fiscal, domanial, and feudal affairs, and the court of the chamberlain, which was the court of first instance for cases raised by the chamberlain.

The court of the auditor had its own place, the second seat in the treasury chamber. A fiscal prosecutor acting for the pope and the chamberlain assisted the chamberlain in all actions relating to the defense of the rights of the Apostolic See. He represented their interests in the auditor's court. The collectors were responsible for summons *in partibus*. The chamberlain represented the Church vis-à-vis its vassals, and received homage and oaths of fidelity. He conferred investiture of fiefs and especially manor seats of the papal State by placing his episcopal ring in the hand of the new beneficiary. As had been the case with the accounts chambers of the temporal princes for a century, the Apostolic Camera started to keep control over the pope's generosity, in order to prevent the obtaining of concessions from the pope in an abusive runner. From 1382 on in Avignon, every Bull referring to a gift, concession, remission, or assignation had to bear the stamp of the chamberlain, who remained the judge of financial appropriateness, even if the pope was still the judge of the political appropriateness of a given act.

On a secondary level, the chamberlain governed the pontifical palace, where he exercised temporal jurisdiction and was resposible for public order in the city. When the pope reserved for himself the bishopric of Avignon without granting it "in administration," it was the chamberlain who administered the diocese and ensured the collection of revenue for the benefit of the Apostolic Camera. The Chamberlain was an administrator, not a financier. He was a jurist, more often than not doctor *in utroque*, that is, in civil and canon law. The fact that he himself was surrounded by jurists conferred an unofficial role of financial adviser upon banking and commercial companies involved in the movement of funds and granting of loans to the pope.

The treasurer, for his part, was usually a bishop, and sometimes an abbot. His immediate role was to manage the funds transferred to Avignon from Rome. He received the voucher from the collectors but was totally unaware of the amount of the assignations, and therefore the overall expenditure. He was more than anything else the cashier of the Curia. Unlike the Chamberlain, whose function ceased with his death, resignation, or promotion to cardinal, the treasurer had to be reappointed if a new pope was elected. In the 14th century, a number of treasurers were promoted to chamberlain: Gasbert de Laval Étienne Cambarou, Guillaume d'Ambussac.

The clerics of the Camera were the chamberlain's closest collaborators. At the beginning of the 14th century, there were always seven, but the number subsequently dropped to three or four. They were jurists, paradoxically more often civil than canonical jurists, as well as experienced administrators, former collectors, or commissaries. Their task was to examine requests, verify accounts (including that of the treasurer), and draw up reports. On the instruction of the chamberlain, they held negotiations with debtors and creditors and drafted the texts that could affect the temporal interests of the pope. The fact that they were responsible for writing the chamberlain's correspondence made them knowledgeable of the financial situation. They were often asked to carry out special diplomatic and financial missions in the provinces.

Promotion to the episcopate put an end to the functions of the clerics in the chamber, but not to their actual service. For some, this promotion was accompanied by a promotion within the chamber. This was the case when a cleric became treasurer. Others remained in service with the title counselor of the Camera. This had no specific content, and was more a position than an actual job. Other clerics, who had no titles, held positions of trust. At any rate, the clerics were simply prelates on whom the chamberlain, or camerlengo, could depend to carry out delicate missions, which required someone of a certain standing in the ecclesiastical hierarchy, not a precise office within the Curia. In carrying out the requests of the chamberlain, they nonetheless played a role comparable to their work when they were clerics of the Camera. The counselors and clerics of the Camera made up the council of the chamberlain or camerlengo. It appears that the treasurer also belonged to that council, which was not an officially recognized body.

The nuncios were specially appointed apostolic collectors and were responsible for local administration. They all enjoyed minor benefices and were chaplains or canons, priests and archdeacons, although we also know that there were some bishops who were collectors. In theory, the collector was chosen from among the members of the local clergy and carried out the practice formerly associated with taxation by a representative of the episcopacy. In reality, the collector was sometimes of foreign, even distant, origin, which was the case of the Italian envoys in Poland or England. A number of collectors come from the Curia and were *a posteriori* provided with a benefice in their collectorship. The first collectors appeared from the beginning of the 13th century for the collection of the *décime*. The duty become permanent in the middle of the 14th century, when taxes followed at such a pace that they could no longer send a special commissary for each tax. At the same time, especially during the papacy of CLEMENT VI, they habitually set up permanent areas for a collector, often an ecclesiastical province (Tours, Bénévent, Miles) or several provinces (Sens and Rouen; Lyon, Vienne, Besançon, and Tarentoise; Grado Zara, Split, and Ber), sometimes a kingdom (Bohemia, Hungry, Poland, Portugal, England). Yet at the end of the century, the Roman collectorships of Italy varied according to each designation. In general, the collector carried out the tasks associated with taxation, inquiry, determining the tax and delivery. For the actual task of collection the collector was assisted by a sub-collector appointed by himself and chosen from among the local clergy. The Camera did not acknowledge the existence of the sub-collector, and held the collector as the sole person responsible. Some collectors even designated a sub-collecting general, who had to assist in a part of the whole of the collectory, or area of collection.

The collectors were clerics. In countries where written laws existed, jurists were generally chosen, with indifference to whether they were civil or canon. The important thing was that they have a passing knowledge of the law and were able to present an argument. They were generally scrupulous accountants, but not financiers. Once the assignations had been paid, they entrusted the transfer of their vouchers to commercial and banking companies chosen by the Apostolic Camera, or to simple merchants chosen by local circumstances and situations. Indeed, during the time of the Great Schism, local circumstances forced the collector of Portugal to send his transfers to Rome via London or Bruges.

From the very beginning, in the time of John XXII, the function of transfer and accounting was carried out by large Florentine companies: Bardi, Peruzzi, Accialiouli. After the banking failures of 1330, Bardi and Peruzzi disappeared from the market. They were replaced by young companies that had been less affected by the crisis because they had not yet been heavily involved in granting loans to the princes and were therefore less vulnerable to the disproportion between mobilizable assets and actual turnover. It was the golden age of the Ricci and especially of the Alberti *antichi*. Following the 1376 crisis, which affected relations between the pope and Florence thanks to the schism, other companies came to the fore. In Rome, it was from Lucca, Guinigi, Moriconi, and Turchi, and the Medici Florentines; for Avignon, from Lucca the

Rapondi, from Pistoia the Tici, and from Asti the Solario and Rici. When the collector came in person to Rome or Avignon to submit his accounts, he paid the balance in cash. However, if, as it sometimes happened, the balance was negative, the collector was unable to bring fresh money to the treasury and had to be reimbursed from the debts pending from the next collection.

The maintaining of a coherent and durable network of collectors was absolutely necessary for the effective functioning of the Apostolic Camera. Before the Schism, there had been cases of collectors who carried out the same function for several decades. This was the case of the Norman Bernard Carit in Paris, who was the collector for the provinces of Sens and Rouen. In 1352 he succeeded his uncle, also named Bernard Carit, who worked as collector until his death in 1383, having previously been appointed bishop of Evreux in 1376. During the time of the Schism, the collectors of Avignon occupied the post for roughly twelve years. Guy de la Roche was the collector for Tours from 1365 to 1390. Sicard de Bourguerol was first counselor to the Camera and nuncio at Languedoc for fiscal affairs, and was appointed collector of Toulouse in 1382. He was transferred in 1386 to the collectory of Narbonne, and did not leave until 1404, when he became cleric of the Apostolic Camera in Avignon. Foulque Périer held his post the longest. He was collector of Toledo for thirty years (1375–1405). Such long periods in office assured a smooth transaction despite the Schism and were naturally precious to the Avignon pope.

Despite this deliberate striving for stability, the Apostolic Camera of the time of the Schism was hampered by improvisation. The collectorates were constantly being redivided. Nominations came in quick succession, without Rome knowing whether these had been accepted or followed up. In a thirty-year period, whereas there were on an average three collectors in each Avignon collectorate, there were seven within the obedience of Rome. Nuncios were asked to double as collectors and the terms of their mission remained vague and ambiguous. Two collectors were appointed simultaneously for Portugal, in the hope that one of them would work. There were many collegial collectorates. In Venice, there were between 1400 and 1404 two simultaneous and independent collectors. Their function was episodic. The future INNOCENT VII, Cosimo di Gentile Megliorato, acted at the same time as cleric of the Apostolic Camera (1379–86), nuncio at Florence, and collector for England. The central administration suffered from the same instability which affected the provinces. The Romans were unable to correct the imbalance in favor of Avignon, where there were competent men in the administration who were already in place before the Schism. Whereas in a given period there were two chamberlains in Avignon, there were at the same time six chamberlains and vice-chamberlains in Rome. As for the clerics of the Camera, none of them had worked previously as collector. They had no experience of working in the field. The prevailing instability in Rome was accompanied by uncertainty in the choice and assignment of the men. Many flatly refused their nomination. Some simply refused to do their job without giving further explanation. In light of these conditions the Camera did not even know with whom it was corresponding. Sometimes the Camera issued instructions to a collector without knowing there had been none in place for a number of years. The most surprising case is that of the bishop of Lübeck, Johann Kleindienst, who died in 1387 and was replaced that same year, with the full knowledge of the Apostolic Camera, which registered the obligation of his successor to pay for the common and petty services rendered. Kleindienst was appointed collector of Bohemia. Six months later he was ordered to submit monies collected. A cleric of the Camera subsequently noted the appointment of Kleindienst and indicated that the bishop had not reported to his post. Naturally, unscrupulous collectors abused this situation. The Italian collector for England, Jacopo Dardani, died without having submitted any accounts over eleven years of tax collecting. He left with his London bankers, the Manini, a personal account of 10,000 florins, which would have been highly appreciated if he had sent them to Rome. It was normal at that time for the collector to have a personal account as the monies collected were in the form of a personal debt. Despite this, Dardani was one of the rare stable elements in the financial administration of the Roman papacy. He was successively collector of Flanders, Holland, Zelande, and England, and he did pay at least some assignations.

The keeping of records is an essential tool in any financial administration. The archives of the Apostolic Camera are particularly rich in information, at least for the Avignon papacy, of the time before and after the Schism. The principal funds are those gained through correspondence. The bulls (registers of Avignon and the Vatican), are the instruments of the decisions of the pope: in the positioning of décimes, the reserving of annates or procurations, the revising of taxes, the maintaining of vacant posts in administration, the appointment of nuncios, and the granting of general quittances. The letters of the camerlengo were recorded separately and were the administrative correspondence which specified nominees and appointees, as well as modes of collection or seizure, notification of deadlines and their revision, and transmitions of assignations and quittances. Special registers (*obligationes et solutiones*) kept record of obligations for common services, with the personal signatures of prelates, quittances for payments made in person or by proxy, deadlines granted after partial payment or after default of payment, and the canonical absolutions governing these time limits. In addition there were letters and deeds drawn up by the Curia and records of petitions addressed to the pope regarding questions of taxation.

The accounts of the treasurer (*Introitus et exitus*) are proofs of payment, recorded within a few days following receipt of the quittance. The treasurer did not include in his records, and therefore in the amount he owed to the pope, a sum of money he had not received. The articles recorded as collected do not refer to the real debt of the payer toward the pope; the account was simply a cashbook. However, for each expenditure the treasurer made a note of the names of the witnesses in the margin of the book. This gave the book the status of proof for the treasurer, who could not then be accused of listing false expenditure. Until 1378, the accounts of the treasury were first kept in the journals, or "manuals," with columns in the margin, and then in the form of large books, with chapters showing the articles, which were similarly listed in columns. From 1378 on, the chronological "manual" was most commonly used. The account was still the annual justification of the management of cash, and could not by itself provide any clues of the volume of papal finances. To have an overview of pontifical finances, one would have to consult the records of the correspondence of the chamberlain, which show the assignations delivered on local collections. Even so, an assignation is not a payment and only the accounts of the receiver or collector could reveal if and when an assignation was followed by actual payment. Moreover the account by the collector makes mention of expenditure that was automatically assigned, such as management and mission expenses, building maintenance, and administration of goods, the cost of which have been accepted by the accountant. The cleric of the chamber required proof that the accountant had indeed approved these costs, and on the basis of these proofs, accepted or rejected the information supplied by the accountant.

The accounts of dominical receivers and collectors made up the series of the *Collectorie*, and were different in nature. They had in themselves no value of proof. The collection receipts did not need to be justified. For every tax, for example, the collector had a general list of the ecclesiastical holders of a benefice, who were debtors of an annate or a décime, with the amount of the tax due. On the same list or on a different one, he made a note of the sums that had been received as well as the expected arrears. Such accounts give a precise view of the rhythm of payment, delays, or nonpayment, whether or not these were justified. On the other hand, the amounts paid and especially the assignations were justified during the rendering of accounts by the producing of the quittances received by the collector. The *Collectorie* series forms the basis for the study of the ecclesiastical geography of the Middle Ages. It provided the principal material for the publication of the *Pouillés*.

One must be cautious in interpreting the record of payments, since the accounts did not distinguish between nonpayment due to real economic hardship and that due to individual ill will. Some procurers within the Curia specialized in infinitely fractionalized payments. This shows that part of the apparent poverty of the Church in the late Middle Ages was due to a systematic resistance to paying taxes. This is quite clear when we see accounts of prelates who owed hundreds of florins for an important benefice but managed to repay only a few florins every three months. The clients of the procurer Thomas le Pourri, in the years 1370–90, had recourse to a practice which protected them from canonical sanctions. The bishop of Bayeux, Nicolas du Bosc, owed 2,200 florins. Even though he was very well off from his pensions as counselor to the king of France, he took twelve years to repay his debt. Out of the eleven main clients of Thomas le Pourri, eight died without having finished paying off their debts.

The councils of the 15th century threw the activities of the Apostolic Camera into disarray. The suppression of the annates and, indeed of all taxation of churches, reduced the role of the Apostolic Camera to one of the financial management of the pontifical State. The Camera also issued INDULGENCES, which were more or less inspired by the jubilees of previous centuries. The suppression of the annates was decreed in 1435 by the Council of Basel and in each country was implemented by means of uncertain concordats and ordnnances, such as the Pragmatic Sanction of Bourges (1438) in France. From the time of the Schism, the pope had been obliged to grant monopolies to financiers to find credit. As from 1462, however, leases for the exploitation and commercialization of the ALUM of TOLFA offered a new source of revenue and led to a new organization of the Camera. One financier, the "depositor" would then play an official role in the financial administration of the Holy See.

Jean Favier

Bibliography

Samaran, C., and Mollat, G. *La Fiscalite pontificale en France au XIV siecle*, Paris, 1905.

Favier, J. *Les Finances pontificales a l'epoque du Grand Schisme d'Ocident (1378–1409)*, Paris, 1966.

See also CAMERLENGO; FINANCES, PAPAL.

APOSTOLIC CONSTITUTIONS. It is most likely that the *Apostolic Constitutions* were written in Syria, around A.D. 380. They provide an essential testimony of the canon law of the ancient Church. At that time, there were a number of works attributed to the apostles or claiming to speak on their authority, on which the *Apostolic Constitution* seems to be based. These would include the *Doctrine of the Apostles* (or *Didache*), written in Greek in the first half of the 3rd century, near Antioch, the *Didascalia*, attributed to the apostles, and the *Apostolic Tradition*, or *Diataxeis of the*

Holy Apostles, written around A.D. 215–18, probably by St. Hippolytus of Rome (d. 235). It would appear that there was an attempt made in the second half of the 4th century to compile these texts, to reaffirm their value, and to ensure their dissemination. This is evident from a manuscript conserved in Verona, written in Greek and Latin.

The *Apostolic Constitutions* appear to date from the very end of the 4th century and are similar to other religious writings of the beginning of that century. The collection, attributed to St. Clement of Rome, includes eight books of detailed descriptions dealing with liturgy, the preparation and dispensation of sacraments, and the discipline of the faithful. This last is more closely related to canon law in the strictest sense, notably to the canons arising from the councils of Nicaea (325) and Laodicea (between 343 and 381). These canons are also reflected in the compilation.

The *Apostolic Constitutions* enjoyed great popularity in some of the non-Hellenic Eastern churches. However, subsequent writers included only fragments of the work in their collections. Dionysius Exiguus, around 500, included the canons at the end of Book VIII of the *Constitutions* at the beginning of his own collection. Gratian reproduced some extracts in his *Decretum*. The *Constitutions* place the bishop at the very heart of the institutions of the Christian community, and provide lengthy arguments to justify their importance within the Church. The work provides a fine example of the so-called pseudoepigraphic law, Had it gained wider acceptance, it may even have been considered as the "code of canon law of the year 380 A.D." (M. Metzger).

François Jankowiak

Bibliography

Bardy, G. "Constitutions Apostoliques," *DDC*, III (1949), 453–460.

Funk, F. X. *Die Apostolische Konstitutionen*, Rotenburg, 1891

Gaudemet, J. *Les Sources du droit de l'Eglise en Occident du IIe au VIIe siecle*, Paris, 1985.

Metzger, M. "Les Constitutions Apostoliques par Clement," *RDC*, XXXII (1982), 130–144.

Metzger M. *Les Constitutions Apostoliques*, I–III., Paris, 1985-7.

Nau, F. *La Didascalie des douze Apôtres,* Paris, 1912.

Schwartz, E. "Die Kanonessamlungen der alten Reichskirche," *ZSSR-KA*, XXV (1936), 1–114.

APPEAL TO THE POPE. Since the pope is the highest authority in the ecclesiastical hierarchy, he has the highest jurisdictional power (*judex ordinarius omnium*) and anyone can make an appeal to him after being sentenced by one of the lower ecclesiastical courts. An appeal made to Rome is not only a procedural technique modeled on Roman law, but also one of the key elements of Roman centralization. It is the means and expression of the *plenitudo potestatis* of the pope as supreme judge. The principles of appealing a bishop's sentence are found as early as the 4th century (Council of Arles, 314, canon 3; Nicaea, 325, canon 5) and the appeal to the pope of a bishop's sentence has been accepted (Serdica, 343, canon 12), but not without some resistance from certain quarters (Churches of Africa and the East). The "False DECRETALS" and CANON LAW of the Gregorian reform sanction this possibility, which became an instrument of government. Usually, the appeal of a sentence must respect the degrees of jurisdiction (*gradatim*), but at the end of the 5th century, direct appeal to the Holy See (an *omisso medio* appeal) was introduced to circumvent the judiciary hierarchy, thus opening this avenue to everyone (Gelasius I, *Cuncta* decretal). Moreover, as opposed to all the usual procedural rules, an appeal to Rome can be made not only after a definitive sentence is rendered, but also at the beginning of a case (*a limine litis*) or during a trial ("in any case" or when an interlocutory sentence, that is, a procedural detail, is decided). The pope does not become involved in all of these matters directly, but designates delegated JUDGES and reserves the most important cases to be judged in his *auditorium*, or entrusts them to the cardinals who have, since the middle of the 12th century, constituted a specialized group of CHAPLAINS, the original ROTA.

The importance of the appeal to Rome, whether normal or direct, is evidenced by the number of decretals that ALEXANDER III made and by the importance of the title concerning it in GREGORY IX's *Decretals* (1234). There are no less than 73 chapters in these documents, which are abundantly commented by doctrine and often reticent regarding the *omisso medio* type of appeal. Since the appeal amounts to a suspended judgment, that is, it prevents the first judgment from been executed, we can understand how a system working in the interest of the plaintiff, who may be unjustly wronged, can lead to abuses favored by a climate of litigation and lawyers representing the parties. This problem led to the creation of a clause in the pontifical decretals during the middle of the 12th century called the *omni appellatione remota* ("all appeals being forbidden") making delegated judges responsible for deciding cases. Truly a "plague" on the papacy during the end of the 13th and 14th centuries, appeals are virulently criticized at the COUNCILS of Basel and Constance. The reorganization of appeals followed the outcome of these councils and at the end of the 15th century, the papacy reaffirmed its power to receive appeals. The practical inconvenience did not overshadow the symbolic strength of the institution. These pretensions were ultimately ruined by GALLICANISM in France and the king's power in other places developing states over the 16th century, during which ecclesiastical civil law was created and the CONCORDATS proliferated. It was thus no longer possible for royal subjects to appeal to an outside power. The *Codex juris canonici* of 1917 and that of 1983 stipulate the uniquely judiciary character of the institution and ignore the appeal "in any case" and *omisso medio*.

Gérard Giordanengo

Bibliography

Amanieu, A. "Appel," *DDC*, 1 (1935), 764–807
"Appellatione remota," *ibid.*, 827–33.
Gazzaniga, J. L. "L'appel *omisso medio* au pape et l'autorité pontificale au Moyen Age," *Revue historique de droit français et étranger*, 1982, 395–414.
Padoa Schioppa, A. *Ricerche sull'appello nel diritto intermedio*, Milan, 1967–70, 2 vols. (Knowledge of the theories of the civilists is indispensable for the comprehension of canonical doctrines); "La delega *appellatione remota* nelle decretali di Alessandro III," *Renaissance du pouvoir législatif et genèse de l'Etat*, Montpellier, 1988, 179–88.

APPOINTMENT OF BISHOPS. The procedure in the general law of the Church for the appointment of bishops in the Latin Church is set forth in canons 377 to 380 of the CODE OF CANON LAW of 1983. In a few lines, the code synthesizes the prescriptions contained in the fifteen articles that made up the "Norms for the Designation of Bishops in the Latin Church" (*Normae de promovendis ad episcopale ministerium in Ecclesia latina*) published on 25 March 1972 by the Council for Public Affairs of the Church under the signature of Cardinal Jean Villot, secretary of state of PAUL VI and prefect of the Council.

As is well known, the procedure used for the Catholic bishops of the different Eastern Churches respects the traditional autonomy of these respective Churches, whose practices may vary on certain points but are still subject to the general law of the CODE OF CANONS OF THE EASTERN CHURCHES of 1990. By the terms of these canons, patriarchs are elected by the SYNOD OF BISHOPS of their church by winning two-thirds of the votes in the first two ballots and an absolute majority in the following ballot; if nobody is elected within fifteen days, the nomination devolves to the Roman pontiff. Once elected, the new patriarch must signal his acceptance within two days, before being proclaimed and enthroned. As soon as possible, the synod sends the pope notification of the patriarch's election and enthronement, together with his profession of faith and his oath; these synodal letters are at once forwarded to the other Catholic patriarchs of the East for their information. The patriarch must also write a letter in his own hand to the supreme pontiff to ask for "ecclesiastical communion." If they are to exercise their office validly from the moment they are enthroned, the Eastern patriarchs should not convene their synod or ordain bishops before receiving the papal reply. These norms apply to six patriarchs: Alexandria of the Copts, Antioch of the Maronites, Antioch of the Melkites, Antioch of the Syrians, Babylon of the Chaldeans, and Cilcia of the Armenians. Although established in the East, the Latin patriarch of Jerusalem is not subject to this procedure since, belonging to the Latin Church, he is logically subject to the Latin Church's rules and thus directly appointed by the pope. As for the bishops of the Eastern dioceses (properly called eparchies), three procedures are possible:

1) The fundamental rule is that the synod of bishops of the patriarchate in question sets up, under secret ballot, a list of priests chosen from among those proposed, after investigation, by the patriarch (all must belong to the celibate clergy). After obtaining the agreement of the pope, to whom the patriarch has forwarded the list, the synod then freely elects the one it considers the most worthy among those short-listed by Rome. The nominee is then informed of his election by his patriarch, who, having received the nominee's acceptance, at once communicates to the Holy See the result of the election and the date of its proclamation;

2) When the patriarchal synod elects a new bishop who is not on the list of candidates accepted by the Holy See, the patriarch immediately and secretly informs Rome of the election so as to obtain the pope's approval. Upon receipt of papal approval, the candidate, in his turn, is informed of his election by the patriarch, who asks for his acceptance before forwarding it to Rome along with the day of publication;

3) In the non-patriarchal Eastern Churches, and in Eastern territories not belonging to a patriarchate, appointments of bishops are made by the Roman pontiff based on a list of at least three names drawn up by the bishops of the same church and sent to Rome. In the election of major archbishops of Eastern non-patriarchal Churches (i.e., those of Lviv of the Byzantine Urkrainians and Ernakulam of the Siro-Malabar Indians) or metropolitans of Churches sui juris, the pope intervenes by confirming the election in the former case, and by granting the pallium in the latter.

In the Latin Church, by contrast, the pope plays a more direct role, even though a distinction should be made between general canon law and exceptions owing to custom or convention.

As a general rule, the bishops of the dioceses of the same ecclesiastical province (excluding any other cleric of non-episcopal rank) draw up and update, at least every three years, a list of priests directly or indirectly known to them and who qualify for promotion to the episcopate, whether they belong to the diocesan or the religious clergy.

The Code of Canon Law sets forth a series of qualities (identical in the Eastern Code) indispensable in each "candidate" for the office of bishop: "[. . .] he should be outstanding in solid faith, good morals, piety, zeal for souls, and endowed with other qualities which make him suitable to fulfill the office in question; of good reputation [. . .]" (canon 378, § 1–2). To which the norms of 1972 added "a sound judgment [. . .]" a balanced and constant character . . . a sense of sacrifice [. . .] a social sense [. . .] an aptitude for dialogue and collaboration," as well as a solid attachment to the orthodoxy of faith, devotion to the Apostolic See, and loyalty to the magisterium of the Church. In addition, objective conditions call for a minimum age of thirty-five, at least five years of priesthood, and a doctorate or license in Holy Scripture, theology, or canon law, or, in the absence of such certification, a competence in one of these areas. After an oral discussion on the merits of each candidate, the bishops vote in secret ballot on each name proposed. All proceedings and steps taken are communicated to the pope's representative (nuncio or apostolic delegate, depending on the country concerned) by the metropolitan of the ecclesiastical province. However, each bishop still has the right to propose, personally and directly, one or more names to the papal representative (canon 377). In any event, these collective or individual lists are merely suggestions that are not binding on the Apostolic See, which has sole and definitive judgment on the fitness of a cleric to be promoted to bishop (canon 378, § 2). That is why it is possible to refer to this bank of names but also to make a choice elsewhere when providing an archbishop, a bishop, or a coadjutor for a diocese.

In such circumstances, the papal representative goes about the selection of the candidate by carrying out a wide-ranging and thorough search. To this end, a detailed questionnaire is addressed to bishops, priests, religious, even members of the laity, but individually and under secret seal. On reading the collected information, the papal legate consults the president of the conference of bishops, the metropolitan archbishop, and the suffragan bishops of the ecclesiastical province to which the diocese in question belongs; he hears the individual opinions of certain priests of the College of Consultors and of the chapter of canons, and he may request, always secretly and separately, the opinion of other members of the diocesan and religious clergy, and, if need be, members of the laity of "outstanding wisdom" (canon 377, § 3). From the diocesan administrator responsible for the provisional government of the diocese, he also solicits a complete, detailed report on the state of the diocese and its needs. The nuncio, or apostolic delegate, then makes a synthesis of these elements, adding his annotations and personal reflections in order to produce a list of three names (called a *terna*) showing, in order of preference, the names of the priests to be promoted or bishops to be transferred whom in conscience he considers most suitable. In certain cases, this personal, secret search is paralleled by a public, collective one. Here the population of the diocese to be provided for is consulted. The Code of Canon Law is silent on this procedure, which therefore remains optional. Recourse to it was had for the first time in 1966, for the diocese of Haarlem, in the Netherlands, and then for the neighboring dioceses of Bois-le-Duc and Breda; the process was repeated in 1967 in the United States in the cases of Manchester and Cleveland, and then in 1968 in New York and in Montreal, Canada. In 1970, similar action was taken in France for the diocese of Marseille, and in 1972 for that of Châlons. That same year, the norms of the Holy See made this empirical initiative official but not mandatory. These consultations must remain impersonal because it is never a question of the faithful proposing names but rather of making an inventory of their diocese's needs and of the qualities—the list of which is often exacting—they expect in their future pastor. Nevertheless, the consultations have a somewhat limited usefulness in the effective choice of a pastor, since as a rule nothing is learned from them that is not known already; at the most, they give free rein to pressure groups and allow certain tensions to be expressed openly.

Once received in Rome, the nunciature's report is taken up by the competent DICASTERY, that is, the Congregation for Bishops in the majority of cases, or the Congregation for the Evangelization of Peoples for the so-called mission countries, or the Congregation for the Oriental Church for those territories that are Eastern but are not patriarchal or extra-patriarchal, and where the nomination of bishops depends on the supreme pontiff. The Roman CONGREGATION examines the report before submitting it to the bimonthly assembly of its member cardinals and bishops (whether they are members of the Curia or diocesan); those unable to attend may send in their observations in writing. Each name on the *terna* is the object of a synthetic report, followed by a discussion that ends in a secret vote. The result is then brought to the Holy Father by the cardinal prefect of the Congregation (or, at times, by the secretary archbishop). In general, the pope ratifies the decision (on the spot or later), but he may just as well decide against it in cases where he has personal knowledge of a candidate or a diocese. Once the nomination is ratified, the candidate is informed by an official, confidential letter from the papal representative of his country, who often takes the trouble to telephone him personally to explain the pressing reasons for his choice. The nominee has very little time in which to reply, as there is but a brief period of time between his acceptance and the publication of his nomination. The latter is juridically effective only with the dispatch of apostolic letters in the form of a papal bull, a parchment calligraphed in Latin and bearing the seal of the Holy See and the signature of the pope. This document, whose personalized style is adapted to each bishop, is read before the College of Consultors at the time the new bishop takes canonical possession of his see. The bishop may already be a bishop, and is simply being transferred or promoted from one see to another; in the case of a cleric who has only priestly rank, three bishops who are co-consecrators of his selection proceed, within three months, to his ordination as bishop, which—like his profession of faith and his oath of loyalty to the Apostolic See—must occur before the taking of canonical possession of his pastoral office.

This procedure, valid for diocesan bishops and coadjutor bishops (that is, bishops having the right of automatic succession to diocesan bishop) is simplified for auxiliary bishops since it is up to each diocesan bishop who wishes an auxiliary to submit a list of three names to the papal representative. The latter then starts the customary inquiry before referring it to the competent Roman congregation. The Code further provides that legitimate measures may entail variations in procedure in the establishment of the *terna*. This is the case, for example, in England and Wales, where the list of three names is first drawn up by the chapter of canons of the diocese to be provided for, then debated and possibly corrected by the bishops of the ecclesiastical province, and finally sent to the nuncio in London, who gives it its definitive form without consulting the president of the conference of bishops. In the Netherlands, the Congregation of PROPAGANDA FIDE in 1858 gave the cathedral chapters the privilege of presenting a *terna* to Rome when their respective episcopal sees became vacant, yet without undermining the pope's full freedom of choice. In countries suffering religious persecution, the Holy See is also accustomed to take exceptional preventive measures in order to ensure the continuity of the apostolic succession at the heart of the local episcopate; the local bishops are therefore entitled to choose and consecrate trustworthy clergy on their own initiative, if need be in secret, provided Rome is informed as soon as possible. This was done in the states of central and eastern Europe and the Far East under Marxist totalitarianism. It is still the case in communist China and other places in similarly difficult circumstances.

Further exceptions to the general law of the Latin Church arise from ecclesiastical traditions or diplomatic conventions.

Ecclesiastical traditions concern episcopal sees provided for through election. These are all to be found in western Europe (Germany, Switzerland, and Austria), not to mention, of course, the unique case presented by the elective seat of Rome.

In Germany, electoral customs were sanctioned by different Roman documents (the constitution *De salute animarum* and the BRIEF *Quod de fidelium* of Pius VII in 1821 for all the Prussian dioceses; the BULL *Ad dominici gregis* and the brief *Res sacra* of Leo XII in 1827 for those of Baden) and confirmed by CONCORDATS or conventions between the Holy See and the states. Today, the German elective seats are as follows: the archdiocese of Cologne and its five suffragan dioceses of Trier, Münster, Limburg, Osnabrück, and Aachen, together with the archdiocese of Paderborn and its two suffragan dioceses of Fulda and Hildesheim (concordat of Prussia of 1929), as well as the diocese of Essen, suffragan of Cologne (agreement between the Holy See and the Land of the Rhineland of North Westphalia in 1957); the archdiocese of Freiburg im Breisgau (concordat of Baden of 1932) and its two suffragan dioceses of Mainz and Rottenburg-Stuttgart (concordat of Germany of 1933). In each of these dioceses of what was once Prussia, the chapter of canons and the bishops of that region send Rome their respective lists, from which or outside of which the Holy See selects the names of three priests, one of whom will be chosen bishop by the canons. The same procedure is followed for the see of Berlin. For the dioceses of Baden, one list is sent to Rome by the chapter when the see becomes vacant, while another is sent each year by the diocesan bishop; the Holy See retains three names—not necessarily from these lists—for the chapter to vote on. These elections apply, however, only to diocesan bishops, not to coadjutor or auxiliary bishops. As for Bavaria, the pope in fact appoints the archbishops of Bamberg and Munich and their respective suffragans of Eichstatt, Speyer, and Wurtzburg, as well as Augsburg, Passau, and Regensburg, but he is limited in his choice by the names retained by the diocesan chapter upon vacancy of the see concerned, and by those mentioned in the triennial lists drawn up by the Bavarian bishops and canons (concordat of Bavaria of 1924).

In Switzerland, the three elective episcopal sees are those of Basel (the bull *Inter praecipua* and the brief *Quod rem sacram* of 1828), Saint Gall (the bull *Instabilis rerum* of 1847, the brief *Prout rerum ac temporum* of 1858), and Chur, the only Latin diocese whose elective privilege is based solely on a Carolingian custom, without written confirmation. Since 1982, the list of candidates drawn up by the canons of Basel has been transmitted to the diocesan conference (the Catholic cantonal representatives), which selects the bishop and forwards his name to the Holy See for pre-publication confirmation; on the other hand, in the case of Saint Gall, the cathedral chapter submits its list to Rome for approval in advance before transmitting it for information, and as a courtesy, to the cantonal Catholic Council; it then proceeds to elect the bishop, whose canonical institution will be requested of the pope. At Chur, in a 1948 decree, the Consistorial Congregation abrogated all elective privileges but granted the cathedral chapter the right to choose its bishop from a list of three names drawn up by the Holy See.

In recent years, certain episcopal appointments depending on the pope or on a capitular election have given rise to demonstrations of hostility of varying intensity depending on the region. The pope has been reproached for forcing electors in a certain direction or for taking their place. In fact, these ecclesial (sometimes even ecclesiastical) disputes have ignored the full governmental powers attached to the primatial and divinely instituted task of Peter's successor, which far overrides what, in the final analysis, depends on nothing more than local traditions, undoubtedly venerable, but based on mere human laws. This Petrine primacy is expressed in the *affectio papalis*, a right peculiar to the Roman pontiff that consists in his power to take the place of any authority instituted within the Church on canonical or liturgical matters. Often applied in the Middle Ages, this right has been invoked above all in the conferring of benefices (promotion, transfer, or deposition), and sometimes been exercised to the point of quashing or prohibiting elections. In our own day, the call from certain electors for respect for local traditions would profit from not forgetting other aspects that would make their case fully convincing.

On the other hand, if the pope is not absolutely bound by diocesan customs, he is bound by the diplomatic conventions set by international law on treaties. Several documents in this category provide for the intervention of political authorities in the process of episcopal appointments. The types of intervention are diverse, from the simplest to the most stringent.

1) According to custom and solely out of courtesy, the Holy See, through the local papal representative, communicates the names of new bishops to certain governments before publication: Spain (for auxiliary bishops), Great Britain (for the Scottish bishops), Belgium, Luxembourg, Ireland, Malta, Switzerland (for the diocese of Lausanne-Geneva-Fribourg), Canada, Mexico, Bolivia, Chile, Paraguay, and Algeria. For two more states, this pre-communication is provided for by a diplomatic convention: Italy (agreements of 1984) and Peru (agreements of 1980).

2) On the basis of bilateral conventions, the Holy See has granted certain governments the benefit of a right of preliminary consultation in the case of the appointment of auxiliary archbishops and diocesan bishops and coadjutors, though never in the case of that of diocesan bishops. Essentially, the Holy See asks the political authorities if they have an "objection of a general political nature" to the nominee. At issue here are not the political opinions of the persons concerned but the attitudes they might adopt in questions of public and constitutional order, state security, or regional separatism, according to a definition contained in a *modus vivendi* of 1928 with Czechoslovakia and which, though lapsed, has set a precedent not in its wording but in its significance. This right of previous consultation is in force in the following countries: France (aide-mémoire of 1921, applicable to

all the metropolitan and overseas departments but not in the three departments of Alsace-Moselle or the overseas territories), Spain (agreement of 1976), Portugal (concordat of 1940), Monaco (convention of 1981), Netherlands (for the military ordinary), Switzerland (for the dioceses of Basel and Sion), Austria (concordat of 1933), Germany (concordats of Bavaria of 1924, Prussia of 1929, Baden of 1932, Germany of 1933), Dominican Republic (concordat of 1954), Haiti (protocol of 1984), Argentina (agreement of 1957), Colombia (concordat of 1973), El Salvador (convention of 1968 for the military ordinary), Ecuador (*modus vivendi* of 1937), Venezuela (convention of 1964), Tunisia (*modus vivendi* of 1964, the only right of consultation granted to an Islamic head of state), and the Philippines (exchange of notes in 1952 concerning the military ordinary). It should be noted that this right of governmental consultation does not correspond to a right of veto. The conventions say nothing of difficulties that might arise, relying on the contracting parties to settle problems in a case-by-case fashion. Thus the Spanish agreement of 1976 leaves it "to the prudent consideration of the Holy See to evaluate these objections." Only the 1964 convention with Venezuela implicitly provides for a right of veto for the president of the republic, since in such a situation the Holy See would have to submit another name.

3) For military ordinaries (bishops of the armed forces), some appointments are made by common agreement between the Holy See and the state in question: Argentina, Ecuador, France, Germany, Paraguay, Peru, and Portugal.

4) The most important political intervention in the matter of episcopal nominations concerns, in our own times, the right of presentation, a relic of the ancient right of patronage. This allowed certain heads of state to choose priests for the office of bishop and present them to the pope so that he could confer canonical institution on them. Granted to the Spanish monarchs in the 16th century and confirmed by the concordats of 1753 and 1851, this privilege was claimed by a number of Latin-American states by right of their status as successor states of former Spanish colonies. But Rome recognized them only on the explicit conventional bases drawn up during the 19th century with Bolivia in 1851, Costa Rica and Guatemala in 1852, Honduras and Nicaragua in 1861, El Salvador and Venezuela in 1862, Peru in 1875, Ecuador in 1862 and 1881, and Colombia in 1887. From a concession of GREGORY XVI (1834), confirmed by PIUS XI (1934), Argentina possessed a "right of recommendation" for four dioceses that had been unilaterally changed by the constitution of 1853 into a right of presentation for all the episcopal sees in the country. Haiti benefited from a right of presentation by virtue of the concordat of 1860. In Europe, the same held true for Monaco owing to the bull *Quemadmodum* of 1886, for Portugal with the con-

cordats of 1778 (for the whole country and its overseas possessions) and 1857 (limiting the patronage to the Portuguese possessions in India and China), and for France on the basis of the concordat of 1801. However, by the end of the 19th century, papal concordatory policy aimed at freeing itself from this exorbitant clause of canonical general law. The 1917 Code prohibited it for the future (canon 1450, § 1) and was echoed by the Code of 1983, according to which, "in the future, no rights or privileges of election, nomination, presentation, or designation of bishops are granted to civil authorities" (canon 377, § 5). In the meantime, the Vatican II Council had recalled the proper and exclusive right of the Roman pontiff to appoint bishops in the universal Church; consequently, it asked the civil authorities "very courteously" to relinquish it "of their own accord in agreement with the Holy See," whether they held it by virtue of a convention or a custom (decree *Christus Dominus*, no. 20). This ordinance was never aimed at the right of consultation, which was not mentioned by the council among the obstacles to Church liberty. Accordingly, the states involved gave up this privilege over the years: Argentina in 1966, Colombia in 1973, Spain in 1976, Peru in 1980, Monaco in 1981, Haiti in 1984. Portugal, for its part, had renounced the right of patronage as early as 1950, and Venezuela in 1964. In most cases, a simple right of consultation took the place of the former right of presentation. Thus, today, there are only two countries where the right of presentation is still in force, and that for only three episcopal sees: Spain, for the bishop of the armed forces, whose name the king presents to the pope based on a *terna* drawn up by mutual agreement between the apostolic nunciature and the minister for foreign affairs and previously approved by the Holy See; and France, for the concordatory dioceses of Strasbourg and Metz.

The case of France is somewhat special in that the government views as a right of appointment what the Holy See views only as a right of presentation. Indeed, on the basis of the concordat of 1801 still in force for the three departments of Haut-Rhin, Bas-Rhin (archdiocese of Strasbourg), and Moselle (diocese of Metz), the procedure is as follows: The president of the Republic signs a decree concerning the "nomination" of a priest to the archdiocese of Strasbourg or the diocese of Metz; he does not publish it, however, since the decree must be followed by the delivery of the papal bull conferring canonical institution. This bull is taken from Rome by the French ambassador to the Holy See, and from there is dispatched to the Quai d'Orsay for delivery to the minister of the interior. Here the Council of State (Section of the Interior) confirms that the papal wording conforms to concordatory rules—but according to the complementary interpretation of the Organic Articles of 1802, which were never recognized by the Holy See, having been unilaterally added to the concordat. If the Council of State replies positively, the text of the bull is transcribed in Latin and French in the Council register. After that, the president of the Republic may sign and publish a new decree concerning the receipt of the bull of canonical investiture. The name of the newly promoted bishop is published simultaneously in Rome and Paris. In actual fact, this type of nomination is reached after an agreement between both parties; otherwise the pope would refrain from issuing the papal bulls, thereby making the governmental candidates canonically invalid, and the head of state would refrain from signing the decree, thereby making the papal candidates legally incapacitated. Hence, this nomination de jure can be seen de facto as a presentation. It will be noted that the French concordat of 1801 does not cover auxiliary bishops, according to the general rule of Roman concordatory policy. Nevertheless, the French government did unilaterally submit these nominations to the procedure provided for in an imperial decree of 7 January 1808, as evidenced by the authorization of the president of the Republic solicited by a priest in order to enable him to receive the papal bull installing him auxiliary bishop of a concordatory bishop; the unpublished decision of the president of the Republic authorizing acceptance of the pope's canonical investiture; the examination of the bull by the Council of State; the decree of the president of the Republic published in the *Journal officiel* and countersigned by the prime minister and the minister of the interior, stating receipt of the bull of nomination. The Holy See ignores this procedure, regarding it as an internal administrative regulation of the French government.

As concerns the implementation of these various modes of political intervention in ecclesiastical affairs, preparation of the canonical dossier and the selection of the candidate fall within the competence of the Roman Congregation for Bishops (Latin Dioceses) or that of the Evangelization of Peoples (Missionary Dioceses), while relations with the states depend on section II of the SECRETARIAT OF STATE of the Holy See, which is precisely empowered to that effect.

Joël-Benoît d'Onorio

Bibliography

Aimone Braida, P. V. "Partecipazione del potere civile nella nomina dei vescovi in accordi conclusi dalla Santa Sede con il governi civili tra il 1965 e il 1976," *Apollinaris*, 50 (1977), and "Partecipazione del potere civile nella nomina dei vescovi (1976–1981)," *Apollinaris*, 54 (1981).

D'Onorio, J. B. *La Nomination des évêques. Procédures canoniques et conventions diplomatiques*, Paris, 86.

"Église locale et choix des évêques," *Concilium*, 157, Paris, 1980.

Fürer, I. "L'élection des évêques de Bâle et de Saint-Gall," *Theologische-Praktische Quartalschrift*, 4 (1977).

Harouel, J. L. "Comment on devient évêque," *Pouvoirs*, 17 (1981).

Harouel, J. L. *Les Désignations épiscopales dans le droit contemporain*, Paris, 1977.

Khoury, J. "La scelta dei vescovi nel Codice dei canoni delle Chiese orientali," *Apollinaris*, Rome, 1992.

Khoury, J. "Le choix des évêques dans les Églises orientales," *Concilium*, no. 77 (1981).

Minnerath, R. *L'Église et les États concordataires (1846–1981)*, Paris, 1983.

APPOINTMENT OF BISHOPS, HISTORY. Two Scripture texts served as the paradigm for the participation of the community in the selection of bishops. In Acts 1:15 Peter proposed to a congregation of about 120 persons that they find a replacement for the apostle Judas, who had betrayed the Lord. Then in Acts 6:5 the twelve called a meeting of all the disciples to select seven men of good reputation to assist in the daily distribution of food. The oldest Christian document outside the New Testament, the Epistle of Clement to the Corinthians, written before the close of the 1st century, testifies to the involvement of the laity in the choice of ministers. Clement warned the Corinthians, that it was not just to remove, without cause, those who had been appointed to the episcopacy "with the consent of the whole church" (44:1–3). At about the same time (ca. 100) the *Didache* of Syrian provenance explicitly directs the people to "choose for yourselves bishops and deacons worthy of the Lord" (no. 15).

At the beginning of the 3rd century HIPPOLYTUS at Rome determined to put into writing the ancient liturgical practices lest they later be distorted. In his *Apostolic Tradition* Hippolytus notes that a bishop is to be ordained "after he has been chosen by all the people." When the candidate has been named and "shall please all," the ordaining bishops "lay hands on him: while all give their consent." In the middle of the century Cyprian, writing from North Africa to various Western churches, especially those in Spain, insists on the necessity of election. He asserts divine authority "for the practice whereby bishops are chosen in the presence of the laity and before the eyes of all." The people "are the ones who are acquainted most intimately with the way each man has lived his life" (Ep. 67:4,5). Again, Cyprian writes that Cornelius was made bishop of Rome "by the choice of God and of his Christ, by the testimony of almost all the clergy and by the vote of the people present, and by the assembly of bishops" (Ep. 55:8,4).

Early Canon Law. With the spread of Christianity the local churches or dioceses, adopting the political organization of the Roman Empire, were grouped into provinces. The development of this structure gave increasing importance to the neighboring bishops. Canon 4 of the First Ecumenical Council of Nicaea in 315 decreed that a bishop must be elected by all (or at least by three) of the bishops of the province. It was the prerogative of the metropolitan (the bishop of the capital city of the province) to confirm the choice. Neither Nicaea nor the Council of Antioch in 341 refers explicitly to any other participants in the election beyond the comprovincial bishops. That the people did continue to have a voice in the process is evident from the warning of the Council of Laodicea at the end of the century that the election was not to be entrusted to the multitude (c. 1). The *Constitutions of the Apostles*, which reflect the customs of the East during the same period, state that the metropolitan is to ask the people and the presbyters if the one nominated is the one they wish to head their church (Bk. 8:8).

The practices of East and West soon diverged, however, as the voice of the laity progressively diminished in the East. In 546 the Emperor Justinian limited lay participation in the electoral process to the leading men of the city who together with the clergy were to draw up a list of three candidates (Novel 123). At the end of the iconoclastic struggles in 787 the Second Council of Nicaea declared that any election of a bishop procured by a ruler was null and void; "the person who is to be advanced to a bishopric should be elected by bishops" (c. 3). Finally the Fourth Council of Constantinople (later rejected by the Orthodox) legislated in 869–70 that "no lay authority or ruler may intervene in the election or promotion" of a bishop. "Any secular authority or ruler, or a layperson of any other status" who violates the canonical method of election is "ANATHEMA" (c. 22).

The West in the Early Middle Ages. The Roman pontiffs of the 5th century on many occasions referred to the involvement of clergy and people along with the neighboring bishops in the election of a new bishop. Pope BONIFACE I in 422 declared it uncanonical to exclude the clergy, the nobility, and the people. Pope CELESTINE I, writing to the bishops of Vienne and Narbonne in 428, insisted that no bishop was to be imposed on a church unwilling to receive him: the consent and wishes of the clergy and people are required (Ep. 4:5). Pope Leo the Great (LEO I) in 445 addressed a letter to the same region reiterating the principle that the bishop who is to preside over all should be chosen by all: "The clergy ought to subscribe to the election, the dignitaries give their testimony, and the rest of the people give consent" (Ep. 10). The *Statuta ecclesiae antiqua* of southern Gaul (c. 480) recapitulated the traditional formula: the bishop is ordained "with the consent of the clergy and the laity and the assembly of all the bishops of the province, especially the metropolitan." Contemporary accounts of elections indicate that the general populace merely acclaimed or ratified a choice made by the local clergy and the neighboring bishops.

Soon after the time of Leo the Great, the Roman Empire in the West gave way to various Germanic kingdoms whose rulers sought to control the choice of bishops. The roles both of the clergy and the people were gradually reduced, though not formally, to acclamation, accepting the one named by the secular power. Canon 10 of the Fifth Council of Orleans in 549 held that no one must accede to a bishopric through purchase or bribery, but only with the consent of the king after election by the clergy and people according to the ancient canons. Pope Gregory the Great (GREGORY I, 590–604) wrote frequently to the Merovingian rulers warning them about the evils of simony and of worldly bishops. In Spain the Twelfth Council of Toledo (681) authorized the bishop of Toledo, if he judged them worthy, to appoint those bishops who had been selected by the king (c. 6).

In the middle of the 9th century some attempt was made to justify the royal appointment of bishops. The archbishop of Lyon, for example, was asked to consecrate for the vacant sees of Autun and Châlons two individuals named by King Charles the Bald. The king acted, it was alleged, because of widespread disorder. The Council of Valence in 855, perhaps by way of compromise with the ancient legislation, required that a license from the ruler be obtained before proceeding to the election by the clergy and people. The instability resulting from the disintegration of the Carolingian empire accelerated the spread of feudalism, in which bishops by reason of their extensive landholdings became vassals of kings or great magnates. These suzerains would obviously seek to control the holders of these offices. To some extent the leading clergy and laymen of the city may have had a voice in nominating candidates for the episcopacy, but the favor of the monarch was decisive. When the ruler invested the new prelate with the ring and crosier, the symbols of office, he was in effect bestowing the bishopric.

Gregorian Reform. The bishop is the key figure in the life of the local church. As far back as the 3rd century, St. Cyprian of Carthage could maintain that the bishop concretized the Church: "the Church is in the bishop" and "anyone who is not with the bishop is not in the Church" (Ep. 66:8). Therefore, bishops who were selected more for their usefulness to the secular power than for their ecclesiastical qualifications gravely threatened the health of the Church. No wonder that the reform movement surging through Western Europe in the mid-11th century focused on the character of bishops. It clearly recognized that the root evil of the age was lay investiture, which fostered both simony (the buying and selling of ecclesiastical offices) and the scandal of clerical incontinence.

Immediately upon his rise to the papacy in 1049 the reform-minded LEO IX sought to restore episcopal elections to the clergy and the people. Under his prodding the synod of Reims threw down the gauntlet in its first canon: "Without the election of the clergy and the people, no one may be promoted to an ecclesiastical office." Cardinal Humbert of Silva Candida, an ardent theoretician of the reform, insisted that the election of the clergy must be "confirmed by the judgment of the metropolitan, and the petition of the nobles and people by consent of the prince." Pope GREGORY VII or Hildebrand, after whom the reform is named, allowed for the election to be confirmed either by the metropolitan or by the Roman pontiff. Eventually a compromise was worked out at the Concordat of WORMS in 1122. The German emperor renounced investiture with ring and crosier and agreed to "canonical election and free consecration" for bishops and abbots. The pope conceded that such elections were to take place in the presence of the emperor or of his representative. After the election the bishop would do homage as a feudal vassal and receive in return the feudal lands and the jurisdiction attached to the office. Similar arrangements were made for England and France.

The Cathedral Chapter. In 1140, shortly after these agreements were signed, the great canonist Gratian in his *DECRETUM* or *Concordance of Discordant Canons* sought to lay out the procedure for free canonical election. In Distinction 63 he first cited eight texts from the 4th to the 12th centuries maintaining that the laity were to have nothing to do with ecclesiastical elections. Then he lined up eighteen texts recognizing lay influence, especially that of the king. He reconciled the texts by arguing that the king's role was only temporary due to crises now happily passed. Lay participation was henceforth limited to acclamation, and the right of "election belonged only to the clergy." It should be noted, however, that during the Middle Ages the Church was never able to completely eliminate royal influence and even recognized the right of the ruler to consent to episcopal elections.

Who precisely among the clergy were entitled to elect? Gratian cites Canon 28 of the just concluded Second LATERAN COUNCIL that the canons of the cathedral are to chose the bishop, but that they are not to exclude other "religious men" (i.e., monks) from the election. If the election is held without the knowledge and consent of these men, it is invalid. The canons, the leading clergy of the diocese, constitute a corporate group, the cathedral chapter. Since they are considered to represent the clergy of the diocese, the canons must consult with the other clergy and with the local monks. While the chapter does not have to follow their advice, the election would be invalid if they were not called upon for an opinion. A few decades later Pope INNOCENT III in deciding a case noted: "It is recognized that according to canonical statutes the election of bishops regularly "belongs to the clerics of the cathedral churches." Pope GREGORY IX emphasized that if laymen took part with the canons in choosing a bishop

the election would be invalid, contrary customs notwithstanding.

The Fourth Lateran Council (c. 24) definitively confided the election of a bishop to the cathedral chapter and laid down the procedure for episcopal elections, referred to by Pope Gregory IX as the *forma canonica* for all elections. It recognized three forms of election: acclamation, compromise, and scrutiny. Election by acclamation occurred when, without previous deliberation, as if by divine inspiration, all agreed upon a certain individual. Apparently the council had in mind the case of St. Ambrose, who, while still a catechumen, was named by popular acclamation bishop of Milan in 374. Since a single elector could object, election by acclamation was a rare occurrence. Election by compromise was equally infrequent since all the electors had to surrender their rights to arbitrators. The usual method, therefore, was by scrutiny. The canons of the chapter in the presence of all were to select three of their number as tellers. The tellers would then solicit individually and confidentially the opinion of each elector. The results were to be put into writing and announced immediately. Clandestine elections were prohibited. The practice, according to a later source, was for the tellers to record the name of the elector and his choice.

The practice of voting, however, had inherent dangers. If there were not unanimity, thus leading to a double election, how was the matter to be decided? Canon law offered no easy solution. The Fourth Lateran Council decreed: "that person shall be elected upon whom all or the greater and sounder part (*maior et sanior pars*) of the chapter agree." The law did not automatically favor the numerical majority; more than the mere counting of votes was required. The Ordinary Gloss or standard running commentary noted that it was necessary to take zeal into account as well as the merits of the person elected and the quality of the electors. The greater and sounder part is that which is "more just and is supported by greater reason and equity." Pope Gregory IX interpreted the "greater" (*maior*) to mean "the absolute majority." The qualitative criterion, however, invited challenge. The numerical minority could well claim to be the more "discerning part" of the electoral body. Eventually the electoral challenges became so burdensome that the First Council of Lyon in 1245 ruled that those who fail to prove procedural objections must pay the expenses of the other side, while those who fail to prove an objection against the character of the person are suspended from ecclesiastical benefices for three years. The Second Council of Lyon in 1274 finally declared that if, after two ballots, one side has twice the number of votes than the other, the minority loses "all power of impugning lack of zeal, merit or authority to the majority or their candidate."

Papal Appointments. Since a numerical majority did not in principle conclusively settle an election, contested elections had to be referred to the judgment of a superior. The appeal process thus resulted in prolonged vacancies in the episcopal office, much to the detriment of the diocese and the people. It was the habitual failure of cathedral chapters to reach agreement that eventually led to direct papal nomination of bishops. From the late 11th century onward the popes or their delegates often settled a dispute by installing their own choice. In perhaps the most famous instance, Innocent III set aside the candidates of both the Canterbury chapter and King John of England by appointing Stephen Langton, a noted English theologian, at the time a cardinal of the Roman curia, as the archbishop of Canterbury. Langton was later responsible for the Magna Carta.

The expansion of papal involvement must be considered in conjunction with the ancient requirement that an episcopal election must be confirmed. Gratian incorporated in his *Decretum* the ancient texts requiring that the metropolitan or archbishop confirm the election of a bishop. Rufinus and Stephen of Tournai, among the first to comment on Gratian, distinguished between the bishop's sacramental power of orders and his jurisdiction. Jurisdiction came only from the superior's confirmation. By the time of the Fourth Lateran Council papal confirmation of metropolitans was the regular practice (c. 26). Steadily the papacy took from the metropolitan the right of confirming the suffragan bishops. The transfer of bishops from one see to another had long been a papal prerogative. In instances where the preferred candidate for a bishopric lacked one or another legal qualification, the chapters increasingly postulated the pope rather than the metropolitan for a dispensation. A decree of Pope ALEXANDER IV, affirmed by the Second Council of Lyon, classifies episcopal elections as major cases and "asserts that their judicial inquiry subsequent to any appeal falls to the apostolic see" (c. 9). From the settlement of disputed elections to the simple confirmation of all bishops was an almost unnoticed step. The chronicler Matthew of Paris, for example, notes that in 1236 Pope Gregory IX confirmed the election of Walter de Cantelupe after his election to the see of Worcester.

As the 13th century advanced, the papacy moved from a role of confirmation of episcopal elections to one of direct appointment. This move was directly connected to the system of "provisions" whereby Rome nominated individuals for certain ecclesiastical benefices. A letter of INNOCENT II to the archbishop of Compostella in 1137 asking that a benefice be conferred on a certain cleric is the first recorded instance of a provision. The practice of provisions soon amounted to the "reservation" of certain benefices for papal appointees. The AVIGNON Pope JOHN XXII (1316–34) reserved a large number of episcopal sees. URBAN V in 1363 climaxed this movement with a general reservation applicable to all sees. The papacy acted by virtue of its plenary power in introducing reser-

vations, but the system did not develop primarily as a means to enhance that power. Rather, the practice was instituted to protect Church offices and property. Oftentimes the ordinary collators, in order to keep revenues for themselves, did not hurry to fill benefices. Abuses did exist and in numerous instances papal reservation sought to alleviate this evil. The extensive exercise of papal power, however, did in turn invite corruption and resentment, which was a contributing factor to the Protestant Reformation.

Absolutist Monarchy. In the last quarter of the 15th century strong monarchs in Europe, especially in England, France, and Spain, succeeded in establishing law and order, putting down feudal rebellion, class war, banditry, and other forms of violence. They laid the basis for the modern national or territorial state. The absolutist monarchy in consolidating its hold sought to exercise control over the Church as well. In 1480 Pope SIXTUS IV conceded to the archdukes of Austria the privilege of nominating bishops throughout the empire. A few years later INNOCENT IV accorded to Ferdinand the Catholic the same privilege for his kingdom of Aragon, which JULIUS II in 1508 extended to all of Spain and to all the lands of the New World. A CONCORDAT (a treaty between ecclesiastical and civil authorities regulating their relationship in matters of common interest) was signed by Pope LEO X and King Francis I of France in 1516 giving the king the right to nominate almost all the bishops in his domain.

In the last period of the Council of TRENT, summoned to meet the threat of Protestantism, a move was made to restore the election of bishops as practiced in the early Church. It was maintained in the conciliar debate that abuses had crept into the three ways that bishops were then chosen, namely by royal nominations, by capitular elections, and by papal provisions. The arguments for retaining the status quo proved persuasive. The decree enacted on 11 November 1563 was content to stress high standards for the episcopacy and to establish a procedure to verify the fitness of the candidates (c. 1 de ref.)

The council exhorted "all who have any right under any title from the apostolic see in the appointment of prelates" to chose "good shepherds who are fitted to guide the church," but insisted that it was the pope who judged "whether the nominees are shown to be suitable by examination and inquiry." While the direct nomination of bishops by the pope may have been the theory, that prerogative was in fact largely relinquished over the next three or four hundred years. The appointment of bishops became a matter of royal patronage in the Catholic countries of France, Spain, Portugal, Bavaria, Saxony, and Austria. This right extended to the possessions of Spain and Portugal in the New World and in the East Indies.

19th-Century Accommodations. Special arrangements had to be made for Protestant states. The papacy could not allow non-Catholic sovereigns to nominate bishops and, on the other hand, Protestant rulers were unwilling to allow the pope a completely free hand in appointing such a significant public figure. One solution was to revive election by cathedral chapter, which had been recognized in law since the 12th century but not practiced in recent times. In agreements worked out with the Protestant states of Prussia and of the Upper Rhine (1821, 1827), cathedral chapters were authorized to conduct elections after ascertaining beforehand the candidates' acceptability to the government. If the election were canonically valid, the pope would then confirm it. In the United Kingdom, in accord with the Catholic Emancipation Act (1829), it was agreed that the cathedral canons and the pastors of the diocese, in an assembly presided over by the archbishop, were to draw up a list of three candidates (a *terna*) to be sent to Rome. Ten days later the comprovincial bishops would be convoked for their opinions of the candidates, which would also be sent to Rome. In England itself, however, the parish priests do not participate in the election.

Toward the end of the 18th century the Jesuit John Carroll was appointed by Rome to head the American mission. In 1788 Carroll persuaded the Holy See that in keeping with the democratic spirit of the United Sates, priests should be permitted to elect their first bishop. Permission for an election was granted for that one occasion only, and Carroll was almost unanimously chosen. When it came time to name a coadjutor bishop, Carroll conducted a consultation of his clergy in the form of an election. That was the last formal participation of the American clergy in an episcopal appointment until the Third Plenary Council of Baltimore in 1888. That assembly rejected a proposal to establish cathedral chapters, approving instead a body of diocesan consultors, half to be freely appointed by the bishop, the other half selected by him from a list proposed by the clergy. The diocesan consultors and the irremovable rectors of parishes were given the privilege of submitting to Rome a *terna*, a list of three candidates for the episcopacy. This provision remained in effect until a new decree in 1916 eliminated any collective consultation of the clergy. Thenceforth, the metropolitan and comprovincial bishops were to meet every other year to compile of list of priests recommended for the episcopacy which would then be transmitted to Rome.

Curtailing Governmental Influence. During the 19th century, as the Church tried to reclaim a stronger role in the selection of bishops, a number of ways to accommodate state interest and involvement in the process evolved. In place of direct nomination or presentation, governments would often settle for the option of veto. At the beginning of the 20th century the Holy See recognized through concordat or other arrangement some role in the selection of bishops for the governments of France, Austria, Germany, Spain, Portugal, Ecuador, Colombia, Bolivia, and Monaco.

The 1917 Code in canon 3 acknowledged that its provisions did not affect any concordats then in existence. But for the first time in history a canonical text of universal import declared the right of the Roman pontiff to freely nominate all bishops (c. 329 §2) and to establish the criteria for their suitability (c. 330). This declaration marked an innovation in Church law. Theoretically the system of elections had always been the rule. While affirming the exclusive competency of the pope, the code recognized that he could concede to others the privilege of electing, presenting, or designating candidates for the episcopacy (c. 331 §2). Through concordats civil authorities did enjoy the privilege of designation, and about twenty cathedral chapters in Western European dioceses had maintained the long tradition of election.

Whereas the 1917 Code first asserted the appointment of bishops as a papal right and then in a separate paragraph allowed for an election by a collegial group as a possible privilege, the 1983 Code treats both procedures together: "The Supreme Pontiff freely appoints bishops or confirms those legitimately elected" (c. 377 §1). This revision is in harmony with the teaching of the Second Vatican Council that the right of nominating and appointing bishops belongs "exclusively to the competent ecclesiastical authority" (*Decree on Bishops* no. 20). The council was most concerned that in the future no rights or privileges be accorded civil authorities and sought to have any existing rights rescinded. By eliminating governmental intervention and providing for the participation of the local churches in the selection process (c. 377 §2 and 3), the 1983 Code has prepared for a possible return to the practice of earlier centuries, an election by clergy and people.

John E. Lynch

English translations of ecumenical decrees are taken from Tanner, N., ed. *Decrees of the Ecumenical Councils*, London, 1990.

Bibliography

Barraclough, G. "The Making of a Bishop in the Middle Ages: The Part of the Pope in Law and Fact," *Catholic Historical Review* 9 (1933–4).

Benson, R. *The Bishop-Elect: A Study in Medieval Ecclesiastical Office*, Princeton, N.J., 1968.

Gaudemet, J., Dubois, J., Duval, A., and Champagne, J. *Les Elections dans l'Eglise latine des origines au XVIe siecle*, Paris, 1979.

Gaudemet, J. "The Choice of Bishops: A Tortuous History," *Concilium* (1996).

Helmholz, R. *The Spirit of Classical Canon Law*, Athens, Ga., and London, 1996.

Kölmel, W. "Episcopal Elections and Political Manipulation," *Concilium* 77 (1972).

Lynch, J. "Some Landmarks in the Development of Papal Reservations up to 1400 AD," *The Jurist* 30 (1970).

Lynch, J. "Co-Responsibility in the First Five Centuries: Presbyteral Colleges and the Election of Bishops," *The Jurist* 31 (1971)

Metz, R. "Papal Legates and the Appointment of Bishops," *The Jurist* 52 (1992).

Pereda, J. *Official Prenotification and Canon 377 § 5*, Rome, 1996.

Schimmelpfennig, B. "The Principle of the *Sanior Pars* in the Election of Bishops during the Middle Ages," *Concilium* 137 (1980).

Trisco, R. "The Variety of Procedures in Modern History," in *The Choosing of Bishops*, ed. W. Bassett, Hartford, Conn., 1971.

APPROBATIONS, PAPAL. We can distinguish *confirmation*, which is not required by law, from an act or a document already perfect in itself, and the *Mandate of the Apostolic See* (called *aperitio oris* in the former style of the Roman CURIA) given to a lower judge in order for him to judge an act or a document, despite previous pontifical confirmation.

Confirmation by the Roman pontiff brings greater stability to a decision already made. It adds an external quality to it, not required by the nature or essence of the juridical act or the document. This is why we can speak of *confirmatio accidentalis*, as opposed to *confirmatio essentialis*, required for the juridical perfection of a given act, often identified with approval. This terminology was first used by Bartolo de Sassoferrato (*In primam Digestii veteris partem commentaria*, Venice, 1575, *De iustitia et iure*, 1, *Omnes populi*, n. 32 *sq.*).

This confirmatio is *utilis* if the act submitted for it is truly valid; otherwise, it is *inutilis*. The canonists distinguish *confirmatio in forma communi* (DECRETALS of GREGORY IX, XII, 30, 7), also called simple or ordinary confirmation. This approval neither adds nor subtracts from the value of the juridical act or document in question, but gives it a greater guarantee and presumption of legitimacy, even though it may be invalid. This is, therefore, an accidental confirmation, for it supposes the act to be valid and can only corroborate such supposed validity, conferring greater authority upon it, if it is the case. The act in question has only the authority of the congregation that produced it, in the name of the pope of course, but not upon his express mandate. Confirmation in *forma communi* is recognizable in clauses such as "*si iuste, canonice aut provide facto sint*," "*dummodo sacris canonibus non adversantur*," "*prout factum est*," "*sicut iuste et pacifice possidetur*," "*sicut provide datum*," or other formulae without any definitive intention such as

"*facto verbo cum Ss.mo*," "*Ss.mus resolutionem Em.morum PP. approbavit et confirmavit*," "*Ss.mus D.N. Papa NN., audita relatione a R.P.D. Segretario eiusdem S.C. supra relatam Em.morum declarationem ratam habere et confirmare dignatus est*"; The canonists also identify *confirmatio in forma specifica, ex certa scientia*, and *in forma speciali*, allowing, if the act had included the impediments of subreptions or obreptions, correction by the Roman pontifical authority. In any case, certain difficulties, those resulting from a misunderstanding of the requirements of natural law or positive divine law, those for which the pope does not usually offer dispensation, and those that cannot be repaired without prejudice for third parties cannot be so concerned. The confirmation in *forma specifica* makes a confirmed act an act of the supreme authority of the Church, who is then legally its author. A lower judge can do nothing against such an act, given the principle that "the First See cannot be judged by anyone else." (Code of Canon Law of 1983, c. 1404). It is for this reason that the *mandatum* of the Apostolic See or *aperitio oris* is indispensable when a lower judge undertakes a new review of a matter or evaluates a document (c. 1405 §2). Consequently, a decree from a provincial council approved *in forma communi* remains a conciliar decree, whereas if it is approved *in forma specifica*, it becomes one of the Roman pontiff's higher laws.

A confirmation is assumed to be have been given *in forma communi*, unless it has been expressly proven that it has already been given *in forma specifica*. There are formal features that make a confirmation *in forma specifica* recognizable: (a) the complete reproduction of the act in the confirmation document (Honorius III's *Venerabilis* in the *Decretals*, Gregory IX: 2. 30. 8); (b) the introduction of the clause "*ex certa scientia*"; (c) recourse to other equivalent clauses such as "*ex motu proprio*," "*de apostolicae auctoritatis plenitudine*," "*ex plenitudine potestatis*," "*non obstantibus quamcumque lege seu consuetudine contrariis*," "*supplentes omnes iuris et facti defectus*," etc.; (d) other words in the act or document proving that the Roman pontiff had full knowledge of the act. It should also be mentioned that a second confirmation of the same act by the same author is always a specific confirmation (*geminatio rescripti habet vim clausulae "ex certa scientia"*: Abbas Panormitanus, *Commentaria absolutissima in quinque libros Decretalium*, Venice, 1708, "*Commentaia tertiae partis in secundum librum Decretalium*," *De confirmatione utili vel inutili*, chap. VI, n. 5).

Confirmation originated in the *corroboratio* of rights, privileges, dispensations, etc. Rather than a confirmation of general norms, it is linked to the principle of *lex specialis derogat legem generalem* (RJ 34). In fact, during feudal times, confirmations were an act by which a prince prolonged—expressly or presumedly, concessions of rights given by his predecessor. Express confirmation is the source of specific confirmation *ex certa scientia* (Valentin Gomez-Iglesias, "*Naturaleza y origen . . . ,*" 114–15). The confirmation of the Roman pontiff in specific form is useful in that it prevents a lower judge from deciding any matter connected with an act or document covered by a confirmation. Indeed, the Roman pontiff wants to protect an act or document against all attempts to nullify or modify it by placing a given act or document under his protection. This is what is called *appositio manuum* in the doctrine. The *mandatum Apostolicae Sedis* or *facultas aperitionis oris* is necessary for an act or administrative decision, guaranteed by confirmation accorded by the Roman pontiff either by *moto proprio* or at the request of the interested party, to be presented before a judge to denounce it. The lower judge in question can be any judge inferior to the Roman pontiff, even the Roman ROTA, as the ordinary court of the Holy See. Moreover, this norm, which does not constitute a *ius novum*, must be interpreted according to the legislation of the decretals. Finally, there is a confirmation *ex certa scientia* or *in forma specifica*. This can only come from the Roman pontiff, never from the Roman congregations which, in the case of a specific confirmation, would need a special *mandatum* from the Roman pontiff. Confirmation must always follow a legal act. It should not precede it because in order to proceed *ex certa scientia*, all the deliberations or facts determining a sentence must have been completed, etc. (Roman Rota, *coram Parrillo* sentence, 30 January 1923, *Acta Apostolicae Sedis*, 115 [1923], 125).

Every juridic act—including acts and administrative decisions confirmed in specific form by the Roman pontiff—can be judged by a lower judge when he is permitted to do so by the *mandatum Apostolicae Sedis*. This is true for conventions, transactions or pacts, concessions of favors by way of rescripts or otherwise, decrees of ordinary or particular councils, etc.

Pontifical approval required for decisions of the *dicasteries* of the Roman Curia is a true essential confirmation, yet nothing prevents the Roman pontiff from approving a dicastery's decision of this type by an accidental confirmation given *in forma generica* or *in forma specifica*. In this last case, it can allow for a *mandatum Apostolicae Sedis*.

The norms of the Code of CANON LAW of 1917 (c. 1683) allowed for extraordinary recourse to the Roman pontiff. This was allowed either to obtain more stability for acts and administrative documents through confirmation in specific form or, in the case of a controversy about a confirmed act, to obtain the mandate of the Apostolic See enabling lower judges to decide.

Generally, decisions of major importance dealt with by the congregations of the Roman Curia have to be submitted to the sovereign pontiff for approval. The only exceptions are in those cases where there has been attribution of special faculties to the presidents of these dicasteries and the sentences pronounced by the courts of the Roman Rota and the Apostolic Signature within the limits of their competence (John Paul II, Apostolic Constitution, *Pastor bonus*, 28 June 1988, art. 18 section 1).

Therefore, decisions not submitted for specific approval concern those of ordinary administrative acts, since they are handled under the ordinary power of a congregation, and those of major importance for which the Roman pontiff has already granted special faculties. With respect to decisions of major importance, congregations have no ordinary power to determine laws or general decrees obliging the ecclesiastical community, or for making administrative decisions derogating from the universal law in effect. Dicasteries can only be empowered for a particular case of this type and with the specific approval of the Roman pontiff, as stated in CIC/83 c. 30 (PB article 18, section 2). The confirmation of the Roman pontiff is required for the authentic interpretation of universal laws brought by the Pontifical Council for the Interpretation of Legislative Texts (PB art. 155).

An act approved by the pope *in forma specifica* becomes an act of the pontiff. It cannot be attacked before an administrative jurisdiction, for there is no appeal or recourse possible against a sentence or a decree emanating from the Roman pontiff (c. 333 §3). The act of a congregation thus approved by the pope can be qualified as a decree-law (*décret-loi*), or a general decree (or legislative degree) by ratification or specific approval (Antonio Viana, "*La potestad . . . ,*" 102). On the other hand, an act approved *in forma communi* can be contested or appealed.

The new general rules of the Roman Curia, which have been in use since 7 June 1992, require that all major administrative decisions be submitted to the Roman pontiff in writing. (This is what constitutes the new part of the rules, since article 136 of the Apostolic Constitution *Regimini Ecclesiae universae* of 15 August 1967 required all decisions to be submitted for papal approval). The petition must be justified, explained, and documented. The same is true for any special mandate and any extraordinary affair. The pope must have the time necessary for personal reflection and study of the matter at hand. The practice of the *ex audientia Sanctissimi* approval seems to have been abolished when matters were settled during a meeting between the Roman pontiff and the president of a dicastery.

The rules also state that decisions with specific approval of the pope bear the mention *Summus Pontifex in forma specifica approbavit*, thus ensuring the legal value of the acts of the Roman Curia. Papal confirmation is required for deliberations of the ECUMENICAL COUNCIL (c. 341 §1), decisions made in a collegial act (c. 341 §2) during an episcopal college, and the legitimate election of a bishop (c. 377 §1). The Roman pontiff must also approve a universal custom for it to have the power of law (c. 23), decrees of the Ecumenical Council (c. 338 §1), and matters that the conciliary fathers want to handle (c. 338 §2).

As for the Holy See, it must approve the building of an interdiocesan seminary and its statutes (c. 237 §2), the program for priests' training established by the conference of bishops (c. 242 §1), the statutes of an international, public association (c. 314), the holding of plenary councils of all the specific Churches of the same conference of bishops (c. 439 §1), and provincial councils of the ecclesiastical provinces that are in a national territory (c. 439 §2), the election of the president of a plenary council (c. 441 §30), the building of an active institute of life dedicated to pontifical law (c. 589), new forms of consecrated life (c. 605), statutes of the conferences of the major superiors of religious institutes (c. 709), catechisms prepared by the conference of bishops for their territories (c. 775 §2), the constitution of universities and ecclesiastical faculties and their statutes (cc. 816 and 817), the publication of books of the Holy Scriptures (c. 825 §1), the constitution of a national sanctuary and its statutes (cc. 1231 and 1232 §1), the abolishment of holy days or their transfer to a Sunday by the conference of bishops (c. 1246 §2), taxes set by the bishops of an ecclesiastical province for acts of executive power for charitable matters or for the request of rescripts of the Apostolic See (c. 1264 §10), new rulings on previously existing ecclesiastical benefices (c. 1272), and the constitution of interdiocesan tribunals (c. 1423 §1).

The term *recognitio* is utilized in a synonymous way with approval and confirmation. Just like approval and confirmation, *recognitio* is an act of the competent superior to authorize the promulgation of a law issued by an inferior authority.

"This *recognitio* is not only a formality, but an act of the power of governance, absolutely necessary (without it the act of the inferior would have no value) and by which it is possible to impose modifications, even substantive ones, to the law or decree presented for the *recognitio*. Nevertheless, the act (law or decree) does not become an act (law or decree) of the supreme authority, but instead remains an act of the inferior authority that made and promulgated it." (*Communicationes,* 15 [1983], 173).

The term *recognitio* (and its equivalents, *recognitus, recognoscendus, recognoscere*) is used in reference to the Holy See for the revision of statutes of an international, public association (c. 314), decrees of particular councils (c. 446), statutes of the conference of bishops (c. 451), general decrees made by the conference of bishops when prescribed by law or with the authorization of the Apostolic See (c. 455 §2), decrees of the plenary assembly of these conferences (c. 456), translations of liturgical books in vernacular language such as those prepared by the conference of bishops (c. 838 §2 and 838 §3), and the rites of marriage developed by a conference of bishops (c. 1120).

Dominique Le Tourneau

Bibliography

Alarcón, A., and Castillo, E. "Las conferencias episcopales en el nuevo Cédigo de derecho canónico," *Universitas canonica*, 3 (September 1983), 41–61.

Amanieu, A. "Aperitio oris," *DDC*, Paris, 1935, I: 633–640.

Baccari, R. "La terapia dell'atto amministrative nel diritto canonico," *Monitor ecclesiasticus*, 99 (1974), 119–32.

Bouix, D. *Tractatus de papa ubi et de concilio oecumenico*, Paris, 1889.

Choupin, L. "Curie romaine (Congrégations). Saint-Office," *Dictionnaire apologétique de la foi catholique*, Paris, 1911, I: 872–83.

D'Onorio, J. B. *Le Pape et le gouvernement de l'Église*, Paris, 1992.

De Luca, L. "Confirmatio apostolica accidentalis," *Studi economico-giuridici*, 31 (1947–8), Rome, 1948, 1–135; "Lo "ius remonstrandi" contro gli atti legislativi del Pontefice," *Scritti in onore di V. Del Giudice*, Milan, vol. I, 19953, 245–73.

Del Rè, N. *La Curia Romana*, 2nd ed., Rome, 1952.

DiFelice, A. "La "confirmatio pontificis" e la "aperitio oris" come ricorsi ed interventi straordinari circa i provvedimenti ed atti amministrativi," *Monitor ecclesiasticus*, 99 (1974), 223–5.

Fedele, P. "La conferma degli atti giuridici nel diritto canonico," *Studia di storia e diritto in onore di Arrigo Somi*, II, Milan, 1941, 345–65; "Il primato del vicario di Cristo," *Ephemerides iuris canonici*, 45 (1989), 199–265.

Gömez-Iglesias, V. "Naturaleza y origen de la confirmación 'ex certa scientia'," *Ius canonicum*, 25 (1985), 91–16; "La "aprobación específica" en la "Pastor bonus" y la Seguridad cientifica," *Fidelium Iura*, III (1993), 361–424.

González del Valle, J. M. "Los actos pontificios como fuente del derecho canónico," *Ius canonicum*, 16 (1976), 245–92.

Kramer, P. "La conférence épiscopale et le siège apostolique," in *Les Conférences épiscopales. Théologie, statut canonique, avenir*, Paris, 1988, 185–99.

Labandeira, E. *Tratado de derecho administrative canónico*, Pampelona, 1988; "Gli atti giuridici dell'amministrazione ecclesiastica," *Ius Ecclesiae*, II (1990), 225–60.

May, G. "Verschiedene Arten des Partikularrechts," *Archiv für katholisches Kirchenrecht*, 152 (1983), 31–45.

Mörsdorf, L. *Die Rechtssprache des Codex Iuris Canonici. Eine kritische Untersuchung*, Paderborn, 1967.

Oesterle, D. G. "Aperitio oris," *Revista española de derecho canónico*, 10 (1953), 25 *sqq*.

Parlato, V. "La 'conferma' pontificia alle deliberazioni del secondo concilio ecumenico di Nicea," *La norma en el derecho canónico. Actas del III Congreso inter-

nacional de derecho canénico, Pamplona, 10–15 de octubre de 1976, Pamplona, 1979, I, 69–77.

Provost, J. H. "Particular Councils," *Le Nouveau Code de droit canonique*, Ottawa 1984, 1986, 537–61.

Strigl, R. "Päpstliche Reservationen in neuen CIC/83," *Recht im Dienste des Menschen*, Graz, 1986, 561–566.

Urrutia, F. J. "De specifica approbatione Summi Pontifics," *Revista española de derecho canónico*, 47 (1990), 543–61; "Quand onam habeatur approbatio in forma specifica?," *Periodica de re morali, canonica, liturgica*, 80 (1991), 3–17.

Van Hove, A. *De rescriptis*, Rome, 1936; *De privilegiis et dispensationibus*, Rome, 1936; *De privilegiis et dispensationibus*, Rome, 1939.

Viana, A. "La potestad de los dicasterios de la Curia romana," *Ius canonicum*, 30 (1990), 83–114; "El Reglamento general de la Curia romana (4.II. 1992). Aspectos generales y regulación de las aprobaciones pontificias en forma específica," *Ius canonicum*, 32 (1992), 501–29.

Wernz, F. X. *Ius canonicum*, Rome, 1938, I: 223–7.

Wernz, F. X. *Ius decretalium*, 2nd edition, Prati, 1914, 550–5.

ARBITRATION, PAPAL. Conceived of as one of the possible solutions appropriate for resolving a conflict, arbitration, here envisioned on the international scale, obeys established rules agreed to in advance by the litigious parties. The essence of the convention is recourse to a third party (as per public international law) to know and judge a conflict at hand. From the perspective of its legal ramifications, the history of international law, in accordance with the political and diplomatic practices of states, has traditionally posited that the result of this procedure, designated by the name "arbitrale sentence," be endowed with a certain authority. Generally, it was binding upon the instances that had recourse to it but did not, in principle, bind third parties. Likewise, the sentence has a definitive character outside of possible cases of nullity, which are also determined by the initial contractual agreement.

Established in positive law by the Convention at La Haye in 1899, the rules relating to arbitration, its existence, and role are largely rooted, along with the heritage of Roman Law, in the originally theological positions adopted by the Church from the 3rd and 4th centuries regarding contentions of all types involving secular powers and threatening Constantine's empire. Under the influence of St. Ambrose and especially St. Augustine, linking kingdoms viewed as "vast banditries" (*De civitate Dei, I*) to the major issue of the origin of evil, the doctrine of the just war was gradually imposed without challenging the evangelical principle of nonviolence. The success of Augustinianism as a political method, influencing the whole of western public institutions up through the dislocation of the Roman Empire, then the Carolingian Empire, made it a *doctrina christiana*. Various popes and bishops attempted, each according to his means, to use it as a foundation for calming the political chaos submerging in the Christian West between the 5th and 11th centuries. It may seem to be exaggeration, as some authors have written, that the papacy functioned throughout the Middle Ages as "a permanent arbitral tribunal." It is nevertheless true that the Church, with various motives and degrees of success, attempted on the whole to rally consciousness to the ideal of peace. It aimed at ensuring the cohesion of peoples within a deliberately well-structured Christian Church for which it acted as the intermediary between local governments and fragmented authorities. Throughout the long and complex Middle Ages, from Gregory the Great (590–604) to GREGORY VII (1073–85) and BONIFACE VIII (1295–1303), the papacy claimed sovereignty and spiritual supremacy. Formulated essentially according to the theory of the two swords to arbitrate conflicts or attenuate their effects, popes and institutions (such as prescriptions given by the COUNCILS of Puy and Charroux in the years 987–994) tended to protect the noncombatants (God's peace) and limit the hostilities between lords (God's cease-fire). As doctrine, the theological heritage of St. Augustine was largely adapted in Gratian's *Decretum*, written in approximately 1140. This synthesis prefigured that of St. Thomas of Aquinas, which was clearly marked by aspects and concepts of Scholasticism, on the theory of the just war, which was founded on the duty of solidarity with a brother unjustly aggressed. Thus, as of the 14th century, William of Ockham (ca. 1250–ca. 1349) promoted the autonomy of the State with regard to the Church. Ockham was responsible for adding the principle of secularism to Marsilio of Padua's *Defensor pacis* (1324). On the doctrinal and institutional levels, this principle tore away at the "seamless robe" of medieval Christianity, previously united under the authority of the pope and emperor.

The Church had to count on its other political powers, which seemed to have changed in nature. During this same 14th century, the first modern configurations of "international" arbitration appeared in connection with the discovery of new worlds and the territorial conflicts these engendered. CLEMENT VI (1342–52) had the Canary Islands attributed to Spain (1344) before NICHOLAS V (1447–55) had decided to entrust the King of Portugal with the monopoly of the trading posts on the West African coast (1452) and proclaimed Portuguese sovereignty over Guinea in 1454. The *Inter coetera* bull (1493) promulgated by ALEXANDER VI (1492–1503) divided possessions in the Indies between the two powers of the Iberian peninsula. More generally speaking, cultural and political mutations during the Renaissance shook up the balance founded until then on the unity of religion and power. The return to classical philosophy and the advent of secular ideas translated into the moral domain made peace appear as the work of reason.

Humanism led to problems linked to the dignity of life on the grounds of natural rights. Similarly, Luther's theory of the two kingdoms privileged individual freedom over the authority of the Church. Thus, in parallel fashion, the new configuration of the known world and juridical and diplomatic issues arising from its conquest incited Spanish theologians such as Francisco de Vittoria (1486–1546)—in particular in his *De potestate Ecclesiae* (V, 13) and Bartholomé de Las Casas (1474–1566), whose *New Laws for the Indies* procured from Charles V were written in 1542—to affirm the doctrinal bases for papal arbitration. There was, therefore, a power confided to the pontiff who was the judge of conflicts of opposing princes because these were motives for starting wars. Moreover, for Francisco Suarez (1548–1617), the pope had the moral and juridical authority to judge the motivations of all conflicts and render a sentence that has to be applied by the princes under penalty of law. At the same time, the concern for the common good introduced into the debate a respect for civilian populations and the consideration of the imputable consequences of wars of conquest.

In a pluralistic world, the Church once again had to readjust the main hypotheses of its peace-keeping mission (G. Dole), especially in order to respond to the rationalist contentions of international law and world peace movements. Whereas 17th and 18th century theologians developed a complex casuistics, Protestants such as Grotius (1583–1645) and Pufendorf (1632–94) defined a naturalistic conception of the internal community in which the States became the primary actors. In 1648 the treaties of Westphalia sanctioned the liberation of Europe through the disintegration of the holy empire. These treaties led to a system of States with complete equality based on the principle of horizontality, itself based on the notion of freely contracted will and no longer on the principle of a higher enlightened authority (J. B. d'Onorio). They therefore succeeded in dissipating the dream of a community unified by the same faith and left Europe thereafter to the hazards of secular politics.

The 19th century brought renewed energy to international ecclesiastical activities. After the Congress of Vienna and the short-lived restoration of the holy alliance, the international conferences attempted to maintain the peace necessary for the expansion of the Industrial Age. Faced with triumphant nationalism, the Church developed a new conception of its mission in a resolutely secular society. Joseph de Maistre contributed to this by setting the problem of peace in its religious dimension. Soon afterward, Taparelli supported the idea of international arbitration as a necessity. His work no doubt inspired positions taken by popes from Pius IX (1846–78) and his successor Leo XIII (1878–1903), who arbitrated the conflict between Haiti and Santo Domingo, creating the basis for a concerted effort to establish a dialogue between the States. There was a break between the Church, a member nation among nations, and this ecclesiastical institution now without temporal power, for which arbitration was gradually transformed into a form of mediation. Leo XIII's declaration that "the Church has never had a more precious occupation than that of interposing its authority to reestablish agreement and pacify kingdoms" (Consistorial allocution, *Nostris errorem sane maximum*, 11 February 1889). This statement expresses a certain nostalgia for the past as well as the Church's way of avoiding being completely erased from the scene of international politics by relying on a voluntary politics of reconciliation and intervention. The Church thus keeps its real moral authority and remains free of any secularization thanks to its extreme neutrality in all matters of a temporal nature.

Table of the Main Good Works Including Papal Mediations and Arbitrations from 1870–1922.

1870—Pius IX proposes to mediate the conflict between France and Germany to avoid war.

Leo XIII mediates between Germany and Spain in order to resolve their differences regarding the Caroline Islands.

Leo XIII mediates between Great Britain and Portugal regarding the Congo.

1891—Portugal and the Congo agree to seek arbitration by Leo XIII if they are unable to directly settle the border dispute they face.

The pope's mediation in Lima in the conflict opposing Peru and Ecuador.

1893–4—The pope's arbitration in Paris between Spain and France regarding customs duties.

1894—The government of Venezuela asks Leo XIII for his mediation in a conflict opposing it to Great Britain.

1895—Leo XIII adjourns his acceptance to arbitrate the border conflict between Haiti and Santo Domingo.

Leo XIII's mediation to prevent a war between Spain and the United States.

1898–9—Despite the invitation of the Holy See to the first conference at The Hague by Russia, Italy refuses the participation of the pope's representative.

Treaty between Colombia and Peru, the terms of which state that when conflicts between them cannot be resolved through direct negotiations, they will submit to the Holy See's arbitration.

1909–10—Tonti then Bavona preside over the mixed arbitration tribunals responsible for determining the amount due in reparations to the citizens of Brazil, Bolivia, and Peru.

August 1st note to the heads of belligerent states.

Treaty between Haiti and Santo Domingo designating Benedict XV as the arbiter in the still pending border conflict.

François Jankowiak

Bibliography

Blet, P., S. J. *Histoire de la représentation diplomatique du Saint-Siège, des origines à l'aube du XIXe siècle*, Paris, 1982.

Brouillet, A. "La médiation du Saint-Siège dans le différend entre l'Argentine et le Chili sur la zone australe," *Annuaire français de droit international*, Paris, 1979, XXV, 49–76.

D'Onorio J. B., ed. *Le Saint-Siège dans les relations internationales*, Paris, 1989.

Dupuy, A. *La Diplomatie du Saint-Siège*, Paris, 1980.

Lefebvre de Béhaine, E. *Léon XIII et le prince de Bismarck*, Paris, 1898.

See also LEO XIII; HOLY SEE OR APOSTOLIC SEE.

ARCARIUS. See **Curia.**

ARCHAEOLOGY, CHRISTIAN. Rooted in a solid secular tradition, Christian archaeology went through many significant changes in the last 20 years of the 20th century. In addition to its definitive orientations and accomplishments, new research and new discoveries have led to a reconsideration of traditional positions. Sometimes new events have left researchers divided. Often, especially in countries or regions where information is not readily and completely available, studies are published that do not include the latest research, and that, therefore, present distorted information to non-specialized audience. Nevertheless, over the past ten years, local work has become more and more sensitive to innovations in progress. Prominent initiatives, to which we will briefly allude, have already led to concrete and extremely interesting results.

Until the 1970s, Christian archaeology limited its chronological horizon to the period beginning with the first evidence of Christianity (rarely earlier than the 3rd century) and ending with the reign of Pope Gregory the Great (590–604). Today, literary and archaeological sources of later periods, up to and including the Middle Ages, are often part of the themes and research subjects of this discipline.

From its origins in the 15th century, and up until the 19th century, Christian archaeology was essentially Roman and papal. In the beginning its principal objective was the study of the CATACOMBS, some of which remained accessible throughout the Middle Ages. The most important of these were St. Sebastian, St. Lorenzo-outside-the-Walls, St. Valentine, and St. Pancrazio. Others were found during the modern era, especially by Antonio Bosio, who died in 1629. His work, *Roma sotterranea*, was published posthumously in 1632.

After Bosio, Christian archaeology experienced an unfortunate period marked by the systematic devastation of the catacombs in the 17th and 18th centuries by those searching for the bodies of saints. At the time, skeletons were removed without respecting the inscriptions, which were often destroyed when attempts were made to remove the bones. This was particularly a problem when moving tiles with tomb inscriptions from closed tombs along the galleries and in the funerary chambers. Inscriptions were removed and added to the collections in many churches in the city, the original collection of Christian epigraphy in the Lateran museums, and, later, collections at the Vatican Museum. This frenetic search for the bodies of saints was motivated by the desire to gather evidence supporting the supremacy of Roman Catholicism, the only denomination with the "right" to the martyrs of the catacombs. The most celebrated and most active in the search were Marc'Antonio Boldetti (1663–1749) and his assistant and successor, Giovanni Marangoni (1673–1753), each of whom wrote a book on the Roman catacombs.

It was not until the 19th century that Christian archeology was founded as an autonomous science through the research and work of the Jesuit priest Giuseppe Marchi (1795–1860). In 1844 he published a volume entitled *Monumenti delle arti cristiane primitive* [Monuments of Early Christian Art], the first methodological and systematic treatise, although limited to Rome, on all types of Christian monuments (not exclusively the catacombs). However, it was Giuseppe Marchi's disciple, Giovanni Battista De Rossi (1822–94), who expanded and established the bases for the methodology of modern Christian archaeology. De Rossi identified and excavated most of the Roman catacombs known today, thanks to PIUS IX's interest and to the Pontifical Commission on Sacred Archaeology, which has supervised and studied them ever since. Also to his credit are three volumes of *Roma sotterranea cristiana*, the incomplete scientific edition of the catacomb inscriptions (later completed by his successors, A. Silvagni, A. Ferrua, D. Mazzoleni, and C. Carletti). He is also the sole original author of the annual review that has become the indispensable reference for all specialists in Christian archaeology, *Bollettino di archeologia cristiana*, which he wrote from 1864 until his death. G. B. De Rossi did not limit his scope of action to Rome, even if the catacombs and Roman BASILICAS constituted the better part of his activities. His skills were solicited wherever new discoveries were made and he was one of the organizers of the first International Congress on Christian Archaeology, held in Split, Croatia, just after his death. It was De Rossi who, in parallel evolution with classical archaeology, firmly established the various specializations, thus founding the basic methodology for Christian archaeology. In addition to editing the *corpus* of Latin inscriptions, De Rossi undertook the editing of all the Christian inscriptions in Rome, followed by a project to do the same over the years for the rest of Italy and other provinces of the Roman Empire, work that continues to this day. He was less systematic with other archaeological documents, however, and it was one of his disciples, the German Joseph Wilpert, who was first entrusted with writing the first of the *corpora* of the paintings, sarcophagi (excluding the rest of the architectural elements, such as sculpture, for example), and the mosaics of Rome alone (except for the sarcophagi). At the time, the Eastern world and Africa were neglected.

At the beginning of the century in Rome, most of the other successors of G. B. De Rossi were not great innovators. The main one among them, Orazio Marucchi, is recognized in archaeological history more for the quantity than for the quality of the work he produced. After a 30-year absence of work after De Rossi's death, a turning point for Christian archaeology occurred when the Pontifical Institute of Christian Archaeology was founded, thanks to initiative of the German Johannes-Peter Kirsch and the support of Pius XI. Pius XI reorganized and reunited the structures handling papal archaeology by founding the institute and linking its destiny to the Pontifical Commission on Sacred Archaeology and the Roman Pontifical Academy of Archaeology. The Pontifical Institute today is well adapted to the times. Originally a school for training the clergy, it has become an international institute, recognized in numerous countries. Scholars of all nationalities come together to study in the institute's advanced graduate degree program. De Rossi's *bollettino* evolved into the *Nuovo bollettino di archeologia cristiana* and later the *Rivista di archeologia cristiana* after the founding of the pontifical institute. It remains today the only specialized review of this type. Numerous collections are published in addition to the *Rivista* and the Pontifical Institute is the headquarters and main organizing committee for the international congresses of Christian archaeology (twelve held since Split in 1894). The subjects taught at the institute cover all possible areas of contemporary Christian archaeology and give an idea of its different fields of application. Thus, there are courses in epigraphy, architecture, iconography, hagiography, the history of religion, patristics, and also topography of both eastern and western provinces in late antiquity and the early Middle Ages.

As of the end of the 19th century, much research had been undertaken in various regions of the Roman provinces of late antiquity. Although the focus was the western provinces, the eastern areas, especially the Holy Land, received attention through an initiative led by the Dominicans of l'École Biblique and the Franciscans of the *Studium biblicum franciscanum*. In Greece the work of Anastasios K. Orlandos later established the bases for the study of eastern monuments, especially those in areas once under Greek influence. Richard Krautheimer is credited with having developed a remarkable body of work on the whole of Christian architecture. Among the

most spectacular discoveries, are those of French archaeologists in North Africa, in particular, Father Delattre. Many early Christian basilicas were uncovered, along with episcopal complexes and some religious centers of the martyrs of one of the first regions of the empire to embrace Christianity.

It is difficult to create a list of the increasingly numerous researchers concentrating on this period and the schools they have created. The discipline has been reaffirmed in countries such as Italy and Spain, through regularly scheduled national congresses on Christian archaeology. Whereas Christian archaeology has practically no traditional following in Great Britain, German researchers, often in addition to theological studies, undergo highly specialized training, particularly in the areas of art history and architecture.

In France, there has been a profound renaissance in Christian archaeology since the work of Edmond Le Blant at the end of the 19th century. This can be attributed to the work of Henri-Irénée Marrou, more of a historian than an archaeologist, and Charles Pietri, his spiritual heir, also a historian, quite sensitive to archaeology. Paul-Albert Février, Noël Duval, and Pietri have greatly advanced the study of Christian archaeology; all three are former members of the l'École Française de Rome, a school that prides itself on a long tradition in the discipline. At the end of the 19th century, Louis Duchesne, one of the first directors at the French School in Rome, collaborated with G. B. De Rossi in the study of literary sources applied to archaeology. Charles Pietri, a successor of Duchesne at the French School (who died an early death in 1991 at the age of 59 years) participated in the revival of Christian archaeology, and founded seminars for its study. Monthly meetings gathered historians and archaeologists interested in common research themes or recent discoveries, including all areas of late antiquity and the Middle Ages.

It was also under the aegis of the three previously cited French scholars that a new discipline was born—Christian urban topography. This field has been especially active with respect to Gaul. Cities are studied by grouping them together by provinces according to the territorial divisions corresponding to the boundaries of the Roman world of late antiquity. These researchers perfected a rigorous method with strict rules developed through collective investigations. This activity is organized through trimester seminars, which serve as occasions for the publication of monographs. Henri-Irénée Marrou, and other researchers of his generation, are primarily responsible for rejecting the idea that the end of antiquity and the early Middle Ages, along with the Christian archaeology of the period, were reflections of a decadent society. On the contrary, Marrou sees the early beginnings of a rich medieval civilization, and the true roots of the modern and contemporary world. It is through this type of approach that one can begin to better appreciate the character of regional fragmentation, the micro-regional splintering of a once homogeneous world, and the formation of the new nations that were the origins of most of the contemporary states. Again, knowledge of the world of Christian archaeology and the study of sources has proved essential.

After having long ignored the methods of stratigraphic excavation, perfected during the first half of the 20th century, Christian archaeology today utilizes these new methods almost universally. A great debate is in progress between researchers of different educational backgrounds concerning Christian archaeology and its right to exist. Some contend that it is not a separate discipline but rather a part of archaeology of late antiquity or early Middle Ages or medieval archaeology in general. For a long time, the history and archaeology of the period from late antiquity to the beginning of the Middle Ages were dominated by the study of monuments or of other evidence directly linked to the history of Christianity, even when historical events were concerned. Although same argue otherwise, it is difficult to ignore the fact that the history of the western world, from the end of antiquity to the Middle Ages, has been influenced by the Christian world, the cities and rural landscapes dotted with Christian monuments. Much of time and space were christianized, and the evidence of Christian archaeology makes it possible to understand social, economic, and political history, as well as of the daily life of men and women in this historical period. This is especially true with regard to the study of their dwellings, their tombs and objects, and the tools they used. Christian monuments such as cathedrals, monasteries, and sanctuaries that became funerary centers where people were buried, have affected the overall look of the cities and countryside, and we cannot ignore their contributions when studying the heritage of Greco-Roman civilization.

Philippe Pergola

Bibliography

DACL

Deichmann, F. W. *Einführung in die christliche Archäologie*, Darmstadt, 1983.

Février, P. A. "Une archéologie chrétienne pour 1986," vol. I, LXXXV–XCXIX, XIth International Congress of Christian Archaeology,

Krautheimer, R. *Early Christian and Byzantine Architecture*, 4th rev. ed., New Haven, Conn., 1986.

Pergola, P. Annual reports of *Rivista di archeologia cristiana,* since 1985.

Testini, P. *Archeologia cristiana. Nozioni generali dalle origini alla fine del sec. VI.*, Rome, Paris, Tournai, and New York, 1958.

Testini, P. "'L'archeologia cristiana,' quale disciplina oggi?" *Atti del V Congresso nazionale di archeologia cristiana* (Piedmont-Val d'Aoste, 22–29 September 1979), Rome, 1982, 17–35.

ARCHCONFRATERNITIES. See **Roman Confraternities**.

ARCHITECTURE, PAPAL. During the Middle Ages, while monasteries, churches, and cathedrals were being built all over Europe, Rome was in a shambles. The authority of the popes was contested, their lives in perpetual danger. Obliged to leave Rome, their absence lasted a century. It was not until the 16th century, once their authority had been recovered, that they were able to undertake the work necessary to make Rome the spiritual capital of the world where more and more pilgrims would congregate and where they would establish the seat of PAPAL THEOCRACY.

In 1275 GREGORY X decided to retreat to VITERBO, the very city where four years earlier a CONCLAVE lasting 22 months had elected him pope. A small town in upper Latium, Viterbo had the advantage of being close enough to Rome—60 kilometers to its northwest—to be a convenient refuge. A familiar papal residence since Mathilda of Tuscany had bequeathed it at the end of the 11th century, popes continued to fortify it against the emperor who aimed at overtaking it. In the 12th century they built the Cathedral of San Lorenzo on the site of the ancient Etruscan acropolis, and in 1267, a palace contiguous to it. The palace was built as a severe and almost impenetrable stronghold, but included on the floor accessible by an outside stairwell, a vast drawing room appropriate for conclaves, and a connecting loggia richly decorated where the pope would appear on solemn occasions. Lodged close together in outlying houses, the CURIA worked on developing the Church's administration during the thirty-five years the popes were in residence in Viterbo.

In 1305 the conclave of Perugia elected CLEMENT V. Returning to Viterbo was a great risk since the emperor was threatening Latium. Returning to Rome, given the rival factions fighting for control over the city, was equally dangerous. After some traveling in Aquitaine in the southwest of France, Clement V chose to establish the papacy in AVIGNON. Seven popes, all French, resided in Avignon over the next 70 years. An enclave within the county district of Venaissin, property of the popes since 1274, Avignon was attached to the kingdom of Naples. It had the advantage of being close to Vienne where a council was to be held. Approximately equidistant from the borders of the western Christian world at the time, the last bridge on the Rhône River, the commercial backbone of the area, Avignon was located on the route linking Italy and Spain, and near the French kingdom. This facilitated resolving differences between the Holy See and Philip the Fair, and ensuring the mediation the pope wanted to offer in the conflict between France and England.

At the risk of displeasing the Romans, who considered this residency in Avignon as a new "Babylonian captivity," Clement V temporarily lived in the Dominican convent. In 1316 his successor, JOHN XXII, bishop of Avignon, established himself in the episcopal palace where he had lived high up on the rock of the Doms, a natural protection. He concentrated his efforts on reorganizing the Church. An able financier, he built up the treasury required for good management. In 1334 BENEDICT XII, his successor, had a complex built to protect the pope, including all basic services. As of 1339 the ARCHIVES of the Holy See were collected in the old palace. Built by Pierre Poisson on the site of the episcopal palace, it was fashioned in the compact and fortified manner of the Cistercian monasteries, the order to which Benedict XII belonged. Elected in 1342, his successor CLEMENT VI had a very different personality. Also a monk, but a Benedictine of La Chaise-Dieu, former chancellor of the kingdom of France, an able diplomat, he spent money lavishly on the Church. During his pontificate, the court at Avignon became one of the most magnificent in all of Europe. Parties, balls, and tournaments were commonplace. Jean de Loubières built the new palace, the Palais-Neuf, for him. This was a more gracious structure, especially inside where there were frescoes painted by Italian artists. The stifling fiscal system necessary to keep the papal court functioning well made it highly unpopular with the powerful Great Companies in Avignon.

In Rome, on the other hand, things were looking up. The 1350 JUBILEE had been a success bringing profits into the city and calming the warring factions, at least on the surface. Rome asked for the return of the pope. Between the announcement of the return in 1365 by URBAN V and the definitive return of GREGORY XI, the popes remained in Avignon for 12 more years. Forty additional years were necessary for the conclave of Constance to reestablish the unity of the Church around the leadership of MARTIN V alone. Construction began on the spiritual and temporal elements for Rome's glorification, but the situation was discouraging. Genoa, Florence, Venice, and many other rival Italian cities had already built their main structures. In Florence, Brunelleschi was erecting the dome of Santa Maria del Fiore, the superb centerpiece of the city at the height of its prosperity, whereas in Rome, no such structures had been built since the 11th century.

Classical monuments had undergone all kinds of abuse due to the passage of time and to wars. Called in 1257 to end the internal wars, Senator Brancaleone of Bologna had torn down more than 100 monuments transformed into strongholds by rival families. Architects were the only ones to gravitate to Rome in order to study tirelessly the composition and details of ancient architecture. The seven major basilicas, including ST. PETER'S, built in the 4th century by Constantine, were in a ruinous state, Rome, a city once boasting of 19 aqueducts, 1,300 fountains, and 5 baths, became a city lacking water and basic hygiene. At the height of the empire, there were as many as 1 million inhabitants; 100,000 during the revival period of the year 800 with the coronation of Charlemagne; then barely 15,000 at the beginning of the 15th century. The population remained stagnant due to lack of work and security. However, the will of the Church remained firm. Despite the GREAT SCHISM, the break with Protestantism, and the SACK of ROME its impetus remained intact; better still, it was even stimulated by this. During the two centuries of transformations leading Rome to its second apogee, more than forty popes would head the Church. Their uneven reigns were sometimes very brief. Their personalities, preoccupations, and circumstances explain the relative dynamism or slow pace of their enterprise. Nevertheless, Rome's continuity remains manifest.

The first task at hand was the restoration or rebuilding of the old basilicas. They had to be cleaned of dirt and deposits accumulated for centuries. Further, certain elements were changed to conform to efforts being made to standardize and clarify the liturgy. Organizing pilgrimages was also an urgent matter. The pilgrimage to Rome, along with Jerusalem and Compostela, continued to attract crowds. The jubilees were well attended for the indulgences they offered, and resulted in a tenfold increase in the population of Rome. Much attention was given to receiving and housing the pilgrims, and to the organization of ceremonies and festivals for them. "Offices" were set up to better manage the Church's administration and in order to house the papal court, if not in luxury, at least comfortably. Rome was thus transformed into the spiritual and aesthetic capital of service to the faith, the goal also pursued by the Holy See.

For a long time, the Romans refused to be ruled by the pope or the emperor. They attempted to organize as a republic and elect a senate. By calling for the return of the pope and welcoming him with open arms, they had abdicated their independence. Very cleverly relying on the validity of the DONATION OF CONSTANTINE, a document that was reputed to be apocryphal and recognized their temporal power over Rome, the popes progressively came to exercise absolute power. For three centuries, nothing was decided upon and nothing was built in Rome without the consent of the pope or his administration. Much like a prince, he had to decide how to go about undertaking all work essential to daily life for the development and good administration of the city. This included guaranteeing its security, cleaning up the dilapidated neighborhoods, maintaining the roads, and ensuring the distribution of water. In order to realize these projects, which had to be magnificent in scope, outside assistance was required. Rome no longer had enough architects, sculptors, painters, or artisans for this lofty enterprise.

The first and constant concern of the Renaissance popes was to reorganize the administration of the Church and its finances. Upon their return from Avignon, they were unable to move into the LATERAN PALACE, their former residence, due to the fire that damaged it in 1309 along with the Basilica of San Giovanni (St. John the Lateran) next to it. Instead, they decided to retreat across the city to the VATICAN inside the "Leonine City," fortified during the 9th and 12th centuries, and housing since approximately the 4th century, St. Peter's Basilica and a few administrative buildings called the *Borgo nuovo*. This is where the papal administration lived during the difficult times of the Great Schism. The resources procured from the pilgrims flocking to Rome for the 1450 Jubilee prompted NICHOLAS V to reorganize the hill of the Vatican. He entrusted the project of creating an isolated, protected, magnificent city capable of housing all the Curia's services to the Florentine architect and humanist, Leon Battista Alberti. He also gave Bernardo Rossellino, who worked with Alberti, the task of coordinating the construction of a gigantic new basilica according to his wish that it be immense and more marvelous than Santa Maria del Fiore in Florence. However, the death of Nicholas V put an end to the two projects and they were never realized. The administrative talents of JULIUS II and the popes who succeeded him—LEO X, CLEMENT VII, PAUL III—were to allow a definitive impetus for realizing these projects, but in a different form.

On the left bank of the Tiber River, set in a bend in the river facing the CASTEL SANT'ANGELO, Julius II favored the construction of a banking and commercial quarter. On the right bank, he consolidated communications between the Vatican and the Castel Sant'Angelo, a papal stronghold, which served as a possible refuge, a secure treasury, a prison, and a tribunal. The Sant'Angelo bridge ensured the connection to this perfectly efficient and repressive administrative and economic compound. At the same time, Julius II entrusted Bramante with the direction of the St. Peter's project. As it turned out, the design and construction of St. Peter's were to take a century and a half to complete. With the authority of the pope restored, the wealth of the ecclesiastical world converged toward Rome. Loans were also contracted by the Holy See, easily covered by the gold arriving through Spain and Genoa from the Americas. Yet, for Rome to once again become the capital of Christianity, a great many workers and master craftsmen were needed. Artists rediscovered that all roads led to Rome. Florentines, for the most part, trained in the Renaissance arts of the day, knew Rome very well due to their studies of classical models. Engineers, architects, painters, and sculptors, exuding humanist ideas and therefore passionate about science, geometry, and literature, came to re-create a city. They developed specifically Roman styles—"classical," "academic," and then,

"baroque"—which marked the different stages of papal architecture in Rome.

At the outset, they were stone masons and carpenters. Then, in order to direct construction sites, they had to belong to a building corporation whose strict statutes and discipline protected them against competition and their clients from all illicit practices. Brunelleschi, a goldsmith by profession—goldsmiths were often selected for the delicate decorations—ended up in jail for neglecting to follow the rules. Sangallo, who directed the construction of St. Peter's, appears in the accounts as a simple carpenter. He was paid by the day and housed with the servants. A few years later, his status of assistant mastercraftsman evolved. It was not only his talent and authority that were recognized within the *bottega* (the workshop where he had learned his art). As the winner of public competitions to which the masters commissioning the work—either princes or municipalities—often had the public at large participate, his fame was sometimes so great that he was offered extensive power. Michelangelo was overwhelmingly famous. Sure of his talent and knowing that he was indispensable, he dared to challenge the pope. A century later, the Cavalier Bernini, was knighted, and arrived at the Court of Versailles as an ambassador. Sought out by princes who were often rivals, the master builder often became their confidant and the privileged interpreter of their will. Instead of a salary, he received pensions, expenses, and benefits. He left the corporation to set up ACADEMIES with his colleagues. The gap then grew larger and larger between the designer and the builder. The independent architect, as he was known in the 18th and 19th centuries, was born.

The construction and organization of St. Peter's took 165 years. Several of the great architects of the 16th and 17th centuries collaborated on it. Their names mark the different stages in its construction or of its embellishment. In 1450 Nicholas V had entrusted Alberti and Rossellino with developing an overall plan for the Vatican renovation. The old basilica, built on the site where the apostle PETER was crucified, had to be rebuilt. The terrain had sunk, and restorations were impossible. Although it was necessary to house the tomb of the first bishop of Rome and his wooden chair, the *seda sancta*, in a dignified manner, CALLISTUS III and PIUS II, who succeeded Nicholas V, were not interested in these projects and the Alberti-Rossellino plan was gradually forgotten. PAUL II seemed to seek a general solution at one point, but it was SIXTUS IV who revived the politics of large-scale projects in bits and pieces, more according to his inspirations than according to a coherent plan. He had the SISTINE CHAPEL built by Giovanni de' Dolci, between 1473 and 1481 and called upon the best Italian painters under the direction of Sandro Botticelli for its decoration.

When Julius II came to power in 1503, the pace was accelerated. He entrusted the project to Donato Bramante, from Urbino. Primarily a painter, Bramante was also the architect for the San Satiro Church and baptistry and for Santa Maria delle Grazie, both in Milan. Established in Rome since 1499, he was a passionate student of the ancient monuments of the city. He was discovered by the powerful Cardinal della Rovere, the future JULIUS II, who much admired his *tempietto*. Bramante had in fact just built this domed and circular Doric temple surrounded by columns at San Pietro in Montorio. Its modest size and exact proportions displayed the purity and nobility appropriate for the future basilica. It was, in a way, a minuscule model of the dome, the ideal form with which to express the power and influence of the Church. Bramante's project for St. Peter's responded to these intentions. He reworked and developed the idea already exploited in Milan of the church on a central plan as per the Byzantine tradition: a Greek cross with two identical naves intersecting orthogonally. At each end of these naves, there would be an apse; and at their intersection, a dome supported by four enormous pillars. Four secondary naves form something of a square ambulatory around the dome's pillars, and in each of the four corners of this square, at the intersection of the secondary naves, there is a dome. In plan, the envelope of the building is thus a square where each corner is characterized by an octogonal chapel. With no orientation privileged over another, this arrangement perfectly represented the intention of embracing the entire universe. As for the immense dome—Bramante dreamed of "setting the dome of Agippa's Pantheon atop the vaults of the Saint-Maxencius basilica"—was it not the best means of representing the infinite space of the cosmos? The vaults of Gothic cathedrals projected toward heaven, whereas the dome of St. Peter's was heaven itself. Bramante also restructured the *borgo* around St. Peter's, and built galleries bordering the St. Damaso courtyard, linking INNOCENT VIII's pavilion to the Vatican palace. Julius II died in 1513 and Bramante the following year.

The four small domes at the intersection of St. Peter's naves were built, but too hastily and of insufficient proportions. When Raphael (Rafaello) received the commission from LEO X to direct the work at St. Peter's, he was 30 years old and was known throughout Italy as a painter, having decorated, in fresco, the pontifical APARTMENTS. Julius II had commissioned him for the celebrated *stanze* in 1508, upon Bramante's recommendation, and the result was breathtaking. However, Raphael's experience as an architect was limited to the Chigi Chapel, a modestly sized structure with a dome, built according to his plan in 1516. When he died in 1520, he left only one plan for St. Peter's. He had chosen to transform Bramante's Greek cross design into a Latin–cross plan to give more importance to the apses by doubling them with circular side aisles, and reinforcing the pillars.

Under Clement VII's pontificate, Baldassare Peruzzi, the noteworthy architect of the Farnesina Palace built on the Tiber River at the foot of the Janiculum hill for the banker Chigi, was called to direct the work at St. Peter's. He returned to Bramante's Greek–cross design. In 1536, Paul III entrusted the work at St. Peter's to Antonio da Sangallo, the Younger. He was building the Farnese Palace that he had begun 20 years earlier for the same PAUL III, then cardinal Alessandro Farnese. Trained by Bramante in the construction site of Santa Maria de Loreto, he was the logical choice to continue his work at St. Peter's. Nonetheless, the necessity of adapting the plan to accommodate the growing number of pilgrims in Rome prompted him to design the basilica with a Latin cross and a very large and richly decorated dome. The model of his plan is preserved at the Vatican. Under his direction, the four pillars for the dome were reinforced and the foundations for the whole site were consolidated. By the time of his death in 1546, the work site was in proper condition. In 1547, Paul III named Michelangelo chief architect of St. Peter's, whose first task was to finish the Farnese Palace begun by Sangallo, a project fraught with conflicts. The disciples of Sangallo felt that they were the only ones to carry on the spirit of their master and felt that both projects rightfully belonged to his workshop, yet Michelangelo refused and had no interest whatsoever in utilizing Sangallo's designs. The construction constraints were quite enough as it was, and Michelangelo was already 72 years old. Early on he had succeeded in overcoming impossible obstacles, and his reputation as a sculptor and painter was unrivaled. However, as an architect, his only experience was the funerary chapel of the Medicis and their library at San Lorenzo in Florence, both his designs, but neither realized under his supervision. Since 1534 he was established in Rome and in 1536, Paul III entrusted him with the decorating of the wall at the back of the Sistine Chapel, where 20 years earlier he had painted the vaulted ceiling. *The Last Judgment* was favorably received by the group of Catholic reformers in the entourage of his patroness Vittoria Colonna. An influential group at the time, their support was certainly a determining factor in the pope's decision to select Michelangelo for continuing the work at St. Peter's. Michelangelo returned to the Greek–cross design, but simplified it. He did away with Raphael's circular side aisles, which Sangallo had maintained, and likewise dispensed with the apsidol chapels and corner rooms, thus opening up and definitively reemphasizing the apses. He enlarged the dome in height and width and produced many models to establish the dimensions and the principle: a dome on pendentives 42 meters in diameter supporting a structure of 16 double ribs in half-elliptical curves. Set on arches, the pressure exerted by these is contained by a very strong vault. Sixteen windows in the drum of the dome provide light, in addition to which there is an oculus at the very top, protected by a lantern, bringing the height of the entire basilica to 120 meters. This design had the advantage of being very luminous and less expensive to build than those of his predecessors. It was also a more successful design in terms of its monumentality, in keeping with Paul III and the Church's politics of opulence at the time. By substituting the superimposed orders planned for the naves by Bramante with a single colossal order, Michelangelo gained a spectacular presentation for what was lost in terms of the human scale. Those preferring a certain architectural truth would often fault him for this, but since there are no reference points at St. Peter's one has difficulty realizing the true size of the entire structure. The colossal order inaugurated by Michelangelo at St. Peter's was repeated, with a few variations, in the composition of the Capitol which he was designing at the same time. In 1564, at Michelangelo's death, the basilica of St. Peter's was rising from the ground. The pillars were finished, the drum was ready to receive the dome, and the transepts had been completed. There were still the four small domes to be built in the four corners of the secondary naves forming an ambulatory around the dome. Vignola built two of them in 1570. With Vasari, he had built a simple, small, and elegant house based on the ancient Roman style for suburban dwellings; situated in the middle of a large garden, the Villa Giulia served as JULIUS III's summer residence. Vignola would go on to build the main church of the Society of Jesus, the Gesù, in 1568. A basilical plan with a single large nave, it was essentially designed for the liturgy of the word. It was to be the model for numerous churches founded by the Jesuits throughout the world. Thanks to the Vatican's treasury, which had grown considerably, SIXTUS V was able to undertake major urban projects and various embellishments. During his pontificate, between 1585 and 1590, Giacomo della Porta and Domenico Fontana raised the dome on St. Peter's according to Michelangelo's plans, with the minor exception of the curve in the ribbing to give more flight to the exterior aspect. St. Peter's roof was closed and covered. One might have thought that the basilica was complete, despite its façade accommodating rather disparate elements.

It was not until 1605 when PAUL V, who spent much energy modernizing and embellishing Rome, had the Acqua Paola built to complete Sixtus V's network of aqueducts that the façade was renovated. He was keen on giving St. Peter's a façade worthy of the dignity, majesty, and wealth of its interior. As the basilica was sometimes too small to handle the crowds of pilgrims—as demonstrated during the previous jubilee—Paul V asked his architect, Carlo Maderna, to enlarge St. Peter's and complete its façade. The Greek–cross plan was modified with the addition of three bays of the nave toward the east, three bays repeating the identical form and decoration of the interior of Michelangelo's barrel vault. The monumental façade in travertine stone, with its colossal pilasters, is crowned at its center with a balcony above the loge where the pope appears on the day of his election and on solemn occasions. The dome of St. Peter's appears to rest on this 115 meter long, 46 meter high, horizontal structure, which by the play of perspective, deprives the pilgrim coming Rome of discovering the building and the overwhelming effect of the elevation, as Michelangelo had wished.

Michelangelo had intended to isolate the basilica in the center of a vast court surrounded by porticos. However, in the beginning of the 17th century, one arrived at St. Peter's by way of a maze of busy, small streets opening onto a large area where Sixtus V had, in 1586, raised the 25 meter high obelisk from Caligula's circus erected in the 1st century. He had it placed in the axe of the basilica allowing for later renovation and extension work. Around Sixtus V's obelisk, Bernini traced an ellipse of 200 meters by 100 meters connected to a trapezoidal open area, which opened up wider and wider toward the façade of the basilica. Porticos supported by quadruple rows of Doric columns surround the whole. There is a gradual slope in the ellipse's pavement, which is higher at the edges than in the center. This allows for one to take in the entire square and the steps leading up the incline to St. Peter's in a single glance. The colonnade was supposed to be continuous with only two narrow openings allowing carriages coming from Rome to enter; however, the ellipse always remained widely open on the city side. The via della Conciliazione, a brutal block effect of modern urbanism, cuts through it and ruins the surprise effect that Bernini's design had prescribed.

The architecture of the popes in Rome was born in rapid fashion. Transplanted artists and artisans from all over, in particular from Tuscany, came to the popes' courts. Thanks to all the new projects they were offered, they were able to create an original type of architecture making Rome distinctive among Italian cities. There are three basic periods, each with its own spirit, each with its own representative architect as chief of the project at St. Peter's. Each reflects the manner in which the Church exercised its power, at first tolerant and then gradually more insistent, when it came to showing its power, pleasant when it sought extension.

At the beginning of the 16th century, during Bramante's time, the quest for harmony was translated by the exact classical proportions inspired by antiquity and tempered to human scale: the cloister of Santa Maria della Pace, the palace court of the Chancellery, the *tempietto* of San Pietro in Montorio, and the St. Damaso court (four major architectural projects realized by Bramante); Raphael's *Stanze*; the court of the Farnese Palace by Sangallo the Younger, the Farnesina and the Massimo Palace by Baldassare Peruzzi; and Santa Maria del Popolo by Baccio Pontelli perfectly illustrate the clear, true architecture characterizing the first Renaissance in Rome.

In the middle of the 16th century, monumentalism triumphed. The period is marked by the "colossal" genius of Michelangelo, the only one capable of allowing himself such license. The dome and naves of St. Peter's, the robust cornice and loggia of the Farnese Palace, and the arrangement of the piazza of the Capitol attest to the freedom and certainty of his talent. Around him and after him, architecture was often stuck in academic formalism, as exemplified by the Lateran Palace and the Quirinale by Domenico Fontana, as well as San Luigi dei Francesi by Giacomo della Porta. The successes of this period were in the suburban residences such as the Villa Giulia by Vignola, the Villa Medici by Lippi, and the Villa d'Este, famous for its gardens.

In the 17th century, during Bernini's times, movement dominates. Lines began to flow invitingly, to accompany the works. Light is in abundance. The precursor of this movement, Vignola had built (in 1568) the Church of Gesù whose elliptical dome served as a model for the period. The best examples of the Roman baroque, the swan song of architecture in the city of the popes, include Sant' Andrea al Quirinale, the baldachin of the central altar and St. Peter's colonnade, the Triton fountain, works by Bernini that added to his fame; Sant'Agnese in Agone, the Falconieri Palace, San Carlo of the Four Fountains by Borromini, by his rival and sometimes associate; San Martino ai Monti by Peter of Cortona.

Attracted by the large-scale projects of the popes, architects, painters, sculptors, and artisans returned to Rome where the signs of its imperial glory had remained dormant for centuries. They freely interpreted these vestiges without actually copying them. If for the Greek architect, homogeneity of materials was proof of truth—from the foundations to the roof tiles, the Parthenon is marble—and if Gothic architecture balanced the economy of materials with the rigorous and extreme structural equilibrium, the builders during the Renaissance were little concerned with truth or technical prowess. Their method could be summarized as follows: build first; decorate later. For these creators, interior and exterior decorations were independent from the structure and could, therefore, be modified almost at any time one wanted to change the appearance of the façades or interiors according to the means at hand and the current styles.

In brick or rubble stone, the wall was coated or doubled with a secondary wall on which, inside and out, the most diverse types of facing were used. During the construction, the bays were left free, ready to receive lintels, casings, and frames which, independent from the wall, were neither compressed nor dilated. The cylindrical or cloister-arched vaults were generally built without arches. Bricks were first assembled in the desired shape; this light frame, which was plastered or on which rubble

was poured to strengthen the whole surface, worked like a monolith without exerting lateral pressure on the supports. The vaults of the Sistine Chapel, the great vaulted hall of the Farnese Palace (which later received frescoes by the Carracci), were built in this way. The domes, most often on pendentives, were built without arches, using corbelled construction. Only the very large domes, such as St. Peter's, used arches. Without the means to ensure that they stay dry, the coverings, without terraces but with a slightly inclined tiled roof, usually receding a bit and hidden by a balustrade or the edge of a cornice, were invisible from the ground floor.

Inside, the walls were covered with mosaics or inlaid marble designs, decorated in stucco or plaster, and painted in fresco, including the ceilings. The floors were often covered with marble tiles in different colors and arranged in rich designs. In order to bring out these richly colored decorations, light was needed. It came through large windows on the upper floor where the reception rooms were located, not on the ground floor at street level, where the openings were very small and well protected. The brick fields of Latium and the convenient exploitation of the reserves of materials from the ruins of the ancient monuments were sufficient for the fabric of the building. Blocks of stone, sometimes enormous, were taken from the ruins and used especially for the larger structural features, such as foundations, corners, and façades, or recut as steps. Marble arrived from the Carrara quarries by sea, where boats carried it up the Tiber, at the time navigable as far as Rome. (This was true of the Tiber River until 1850 when an accumulation of silt creating rapids made it impossible to navigate.)

Alberti had restored and ennobled the use of columns; Bramante differentiated them according to their character, reserving the very robust Tuscan and Roman Doric for the foundations, and the lighter Ionic order for the upper floors. The architects of the time used orders more for their specific character and their proportions than for the artistic value of their distinctive features. Moreover, Bramante enlivened the orders to underscore the projecting parts of the construction by using ornate columns and moldings throughout to indicate the various floors, thus clearly expressing the great horizontal and vertical divisions of the building. Other examples are the Palace of the Chancellery and the Pigna court of the Vatican. In any case, verticality especially affirmed power, and to express it Michelangelo created a colossal order, first applied in an entirely justified manner in the composition of the relatively cramped Capitol complex. Simple relationships governed all the compositions. Their exactness could be checked in plan, in section, and in elevation, with regulating lines drawn in, which the architects did not, however, need, given how knowledgeable they were of them and how they applied them to their buildings after the fact. They were not afraid to publish their designs in manuals beside the greatest ancient examples, for the instruction of their successors.

Triumphant Catholicism neither detested the ancient classical sites nor respected their archeology. In the 18th century, Winckelmann, "antique dealer for His Holiness," was forced to demand that they be protected. By recovering them, they were purified and "appropriated from paganism." Thus, the fate of the obelisks: Augustus and the Caesars had erected more than 40 of these all over Rome, brought back from Egypt, to mark their triumph. They were abandoned in the Middle Ages. Later, Sixtus V had several of them restored, including the one at St. Peter's. He had it surmounted by a cross and solemnly inaugurated it after having exorcised it, in the name of God, of all pagan contamination. Thus, when architects reused these structures, and brought out the elements of beauty they judged worthy, they had no concerns, as they were working for the glory of God.

The originality of the architecture of the popes in Rome was especially manifest in its conception of space. The free medieval arrangement and juxtaposition of elements according to their function was substituted by a theatrical use of space according to the new laws of perspective and according to their importance and the hierarchy of their symbols, in order to bring out their optimal value. The central plans are expressly designed to achieve this result. Domes lent themselves admirably to the play of perspectives they enclosed in their fluid, uninterrupted continuity. The ellipse was even more appropriate thanks to its greater dynamism and the possibility of exploiting its two centers. The ellipse thus became the favorite form of the baroque period, both for the shape of domes and for the design of public squares. The baroque was also replete with circular or elliptical curves, used even on façades, by such architects as Borromini, who invented wavy walls.

Whereas humanist architects still dreamed of ideal cities with regular shapes where life would harmoniously unfold, and even found princes to finance these projects, Cardinal Felix Peretti, the future Sixtus V, took advantage of his forced retirement from Montalto to reorganize the Church and urban plans for the city of Rome. During his pontificate, which lasted only five years (1585–90), thanks to his financial genius, he was able to find the means with which to undertake the indispensable work necessary for the proper functioning of the city. Aided by his architect, Domenico Fontana, he modernized the urban roadways by piercing the strada Felice from Santa Croce in Gerusalemme to the Piazza di Spagna by way of Santa Maria Maggiore, with the plan to extend it through to Piazza del Popolo. On this four kilometer long backbone, where five horse-drawn carriages could pass through at a time, the usable roads had to be grafted together to link the seven main churches and basilicas. He sketched an obelisk in the center of each *piazza*: St. Peter's Square, Piazza del Popolo, Maggiore, San

Giovanni, and Santa Croce all owe their obelisks to him. Likewise, he had Trajan's Column uncovered. In 18 months, Rome was being provided with enough water, tapped from the Palestrina sources and channeled by aqueduct above and below ground, over 20 kilometers. The *acqua felice*, or "happy water," as it was baptized, soon flowed into 27 fountains he had had spread about the city. Thus, water was at the same time distributed to public baths and to the wool workers.

Robert-Jean Vinson

Bibliography

Burckhardt, J. *The Civilization of the Renaissance in Italy*, New York, 1958.

Choisy, A. *Histoire de l'architecture*, Paris, 1899.

Christophe, P. *L'Eglise dans l'histoire des hommes*, 1983.

Gromort, G. *Histoire abrégée de la Renaissance en Italie*, Paris, 1913.

Insolera, I. *Le Città nella storia d'Italia, Rome*, 1980.

Labande, L. H. *Le Palais des Papes et les monuments d'Avignon au XIVe siècle*, Marseilles, 1925.

Letarouilly, P. *Le Vatican et la basilique Saint-Pierre*, Paris, 1882.

ARMIES, PAPAL. The presence of military forces directly in the service of and available to the popes is inextricably linked to the existence of the PAPAL STATES as they gradually developed over the centuries during the Middles Ages.

Even after the Edict of Milan in 313 and throughout the middle of the 4th century, although popes owned very large proprietary domains, it was not up to them to ensure the defense of their properties. Emperor Justinian's pragmatic sanction of 554 expanded the popes' temporal jurisdiction which allowed them to exercise greater control over their patrimony. PELAGIUS I (556–61) is considered to have played an important role in organizing this change. A letter from St. Gregory the Great addressed to Empress Constanza on 1 June 595 mentions, among the expenses he was to manage (with little choice in the matter), payment for troops along with provisions for the population and tributes to be paid to the Lombard invaders. It would nevertheless be erroneous to consider these troops as constituting the first form of a pontifical army since they depended on the Byzantine emperor and formed, according to the expression used at the time, an *exercitus romanus*. In 638, upon the death of HONORIUS I, even before the succession of SEVERINUS (640), the charter custodian (*chartularius*) Maurice, who represented the emperor, confiscated part of the papal treasury, under the pretext that the money was owed to the army.

Both in 730 and again in 739 Liutprand, king of the LOMBARDS, attempted to capture Rome. St. GREGORY II

(715–31) and St. GREGORY III (731–41) managed to prevent him from doing so, more thanks to negotiations than to the force of arms. In any case, the walls of Rome were rebuilt, given the circumstances, which implies that they were also defended. The powerful Byzantine protectorate collapsed, and the pope was still unable to defend himself and his people against the Lombard threat with his own forces alone. Therefore, during STEPHEN II's pontificate (752–57), an appeal was made to Pepin the short (king of the Franks), who then received the title Patrician of the Romans. Consecutively, Pepin granted to the pope two supposedly Byzantine territories: the exarchat of RAVENNA and the duchy of Rome. On this occasion, the king of the FRANKS obliged numerous cities to turn over their keys, which he then deposited in St. Peter's. In 773, HADRIAN I defended the city of Rome threatened by Didier, king of the Lombards. Troops were raised for this purpose in the Roman countryside. A short time after Charlemagne confirmed the donation of Pepin in 774, papal troops were at war against the rebels of Campagna.

According to the new order, popes should not have had to worry about military problems: the Carolingian sovereigns had, in theory, succeeded the Byzantine emperors as their appointed protectors. Circumstances decided otherwise. During the reign of SERGIUS II (844–7), in August 846, a flotilla of SARACENS with, reportedly, 73 boats and more than 10,000 men, appeared at the mouth of the Tiber River. Ostia and Porto were occupied. The castle of Gregoriopolis was quickly abandoned by its defenders. The Saxons' *scholae*, Frisons and Franks, were beaten in the countryside. ST. PETER's and St. PAUL's, both located outside the walls of the city, were devastated while Romans retreated behind the Aurelian wall perimeter. *In extremis*, Louis II, king of Italy, son of the Emperor Lothair, saved the day. But it was a narrow escape, and the new pope, LEO IV (847–55), actively took up the defense of the Church's patrimony. The renovation of the Aurelian wall included the construction or reconstruction of 15 towers. In six years, the "Leonine city" was built, in part thanks to the financial contribution made by Christians all over the world. A warrior pope as much as a builder, Leo IV leagued the flotillas of Naples, Gaeta, and Amalfi against the Saracens, who suffered a serious naval defeat in 849: survivors of the battle were obliged to work on fortifications. The military role of the popes was also highly visible during the period of JOHN VIII (872–82), as evidenced by the veritable victory message he sent to Emperor Louis II upon his return from a military campaign he led against the infidels. Likewise for JOHN X who, in August 916, drove the Agareni from their stronghold in Garigliano. During the battle, John X himself was seen charging against the enemy on several occasions.

Constantly endangered and under attack, the popes main concern then became military problems in a context that can already be qualified as feudal. It was written about BENEDICT VIII (1012–24), former count of Tuscu-

lum, that "helmut on his head, hauberk on his back, he policed his States himself" (Emile Amann). Norman mercenaries were in his service. On at least one occasion, Emperor Henry II asked him for troops. It was he who led the military effort against a new Saracen invasion in 1016. Among the booty obtained after victory, the pope kept the diadem decorated with precious stones that had belonged to the emir Abu Hussein Mogehid. St. LEO IX (1048–54) advocated what can be called a holy war against the Normans in the south of Italy—the new Agarens. On 18 June 1053, leading the German and Italian contingents, he fought a them, was beaten, and taken prisoner. For two days afterward, he remained on the battlefield to pray for the dead, ordering the construction of a monument in memory of the victims who, having fought for the Church, could be considered martyrs. Recognized and supported by Henry III, the bishop of Parma, Cadalus (ANTIPOPE CLEMENT III), arrived near Rome and defeated Alexander II's troops on the campus Leonis on 14 April 1062. GREGORY VII's reign also had a significant military dimension. When threatened by Henry IV, he took refuge in the CASTEL SANT'ANGELO, the most secure of the Roman fortresses until Robert Guiscard arrived with reinforcements.

PASCHAL II (1099–1118) had a conflict with Henry V during the quarrel over INVESTITURES. He had his own militia and on occasion also called upon Norman troops for his defense. Between 1120 and 1121 his successor, CALLISTUS II felt strong enough to expel antipope GREGORY VIII from the Roman campaign, thanks to the backing of an army led by Cardinal Jean de Crème.

The presence of armed forces at the pope's side was evident, for example, in 1124, on the occasion of the election of HONORIUS II. At first the cardinals assembled at the LATERAN had elected one of their own, Theobald, using the name CELESTINE II. However, the Frangipiani faction refused this choice. While the *Te Deum* was being sung in honor of Celestine II, Robert Frangipiani, chief of the papal guard, charged in with his men. Celestine II was expulsed and replaced by Lambert, bishop of Ostia, who then became Honorius II. He and HADRIAN IV (1154–9) after him, both had troops. These were in use, for example, during the episode concerning Arnold of Brescia. Hadrian IV made a concerted effort to reorganize the Church's PATRIMONY. Barons had to turn over their usurpations, which were then returned to them as fiefs. Once vassals of the Roman Church, they pledged homage and fidelity to the pope, swearing to fight according to his orders for the unique defense of the Apostle and to obey the Truce of God (respect for churches, hospitals, clerics, monks, and merchants). In theory, then, the pope's army thus acquired statutory feudal character.

On 14 July 1167 Frederick Barbarossa attacked the Castel Sant'Angelo where ALEXANDER III and his entire "family" or "mesnie" (*masnada*) were taking refuge.

During the resulting vicissitudes, not only did Alexander III dispose of castles and fortresses (the Coliseum, Segni, Anagni, Ferentino, etc.), which in itself implied the existence of several garrisons, but became the soul of the Lombard League. Manor lords, marshals, and other dignitaries of castle life were all mentioned as having been part of his entourage. The popes counted more on strong fortifications than on men to protect themselves from the worst, thus the importance of the agreement concluded between the commune of Rome and Clement III in 1188. Papal participation in the maintenance of the city walls was specified at the same time as the military obligations of the Romans were recalled. With INNOCENT III (1198–1216), the ambitions and temporal preoccupations of the papacy were accentuated. GREGORY IX (1227–41) and Frederick II were in conflict for a long time. For the first time, the pope handled the financing of his troops by levying a subsidy on all Christians. As of the middle of the 13th century, documentation concerning the pope's armies increased significantly. The armies were basically the result of a more or less direct contribution from the urban communities and the state barons of the Holy See. In 1287, for example, the rector of the Ancona *march*, asked Macerata for 10 horsemen, each with two horses, 500 foot soldiers, 25 carefully selected crossbowmen, and 100 *guastatores* who specialized in the devastation of enemy territory. This army was to be in Fano in five days to serve for ten days (only!) against Pesaro, a city in revolt. In addition, many mercenaries were recruited either locally, from other parts of Italy, or from foreign lands. All of these expenditures amounted to a great deal of money.

On 7 October 1243, INNOCENT IV sent Cardinal Rainier 2,500 ounces of gold (Roman weight) intended for the monthly salaries of 500 *milites* and 1,000 *pedites* hired to defend Viterbo. URBAN IV (1261–64) was supposed to have spent as much as 200,000 pounds on his wars. Contemporary sources indicate that BONIFACE VIII (1294–1303) spent anywhere from 600,000 or 1 million florins in his conflict against the Colonna. All this explains the a fiscal system established inside and outside the Church States even before luxury spending.

The papacy of AVIGNON did not innovate anything in this area. It simply intensified the existing phenomenon during a time when war was spreading like wildfire all over Europe. CLEMENT V led the War of Ferrara (1308–13) against Venice. Under the unbeatable and ambitious JOHN XXII, Cardinal Bertand du Pouget fought intensively in Lombardy. The papal armies were dispatched on many occasions, especially between 1320 and 1323. The combined total military expenses of the Papal States reached 3 million florins, or two-thirds of the Church's revenues. After the more pacific interval of BENEDICT XII's pontificate (1334–42), when only 6 percent of expenditures went for military purposes,

CLEMENT VI (1342–52) returned to John XXII's politics. In the same way and according to the same stipulations as other powers, he engaged *condottieri*, who were very expensive, despite their dubious efficacy and fidelity. Thus, by 1350, the German, Werner von Urslingen had 200 cavalrymen and 400 infantrymen.

INNOCENT VI (1352–62) further developed this practice. His plan was to reestablish papal authority in the *Patrimonium Crucifixi*. This was an overwhelming task entrusted to an aggressive prelate of Castilian origin, Cardinal Gil Albornoz. People at the time facetiously referred to him as the Angel of Peace. Among the many military leaders employed, were Rodolfo da Camerino and Galeotto Malatesta—this latter promoted, for a time to *gonfalonier* of the Church. Mercenaries from many different places appeared by the hundreds and thousands in the papal accounting. Perhaps as much as half the resources of Innocent VI were absorbed by the war. It is true that at the beginning of his pontificate, circumstances were such that he immediately faced having to make great expenditures to defend Avignon and his palace-fortress ("the citadel of an Asian tyrant, more than the residence of the vicar of the God of peace," wrote Prosper Mérimée).

URBAN V (1362–70) and GREGORY XI (1370–78) followed the same path. In 1373, for example, troops of "Briganti" (*briganti*) of varied geographical origin were responsible for defending Avignon. Support came from numerous dioceses of southern France, northern Italy, and Aragon. The following year, Gregory XI named captain general Juan Ferdinand de Heredia as manor lord of Emposte with full powers for visiting the towns, castles, and fortresses in the Comtat. In Italy the popes waged war in Milan as well as in Florence. Another crucial Italian campaign led to the submission of Bologna. On several occasions, the famous English *condottiere* John Hawkwood (Giovanni Acuto) fought for the Church. Moreover, the papal legate, Cardinal Robert of Geneva (the future antipope CLEMENT VII), bought the services of mercenaries from Brittany and Gascony. Among the first of these were Sylvester Budes and Jean, lord of Malestroit followed by Bernardon de la Sale and others. Thus, in 1376, the Bretons were recruited at a pay rate of 18 florins per lance and per month. They left the region of Avignon, which they were threatening, crossed the Alps, and attempted to retake Bologna. At one point, a struggle between the butchers of Cesena and the Bretons led to many deaths: "*Moriantur Britones, moriantur pastores Ecclesie.*" The survivors took refuge in the Castle of Cesena. With John Hawkwood's support, they went out on a counterattack and massacred the civil population with a savagery that raised general indignation in Italy. "*Sangue e sangue,*" said the Cardinal of Geneva in encouragement while the Bretons exclaimed: "Go, go, kill, kill!" (1 February 1377).

At the time of the GREAT SCHISM, the popes of Rome, according to their means, recruited soldiers. Thus, under URBAN VI (1378–89), the Englishman John Beltoft was rector of the duchy of Spoleto. Later, his successor BONIFACE IX (1389–1404) hired *condottieri* such as Paolo Orsini, Braccio da Montone, and Ludovico Migliorati. The same phenomenon occurred with Clement VII (1378–94) and BENEDICT XIII (as of 1394), but with mercenaries of mainly French origin, in the wide sense of that term. We know how, with very weak forces, Pedro de Luna resisted in the palace of the Doms for several years at the end of the 14th century and later in his citadel of Peñiscola. As for JOHN XXIII, he was himself a military man (even, it was said, something of a pirate) before his election in 1410. We are, therefore, not surprised to learn that, in the night of 20 and 21 March 1415, he escaped Constance disguised as a crossbowman, behavior unusual for a pope.

The pontiff of the reestablished unity, MARTIN V, Colonna (1417–31), was intent on reestablishing sovereignty in his States. He mainly led two wars: one in the kingdom of Naples in 1421 and 1422 and the other against Bologna in 1428 and 1429. In the first case there were 3,500 horsemen and 400 foot soldiers, totaling expenditure of 170,000 florins annually. In the second case there were 3,000 horsemen and 1,100 foot soldiers, costing 160,000 florins. In his use of *condottieri*, Martin V was much more firm than his predecessors, significantly reducing their margin of independence. Thanks in part to his army, Braccio da Montone, one of the most prestigious warlords, was defeated in June 1424. EUGENE IV (1431–47) employed famous captains such as Niccolò Fortebraccio, Guidantonio di Montefeltro, Giovanni Vitteleschi, and Francesco Sforza. In 1435 Vitteleschi's army boasted 481 lances (or 1,555 horses) and 1,152 foot soldiers.

The popes during the 2nd half of the 15th century acted more and more like territorial princes within the peninsula. Their armies ranked honorably behind those of Milan and Venice. NICHOLAS V (1447–55) sought, perhaps in imitation of Charles VII, to create a permanent army. PAUL II (1464–71) lent forces to Frederick of Urbino. SIXTUS IV (1471–84) reestablished order in his States thanks to the military talents of cardinals Pietro Riario and Giuliano della Rovere, then led the war of Tuscany (1479–80) and the war of Ferrara (1482–4). Here again we can quote specific numbers: military expenses accounted for 40 percent of annual revenues amounting to approximately 240,000 ducats. As for INNOCENT VIII (1484–92), even the weakness of his government did not prevent him from hiring *condottieri* such as Robert Sanseverino.

Although war was a standard practice of papal government, as opposed to many powerful secular leaders, not a single pope died in battle. The Church at the time had many cardinal war chiefs on the battlefield, but it appears their role was more to give orders than to fight, since the actual shedding of blood by a man of the Church was frowned upon. The papacy was never a great military power, and its objective, even if misunderstood by contemporaries, was generally of a defensive nature. Due to the evolution of political structures and social realities, the papacy was not able to only appeal to the inhabitants of its States. This is where, especially at the end of the Middle Ages, the use of mercenaries came into play, with all the financial, political, and human toll such a recruitment incurred.

The papacy's repeated recourse to temporal arms throughout its long medieval history made it the object of a significant number of critical reactions. In the middle of the Gregorian Reform a council met in Rome in May 1082 to condemn the use of Church wealth for the financing of troops. For the assembled prelates, Church wealth was supposed to be exclusively used for helping the poor, for ensuring the celebration of divine service, and for ransoming prisoners. The same opinion was held by St. Pierre Damian and Bruno de Segni. St. Bernard in *De consideratione* criticized the pope for using the sword against the commune of Rome and for living surrounded by military men. Afterward, criticism became more rare, but did appear occasionally at the beginning of the 15th century, during the council of Constance. In fact, another system could certainly have been envisaged which would have meant entrusting the pope's security to a secular protector: a Byzantine emperor, a western emperor, a feudal lord of Latium, even the commune of Rome. This is what Pierre Dubois proposed at the end of the 13th century, but this time in favor of the king of France. Nevertheless, the popes, due to the historical evolution as well as the development of a certain political theology, categorically refused such arrangements, which would have put their independence in jeopardy. No doubt, there were pontiffs, such as GREGORY VIII (1187) who decided from the beginning of their reigns not to have recourse to arms. Yet even these men of peace did not go so far as to legally condemn recourse to arms on the part of the Church. Moreover, theologians and canonists, reflecting on the concept of just war at the time, came to feel that only a "Roman" war could be fully considered a just war, in other words, one led by and for the Church (John de Legnano, jurist in Bologna of the 14th century).

One must consider that papal armies were not only those that, for better or worse, defended the integrity of the PATRIMONY OF SAINT PETER. They were also the armies that in the name of the Church and the pope, participated in the successive CRUSADES. As early as 1066, ALEXANDER II had supported the expedition led against Harold, king of England, by William, duke of Normandy by sending him a gonfalon and a hair from the apostle Peter's head. Likewise, he encouraged—in particular, by sending blessed gonfalons—the Normans' war against the Saracens in Sicily and the French against the Saracens of Spain. The "faithful of Saint Peter," the "knights of Christ," and the Church appeared at this time. When Urban II launched his appeal for the crusade at the council of Clermont in 1095, this tendency was evidently extended. Very explicit in this respect is his letter to the Flemish in which he explained that the expedition was to leave from Puy 15 August 1096 and that it would reunite all the Christian knights with the legate Adhemar de Monteil as its chief. It is, therefore, no exaggeration to consider all the later crusades directed against the infidels, heretics, temporal powers (the emperor, the king of Aragon, the king of Sicily, etc.) as uniting the papal armies, in the broad sense of the term. It was the Holy See that legitimized them, gave them their status in the temporal and spiritual order, and foresaw the financing (decime), as well as placed them in the care of its legates. From the victory in Nicaea on 16 May 1097 to the defeat of the papal zouaves in Lamoricière at Castelfidardo on 18 September 1860, by way of the galleys entrusted to Jacques Coeur, by CALLISTUS III for use against the Ottoman Turks, the approach remained coherent.

Philippe Contamine

Bibliography

Da Mostro, A. "Ordinamenti militari delle soldatesche dello Stato Romano dal 1430 al 1470," *QFIAB*, 5 (1903), 19–34.

Partner, P. *The Papal State under Martin V. The Administration and Government of the Temporal Power in the Early Fifteenth Century*, London, 1958; *The Lands of St. Peter. The Papal State in the Middle Ages and the Early Renaissance*, London, 1972.

Storia d'Italia, edited by G. Galasso, VII, Turin, 1987 ("Le origini del Patrimonio di S. Pietro," by G. Arnaldi; "Il Patrimonio di S. Pietro fino alla metà del secolo XI," by P. Toubert; "Lo Stato papale dal periodo feudale a Martino V," by D. Waley), and XIV, 1978 ("Lo Stato pontificio da Martino V a Gregorio XIII," by M. Caravale).

See also NAVY, PAPAL.

ARMS, PAPAL. Armorial bearings or coats of arms are colored emblems whose compositions conform to the specific rules of heraldry. Popes only began displaying coats of arms during the second half of the 13th century. Before that time they had borne their personal or familial coats of arms, but not specific papal arms.

Heraldry is a system of symbols that originated and developed independently of the influence of the Church. The Church, suspicious at first, finally became involved with this system, although approximately a century went by between the appearance of the first knightly coats of arms on battlefields and in tournaments, and the appearance of those first used by bishops on official seals. It was the use of the seal throughout the 13th century that gradually extended the use of coats of arms by the clergy. By the middle of the 14th century, the familial shield began to be accompanied by two symbols indicating the pontifical dignity: the KEYS and the TIARA.

BONIFACE VIII was the first pope whose coat of arms is known to us, thanks to a document contemporary to his reign. His armorial bearings are represented twice in the cathedral of Anagni on inlaid mosaic marble. It was not until the reign of JOHN XXII (1316–34) that the papal arms crowned with the tiara were seen for the first time in the cathedral of Avignon. Under CLEMENT VI (1342–52), the definitive tripartite structure of the papal coat of arms was introduced: a shield with the arms of the pope's family, with two crossed keys (joined by a cord) and the tiara above the whole composition. The tiara became a three-tiered crown during the reign of John XXII; one of the keys is Or (*gold, yellow*) and the other Argent (*silver, white*); the cord connecting them is Gules (*red*). This simple composition was not altered until the 20th century, although during the Renaissance and baroque periods, superfluous decorative elements were often added. During the modern period, some pontiffs who had belonged to a religious order before ascending to the chair of St. Peter made use of armorial bearings that included their order's arms and those of their family (BENEDICT XIII, CLEMENT XIV, PIUS VII, GREGORY XVI). During the contemporary period, the four popes who had no familial arms used those adopted or received when they became prelates.

Although Boniface VIII is the first pope with an identifiable coat of arms, this does not mean that his immediate predecessors did not make use of heraldry. URBAN IV, NICHOLAS III, HONORIUS IV, and NICHOLAS IV probably used arms, but their coats of arms are only seen on documents subsequent to their pontificates. It is less likely that arms were used by the other sovereign pontiffs of the 13th century, (especially those who reigned before Urban IV). There is no evidence that the popes who preceded INNOCENT II used coats of arms.

During the 15th century, collections of papal coats of arms were compiled, at first in the form of simple blazoned lists, then in the form of illuminated rolls of arms that are full of errors and contradictions. Some of these accountings attempted to attribute coats of arms to all the popes since St. Peter! This imaginary papal heraldry became commonplace during the 17th century and led to the publication of several printed repertories which, despite their errors, are very interesting for the historian. In studying the meaning of the symbols and colors of the coats of arms, these repertories are helpful for comparing what we know or believe we know about the popes who lived during pre-heraldic times and the symbols and colors incorrectly attributed to them during the 15th through 17th centuries. This is a very difficult, if not practically impossible, exercise for authentic coats of arms, whoever their possessor.

Given the present state of our knowledge, the following are descriptions of the coats of arms of the popes, as supported by authentic documents and rigorous historical research. As of the pontificate of PIUS II (1458–64), clearly written and illustrated evidence is available and the information furnished is incontestable.

Urban IV (1261–64): Quarterly I and IV, Azure (*blue*) a fleur-de-lis Or (*gold, yellow*); II and III, Argent (*silver, white*) a rose Gules (*red*). (No contemporary evidence.)

Clement IV (1264–68): Argent an eagle Gules holding a dragon Vert (*green*). (Mythic coat of arms attributed to this pope between 1330–40.)

Gregory X (1271–76): Azure a chief embattled Or. (No contemporary evidence.)

Innocent V (1276): Argent a pile throughout issuant in base Sable (*black*). (Arms of the Dominican order that this pope perhaps adopted; no contemporary evidence.)

Hadrian V (1276): Bendy Azure and Argent. (No contemporary evidence.)

John XXI (1276–77): Quarterly I and IV, Argent three crescents Gules; II and III, Sable two pales Or. (No contemporary evidence.)

Nicholas III (1277–80): Bendy Gules and Argent, on a chief Argent a rose Gules seeded Or. (No contemporary evidence but this pope's coat of arms was displayed at the beginning of the 14th century.)

Martin IV (1281–85): Argent a bend vairy Or and Gules. (No contemporary evidence; these are the arms of the Brion family, from Champagne. They were later attributed to this pope.)

Honorius IV (1285–87): Bendy Or and Gules, on a chief Argent a rose Gules surmounted by a bird between two lions affrontés all Gules. (No contemporary evidence.)

Nicholas IV (1288–92): No known coat of arms; as of the 15th century, tradition attributed to him a shield Argent a bend Azure between two mullets Azure, on a chief Azure three fleurs-de-lis Or.

Celestine V (1294): No known arms; a late tradition attributes to him a shield Or a lion Azure debruised by a bend Gules.

Boniface VIII (1294–1303): Or two bends undy Azure.

Benedict XI (1303–04): Per pale Argent and Sable. (No contemporary evidence.)

Clement V (1305–14): Or three fess Gules.

John XXII (1316–34): Quarterly I and IV, Argent a lion Azure between an orle of torteaux (*red roundels*); II and III, Gules two fess Or. (No contemporary evidence.)

Benedict XII (1334–42): Argent a bordure Gules. (No contemporary evidence for colors.)

Clement VI (1342–52): Argent a bend Azure between six roses Gules seeded Or in orle.

Innocent VI (1352–62): Gules a lion Argent debruised by a baton couped Azure, on a chief Gules supported by a barrulet Azure three scallops Argent.

Urban V (1362–70): Gules a chief indented Or.

Gregory IX (1370–78): Argent a bend Azure between six roses Gules seeded Or in orle.

Urban VI (1378–89): Or an eagle displayed Azure.

Clement VII, antipope (1378–94): Or a cross counterpierced Azure.

Boniface XI (1389–1404): Gules a bend checky Argent and Azure.

Benedict XIII (1394–1417): Per fess Gules and Argent a crescent reversed Argent in chief.

Innocent VII (1404–06): Or on a bend cotised Azure a comet Vert.

Gregory XII (1406–15): Per fess Argent and Azure a lozenge throughout counterchanged.

Alexander V (1409–10): Azure a sun in splendor Or between eight six-pointed mullets Or.

John XXIII, antipope (1410–29): Per fess Gules and Vert, in chief a leg Argent, in base three bends Argent, overall a bordure indented Or and Azure.

Clement VIII, antipope (1417–29): Quarterly I and IV, Gules a cross flory Or pierced of the field; II and III plain Or.

Martin V (1417–31): Gules a column Argent ducally crowned Or.

Eugene IV (1431–47): Azure a bend Argent.

Felix V, antipope, (1439–49): Gules a cross Argent.

Nicholas V (1447–55): Gules two keys in Saltire Argent (or Or). (Out of humility, Nicholas V did not use his familial arms, Parentucelli de Sarzana, Argent two bends undy Gules, but made use of the mythic arms of Saint Peter.)

Calistus III (1455–58): Or a bull Gules grazing on a mound Vert, on a bordure Or eight tufts of grass Vert.

Pius II (1458–64): Argent on a cross Azure five crescents Or.

Paul II (1464–71): Azure a lion Argent debruised by a bend Or.

Sixtus IV (1471–84): Azure an oak tree eradicated Or its branches in saltire.

Innocent VIII (1484–92): Gules a bend checky Argent and Azure, on a chief argent a cross Gules.

Alexander VI (1492–1503): Per pale, I a bull Gules grazing on a mound Vert, on a bordure Or eight tufts of grass Vert; II barry Or and Sable.

Pius III (1503): Argent on a cross Azure five crescents Or.

Julius II (1503–13): Azure an oak tree eradicated Or its four branches per saltire.

Leo X (1513–21): Or with five torteaux in chief a roundel Azure charged with three fleurs-de-lis Or.

Hadrian VI (1522–23): Quarterly, I and IV, Or three wolf's hooks Vert; II and III, Argent a lion Vert crowned Or.

Clement VII (1523–34): Or five torteaux, in chief a roundel Azure charged with three fleur-de-lis Or.

Paul III (1534–49): Or six fleurs-de-lis Azure 3, 2, 1.

Julius III (1550–55): Azure on a bend Gules a trimount Or between in chief and in base two laurel branches entwined also Or.

Marcellus II (1555): Azure nine bullrushes Or growing from a base Vert and a fawn Or lodged in base.

Pius IV (1559–65): Or five torteaux, in chief a roundel Azure charged with three fleurs-de-lis Or.

Pius V (1566–72): Bendy Or and Gules.

Gregory XIII (1572–85): Gules a demi-dragon Or.

Sixtus V (1585–90): Azure a lion Or holding a pear tree branch Or overall on a bend Gules a six pointed mullet Or in chief and a trimount in base also Or.

Urban VII (1590): Bendy Argent and Gules, on a chief Gules supported by a barrulet Or a chestnut branch stemmed, leaved and fructed Or.

Gregory XIV (1590–91): Quarterly, I and IV, Or on a bend embattled Azure two mullets of six points Or; II and III, Argent a tree eradicated Vert.

Innocent IX (1591): Argent a walnut tree eradicated Vert.

Clement VIII (1592–1605): Azure a bend embattled Or between six six-pointed mullets Or.

Leo XI (1605): Or five torteaux, in chief a roundel Azure charged with three fleurs-de-lis Or.

Paul V (1605–21): Azure a dragon Or, on chief Or an eagle displayed Sable.

Gregory XV (1621–23): Gules in chief three bends Or retracted.

Urbain VIII (1623–44): Azure three bees Or.

Innocent X (1644–55): Gules a dove Argent holding in its beak an olive branch Vert, on a chief Azure three fleurs-de-lis between two demi-pales Gules.

Alexander VII (1655–67): Quarterly, I and IV, Azure an oak tree eradicated Or the four branches per saltire; II and III, Gules a sextuple mount issuant from the base surmounted by an eight-pointed mullet Or.

Clement IX (1667–69): Quarterly Or and Azure four lozenges counterchanged.

Clement X (1670–76): Azure six eight-pointed mullets argent, a bordure indented Argent and Azure.

Innocent XI (1676–89): Argent, between three fess Gules six cups Gules 3, 2, 1, in chief a lion passant Gules, on a chief Or an eagle displayed Sable.

Alexander VIII (1689–91): Tierced in bend Azure and Vert overall a bend Or, on a chief Or a double-headed eagle displayed Sable.

Innocent XII (1691–1700): Or three pitchers Sable those in chief addorsed.

Clement XI (1700–21): Azure between a fess Or, in chief a mullet of eight points Or, in base a trimount Or.

Innocent XIII (1721–24): Gules an eagle displayed checky Or and Sable crowned and armed Or.

Benedict XIII (1724–30): Per pale, I, bendy Gules and Argent, on a chief Argent supported by a barrulet Or an eel Azure surmounted by a rose Gules; II, Azure a tower Argent on a terrace Vert, on a chief the arms of the order of Saint Dominick.

Clement XII (1730–40): Bendy Argent and Gules overall a fess Azure.

Benedict XIV (1740–58): Or paly of four (or three) Gules.

Clement XIII (1758–69): Quarterly I, Gules a cross Argent; II and III, Azure a tower Argent; IV, Gules three bends sinister argent; overall on an escutcheon a double-headed eagle displayed, crowned Sable, a coronet Or over the escutcheon.

Clement XIV (1769–74): Azure a fess Gules between in chief three mullets of six points Or surmounted by the arms of the order of Saint Francis, in base a trimount Or.

Paul VI (1775–99): Gules a representation of the North Wind in dexter chief blowing on a lily Proper issuant from a mound Vert, on a chief Argent three eight-pointed mullets Or.

Pius VII (1800–23): Per pale I, Azure a double-traversed cross issuant from a trimount in base overall in fess the word PAX all Or (order of St. Benedict), II, per bend Or and Azure on a bend Argent three Moor's heads Sable, on a chief Azure three mullets of six points Or.

Leo XII (1823–29): Azure an eagle displayed, crowned Or.

Pius VIII (1829–30): Gules a lion Argent holding a Tower Or.

Gregory XVI (1831–46): Per pale I, Azure a chalice Or between two doves Argent armed Gules drinking from the chalice and surmounted in chief by a comet Or pale-wise (Camaldolese); II, per fess, Azure and Argent in chief a priest's hat Sable, on a overall Gules three mullets Or.

Pius IX (1846–78): Quarterly I and IV, Azure a lion crowned Or on a bezant (*gold roundel*); II and III, bendy Argent and Gules.

Leo XIII (1878–1903): Azure a pine tree Vert issuant from a mound Vert, between a comet Or in dexter chief and in base two fleurs-de-lis Argent, overall a fess Argent.

Pius X (1903–14): Azure on water in base Proper a triple pronged anchor fouled Argent in bend, a mullet of six points in chief, on a chief the lion of Saint Mark.

Benedict XV (1914–22): Per bend Azure and Or overall a church Argent with its tower to the sinister roofed Gules, on a chief Or a demi-eagle displayed Sable.

Pius XI (1922–39): Argent three torteaux, on a chief Sable an eagle displayed Sable.

Pius XII (1939–58): Azure on a trimount Argent issuant from a terrace Vert placed on a sea Proper a dove reguardant Argent holding an olive banch Vert in its beak.

John XXIII (1958–63): Gules a fess Argent, overall in pale a tower between in chief two fleurs-de-lis all Argent, on a chief the lion of Saint Mark.

Paul VI (1963–78): Gules a sextuple mount Argent, in chief three fleurs-de-lis Argent 1, 2.

John Paul I (1978): Did not use a papal coat of arms.

John Paul II (1978–): Azure a cross Or issuant from dexter flank the bar extended to sinister flank, in sinister base the capital letter M Or.

Michel Pastoureau

Bibliography

Galbreath, D. L. *A Treatise on Ecclesiastical Heraldry. Part I: Papal Heraldry*, Cambridge, 1930, 72–107.

Galles, D. L. C. M. "Papal Armory—A Brief Survey," *Heraldry in Canada*, December 1997, 6–15.

Heim, B. B. *Coutumes et droit héraldiques de l'Église*, Paris, 1949.

Heim, B. B. *Heraldry in the Catholic Church, its Origin, Customs and Laws*, Gerrards Cross, 1978.

Neubecker, O. *Heraldry Sources, Symbols and Meaning*, 1977 (1997 ed. Twickenham, 236–239).

Pasini-Frassoni, P. "Essai d'armorial des papes," *Rivista Araldica*, 1905, 705–717; 1906, 17–32 and 81–96.

ARTISTS, FOREIGN, IN ROME. Giulio Mancini, in *Considerzioni sulla pittura*, written circa 1620, wrote that he was unable to count all the "Frenchmen and Flemish who come and go" in Rome, a multitude that the parish books of the *status animarum* were to have kept in check. Foreign artists had not ignored the road to Rome before this. Indeed, in 1437, Jean Fouquet painted EUGENE IV's portrait there and Roger van der Weyden, on the occasion of the 1450 jubilee, went to Rome from Ferrara, where he worked for the court. Whether as pilgrims or travel companions to great lords, artists had long found the discovery of Rome to be a special occasion and an individual exploit. However, despite the wars that ravaged the Netherlands and the rupture in Christianity caused by the REFORMATION—or perhaps because of them—travel in the 16th century came into its own with the awareness of the splendor of Italian art. This recognition implied the idea of Italian art as the model to follow to recover from the torpor of medieval tradition. Founded on a renewed vision of antiquity, the Renaissance transformed Rome, its incontestable heir, into an artistic capital. This precedence was for a time thwarted by the troubles that were disturbing the papacy, but ultimately, it was strengthened. The spiritual revival after the COUNCIL OF TRENT called on all vibrant forces and made art into a privileged medium for the Church. Once a mere attraction, the trip to Rome gradually became an obligatory part of an artist's training.

The Voyage. As time passed, artists went over the Alps in droves, despite the fear this difficult border held for them. The first transalpine travelers were the Flemish, a term that included all the people from both north and south in the Low Countries. There were more than five hundred such visiting artists in the 17th century. They were more numerous than the French, to judge from their respective financial participation in the Festa di San Luca. Next, there were the Bourguignons, French from the Franc-Comté region who were generally escaping Louis XIV's armies, and Lorrains and southern Germans from the Germanic empire. They often received the title of "Monù," a deformation of the term "Monsieur" originally reserved for Frenchmen and usually followed by the first name alone or a nickname because of the difficulty of pronouncing foreign surnames.

The Spanish enjoyed a privileged relationship with the Italian peninsula through the intermediary of the vice-kingdom of Naples that in 1734 became an independent monarchy governed by a Spanish dynasty. In the 16th century, there were already many Spaniards in the fraternity of painters, the greatest of which did not neglect their Roman education. Velasquez made two trips to Rome and left his portrait of INNOCENT X, and Goya spent a few months in Rome, enough time, it was said, to collaborate briefly on the decoration of the Church of the Trinity on the via Condotti.

Religious affiliation was a significant factor in the arrival of artists in papal lands. Instituted by the Council of Trent, the annual census of the population was both a civic and religious exercise. Each person had to prove his regular practice of the Catholic faith by presenting a bill of confession at Easter. A tempered severity due to negligence protected artists who were disobedient, yet some artists with more liberal mores preferred to distance themselves from the city, at least during the bishop's visit. Threatened with denunciation from the HOLY OFFICE the artist Sebastien Bourdon, a Protestant from Nîmes, was forced to leave Rome altogether. The German archeologist and art historian Johann Joachim Winckelmann converted, and the Saxon Anton Raphael Mengs recanted before undertaking a Roman career. Protestants did not have the right to the king's pension. François-André Vincent, who was considered a brilliant artist, was one of the only exceptions. He stayed in the Academy of France in Rome from 1771 to 1775 with the bishop's and director's complicity. Artists devised ways to avoid difficulties on specific occasions, such as "eating during lent." Yet the very obligation of being under papal authority provoked revolts. Adrien Mouton, the architect, argued that he refused to submit to the pope since he was a subject of the king of France. He was then excluded from the Academy, but brought the matter before the jurisdiction of the Châtelet, which gave him a favorable judgment without calling upon Rome. During the century of the Enlightenment, the rigor with which Catholic orthodoxy was imposed on foreign artists in Rome dissipated with influx of Protestants, who were preponderantly English. Although they were mentioned in the parish registers as heretics, the "eretico" written after their names had little consequence.

Artists often came to Rome very young, sometimes as adolescents. The Catalan Michel Serre, who later settled in Marseilles, is an example. According to what has been said, Nicolas Pinson de Valence en Dauphiné was only twelve years old when he came to Rome, although he passed for seventeen. However, most artists waited to come to Rome until after completing their first apprenticeship and deciding on their vocation. Before the trip had become institutionalized, they depended on their personal savings or on a patron whose support they were to recognize through the production of works of art. The luckiest benefited from the support of a great lord. Thus, Nicholas Mignard from Avignon left in 1635 on the royal ships in the entourage of Cardinal Alphonse de Richelieu, who departed for Rome as Louis XIII's ambassador to URBAN VIII. Joseph Vernet, like most artists from the south of France, traveled by sea. Those who did not descend the Rhône by boat to then sail through the Mediterranean arrived in the small town of Pont-de-Beauvoisin, the border with Savoy, and then climbed to the top of Mont-Cenis. The Flemish and the Lorrains preferred the road from Germany to cross the Alps more easily at Brenner. The initiation path was thus established, as it led from town to town, each place retaining a particular revelation.

Artists entered Rome through the Porta Flaminia at the north of the city and discovered the new quarter bordering the Pincio, urbanized in the 16th century by Popes SIXTUS V and PAUL III. The via Sistina, the Paolina, and its extension, the Babuino, which takes its name from a Roman statue still on that spot, were at that time bordered by low houses flanked by a garden. In or near this park, the poorest of the travelers easily found a room to share with other artists, preferably compatriots, before being able to rent lodging on a top floor with rooftop studio space. There were many sculptors living near the Quirinale, occupying the courts of ancient palaces. In this marginal neighborhood full of raw charm, transalpine foreigners and Italians lived side by side, barely strangers to one another.

In the capital of Christianity, nations maintained their identities, attached to their respective brotherhoods and languages, which for many peninsular Italians meant a dialect of Italian. Flemish artists formed an association without any religious context in 1620 called the *Schilldersbent*. The "birds of the band," the *Bentvueghels*, were bons vivants whose banquets and drinking parties were criticized by the public. Each new arrival received, in a parody of a baptism, a new surname evoking his personality or artistic habit. A true social force, the *Bent* clashed with the Academy of San Luca, mostly over the right to tax artists for exercising their profession. They won, in part, but their influence declined with the onset of the century of academicism and disappeared in 1720, when CLEMENT XI forbade parties and night parades outside of carnival time. The French cultivated their independence, supporting artists with the power of their official diplomatic and religious institutions.

Most artists eventually returned home, where their Roman education meant new consideration and commissions. The epithet of "Roman" was added to some of their surnames and accredited with value. However, the lengths of visits to Rome were very unequal—sometimes months, sometimes years–depending on the forces of homesickness and fascination. Some foreign artists settled permanently in Rome due to their success there; some married Italian women and founded families in Italy. The French painter Claude Lorrain enjoyed glory and fortune whereas Nicolas Poussin, also French, preferred the humility of his Roman life to the splendor of court life and felt that the serenity offered him independence.

The Era of the Academics. Since 1593, as the successor institution to the *universitas* of painters, the Academy of San Luca ruled artistic life in Rome under the authority of the pope who delegated a CARDINAL PROTECTOR for it. Open then to all those who exercised some type of artistic profession—painters, sculptors, and architects, but also embroiderers, restorers, and merchants—it was originally composed mainly of Italians and some Spaniards. Isolated Frenchmen appeared toward 1620 and increased in number between 1624 and 1627, when Urban VIII entrusted the "principat," that is, the direction, to a Parisian, the painter Simon Vouet. Vouet's return to France meant a decline in the French presence in Rome whereas the Flemish, contigent—Abraham Breughel, David de Coninck—despite the *Schildersbent*'s hostility, maintained its membership. One of the obligations of the Academy of San Luca had always been to train youths, but this practice had fallen into disuse when Carlo Maratta revived it in 1664, instituting courses and competitions.

During this short-lived boom, the institute overflowed with students. For a group of one hundred students whose passage there can be documented, we see that the French were preponderant and that most of them came from the south of France. France's influence culminated in a joint project with the young Royal Academy of Paris, conceived of by Charles Le Brun upon Colbert's request. It marked a high point in the quest for a balance between inspiration and education, that obeyed an ideal of order and reason. Yet the imperial objectives of Louis XIV and his conflict with INNOCENT XI destroyed this illusory attempt. The Academy of San Luca rediscovered its independence, but it had already to contend with the new power of the Académie de France in Rome, founded by Colbert in 1666.

After an era of freedom, institutions brought security and constraints. Foreign sovereigns wanted to support their artists while also gaining better control over them and more glory for themselves. Pensions were used as a means to motivate artists and to prevent them from living in misery. Teaching, once pragmatic training dispensed in studio workshops, now took a theoretical turn. The Colbert foundation was durable, although its objectives had always been linked to a great political plan. It has lasted throughout the 18th, 19th, and 20th centuries, as a citadel sure of its force. The experience acquired by artists has

had to serve the monarchy in many ways. Copies of classical works of art and the paintings of the great masters of the 16th and 17th centuries, Raphael and the Bolognesi, decorated parks and royal dwellings. Frescoes from the gallery of the Carraccio in the Palazzo Farnese were transported to the Tuileries in France as a model for those who would not make the trip. The pensioners themselves had to return to their homelands to attempt to equal, if not surpass, works they had studied for years during their Roman stay. Thus, a "French school" appeared that was, without any trace of servility, the reflection of the Italian school.

France had given itself the means for its success. To direct the new institution, it selected distinguished artists from the recent Royal Academy of Paris who were also familiar with Rome and the complexities of its social life. A regular correspondence with the superintendent of buildings maintained the Academy of France in Rome under the attentive supervision of the royal power. In time, a headquarters up to its dignified standards was obtained by renting and then purchasing in 1737 the Corso Palace from the Duke of Nivernais, nephew of Cardinal Mazarin. Such care and concern were not without political motives. The luxuriously furnished Mancini Palace became the "House of France" where ambassadors were received during the Carnival. Directors, such as Nicolas Vleughels, had a reputation in high society that opened important doors—those of the palaces—the necessary rights of way in a country where human relationships were founded on protection and recommendations.

Young artists admitted to the king's residence were recruited through competitions, which were somewhat irregularly conducted, although the rules became more stringent over time. Thus, the artists arriving in Rome were not as young as in earlier times. They were already trained and more apt to benefit from the experience, but also more inclined to the pride and scornfulness that some directors encouraged with regard to contemporary painting in Rome. The critique on the theme "the knowledge and simplicity of the Ancients are rarely followed and imitated" tended to keep them in the current of an intangible classicism. For these ideological reasons, and other political reasons, the residents did not participate in the competitions at the Academy of San Luca. Charles Natoire was the last of the rare exceptions in 1725 and, although Jean-Baptiste Pigalle participated as an outside competitor in 1738, he did so in secret and had to pretend to be from Avignon. This self-sufficiency was long justified by the merit of those who were sent to Rome. Eighteenth-century French art owes its flourishing to the Academy, even if some of the greatest painters of the period, such as Watteau and Chardin, never went to Rome.

The sculptors of the Academy proved to be particularly brilliant. Rome is the city of marble and is founded on a long tradition of masterworks relying on vocational craftsmanship. Pierre Legros belonged to the first generations completely in the service of the king. Anxious to become famous, he accepted a major commission from the JESUITS at the end of the 17th century—the chapel of St. Ignacio—which was for him the beginning of a fabulous Roman career. Michel-Ange Slodtz, a tireless worker, made a specialty of creating funerary monuments including the imposing mausoleum dedicated to the bishops of Montmorin and La Tour d'Auvergne. Clodion and Antoine Houdon, who lived at the Academy at the same time, bore the promise of new times to come, the former cultivating a gracious style reminiscent of classical art, and the latter prefiguring the somewhat cold rigor of neoclassicism to come, as, for example, in his *Saint Bruno* at Santa Maria degli Angeli.

Only historical painters and sculptors were admitted to the Academy. Portraitists and landscape painters had no place there, and those who desired to know Rome traveled at their own expense. Among them were Joseph Vernet, whom the director sent "out to the seaports to study," and Jean-Baptiste Lallemand from Dijon. Many recommendations and great talent were required for Hubert Robert to be accepted under the Academy's roof.

The painters of the Academy were destined to have brilliant careers upon their return to Paris. Some returned to Rome as directors; Poerson, Jean-François de Troy, and Charles Natoire all died in Rome. But many remained in France and left many works there. The Van Loo, for example, brought the young Boucher with them and the class of 1728. This was a successful year since Trémolières, Blanchet, and Subleyras attended together, the latter two refusing to return. Doyen, whose *Miracle of the Faithful* (*Miracle des ardents*) is the most celebrated work of the period and who emigrated to St. Petersburg in 1791, also attended. Fragonard's reputation eclipsed perhaps all the others.

France had its imitators. During the reign of John V, Portugal's prosperity incited it to train its own artists, instead of depending upon imports. Yet what was supposed to be an official academy only lasted thirteen years, from 1720 to 1733. The directors of the Academy of France considered the attempts of other countries to be mere imitations, referring to them as "espèces d'académies." In fact, there were national residences paid for by the sovereigns of various countries, but none had the official rules and structure of the French institution. The Great Duke of Tuscany, showing thusly the vitality of the idea of a nation, maintained three painters whom he housed in his palace at the Piazza di Firenze. In 1709, the Duke of Lorrain had nine artists, among them "a young man to teach music," four painters, and a sculptor. "These young people are living here and there, each doing what he pleases," wrote Vleughels. Spain did not found an academy, but sent its artists to learn drawing at the Academy of France, which, due to the political climate, pampered them in due

fashion. However, in 1758, Spain designated Francisco Preciado, who had been established in Rome for many years, to direct the students sent from the Academy of San Fernando. The Count of Cobenzl, minister of the Empress Maria-Theresa in the Netherlands, dreamed before his death in 1770 of founding a veritable academy in the French manner. After 1772, Anton von Maron, Mengs's brother-in-law, then administered a less formal direction of the imperial residents.

The Academy of San Luca lost some of its original good-naturedness to gain in dignity. It eliminated embroiderers and restorers from its ranks to distinguish between craftsmen and artists, and even refused entry to decorative painters because their art was judged to be too "mecanical." It reduced its recruitment to three great disciplines, among which it established a balance reflecting the components of the artistic community in Rome, where painters were in the majority, and, as in the Academy of France, it only admitted those practicing "*la grande manière.*" Flemish landscape painters, who during Paul Brill's time were highly acclaimed, had difficulty imposing themselves. Gaspard van Wittel waited until 1712 to be elected, and Jan Frans van Bloemen was not admitted until 1742. The title of academician defined an elite. The directors of the Academy of France were automatically admitted, an indication of how inconceivable it was to counter a choice made by Paris. For established foreign artists, this title was less an honor than a necessity. Without it, it was difficult to gain access to prestigious commissions: Pierre Subleyras, BENEDICT XIV's painter; Antoine Derizet, the architect of the Holy Name of Mary Church; and Etienne Parrocel from Avignon were among those admitted. The Academy was most accessible to artists who planned to leave Rome. Such was the case of the sculptors such as Adam and Bouchardon, the architect Soufflot, and even artists of minor genres, such as Joseph Vernet, Jacques Volaire, and Jacques Gamelin de Carcassonne, the battle painter. The Academy of San Luca was above all an institution for Italians. Through it, Rome was able to resist being taken over by foreigners.

New Situation. The Academy of France grew increasingly hermetic. Wars and financial difficulties contributed to impeding its expansion, and the vigorous attempt at reviving it in 1775 was without any positive effect, despite the quality of the young artists sent—David, Drouais, and Peyronn—and despite all efforts made by Joseph-Marie Vien, the director who instituted the exhibition of works for the Saint-Louis fest. Directors displayed a growing indifference to artistic life in Rome and remained more tuned in to Paris. In the last two years before the French Revolution, Lagrenée the Elder and Ménageot neglected to occupy their seats at the Academy of San Luca. The states of Burgundy stole the monopoly of training residents in 1776 by instituting a Rome prize. Two valuable painters, Bénigne Gagneraux and Pierre-Paul Prud'hon, won this award. Whereas the Academy of France had for a very long time been the model, freely welcoming foreigners into its drawing classes, in 1754 Benedict XIV created a new academy. The Accademia del Nudo was placed under the direction of the Academy of San Luca, which thereby reasserted one of its statutory functions. Prizes ensured that courses were open to all, and the awarding of prizes was an occasion for a solemn ceremony on the Capitol. Prizes such as the Clementine, whose existence went back to Clement XI, and a more recent prize, the Balestra, both intended for advanced artists, took on new luster. The papacy thus boldly reaffirmed its authority over the arts.

The ideology of a return to the ancients was dominant. In 1785, David's *Serment des Horaces* was a thunderous event. The painter proved his allegiance to Rome, since he came to Rome to paint the painting. He was no longer a resident at the Academy, and was one of many artists of the time who were fascinated by antiquity. This is reflected in the registration list at the Accademia del Nudo. The range of nationalities in this cosmopolitan city had enlarged to include South Americans, Russians, and Scandinavians. The esteemed artists who were laureats of the Clementine and Balestra prizes came from all over the world. There were the sculptor Nollekens from England, the architect Robert Mylne and the painter David Allan from Scotland, the architect Francisco La Vega and the painter Antonio Carnicero from Spain, and the architect Stanislas Zawadzki and the painter François Smuglewicz from Poland. Rome remained faithful to its vocation as the *communis patria*.

On the fringe of the Academy, young French people competed well. Sculptors Claude-François Attiret and Luc Breton from Franche-Comté and, Etienne Dantoine from Carpentras, and painters Laurent Pécheux from Lyon and Laurent Blanchard from Valence were some of these French provincials, who expected nothing from Paris and frequented Grand Prize losers who managed to hold on to their dreams, such as the sculptor from Lyon, François-Maris Poncet and the painter Jacques Gamelin from Carcassonne. Guillaume Ménageot, attached to the past and to institutions in general, wrote to Paris: "What hurts me the most here is to see legions of young French artists who believe that it is enough to be in Rome to become a great painter. Most of them, without assistance and without fortune, lead miserable lives and embarrass both art and the nation. But this was inevitable with the free schools and painting colleges that all artists have today. . . ."

Germans and "Englishmen" then occupied a dominant position. Artists from the Germanic Empire were proud to have a theoretician in the new in Winckelmann, and found in Mengs a true leader—a member of the Academy

of San Luca, "prince" in 1772, and well-appreciated by popes and the king of Spain, who brought him for a time to Madrid. The fresco of *Parnasse* in the villa Albani is a kind of manifesto of his art. The death of Mengs in 1779 made way for the predominance of two who were generally called the "Englishmen," even if one was Scottish and the other Irish. Artists like Hogarth and Gainsborough, who found their inspiration in the imitation of nature, were not tempted to go to Rome, but others who believed in theory came to Italy seeking masters and models. Paradoxically, Josuah Reynolds's stay ended up in the creation of the Royal Academy and the formation of a national school against an all-invasive Italy. Without official institutions on which to rely, the new arrivals, for example, Gavin Hamilton, James Byres, Thomas Jenkins, and the more and more numerous gentry who made the trip, sought aid from those who had managed to establish themselves. Despite their independent spirit, they belied their solitude, as the Flemish had in the past, by getting together. James Russel speaks of a group of sixteen Englishmen and Scotsmen who met regularly and formed a small academy among themselves. Outside of work, they met at the Piazza di Spagna at the English café, which was decorated in the Egyptian style by Piranese.

The Academy of San Luca also reflected these mutations. It became more liberal with the arrival of Protestants who had to obtain a papal dispensation in order to be elected. Thus it was for the Scottish architect Robert Adam in 1756. The most representative of the tenants of English neo-classicism followed, such as Robert Mylne, George Dance, and Thomas Harisson, who was imposed by the pope himself. The British formed the most numerous group in the 18th century, but their respective admissions, most prevalent from 1756 to 1796, were not followed by any participation in the life of the Academy. They had an honorary character, as the title of "Arcade" always had been sought out by great artists. Numerous architects had to go through Rome on the road to Campagna, Sicily, and even Greece. The tradition of electing women painters as academicians of merit was perpetuated without any particular consequences; three French women were elected in the last quarter of the century: Marie-Thérèse Vien, Geneviève Brossard de Beaulieu, and Elisabeth Vigée-Lebrun.

Was Rome then just a school for all these foreign artists? Was it a place to pillage shamelessly and denigrate occasionally? Was it a place from which to take ancient models while ignoring its contemporary creations? It was for many a market overflowing with institutions, but necessary to those who came to the city without resources. Views of Rome, landscape painting, and copies of classic works were sold as souvenirs for tourists. Foreign painters also maintained a foreign clientele. Patronage had national character to it. Religious communities, princes of the Church, and diplomats generally protected their compatriots, without being exclusive about it. Thus, the decoration of St. Louis in the 18th century was entrusted to the French, but two essential themes went to celebrated Italian sculptors: Filippo Della Valle and Giovanni Battista Maini. A cosmospolitan city, Rome had become an incontestable artistic center. Artists who were proven and solicited by foreign sovereigns did not refuse to expatriate themselves a second time, tempted by the bait of wealth. El Greco came from Crete and passed through Rome before establishing himself in Spain. The French sculptors Jacques Saly and André Lebrun went to Denmark and Poland, and, more modestly, the painter Laurent Pécheux went to the court of Turin. Artists, great connoisseurs of art in general, became art merchants. This commercial activity was one of the main reasons for British travel to Rome at the end of the century. The aura of Rome became greater as the city itself became impoverished.

A Center is Extinguished. In 1789, the Academy of France entered into turmoil. Artists were routinely accused of being freemasons and Jacobins. In 1792, two sculptors, Chastel and Chinard, and the architect Ratter, were accused of subversion due to their symbolically contentious works of art, and were imprisoned. An agitator, the emissary from the Republic Hugou de Bassville, was assassinated on 13 January 1793. The Mancini Palace was pillaged and all the artists were hunted down. En masse, they took refuge in Florence, living luxuriously on their subsidies. During the empire, the Academy of France took on new life at the Villa Medici, purchased from the Grand Duke of Tuscany. This splendid isolation distanced young French artists more than ever before from the city, although the courses of instruction and recruitment remained as they had been, with the sole exception of the inclusion of musicians in the Academy. Musicians such as Berlioz and Gounod, more than painters, supported the Academy's reputation during this period, despite the celebrity of some of its directors such as Ingres, Horace Vernet, and Hébert.

Rome continued to attract artists. Danish artists formed a coherent group distinguished by particularly strong personalities such as Christoffer Wilhelm Eckersberg and Bertel Thorvaldsen, Canova's rival. The Café Greco was their habitual meeting place, and was also frequented by Germans and other Scandinavians. Toward the year 1850, however, this activity abated, as many artists departed and fewer arrived. Roman artistic life remained vibrant outside of traditional paths. Mysticism, after centuries of decline, was revived in the Nazarenes' art. There was a group of German artists who led the lives of monks, exploring early 15th-century sources. The frescos at the Villa Massimo are their masterwork. The English Pre-Raphaelites came to be inspired and seduced by Rome as well.

When the *pittoresco* was rediscovered in the 19th century, Léopold Robert, a Swiss close to the French, raised

it to the ranks of historical painting. It represented large folk celebrations in all their majesty with a romantic backdrop of hostile mountains and dramatic scenes taking place in which the outlaw becomes the antihero. Rome was not his only mediator. Naples and Venice where he worked were equally important. Landscape painting itself turned away from monumental beauty in search of modes of enchantment in the neglected detail and the fleeting instant. The artist varied his impressions by distancing himself farther and farther from the city. He cultivated travel. The myth of Romanita spread throughout Italy. The papacy never abandoned its interest in the arts, but PIUS IX, who was a great patron, blazed no new trails; the artists to whom he entrusted the invasive decoration of churches used formulae that were already outmoded.

Olivier Michel

Bibliography

Bodard, D. *Les Peintres des Pays-Bas méridionaux et de la principauté de Liège à Rome au XVIIe siècle*, Brussels-Rome, 1970, 2 vols.

Bousquet, J. *Recherches sur le séjour des peintres français à Rome au XVIIe siècle*, Montpellier, 1980.

Boyer, F. "Les artistes français, étudiants, lauréats ou membres de l'Académie romaine de Saint-Luc entre 1660 et 1700," *Bulletin de la Société de l'histoire de l'art français*, 1950, 117–132; ". . . dans la première moitié du XVIIIe siècle" ("in the first half of the 18th century"), *ibid.*, 1955, 131–142; ". . . dans la seconde moitié du XVIIIe siècle" ("in the second half of the 18th century"), *ibid.*, 1957, 273–288.

Coekel-Berghs, D. *Les Peintres belges à Rome de 1700 à 1830*, Brussels-Rome, 1976.

Dacos, N. *Les Peintres belges à Rome au XVIe siècle*, Brussels-Rome, 1964.

Salerno, L. *Roma communis patria*, Bologna, 1968.

ASSASSINATION ATTEMPTS AGAINST THE POPE.

Antiquity. The historical writing that developed gradually during the Early Middle Ages traditionally and frequently referred to the figure of the martyr pope to the extent that it became something of a cliché. The historical reality of such assaults is, however, rarely evidenced, and it is very difficult to assimilate certain types of suffering into the category of assassination attempts. An assassination attempt is by definition perpetrated against an established and recognized authority, a definition inapplicable to the early pontiffs. The first admissible case of an attempt on the life of a pope concerns CALLISTUS I (217–22), mentioned as a martyr in a 4th-century calendar. However, a Passion reporting events of his pontificate indicates that he suffered a violent death, perhaps during a popular uprising in Rome. Valentinian II's soldiers, following a mandate to persecute the pope, decapitated SIXTUS II (257–8) on 6 August 258, while he was celebrating mass in the Praetextan cemetery. There are no other indications of a physical attempt of this type against later popes from antiquity and the early Middle Ages.

François Jankowiak

Middle Ages. (This list does not include recognized ANTIPOPES, such as JOHN XVI, who in February 998, while Emperor Otto III was reestablishing GREGORY V in Rome, was blinded, mutilated, and dragged by a donkey through the streets of the city.)

MARTIN I (649–53) was brutally captured (17 June 653) by the exarch Theodore Calliopas on imperial orders. He was then taken prisoner and deported to Chersonesus, where he died.

LEO III (795–816) was attacked on 25 April 799 by his adversaries in the Roman nobility while he was walking in procession during a mass. These nobles attempted unsuccessfully to blind him and then forced him into a deposition ceremony, after which the pope escaped to Paderborn under the protection of Charlemagne.

FORMOSUS (891–6) was judged nine months after his death (January 897) in what constituted more a posthumous execution than an assassination. The pope's body was exhumed on the order of his successor, STEPHEN VI, dressed in papal vestments, set on the throne, judged, condemned, and degraded. The body was then thrown into the Tiber River after the amputation of three fingers of the right hand—those used for blessings and taking solemn oaths.

JOHN X (914–28) was imprisoned in May 928 at the instigation of the patrician and senatrix Marozia. He died in prison in mid-929 apparently suffocated.

JOHN XI (931–5/6) was captured in December 931, along with his mother, Marozia, by his half-brother Alberic II. The pope was then kept under house arrest until his death, his activities restricted to ecclesiastical ones.

STEPHEN VIII (939–42) was imprisoned, mutilated, and then killed in October 942 for having participated in a plot against Alberic II.

JOHN XIII (965–72) was brutally captured during an anti-imperial riot in Rome in December 965. He took refuge under the protection of Otto I.

JOHN XIV (983–4) was seized and assaulted during an anti-imperial riot in Rome in April 984. He was imprisoned in the Castel Sant'Angelo, where he died in August, probably of starvation.

BONIFACE VII (considered an antipope by modern historians) was probably assassinated on 20 July 985. His body was dragged through Rome and exposed naked beneath Marcus Aurelius's statue, which was then in front of the Lateran (today on the Capitol).

Olivier Guyotjeannin

Modern Period. On 4 June 1434, EUGENE IV, disguised as a Benedictine monk, escaped from Rome to avoid being taken by force to the Capitol where, a few days earlier, the Roman Republic had been proclaimed. This proclamation meant that the commune had become independent from the direct authority of the Holy See. Aboard a boat in the port of Ripa Grande, the pope was soon recognized; Romans pursued him as far as St. Paul's Outside the Walls, throwing rocks and shooting arrows at his small craft. Eugene IV, lying on the bottom of the boat and protected by a shield, nonetheless managed to escape to the vessel awaiting him at Ostia, whence he departed for Pisa the following day. Afterward, he went to Florence. In the meantime, the Romans had taken the pope's nephew hostage. The camerlengo, Cardinal Francesco Condulmer, was not liberated until October, after the pope regained control of the city.

This episode was part of the overarching crisis the papal state was undergoing at the time. Pressure was coming from various sources: the activities of the duke of Milan, the rancor of the Colonna party persecuted since Martin V's death, difficulties created for the pope by the council meeting in Basel and, finally, the exasperation of Romans weary of interminable war. It is possible that the plan had been to take the pope hostage on behalf of the council in the hope of having the assembly transferred to Rome.

François-Charles Uginet

Contemporary Period. Of the fourteen popes in the 19th and 20th centuries, two were physically attacked. The first attempt made was against PIUS VII, but it was aimed more to remove this particular pontiff than to strike at his office. The other assassination attempt, against JOHN PAUL II, seems to have been intended purely and simply to murder the head of the Universal Church. The attempt against the life of PIUS VII (1800–23) occurred on the night of 5–6 July 1809 and revealed a politics of violence against the papacy already experienced by his predecessor, PIUS VI. After a popular insurrection in Rome in December 1797, fomented by General Duphot and repressed by the Holy See, General Berthier took Pius VI prisoner on 20 February 1798. Berthier was part of the forces occupying Rome, where the Republic had been proclaimed on 15 February. Anecdotes from history suggest that Pius VI expressed a wish to die in Rome, and that a high-ranking French officer replied, "Dying can be done anywhere" (*"Mourir, ça peut se faire partout"*). Deported to Siena, then imprisoned in Florence, Pius VI—owing to the Directory's fear of his being kidnapped—was transferred to France by stages. He died in Valence on 29 August 1799.

As for Pius VII, he was arrested in the Quirinal palace on the night of 5–6 July 1809. The Papal States had been incorporated by Napoleon I into the French Empire as of

March 1809. The pope excommunicated the emperor on 10 June. Pius VII was then captured and taken to Grenoble, where his predecessor had stayed, then on to Savona; he was secretly transferred to Fontainebleau on 19 June 1812. Napoleon I obtained advantages from the pope (the Concordat of Fontainebleau, 1813) that led to his sending the pope back to Savona preceding Pius's triumphal reentry into Rome on 24 March 1814.

The assassination attempt against John Paul II (1978–) was a completely different matter. On Wednesday, 13 May 1981, there was a public audience outside on St. Peter's Square, favored by good weather. At 5:12 P.M. Pope John Paul II, riding in an open car, was hit by several bullets just as he was driven up to the Bronze Door. Despite general confusion, the assassin was caught by the faithful present and handed over to the Italian police, in accordance with the LATERAN ACCORDS (articles 8 and 22). The sovereign pontiff was treated by the emergency services set up for pilgrims under the Bell Tower Arch and was quickly transported to the Gemelli Hospital, where he underwent several hours of surgery. His death was even announced on Italian radio at 6:50 P.M. but the error was soon retracted. The city of Rome was paralyzed as the entire world listened to the news, which became more and more reassuring as the days went by. The pope remained under observation for one month and gradually recovered. A book relating the event, with photos of the pope in private life as a patient, appeared in 1983. This media event broke down traditional barriers regarding the personal life of the pope that had been strictly adhered to since the scandal of the pirated photos of Pius XII on his deathbed. The image of vulnerability—the very opposite of the image of eternity expressed in the sacred character of the pope as the bishop of Rome—had nonetheless penetrated public consciousness.

The assassin, Ali Agça, was born in 1958 in Hekimhan in Turkey into a modest family. He studied at the University of Ankara, where he was part of the Grey Wolves, a youth organization advocating nationalist, anticommunist, and anticapitalist politics along with the dream of a pan-Turkic empire from the Mediterranean to Mongolia. On 1 February 1979, in the heart of Istanbul, he had assassinated Abdi Kebei, director of the liberal daily newspaper *Milliyet*. Arrested, he escaped on 23 November and four days later sent a letter to the same newspaper indicating his intentions of killing "the Commander of the Crusades." John Paul II was on a very difficult and controversial trip to Turkey at the time.

As soon as John Paul II recovered consciousness, he pardoned the act. The trial was long and complicated: Had this been the act of a psychopath, or part of a political plot? In the beginning, Ali Agça spoke a great deal and appeared to be insane, although it was not clear whether this state was real or simulated. In 1982, however, he revealed information indicating that he had not acted alone but was supported by the secret service of the Bulgarian embassy in Rome. The press (for example, the newspaper *Libération* in France) attempted to unravel the "Bulgarian plot" down to its KGB sources.

A first trial took place in July 1981, and a second one from May 1985 to March 1986. In the meantime, the contradictory statements made by Ali Agça, added to information stemming from the investigations and inquiries, led to 128 different versions of the purported plan to assassinate the pope. The thesis of a Soviet-ordered assassination attempt through the intermediary of the Soviet embassy in Sofia emerged as plausible. However, the time that had passed and the nature of acquaintances made by Ali Agça in prison—from Mafia bosses to Italian secret service agents—raised uncertainties. Was his argument a confession, or had it been suggested to him for anticommunist political reasons, or was his main interest in saving himself (given the law regarding confessed and repented criminals)? The hypothesis of combining these motivations is not to be rejected.

The affair had widespread consequences beyond the Catholic world, owing in part to the constant media attention. The pope returned to his public activities on 7 October 1981, the day after the assassination of Egyptian president Anwar Sadat. On 29 December of the holy year of 1983, John Paul II visited Ali Agça in his prison cell at the Rebbibia penitentiary in Rome and reiterated his declaration of pardon in front of television cameras. Some denounced this public gesture as overly ostentatious, but it nevertheless underscored the role played by the media and social communication in translating apprehension and reporting the assassination attempt.

In addition, the affair inspired literary and cinematic productions, such as "The Man Who Shot the Pope" on the American network NBC, in which Ali Agça is portrayed as an extremist working for the Soviet secret service. The trial also led to a televised film on Italy's RAI/network, which reconstituted the legal investigation, the trial, and the Bulgarian plot theory. Literature—in particular, Philippe Soller's novel *Le Secret*, published in France in 1993—shows how the theme of the assassination (or attempted assassination) of the pope relates to an anthropology of death in contemporary societies.

Philippe Levillain

Bibliography

Das Attentat auf den Papst im Lichte Fatimas und im Schatten der Oktober-Revolution 1917, Rome and Koblentz, 1984.
Henze, P. B. *The Plot to Kill the Pope*, New York, 1983.
Labo, S. *L'attentato al papa nella luce di Fatima*, Rome, 1983.
Mulisch, H. *L'Attentat*, Paris, 1984.
Sollers, P. *Le Secret*, Paris, 1993.

Sterling, C. *Anatomia di un attentato: L'indagine sul complotto, oltre la verità ufficiali*, Milan, 1984.

ASSUMPTION OF THE VIRGIN MARY. On 1 November 1950, Pius XII defined the dogma of the Assumption of the Virgin Mary in the APOSTOLIC CONSTITUTION *Munificentissimus Deus*, using the following terms:
"After having addressed constant and beseeching prayers and invoked the enlightenment of the Spirit of truth, for the glory of all-powerful God who blessed the Virgin Mary with especial benevolence, in honor of his Son, immortal King of the centuries and Vanquisher of death and sin, in order to enhance the glory of his august Mother and for the joy and exultation of the entire Church, by the authority of Our Lord Jesus Christ, the blessed apostles Peter and Paul and by Our own, We proclaim, declare and define that this is a divinely revealed dogma that Mary, the Immaculate Mother of God always a Virgin, at the end of her life on earth, was in body and soul assumed into heavenly glory."

Pius XII thus consecrated into Church dogma what had been a traditional belief linked to the logic according to which the Virgin, preserved from original sin (the immaculate conception and being the mother of God, or Théotokos (council of Ephesus, 431), had not known the corruption of burial after death. The Marian feasts instituted by SERGIUS I in the 7th century celebrated, among other events, her Assumption.

The orthodox Churches celebrate the Assumption and call it the "Dormition of the Blessed Virgin Mary" (that is, the feast of "Falling Asleep"). Established according to the Julian calendar, this celebration takes place on 23 August, thirteen days after 15 August in the Gregorian calendar. The Churches of the Reformation do not practice any devotion on 15 August because the Assumption is mentioned only in apocryphal writings.

The Assumption is a holiday in many countries of Catholic tradition. In Italy, it has remained a holiday despite the revision of the CONCORDAT of 1929, upheld on 18 February 1984, which abolished some religious holidays. In France, until the revolution, the Assumption was a national holiday linked to the memory of Louis XIII's vow consecrating France to the Virgin Mary in 1638. This holiday, reestablished by the concordat of 1802, did not disappear with the separation of Church and State in 1905. With Christmas, Ascension, and All Saint's Day, the Assumption is one of the four great religious holidays observed in France.

Philippe Levillain

Bibliography

Balic, C. "De proclamato assumptionis dogmate prae theologorum doctrinis et Ecclesiae vita," *Antonianum*, 26 (1951), 3–39.

Bennett, V., and Winch, R. *The Assumption of Our Lady and Catholic Theology*, London, 1950.

Echi e commenti della proclamazione del dogma dell'Assunzione, Rome, 1954.

Healy, K. *The Assumption of Mary*, Wilmington, Del., 1982.

Jugie, M. *La Mort et l'Assomption de la Sainte Vierge*, Vatican City, 1944.

van Esbroeck, M. *Aux origines de la Dormition de la Vierge*, Brookfield, Vt., 1994.

ASTERISK. See **Mass, Papal: Liturgical Objects**.

ASYLUM, RIGHT OF. Since Greek and Roman antiquity, protection has been granted to criminals seeking refuge in a religious or sacred place (in a church or its surrounding buildings, in an oratory, or near an isolated cross). This practice was naturally continued by the Christian Church and asylum was recognized and regulated in the Near East by the constitutions of 392 and 431. The West also practiced the granting of asylum. The BARBARIANS granted asylum and also added several innovations. For example, if eventually turned over to the authorities, the criminal who had sought asylum could not be executed and his punishment was reduced or waived. The Carolingians attempted to limit abuses of the right of asylum and enforce peace in the 10th and 11th centuries by emphasizing asylum as a means of preventing violence against the weak. Whereas the DECRETUM OF GRATIAN (1140) specified the laws in effect and reiterated that excommunication would be the means to punish the guilty, the popes began to define the right to asylum and except certain delinquents from the protection (for example public thieves, brigands, and murderers who committed their crimes in churches). GREGORY IX's *Decretals* (1234) determined these *casus excepti* (exceptions), while the development of courts of justice made this special judicial treatment less useful and a source of conflict with secular authorities. Up until the 16th century, the number of excluded cases continued to increase and the institution, a source of scandals, was in total decadence. It is briefly mentioned in the CODE OF CANON LAW OF 1917. On the other hand, the idea of asylum was not forgotten over time. Hunger strikes for political or humanitarian reasons still take place in churches or their annexes and unambiguously attest to the survival of this practice.

Gérard Giordanengo

Bibliography

Baker, J. H. "The English Law of Sanctuary," *Ecclesiastical Law Journal*, 2 (1990), 8–13.

Ducloux, A. "L'Eglise, l'asile et l'aide aux condamnés d'après la constitution du 27 juillet 398," *RHD* (1991), 141–176.

Gaudemet, J. "Asylum," *Augustinus-Lexikon*, Wurzburg, 1990, 490–493 (bibliography).

Herman, E. "Asile dans l'Eglise orientale," *DDC, 1* (1935), 1084–1089.

Le Bras, G. "Asile," *DHGE*, 4 (1930), 1035–1047.

Misserey, L. R. "Asile en Occident," *DDC*, 1, 1089–1104.

Timbal-Duclaux de Martin, P. *Le Droit d'asile*, Paris, 1939.

AUDIENCE. The term "audience" designates any and all meetings with the sovereign pontiff that have been the object of an approved request. Contrary to what the courtly term might imply, today an audience with the pope covers a great variety of modes of access to the sovereign pontiff, from a meeting between the pope and a large group (for example, in PAUL VI's *aula* or in St. Peter's Square) to a one-on-one meeting in the Vatican or at Castel Gandolfo. Until 1870, the pope's role as a sovereign included some practices such as PIUS IX's habit of strolling the streets of Rome without much of an entourage, even joining a funeral procession he encountered on his way. The end of the papal state, however, isolated the pope and made access to his person a more complicated matter. He became secluded in his Vatican palace, which reinforced the sacred character of approaching him. The strict protocol maintained under LEO XIII (1878–1903) increased the reputation of the audience as an extraordinary event.

It is necessary to distinguish between audiences granted in various forms to pilgrims and visitors, and those held by the HOLY SEE to maintain relations with various functionaries dealing with administrative matters. Until the reform of the CURIA in 1967, a yearly table of audiences granted to functionaries (*udienze di tabella*) was established and made public. This system, though laborious, had the advantage of ensuring the regularity of meetings between the sovereign pontiff and members of the Curia. It avoided the total isolation of the pope from his close advisors and kept him from becoming a "prisoner" of the Vatican. The abolition of this system gave the Curia a new kind of autonomy regulated by entrusting relationships to the heads of the DICASTERIES and the SECRETARIAT OF STATE. These relationships, by definition, were not uniform. The result is that the pope no longer has a constant overall view of the activities of the Curia and the life of the state of Vatican City.

Visitors obtain audiences with the pope through rules of protocol or through the pope's own spontaneous gestures. The pope must receive ambassadors at the beginning and end of their missions. Likewise, he receives all political leaders who request an audience. This explains why, without any general political considerations, JOHN PAUL II has received Alexis Adjoubeï, Golda Meir, Yasser Arafat, Wojeiech Jaruzelski, and Kurt Waldheim at the Vatican. The principle of deferring to the expression of the wish to meet is part of the nature of the Holy See, but it is sometimes misunderstood by public opinion in Western democracies.

There are several types of audiences and meetings with the pope, and these constitute a significant part of his regular activities. The one-to-one private audience occurs in the papal library; its duration depends upon the atmosphere of the exchange. The *Osservatore romano* usually records such events in the following day's edition. Ambassadors, important politicians, and well-known intellectuals benefit from this type of audience, which can be extended to their family and colleagues. The term "private audience with the pope" is also used to indicate a pope's meeting with a group of pilgrims or participants at a colloquium, for instance, with or any other collectivity whose request through an intermediary has been accepted. This type of audience generally takes place in one of the rooms of the papal apartments (the Consistory hall or Clementine room). At this type of audience, the pope honors his guests with a discourse relevant to their trip to Rome and their relationship with the Church. The discourse is published the following day in the *Osservatore romano*. The pope, once his speech is over, gives his blessing and personally greets all the participants, who are presented to him one at a time. The audience finishes with a group photograph including the pope.

Public audiences take place either in Paul VI's wing or in St. Peter's Square, depending on the season and the weather. These can also take place in St. Peter's basilica, as was usually the case before the construction of the Paul VI wing. One needs a ticket to attend a public audience, since all participants are seated. Every audience takes place in almost identical fashion. After the prayers, the pope gives a speech whose general content is then translated into several languages. Afterward, the pope greets the main groups in their own languages and receives ovations, songs, and fanfare when he does so. Once the blessing is given (when in the Paul VI hall), the pope moves up the central aisle and stops every five meters or so, going left to right, accompanied by his secretary and the prefect of the papal house. These men gather the various offerings made (books, statues, paintings, creches, clothing, letters, etc.). The pope shakes hands and allows himself to be photographed with families by one of two authorized Vatican photographers. When the public audience takes place in St. Peter's Square, the pope makes one or several trips by car around the square in the areas where the participants are seated. There are always special seats reserved for noted personalities passing through who were unable to arrange a private audience. These special guests are admitted, after the public audience, to a meeting once called the *bacciamano* ("kiss on the hand") which does not normally last as long as a private one-on-one audience, but which can become, on occasion, a valuable conversation with the pope. This type of meeting, as opposed to an officially pre-arranged private audience, can be more spontaneous and relaxed and offers the possibility of surprising the pope with a subject for discussion. Although the private audience with the pope is a more solemn occasion, contrary to widespread public opinion on the matter, a meeting with the pope does not depend only on his interest level, apparent in the questions he might ask; it is also a matter of the visitor's skill in stimulating an intriguing conversation. The reason is simple and relates to the core responsibility of the papal role: the sovereign pontiff, more than any other chief of state, sees a parade of people registering their varying interests and concerns within the universal Church and in the world. Each meeting stipulates that the pope focus his attention on these people and their concerns before the photographer's lens. It is a cruel illusion to believe that the pope recognizes everyone who is introduced to him and that he has consulted a kind of file to prepare appropriate words for each visitor.

Philippe Levillain

Bibliography

Del Re, N. *La Curia romana: Lineamenti storico-giuridici*, Rome, 1970.

Willi, V. J. "Les audiences," *Le Vatican*, Paris, 1979.

AUDITOR, ROTA. To assist him in the exercise of his judicial, spiritual, and temporal authority, the Roman pontiff since early antiquity has retained in his immediate entourage counselors competent in both civil and CANON LAW. These advisors are called *capellani papae*; their role is to prepare papal decisions in trials submitted from all corners of the Catholic world for the judgment of the head of the Church. These advisors come from the countries whose cases are submitted to the Holy See in order to facilitate and clarify decisions made. Because of a growing number of appeals and cases, JOHN XXII (1316–34) in 1326 instituted a body of prelates to accelerate and better regulate these procedures. This group, composed of members with the necessary qualifications and legal power, bore the official title of Auditores Sacri Palatii Apostolici.

For about a century, the number of these auditors varied according to the number of appeals addressed to the pope. In the late 15th century, SIXTUS IV (1471–84), in the bull *Romani pontificis indefensa sollicitudo* (14 March 1472), established that there would be twelve auditors. He decided that there would be eight Italians—three from Rome, one from Bologna, one from Ferrara, one from Venice, one from Milan, and, alternately, one from Florence or Perugia. The other four auditors would be from the other side of the Alps: a Frenchman, a German, a "Castilian subject," and a "subject of the king of Aragon." The list of French titularies has continued uninterrupted since 1230, when Pierre Colmieu first assumed the role; he has had 59 successors up to the 1990s.

The cases handled by the auditors at the time extended to all matters submitted to the Holy See, including rites and procedures related to BEATIFICATIONS and CANONIZATION. In time, these types of cases were entrusted to specialized CONGREGATIONS, limiting the jurisdiction of the auditors of the Rota to special cases of civil and canon law, such as annulling marriages.

The auditors of the Rota, named by the pope, began their mission on the day they were named by the dean's pronouncing the formula *Esto auditor*. Since the apostolic constitution *Pastor bonus* (29 July 1988), the title "auditor" has been replaced by the term "judge." Now, a judge begins to exercise his duties after taking an oath before the College of Judges in plenary session. The judges of the Rota are now required to retire at the age of 75.

The gravity and importance of their functions in papal Rome meant that the Rota's prelates had to reside in Rome. After the ambassadors, these were the most important representatives of their respective nations. They greatly influenced the development of foundations aiding the spiritual and temporal needs of their compatriots who were pilgrims or residents in the city of Rome. They benefited from various privileges and occupied a special place in processions during papal ceremonies. They were also involved in the blessing ceremony and the distribution of the *pallium*.

Bernard de Lanversin

See also ROTA, TRIBUNAL OF THE.

AUTOMOBILES, PAPAL. The appearance of the automobile, replacing the horse-drawn carriage, and the creation of a papal garage followed the normalization of relations between the Holy See and Italy after the LATERAN ACCORDS. The automobile had not theretofore been a means of transportation at the Vatican, but until then popes had little need for automobiles. Even though the archbishop of New York gave PIUS X a custom-built black-and-white 1909 Itala 20/30, fresh out of the Locati e Torretta workshop in Turin, the pope never used it. He also had a Fiat, received in 1914, but never used it either, apparently disdaining carriages that made noise. PIUS XI, more sporty and modern, received a 1922 Bianchi on the occasion of his election to the papacy. This gift from the ladies of his former archbishopric of Milan was inaugurated into use in an official ceremony to transport the statue of the Virgin of Loretto, patron saint of aviators, on 1 September 1922. The car traveled with diplomatic license plates bearing the insignia of the king of Italy. Pius XI received a second

Bianchi in 1926. In the same year, twenty-five small trucks were acquired from Fiat to replace the mules used at the Vatican, and four limousines were rented for ceremonies. Traffic issues concerning automobiles, planes, and boats in Vatican City are mentioned in article VI of the Lateran Accords. The Holy See followed up these agreements by setting up a service to register all vehicles. The automobile garage was divided into two categories: cars reserved for the pope and high-ranking dignitaries were to bear license plates with red letters and numbers on a white background; service vehicles or residents' cars were to bear license plates with black letters and numbers on a white background. The registration of cars was simple: the three letters SCV (Stato della Città del Vaticano), followed by a registration number. All the pope's vehicles bear the first numbers in red. It was long an enviable distinction to have Vatican City license plates—something like an access card to the ANNONA. Today that is no longer the case, given Holy See functionaries' preference for anonymity and the fiscal complications connected with temporary export license plates.

The pope, who had been a "prisoner of the Vatican" since 1870, went out again into the city of Rome on 22 December 1929, to attend the jubilee celebration of his priesthood at the St. John Lateran Church. The automobile he used was a Graham-Page, offered a few months earlier as a gift from the Graham brothers, pious Catholics from the United States. After this, cars became the usual means of transportation for the sovereign pontiff. Images of popes in cars were not, however, very frequent until PAUL VI and the increase in papal TRAVELS. Paul VI always borrowed cars lent to him abroad by his official hosts in different countries. In Bogota in 1968, he traveled through the crowd aboard an open Land Rover, the modern version of the SEDIA GESTATORIA. In the holy year of 1975, the pope regularly began to move around St. Peter's Square in a motorized vehicle as when JOHN PAUL II held open-air AUDIENCES. On 13 May 1981, John Paul II was injured in an ASSASSINATION ATTEMPT while riding in a Fiat convertible with the top open. When he came back out in public on 7 October of that year, he rode in the same car.

Nonetheless, security measures began to be imposed, and the pope accepted a gift from Mexican Catholics especially designed for his protection. The so-called popemobile is a bullet-proof vehicle in which two people can ride standing up. This famous car has since been as closely connected to the pope as is the Rolls-Royce belonging to the queen of England.

Philippe Levillain

Bibliography

Moretti, V. *Le auto dei papi*, Rome, 1981.

AVIGNON, PAPACY OF. The establishment of the papacy in Avignon was the choice of Pope CLEMENT V—the former archbishop of Bordeaux, Bertrand de Got—elected on 5 June 1305. He decided not to return immediately to Rome out of fear of conflict with violent factions that had been warring since BONIFACE VIII's pontificate (1294–1303). Moreover, he wished to stay close to France, yet outside territory controlled by the French, in order to negotiate a reconciliation between the kings of France and England, which he deemed essential for resuming the crusades. Clement V was crowned in Lyon and convened a COUNCIL at Vienne in order to deal with a controversy surrounding the Knights Templars. He found it convenient to settle temporarily in an imperial city, near France and not far from the Venaissin county, which the Holy See had purchased in 1229. Clement V went to Avignon on 9 March 1309 and set up temporary residence at its Dominican convent and in the Comtat castles. The agitation provoked in Italy by Emperor Henry VII's expedition there, as well as the pope's illness, were sufficient to dissuade Clement from leaving the shores of the Rhone for Italy.

The City and the Lordship. An ancient Roman city and since the 4th century, the seat of a bishopric, Avignon is notable for its strategic geographic position high on a rocky plateau dominating the Rhone Valley trade route. A site of political unrest since the 5th century, it was coveted by the Burgunds, the Ostrogoths, and the Franks. The city then became part of the county of Forcalquier. In 1129, it was designated as a *commune* ("municipality"), with the count's agreement. The importance of Avignon for regional commerce was such that a bridge was built there to span the Rhone River, inaugurated in 1180 by the bishop, St. Bénézet.

During the crusade against the Albigensians, the bourgeois residents of Avignon backed the count of Toulouse. After a siege of three months, the city was taken on 12 September 1226 and destroyed. Charles d'Anjou, who then became the lord of this county through his marriage to Béatrice de Provence, brought Avignon under his control by abolishing the commune (1251). (It should be noted that Avignon is not part of the nearby county of Venaissin, whose capital is Carpentras.) For generations this region had been divided between the count of Provence, at this time Charles d'Anjou, and the count of Toulouse, then Alphonse de Poitiers, later succeeded the king of France, his heir. Avignon was reunified when king Philip the Fair of France ceded his share in 1290 to his cousin, Charles II of Anjou. It was his great-granddaughter, Queen Joanna I of Naples, who finally sold Avignon to CLEMENT VI for 80,000 florins on 19 June 1348.

Seat of the papacy from 1309 on and seat of one of the popes during the GREAT SCHISM OF THE WEST, Avignon remained Holy See property, with the inclusion of the

Venaissin county and its capital, Carpentras, after 1274. The inhabitants of Avignon opposed the plan of ceding it to Louis XI, a proposal put forward by Pope EUGENE IV' in order to gain favor with the king of France. The papal presence was ensured by a cardinal LEGATE and then, after the 16th century, by an archbishop bearing the title of vice-legate.

The university created by Boniface VIII in 1303 was splendid evidence in the 14th century of advances in law and medicine. During the period of the Avignon papacy, it also served as a curial school and benefited from the presence of celebrated theologians attached to the papal court.

Avignon has several abbeys. Most of these were founded before the arrival of the popes: Saint Agricol, founded in 680 by Bishop Agricol with the Benedictines from Lérins; Saint-Laurent (Benedictines), founded in 951 by Count Amelio; Notre-Dame-des-Doms, Regular Canons of Saint Augustine, 1068; Saint-Catherine, founded in 1254 for the Cistercians by Bishop Zoen Tencarari and joined to Saint-Véran in 1436; Saint-Claire, Claritians or "Poor Clares," founded in 1250; and Saint Véran, Benedictines, founded in 1140 by Count Guy de Forcalquier and joined to Saint-Catherine in 1436. The papal residence in Avignon prompted the foundations of new abbeys, such as Notre-Dame, transferred from Tours to Avignon by Cardinal Anglic Grimoard (Benedictines, 1368; suppressed in 1428) and Saint-Pierre-de-Luxembourg (Celestines, 1390). The College of Saint-Martial, created in 1362–79 for the Cluny monks studying in Avignon, was established in Queen Joanna's former palace.

The Avignon Popes. When Clement V died (6 April 1314), a CONCLAVE was held at Carpentras, where the pope had spent the winter and where the Curia was still in residence. It then transferred to Avignon and finally to Lyon. There the cardinals, after two years of debating candidates in vain and many upheavals, interruptions, and temporal pressures, finally decided on an old cardinal, Jacques Duèse, who was considered a "transition pope" (7 August 1316). Duèse, who took the name JOHN XXII (1316–34), decided to settle in Avignon, where he had been a bishop (March 1310–February 1313) and where the bishop at the time was his nephew, Jacques de Via. He set up his home within the episcopal palace, kept the bishopric and the revenues, and organized the Curia around his residence. The major structures for handling administrative matters and spiritual and temporal justice at Avignon were definitively set forth during his pontificate.

The pope enjoyed precious independence in Avignon while he and Emperor Louis of Bavaria were in the throes of the last episode in the struggle between the Church and the empire. John XXII was declared deposed by an emperor he excommunicated and faced the inauguration of

the antipope NICHOLAS V (1328–30). He was also shaken by his blunder in the affair of the Beatific Vision and was prey to the unrest of the Spiritual faction of the Franciscan order. Nonetheless, John XXII took good advantage of his borderline position with the empire, which guaranteed his safety and independence.

The Avignon papacy was temporary in John XXII's view, but he was content to renovate the episcopal palace. Well-placed on the economic and political arteries of western Christianity, until the arrival of the Great Companies in the 1360s Avignon remained a small, tranquil town. Pope BENEDICT XII (1334–42), a former Cistercian monk born Jacques Fournier, undertook several theological and moral reforms. He taught theology, and, as bishop of Pamiers, bishop of Mirepoix, and finally cardinal of the Curia under John XXII, he enthusiastically directed the INQUISITION against burgeoning heresies. As pope, he repressed the abuses of pontifical administration, forced bishops to stay in residence, and reduced the practice of EXPECTATIVES. He was a model of personal rectitude and refused to practice any type of nepotism.

Benedict XII led an important reform of religious orders. He reestablished the original requirements of austerity for the Cistercians, unified the Order of St. Benedict, and revived strict discipline in intellectual activities, which had fallen by the wayside since the emergence of the mendicant orders and the establishment of universities. Despite the resistance and discontent freely expressed after his death, he managed to bring the Franciscans to obedience and curbed the anarchical evangelism of the smaller brotherhoods.

This wave of reforms, led with a constant refusal of any concessions to certain common practices of the time, did not win over the Curia and the clergy, and public opinion even less. The pope was accused of authoritarianism, contempt, egotism, and avarice. Deeply involved with the internal workings of the Church, he proved to be little suited for ensuring a leadership role in the political life of Christianity. He did not understand events in Italy and made multiple failed and awkward gestures at reconciliation. Likewise, he failed to end quarrels that had opposed the papacy to Emperor Louis of Bavaria since the time of John XXII. In order to ensure his authority over the Church through efficient government, Benedict XII organized a comfortable pontifical seat by building his palace as an austere fortress. This was conceived as a useful setting for rapidly developing administrative needs and for the stability sought for the Curia outside Italy.

The court of Avignon had five hundred curialists, half of whom were administrators and judges. Domestic services increased with the needs of so many people, both in the papal palace and in the cardinals' quarters. The size of the apostolic chamber grew with the development of a fiscal system extending to all church revenues. The CHANCERY increased the number of its offices to deal with the policy of automatically reserving collations. This led clerics, bishoprics, and abbeys throughout Christianity to address their requests directly to the pope to obtain even the most modest benefices. In addition, it was necessary to manage the surplice fees and to record the collations and deferred collations called expectatives. All this engendered countless disputes which were brought to the attention of the CONSISTORY and AUDIENCES, not to mention the PENITENTIARY.

CLEMENT VI (Pierre Roger, 1342–52) was a Benedictine from Limousin. A theologian known for his sacred learning and talent as a preacher as well as for his background in classical culture, he was also a statesman whose behavior often recalled that of a temporal prince. Richly funded in BENEFICES (as the abbot of Fécamp, bishop of Arras, and then archbishop of Sens and finally Rouen), he served the interests of King Philip VI. He acted as the spokesman for the clergy at the assembly of Vincennes in 1329 and sat on the royal council. The king used him as an ambassador on numerous occasions, notably in England and in Avignon. During his pontificate, there was collusion between the papacy and the French king's government, so obvious that it provoked severe criticism and hostile reactions up to and including the Great Schism, the ultimate result of this conflict. Clement VI's nepotism offended his contemporaries, who saw the pope make four of his nephews cardinals; one of them became Pope GREGORY XI, and a fifth nephew became an archbishop and another an officer in the Roman court. After buying the lordship of Avignon from Queen Joanna I of Naples in order to be "at home" when in residence, Clement VI considered Avignon as the proper residence for the pope. In order firmly to establish the papacy on the banks of the Rhone, the pope doubled the papal palace in size and grandeur, with a definitive intention to create and maintain a luxurious bastion for the papacy. He held a brilliant court there which attracted literary and artistic figures as well as businessmen. Avignon then drew many immigrants, mainly from the south of France and from the Rhone Valley area. As the city grew and construction projects proliferated, religious foundations began to take on more importance and the university flourished. Business intensified, both in order to fulfill the new, larger city's needs—it had 30,000 inhabitants in 1376—and to benefit from the influx of capital resulting from the fiscal exploitation of Christiandom.

Clement VI was the last pope to act as an arbiter in European affairs, but this ended in more disappointments than prestige. In particular, he failed in his attempts to impose mediation and forge a peace between France and England. He also failed to be recognized as the arbiter in the conflict between Aragon and Mallorca. After the death of King Robert I of Anjou, he lost himself in the imbroglio of Italian quarrels and reacted with difficulty to the Roman revolt in Cola di Rienzo. Nevertheless,

Clement VI courageously and intelligently confronted the Black Plague of 1348 and its consequences. A merchant friend of Petrarch's wrote that the epidemic had killed half the population of Avignon. Clement VI especially protected the Jews, who were threatened by the populace who believed that they were guilty of spreading the epidemic. The pope also reacted firmly to the expansion of the Flagellant movement, fanatic groups who did penance by whipping themselves and begging for divine pardon. These groups had come from the Rhine Valley to Avignon in 1349, but they mostly dispersed after the pope's condemnation; those who remained ended up in prison or were executed.

INNOCENT VI (Etienne Aubert, 1352–62) was a law professor, loyal to the king of France. He had been a judge in the seneschal's court in Toulouse. A sick and indecisive man, he never even thought of returning to Rome, but he intended to reestablish order in papal Italy through the work of his legate, the remarkable Cardinal Albornoz. Simultaneously, he redoubled efforts to bring peace between France and England. He suffered the consequences of the dispersion of mercenary companies when they were left without work after the treaty of Brétigny, especially the company of the "Archpriest" Arnaud de Cervole, who ravaged the south of France and threatened Avignon. Convinced of the need to reform the Church, Innocent VI restricted pontifical luxury and brought the Franciscans to obedience, curbing the prophetic and evangelical tendencies of certain members of the order. He also attempted to reform the order of the Hospitalers, who had been unwilling to submit to the Holy See.

URBAN V (Guillaume Grimoard, 1362–70) initiated a different politics. This pious and erudite Benedictine, who had been abbot at St. Victor's in Marseilles and NUNCIA in Naples, became the protector of the universities and created new faculties and colleges. Nonetheless, his politics was marked by awkwardness. He impeded the efforts of his legate Gil Albornoz against Bernabo Visconti, and he treated the problem of the mercenary companies invading the south of France and the Rhone Valley with naïveté. Urban V dreamed of reestablishing the Holy See in Rome yet underestimated the difficulties of such a return when he affirmed the principle that St. Peter's seat is in Rome. He left Avignon on 30 April 1367 with only a part of the Curia, but he returned disappointed and exhausted on 27 September 1370. He died in Avignon on 19 December of that year.

Gregory XI was the nephew of Clement VI and had been created cardinal at the age of nineteen. He was an excellent jurist and a member of the Church's government. One of his major preoccupations was the fate of the religious orders, whose reforms he organized and supported. However, lacking clear vision regarding the deep causes for the success of heretical preaching, he attempted more or less in vain to give the Inquisition an efficacy it had lost owing to a lack of support from the temporal powers.

The pope was especially concerned with the CRUSADES necessitated by the advance of the Turks. He managed to end several conflicts that had been immobilizing Europe in its confrontation with the Turkish invaders. His diplomatic successes won him true prestige, especially when he resolved the conflict between Emperor Charles IV and King Louis of Hungary and that between Bavaria and Savoy. Moreover, he had experience in Italian affairs, something his predecessor Urban V lacked. He therefore decided to reestablish the papal presence in Rome, whatever the cost. He did so despite a dramatic conflict with Florence, for whom the pope's return to the peninsula countered its claims to control central Italy. Gregory XI left Avignon on 13 September 1376 and entered Rome on 17 January 1377, but he died the following year (27 March 1378) without having achieved his political goals.

At this point, the Great Schism exploded the West. CLEMENT VII (Robert de Genève, 1378–94), the antipope elected by the conclave at Fondi, naturally found in Avignon a Holy See with most of Gregory XI's adherents still in residence. His successor, BENEDICT XIII (1394–1417) abandoned Avignon only in March 1403 when threatened by an armed force. After his departure into exile in Peñiscola, Avignon welcomed the antipope JOHN XXIII, elected successor to ALEXANDER V (1409–10). By ending the schism with the election of a single pope (November 1417), the Council of Constance finally ended the Avignon papacy, which had lasted more than a century.

The Legacy of the Avignon Period. Avignon then became a mere possession of the Holy See. A local administration governed by vice-legates was established, and this delegation continued as a royal but nonpolitical court until the French Revolution. Considerably strengthened during the Avignon period to handle the responsibilities of the pope's expanded role, the papal administration reflected increased centralization in the Church that began at the time of the Gregorian REFORM. The pope was increasingly involved in the affairs of local churches as a result of the dormancy of the conciliar institution after the Councils of Lyon (1274) and Vienne (1312) and the increasingly extensive reservation of even minor benefices to the pontifical collation. In addition, there was the sheer weightiness of the fiscal system established since the 13th century for churches and clerics. John XXII and his successors were thus led to organize and lodge smaller jurisdictions and administrations with an itinerant Curia of few members, who followed the pope's moves among his residences in the area of Rome. Thus, it was the fact that the administration handled matters with both secular governments and the clerics of all of western Christianity that made Avignon a true capital.

The administrative institutions developed in Avignon, included the Consistory, where cardinals and certain high prelates close to the pope met; it acts as both a political and ecclesiastical advisory committee and the supreme arm of papal jurisdiction. The Curia also includes the Chancery, responsible for the diplomatic form of decisions and judgments made by the pope in the form of BULLS; the APOSTOLIC CAMERA, which organizes and controls the financial management of the papal state and its accounting; and the Penitentiary. It also has a number of specialized tribunals responsible for judging cases that are not brought before the pope himself but judged in the Consistory. For example, forbidden literature goes through an audience, a preliminary hearing, before the examination of the matter in depth; in particular, the validity of the evidence produced and the ecclesiastical quality of the plaintiffs are reviewed. Created in Rome in the 13th century, the institution of the audience was reorganized in Avignon under John XXII (with the constitution *Qui exacti temporis* of 1331). The auditor of forbidden literature is assisted by readers responsible for the public reading of the documents in question. He must also attend to the publication through public reading of all bulls that can be opposed.

Auditors of cases from the apostolic palace know the substance of all matters referred to them by the pope, but the audience's particular area of competence is the countless cases involving benefices. Organized in Rome as early as the 1270s, the audience did not receive a permanent delegation from the pope until the first years of the 14th century. It received its definitive status through the constitution *Ratio juris* (1331). From 1330 on, it is often called the ROTA tribunal, a reference to the circular bench on which the judges, called auditors, are seated. These auditors have increased in number over time (eight in the 14th century, twelve at the end of the 15th) and are selected from among the best jurists of the Curia. No appeal is possible after their judgment.

The Penitentiary, already active in Rome in the 13th century, was also reorganized by John XXII (constitution *In agro dominico*, 1338). It specializes in the judgment of spiritual matters and conflicts relating to the sacraments. It instructs and judges requests for absolution following canonical punishments. The abuse of excommunication practiced at the end of the 14th century by the Apostolic Camera—which sometimes excommunicated bishops and abbots for payments of common services made a day late—led to the dismantling of the canonical competencies of the Penitentiary. The Apostolic Camera then took on the responsibility of judgments against prelates who finally paid their debts. The cardinals' tribunals, presided over by an auditor, are often responsible for giving summary instruction on matters later deferred to the pope.

Crises in the Church. The history of the Avignon papacy was marked by several political and ecclesiastical crises. The first was a result of the conflict between Boniface VIII and Philip the Fair. The king threatened to revive litigation against the memory of Boniface, and Nogaret pursued his absolution for his participation in a skirmish at Anagni, as well as in a new matter, the affair of the Templars. Clement V had vacillated for a long time before reforming the military orders and had dismissed denunciations of the Templars as bothersome. King Philip arrested the French Templars on 13 October 1307; among those seized were high dignitaries of the order. Later, royal justice, the cardinals' commission, and the dioceses conducted investigations whose conclusions indicted the Templars, but they were never able to make any charge stand against the order.

The Council of Vienne, opened on 1 October 1311, hesitated to support an order crippled by unpopularity and incapable of refuting accusations against it. Nonetheless, it decided not to condemn it for alleged acts committed by only some of its members. Clement V hesitated once again and refused to allow dignitaries to appear who would certainly have convinced the council, but he refused to make a formal condemnation. King Philip came to Vienne to urge a decision whereby the pope chose to suppress the order—not as guilty, but because it would prompt a scandal—without consulting the council (bull *Vox in excelso*, 3 April 1312). The Templars' possessions and wealth were allocated to the Order of Hospitalers, in order to facilitate the organization of a future crusade. Not forgetting that it had been convened to reform the Church, the Council of Vienne made various specific decisions concerning the Beghards and Beguines and the Inquisition, as well as a response to the "evangelical" tendencies of the Spiritual Franciscans. For the most part, the reform was put off, and the Church went through many crises before the Councils of Constance and Basel in the 15th century resolved these issues.

By 1312, relations between the papacy and France had calmed down. This was favored by the inclusion of many French clerics in the Curia at all levels, from the Sacred College to the institutions of financial administration. Although the association between the popes at Avignon and the king of France was not as close as was claimed by the clergy in England or Italy at the time, the Holy See was ever ready to hear the preoccupations and wishes of the French clergy. This was favored by the distribution of benefices the papacy reserved in collation.

With England, difficulties arose during the time of John XXII over the same practice, the collation of benefices. The king had no intention of sacrificing his royal rights. The French–English war exacerbated the conflict, since the English clergy saw that the revenues the popes reaped from England served to finance politics favorable to the king of France. By the reign of Clement VI, the conflict was openly declared. Parliament voted a statute on provisors (1351) that took away practically all prerogatives from the pope in matters of benefices, and then a statute of *praemunire* (1353) that removed all jurisdiction from him. In 1375, Gregory XI reached a limited agreement, which nevertheless left a hostile climate encouraging England to adhere to Rome during the Great Schism.

With the Holy Roman Empire, there were successive crises. Henry VII's 1312 expedition to Rome to be crowned emperor in the absence of the pope reinforced the GHIBELLINE party in Italy, which was hostile to papal power and to the influence of an ally of the papacy, the ANGEVIN king of Naples. On the occasion of the coronation, there were battles in Rome; the Orsini blocked the road to St. Peter's to prevent the emperor from passing through, although he was finally crowned at the Lateran. The death of Henry VII allowed Clement V to proclaim the superiority of the pope over the emperor (decretal *Pastoralis cura*). Later, John XXII entered into conflict with Emperor Louis of Bavaria, who nurtured the hostility of the Angevins in Italy. Louis had an antipope elected in 1328, the Franciscan Pietro Rainalducci da Corvaro (Nicholas V), whose party was composed mainly of brothers of the mendicant orders and who died in prison in Avignon (1333). From 1327 to 1346, war ravaged Italy. Supported by France and Bohemia, the pope pushed Louis of Bavaria to abdicate (1333), an abdication he then recanted. The pope also placed Germany under interdict just at the time a new imperial dynasty was rising in Luxembourg.

This conflict with Louis of Bavaria gave rise led to a whole body of political and juridical literature. The *Defensor pacis* is a long treaty justifying imperial independence and combating the political Augustinianism on which papal pretensions to universal sovereignty were founded. The authors were two Parisian academics, Jean de Jandun from Champagne and Marsilio of Padua, Italy. Both theologians were influenced by the writings of French legislators, by treatises written by Italian civilists, by Ghibelline literature, and by the Averroist current in philosophy. Opposing the views developed by Boniface VIII in the bull *Unam sanctam* and even the theses of moderate partisans of pontifical power such as Giles of Rome and James of Viterbo, the authors of the *Defensor pacis* defined the state as a natural reality. As such, it should be ruled by the consent of the people, who delegate powers to the prince without the intervention of the Church. They even denied the origin of divine power in the Church and ecclesiastical hierarchy. Pontifical power was seen as the result of a long series of usurpations at the expense of the community of the faithful. The supreme authority of the Church could only belong to the assembly of clergy and the faithful—that is, a council situated outside all hierarchy. As for secular affairs, the pope should not be involved. Louis of Bavaria had Marsilio of Padua come to act as his doctor and advisor, and Nicholas V was for a time archbishop of Milan.

In 1346, Louis of Bavaria was dethroned by the election as emperor of Charles IV of Luxembourg, son of the king of Bohemia, John of Luxembourg. This led to an imperial decree, the "Golden Bull" (13 January 1356), which definitively ended the imperial crown's manipulation by papal intrigues through the establishment of organized elections of emperors. Innocent VI accepted this fait accompli. For the papacy, this had the double advantage of making the split between the two parts of the empire (German and Italian) both official and permanent, and of precluding for a time the hereditary succession to the imperial crown. The conflict nonetheless continued in Italy, especially in Tuscany, Emilia, and Romagna. It represented one of the main preoccupations and one of the most burdensome financial responsibilities of the Avignon papacy.

Clement V responded successfully to a move by Venice to take over Ferrara (1308–13). John XXII managed to resist the league of Ghibelline cities in Lombardy (1316–34). The battles were directly fought by the papal legates Bertrand du Pouget and Giovanni Orsini. Benedict XII contended with an insurrection in Bologna, then the chaos perpetuated by the lords of Romagna and in the Marches with their old autonomist tradition. Clement VI experienced the loss of Bologna to the Visconti. Peace in Tuscany was reestablished with the treaty of Sarzana (1353), and the legate Gil Albornoz was then able to attempt pacifying relations between the papal state and Bernabo Visconti. Urban V finally chose to yield to Visconti in order to be free to organize a crusade (1364), but this did not create a lasting peace. Urban V's vain attempt at returning to Rome and his less than glorious return to Avignon only served to aggravate the anarchy in Italy and to consolidate the Avignon papacy. The uprisings in Florence and Bologna were evidence of the all-out war against the papacy that had existed since 1375. The "War of Eight Saints" seriously disturbed economic life for western Christianity when a papal ban was inflicted on the commercial and banking companies headquartered in Florence. Gregory XI assumed the battle fought by Urban V and died in Rome (1378). An election in Rome resulted from the pressure of the Roman people, tired of French popes and the exile of the seat of St. Peter.

More or less in response to this popular pressure, the cardinals meeting in Rome took advantage of the occasion to end French control of the Holy See. They elected an Italian archbishop, Bartolomeo Prignano (Urban VI). With the support of the French party, a new conclave was held in Fondi, where the son of the count of Geneva was elected. A relative of the king of France, Cardinal Robert of Geneva (Clement VIII) was not well loved in Italy, where he had brutally managed the interests of the Holy See as its legate in the conflict with Florence and in Roman affairs. After a deliberately anti-French election, the choice of Robert of Geneva was clearly an anti-Italian provocation. Positions hardened and the Great Schism of the West took on a nationalist dimension from which the Church suffered until the Council of Constance. Each pope sought his own faithful and attempted to organize his obedient followers. France and the Spanish kingdoms constituted the majority of Clement VII's followers. When he returned to Gregory XI's palace, he found a good part of the administration, archives, and treasury intact in Avignon. This inheritance counted as an especially important political and financial advantage while the pope in Rome failed miserably at improvising an effective administration owing to the absence of experienced men. This was one of the main reasons for the long duration of the Avignon papacy after 1378. However, this papacy was connected to the Angevin dynasty in Naples, also in difficulty. Both military force and diplomacy failed to reconcile the popes from the time of Benedict XIII (a cardinal from Aragon, Pedro de Luna), elected hastily in 1394, by cardinals who feared the schism would be resolved by a general rallying behind the sole surviving pope in Rome. Thereafter, the Church began to pressure the popes in a context of aggravated violence in Avignon, but the presence there of a good number of mercenary companies preserved the pope. The French clergy—strongly influenced by the University of Paris, disapproved of by the University of Toulouse, and supported by the government of Charles VI, which was dominated by the Burgundy party—twice declared its "subtraction from obedience." Castille followed France, while other kingdoms kept their distance. The Church of France thus learned to live without a pope, without realizing that it thus played into the hands of the king, and GALLICANISM began to take shape.

The solution imagined in 1409 would not come from the cardinals. Defeated on both sides, they finally agreed to meet at the Council of Pisa to elect a third pope, Alexander V (a Greek, Peter of Candia, 1409–10), succeeded by Cardinal Baldassare Cossa as John XXIII (1410–15). The latter was the main architect of the abandonment of the Roman pope Gregory XII by his own cardinals. The only result of the Council of Pisa was to provide the Church with three popes instead of two. In any case, Gregory XII had few followers, and Benedict XIII remained a refugee in his own country in Peñiscola. Thus, the paths to unity were opened, and the Council of Constance in 1415 dismissed the three warring popes and reunited the Church around a single pontiff. Martin V (Oddone Colonna, 1417–31) definitively reestablished the Church in Rome.

Matters of Doctrine and Morality. Theological reflection flowered after debates that, up through the 1270s, were the fruit of western Christianity's discovery of Aristotelian metaphysics, often through Arab philosophers, such as Avicenna and Averroes. In the 14th century, Thomism was little regarded and only taught discreetly in Dominican convents. The universities were more concerned with law and logic than with metaphysics. This was the time when, in both Paris and Oxford, a new approach to the material world was being founded (e.g., by William of Ockham), and French and Italian jurists worked to comment on the decretals, the last book of which was published by John XXII. Thus, it was completely unintentional when, during a sermon in 1332, the pope ignited a vicious quarrel on the subject of the "Beatific Vision." Traditional doctrine admitted that the just could see God and therefore enter paradise as of their particular Judgment Day—that is, the day of their death. John XXII shocked theologians and worried the faithful when he suggested that the elect were not really chosen until the Last Judgment, at the end of the world. After long consultations, the pope retracted this statement on his deathbed; his successor, Benedict XII, returned explicitly to the traditional doctrine in the bull *Benedictus Deus*, 29 January 1336.

During the 1300s, spiritual movements influenced theology and morality. Influenced by Joachim of Flora's eschatological prophetism and marked by the heritage of Cathar thought, some clerics—specially Franciscans—denounced the Church's compromises with the temporal world. One part of the Franciscan order, in northern Italy and southern France, came to advocate a return to absolute poverty. The "Fraticelli" also condemned community possession of places of worship or provisions and personal possessions. The "Spirituals" thus opposed the laxer attitude of the "Conventuals," who saw no contradiction in St. Francis's doctrine that mendicant brothers might exercise some power in the church and in society, as long as this power and its financial bases remained collective.

John XXII thought that he would be able to end this quarrel by being decisive. He decided that it was licit to possess a roof over one's head and provisions necessary to live on, and that it was heretical to place the ideal of poverty at the level of a tattered robe; moreover, poverty dispensed one neither from obeying the pope nor from internal discipline. The Fraticelli and Beguines were excommunicated unless they reentered their the order (7 October and 30 December 1317; 23 January 1318). The Franciscan Order then took a stand of solidarity in an attempt to defeat the papal call for control. Debate arose on subjects such as Christ's way of life with the Apostles: Did they possess anything, and was it collectively or individually? In 1322, the general chapter of the order issued a declaration in favor of absolute poverty. The bull *Cum inter nonnullos* (8 December 1322) declared the doctrine of the general chapter a heresy. The affair became even more complicated as a result of its interaction with Nicholas V's schism. The master general, Michael of Cesena, was taking refuge with Louis of Bavaria and backing the antipope, a former Fraticello. The Spirituals supported *Defensor pacis*, and the secular world took positions in the affair according to their political attitudes toward papal power. This long repression would finally succeed in stopping the Spirituals and their doctrine, often through the rigors of the Inquisition. The last of the Spiritual Franciscans disappeared in the 1350s, although some preachers such as Wyclif, revived their ideas through the end of the century. In much more modest form, these ideas are the basis of much university research and writing on the subject of Church reform.

Jean Favier

Bibliography

Guillemain, B. *La Cour pontificale d'Avignon, 1309–1376: Étude d'une société*, Paris, 1966.

La Papauté d'Avignon et le Languedoc (1316–1342) Cahiers de Fanjeaux, 26, Toulouse, 1991.

Mollat, G. *The Popes at Avignon (1305–1378)*, J. Love, trans., London and New York, 1963.

Mollat, G. *Vitae paparum avenionensium (1305–1394)*, new ed., 4 vols., Paris 1914–27.

Renouard, Y. *The Avignon Papacy, 1305–1403*, D. Bethell, trans., London, 1970.

B

BANKING AND THE PAPACY.

Antiquity. We do not know whether the popes of antiquity had recourse to the services of professional bankers or other private financial agents in order to make deposits, borrow money, or transfer it from one city to another. It is highly improbable that they did, except perhaps for very occasional transactions of which no record remains. One of St. Augustine's letters, discovered recently by J. Divjak, indicates that in A.D. 420, the count Boniface deposited with a money changer–banker (*collectarius*) a certain number of gold coins that he designated for the Church of Hippo; at that time, however, the money was not yet the property of the Church, and, in any event, the affair did not in any way concern the bishop of Rome. Four letters by Ennodius (3, 10; 4, 8; 5, 13; 6, 33) indicate that Pope SYM-MACHUS, at the very end of the 5th century, was led into debt, undoubtedly on account of the rules imposed on him by the Senate regarding finances and inheritances; his creditors were not financial specialists. GREGORY I intervened in 600 on behalf of Johannes, the last banker still working in Rome (*Letters* 11, 16), but that intervention is not a clear indication that the pope had been his client. It was in the nature of his trade that Johannes served everyone, and Gregory writes that often he served as guarantor for people without means.

CALLISTUS I (217–22), one of the popes at the beginning of the 3rd century, as a young man, worked in Rome as a money changer–banker (then called *argentarius* or *nummularius* in Latin, and *trapézite* in Greek). But the antipope HIPPOLYTUS of Rome, who recounts the history of Callistus in his *Refutatio omnium haeresium* (9, 12, 1–12), was very hostile toward his subject, whom he considered a heretic and personally dishonest; there is reason, therefore, to distrust what Hippolytus wrote about him.

During the reign of Commodus, Callistus, who was a Christian slave, had as his master one of the emperor's freedmen, Carpophorus (Marcus Aurelius Carpophorus),

from whom he received a sum of money for the purpose of developing a banking business. At one point, he refused to return their deposits to his clients (many of whom, it seems, were Christians or Jews); there was no more money in the bank, he said, and gave as reason that his debtors had not repaid their loans. After some clients alerted Carpophorus, Callistus tried to flee but was captured at Portus, near Ostia. Having made his way to the synagogue one Saturday (perhaps to harass some debtors), he caused such an uproar that finally the city prefect, Fuscianus, who held the office from 185 to 189, condemned him to forced labor in the mines of Sardinia. When free once again, Callistus no longer worked at banking. He served as an adviser to Pope ZEPHYRINUS, no doubt as a deacon, and succeeded him in 217.

As a banker, was Callistus guilty of imprudence in lending money to people with insufficient guarantees or in failing to keep enough reserves in the bank? Or should his insolvency be related to the financial crisis that seems to have raged during the reign of Commodus? Or did he waste his clients' money, as Hippolytus suggests? An answer can hardly be arrived at; the little banking "boutiques" of ancient Greece and Rome were highly vulnerable, and cases of bankruptcy surely were not infrequent.

Jean Andreau

Bibliography

Andreau, J. "La letter 7, document sur les métiers bancaires," *Les Lettres de saint Augustin découvertes par Johannes Divjak*, Paris, 1983, 165–76.

Bogaert, R. "Changeurs et banquiers chez les Pères de l'Église," *Ancient Society*, 4, 1973, 239–70.

Piétri, C. *Roma christiana*, Rome, 1976, 2 vols.

Middle Ages. The development of a true system of taxation in the Church gave rise in the 13th century to a movement of funds in amounts far exceeding the meager returns from the provinces of the Papal State. The revenues raised on taxes levied in England were not necessarily spent there, and from the holders of small benefices who were subject to the ANNATES, the pope could not demand a CURIA payment, which he could expect from the bishops and abbots for their common and everyday services.

The first bankers of the Holy See were the religious orders immediately under pontifical authority: the Templars, of course, for the TITHE designated for the CRUSADES, and the Hospitallers and the mendicant orders for other revenues. One or the other saw to the security of the funds collected, but they did a poor job of handling transfers, and hardly had the capability to establish the exchange rates that were necessary, given the diversity of the coin collected in the different provinces of Roman Christendom. Accordingly, from the time of the pontificate of INNOCENT IV, in the middle of the 13th century, financial companies became involved. They were known as "papal agents" or "money changers of the papal Camera." Without seeming to favor any one of them, the popes made use of the large Tuscan companies such as the Buonsignori of Siena, the Chiarenti of Pistoia, and the Riccardi of Lucca—who were also the bankers of the king of England—and, above all, of numerous Florentine companies—the Frescobaldi, the Mozzi, the Scali, the Spini. By the end of the century, in papal business as in all the European markets, the Florentines had relegated the other Tuscans to second place. Profiting largely from the political alliance of the popes with the GUELPH seignorial government, the Florentine banks monopolized the movement of papal funds for a century. In the other direction, they profited from the currency that was left liquid in the various banking centers of the West by a fiscal system the growth of which accelerated from 1320 on. The service consisted in the safekeeping of large deposits in branches at Bruges, Paris, London, Barcelona, Genoa, and Venice. The banks were suitably rewarded for the service by having at their disposal a mass of capital for commercial purposes. For the pope that also meant open credit from these companies, at rates more favorable than on deposits made elsewhere, and even better, the revenues could be counted on. Everyone, accordingly, was satisfied with a system in which the material transfer of funds to Rome was compensated for by the availability in all regions of credit that could be used for the pope's political purposes, whether to finance diplomatic actions, remunerate the faithful, or pay off companies and garrisons. From then on, the bankers profited from their position to concern themselves with very different functions belonging to the administration of the Papal State, and even to that of the Church. This was the start of a phenomenon that, in the 16th century, led those descendants of bankers who became the Medici and the Chigi toward princely titles, cardinal's hats, and even the tiara.

Reliance on Tuscan banks was interrupted by the wanderings of CLEMENT V and later his temporary installation at AVIGNON, and by the evident weakness of companies over-specialized in banking. More and more bankruptcies occurred. The Buonsignori collapsed in 1298 and were soon followed by the Mozzi, the Frescobaldi, and the Scali. Clement V's financial managers once again turned to the reserves of the mendicant orders. And the collectors once again transported sacks of money.

The Avignon papacy, well established from the time of JOHN XXII, distinguished in the nature of the things between the pope's ordinary FINANCES, essentially based in Italy and scarcely sufficient for Italian papal policy even without taking into account the regular transfers to the new Curia, and the revenue from the taxes levied on all the Western Churches. The latter promoted the establishment around Avignon (a location more central than Rome on the economic map of Europe) of a new money transfer industry that developed between 1300 and 1340, following the collapse of banking in Florence. First came the triumph of new companies such as the Bardi and the Peruzzi, and then that of the Alberti *antichi*, with which were associated some families of Lucca, such as the Guinigi, the Interminelli, and the Spifame, and, later, Andrea di Tici of Pistoia. Several factors contributed to these choices among financial companies, the primary one being the papacy's political relations with the large financial centers, Florence, Genoa, Venice, and Milan. This can be seen clearly at the point at which, beginning with the "War of the Eight Saints" (1376), the Florentines ceased to be welcome at the Curia. Second, the pope counted on the existence of permanent European networks. The best was the one that assured the greatest flow of money. But Avignon was not indifferent to the commercial basis of the banking powers, a basis that had been lacking in the companies ruined by the troubles of the 1300s. Because they maintained a presence as merchants in Europe's principal commercial centers, the pope's bankers could make use everywhere of the funds procured by the papal collectors, and could make available everywhere the funds necessary for political, diplomatic, and military relations. The wide commercial base allowed for equalization, freeing the administrators of the APOSTOLIC CAMERA from any constraint upon having receipts in one locality and disbursements in another. As for the companies, they fully trusted the curial and urban market of Avignon, with its concentration of men and fortunes, its need for luxury goods, and its recourse to commercial credit—cash payments were good for the owners of boutiques—and bank credit. Only the large companies could both offer credit and provide major commercial products. Finally, the pope was attentive to the foreseeable stability of these companies. It was a case of playing with credit, since every money transfer is a credit operation until payment is made, and therefore a gauge of confidence for the period concerned. That explains the monopoly, total or partial, given to certain very large companies. Until the banking crisis of 1342–6, four of them shared the papal business among them: the Scali, the Bardi, the Peruzzi, and the Acciaiuoli. These were used also by kings in the temporal sphere, notably the kings of England and Naples. The close links forged between these princes and their bankers led the latter to bankruptcy: the security of creditors was of less concern than political alliances and military successes. It was then that the Alberti *antichi* took over. Their agents at Avignon knew better than others how to make the most of the services the pope might expect from a well-balanced company. Thus, until the falling out of 1376, the Alberti *antichi* retained control of the papal business, except for an interlude that saw the return of the non-Florentines, the Spifame and the Guinigi of Lucca and even the Astesano of Malabayla, and occasional services by the small merchants of Lucca, Asti, Genoa, and Montpellier.

The falling out brought the Luccans back into the picture. Except for a few interventions by Andrea di Tici, they held the terrain until France withdrew obedience from the pope in 1398. In first place, naturally, was a company that had skillfully obscured its connections with the Tuscan city: that of Dino Rapondi and his brothers, whose position at Avignon was owing above all to their having won the business and the protection of the duke of Burgundy at Paris and Bruges. Next came the small Asti companies, like the Solario and the Ricci. In Rome, however, the best of the Luccans remaining in Italy were favored, such as the Guinigi, the Moriconi, and the Turchi, and some small Florentine companies such as the Caponi and the first Medici associated with the last of the Bardi. The company of Giovanni di Bicci de' Medici profited in 1409 from a clear case of embezzlement. For several years, considerable subsidies had been withdrawn from the Apostolic Camera in Rome by Cardinal Baldassare Cossa, LEGATE at Bologna and in Romagna, justified, he maintained, by the enormous amounts the Papal State had to pay for the defense of this admittedly insecure province. While he was alleging this financial hardship, between 1404 and 1409, Cardinal Cossa deposited nearly 43,000 florins with the Medici. On 22 March 1409, three days before the opening of the council of Pisa that would dethrone Pope GREGORY XII, Cossa withdrew the full amount. He financed the council, which elected one of his henchmen, an old Greek Franciscan who became ALEXANDER V. The following year, Cossa succeeded him as JOHN XXIII. Giovanni de' Medici turns up again at the council of Constance. He swung a deal by being party to a misappropriation.

The breakdown in papal revenues during the conciliar period made rather useless the services of the "money changer of the Apostolic Camera," an office held by a succession of small Roman or Florentine bankers. It was not until the discovery, in 1462, of the ALUM OF TOLFA, in the Papal State, that the Curia would once again see the need for high-level economic mediation. A company would take charge, by lease agreement, of all production of the mineral, essential for the drapery industry and all the more precious after Turkish advances made it impossible for traders from Genoa to exploit the alum of Phocaea, in Asia Minor. Alum now had to be extracted at Tolfa, and its transport and sale ensured all the way to Bruges and London. From 1463 on, the Medici got their hands on the largest part of this trade. Their company in Rome was called "depository of the Apostolic Camera," meaning that a banking function had been grafted onto the commercial operation. In 1471, a new contract gave the Medici a virtual monopoly. Other companies took their place after 1476. First were the Pazzi of Florence (1476), then the Centurioni of Genoa (1478), the Medici once again (1485), and then the Gentili of Genoa and the Ruccellai of Florence (1489). In 1501, the lease was taken over by Agostino Chigi of Siena, and he and then his three sons retained the business until 1530. The fortune brought to Chigi by the lease is well known; he came to be called Agostino the Magnificent, in a jesting allusion to the reputation of the Medici Lorenzo the Magnificent. This, finally, was Siena's revenge upon Florence.

The modern era saw all the large Italian financial companies, more or less associated with other bankers and notably with Roman banks chosen for convenience, succeed one another in the role of depository of the Apostolic Camera: the Grimaldi (1531–53) and Pallavicini (1566–78) of Genoa, the Ridolfi (1578–1614) and Acciaiuoli (1636–59) of Florence, the Torre (1677–1701) of Genoa, the Gangalandi (1719–43), and the Lepri of Milan (1751–87).

Jean Favier

See also FINANCES, PAPAL.

Bibliography

O'Sullivan, M. D. "Italian merchant bankers and the collection of papal revenues in Ireland in the 13th century," *Galway Archeological Association Journal*, 22 (1946–7), 132–63.

Renouard, Y. *Les Relations des papes d'Avignon et des compagnies commerciales et bancaires de 1316 à 1378*, Paris, 1941.

BANNERS. Papal vexillology, like HERALDRY, is governed less by rules than by practices that have changed with the times. Only the most important banners can be referred to here. For early periods, it is often impossible to say whether a banner is that of the Church, the pope, the HOLY SEE, or the PAPAL STATES, even if a distinction is regarded as existing among these four. The *vexillum* of the 12th and 13th centuries had a CROSS and probably was used both to accompany the pope and to represent the Church. Later, perhaps from the 15th century on, the banner carried near the supreme pontiff at major events displayed his personal coat of arms. This practice figures prominently in 16th-century iconography. The cover of a 1571 *biccherna* from Siena, representing the signing of the Holy League before PIUS V, shows a white banner with the arms of the Ghislieri; Titian had already shown ALEXANDER VI with Cardinal Francesco Pesaro, the "captain general" of the Church, beside him holding in his hand a banner with the Borgia coat of arms, without indicating whether it is a papal banner or an insignia of office. On another Siena *biccherna*, dating from 1595, the banners on the trumpets of the cortege bear the arms of the Aldobrandini (CLEMENT VIII).

In the 15th century, paralleling the practices of heraldry, the cross gave way to the KEYS of St. PETER. The manuscript *Entrée d'Espagne* (first half of the 14th century, Marciana library in Venice) shows the red banner bearing silver keys. The same banner is found in the chronicle of Giovanni Sercambi (1347–1424). The flag of the *milicia* on Filarete's bronze door at ST. PETER'S in Rome has the crossed keys to the right of the Condulmaro arms of Eugene IV. In 1512, the papal LEGATE, Cardinal Schiner, once again "honored" the banner of the Swiss city of Mellingen by adding the keys, and in 1520, Raphael executed a design with a banner decorated with the keys alone. But from the 15th century on can be found banners decorated with the TIARA. A 1479 *biccherna* shows such a banner in red, carried by the papal army during the war with the Florentines. A contemporary representation of the battle of the Colle di Val d'Elsa, during that same war, shows an identical banner. Toward the end of the 16th century, for unknown reasons, the background color of the standards was changed from red to white, and the figure of the apostles Peter and PAUL was added. The latter were represented also on the banner that thenceforth flanked the personal arms of the popes, such as those of CLEMENT IX in 1669 (whose banner still had a red background).

The papal NAVY made use of white flags decorated with the figure of the apostles, but also raised the personal arms of the popes with keys and tiara (PIUS VI). It is difficult to establish fixed rules for banners before the beginning of the 19th century. In 1825, LEO XII decreed that thenceforth the standard of the Church would display the apostles Peter and Paul grouped around the crucified Christ; that battleships would hoist the apostles surmounted by the keys and the tiara; and that boats for civilian use would fly a white flag bearing the keys and the pavilion (*ombrellino*), whereas the merchant navy would fly the same flag but with the tiara instead of the

pavilion. It was also established that, when the pope was aboard a battleship, it would raise the banner with the personal coat of arms of the supreme pontiff. However, if the pope were staying in a fortress, the white flag with the keys and tiara would be raised—a nuance with no known explanation.

The colors yellow and white, which later would prevail on papal banners, appeared for the first time on 16 March 1808, on the cockade prescribed by the secretary of state to distinguish the troops that had remained faithful to PIUS VII (SWISS GUARD, NOBLE GUARD, Capitol militia, financial guard) from those that had rallied to the French army occupying Rome and had kept the yellow and red cockade of the former papal army. The choice of the new colors perhaps was inspired by the colors of the keys (gold and silver) on the papal coat of arms. They were featured on the flag assigned to the civic guard in 1823 by Galeffi, the cardinal CAMERLENGO. At present (the 7 June 1929 annex to the Vatican City constitution, completing the Lateran pacts of the previous 11 February), whereas the Vatican City coat of arms is a red shield bearing the keys of Peter surmounted by the tiara, the flag, similar to that assigned to the troops of the Holy See in 1859, is divided into two gold (yellow) and silver (white) fields, the white part having in its center the crossed keys surmounted by the tiara. This arrangement (as noted by the heraldic expert Bruno Heim) does not conform to the rules of heraldry, according to which the keys and tiara should be on a gules (red) shield, placed on the line dividing the gold and the silver.

Wipertus Rudt de Collenberg

BAPTISTRY. In the Christian LITURGY of the first centuries, the administering of baptism was the activity that gave rise to the most varied architectural arrangements. At no time was there a single model for the baptismal font, and still less a baptismal building adopted universally by the different Christian communities. The baptistry could as easily be a secondary room attached to a church as a separate building with the baptismal font at its center.

The administering of baptism long remained the privilege of the bishop, in spite of the great number of baptismal fonts or baptistries associated with churches that never had the status of cathedral. The oldest known baptistry (before the year 257) is at Dura Europes, in Syria. It consists of a room like the room of a *domus* adapted for the Christian rite, with a rectangular font on small columns integrated into it. On the walls were frescoes decorated with scenes taken from the New Testament and relative to Christian salvation. These frescoes have been reconstructed at the Yale University Art Gallery, where they can be seen today. Rooms for the administering of baptism, already clearly defined by their architectural features, would have existed at the same period elsewhere in the empire, and certainly in the principal centers of the Christian world. It is only from the beginning of the 4th century, and from throughout the 5th and 6th centuries, that the concrete evidence of the structures themselves has come down to us (in Rome, Milan, Aquileia, Liguria, Provence, the Iberian Peninsula, Germany, Africa, the East). No evidence of the apparatus used in baptism in the catacombs exists for earlier than the 6th century. The most typical form of baptistry throughout the Christian world seems to have been derived from Roman buildings, with a center plan and often covered with a cupola. This design is based on that of the mausoleums, or of rooms found in baths, or the vestibules of palaces. The baptistry usually has a design that highlights its focal point, the *piscina* (pool), the center of the religious ceremony; the font is sometimes emphasized by a row of columns that sets it apart from the ambulatory. The architectural structure also gives evidence of the formal variations that were adopted and confirmed along with the evolution of the rite. From simple baptism with running or still water, but always on private property, there developed a structured procedure that took place essentially in three phases—catechesis, baptism, and *confirmatio* (Tertullian, *De baptismo*) during the season of Easter or Pentecost.

Among the various designs for baptistries (circular, quadrangular, polygonous), the octagon was probably the most widespread. There also were more complex structures resulting from the elaboration of different geometric figures, sometimes embellished with niches. Liturgical requirements seem to have been at the origin of the adding on of rooms, such as apsidal rooms perhaps for the bishop's throne, vestibules, or heating structures. One of the most exemplary of these buildings is the baptistry at Split, for which the archaeologist Dyggve has hypothesized a development linked to liturgical function. This is also the case with several other complex structures from the ancient world. The baptismal font itself also shows an evolution over time, in the modification of its exterior perimeter (different from the interior perimeter). The circular, quadrangular, or simply polygonal font of the 4th century took on many curved projections or adopted more complex polygonal forms. From the following century, there are several varieties of cruciform font, though these were not widespread. Hollowed out below ground level, the font was usually of masonry or stone and was covered with waterproof material, sometimes with decorative intent, as in the cases where marble or mosaic was used. A canopy supported by columns sometimes covered the font. The depth of the font could vary from several dozen centimeters to 6.5 feet/2 meters, with the variation usually indicating whether a rite of infusion or a rite of immersion was used. A system of ducts, for the inflow (rare) or drainage of water, allowed, in the first instance, for the font to be filled with an often symbolic amount of water, and, in the second, for it to be emptied. In one case, that of the baptistry at Lyon, there is an underground furnace that probably had to do with the rite of immersion.

The typical design of baptistries remained unchanged until the 8th century in the West and the Arab invasion in the East. In some places (for example in Spain), two basins can be found that are difficult to account for unless they can be seen as having different uses in the rite. There are two main hypotheses on the subject: that two forms of the rite were used, immersion and infusion; or that both basins were used for immersion, one for adults and the other for infants. Recent archaeological discoveries show that there were no precise rules for the placement of the baptistry, which was situated either inside the place of worship (in the narthex, transept, or nave) or outside it, in an adjoining room or a quite separate structure. The presence of a baptistry, long taken as proof of a cathedral church, instead indicates only that baptism was administered at the place of worship, which could be an urban parish, a suburban *martyrium*, or a rural *pieve*.

Venerated relics sometimes were deposited in the baptistry, and later it became also a burial place, at the time of the first interments inside the city (in several cases, beginning in the 5th century).

Rossana Martorelli

Bibliography

Apolloni Ghetti, B. "Le cattedrali di Milano ed i relativi battisteri. Nota sulla basilica di S. Lorenzo Maggiore," *Rivista di archeologia cristiana*, 63 (1987), 23–89.

Bonnet, C. "Baptistères et groupes épiscopaux d'Aoste et Genève: évolution architecturale et aménagement liturgiques," ibid., 1407–26.

De Palol, P. "El baptiserio en el ambito arquitectonico de los conjuntos episcopales urbanos," ibid., 558–606.

Duval, N. "Edificio di culto—IV—Il battistero," *Dizionario patristico e di antichità cristiane*, I, Casale Monferrato, 1983, 1088–91.

Episcopo, S. "L'ecclesia baptismale nel suburbio di Roma," *Atti del VI Congresso nazionale di archeologia cristiana (Pesaro-Ancona, 19–23 settembre 1983)*, Ancona, 1985, 297–308.

Falla Castelfranchi, M. ΒΑΠΤΙΣΤΗΡΙΑ (*Intorno ai più noti battisteri del Oriente*), Rome, 1980.

Février, P. A. "Baptistères, martyrs et reliques," *Rivista di archeologia cristiana*, 62 (1986), 109–38.

Khatchatrian, A. *Origine et typologie des baptistères paléochrétiens*, Mulhouse, 1982 (2nd ed.).

Krautheimer, R. *Early Christian and Byzantine Architecture*, 4th ed., New Haven, Conn., 1986.

Picard, J. C. "Ce que les textes nous apprennent sur les équipements et le mobilier liturgique nécessaire pour le baptême," ibid., 1451–68.

Saxer, V. *Les Rites de l'initiation chrétienne du IIe au VIe siècle*, Spoleto, 1988.

Testini, P. *Archeologia cristiana*, 2nd ed., Bari, 1980.

Testini, P., Cantino Wataghin, G., and Pani Ermini, L. "La cattedrale in Italia," *Actes du XIe Congrès international d'archéologie chrétienne (Lyon-Vienne-Grenoble-Genève et Aoste, 21–28 septembre 1986)*, II, Vatican City, 1989, 861–915.

BARBARIANS. What are called the "barbarian invasions" but instead should be called "migrations of peoples" is a historical phenomenon that extended over several centuries. After an initial wave that was arrested by the 4th-century emperors, the movement resumed around 370 with the arrival of the Huns in eastern Europe. The Germanic barbarians, who did not share the way of life of the peoples of the steppes, fled toward the west. The Visigoths asked for asylum in the empire, and then spread in both the East and the West. The Vandals, the Swedes, entered Gaul on the last day of 406. The Burgundians made their way into the valleys of the Doubs and Saône rivers; the Alemanni toward the Middle Rhine; the Angles, Jutes, and Saxons crossed the North Sea and invaded Roman Britain, that is, present-day England; and the Franks settled in the Lower Rhine, awaiting an opportunity to slide toward the south.

The barbarians were either Arians or pagans. After contact with the eastern Roman world, the Goths, or at least their aristocracy, had been converted by Arian missionaries. Bishop Ulfila had translated the Bible into the Gothic language and adopted the teachings of the priest Arius. Whereas the Catholic *credo* professed the consubstantiality of the Father and the Son, the Arians held that the Word was not of the same substance as the Father, and that the Son was subject to the Father. The spread of Arianism was facilitated by the use not only of the Germanic language in the liturgy, but also of a particular calendar and nocturnal ceremonies. It represented one of the elements of barbarian nationalism. The Visigoths, the Ostrogoths, the Vandals who settled in Africa in 439, the Burgundians, and the LOMBARDS were Arian Christians and therefore, for the Roman Church, heretics.

The other Germanic barbarians were pagans. They worshiped the forces of nature, a nature they saw as the field of battle on which the gods contend—Woden the god of war, Thor who battles giants, and other secondary divinities. Sacrifices of animals and especially of horses would bring blessings from the gods. The pagan Germanic peoples won the favor of the gods by means of magical practices, the wearing of phylacteries, and inscriptions in runic characters.

The arrival of the barbarians caused panic among the Catholics. Many thought the end of the world had come. The happy equilibrium that had been achieved after the conversion of CONSTANTINE, with the establishment of a Christian empire, seemed threatened. These barbarians, who had neither the same culture, nor the same laws, nor the same language, seemed to some unworthy of being called human. A Christian poet even wrote that between a Roman and a barbarian there is as great a difference as between a biped and a quadruped. The papacy had no cause to concern itself with the barbarian problem until Alaric, king of the Visigoths, laid siege to Rome and took it (409–10). Terrified by the arrival of the barbarians, some Romans who were still pagans wanted to offer sacrifices. Pope Innocent I (402–17) accepted, on condition that they did so in private; then he left Rome for RAVENNA. Just in time, for Alaric seized the city on 24 August 410. The leader of the Visigoths allowed his troops to pillage Rome, except for the basilicas of ST. PETER'S and St. Paul's Outside the Walls. He remembered that he was a Christian. But the Lateran palace was not spared.

From Leo the Great to Gelasius. When the Visigoths left Rome and even Italy to settle in southern Gaul and in Spain, the emperors, installed at Ravenna, maintained their authority as best they could. However, in 452, Attila, leader of the Huns, invaded northern Italy. The emperor Valentinian left Ravenna to take refuge in Rome. He asked Pope Leo I to accompany a delegation of Roman officials mandated to negotiate with Attila. The encounter took place near Mantua and was a complete success. Attila, persuaded by the pope, agreed to withdraw upon payment of a large tribute. This famous meeting, which Raphael would represent in one of the Vatican loggias, reinforced the pope's popularity. Three years later, the Vandal Genseric landed at Ostia and occupied Rome. Leo the Great, the only authority remaining in Rome, went to meet him, presented him with some liturgical vessels, and won his agreement to order his soldiers not to murder or set fires in Rome. Leo sang the praises of the apostles Peter and Paul as defenders of Rome, "capital of the world" and guardian of the orthodox faith. After the death of Leo the Great (10 November 461), the popes who succeeded him saw the imperial power crumble to the point where, at Ravenna, the last Western emperor was deposed by the barbarian Odoacer. Until 800, when the Western Empire was restored by a pope, there was only one emperor, in Constantinople. As a result, the pope, remaining in Rome, sometimes had the impression that he held the place of the former Western emperor, but for the most part the bishop of Rome was under the control of the barbarian sovereign, who ruled Italy. The senators rallied to the support of Odoacer. The prefect of the praetorium presided in the name of the king over the assembly of aristocrats and clerics who chose the successor to Pope Simplicius (468–83) by electing the deacon Felix, who was pope until 492. The following year, under the pontificate of

Gelasius I (492–6), one of the great popes of late antiquity, King Odoacer was defeated, killed, and replaced by the Ostrogoth Theodoric I, who earned the title the Great. He settled in Ravenna but kept an eye on affairs in Rome. Although of the Arian religion, he was tolerant during most of his reign. He was not displeased to know that there was a Schism between the Church of Constantinople and that of Rome. Gelasius sent Emperor Anastasius a letter that was to become famous, for it recalled that the auctoritas (authority) of the spiritual power was superior to the potestas (power) of princes. As for the barbarians, Gelasius deplored the ravages caused by the war between Odoacer and Theodoric, and the persecutions endured by the Catholics in the kingdom of the Vandals. He also pleaded in favor of Italian peasants deported to the kingdom of the Burgundians.

The Popes Between the Goths and the Byzantines. The incidents surrounding the succession of Pope ANASTASIUS II (496–8) forced Theodoric to intervene in Rome. One party among the Roman clergy had elected LAWRENCE and another had chosen SYMMACHUS. Years of disorder marked what has been called the "Symmachan schism." Theodoric began by bringing the two rivals to Ravenna and recognizing Symmachus as pope. Then, in 500, he went to Rome himself to pray at the tomb of the apostle Peter and have himself acclaimed by the people of Rome. After his departure, the supporters of Lawrence accused Symmachus of immorality. The king summoned the pope to Ravenna, but Symmachus barricaded himself in St. Peter's at the Vatican. Theodoric sent Peter, the bishop of Altinum, to intervene, and then called a council to judge the pope (May 501). Symmachus refused to appear, and thanks to the support of the people and of certain senators who were hostile to Theodoric, the pope regained his position and called a council at St. Peter's. Soon afterwards, Lawrence was abandoned by his partisans. These details of the affair are known from the LIBER PONTIFICALIS, of which the first chapters were drafted at the time itself; later they were expanded and completed.

Pope HORMISDAS (514–23), who succeeded Symmachus, had the joy of seeing union reestablished between Constantinople and Rome. But the ending of the schism, which satisfied the senators who were partisans of the Western emperor, was not pleasing to Theodoric. He began to show less favor to the Catholics. Even more, when he learned that Emperor Justin I had had the Arian churches in Constantinople closed, he forced Pope JOHN I (523–6) to lead a delegation of bishops and senators to have the measure revoked. Having failed, the pope was imprisoned upon his return to Rome and died shortly afterwards (18 May 526). The king had FELIX IV elected, but died himself within a few weeks. Rumors concerning the death of the king made the rounds. In Book IV of his *Dialogues*, Gregory the Great pictured the king hurled into the crater of a

volcano, that is, into hell, by Pope John and the senator Symmachus, another of Theodoric's victims.

Theodoric's successors were reconciled with the Byzantines, but Justinian, the new emperor, had firmly decided to reconquer the barbarian West. The Ostrogothic king Theodahad sent AGAPITUS I as ambassador, but to no avail; and Agapitus died during the course of his mission (August 536). The general Belisarius landed in Italy and retook Rome. Pope SILVERIUS, having been accused of treating with the Goths, was deported to an island and replaced by VIGILIUS (537–55): the popes had a new master and now had to submit to the control of the Byzantines. Vigilius was forced to go to Constantinople to approve the theological initiatives of the emperor and, after strong resistance, subscribed to the acts of the fifth ecumenical council, the council of Constantinople II, which condemned the "Three Chapters," that is, some allegedly Nestorian writings. But the council had repercussions in Merovingian Gaul and especially in northern Italy, which had been occupied by the Lombards beginning in 568. This was what is known as the "schism of the Three Chapters." The metropolitans of MILAN and of Aquileia separated from Rome.

The successors of Vigilius were subject to the Byzantines, while the establishment of the Lombard kingdom continued in the north and in the duchies of Spoleto and Benevento. Another danger for the papacy presented itself; it would last for a century and a half.

Gregory the Great and the Barbarians. GREGORY I, the first monk to become pope and the greatest pope of the early Middle Ages, showed great interest in the barbarian peoples. Paradoxically, this Roman, who in a letter to the Byzantine emperor Phocas had contrasted the barbarian kings "who are masters of slaves with the emperors who rule over free men," turned to these barbarians, the Visigoths, Lombards, Anglo-Saxons, and FRANKS.

During the 6th century, the Visigoths in Spain had remained Arian. What is more, King Leovigild had sought to convert all Spain to his faith. But the Hispano-Roman aristocracy remained Catholic, and Hermenegild, Leovigild's son, converted to Catholicism under the influence of Leander of Seville. He was seized and executed by his father. Reccared, Leovigild's successor, was also influenced by Leander, and abjured heresy in 586. At the council of Toledo III (589), the Visigothic kingdom became Catholic. Gregory the Great rejoiced at this and congratulated the king and his friend Leander, whom Gregory had met in Byzantium when he was papal legate in 582. He devoted chapter 31 of Book III of his *Dialogues* to "the martyrdom of Hermenegild," who was thereafter considered a saint.

With the Lombards, Gregory had more difficulties. Rome was threatened by these barbarians, who had settled in northern and central Italy. The pope had to defend the city in the absence of Byzantine troops. Two hundred bishops of the Italian peninsula, of which the pope was metropolitan, disappeared. Although the archbishop of Milan returned to communion with Rome in 573, three of his suffragan bishops persisted in the schism of the Three Chapters. At Aquileia, under pressure from the Lombard duke of Friuli, the bishop, who was a schismatic himself, resided at Cividale. The pope wanted the exarch of Ravenna to make peace with the Lombards, and, for his own part, he negotiated with King Agilulf. "If I had wished to devote myself to destroying the Lombards," wrote Gregory, "this nation today would no longer have either king or dukes or counts, and would be prey to irremediable confusion; but because I fear God I have not sought to involve myself in the destruction of anyone." Gregory looked for the conversion, not the destruction, of the Lombards. One blessing of chance smiled on him: the marriage of Agilulf to the Bavarian princess Theodolinda, who was a Catholic. Thanks to Secundus, the bishop of Trent, the pope intervened in the royal court. The heir to the throne, Adaloald, was baptized in the Catholic rite. The king himself was close to being converted under the influence of the Celtic monk Columbanus, who had settled at Bobbio. The pope sent Theodolinda some gifts, which she placed in the church at Monza, and a manuscript of his *Dialogues*. In this way, northern Italy became acquainted with Hermenegild's martyrdom as well as with the life of BENEDICT II. Unfortunately, upon the death of Adaloald (626), the Lombard kings returned to Arianism. Gregory the Great had at least hoped for the conversion of this people.

Gregory also met with some success among the Anglo-Saxons. The Celts, who had been driven back by the Germanic invaders, refused to convert the Anglo-Saxons, "so as not to meet them again in paradise," according to the Venerable Bede. In 595, Gregory asked the rector of the patrimony of Provence to ransom some Anglo-Saxon slaves being sold in Marseille, and to convert them. Undoubtedly he was already thinking of the mission he would send to Kent in the spring of 596. Augustine, the prior of the monastery of St. Andrew, and a dozen monks succeeded in converting King Ethelbert, whose wife, a Merovingian princess, was a Catholic. Augustine was installed in Canterbury, and became bishop of the Angles. The pope congratulated the "new Constantine" and rejoiced in the conversion of his people. He sent Augustine some reinforcements, led by the priest Mellitus. He advised Augustine not to destroy the pagan temples, but to rid them of idols and transform them into churches, so that the people who were accustomed to come to these places of worship would "feast on the occasion of the dedication of a church or of the feast days of the martyrs whose relics the church would have received. It is impossible to forbid everything at once to such uncultivated people; one who seeks to attain the summit must strive step by step, and not leap there in one bound."

This letter would often be quoted as a model for the pastoral approach to be taken in missionary work. The pope sent replies to Augustine's questions concerning conduct toward bishops, the Celts, and the Merovingians, and concerning the organization of the liturgy. These *Responsiones*, the text of which was preserved only by the English monk the Venerable Bede, seem unquestionably authentic. In the fifth response, the pope writes: "Holy Church corrects with love, tolerates with leniency, permits and supports with reflection." It was Gregory's desire that the new English Church have two metropolitans, of London and of York, as in the 4th century. Instead, Augustine remained the sole metropolitan, with his see at Canterbury, and in 604 he had two suffragans, at London and Rochester. Gregory also hoped that the Celtic bishops would rally to Augustine, but that did not come about.

It was on the Continent that Gregory had dealings with the Celts, in the person of the Irish Colombanus. Installed at Luxeuil in 590, Colombanus, who was proud of his orthodoxy and the good relations between the Irish Church and Rome, wrote to the pope asking him to send some exegetical works, and he also received a copy of the *Dialogues* and probably the Rule of St. Benedict from him. In one letter, he called Gregory "the most august flower of a softened Europe" and asked him to adopt the Easter practices of the Irish.

The Papacy and the Barbarians of the 7th and 8th Centuries. After the death of Gregory the Great (604), the popes continued to follow the progress of the Anglo-Saxon Church closely. The letters exchanged with the English bishops far outnumber those sent by the popes to Gaul or Spain. BONIFACE IV (d. 615) invited Mellitus of London to come to Rome. BONIFACE V wrote to King Edwin of Northumbria to urge the conversion and protection of Paulinus of York. In 653, Wilfrid, a former monk of Lindisfarne, came to Rome to learn the Roman LITURGY, and, having returned to England, he contributed to the victory of Roman practices over Celtic practices at the synod of Whitby (664). Five years later, Rome sent Theodore and Hadrian to England, the one as bishop of Canterbury and the other as abbot of the monastery of Sts. Peter and Paul in the same city. The Roman influence was decisive for the organization of the Church and for culture in England. The Venerable Bede, a disciple of Benedict Biscop, who had many sojourns in Rome, gives the best portrait of this culture. In his *History of the English Church and People*, he attributes the success of the Anglo-Saxon Church to the activity of the popes.

The Lombard princes returned to the Arian faith beginning with the reign of Arioald (626–36), but they were more or less tolerant. Rothari (636–52) was able to profit from the struggle between the Byzantines and Pope MARTIN I (d. 655). King Aripert (652–62), a grand-nephew of

Theodolinda, restored Catholicism, and in 698, the schism of the Three Chapters ended at the synod of Pavia. Lombard Catholics continued to dream of unifying all Italy by expelling the Byzantines, and the popes lived in dread of this eventuality: accordingly, they were led to call on the Franks. As for the Visigoths, relations with them were good but almost nonexistent. The Spanish Church was subject to the king, and the metropolitans of Toledo called councils that played as much a political as a religious role. Between 604 and 711, only eight letters were exchanged between the popes and the Spanish bishops, whereas forty-seven were addressed to the Anglo-Saxons. Although they acknowledged the pope, the bishops did not accept the criticisms he directed at them, as witnessed by the letter sent by Braulio of Saragossa to Pope HONORIUS I (625–38). LEO II (682–3) and his successor BENEDICT II (684–5) sent the decisions of the sixth ecumenical council, the council of Constantinople III, to the Spanish bishops, but Julian, the metropolitan of Toledo, undertook to comment on the Christological teaching. In 711, a Berber-Arab army invaded Spain. The Church was in disorder, and the Christian aristocrats fled to the north to form a small kingdom. There is no text indicating how Rome reacted to this invasion; the papacy was concerned above all with the Lombard threat and drew closer to the barbarian Franks.

Pierre Riché

Bibliography

Bertolini, O. *Roma di fronte a Bisanzio e ai Longobardi*, Bologna, 1941 (*Storia de Roma*, IV).

Demougeot, E. *L'Empire romain et les Barbares d'Occident, IVe–VIe siècle*, Paris, 1988 [collection of articles].

Fliche-Martin, IV and Riché, P. *Grandes Invasions et Empires, fin IVe–début XIe*, Paris, 1968.

Musset, L. *Les Invasions*, 2nd ed., Paris, 1969, 2 vols. [bibliography].

BARBER, POPE'S. The popes have not always been clean-shaven. St. PETER, according to ancient iconographic tradition, wore a beard, and abundant rough hair grew on the face of the fisherman of Galilee. The canons of masculine elegance that prevailed among the upper public administration of the Roman and then Byzantine Empire put a quick end to the fashion for papal hair, but it returned with vigor during the Renaissance. JULIUS II, both under the tiara and in armor, wore mustache and beard; PAUL III, SIXTUS V, PAUL V, URBAN VIII, INNOCENT XI, and all the popes of the 16th and 17th centuries wore either a goatee, growing as nature provided or else carefully tapered to a point, or a mustache, abundantly covering the upper lip or else artfully trimmed. It was in the 18th century, with its powdered wigs and affected proprieties, that hair once again disappeared from the face of the successor of Peter: from BENEDICT XIV to JOHN PAUL II, the pope has been clean-shaven.

This brief excursus shows the historical importance of the functions of the pope's barber: a distinguished member of the papal family, usually furnished with title *ajutante di studio* of His Holiness, he did the pope's hair, shaved him, helped him dress, and, if necessary, powdered the often wrinkled face of the venerable pontiff, whom he was one of the first to see early in the morning, and with whom he would not have failed to exchange a few words every day. The exceptional destiny of Gaetano Moroni (1802–83), the barber of GREGORY XVI and author of the *Dizionario d'erudizione storico-ecclesiastica da S. Pietro ai nostri giorni* (1840–61), grew out of this signal privilege of daily familiarity with the supreme authority of the Church. At the age of fourteen, Moroni was taken into the service of Abbot Mauro Cappellari, then procurator general of the Camaldolese order at the monastery of S. Gregorio al Celio; when Cappellari was made cardinal in 1826, and then prefect of the Propaganda, he kept Moroni in his personal service as barber, private secretary, and, finally, conclavist in 1829 and 1830. When elected pope on 2 February 1831, he named Moroni his first *ajutante di camera*. "I want to live as long as it takes to make Gaetano a gentleman (*un signore*)," the pope confided to Bernetti, the cardinal secretary of state. Although his brother Vincenzo gradually freed him of his duties as barber, Gaetano Moroni remained closely attached to the person of the pope. Conscientiously self-taught but somewhat dissolute, he undertook, under the pope's direction and at the instigation of the Venetian editor Battaggia, an immense compilation of the history of the CURIA and of the Roman Church, based on the scholarly works of Novaes and Cancellieri. There is reasonable doubt as to whether he was the sole author of the 103 volumes and 133,122 articles of his gigantic encyclopedia; probably others, perhaps even the pope himself, made suggestions, contributions, additions, and corrections. However, the unity of style that characterizes his work—wordy, unsystematic, pious and apologetic—and above all his notes and personal papers, bequeathed by his heirs to the Vatican Library, prove beyond possible doubt that he was the principal author of the compilation. Derided because of his common origin and the reason for his familiarity with the pope (Giuseppe Belli devoted many vengeful sonnets to *Ghitanino* and his family), sharply criticized by many learned contemporaries, plagiarized unscrupulously by numerous rivals and successors, Gaetano Moroni nevertheless brought his work to a successful conclusion, encouraged by Gregory XVI and, later, PIUS IX; toward the end of his life, he completed a valuable *Index* (1878–9) in six volumes of his *Dizionario*, including in it a naive and engaging, somewhat self-justifying, autobiography. Gregory XVI's barber thus has his place in history.

Philippe Boutry

Bibliography

Carusi, E. "Nuovi documenti sul Dizionario di Gaetano Moroni tratti dal suo archivio privato," *Aevum*, VII, 1933, 245–78.

Croci, E. "Gaetano Moroni e il suo Dizionario," *Gregorio XVI, Miscellanea commemorativa*, Rome, 1948, II, 135–52.

BASILICAS. See **St. John Lateran, Basilica of; St. Mary Major, Basilica of; St. Paul's Outside the Walls; St. Peter's Basilica.**

BASILICAS, MAJOR. The canonical definition according to which "no church can be honored with the title of basilica except by apostolic permission or immemorial custom, the related privileges deriving from one or the other" (canon 1180 of the CODE of 1917) determines the juridical status of these churches independently of the special favors and privileges accorded them in matters of liturgy or protocol. It is these latter that distinguish major basilicas, which share several characteristics, from their minor counterparts. Major basilicas are headed by a CARDINAL archpriest representing the pope, and a chapter whose members, as a body, have all the privileges of apostolic PROTONOTARIES (whose insignia they wear). Major basilicas are open all day to the faithful (unlike some other buildings), and all have five naves and five doors, one of which, usually closed, is called the "holy door" and is reserved for the jubilee year. Also, their main altar, called a "papal altar," is reserved for the pope; it can be dispensed from this restriction for the celebration of the Mass only through a special indult specifically naming a cardinal. Among the major basilicas, there are four patriarchal (or primary) ones: ST. JOHN LATERAN, the cathedral church of the pope in his capacity as Western patriarch, with precedence over all the others; and St. Peter's, St. Paul's on the road to Ostia (entrusted to the Benedictines), and the Liberian basilica, which traditionally represent the sees of Constantinople, ALEXANDRIA, and Antioch respectively. The anniversaries of their consecration (9 November for the Lateran; 18 November for St. Peter's and St. Paul's; 15 August for ST. MARY MAJOR) are observed as feast days throughout the Catholic world.

François Jankowiak

Bibliography

Molien, A. "Basilique," *DDC*, II (1937), 224–49.

BASILICAS, MINOR. In the same manner as the major BASILICAS, churches are raised to the rank of minor basilica by express papal decision conferring on them the title and the related privileges. Minor basilicas accordingly have the right to display the PAVILION, a sort of umbrella banded in red and yellow silk (the hereditary colors of the former Roman Senate), topped by a gilded copper globe with a cross. They are endowed with a special bell, the use of which is attested beginning in the 14th century on the occasion of the canonization of St. Bridget of Sweden (7 October 1391). The canons of minor basilicas may bear the *cappa magna*, made of purple wool and carried folded under the left arm. Without recourse being had to any special precedence except for churches of the same rank (parish, collegiate, or cathedral), the decision to erect a minor basilica is based on the criteria of the age of the church (for example, the cathedral of Albano, dating from the era of Constantine) and its historical, cultural, or symbolic importance (Paray-le-Monial, elevated in 1875, Lourdes, in 1874 and 1926, or Sacré-Coeur of Montmartre in 1919, all in France), and can be accompanied by affiliation with a major basilica, as when the cathedral of Nevers was linked with St. John Lateran on 9 February 1868. The city of Rome alone has eleven minor basilicas, and France had seventy-nine in 1934 (the cathedral of St. Sernin in Toulouse was granted the title in 1642). Far from declining today, the practice of erecting minor basilicas is clearly part of a strategy to strengthen the links between the local Churches and Rome, and can take place in the context of larger projects, as when JOHN PAUL II consecrated the basilica of Our Lady of Peace at Yamoussoukro, Ivory Coast (10 October 1990) as part of the preparations for the African synod of 1994.

François Jankowiak

Bibliography

Molien, A. "Basilique," *DDC*, II (1937), 224–49.

BEATIFICATION

Middle Ages. A slow development of canon law that took its final form only in the modern era led to what today is called beatification—that is, a papal decision that, at the end of a complex process, grants the title of blessed to a deceased servant of God, thereby placing that person with great precision at the intermediary stage between venerable and saint. The first centuries of Christianity were not encumbered with procedures for recognizing the holiness of an individual, especially when the end of earthly life was crowned by martyrdom. The medieval papacy very slowly established the notion of reserving CANONIZATION to the pope, and it was affirmed at the end of the 12th century. But, beatification, which had no basis in canon law, continued as the result of a changing and fluid practice, to which the popes began to give some order only during the last centuries of the Middle Ages.

The adjective *beatus* and its superlative form, *beatissimus*, were used freely to describe the Roman emperors and, later, ecclesiastical dignitaries, and frequently were associated with the title of martyr, always as adjectives. In the early Middle Ages, *beatus* appears as a noun, but always as the exact synonym of *sanctus*. Thus, Gregory of Tours (d. 594) used *sanctus*, *beatus*, or *domnus* without distinction when referring to his hero, St. Martin.

This absence of distinction persisted until the middle of the 13th century, even when the matter of canonization was reserved to the pope. Toward the middle of the 14th century, a distinction between saints and the blessed appears in both iconography and texts. Saints, officially canonized by the Roman Church, had the right to be called *sancti* and furnished with a halo; the blessed, about whom the HOLY SEE had made no pronouncement, were called *beati* and were entitled only to simple rays of light. Even as he set forth this principle, André Vauchez revealed that it was got round by countless infringements and exceptions in the reality of the local cults, and underlined the little attempt by the Holy See expressly to combat these obvious breaches of its prerogatives. The GREAT SCHISM (1378–1417), by weakening papal authority, only served to increase a disorder arising naturally from popular local devotions, the leniency of the bishops concerned, and the determination of the various religious orders—especially the mendicants—to promote the fame of their saints. In this way, deceased persons on whose sanctity the Holy See had given no opinion came to be honored in special offices and in churches, chapels, or altars dedicated to them.

The divorce between theory and practice was not definitively resolved until 1634, with the institution by URBAN VIII of what is called equivalent beatification, to the definition of which BENEDICT XIV added the clarification that it would apply only to persons who had been venerated without authorization prior to 1534. Accordingly, during the 17th, 18th, and 19th centuries, by means of this process less rigorous than that for formal beatification, many well-established medieval cults were regularized that until then had been unofficial, if not illegal. The history of equivalent beatification belongs to the modern period. The processes involved in the beatifications, however, are of particular interest for medieval history, to the extent that they brought to light many hagiographical texts, traces of ancient cults that otherwise would have been lost. But in dealing with these texts, it must be remembered, on the one hand, that local piety sometimes forced the hand of the authentic witnesses, and, on the other, that even if there is no clear evidence that the historical sources were manipulated, the image given of these medieval *beati* often is more typical of the piety of the Counter Reformation than of genuinely medieval spirituality.

Jacques Dalarun

Bibliography

Delehaye, H. *Sanctus. Essai sur le culte des saints dans l'Antiquité*, Brussels, 1927 (*Subsidia hagiographica*, 17).

Garampi, G. *Memorie ecclesiastiche appartenenti all'istoria e al culto della b. Chiara di Rimini*, Rome, 1755, 428–36.

Kemp, E. W. *Canonization and Authority in the Western Church*, Oxford, 1948.

Naz, R. "Causes de béatification et de canonisation," *DDC*, 3 (1942), 10–37.

Ortolan, T. "Béatification," *DTC*, 2 (1936), 493–97.

Vauchez, A. *Sainthood in the Middle Ages*, New York, 1997.

Modern and Contemporary Eras. Following is a list of those beatified since the creation in 1588 of the Congregation of Rites, now the Congregation for the Causes of Saints (giving the date of beatification), as well as those declared blessed by the confirmation of their cult (giving the date of the decree confirming cult).

CLEMENT VIII (1592–1605): John of St. Facundo Gonzales (19 June 1601), Colette Boilet (1604). PAUL V (1605–21): Stanislaus Kostka (1605), Aloysius of Gonzaga (1605), Sauveur d'Horta (5 February 1606), Louis Bertrand (19 July 1608), Ignatius of Loyola (27 July 1609), Margaret of Citta di Castello (19 October 1609), Seraphin of Montegranaro (1610), Teresa of Avila (24 April 1614), Philip Neri (11 May 1615), Thomas of Villanova (7 October 1618), Paschal Baylon (29 October 1618), Isidore the Farmer (2 May 1619), Francis Xavier (25 October 1619). GREGORY XV (1621–3): Peter of Alcantara (18 April 1622). URBAN VIII (1623–44): James of Marca Gangali (12 August 1624), Francis Borgia (23 November 1624), Andrew Avellin (10 June 1625), Felix of Cantalice (1 October 1625), Mary Magdalene dei Pazzi (8 May 1626), Paul Miki and his twenty-six Japanese martyr companions (14 and 15 September 1627), Gaetano of Thiene (8 October 1629), John of God (21 September 1630). *Confirmation of cult*: Matthew Carreri (2 December 1625), Colombe of Rieti (25 February 1627), Josaphat Kuncewicz (16 May 1643), Bernard Tolomei (26 November 1644). INNOCENT X (1644–55): *Confirmation of cult*: Philip Benizi (8 October and 9 December 1645), Nicholas of Flue (1 February 1649), John of Capistrano (19 December 1650), Bernardine Tomitano of Feltre (13 April 1654). ALEXANDER VII (1655–67): Francis de Sales (8 January 1662), Peter of Arbues (20 April 1664). CLEMENT IX (1667–9): Rose of Lima (15 April 1668). *Confirmation of cult*: Margaret of Savoy (8 October 1669). CLEMENT X (1670–6): Pius V (1 May 1672), John of the Cross (21 April 1675), Francis Solano (30 June 1675), Nicholas Pieck and his 18 martyr companions of Gorcum (24 November 1675). *Confirma-*

tion of cult: Peter Paschase (4 June 1670), Louise Albertini (28 January 1671), James Bianconi of Mevania (18 May 1672), Salome of Galicia (17 May 1673), Catherine of Genoa (6 April 1675), Hildegard (25 May 1675), John of Kenty (28 March 1676). **INNOCENT XI (1676–89)**: Turibius Alphonse of Mogrovejo (2 July 1679). *Confirmation of cult*: Amadeus IX of Savoy (3 March 1677), Julienne of Falconieri (21 July 1678), Simon of Lipninza (24 February 1685), Peter Armengol (28 March 1686), Anthony of Stroncone (28 June 1687). **ALEXANDER VIII (1689–91)**: *Confirmation of cult*: Cunegonde of Poland (11 June 1690). **INNOCENT XII (1691–1700)**: *Confirmation of cult*: Joan of Portugal (31 December 1692), Peter Gambacorta (9 December 1693), Humilienne of Cerchi (24 July 1694), Helen Enselmine (29 October 1695), Marie della Cabeza (7 August 1697), Augustine Kazotic (17 July 1700). **CLEMENT XI (1700–21)**: John Francis Regis (24 May 1716). *Confirmation of cult*: James of Bitetto (29 December 1700), Peregrin Laziosi (11 September 1702), John of Perouse and Peter of Sassoferrato (31 January 1705), Lucy Broccadelli of Narni (1 March 1710), Ceslas Odrovaz (27 August 1712), Gregory X (8 July 1713), Liberat of Lauro Brumforti (2 September 1713), 7 servants of the Order of Servites (1 December 1717), Humilite of Faenza (27 January 1720). **INNOCENT XIII (1721–4)**: *Confirmation of cult*: John Nepomucene (31 May 1721), Andrew Conti (11 December 1723). **BENEDICT XIII (1724–30)**: Hyacinth Marescotti (1 September 1726), John of Prado (24 May 1728), Fidelis of Sigmaringen (24 March 1729), Vincent de Paul (21 August 1729), Peter Fourier (29 January 1730). *Confirmation of cult*: 7 servants of the Order of Servites (30 July 1725), Dalmace Moner (13 August 1721 and 19 June 1726). **CLEMENT XII (1730–40)**: Catherine Ricci (23 November 1732), Joseph of Leonessa (22 June 1737). *Confirmation of cult*: John of Dukla (21 January 1733), Benedict XI (24 April 1736), Micheline of Pesaro, Claire of the Cross of Montefalco (13 April 1737), Jean-Ange Porro (15 July 1737), Andrew Cacciola (25 July 1738). **BENEDICT XIV (1740–58)**: Alexandre Marie Saoli (23 April 1741), Camillus of Lellis (7 April 1742), Jerome Emiliani (29 September 1747), Joseph of Calasanz (18 August 1748), Joan-Frances Fremiot (21 November 1751), Joseph of Cupertino (24 February 1753). *Confirmation of cult*: Stephanie of Quinzanis (14 December 1740), Alvarez of Cordova (22 September 1741), Peter Conzalez (13 December 1741), Joan of Valois (21 April 1742), Benedict of Saint-Philadelpe Manassari, called the Moor (15 May 1743), Francis Patrizi (11 September 1743), Nicholas Albergati (25 September 1744), Pacific of Cerano Ramati (7 July 1745), Aegidius called Giles of Vaozela, Albert of Bergamo (9 May 1748), Ladislas of Gielnow (11 February 1750), Marcolin Amanni of Forli (9 May 1750), Henry of Bolzano (23 July 1750), Ange of Clavasio Carletti, John Liccio (25 April 1753), Julienne

of Collalto (30 May 1753), Gabriel Ferretti (19 September 1753), Seraphine Sforza (17 July 1754), Joan Vanna of Orvieto (11 September 1754), Fort de Gabrielli (17 March 1756), Odoric Matiuzzi of Pordenone (2 July 1755), Hugh of Actes (27 July 1757). **CLEMENT XIII (1758–69)**: Gregory Barbarigo (20 September 1761), Simon of Roxas (19 May 1766), Bernard of Corleone (15 May 1768). *Confirmation of cult*: Anthony of Amandola Migliorati, Anthony of Aquila Torriani, Augustine Novelli (11 July 1759), Sebastian Maggi (15 April 1760), Peter Corradini (10 August 1760), Ange Augustine Mazzinghi (7 March 1761), James Philip Bertoni (22 July 1761), Clement of Osimo (16 September 1761), Andrew of Monte Reale, Vincent Kadlubek (18 February 1764), John Marignoni (5 December 1764), Bienvenue Bojani (6 February 1765), Matthew of Nazareis (27 July 1765), Elizabeth Achlin (19 July 1766), Philip of Plaisance (27 August 1766), Anthony Neyrot, Matthew Guimera (22 February 1767), Angela Merici (30 April 1768), Thomas of Urbeveteri Corsini (10 December 1768). **CLEMENT XIV (1769–74)**: Francis Caracciolo (10 September 1769), Paul Burali (8 June 1772). *Confirmation of cult*: Catherine of Pallanza and Julienne of Busto Arsitio, Bernard II of Bade, Gregory Celli (16 September 1769), Sanctes of Urbino (18 August 1770), Joan Scopelli, Nicholas of Furca Palena, Thomas Bellacci (24 August 1771), Anthony Primaldi and his 800 companions (14 December 1771), John a Baculo (29 August 1772), Beatrice II of Este (3 July 1774). **PIUS VI (1775–99)**: Bonaventure of Potenza (26 November 1775), Sebastian of Jesus Sillero (19 June 1776), Michael of Saints Argemir (2 May 1779), Mary-Anne of Jesus of Guevara (25 May 1783), Lawrence of Brindisi (1 June 1783), Joan-Mary Bonomi (9 June 1783), Pacifique of San Severino Divini (13 August 1786), Nicholas Factor (27 August 1786), Thomas of Cori (3 September 1786), Gaspard of Bono (10 September 1786), Nicholas Saggio, called Nicholas of the Lombards (17 September 1786), Sebastian of Apparizio (17 May 1789), John-Joseph of the Cross Calosinto (24 May 1789), Andrew Hibernon (22 May 1791), Marie of the Incarnation Avrillot (5 June 1791), Catherine Thomas (12 August 1792), Bartholomew of Bragance (11 September 1793), Bernard of Offida (25 May 1795), Leonard of Port Maurice Casanova (19 June 1796), John of Ribera (18 September 1796). *Confirmation of cult*: Francis Venimbeni, Jerome Ranucci (1 April 1775), Aime Ronconi (17 April 1776), John of Parma (1 March 1777), Gondisalve of Lagos (2 May 1778), John of Salerno (2 April 1783), Peter Jeremie (12 May 1784), Claire Agolanti of Rimini (22 December 1784), Vincent of Aquila (19 September 1787), James Rukem de Waldonna, of Strepa (11 September 1790), Mafalda of Portugal (14 March 1792), Bienvenu of Recineto (17 September 1796), Andrew Gallerani (13 May 1798), Joan of Signa (21 September

1798). **PIUS VII (1800–23)**: Veronica Giuliani (17 June 1804), Francis of Hieronimo (11 May 1806), Joseph Oriol (21 September 1806), Alphonsus-Mary Liguori (15 September 1816), Francis Posadas (20 September 1818), Jean-Baptiste de la Conception Garcia (26 September 1819). *Confirmation of Cult*: John of Vespiniano (1 October 1800), Peter Pectinarii (18 August 1802), Raynier de Marianis of Arezzo (18 December 1802), Joseph Mary Tomasi (29 September 1803), Anthony Patrick of Monticiano (1 March 1804), Jerome of Ghirardutiis or of Recineto (4 July 1804), Mary Bartholomew Bagnesi (11 July 1804), Elizabeth of Picenardis (10 November 1804), James of Castro Plebis (17 May 1806), Philippine Mareri (30 April 1806), Crispin of Viterbo Fioretti (7 September 1806), Andrew Dotti (29 November 1806), John of Penna (20 December 1806), Sadoc and his 48 Polish martyr companions (18 October 1807), Catherine Matteis of Raconixio (9 April 1808), Peter Cappucci of Tipherno (11 May 1816), James of Voragine (7 September 1816), Conrad of Ophyda (21 April 1817), Nevolon (4 June 1817), Anthony of St. Germain (15 May 1819), Julie de la Rena (18 May 1819), Simon Blacchi of Saint Archange (14 March 1820), Andrew of Peschiera, Lawrence of Portugal (26 September 1820), Ubald of Adimari (3 April 1821), Peregrin of Falerone (31 July 1821), Constant of Fabriano (25 September 1821), Bonaventure Bonaccorsi (23 April 1822), Joan of Bagno di Romagna (15 April 1823). **LEO XII (1823–9)**: Julian of Saint Augustine Martinet (23 May 1825), Hippolyte Galantini (19 June 1825), Ange d'Acri (18 December 1825), Mary Victoria Fornari (21 September 1828). *Confirmation of cult*: Villana of Bottis (27 March 1824), John Sordi called Cacciafronte (30 March 1824), Angela of Marsciano, Bernard Scammacca (8 March 1825), Ange of Valido, James of Ulma (3 August 1825), Jordan of Saxony (10 May 1826), Imelda Lambertini (20 December 1826), Yolande Madeline Panatieri (26 September 1827), Bernadine of Fossa, Helen Duglioli, Nicholas Paglia (26 March 1828), Joan of Aza, Joan Soderini (1 October 1828), Benincasa of Monticchiello (23 December 1829). **PIUS VIII (1829–30)**: *Confirmation of cult*: Claire Gambacorti (24 April 1830). **GREGORY XVI (1831–46)**: Sebastian Valfre (31 August 1834), John Macias (22 October 1837), Martin de Porres (30 October 1837), Marie Francoise of the Five Wounds of Our Lord Jesus Christ Gallo (12 November 1843). *Confirmation of cult*: Henry of Suse (22 April 1831), John of Dominique, John of Reate (9 April 1832), Lucy Bufalari (3 August 1832), Simon Rinalducci (18 March 1833), Jordan of Pisa (23 August 1833), Mammed (2 June 1834), Christine of Spoleto (19 September 1834), John and Peter Becchetti (28 August 1835), Arcange of Calatafini (9 September 1836), Albert of Sassoferrato (30 September 1837), Evangeliste (17 November 1837), Boniface of Savoy, Hubert III of Savoy (7 September 1838), Rizzeri of Muccia (14 December 1838), Louise of

Savoy (12 August 1839), Bronislav (23 August 1839), Mark of Monte Gallo (20 September 1839), Camille Gentili, Christine Cicarelli of Aquila, Fortunat (15 January 1841), Louis Rabata (10 December 1841), Ange of Sassatio (22 April 1842), Romeo (29 April 1842), Louis Morbioli (24 October 1842), Baptiste Varano (7 April 1843), Francis Piani (1 September 1843), James of Canepaciis (5 March 1845), Ange of Aquapagana (24 July 1845), Paula Gambara (14 August 1845). **PIUS IX (1846–78)**: Peter Claver (21 September 1851), Paul of the Cross Danei (1 May 1853), John of Britto (21 August 1853), Andrew Bobola (30 October 1853), John Grande (13 November 1853), Mary Anne of Jesus of Paredes y Flores (20 November 1853), Germaine Cousin (7 May 1854), John Sarkander (6 May 1860), John Baptist of Rossi (13 May 1860), Benedict Joseph Labre (20 May 1860), John Leonard of the Mother of God (10 November 1861), Margaret Mary Alacoque (18 September 1864), Peter Canisius (20 November 1864), Marie des Anges Fontanella (14 May 1865), John Berchmans (28 May 1865), Alphonsus Rodriguez (5 June 1865), Benedict of Urbino (10 February 1867), Alphonsus Navarrete (7 July 1867). *Confirmation of cult*: Peter of Gubbio (5 March 1847), Antoinette of Florence, Marguerite Colonna (17 September 1847), Damian Furchere of Venario (4 August 1848), Helen of Udine, Peter Jacob of Pesaro (27 September 1848), Lawrence of Ripafratta (4 April 1851), Raynald of Concoregio (15 January 1852), Bentivoglio of Bonis (30 September 1852), Bartholomew Cerveri, Guido or Wido, Roland of Medici (22 September 1853), Dominic Vernagalli, Gregory and Dominic, Sibylline Biscossi (17 August 1854), Mary Mancini (2 August 1855), Stephane Bandelli (21 February 1856), Aymon Taparelli, Gherardesca (29 May 1856), Anthony Pavoni, Hugolin Magalotti, Peter Cambiani (4 December 1856), Bartholomew of Pisa, John of Pace, Marc Scalabrini (10 September 1857), Varmundus of Arboreis (17 September 1857), Cicco of Pesaro, Odon of Novare (31 March 1859), Thomas Helyas (14 July 1859), James Benfatti (22 September 1859), William of Fenoliis, Hercule of Piegaro (29 March 1860), Ayrald (8 January 1863), Frances of Amboise (16 July 1863), John of Hispanus (14 July 1864), Arcangela Girlani (1 October 1864), Cherubin Testa (21 September 1865), John Soreth, Peter Levite (3 May 1866), Paule Montaldi, William Arnaud and 10 martyr companions (6 September 1866), Lawrence Sossius, Panacea of Muzzi (5 September 1867), Mark Fantuzzi (5 March 1868), Guala (1 October 1868), Beatrice of Ornacieu (15 April 1869), Timothy of Monticchio, Urban V (10 March 1870), Jeanne-Marie of Maille (27 April 1871), Augustine of Biella, Peter Favre (5 September 1872), Alpaix of Cudot (26 February 1874), Agnes of Bohemia (3 December 1874), Christopher of Mediolano, Oglerius (3 April 1875), Reginald (8 July 1875), Vullermus of Leaval (15

February 1877). **LEO XIII (1878–1903)**: Alphonse of Orozco (15 January 1882), Louis-Marie Grignion of Montfort, Charles of Sezze Melchiori (22 January 1882), Humble of Bisagnano (29 January 1882), John Fisher and Thomas More (9 December 1886), Clement Marie Hofbauer (29 January 1888), Egidio Marie of St. Joseph Pontillo (5 February 1888), Felix of Nicosie (12 February 1888), Jean-Baptiste of Salle (19 February 1888), Joseph Marie of St. Agnes of Beniganim (26 February 1888), Grace of Catharo (6 June 1889), John Gabriel Perboyre (10 November 1889), Pierre-Louis Marie Chanel (17 November 1889), Anthony Marie Zaccaria (3 January 1890), John Juvenal Ancina (9 February 1890), Pompilius Marie Pirotti of St. Nicholas (26 January 1890), Francis Xavier Marie Bianchi (22 January 1893), Gerard Maiella (29 January 1893), Leopold of Gaiche (12 March 1893), Anthony Baldinucci (16 April 1893), Rudolph Acquaviva (30 April 1893), Peter Sanz (14 May 1893), John of Avila (15 April 1894), Didier Joseph of Cadiz Lopez-Caamano (22 April 1894), Bernadine Realino (12 January 1896), Theophilus of Corte Signori (19 January 1896), Ignatius Delgado Cebrian (27 May 1900), Mary Magdelene Martinengo (3 June 1900), Denis of the Nativity Berthelot (10 June 1900), Joan of Lestonac (23 September 1900), Anthony Grassi (30 September 1900), Mary Crescentia Hoss (7 October 1900). *Confirmation of cult*: Bartholomew Pucci Franceschi, John of Alverna (24 June 1880), Egidio of Laurenzana de Bello (27 June 1880), Emeric of Quart, Urban II (14 July 1881), Charles the Good (9 February 1882), Simon Fidati (23 August 1883), Baptiste Spagnoli (17 December 1885), Cuthbert Maine and his 39 English martyr companions (9 December 1886), Sancte of Cora (1 February 1888), Diane of Andalo (8 August 1888), Ange of Furci (20 December 1888), Nicholas Tavelic and his 3 companions (6 June 1889), Boniface Valperga (28 April 1890), Christopher Macassoli (23 July 1890), Angela of Foligno (11 March 1891), Cecile and Aimee (24 December 1891), Agnel of Pisa (4 September 1892), Lanuinus (4 February 1893), William of Tolosa (18 April 1893), Justine Francucci Bezzoli (14 January 1894), Idesbaldus (23 July 1894), Joan of Tolosa (11 February 1895), Hugh Faringdon (13 May 1895), James of Cerqueto (10 June 1895), Thaddeus Machar (26 August 1895), Pons of Faucigny (15 December 1896), Hrosnate (16 September 1897), Innocent V (14 March 1898), Raymond of Capoue (15 May 1899), Mark Criado (24 July 1899), Anthony Bonfadini (13 May 1901), Eurosie of Jaca (1 May 1902), Andrew Abellon (19 August 1902). **PIUS X (1903–14)**: Gaspard of Bufalo (18 December 1904), Stephen Bellesini (27 December 1904), Agathange of Vendome and Cassien of Nantes (1 January 1905), Jean-Baptiste Marie Vianney (8 January 1905), Mark Crisinus and his 2 martyr companions (15 January 1905), Julie Billiart (13 May 1906), Francis Gil of Federich and his 7 martyr companions of Tonkin (20 May 1906), Therese of St. Augustine Lidoine and her 15 martyr companions of Compiegne (27 May 1906), Bonaventure of Barcelona Gran (10 June 1906), Marie-Madeleine Postel (17 May 1908), Gabriel of Addolorata Possenti (31 May 1908), Joan of Arc (18 April 1909), John Eudes (25 April 1909), Francis of Capillas and his 33 Indochinese martyr companions (2 May 1909). *Confirmation of cult*: Jean-Baptiste of Fabriano, John of Vercellis (7 September 1903), Charles of Blois (14 December 1904), Mark of Marconi (2 March 1906), Benedict of Coltibuono (29 May 1907), Zdislava Berka (28 August 1907), Madeleine Albrici (11 December 1907), Christine, Potentinus, Felicien and Simplice (12 August 1908), John Ruysbroeck (9 December 1908), Bartholomew Fanti (18 March 1909), Frederick of Ratisbonne (12 May 1909), Uthon and Gamelbert (25 August 1909), Julienne Cesarello (23 February 1910), James Capocci (14 June 1911), Bonaventure Torinelli (6 September 1911). **BENEDICT XV (1914–22)**: Joseph Benedict Cottolengo (29 April 1917), Anne of St. Barthelemy Garcia (6 May 1917), Louise of Marillac (9 May 1920), Anne-Marie Taigi (30 May 1920), Charles Lwanga, Matthias Mulumba Kalemba and their 20 Ugandan martyr companions (6 June 1920), Marie-Magdeleine Fontaine and her 14 martyr companions (13 June 1920). *Confirmation of cult*: Augustine Cennini and his 63 Prague martyr companions (26 June 1918), John Pelingotto (13 November 1918), Hugolin of Gualdo, Isnardus of Chiampo (12 March 1919), Oliver Plunkett (23 May 1920), Dominic Spadafora (12 January 1921), Marguerite of Lotharingie (20 March 1921), Ange Scarpetti (27 July 1921), Andrew Franchi (23 November 1921). **PIUS XI (1922–39)**: Theresa of the Child Jesus (29 April 1923), Michel Garicoits (10 May 1923), Robert Bellarmine (13 May 1923), Antoine-Marie Gianetti (19 April 1925), Vincent Marie Strambi (26 April 1925), Joseph Calasso (3 May 1925), Iphigenie of St. Matthew of Gaillard de Lavaldene and her 31 martyr companions of Orange (10 May 1925), Marie Michelle of Saint-Sacrament Desmaisieres (7 June 1925), Marie Bernadette Soubirous (14 June 1925), Jean de Brebeuf and his 7 Canadian martyr companions (21 June 1925), Andrew Kim, Paul Chong, Lawrence Imbert and their 72 Korean martyr companions (5 July 1925), Pierre Julien Eymard (12 July 1925), Andrew Hubert Fournet (16 May 1926), Jeanne Antide Thouret (23 May 1926), Bartholomew Capitanio (30 May 1926), James Sales and William Saultemouche (6 June 1926), Lucie Filippini (13 June 1926), Michel Ghebre (3 October 1926), Emmanuel Ruiz and his 10 martyr companions from Damas (10 October 1926), Jean Marie du Lau of Alleman and his 190 September martyr companions (17 October 1926), Natalis Pinot (31 October 1926), John Bosco (2 June 1929), Theresa Margaret of the Sacred Heart of Jesus Redi (9 June 1929), Claude de la Colombiere (16

June 1929), Come of Carboniano (23 June 1929), Francis Marie of Camporosso (30 June 1929), Cuthbert Mayne and his 39 English martyr companions, Thomas Hemerford and his 135 campanions (15 December 1929), John Ogilvie (22 December 1929), Paula Frassinetti (8 June 1930), Conrad of Parzham Birndorfer (15 June 1930), Albert the Great (equipollent bull 16 December 1931), Mary of St. Euphrasie Pelletier (30 April 1933), Catherine Vincentia Gerosa (7 May 1933), Gemma Galgani (14 May 1933), Joseph Marie Pignatelli (21 May 1933), Catherine Laboure (28 May 1933), Roch Gonzalez and his 2 martyr companions (28 January 1934), Anthony-Marie Claret (25 February 1934), Pierre-Rene Rogue (10 May 1934), Joan Elizabeth Bichier of Ages (13 May 1934), Mary Josephine Rossello (6 November 1938), Frances Xavier Cabrini (13 November 1938), Marie-Dominique Mazzarello (20 November 1938). *Confirmation of cult*: Lawrence of Villamagna (28 February 1923), Beatrice de Silva Meneses (28 July 1926), Stilla (12 January 1927), Luke Belludi (18 May 1927), Hugh of Fosses (13 July 1927), Hosanna of Kotor (21 December 1927), Simeon and 7 companions (16 May 1928), Irmengarde (19 December 1928), Balthazar Ravaschieri of Chiavari (8 January 1930). **PIUS XII (1939–58)**: Emilie of Vialar (18 June 1939), Justin of Jacobis (25 June 1939), Philippine Duchesne (12 May 1940), Joachim of Vedruna (19 May 1940), Marie Crucifiee di Rosa (26 May 1940), Marie Guillaumette, Emilie of Rodat (9 June 1940), Ignatius of Laconi Cadello Peis (16 June 1940), Madeleine of Canossa (7 December 1941), Margaret of Hungary (equipollent bull 19 November 1943), Mary Theresa of Soubiran La Louviere (20 October 1946), Theresa Eustochium Verzeri (27 October 1946), Gregory Grassi and his 28 Chinese martyr companions (24 November 1946), Contardus Ferrini (13 April 1947), Maria Goretti (27 April 1947), Mary Theresa of Jesus Le Clerc (4 May 1947), John of the Cross (9 November 1947), Benilde Romancon (4 April 1948), Vincent Pallotti (22 January 1950), Marie de las Dolores Torres Acosta (15 February 1950), Vincentia Maria Lopez Vicuna (19 February 1950), Dominic Savio (5 March 1950), Paula Elizabeth Cerioli (19 March 1950), Mary of Mattias (1 October 1950), Anne Marie Javouhey (5 October 1950), Marguerite Bourgeoys (12 November 1950), Alberic Crescitelli (18 February 1951), Francis Anthony Fasani (15 April 1951), Joseph-Marie Diaz Sanjurjo and his 24 martyr companions of Tonkin (29 April 1951), Placide Viel (6 May 1951), Julien Maunoir (20 May 1951), Pius X (3 June 1951), Theresa Couderc (4 November 1951), Rose Venerini (4 May 1952), Raphaelle Marie of the Sacred Heart of Jesus Porras (18 May 1952), Marie Bertilla Boscardin (8 June 1952), Anthony Marie Pucci (22 June 1952), Marie Assomption Pallotta (7 November 1954), John Martin Moye (21 November 1954), Placide Riccardi (5 December 1954), Leo Ignatius Mangin and his 55 Chinese martyr companions (17 April 1955), Marcellin Joseph Benedict Champagnat (29 May 1955), Jean-Baptiste Turpin of Cormier and his 18 martyr companions (19 June 1955), Innocent XI (7 October 1956), Marie de la Providence Smet (26 May 1957), Theresa of Jesus Jonet Ibars (27 April 1958). **JOHN XXIII (1958–63)**: Helen Guerra (26 April 1959), Mary Margaret Dufrost of Lajemmerais d'Youville (3 May 1959), Innocent of Berzo (12 November 1961), Elizabeth Anne Bayley Seton (17 March 1963), Louis-Marie Palazzolo (19 March 1963). **PAUL VI (1963–78)**: John Nepomucene Neumann (13 October 1963), Dominic of the Mother of God Barberi (27 October 1963), Leonard Murialdo (3 November 1963), Vincent Romano (17 November 1963), Nunzio Sulprizio (1 December 1963), Louis Guanella (25 October 1964), Jacques Berthieu (17 October 1965), Chabel Makhlouf (5 December 1965), Ignatius of Santhia (17 April 1966), Marie Fortunee Viti (8 October 1967), Francis Simeon Berneux and his 23 martyr companions of Korea (6 October 1968), Mary of the Apostles Wullenweber (13 October 1968), Clelia Barberini (27 October 1968), Maxmilian Marie Kolbe (17 October 1971), Michel Rua (29 October 1972), Augustine Pietrantoni (12 November 1972), Liborius Wagner (24 March 1974), Mary Frances Schervier (28 April 1974), Cesar of Bus (27 April 1975), John-Henry Charles Steeb (6 July 1975), Marie-Eugenie of Jesus Milleret of Brou (25 August 1975), Arnaud Janssen, Charles-Joseph Eugene de Mazenod, Joseph Freinademetz, Mary Theresa Ledochowska (19 October 1975), Ezechiel Moreno y Diaz, Gaspard Bertoni, Joan Frances of the Visitation Michelotti, Mary of the Divine Heart of Jesus Droste zu Vischering, Vincent Grossi (1 November 1975), Joseph Moscati (16 November 1975), Leopold of Castelnovo (2 May 1976), Mary of Jesus Lopez de Rivas (14 November 1976), Mary Rose Molas y Vallve (8 May 1977), Mucianus Maria Wiaux, Michel Febes Cordero (30 October 1977), Mary Catherine Jasper (16 April 1978), Marie-Henriette Dominici (7 May 1978). *Confirmation of cult*: Nicholas Tavelic and his 3 companions (12 June 1966), Dorothy of Montau (9 January 1976). **JOHN PAUL II (1978–)**: Francis Coll, Jacques Desire Laval (29 April 1979), Henry Osso Cervello (14 October 1979), Kateri Tekakwitha, Francois de Montmorency-Laval, Joseph of Anchieta, Marie of the Incarnation Guyart, Peter of St. Joseph of Betancour (22 June 1980), Louis Orione, Bartholomew Longo, Mary Anne Sala (26 October 1980), Dominic Ibanez of Erquicia, Lawrence Ruiz of Manilla and their 7 Japanese martyr companions (18 February 1981), Alain of Solminihac, Louis Scrosoppi, Mary Repetto, Mary of St. Ignatius Thevenet, Richard Pampuri (4 October 1981), Andre Bessette, Angele-Marie Astorch, Mary Anne Rivier, Mary Rose Durocher, Peter Donders (23 May 1982), Mary of the Cross Jugan, John Faesulanus, savior of Cappadocia, and his 7 companions (3 October 1982), Angela of the Cross Guerrero Gonzalez (5 November 1982), Mary Gabrielle Sagheddu (25 January 1983), Louis Vesiglia and Calixtus Caravario (15 May 1983), Ursula Ledochowska (20 June 1983), Albert Chmielowski, Raphael of St. Joseph Kalinowski (22 June 1983), Dominic of the Blessed Sacrament Zubero, James Cusmano, Jeremy of Valachia (30 October 1983), Mary of Jesus Crucified Baouardy (13 November 1983), William Repin and his 98 martyr companions of Angers, Jean-Baptiste Mazzucconi (19 February 1984), Marie-Leonie Paradis (11 September 1984), Clement Marchisio, Frederick Albert, Isidore of St. Joseph of Loor, Raphael Ybarra (30 September 1984), Elizabeth of the Most Holy Trinity Catez, Joseph Manyanet Vives (25 November 1984), Mercedes of Jesus Molina (1 February 1985), Anne des Anges Monteagudo (2 February 1985), Mary Catherine of St. Rose Troiani, Pauline von Mallinckrodt (14 April 1985), Benedict Menni, Peter Friedhofen (23 June 1985), Clementine Anuarite Negapeta (15 August 1985), Virginia Centurione (22 September 1985), Didier Louis of St. Victor, Francis Garate, Joseph-Marie Rubio Peralta (6 October 1985), Titus Brandsma (3 November 1985), Mary Theresa of Jesus Gerhardinger, Pius of St. Louis Campidelli, Rebecca Ar-Rayes of Himlaya (17 November 1985), Daniel Brottier (25 November 1985), Alphonsine of the Immaculate Conception Muttathupandatu, Cyriaque Elie Chavara (8 February 1986), Andrew Dung Lac, Thomas Thien, Emmanuel Phung, Jerome Hermosilla, Valentin Berrio Ochoa, Theophane Venard and their 111 Vietnamese martyr companions (18 April 1986), Antoine Chevrier (4 October 1986), Theresa Mary of the Cross Manetti (19 October 1986), Maria del Pilar of St. Francis Borgia Martinez Garcia, Theresa of the Child Jesus and of St. John of the Cross, Emmanuel Domingo y Sol, Marcel Spinola y Maestre (29 March 1987), Theresa of Jesus of the Andes Fernandez Solar (3 April 1987), Theresa Benedicta of the Cross Stein (1 May 1987), Rupert Mayer (3 May 1987), Andre-Charles Ferrari, Louis-Zephyrin Moreau, Peter-Francis Jamet, Benedicta Cambiagio Frassinello (10 May 1987), Caroline Kozka (10 June 1987), Michael Kozal (14 June 1987), George Matulewicz (28 June 1987), Marcel Callo, Antoinette Mesina, Pierrette Morosini (4 October 1987), Arnold Reche, Ulrich Nisch, Blandine Merten (1 November 1987), George Haydock and his 84 English martyr companions (22 October 1987), Joseph Nascimbeni, Joan Calabria (17 April 1988), Peter Bonilli, Francis Palau y Quer, Gaspard Stanggassinger, Sabine Petrinelli (24 April 1988), Joseph Gerard (15 September 1988), Laura Vicuna, Michael Augustine Pro, Joseph Benedict Dusmet, Francis Faa' di Bruno, Junipero Serra, Josephine Naval Girbes, Frederick Janssoone (25 September 1988), Bernard-Marie Silvestrini, Charles Houben, Honorat

Kozminski (16 October 1988), Niels Stensen (23 October 1988), Samuel Marzorati, Liberatus Weiss, Michael Pie Fasoli, Katherine Drexel (20 November 1988), Victor Rasoamanarivo (30 April 1989), Martin of St. Nicholas, Melchior of St. Augustine, Mary of Jesus the Good Shepherd Siedliska, Mary Margaret Caiani, Mary Catherine of St. Augustine (23 April 1989), Brother Scubilio (2 May 1989), Anthony Lucci, Elizabeth Renzi (18 June 1989), Nicefor Diaz Tejerina and his 25 Spanish martyr companions, Lawrence Marie Salvi, Gertrude Catherine Comensoli, Frances Anne Cirer Carbonnel (1 October 1989), Philip Siphong, Agnes Phila, Lucy Khambang, Agatha Phutta, Cecile Butsi, Vivian Khampai, Marie Phon (22 October 1989), Timothy Giaccardo, Marie Deluil-Martiny (22 October 1989), Joseph Baldo, Innocent of the Immaculate, Cyril Bertan and his 7 Spanish martyr companions, Mary Mercedes Prat y Prat, James Hillary Barbal Cosan, Philip Rinaldi (29 April 1990), Christopher, Anthony and John, Mexican martyrs, Jean Diego, Joseph Marie of Yermo y Parres (6 May 1990), Peter George Frassati (20 May 1990), Joseph Allamano, Hannibal Marie di Francia (7 October 1990), Elizabeth Vendramini, Louise Therese de Montaignac of Chauvance, Mary of the Sacred Heart of Jesus Schinina, Martha-Aimee le Bouteiller (4 November 1990), Annonciade Cocchetti, Mary Therese Haze, Claire Dina Bosatta (21 April 1991), Edward Joseph Rosaz (14 July 1991), Angela Salawa (13 August 1991), Pauline Visintainer (18 October 1991), Adolph Kolping (27 October 1991), Josephine Bakhita, Josemaria Escriva de Balaguer (17 May 1992), Francesco Spinelli (21 June 1992, Caravaggio, Italy), 17 Irish Martyrs, Rafael Arnaiz Baron, Nazaria Ignacia March Mesa, Leonie Francoise de Sales Aviat, and Maria Josefa Sancho de Guerra (27 September 1992), 122 Martyrs of the Spanish Civil War, Narcisa Martillo Moran (25 October 1992), Cristobal Magellanes and 24 companions, Mexican martyrs, and Maria de Jesus Sacramentado Venegas (22 November 1992), Dina Belanger (20 March 1993), Mary Angela Truszkowska, Ludovico of Casoria, Faustina Kowalska, Pauls Montal Fornes (18 April 1993), Maurice Tornay, Marie-Louise Trichet, Columba Gabriel and Florida Cevoli (16 May 1993), Giuseppe Marello (26 September 1993), Eleven Martyrs of Almeria, Spain, during the Spanish Civil War (2 bishops, 7 brothers, 1 priest, 1 lay person), Victoria Diez y Bustos de Molina, Maria Francesca (Anna Maria) Rubatto, Pedro Castroverde, Maria Crucified (Elizabetta Maria) Satellico (10 October 1993), Isidore Bakanja, Elizabeth Canori Mora, Dr. Gianna Beretta Molla (24 April 1994), Nicolas Roland, Alberto Hurtado Cruchaga, Maria Rafols, Petra of St. Joseph Perez Florida, Josephine Vannini (16 October 1994), Magdalena Caterina Morano (5 November 1994), Hyacinthe Marie Cormier, Marie Poussepin, Agnes de Jesus Galalnd, Eugenia Joubert, Claudio

Granzotto (20 November 1994), Peter ToRot (17 January 1995), Mother Mary of the Cross Mackillop (19 January 1995), Joseph Vaz (21 January 1995), Rafael Guizar Valencia, Modestino of Jesus and Mary, Genoveva Torres Morales, Grimoaldo of the Purification (29 January 1995), Johann Nepomuk von Tschiderer (30 April 1995), Maria Helena Stollenwerk, Maria Alvarado Cordozo, Giuseppina Bonino, Maria Domenica Brun Barbantini, Agostino Roscelli (7 May 1995), Damien de Veuster (4 June 1995), 109 Martyrs (64 from the French Revolution—Martyrs of La Rochelle—and 45 from the Spanish Civil War, Anselm Polanco Fontecha, Felipe Ripoll Morata, and Peitro Casini) (1 October 1995), Mary Theresa Scherer, Maria Bernarda Butler and Marguerite Bays (29 October 1995), Daniel Comboni and Guido Maria Conforti (17 March 1996), Cardinal Alfredo Ildefonso Schuster, O.S.B., Filippo Smaldone and Gennaro Sarnelli (priests) and Candida Maria de Jesus Cipitria y Barriola, Maria Raffaella Cimatti, Maria Antonia Bandres (religious) (12 May 1996), Bernhard Lichtenberg and Karl Leisner (23 June 1996), Wincenty Lewoniuk and 12 companions, Edmund Rice, Maria Ana Mogas Fontcuberta and Marcelina Darowska (6 October 1996), Otto Neururer, Jakob Gapp and Catherine Jarrige (24 November 1996), Bishop Florentino Asensio Barroso, Sr. Maria Encarnacion Rosal of the Sacred Heart, Fr. Gaetano Catanoso, Fr. Enrico Rebuschini and Ceferino Gimenez Malla, first gypsy beatified (4 May 1997), Bernardina Maria Jablonska, Maria Karlowska (6 June 1997), Frederic Ozanam (22 August 1997), Bartholomew Mary Dal Monte (27 September 1997), Elias del Socorro Nieves, Domenico Lentini, Giovanni Piamarta, Emilie d'Hooghvorst, Maria Teresa Fasce (12 October 1997), John Baptist Scalabrini, Vilmos Apor, Maria Vicenta of St. Dorothy Chavez Orozco (9 November, 1997), Bishop Vincent Bossilkov, Maria Salles, Brigida of Jesus (15 March 1998), Fr. Cyprian Tansi (22 March 1998), Nimatullah al- Hardini, 11 Spanish Nuns (10 May 1998), Secondo Polla (23 May 1998), Giovanni Maris Boccardo, Teresa Grillo Chavez, Teresa Bracco (24 May 1998), Jakob Kern, Maria Restituta Kafka, and Anton Schwartz (21 June 1998), Giuseppe Tovini (20 September 1998), Cardinal Alojzije Stepinac (3 October 1998), Antonio de Sant' Anna Galvao, Faustino Miguez, Zeferino Agostini, Mother Theodore Guerin (25 October 1998), Vicente Soler, and six Augustinian Recollect Companions, Manuel Martin Sierra, Nicolas Barre, Anna Schaeffer (7 March 1999), Padre Pio (2 May 1999), Fr. Stefan Wincenty Frelichowski (7 June 1999), 108 Polish Martyrs, Regina Protmann, Edmund Bojanowski (13 June 1999), Bishop Anton Slomsek (19 September 1999), Ferdinando Maria Baccilieri, Edward Maria Joannes Poppe, Arcangelo Tadini, Mariano da Roccacasale,

Diego Oddi, Nicola da Gesturi (3 October 1999), Andre de Soveral, Ambrosio Francisco Ferro and 28 Companions, Nicolas Bunkerd Kitbamrung, Maria Stella Mardosewicz and 10 Companions, Pedro Calungsod and Andrew of Phu Yen (5 March 2000), Mariano de Jesus Euse Hoyos, Francis Xavier Seelos, Anna Rosa Gattorno, Maria Elisabetta Hesselblad, Mariam Thresia Chiramel Mankidiyan (9 April 2000), Jacinta and Francisco Marto of Fatima (13 May 2000), Pope John XXIII, Pope Pius IX, Archbishop Thomas Reggio, William Joseph Chaminade, Dom Columba Marmion (3 September 2000). *Confirmation of cult*: Margaret Ebner (24 Feruary 1979), John Duns Scotus (20 March 1993), Stanislaus Kazimierczyk (18 April 1993).

Dominique Le Tourneau

See also CAUSES OF CANONIZATION.

Bibliography

Congregation of Rites, *Index ac Status causarum beatificationis servorum Dei et canonizationis beatorum*, Vatican City, 1953 (earlier editions of 1890, 1895, 1901, 1909, 1931, and 1941).

Congregation for the Causes of Saints, *Index ac Status causarum* (Editio particularis cura P. Galavotti), Vatican City, 1988; *I Supplementum (1988–1989)*, Vatican City, 1989; *II Supplementum (1989–1990)*, Vatican City, 1991.

Jombart, E. "Beatification," *Catholicisme*, Paris, I, 1968, 1339–42.

Löw, G. "Beatificazione," *EC*, II, Vatican City, 1949, 1090–1100.

Woodward, K. *Making Saints: How the Catholic Church Determines Who Becomes a Saint, Who Doesn't, and Why*, New York, 1990.

BELLS. It has traditionally been thought (and wrongly so) that bells first appeared in Campania during the 5th century and that Pope SABINIAN (604–6) introduced them into Roman churches. However, they were used in Rome as early as the 1st century. Martial writes that they were used to announce the opening hours of public baths (L14. Epigr.163), and according to Plutarch, they announced the sale of fish at the markets (L4. *Symposium* q.5). During the 6th century, in the West, monastic life was punctuated by the ringing of bells, and in the 8th century they were used in Rome during Christian worship. Pope STEPHEN II (752–7) had a bell tower built near St. Peter's Church and had three bells placed in it (LP1, 454). At the same time, the art of smelting and the range of tones were both improving. From two simple curved and riveted metal sheets, bells had become solid objects made of cast bronze (three parts of copper to one of tin).

They began to take on the more rounded form of an overturned goblet. The thickness of the metal sides and the composition of the alloy used determined the sound produced. Soon their use in Christian worship became more precise and widespread.

The origin of the ceremony of the blessing of the bells is attributed to Pope JOHN XIII (965–72). He gave his name to the large bell of ST. JOHN LATERAN. This practice was already common in the 8th century, since Charlemagne fought against the beliefs that tended to equate this ceremony to a baptism (789). At the council of Clermont, in 1095, Pope URBAN II promulgated the ringing of bells at dusk each day as "encouragement to embark on the first crusade." In 1316, JOHN XXII established the terms of the *Angelus*. BENEDICT XIV, in a decree of December 19, 1740, ordered that the bells of Rome were to be rung at 3:00 p.m. on Fridays to recall the death of the Savior. Elsewhere, a bell was usually rung during mass at the moment of elevation, except in Rome during the masses said by the pope. Also in Rome, the bell of the Capitol was rung at the death of a pope and at the beginning of a conclave. A pontifical dating from the 8th century, and found in the Saint Lucien Monastery in Beauvais, mentions the silence imposed on the bells for the three days of Holy Week, when "the bells 'go to' Rome" (Martène, De Antiquis Ecclesiae ritibus, III, lib. 4, chap 22).

Bells were often sounded during processions, and for the mourning of the dead also. The bell, a musical instrument and an object of artistic and liturgical value, very soon acquired a symbolic value, as evidenced by inscriptions made on them. It does not seem that a tithing duty was imposed for owning a bell, or that any ecclesiastic duty had to be paid for the smelting of the bronze. Bells could be ordered by the clergy or donated as gifts. Their presence in a church was often only an indication of the financial means of the clergy or of the church members. Indeed, to facilitate matters, the smelting often took place in the church itself. Itinerant smelters eventually replaced the monks who in earlier centuries had done the smelting. They often also inscribed their own name, the date, the circumstances of the smelting and the weight of the bell.

Some Roman bells from the Middle Ages have been preserved, the oldest being the one at St. Benedict in Piscinula, made in 1064. The four bells at St. Mary Major have, since the 16th century, been reputed to be the most melodious in Rome. The bells of St. Peter's basilica, which date from 1289, have been preserved in the Lateran museum. They both come from the workshop of Guido of Pisa, as do five others in Rome. The bell of St. Mary Major was donated to the church by Alfanus, a secretary to CALISTUS II, then repaired at the request of Pandulfus of Sabello, brother of HONORIUS IV, and a Roman senator. The name of Honorius also appears on the bell of St. Peter's in Rome, as well as on two others in St. Angelo

in Pescheria (smelted by Guido of Pisa in 1291). It is also inscribed on the bell of St. Nicholas of Lateran (dated in 1286, from the same foundry). Sometimes the popes made donations of bells. In the 8th century, St. Peter's received three bells from Stephen II, (the three bells which had replaced them in the meantime were re-smelted in 1353 after being struck by lightning, and in the 17th century their number was increased). At the Capitol, one of the two bells of the dispensary of J. Spagne and A. Casini (1803) bears a long inscription testifying to the munificence of PIUS VII. Most of the existing Roman bells date back to the 18th and 19th centuries.

Agnès Etienne-Magnien

Bibliography

Bayart, P. "Cloche, droit ecclésiastique," DDC, 3 (1938), 882–87.

Roccha, F. *De campanis commentarius*, Rome, 1612.

Sefafini, A. *Torri campanarie di Roma e del Lazio nel medioevo*, Rome, 1927.

Thiers, J. B. *Traitez des cloches . . .*, Paris, 1602.

BENEDICT I. *(b. Rome, ?, d. Rome, 30 July 578). Ordained on 2 June 575. Buried at St. Peter's in Rome.*

Of Roman origin, the son of a certain Boniface according to the *Liber pontificalis*. Few traces remain of his brief pontificate, during one of the most confused periods of the 6th century.

After the death of JOHN III, Benedict was ordained pope on 2 June 575, ending a very long vacancy of ten months and nineteen days. The delay was undoubtedly prolonged less by internal difficulties among the Roman clergy than by the serious military situation: after the death of King Cleph in 574, the LOMBARD dukes did not elect a successor; instead, each on his own account set out on pillaging raids that left Italy with many bitter memories.

However, the few facts that emerge about Benedict's pontificate show that one should not exaggerate the impression of chaos given by a superficial reading of the *Liber pontificalis*. Benedict was able to manage the affairs of the Church, for he intervened in the dispute between a monastery and the Church of Spoleto. During his pontificate, he ordained 15 priests, 3 deacons, and, most important, 21 bishops, among whom was the bishop of Ravenna, John III: he chose a Roman deacon on whom he conferred the *pallium*, thereby affirming the direct authority of Rome in that diocese.

According to accounts by the Venerable Bede, and Paul the Deacon, it was during Benedict's pontificate that GREGORY, then a monk, felt the stirrings of his vocation to evangelize in Britain. To prevent Gregory's departure, the people of Rome put pressure on the pope to recall him, and Benedict ordained him a deacon of the Roman Church.

No matter how one might nuance the traditional account of the ravages by the Lombards, the situation was grave at the end of Benedict's pontificate. Menander the Protector speaks of a delegation sent from Rome to Constantinople in 577, bearing a considerable sum of money, to sue for the emperor's assistance. Pamphronius, the patrician who headed the mission, obtained from Justin only the authorization to take the money back to Rome and use it for political purposes: to buy out the Lombards by proposing that they enlist in the service of the Byzantines against the Persians, or else to persuade the Franks to attack the Lombards. Perhaps it was this embassy that prompted the shipment of Egyptian grain to which the *Liber pontificalis* refers, a shipment that arrived safely to relieve the famine raging in Rome. Pressure on the city by the Lombards was so severe that the author of the *Liber pontificalis* speaks of a siege.

Benedict died during the summer of 578, "in pain and sorrow" according to the *Liber pontificalis*. He is buried in the *secretarium* at St. Peter's basilica.

Claire Sotinel

Bibliography

JW, 1, 137; 2, 699.

LP, Vita Benedicti, 308.

Agnellus Rav., *LP, Vita Johanii*, III, *MGHsrl*, 342.

Bain, F. "Benoît Ier," *DHGE*, 8 (1939), 7, 9.

Bedus, *Hist. Eccl. Anglorum*, II, 1.

Bertolini, O. "Benedetto I," *DBI*, 8, (1966), 324.

Gregorius I Papa, Epist. IX, 87, *MGH*, Epist. II, 101.

Johannes Diac., *Vita Gregorii*, 1, 21–5.

Ménandre le Protecteur, *Historia. Corpus scriptorum hist. Byzantinum*, 15, 327–8.

Paulus Diac., *Vita Gregorii*, 17, 20; *Historia Longobardorum*, III, 11, *MGHsrl*, 98.

BENEDICT II. *(b. Rome, ?, d. Rome, 8 May 685). Ordained pope on 26 June 684. Buried at St. Peter's in Rome.*

Benedict II made an important contribution to the evolution of the papacy in spite of his very short pontificate, like that of his predecessors and immediate successors. The clergy of Rome chose in him, the son of a certain John, an ordinary city priest who had spent part of his career in the *Schola cantorum*. Almost a year separated his election and its confirmation by the emperor. Then Benedict, whose position was very strong in Rome, won agreement that henceforth confirmation would be given not by the emperor but by the exarch of RAVENNA. A profound innovation followed from this modification of the procedure. The real reason for it had less to do with shortening the lines of communication—people were able to cover great distances rapidly when they wanted to—than with the weakness of the exarch: it was clear that he would be content to go along with what Rome decided. As for the emperor, he was too busy with his eastern wars to withhold his agreement. So a temporary improvement of the relations between Rome and Constantinople was gained.

In Rome, Benedict was the unquestioned leader. He loved "the poor" and showed himself tender-hearted to all, signifying a policy favorable to the people, even demagogic. He presided not only at religious ceremonies but also at major civil celebrations: it was he who, as head of the clergy and the army, in the name of the entire city received the locks of hair from the heads of the emperor's sons, sent as a sign of recognition. Accordingly, higher than the duke, he ranked first among all the notables who represented Rome. In particular, he was in charge of finances, and, without any imposition of control by the agents of the imperial treasury, he was able to distribute the large sum of thirty pounds of gold to the clergy, the monasteries, the bishop's charitable services (the *diaconia*), and those responsible for maintaining the churches (the *mansionarii*).

In the West, he continued the policy of Agatho and LEO II even though the *Liber pontificalis*, reflecting the preoccupations of the local priests, who were concerned above all with their own welfare and relations with the Empire, does not say a word about this. The power of the local Churches is evident here. They were ready to support the pope in his confrontations with Constantinople and to receive the texts of the councils from him. There was no question, however, of unconditional obedience. For example, Julian, bishop of Toledo, and his council discussed the acts of the council *in Trullo* and sent Benedict their own profession of faith. Similarly, when Benedict sought to impose the reestablishment of Wilfrid on the diocese of York, he met with refusal. Thus began a difficult dialogue between Roman pontiffs and national Churches that lasted more than a thousand years.

Jean Durliat

Bibliography

PL, 96, 423–4.

JW, 1, 241–2; 2, 699–741.

LP, 1, 363–5.

Bertolini, O. "Benedetto II," *DBI*, 8 (1966), 325–9; *Roma di fronte a Bisanzio e ai Longobardi*, Bologna, 1971.

BENEDICT III. *(b. Rome, ?, d. Rome, 7 April 858). Elected pope in July 855 (after 17 July), ordained on 29 September 855. Buried at St. Peter's, in Rome.*

Born of a Roman father, educated at the Lateran, and having a strong reputation as a scholar, Benedict was cardinal priest of the title of S. Callisto at the time of the death of LEO IV (17 July 855). He was elected pope only by default, because Cardinal Hadrian, the preferred candidate, declined election. The constitution of Lothair promulgated in 824 required that a pope's election be ratified by the emperor, and that he be consecrated before the imperial representatives; the civil authority, therefore, was asked to confirm the CONCLAVE's choice. However, the embassy entrusted with this mission was circumvented by the partisans of another candidate, Anastasius, who had the support of Emperor Louis II. This support enabled Anastasius to impose himself on Rome with the help of the imperial *missi* on 21 September 855, after having imprisoned Benedict III. His takeover was short-lived, however: of the three bishops required for the papal consecration, two refused to accept the usurpation; facing pressure from the clergy and the people, Anastasius and the *missi* had to back down. No doubt on the strength of a discreet agreement with them, one of the first acts of the newly consecrated Benedict III was to pardon Anastasius, for whom the excommunication imposed on him during the time of Leo IV was partially remitted. Benedict's firmness toward the Frankish empire, the need for which was evident at the beginning of his pontificate, was confirmed during his two-and-a-half-year reign. Here, the advice of his close friend, the future NICHOLAS I, can be seen clearly. Benedict made every act of agreement on his part to requests from the other side of the Alps subject to express recognition of the rights and prerogatives of the Holy See and to the Holy See's examination of the content of texts circulated by the local ecclesiastical authorities; this requirement in particular affected Hincmar, the archbishop of Reims. Benedict also applied himself to emphasizing Rome's precedence over Constantinople in matters of jurisdiction, by recalling for his own examination the case of the archbishop of Syracuse, a refugee in the East who had been deposed by the patriarch, Ignatius, owing to a personal conflict.

The pope also was active in matters of Christian morality, making energetic but fruitless interventions against the behavior of Lothair II's brother-in-law, the subdeacon Hubert, who had taken over the abbey of St-Maurice d'Agaune (Valais, Switzerland) and was leading a most dissolute life. But it was also during his pontificate that there arose the prickly question of Lothair II's remarriage, which would so preoccupy Nicholas I.

In Rome itself, Benedict III made his mark by restoring many churches, undoubtedly aided in this work by the generosity of Ethelwulf, king of Wessex, who, following a pilgrimage to Rome in 855–6, had instituted an annual contribution to St. Peter from the royal treasury.

François Bougard

Bibliography

LP, 2, 140–50.
JW, 1, 339–41; 2, 703, 744.
Baix, F. "Benoît III," *DHGE*, 8 (1935), 14–27.
Bertolini, O. "Benedetto III," *DBI*, 8 (1966), 330–7.
Fliche-Martin, VI, 288ff.

BENEDICT IV. *(b. ?, d. end of July or beginning of August 903). Elected pope in January 900. Buried at St. Peter's in Rome.*

A Roman cleric, the son of Mammalus, he was elected pope probably in January 900. He had been ordained priest by Pope Formosus, and so was taken to be a member of the party supporting Formosus. There are a few more sources of information about his pontificate than about those of the popes who preceded or followed him. He used his papal authority to intervene in various affairs, especially in Italy and the Western Francia: a confirmation of property for Berceto (document lost), a donation and intervention on behalf of Arezzo, a recommendation for the ransom of Bishop Malacenus of Amasea, a prisoner of the SARACENS, the settling of the dispute between Capua and Naples, the excommunication of Winemar of Reims. During a synod at the Lateran, he resolved the question raised by the removal from office of Bishop Argrinus of Langres, a matter that had preoccupied JOHN IX in his time. The death of Emperor Lambert (15 October 898) created a power vacuum in Italy that Benedict tried fill with the grandson of Emperor Louis II, Louis of Provence, called Louis the Blind (887–928). When Louis was elected emperor (February 901), a *placitum* seemed at first to promise a certain political success; however, the initiative was without an appreciable sequel, for Berengar I of Friuli soon regained supremacy over Italy and drove Louis north of the Alps (August 902). When Benedict died, the factional struggles in and around Rome still had not been settled. He is described in numerous sources as a pious man, preoccupied with the welfare of the needy.

Klaus Herbers

Bibliography

JL, 1, 443–4; 2, 705.
LP, 2, 233.
Baix, F. "Benoît IV," *DHGE*, 8 (1935), 27–31.
Bertolini, O. "Benedetto IV," *DBI*, 8 (1966), 337–342.
Hartmann, W. *Die Synoden der Karolingerzeit in Frankenreich und in Italien*, Paderborn, 1989 (*Konziliengeschichte Reihe A, Darstellungen*), 395–6.
Pokorny, R. "Ein unbekanntes Brieffragment Argrims von Lyon-Langres aus den Jahren 894/95 und zwei umstrittene Bischofsweihen in der Kirchenprovinz Lyon. Mit Textedition und Exkurs," *Francia*, 13 (1985), 602–22.

Schieffer, R. "Benedikt IV.," *LexMA*, 1 (1980), 1858.

Zimmermann, H. *Papsturkunden*, 23–9.

Zimmermann, H. *Papstabsetzungen des Mittelalters*, Graz-Vienna-Cologne, 1968, 63.

BENEDICT V. *(b. Rome, ?, d. Hamburg, 4 July 965/6). Elected and consecrated at the end of May 964, deposed at the end of June 964. First buried in the Hamburg cathedral, his remains were transferred probably in 988, by Otto III, to Rome, where his place of burial is unknown.*

Roman by birth, he was the son of a certain John, originally from the *regio Marcelli*. When JOHN XII died on 14 May 964, the Romans sent a delegation to Otto the Great to ask for his authorization of the election of the Roman DEACON Benedict. Noted for his piety and learning, which earned him the name *Grammaticus*, Benedict had been won over to the ideas of the church reform and could be regarded as the candidate of those eager for compromise. Perhaps he had been in the competition with LEO VIII during the papal election of 963. Otto rejected the delegation's request and instead demanded the reinstatement of Pope Leo VIII, whom he was sheltering as a refugee. At the end of May 964, the Romans nevertheless elected Benedict, had him ordained, and solemnly promised him their support. However, they did not long resist the siege of Rome by the imperial troops: overcome by hunger, they opened the gates on 23 June 964 and delivered up Benedict to Otto I. At the end of the month, Benedict was deposed at a synod in the LATERAN at which the emperor and Pope Leo VIII presided. At Otto's insistence, he was allowed to retain the rank of deacon, but he was banished from Rome. At the end of 964, the emperor took Benedict with him to Germany and, in April 965, entrusted him to Archbishop Adaldag of Hamburg-Bremen. Shown every mark of honor by the archbishop, he lived an exemplary life in Hamburg. His reinstatement seems to have been contemplated in 965, after the death of Leo VIII.

Rolf Grosse

Bibliography

LP, 2, 251.

Baix, F. "Benoît V," *DHGE*, 8 (1935), 31–8.

Delogu, P. "Benedetto V," *DBI*, 8 (1966), 342–4.

Schieffer, R. "Benedikt V.," *LexMA*. 1, (1977–80), 1858.

Wolter, H. *Die Synoden im Reichsgebiet und in Reichsitalien von 916 bis 1056*, Paderborn-Munich-Vienna-Zurich, 1988, 83–6.

Zimmermann, H. *Papstregesten*, 139–44, 149–51.

Zimmermann, H. "Parteiungen und Papstwahlen in Rom zur Zeit Kaiser Ottos des Grossen," *Römische historische Mitteilungen*, 8–9 (1964–6), 59–66 (repr. in *Otto der Grosse*, Darmstadt, 1976, 370–81); *Papstabsetzungen des Mittelalters*, Graz-Vienna-Cologne,

1968, 92–5, 235ff.; *Das Dunkle Jahrhundert*, Graz-Vienna-Cologne, 1971, 151–2.

BENEDICT VI. *(b. Rome, ?, d. Rome, July 974). Probably elected pope in September or December 972 and enthroned on 19 January 973. Perhaps buried at St. Peter's in Rome.*

A Roman by birth, he was the son of one Hildebrand *monachus* from the region of the city below the Capitoline hill *(sub Capitolio)*. Cardinal deacon of S. Teodoro, Benedict was elected pope after the death of JOHN XIII (6 September 972), and it is probable that Otto the Great was asked for approval before his enthronement. DEACON Franco, the future antipope BONIFACE VII who enjoyed the support of the Crescentii, seems to have been his rival. Benedict, for his part, was a member of the faction hostile to the Crescentii. He may have been a descendant of the noble family of the Hildebrandi-Aldobrandeschi, who were vassals of the emperor. During his pontificate, he did his best to confer favors on members of his family by ceding them the cities and counties. Hildebrand undoubtedly had retired to a monastery by the time his son was elected pope. Benedict confirmed the founding of the diocese of Prague by Otto the Great (973). However, two acts purportedly drawn up in his name concerning diocesan rights in Hungary for Passau and Salzburg are not authentic. Besides having dealings with Churches in Italy and the German lands, Benedict maintained relations as far away as France and Spain. A revolt erupted in Rome at the end of June 974, stirred up by the Crescentii and led by Crescentius of Theodora; it is not known whether the rioters had links with BYZANTIUM. After being arrested and deposed following various accusations, Benedict was locked up in Castel Sant'Angelo. The Romans elected as his successor the deacon Franco, who became Pope Boniface VII. Otto II, the emperor, could not intervene personally, but Count Sicco of Spoleto, as imperial *missus*, demanded Benedict's release. Boniface VII did not grant this request, and had the imprisoned pope strangled in July 974 by a priest, Stephen, with the help of Stephen's brother.

Rolf Grosse

Bibliography

LP, 2, 255ff.

Baix, F. "Benoît VI," *DHGE*, 8 (1935), 38–43.

Delogu, P. "Benedetto VI," *DBI*, 8 (1966), 344–6.

Schieffer, R. "Benedikt VI," *LexMA*, 1 (1977–80), 1858–9.

Zimmermann, H. *Papstregesten*, 203–12; *Papsturkunden*, 1, 433–60.

Zimmermann, H. "Parteiungen und Papstwahlen in Rom zur Zeit Kaiser Ottos des Grossen," *Römische his-*

torische Mitteilungen, 8–9 (1964–6), 81ff. (repr. in *Otto der Grosse*, Darmstadt, 1976, 403–6); *Papstabsetzungen des Mittelalters*, Graz-Vienna-Cologne, 1968, 99ff.; *Das dunkle Jahrhundert*, Graz-Vienna-Cologne, 1971, 202ff.

BENEDICT VII. *(d. 10 July 983). Elected pope in October 974.*

Compared with other popes of the 10th century, Benedict VII had an unspectacular reign, without dramatic incidents. His pontificate is noted for his close and trusting collaboration with Emperor Otto II, whose reign (973–83) extended almost throughout the whole of Benedict's time as pope. He had served as Bishop Benedict of Sutri, and was related through his family to the Roman prince Alberic. A first proof of his link with the emperor was given when his election took place in the presence of Count Sicco of Spoleto, the imperial LEGATE, and with his permission. The emperor's support was of capital importance, because the ANTIPOPE BONIFACE VII posed a constant threat, as shown by his brief return to Rome in the summer of 980.

The close collaboration between emperor and pope is witnessed by the many privileges and EXEMPTIONS granted to German monasteries, the requests often coming from the emperor himself. It was certainly at Otto II's initiative that Gerbert of Reims, whose reputation for learning was already well known and would continue to flourish when he became Pope SILVESTER II, was named abbot of the ancient monastery of Bobbio, founded by St. Columbanus. The close collaboration between Benedict VII and Otto II was evident also when the entire suffragan diocese of Merseburg was detached from the archdiocese of Magdeburg, a measure much contested on juridical grounds. But many Italian and French monasteries also benefited from privileges conferred by the pope, among them Fleury, Charroux, Vézelay, and Micy, as part of the major movement for monastic reform and renewal in the second half of the century. The relations between the pontifical see and the Christian Churches of Europe, which were strengthened during Benedict VII's era, have a special historical interest, but were relatively marginal from a geopolitical point of view. For example, a number of privileges were established for churches and monasteries (Vich, Gerona, Urgel, Besalu, Cuxa) situated in the Pyrenees, that is, in the old Spanish march founded and designated as such by Charlemagne. The monastery of SS. Bonifacio e Alexico, founded in 977 on the Aventine, in Rome, brought together Benedictines of the Western tradition and Basilian monks of the Eastern: it became an important center for Rome's external relations in AFRICA and the territories of BYZANTIUM. The policy of the emperor and of the pope toward Byzantium, as it was revealed at the beginning of the 980s when they had a common aim, can thus be more clearly understood. It was evidently meant to weaken once and for all the Byzantine influence in southern Italy. In the realm of ecclesiastical policy, Benedict tried to detach Trani from the influence of the metropolitan of Bari by establishing a new archdiocese; at the same time, Otto II launched an armed offensive in southern Italy. His severe military defeat at Cape Colonna on 13 July 982 brought these projects to nothing.

Hans-Henning Körtum

Bibliography

LP, 2, 256–8.
Baix, F. "Benoît VII," *DHGE*, 8 (1935), 46–61.
Delogu, P. "Benedetto VII," *DBI*, 8 (1966), 346–50.
Schieffer, R. "Benedikt VII.," *LexMA*, 1 (1977–80), 1859.
Zimmermann, H. *Papstregesten*, 213–250; *Papsturkunden*, 1, 461–548.
Zimmermann, H. *Das dunkle Jahrhundert*, Graz-Vienna-Cologne, 1971.

BENEDICT VIII. *Theophylact of Tusculum (b. ?, d. Rome, 9 April 1024). Elected on 17 May 1012, ordained on 21 May.*

After the death of the Roman patrician John II Crescentius, the Crescentii had one of their partisans elected canonically under the name GREGORY (VI). He, however, had to flee to Sabina, unable to remain in Rome after the Tusculan party, on 17 May, elected Benedict VIII, the second son of Gregory, count of Tusculum, and his wife Mary. Benedict VIII managed to establish himself in Rome and was ordained on 21 May. As a distinctive mark of the new papal policy, Benedict VIII no longer provided for the Roman patricians, and through intense activity tried to extend the influence of the Church into areas belonging to the temporal order. The Crescentii, who until then had been all-powerful, were largely dispossessed, and the pope's own family had only a marginal share of power. His summer campaign in Sabina ended with victory for Benedict, and Gregory (VI) took refuge in the German lands. But Benedict had already established contacts with Henry II, king of Germany, and on 21 January 1013 had confirmed to him the diocese of Bamberg, to which the king was partial, and had opened talks with him in anticipation of Henry's coronation as emperor. Gregory (VI), the pope's adversary, disappeared into the mists of history.

Benedict VIII solemnly crowned Henry II emperor in Rome on 14 February 1014, the event marking the beginning of close collaboration with the empire. That same year, at Ravenna, during a synod that condemned SIMONY, among other things, the emperor and the pope tried to remedy some obvious shortcomings in the internal organization of the Church. In the spring of 1016, with the aid of a coalition from Genoa and Pisa, the pope succeeded in defeating SARACEN pirates off the coast of Sardinia. The following year, he sent NORMAN mercenaries to assist the LOMBARD princes of southern Italy, who had been his allies since 1014, in maintaining their uprising against BYZANTINE rule. When the uprising was defeated in Apulia in October 1018, the pope sought German help from Henry II: the two met at Bamberg on 14 April 1020. There the pope consecrated the collegiate church as well as the chapel of the imperial palace, and confirmed the privileges of the diocese. By 1 May at the latest, Henry II had sent the pope at Fulda a renewed and updated version of the privileges established by Otto I for the states of the Church (see PAPAL STATES), including the transfer of Bamberg to the Holy See. The chief outcome of the meeting was surely the agreement to launch a military attack on southern Italy. The campaign during the summer of 1022 was disappointing: it succeeded in overcoming the Lombard allies of Byzantium at Salerno and Capua, and a dependable abbot was installed in the monastery of Monte Cassino, but, after the departure of the imperial army, instability reigned as before.

Having concluded the campaign in southern Italy, the pope and the emperor continued their series of reforming councils at the 1 August 1022 synod in Pavia. They agreed to punish concubinage by clerics and the enfranchisement of clerics' children, as well as the free sale or purchase of church properties; once the synodal decrees had been published, Henry incorporated them in public law. This was a modest beginning of a reform that continued the thrust of the decisions made in 1014 at Ravenna. Benedict and Henry clearly had other reforming synods in mind, but these were prevented by their deaths, in the spring and early summer of 1024 respectively.

In 1023–4, the pope found himself in violent conflict with Archbishop Aribo of Mainz over the affair of the Hammerstein couple: by decrees adopted on 12 August 1023 at a synod at Seligenstadt, the archbishop wanted to prohibit Benedict VIII from making the final decision in the case of Irmingard von Hammerstein, who came to Rome in person for a settlement. Benedict VIII reacted sternly: For his arrogance, Aribo saw himself stripped of the *pallium*, the outward sign of his rank as archbishop, and it was never restored to him, even after he went to Rome in 1031 to do penance before Benedict's successor, JOHN XIX.

Benedict VIII maintained very close ties with French monastic reformers after the imperial coronation in Rome in 1014, in which Abbot Odilo of Cluny also participated. Benedict intervened many times in favor of the celebrated monastery, the ecclesiastical policy of the Tusculans in France always having been marked by the friendly character of the relations maintained with monastic circles.

In the affair of the election of Abbot Gozlin of Fleury

as archbishop of Bourges in the spring of 1012, the pope took the abbot's side against episcopal opposition. But despite his intervention, another five years would pass before the archbishop was enthroned at Bourges, at the instigation of Abbot Odilo of Cluny.

In his relations with the monasteries and bishops of Catalonia, Benedict was more inclined to react than to act in order to pursue, in the footsteps of his predecessor SERGIUS IV, the consolidation of ecclesiastical institutions.

Benedict VIII died on 9 April 1024. His pontificate was marked by a close personal collaboration with Henry II; by a real policy of expansion, unsuccessful in the short term, of the Roman Church in southern Italy; and by a struggle to reinforce the papacy, which he was able to detach from its very close ties to the Roman nobility, including his own family. Although he did not intentionally aim at a plan for reform of the Church, his policies laid the foundations for the program of the future reform-minded papacy.

Klaus-Jürgen Herrmann

Bibliography

JW, 1, 506–14.

LP, 268.

Herrmann, K. J. *Das Tuskulanerpapsttum, 1012–1046*, Stuttgart, 1973.

Schieffer, R. "Benedikt VIII.," *LexMA*, 1 (1977–80), 1859.

Tellenbach, G. "Benedetto VIII," *DBI*, 8 (1966), 350–4.

Wappler, P. G. *Papst Benedikt VIII.*, Leipzig, 1897.

Wolter, H. *Die Synoden im Reichsgebiet und in Reichsitalien im 916 bis 1056*, Paderborn, 1988, 242–312.

Zimmermann, H. *Papstregesten*, 1075–1276; *Papsturkunden*, 2, 464–549.

BENEDICT IX. *Theophylact of Tusculum (d. Grottaferrata between 18 September 1055 and 9 January 1056). Pope from 21 October 1032 to September 1044; from 10 March 1045 to 1 May 1045; and from 8 November 1047 to 16 July 1048. Buried in the abbey church at Grottaferrata.*

After the death of JOHN XIX on 20 October 1032, Alberic III, at the cost of concessions to the electoral college and the nobility, managed to have his son Theophylact elected on 21 October as Pope Benedict IX. Very young and a layman besides, Theophylact was crowned the next day. Although the sources later would depict him as depraved, the young pope was able to direct the Church skillfully throughout the twelve years of his pontificate. At Rome and in the Papal States he pursued a policy of appeasement with other factions of the nobility; his father, Alberic III, withdrew from official political life, and his brother, Gregory II of Tusculum, assumed judicial functions in particular cases. The new pope seems not to have sought immediate contacts with the imperial German court; only after the quarrel erupted over the emperor's decision to depose Archbishop Aribert of Milan (1018–45) did Conrad II think of making use of the pope as a docile instrument. At a meeting with Benedict IX at Cremona in 1037, Emperor Conrad II tried to win the pope's agreement to the deposition of Aribert. Benedict IX, who hoped to negotiate a compromise, did not bend to the emperor's political wishes. Conrad II had to face the fact that Benedict IX, unlike his uncle and predecessor John XIX, would in no way submit to his demands. The next year, in a new political context, while he was at Spello for the Easter celebrations and probably during another meeting with Conrad, Benedict IX did excommunicate Aribert. At the time, Benedict IX was supporting the emperor's campaign in southern Italy: his aunt or his sister Theodora, having married into the dynasty of the counts of Salerno, it became possible to form an alliance directed mainly against the dynasty of Pandulf IV of Capua, who favored BYZANTIUM. The chief beneficiary of the campaign in southern Italy and of the whole policy conducted jointly by the pope and the emperor in the southern part of the peninsula was the monastery of Monte Cassino, the autonomy of which Conrad II and Benedict IX reestablished. As a result of skillful diplomacy, the pope succeeded in strengthening the position of the Roman Church in the Byzantine sphere of influence, and laid the foundations of extensive church reorganization.

Departing from his father's ways, the new German king Henry III (1038–56), sought the pope's help, especially in order to have removed the obstacles to his marriage to Agnes of Poitou. Benedict IX, for his part, guarded his complete freedom of choice: at a synod in April 1044, he quashed the decision earlier imposed by Conrad II on his uncle John XIX regarding the patriarchate of Aquileia, and restored the title of patriarch to Grado. In ecclesiastical matters, the pope, who had ties to reforming circles, was able, within very clear limits, to correct some evils, without having undertaken an active project of reform. At a synod in Rome at the beginning of 1036, Benedict extended his support to a convent of canons in Florence, which he placed under papal protection, and he defended the monastery of S. Pietro di Calvario against its bishop. Prodded by the reformer Peter Damiani, Benedict IX deposed and excommunicated the bishops of Pesaro and Fano, found guilty of simony. The pope seems to have enjoyed particular prestige in France. Undoubtedly it was at his prompting that the archbishops of Vienne and Besançon met in 1037 near Lausanne together with the bishop of that city to promote a peace initiative, the Truce of God. While it is difficult to support the theory that Benedict IX himself went to Marseille in October 1040 to discuss extending the Truce of God, he would certainly have had contacts with the project.

In the German lands, the pope supported Archbishop Poppo of Trier in his 1035–36 struggle with the dukes of Lützelburg (Luxemburg) by sending him a coadjutor, and he canonized the Syrian monk Symeon, who had died a recluse in a cell of the *Porta Nigra* at Trier.

At the beginning of September 1044, a riot brought on as a result of discontent stirred up by the Tusculan government incited a group of Roman citizens and the Stephanians, a branch of the Crescentii, against the reigning pope, Benedict IX, who was forced to flee Rome. On 10 January 1045, he was able to return with troops to the Trastevere area and defeat the insurgents. The Romans, egged on by the Stephanians, elected their Sabine bishop John as the new pope, under the name SILVESTER III, and enthroned him on 13 or 20 January 1045. Benedict IX excommunicated the ANTIPOPE and, on 10 March 1045, reentered the Leonine city by force of arms. Silvester III fled to Sabina, where, until March 1046, he refused to renounce papal status. Back in Rome, Benedict IX was no more than a pawn of the noble factions: on 1 May 1045, undoubtedly for personal reasons as well, he resigned in favor of the archpriest John Gratian, who took the name GREGORY VI. The sums of money evidently raised for the papal abdication did not profit Benedict IX personally, but were taken by the still active Tusculan party as compensation for their interests. After abdicating, Benedict retired as an ordinary citizen to his estates near Tusculum, and he did not appear at the 20 December synod at Sutri or the 24 December synod in Rome, at which the three popes were deposed at the urging of the German king, who was there in person. After Emperor Henry III had Bishop Suidger of Bamberg elected pope as CLEMENT II, and had returned to Germany with the deposed Gregory VI, the Tusculans renewed their attacks on Rome. They had to wait for Clement II's death at Pesaro on 9 October 1047 before they were able to reestablish Benedict IX, on 9 November, in Rome. Only one pro-imperial faction appealed to the emperor, taking a definite stand against Benedict IX by electing Poppo of Brixen as Pope DAMASUS II. He was installed in Rome by a reluctant Marquess Boniface of Canossa, on orders from the emperor. Benedict IX fled Rome on 16 July 1048; the next day, his adversary, Damasus II was officially introduced to Rome, only to die of malaria at Palestrina just twenty-three days later. When the new Pope LEO IX came to Rome with the emperor's backing, he was exposed to daily military opposition from the Tusculans. Leo IX replied by destroying the Tusculan territories and excommunicating Benedict and all those who had aided him. After the death of Leo IX on 19 April 1054, Benedict IX apparently made one last vain attempt to regain papal status. During the course of the year 1054, he retired to the monastery at Grottaferrata, which supported the Tusculans, and he died there between 18 September 1055 and 9 January 1056. The story that he died at Grottaferrata after becoming a monk as a penitential act has no basis in fact. He was buried in the abbey church at Grottaferrata.

Klaus-Jürgen Herrmann

Bibliography

JW, 1, 519–23; 2, 709 and 748 ff.

LP, 2, 270–2.

Baix, F. and Jadin, L. "Benoît IX," *DHGE*, 8 (1935), 93–105.

Borino, G. B. "L'elezione e la deposizione di Gregorio VI," *ASR*, 39 (1916), 141–252, 295–410.

Borino, G. B. "Invitus ultra montes cum domino papa Gregorio abii," *Studio gregoriana*, 1 (1947), 3–46.

Ghirardini, L. L. *Il papa fanciullo Benedetto IX (1032–1048)*, Parma, 1980, (cf. Jaspers, D. *Deutsches Archiv*, 38 [1982], 273).

Herrmann, K. J. *Das Tuskulanerpapsttum, 1012–1046*, Stuttgart, 1973.

Luccicchenti, L. "Benedetto e la sua tomba," *Bollettino della badia greca di Grottaferrata*, n.s. 28 (1974), 37–64.

Mathis, A. "Il pontefice Benedetto IX. Appunti critici di storia medievale," *La Civiltà cattolica*, 66 (1915), 549–71; 67 (1916), 285–96, 535–48.

Messina, S. *Benedetto IX, pontefice romano, 1032–1048: studio critico*, Catania, 1922.

Schieffer, R. "Benedikt IX.," *LexMA*, 1, (1977–80), 1859–60.

Wolter, H. *Die Synoden in Reichsgebiet und in Reichsitalien von 916 bis 1056*, Paderborn, 1988, 358 and 374ff.

Zimmermann, H. *Papsturkunden*, 2, 598–623.

Zimmermann, H. *Papstabsetzungen des Mittelalters*, Vienna-Cologne-Graz, 1968, 120–39.

[BENEDICT X]. *John Mincius (b. Rome, ?, after 1073). Antipope elected and enthroned in Rome on 5 April 1058, resigned in 1059, deposed at the Lateran in April 1060.*

The son of a certain Gui from the *regio* of ST. MARY MAJOR, he was related to the counts of Tusculum and, by the same token, to the party of the Roman NOBILITY, to whom he undoubtedly owed the honor of being named bishop of Velletri. It is not known to what extent he was tied to the Roman reform group, and whether it was he or his predecessor as bishop of Velletri who was proposed in 1057 as papal candidate by Frederick of Lorraine (STEPHEN IX). He certainly took the oath required by Stephen IX of the Roman clergy and people not to elect a successor after his death until Hildebrand's return from his mission to the German court. However, scarcely a week after the death of Stephen IX, though making a show of protest, he allowed himself to be persuaded by the leaders of the Roman nobility to assume the papacy.

Peter Damian, called on as CARDINAL bishop of Ostia to direct the enthronement—Benedict X was already a bishop—fled Rome with the rest of the cardinals, thereby escaping the curse of the *intrusus*. So that the enthronement could proceed, a priest from Ostia was called on, an uneducated and incompetent cleric according to the invectives of Peter Damian, who was carried away by passion to use the language of the streets. Later, Benedict X's opponents refused to pay the money traditionally thrown to the people during the procession, speaking of electoral corruption or, according to the language of the times, SIMONY. With the election of this pope, the aristocracy that had dominated the Roman church during recent decades was attempting once again to regain control of the papal see. Facing the weakness of the imperial government of Empress Agnes, and in the absence of most members of the Roman reform group, Gregory di Alberico of Tusculum, Gerard of Galeria, and Ottaviano Crescenzi of Monticelli judged that the situation was opportune for recovering, by installing a pope of their choice, their former dominant position in Rome; the question of the reform of ecclesiastical life undoubtedly played a minor role in bringing their faction together. Their sudden initiative at first met with full success. Until January 1059, Benedict X was able to live peacefully in the Lateran. Little else is known about his administration. He allotted a hospice near St. Peter's to the Hungarian pilgrims, sent the *pallium* to Archbishop Stigand of Canterbury, and, in return for the payment of an annual tax, ceded some fiefs to several nobles from the Marches of Ancona; at the request of Bishop Hezilo of Hildesheim, with a formula of privilege, he confirmed property rights for a women's convent at Hildesheim, in the German lands. All these activities point to a routine conduct of papal affairs.

The reform group around Hildebrand met only in December 1058 to affirm their opposition by electing Bishop Gerard of Florence as Pope NICHOLAS II. At the approach of his rival, Benedict X fled Rome and sought the protection of his allies, first in the fortress of Passerano to the east of Rome, and then in the fortified castle of Galeria, north of the city. In January 1059, a synod called by Nicholas II at Sutri pronounced excommunication against Benedict X. The subsequent sieges of Galeria had no real success, despite aid from the NORMANS. Benedict decided to renounce the papal honor and take up residence in his private house in Rome only after some leading Romans guaranteed his safety. During another synod held at the Lateran in April 1060, he was deposed on charges of perjury and simony, declared an ANTIPOPE, and duly and ceremoniously degraded. The diocese of Velletri was placed under the administration of Peter Damian and remained united to Ostia until the modern era. Stripped of all his ecclesiastical honors, the deposed pope probably lived in retirement, until the pontificate of GREGORY VII, with the religious at Sta Agnese on the Via Nomentana, where he was also buried. His pontificate, though only a brief episode, gave rise to the 1059 decree on papal elections, by means of which the reform group sought to ensure its controlling influence and to present the election of Nicholas II as legitimate even though it barely conformed to the rules in force until then.

Tilmann Schmidt

Bibliography

Capitani, O. "Benedetto X," *DBI*, 8 (1966), 366–70.

Hüls, R. *Kardinäle, Klerus und Kirchen Roms 1049–1130*, Tübingen, 1977 (*Bibliothek des Deutschen Historischen Instituts in Rom*, 48), 144.

Schmidt, T. *Alexander II. (1061–1073) und die römische Reformgruppe seiner Zeit*, Stuttgart, 1977 (*Päpste und Papsttum*, 11), 78–80.

Schieffer, R. "Benedikt X.," *LexMA*, 1 (1980), 1859.

Tellenbach, G. *Die westliche Kirche vom 10. bis zum frühen 12. Jahrhundert*, Göttingen, 1988 (*Die Kirche in ihrer Geschichte*, 2, F 1), 134.

BENEDICT XI. *Niccolò Boccasini (b. Treviso, 1240, d. Perugia, 7 July 1304). Elected pope on 22 October 1303, crowned on 27 October in Rome. Buried at S. Domenico in Perugia. Beatified on 26 April 1736.*

The pontificate of BONIFACE VIII's successor was too short to influence the directions taken by the Church, but at least "the Dominican pope" did not shy away from the difficult questions facing the Church at that time.

The son of a notary, educated by an uncle who was a priest, he spent his entire career in the Dominican order, first at Treviso and then at Milan, Venice, and Genoa. He was given a theological formation (he left a *Commentary* on the Bible), but he was above all an administrator: after serving as prior and then provincial (in 1289 and 1293–6, in Lombardy), he became master general of the Dominicans on 12 May 1296. Boniface VIII named him CARDINAL (December 1298) and then bishop of Ostia (1300), and sent him on missions to France and Hungary. He returned to Italy in 1303. The outrage at Anagni, followed by the dramatic death of Pope Boniface VIII, caused such a shock that the CONCLAVE, overcoming its divisions, unanimously chose Boccasini, who had remained faithful to Boniface, but been kept away from the latter's conflicts by missions far from Rome. Belonging to no faction, Benedict had to look elsewhere for support: the three cardinals he had time to name were Dominicans.

He found himself immediately facing the consequences of the Anagni affair. Like the reed, Benedict XI bent (he remitted the excommunication of Philip the Fair and annulled the proceedings of his predecessor) but did not break, and he refused to make any gesture in favor of Nogaret, the instigator of the Anagni affair, and his Italian allies, the Colonna. The gain was slight: the king no longer demanded the calling of a COUNCIL, but he continued to insist that Boniface VIII be condemned; as for the Colonna, they controlled Rome and forced the pope in May 1304 to take refuge in Perugia.

As for other problems—the conflict over Sicily between the Angevins of Naples and the Aragonese, the crisis of the GUELPH party at Florence, the division among the Franciscans—Benedict XI died too soon to bear any blame for failing to resolve them. Whether he would have had the means and strength of character necessary for dealing with them is an open question. He was buried at Perugia; visitors to his tomb reported miracles.

Alain Demurger

Bibliography

Ferrero, A. M. *Benedetto XI, papa domenicano*, Rome, 1935.

Finke, H. and Gaibrois y Ballesteros, *Roma despuès de la muerte de Boniface VIII*, Rome, 1924.

Grandjean, C. "Recherches sur l'administration financiere du pape Benoit XI," *MAH*, 3 (1883), 47–66; "Benoit XI avant son pontificat," *MAH*, 8 (1888), 219–291; *Le Registre de Benoit XI*, Rome, 1905.

Jadin, L. "Benoit XI," *DHGE*, 8 (1935), 106–16.

Nuske, G. F. "Untersuchungen über das Personal der papstlichen Kanzlei, 1254–1304," *QFIAB*, 21 (1975), 249 ff.

Schwaiger, G. "Benedikt XI.," *LexMA*, 1 (1980), 1860–1.

Walter, I. "Benedetto XI," *DBI*, 8 (1966), 370–8.

BENEDICT XII. *Jacques Fournier (b. Saverdun, Ariège, 1285, d. Avignon, 25 April 1342). Elected on 20 December 1334, crowned on 8 January 1335. Buried in the cathedral of Notre-Dame-des-Doms at Avignon.*

Arnaud Nouvel, the maternal uncle of Jacques Fournier (*de Furno*), the future Benedict XII, built a hospital at Saverdun (Ariège), their birthplace, in 1285, the very year his nephew was born. After 1289, this professor of law took the Cistercian habit at the monastery of Boulbonne, where he later received his nephew as a *nutritus* (novice). Having become abbot of Fontfroide (Aude), Arnaud Nouvel soon was named CARDINAL, in 1310, and died on 14 August 1317. His nephew Jacques, a monk of Boulbonne, was called to succeed him as head of Fontfroide, after studying theology with brilliant results at the Cistercian college of St-Bernard in Paris.

Named to the diocese of Pamiers, Jacques Fournier was ordained bishop at AVIGNON on 22 August 1317, eight days after his uncle's death. Thus began the well-known period of his life, popularized by Emmanuel Le Roy Ladurie in his *Montaillou*. On 3 March 1326, Fournier was transferred to the diocese of Mirepoix.

At Christmas the following year (1327), he was called, as cardinal of the TITLE of Sta Prisca (which had been that of his uncle), to join the Roman CURIA in residence at Avignon, where he took up the resposibility of counselor to JOHN XXII. When John XXII died, Jacques was elected to succeed him, ushering in the shortest reign of the Avignon popes, from 20 December 1334 to 25 April 1342, the date of his death. His career as Benedict XII was marked from the outset by originality. With more depth and constancy than his two predecessors, CLEMENT V and John XXII, he grasped the essentially religious aspect of his position. He remained a monk; as cardinal, he had kept the white habit of his order. Once elected by the CONCLAVE, he chose the name Benedict because he lived by the rule of Benedict, the patriarch of his order. He was not the least preoccupied with personal comfort; art, as such, scarcely interested him. The château that he had built, because he needed better and safer lodging, was neither large nor elegant, and he lived in it as in a monastery. Education, which he encouraged, in his view ought only to assist the one who received it in carrying out his vocation: what good did it do a young Cistercian to study either civil or church law at a UNIVERSITY? It was enough to attend the faculty of arts so as to move on to studies in theology. In his sermons, Benedict XII sought after neither the easy success of eloquence, nor the charm of anecdotes, nor the appeal of doctrinal novelty. He regarded his sermons as lessons in dogma. His *Postille* on St. Matthew, which he had checked by the experts but left unfinished, touched on simple moral questions.

Modest in his private life—his election had surprised him—Benedict XII showed himself energetic and sometimes even brutal in his handling of papal affairs. He did not hesitate in CONSISTORY to revoke benefices held *in commendam* (yielding revenues even if vacant), though he did not go so far as to apply that decision to members of the SACRED COLLEGE. He left political questions to the college. Having personally decided, in July 1335, to return to Rome, he temporized in the face of opposition from the cardinals, who thought the move inopportune, and in the end he decided, in July 1337, that the papacy would remain at Avignon.

His proposals for reform, set forth beginning on 17 June 1335 with the constitution *Pastor bonus*, would put him at odds, on several fronts, with the principal religious orders for the seven years of his pontificate.

The Cistercians were the first object of the papal concern, with the constitution *Fulgens sicut stella* of 12 July 1335, and were soon followed by the Benedictines, on whom, with the bull *Summi Magistri* of 20 June 1336, he attempted to impose a plan for centralization that the black monks had not asked for, and that they resisted vigorously. He was very reserved toward the Franciscans, to whom, beginning with his first consistory, held just three days after his election, he had addressed severe criticisms, Benedict XII broke with them in what could be called a definitive way with his bull of 28 November 1336, *Redemptor noster*; this text, according to J. B. Mahn, "today still earns him the stubborn hostility of all the sons of St. Francis, no matter which branch they belong to."

His interest in intellectual matters no doubt explains his high regard for the DOMINICANS, shown even before his election as pope. In the inaugural consistory of his pontificate, he praised the sons of St. Dominic "as being at the head of all the other orders," paying public homage to their theological learning as well as to their apostolic courage in lands infected with the poison of HERESY. Yet it was from them that his most bitter disappointments would come. The order of preachers had elected as their head Hugh of Vaucemain, a native of Burgundy, who, for Pentecost in 1336, was presiding over their annual general chapter at Bruges. The pope asked members of the chapter to prepare for his use a detailed census of the whole order. This did not bode well. The pope's 18 December 1337 letter to the head of the order opened up a five-year struggle between him and the Dominicans. In 1338, a general chapter having been called at their convent at Metz, Benedict XII asked that it be moved to Avignon, thinking he could thereby influence the chapter's decisions. Hugh of Vaucemain refused to change the location, preferring that there be no chapter at all. Benedict XII went so far as to contemplate the suppression of the order of St. Dominic. But it was his own death, following that of Hugh of Vaucemain, that ended the conflict.

Tall, of ruddy complexion, with a sonorous, high-pitched voice, Benedict XII seemed formidable to those around him. Few popes have been more disparaged than he: witness the writings of Petrarch, who never stopped gibing at the pope. Of proven integrity, hostile to every form of favoritism, Benedict XII surrounded himself with remarkable collaborators who, through excellent management, filled the coffers of the papal treasury. This sound economy enabled the pope to come to the aid of the most impoverished. The ASSISTANCE given to the poor during Benedict XII's pontificate was particularly effective, amounting to 19.4 percent of the total budget for the expenses of the apostolic almoner—undoubtedly a level never reached elsewhere. This was a major component of the activity of this over-vilified pope, and can only be set down to his credit.

Paul Amargier

Bibliography

Amargier, P. *Benoît XII, pape cistercien; Cîteaux après l'âge d'or*, Sénanque, 1987, 37–58; "*Nullus in jure peritus in utroque*: Benoît XII–Urbain V," *Aux origines de l'État moderne. Le fonctionnement de la papauté d'Avignon*, Rome, 1990, 33–39 (*CEFR*, 138).

Guillemain, B. *La Cour pontificale d'Avignon (1309–1376)*, Paris, 1962.

Jadin, L. "Benoît XII," *DHGE*, 8 (1935), 116–35.

Jadin, L. *Benoît XII*, Paris, 1964, 72–88.

La Papauté d'Avignon et le Languedoc (1316–1342), *Cahiers de Fanjeaux*, 26 (1991).

Mollat, G. *The Popes at Avignon*, New York, 1963.

Trottman, C. *La vision béatifique: des désputes scolastiques à sa définition par Benoît XII*, Rome, 1995.

[BENEDICT XIII] *Pedro de Luna (b. Illueca, Aragon, 1342 or 1343, d. Peñiscola, 27 November 1422). Elected pope of the Avignon obedience on 28 September 1394, ordained on 11 October, deposed, along with his rival, by the council of Pisa on 5 June 1409, deposed again by the council of Constance on 3 September 1417, rebellious until his death. Buried at the Castle of Illueca, tomb destroyed in 1811.*

The second son of Juan Martinez II de Luna and Maria Pérez de Gotor, Pedro de Luna was born at Illueca (in the kingdom of Aragon), in the maternal castle, at the end of 1342 or the beginning of 1343, and not in 1328 as has often been said. The Luna family was allied to the royal family of Aragon and to other great lineages, those of the marquesses of Saluzo, the counts of Foix, and the Albornoz. The Gotor were descendants of a Moorish king of Majorca whose son was baptized in 1229.

Already described as counselor of the king of Aragon when he began studies in CANON LAW at the University of Montpellier in 1361, Pedro de Luna took the whole *cursus* up to the licence and the doctorate before becoming a teacher himself, around 1370. The only one of his scholastic works to survive (*Repetitio c. Sicut stellas*) probably is from these years. To the advantage of noble birth he added a fine education in the discipline most likely to promote a brilliant clerical career. First named canon of Calatayud, the city closest to Illueca, he became canon and precentor of Lerida (1361), and then obtained prebends, or the prospect of prebends, in several Spanish cities, though current research cannot be more precise about these.

When he was named CARDINAL by GREGORY XI in December 1375, he was provost of Valencia and had never held episcopal rank: as cardinal of the TITLE of Sta Maria in Cosmedin, he was allowed to remain a simple deacon.

Known as the cardinal of Aragon, he scarcely had time to settle in AVIGNON because, in September 1375, he followed Gregory XI, who was departing for Rome in order to reestablish the Holy See there. Like the pope, he was determined to remain in Rome and quickly became associated with the friends of Bridget of Sweden, who were in Rome in anticipation of her canonization. Along with two other cardinals, he was given responsibility for examining the revelations associated with her, and the opinion he gave was favorable.

Gregory XI died on 27 March 1378. The grave responsibility of choosing a successor fell on the sixteen cardinals who had followed him to Rome. Tumult reigned, in the skies and in the spirits of those voting. The cardinal of Aragon received communion from the hands of Alphonsus of Vadaterra, the former confessor of Bridget of Sweden, before entering the CONCLAVE, and he decided to support an Italian, Bartolomeo Prignano, the archbishop of Bari. Thus, it was not the uproar of the Roman crowd that dictated his choice, and many witnesses report that he was calm and resolute in the midst of the general panic.

Bartolomeo Prignano took the name URBAN VI and began his reign with a series of measures that turned his electors against him. The argument began to spread that he had been elected invalidly, by men certainly of sound mind but in the grip of terror. It was based on a DECRETAL (*De his quae vi metusve causa fiunt*, I, 40); Pedro de Luna, an eye-witness of the election and an expert in canon law, took his time examining it; his judgment was irrevocable and sealed the pope's fate. He himself had explained to Alphonsus of Vadaterra, distraught by his decision to break with Urban VI, "that no man on earth may go counter to what he believes to be true."

At the end of June, he joined the protesting cardinals. He signed the manifesto denouncing the election of Bartolomeo Prignano (9 August) and took part in the conclave of Fondi, at which Robert of Geneva was elected on 20 September 1378. To finish off their initiative, the cardinals had only to organize the effort to dislodge the "*intrus*" and his partisans, and to persuade the world of the clear right of the new pope, CLEMENT VII. More than anyone else, Pedro de Luna went about the task with talent and charm: his mission to the kingdoms of Aragon, Castile, Portugal, and Navarre, which began on 18 December 1378, drew to a close on 15 December 1390.

The Iberian Peninsula was slow to be convinced, and the kings of Castile and Aragon were unwilling to accept the word of a single LEGATE: they sent commissions to make inquiry of the cardinals and their conclavists concerning the circumstances of the election. During this period, Pedro de Luna took advantage of his many connections to go ahead with a major project among the clergy. Anxious to promote education, he intervened with Clement VII for the creation of a faculty of theology at Salamanca and a *studium generale* at Perpignan. The religious houses of his native region benefited from his largesse, and he refitted the church of St. Peter the Martyr at Calatayud as a family cemetery. With several eminent figures, he formed solid alliances that, fostered by the heat of the controversy, developed into ties of esteem and friendship. Among others, he won the spoken and written support of Vincent Ferrier, whose personal reputation already extended beyond Valencia. And in

Navarre, from the outset, he had the support of Martin of Zalba, who, while not a saintly miracle worker, was a man with connections, a competent canonist, discreet, efficient, and loyal.

His mission bore its first lasting fruit in Castile. At Medina del Campo, Pedro de Luna was opposed by Francesco Uguccione, a champion of Urban VI, in interminable contests in eloquence. Then the clergy took his side, and King John I made a profession of faith for himself and his people in support of Clement, in the cathedral of Salamanca (1381). The legate even had the satisfaction of convincing an eminent supporter of Urban: Gutierre Gomez made his act of submission, returning the cardinal's hat he had received from Urban VI. Magnanimous, Pedro de Luna intervened to have him integrated into the SACRED COLLEGE that supported Clement.

As long as he lived, Peter IV of Aragon was unwilling to take sides between Urban and Clement, but this balancing came to an end in 1387 with the succession of his son, John. An assembly called at Barcelona counseled the new king to recognize the Avignon pope, Clement. To seal this alliance, the legate made James of Aragon, the bishop of Valencia and the king's cousin, a cardinal. Two months later, King John chose Pedro de Luna to be the executor of his will, and the latter had many occasions on which to exert his influence in the familial and political intrigues of the Aragonese court.

At Navarre, a change of sovereign enabled the legate to score a victory for the Avignon cause. Despite a long stay at Pamplona in 1385, he had been unable to persuade Charles the Bad to join Clement's camp, though a number of clerics close to the crown had already done so. Then Charles III came to the throne in 1387, and, on 6 February 1390, Pedro de Luna was able to deliver a fine speech announcing that Navarre had entered into the obedience of Avignon. The king was then crowned by the legate, and Martin of Zalba, the bishop of Pamplona, was rewarded for his zeal by being named cardinal.

The dynastic vicissitudes in Portugal, together with the fickleness of its kings, created a confused situation that Pedro de Luna was unable to master. The Portuguese clergy were deeply divided, and the discussions at Santarém came up against the problem of the independence of the kingdom with respect to Castile. The legate emphasized the personal bonds between the two royal families, but Portuguese nationalism was strong enough to ensure the victory of another lineage, that of Avis. The latter turned to England for support, which resulted in Portugal's being tipped into Urban's camp.

When he returned to Clement VII, now installed in Avignon, the legate accordingly had not triumphed on all fronts but he had considerably expanded the borders of the obedience. His prestige reached beyond the frontiers of his native land; he had acquired vast diplomatic experience and a reputation as an excellent orator. Some of his appeals (at Santarém in 1380 and at Medina del Campo in 1381) have come down to us, along with the outline of the speech he gave, in the Aragonese dialect, before Charles III of Navarre in 1390.

To consolidate the gains France had made in countries supporting Urban, Clement VII decided to call again on the energy and skill of the cardinal of Aragon. By means of a series of bulls issued over six months, the pope entrusted Pedro de Luna with a new mission, in the countries extending to the north of France, from the Low Countries to England and Scotland.

In February 1393, Pedro de Luna therefore set out for Paris. He arrived in time to be brought up to date on the situation, before taking part in the meetings at Leulinghen, where the problems of the SCHISM still complicated the peacemaking between France and England. They agreed to meet again the next year. During the year he spent in France, the legate could assess the complexity of the political situation. Charles VI had already been struck by his first attack of insanity, but his young brother, Louis of Orléans, was available to lead an armed expedition designed to install Clement VII in Rome. At the same time, in the University of Paris, opinion favoring a union of the two obediences developed. While the king's counselors dreamed of exploits, the doctors talked of a COUNCIL or of "the path of cession," that is, the joint resignation of the two pontiffs.

During the summer of 1394, though new talks at Leulinghen still had allowed no definite advance, the legate left for Avignon. He had made a reputation in Paris as a prelate favorable to union. That did not preclude his being one of the four cardinals let in on the secret of the kingdom of Adria, that it should be carved out of the PAPAL STATES as repayment to Louis of Orléans for his services. Then the unforeseeable happened: Clement VII died suddenly of apoplexy on 16 September 1394.

Following the example of their opponents, who had rushed to name another pope after the death of Urban VI in 1389, the Avignon cardinals quickly met in conclave; but their concern for union also prompted them to sign a "promise" that bound each of them, if elected, to make every effort, including that of the "path of cession," to unite the church. Pedro de Luna also signed this oath, and he was elected unanimously except for one vote. Ordained priest on 3 October 1394, he took the name Benedict XIII and was crowned eight days later. His history thus is inseparable from that of the GREAT SCHISM OF THE WEST.

The new pope informed the world of both his election and his intentions with respect to union. At the French court, this was taken all the more seriously because the time seemed right for a change of policy and the abandonment of daring Italian expeditions. Charles VI called together the prelates of the kingdom, who voted massively in favor of the path of cession. The king's uncles and brother were sent to present the motion formally to the pope. But the initiative did not suit Benedict XIII, who was steeped in theocratic principles. He received his august visitors but, wanting to keep his options open on the manner of achieving union, made no commitment. They parted, annoyed and deeply hurt (July 1395): from that day, France ceased to be the unconditional ally of the Avignon papacy.

Benedict XIII had other trump cards: first of all, in Spain, where the pope had been so successful in winning the favor of his compatriots; and also more widely, in that he had many devoted partisans who saw in the reign of this man, who was well educated, pious, and concerned with his pastoral duties, an unhoped-for opportunity to regenerate the Church. In France, such figures as Pierre d'Ailly, Jean Gerson, and Nicholas de Clamanges refused to ally themselves with the more "political" position of the majority of the clergy. No doubt they were also attracted by the pope's immense intellectual appetite. Benedict XIII attracted humanists, scholars, and artists. Under his inspiration, the papal library was enlarged and took on new importance. His personal collection also was impressive: several hundred volumes, constantly brought up to date, were chosen for his working office, and thereafter followed him wherever he went.

While the pope was beginning to put his personal stamp on the Avignon obedience, revolt was brewing in France. At the 1398 assembly of the clergy, Benedict XIII had to count on the loyalty of some prelates to come to his defense. When the resolution to withdraw obedience was proclaimed at Avignon on 1 September, five of the twenty-three cardinals remained at his side to withstand the siege of the palace.

The CURIA was emptied of French functionaries, and the pope organized his resistance with a small band of supporters from Catalonia and Aragon. The chronicle written by Martin of Alpartil conveys the atmosphere that prevailed: the captive Pedro de Luna remaining as pope and making that clear by his courage and his faith in his own legitimacy. He tried to demonstrate this once again in the treatise *Quia ut audio*. In Spain, an effective network of solidarity was organized around Francesco Climent. The guard put in place by the duke of Orléans, who opposed the withdrawal of obedience, allowed many messengers to get through. Benedict XIII was kept fully apprised of the rallying; when he escaped from the palace, on 11 March 1403, he knew better than before on whom he could count.

With all the former rebels having returned to obedience, he could have taken up his former ways in Avignon. On the contrary, he arranged his affairs so as to be completely mobile, and assembled an efficient and loyal group of Aragonese collaborators, leaving behind most of the cardinals and the bureaucratic apparatus of the papacy, and keeping in touch with Avignon by means of endless messages. Everywhere he went, the pope paid scrupulous attention to the conduct of liturgical ceremonies or practices hallowed by customary use. He continued to collect books, to order repairs in his castles or improvements in his favorite places of worship, and to commission liturgical ornaments and plate. The magnificent bust containing relics of St. Valerius that he gave to the Saragossa cathedral is thought to be his likeness.

But what was above all expected of him was personal effort to reestablish the unity of the Church in the West. True to himself, he followed his own preferred path, the path of "coming together" or agreement, and sent a delegation to BONIFACE IX in order to propose a meeting. He was able to turn to his own advantage, in public opinion, the snubs suffered by his ambassadors, and show that the solution of a double resignation would be difficult to implement because his competitor refused to hear it spoken of. But fortune seemed to smile on him once again when the "conversion" of the Genoese opened wide the gates of Italy to him. For a march to Rome, he needed only some armed standard-bearers to clear the way; but none of the French princes he approached came forward to lead the expedition.

Already the situation was turning less favorable, and Benedict XIII had to fall back to Provence. At Marseille, he met the envoys from his new rival, GREGORY XII, bearing their own proposals for a meeting (April 1407). He welcomed them warmly, and was able to put off a large French delegation that arrived at the same time by showing them the agreement that had been reached on the details for a meeting at Savona. The French, therefore, had to give him credit once again, and he made the scrupulous fulfilling of his engagements a point of honor.

Gregory XII turned to delaying tactics to avoid going to Savona. Benedict might have used this completely to his advantage, if observers had not begun to suspect the continual shuffling of missions between the two rival camps, only a day's journey apart. Some thought there was reason to suspect that Benedict XIII in fact had reached an agreement with his rival never to meet. He replied to the increasingly impatient pressure from France by issuing BULLS of INTERDICT against the kingdom and of excommunication against the king (May 1408). His very security being at risk if he remained on French territory, he left hastily for Aragon after announcing the opening of a COUNCIL in territory obedient to him.

On 15 November 1408, at Perpignan, Benedict XIII again had the satisfaction of presiding over an assembly of nearly three hundred participants, most of them Spaniards. During the previous year, he had examined, in a theoretical treatise, the modalities of holding a council that would settle the various disciplinary problems in the pope's favor. His supporters, however, were being won over to the idea of union, and obliged him to send a delegation to the council assembled in Pisa at the call of the unionist cardinals from the two obediences. Nothing could be more repugnant to Benedict XIII than the idea of having to appear in their presence; he delayed the preparations for the embassy so long that it arrived only to hear that the one whom they represented had been deposed (June 1409).

Still recognized as legitimate pope in Aragon and Castile, as well as in Scotland and several counties in the middle of France, Pedro de Luna set out to battle the decision at Pisa. He printed and distributed many copies of his treatise *Quia nonnulli*, and occupied himself with replying to a refutation published by a former supporter (the treatise *Inter distractionum*). His courage when an epidemic of the plague swept through Barcelona, and the return of Vincent Ferrier to his side, helped him maintain his authority in areas loyal to him. Also in his favor was the compromise of Caspe (1412), which settled on Ferdinand d'Antequerra as successor to King Martin of Aragon. From February 1413 to November 1414, at the prompting of his doctor, a converted Jew, he organized at Tortosa a remarkable discussion between rabbis and Catholic scholars.

In September 1415, he made his way to Perpignan to meet with Sigismund, the "king of the Romans," who had come from the council assembled at Constance in search of an acceptable solution, but Benedict XIII clung to the argument of his legitimacy, a legitimacy he alone could judge, as the sole survivor of the election of 1378. This spelled the end of his support, reduced to a few die-hards after the council of Constance deposed him once again and elected MARTIN V (1417). He shut himself away in the fortress at Peñiscola, where, in a little closed world, a few faithful followers kept up around him the fiction of a papal court. He continued to devote himself to study and to the collection of books until his last breath.

On 22 November 1422, feeling his strength failing, he organized his own succession by elevating four of those around him to the rank of cardinal. According to one of them, Jean Carrier, who tried to maintain little groups of partisans in Rouergue, Benedict XIII died five days later, but the three other "cardinals" concealed the death and did not make it public until 23 May 1423. The split of this little remnant between two pretenders gradually wore down their tenacity. In 1429, the dead pope's remains were transported to the castle of Illueca by his nephew, and his ashes were scattered by soldiers in 1811. His splendid library had disappeared before that; it was used partly to pay the wages of his servants.

Hélène Millet

Bibliography

Baer, F. "Die Disputation von Tortosa (1413–1414)," *Gesammelte Aufsätze zur Kulturgeschichte Spaniens*, 3 (1931), 307–36.

Baix, F. and Jadin, L. "Benoît XIII," *DHGE*, 18 (1935), 135–63 [in preference to biographies, often to be read with caution].

De Moxó, F. *La Casa de Luna (1276–1348)*, Münster, 1990 (*Spanische Forschungen der Görresgesellschaft*, 24).

Ehrle, F. "Aus den Acten des Afterconcils von Perpignan 1408," *Archiv für Literatur- und Kirchengechichte des Mittelalters*, 5 (1889), 387–492 and 7 (1900), 576–696; "Die kirchenrechtlichen Shriften Peters von Luna (Benedikts XIII.), ibid., 7 (1900), 515–75; *Martin de Alpartils chronica actitatorum temporibus domini Benedicti XIII*, Paderborn, 1906 (Quellen und Forschungen aus dem Gebiete der Geschichte, 12).

Girgensohn, D. "Ein Schisma ist nicht zu beenden ohne die Zustimmung der konkurrierenden Päpste," *AHP*, 27 (1989), 197–247.

Glasfurd, A. *The Antipope: Peter de Luna, 1342–1423; A Study in Obstinacy*, London, 1965.

Jullien de Pommerol, M. H. and Monfrin, J. *La Bibliothèque pontificale à Avignon et à Peñiscola*, 2 vols., Rome, 1991 (*Collection de l'École française de Rome*, 141).

Lapeyre, H. "Un sermon de Pedro de Luna," *Bulletin hispanique*, 49 (1947), 38–46 and 50 (1948), 129–46.

Puig Y Puig, S. *Episcopologio Barcinonense. Pedro de Luna, ultimo papa de Aviñon (1387–1430)*, Barcelona, 1920.

Seidlmayer, M. "Peter de Luna (Benedikt XIII.) und die Entstehung des Grossen Abendländischen Schismas," ibid., 4 (1933), 206–47.

Sesma Munoz, J. A. et al., *La vida y el tiempo del Papa Luna*, Saragossa, 1987.

BENEDICT XIII. *Pierfrancesco Orsini (b. Gravina di Puglia, Bari, 2 February 1650, d. Rome, 21 February 1730). Elected pope on 29 May 1724. Buried at Sta Maria sopra Minerva.*

In the history of the papacy of the 18th century, the government of the DOMINICAN, Orsini, shows some rather unusual features. He introduced into the institution a great spiritual and religious orientation, which issued from his personal piety and, above all, from his long experience as bishop in different Italian dioceses.

His career and ascent only partly followed the model for that of a high-ranking prelate. He belonged to a southern Italian family, of the very old nobility, who had given two popes to the church. As the eldest in the family, he inherited the fiefs of Gravina and other small estates in Apulia when his father, Duke Filippo Orsini, died. But just when he seemed destined to lead the life of a local notable, he changed course. He entered the Order of Preachers (under the name Vincenzo Maria) and renounced his inheritance. Having first made his profession at the Roman convent of Sta Sabina, he subsequently took courses in philosophy and theology at Naples, Bologna, and Venice. On 24 March 1671, he was ordained priest at the age of twenty-two, and a few days later his family requested and obtained from CLEMENT X Altieri his nomination as cardinal. On 4 January 1673, he was named prefect of the CONGREGATION of the Council and a member of other Roman congregations. However, CARDINAL Orsini quickly learned how to free himself of bureaucratic constraints in order to devote himself to tasks more in line with his religious and pastoral inclinations. On 28 January 1675, he took possession of the diocese of Siponto (Manfredonia), where he remained until 1680, when he went to Cesena. His ideal as to what he ought to be as a bishop is evident: pastoral visits and diocesan synods, the restoration of seminaries, the creation of charitable works with social goals, the discipline of the clergy and the Christian people, the encouragement of the teaching of CATECHISM and of popular missions. Such was the synthesis of an episcopate lived in fidelity to the model of a good bishop defined by the council of TRENT. On 18 March 1686, he left Cesena for Benevento, a diocese that, because of its difficult economic conditions and proximity to Naples, posed a rather severe test for an ordinary bishop. He remained there for forty years, surprising everyone by the tenacity with which he faced up to a very impoverished situation. Cardinal Orsini's work had a number of constant elements: firm opposition to the prerogatives of the local and Neapolitan aristocracy (which ranged from usurping church properties to interfering in matters entirely within the competence of the church, such as ordinations); the reestablishment of the episcopal authority following the bad management of his predecessor, Cardinal Giolamo Castaldi; the reform of ecclesiastical customs and organization. On this latter point, he worked tirelessly, not only within the framework of synods (of which he brought fifteen to a conclusion, an exceptional number), but also by courageously overhauling the office of canons and the network of parishes. The establishment of a registry of revenues and of the inheritance of the Church of Benevento was typical of his approach, which sought to restore a minimum of rationality to the system of benefices. Very close to the humblest classes, such as the country folk, he tried to anticipate and to resolve their problems. On their behalf, he instituted (14 February 1694) the annonarian reserve (a tested form of land credit) and undertook a series of economic measures aimed at relieving the most indigent workers and bringing a little prosperity into a backward and stagnant economy.

At Rome and in the Curia, this unusual activism was looked upon with a certain mistrust. There was even some criticism, and great reservations about his ability to manage large-scale diplomatic and political issues, about the distance he kept from the courts and the factions, about the frankness of his opinions, and about his want of taste for the ceremonial. There was no surprise, then, when his name was not among the favorites after the death of INNOCENT XIII (7 March 1724), and that it took two months in CONCLAVE before his eventual candidature was considered. It was only after the rejection of candidates proposed by the major powers (Cardinals Imperiali and Piazza), by the Bourbon court (Olivieri and Paolucci), and by the 'zelanti,' that the members of the conclave decided to combine their votes in favor of Cardinal Orsini, who was elected pope on 29 May 1724.

Having acceded to the throne of St. Peter, he sought to govern the Church in keeping with the asceticism and the solicitude of the pastor of souls he had always striven to be. He tried to give greater room to religion than to politics. Still, an assessment of his pontificate cannot fail to mention choices and strategies that left his contemporaries perplexed or critical.

Hoping to renew the curial milieu, he turned to people who had his complete confidence. The SECRETARIAT OF STATE was entrusted to Cardinal Paolucci—a person of great moral and religious merit. But Benedict XIII also gathered around him numerous friends and collaborators from his former diocese (in which he continued to play an active role) who were not slow to profit from their situation in disgraceful ways (including the secretary Niccolò Coscia, later condemned for a considerable series of indiscretions) and shamelessly took over the government. As for the problems of the PAPAL STATES, Benedict XIII tried to ease the grave social needs rather than to give serious study to causes and appropriate remedies. Such was the case when he sought to develop an economic policy based on tax exemptions and easy loans. Without bringing real benefits to those concerned, he ended up by emptying the state treasury. In the strictly political realm, the CONCORDAT signed (1727) with Victor Amadeus II, king of Sicily and Sardinia, at the price of numerous jurisdictional concessions, was considered a setback. But his detractors failed to take sufficient account of the fact that there were no bishops in the dioceses of Sardinia and Piedmont, and that the pope had to use every means possible of re-establishing a normal situation by eliminating the underlying points of contention. The episcopate was at the center of his attention. Similarly, his compromise with Emperor Charles VI, on the question of the apostolic legation in Sicily and the royal court, was considered no masterpiece of shrewdness. Apparently favorable to the Holy See, it was in fact largely to the advantage of the other party. It restored to the ruler of Sicily some of the old autonomy in ecclesiastical matters that CLEMENT XI had sought to abolish.

Moderate and tolerant by nature, Benedict XIII endeavored not to increase the tensions among religious groups and currents of opinion, and strove above all to reconcile anti-Roman tendencies. This was evident during a new phase of the controversy over acceptance of the BULL *Unigenitus* of Clement XI, against JANSENISM. The French clergy contested it strongly. In the brief *Demissas preces*, Benedict XIII accepted and proposed anew the doctrine on efficacious grace and on predestination without the provision of merits, in the terms upheld by the Thomist school. It was a doctrinal base on which the rigorist theologians and the bishops who challenged them could easily find some common ground. The pope's aims were obvious, regardless of the fact that things later took another direction, partly because they slipped from his control. In fact, the bull *Pretiosus*, drafted by the INQUISITION and published in 1727, brought about a stiffening in favor of the positions of the Molinists and a fresh confirmation of the bulls *Unigenitus* and *Pastoralis officii*. With this document, which clearly did not take the pope's thinking into account, the traditional line of the Curia was reaffirmed, one close to the Molinist positions. In a sense, the pope was isolated. It must have been very painful for him to feel himself hampered in what was dearest to his heart: an end to the factions and the opening of dialogue with people and groups in difficulty with the Holy See.

Benedict XIII was not a celebrated pope. The entry into the papal court of his old friends—a masked form of nepotism—did not make him popular among the Romans or in curial circles. Except for biographers belonging to his own order, historians have paid little attention to him. There is common agreement that his pontificate was religious. This is a judgment shared, curiously enough, by partisans and adversaries of the Curia: by the one group in order to reproach him for lack of political ability, and by the other in order to present him as the victim of a childish bigotry. More penetrating and thoroughgoing studies would be able to show the part of this judgment that corresponds to the real qualities of the man and the pope, and whether his profound religious engagement was harmful to the initiatives taken during his brief pontificate. It is in this context that a purely religious decision such as the convoking of a SYNOD of the Roman province in 1725, when there had not been one at Rome for centuries, was an original and important action. In its singularity, this initiative sought to reaffirm the pastoral dimension of the pontiff and his close relations with the diocese of Rome, and to show that even what was called the Holy City suffered from numerous disorders and accordingly had a need for a serious examination of conscience. Obeying an intuition, the sculptor called upon to commemorate the dead pope in marble did not hesitate to represent him in the act of convoking the synod.

Luigi Fiorani

Bibliography

De Caro, G. *DBI*, Rome, 1966, VIII, 384–393.
De Spirito, A. "Personalità e stile di vita di Benedetto XIII vescovo e papa meridionale," *Campania sacra*, 21 (1990), 205–279.
Fiorani, F. *Il concilio romano del 1725*, Rome, 1978.
Giordano, G. *L'impregno missionario del card. Vincenzo Orsini*, Benevento, 1982.
Pastor, 34.
Savoia, P. *L'episcopato beneventano di papa Orsini*, Acerra, 1973.
Vignato, G. B. *Storia di Benedetto XIII dei frati predicatori*, 8 vols., Milan-Rome, 1952–74.

[BENEDICT XIV]. *Bernard Garnier (b. ?, d. ?). Antipope, elected secretly on 12 November 1425.*

A native of Guyenne, Bernard Garnier and others were condemned by default on 24 July 1420 by the NUNCIO sent by MARTIN V to the middle region of France to punish the hardened partisans of the antipope BENEDICT XIII (Pedro de Luna). He was one of a group of these partisans who enjoyed the favor of John IV, count of Armagnac, who remained faithful to the Aragonese pope. When Benedict XIII died, three of the four cardinals he had created on 27 November 1422 elected Gil Muñoz as his successor (10 June 1423), under the name CLEMENT VIII. The fourth cardinal, Jean Carrier, refused to accept this election in which he had not participated, and, regarding himself as making up the entire SACRED COLLEGE, he secretly elected Bernard Garnier as pope, on 12 November 1425, in the presence of a notary. Garnier had been a subagent of Jean Carrier and remained his confidant. For security reasons, the election was kept secret until January 1429, when Jean Carrier sent a lengthy manifesto to the count of Armagnac. The count, no doubt embarrassed by this proliferation of pontiffs, sent a message to Joan of Arc asking her which was the true pope, Martin V, Clement VIII, or Benedict XIV. The Maid of Orléans, knowing only Martin V, avoided the question (22 August 1429). The next year, John IV was reconciled with Martin V, and Bernard Garnier disappeared into the shadows.

As for the activity of Benedict XIV, it can be said only that he had some authority over the members of the little schismatic Church. He appointed a bishop of Hebron in the person of a Franciscan named Bernardulus, and he promoted to cardinal a certain Jean Farald. After Bernard Garnier died, which must have been soon after 1430, Farald elected Jean Carrier as pope, and he too took the name BENEDICT XIV.

François-Charles Uginet

Bibliography

Aubert, R. *DHGE*, 19 (1981), 1294–95.
Tribout de Morambert, H. *DBF*, 15 (1982), 473.
Valois, N. *La France et le Grand Schisme d'Occident*, IV, Paris, 1902, *ad indicem*.

BENEDICT XIV. *Prospero Lambertini (b. Bologna, 31 March 1675, d. Rome, 3 May 1758). Elected pope on 17 August 1740, crowned on 21 August.*

Benedict XIV was a central figure in the history of the 18th-century Church: during his long pontificate, he gave proof of an open-mindedness marking Catholicism. In electing him, the CONCLAVE cleared the way for the Church's difficult transition from the politico-religious conditions of the first half of the 18th century and from the long series of popes belonging to the great aristocratic families of Italy, Tuscan and Roman, toward a more constructive fashion, on the part of the papacy, of tackling the major problems of the times. Of a very modest patrician family, his personality evolved in the middle ranks of the curial bureaucracy, but his cultural sensibility derived above all from the government of an important archdiocese like that of Bologna. His stay in Rome (1688–1727) began with education in theology and canon law. A career in the CURIA, extending from his youth to his mature years, opened into a creative exchange between his work and his participation in the academies and learned circles of Rome. In the CONGREGATION of Rites, he rose to the position of promoter of the faith, and in the Congregation of the Council he was secretary from 1720 on. At the same time, he was in contact with those interested in archaeological studies, open to Maurist learning, and attentive to the philosophical and scientific culture inspired by Locke and Newton.

His long experience in the congregations is apparent in his two most celebrated works. The first was a long historical and critical study of the CANONIZATION of saints, *De servorum Dei beatificatione et beatorum canonizatione*, published in Bologna (1734–38) and often reprinted. The other was *De synodo dioecesana libri tredecim*, which was published in Rome (1748) after his election as pope had eliminated certain difficulties standing in the way of publication; it dealt with the need, felt at the beginning of the 18th century, for a renewing of the tradition of diocesan synods inspired by the council of TRENT and Charles Borromeo, while remaining within the framework of the control of the Curia that had arisen out of Roman centralization. Other writings, such as the *Raccolta* (5 vols., 1733–40), and some pastoral letters and notes for the governing of the archdiocese of Bologna, reflect his preoccupations when, after having headed the archdiocese of Ancona (1717) and been made a cardinal (1728), he was named to his native city in 1731. At Ancona, his relations with the large Jewish community had been good, especially during difficult negotiations over the establishment of a free port. At Bologna, his interest in institutions arising from the Council of Trent, particularly regarding parishes and women's convents, was increased as the result of a personal style whereby he was readily available to the faithful, who seemed to benefit from both the "modern" instrument of

the popular MISSION (whence his interest in St. Leonard of Port-Maurice and St. Paul of the Cross after he was named pope) and the taste for education typical of the end of the 17th and the beginning of the 18th century. These topics recur in his two liturgical and devotional works, *Annotazioni sopra le feste di Nostro Signore e della beatissima Vergine* (Bologna, 1740) and *Della Santa Messa* (Padua, 1747), reprinted several times, translated into Latin, and included in the complete editions of his works (Rome, 1747–48; Venice, 1787; Prato, 1839–56).

Despite his experience, Cardinal Lambertini was not among the *papabili* at the conclave following the death of CLEMENT XI (1740). Indeed, his status as a compromise candidate did not develop until the 255th vote, after six months of interminable negotiations between the group of cardinals led by the ex–CARDINAL NEPHEW Neri Corsini and the opposition allied to Albani, the CAMERLENGO. Be that as it may, and as the election difficulties showed, this obstinacy was the outcome of a long crisis. The crisis began in the first decades of the century with the War of the Spanish Succession and the new balance of power in Europe, especially in the Italian peninsula, owing to the rise of Austrian influence. It had not been resolved, despite various efforts made during the pontificates of BENEDICT XIII and CLEMENT XII. Although he had chosen the name Benedict out of gratitude to the former pope who had named him cardinal, Benedict XIV did not want to walk in his predecessor's footsteps, save for his attitude toward religious tension, which, with all the limitations of a government that was weak and dominated by groups of unscrupulous hucksters, nevertheless was a real mark of the controversial pontificate of the Orsini pope. A new era had opened; although intellectually linked to tradition, Benedict XIV was a "new" man, and a powerful spirit of renewal seemed to spread through the Curia and the Church, especially in the early years of his pontificate. Benedict XIV was resolved to reinvigorate ecclesiastical institutions, recapture lost ground, and promote new possibilities for encounter between Catholicism and a society undergoing profound transformations. Faced with no lack of opposition to the realization of his plans, Benedict XIV, with indubitable skill, was able to counter the resistance of the Sacred College and of certain influential cardinals, and bring to an end the latent opposition favored by the slow working of the congregations; this is often emphasized in his letters to Cardinal de Tencin, which are among the most important sources for direct acquaintance with the pope's psychology and with numerous facets of his pontificate. Above all, he was able to surround himself with excellent collaborators, such as the secretary of state, Silvio Valenti Gonzaga, and the pro-datary, Aldrovandi; they were among the chief architects of the concordatory policy that, on the political level, represented one of the principal developments of the beginning of the pontificate.

Not that there was novelty in attempts at CONCORDATS between Rome and the various Italian and European states. Such an accord had been signed in 1727 with the kingdom of Sardinia (but it had been denounced by Rome in 1731) and with Portugal (1736), and difficult negotiations with Naples and Spain had been carried out during the previous pontificate. What was new was Benedict XIV's conciliatory spirit, the importance he accorded the truly religious aspect when facing issues that were principally ecclesiastical and institutional, his clear awareness of the new historical trends affecting European society, and his determination to move the Church out of an isolation that was both sterile and dangerous. Having completed a new agreement with the kingdom of Sardinia in 1741, thanks to direct dealings with the king and his minister, the marquess of Ormea, Benedict XIV found negotiations with the kingdom of Naples more complex. But there, too, and in the same year, a conclusion acceptable to the Papal State on matters of church immunities was arrived at, after the three final meetings, held in the presence of the pope himself, had overcome some of the juridical objections to which Naples had clung most rigidly. The accord with Portugal (1745), which replaced that of 1736, and the concordat with Spain, for which negotiations begun in 1740 were not completed until 1753, made major concessions to the regalist tendencies of the two governments in the area of church benefices. They had important consequences for the Curia itself, in eliminating once and for all the network of interests and abuses that had long prevailed in the DATARY regarding Spanish prebends. The concordat for Austrian Lombardy, the last of its kind, settled the modalities of the taxation of ecclesiastical properties by applying Maria Theresa's cadastral plan (1757).

Benedict XIV put equal energy into problems touching religious and ecclesiastical life. In his first encyclical, *Ubi primum* (3 December 1740), in which he made use for the first time of this modern form of "colloquy" with the episcopate, he reminded the bishops of the importance of formation for the clergy (one of the major intellectual preoccupations of the 18th-century Church, promoted in a particular way by Benedict XIV), of pastoral visits, and of the obligation of residence. He created a CONGREGATION with special responsibility for choosing bishops, and delegated to another extraordinary congregation (1740) the prompt resolution of complex questions addressed to Rome by the dioceses. These two initiatives amounted to a real transfer of competence and power of intervention from the Consistorial Congregation to the one for bishops and religious clergy.

In other areas, Benedict XIV acted on a great number of historiographical requests and criticisms from the Maurists and Bollandists, as well as on many requirements of the "dévotion réglée" (prescribed devotion) that for several decades had been called for in the work of the great scholar and historian Muratori. Even though the work on modification of the Roman BREVIARY, assigned to a special commission, was not concluded, it was nevertheless crucial for the development of the studies in hagiography, ecclesiastical history, and liturgy that marked the pontificate.

His measures against the "baroque" pomp of sacred music and against public flagellations, and those attempting to reduce the number of church holidays in Italy (1742) and in various European countries (1748), were in line with a more vigorous appeal to the interiority of the Christian message, and also, from the perspective of an active Christianity, a herald of the major themes of the Catholic *Aufklärung*, or Enlightenment, of the century's end. Attentive to the liturgy and to devotion, Benedict XIV, in agreement with the rigorists and the Jansenists, was no less vigorous in rejecting demands for a more direct relationship on the part of the faithful with the biblical and patristic texts, in particular with the Scriptures through translations of the Bible. In this area, in 1748 he renewed the interdictions pronounced after the council of Trent, and only belatedly (1757) granted a dispensation. The position was not easy, between the rigorists and the Jansenists on the one hand and the Jesuits and their partisans on the other, with the two tending more and more to become antagonistic battle lines.

However, two almost simultaneous decisions showed Benedict XIV's capacity for mediation and impartiality. The first concerned the "Chinese and Malabar rites," which were dealt with in the bulls *Ex quo singulari* (1742) and *Omnium sollicitudinum* (1744), and the second had to do with usury, which was dealt with in the encyclical *Vix pervenit* (1745) addressed to the Italian bishops. He renewed the condemnation of the "Chinese rites," that is, the methods adopted by the JESUITS in China, but in terms more open to the Jesuit practice of "accommodation" to local cultures in their missions in southern India. In the quarrel between the Utrecht Jansenist Broedersen and the learned Maffei of Verona about the charging of interest, while he confirmed the traditional idea that money should not earn interest, the pope did not reject the "laxist" position—which was supported by widespread practice—that receiving interest in financial and business transactions was justified.

Benedict XIV's interest in ecclesiastical and religious questions seemed to decrease toward the middle of the first decade of his pontificate. His attention was drawn to other matters by the War of the Austrian Succession and by international political problems, including the fate of the PAPAL STATES themselves, which were being crossed by warring Austrian and Spanish armies. In this area, the pope's uncertain and contradictory policy contributed to the secondary role played by the Holy See for almost a century, with the negative outcome of the treaty of Westphalia; Benedict XIV's lack of direct political and diplomatic experience on the European chessboard was perhaps also a factor. First, his too hasty recognition of Maria Theresa's hereditary rights to the imperial throne (1740) provoked violent reactions. Then, he accepted as a fait accompli the imperial election of her rival, Albert of Bavaria (1742). Later, he succeeded in returning to a more convincing position of neutrality until the recognition in 1746 of Francis of Lorraine, Maria Theresa's husband. However, with the end of the war (1748), the pope faced new problems, in particular with regard to Protestant Prussia, where Frederick II had annexed Catholic Silesia and was pursuing a policy of absorbing ecclesiastical jurisdictions into the administration of the state. In this case as in the negotiation of concordats with Catholic states, the diplomatic flexibility and patience of the Curia and the personal qualities of the pope won out on the most contentious points. In 1747, there was a development, without precedent since the Reformation, in the relations between the papacy and a Protestant country: the nomination, unofficial to be sure, of the representative of the Palatinate in Rome as diplomatic agent for Prussia. A general agreement with particular reference to ecclesiastical benefices and matrimonial laws was signed the next year. Thus, in the relations between Benedict XIV and Frederick the Great, there was an intersection of diplomacy and political realism, of the art of governing and concrete openness to negotiation. These relations were subsequently carried forward indirectly by the mediation of the mathematician Maupertuis, who was secretary of the Royal Academy of Prussia, and Algarotti, the cosmopolitan Italian man of letters of whom Frederick was very fond. They established once and for all the pope's reputation across Europe as wise and tolerant. As the priest Galiani wrote with pleasure in 1758 in his eulogy of the pontiff, Benedict XIV came across to his contemporaries as a man who was compassionate, humane, and given to laughter, and as not at all surly, threatening, or severe. This reputation, which extended even into a vigorously antipapist England, had also benefited a few years before from Voltaire's dedication of his *Mahomet* to Benedict XIV. The pope had replied with the greatest kindness to the writer's nonconformist overture (1745), in particular because of pressure coming all at once from Cardinals Passionei and Querini, from his own doctor, Leprotti (who corresponded with Voltaire), and from Canillac, the French representative in Rome. After his reply, skillfully exploited by its recipient, had stirred up new and violent polemics, the pope himself explained in a letter to Cardinal de Tencin the reasons, in a certain sense illusory, for his behavior toward the abrasive writer: he had acted thus in order to link to the Church in some fashion a writer who held an extraordinary position in the world of letters, "the Holy See having," he said, "suffered considerable damage at the hands of rejected people who, if they had remained with us, would not have caused so much harm later on."

The idyll with the Enlightenment had ended when it had scarcely begun, the distance being too great between the new ideas and a personality, open as it was, like that of Benedict XIV. The pope confirmed this with the bull *Providas Romanorum Pontificum* (1751), which renewed Clement XII's condemnation of FREEMASONRY (1738); with the decision, after a long discussion, to place Montesquieu's *Esprit des lois* on the INDEX (1752); with the brief that same year against the theses upheld at the Sorbonne by the Abbé de Prades, which led to the first crisis of the *Encyclopedia*; and by the decision, again in 1752, to place on the Index the entire Dresden edition of the collected works of Voltaire. A proof would be given later of the limits of this pope's celebrated tolerance. But it must be stressed that this reputation rested, in his own day and especially later on, on the "myth" that Benedict XIV's image, in contrast to that of his immediate successors, CLEMENT XIII and PIUS VI, helped to feed. His was a tolerance that could recognize situations of fact, but that did not prevent him from showing himself hostile toward other Christian confessions. Accordingly, he opposed the ecumenical and irenic overtures made by Cardinal Querini toward German Protestant scholars, and the effective religious tolerance advocated by Cardinal Zinzendorf, the archbishop of Breslau. True, the encyclical *A quo primum* (1751) indeed enjoined the Polish bishops to respect the juridical norms—even though restrictive—in force in Poland, in order to limit the excesses of the anti-Jewish persecutions that had taken place there; but, in an unexpected way, the encyclical remained a dead letter in Rome and in the Papal States, where, from the 1750s on, the repressive aspects of the traditional legislation prevailed, even in the framework of a policy of "conversions."

The turning point of the pontificate came with the mid-century jubilee (to which Benedict XIV gave its present form, and which he extended to the whole Catholic world) and with the preoccupations caused by the Enlightenment, which the pope tried to counter by promoting Catholic APOLOGETICS, with some success. This did not exclude, and even reinforced, the second orientation of the pontificate, in the calm years from the peace of Aix-la-Chapelle (1748) to the start of the Seven Years' War (1756). This time, instead of ecclesiastical reforms, the pope attempted a series of measures in the States to promote letters and the arts, scarcely hinted at in the preceding years.

First came the business of improving a very grave financial situation. On the advice of Valenti Gonzaga, Aldrovandi, and the Roman banker Belloni, Benedict XIV did not settle for selective interventions, as had been the custom. He instituted unified measures, inspired by a mercantilist conception, which he spelled out in the constitution *Apostolicae Sedis aerarium* (1746). The pope rationalized the accounting procedures of the Apostolic Camera, opening the path, by means of a *motu proprio* and a bull of 1748, to a liberalization of the internal wheat trade and of trade in general—except for the region of Rome, however, because of the prevailing contingencies in that center of consumption. To crown these first steps, two constitutions that were central in Benedict XIV's plan of action appeared simultaneously a few years later (1 October 1753). The first, *Super bono regimine communitatum*, instituted a special congregation to deal not only with problems of internal and external trade, but also with the development of agriculture and manufacturing. The second, *Ad coercendum delinquentium flagitia*, laid down a plan for the reform of procedures. In substance, they were attempts at modernization rather than true reforms. They eliminated or reduced dysfunctions and introduced more rational criteria for administrative control, but they made no attempt to challenge structures and left open the debate on the particular character of the reform of the ecclesiastical state until the end of the century.

In the climate of peace at the beginning of the 1750s, Benedict XIV's pontificate also seemed marked by privileged developments in the area of culture and patronage. Along with the activity of the Roman ecclesiastical ACADEMIES, there was a blossoming of archaeological studies, both classical (where the influence of Winckelmann began to be felt) and Christian, following a reawakening of interest in the CATACOMBS and, more generally, in the early Church. This period lasted from the publication of *Magnificenze di Roma* (1747–61) by Guiseppe Vasi to the foundation (1755) of the Museum of Christian Antiquities, which was first attached to the VATICAN LIBRARY, and to the printing of *Antichità romane* (1756) by Piranese. Benedict XIV extended the Vatican Library, which he enriched with new books and manuscripts. He reformed the university of Rome and, in the Papal State, enlarged the University of Bologna, which he endowed with new chairs of science and medicine; at Bologna, he also developed the Institute of Sciences, for which he had a special fondness and to which he bequeathed his private library, opened to the public in 1756.

It was at the end of the pontificate that the principal political and religious problems came along, those that would shake the church in the second half of the century. The balance maintained by the pope became all the more precarious in that he sought until the end to control tensions without suppressing the many ferments agitating ecclesiastical institutions and, more generally, religious life. It is significant that, faced with the draconian condemnations by the congregations concerning mainly Jansenist writings, there ripened in the pope the profoundly juridical conviction that a Catholic author whose work was subject to examination by the Congregation of the Index must

be allowed a defense. This conviction was manifest by the reform of the congregation by the constitution *Sollicita ac provida* (1753)—subsequently neglected and recalled only in 1965 in the *motu proprio* of PAUL VI for reform of the HOLY OFFICE—and by reform of the Index (1757). It is also rather significant that one of Benedict XIV's last important gestures had to do with the political and religious situation in France. This had been severely unsettled by the differences that had arisen between the Jansenists and the parliaments on the one hand and the monarchy on the other, especially in 1750–55 by the question of the *billets de confession* that would sanction the refusal of the sacraments to those on the point of death who did not acknowledge the 101 propositions of the papal bull *Unigenitus*. The problem of JANSENISM thus having returned to center stage at mid-century, Benedict XIV, seconded by his closest collaborators, especially Cardinals Tamburini and Besozzi, tried successfully, with the encyclical *Ex omnibus Christiani orbis* (1756), to steer the whole affair into the harmless context of a more correct procedure in ecclesiastical discipline. The discussions that followed the encyclical, which was accepted unanimously by the general assembly of the French clergy (1760), seemed to open wider perspectives for an eventual reduction of the Jansenist split, thanks to an old, never-abandoned project for explaining *Unigenitus*. Some of the best-known French and Italian representatives of Jansenism involved themselves in this project, and certain prestigious members of the Curia itself, such as Tamburini, were not indifferent to it.

However, parallel with this development, was the problem of the Jesuits. It reached its climax in the later years, when Benedict XIV, with death approaching, named the patriarch of Lisbon, Saldanha, as visitor and reformer of the Portuguese Jesuits (1758). He thereby gave in to pressure from the Portuguese minister Pombal, and perhaps he was not himself opposed to interventions in the internal organization of the Society of Jesus. Thus, for opposite reasons, made more complex by the spread of ecclesiastical reforms set in motion in that era by enlightened despotism, from then on the Church had to battle on two fronts, Jansenism and the Jesuits. Once the pope had died, the still uncertain lines of a new face for the Church and of a different organization for the ecclesiastical state, and the political and religious perspectives and alternatives that Benedict XIV had indicated during his twenty-year pontificate and in the constructive climate of the mid-century, were submitted by his successors to a much more rigid logic of self-protection. In this way, a whole spirit of enclosure and rejection in the Church of the 18th century, which Benedict XIV had sought to moderate and to a certain extent had overcome, would be given a vigorous new birth and, historically, would suppress the full first fruits of the Lambertinian pontificate.

Mario Rosa

Bibliography

Up to 1966, cf. *DBI*, VIII, s.v. (by M. Rosa).

Among the sources, *Le lettere di Benedetto XIV al cardinale de Tencin*, pub. by E. Morelli, III, *1753–1758*, Rome, 1984.

Many other letters from Benedict XIV to his family, and especially to his friend Filippo M. Mazzi, are published in *Due carteggi inediti di Benedetto XIV*, pub. by I. Folli Ventura and L. Miani, Bologna, 1987.

For the enduring interest on the part of Anglo-Saxon culture in Benedict XIV, see the portrait by Haynes, R. *Philosopher King: The Humanist Pope Benedict XIV*, London, 1970.

For interventions in the ecclesiastical and religious domains: Brandolini, L. "Benedetto XIV di fronte ad alcuni movimenti riformistico-liturgici del secolo XVIII," *Ephemerides liturgicae*, 88 (1974), 447–70.

Hermans, J. *Benedictus XIV en de liturgie: Een bijdrage tot de liturgiegeschiedenis van de moderne tijd*, Bruges-Boxtel, 1979.

Bertone, T. *Il governo della Chiesa nel pensiero di Benedetto XIV (1740–1758)*, Rome, 1977.

Sabbioneta Almansi, C. "Il papato di Prospero Lambertini e la 'Scrittura' sulla diminuzione delle feste di precetto," *Studi in onore di Ugo Gualazzini*, III, Milan, 1986, 151–84.

Paarhammer, H. "*Sollicita ac provida, Neuordnung von Lehrbeanstandung und Bücherzensur in der katholischen Kirche im 18. Jahrhundert*," *Ministerium Justitiae. Festshrift für Heribert Heinemann*, pub. by Gabriels, A., Reinhardt, H. J. F., Essen, 1985, 343–361.

Van Kley, D. "The Refusal of Sacramental Controversy and the Political Crisis of 1756–1757," *Church, State, and Society under the Bourbon Kings of France*, ed., Golden, R. M., Lawrence, Kans. 1982, 284–326.

For cultural interests and attention paid to culture, *La raccolta delle stampe di Benedetto XIV Lambertini nella Pinacoteca nazionale di Bologna*, ed. Emiliani, A., and Bertela, G. G., Bologna, 1970.

Morello, G. "Il Museo "cristiano" di Benedetto XIV," *Bollettino. Monumenti, Musei e Gallerie pontificie*, 2 (1981), 53–89.

A series of very detailed studies, without any essential new information on Benedict XIV, in *Benedetto XIV (Prospero Lambertini). Convegno internazionale di studi storici. Cento, 6–9, dic. 1979*, ed. Cecchelli, M. Cento (Ferrara), 1981–1982, I and II.

BENEDICT XV. *Giacomo della Chiesa (b. Genoa, 21 November 1854, d. Rome, 22 January 1922). Elected pope on 3 September 1914, crowned on 6 September. Buried at St. Peter's in Rome.*

Viewed by his contemporaries essentially as the pope who presided over the destiny of the Church during the First World War, Benedict XV nevertheless has long remained in the collective memory as an "unrecognized" pope (F. Hayward). Born in the parish of St. Mary of the Vines (archdiocese of Genoa) to the marquis Giuseppe della Chiesa and Giovanna Migliorati, he thus belonged to a family of very ancient Lombard origin, the same stock as CALLISTUS II and Berengar II: the family name della Chiesa (of the Church) derived from the fact that during the time of St. Ambrose the pope's distant ancestors had stood up for orthodoxy against the Arians, who then were very powerful in Milan. After his initial classical studies at the Danovaro e Giusso college, he followed his father's wishes and enrolled in the faculty of law at the University of Genoa, where he obtained (5 August 1875) his doctorate in civil law. His stay at the university gave him time and opportunity for intellectual pursuits. In the anticlerical and anti-Catholic climate that followed the taking of Rome, under the influence of Fr. Giacomo of Genoa, his Capuchin uncle, he became president of the local Catholic Action association; the association supported his work on *Il Cittadino*, a publication in the founding of which the future pope's family had taken an active part. In November of the same year (1875), he entered the Capranica College in Rome, an establishment for the formation of young elite priests.

Ordained on 21 December 1878 in the basilica of ST. JOHN LATERAN by Cardinal Monaco La Valetta, vicar of LEO XIII, Giacomo della Chiesa celebrated his first mass the next day at ST. PETER's, then at the church of the Gesù, and finally at ST. MARY MAJOR. The following year he entered the ACADEMY for Noble Ecclesiastics, the prestigious Roman institution responsible for training students of noble lineage (a condition later suppressed by PIUS XI) for practical diplomacy and the law of international relations. There he earned a doctorate in canon law in 1880, and he accepted a chair in diplomatic protocol at the Academy itself.

This position put him in contact with the functioning of the SECRETARIAT OF STATE, which he frequented assiduously from then on, and where he met Mariano Rampolla del Tindaro, who was made a cardinal on 8 December 1882, and who would have a great influence on him. As special secretary of the nuncio, he went to Spain with the cardinal and Msgr. Segna, auditor at the NUNCIATURE. He witnessed the earthquake that ravaged the provinces of Malaga and Granada in 1884, and also the cholera epidemic that ravaged Madrid during the summer of 1885. Then, after Rampolla was named secretary of state in 1887, Giacomo della Chiesa served as *MINUTANTE* for ordinary affairs, a relatively minor post but one that enabled him to deepen his knowledge of the workings of power within the Roman bureaucracy; his experience was rounded out by his being sent on a special mission to the nunciature at Vienna (1889–90). Named SUBSTITUTE OF THE SECRETARIAT OF STATE in 1901 and apparently headed for great things, he continued his task under PIUS X, until he was unexpectedly named archbishop of Bologna in October 1907. The post of nuncio at Madrid was vacant, but the pope seemed to have other things in mind for him.

The future Benedict XV was ordained archbishop in the SISTINE CHAPEL by Pius X on 22 December 1907. The following 10 February, he published a pastoral letter, the first to be noted, on "The Office and Duties Proper to a Bishop." His elevation to the cardinalate was clearly expected (for seven years), since by long tradition the archbishop of Bologna, often throughout history a valuable ally of Rome, was a member of the SACRED COLLEGE; finally named during the secret CONSISTORY of 25 May 1914, he was enthroned on 28 May, and named titular of the church of SS. Quattro Coronati on the Celian, of which he took solemn possession on 4 June. After that, everything accelerated: scarcely three months after being made a cardinal, Giacomo della Chiesa was elected pope, on 3 September 1914. The fact, reported by some witnesses, that he showed little hesitation in accepting the supreme responsibility was interpreted by some as a sign of presumption, by others as a sign of great courage, even of a spirit of sacrifice (in view of the Church's immense internal problems, only partly resolved by his predecessor, and of the clouds gathering in the skies of Europe)—but perhaps that was pushing things too far. What remains true is that the moral portrait drawn by the contemporaries of the new pope emphasized his rationality, his ability to make decisions, and his critical mind, which tended toward an ironic manner and a capacity for anger; this generous steadiness contrasted with a physical appearance that was rather frail and unsure.

The new pope's choice of the name Benedict seems to have been—as he said himself—a reference to "the great lawmaker of the modern Church" (Ulrich Stutz) that had been BENEDICT XIV (Prospero Lambertini); and this was the personality and the line of conduct of the whole pontificate, both in an immediate sense (with the promulgation of the CODE OF CANON LAW in 1917) and in a more lasting sense (notably, by the attitude of the Church during the First World War and the organization of the MISSIONS).

Because of what was happening, Benedict XV, trained by his education and experience in the techniques and practices of diplomacy, was to be remembered as the pope of the Great War. The Holy See was barely emerging, thanks to the efforts of Pius X, who sought to "restore all things in Christ," from the most difficult phase of its struggles against the extreme forces of secularism in the form of social and political anticlericalism, particularly strong in France, as well as against MODERNISM in intellectual and scholarly circles. However, some of its

important gains, such as the reawakening of Eucharistic fervor and the general vitality of the PILGRIMAGES, did not play a big part in the tenor of the relations—at best distant and sometimes frankly hostile—that Rome had with secular states. On the eve of 1914, the Vatican had accredited diplomatic representatives from fourteen nations, which were acting more for the opportunity for observation or control than by virtue of a tradition of respect or even cordiality; the Church's loss of all civil sovereignty and of all its temporal possessions deprived it of many means of action, and had already led it, on other topics, to elaborate a discourse that was characterized increasingly by its abstractness. While such circumstances help to explain Benedict XV's attitude toward the war, in the stance taken by the Vatican there could also be seen unmistakably the pope's own personality, that of "a first-rate political brain" (J. Droz).

Of major importance was his 13 October 1914 appointment of Cardinal Pietro Gasparri to head the Secretariat of State. Gasparri, a diplomat and skilled canonist, was already head of the project for the codification of the law of the Church, initiated ten years earlier by Pius X. In his first ENCYCLICAL, *Ad Beatissimi*, dated 1 November, the pope outlined as the program for his pontificate a Church who was mother and guide (*Mater et Magistra*), accompanying humankind through all stages of individual and collective life—a life for which religious discipline was considered the sole guarantee of a moral and fraternal world. War, on the contrary, according to a line of argument taken up again in later acts of the pontiff, by feeding on blood and tears and by transforming Europe into "a field of death," demonstrated "the confrontation of the deadly elements brewed in materialism," and consequently ought to be ended by restoration of "the rights of God."

These analytical statements, into which were blended elements of moral theology, were coupled with positions that took more account of the material situation engendered by wars and their results; Benedict XV pleaded for a peace that would be "just and lasting," bringing dishonor to none of the belligerents, and emphasized the absolute need to "humanize the war" and relieve the suffering. Descending, according to its own terminology, "to more concrete and practical matters" in a message of peace to the heads of the warring states ("Dès le début," 1 August 1917), the Holy See proposed the institution of an international arbitration procedure that would substitute for armed force and reestablish the "supreme power" of the law. Respect for law would also ensure a "real freedom and community of the seas," the absence of which was seen to be the cause of conflicts. On the economic and financial question raised by the reparations for war damages, Benedict XV called for a wholesale and reciprocal "condonation," except in the case of Belgium, which ought to be guaranteed independence;

Germany at the same time ought to leave French territory, and in return have its former colonial territories restored. And, in his view, the settlement of other land questions (the Rhineland, Austria, Armenia, the Balkan states) ought to take into account the aspirations of the peoples involved.

A number of authors have called this 1 August 1917 document the most important act of Benedict XV's pontificate; a diplomatic note, initially classified as secret, it was not made public until well after it had been sent, and was then first published by British newspapers only after the agreement of the various censors, and without the pope having done anything toward its publication. It nevertheless unleashed a violent campaign against the pope in France and especially in Italy. He was accused of having sought to weaken the morale of the combatants, and of having pronounced ignominious words by calling the war "a useless massacre" (*inutile strage*). Starting with his 28 July 1915 message, Benedict XV had spoken of "the horrible butchery that has dishonored Europe for a year." Clemenceau (*L'Homme enchaîné*, 18 August 1917) affirmed notably that the pope wanted "a German peace," and Stephen Pichon saw in it the danger of a peace that would establish Austro-German power on a still stronger footing, by dispensing those countries from all reparation for damages. The steadfast and often reiterated neutrality of the Church was taken by the belligerents on each side to show a lack of the political courage to denounce the odious acts of the adversary; Clemenceau's "German pope" was balanced perfectly by Ludendorff's "French pope."

Initially, historical reality took other paths. Benedict XV's attention turned first to the condition of the wounded and the prisoners of war. A pontifical aid service set up specifically for this intention was entrusted in December 1914 to the direction of Eugenio Pacelli, then secretary of the Congregation for Extraordinary Ecclesiastical Affairs and the future PIUS XII. At the same time, the pope sent telegrams to the heads of the warring nations, begging them to end "this disastrous year" and begin the new one by generously accepting his suggestion for an exchange between the warring armies of all prisoners invalided by injury or sickness and deemed unfit for service. Almost all the recipients of this message responded positively, from George V to Czar Nicholas II and from Count Hering (president of the Bavarian Council) to Poincaré. The first exchanges were made at the beginning of 1915, and Benedict XV was later given official credit for the initiative. More than thirty thousand French, Belgian, English, and Austrian soldiers were thus able to receive hospital care in Switzerland; among other initiatives, Sunday rest was granted to prisoners (1915), and a monument was dedicated to the Christians who had fallen in the Dardanelles (1916). A decree dated 15 January 1915 announced a universal day of prayer for the reestablishment of peace, set for 7 February throughout Europe and 21 February in dioceses outside Europe; similarly, the celebration of three masses on All Souls' Day was extended to the universal church (1915). The Missing Persons Bureau, opened at the Vatican Palace, received 170,000 requests for information, assisted in 40,000 repatriations, and communicated with 50,000 families.

Benedict XV's other interventions had less success and fewer results. Multiplying his calls for peace (8 September and 6 December 1914; 25 May, 28 July, and 6 December 1915; 4 March and 30 July 1916; 10 January and 5 May 1917), the pontiff was especially impeded by the refusal of the powers involved in the war to observe a cease-fire for Christmas 1914, and to guarantee burial for soldiers killed on the field of battle (1915). Through messages sent to Belgium (1920) and then Russia and the countries of central Europe (1921), the pope made himself the herald-defender of "martyred and devastated" children, developing the argument that "for a new person to be born, another must die" (1921). Gasparri noted that it took 82 million gold lire to finance this personal work of charity, which made the Vatican a kind of "second Red Cross," as it was described by Romain Rolland. Added to this sum was the amount spent to relieve the sufferings caused by the catastrophe, a natural one this time, of the earthquake at Avezzano, in the Abruzzi, in January 1915: several thousand victims were housed and cared for in the St. Martha hospice, in the neutral enclosure of the Vatican.

For Benedict XV, diplomatic and political questions were necessarily the other aspect of the war that was of basic concern to the Church. As early as the end of 1914, certain people in London realized that the Allies had much too weak a position in Rome, which was seen as a unique listening post. The French embassy to the Holy See having been closed in 1906, the need for relations was all the more urgent: Sir Henry Howard, a relation of the duke of Norfolk, was accredited as head of an extraordinary mission to the Holy See, its members forming Great Britain's legation after the war. Italy's entry into the war, on 24 May 1915, raised fear of a socialist revolution in Rome in the case of a defeat, and somewhat changed the diplomatic balance; the representatives at the Vatican of the Central powers had to quit Italian soil and install themselves in Switzerland, as close to the Italian border as possible. The difficulties of communication between the pope and his nuncios grew, undermining chances for any sustained effort at mediation; one such message, to the Secretariat of State from Msgr. Scapinelli, the Holy See's spokesman in Vienna, routed through Zurich, was stopped at the Austrian border and returned to its sender on the ground that it came from enemy territory. The Church considered Austria a bastion of Catholicism on the fringes of the Orthodox zone of influence, and also as a stable element in a Europe in turmoil. Following the same line of thought (that a ruined Europe risked losing its role as torchbearer for Christian civilization), Msgr. Tacci, the nuncio accredited to the king of Belgium, followed the refugee government to Le Havre. Benedict XV entrusted a special mission in Switzerland to Count Carlo Santucci, who was welcomed by the counselor Giuseppe Motta, responsible for foreign affairs and a model Catholic, with whom he got along very well, as he did with Gustave Adar, then president of the International Red Cross. But given the tensions during the previous pontificate, it is not really surprising that nothing came of Msgr. Baudrillart's September 1915 mediation attempt with the French government, proposing a compromise peace with Germany. Other discussions, this time secret, were opened in March 1918 between Gasparri and the minister Nitti, aimed at a negotiation between Italy and Austria. The pope also took an interest in several individual cases, including those of Princess Marie of Croÿ-Solre and of Mme Carton de Wiart, the wife of the Belgian minister of justice, who had been condemned to detention and later was able to find refuge in Switzerland; he also had Msgr. Ladeuze, the rector of the University of Louvain, set free.

At the same time, Eugenio Pacelli was sent to Munich in May 1917 as nuncio, and the pope took the step of naming a chaplain in chief for the Italian army, in the person of Angelo Bartolomasi, the coadjutor archbishop of Turin. Under this "bishop of the camps" and his counterparts for the Belgian, French, English, German, and Austrian armies, an entire ecclesiastical-military system was developed, with special faculties delegated to priests serving in the front lines.

By the London accords, signed in April 1915, Italy won agreement from its allies that the Vatican would not be represented in the international bodies that were to be established to decide on the settlement of the peace at the end of the war. During the summer of 1918, Rome exercised its ingenuity in order to obtain the suspension of this Article 15, which it judged injurious in applying only to the Vatican and not to neutral powers in general; the powers participating in the peace conference of Versailles, following the reception of President Wilson in solemn audience at Rome on 4 January, accepted the appointment to their body of Bonaventura Cerretti, the archbishop of Corinth. Although excluded from the new League of Nations, the papacy inaugurated a new round of concordats with the secular powers immediately after the war. In his encyclical *Pacem Dei munus* (23 May 1920), the pope announced that the Church was disposed to ease the restrictions upon official visits to the QUIRINAL by Catholic princes and heads of state. In his consistorial allocution of 21 November 1921, Benedict XV sketched the line of action the Vatican wanted to follow in international negotiations; arguing from the clause *res inter alios acta*, the pope refused a pure and simple transfer of

the privileges accorded in his time to Austria in the person of the emperor to the new states born of the dismemberment of the Austro-Hungarian Empire. The heads of the states were, in the eyes of the Vatican, new partners representing entities that were themselves new, with which the Holy See had no juridical ties; Benedict XV intended in this way to guarantee the greatest possible freedom for the Church, by reserving in particular the exclusive right to appoint bishops, which the CONCORDAT of 1855 had granted to the emperor. This position constituted, among other things, the foundation of later concordats; the first of these, with Latvia, was signed on 30 May 1922.

During the secret CONSISTORY of 4 December 1916, Benedict XV was able to make official announcement that the codification of canon law, a project launched twelve years earlier by Pius X and pursued, indeed directed, by Cardinal Pietro Gasparri, was complete. Promulgated on Pentecost 1917 (constitution *Providentissima Mater Ecclesia*) and due to come into force after a one-year transitional period, the new *Codex iuris canonici* was published on 28 June 1917; the same day, the members of the two codification commissions placed in the hands of Benedict XV a copy of the Code, which they presented as the accomplishment of an undertaking both magnificent and of great practical value. By the *motu proprio Cum iuris canonici Codice* (15 September 1917), Benedict XV instituted a Pontifical Commission for the Authentic Interpretation of the Code of Canon Law, which would have the exclusive power to determine the meaning or scope of the various canons, and he assigned precise limits to the legislative power of the Roman congregations, in order to preserve the newly constituted normative unity.

The 1916 occupation of the Palazzo Venezia by the Italian state, and the exile to Lugano of diplomatic representatives accredited to the Holy See, had served only to aggravate the situation in the peninsula, centered on the Roman question. Gasparri, in an interview published on 28 June 1915 by the *Corriere d'Italia*, pleaded for respect for the "true" interests of the Italian people; in 1919, he had a defense of "the politics of Benedict XV" against attacks by some French journalists published, under the byline Henri Le Floch, the rector of the French seminary of Rome. Thanks to Benedict XV's experience and conciliatory approach, the postwar years were marked by a clear rapprochement between the Italian government and the papacy. The formation, accepted by the pope, of the Italian Popular party (PPI), with Don Luigi Sturzo, a Sicilian priest, Count Grosoli, Count Santucci, and a journalist, Montini, as its moving spirits, put an end to the rigors of the *non expedit*, the principle of which, upheld by Leo XIII and eased by Pius X, prevented Catholics from participation in Italian politics. Nonconfessional in the sense that it formed no part of a diocesan organization (R. Aubert), the movement quickly drew Catholics of all political tendencies and won 103 seats in the November 1919 legislative elections. The emergence of these new forces, which were secular and lay, helped to roll back anticlericalism and allowed the formation of Catholic networks, until the arrival of fascism in 1922.

The pontificate of Benedict XV was marked likewise by a renewal of interest in other questions of international scope, a field that had become manifestly essential during the period. Immediately after the war, Benedict XV had clearly emphasized two aspects he considered of capital importance if the Church was to be heard and eventually to grow: one was relations with the Eastern Churches, and the other was missionary activity. Out of the Congregation for the Oriental Churches, created by PIUS IX on 6 January 1862 within the Congregation for the Propagation of the Faith and having responsibility for matters concerning the Eastern Church, Benedict XV created an independent body called the Congregation "for the Oriental Church" (*motu proprio Dei providentis* of 1 May 1917); it was designated by this title beginning with the 1917 Code (canon 257, § 1) and placed under the aegis of Cardinal Martini. It was responsible for dealing with issues relevant to the Alexandrian, Chaldean, Byzantine, Armenian, and Antiochene Churches, representing about 8 million faithful, without counting the 150 million dissidents scattered across the entire Eastern world. It was established out of concern over the growing respect for the UNIATE Churches, seen as counterweights in an area deemed chaotic and uncertain for Catholicism. Another *motu proprio*, devoted expressly to the *Orientis catholici* and dated the following 15 October, announced the foundation in Rome of a Pontifical Oriental Institute, which Benedict XV said he would "oversee personally." Roman unionist hopes—the forerunners of the ecumenical movement—were disappointed initially by obstacles placed in the way by the new Soviet power (the fruitless attempt by Msgr. d'Herbigny to establish a Catholic hierarchy in Russia), and by the secular aims of Kemalist Turkey, the intrigues of which encroached on the sphere of influence of the patriarchate of Constantinople. On the border of the Orthodox region, Rome had to deal with the Czech schism, at the heart of a much weakened central Europe, and in the end, on 16 December 1920, condemned the adherents of a patriarchate of Prague that enjoyed a relative autonomy and those of an independent national Church of the Presbyterian type (R. Aubert), which was recognized by the state.

In a related way, the pontificate of Benedict XV was a turning point for the missionary activity of the Church. It was given a new direction by the 30 November 1919 encyclical *Maximum illud*, in which the pope announced the Holy See's intention to separate the missionary cause and the apostolate from the colonial intrigues of the European powers; it rebuked the "indiscreet zeal" of which many missionaries had been guilty in serving the national interests of their homelands. To counteract this tendency, and out of an even greater desire to revitalize the spirit of evangelization, some special recommendations were made to the Propaganda for the creation of regional seminaries that would produce an indigenous clergy; a decision was made conjointly to establish colleges in Rome, throughout Italy, and in Switzerland and Germany.

Religious life and piety, in the new contexts essentially determined during the pontificate of Pius X, continued to be developed during that of Benedict XV, though they took on a sometimes tragic cast in their mindfulness of the war. This was reflected in the extension to the universal church of the feast of the Holy Family and in the development of devotion to the Sacred Heart, the Precious Blood, the ROSARY, Our Lady of Sorrows, Our Lady of Peace, and Our Lady of Loreto. The canonization of Joan of Arc (decree *Divina disponente clementia* of 16 May 1920) had identical roots, in exalting the ideal of a holiness that was at least combative if not warlike, for the benefit of a battered but victorious France, a kind of engulfing cathedral capable of becoming once again a pillar of Catholicism in the modern world born of the war. Benedict XV also proclaimed the beatification of Joseph Cottolengo, Anna of San Bartolomeo (1917), Anna-Marie Taigi, Oliver Plunkett, Louise de Marillac, the twenty-two Ugandan martyrs, and the Ursulines of Valenciennes (1920).

The ecclesiastical sciences in general, and biblical studies in particular, were resumed only with difficulty after the trauma provoked by the modernist crisis (Charles Wackenheim). Even though the number of condemnations and rejections tended to diminish under Benedict XV, who was obsessed by the specter of an Alfred Loisy, the Holy Office and the Biblical Commission made it a point of honor to exercise the closest kind of surveillance. The disciplinary norms required by the oath against modernism were maintained, as were the Committees of Vigilance. In April 1920, a decree from the Holy Office contested the rather moderate opinions of the Sulpician Jules Touzard, who was reproached for being too daring in his writings about whether Moses was truly the author of the books of the Pentateuch. The encyclical *Spiritus Paraclitus* of 15 September of the same year only reinforced the conservative position in these matters, the pope challenging especially the thesis that the inerrancy of the Bible applied only to religious truths and not to the events of the secular order. Under the influence of such signs of heterodoxy, emphasis was placed on the "meticulous and active" formation of seminarians, along with the institution of a Congregation for Studies, Seminaries, and Universities (1915), which developed a rule that was praised as "pedagogically perfect and doctrinally admirable," intended first of all for Italian seminaries. Still, the suspension, followed by the definitive suppression in November 1921, of the traditionalist *Sapiniere* organization directed by Msgr. Begnini, contributed to some change in the climate of studies. In the domain of culture and the arts, Benedict XV inspired the foundation of Milan's Catholic University of the Sacred Heart (1920) and financed the reconstruction of the library at the University of Louvain (1918) and of the Petriano MUSEUM (1917); inside Vatican City, he ordered the continuation of the restoration of the ducal hall and of the new center for papal administration (1917), opened the astrophotography office of the Vatican OBSERVATORY, and, in the last days of his pontificate, opened new quarters for the Noble Guard (1922).

Having been struck suddenly by a flulike bronchitis on 18 January 1922, Benedict XV died within four days, at age sixty-eight. His pontificate, which played its part in effecting the transition between the prewar and the postwar world, had lasted seven years, four months, and twenty days.

Benedict XV promoted his two successors to the episcopate: the first was Achille Ratti (6 June 1919), who was sent as apostolic visitator and then as nuncio to Poland, and was named cardinal by Benedict XV; the second was Eugenio Pacelli (23 April 1917), who was ordained bishop (13 May 1917) by Benedict XV himself and later sent as nuncio to Bavaria and then Germany. Benedict XV created 32 cardinals, 8 archdioceses, 26 dioceses, 3 abbeys and PRELATURES *nullius*, 2 apostolic delegations (in Japan and Albania), 28 apostolic vicariates, and 8 apostolic prefectures.

François Jankowiak

Bibliography

The archives of Benedict XV in the Vatican Secret Archives [ASV] have been open since 20 August 1985 to qualified researchers.

Carcel Orti, V. "Benedicto XV y los obispos españoles. Los nombriamentos episcopales en España desde 1914 hasta 1922," *AHP*, XXIX (1991), 197–254.

Conzemius, V. "L'offre de médiation de Benoît XV du ler août 1917. Essai de bilan provisoire," *Religion et politique*, Lyon, 1972, 303–26.

Degli Occhi, L. *Benedetto XV*, Milan, 1921.

Della Torre, G. "Benedetto XV," *EC*, II (1949), 1285–94.

Epp, R., Lefebvre, Ch., and Metz, R. *Le Droit et les institutions de l'Église catholique latine de la fin du XVIIIe siècle à 1978*, Paris, 1981.

Fontana, J. *Les Catholiques français pendant la Grande Guerre*, Paris, 1990.

Rumi, G. (ed.), *Benedetto XV e la pace 1918*, Brescia, 1990.

Hayward, F. *Un pape méconnu: Benoît XV*, Paris-Tournai, 1955.

Kovacs, E. "Papst Benedikt XV. und die Restaurationsbemühungen des Kaisers und Königs Karl von Österreich," *AHP*, XXVII (1989), 357–99.

Le Floch, H. *La Politique de Benoît XV*, Paris, 1919.

Pollard, J. *The Unknown Pope: Benedict XV (1914–1922) and the Pursuit of Peace*, London, 1999.

Rumi, G. "Benedetto XV. Un epistolario inedito," *Civitas*, XLII (1991), 3–83.

Thévenin, N. "La note de Benoît XV du ler août 1917 et les réactions des catholiques français," *Revue d'histoire diplomatique*, CIII (1989), 285–338.

BENEDICTIONS, PAPAL. The papal benedictions are also called apostolic blessings, because they are given by those whom the LITURGY and the Christian people call the successors of the apostle Peter, the Roman pontiffs. The pope gives his blessing with the first three fingers of his right hand, in honor of the Holy Trinity, while folding the other two fingers.

1) Ordinary or common blessing. This is given privately, for example at the end of an AUDIENCE or liturgical ceremony, or in the formal conclusion of a letter to Catholics: "with my greetings and apostolic blessing," *salutem et apostolicam benedictionem.*

2) Blessing *urbi et orbi* (to the city [of Rome] and to the world). This is given solemnly and extended to the whole world, for example on the day of a pope's election, at his enthronement, at Christmas, at Easter, etc. It is given from the balcony (*loggia*) of ST. PETER's basilica.

Until the disappearance of the PAPAL STATES (1870), this blessing was given four times a year: on Holy Thursday and Easter Sunday from the balcony of St. Peter's; on Ascension Day from the balcony of ST. JOHN LATERAN; and on the feast of the Assumption from the balcony of ST. MARY MAJOR. Popes LEO XIII, PIUS X, and BENEDICT XV gave the blessing *urbi et orbi* only inside St. Peter's basilica, in protest against the situation of the HOLY SEE after the taking of Rome. On 6 February 1922, the day of his election, PIUS XI again gave this blessing from the balcony of St. Peter's.

A pontifical blessing ordinarily carries a plenary INDULGENCE, which can also be obtained by those who receive the blessing by radio or television.

3) Papal blessing. This is given by a bishop, or even a priest, by delegation in the name of the pope. The delegation is not given to anyone in Rome owing to the presence of the Roman pontiff in the Eternal City.

4) Apostolic blessing for a special occasion. This can be obtained on the occasion of an assembly, a marriage, etc., by a request sent to the SECRETARIAT OF STATE.

5) Apostolic blessing *in articulo mortis*. This is given to someone who is sick and in danger of death, even if death is not imminent, and carries a plenary indulgence applicable to the moment of death. For that reason, the blessing cannot be repeated during the same illness.

Dominique Le Tourneau

Bibliography

Lesage, R. "Bénédictions données par le pape," *Catholicisme*, I, Paris, 1948, 1409–10.

Opperheim-Celestino Testore, F. "Benedizione impartite dal Papa," *EC*, II, Florence, 1949, 1301–2.

BENEFACTION. In the early days of Christianity, generosity was the primary source of income for the Church, whose expenses were split between maintenance of buildings, religious exercises, assistance to the poor and foreigners, and support of the clergy. Benefaction was almost nonexistent at the level of the papacy, but the BISHOP OF ROME, undoubtedly more than others, benefited from the practice. Originally it came in modest quantities from individuals, then from imperial largesse, which, in the 4th century, founded the patrimony of the Roman Church, and the aristocratic generosity that took over at the beginning of the 5th century.

It is impossible to calculate how important a role benefaction played in the life of the Church before CONSTANTINE's victory, either in Rome or elsewhere. Not that the faithful were not generous: some of the *ex-votos* found in the CATACOMBS, the rare churches founded before the 4th century, and the riches that the deacon Lawrence refused to hand over to a persecutor show this well. But before 313, the Church was not juridically qualified to own goods, since Roman law had no concept of individual legal entities. It was thus impossible to estimate its wealth, which was modest in any case, and was greatly depleted at the end of the 3rd century by confiscations. Everything changed with Constantine's victory, as he authorized the Church to receive donations and bequests, and the emperor was the first to distribute his largesse.

In the first half of the 4th century, imperial generosity changed the material situation of the Church of Rome. The breadth of imperial benefaction can be estimated through the charts of donations preserved in the *LIBER PONTIFICALIS*, the authenticity of which Msgr. Duchesne has shown; it would serve no purpose here to review Constantine's generosity in detail, but the donations connected to the Constantinian basilica (St. John Lateran), to the BAPTISTRY, to the basilica on Via Labicana, to the *martyria* (St. Lawrence, ST. PETER, and ST. PAUL) come to a total of nearly 21,000 *solidi* in revenue, on lands located in Latium, in Campagna, in Sicily, in Asia, and in Africa. To these direct donations should be added those that the emperor inspired: Constantine's own daughter endowed the basilica on Via Nomentana, along with its functionaries and servants, who were undoubtedly hoping to succeed in winning imperial favor for themselves. This wealth of donations was to a certain extent transformational for the Church of Rome. The buildings themselves changed the conditions of worship: in much larger basilicas, crowds of Christians could gather together for the great episcopal celebrations. But above all, imperial benefaction changed the economic status of the Church. With nearly 26,000 *solidi* in revenues, the bishop of Rome became an economic power, albeit a second-class one who could not manage his patrimony with complete freedom. Actually, the Church of Rome's fortune remained modest when compared to senatorial fortunes: even the least wealthy senators received incomes ranging from 72,000 to 108,000 *solidi*, and the greatest fortunes reached as high as 288,000 in revenue. The bishop of Rome was still far from being able to compete with senators. Besides, several restrictions were imposed upon donations. Most of the revenues were allocated for particular expenses specified on the deeds of gift, such as lighting and building maintenance. In some cases, the most blatant of which was the basilica of Helen, Santa Croce in Gerusalemme, the donor kept substantial rights over his donation: Holy Cross remained a Palatine chapel until the 6th century, and the bishop had no intervening power. After 377, the word *titulus*, appearing in the charts, refers simultaneously to the church, the revenues, and a treasury over the uses of which the new owner—the bishop—had no leverage. Moreover, the patrimony itself was inalienable. Thus, the Church of Rome was a real but very limited economic power.

Beginning at the end of the 4th century, the sources of Roman wealth began to diversify: after a half-century hiatus, private benefaction came back into prominence, and the generosity of the aristocracy took the place of imperial largesse. New problems arose between donors and the bishop of Rome, who began increasingly to seek ways of escaping from their supervision.

After the prosperous period of Constantine's reign, the generosity of the princes manifested itself more discreetly; the reconstruction of San Paulo fuori le Mura should be mentioned, along with the contributions of Theodosius II and Eudoxia for San Pietro in Vincoli, and those of Valentinian III for San Lorenzo in Damaso. In a number of places, the *Liber pontificalis* also mentions the reconstitution of pillaged treasuries. The sources of benefaction multiplied: Anicia Faltonia Proba offered revenues "for clerics, the poor, and monasteries," and delegated to pope Innocent the establishment of the *titulus Vestiniae* (St. Vitalian); Demetrius, also a member of the Anicia family, founded a basilica on Via Latina in honor of St. Stephen during the time of Leo's papacy. An *illustris femina*, Firmina, gave all her possessions to pope Gelasius, who accepted them. There were also clerics who practiced benefaction: perhaps a few priests, to whom the management of foundations had been entrusted, took on the responsibility of paying for part of the work, like the priest Leopardus, during the time of Innocent's papacy, for Santa Pudenziana, or Peter of Illyria for Santa Sabina. The bishop himself began to practice benefaction: Damasus founded San Lorenzo in Lucina, probably on family property, and SIXTUS III founded SANTA MARIA MAGGIORE. But it is not easy to distinguish between benefaction and mobilization of the Church's resources, while in the previous century church building and the foundation of institutions by popes was clearly due to private generosity. Throughout this period, the Church's wealth eroded almost as quickly as it had grown: changes in the boundaries of the Empire caused the loss of lands in the East, and then in Africa; invasions and raids in Italy after 410, ruined a treasury that was only partially reconstituted later on. But because the situation was similar for the aristocracy—sometimes even worse, since there were no gifts to compensate for the losses—the bishop of Rome progressively became a true rival of the Roman elite, and relationships began to be strained. After Leo's papacy, the popes attempted to acquire more control over their patrimony, while the aristocracy attempted to restrict the pope's freedom. The popes applied themselves to managing their wealth in various ways: by organizing collections, setting up regulations for paying expenses, by registering and coordinating information about the revenue from church property, and by instituting *conductores* entrusted with the task of travelling through church estates and drawing up reports. Gelasius gathered all this information in a polyptych that was later reformed by Gregory the Great. If the prohibition against ceding lands remained, a certain flexibility did set in: pope Leo decided, probably after 452, that the bishop could sell lands when it was required by community interest and backed by the unanimous approval of the clergy. Pope Hilary replaced the unanimity of the clergy with agreement by a SYNOD, the composition of which was not specified. This new ambition did raise conflicts with the aristocracy who made donations. This was felt clearly in 487 when the prefect of the praetorium, Basilius, took advantage of the weakening of papal authority at the time of Simplicius's death by adopting a *scriptura*: not only was it absolutely forbidden to cede the lands of the patrimony, but it was also forbidden to accumulate personal property that could not be put to liturgical use (precious stones or metals, fabrics, etc.). Significantly, the text was voted on by an assembly composed of members of the clergy and the SENATE. Without abolishing the legislation, Gelasius set up, perhaps as a means of revenge, strict rules for donors; it may be presumed that the rule he proclaimed for the bishops of Lucania in 494 applied to Rome as well: donors were to present a *petitorium* through which they lost all rights to their gifts. If donors could not agree to such a commitment, the bishops were to refuse all gifts. This is perhaps the reason why the generosity of donors tended to turn elsewhere in the 6th century. Gelasius's correspondence shows members of the aristocracy to be concerned primarily with building churches and founding monasteries on their great domains, a movement that was confirmed in the fol-

lowing decades: Faustus the senator, Liberius the prefect of the Gauls, and Cassiodorus practiced these new forms of benefaction themselves as they allowed the donor to avoid the bishop's control. In any case, benefaction was no longer as significant as it had been in the 4th and 5th centuries: the Church was henceforth an economic power that drew its wealth from the revenues of its patrimony, and no longer from the generosity of the prince or the aristocracy. Gregory the Great's correspondence makes this clear: whenever the pope had a concern over donations made to the Church, it was because he feared that resources allocated for the construction of buildings would be insufficient to assure their upkeep. In the other churches of Italy, the problem of patronage was raised more sharply, but for a while, at least, the bishop of Rome had gained control over his own patrimony.

Claire Sotinel

Bibliography

Pietri, C. "Évergetisme et richesse ecclésiastique dans l'Italie du IVe à la fin du Ve siècle," *Ktéma*, 3 (1978), 317–37; "Aristocratie et société cléricale dans l'Italie chrétienne au temps d'Odoacre et de Théodoric," *MEFRA*, 93 (1981), 417–67.

BENEFICES. See **Finances, Papal**.

BENEFICES, VACANT. This term refers to income from churches and ecclesiastical benefices that is unpaid because of the death or change of titular, and has fallen due between the vacancy and the collection of the new beneficiary. The vacants of any benefice where the collection was paid to the pope were given to the Holy See in the 14th century. In fact, the only vacants collected were those of the major benefices, that is, bishoprics and abbeys. By contrast, the Avignon popes, and especially those of the Great Schism, maintained some benefices vacant, especially in the south of France. The idea was either to give, on a more or less long-term basis, "financial assistance" to prelates insufficiently provided for, in consideration of the services they rendered the papacy or temporal rulers; or to have the vacants collected for a few months by the Apostolic Camera and its collectors. The vacants created illusions. The beneficiary who was provided for during a year and found his income cut off was hard put to pay off the debt (the annate, or rather community service) he owed for his collection. As for prolonged vacancy, which provided the pope with a means of remuneration, it deprived him of the taxes that a new titular would normally have paid. Vacant benefices obviously did not pay annates, tithes, or proxies. Finally, the financial costs of managing the vacant benefice were borne by the collector, leaving only a limited profit for the pontifical treasury. An administrator had to be appointed and compensated. Reserving vacants competed with the temporal regalia, which gave the king the income of the so-called royal churches while they were vacant. In contrast to the tithe, in which the king had an interest, and the annate, to which the temporal rulers were indifferent, the vacants encountered open hostility. The history of vacant benefices is therefore ambiguous, with each one trying not to embarrass the other so as to avoid arousing a reaction of which the clergy would take advantage. The pope was particularly prudent with regard to the vacants of the most important churches in France, which were given, as soon as possible, by the pope to prelates on the recommendation of the king.

Jean Favier

See also FINANCES, PAPAL.

Bibliography

du Pasquier, G. "Réserve des bénéfices ecclésiastiques," *Dictionnaire de Droit Canonique*, Paris, 1935–65, 7, 648–49.

BIRETTA, CARDINAL'S. The biretta, the name of which is of Latin origin (*biretum* or *bireta*), is mentioned as church headdress for the first time in 956, at the ceremony in which JOHN XII degraded the bishop of Cahors. Made of red wool or velvet, square and furnished with three or four peaks, worn both by nobles (15th century) and as the distinguishing mark of doctors of theology or CANON LAW, it was granted as a privilege to CARDINALS by PAUL II in 1464. In 1888, LEO XIII recognized the purple biretta as an insignia of bishops and archbishops. In the CODE OF CANON LAW promulgated by BENEDICT XV in 1917, canon 234 specified that "the cardinal's biretta is worn by a special legate. So-called cardinals of the crown, that is, those presented by a secular monarch, receive the biretta from the monarch and the skullcap from the papal legate." Although the biretta is still used, current law (CODE OF CANON LAW of 1983) no longer mentions it.

François Jankowiak

Bibliography

Henry, W. "Barrette," *DACL*, II (1910), 495–6.
Naz, R. *Traité de droit canonique*, I, Paris, 1946.

BISHOP OF ROME. Even if, in pure CANON LAW, it could be otherwise, the history of the Church shows us that, in the modern era, whenever a new bishop of Rome is elected, he is already a bishop, and must thus leave his diocese (or his other functions) to head the Church of Rome. Things were very different in the early Church,

and it was only toward the end of the 9th century, with the choice of MARINUS I (882–884), who was the bishop of Civitavecchia at the time of his election, that we find the first example of what was to become a habitual practice. And yet, the election of Marinus was contrary to the decisions of a Roman council in the year 769, which stated that "*summus pontifex, quando benedicetur, eligitur unus de cardinalibus* [that is, a member of the Roman clergy], *aut presbyter aut diaconus; nam episcopus esse non poterit.*"

The bishop of Rome was thus elected, while a priest or a DEACON was chosen from the local clergy. And this custom is widely confirmed by notices in the *LIBER PONTIFICALIS*. Of the ninety-four bishops of Rome, from Eleutherius, elected in 175, to Nicholas I, elected in 858, we have information on the ecclesiastical careers of fifty-two, and there are only two exceptions, that of Fabian, who at the time of his election in 236 was simply a layperson, and that of Silverius in 536, who was a subdeacon. But it must not be forgotten that Fabian's election took place thanks to the miraculous intervention of a dove, and that Silverius was imposed on Rome by the Gothic king Theodahad. (Another layman, Constantine, was elected bishop of Rome in 767, but he was an ANTIPOPE.)

Insofar as we can trust the incomplete list in the *Liber pontificalis*, there is a second aspect of the selection of bishops of Rome that seems important. At least up until the middle of the 7th century, there seemed to be a preference for deacons: from 175 to 642, we find 23 deacons elected, as opposed to only 6 priests. And, in the case of at least two of the latter, Cornelius, in 251, and Dionysius, in 259, the exception is explained by the circumstances, since persecutions had apparently wiped out the college of deacons. As for the next two, Marcellinus and Marcellus, in 296 and 308, they were in all likelihood the same person. At the end of the 7th century the tendency appears to reverse, since from Benedict II, who was a priest when he was elected in 682, up to Nicholas I, elected in 858 while he was a deacon, we count 12 priests versus 8 deacons at the time of their election. When a deacon was chosen, he was immediately ordained a bishop, without receiving presbyterial ordination. It is not until the 11th century that we see the first mention of a deacon being elected bishop of Rome, and having to be ordained a priest before receiving his episcopal ordination: Gregory VII, elected 22 April 1073, was ordained priest on 22 May and bishop on 30 June of the same year.

The new bishop was elected by the community over which he would become head. Such was the case for Rome as well as for all the other churches. If we are to believe the account of Fabian's election (in 236), the faithful played an important role in the choice. But it must be remembered that this account gives ample space to the marvellous (as was also the case for Ambrose's election in Milan, where once again the people played a predominant role). What is more likely, and has been confirmed over time, is that the main figures in the election were members of the clergy, the role of the faithful being to confirm or invalidate the choice. This seems to be clearly shown by the fact that when the choice fell upon a deacon, it was almost always an archdeacon; and especially by the fact—although this came at a later date—that when the delegation of a local church came to submit to the bishop of Rome the name of the one they had just chosen as their new pastor, it was only the members of the clergy that the pope would subject to a long interrogation on the qualities of the newly elected.

Chosen by the members of the clergy, accepted by the faithful, the newly elected had to be only one of the members of the community for which he had just been chosen. Thus, all these bishops would come from the clergy of the City, which does not mean that they all needed to be native Romans. Thus, of the fourteen names of bishops of Rome in the first two centuries that tradition has preserved for us, ten are Greek-sounding names, and, at the other end of the chain, of the twenty-five popes elected between Honorius I (d. 638) and Hadrian I (elected in 771), nine were still from the East: three from Greece, three from Syria, two from Antioch, and one from Thrace. But they had all taken up residence in Rome and were part of the local clergy. This electoral system was not without risks, since an unfortunate "candidate" could attempt to get into office by force, or create a SCHISM. There is no lack of examples in Rome, the most spectacular of which is undoubtedly that of Ursinus who, in 366, opposed the election of Damasus: at the end of the quarrel that ensued between the two factions on the Esquiline Hill, some twenty had died. But even without going to these extremes, the examples of Hippolytus opposing Pontian in 230 (even though it is likely that he did not go so far as to create a schism), NOVATIAN, who stepped over the limit in 251, Eulalius in 418, and Lawrence in 498, have become famous. It might be interesting to point out that of these four "antipopes," three were priests, which might be a sign of tension between the college of deacons and the college of priests.

Chosen from among the deacons or from the priests in the Church of Rome, the newly elected pope needed to be ordained a bishop: this ordination marked his true ascent to office. Ecclesiastical law soon specified that this ordination could be conferred by only three bishops: as early as 251, in opposing Cornelius, who had been regularly elected and ordained, Novatian was obliged to bribe three bishops so that his ordination would appear valid. When he was ordaining one of his suffragans, it was one of the bishop of Rome's privileges to be able to perform this ordination alone, without the assistance of other bishops in the consecration. The *Ordines* of the High Middle Ages, which often make use of older texts, have provided a description of the bishop of

Rome's ordination rites. First, the three consecrating bishops may not be chosen at random, but should be well established by tradition: the bishop of Ostia, who played the most important role, was assisted by his colleagues from Albano and Porto. When, for one reason or another (vacancy of the bishop's seat, illness, etc.), one of these three bishops could not be present, it appears as though he was replaced by the bishop of Velletri. The ordination took place in St. Peter's, always on Sunday. In fact there was little difference between it and the ordination of a bishop from another see. The only point that was specific to it was the archdeacon's placing of the *pallium* on the newly ordained bishop as the sign of his function and his authority. Reserved for the bishop of Rome from very early times, this ornament quickly spread after Symmachus, in 513, gave Caesarius of Arles the privilege of wearing one. In contrast to the great majority of other bishops, the bishop of Rome was not ordained in his cathedral, but in a funerary basilica. The ordination was followed by the newly ordained bishop taking possession of the mother church of his diocese, in this case the Lateran basilica. Also, at the very end of the ordination ceremony, a full procession—one might almost say a cavalcade—was organized, in which the new bishop rode a richly harnessed mount from the Vatican to the Lateran, to the acclamation of the populace. Once inside his cathedral, the newly ordained *sedet in sede magna* takes possession of his diocese to officially begin his ministry.

Without going too far into theological considerations, it is nevertheless important to note that from very early times, the bishop of Rome has insisted on showing his primacy over the other bishops, and for the most part they have recognized this prerogative, connected not only to the fact that this church had connections to Peter and Paul, but also to the fact that its see was, precisely, in Rome. Although the relationships between Rome and the other churches have always existed in a climate of considerable liberty, examples of Roman primacy could be multiplied with the respect shown by Ambrose of Milan and Augustine of Hippo. But it is undoubtedly between Carthage and Rome that this phenomenon is clearest. After the close and quite fraternal ties that Cornelius and Cyprian maintained throughout their extensive correspondence, the election of Stephen in Rome seemed to create a distance between the two churches. In councils held in both cities as well as in his correspondence with his predecessor, Cyprian never hesitated to tell the new bishop of Rome what he thought of his actions. But he would never forget that while he was only the bishop of Carthage, Stephen was the bishop of Rome.

Patrick Saint-Roch

Bibliography

Andrieu, M. "La carrière ecclésiastique des papes et les documents liturgiques du Moyen Age," *Revue des sciences religieuses*, XXI (1947), 90–120.

BLESSED OR HOLY HAT AND SWORD. The blessed hat and sword are ceremonial regalia, blessed each year by the popes, and offered exclusively, with rare exceptions, to emperors and kings to encourage them to defend the rights of the Church.

The handle of the sword formed two crossed hands, the whole (handle, pommel, hilt, and blade) was worked in chased silver. The scabbard, equally richly decorated, was a great opportunity for silversmiths to demonstrate their ingenuity and skill. The sword belt was as magnificent as the rest of this costly gift.

The hat, high and rigid, was encircled with a deep brim, which curved upward toward the front, with two lappets falling at the back, somewhat in the style of a bishop's miter. It was normally of a deep crimson velvet, although at times it could be gray or even black, and was lined with ermine. A dove, symbol of the Holy Spirit, embroidered in gold thread and ornamented with pearls, was placed on the right side of the hat. Alternate straight and wavy lines in gold thread, ornamented with seed pearls, descended from the top of the hat toward the brim.

The sword and the hat were indisputably a costly gift, as evidenced by the payments carefully registered by various ateliers. In the 15th century, the cost was as high as 250 gold florins. The accounting ledgers of different periods provide detailed information on the approximate cost of the different elements required for its design. In the 16th century, the price had almost doubled to close to 500 florins. Like the Golden Rose, the first of the blessed swords and hats have not survived, which is understandable for the hat given the fragile nature of the material. More of the swords have survived the ravages of time, with ten 15th-century and around a dozen 16th-century swords still existing in a number of museums and private collections. The sword given by EUGENE IV (1431–47) to John II, king of Castile, is the most antique piece still extant. Two hats, along with swords, presented to Archduke Ferdinand of Tyrol in 1567 and 1581 are conserved in the Kunsthistorisches Museum in Vienna.

The origins of this pontifical gift cannot be understood without bearing in mind that throughout the Middle Ages, the sword was associated with liturgical ceremonies with accompanying chivalry, and the coronation of kings. According to Gregorovius, the tradition goes back to the sword that PAUL I (759–67) gave to Pepin, king of the Franks, in 758 as a symbol of royal duty in the defense of the Church against oppressors. Matthias von Neuvenburg relates in his chronicle that in 1347, the future emperor, Charles IV of Luxemburg proclaimed the gospel, sword in hand, at the Christmas midnight mass. He does not say explicitly that the pope blessed the sword before entering the choir for the sung office (probably because the ceremony was not familiar to him). For this reason historians hesitate to consider his story incontestable proof that a sword was blessed and offered by the pope on this occa-sion. The first written proof of a sword and hat offered by the pope is provided by the notation of a payment of 62 florins 12 cents and 9 denarii *"pro ense cum zona de serico minuta de argento, data per papam in vigilia nativitatis Domini, cum capello . . ."* which appears in the 1357 account ledger. Confirmation can be found in a somewhat similar inscription of 1365, during the pontificate of URBAN V (1362–70), when it appears the practice had been in existence for a long time. Whatever the real origin of the blessed sword and hat, by the 16th century they rested on several hundred years of tradition and were invested with the purest ideals of chivalry.

The significance of the blessed sword and hat indicated the pope's confidence in the chosen individual to defend the rights and freedoms of the Church, particularly of the Apostolic See. In some cases, the gift was sent to the individual in recognition of services already rendered; in others, the honor was granted to encourage taking up the sword in defense of the Church. Political motivations played their role.

The spiritual symbolism attached to the sword and hat rested on their ritual benediction, which guaranteed divine protection. This blessing always took place at Christmas and was included in the liturgical ceremonies of the celebrations. Even when the pope had no intention of presenting the sword and hat, the ritual was observed and they were given, for safekeeping, to the pope's sacristan to be presented later if the opportunity arose. The ceremony took place in one of the chapels or in the *aula dei paramenti* of the palace early on Christmas Eve, before the solemn procession to St. Peter's for Matins.

The sword represented the temporal power claimed by the pope by virtue of his supreme jurisdiction over the world, which he entrusted to secular leaders to exercise in his name. [This supreme jurisdiction, based on Medieval canonist theories, alludes to the two swords mentioned in Luke's gospel (22.38) as well as Peter's sword in John's (18.11).] The blessed hat apparently represents the infallible protection of the Holy Spirit, which accompanies every valiant defender of the Catholic faith. If the individual whom the pope wished to honor was present during the blessing, investiture with the sword and hat took place immediately and a special place was accorded him in the procession. Most often, however, the honor was bestowed from Rome, and a special envoy was charged with its conferral during a highly precise ceremony. In the list of swords and hats presented throughout the centuries which is far from complete, it appears that at least a dozen were bestowed on the emperors of the Germanic Holy Roman Empire, ten to the Most Christian kings of France, seven to the kings of Poland, six to their Most Catholic Majesties of Spain, three (or perhaps four) to the kings of England, three to the kings of Hungary, Portugal, and Scotland (perhaps only two), and one each to the kings of Bohemia and Naples. The others were offered to various princes, including the heirs-apparent; to archdukes, dukes, nobles, and grand captains; and to the city-states and to republics.

Charles Burns

Bibliography

Burns, C. *Golden Rose and Blessed Sword: Papal Gifts to Scottish Monarchs*, Glasgow, 1970: "Papal Gifts and Honours for the Earlier Tudors," *MHP*, 50, (1983), 173–97.

Cornides, E. *Rose und Schwert im päpstlichen Zeremoniell*, Vienne, 1967.

Modern, H. "Geweihte Schwerter und Hüte," *Jahrbuch der Kunsthistorischen Sammlungen des Allerhochsten Kaiserhauses*, 22, 3 (Vienne, 1901), 127–68.

Muntz, E. "Les epees d'honneur distribuees par les papes pendant les XIVe, Xe et XVIe siecles," *Revue de l'art chretien*, 39 (1889), 408–11; 40 (1890), 281–92.

BOLLATICA. The *bollatica* or *littera santi Petri* is the form of script used by the papal CHANCERY from the 16th to the 19th century for making extra copies of the pontifical ACTS sealed with lead seals or BULLS. This writing, entirely artificial, resulted from the transformation or rather the deformation of that used at the end of the Middle Ages, the bastard Gothic, itself derived in the 14th century from the curial lowercase of the 11th to 13th centuries.

Toward the end of the 15th century, on the original copies sealed on knots of silk, there appeared some floral decorations on the initial of the pope's name (written in an uppercase character that was thicker than the rest of the text). Later, the other words making up the formulas of superscription, address, and salutation were likewise decorated. Beginning in about 1550, two new factors came into play and modified the appearance of all the bulls, whether they were sealed with silk knots or hemp cords: first, a change in the system of abbreviations, and then, around 1600, a change in the writing itself.

First, the system of abbreviations became more complex. More and more words were contracted, and the contractions became more severe, giving rise to sequences of letters unused until then: for example, *coodus* for *commodus*, *beneij* for *beneficii*, *impedtum* for *impedimentum*. Sometimes the horizontal strokes indicating the abbreviations were excessively shortened, sometimes hardly visible, or even omitted. In the 18th century, new abbreviations by suspension appeared, so that *–an* or *–en* was used for all the forms of the present participle and the gerund. Some abbreviations stood for several words: for example, *proxto* for *proximo preterito* or *quadris* for *quoad vixeris*. To this sophistication in the system of abbreviations was added, around 1600, an evolution of the form of the letters, often excessively stylized. The writing became up-right, or slightly slanted to the left. A heavy stroke was used. The disproportion between the thick strokes and the thin strokes was accentuated to the point where some parts of letters completely disappeared; and some letters were remodeled (the letter *e*, for example, became "two-storied" and climbed into the space between the lines). Punctuation marks were neglected.

In the 18th and 19th centuries, the *bollatica*, which only a few specialists could read, gave the papal bulls an undeniably aesthetic appearance, reinforced by their luxurious ornamentation. But they had become so difficult to read that the Chancery had to send with each original another certified copy of it, the *transumptum*, provided at the expense of the one to whom the bull was addressed. However, these *transumpta*, drafted on paper in ordinary Latin writing, also used abbreviations that sometimes made them difficult to read. The system had become so complicated and costly that LEO XIII, as soon as he was elected, suppressed the *bollatica* by a *motu proprio* of 29 December 1878. Since then, papal bulls have been drafted in normal Latin script.

Bernard Barbiche

Bibliography

Frenz, T. "Littera Sancti Petri. Zur Schrift der neuzeitlichen Papsturkunden 1550–1878," *Archiv für Diplomatik*, 24 (1978), 443–515.

BONIFACE I. (*b. ?, d. 4 September 422*). *Elected pope on 28 December 418, ordained on 29 December. Buried in the cemetery of St. Felicity on the Via Salaria.*

A Roman priest, the son of a priest named Iocundus according to the LIBER PONTIFICALIS, Boniface had become familiar with the East: during the summer of 406, he was a member of a delegation sent by Pope INNOCENT I and the Western council to meet Emperor Arcadius in Constantinople to protest against the deposition of John Chrysostom. Their mission was to call for the reestablishment of John in his see before any judgment was made against him. The mission failed: once Boniface and his companions arrived in the states of Arcadius, they were prevented from moving about freely, and subjected to heavy pressure to agree to abandon John's cause; they returned to Italy without having met the emperor, and without even having been able to get information about the exiled bishop. However, they received letters from John congratulating them on the action they had taken. Boniface would return to the East: he is certainly the priest to whom Pope Innocent wrote—probably in 415—to tell him of the return of Bishop Alexander of Antioch to communion with Rome; he was then made responsible by the pope for informing Atticus, John Chrysostom's second successor in the diocese of Constantinople, of the conditions for his reintegration into the Roman communion.

Boniface returned to Italy before the death (26 December 418) of Pope ZOSIMUS, whose contested pontificate presaged a difficult succession. When Zosimus died, the archdeacon EULALIUS was elected by the deacons on 27 December in the episcopal church of the Lateran, while Boniface was elected on 28 December in the church of Theodora (unknown today) by the majority of the college of presbyters, who favored him for his mature age, his good morals, and his reputation for learning (*doctissimus in lege*). On Sunday, 29 December, Boniface was ordained in the *ecclesia Marcelli* and from there brought to ST. PETER'S in the Vatican, while his rival was ordained the same day in the church of the Lateran by the bishop of Ostia.

On the basis of a report by Symmachus, the prefect of the city, who favored Eulalius, on 3 January 419 Emperor Honorius confirmed the election of Eulalius and ordered the expulsion of Boniface from Rome. According to the *Liber pontificalis*, Boniface installed himself in the cemetery of St. Felicity. But his supporters protested to the emperor against the partiality shown by Symmachus, and made the most of the fact that Boniface had the support of seventy Roman priests as well as nine Italian bishops. Honorius convoked a council at RAVENNA on 8 February to decide between the two contenders. When the debates failed to reach a conclusion, Honorius decided on 15 March to assemble a larger council in Spoleto for Pentecost. He expelled the rival popes from Rome, where riots were occurring, and named Bishop Achilleus of Spoleto, who favored neither side, to conduct the Easter ceremonies in Rome. Boniface obeyed the emperor's order, but Eulalius returned to Rome on 18 March and occupied the church of the Lateran (29 March) before being expelled from the city once more, with difficulty, on orders from Honorius. The show of force by Eulalius failed: in a letter dated 3 April 419, received in Rome on 8 April, Honorius came down in favor of Boniface, who, recognized as the legitimate bishop of Rome, was allowed to return to the city.

Boniface, who owed his confirmation to the emperor's intervention, pursued a policy that was prudent and, at the outset, unassuming. He sought the support of Honorius without, however, disavowing his predecessor's initiatives.

In AFRICA, he inherited the conflict created by the interventionist policy of Zosimus, who had received the appeal of Apiarius, a priest of Sicca Veneria, who had been excommunicated by his bishop, Urbanus. On 26 April 419, Boniface appointed two new representatives in Africa, without modifying in any essential way his predecessor's directive to the LEGATES dispatched to the place, Bishop Faustinus of Potenza and the Roman priests Philip and Asellus. But he came up against the opposition of the African Church, which, in a letter of 26 May 419, protested against this Roman interference. The Apiarius

affair had been settled locally by the council, with the reluctant accord of the legates, and the canons presented by Rome as being those of the council of Nicaea (in fact they were those of the council of Sardica), and on which the Apostolic See based its case for intervention, had been accepted only provisionally; the African bishops, taking the view that Rome was not the only source of law, decided to have the canons verified by the major Eastern dioceses, and invited Rome to follow the same course.

In Gaul, Boniface I at first refrained from directly questioning the primacy of Arles, established by his predecessor. He ordered Patroclus of Arles, with other bishops of Gaul, to call a council before 1 November 419 to settle the question, long pending, of Maximus of Valencia, an unworthy prelate; however, he reserved the right to confirm the sentence (JK, 349). In Illyricum, he attempted to continue the policy of Innocent I and to consolidate his authority by giving Bishop Rufus of Thessalonica the authority of a vicar. He took advantage of the contested election of Bishop Perigenes of Corinth to intervene in the affair; he accepted the petition addressed directly to Rome by the supporters of Perigenes, and charged Rufus of Thessalonica to settle the dispute in the name of the Holy See. After a first fruitless attempt, in September 419 he invited Rufus to confirm the election of Perigenes, but that decision ran into opposition from some of the bishops of Illyricum, who appealed it to the Eastern emperor, Theodosius II.

Boniface I, who kept in the background in the struggle by Emperor Honorius and the African bishops against the Pelagian HERESY, sought the help of Augustine in order to refute the two pamphlets of Julian of Eclanum, who appealed to Rome and to Thessalonica not to condemn the Pelagians; the bishop of Hippo dedicated to Boniface his *Contra duas epistulas Pelagianorum*. However, sick and worried about the disturbances that could arise again after his death, Boniface asked for help from Honorius in July 420, and obtained from him a rescript declaring that in the case of a rivalry between two candidates, both would be rejected.

The pope was able to reinforce his authority in the last year of his pontificate. He successfully opposed encroachments by the Church of Constantinople, which in July 421 obtained from Theodosius II a decree recognizing its jurisdiction over the entire diocese of Illyricum. He made an official protest to the court of RAVENNA, denouncing the intrigues of the bishops of Illyricum as well as the pretensions of Atticus, as contrary to the canonical rules, and Honorius successfully intervened with Theodosius II to have the prerogatives of Rome respected. The emperor, without abrogating his decree, declared that he wanted the privileges traditionally recognized at Rome to be upheld. At the beginning of 422, in reply to objections by some bishops of Illyricum, among them unwavering opponents of Perigenes, Boniface I sent a legate to Rufus of Thessolonica with three letters that reinforced the powers of his vicar. Rufus was given responsibility for overseeing episcopal elections and councils in the whole of Illyricum, and for ruling in particular on the conflicts caused by the bishops of Thessalonica; those who rejected Rufus's authority were threatened with excommunication. Boniface should probably also get the credit for an intervention, relayed by Rufus of Thessalonica, in support of Bishop Felix of Dyrrhachium (Durres), who had encountered some difficulties—a situation that gave the pope an opportunity to reaffirm the Roman authority over all ecclesiastical affairs in Illyricum by inviting the metropolitan bishops to recognize the powers delegated to Rufus.

Boniface also intervened in Gaul in 422 to place limits on the primacy of Arles. Following a complaint from the Church of Lodève, on which Patroclus had imposed a bishop, the pope invited Bishop Hilarius of Narbonne—of which Lodève was a suffragan—to put an end to interference by Arles and to use his powers as a metropolitan to reestablish order in the name of the Apostolic See.

In Africa, on an unknown date, Boniface agreed to an appeal from Antony, the elected bishop of Fussala, who was protesting against a synodal decision condemning him; however, the pope asked for fuller information before getting involved.

According to the *Liber pontificalis*, Boniface I ordained thirty-six bishops. He also instituted various liturgical prohibitions concerning women, and prohibited *curiales* and slaves from becoming clerics.

Christiane Fraisse-Coué

Bibliography

Bardy G., *DHGE*, 9 (1935), 895–7.
Bonfatius, *Epistulae, PL*, 20, 750–84 (*Epistulae*, 4–5, 10–11, and 13–15; *Collectio Thessalonicensis*, 6–10, 27.
Caspar, E. *Geschichte des Papsttums*, I, Tübingen, 1930, 361–599.
Collectio Auellana, 14–38; *CSEL*, 35, 1, 59–88.
Duchesne L., *Fastes épiscopaux de l'ancienne Gaule*, I, Paris, 1907, 108–11.
Epistula, in Turner, Eomia, 1, II, 3, Oxford, 1930, 565.
Palladius, *Dialogus*, 3–4, Colemann-Norton, 21–4.—*Liber pontificalis*, I, 227–9.
Piétri C., *Roma christiana*, II, *BEFAR*, 224, 1976, 948–54, 1254–70.
Silva Tarouca, 23–36, 64–5).

BONIFACE II. (*b. ?, probably before 476, d. 17 October 532). Elected pope on 22 September 530. Buried at St. Peter's in Rome.*

His episcopate of two years and twenty-six days was marked by the SCHISM in which he was opposed by his rival, DIOSCORUS, and by his continuation of the policy of détente with RAVENNA pursued by his predecessor, FELIX IV. The son of Sigibuld, perhaps a descendant of the consul of 438, he was of Germanic origin, according to the *Liber pontificalis*. He must have been born before the establishment of the monarchy of Odoacer (476), for his epitaph presents him as an old man (*senex*). Perhaps of a barbarian family that had attained a prominent position in the empire, he was highly romanized: he was trained from youth in the government of the Roman Church (*sedis apostolicae primaevis miles ab annis*); in 530, he was an archdeacon. In addition, he had at his disposal a large personal fortune, which made him the ideal candidate to succeed Felix IV. The latter, when sick, conferred the *pallium* on him after 30 August 530, in the presence of some clerics and senators. The *contestatio* of the SENATE, which was posted in the titular churches of Rome, recalled the ordinary rules for succession, but did not have in view the choice made by the dying Felix or the election that ought to take place after his death. Boniface was acclaimed and ordained on 22 September 530, in the great hall of the Lateran (the Julian BASILICA) by those who remained faithful to the last wishes of Felix, while the DEACON Dioscorus was ordained the same day in the Constantinian basilica itself by a majority of the priests and senators. The schism came to an end when Dioscorus died suddenly on 14 October 530. Boniface required the sixty priests who had supported Dioscorus to take a solemn oath recognizing the legitimacy of his own election and regarding that of Dioscorus as nothing but a revolt against the established authority. On 27 December 530, he was in possession of the act that declared Dioscorus ANATHEMA and placed his own election above suspicion.

At the end of 530, Boniface received the acts of the COUNCIL of Orange that Cesarius, bishop of Arles, had sent him by the priest Arminius in order to ask him to obtain Felix IV's confirmation of the decrees condemning the semi-Pelagians. Having been ordained pope in the meantime, Boniface was able to satisfy Cesarius: in his decree of 25 January 531, he confirmed the conclusions of the Council of Orange, giving its canons the force of law. He convened a synod in Rome, on 7 and 9 December 531, after an appeal to the pope by Bishop Stephen of Larissa, whose election had been revoked by Bishop Epiphanius of Constantinople. This synod gave the pope an opportunity to show the legitimacy of recourse to Rome by a bishop in the vicariate of Thessalonica, and to oppose the attempt by the bishop of Constantinople to place Illyricum under his authority.

It is not known what event gave rise to the *relatio* (brief) of the African bishops mentioned in the *LIBER PONTIFICALIS*.

Imitating his predecessor, Boniface II wanted to name his own successor: without reasons of health, without bothering to seek the advice of the Senate, he convened a synod in St. Peter's basilica during which he imposed the choice of the deacon Vigilius. Soon afterwards, undoubtedly under pressure from Athalaric, he convened a new assembly: accusing himself of having overstepped his rights, he burned the decree nominating VIGILIUS in front of the assembled priests and senators—a serious action that indirectly recognized the legitimacy of Dioscorus. The Senate had registered its disapproval, as is proved by Athalaric's rescript of 533 referring to the decree of the Senate published in Boniface's time that declared null any promise or contract to secure votes for the episcopacy. He died in 532, much mourned by the poor according to his funeral eulogy, which recalled his generosity.

Janine Desmulliez

Bibliography

LP, I, 57, 281.

"Boniface," *LTK*, 2, 588 and *DHGE*, 9, 897–8.

Bonifativs, *Ep. ad Caes.*, in Gaudemet, J. *Les canons des conciles mérovingiens, SC*, 353, 1989, 176–85.—*Coll. Thessalonicens*, in Silva Tarouca, G. 1937, 1–16.—*ICUR*, n.s. 2, 4153.

Cassiodorus, *Variae*, 9, 15, *CC*, 96, 362, 363.

Piétri, C. "Aristocratie et société cléricale. . ." *MEFRA*, 93, 1981, 461–7.

Pontal, O. *Histoire des conciles mérovingiens*, Paris, 1989, 75–99.

Schwartz, E. *ACO*, IV, 2, 96–7.

von Harnack, A. "Der erste deutsche Papst und die beiden letzten Dekreten des römischen Senats," *SAB*, 1924, 24–42.

BONIFACE III. (*b. Rome, ?, d. Rome, 12 November 607). Elected pope on 19 February 607. Buried at St. Peter's in Rome.*

This short-lived pope is known almost exclusively from a brief entry in the *Liber pontificalis* and a very vague epitaph. His father was one John, called *kataadioces*, a term that is unexplained but that strongly suggests a Greek origin. Boniface was "of Roman nationality," which gives evidence of rapid integration in the city in which he was born. Among those closest to GREGORY the Great, he must be identified as the one who was chief of the "defenders" of the pope (*primus defensorum*), and then was ordained DEACON (603) before being *apocrisarius* at Constantinople, like his predecessor, Sabinian. Be that as it may, Phocas's (602–10) delay in confirming Boniface's election—nearly a year passed between his being chosen by the Romans and his ordination as bishop of Rome—suggests that there were tensions between the partisans and the adversaries of Gregory's policies: the diocesan clergy might resist, but the emperor won approval for the man the capital knew, and who knew the capital well.

For one of the biennial SYNODS that regularly brought together all the bishops of the part of southern Italy that remained Byzantine, thirty-three Roman priests and seventy-two bishops responded to the convocation; their number attests to the authority of the pope over his suffragans. There was a prohibition, it should be recalled, against campaigning, before the death of a pope, to succeed to his office. Three days after the death of the pontiff, there would be a meeting of the clergy and the "sons of the church," evidently the elite of society, that is, certain members of the senatorial class. Each would vote according to his conscience.

Boniface showed his support for Phocas. He had a statue erected with a highly laudatory dedication in honor of the emperor. The latter, having considerable difficulties in the East, was seeking support in the western areas, where he faced the LOMBARDS. Events that came to pass under BONIFACE IV show that his wishes were met. In exchange, the papacy won a lasting victory in its conflict with the patriarch of Constantinople, which had gone on since PELAGIUS II. Phocas declared that "the Apostolic See of the blessed apostle PETER would be head of all the Churches." The repetition of the words "Apostolic" and "apostle" indicates the argument used by the emperor: the patriarchate of Constantinople, made the capital only in 381 by imperial decree, could not pretend to be "ecumenical," while the patriarchate of Rome reached back to Peter himself.

Jean Durlait

Bibliography

JW, 1, 220; 2, 698.

LP, 1, 316.

Bertolini, O. "Bonifacio III," *DBI*, 12 (1970), 136–7.

Schneider, E. 17.—*ICUR*, 4158.

BONIFACE IV. (*b. in the city of Marses in the Italian province of Valeria, ?, d. Rome, 8 May 615). Elected pope on 25 August 608. Buried at St. Peter's in Rome. Saint and confessor (cult promoted at the time of the discovery of his tomb during the pontificate of Boniface VIII).*

"He invariably followed the counsel and example of his master, GREGORY [the Great]," continuing the latter's policy of fidelity to the emperor, no matter who, of contact with the Franks and the English, and of religious reform at Rome.

Nothing is known about his social origin or his life until his ordination as deacon, before 591. Gregory the Great's correspondence shows that Boniface carried out many missions in Italy. Above all, he is to be identified as the Bonifatius who, according to the *Dialogues*, acted as *dispensator*, that is, papal treasurer-paymaster for religious operations. Very close to Gregory, as were his two predecessors, he played a role in history that clearly was more important than might be believed from the brief note in the *Liber pontificalis*, some letters, and the few allusions in various chronicles.

Imperial confirmation of his election was undoubtedly delayed to enable the EXARCHATE OF RAVENNA to be present at his ordination and at the same time at the erection of the column bearing the statue of Phocas (1 August 608). The alliance among the emperor, his representative in Italy, and the city of Rome—which they no doubt wanted to last forever—then seemed triumphant. This position of strength led the Lombard king, Agilulf, into multiple truces, sometimes signed by the emperor himself. Despite the backing of Columbanus and of the LOMBARDS, supporters of the Three Chapters could not count on the traditional opposition between the pope's more pastoral aims and the purely political ones of the kings of Constantinople.

In the part of Italy that remained Byzantine, Boniface carried on as his illustrious predecessor had done. He won from Phocas the right to transform the PANTHEON, a pagan temple, into a church dedicated to the Virgin Mary, and proceeded to consecrate it, undoubtedly on 13 May 609. Imitating Gregory, he transformed his family home, clearly Roman, into a monastery. As metropolitan, he regularly convened SYNODS, and under his influence they took the decision that monks could be ordained priests and fully exercise their ministry.

At the same time, the prestige of the Roman patriarch spread farther west. Mellitus, a former monk sent out by Gregory the Great and now archbishop of London, gave the synod an international dimension by his participation in it. He returned to London with letters from the pope addressed to the king and to the "people." In Gaul, Boniface conferred the *pallium* on the bishop of Arles, chosen by the king of the FRANKS.

In this way, Boniface benefited from the last instances of the convergence of the general policy of the empire, the Italian policy of Rome, and the ambitions of the patriarch of the West.

Jean Durliat

Bibliography

JW, 1, 220–2; 2, 698, 739.
LP, 1, 317–18.
MGH, Epist., 3, 163–4, 170–7.
Bede, *HE*, 2, 4.
Bertolini, O. "Bonifacio IV," *DBI*, 12 (1970), 137–40; *Roma di fronte a Bisanzio e ai Longobardi*, Bologna, 1971.
Mansi, X, 504–8.
Schneider, E. 18.—*ICUR*, 4159.

BONIFACE V. (*b. Naples, ?, d. Rome, 25 October 625*). *Elected pope on 23 December 619. Buried at St. Peter's in Rome.*

This cleric, who clearly spent his entire career in the Church of Rome, felt the effects of the very grave crisis that swept over the Byzantine Empire and, powerless, shared in the first repercussions in Italy of the new situation, yet drew from it every favorable result for the clerical class from which he came, and which no doubt manipulated him. That is why his epitaph, written by a cleric from his own entourage, is so laudatory.

The son of a certain John whose social situation is unknown, Boniface belonged to a milieu sufficiently well off to enjoy the kind of ecclesiastical career that presupposed the choices he made after being elected pope. Nothing is known of what he did before that. After his election as bishop of Rome, his activities reveal the general evolution of the papacy during the 7th century. He was a faithful citizen of the empire; during the course of a SYNOD which he convened in accordance with the civil law calling for two annual COUNCILS under the metropolitan's authority, he won confirmation that all texts should be drafted "according to the prince's orders." Similarly, he does not seem to have taken any part in the revolt by the exarch, Eleutherius. The latter, sent in 616 to avenge the death of his predecessor and eliminate a usurper at Naples, had himself proclaimed emperor in 619. The archbishop of RAVENNA refused to crown him, and advised him to seek consecration in Rome, the cradle of the empire. But he was killed on the way by soldiers faithful to Heraclius, and the head of the "rebel" was sent to the "most pious" emperor. The descriptive terms used in the *Liber pontificalis* leave no doubt about Boniface's choice. He condemned it, but for want of means did nothing. The pope did not yet represent a political power in Italy as a whole, or even in the Byzantine part of it. His role in Lombard-Byzantine relations remained insignificant.

On the other hand, as head of the church of Rome, he had at his disposal increasing autonomy in the management of clerical affairs. Given the social power of the bishop and clergy in all the cities of the West and the East, that meant that he progressively became the master of Rome. Both the entry in the *Liber pontificalis*, and his epitaph describe him as munificent and solicitous for the common good, inclined to regard his own wealth as public revenue. Above all, they note his compassion for everyone, immediately before adding that he "gave the clergy their full salary." In other words, Boniface had control over his priests and, through them, those who benefited from public salaries, several thousand persons in all. Moreover, he reserved to the religious communities the right to transfer relics, and responsibility for the right of asylum. He continued the anti-Gregorian policy of Pope ADEODATUS and, either before his election or after his death, arranged for an annual salary supplement to be paid to the clergy of Rome. That is an example of the shrewd operating that characterized the Church of Rome, for, in places removed from the capital, the pontiff did not always respect the law.

Nothing is known of his relations with the Western Churches, except in England. He wrote to King Edwin of Northumbria, whose wife was a Christian and whose conversion he hoped for, as well as to Mellitus, the archbishop of Canterbury, and his successor, Justus. The states hostile to England were inclining more and more to Christianity. But a struggle for influence between the Irish and the "papists" began. Boniface tried to hold on to the gains made by Gregory the Great. Thus was confirmed, during this pontificate, a reciprocal ignorance on the part of the papacy and the monarchies, except for that of England, which would play a key role in the religious history of the West from the 8th century until the beginning of the Carolingian era.

Jean Durliat

Bibliography

JW, 1, 222–3; 2, 698.
LP, 1, 321–2.
RI, 80, 429–40.
Bede, *HE*, 2, 7–11.
Bertolini, O. "Bonifacio V," *DBI*, 12 (1970), 140–2; *Roma di fronte a Bisanzio e ai Longobardi*, Bologna, 1971.
Schneider, E. 20.—*ICUR*, 4162.

BONIFACE VI. (*b. Rome, ?, d. end of April or beginning of May 896). Elected around mid-April 896.*

After the death of FORMOSUS, Boniface was rather quickly elected pope by the people of Rome, around mid-April 896 (ordination 11 April?). About his origins, it is known only that he was a Roman, supposedly the son of a bishop named Hadrian, whose see has never been identified. Other important historical sources besides the *LIBER PONTIFICALIS*, mention this brief fourteen-day pontificate, above all the *Annales de Fulda* and Liutprand of Cremona. No authentic basis can be found for the claim, sometimes found in historical works, that Boniface was elected while Formosus was still living. His career before his election is also a subject for debate. In general, it is thought that canon 3 of the council of Ravenna (898) refers to the election of this pope. Consequently, at some earlier time Boniface must have been deposed (*ejectum*) as both a deacon and a priest; his rise to the higher orders must have been owing to the tumult of the people. Because of the brevity of this pontificate, no precise orientation can be discerned, a state of affairs that fosters the debate as to whether or not Boniface belonged to the Formosan party. Almost all the sources attribute his death

to gout. It is possible that he was buried at St. Peter's; according to Petrus Mallius, there was also some confusion with another pope. Since 1751, he has no longer been included in the official list of popes.

Klaus Herbers

Bibliography

JW, 1, 439.
LP, 2, 228.
Baix, F. "Boniface VI," *DHGE*, 9 (1937), 899–900.
Bertolini, P. "Bonifacio VI," *DBI*, 12 (1970), 142–3.

[BONIFACE VII]. *Franco (b. Rome, d. July 985). Antipope elected in June 974.*

The pontificate of Boniface VII has contributed largely to the formation of the extremely negative image of the papacy during this "dark century." His name remains linked to the assassination of his predecessor, BENEDICT VI (973–4), captured by the Romans and killed in July 974. A month earlier, at the end of June 974, thanks to the preponderating influence of the noble Roman Crescentius, who had already played a leading role in the arrest of Benedict VI, the Roman DEACON Franco *ex patre Ferrutio* was elected pope under the name Boniface VII. The assassination of Benedict VI was carried out on orders from Boniface VII by a priest, of whom we know only that his name was Stephen, with the assistance his brother. Before the crime was committed, the imperial legate, Count Sicco of Spoleto, had tried to intervene. He had demanded, in vain, that the pope, detained in CASTEL SANT'ANGELO, be set free. The assassination of Benedict VI clearly was carried out with the assurance that the Roman people and, at their head, Crescentius of Theodora would continue to give Boniface VII unreserved support, and that the emperor, Otto II, probably would have no intention of intervening militarily. But the course of events showed that Boniface VII had badly misjudged the situation, for the Romans, at least the greatest number of them, did not accept the fait accompli. With Sicco's backing, Boniface was chased out of Rome; he fled (July–August 974), probably to southern Italy, then under Byzantine rule, and the bishop of Sutri was elected pope in October 974 at Rome under the name BENEDICT VII.

A synod, convened probably at the end of 974, condemned Boniface VII. He turns up again only in 980: he returned to Rome and managed to drive out Benedict VII, who, for his part, appealed to Otto II for help (summer of 980). With the aid of the emperor, who had hastened to Italy in the meantime, Benedict VII succeeded in expelling Boniface from Rome, but not until March 981. Boniface then fled to Byzantium.

At the end of April 984, Boniface VII was able to impose his power at Rome once more. The pope at that time, JOHN XIV (983–4), the legitimate successor of Benedict VII, suffered the same fate as Benedict VI: captured and imprisoned in Castel Sant'Angelo toward the end of April 984, he died a violent death there on 20 August 984. Boniface VII then reigned at Rome until the end of July 985. With the weakening of the imperial power—Otto II had died in 983 of the effects of malaria—there was no imperial intervention at Rome. Although certainly opposed by some of the clergy and people of the Eternal City, Boniface VII managed to hold on until he died suddenly at the end of July 985. After he was gone, the Romans gave vent to their hatred and outrage by profaning his corpse and subjecting it to the enactment of a posthumous deposition.

The pontificate of Pope Boniface VII, sullied from the outset by the defamatory epitaph *maleficius*, thus belongs to one of the darkest chapters in the history of the papacy of the 10th century. He had detractors even among his contemporaries, for example the celebrated Gerbert of Aurillac, archbishop of Reims, who was himself later called to ascend the throne of St. Peter. Boniface VII's detractors did not have words strong enough to denounce his administration. The criticism resurged at the time of the Reformation in the polemical confrontations between Protestants and Catholics. However, as shown by his two attempts to take over in Rome, Boniface VII was able, for a while at least, to count on the support of a large part of the Roman NOBILITY, even if, in the absence of sources, it is impossible to identify more precisely the different factions that gave him their backing. As had already been the case for earlier popes, southern Italy under Byzantine domination was the ideal place of refuge for popes who could not count on Emperor Otto's political support.

Hans-Henning Körtum

Bibliography

LP, 2, 255–9.
Baix, F. "Boniface VII," *DHGE*, 9 (1937), 900–4.
Delogu, P. "Bonifacio VII," *DBI*, 12 (1970), 143–1.
Schieffer, R. "Bonifaz VII." *LexMA*, 2 (1981–3), 414.
Zimmermann, H. *Papsturkunden*, 1, 553–4.

BONIFACE VIII. *Benedetto Caetani (b. Anagni, 1235/40, d. Rome, 11 October 1303). Elected on 24 December 1294 at Naples, crowned in Rome on 23 January 1295. Buried at St. Peter's in Rome.*

Boniface VIII was the last pope of the Middle Ages, the one who saw the notion of a temporal power subject to papal authority shattered by a state mindful thereafter of its own autonomy. His name is documented in 1260 when, already a canon in Anagni, he was also named a canon in Todi, where his uncle was bishop, and where he studied law under Bartole. From that time on, there were concerns about his morals. He continued the study of law

at Spoleto and Bologna. A papal NOTARY and CONSISTORIAL ADVOCATE, he began in 1264 in Paris, and continued the next year in England, a diplomatic career in the service of two LEGATES who would become popes and help him in his career. The first, HADRIAN V, sent him back to Paris in 1276 to receive the tithes for the CRUSADE; the second, MARTIN IV, made him CARDINAL deacon of St-Pierre-aux-Liens in 1281, authorizing him to keep all the prebends. Over the next ten years, the most varied diplomatic missions were entrusted to him and brought him incomparable experience. At Paris in 1290, along with Cardinal Gerard of Sabina, he settled the conflict between diocesan and religious clergy with both skill and authority, but also with polemical gibes that left the French capital with lasting bad feelings toward him. He also took part in the Tarascon accords in February 1291 between the houses of Anjou and Aragon.

On his return to Rome, after being ordained a priest at Orvieto, he was promoted to cardinal priest of S. Martino ai Monti in the summer of 1291, once again without having to give up any of his benefices. The same year, his brother Roffredo was elected a Roman senator. The Caetani, who belonged to the minor nobility of southern Latium, from then on could aspire to rival the Roman barons. Thanks to his large income from the accumulation of prebends, and to a purchasing policy as judicious as it was unscrupulous, the cardinal amassed a considerable landed estate over a dozen years, especially around his birthplace, but also in the kingdom of Naples and the Patrimony of St. PETER. Accumulated bad feelings among those who, under skillful constraint, had been forced to give up their family domains, played a large part in the events that led to the pope's tragic end.

A long vacancy began in April 1292 with the death of NICHOLAS IV, during which Cardinal Caetani kept his distance from both the Colonna and the Orsini, whose rivalry prevented the election of a successor. When, finally, at Perugia, on 5 July 1294, the hermit Pietro del Morrone was elected and took the name CELESTINE V, Caetani gave him his vote without hesitation. However, the new pope quickly saw that he was not the man for the position and considered renouncing it. Despite the legends that would circulate on the subject, he was not led to this decision by Caetani's stratagems, though it seems that the latter was consulted and that his advice played a decisive role in the affair. Celestine abdicated on 13 December 1294, and on 24 December at Naples the cardinal of the title of S. Martino ai Monti succeeded him, taking the name Boniface VIII.

One of the new pope's first decisions was to revoke or suspend the measures adopted by his predecessor—suspected of having been extorted from him in his excessive simplicity—and to put under surveillance the man who had become once again simply Pietro del Morrone;

he was later imprisoned in the fortress of Fumone, where he died. The new pontificate was marked by firmness, and Boniface's determination to control things himself was quickly confirmed by an almost complete change of personnel in the CURIA, in favor of men more devoted to him.

On the political level, Boniface inherited the difficult matter of Sicily. One of the aims of his pontificate was to bring the island back to obedience to the church and return it to the house of Anjou. On 20 June 1295, a group of accords known as the peace of Anagni seemed to resolve the major problems, but displeased the most interested party, the Sicilians themselves, who on 15 January 1296 declared Frederick of Aragon king of Sicily. Boniface recognized him as such after the peace of Caltabellota, which gave the island independence on 31 August 1302. Meanwhile, the pope's efforts to regain control of this fief of the Church had been unceasing, with the concurrence of Charles II of Anjou and Charles of Valois. His policy in this area ended in failure.

The HOLY ROMAN EMPIRE was his second major political challenge. Adolph of Nassau, elected king of the Romans in 1292, was not supported by the pope, who thought little of him and never crowned him. However, after the king was deposed by the diet of Mainz on 23 June 1298, and then died on 2 July, Boniface took his part and excommunicated the newly elected Albert of Austria for felony against his dead lord. It was only on 30 April 1303 that the pope, forced to switch alliances by his conflict with France, recognized Albert's election and accepted his oath of office. This about-face would be one of the grievances against the pope when he himself was accused.

Also of note, on a purely political level, were the truces Boniface succeeded in imposing on France and England in May 1295 and June 1297, and his interventions in the successions to the thrones of Hungary and Poland in 1295. The pope thereby affirmed an integral part of his conception of the papacy, that of its role as arbiter of crowns. It was precisely this conception of a pope to whom every creature on earth is subject that, in opposition to the conception that was developing in the court of Philip the Fair, would transform a financial dispute that at the outset was like any other of its kind into a dramatic conflict. Inseparably linked to the differences that pitted the pope and the Colonna against each other, it increasingly dominated his pontificate and led to his tragic end. At its origin was the old and thorny question of the EXEMPTION of priests from the taxes levied by the temporal sovereigns. This was a privilege supported by long tradition. Boniface's innovation was not in claiming the exemption, but in demanding that all taxes affecting the clergy should be subject to prior authorization by the HOLY SEE and thereby denying the sovereignty of the states in fiscal matters. The claim, set forth in the bull *Clericis laicos* of 24 February 1296, ran into fierce opposition from the two kingdoms at which it was especially aimed, England and France, which had the greatest need of new sources of revenue because they were at war with each other. France in particular reacted violently, and Philip the Fair in reprisal, ordered that no valuable exports should leave the kingdom, and so none would find their way to Rome. Boniface responded with his letter *Ineffabilis amoris* of 20 September 1296, the first of his major polemical writings against France. However, at that stage nobody wanted to break off relations, so, without retracting *Clericis laicos*, Boniface authorized, on 7 February 1297, an interpretation of it that, for the moment, ended the conflict.

The same year there began the other crisis that would shake the pontificate: the rupture between Boniface and two of the most influential cardinals in the Curia, Giacomo Colonna and his nephew Pietro, members of a great Roman baronial family that was seriously threatened by the expansion of the estates of the Caetani. On 3 May 1297, Stefano Colonna, Pietro's brother, seized a considerable sum of money being transferred from Anagni to Rome for some new purchases. Boniface cited the two cardinals, who restored the money but refused to deliver up their kinsman and to hand over their castles as surety. The pope convened a CONSISTORY for 10 May for the purpose of examining their case, but as that day dawned they signed a manifesto at Lunghezza that questioned the legitimacy of Boniface's election and appealed to a COUNCIL. Boniface then declared that all ecclesiastics of the Colonna were stripped of their honors and benefices, and soon afterwards excommunicated them; for their part, the two cardinals issued other statements that enlarged the scope of their accusations, denouncing Boniface's absolutism and his financial activities, but without mentioning either HERESY or immorality. Before the end of the year, Boniface launched a military action against the Colonna that turned into a crusade. After the surrender of Palestrina, their principal fief, the two cardinals and their relations made an act of submission at Rieti, but after being sent into forced residence at Tivoli, they escaped and began a clandestine existence that later would lead them to France, where the king took up their cause.

Meanwhile, the situation between Rome and the court of Philip the Fair had eased. The CANONIZATION of St. Louis (11 August 1297) was a sign of this, and for the next three years there were no open hostilities, even if the fundamental disagreement continued. Two events that remain linked to Boniface's memory occurred during this period of calm: the publication of a sixth book of the *DECRETALS*, the fruit of his experience as a jurist, and above all his proclamation of the first jubilee year in history, that of 1300. The repercussions of this unexpected initiative would reinforce the prestige of the pontiff and refill his coffers. However, the Colonna and those who gave them asylum remained excluded from the benefits of the INDUL-GENCE. The fire smoldered under the ashes.

The situation became inflamed once more when Boniface, without consulting the king, raised the city of Pamiers to the rank of a diocese and named to it a monk he favored, Bernard Saisset. The king had the new bishop arrested, which drew a severe admonition from the pope (the letter *Ausculta fili* of 5 December 1301). The court of France replied by accusing Saisset of heresy. Boniface opposed his having been placed on trial, and called a SYNOD of the French bishops in Rome for the end of 1302. A number of them attended, and heard the famous bull *Unam sanctam* (18 November 1302), in which, after recalling that the Church held both the temporal and the spiritual sword, Boniface made the statement that "every human creature, as a necessity of salvation, is subject in all matters to the Roman pontiff." By way of conclusion to the synod, the king was sent a series of urgent requests concerning the administration of the kingdom and the Church. The response of Philip the Fair was cautious, as he played for time, but positions hardened when, soon afterwards, Pierre Flote was succeeded as adviser to the king on religious affairs by Guillaume de Nogaret, an unscrupulous jurist. Instead of remaining on the defensive, Nogaret attacked and, on 12 March 1303, read in the Royal Council an indictment that denounced Boniface for usurpation, heresy, and simony, and demanded that the king call a council to judge the matter. Soon afterwards, armed with a very large mandate, he left for Italy, determined to persuade the pope to accept the council's decision. On 13 and 14 June, the accusations were renewed and expanded at a meeting at the Louvre; the king espoused the council's appeal, to which the French clergy began to rally. On 15 August, Boniface rejected the accusations and announced steps against Philip the Fair. A bull of excommunication was prepared, to be published on 8 September. The day before, Nogaret, accompanied by a small armed force and aided by accomplices, entered Anagni, where the pope resided. The intention was clearly to force the pope's hand, but Sciarra Colonna and various representatives of the nobility of southern Latium, whom Boniface had despoiled and humiliated, were likewise present. The raid degenerated into rioting and pillage. Boniface was arrested and held under armed guard for two days. An about-face by the people of Anagni then forced the French to free the pope and flee. Boniface left for Rome a few days later, and died there on 11 October. The French court, and especially Nogaret, wanting to be cleared of their role in the outrage, persuaded CLEMENT V to open heresy proceedings against the dead pope. They began in 1310 and were never concluded, but they made for a gathering of testimonies that historians can neither accept nor reject as a whole.

Boniface had superior intelligence and therefore a keener critical faculty than many of his contemporaries; he combined a lofty idea of the pontifical authority with an evident will to power, turned to the service of his own family; he was endowed with a sure sense of government, but also with a cynicism to which the management of other mortals often leads. He was beyond doubt an important pope, but the man of God could not be seen in him. To many who approached him, he gave the impression of being what later came to be called a free spirit, and an unscrupulous man. In the circumstances, it is not improbable that his morals were not those of a saint. If, as noted earlier, he can be called "the last pope of the Middle Ages," it was certainly because, first of all, he was the last defender of papal absolutism; but perhaps the title fits him even more because of the way his life announced the crisis of a certain kind of Christian world, undermined from within by the emergence of another world whose logic was no longer that of the faith.

Jean Coste

Bibliography

Boase, T. S. R. *Boniface VIII*, London, 1933.

Caetani, G. *Regesta chartarum*, I, Perugia, 1922.

Courtenay, W. "Between Pope and King: The Parisian Letters of Adhesion of 1303," *Speculum*, 71 (1996), 577–605.

Denton, J. H. *Philip the Fair and the Ecclesiastical Assemblies of 1294–1295*, Philadelphia, 1991.

Digard, G., et al., ed. *Registres des papes du XIIIe siècle* [Urban IV, Martin IV, Honorius IV, Nicholas IV, Boniface VIII], Paris, 1884–9, 4 vols.

Digard, G. *Philippe le Bel et le Saint-Siège de 1285 à 1304*, 2 vols., Paris, 1936.

Dupré-Theseider, E. "Bonifacio VIII," *DBI*, 12 (1970), 146–70 [important bibliography up to 1967].

Dupuy, P. *Histoire du différend d'entre le pape Boniface VIII et Philippe le Bel roy de France*, Paris, 1655.

Favier, J. *Philippe le Bel*, Paris, 1978.

Fawtier, R. "L'attentat d'Anagni," *MAH*, 60 (1948), 153–179.

Frugoni, A. "Il giubileo di Bonifacio VIII," *Bollettino dell'Istituto storico per il Medievo*, 62 (1950), 1–121.

Holtzmann, R. *Wilhelm von Nogaret*, Freiburg im Breisgau, 1898.

Izbicki, T. M. "*Clericis Laicos* and the Canonist," in *Popes, Teachers and Canon Law in the Middle Ages*, ed. Sweeney, J. R. and Chodorow, S., Ithaca, N. Y., 1989, 179–90.

Le Bras, G. "Boniface VIII symphoniste et modérateur," *Mélanges d'histoire du Moyen Âge L. Halphen*, Paris, 1951, 383–94.

Menache, S. "Un peuple qui a sa demeure à part. Boniface VIII et le sentiment national français," *Francia*, 12 (1984), 193–208.

Muldoon, J. "Boniface VIII as Defender of Royal Power," in *Popes, Teachers and Canon Law in the Middle Ages*, ed. Sweeney, J. R. and Chodorow, S., Ithaca, N. Y., 1989, 62–73.

Rivière, J. *Le Problème de l'Église et de l'État au temps de Philippe le Bel. Étude de théologie positive*, Louvain, 1926.

Schmidt, T. "Bonifatius VIII," *LexMA*, 2 (1985), 414–16; "Papst Bonifaz VIII. und die Idolatrie," *QFIAB*, 66 (1986), 75–107, *Der Bonifaz-prozess*, Cologne-Vienna, 1989, (bibliography 444–65).

Schmidt, T. *Libri rationum Camerae Bonifatii papae VIII*, Vatican City, 1984.

Sibilia, S. *Bonifacio VIII*, Rome, 1949.

Wenck, K. "War Bonifaz VIII. ein Ketzer?," *HZ*, 94 (1905), 1–66.

Wolter, H. *Storia della Chiesa*, ed. M. Jedin, V, 1, 1983, (bibliography 401–4).

Wood, C. T., ed. *Philip the Fair and Boniface VIII*, 2nd ed., 1976.

BONIFACE IX. *Pietro Tomacelli (b. Naples, mid-14th c., d. Rome, 1 October 1404). Elected on 2 November 1389, crowned on 9 November 1389.*

Of a family of old Neapolitan stock, Pietro Tomacelli seems to have launched himself early into an ecclesiastical career. He had little education, but, according to some contemporaries, very high morals combined with real political intuition. He made progress in the circles of the CURIA and while still an adolescent obtained from his compatriot URBAN VI the rank of cardinal deacon of S. Giorgio and, in 1385, the title of cardinal priest of Sta Anastasia. Against the two rival parties of Poncello Orsini and of Angelo Acciaiuoli, supported by Florence, the rump CONCLAVE made up of thirteen cardinals, convened hastily after the death of Urban VI (15 October 1389), on 2 November elected the man who was called "the cardinal of Naples." He was only thirty-five or forty years old, which promised a long reign.

Crowned on 9 November, Boniface IX inherited with a vengeance the immense difficulties linked to the Great Schism of the West and to the changing political configurations on the Italian peninsula, toward which his predecessor had adopted a brusque and authoritarian attitude.

A scarcely tolerated guest in Rome rather than the ruler of the city, which was governed by a commune, the pope saw the pontifical patrimony pass from his authority to benefit the party supporting CLEMENT VII, who had the see in Avignon. One of his first acts was to restore the purple to the four cardinals who had been deposed by Urban VI, thereby winning their backing. In the kingdom of Naples, he took a stand against the Angevin domination, reestablished peace with Margaret of Durazzo, the widow of King Charles III and a refugee at Gaeta, and

crowned her son Ladislas, who was barely seventeen years old, and to whom he gave Cardinal Acciaiuoli as counselor. Undertaking to reconquer large portions of the PAPAL STATES from Gascon and Breton mercenaries in the pay of the Clementines, he recovered sovereignty over Bologna, thereby thwarting the designs of John Galeassi Visconti, the master of Verona and Padua, who coveted the city. After the assassination of Rinaldo Orsini (14 April 1390), he entrusted Spoleto to the care of his own brother, Marino Tomacelli. At Rome, by threatening to move the Curia, he obtained the commune's recognition of ecclesiastical immunities. Subsequently, he contracted with the city to renew its defense system (11 September 1391). The papal army, defeated in a first battle by Giovanni Scarria of Vico, who held Viterbo, in the end overcame him (15 June 1393).

The jubilee of 1390, decreed by Urban VI, who had wanted to celebrate it every thirty-three years, was above all a financial success. Boniface IX himself took as a cut nearly half of the sums collected, and he speculated widely in indulgences. The jubilee of 1400, though involving only the obedience of Avignon, provided another opportunity to levy on the pilgrims who had flocked to Rome. The cost of the pope's external policies was also partly financed by the sale of privileges. The very evening of his coronation, Boniface decreed that henceforth the ANNATES would be paid by all benefices, religious or diocesan, with or without *cura animarum* (the cure of souls). His pontificate was punctuated by resistance—isolated, except in the northeast of the empire—condemnations, and lawsuits against the *ius spolii*. Boniface IX cannot be totally exonerated of the charges of nepotism made by historians: even if there were justifiable security reasons for naming his brothers to the duchy of Spoleto and the marquessate of Ancona, there was evident abuse in the appointment of his nephew Ceccho as administrator of the monastery of Rieti and of his cousin Arrigo as abbot of Monte Cassino.

With regard to Western Christianity, Boniface seemed never to doubt his legitimacy. He was "Pope of Rome, therefore true pope," according to his own expression; the only acceptable solution for ending the SCHISM was the pure and simple abdication of his rival, a view in line with the intransigent views of his predecessor Urban VI. In fact, he made efforts to facilitate a coming together, but it took second place in his thinking to a strategy aimed at strengthening the loyalty of the German lands and England, while exploiting the French desire for a restoration of unity. In 1391, at the suggestion of two envoys sent by Clement VII, Bartholomew of Ravenna and, especially, Peter of Mondovia, the prior of the Carthusian monastery of Asti, Boniface IX sent a letter himself to Charles VI, who received the papal message in December 1392. The king, after hinting at a double resignation, was struck by fit of insanity and cut short the discussions;

from then on, he was advised by the University of Paris, which, in a brief probably written by Nicholas de Clamanges (3 June 1394), proposed two other paths: compromise or a general COUNCIL. The death of Clement VII (16 September 1394), far from settling the division, gave rise to the election of BENEDICT XIII (Cardinal Pedro de Luna). He immediately took a hard line, by refusing conciliation and developing networks of influence on the frontiers of the empire (Metz, Toul, Verdun, Cambrai). The empire was still essentially Roman, thanks to King Wenceslas, a pillar of Boniface IX's policy, and so it remained until Wenceslas's encounter with the king and regents of France at Reims (23 March 1398) and his deposition (20 August 1400) by Robert of Bavaria, whom Boniface IX, after a number of delays, finally recognized at the consistory of 10 July 1403. After having left Rome for eleven months (2 October 1392 to 10 September 1393)—during which he stayed in Perugia, where he took over the direction of the commune, and then, under armed pressure from Biordo, in Assisi—the pope managed to destroy the Roman communal government by uncovering the plot fomented by Onorato Gaetani to reestablish the domination of the nobility (1399). From then on *rigidus imperator* (in the words of Gobelinus Persona), he proceeded to reconstruct Castel Sant'Angelo (1403), which symbolized the triumph of the papal power.

Having regained the obedience of France the same year (it had been withdrawn in 1398), Benedict XIII sent four envoys to Rome in September 1404, without results; the conference ended on 29 September in an exchange of virulent reproaches. That evening, sick with kidney stones, Boniface IX suffered violent pain, and then a fever that ended his life on 1 October 1404.

In religious matters, the pontificate was that of one who acted more as "an Italian prince" (M. Jansen) than as head of the Church; it was noted for little except the 7 October 1391 canonization of Bridget of Sweden (who had died in Rome on 23 July 1373), and the provision (1402) that in times of interdict the religious clergy could celebrate mass behind closed doors. Several favors granted to UNIVERSITIES in the empire (Prague, Heidelberg, Erfurt, Cologne), and the granting of an indulgence for recitation of three Hail Marys at the sound of the morning bell, were political decisions; the pontificate of Boniface IX and, to a certain extent, the very personality of the pope were markedly political.

François Jankowiak

Bibliography

Esch, A. *Bonifaz IX. und der Kirchenstaat. . .*, Tübigen, 1969 (Bibl. der Deutschen hist. Instituts in Rom, 29).

Fantasia, M. *I papi pugliesi: Bonifacio IX, Innocenzo XII, Benedetto XIII*, Fasano, 1987.

Jansen, M. *Papst Bonifazius IX. und seine Beziehungen zur deutschen Kirche*, Freiburg im Breisgau, 1904.

Rapp, F. *L'Église et la vie religieuse à la fin du Moyen Âge*, Paris, 1981.

Vansteenberghe, E. "Boniface IX," *DHGE*, IX (1937), 909–22.

BONNET OF THE HOLY SPIRIT. See **Blessed or Holy Hat and Sword.**

BREVIARY, ROMAN. The breviary in use in the Roman Church at the beginning of the 16th century, spread by the development of printing after 1474, derived from the abridged breviary of the CURIA, propagated by the Franciscans in the 13th century, with a sanctorale that had been enriched over the course of time. A new breviary favoring private recitation, put together in 1535 by Quiñones, was given a lukewarm reception. The council of TRENT entrusted the reform of the breviary to the pope. The text published by PIUS V in 1568 was meant to be definitive. However, it underwent revision until 1632.

Quiñones and the Reform of the Breviary in the 16th Century. Under the influence of various trends, both humanist and traditional, a need for reform made itself felt. CLEMENT VII asked the CARDINAL of the title of Sta Croce, the Spanish Franciscan Francisco Quiñones, to undertake the desired reform, and to return the office to its ancient form, while removing long passages, errors and complexities. The new breviary, *Breviarium romanum ex sacra potissimum scriptura et probatis sanctorum historiis collectum et concinatum . . .*, appeared in 1535 at Rome, and enjoyed quick success. Three principles had guided Quiñones: the weekly recitation of the psalter, with a new distribution of psalms among the hours; the reading once a year of at least the major parts of the Holy Scriptures; an office of equal length for each day. Each hour had three psalms, with the *Benedictus* at lauds, the *Magnificat* at vespers, and the *Nunc dimittis* at compline. The psalms followed one after the other for each hour and each day in such a way that there would be no repetition during the week. The number of readings at matins was set at three once again, and the short readings at the little hours, at lauds, and at vespers were eliminated. The first reading at matins was taken from the Old Testament, the second from the New Testament, and the third, for the feasts of saints, from various accounts of their lives. For certain days (Sundays, weekdays, feasts of the Lord and of the Virgin, etc.) a homily from the Fathers on the Gospel or the New Testament would be used. The legends of the saints were not retained unless their veracity was assured. Only the invitatories, the hymns (matins and vespers), the antiphons of matins, lauds, and vespers (reintroduced in 1536), and the prayer of the third lesson of vespers would vary. Verses, chapters, and responses disappeared. The reform was radical. The breviary, conceived as an instrument for the education of priests, was well received by a clergy who more and more favored private recitation over the singing of the hours in choir; but it was rejected by others. If the idea of a breviary better adapted for private recitation was good, its realization was less successful, and the solemn celebration of the hours could not be dissociated from its private recitation.

The Reform of Pius V. In 1556 PAUL IV forbade the use of the Quiñones breviary, but he died before being able to take up his old project for revising the book. The council of Trent took it up under PIUS IV, but the work was far from finished when the council ended on 4 December 1563. The reform of the breviary was therefore entrusted to the pope. The commission took a direction opposite to that of Quiñones. It was no longer a question of making a new liturgy of the hours, but of returning to a primitive form and adapting the old breviary, while still taking into account the changes introduced over the years. In the end, no difference would be made between the private recitation and the solemn, public office. The legends of the saints fell special victim, and a more judicious choice was made of lessons from the Fathers. The passages drawn from the Scriptures were sometimes divided and regrouped. The prayers were corrected using the best manuscripts. The liturgical year kept its three major cycles: Christmas, with Advent and Epiphany; Easter, from Septuagesima Sunday to the octave of the Ascension; Pentecost and the feasts that followed. In compensation, the number of saints' feast days was reduced, to avoid too much curtailment of the office for Sundays and weekdays, but particular Churches and monasteries were authorized to make up for this reduction by introducing their own offices. The new breviary was published in Rome in 1568: *Breviarium romanum, ex decreto sacrosancti concilii Tridentini restitutum, Pii V Pont. max. jussu editum.* The BULL *Quod nobis* of 9 July 1568 contained the reminder that thenceforth the Quiñones breviary and any other breviary that could not be proved to have been in existence for two hundred years, or that had not been expressly approved by the pope, could not be used. Bishops and their chapters were therefore left free either to adopt the *Breviarium Pianum* or to keep using their ancient version, if they had one (Milan, Aquileia, Toledo, Lyon, etc.). The success of the new breviary was rapid, and a series of synods held after 1569 decided to adopt it. In France, only the provinces of Lyon and Besançon and the dioceses of Vienne, Paris, Meaux, Chartres, Sens, Bourges, and Arras preserved their old books, while correcting some texts and rubrics.

From Pius V to Urban VIII. The text of Pius V's breviary was not to be modified. GREGORY XIII authorized only the celebration of the feast of the ROSARY in 1573 (in thanksgiving for the victory of LEPANTO) and the transformation of the feast of St. Anne into a universal feast, and introduced, beginning in 1583, the calendar he had reformed the previous year. However, from 1588 on, SIXTUS V made some changes, by adding certain feasts and reestablishing some feasts that had been suppressed, such as the Presentation on 21 November. The texts of the Scriptures were made to conform with the Vulgate edition of the Bible that he had had established. GREGORY XIV set up a commission to finalize the reform undertaken by Sixtus V, but it was under CLEMENT VIII that the work bore fruit: double majors were instituted, and some feasts were elevated to double of the second class. The corrected breviary appeared in 1602. From then on, it could not be printed without the authorization of the local ordinary, and only in conformity with the Vatican edition. A final revision was made under Urban VIII, in particular of the historical lessons and the sermons and homilies, but also of the hymns, some of which were composed by the pope. No further corrections were made, except for a few changes in the calendar of saints. The breviary of Urban VIII, published in 1632, in its principal parts—psalter, proper of the season, common of the saints—remained the *vulgata recensio* of the breviary until the reform of PIUS X and the promulgation of a new breviary in 1913.

Jean-Loup Lemaitre

Bibliography

Batiffol, P. *Histoire du bréviaire romain*, 3rd ed., Paris, 1911.

Baumer, S. *Histoire du bréviaire*, Fr. trans. Biron, Paris, 1905.

Bergel, A. "Die Emendationen des Römischen Breviers unter Papst Clemens VIII. in handschriftlichen Quellen dargestellt," *Zeitschrift für katholische Theologie*, 8 (1884), 289–343.

Bohatta, H. *Bibliographie der Breviere*, Leipzig, 1937, 1–80, nos. 1–948.

Bouchère, M. "Bréviaire," *Catholicisme*, 2 (1949), 253–8.

Oppenheim, F. "Breviario," *EC*, 3 (1949), 81–6.

Salmon, P. *L'Office divin. Histoire de la formation du bréviaire,* Paris, 1959; *L'Office divin au Moyen Âge,* Paris, 1967.

BRIEF. A brief is a papal letter with characteristics both external (medium, script, seal) and internal (form) that distinguish it from a BULL, which is much more solemn. The oldest preserved brief (7 October 1390) is in the Archivio di Stato of Mantua, and emanated from Pope BONIFACE IX. In a brief, the pope's name, at the top and center of the page, is followed by his ordinal number. The person to whom the brief is addressed is designated by a vocative (*Dilecte fili*), and the date is expressed in days of the month, as is the current custom, and not in the *calends, nones*, and *ides* of the Julian CALENDAR, used in bulls. The document, always written on a very white and very fine vellum, in an elegant italic script, is sealed with red wax with the seal of the pope known as the FISHERMAN'S RING, mentioned in the final phrase (*sub anulo piscatoris*). In 1842, GREGORY XVI substituted a red ink stamp with an analogous representation for the seal of stamped wax—very few of which have been preserved intact, because opening the document broke the seal. The number of briefs increased in the 15th century, and in the modern period, the brief has become the main instrument of correspondence for political affairs and ecclesiastical discipline. In many cases, the Holy See has used briefs or bulls indifferently: it was by a brief that PIUS IX in 1850 reestablished the English hierarchy; it was by a bull that LEO XIII in 1878 reestablished the Scottish. The Society of Jesus was instituted by a bull of PAUL III, suppressed by a brief of 1773, and reestablished by a bull of 1814. Briefs are now classified in different collections in the Vatican Archives according to date, content, and addressee. Until 1487, all briefs, without distinction, were written and dispatched by the secretaries of the pope; a number of their minutes and registers are preserved in the *Armaria* XXXIX and XL. By the bull *Non debet* of 31 December 1487, INNOCENT VIII distinguished between apostolic secretaries and domestic secretaries: the former were regrouped in the apostolic secretariat and given responsibility for so-called common briefs (general concessions of favors); the latter were responsible for political and ecclesiastical affairs, and their briefs were called secret or of the Curia (*brevia secreta* or *de Curia*). There resulted two distinct series of briefs, which later underwent further divisions. In the years 1560–6, the secret briefs were entrusted according to subject, to different secretaries, themselves forming two secretariats: the SECRETARIAT OF BRIEFS and the SECRETARIAT OF BRIEFS TO PRINCES. In 1678, the former apostolic secretariat was disbanded, and the drafting of the briefs for which it was still responsible was passed to the DATARY.

François-Charles Uginet

Bibliography

de Witte, C. M. "Notes sur les plus anciens registres de brefs," *Bulletin de l'Institut historique belge de Rome*, 31 (1958), 160.

Moroni, G. *Dizionario di erudizione storico-ecclesiastica*, VI, Venice, 1840, 115–25.

Rabikauskas, P. "De significatione verborum 'bulla,' 'breve,'" *Periodica de re morali, canonica, liturgica*, 55 (1966), 85–92.

BULL. The term "bull" designates the lead seal attached to certain pontifical ACTS and, by extension, to the documents themselves. The use of this type of seal, borrowed from the Roman and Byzantine emperors, is not peculiar to the papacy. In the Mediterranean basin, it was widespread very early (from the 4th century on). The emperors and kings of Italy in the 9th century, the Spanish sovereigns, the doges of Venice (until the fall of the Most Serene Republic in 1797), many archbishops and bishops, counts and dukes, judges and notaries, and cities all sealed their acts with bulls in this way.

The popes used the lead bull at least from the 6th century. The oldest known example is a bull of ADEODATUS I (615–18), with a representation of the Good Shepherd on the obverse side and the name of the pope on the reverse. Then, until the middle of the 11th century, bulls had only inscriptions in capital letters: the name of the pope on the obverse, his title on the reverse, in the genitive case and accompanied by crosses. At first, the pope's name was set out horizontally in two or three lines; then, under LEO IV (847–55) and BENEDICT III (855–8), in monogram; and finally, beginning with Benedict III, in a circle around a decorative element (flower or star). LEO IX, in 1049, added the pope's ordinal number to his name. VICTOR II (1055–7) put on the obverse side the figure of ST. PETER receiving the KEY, handed to him from heaven by Christ, with the phrase *Tu pro me navem liquisti, suscipe clavem*, and on the reverse a building symbolizing the Church with the inscription *Aurea Roma* and the pope's name in the genitive case. His successors retained the principle of these figured representations, but modified them according to their liking, and added various phrases that recalled the PRIMACY of the Apostolic See. Finally, PASCHAL II (1099–1118) established a definitive style: on the obverse, the heads of the apostles ST. PAUL and ST. PETER (recognizable by their hair and their beard, sketched with lines and dots respectively) separated by a cross and surmounted by the abbreviated phrase *SPA SPE* (*Sanctus Paulus, Sanctus Petrus*), the whole inscription surrounded by dots; on the reverse, the pope's name in the nominative case, with his ordinal number. The seal was about 1.37 inches/3.5 centimeters in diameter, and 0.2 inches/0.5 centimeters thick. Allowing for a few minor variations, this design was not changed in any major way after the 12th century except by the Venetian pope PAUL II (1464–71), who had placed designs inspired by the bulls of the doges of Venice on both sides of the bull (on the obverse, the apostles seated, on the reverse, a scene of papal audience). On 18 January 1931, PIUS XI increased the diameter and the weight of the bull, and changed the image of the apostles.

In the 13th, 14th, and 15th centuries, between their election and their coronation the popes used an incomplete lead seal, the half-bull (*bulla dimidia, blanca, defectiva*), not bearing their name on the reverse. The acts sealed in this way were drafted with some particular features: in the superscription, the pope's name was followed by the word *electus*; for the date, the formula *suscepti a nobis apostolatus officii* replaced the words *pontificatus nostri*; and a special clause set forth the reasons for the use of the half-bull. The oldest known original sealed in this way is an act of GREGORY X of 4 March 1272. The bull was used to seal pontifical acts only until the 13th century (when mention is first made of the FISHERMAN'S RING, used from the end of the 14th century to validate BRIEFS). Privileges, solemn letters, and letters conferring favors were sealed with silk cords (red and yellow from the time of ALEXANDER III), and pastoral and closed letters were sealed with hemp cords. The silk or hemp cords passed through two holes in the fold made at the bottom of the page of parchment, except in the case of closed letters, which had no such fold but were folded on themselves and which the bull served to close, and in the case of bulls *in forma libelli*, where the attachments of the seal went through the full thickness of the document at its lower left corner. Apart from the acts of the popes, those of the councils of Constance (1414–18) and of Basel (1431–7) were sealed with bulls.

The lead seal was attached to documents by two *bullatores* (later called *plumbatores*), whose existence is attested for the first time in 1198, and who worked directly under the CAMERLENGO. Chosen originally (13th and 14th centuries) from among the lay brothers of the Cistercian order (usually from the abbey of Fossanova when the popes resided in Italy, and from the abbey of Fontfroide when the Curia was at Avignon), they were familiarly nicknamed *fratres barbati*.

By a *motu proprio* of 29 December 1878, LEO XIII reserved the use of the lead seal to a limited number of pontifical acts: PROVISIONS, the erection, suppression, or division of large benefices (dioceses and major abbeys), and solemn acts of the HOLY SEE (for example, the calling of councils). The other letters formerly sealed with the bull, notably the acts dealing with minor benefices and marriage dispensations, were authenticated thereafter by a red stamp representing the heads of the apostles.

Like other sovereigns (beginning with the Byzantine emperors), popes sometimes sealed some of their acts with gold bulls instead of lead ones. This practice, always exceptional, is attested by Conrad of Mure at the end of the 13th century, but the oldest known example dates from 1524.

Bernard Barbiche

See also BOLLATICA.

Bibliography

Frenz, T. *Papsturkunden des Mittelalters und der Neuzeit*, Stuttgart, 1986 (*Historische Grundwissenschaften in Einzeldarstellungen*, 2), 42–4; Ital. Trans., Vatican City, 1989, 48–9, with earlier bibliography.

Sella, P. *Le bolle d'oro dell'Archivio Vaticano*, Vatican City, 1934.

Serafini, C. *Le monete e le bolle plumbee pontificie del medagliere Vaticano*, Milan, 1910–28, 4 vols.

BYZANTINE POPES, 534–715. The Byzantine reconquest of Italy, undertaken by Justinian, lasted from 534 to 552, but was challenged three years after the death of the great emperor when the LOMBARDS occupied Italy (568). Inconclusive wars gave rise to the following situation: The empire retained a rather large territory around RAVENNA, home of the exarch, who was the head of the civilian and military administration in Italy, the region of Rome and the Campania, and some possessions along the coast. These territories were linked only by sea, except for the first two, for despite hard combat, the Lombards were not able to cut the Rome–Ravenna road and unify their own territories: their kingdom, in the north, and the two duchies of Spoleto and Benevento in the south. Sicily formed a province directed by a praetor who was under the direct authority of the emperor. From the end of the 6th century, occupied in the east with the Slavs, the Persians, and then the Turks, the emperor left the exarchs to fight their battles using local resources. Lacking means, most of them tried only to maintain the status quo. Those who had favorable situations took advantage of them to revolt against the central power, instead of trying to expand the Byzantine territory. The popes, therefore, lived under the constant threat of the Lombards, and often collided with the exarch, who was not much inclined to help them. Like all bishops from the time of CONSTANTINE, the popes followed the public liturgy of the official cult, then called "orthodox." They also participated directly in political life. The naming of popes was of such importance that sometimes it was the result of a simple imperial decision. Even when named by the priests and "the people," that is, the heads of the senatorial nobility, a pope could not be consecrated without official confirmation, which was often slow to arrive. For convenience, the exarch acted in the name of the emperor with increasing frequency, but, from a purely institutional point of view, the Byzantine popes are distinguished by the fact that all of them exercised the fullness of their authority by order of the emperor in Constantinople. This right of oversight, unchallenged for more than a century and a half, presupposed that the civil power was superior to the spiritual power. That is why the emperors had the right, recognized even by victims of the procedure, to judge and depose popes who did not follow their policies: that was the case with SILVERIUS, VIGILIUS, and MARTIN I. The situation required the presence of a strong man in Rome, for the pope, like other prelates, was responsible for the civil administration. Undoubtedly the popes took part in the choice of civil bureaucrats, though this cannot be documented. Until the pontificate of SABINIAN, the pope distributed the public annona. He also paid their salaries to the agents of the state, in particular the soldiers. He negotiated with the Lombards, and even signed peace accords when other authorities were unable to intervene. From the civil revenues of Rome, he paid the tributes exacted by the enemy. These civil duties were added to the customary responsibilities of a prelate: the selection and direction of the diocesan clergy, the supervision of the monasteries, the maintenance of buildings, aid to the poor. In a city already large for its period, that gave the pope great power. But the pope of Rome was also the metropolitan of all the Byzantine bishops of Italy, a fact that sometimes provoked violent conflicts with the bishop of Ravenna. Above all, the pope was patriarch of the West, and under this title could intervene in any state, provided the sovereign sought such intervention. His principal activity was settling affairs in which his intervention had been asked for. All these responsibilities presupposed vast resources. For the most part, they came from patrimonies made up of taxation rights, the management of which, in conformity with the principles of Roman public management, is well known from the correspondence of GREGORY the Great. The position of the pope was therefore particularly ambiguous. As a Byzantine bishop, he was a citizen of the empire, and this considerably hampered him in carrying out his activity as patriarch, for example, during the many conflicts between the emperor and the Lombards, who saw in him only the citizen of a hostile state. They had good reasons for that. As bishop of Rome, the pope ensured the safety of the population and fought against the Lombards. He was thus involved in political choices that brought him into conflict with those in Rome who saw things differently. Attempts to influence his policies were made by various pressure groups, including nobles of senatorial rank, diocesan clergy accustomed to the handling of business, monks full of their own prestige, and, later, refugees from the East. As a man of the Church, he had to take a position in the theological disputes that divided the empire. If he resisted the emperor, he deprived himself of the emperor's material assistance at moments that sometimes were crucial. There was therefore a slow slipping away rather than any clean breaks. Until the Lombard invasions, the popes obeyed the emperor completely. Contacts with the national Churches were insignificant. Then a rapprochement with the FRANKS began, for the papacy sought an ally on the other side. The general peace among the states—except for the Lombards—in the 7th century, and the conversion of all the sovereigns to "orthodoxy," accounts for the normalization of these relations, though it did not mean that the sovereigns allowed the pope to intervene directly in their Church. The Anglo-Saxon clergy, however, showed the greatest respect for the papal institution. At the same time, the reverses of the Byzantine army, unable to intervene in the West, the theological disputes, and the increasing particularism of Ravenna sanctioned the estrangement of the papacy from the empire: the pope could not impose his theology any more than the emperor his political authority. As for the many Easterners who settled in Rome in flight from the Arab invasions, they were traditionally hostile to the emperor. They would play a major role in religious life, occupying the see of Peter without interruption from 686 to 715. The evolution accelerated at the beginning of the 8th century. The isolated missionaries working to convert the

peoples on the margins of the Frankish kingdom placed themselves under the direct authority of the popes. The new outbreak of danger from the Lombards led to ever more direct requests for intervention by the Franks. Above all, the rejection of the iconoclast heresy adopted by the emperor entailed the rupture with Constantinople. As a sign of the times, papal elections from the time of GREGORY II were confirmed not by the emperor but by the duke of Rome, a noble favorable to local interests. The real break therefore took place during the pontificate of Gregory II, when the pope drew the definitive consequences of the new state of affairs.

Jean Durliat

Bibliography

JW, 1, 113–249.

LP, 1, 290–395.

Agnellus, *Liber pontificalis ecclesiae Ravennatis*, ed. O. Holder-Egger, Hannover, 1878 (*MGH, SS, cit.*), 275–391.

Bavant, B. "Le duché byzantin de Rome. Origine, durée et extension géographique," *MEFRM*, 91 (1979), 41–88.

Bede, *Kirchengeschichte der englischen Völker*, ed. and trans. Colgrave, B., Mynors, R. A. B., and Spitzbart, G., Darmstadt, 1982.

Bertolini, *Roma di fronte a Bisanzio e ai Longobardi*, Bologna, 1971 (*Storia di Roma*, 9).

Conte, P. *Chiesa e primato nelle lettere dei papi del secolo VII*, Milan, 1971.

Förster, H. *Liber diurnus romanorum pontificum*, Berne, 1958.

Storia d'Italia, ed. Galasso, G., Delogu, I. P., Guillou, A., Ortalli, G. *Longobardi e Bisantini*, Turin, 1980.

Guillou, A. *Régionalisme et indépendance dans l'Empire byzantin au VIIe siècle. L'exemple de l'Exarchat et de la Pentapole d'Italie*, Rome, 1969.

Paul the Deacon, *Historia Langobardorum*, ed. Bethmann, L., and Waitz, G., Hannover, 1878 (*MGH, SS, rerum langobardicarum et italicarum saec. VI-IX*), 12–187.

Richards, J. *The Popes and the Papacy in the Early Middle Ages*, 476–52, London-Boston-Henley, 1979.

Schneider, E. 13–23.—*ICUR*, 4156–62.

BYZANTIUM AND THE PAPACY.

The Empire at the Beginning. The *Prima Petri*, or First Letter of Peter, is undoubtedly one of the scriptural texts most frequently cited during the long history of the Byzantine Church: it contains the commandment "Honor everyone. Love the family of believers. Fear God. Honor the emperor" (1 Pt 2:17), using the same Greek word, *basileus*, that designated the Roman emperor, whose seat had been at Constantinople since 330. And the Greek FATHERS only emphasized this organic relationship between Christianity and Roman power perpetuated by Byzantium, each power providing the support neceessary to the other, for, as Gregory of Nazianzus wrote, "to attack Christianity is to weaken the power of the Romans and endanger public order" (*Homilies*, I, 74). There lies the root of the misunderstandings, and then the ruptures, that marked the relations between the Roman papacy and the head of the CHURCHES OF THE ORIENT until the demise of Byzantium: the Byzantine Church never lost the indispensable support that was the imperial throne, even though it accepted a mighty degree of subordination, whereas the decline of the Western Empire liberated the patriarch of Rome from the imperial power beginning in the 5th century.

In Byzantium, where the imperial reality of Rome was seen as obviously providential, it was also evident that the emperor, God's lieutenant, had the essential mission of defending the universal Church, especially against inside enemies who sought to call the content of the faith into question. It was on the strength of this function that the emperor, following the example of CONSTANTINE at Nicaea in 325, convened and presided over the ecumenical COUNCILS, and then ratified the canons. The fact was that the great formative councils, Nicaea I, Constantinople I, Ephesus, and Chalcedon, unchallenged by Rome in their deepest sense, had been called at the initiative of the imperial power and, each time, called to reject HERESIES judged to be such by both the pope and the emperor.

Like it or not, wherever the empire survived, these precedents gave the sovereign an enormous power of intervention in the Church, despite the doctrine, enunciated clearly from the 4th century by St. Athanasius of Alexandria, that reserved to the emperor the conduct of the things of this world and to the Church the things not of this world. But the Church, it was argued, belonged to this world, especially in an empire in which, even before Christians had the right to express themselves, the organs of the Church had slipped into the administrative mold of the state. The doctrine of the two powers would be constantly and forcefully recalled in Byzantium, from John Chrysostom (5th century), to the deacon Agapitus under Justinian the Great, and then to John of Damascus and Theodore the Studite; it was also the doctrine of all patriarchs worthy of the name, who sought to "have a share in" the imperial power. Such efforts, however, were more or less in vain, given that the throne was increasingly regarded as sacred (under the reign of the weak Theodosius II, just before 450, some were already daring to compare the dead emperor with Christ himself, emphasizing that both of them had risen toward their divine essence) and that, after the iconoclast crisis, it arrived at its most perfect expression in an authentic theocracy.

Under Justinian, imperial law made doctrine official, but in order to add to it an important nuance, namely, the necessary cooperation of the two powers, the source of a happy harmony; it meant, furthermore, that the clergy had

to be above all criticism, and that if not, it was the emperor's duty to correct its dignity and moral bearing, a state of affairs that clearly could lead to every imaginable abuse. In the 880s, the Epanagôguè of Basil I made the sovereign not only the tutor of the Church, since it was he who, by the civil law, set the limits of the patriarchal power, but also the "conservator" of the body of doctrine—the Scriptures, the canons of the seven ecumenical councils, and those Roman laws confirmed by experience (which guaranteed, for example, that the liturgical and cultural practices of the Byzantine Church were untouchable)—and at the same the defender against heresy.

This doctrine of the "limited autonomy," of a Church under the moral tutelage of the throne went unchanged until the fall of the empire; in the long run, it did not suit Rome, since it was easy to move from disciplinary tutelage to the imperial interpretation of dogma. It must not be forgotten that St. Athanasius enunciated his doctrine at the time of an Arian emperor, Constans II, many of whose successors had sympathies for the Nestorians or the Monophysites, long before defining the "imperial heresy" that was iconoclasm.

Primacy, Heresies, and Imperial Power. However, Rome did not immediately denounce the view whereby the structures of the Church were equivalent to those of the empire, which was at the origin of the subordination of the spiritual to the political. The principle having been enunciated in canon 4 of Nicaea and reiterated by the synod of Antioch in 341, Popes INNOCENT and BONIFACE twice recalled, at the beginning of the 5th century, that there should be only one metropolitan for each province, to whom all suffragan bishops should submit. Rome could also do nothing but accept a more challenging consequence of this "principle of accommodation": that just as the provinces, in the 4th century, were grouped in vast territorial units, called dioceses, so the fathers of Nicaea had found it natural that the ecclesiastical hierarchy should be headed by a limited number of metropolitan "superiors," each of whom would exercise the same power within his territorial limits.

In addition, canon 6 of Nicaea gave the metropolitans of ALEXANDRIA and of Antioch, and likewise, without naming them, the Churches of the other eparchies (which supposed, in theory, the attribution of a higher right to the metropolitans of each diocese), "a supreme power over all [their] territory, as is the case for the bishop of Rome, who has the same power." Thus, it was Nicaea that fixed the geographical limits and powers, of the same scope if not the same nature, of what would become the patriarchates, apparently without the fathers seeming to envisage that effectively they were putting a "patriarch" at the head of every civil diocese, as the versions of the canons that come down to us no doubt assert. And Rome, although it had been represented at

Nicaea only by two priests, obviously never expressed the least reservation regarding this canon from the founding council. In any case, at least for Antioch, a letter from Innocent I indicates that, at the beginning of the 5th century, Rome admitted the principle of these "metropolitan superiors," and indeed gave canon 6 the meaning it is given today.

For the rest, the boundaries were fluid, especially between Antioch and Alexandria, and a letter of St. Jerome, dated 396 or 397, shows that this Father was preoccupied with the rights of Antioch, which were being nibbled away at by its rival. Moreover, such a redistribution of powers could not disturb Rome, to which the Eastern Churches accorded, among other things, a supreme jurisdiction over all the Churches. The synod of Sardica (343), the canons of which the Western Church did not accept, invited priests to appeal to the bishop of Rome "to honor the sacred memory of the apostle PETER." This is no doubt the origin of what Rome considered its effective PRIMACY, whereas the Byzantine and other Eastern Churches saw in Rome only a primacy of honor, supreme, to be sure, but little different in nature from what Nicaea, in its canon 7, had accorded to Jerusalem when providing for the authority of the metropolitan of Caesarea.

Yet it is true that in the 4th and 5th centuries the reverence due to the first apostles was evident throughout the Christian world and was translated into a vague but incontestable superiority. Even Eusebius of Caesarea, who, in his *Ecclesiastical History*, had declared, following the ancient tradition, that the see of Rome had been founded by Peter and PAUL, in his *Chronicle* speaks only of Peter; this seems accordingly to reflect some adaptation to a recent evolution, to which the *Catalogue* of Pope LIBERIUS attests in 354.

In the relations between Rome and Byzantium, the preeminence and soon the exclusivity of Constantinople, the fruit of the imperial reality, therefore played a determining role, Byzantium considering it natural to accord first place to the sole capital of the empire, whereas the popes stressed the apostolic tradition that based on Peter the primacy of the Roman see, and that could not long accept the political tradition of Byzantium. Equivocation therefore, from an early period began to tie up in knots the discussion of two closely related themes: the power of the *basileus* to intervene in the Church, which Rome judged intolerable, and the place to be accorded Constantinople in the hierarchy of the universal Church, which Byzantium thought incontestable, since it never claimed that its see occupied the highest place in that hierarchy. It was indeed, because Constantine let himself be convinced by the Arians that Athanasius was exiled to Trier in 335, and it was indeed the imperial decision that Pope JULIUS I challenged, in 337, in declaring Athanasius the sole legitimate bishop of Alexandria. Despite appearances, the dogmatic quarrels that tormented the Eastern Churches and allowed Rome to see in them the beginnings of heresies, and even of SCHISMS, were utterly secondary to the fundamental problem, which was disciplinary, and so things would continue at least until the end of the 11th century.

In truth, the times lent themselves to imperial intervention, which played with religious options in order to have the last word, while Rome, for its part, resisted, bringing upon itself a long series of violent acts that reinforced its image as a religious authority unyielding to the whims the imperial power. Still, Pope Liberius, exiled to Thrace by the Arian Constantius II in 356, in the end accepted a formula of faith strongly tinged with Arianism, and it was Hilary of Poitiers, Eusebius of Vercelli and then Ambrose of Milan who, long before Rome, began the Western reaction against the triumphant Arianism, for the world waited until the Roman synod of 377 to see Pope DAMASUS condemn it formally.

In reality, however, this was not an East-West quarrel: at the same time, Greeks such as St. Basil and St. Gregory of Nazianzus were struggling just as vigorously against the heresy, an effort that amounted to refusing the emperor any initiative in questions of dogma. And yet it was a decree of Theodosius the Great that, in 380, ordered a general return to orthodoxy as professed in Rome and Alexandria, while, soon afterwards, a synod in Constantinople convened by the same emperor had no other aim than to ratify this return to the tradition of Nicaea: only some Eastern fathers attended it, while the Western emperor, Gratian, convened another synod at Aquileia, which the pope did not even attend. Besides, the acts of Constantinople—including canon 3, the triumph of the current policy, by which the see of Constantinople, a simple diocese as Gregory of Nazianzus had just shown, received the primacy of honor, just behind the pope, "because the city is the new Rome," an expression not used until then—were not even communicated to Rome, as LEO the Great confirmed later. He well understood that what was involved was a putting affairs in order inside the Eastern Churches, directed against Alexandria and not against Rome.

Apostolicity and Pentarchy in the 5th Century. Since, at the time, the synod of 381 obviously was not perceived as ecumenical, any real dispute was avoided: Chalcedon would bring such a dispute, and fresh exchange of fire between Rome and Byzantium, originating with the doctrine of Nestorius, patriarch of Constantinople after 418. Facing opposition from Cyril of Alexandria, who was backed by Pope CELESTINE, Theodosius II convened at Ephesus in March 430 what was to have been only another Eastern SYNOD. What is especially remembered of its complex history is the presence of Roman legates and their action in favor of Cyril, which made the 431 synod the third ecumenical council and a defeat for the imperial power.

The appeal to the pope became from then on a normal procedure, and for many years to come, a way of depending on him, as emerges clearly from the efforts of Eutyches who, with Dioscorus of Alexandria, hardened the theses of Cyril in giving birth to the monophysite doctrine: after his excommunication by a synod of Constantinople in 448, he sought the support of Pope LEO before urging Theodosius II to convene a new council. At this council, the "plundering of Ephesus," as St. Leo himself called it, the papal legates, who were carrying the *Tome*, the letter to Patriarch Flavian of Constantinople summing up the orthodox teaching, were not even heard, and the Monophysites triumphed by violence to the emperor's satisfaction, even if a Roman synod condemned their action in September 449. The pope could not speak out until Theodosius died; then he took up once again the idea of a general council, which he hoped would assemble in Italy. When Pulcheria and Marcian called it for Nicaea, the pope protested only feebly; it was the time of the Hun invasions in the West, and, all things considered, he was right. In addition, he sent envoys to the council that met at Chalcedon in October 451. It was at Chalcedon, then, that the latent conflict flared up.

We know that the famous canon 28, which ensured the precedence of Constantinople over Alexandria and Antioch and, above all, gave the city jurisdiction over the dioceses of Thrace, Pontus, and Asia, as well as all the territories that future missions might win for Christianity, was voted in the absence of the Roman legates, who protested at once, followed by Leo himself. Was there equivocation? It would be wrong to believe that at Rome the Eastern realities were misunderstood. Leo knew very well that, once again, a canon had been passed against monophysite Alexandria, which Theodosius had constantly favored; the Chalcedon fathers not only did not scorn Rome, but had Leo's *Tome* read in council and sanctioned it as the best summary of the orthodox teaching.

Besides, Rome did not protest against canon 17, which finally acknowledged the need for the Church to adapt its structures in accordance with the eventual remodeling of the civil districts. What Rome could not accept was the territorial inflation of the new diocese, and, even more, the pledging away of the future of the territories still to be converted, over which Rome firmly intended to keep the initiative; from that pledging stemmed the problem of Illyricum, that vast territory in the Balkans where the two authorities imposed themselves, and where the pope kept a vicar, seated at Thessolonica, until the 8th century. With great clarity this time, Chalcedon illustrated well the two, increasingly divergent, conceptions of the supreme management of the Churches: that of Rome, which made no distinction between primacy of honor and effective direction in the hands of the successor of Peter, and that of Byzantium, which conceived the Church as a juxtapositioning of five patriarchates, each master of its own affairs but together in charge of the Christian world. Byzantium here made exception for the practice of appeal, invariably admitted, to Ancient Rome, which, however,

ought not abuse what for the Easterners was only a primacy of honor. Hearing it in this sense, the Chalcedon fathers had no objection to canon 6 of Nicaea, solemnly read before them in a Latin version that differed from the Greek, and which underlined that "the Roman Church has always held the primacy." In any case, the imperial power did not seem to be involved in the voting on canon 28: the vote was taken in the absence of the imperial representatives and was to be considered a matter internal to the Byzantine Church.

Already confronting the "pontifical monarchy," then, was what rightly could be called the pentarchy, to which almost all of Eastern orthodoxy rallied. Rome reacted all the more negatively when, in the 5th century, it scarcely could take advantage any longer of imperial support, which disappeared in 476. That is why Leo the Great insisted so strongly on the apostolic character of the see of Rome, and why he was so mortified to see no mention of it in the canons of the council. From then on, Rome had only the principle of apostolicity with which to shore up its universal authority, while the see of Constantinople increasingly prided itself on being the religious face of an empire united once more. Leo therefore invoked in all its rigor a principle that gave precedence, in order, to Rome, Alexandria, and Antioch, by reason of their apostolic origin; however, proof of the Byzantine wish for appeasement, canon 28, rejected by Rome, was not included in the official collections until the 6th century.

Byzantium, however, had only seemed to bend; in fact, Constantinople never again let go of the dioceses that had come under its control. Both Rome and Byzantium had reasons for wanting to calm the situation: faced with patriarchates at Antioch and Alexandria that were increasingly being won over to heterodoxy, the pope had scarcely more than one ally, Constantinople, while Constantinople was preoccupied with rallying its eastern provinces, where secession threatened.

The Estrangement: From the Schism of Acacius to Iconoclasm. In 482, Patriarch Acacius endorsed the *Henoticon* (Union), a decree of Emperor Zeno that made some concessions to the Monophysites but above all showed, once again, the will of the imperial power to intervene in matters of dogma. Pope FELIX excommunicated Acacius in 484. From that date, the first real schism began, dividing the orthodox Churches; it lasted until 519. It was then that Pope GELASIUS pushed to its extreme the Roman principle of apostolicity, going so far as to refuse Constantinople the status of metropolis, even as, throughout this major rupture, the Byzantine Church showed itself increasingly open to the apostolic arguments of this pope and of his successor, SYMMACHUS. But Gelasius, relying on the support of a sovereign considered a "BARBARIAN" in Constantinople, the king of the Ostrogoths Theodoric, was the first pope to dare openly to deny the emperor any right to involve himself in religious matters, on the strength of a doctrine that Rome would never again abandon, that of the "two powers," distinctly independent. Here, Byzantium, which had always admitted a division of responsibility between spiritual and temporal powers, was certainly not ready to see the throne stripped of a supreme power of control that, for its Church, was also a form of protection: soon, in opposition to the Roman doctrine, which reserved to priests the moral censorship of worldly matters.

Justinian would promote the notion of an imperial power that was essentially divine and had as its proper task the redressing of the errors of the clergy. It was Justinian himself, from then on the true holder of imperial power, who helped to denounce the schism by forcing the Byzantine Church in 519 to sign the *Libellus Hormisdae*, in which Pope HORMISDAS set forth unequivocally the apostolic principle of the Roman primacy: all the reserve of the upper Eastern clergy can be felt in Patriarch John's insistence that the text should be preceded by an explanation in which he emphasized that, in truth, the two Romes were nothing but one and the same diocese. The question is whether Rome and Byzantium were headed toward a synthesis of the principles of apostolicity and of accommodation. The correspondence between Hormisdas and the patriarch suggests that they were: the pope admitted at least tacitly the validity of the "first four councils," thereby including that of Constantinople, with its famous canon 3; this became clear when his legates to Constantinople, rejoicing in the union that had been restored, declared on 29 June 519 that they "admitted nothing outside the four councils and the letters of Pope Leo, nothing not mentioned in the aforementioned councils or not written by Pope Leo."

The universal Church accordingly seemed to accept the equality of the two traditions, that of the apostolic Rome and that of the mostly Eastern councils that represented the Church accommodated to civil structures. In any case, the *Prisca*, the first preserved Latin collection of canons, put together in Italy at the turn of the 5th and 6th centuries, included all the canons of 381, as did other later collections such as the *Dionysiana* and the *Hispana*, some 6th-century Italian collections going as far to include canon 28 of Chalcedon. Not only was the papal rigor lessened, but a number of Roman Catholic coteries in southern Italy seem to have been moved by a more sympathetic understanding of the Byzantine positions. Such a reconciliation would not have been possible without Justinian, for whom the unity of the faith and of the Church went hand in hand with his plan to restore the Roman Empire. Rome understood, and therefore did not protest when the emperor, passionately interested in theology, risked dogmatizing; indeed, little could be said against a sovereign who had just reconquered a good part of the Roman Empire, fully intended to restore unity therein, and had written in his novella IX, in May 535: "The ancient city of Rome has the honor of being the mother of laws, and no one could doubt that in Rome the

summit of the sovereign pontificate is to be found."

At the beginning of his reign, in 533, when the emperor ventured onto theological ground, Pope JOHN II approved his decree. All the same, Agapitus asked him to be wary, for preaching the faith remained the preserve of the clergy. As for the 15 "Origenist" propositions that Justinian detected in the teaching of the Palestinian monks, they did not alarm Pope VIGILIUS, though the enterprise was more than questionable.

The emperor, for his part, did not hesitate to draw back when he perceived that his religious initiatives were displeasing to Rome, whose support was so important for him in an Italy retaken by the Ostrogoths. In 544, still animated by a desire to purify the faith once and for all, he issued a decree condemning the work of three 5th-century theologians, Theodoret of Cyrrhus, Theodore of Mopsuestia, and Ibas of Edessa, whom he accused of Nestorianism. Vigilius, who had gone to Constantinople and allowed himself be circumvented there, perhaps in a rather rough way, in 551 condemned a still sharper imperial decree, while agreeing to submit the question to an ecumenical council that he wanted to have meet in the West. However, he gave in once again: the council met at Constantinople, in May 553. It is known that, even though his first *Constitutum*, by which the pope refused to condemn the errors of dead doctors of the faith, was rejected, and his name struck from the diptychs on 26 May, the emperor's will prevailed over Vigilius: in February 554, the pope had to acknowledge that he was mistaken and ratify the council's decisions. However, they had brushed up against a schism, and it was solely because it had reaffirmed the doctrine of Chalcedon that Rome did not call into question the ecumenical character of the fifth council, in contrast to the monophysite Churches and despite the resistance of a part of the West, in Italy and in Illyricum.

For future relations between Rome and Byzantium, therefore, the essential question was not dogma; it was to be found, rather, in the edict that convened the council, in which Justinian risked an official formulation of the respective roles of the *imperium* as supervisor of the "most zealous priests, assembled in council," and of the *sacerdotium*, which he could legitimately "use" to "combat every heresy [. . .] and thus preserve the peace of the Church by the proclamation of the true faith." It goes without saying that such a teaching, which only made the imperial tradition explicit, was more and more clearly opposed to the idea of a collegial, pentarchial *sacerdotium*, within which Rome could claim only a preeminence of honor owed to it, in the opinion of all those in the East, on account of its apostolic origin; this synthesis of the political and the apostolic could not be accepted in the long run by the Church of Rome, to which violence clearly had been done.

The show of strength of 553–4 was the achievement of an apparently triumphant empire. However, the empire was drastically weakened, at the turn of the 6th and 7th centuries: the monophysite Churches of Syria and Egypt openly seceded right after the council, and when the borders were assaulted by the Slavs and then the Muslims, Constantinople, facing peril from without, thought that by giving guarantees to religious dissidents it would better ensure the state's ability to resist a threat to its very existence. Rome, left to itself in Italy, did not take advantage of this state of affairs to speak with a louder voice: GREGORY the Great, who regarded himself as subject to the emperor, never conceived of a *sacerdotium* without the *imperium* whose power of decision was limited only by the canons, but continued to maintain that the Roman see, "whatever is said of it," was well and truly superior to that of Constantinople, as "has always been recognized by the most pious emperor and by our brother the bishop of that city."

Now, that "bishop" was none other than the patriarch John IV, called the Faster (582–95), of whom the claim is made that he was the first to give himself the title of ecumenical patriarch, though it had appeared much earlier in Alexandria as well as in Constantinople, indicating simply conformity with the tradition that emphasized the supreme powers of each patriarch in his own patriarchate. No real crisis therefore resulted, only a simple irritation on Gregory's part at what he considered immodesty on the part of John IV. The *Liber pontificalis* attests that, under BONIFACE II, in 607, Byzantium recognized the primacy of Rome, even if thenceforth the see of Constantinople regularly decked itself with the title ecumenical.

In any case, it is known to be completely false to situate in this period the development of the myth according to which the apostle Andrew passed through Byzantium and there ordained a bishop, Stachys. Later, in the 9th century, Photius himself judged these legends to be aberrations, because they were based on the *Acts of Andrew*, notoriously apocryphal, compiled in Greece beginning in the 3rd century. If they circulated until the 7th century, they attested to the progress made, in the East, by the idea of apostolicity, of which Rome had always been the champion; but they did nothing to shore up Constantinople's pretensions to equal, indeed to surpass, Rome in dignity. Certainly, Constantinople sought to have recognized an apostolic origin of its own, but at that time it preferred to present itself as the heir of Ephesus, a see indisputably founded by John, the favorite apostle of Jesus.

Thus it was invariably imperial action, not action by the Eastern Church, that widened the gap by endeavoring to conciliate the monophysite communities: under Heraclius, monoenergism, which in 634 allowed in Christ a double nature animated by a single energy, and monothelitism, defined by the *Ekthésis* of 638 and which saw the two natures as informed by a single will, were clearly only monophysitism dressed in new clothes. Rome violently opposed them, especially Popes JOHN VI and THEODORE I; prompted by the revolt of the Western Churches, especially the African, Theodore I even excommunicated the patriarch Paul in 647. In fact, opposi-

tion to monothelitism was as strong in the East as in the West. That was the origin of an imperial avowal of powerlessness, the *Typos*, an edict of Constans II that in 648 prohibited all controversy on the single or the double will; the fate of St. Maximus, tortured to death in 662, had nothing over that of Pope MARTIN I, who had condemned the *Ekthésis* and *Typos* in 649, and was abducted from the LATERAN by the exarch of RAVENNA, then led to Constantinople in order to be condemned and deposed there before a lay tribunal, and then was exiled to the Crimea, where he died a martyr in 655. It is significant that in his letters St. Maximus recognized clearly that Rome had "the power to rule over all the holy Churches of God in the entire universe."

Once again, the general crisis forced Constantine IV, after renewing ties with Pope AGATHO, to have recourse to Byzantium's traditional action: the calling of a new ecumenical council that, in September 681, meeting in the rotunda (the *Troullos*) of the imperial palace, solemnly condemned monothelitism. The crisis, though grave, had apparently ended, and without doubt no other council has more clearly affirmed the submission to Rome of the universal Church, naturally admitted by the emperor to whom the council fathers wrote: "It was our head, the chief of the apostles, who fought with us. To strengthen us, we had with us his disciple and successor, who, in his letters, explained to us the mysteries of the knowledge of God. This ancient city of Rome sent you a confession written by God [. . .] and it was Peter who spoke through Agatho." Without, however, abandoning its rights in its own area of competence, Byzantium seemed to have clearly adopted the apostolic doctrine that justified the primacy of Rome. But the council, in which the papal LEGATES participated, also condemned the memory of Pope HONORIUS I, who seemed to have had in his day some weakness for the rejected doctrine. From then on, Byzantium accordingly could take pride in a council, accepted by everyone as having been ecumenical, that had taken proceedings against a Roman pontiff.

Now, if the whole church had added a number of aberrant practices, the products of a popular piety exacerbated by the sufferings of the times, to the old traditional pagan roots, still alive with magical practices and incongruous rites, only the Church of Byzantium felt the need to recall priests and laity to the discipline that the latest councils had had neither the time nor, above all, the will to reaffirm. Therefore, in a gesture typical of Byzantium, Justinian II convened in 691 a new ecumenical council given responsibility for codifying the LITURGY and the discipline of the Churches while recalling the Christian people to a religious, moral, and sexual life more in conformity with the old canons. Rome and Byzantium undoubtedly would have agreed on the moral reform of the laity; but, in its determination to define a single discipline and one liturgy for all Christian priests, the council, called "Quinisext" (because it completed the decisions of the fifth and sixth councils) or *in Trullo* (because it was held in the same hall as that of 681), did not want to see the development of a great division in the practices of Churches now highly individualized. Accordingly, when it adopted a set of canons intended for the universal Church, it was seeking to impose an ecclesial model very close to the one already defined by the legislation of Justinian the Great, with married clerics who were not impeded from going on to the priesthood, its own liturgical calendar, and its specific disciplinary rules, in particular those affecting Lent and the practice of fasting.

It became clear that Rome was incapable of accomplishing such a reform, or of sending a sufficient number of representatives to Constantinople. Pope SERGIUS I then refused to subscribe to the decisions of Quinisext, perhaps because that council reaffirmed the equal power of the two sees by repeating Chalcedon's famous canon 28 word for word, but more likely because two religious universalisms, which no longer coincided with political boundaries, had now defined themselves. Rome held that only Western practices were valid, even if it no longer could impose them on others. Constantinople, believing itself still to have the means—even though its forces, since the end of the 6th century, had been more than compromised by administrative disorganization and by the Slavic and Muslim invasions—intended to have its own way accepted even in the Latin West, where it had lost Carthage in 698. There was accordingly a great scandal at Constantinople when the imperial envoy was chased from Rome by the combined efforts of the local militia and that of Ravenna, the seat of the Byzantine exarchate of Italy; calm apparently having been restored after the violent eviction of Justinian II in 694, Tiberius III sent a new expedition to put down the Roman "rebels," and only Pope John VI himself was able to calm the zeal of his militia. A political crisis ensued, because Rome still had no idea of repudiating a politico-religious system in which the emperor could do Rome damage but remained its sole protector.

After Justinian II succeeded in regaining the throne in 705, he invited Pope Constantine and received him in 710–11 with great honor in his capital; in front of the pope, according to the *Liber pontificalis*, the emperor "renewed all the privileges of the Church," which could be interpreted only as new Byzantine acknowledgment of Rome's primacy. Nothing was taken back from the Quinisext canons, while the Byzantine Church was already applying itself to get under way a reform that Rome would not really see until the 11th century.

The First Great Rupture: Iconoclasm. The Quinisext had ratified the veneration of the sacred images, or icons, that had overtaken Byzantium: thence arose a crisis that seemed irremediable, while the West remained rather reticent about the cult. Today it is regarded as absurd to reduce the action of sovereigns such as Leo III the Isaurian

and, especially, his son, Constantine V, to a matter of religious policy: even in relation to Rome, what would be called iconoclasm was also translated into political actions recalling that, if the imperial power admitted the Roman primacy, it was always in the restricted sense of a primacy of honor within a pentarchial Church. However, this time the emperor attacked practices to which a number of Byzantine clergy, along with the people, were strongly attached, and their reaction demonstrated that, feeling violence had been done them by the imperial power, they thought it natural to appeal to the apostolic authority of Rome, thereby illustrating the progress, in the East, of a conception that once and for all subordinated the throne to the altar.

At first, the crisis seemed a repeat of those of the 7th century. In 727, Leo III, with the help of threats, tried to persuade GREGORY II to agree with his opposition to the veneration of images, and the pope, energetically refusing to do so, reaffirmed his attachment to the universal Christian edifice, of which the emperor was the keystone. Gregory even wrote to Leo III that Rome constantly urged the "new kings" to obey the highest throne, but on the condition that the emperor, to whom he would not refuse even the title of priest if he remained in dogmatic agreement with the church, not confuse the privileges of the *imperium* and of the *sacerdotium*. But this pope, isolated from almost everyone by the attacks of the SARACENS and LOMBARDS, also took advantage of the situation to highlight the moral prestige of his diocese, the see of Peter, whose image was threatened by the emperor while "the kingdoms of the West continue to consider it as God on earth." The pope was blocking the development of the resolutely theocratic Byzantine power to which Leo III added the final touch when, in 740, he affirmed in the preamble to his *Ekloguè* that "God put imperial power in our hands, according to his good pleasure [. . .] assigning to us, as to Peter, the head and leader of the apostles, the responsibility for feeding his most faithful flock . . ."

Accordingly, when, in January 730, Leo, after deposing Patriarch Germanus, obtained from the synod an edict condemning images, deemed to be responsible for a new idolatry, the new pope GREGORY III convened a Roman council that condemned these theses. Byzantium knew very well that, this time, there was a risk of defection by all the Latin West, including its own Balkan and Italian provinces. Even if there is no textual evidence from the period, it was most probably around that time that the emperor decided to attach to the patriarchate of Constantinople the Churches of Sicily, Calabria, Illyricum, and Crete, which were still officially under Roman power. On the pretext of a natural accommodation to new political realities, Byzantium added an irreparable territorial dispute to the old disciplinary quarrels and the new doctrinal disagreement.

Until Leo's death in 741, iconoclasm was not a true heresy, but at most a return to ancient forms of piety, and above all a reclaiming of the Church by a power being fully restored. At the beginning of Constantine V's reign, the great organs of the state, including the upper echelons of the Church, were clearly behind the throne, and the victories won against the Muslims also rallied a number of popular elements and even some monasteries to his support. Over against this "imperial party," an opposition developed, dominated increasingly by the majority of the monks, who were generally sincere about the new piety, which brought them, among other things, the benefits of offerings and pilgrimages, especially in the countryside, the majority of the people remained iconophiles. To meet this opposition, there was only one recourse, Rome, where initially there were few echoes, the popes first having to face the Lombard invasion, so that for a long while they maintained normal relations with the emperor, their traditional protector; in 741–2, Pope ZACHARIAS even obtained from King Liutprand a territorial *statu quo* favorable to both Byzantium and Rome.

However, from the reign of Leo III, a number of opponents turned to Rome, where they were welcomed by the several Greek monasteries in the city, which had appeared over the course of the 7th century, perhaps around figures hostile to monothelitism such as Maximus the Confessor, who was in Rome in 645–6; there thus existed an ardently iconophile GREEK milieu in Rome, with which the popes often had close relations. The Lombard offensive, with Ravenna's support, ended in 751 all that remained of real Byzantine power in central Italy. At the meeting at Ponthion, STEPHEN II found another protector in Pepin, the king of the FRANKS, who, in regaining the conquered territories for the Holy See, established its independence from the empire in law and in fact.

But if the empire, after 731, no longer ratified any papal election, the Roman CHANCERY stopped referring to the imperial reigns only in 775, maintaining until then the semblance of respect for Constantine, who died that same year. He made of iconoclasm a true doctrine that went beyond a simple struggle against idolatry, establishing between the image and its prototype a substantial relationship that implied a blasphemous intention to circumscribe the divine nature, contrary to the canons of Ephesus and Chalcedon; even more, he denied the perpetual virginity of the Virgin Mary, and also the mediation of saints and relics. True, the council he convened in his palace at Hiereia in 754 did not support him on the latter points; still, this synod of 338 Eastern bishops, which regarded itself as ecumenical, established iconoclasm as an official doctrine of the empire and, according to tradition, even claimed to make it an article of faith for all Christians.

The West did not go along with this, even if the council of Gentilly in 767 adopted some clearly iconoclastic views. Iconophile refugees flourished at Rome, especially after 760, when Constantine had become their persecutor, and they undoubtedly played a not insignificant

role around Pope STEPHEN III, who, in 769, resolved to call the council that finally proclaimed the legitimacy of the veneration of images. One wonders whether, in Byzantium itself, there were voices raised in outcry to the pope. His *Life* has Stephen the Young, who died as a martyr in 760, saying that "according to canonical directives, religious matters cannot be defined without the participation of the pope of Rome," but this work, in fact, could hardly have been written before 808.

A False Union? Around 775, the rigorist iconoclasm had exhausted the patience even of certain of its partisans, while many iconophiles hoped to find a ground on which there could be agreement. Irene, the regent since 780, was certainly close to the most intransigent among them, as well as those closest to Rome (the "zealots"), to the point of asking for Pope HADRIAN'S support when, in 785, she contemplated calling an ecumenical council to put an end to the iconoclast question. It is significant that this plan was opposed by the moderates on both sides, who united around the idea of compromise ("economy" or *oikonomeia*). At that same time, these moderates also carried the day when a well-educated layman acceded to the patriarchal throne of Tarasius, and it was they who dominated the council of Nicaea II, in 787. In the presence of the papal legates (including the abbot of the "Greek" monastery of S. Saba in Rome), the legitimacy of the veneration of images was affirmed, and Rome was exalted as the norm of orthodoxy, as Patriarch Nicephorus would recall later.

But, to the fury of the zealots, the former iconoclasts were also reconciled. Except for the fact that the Greek versions of the acts of the council were discreet about papal primacy, from then on there was a Byzantine party that was more Roman than Rome itself, in which the disappointed zealots continued to hope it: Hadrian, no doubt influenced by them, hesitated to sanction the election of Tarasius. The rigorists, however, hardly risked finding an echo at Rome: since 800, the pope had had his own emperor, Charlemagne, and took little interest in Byzantine "schisms," which were simply disciplinary disputes. The chief of the zealots at that time was Theodore, abbot of Studios, who, in 806, sought in vain to rally Rome against the new patriarch, Nicephorus, who had come from their ranks and was closely linked to Rome, but was guilty of having reconciled a priest who, not long before, had blessed the union of Emperor Constantine VI with his former mistress; what was important is that Theodore then formulated an orthodox doctrine of the appeal to Rome, which he did not cease to refer to as "apostolic," all the while remaining directly in line with the pentarchial tradition.

Others, however, tried to use Rome to bring about victory for their own partisan causes, and it was indeed the excesses of the zealots that provoked the return, more moderate, of iconoclasm: in 815, LEO V had it approved by a local synod, and Theodore the Studite, exiled, appealed to Rome several times, while the emperor tried to come to terms with the West. Rome was listening to Theodore when, in 825, PASCHAL I refused to approve the compromise arrived at by a council in Paris, with the approbation of Louis the Pious, who, like Charlemagne, was not well disposed to images. Relations resumed with Rome only in March 843, when a local synod, convened by the regent, Theodora, put back into force the canons of 787, but the pope long remained attentive to the zealots, who formed a close presence around him and awaited their moment.

They thought it had arrived in 847 when, after the death of the moderate patriarch Methodius, Theodora chose one of their party, the eunuch Ignatius, the son of Emperor Michael I, who had been deposed in 813. It was he who would furnish the best proof that the zealots, who appealed so often to Rome, were quick to repudiate Rome when it did not serve their interests; besides, it was under his patriarchate that the see of Constantinople undertook the conversion of the Slavic peoples, whom the pope considered as in his sphere of influence, recalling the violent annexation of Illyricum to the orthodox patriarchate. It would be a mistake, therefore, to believe that, around 858, Ignatius and the zealots were highly regarded in Rome. The main lines of what would become the "schism of Photius" were entirely political.

Ignatius, the creature of Theodora, who named him without consulting the synod, began his patriarchate by condemning the bishops who had opposed his "election" and, in particular, their leader, Gregory Asbestas, the archbishop of Syracuse; logically, and as an example of the regularity of the appeals to Rome, these holders of the idea of "economy" complained to Popes LEO IV and BENEDICT III, both of whom disapproved of Ignatius's prohibitions, and they clearly placed his legitimacy in doubt. In sectarian policies, the patriarch went further: he opposed the young Michael III and his all-powerful minister, Bardas, and then defended Theodora, whom her son claimed to have had tonsured, before sending her into exile. What followed was logical: Ignatius was forced to resign, and to replace him, a perfectly regular synod elected Photius, a leading lay bureaucrat, to whom, in conformity with the Eastern canons, all orders were conferred at the same time (as already had been the case, for example, with Tarasius and Methodius). However, Photius, in order to secure Ignatius's resignation, had to promise that his respect and honor for him would remain intact, an entirely formal gesture, which the zealots interpreted as support for their cause: when they saw that the new patriarch remained faithful to his moderate principles, they met in February 859 to declare him deposed. Photius in response had the illegitimacy of Ignatius proclaimed by a solemn synod held in the Church of the Holy Apostle.

A general revolt of the zealots followed, with the monks of Studios at their head. They went so far as to claim that a return to iconoclasm was being prepared, and the political power, openly defied, reacted with violence, which forced Photius to ask Rome to convene an ecumenical council for the purpose of reestablishing harmony. Thus, it was the moderate patriarch who was appealing to Rome, doing what Irene had done in 785. Until that time, NICHOLAS I had never questioned the legitimacy of Photius, but he took the opportunity to have Rome's primacy recognized once and for all, at a time when the grave problem of conversions was at issue. He agreed to send legates to Constantinople, but only to verify the contested patriarchial elections, and without prejudging the fundamental problems, including respect for the primacy, the question of Illyricum, and, above all, Rome's right to seek conversions in the new mission territories.

Indeed, the council held in May 861 should have satisfied Rome fully. Ignatius did not appear at it except bound and guarded, his condition rightfully emphasizing that he had never appealed to Rome, and, in the most dramatic manifestation of the Roman primacy, the papal legates took part for the first time ever in the trial of a patriarch of Constantinople, who was sent off to a monastery. The legates then seized the occasion and participated in the condemnation of Ignatius, even if, as good canonists, they knew very well that they were overstepping their mandate.

In fact, it was the pope who had not sized up the situation very well, in particular failing to see that he was dealing with an empire enjoying full rebirth. He allowed himself to be circumvented by a delegation of zealots, bearing a pseudo-appeal by Ignatius to Rome. He ended up in April 863 by calling a council at which he both anathematized Photius and recognized the legitimacy of Ignatius, but not without renewing the former ANATHEMAS against iconoclasm; the zealots had peddled the old rumors of 858 as far as Rome. Nicholas then thought himself strong enough to have Byzantium renounce the obedience of Bulgaria, of which, however, the khan, Boris, was converted at the hands of Orthodox missionaries in 864. Ten years later, JOHN VIII would recall that Ignatius had been reinstated only on the condition that he would cease all anti-Roman proselytizing in Bulgaria. It was this 863–6 struggle in Bulgaria between Rome and Constantinople that led to the rupture. It had to do mainly with rites and discipline, the question being how best to seduce Boris to one way or the other.

In the autumn of 867, Photius, who had already had Nicholas condemned by a local synod, had this measure confirmed by a council in which legates from the three other Eastern patriarchates participated, a clear illustration of the old doctrine of the pentarchy. For this so-called Photian council, of which the acts have been destroyed, Rome's primacy of honor was not questioned and only Nicholas, first among the five pentarchs but unworthy, was personally condemned. It was the pope, who was very sick (he died in November), who thought a doctrinal condemnation was involved and who, for the first time, accused the Easterners of having questioned the Roman doctrine of the *Filioque*. In fact, even if that formula was rarely used in Byzantium, at that time they found nothing heretical in the idea that the Spirit proceeded from both the Father and the Son, and there would always be Orthodox believers who accepted it. The "schism" of Photius was therefore a *quid pro quo* affair, since it was essentially about disciplinary differences and, above all, the political designs of the two Churches.

At Rome, HADRIAN II scarcely understood the situation when, soon after his triumph, Photius was driven from the throne by the usurper Basil I, the assassin of Michael III, who counted on being pardoned by the zealots. Ignatius, now restored to power, led such a policy of revenge that Basil, like Photius earlier, was forced to ask Rome to call a new council, an apparent avowal of submission that led the pope to condemn Photius unilaterally in June 869. But the imperial fact remained. Basil ordered Photius to appear before what the West considered the eighth ecumenical council, thereby underlining that condemnation by Rome was insufficient. As for Ignatius, his policy toward Rome was much more intransigent than that of Photius. From 870 on, Bulgaria was definitely under the control of Constantinople, and Rome, its protests constantly rejected, was ready to condemn the emperor when he died in October 877.

The return of Photius, on the other hand, was in fact a reconciliation. The council that in 879–80 recognized his legitimacy in the presence of the legates of John VIII had indeed been approved by the pope, who got something out of it. True, it proclaimed the Nicene-Constantinopolitan creed, which avoided the *Filioque* clause, but it also recognized the validity of the reciprocal excommunications by pope and patriarch, which, for Byzantium, amounted to recognition that Rome had an effective right to intervene in the internal affairs of the Eastern patriarchate. The "second schism of Photius" is therefore just a legend, owed to the zealots, of whom a later Roman tradition would become the echo.

From True to False Schism. Until the middle of the 11th century, the empire was at the height of its power, while Rome passed through a long crisis that in Eastern eyes devalued it and rendered it ineffective. In that situation, then, the legend of the apostle Andrew lodged itself in Byzantium, without, however, challenging the primacy of the Western see. Appeals continued to be made to Rome, even if the sole purpose was to use it for ulterior and sometimes dishonorable ends; examples are LEO VI's request that the pope approve his fourth marriage, contrary to the Eastern canons,

which request led to what is called the "tetragamy" crisis between 906 and 920; and JOHN XI's approval in 933 of the elevation to the patriarchate of the young Theophylact Lecapene, only thirteen years old but the emperor's son. The Byzantines certainly thought ill of Rome and its practices, and were supported in their view by the low moral tone of the papal court, but they made no further reproach against Rome for dogmatic deviance until around 1050.

Then, once again, a crisis arose out of a political problem, this time in southern Italy. Even if they had begun to reform their Church, the popes from the beginning of the 11th century were the political allies of Byzantium, which defended Calabria and Apulia against the NORMANS, unrelenting enemies of Rome. But this alliance with the emperor hardly hid the conflict over obediences: Constantinople, at the height of its power, and Rome, striving for renewal, both wanted to impose their rites on the southern provinces. Added to this was the authoritarian personality of the patriarch Michael Keroularios ("Cerularius") (1043–58), who had no fear of opposing the emperor, Constantine IX Monomach. It was Michael who, sabotaging the imperial enterprise in order to shatter Roman reform in Italy, ordered Archbishop Basil of Ochrida to write an inflammatory letter to the bishop of Trani in which, for the first time, along with a traditional critique of Latin practices, a full polemic against the dogma of the *Filioque* was developed. In reply, LEO IX, with imperial support, sent two legates to Constantinople, Cardinal Humbert and Frederick of Lorraine, the future Pope Stephen IX. Welcomed at the palace but rebuffed by Cerularius, they saw fit to place on the main altar of St. Sophia, on 15 July 1054, a sentence of excommunication against the patriarch. In response, Michael called his synod, which, in its turn, excommunicated the Romans on 25 July.

The Reality of the Rupture: The Period of the Crusades. This crisis, which changed very little in the relations between the two Churches has been greatly inflated; besides, it could be emphasized that the two excommunications were invalid since, on 15 July, the pope died, which annulled the powers of his legates. Politically, the alliance against the Normans lasted until 1059, and GREGORY VII himself, in 1073–74, thought of renewing it. What changed everything was the brutal weakening of Byzantium, conquered all at once by both the TURKS and the Normans in 1071. From then on, Rome could assert itself, adopting an attitude it would maintain until the death of Byzantium: the price of Western aid was the "Union," understood as the adoption by Constantinople of Latin practices and dogma. For Byzantium, this could only be understood as a renunciation of its whole religious culture.

To this a new fact was added, the CRUSADE, which clashed with both the traditions and the political realities of the East: not only was a holy war an abomination for which Byzantium had invariably reproached the Muslims, but, in 1096, Alexis I believed that the crusaders, like any other mercenaries, would win back for him the territories taken by the Turks, and they failed to do so. To be sure, the two thrones did not break off negotiations, which centered around three issues: in order of importance, the Roman primacy, the Latin use of unleavened bread, and the *Filioque*. Delegations sent by PASCHAL II (1100–01, 1112) and EUGENE III (1136) resulted only in courteous debates.

In hindsight, more must be made of a growing reciprocal aversion between Latins and Greeks, a product of the crusades and Western economic imperialism, at the time when the Byzantium of the Comnenes seemed to get a new foothold in Anatolia, the Balkans, and even Italy: in 1155, a new Roman delegation drew from Manuel I a definite rejection of the primacy. From then on, this rejection underwent progressive theoretical development in the name of the pentarchy: PETER, never having received any effective primacy over the other apostles, Rome could have none over the other patriarchates, which, all five of them, should govern the universal Church; even more, Rome had lost its title with the transfer of the empire to Constantinople, and the origin of the mission to preach should be sought in Jerusalem, not Rome.

When Byzantium once again lost strength, the very idea of accepting the Roman primacy amounted to political capitulation before the enemy. In 1193, the weak Isaac II had a letter drafted to CELESTINE III in which, for the first time, doubt was cast on the Petrine origin of the see of Rome. There remained in Byzantium, however, a number of sincere partisans of the union of the Churches, who regarded the dogmatic and disciplinary issues as surmountable. At the beginning of the 13th century, that was the position of a great Greek canonist, Demetrios Chomatenos. But the majority was increasingly anti-Roman, as was another canonist of repute, Theodore Balsamon, who, at the end of the 12th century, wrote that an Orthodox believer could neither hear the Latin mass nor receive communion at it. The enemy was the West, as proved by the Fourth Crusade, preached by INNOCENT III against Egypt, which resulted in the bloody capture of Constantinople in 1204 and the carving up of the great Christian empire by Westerners. The religious problems between Byzantium and Rome became secondary, compared to their insurmountable political and cultural estrangement.

The Impossible Union. The shock of 1204 must always be kept in mind to account for why, until 1453, union was attempted several times but never realized. Rome certainly was not responsible. Innocent III, learning of the taking of Constantinople, excommunicated the perpetrators though he soon repented of it on the ground that the crusade, in the end, had been profitable for Christianity. For Byzantium, it would thenceforth be impossible to distinguish the papacy from a West that was bent on its destruction; moreover, Innocent had placed on the throne of conquered Constantinople a Latin patriarch who imposed his rite there. Rome had destroyed at one stroke the two foundations of Orthodoxy,

the empire and the Orthodox see.

Accordingly, it was at Nicaea in 1208, alongside an exiled empire, that the patriarchate of Constantinople was reconstituted; from it would flow a polemical literature, using the legend of Andrew, the first of the apostles since he introduced Peter to Jesus, to prove that Constantinople was indeed the first of all dioceses; it was undoubtedly in this atmosphere of exile that the lampoon long falsely attributed to Photius was written, "Against Those Who Say Rome Is the First See." In fact, its real themes are the despoiling of the Greek churches and the shame cast on them by the naming of a Venetian patriarch, and the story circulated that from the time of the Latin conquest the protectress of the city, the Mother of God of the Blachernes, no longer performed miracles. It is worth noting that this text, written in Greek for Greek readers, proves that it was still necessary to convince many Byzantine partisans of the Roman primacy; it would always remain so, to the extent that one would hardly dare question the conciliar decisions, especially those of Chalcedon, or the legislation of Justinian.

The reference to Andrew was therefore dangerous, since it confirmed the Latins' claim by simply outbidding it, and even before 1230 it was completely abandoned. From then on, theologians aware of the traditions preferred to emphasize the apostolic idea, by demonstrating that it was compatible with their pentarchial conceptions. They stressed that the apostles, far from having been attached to a particular see to which they gave greater or less luster, each without distinction fulfilled a mission directed to the universal Church, as John Kamateros, the last patriarch before 1204, had already underlined. Speaking in front of Tommaso Morosini, the Latin titular of Constantinople, Nicholas Mesarites went further in 1206 by affirming that, in consequence, attaching Peter exclusively to the see of Rome was a Jewish idea. It was, then, a sacrilege to substitute another primacy for the only one of value, that of Christ, and the Roman claim flouted the apostolic mission, directed to all Christians, as Patriarch Germanus II (1222–40) strongly affirmed.

The Byzantine Church therefore made increasingly less claim to its own primacy, preferring a collegial vision then brought to its perfection: in the 14th century, Barlaam of Calabria, before joining Roman Catholicism, stressed that Peter had passed on the function of leader of the apostles to the ensemble of the bishops and not to Clement alone, something that denied the pope any ground on which to claim he was leader of all the bishops. At the same time, a certain Nil Kabasilas went even further, in maintaining that the real foundations of the ecclesial edifice are the bishops, all equal as "guardians of the profession of Peter."

It is clear that the Byzantines arrived in that period at a communitarian conception of the Church that could not have emerged while the imperial institution retained all its power. With the weakening of that power was born the idea of a universal Christianity able to survive on its own, under the protection of bishops collegially responsible for its administration, a conception that enabled Orthodoxy to adapt, after 1453, to a tough earthly reality, the Ottoman domination. Nevertheless, this doctrine, which continued to deepen until the 15th century, still preserved, theoretically, the old idea of the primacy of honor reserved to the pope. John Mesarites and his son, Nicholas, proved this in 1206 and 1214, and the patriarch Nil still admitted it around 1380, in a letter to URBAN VI, the pope of Rome and not that of Avignon.

But from then on the doctrinal aspect took over: the pope could, in principle, receive the appeals of a decision of the patriarch, but he nevertheless had to profess the true faith, which was no longer the case with Rome's adoption of the *Filioque*. In the 15th century, Simeon of Thessalonica emphasized this clearly: "When the Latins say that the bishop of Rome is the first, they must not be contradicted . . . His throne is apostolic, and the pontiff who occupies it, as long as he professes the true faith, is named successor of Peter. No one who judges and expresses himself correctly could deny it . . ." However, it is clear that the dogma was only an alibi, for the real clash now was between two radically divergent conceptions of the Church, the one more and more monarchical and hierarchical, the other resolutely communitarian and less and less subject to the imperial power.

Whence the uselessness of the attempts at union in the 14th and 15th centuries, the sincere artisans of which, such as John Vekkos, Demetrios Kydones, and Bessarion, never managed to convince either their Church or the faithful of its propriety. These efforts, in effect, were the fruit of a political will that, in order to succeed, would have had to change mentalities, but that in reality did nothing but beg for Western aid, accepting all the conditions attached to it. In 1274, it was to avoid the offensive of Charles of Anjou that Michel VIII Palaeologus subscribed to the union of Lyons, rejected by the great majority of the Orthodox, despite the proofs of moderation given by a number of Latin theologians, such as Humbert of Romans. Andronicus II repudiated it in 1282, and the conversion of John V in 1369, in the midst of the Turkish invasion, was never more than a personal act without consequences.

More than ever, any acceptance of the doctrine and, above all, the hierarchy of the Latins was felt to be a cultural capitulation, with the result that the GREAT SCHISM OF THE WEST which brought the conciliar reality back to center stage, had little echo in Byzantium, which, all things considered, would never opt either for Avignon or for the council of Constance. The union of Florence, signed on 5 July 1439, was the work of an emperor in distress, John VIII, surrounded by a lofty hierarchy away from home, and the fact that it corresponded to the reaffirmation of a Roman papal power freed from conciliar oversight was not

in its favor. Disobeyed and even ignored by a great many, since it had to be imposed by force on Constantinople, and then only on 12 December 1452, its sole real consequence was a schism in the Byzantine Church. After 1453, it was weakened by the Turkish conquest and the flight of the "Uniates" to the West.

Alain Ducellier

Bibliography

Ducellier A. et al., *Byzance et le monde orthodoxe*, Paris, 1986; *L'Église byzantine. Entre pouvoir et esprit*, Paris, 1990.

Dvornik, F. *Le Schisme de Photius, Paris*, 1950; *Byzance et la primauté romaine*, Paris, 1964; *Photian and Byzantine Ecclesiastical Studies*, London, 1974.

Geanakoplos, D. J. *Byzantine East and Latin West*, rev. ed., New York, 1983.

Gerö, S. *Byzantine Iconoclasm during the Reign of Leo III with Particular Attention to the Oriental Sources*, and *Byzantine Iconoclasm during the Reign of Constantine V*, Louvain, 1973–77.

Gill, J. *Byzantium and the Papacy, 1198–1400*, New Brunswick, 1979; *Church Union, Rome and Byzantium, 1204–1453*, London, 1979 (collection of articles).

Grumel V. "Les préliminaires du schisme de Michel Cérulaire ou la question romaine," *Revue d'études byzantines*, 10 (1952).

Hannick, C. "Die byzantinischen Missionen," *Kirchengeschichte als Missionsgeschichte*, Munich, 1978.

Leib, B. *Rome, Kiev et Byzance à la fin du XIe siècle*, Paris, 1924.

Maccarrone, M. "Cathedra Petri und päpstlicher Primat von 2. bis 4. Jahrhundert," *Saeculum*, 13 (1962).

Magi, L. *La Sede romana nella corrispondenza degli imperatori e patriarchi bisantini, VI–VII sec.*, Rome-Louvain, 1972.

Nicol, D. "Byzantium and the Papacy in the Eleventh Century," *JEH*, 13 (1962).

Patlagean, E. "Les stoudites, l'empereur et Rome: figure byzantine d'un monachisme réformateur," ibid., 429–60.

Runciman, S. *The Byzantine Theocracy*, Cincinnati, 1973.

Sansterre, J. M. *Les Moines grecs et orientaux à Rome aux époques byzanine et carolingienne (milieu du VIe–fin du IXe s.)*, Brussels, 1983, 2 vols.; "Le monachisme byzantin à Rome," *Bisanzio, Roma e l'Italia nell'alto Medioevo. Settimane di studio del Centro italiano di studi sull'alto Medioevo XXXIV*, 1986, I, Spoleto, 1988, 701–40.

Setton, K. M. *The Papacy and the Levant, 1207–1571*, 1976–84.

Spiteris, J. *La critica bisantina del primato romano nel secolo XII*, Rome, 1979.

C

CAIUS. *Pope from 17 December 283 to 22 April 296.*

Caius succeeded EUTYCHIAN during the reign of Numerian. He held the episcopate for twelve years, four months and seven days—according to the *Liberian Catalogue* (MGH AA, 9/1, 75), between 17 December 283 and 22 April 296. Euseius (*Ecclesiastical History*, VII, 32) assigns him fifteen years. This pope is as little known as his predecessor, Eutychian. Most of his pontificate was contemporary with the first part of the rule of Diocletian (284–305), when this emperor slowly reestablished the stability of the Roman state. Eusebius mentions that at that time, before the unleashing of the great persecution, the tolerance of the authorities had never been so great, and that Christians were able to advance to high levels in the administration. Caius was buried in the CATACOMB of Callistus on the Appian Way.

Michel Christol

Bibliography

LP, 1, 161 = *MGH, GPR,* I, 40: *MGH, AA,* 9/1, 70.

CALENDAR. A calendar is any system of the division and arrangement of time. The ecclesiastical calendar, established in the domain of LITURGY, soon moved beyond it to regulate the Christian world.

Divisions of Time and Their Denominations. From their foundation, the Churches inherited the Jewish lunar calendar. Their expansion within Greco-Roman civilization brought them into contact with the civil solar calendar, which gained ascendancy within a few centuries and endured in a Christianized form. The liturgical year is therefore based on an approximation, fixed at 365 to 366 days by the Julian calendar and slightly rectified by the Gregorian calendar (see the following entry). The liturgical day, however, begins at the sunset preceding the corresponding civil day. From the lunar base of the Jewish calendar, only the movable character of the date of Easter, as well as the cycle of feasts and seasons dependent upon it, has been preserved; its determination gave rise to the EASTER-DATE CONTROVERSY.

The division of days into twelve months of unequal length and the denomination of these were derived from the Roman calendar. The calculation of days within months was modified by many other influences than that of the Church. From the third century, the Classical Roman system (with its *calends, nones,* and *ides*) lost ground to a simpler method of calculating the day of the month by numbering the days within each month, sometimes with intermediate periods (halves or thirds of months). But the Roman system was still widely used in the Middle Ages, once there was sufficient knowledge of antiquity. Traditionally, it was preserved in the most solemn papal ACTS, even though BRIEFS were dated by the day of the month. From the 2nd century on, a concurrent cycle of seven days became widespread: the week (*hebdomada, septimana*), the origins of which go far back in Middle Eastern astrological tradition, which names the days after planets. The Jewish religion adhered to the same cycle, placing the Creation within seven days. The Church accepted the system, though it was not able to replace the old "pagan" appellations with the numbering of *feriae* (*feria prima* = Sunday, *feria secunda* = Monday, etc.), which has been preserved only in Portuguese. Very soon the Church replaced the Jewish Sabbath on Saturday (*sabbati dies,* or "day of Saturn," *Saturday*) with Sunday, the Lord's day (*dominica dies*), a day of rest and of celebration of the resurrection of Christ, occurring on the day following the Sabbath and a day which is that of the sun in the Middle Eastern tradition (*Sunday, Sonntag*).

In the empire, at Rome and later at BYZANTIUM, the years were designated after the names of incumbents of the consulate, then, from 567, after the years of the emperor's reign and (fictive) consulate. The papal chancery immediately adopted this usage, which prevailed in public and private acts. Pope ADRIAN I demonstrated his independence by substituting his own year of pontificate. The system continued under Frankish tutelage; the regnal year of Charlemagne and that of his successors was added from 798 on. This system's precision faltered in the 10th century, though it was reinstituted in the East under the Ottomans, and it disappeared definitively from Western usage in the first decades of the 11th century. From 957 on, not without some confusion, the date was fixed from the birth of Christ. Its computation had been fixed around the middle of the 6th century at Rome, independent of the papacy, by a Scythian monk, Dionysius Exiguus; based on calculations that were no doubt slightly inexact, Dennis placed the birth of Christ on 25 December of the year 753 from the foundation of Rome. As Christian era as a method of dating slowly spread, so did the Easter tables of Dionysius. The calendar crossed over with the missions to England, returned to the Continent, and was adopted in 741 by the annals of the Frankish kingdom, and later by the papal chancery.

Liturgical Cycles of the Year. Commemorated on a Sunday, Easter, from the 2nd century on, highlighted the year with the most important of all anniversary celebrations. Little by little, an increasing number of days were associated with it, which came to form the Easter cycle, seven weeks before and fifty days after Easter. The feast began with a vigil when the Easter candle was lighted and marked with the indication of the year, which gave rise to the custom—widespread until the 16th century—of beginning the civil year not on 1 January but at Easter. Soon the vigil was preceded by celebration of the *tridium* (Holy Thursday, Good Friday, and Holy Saturday). The prolongation of the cycle at beginning and end, linked to the catechesis preceding and following Easter baptisms, came into effect around the second half of the 4th century. It was then that the institution of Lent, well documented from the early 4th century in Egypt, spread to Rome, where it increased from two weeks to forty days. However, Palm Sunday is not solidly documented in the West before the 9th century, and even at Rome not until the 11th century.

Developed in counterpoint, the shorter Christmas cycle also appeared later. The first evidence of this feast is seen in a calendar drawn up at Rome around 336. December 25 was the festival of the glorification of the emperor (*natalis invicti*) as well as that of the triumph of the sun at the solstice. Even in the mid-5th century, Pope LEO I reprimanded the faithful who, in a dubious syncretism, greeted the rising sun from St. Peter's Square. The period of Advent seems to have been introduced at Rome in the second half of the 5th century. On Epiphany (6 January), the papacy emphasized the Adoration of the Magi (the revelation to the pagans), whereas the Eastern Churches made that date the great feast of the Baptism of Christ.

A final cycle, of decidedly Roman origin, placed one week of fasting and prayer at the opening of each season. These were the "Three Seasons" (June, September, and December), then, on the addition of the beginning of spring, the Ember Days. Exported throughout the West, they were always of lesser importance.

Feasts and Calendars. Outside these cycles, time was said to be "ordinary"; however, feasts multiplied rapidly, dedicated to Christ, to the Virgin, to saints, or even to certain historical events (Finding of the Cross by St. Helena) or local events (dedication of a basilica). In the beginning, each Church developed in its own fashion the cult of martyrs, and then of witnesses of the faith in a larger sense. The celebration of this cult at the martyr's tombs, first documented in Asia, is documented at Rome from the 3rd century. It was necessary to preserve the memory of name, place, and date (anniversary of death and birth in Heaven, or *dies natalis*; for a nonmartyr, *depositio*): *nomen, locus, dies*. Thus were created the purely local calendars, in the strictest sense of the word. In Classical Latin, "calendar" meant a table of beliefs and of interests to be noted on the *calends*, the first day of the month. The first known Roman Christian calendar, drawn up around 336 and kept as a luxurious private almanac, is the "Chronograph" of 354, attributed to a no doubt pseudonymous Philocalus. It registers about twenty celebrations, concentrated between July and December. Its first expansion, in terms of the year as well as the area of the city, is attributed to Pope DAMASUS I.

Soon attempts at a universal compilation—the "martyrologies"—appeared. The first worthy of the name was drawn up in the 430s and is attributed to St. Jerome (the Hieronymian Martyrology). It is known to us only through a revised version made at Auxerre at the end of the 6th century. At Lyons and at Vienne, a succession of Frankish clerics developed a new martyrology—the Martyrology of Ado—riddled with interpolations and misreadings, that was passed off as a text discovered at Rome. Invested with papal authority, and not without new modifications, it passed into the martyrology composed in the 860s by Usuard at Saint-Germain-des-Prés, which was widely distributed as late as the 16th century. GREGORY XIII had it inserted within the framework of the Roman martyrology. The first printed edition (1584) was reprinted under the auspices of Cardinal Baronius in 1586, 1589, 1598. The edition of 1681, personally revised by BENEDICT XIV in 1748, serves as a basis for the last official edition (1922). Because of its textual problems, an inscription in the Martyrology of Ado is not sufficient proof of sanctity.

The celebrations did not cease to multiply in the Middle Ages, when a principal feast was coupled with the evening before it—the "vigil"—and its recall a week later during the "octave." There was great confusion: several saints honored on the same day, several feasts for the same saint held on different dates, saints with the same names. Papal intervention progressed slowly, together with interventions related to the liturgy and CANONIZATION. In the last centuries of the Middle Ages, the calendar was expanded to include the celebration of contemporary saints. Through its prestige, and indirectly through pilgrimages that diffused Roman feasts, as well as by the official proclamation of new feasts throughout the Christian world, the papacy, with increasing success, juxtaposed new celebrations to those that had been instituted locally. The papal initiative was sometimes decisive; thus, in 1264 URBAN IV brought the feast of Corpus Christi with him from his diocese of Liège, and that of Christ the King was inaugurated in 1925 by PIUS XI. At other times, the papacy extended primarily local feasts to the wider Christian world: the Trinity, promulgated by Cluny, was spread by JOHN XXII in 1334, long after the reservations expressed about it by ALEXANDER II and ALEXANDER III. The Sacred Heart, generalized in 1856 by PIUS IX, had at first been granted to local, then national, Churches (Poland and Portugal in 1765, Austria and Spain in 1778). In effect, only at the end of an evolution stretching from the council of TRENT to VATICAN II has the papacy been able to directly effect standardization. In the Roman calendar of 1568, the number of feasts was reduced to approximately 200 (130 for saints). This was widely adopted, subject to the addition of local or national celebrations. It continued to mushroom, however: 13 new feasts (12 of them for saints) up to 1600; 49 (46) in the 17th century; 32 (31) in the 18th century; 25 (23) in the 19th century; 26 from 1901 to 1960. A major revision promulgated on 14 February 1969 is still applied by national Churches, with a few additions. Seeking greater universality, the revision modified dates and excised a number of saints, leaving only 180. The protests these modifications engendered demonstrate the strong influence, social and psychological, of tradition in the calendar.

Liturgical Calendar.

I. The medieval and modern Easter cycle

9th Sunday before Easter: Septuagesima, *Alleluia clausum* (since 1072 the Alleluia is not sung), Sunday of *Circumdederunt* (after the first word of the Introit of the day).

8th Sunday before Easter: Sexagesima, Sunday of *Exsurge*.

7th Sunday before Easter: Quinquagesima, Sunday of *Esto mihi*.

Ash Wednesday: "Great fasting," beginning of Lent ("Great Lent") of 40 days, or Quadragesima, definitively fixed at the council of Benevento, 1091.

6th Sunday before Easter: 1st Sunday of Lent, Sunday of *Invocavit me*, of the Bones, quintain. Week of the Watch, of the Bones.

5th Sunday before Easter: 2nd Sunday of Lent, Sunday of *Reminiscere*, of the Canaanite woman.

4th Sunday before Easter: 3rd Sunday of Lent, Sunday of *Oculi*.

Thursday of Mid-Lent (since the late Middle Ages).

3rd Sunday before Easter: 4th Sunday of Lent, Sunday of *Laetare Jerusalem*, of mid-Lent (before its shift to the preceding Thursday).

2nd Sunday before Easter: 5th Sunday of Lent, Sunday of the Passion, of *Judica me*.

1st Sunday before Easter: Palm (*Osanna*, Palm Sunday, *Festum olivarum* in Italy).

Holy Week, (Sorrowful, great, etc.).

Holy Thursday, (Thursday of absolution), Last Supper.

Good Friday, Friday of Adoration.

Holy Saturday, Great Saturday.

Easter Sunday: Resurrection (the German name *Ostern* and the English name *Easter* are named after a pagan Germanic feast).

Easter Week, white, (the newly baptized wear white garments) *authentica*.

1st Sunday after Easter: White Sunday, of *Quasimodo*; *Antipascha*, Low Sunday.

2nd Sunday after Easter: Sunday of the Good Shepherd, of *Misericordia Domini*.

3rd Sunday after Easter: Sunday of *Jubilate*.

4th Sunday after Easter: Sunday of *Cantate*.

5th Sunday after Easter: Sunday of litanies, of *Rogate*.

Rogation days (from Monday to Wednesday; days on which special litanies are recited).

Ascension Thursday.

6th Sunday after Easter: Sunday after the Ascension, of *Exaudi Domine*.

7th Sunday after Easter: Pentecost, May Passover.

[Data simplified from A. Giry (1894), esp. "Glossaire des dates," 259–73.]

II. The great Marian feasts

The four major feasts, in boldface, were promulgated at Rome during the course of the 7th century and made solemnities at the end of the 20th century; the feasts in italics are of modern origin.

1 January: "Natale Sanctae Mariae" (Birth of Mary), the oldest feast, well documented in the 7th century, later relegated to secondary importance by the Christmas octave and the Circumcision.

2 February: **Purification** (Candlemas), originally, and again since 1969, a feast essentially consecrated to the Lord (Presentation in the Temple).

11 February: *Apparition of the Immaculate Conception*, granted to the diocese of Tarbes by Leo XIII in 1890, extended to the Roman Catholic world by Pius X in 1907.

19 March: Nuptials, a feast of St. Joseph developed in the 15th century and extended to the Roman Catholic world in 1621.

25 March: **Annunciation**, with the same evolution as Purification (Annunciation of the Lord).

Friday before Palm Sunday: Compassion of Mary, promulgated by the Cistercians and registered in the Roman calendar in 1727.

31 May: *Mary, Queen*, instituted by Pius XII in 1954.

2 July: Visitation, of Eastern origin, promulgated by the Franciscans and instituted for the universal Church by Urban VI in 1389 to put an end to the Great Schism.

16 July: Our Lady of Mount Carmel, promulgated by the Carmelites in the 14th century and registered in the Roman calendar in 1726.

5 August: *Our Lady of the Snows*, feast of the dedication of ST. MARY MAJOR, registered in the Roman calendar in 1568.

15 August: **Assumption**, of Eastern origin (Dormition).

22 August: *Immaculate Heart of Mary*, promulgated by the Eudists; instituted for the diocese of Rome by Leo XIII in 1880, and for the Roman Catholic world by Pius XII in 1942.

8 September: **Nativity** of Mary, Our Lady of September.

12 September: *Holy Name of Mary*, first celebrated the Sunday after the Nativity; granted by Julius II to the diocese of Cuenca, and registered in the Roman calendar in 1683.

15 September: *Seven Sorrows of Mary*, first celebrated the 3rd Sunday of September, extended to the Roman Catholic world by Pius VII on his return to Rome in 1814.

24 September: *Our Lady of Mercy*, developed by the Mercedarians and extended to the Roman Catholic world by Innocent XII in 1696.

7 October: *Rosary of the Virgin Mary*, first celebrated the first Sunday of October under the name Our Lady of Victory, as thanksgiving to God after the battle of Lepanto. Instituted for the city of Rome by Gregory XIII in 1573, and for the Roman Catholic world by Clement XI in 1716.

11 October: *Maternity of Mary*, granted to Portugal by Benedict XIV in 1751 and instituted by Pius XI in 1931. Anniversary day (erroneous) of closure of the council of Ephesus; inaugural day of the Second Vatican council.

21 November: Presentation of Mary in the Temple, of Eastern origin, approved by Gregory XI in 1372.

8 December: Conception of Mary, introduced in England in the 11th century, transported to the Continent, and promulgated by the Franciscans; instituted for the diocese of Rome by Sixtus IV in 1477, and for the Roman Catholic world by Clement XI in 1708; became the Immaculate Conception in 1854.

Oliver Guyogeannin

Bibliography

Dalmas, I. H., Jounel, P., and Martimort, A. G. *La Liturgie et le temps*, Paris, 1983 (*L'église en prière*, 4).

Del Piazo, M. *Manuale di cronologia*, Rome, 1969 (*Fonti e studi del corpus membranarum italicarum*, 4).

Giry, A. *Manuel de diplomatique*, Paris, 1894, repr. Geneva, 1975, 79–314.

Le Temps chrétien de la fin de l'Antiqueté au Moyen Age (IIIe-XIIIe siècle), Paris, 1984 (*Colloques internationaux du CNRS*, 604), especially C. Pietri, "Le temps de la semaine à Rome et dans l'Italie chrétienne, IVe-VIe siècle," 63–93.

Maurice Denis-Boulet, N. *Le Calendrier chrétien*, Paris, 1959.

Styrubbe E. J., and Voet, L. *De chronologie van de Middeleeuwen en de moderne Tijden in de Nederlanden*, Anvers-Amsterdam, 1960.

Talley, T. *Origins of the Liturgical Year*, New York, 1986.

CALENDAR, GREGORIAN. Promulgated by GREGORY XIII on 24 February 1582 (bull *Inter gravissimas*), the Gregorian calendar reformed the Julian calendar by narrowing the gap between the length of the average civil year (365.245 days) and that of the tropical year (duration of the revolution of the earth around the sun, 365.2422 days). The Julian reform of the calendar in use in 46 B.C., on the initiative of Julius Caesar, made a leap year of 366 days follow three common years of 365 days; this led to an average year (365.25 days) that was slightly longer in relation to the movement of the planets with an annual surplus of approximately 11 minutes 14 seconds—almost one day every 128 years. The spring equinox, which fell on 25 March in the time of Julius Caesar, was thus observed on 21 March in 325, the year when, according to medieval tradition, the council of Nicea chose this period as a point of departure for the calculation of the date of Easter.

From the 13th century on, astronomers were capable of explaining the time difference and of proposing corrections, even though it was necessary to wait for Copernicus to arrive at a precise measurement of the tropical year. Naturally, the papacy was both source and target of the reflections of astronomers such as John of Holywood, Robert Grosseteste, and Roger Bacon in the 13th century, or Jean des Murs and Fermin of Belleval in the 14th. Councils took up the cause in the 15th century—Pierre d'Ailly at Constance, and Nicholas of Cusa at Basel. The question was still under discussion under SIXTUS IV, Julius II, and LEO X, and at the Fifth Lateran Council.

On its adjournment on 4 December 1563, the council of TRENT charged the pope with the writing of a new MISSAL and a new BREVIARY. Gregory XIII, in a far-ranging interpretation, linked the reform of the calendar to the redrafting of the liturgical books, which had been approved by PIUS V. A first commission met around 1575 and determined that since the true equinox henceforth fell on 11 March, it would to reduce to 10 days the interval between the civil year and the tropical year, without advancing any practical solution. In 1577, the pope consulted the princes and the universities, without any better result.

The papal commission resumed its work. Under the chairmanship of the prefect of the Vatican Library, Cardinal Guglielmo Sirleto—who had already worked on the reform of the missal, the breviary, and the martyrology—it recruited curialists such as the Frenchman Seraphin Olivier, judge of the Rota, and intellectuals including the Calabrian Antonio Giglio, the Bolognese Dominican Ignazio Danti, the German Jesuit Christof Clavius, and the Spaniard Pedro Chaco. The commission proposed to slash 10 days from the civil calendar and to reduce three leap-year intercalations every 400 years: when the first two numbers of century years could be multiplied by four (1600, 2000, etc.), these would be leap years, as in the Julian calendar; but the others (1700, 1800, 1900, 2100, etc.) would be common years.

Gregory XIII prescribed the measure without hesitation: the day following Thursday, 4 October 1582, was to be designated Friday, 15 October. Only Italy, Spain, and Portugal, together with their colonies and Poland, applied the reform to the letter. The other Catholic countries followed with a slight time lag: thus, there was a jump from Sunday, 9 December, to Monday, 20 December 1582 in the king-dom of France and in Lorraine; from Friday, 21 December 1582, to Saturday, 1 January 1583 (thereby omitting Christmas) in the Savoy and in the Catholic Low Countries; Holland (for an unequal application), waited for February–March 1583; Peru complied in March 1583, Catholic Switzerland, Bohemia, and Monrovia in January 1584, and Hungary in 1587. The empire demonstrated its divisions: Habsburg adopted the new calendar in February 1583, a part of Austria and Bavaria in October, the towns of Wurzburg, Münster, and Mainz at different times in November, and the rest of Austria in December.

The Gregorian calendar met with vehement opposition in the Protestant and Orthodox countries, which persisted in some places up to the beginning of the 20th century. The chronological differences between countries complicated the work of diplomats and merchants, besides bedeviling historians. The revision of the calendar, launched from Rome, had been squarely placed under the rubric of the Catholic Reformation. Whatever the authenticity of the witticism "better to live in disharmony with the sun than in harmony with the pope," comparisons of the introduction of the Gregorian calendar with that of the Trojan horse in the Reformed citadel flourished in polemic literature. The smallest differences in the opinions of astronomers, such as Tycho Brahe and Johannes Kepler, combined with practical barriers to delay the new calendar's adoption by civil authorities. Reformed Germany and Denmark adopted the Gregorian calendar only in February 1700; the Protestant Swiss cantons followed in 1701, the Grisons in 1811. Sweden decided to move closer to the Gregorian calendar by one day, making the year 1700 a common year. It reverted to the strict Julian calendar by adding a day (30 February) to the year 1712 and adopted the Gregorian calendar only in 1753. England and its colonies, after ferocious opposition to the "papist" calendar, adopted it by moving from 2 to 14 September in 1752. In the modern era, the predominance of the Gregorian calendar facilitated its adoption even by countries opposed to westernization: Japan in 1873, at the time of the legislation of the Christian cult; China in 1912 , then 1929; Turkey in 1914. The countries of Orthodox tradition were the last to resist, until the time lag with the Julian calendar was 13 days. In 1918, this was one of the first acts of the Bolshevik government in the Soviet Union, made definitive in 1940 after trials with a perpetual calendar launched in 1923. The move was made in 1923 in Greece (predetermining leap years in 2900 and 3300 instead of 2800 and 3200), in 1927 elsewhere. The Orthodox churches have progressively adjusted their feasts. The Gregorian calendar has also become the only solar calendar of worldwide use, as opposed to traditional lunar or other systems of calculating long periods of time, such as the Muslim and Jewish lunar calendars.

Olivier Guyotjeannin

Bibliography

Coyne, G. V., Hoskin, M. A., and Pedersen, O., eds. *Gregorian Reform of the Calendar: Proceedings of the Vatican Conference to Commemorate Its 400th Anniversary (1582–1982)*, Vatican, 1983.

Giry, A. *Manuel de diplomatique*, Paris, 1894, repr. Geneva, 1975, 159–68.

Maiello, F. H. "Tempo, potere e cosmologia: La riforma gregoriana del calendaro," *Dimensioni e problemi della ricerca storica*, 1989, 102–37.

CALLISTUS I. *(born in Rome, ca. 153, died in Rome, 222). Elected pope in 217. Saint.*

The life of Callistus (or Calixtus) I is fairly well known through HIPPOLYTUS's *Philosophumena*, but this testimony comes from one of the pope's greatest adversaries and should be interpreted accordingly. Other sources give only sparse bits of information. We know that Callistus was Roman, born on the right bank of the Tiber in the Transtiberina. He was a slave of a Christian, Carpophorus, and served as his financial steward. According to Hippolytus, Callistus compromised the interests of his master by embezzlement. To avoid prosecution, he probably fled to Ostia and tried to board a ship. Caught, he was sentenced to work on a treadmill, but was pardoned. One Sabbath, he disturbed the sacred reading in a synagogue. He was handed over to the prefect of the city, Seius Fuscianus, who had him whipped and deported to the mines of Sardinia, where other Christians were already enslaved (c. 186–9).

Following an agreement between Pope VICTOR and the mistress of Commodus, Marcia, many Christians were released from Sardinia, including Callistus (between 190 and 192). Victor may not have wished for his release; he sent him to Anzio and gave him a monthly pension for what may have been a mission in the service of the Church. The new pope, ZEPHYRINUS, recalled Callistus to Rome, where he rose rapidly in the ecclesiastical hierarchy. As a deacon, he was appointed administrator of the cemetery on the Appian Way, the first officially owned by the Church, which later bore his name. When Zephyrinus died, Callistus was chosen as his successor, but among the clergy of Rome he already had many adversaries; some refused to recognize him and instead designated Hippolytus bishop of Rome (217). This schism would last until 235. Callistus governed the Church of Rome for five years, two months, and ten days, if Eusebius of Caesarea and other sources are to be believed.

Precise knowledge of Callistus's philosophy and actions is problematic. Hippolytus gives us the most information, but he portrays Callistus as the most unworthy of popes since the origin of the Church. It is, however, through this biased account that we must try to define the positions taken by Callistus. During his pontificate, conflicts of doctrine constantly arose, and Callistus made important decisions. Hippolytus accused him of having taught and defended the theories of modalism (theory that explained Father and Son as "modes" of divine being), spread by Epigonius, Cleomenius, and Sabellius. It appears, however, that even if Callistus at some time in his youth had espoused these doctrines, he did not, as pope, defend this radical position, which claims that, except for the incarnation, the difference between Father and Son is purely nominal: that there is only a single being, whose visible and human element is Christ and whose invisible and divine element is the Father. Callistus, in fact, even condemned Sabellius and the Sabellians, but he did not accept the theories of Hippolytus, which emphasized the distinction between the Father and the Word, from which follows the subordinate nature of the Word in relation to the Father (subordinationism). It was for this position that Hippolytus, driven from the Church for "ditheism," could not forgive him, even though Callistus only continued to affirm the unity of God in the distinction between Father and Son.

Callistus thus found himself exposed to attacks by Hippolytus based on morality and discipline. Hippolytus accused him of having been the first to "give full reign to human passions, saying that he pardoned everyone's sins." Callistus's indulgence was a way to reintegrate into the Church those whom harsh churchmen had driven out and to allow them ecclesiastical reconciliation after a penance that Callistus had never wished to suppress. The *Philosophumena* also accuses Callistus of not having deposed corrupt bishops and of having admitted to the episcopate, priesthood, and diaconate men who had been married two or three times; he might even have retained in their offices clerics who were married. This is probably calumny or a generalization from a few cases. In regard to matrimonial discipline, Callistus may have permitted Roman ladies of noble birth to contract marriages with men of inferior status. Such a measure would have been of great importance: Callistus thus approved marriages that civil law regarded as disgraceful to the women and he affirmed the authority of the Church in matrimonial matters. Hippolytus also claimed that during this pontificate, the abuse of rebaptism was widespread, but he attributes to Callistus a practice that existed in the Churches of Africa and of Cappadocia, for which he was not responsible. In fact, Hippolytus could not support the success of a policy of leniency while he adhered to the principle of rigor. It is evident that the positions he ascribed to Callistus are false and should be corrected, particularly because, in the tradition of the Church, this pope is without blemish. He has even been credited with the institution of fasting on Ember Days and with the construction of a basilica near the future St Mary's of Trastevere.

In fact, Callistus remained faithful to the traditions of the ancient Church, but he adapted them to his time and to the spread of Christianity in his society, which was raising new and acute problems. His success, for which Hippolytus reproached him and which is acknowledged by the formation of a "school" of doctors and theologians, allowed the Church to experience a period of prosperity and well-ordered effectiveness.

Callistus seems to have died during a local anti-Christian riot. He may have been thrown from a window into a well in Trastevere. His remains were interred in the cemetery of Calepodius on the Via Aurelia. His tomb was discovered in 1960 under the ruins of an oratory erected by Pope JULIUS I. Callistus was counted among the martyrs of the 4th century.

Jean-Pierre Martin

Bibliography

Altaner, B., and Daly, C. B. "The Edict of Callistus," *TU*, LXXVIII (1962), 176–82.

Bardy, G. *DHGE*, XI, 421–4. *Catholicisme: Hier, aujourd'hui, demain*, Paris, 1949, II, 387–8.

Bareille, G. *DTC*, II, 2, 1333–42.

Buruffa, A. *The Catacombs of St. Callixtus: History, Archaeology, Faith*, W. Purdy, trans., Vatican City, 1993.

Chapin, J. *NCE*, II, 1080–1.

Dáles, A. *L'edit de Calliste, Étude sur les origines de la pénitence chrétienne*, Paris, 1914.

Eusebius, *HE*, VI, 21, 2: 26, 2.

Galtier, P. "Le veritable edit de Calliste," *RHE*, XXIII (1927), 465–88.

Harrington, T. J. "The Local Church at Rome in the Second Century: A Common Cemetary Emerges Amid Developments in this 'Laboratory of Christian Policy,'" *Studia Canonica* 23 (1989), 167–88.

Heine, R. E. "The Christology of Callistus," *The Journal of Theological Studies*, 49 (Apr. 1998), 56–91.

Hippolytus, *Ref.*, IX, 11–13; 10, 27.

Leclerc, H. *DACL*, II, 2, 1657–64.

CALLISTUS II. *Guy de Bourgogne (b. Quingey, France, ca. 1050–d. Rome, 13 December 1124). Elected pope 2 February 1119, consecrated at Vienne 9 February 1119. Buried at St. John Lateran.*

In 1119, soon after the death of GELASIUS II in his refuge at Cluny, the papacy—engaged for half a century in the INVESTITURE conflict—found itself in a critical situation. The two cardinal bishops who had accompanied the pontiff in his exile took it on themselves to designate as his successor the archbishop of Vienne, Guy of Burgundy. They notified the cardinal bishop of Porto, Pierre, in Rome, who had their choice approved by acclamation of the clergy and the people in the cathedral of St. John Lateran on 1 March. The newly elected pope had already received episcopal consecration in the cathedral of Vienne, taking the name Callistus II.

This precipitous "election," accomplished with questionable regularity, resulted from the need to minimize the duration of the vacancy. The cardinals advocating it were eager to put on Peter's throne a person who on the one hand had enough authority either to resist Emperor Henry V or to negotiate without compromise, and who on the other hand was unfamiliar to the cardinalate factions linked to the rivalries of the great Roman families and above the divisions of the Sacred College concerning the position to adopt in relation to the Empire. Some cardinals believed that since PASCHAL II and the "concordat" of Sutri, no agreement was possible, and that it was necessary to impose free election of bishops without the intervention of lay authority. Others considered that a compromise was desirable in order to reestablish cooperation. These factors explain the choice of Guy, born at Quingey in present-day Franche-Comté, son of the count of Burgundy, related to the emperor, and allied to the most powerful families. His origins, career, metropolitan function, and relations with episcopal circles had given him perfect knowledge of the workings of the imperial Church, in which the bishops exercised by delegation certain state prerogatives (*regalia*), which provided them with revenue. He was, in fact, a man of the highest caliber, as well as a committed Gregorian bent on following the reform initiative in order to liberate the clergy from the too-firm hold of the laity on churches, and to consolidate Roman ecclesiastical power. In addition, he was a prelate from the secular orders (in contrast to his predecessors, who all came from the monastic milieu) and well informed about its problems—a metropolitan archbishop who was not a cardinal.

Callistus II inherited a burdensome legacy. Emperor Henry V, who had tried a few years before to force the hand of Paschal II and in response had been excommunicated in 1115, intended to maintain his privilege of controlling the designation of bishops in the Empire in order to grant them the regalian rights to which they were very attached. In 1116, after a SYNOD at Rome solemnly recalled that the Roman Church condemned this method of designation as well as the investiture of bishops by the sovereign, Henry V marched on the city and occupied it. Paschal II lay dying at that time (January 1118), and the cardinals replaced him with Gelasius II, who was one of the men most opposed to Henry. Thereupon, Henry had a few docile prelates elect an ANTIPOPE who shared his views and who took the name GREGORY VIII. This brought Henry a new sentence of excommunication from the legitimate pontiff, Gelasius II, who then fled Italy and died at Cluny after a very short pontificate.

Callistus II, thus faced the emperor and an antipope supported by several German bishops. He enjoyed, however, the favor of the majority of the French clergy and a good part of the Italian episcopate. He was the beneficiary of procedures developed in France and elsewhere for the recruitment of bishops that allowed for free election by chapters, while maintaining a certain royal prerogative. Moreover, the Church was pervaded by the exhaustion born of an endless conflict and a profound desire for peace on the part of a large number of Germanic prelates. This allowed Callistus, soon after a meeting of the diet of the empire at Mainz (June 1119) during which these bishops expressed their wish, to make contacts and to open negotiations. The pope and his legates unambiguously demanded the emperor's renunciation of the investiture of bishops with the cross and the ring, as well as the recognition of the elective principle (which Henry V had agreed to during conversations at Sutri). They accepted, however, that bishops—though elected and consecrated bishop by the Church alone—would remain linked to and under monarchical authority (even though Callistus preferred to create bishops by the canons' choice, investiture.)

The negotiations began at Strasbourg, where two legates were received by the monarch. They continued in the summer at Lorraine and seemed about to be concluded in October, when the pontiff—who had convened a council at Reims to settle the details of the conciliation—arrived at Mouzon to meet the emperor. The latter, however, hardened his position and caused a new rupture. The pope traveled to Rome. In the following months, Henry V, influenced by his entourage, resumed the talks; meanwhile, the antipope, imprisoned by the Normans of Sicily, submitted to Callistus (April 1121). In September, contact was reestablished, and in February 1122, the agreement was practically concluded. The final negotiations took place at Worms and ended on 23 September with the concordat of WORMS, which brought the investiture controversy to an end. In the future, according to this treaty, bishops would be elected by the canons in the presence of a representative of the king (or emperor); the elected would then receive the *regalia* from the monarch and would swear allegiance to him (which can allow the monarch to refuse to accept the one chosen by the canons), after which the bishops would be consecrated by the metropolitan. The agreement on these provisions constitutes a compromise by instituting elections while granting to the civil power means of intervention that were judged by some to be excessive (even though an analogous method had been established in the whole of Christiandom). The compromise would soon reveal itself to be, in practice, favorable to ecclesiastical jurisdiction, which was in fact the only judge of the canonical validity of the choice agreed on by the electors.

It was no doubt to strengthen this success and to manifest the preeminent authority of the papacy in the Church—an essential element of the Gregorian REFORM—and certainly also to translate those accomplishments into juridical norms, that Callistus II on 18–27 March 1123 convened the First LATERAN COUNCIL. This was the first congress of all bishops to be held in the West, previous ecumenical councils having all been held in the East, the last in 867. This illustrated both the sovereign PRIMACY of the pope and the acceptance of the Eastern SCHISM of 1054. In a few days the assembly, following the plan conceived by the pontiff who promulgated it, passed a series of decisions that can be grouped under two headings: (1) canons refining the previous great initiatives against SIMONY and NICOLAISM, on the Truce and Peace of God, and for the protection of the crusaders; and (2) rules aimed at consolidating, according to the principles of the reform, the parochial structure under the control of bishops (appointment for the *cura animarum* by the ordinary; prohibition of monks from filling curial offices without being instituted by the ordinary; constitutions concerning discipline and morals of the laity, marriage, inheritance, counterfeit money, etc.).

In 1122, Callistus II had to intervene in a serious debate among the Cluniacs about the position to be adopted in relation to bishops who protested against the management of parishes by the monasteries and against the collection of revenues and tithes which, in their view, were allocated to them. Some religious believed that the prerogatives juridically deemed theirs should be preserved, others that it was better to come to some agreement with the episcopate. In this dispute, the financial difficulties of the abbey were also considered, as well as the need to reform the congregation and the aims of monasticism. The abbot Pons de Melgueil was also deeply involved. The pope leaned firmly toward restoring episcopal rights and held the monastic life as an ideal whose values, to be aspired to by all, should be practiced primarily in retirement from the world, without involvement in the hierarchical organization of the Church. He took a position against the Cluniac leader and forced him to abdicate. This caused a crisis in the order, which Peter the Venerable would seek to alleviate by restoring discipline and cohesion, though without success in reestablishing the order's former dynamism. The future thus belonged to the new monasticism, in particular to the young congregation at Cisteaux, for which the pope had great admiration and whose first statutes he approved.

The relative brevity of Callistus II's pontificate in no way prevented him from intervening efficaciously in major problems faced by the Church. However, this great Franche-Comté aristocrat was quite unable to influence the traditional rivalries of the great families of Rome, where he stayed semipermanently from 1121. There, he collaborated with the Pierleoni clan against the Frangipanis, and as a result, problems arose with the election of his successor.

Marcel Pacaut

Bibliography

JW, I, 780–821; 2, 714–15, 755.

PL, 163, 1093–1358.

Fliche-Martin, VIII.

Jordan, E. "Calixte II," *DHGE*, 11 (1949), 424–38.

Maleczek, W. "Calixtus II," *LexMA*, 2 (1981–3), 1379–98.

Miccoli, G. "Callisto II," *DBI*, 16 (1973), 761–8.

Robert, U. *Bullaire du pape Calixte II*, 2 vols., Paris.

Robert, U. *Histoire du pape Calixte II*, Paris, 1891.

Stroll, M. "Calixtus II," *Studies in Medieval and Renaissance History*, 3 (1980), 1–53.

Stroll, M. *Symbols as Power: The Papacy Following the Investiture Contest*, Leyden, 1991.

Waaterich, J. B., 2, 115–53.

[CALLISTUS III]. Giovanni (d. before 1184). Antipope. Elected 20 September 1168, abdicated 20 August 1178.

Little is known of this man's life before he became abbot of Struma, near Arrezzo. He was elected antipope at Rome on the death of the antipope PASCHAL III, who had succeeded VICTOR IV, himself elected in 1159 at the same time as ALEXANDER III with the approbation of Emperor Frederick Barbarossa. Like his two predecessors, Callistus III put himself at the service of Frederick to help him bring the kingdom of Italy and the peninsula under his authority. At the date of his election, fortune had temporarily ceased to smile on the German monarchy, which was now supported only by a part of its episcopate and by a few Italian bishops. All the rest of Christianity outside of the empire, and even within it, was firmly ranged in Alexander III's camp, which had just been considerably reinforced by the formation of the Lombard League, reuniting the principal towns in the north of Italy in an antiimperial political and military alliance.

Conscious that the force of this response profoundly modified the characteristics of the struggle between Church and Empire, Frederick sought to separate the League from Pope Alexander III. He did not succeed, and failing in a final military exercise (the Lombard victory at Legano in May 1176), he decided to negotiate with the pontiff and to recognize him as the sole head of the Church, as well as to conclude a truce with the towns and with the king of Sicily. The "so-called Callistus" would receive in compensation only the administration of an abbey (preliminaries of Anagni in October 1176, confirmed by the treaty of Venice in July 1177). The antipope, to his grave disappointment, had not even been consulted. This explains the refusal of his most ardent partisans—the counts of Tusculum, a few barons of Campania, and a few Roman clerics—to bow to his decision, as well as his desire to remain in the Roman region for a last, hopeless battle. Archbishop Christian of Mainz, chancellor of the empire, put an end to this on instruc-

tions from Frederick Barbarossa, reinstalling Alexander III in Rome and forcing poor Callistus to submit and then to abdicate (20 August 1178). Alexander compensated him by naming him papal governor of Benevento; his successor was installed in 1184, so Callistus must have died shortly before that.

Marcel Pacaut

Bibliography

JW, 2, 42–430.

Fliche-Martin, IX-2.

Jordan K., "Calisto III," *DBI*, 16 (1973), 768–9.

Maleche, W. "Calixtus III," *LexMA*, 2 (1981–3), 1398.

Watterich, 2, 411 *sq.*, 577, 640-2.

CALLISTUS III. Alfonso de Borja, Borgia in Italian (b. Jativa, near Valencia in Spain, 31 December 1378, d. Rome, 6 August 1458). Elected pope 8 April 1455, concecrated 20 April. Interred in the Rotunda of St. Andrew, close to St. Peter's Basilica; transferred in 1610 to the Spanish church of St. Mary of Montserrat, Rome.

Alfonso de Borja began his studies at Valencia and continued at the University of Lerida, where he obtained his doctorate *in utroque jure* and taught for some years. BENEDICT XIII granted him a sinecure at Lerida. In 1412, on the death of Bishop Pedro of Cardona, he was named apostolic vicar. His reputation as a great jurist and as a man of integrity won him the post of counselor and private secretary to Ferdinand V, king of Aragon. He played a decisive role in the abdication of the antipope Gil Munoz, (CLEMENT VIII) on the death of Benedict XIII and in the reconciliation between Alfonso V, king of Naples and of Aragon, and Pope MARTIN V, on terms favorable to the succession to the throne of Naples of Louis d'Anjou. Martin V rewarded him for his efforts by naming him bishop of Valencia on 20 August 1429. Alfonso de Borja continued to assist the king in resolving disputes that divided Aragon and Castille, educating the king's natural son Ferrante, and organizing the Neapolitan kingdom. However, his loyalty to the sovereign pontiff led him to refuse to represent Alfonso V at the schismatic council at Basel. He confirmed his diplomatic skill as the author of the reconciliation between the king and EUGENE IV, validated by the signing of an agreement with Cardinal Scarampo on 14 June 1443 at Terracina. The pope showed his gratitude by naming Alfonso de Borja cardinal on 2 May 1443, while allowing him to retain the bishopric of Valencia. Alfonso then established his residence at Rome, where he became famous for his juridical competence, his honesty, and his piety.

On 8 April 1455, after the death of NICHOLAS V during the night of 14–25 March, the sixteen cardinals of the CONCLAVE, divided between the Orsinis and the Colonnas, finally opted—influenced by Alan de Caetivy and

Scarampo—for a caretaker pope in the person of Alfonso, then seventy-seven years old. Initial discontent aroused by his foreign origin soon disappeared in response to his honesty, virtue, and impartiality, which were recognized and praised by his contemporaries Vespasiano da Bisticci, St. Anthoninus of Florence, and Enea Silvio Piccolomini. One of the first acts of his pontificate, in which he took the name Callistus III, was the canonization, on 29 June 1455, of his compatriot St. Vincent Ferrer, known for having prophesied the accession of Callistus to the Holy See.

The principal objectives of Callistus III's government were peace and a concordat among the Italian princes and a CRUSADE against the Turks. The first supposed the maintenance of the balance attained in 1454 after the peace of Lodi. To succeed, Callistus showed his independence from his former protector, Alfonso the Magnanimous, who sought to add to his kingdoms of Aragon, Baleares, Sardinia, Sicily, and Naples that of Milan on the death of Filipino Maria Visconti (1447), in order to ensure his absolute control over the Italian peninsula. Callistus III favored the succession to Milan of Francesco Sforza. Equally, he opposed by force and spiritual sanctions the condottiere Giacomo Piccinino, who had undertaken the conquest of Siena and threatened the city of Bologna and the whole of Romania before finally retreating to the kingdom of Alfonso V.

This struggle to maintain equilibrium in the Italian peninsula seriously compromised the success of the second papal objective: the crusade against the Turks. In response to the conquest of Constantinople in 1453 and the persistent danger of expansion of the Ottoman Empire, the pope cherished the medieval ideal of a crusade of all the Christian princes, and during the conclave of his election he solemnly vowed to pursue it. On 15 May 1455, he published a bull ordering the crusade and fixing the departure of troops for 1 March of the following year. His enterprise collapsed, however, under the indifference of all the states. The dispatch of his nuncios to various countries proved fruitless: Cardinal Dionysio Szechy, bishop of Gran, to Hungary; Cardinal Nicholas of Cusa to England and Germany; Cardinal Alan de Caetivy to France; and Cardinal Juan de Carvajal to Germany, Hungary, and Poland. Callistus also dispatched preachers of the crusade, principally Franciscans, to each country of Europe. But in the end he could count only on his own forces, as well as on the not entirely disinterested support of the king of Naples, Emperor Frederick II of Germany, and the king of Hungary and Bohemia, who rallied to his cause through the intervention of Cardinal Juan de Carvajal.

The pope spent enormous sums, seeking to arm a fleet of sixteen galleons which, aided by Neapolitan reinforcements and under the command of Cardinal Scarampo, routed the Turkish fleet at Metelino (1457). The greatest success of this crusade was the liberation of Belgrade (1456) in the presence of Cardinal Carvajal, St. John of Capistrano, and Mathias Corvin (John Hunyadi), the new king of Hungary. To commemorate this victory, the pope in 1456 instituted the feast of the Transfiguration (6 August). In 1457, George Gastriota (Skanderberg), a protégé of Callistus III, conquered the Turkish army at Tomoniza, Albania. But these successes were partial and did not live up to the great ideal of Callistus III.

One disastrous consequence of his papal politics was the rise of anticlericalism in Germany, leading to the proclamation, in 1456, of *gravamina nationis germanicae* (a list of complaints against exercise of papal authority in Germany). The pope's concerns about the Turkish menace prevented him from dealing seriously with ecclesiastical discipline and doctrine. The following must, however, be noted: the publication of the constitution *Regimini* in response to a request from the bishop of Merseburg concerning the legislation of a type of annuity contract in use in Germany; and the pope's protests against the custom, prevalent in Salzburg, of bringing clerics before the civil courts, a practice at variance with canonical immunity. In addition to the beatification of Vincent Ferrer, Osmond, bishop of Salisbury, and Rose of Viterbo, Callistus III ordered the revision of the trial of Joan of Arc (11 June 1455). He held two CONSISTORIES, on 17 September and 17 December 1456, during which he named nine cardinals: Enea Silvio Piccolomini during the second, and two of his nephews, Luigi-Giovanni of Milan and Rodrigo Borgia (the future ALEXANDER VI) during the first. Callistus III was reproached for his excessive nepotism: apart from these two cardinals, he employed a good number of his compatriots, notably the brother of Rodrigo, Pietro-Luigi of Borgia, on whom he conferred the Castel Sant'Angelo and who was named captain-general of the Church. It must be pointed out, however, that this was a common practice of all the popes both before and after him, and the "Catalans" present in the Roman curia had been appointed, for the most part, by Alfonso V of Naples and Aragon.

Elected at an advanced age, with strictly legal training, Callistus III was not a pope in the mold of Nicholas V, influenced by the humanists. On the contrary, he attracted their hatred to the point where they accused him—unjustly—of having destroyed the library of Nicholas V. However, Callistus was not in any way prejudiced against them, as is evident in the protection he granted to Lorenzo Valla, named papal secretary and canon of St. John Lateran, as well as to Cardinal Enea Silvio Piccolomini, who would succeed him as Pope PIUS II. Callistus III died piously, and his nephew, Rodrigo Borgia, had constructed in his honor a grandiose tomb, important vestiges of which survive.

Just Fernandez Alonso

Bibliography

Albareda, A. M. "Il Bibliotecario de Callisto III," *Miscell. G. Mercati*, IV, Cité du Vatican, 1946, 177–208.

Altisent, J. B. *Alfonso de Borja en Lerida*, Lerida, 1924.

Babinger, F. *Mehmed der Eroberer und seine Zeit*, Munich, 1943.

Baillori, M. *Dice. Hist. Ecles. de Espana*, Madrid, 1972, 319–20, 275–6.

Brezzi, P. "La politica di Callisto III," *Studi romani*, 7 (1959), 31–41.

Canedo, L. G. *Un español al servicio de la Santa Sede, don Juan de Carvajal*, Madrid, 1947.

de la Serviere, J. and Croupin, L. *DTC*, II 1345–62.

Paschini, P. "La flotta de Callisto III," *Arch. Società di Storia Patria*, 53–5 (1930), 177–254.

Pastor, 1, 649–786.

Rius, J. "Catalanes y aragoneses en la corte de Calixto III," *Anal. Sacra Tarraconensia*, 3 (1927), 193–330.

Ruis, K. *Regesto ibericao de Calixto III*, 2 vol., Barcelona, 1948–58.

Schuller-Piroli, S. *Die Borgia Papiste: Kalixt III, und Alexander VI*, Vienna, 1979.

Schweiger, P. *LTK*, 11, 884–5.

Silvera, J. S. "El ob. De Valencia, Alfonso de Borja (Calixto III)," *Bol. Real Acad. de la Hist.*, 88 (1926), 241–313.

Vansteenberge, E. *DHGE*, XI, 438–43.

CAMAURO. See **Vestments, Pope's Liturgical.**

CAMERLENGO.

This important officer of the papal administration is known by the Italian word for the bursar of a religions institution. Historians of the medieval papacy, however, employ the English word "chamberlain" (French, Camérier, from Latin *camerarius*).

Middle Ages. The title first appeared in 1105. The function replaced the old offices of *arcarius, sacellerius,* and *vestarius* of the Lateran palace, which seems to have been drastically changed during the reorganization and development of the papal administration in the second half of the 11th century. The office took its classic form with Cardinal Censius, named chamberlain in 1188, author of the masterly compilation LIBER CENSUUM, and the future pope HONORIUS III. In the 13th and 14th centuries, in concert with the extension of the papal tax system, the office assumed increasing responsibilities within the CURIA. The chamberlain received verbal orders from the pope (by extension, all his acts were seen as legitimate), and administered the oaths of almost all officials of the Curia. He was often a cardinal, but not systematically so before the 15th century, and the Avignon popes avoided combining these ranks: Gasbert de Laval (Chamberlain 1319–47), Etienne Cambarou (1347–61), and Arnaud Aubert (1361–71) were not cardinals, and when Pierre de Cros, chamberlain from 1371, donned the red hat in

1383, he gave up his other post. Because the Camera was also a tribunal, the chamberlain was above all an administrator, sometimes a high-ranking counselor—in essence, a jurist—assisted by a *vice-camerarius*. The actual accounting, like the custody of the papal treasury, was under the jurisdiction of the treasurer. A body for the administration of the finances of the SACRED COLLEGE, the *Camera collegii*, founded at the end of the 13th century, was directed by a cardinal chamberlain.

14th Century Onward. The transfer of the Roman curia to Avignon did not fundamentally transform the rank and duties of the chamberlain, but it would make the head of the APOSTOLIC CAMERA into a pillar of papal administration. The extent of his competence remained far above that of the officials who surrounded him, who were clerics and counselors often with vaguely defined duties. The treasurer, second in importance after the chamberlain within the Camera, was much less influential: as head of the Treasury, he was in reality only a cashier, a keeper of funds, without administrative autonomy. The pope's adviser, the chamberlain, was the key man of the entire Avignon papal administration until the end of the GREAT SCHISM. The custom of separating the roles of chamberlain and cardinal in Rome in this period was not observed where three of the six chamberlains were cardinals.

The chamberlain, chosen by the pope, designated on his own authority the officials of the Apostolic Camera from treasurer to NOTARIES. Only the nomination of tax collectors, done by a bull because of the powers attributed to them as apostolic NUNCIOS, required the intervention of the pope and his advisers. The chamberlain administered the oaths of all officials of the Curia, from the Chancery to the kitchens. He was responsible for the revenues of the Church, and coordinated the papal financial administration; the tax collectors deployed throughout Christendom could dispose of their receipts only on his orders. It was around him, the most knowledgeable about the availability of funds, that the system of allocations turned. In charge of overseeing public receipts and expenditure, the chamberlain supervised the work of the accountants and certified the payment of debts.

The responsibility of governing the Papal States went hand in hand with the administration of finances, and that of the administration of the apostolic palace implied the designation of officials of the temporal administration, the reception of homage from vassals, the administration of the pope's personal property, and the exclusive capacity (apart from that of the pope) of committing the Holy See to financial liability. Finally, the chamberlain had judiciary power in all causes where the interests of the Apostolic Camera were implicated. In the latter responsibilities, which were always interpreted very extensively, the chamberlains soon delegated their powers to the auditor of the Apostolic Camera, whose importance continued to increase until the end of the Papal States. For the numerous cases that were not judged in the Curia, the chamberlain delegated the appropriate collector or even a diocesan official. However, in Avignon as in Rome, the auditor's court did not preclude the existence of the chamberlain's own court, which was both a court of appeal to that of the auditor and a magistrate's court for cases that the chamberlain reserved to himself. He had at his disposal a "tax prosecutor of the pope" who petitioned in the name of the pope and of the Church, thus preventing the chamberlain from acting as both judge and plaintiff. At the auditor's court, a "tax prosecutor of the chamberlain and of the court of the Apostolic Camera" was responsible for representing the chamberlain.

To deal with the growing need for money, the papal tax system grew steadily from the time of JOHN XXII. It had already generated a well-developed system and personnel in 1378, when the schism occurred. The Avignon papacy inherited the funds of the Apostolic Camera and the personnel. At Rome, URBAN VI had to hastily create a new administration, but he had neither the men nor the means of his transmontane rivals. At the beginning, a great deal of improvisation and instability of personnel ensued. Therefore, it is not astonishing that, at the end of the schism, MARTIN V confirmed (27 July 1418) as chamberlain François de Conzié, who occupied the post from 1384 in the Avignon establishment and kept it until his death under the pontificate of EUGENE IV, on 31 December 1432. Conzié did not follow the Curia to Italy, nor did he go to the council of Constance, where he was represented by a vice-chamberlain. This practice of delegation became fixed and, from the middle of the 15th century, with the exception of the pontificate of SIXTUS V, the office of vice-chamberlain (or vice-camerlengo, as custom henceforth designated it) merged with that of governor of Rome, responsible for public order and having for that end a mainly criminal court.

The return of the papacy to Rome, the gradual refinement of the local administration, and the increasing specialization of offices all joined slowly to erode the broad jurisdiction of the chamberlains at the end of the 14th century. In 1481, SIXTUS IV gave independence to the treasurer of the Apostolic Camera, and at the end of that century, the auditor's court acquired a juridical function that surpassed the traditional competence of the Camera (bull *Apprime devotionis* of Innocent VIII, 22 December 1485). The camerlengo, as he was henceforth called (in French, camerlingue) and the clerks of the Apostolic Camera retained within their jurisdiction everything that related to public administration, trade in grain and supplies, bridges and roads, water, the minting of coins, and so on. Until the beginning of the 18th century, a system of annual rotation of clerks of the Camera heading each section of the administration remained formally in force;

however, specialization and the greed of incumbents obstructed global control by the camerlengo, who ended up having his own domain restricted.

From the middle of the 16th century; the clerks, although reproved by the pope, assumed the custom of executing privately, without the seal of the camerlengo, acts related to their own spheres of activity, each taking the name of the presidency or of the prefecture. In 1612, PAUL V officially granted to the clerks of the Camera the power to execute, under their own seals, business that had been delegated to them in plenary sessions of the Camera (*plena Camera*) and those concerning matters during their presidency. This measure was rescinded in 1621 by GREGORY XV, but at that time the competence of the camerlengo was precisely defined—an attempt to put an end to the far-from-honorable conflicts between the camerlengo and the clerks of the Camera. Gregory XV's bull, prepared by a committee of cardinals, reserved wide powers to the camerlengo—at that time, Cardinal Ludovico Ludovisi, the pope's nephew—but the list was exhaustive. On the one hand, the bull stated that the camerlengo must have cognizance of all matters under the jurisdiction of the Camera, concurrently with the other officials. In other words, the clerks and the treasurer, while recognizing the superior authority of the camerlengo, were now endowed with a legal competence that had been denied them until then. Limited terms of office had not been respected for a long time, and the annual rotation remained permanently entrusted to the same official, answerable directly to the pope.

In 1741, BENEDICT XIV restored the supreme authority of the camerlengo, but a *motu proprio* of 1 March 1742 defined the specific domains of the camerlengo and of the treasurer, reserving to the latter and his court everything related to fiscal and national administration. The camerlengo himself retained concurrent jurisdiction with the clerks of the Camera on all matters related to the different presidencies and prefectures. In addition, he received "private" (exclusive) jurisdiction, over the postal services of the papal state, granting the concession of letters patent for hoisting the papal flag on ships, the nomination of consuls in Mediterranean and Adriatic ports, and the execution of papal concessions of fiefs and new fairs under state jurisdiction. Thereafter, the treasurer was a real minister of finance, while the camerlengo continued to have complex relations with the clerks of the Camera within the framework of the presidencies. At the end of the 17th century, the acts of the presidents no longer bore the *visa* of the camerlengo, although the title mentioned him as the superior authority. The plenary meeting of the Camera, often cited as a deliberative organ in the earliest decisions, had become a solemn formality required for certain types of acts (e.g., tax exemptions for the fathers of twelve children, decrees for the registering of papal documents). The reforms of PIUS VII, followed by those of the Restoration, even further restricted the camerlengo's jurisdiction. Under Pius IX, (*motu proprio* of 12 June 1847, which established the Council of Ministers), the camerlengo was called on to form part of the new body as minister of trade, fine arts, industry and agriculture—functions he had to give up in February 1848 to make way for a lay minister.

The Apostolic Camera and its judiciary and administrative functions, having lost their raison d'être after 1870, preserved only those attributes that had always been their own during a vacancy of the Apostolic See. The successive reforms of the Curia confirmed the Camera's existence, maintaining as a particularly striking anachronism, the office of vice-camerlengo), along with the auditor-general, the treasurer, and the clerks of the Camera joined collegially under the presidency of a dean, as well as the notary. The constitution *Pastor bonus* (29 June 1988), taking note of the measures decreed by Paul VI, provides for the camerlengo, like all the heads of the DICASTERIES, to submit his resignation to the pope at the age of 75. However, only he and the Cardinal Penitentiary do not lose their posts on the death of the pontiff.

During a vacancy of the Holy See, the camerlengo immediately takes possession of the apostolic palace. It is his duty officially to certify the death of the pope, have the certificate drawn up, and notify nuncios and ambassadors of various countries. The prefect of the PAPAL HOUSEHOLD (formerly the master of the chamber) hands over to him the FISHERMAN'S RING, which a *ceremoniarius* breaks during the first meeting of the cardinals. Money and postage stamps issued by the Vatican may bear the camerlengo's coat of arms. He presides over the general organization of the conclave and gives a report of the general state of finances. His authority is therefore very high, but it is limited to current matters, and the majority of decisions are made during meetings of the cardinals who, as a body, exercise the prerogatives of apostolic authority during a vacancy. At the 1958 conclave, the cardinals had to elect a camerlengo, Cardinal Aloisi Masella, because the post was vacant since Pius XII (who himself had been a camerlengo) had not replaced the camerlengo Cardinal Lorenzo Mauri, who had died in 1941.

Olivier Guyotjeannin
François-Charles Uginet

Bibliography

Del Re, N. *La Curia romana*, Rome, 1970, 307–9.
Favier, J. *Les Finances pontificales à l'époque du Grand Schisme d'Occident (1378–1409)*, Paris, 1966, 42–59.
Pastura Riggiero, M. *La Reverenda Camera apostolica e i suoi archivi (secoli XV–XVIII)*, Rome, 1984, 63–75.

CAMPO SANTO TEUTONICO. See Churches, National, in Rome.

CANON. Derived from the Greek word *kanōn*, this word is taken from an original meaning a "stem of a reed." Its first known figurative meaning applied to the rule related to a profession, an occupation, or an art—that is, a principle, type, or catalog. The word was widely used from the beginnings of Christianity, as its polysemy attests. In fact, "canon" then meant primarily the list, intentionally definitive, of the sacred books whose inspired or "authentic" character the Church recognized and on which it consequently conferred a normative value. Soon, however, the term was extended to liturgical rules (including the consecration of species in the liturgy of the Mass), to norms of behavior and of life inscribed in the truths of the faith and the prescriptions of divine law, and finally to rules applicable to monks and clerics in their consecrated life.

The word "canon," therefore, originally denoted any rule, without distinction of source; however, it came to be applied by antonomasia to strict ecclesiastical laws, which according to Isidore of Seville (*Liber etymologiarum*, VI, 16) were alone capable of "leading to the strait way," and thus to guarantors of orthodoxy vis-à-vis the precisely "canonical" original. In the year 325, the council of Nicaea had already designated as "ecclesiastical canons" the disciplinary measures of the Church (c. 2, *kanona ton ekklesiastikon*; another mention at c. 5). The novella CXXXVII of Justinian (c. 483–565) adopted this interpretation by designating civil laws by the word *nomos*, declared to be inapplicable to ecclesiastical prescriptions. In the spirit of the DECRETUM OF GRATIAN, this collection of norms, called *ordo canonicus* or *jus canonicum*, tended toward a specialization that was fluctuating and not easily defined. The canon covers disciplinary as well as theological or dogmatic decisions (as well as heresy in the meaning given to the term by the council of Trent); it also notes other criteria distinguishing codified or uncodified acts of universal or partial scope, either collective or individual.

This widening and concomitant specialization of signification led "naturally" (M. Lalmant) to a double contemporary meaning: dogmatic and disciplinary. Although the codification of Church law in the 20th century has expressly excluded from its domain the customary liturgical dispositions (*Codex iuris canonici* of 1917 and 1983 Code, c. 2), the notion of the canon as a primordial germ of truth guarded by the codification, or as the general normative corpus of the Church, persists, if in a complex and sometimes confusing way.

François Jankowiak

Bibliography

Köstler, R. *Wörterbuch zum Codex Iuris Canonici*, Munich, 1927.
Künneth, W. "Kanon," *Theologische realenzyklopädie*, XVII (1988), 562–70.

La norma en el derecho canonico, Proceedings of the 3rd Congress of Canonical Law, Pamplona, 1979, 2 vols.

Lalmant, M. "Canon," *DDC*, II, (1937), 1283–8.

CANON LAW.

Definition. Canon law, or ecclesiastical law, is the law of the Church, a complete society (formerly called "perfect") of divine origin, designed to assure order for the common good of its members, clerical and lay, and to help them advance toward salvation. The term comes from the Greek *kanon* (κανων, *canones* in Latin), which designates a rule, and is different from *nomoi* (νομοι), or civil laws (*leges* in Latin). Among the main divisions of canon law one must distinguish between divine law and disciplinary law, the first being of divine origin and, therefore, unalterable, and the second introduced for reasons of discipline, and from which the pope or his delegates can dispense, reform, limit, or abrogate. Since the 16th century it has also been customary to designate as ecclesiastical law (in France, civil ecclesiastical law), laws made by lay authorities on religious matters agreed to by the papacy in a CONCORDAT. Canon law concerns matters that touch upon the interests of the Church and of society, in general, as distinct from ethical and moral issues involving the individual conscience. As in Roman law, canon law has no clear-cut separation between constitutional, public, private, administrative, or procedural law. It was only with the decree *Sapienti consilio* of 1908 that the legislative, administrative, and judiciary organs of the CURIA were clearly established as the pope concentrates all these powers in his person. It is difficult to get an overview of the history of canon law because its evolution has been formidable and nuanced. It is still no less true that its history is that of the reinforcement of the power of the Roman pontiff, who from being bishop of Rome became the universal pastor, and from St. Peter's successor, the vicar of Christ, superior to the COUNCIL, the source of all law ("he has all law in the archive in his breast"), exercising the fullness of his power over all Christianity without any intermediary (*plenitudo potestatis*), although doctrine and law bar any unreasonable application of it.

The overriding doctrinal and disciplinary necessities explain the grasp for power that accompanied an ever-strengthened centralization, and which is based much less upon pontifical politics than the demand for a firm foundation, for various reasons, most often legitimate. There are few common points between the exaltation of the powers of the pope by the forgeries of Carolingian clerics in the middle of the 9th century, the regrouping after the crisis of the REFORMATION of the 16th century, and the adulation of prelates and French faithful at the time of the triumphant ultramontanism of the 19th century, except the results. Counterreactions, when central-

ization was too insupportable, such as GALLICANISM and JOSEPHISM, slowed the movement but did not stop it. Canon law defines the organization of the Church in a legal way; it places the Roman pontiff at the summit of the hierarchy of all the faithful, emperor and kings included, which did not occur without protests to define the nature of pontifical power, to fix the modalities of choosing the pope, to determine the formal sources (documents, rescripts, DISPENSATIONS, privileges, CUSTOM) and the extent of his normative power and that of other deliberating assemblies (ecumenical, general, or provincial councils and more recently, episcopal conferences and SYNODS OF BISHOPS), which are all subordinate. From the minor cleric to the bishop, all clerics can see their rights and duties laid out according to a functional hierarchy (major and minor orders, episcopate), jurisdictional hierarchy (archdeacon, canon, curate), or territorial hierarchy (provinces, bishoprics, parishes), the access to which (postulation, election, compromise, nomination, presentation by virtue of the right of patronage) is determined by qualities and conditions (age, knowledge, income).

The material life of clerics was not forgotten (oblations, tithes), nor was their conduct (dress, relationships with women and money). Laypersons are reminded of their duties: obedience, the payment of tithes, assistance at mass and, to make certain points of discipline clear, paschal communion, annual confession, matrimonial legislation (degrees of relatedness, banns, validity, indissolubility, and annulment). The diffusion of these norms and disciplinary controls are handled by provincial councils, diocesan synods, and pastoral visits. A very sophisticated, contentious, and punishing penal procedure, laid out in numerous *ordines judiciarii* (manuals of procedures) that influenced lay courts, whose quality attracts defenders, allows officials to regulate differences between clerics or particulars and to punish derelictions of duties with ecclesiastical punishments such as CENSURE, excommunication, or INTERDICT.

Sources and History. The history of canon law is tightly linked to the knowledge of its sources, a faithful reflection of the place given to law in the history of the people of God. It changes, between its origins and the 20th century, from a law inextricably linked to theology in the early centuries of the Church to a contemporary law completely subordinated to pastoral work, and which has only nostalgic shadows of its former dominance that it exercised in the centuries during the Middle Ages, when the Church thought itself above all others in terms of law and administration. The historiographic inequality that concentrates most on the Middle Ages may, therefore, be explained with good reason: the researchers have been seduced by the brilliance, the capacity for innovation, the rigor, and the influence of a law that then attracted the shining intellects, destined for a European intellectual dissemination, and for prestigious ecclesiastical careers that would permit them to put their theories into practice.

"Apostolic Tradition." From the beginning, the early Church needed to set rules, as certain passages of the New Testament show. There, as well as in the Old Testament, it found answers to some questions, but it also had to resolve new problems (e.g., the "council" of Jerusalem, A.D. 49). Several succinct texts, often attributed to the patronage of the apostles and whose dating and localization are sometimes debated, reflect these new preoccupations, as much theological as legal. The *Didaché* or *Doctrine of the Twelve Apostles* (*Doctrina duodecim apostolorum*, ed. SC, 248) written in Syria or Palestine at the end of the 1st century deals with baptism, the Eucharist, the clergy, and fasting in 16 chapters. Rome was where the *Pastor* of Roman Hermas originated (around 140, ed. SC, 53b) and the *Apostolic Tradition* attributed to Hippolytus (215–18, ed. SC, 11b), not without controversies. Between the middle of the 3rd century and the beginning of the 5th, still in Syria or Palestine, there were the *Didaskalion* (about 230 or after A.D. 250) and the *Apostolic Constitutions* (late 4th or early 5th century, ed. SC, 320, 329, 336), a well-articulated work eight books long, which surpasses the preceding ones in both size and influence (although it used them) but was condemned, except for the apostolic canons, by the council of Constantinople of 691. They also influenced the *Statuta ecclesiae antiqua* written in southern Gaul between 476 and 485, perhaps by Gennadius of Marseille, preserved in more than forty manuscripts: proof of their dissemination. The subjects included in these collections deal as much with worship and rites as with juridical organization, from which they get their name of "canonico-liturgical collections": church hierarchy (bishops, priests, deacons, subdeacons, deaconesses, widows), provincial synods, marriage, penitence, the liturgical year, morals, and Christian initiation. It was not, however, these anonymous texts, all written in Greek, (except the Gallic collection) that would have a future, but rather collections in Latin of the canons of councils that multiplied during the 4th and 5th centuries such as those in Gaul, the *Collectio arelatensis* from the middle or late 5th century, and the later collections of letters of the popes, which the canonists called "decretals." It is, by the way, only due to the single method of canonical collections that the canons of the councils and the pontifical letters from this time period are known today.

Canonical Collections of the 5th to 11th Centuries. Almost all the canonical collections of this time are anonymous compilations, and none had any official character. They present the texts by categories: eastern, African and Gallic councils, letters of popes, and other miscellaneous texts (extracts from the Fathers, Augustine, Jerome, Am-

brosius, and Isidore, Gregory the Great, ecclesiastical authors; Roman law from the Code of Theodosius, in 438; in the 9th century, extracts of the Carolingian *Capitularies*). In these great masses, the texts are copied according to their chronological order, not without errors. The compilers allowed themselves to abridge, rearrange, and sometimes even to distort texts, and some forgeries escaped their vigilance or were even fabricated by them. This presentation does not make research easy, and the systematic attempts to organize them are rarely good: for example, the *Vetus Gallica*, compiled in Lyon around 600 and rewritten at Autun and Corbie (first quarter of the 8th century). In addition, the capacity for memorization then encouraged by the methods of teaching made systematization less necessary. It was the origin of the text, letter from a pope, or canon of a council that gave the text its value, its legal authority, no matter which canonical collections it came from. But in fact, several collections dominated. These were recopied, totally or in part, according to the interests of the copyist (a monk does not recopy the same portions as a cleric would), augmented, and regrouped. The proliferation of collections characteristic of canonical law until the middle of the 12th century, is the proof of the importance of authorities in the formation of Church law: each action must have a text as its justification. And so in Rome, at the time that was called the Gelasian renaissance, a collection that wasn't the first or the only one (cf. the collection of Freising, the *Quesnelliana*, around 495) took over: the one by Dionysius Exiguus, a Scythian monk, who translated the Greek councils and added some pontifical decretals to them (from 384 to 498). The popes used it from the beginning of the 6th century, and it was this collection, with decretals from later pontiffs, that Pope HADRIAN I sent to Charlemagne in 774: this *Collectio Dionysio-Hadriana* was the favored one, semiofficial, of the Carolingian reformers, that they would soon combine with a Hispanic collection before turning to the *False Decretals* in the mid-9th century.

The Iberian peninsula was the other important center of canonical activity. An important collection (67 councils, 103 decretals) was compiled in Seville between 630 and 636, "the richest and best of the collections of the high Middle Ages," whose traditional attribution to Bishop Isidore (570–636) must be maintained. Completed around the end of the 7th century, it was added, in Spain, to the law of the Visigoths in sumptuous manuscripts. It spread throughout all civilized Europe of that time, Italy and Gaul, where it gave way, among other adaptations, to two important systematic orderings, setting the stage for the future: the *Hispana Gallica* (late 8th century) and the collection called the *Dacheriana*, which is a combination of the *Hispana* and the *Dionysio-Hadriana* completed around 813–31, perhaps by Agobard, archbishop of Lyon.

Nothing portrays the concrete, living, and eminently practical character of these collections better than an examination of the manuscripts, whose variety made editors despair. Although he left no purely canonical writing, Archbishop Hincmar of Reims (845–82) was an excellent example of the new attitude of certain Carolingian bishops toward law. His reasoning abandoned the moralizing verbiage of his contemporaries in favor of a perfectly mastered juridical form. He may have been the target of certain reformers responsible for the collection of Pseudo-Isidore or the *False Decretals* (847–52/7). This was the largest compilation of its time, which put diverse sources to good use with intelligence—*Hispana, Dionysio-Hadriana, Quesnelliana*, decretals and canons from isolated councils and ecclesiastical writers—but especially forged papal decretals attributed to the first popes (CLEMENT to MILTIADES). The object was to promote the reform of the Carolingian Church by freeing it from subjection to the secular powers and by strengthening the position of the bishop with respect to the metropolitan or archbishop. Because traditional canon law had not dealt with their concerns, the reformers forged the needed texts. To give them the highest authority they attributed the text to the ancient popes who, in fact, had written nothing on the matter. In so doing the forgers exalted the prestige of contemporary Roman pontiffs through well-phrased text. In Rome, the collection was used beginning with NICHOLAS I (858–67), but its finest days were during the reform of the 11th century. Regardless of rich, new collections, that were more easily manipulated, this one had the incomparable advantage of being ancient.

Of the canonical activity of the 10th century, two collections deserve attention. The collection of Abbo of Fleury, dedicated to king Hugh Capet and his son Robert the Pious in 988–96, bases, for the first time, the *auctoritates* on a personal commentary by the author (ed. *PL*, 139). Despite the novelty of the presentation, the alliance of canonical sources with lay sources, and the quality of the commentaries, the work seems to have had little circulation but remains a document of the highest rank in the political history of its time. Conversely, the *Decretum* (1008–12) by Burchard, bishop of Worms, (1000–25) was widely circulated and had a lasting success until the early 12th century, as evidenced by about 80 preserved manuscripts (ed. *PL*, 140). In twenty books, 1,780 canons methodically present Church law, without commentary from the author, a realistic prelate who was conscious of the shortcomings of clerics and laypersons. When the evolution of the law caused certain of the bishop's opinions to appear superfluous or suspect, the imperial prelates, concerned about the marriage of priests or the indissolubility of marriage for laypersons, added texts to his collection to bring it up to date in the spirit of reform.

"Canonical Preparation" for Gregorian Reform (11th–12th Centuries). To reform the Church and return it to its former state, was to wish it once again "chaste and free": This involved condemning simoniacal and unchaste clerics and limiting laypersons to specific and subordinate jobs. It was no longer a question of displaying the faults of the clergy; on the contrary, they were to occupy a superior position, shielded from accusations by laypersons. The PAPAL ONOMASTIC was then an entire agenda unto itself: LEO, GREGORY, and the first popes. The papacy then played the leading role in establishing canon law. In conjunction with a parallel and intensive diplomatic action, the sending of LEGATES or JUDGE DELEGATES, there had to be a secure juridical basis for their world-encompassing pretensions, and so they compiled texts and assembled new canonical collections. GREGORY VII boldly affirmed his legislative power in the DICTATUS PAPAE (1076): "Only the pope may promulgate new laws." But in fact, more recent texts were rare in the new collections compiled by the pope's entourage; they preferred the ancient authorities. These were, however, arranged according to new needs: they rediscovered texts that exalted the authority of the Roman pontiff and regrouped them in the following manner into collections reflecting on: tradition, which they were wary of; public usefulness, which is highlighted; reason, with which one must conform; but also on the necessity to ask for advice. To the strictly juridical texts were added extracts from the Church fathers, more numerous and well chosen, which expanded them and exhibited the anchoring of juridical reasoning in a very broad religious vision. But the compilers always hid behind the *auctoritates*, adding no personal commentary and making these very elaborate compilations so arid and difficult to interpret that historians wrongly avoid them. Among these important collections, several were written by or under the direction of prelates very close to the pontiffs, men of property as well as intellectuals: the Breviarium of Cardinal Atto (1070?), *Collection canonum* by Bishop Anselm of Lucca (around 1083), 12 manuscripts by Cardinal Deusdedit (around 1083–87), *Liber de vita christiana* by Bonizo of Sutri (1089–95), *Polycarpus* by Cardinal Gregory (1109–13); others are anonymous, such as *Collection in II Books* (around 1051), *Collection in LXXIV Titles* (1073–75), doubtlessly one of the most typical, and *Collection of CLXXXIII Titles* (1063–85), but none is official. Canonical activity was not limited to Rome or even the Italian peninsula; Gaul also participated in this intellectual effervescence (*Collection of Semur*, after 1059), principally central France from Poitiers to Chartres, with the *Collections in XVII Books, in XIII Books, in VII Books, in IV Books*(?), the *Collectio tarraconensis* and the *Collection of Bordeaux*, all originating in Poitiers or its region (late 11th century).

But it was the Chartres collections that would exercise considerable influence, as much in France as in Italy, until around 1140. Between 1090 and 1095 three works came from the workshops of the team directed by Bishop Yvo (1090–1116), an active prelate. The *Tripartita*, the *Decretum*, and the *Panormia* (ed. *PL*, 161) are still awaiting a critical edition. If the first collection was more of a working file, while the second is a vast compilation in 17 books and 3,960 chapters—a more usable *compendium* that remedied the faults of its original (100 manuscripts). What characterizes these works is a loftiness of viewpoint on the big problems of the time, excluding polemics and solutions that were too radical, a juridical analysis that went straight to the essential problem of investitures. Yvo had previously stated his views on the sources of law, their authority, and their application in a famous preface that influenced later developments in canonical law. It was these moderate ideas of the bishop of Chartres that later triumphed at the CONCORDAT OF WORMS in 1122. The success of his collections would be considerable, as we see by the number of manuscripts, adaptations, borrowings, as much in Gaul (Châlons) as in Italy. Across the English Channel, Lanfranc, the former abbot of Bec, now the archbishop of Canterbury (1070–89), made a collection of canons that became the "code for the reform in England" (ed. *PL*, 150). According to Burchard, the imperial Church was not particularly fertile in canonists, but quality replaced quantity because the *Liber de misericordia et justicia* (1095–1121) by Alger of Liège, a moderate Gregorian, deserves to be ranked with the great works of this time. Like the Abbot of Fleury, he situated the authorities within a personal commentary. Like Hincmar, he believed in the efficacy of law and that the sad state of the Church resulted from the ignorance of the canons or from a poor interpretation of texts, but his juridical order is filled with charity, and in this way is completely representative of partisans of reform.

The reformers would also express their ideas through short polemic treatises that were easier to access than the collections, but where law occupied an even greater place: this is how the *Liber de regia potestate et sacerdotali* (1103–04) successfully implemented Yves of Chartres' ideas on investiture. Their opponents were no less hostile, and used the same sources. These treatises, as well as correspondence where canonical arguments were customary, such as those by Yvo of Chartres; the poet Hildebert de Lavardin (d. 1134), who had also made a compilation, now lost; and Geoffroy of Vendôme (d. 1132), allow us to see canon law put into practice and its great importance in the debate of ideas of the time. Although this has been a geographical presentation, it should be noted that there was remarkable unity throughout this production that circulated very quickly and had Rome as its true center. Yvo of Chartres got his texts from the newly rediscovered *Digest of Justinian* which he integrated into his compilation. A large number of collections depended upon these great works, and this infatuation with law was translated to the local level. There was a utopian hope in returning to these austere texts, which, in their way, translated the ideal of reform so well: Peace and agreement should be guaranteed by juridical order, which determines the place, rights, and duties of each person. We can also comprehend the potential risks of such a vision: It is too easy to progress from "putting the world in order" to the problems of a tentative and petty implementation on the practical level, and there is evidence of worrisome procedural stubbornness.

From Gratian to the Great Schism, 1140–1378: The Alliance of the Papacy and the School. The *Decretum* by Gratian is the pivotal point between two eras: a nonofficial work, it fits into the tradition of earlier collections, and is the last of the collections of the Gregorian reform. It became the main textbook in all the canon law school of Europe. All we know about Gratian is that he taught in Bologna and that his work appeared about 1140. It was not until the 13th century that university manuscripts took their definitive form, and many questions on the genesis of the work are still the object of lively discussions (*paleae*, texts of Roman law, divisions). Originally in two parts (the third, *De consecratione*, was an early addition, as was *De penitencia*), the *Decretum magistri Gratiani* or *Concordia discordantium canonum* had the twofold purpose of compiling all ecclesiastical law and of resolving contradictions in the law. The size of the text made it a university work of the first order (between 3,500 and 4,000 canons: 718 pages in the edition by E. Friedberg, Leipzig, 1879). It is the amplitude and quality of the commentary by the master that partially explains its success, although it is not well organized: despite unequal parts, and widely scattered subject matter, it is all there. The other important reason for the circulation of the work is the intellectual milieu in which it was written: in the 1140s, Bologna had become the center of legal studies, both ecclesiastical and civil, and from there the *Decretum* spread throughout Europe. Although it was never officially approved by the papacy—which used it, nevertheless, from the reign of ALEXANDER III—it would be commented upon in the UNIVERSITIES where canon law was eventually separated from the teaching of theology and liberal arts. Those who are called the decretists critiqued and commented upon the work of the Bolognese teacher: *Paucapalea*, master Rolland (who is not, as was believed, the future Alexander III), *Omnibonus* at mid-century, Rufinus, Simon of Bisignano a bit later, and finally the most important, Huguccio of Pisa (d. 1210). The schools of Paris also quickly commented on Gratian, but the original Parisian school flourished about 50 years before fading away. It is famous for the *Summa Decreti* (1165) by Stephen of Orleans, abbot of Sainte-Geneviève, the future bishop of Tournai (d. 1203), and by anonymous works such as *Summa* "Elegantius in jure divino," written in Cologne, 1169; *Summa Parisiensis*, around 1170; *Summa* "Imperatorie majestatis," 1175–78; *Ecce vicit leo*, 1202–10; and *Animal est substancia*, 1206–10, to mention the most important. The Anglo-Normans also were a vigorous and creative group, in close contact with Parisian teaching. The Loire valley and Chartres also maintained tradition, but in works of lesser importance, and attention has been drawn to the juridical activity at Reims during the 1170s. In contrast, Provence, which knew of the *Decretum* very early (*Abbreviato "Quoniam egestas"* around 1150) turned more toward civil law to promote its ideal of peace between prelates and princes.

As the *Decretum* was spreading, papal decretals on juridical matters were multiplying. This massive augmentation was the result of two currents. The papacy thought of itself more and more juridically and aspired to dictate the norms for all Christianity, but the demands of the faithful could not be neglected either. As soon as a problem arose, concerned parties wrote or sent agents to Rome so that Roman centralization was as much a basic goal as it was a desire of the reigning pontiff. The papal chancellery refined its methods, and each response to a petition was very carefully written; even for an issue that appeared to be quite secondary, it tried to generalize the answer to apply the solution to all the Christian world, in imitation of the rescripts by the emperors of antiquity. The decretals on matrimonial questions are typical of this series. To this casual legislation were added the decisions of the councils of the Second, Third, and Fourth LATERAN COUNCILS (1139, 1179, 1215), whose canons are more general and essential regarding canonical matters. But it was not enough to legislate; they also needed to disseminate this new legislation. At first, it was the clerics who worked independently to bring together the decretals of which they were aware; a few more than seventy collections between 1140 and the end of the century are known. The English clerics distinguished themselves in the quest for papal rescripts, to the indifference of the French, a likely reason for the irremediable decline of the Parisian canonical school. At Bologna, one private collection immediately dominated (127 manuscripts), sealing the alliance of the papacy and the school for more than two centuries: the *Breviarium extravagantium* of Bernard of Parma, provost of Pavia (1190). The collection was divided into five books: (1) ecclesiastical jurisdiction and hierarchy, (2) canonical procedure, (3) clerics and religious orders, (4) marriage, (5) criminal procedure and penalties subdivided into titles modeled after Justinian compilation. By 1226 this collection was followed by four others, the *Quinque compilationes antiquae*, which included the decretal of later popes. Since this multiplicity of collections was inconvenient, GREGORY IX decided to commission the Dominican Raymond of Peñafort, a former professor of Bologna, to compile an official collection. He was given authority to abridge, modify, and

harmonize the texts, and to fill lacunae by inserting 65 new papal decretals. Raymond borrowed the organizational model of the *Quinque compilationes*, adopting 179 out of 185 titles and 1,756 out of 2,139 canons. The compilation, promulgated on 5 September 1234 by the bull *Rex pacificus*, was sent to the teachers and students of Bologna. Along with Gratian's *Decretum*, it alone was to be taught in the schools and used in the courts of justice. This collection was immediately named the *Liber extravagantium* "beside the *Decretum of Gratian*" or more simply, *Extra*, abbreviated as *X*. This collection was the triumph of the jurists and reinforced the juridic role of the papacy.

Shortly thereafter, leaders such as St. Bernard denounced this collection. Other detractors included those who saw their positions being dissolved, or who, having been ignored, had time to meditate on their situations. The heavy-handed takeover by the jurists was accomplished despite the efforts of the popes against it. The jurists, many of whom were not canonists, were threatened by the clerics' fascination with juridical studies, and had intentionally limited their involvement, especially in matters of Roman law. HONORIUS III had, in fact, forbidden the teaching of Roman law in Paris in 1219 as a result not only of demands made by liberal arts teachers, but in favor of theology; this resulted in a condemnation of canon law, whose study had already diminished significantly. Eventually, the political climate coupled with the desire to maintain doctrinal unity won out over the desire for equity. The *Liber Extra* of GREGORY IX was the result of over a century of legislative rather than jurisprudential activity by the pontiffs, and the legislative corpus of the Church was formed.

The great canonist Sinibaldo dei Fieschi, who became Pope INNOCENT IV (1243–54), convoked the First Council of Lyon (1245) and promulgated its canons as well as some of his own decretals in three small collections, the *Novelles*. GREGORY X's *Novissimae*, promulgated after the Second Council of Lyon (1264), treated important issues such as elections, benefices, and usury. NICHOLAS III (1280) and other popes imitated it because these small collections and private compilations of new decretals presented the same inconveniences present at the beginning of the century, and the University of Bologna requested a new official collection from Boniface VIII. This was promulgated on 3 March 1298 as the *Sextus liber* (the "*Sextus*"), modeled on the *Decretals* of Gregory IX but much smaller in size (5 books, 76 titles, and 359 chapters: 96 pages in the Friedberg edition). Later official or semiofficial papal collections merely refined points of detail and were more administrative than juridical: the *Clementines* promulgated by JOHN XXII on 25 October 1317 (106 chapters, integrating the canons reworked from the Council of Vienne, 1311–12); the *Extravagantes* of John XXII, 1319 (20 chapters, ed. J.

Tarrant, 1983, MJC, B, 6); and, finally, the *Extravagantes communes*, which were added during the 14th and 15th centuries (70 chapters).

It would be incorrect to use these official texts apart from their learned commentaries. Even as the *Quingue Compilations* were being shaped, activity was considerable. Stephan Kuttner has been able to account for 1,109 manuscripts of works written between the DECRETUM of Gratian and the promulgation of the *Decretals* in 1234, which rendered them obsolete. Canonists immediately commented the legislation of the Fourth Lateran Council in 1215 (ed. A. Garcia y Garcia, 1981, *MJC*, A 2). Johannes Teutonicus composed the *Glossa Ordinaria* (the basic commentary) on Gratian's *Decretum* about 1215; it was updated by Bartholomew of Brescia (d. 1258). The ordinary commentary on the *Decretals* of Gregory IX was finished in 1241 by Bernard of Parma, who reworked it until his death (1266). Among the decretalists, two personalities with similar careers stand out. Hostiensis, archbishop of Embrun (1250–61) and, later, cardinal-bishop of Ostia (d. 1271), was the author of a Summa on the decretals. (1252) that had immense success (called the Golden Summa, *Summa Aurea*, in the editions printed during the 16th century). Sinibaldo dei Fieschi completed his works after he became Pope Innocent IV: the *Apparatus in quinque libros decretalium* (1246–53) and *Commentaries* to his two earlier collections of *Novellae*. Whatever their qualities, Raymond de Peñafort (d. 1275), Godfrey of Trand (d. 1245), Bernard of Parma, (d. 1266), Petrus de Sampsone (1246–50), Bartholomew of Brescia (d. 1258), and Bernard of Montemirat (d. after 1261) were reduced to secondary roles. The promulgation of the Sextus, the *Clementinae* and the *Extravagantes* of JOHN XXIII renewed the activity of the commentators: in Italy, Guido da Baiso (d. 1313) and Johannes Andrese (d. 1348) at Bologna; in France, Cardinal Jean Le Moine (d. 1313) and Henri Bohic (d. around 1349) in Paris, Guillaume de Montlauzun (d. 1343) in Toulouse, Jesselin de Cassagnes (d. 1334) in AVIGNON, and Pierre Bertrand (d. 1349), better known for his diplomatic activity. The end of the century produced several new, rather lengthy works, but university teaching became atrophied. There were no new texts to comment and the Great Western Schism was not very favorable toward the vast apparatuses that were attempted by Johannes de Legnano in Bologna (d. 1383) and Baldus de Ubaldis, (d. 1400), but it didn't end their commentaries. Gilles Bellemère (d. 1407), a better scribbler than a diplomat, commented on the whole corpus of canon law at Avignon for 20 years, in 30 volumes and 11,000 folios.

From the Great Schism to the Council of Trent: The Lowest Ebb of the "Scientia Canonica."

The beginning of the GREAT SCHISM dealt a very hard blow to the jurists who had almost exclusively dominated the Avignon period. They saw themselves blamed for Christianity being torn asunder. It was the theologians turn, with those of the University of Paris at their head, although it is difficult to pretend that they shone brilliantly. At the councils of Constance (1414–18) and Basel (1431–37), they discredited themselves and the canonists rose again, but without being able to regain the prestige or skill that was previously theirs: It was truly the arrival of "a generation with no genius." These legal experts were more numerous than ever after the creation of new universities a century earlier, but this diversity and emulation were in no way an intellectual stimulant: it was an era of short polemic treatises, consultations, and practical works. The lack of ingenuity and the habit of consulting—a source of great profit but a poor approach to life—led them to prefer the common opinion of the professors to original thought, and the accumulation of authorities took the place of demonstration. More and more weighty, multiplying subtleties, the university works turned upon themselves and were only destined for specialists now. The sterilization of juridical thought, which brought about parroting, confusion, and the intrusion of the irrational in a domain seamingly exempt previously was truly a sign of the unhappiness of the times. Still, the jurists had returned to their place within the Church, which their lack of knowledge hardly justified. They even had the pretension to enjoy an official interpretive authority, imitating those in Roman antiquity, and it was often the authors of these fat, unreadable tones who were called to positions of responsibility. It is not surprising that they were unable to seize the chance to save the Church from ruin by weighing pros and cons and scrutinizing opinions. At the end of the century, printing played a considerable role in the diffusion of official texts and their commentaries, but teaching and cannonical science hardly profited, being almost reduced to a unique beneficed discipline.

The Period of Administration and Regulation (mid-16th to late 18th Century).

The history of secular law is marked by the official recording of already-established customs after the late 15th century, intense legislative activity from the middle of the 16th to the end of the 18th century, and inserted consolidations or codifications done in a sustained manner between the 1750s and the end of the 19th century in Europe, and the papacy had no new compilations or official codifications until 1917. The COUNCIL OF TRENT (1545–63) marked the triumph of papal authority and began what has been called the second Roman centralization. After the relative lack of direction in the preceding period, reorganization relied upon the multiplication of legislative documents. Although the law and the juridical institutions were brought to the forefront, no new reference collections came out of this. The ancient compilations were officially promulgated under the name *Corpus juris canon-*

ici (1 July 1580), but the complementary volumes were missing (*Institutiones juris canonici* by G. P. Lancelotti, 1563; *Liber septimus* by P. Matthieu, 1590) and more than ever, the pope served as the only legislator and interpreter of his laws. The bull of promulgation of the Council of Trent prohibited any translation or commentary on its canons. It is difficult to say if the scholars heeded this edict for other legislative documents or if it was the lamentable state of the university from the 17th through 19th centuries, in civil law as well as in canon law, that ended the alliance between the papacy and the university, which no longer had a role of selection and compilation of texts indispensable to juridical knowledge. When the congregations created by the council replaced the schools of law, it became a question of administrative law and regulation. It was not that texts were lacking, rather they were too numerous and too widespread despite (or because of) a considerable editorial effort, mostly on private initiative, too often disserved by its mediocre quality (*bullaris concilur* enactments). Popes legislated abundantly, but only BENEDICT XIV (1740–58) was interested in canon law and decided to officially publish (1746) a compilation of his own legislation in the order of the *Decretals* and to dictate a treatise on the diocesan synod.

Tests, Reconstruction, and "Ignorancia Juris" Assumed. Reconstruction after the trials of the revolutions took place without canon law and even against it, especially in France: The episcopate felt that an obedient and defenseless clergy was better than priests who resisted, *Corpus* in hand. They wanted no more officialities, but they preferred, discretely, transaction and pressures to trials. Several independent spirits such as Abbot J. F. André (1809–81) denounced this ignorance of canon law, while Abbot J. P. Migne (1800–75) edited his *Patrologia latina* (1844–55), which included most of the canonical collections until Gratian, and his *Encyclopédie Theologique*, which included R. Prompsault's treatise and the alphabetical listings of Abbot M. André. The course on the history of canon law created at the Royal School of Chartres in 1846 did not worry anyone. Once the time of reconstruction was over, the indispensable reorganization, in a world that had indisputably changed, made the completion of a new legislative system inevitable and feasible. In 1865 the *Acta Sanctae Sedis* became the semiofficial record for the papacy (before becoming official in 1904, since 1908, the *Acta Apostolicae Sedis*), the first attempt at a rationalization. At the First Vatican Council (1871), this desire for a new code for the Church was unanimous: "We are buried under laws" cried the French bishops, in the unanimity of a brand new ultramontanism, and the Neapolitans ironically discussed the number of camels necessary to transport all the law books. More realistically, certain bishops insisted on the burden of the task. There-

fore, although a code was desired, no one wanted to have to provide a place for canonists. For example, it took threats from Rome before a course on canon law was created within the brand new department of theology in Paris (1880); but at last they found a professor in Italy, Abbot Pietro Gasparri. While awaiting the new code, several canonists audaciously published private codes, such as the Frenchman A. Pillet (1890) and the Italian H. M. Pezzani (1893–1902), who also participated in the official writing. The popes themselves must not have felt any real urgency for a codification since it took more than 30 years before the project was completed.

The "Codex Juris Canonici" (1917): A Belated Child to the Code Napoleon. Right after his election, PIUS X (1902–14) took on this endeavor. By the *motu proprio Arduum sane munus* of 19 March 1904, he ordered the codification of Church law, probably at the insistence of Pietro Gasparri (1853–1934) who was the key person dealing with the work until its completion. Given to a commission composed of cardinals assisted by consultants, the plans for the new code were sent to the bishops and to certain religious superiors for their opinions, then sent back to the workplace. This took time and it was not until 17 May 1917 that BENEDICT XV promulgated the *Codex juris canonici*. In its presentation and form, the code differed completely from the ancient compilations. The organization in five books, subdivided into titles, was copied from that of the *Decretals*, but the division of the matters was inspired by the *Institutiones juris canonici* of Lancellotti (1563), which was similar to that of the civil code of the French in 1804. The abstract general style, and brevity of the articles, numbered continuously (2,414 canons), were like those of the code issued during the revolution, which had also dealt with procedures for canonization, contentious, and criminal cases. Basically, it was a clear representation of the whole heritage of ancient law, with the contradictions and obscurities eliminates. It was authentic and exclusive for the worldwide Latin Church, that is to say all the canons had the same authority and the ancient collections no longer had any legislative value.

For the first time in Church history, all canon law was encompassed in one code, with the exception of concordat law. Though specialists may have had some criticism of detail, the code was well received by the episcopate, which finally had an easy-to-consult text. The age of canon law extending its doctrinal influence beyond the religious circle was over; its role was limited strictly to church matters as the framers had wanted. Even if promulgation brought about a renewal of canonical studies and the creation of several school or institutes, it cannot be said that this code made a mark on Western juridical thought. Law was no longer the only method for analyzing society and acting to direct or control it. Secular norms were viewed more as "requests" than obligations, as seen in the ecclesiastical world. In 1917, although governments had other preoccupations, it was still significant that they had no reaction to the code. Attempts to attribute this silence to the delicate relations between church and state is hardly convincing. Furthermore, the rapid evolution of Catholicism beginning in the 1930s was not followed by an updating of the *Codex* (in imitation of the French civil code), and it therefore no longer served expected needs. This continued to be the case as the commission for interpretation, active until the 1940s, never fulfilled its task of updating. As for theology, which had done so much to promote canon law in the Middle Ages, it played only a very small role, despite an undeniable renewal of interest. Once again, the authority of the pope prevented this obsolescence of the *Codex* from being harmful to the Church.

The New "Codex juris canonici" (1983): The Spirit of the Second Vatican Council? At the very opening of the council, JOHN XXIII (1958–63) announced "l'aggiornamento" of the Code of canon law on 25 January 1959. This explains why the preparatory drafts of conciliar documents that dealt with canonical issues had been definitively put off between the two first sessions, while John XXIII was setting up a commission charged with revising the *Codex*. The commission was originally made up of 31 cardinals and 70 consultants (including one lay member, in June 1964). After the closing of the council on 20 November 1965, PAUL VI officially inaugurated the work of the commission. Canon law was thus confirmed as subordinate to pastoral concerns. The principles of revision agreed upon in 1967 show the desire to incorporate the ecclesiology of the Second Vatican Council and its desire for ecumenism. The drafts of the new code in 1979 and 1980 show a return to a more hierarchical and juridical vision of the Church. The changing of certain titles between 1977 and 1980 confirms the orientations of the new pope, JOHN PAUL II, as well as the abandonment of the writing of a basic law (*Lex Ecclesiae fundamentalis*) containing the constitutional law of the Church. Promulgated on 25 January 1983, to go into effect at the beginning of the liturgical year (November 27), the new *Codex juris canonici* was divided into seven books, subdivided into parts, titles, and chapters. It is shorter than the preceding one (1,752 canons). Its organization, clear and well articulated, underwent some changes. The laypersons are at the beginning of Book II: *The People of God*, and procedure has been relegated to the two final books.

It is difficult to measure the impact of the new *Codex*, perhaps because its goals were to correct admitted defects, to abolish practices that had already fallen into disuse, to give legal sanction to practices already in effect, to introduce new practices desired by everyone, to be a reminder of precepts while not overthrowing a legislation and its routine, and to resolve or innovate on very controversial points. It also seems that some had expected too much from this code, which explains the disappointment when it was promulgated and seen as the consecration of "maintaining a clerical system" (Jean Schlick, *Le Monde*, 2 March 1983). Regarding the collegiality of the parochial organization and the place of laypersons and women, the changes are so restrained that they were upsetting for those involved; on the burning problems of the ordination of married men or the marriage of priests, there was nothing at all to be expected. Alone or almost so, the freemasons expressed their satisfaction at no longer being excommunicated *ipso facto*. That the *Codex* was criticized should not be discouraging to its creators: William of Ockham (around 1290 to 1350) blasted the *Decretals*; the Code of 1917 did not please all the canonists, and the councils of Trent and the Second Vatican Council unleashed passions. It is, in fact, the massive indifference outside the narrow confines of the canonists and perhaps part of the hierarchy that deserves attention. Even more than in 1917, the law has ceased to be a supporting structure of Church society, which no longer defines itself with regard to it. The *Codex juris canonici* of 1983 does not seem to have opened a new golden age for canon law but, more modestly, is "at least a work of reference on the situation of official legislation of the Catholic Church at the end of the 20th century" (R. Metz), a sad end for a text that was to have ruled the future. It had been anticipated, in 1927, that a code would be made for the eastern churches united with Rome. After many interruptions, one was promulgated on 25 October 1990; the first reactions have not been very favorable.

The deep problems and crises of today should not make us forget the considerable influences of yesterday. To neglect the importance of canon law and canonists is to ignore a prime indicator for understanding major phenomena like the Gregorian reform in the 11th and 12th centuries, the establishment of the papal monarchy in the 13th and 14th centuries, and the crises of the 15th, 16th, and 19th centuries. The influence of canon law has long been felt, often in conjunction with Roman law (*jus commune*), in civil legislation, administration and procedure, up to the contemporary era, with administrative procedure and electoral techniques being the clearest examples.

Gerard Giordanengo

Bibliography

L'Année canonique, Paris, since 1953.
Bulletin of Medieval Canon Law (with bibliographic listings), Berkeley, since 1955 (14, 1984; index 1955–83). *HDIEO*, 16, 1981, 214, 144, 341.

Congress: International Congress of Medieval Canon Law, since 1958, published in the *Monumenta juris canonici*, series C, since the second (1965, last volume publ. in 1988).

Corpus christianorum, Continuatio mediaevalis.

Fournier, P. *Mélanges de droit canonique*, Aalen, 1983, 2 vol.

Fournier, P., and Le Bras, G. *Histoire des collections canoniques en Occident depuis les Fausses Décrétales jusqu'au Décret de Gratien*, Paris, 1931–32, 2 vol., repr. Aalen, 1972.

Fransen, G. *Les Décrétales et les collections de décrétales*, Turnhout, 1972 (*Typologie occidentale des sources du Âge*, 2); *Les Collections canoniques*, Turnhout, 1973 (*ibid.*), 10).

Friedberg, E. ed. *Corpus juris canonici*, official edition, Rome, 1582, Leipzig, 1879–81 (reprint Graz, 1959), 2 vol.

Gaudemet, J. *Droit canonique*, Brussels, 1963 (*Introduction bibliographique à l'histoire du droit et à l'ethnologie juridique*, B/9).

Gaudemet, J. *Les Sources du droit de l'Église en Occident du IIe au VIIe siècles*, Paris, 1985 (*Initiation au christianisme ancien*).

Gaudemet, J. *Les Sources du droit canonique, VIIIe-XXe siècles. Repères canoniques. Sources occidentales*, Paris, 1993.

The Jurist, Washington, D.C., since 1941.

Kuttner, S. *Repertorium der Kanonistik (1140–1234)*, Vatican City, 1937 (*Studi e testi*, 71).

Le Bras G., and Gaudemet, J., dir., *Histoire du droit et des institutions de l'Eglise en Occident*, Paris, since 1955 [*HDIEO*], 15 volumes to date.

Metz, R. "La nouvelle codification du droit de l'Église (1959–1983)," *RDC*, 33 (1983), 110–68.

Monumenta juris canonici, Vatican City, since 1965, series A and B.

Naz, R. dir., *Dictionnaire de droit canonique*, Paris, 1935–65, 7 vol.

Naz, R., dir. *Traité de droit canonique*, Paris, 1954, 4 vol.

"Regards sur l'histoire du droit canonique antérieurement au Décret de Gratien," *Studia et documenta historiae et juris*, 51, 1985, 73–130.

Revue de droit canonique, Strasbourg, since 1951.

Stickler, A. M. *Historia juris canonici latini, I, Historia fontium*, Turin, 1950, repr. 1984.

Studia Canonica, Ottawa, since 1967.

Valdrini, P., Vernay, J., Durand, J. P., Échappé, O. *Droit canonique*, Paris, 1989 (*Précis Dalloz*).

The editor *Variorum* reprints (Aldershot) has reprinted a selection of articles by S. Kuttner, J. Gaudemet, R. Metz, C. Munier, and A. Vetulani.

Volumes 7, 1965 [period from 1140–1378], 13/1, 1971 [1378–1500], 14, 1990 [1500–63], 15/1, 1976 [1563–1789] and 16, 1981 [1789–1978] of the *HDIEO*.

Zeitschrift des Savigny Stiftung für Rechtsgeschichte. Kanonistiche Abteilung, Berlin and then Weimar, since 1910.

See also CANONICAL COLLECTIONS.

CANONICAL COLLECTIONS. The canonic collections came into being largely due to the need to conserve those texts that were deemed important because of their content or simply because the authorities that produced them judged them to be so. They are collections of essentially disciplinary and liturgical instructions, and their preservation was intended to protect them from being dispersed and falling into oblivion. Furthermore, the judiciary, administrative, and pedagogical practices of the Roman Church (here we refer specifically to the Western collections) made it necessary very early to divide the collections into groups by subject. This went a long way toward making the juridical material more coherent, despite the vast diversity of the sources. However, the texts as a whole were far from being homogenous and were divided within the collections according to certain criteria. The first was the structure of the collection (whether the material was placed in chronological order, or whether another system was used). Second was the nature of the norms observed (whether norms of divine law or ecclesiastical law). Another consideration was the legal authority of the documents (whether the collections were acknowledged as authentic or recognized only as private works). Finally, the nature of the texts themselves was deemed to be original, interpolated to various degrees, or simply apocryphal.

The history of the canonical collections, which have been a means of preserving and documenting various legal sources, helps us to trace the gradual increase of pontifical authority. The Milan Edict of Tolerance (313) allowed the Church to emerge from relative clandestinity. Other events allowed for the preliminary gathering of canonical texts and information, such as the passages of the New Testament and the writings of the FATHERS, as well as pseudo-apostolic texts and imperial constitutions. The increased number of council meetings and decisions of local and universal scope all played a role in promoting the accumulation of canonical information. (Councils included that of Elvira, in Spain, in 300, up to the Carolingian council of Cologne in 887.)

Conciliar canons were the basis for the collections, which at first were chronological and listed as inventories. Other vital sources for the collections were the papal decretals, recorded starting with the pontificate of DAMASUS I (366–84), or SIRICIUS (384–99) and reaching a peak in the time of GELASIUS (492–96). Some instructions of a civil nature, drawn from Roman law, were also important sources for canonic collections.

From the middle of the 4th century, in the East, the so-called collection of *Antioch* (*corpus canonum*) was formed. It was a collection of canons that was regularly updated, and mentioned in the ecumenical Council of Chalcedon in 451. The churches of Africa contributed to the compilation of several important collections between 397 and 418 (*Breviaire d' Hippone, Codex Apiarii causa, Registri ecclesiae carthaginensis excerpta*). The movement, however, did not reach the West until later.

At the beginning of the 6th century, in Rome, the Scythian monk Dionysius Exiguus drafted a widely distributed collection entitled *Dionysiana*. It contained many canons from Greek councils translated into Latin. Shortly afterwards, several papal decretals were added, and the collection, with these additions, became known as *Dionysiana* III (a). HADRIAN I (772–95) added to the collection and sent it to Charlemagne, giving it the name *pseudo-isidoriana*. It soon became the major reference work in the West, overshadowing other collections. One of these was the compilation known as the Freising collection, named after an abbey in southern Bavaria where a single handwritten copy was found. It was of French origin, included 109 canons, and was ostensibly written around 495. Another collection, the *Quesnelliana* (Rome, ca. 497), was important up until the beginning of the 10th century. The *Collectio Avellana* (ca. 553–5) was a set of 244 pieces, including, notably, papal letters from INNOCENT I (401–17) to Vigilius (537–55). The collection was intended to fill the remaining gaps in the available information. Other local collections included the *statuta ecclesiae antiqua* of the 5th century. This was a compilation of instructions regarding dogma as well as legal and liturgical matters, intended for use in Gaul. The *Hispana* (ca. 633–6), was a work attributed by most of the authors to Isidore of Seville. It quoted from 67 councils and some 500 decretals. All of these works paved the way for the development of another type of collection, organized according to a thematic plan.

The East acted as the catalyst for the movement toward a better organization of the collections. The *synagogue* of the patriarch of Constantinople, John the Scholastic (ca. 550), was a prime example of this. This collection listed the canons of the special Eastern councils. In Africa, the *Breviatio canonum* of Fulgence Ferrand was revised around 546, and used a methodical classification as well as technique of summarizing (*tituli*) the canons. The *tituli* referred back to original texts, which could be consulted elsewhere in the collections. The *Concordia canonum* of Cresconius (6th or 7th century), which used the two series (council decisions and decretals) used in the Dionysiana, explored the canons in 301 systematic chapters. In Spain, there was the Capitula (attributed to Martin de Braga, ca. 570) and a thematically revised version of the *Humana* in 1,630 chapters (ca. 680). Among other collections, the *Vetus Gallica* (400 canons grouped under 64 headings) was drafted several times between 600 and 730. There was also the *Dacheriana*, compiled around 800, which had considerable influence on the juridical

sources used by the Carolingian Church as well as on the GREGORIAN reform.

The 9th century marked the third stage in the development of canonic collections. There was widespread use of false canonic collections, which were intended to defend the privileges and justify the demands of the ecclesiastical authorities, in the face of encroachment on their rights by civil authorities. Some capitularies made generous use of these false canonic collections, including that of Benedict the Levite (ca. 847), the collections of Angilramme, and the most important collection of the time, the *pseudo-isidoriana* or "False Decretals," written in Lyon or Tours between 847 and 852.

Other collections may be said to belong to a the later stage, described by P. Valdrime as one of "intensive maturation" of canon law, as a result of the reform led by GREGORY VII (1073–85). The Italian collection known as the *Anselmo dedicata*, compiled around 885, and the 64-part collection of Anselm of Lucca are typical examples of the works of this period. German collections also reflected this stage of "intensive maturation." The most notable examples are the *Livre des causes synodales* (*Book of Synodal Causes*) by Reginon de Prüm (ca. 906), and the Decretum of Burchard of Worms, written around 1012. The three-part collection (*Tripartita, Decret, Panormie*) compiled by Yves de Chartres in 1090–5 marked the culminating point for the works of that period, which saw a new, promising trend toward clarity and practicality. It was also a harbinger of the method of reconciling texts exemplified by the work of GRATIAN, the *Decretum*, around 1140.

After the 12th century, decretals were regularly and methodically collected and compiled to form the major part of canonic collections. They highlighted the increased importance of pontifical legislation, which had by then developed into a full-fledged legal system. In 1187 the first collection of decretals under GREGORY IX, compiled by Bertrand of Pavia, appeared. The period of development and consolidation of decretals lasted until 1580, the date of the official edition of *Corpus iuris canonici*, promulgated by GREGORY XIII (1572–85). BONIFACE VIII (1294–1303) was the author of several collections, and his sixth book of decretals, the *Sextus*, was promulgated on 3 March 1398. CLEMENT V (1305–14) compiled the *Clementines*, published by JOHN XXII (1316–34). The latter also compiled the *Extravagantes*, which came to complement the Clementines. The *Extravagantes Communes* was from 1503. The two *Extravagantes* were private works, as were the *Institutiones juris canonici* (1563) by Lancellotti and the *liber septimus decretalium* (1590) by Pierre Matthew. They completed the corpus.

From 1524 on, decisions of the council were also systematically compiled to be published as collections. One of these was the *amplissima* collection by Mansi, which was published in several editions from 1759 to 1798. The last collections to include papal acts and decrees were the *Roman Bullary* and a first volume of the Bullary of BENEDICT XIV (1740–58). There were several successive editions of the *Roman Bullary* between 1586 and 1830, while the framework for the Bullary of Benedict XIV coincided with the titles of the Corpus.

The CODE OF CANON LAW 1917 was completed during the papacy of BENEDICT XV (1914–22). The code recognized the value of the canonic collections as a necessary source of knowledge of the law *fondes cognescent iuris canonici*, even though they no longer had a valid binding power. Pope PIUS X (1903–14), was the author of the acts promulgated between 1905 and 1908, compiled in five volumes. These were proclaimed authentic on 26 December 1913, by the SECRETARIAT OF STATE, (acta Pii X), and it was these acts of PIUS X that helped promote the canonic collections as a viable source for understanding the law. The Holy See gave its permission for a new edition (canon 1389 of the codex of 1917), retaining the right to set other conditions in keeping with a general need for protection and authenticity. The contemporary codes have undoubtedly put an end to the compiling of canonic collections. However, they continue to borrow some of their formal methods and substantive arrangements and acknowledge their debt to a tradition of which they are the direct heirs.

Francois Jankowiak

Bibliography

Andrieu Guitrancourt, P. *Introduction a l'étude du droit canonique contemporainen particulier*, Paris, 1963.

Buisson, L. "Die Entstehung des Kirchenrechts," *Zeitshrift der Savigny-Stiftung fur Rechtsgeschichte.*

Fournier, P., and G. LeBras, *Histoire des Collections canoniques en Occident*, vol. 2, Paris, 1931.

Gaudemet, J. "Collections Canoniques et codifications," *RDC*, XXXIII (1983), 81–109.

Gaudemet, J. *Les sources du Droit de l'Eglise en Occident du IIe au VIIe siècle*, Paris, 1985.

Kanonistische Abteilung, LII (1966), 1–175.

Massen, F. *Geschichte der Quellen und Literatur des canonisches Rechts im Abendlande bis zum Ausgang des Mittelalters*, Graz, 1870.

Motta, J. (ed), *Liber canonum diversorum sanctorum Patrum sive Collectio in CLXXXIII titulos digesta*, Vatican City, 1988.

Stickler, A. *Historia iuris canonici latini*, Turin, 1950.

van Hove, A. *Prolegomena*, 2nd edition, Malines-Rome, 1945.

Wojtewytsch, M. *Papstum und Konzile von den Anfangen bis zu Leo I.* (440–461), Stuttgart, 1981.

CANONIZATION. The canonization of a saint is one of the fundamental rights that the sovereign pontiff exercises in spiritual matters. The range of solemn decrees by which the pope recognizes the sanctity of a servant of God and grants a universal public cult to him or her is considerable: it involves both recognizing and confirming spontaneous devotions already expressed in relation to the individual and of proposing to the Christian people, models of spirituality in conformance with the teachings of the Church.

Following a complex development, canonization became a right reserved by the pope and a critical procedure of examining the reputed sanctity of the individual. During this development, the concept of canonization, and consequently the very idea of sanctity, gradually acquired an increasingly precise and restricted sense. First, the examination of proof of sanctity was separated from its liturgical recognition; then there was a distinction in the hierarchical degrees between canonization and BEATIFICATION, in which the latter concept was gradually separated from the former and then specified. Thus, the history of the idea and the procedure for canonization may be divided into three essential stages: the affirmation of the papal reservation; the specific examination of the cause in the CURIA, instituted during the 11th and 12th centuries; and the strict definition of a judicial procedure by URBAN VIII at the beginning of the 17th century. The canonical treatise of Pope BENEDICT XIV (*Prosper Lambertini*), *De Servorum Dei beatificatione et beatorum canonizatione* (1734–8), constituted the reference for this codification until immediately following VATICAN II. The edition of CANON LAW completed in 1983 grants a greater initiative to bishops in the domain of canonization.

The verb *canonizare* was used for the first time by BENEDICT VIII at the beginning of the 11th century in relation to the recognition of St. Simon of Polirone; it came into general use in the following century. But the act of canonizing—recognizing and glorifying individuals rewarded by God because of exceptional merits and virtues—is a fundamental component of the organization of the Roman Catholic Church. From the 2nd century in the East and the 3rd in Rome, the apostles and the first martyrs were the object of a spontaneous cult, quickly observed and confirmed by the bishops of dioceses where their remains were conserved. Sanctity was officially recognized by the organization of a solemn liturgy on the anniversary of the death of the saint, or more often—because the exact date was not always known—on the anniversary of the recognition and solemn translation of the saint's relics. To better ensure the permanence of the devotion, the bishops encouraged the local communities to inscribe their saints in a martyrology; from the 4th century, accounts were written of the lives of the martyrs, specifying the details of their deaths. The existence of these *Acta* or *Vitae* constituted proof of the *fama sanctitatis* and a means of spreading the saint's cult. From the

5th century, within the context of spirited controversies about the authenticity of certain martyrs, particularly in North Africa, it became customary to examine the veracity of the *Acta Martyrum* during SYNODS or provincial COUNCILS. Afterward, the decision on the authorization of the public cult was announced, often by the metropolitan; it designated the *martyrs* as *vindicati*, or recognized by the judgment of the Church. After that, the circulation of the texts from one diocese to another ensured the universalization of the cult to the entire Church. After this time, the affirmation of sanctity ceased to be the simple confirmation of a de facto popular cult and became a prerogative of the ecclesiastical hierarchy. However, the body of conciliary legislation (notably that of the council of CARTHAGE in 401) until the 8th century, shows that the decision reverted to the bishops and metropolitans to the exclusion of papal intervention.

The legislative and unifying work of the Carolingian Church also treated the recognition of sanctity. It was all the more influential because, since the time of St. Martin and the *Desert Fathers* of the Eastern Church in the 4th century, a cult of confessor saints (saints who were not martyrs) had developed. The asceticism of their lives and their virtues did not, however, constitute criteria for sanctity as strong as did evidence of violent death accepted for affirmation of the faith. During the same era, the honorary title *sanctus* was frequently attributed to prelates because of their spiritual function. It then became necessary to specify the criteria of true sanctity and, therefore, to be better acquainted with the lives of individuals whose virtues truly destined them for divine *election*. The legislation of Charlemagne and of Louis the Pious instituted what may be considered a veritable "episcopal canonization," which was practiced exclusively until the end of the 11th century: it was thereafter forbidden to venerate saints without the agreement of the ordinary, (local bishop) who alone could examine the *Acta* and proceed, together with the lay princes, to the solemn ceremonies of the translation of the relics that officially instituted the cult.

During the 11th and 12th centuries, the progressive institution of papal reserve in matters of canonization was inseparable from the pontiffs' wish for independence from the secular powers within the framework of the Gregorian REFORM. That reform established the medieval procedure for the canonization of saints, the determination of which belonged exclusively to the Holy See.

Historians of canon law long ago discovered authoritative texts about this process. The first documented proof of papal intervention in relation to cults dates back to 978: the bishop of Trier asked the pope to fix the date for the celebration of St. Celse on 23 February. In 993, JOHN XV proclaimed, as a saint, Ulrich, bishop of Augsburg, who had died in 979. However, canonization was still only a matter of confirming the decision of a bishop; numerous saints were still canonized without the intervention of the pope in the 11th century. The increasingly frequent practice of solemnly confirming the cult of a servant of God during the general synods or councils presided over by the pope, according to the recommendations of URBAN II or of CALLISTUS II, favored the transfer of this right. EUGENE III (1145–53) took a decisive step when he decided on his authority alone to canonize Emperor Henry II. A prerogative exercised jointly by the body of prelates and by the bishop of Rome ultimately reverted exclusively to the latter, at the very moment when he affirmed his universal preeminence over the Church. It is not surprising, then, to see the papal privilege of canonization defined with increasing force by ALEXANDER III, INNOCENT III, and INNOCENT IV. However, when Alexander III wrote in *Aeterna et incommutabilis*, his 1172 letter to King Kol of Sweden, "that it is not in the bishops' power to venerate a particular saint without the authority of the Roman Church," he did not claim to establish a general principle: the prohibition applied specifically to King Eric of Sweden, who could not be considered a saint, since he had died in a state of drunkenness. But under Innocent III, the Fourth Lateran council (1215), in its canon 62, forbade any new recognition and veneration of relics without the authorization of the pope. Finally, Innocent IV reviewed the brief *Audivimus* of Alexander III and glossed it in the *Decretal* collection in 1234. He justified the absolute reserve of the papal right because of the solemn and universal character of the liturgical cult of the saints.

The papal decision had to be accepted, without contest, by the entire Church. Henceforth, canonizations were promulgated after a strict process of probatory investigation that developed in parallel with the evolution of the doctrine and acquired its classic organization in the first half of the 13th century. The procedure did not evolve further until the end of the 16th century. It was justified by the idea that the examination of the acts of the life of the servant of God and the liturgical solemnities that identified his relics did not in themselves provide sufficient proof of the sanctity of his life. It was on the occasion of the canonization of St. Hugh, abbot of Cluny, that Callistus II, in 1120, officially demanded the interrogation of witnesses who had known Hugh when he was alive. The inquiry—entrusted to the authority of the diocesan bishop in the 12th century, then controlled in the 13th century by the Roman curia—responded to a concern to avoid a too exclusively thaumarturgical concept of sanctity. Examples of a saint's virtues evidently had a pastoral and spiritual value superior to that of miraculous wonders.

The medieval procedure was fixed from the canonization of St. Philip Berruyer, archbishop of Bourges (1265–8). It fell to the diocesan clergy and to its bishop to request the opening of the inquiry on the virtues of an individual whom they wished to have canonized. The request was supported in the Curia by increasingly influential lobbyists (prelates, cardinals, princes, and kings) who funded this long and costly procedure. A preliminary inquiry, the diocesan informative process, directed by the ordinary, brought together written and oral proof of the *fama sanctitatis*. Then began the *informatio in partibus*, entrusted to three commissioners named by the Roman Curia. One of the commissioners had to be a bishop; however, from the end of the 13th century, the ordinary was excluded in order to guarantee the impartiality of the investigators who interrogated the witnesses where the servant of God had lived or where his miracles had occurred. The commissioners were surrounded by a growing number of notaries, prosecutors, and interpreters; during the 14th century, they formed a veritable itinerant court of justice. A copy of the acts was sent to the Curia and entrusted to the examination of three cardinals. The curial phase of the procedure is thereafter essential: it decides the outcome of the canonization and consequently ensures the selection of the criteria of sanctity. The report of the cardinals and their chaplains—a *summarium* containing the synthesis of the documents and testimony, as well as any reservations and doubts about the sanctity of the individual—was successively examined in three consistories, presided over by the pope. The first two were secret, one assembling cardinals of the SACRED COLLEGE, then the other bishops and archbishops present at the Curia. If the opinions of the two consistories were positive, the pope then convoked a third, public one, which solemnly decided on the registration of the servant of God in the catalog of saints.

In the last centuries of the Middle Ages, the procedure underwent only modifications under the influence of administrative customs of the Curia at Avignon or Rome. The most significant consisted in providing more systematic criteria of sanctity, whatever the circumstances of the procedure; it also contributed appreciably to the establishment of a *formula interrogatorii*, then of *articuli* aimed at ensuring the veracity of testimony about miracles and of a classification of the virtues of sanctity that departed from the Benedictine model to adopt a schema of theological and cardinal virtues. The last modification occured in 1482 on the occasion of the canonization of the Franciscan St. Bonaventure.

The complexity of the procedure, as much as the desire of the pope to proclaim with infallible certainty the sanctity of the servants of God, considerably reduced the number of canonizations at the end of the Middle Ages. A contradictory situation resulted, which aggravated the fluctuating use of the words *beatus* and *sanctus*. Although in principle, since Innocent IV, only saints canonized by the pope could benefit from a public cult and recitation of a solemn office, the privilage of religious orders to inscribe the blessed in prayers encouraged the expression of a liturgical veneration, sometimes confirmed by epis-

copal indulgences, in favor of numerous individuals reputed to be blessed by the faithful even though their sanctity had not yet been recognized, perhaps for reasons external to the validity of the cause (such as the death of a pope). In addition, in the 15th century, the apostolic reserve on matters related to sanctity did not prevent the blossoming of spontaneous and "popular" cults.

Absolute papal reservation was reestablished in practice only at the end of the 16th century, following the reorganization of the Curia during the Catholic REFORM, when it was felt necessary to defend the cult of saints against Protestantism. On 15 January 1588, Sixtus V created the Congregation of Rites, which was entrusted exclusively with canonization proceedings, the Sacred College having been divested of this responsibility. Urban VIII, in the decrees of 13 March and 2 October 1625, and the brief *Coelestis Jerusalem cives* (15 July 1634), forbade any public cult of non-beatified or non-canonized individuals. At the same time he established the difference between "blessed" and "saint" on which still rest the procedures for beatification and canonization, as defined by canon law. Henceforth, canonization could be granted only to an individual already proclaimed blessed, if new miracles had been attributed to his intercession since the beatification.

The present process of canonization is consequently the final stage of a procedure that first verifies that no spontaneous public cult has been granted to a blessed whose existence postdates the decrees of URBAN VIII. In principle, the heroic virtues established during the beatification process are no longer to be proven; only miracles are of interest. The canonization is announced after the meeting of the three consistories, of which the third, a public one, is open to bishops, members of the Curia, and representatives of Catholic sovereigns in Rome. It concludes with the solemn proclamation of the saint in the Vatican basilica.

The creation by PIUS X in 1930 of a "historical section" in the Congregation of Rites and that by PIUS XII in 1948 of a "medical college"—the latter is consulted on the candidate's miracles and psychic manifestations, of asceticism—reflect the concern to define sanctity with the help of modern methods of scientific investigation. Within the framework of a specialized congregation for the cause of saints, redefined in 1969, the constitution *Divinus perfectionis Magister* of JOHN PAUL II (25 January 1983), seems to conclude the modern papal phase of canonization by restoring to the ordinary the initial responsibility for establishing the dossier on proof of sanctity.

List of Canonized Saints. The list begins with the creation, in 1588, of the Congregation of Rites, and also includes the Congregation for the Causes of Saints (given by date of canonization), as well as saints by confirmation of cult (given by date of decree of confirmation of cult).

Sixtus V (1585–90): Didacus d'Alcalia (1588).

Clement VIII (1592–1605): Hyacinth Odrowaz (17 April 1594), Raymond of Peñefort (29 April 1602).

Paul V (1605–21): Frances of Rome (29 May 1608), Charles Borromeo (1 November 1610).

Gregory XV (1621–3): Francis Xavier, Ignatius of Loyola, Isidore the Farmer, Philip Neri, Teresa of Avila (12 March 1622).

Urban VIII (1623–44): Elisabeth of Portugal (24 June 1626), Andrew Corsini (22 April 1620); *recognition of cult*: Peter Nolasco (30 September 1628).

Alexander VII (1655–67): Thomas of Villenova (1 November 1658), Francis de Sales (19 April 1665); *confirmation of cult*: Ferdinand II of Castille (31 May 1655), John of Malta and Felix of Valois (21 October 1666).

Clement IX (1667–9): Maria Maddalena dei Pazzi, Peter of Alcantara (28 April 1669).

Clement X (1670–6): Cajetan of Thiene, Francis Borgia, Louis Bertrand, Philip Benizi, Rose of Lima (12 April 1671).

Alexander VIII (1689–91): John of Capistrano, John of God, John of Facundus González, Lorenzo Giustiniani, Paschal Baylon (16 October 1690).

Innocent XII (1691–1700): *Confirmation of cult*, Mary of Cerevellon or of Help (13 February 1692), Zita (5 September 1696).

Clement XI (1700–21): Andrew Avellino, Catherine Vigri of Bologna, Felix of Cantalice, Pius V (22 May 1712); *confirmation of cult*: Teresa and Sanchia of Portugal (30 May 1705).

Benedict XIII (1724–30): Agnes Segni of Montepulciano, James of the March Gangale, Turibius Alfonso of Lima (10 December 1726), Francis Solano, John of the Cross, Peregrine Laziosi (27 December 1726), Aloysius Gonzaga, Stanislaus Kostka (31 December 1726), Margaret of Cortona (16 May 1728), John Nepomucene (19 March 1729); *confirmation of cult*: Serapion (14 April 1728).

Clement XII (1730–40): Catherine of Genoa, John Francis Regis, Juliana Falconieri, Vincent de Paul (16 June 1737).

Benedict XIV (1740–58): Camillus de Lellis, Catherine dei Ricci, Fidelis of Sigmaringen, Joseph of Leonessa, Peter Regalado (29 June 1746); *confirmation of cult*, Gerard of Monte Santo (1 August 1742).

Clement XIII (1758–69): Jerome Emiliani, Jane-Frances de Chantal, John of Kanti, Joseph Calasanz, Joseph of Cupertino, Seraphino of Montegranaro (16 July 1767), Emily of Vercelli (19 July 1769).

Pius VI (1775–99): *Confirmation of cult*: Christine Menabuoi of Santa Croce (15 June 1776).

Pius VII (1800–23): Angela Merici, Benedict of St. Philadelphus Manassari called the Moor, Colette Boilet of Corbie, Francis Caracciolo, Hyacintha of Marescotti (24 May 1807); *confirmation of cult*, Berard (10 May 1802).

Gregory XVI (1831–46): Alphonsus Maria Ligouri, Francis Girolamo, John-Joseph of the Cross, Pacifico of San Severino, Veronica Giuliani (26 May 1839); *confirmation of cult*, Cecard, Conrad (9 April 1832), Gerard Mecatti (18 March 1833), Artaldus (2 June 1834), Albert of Sassoferrato (30 September 1837), Louis Rabata (10 December 1841).

Pius IX (1846–78): Michael of the Saints, Argemir, Peter Baptist and 22 companion martyrs of Japan, Paul Miki and 2 companion martyrs of Japan (8 June 1862), Germaine of Pibrac, Josaphat Kuncewicz, Leonard Port, Maurice Casanova, Mary Frances of the Five Stigmata of Our Lord, Jesus Christ Gallo, Nicholas Pieck and 18 companion martyrs of Gorkum, Paul of the Cross Danei, Peter of Arbues (29 June 1867); *confirmation of cult*: Maura (4 August 1848), Juliana and Sempronia (13 September 1850), Prosper (4 May 1854), Ignatius Azevedo and 39 companion martyrs (11 May 1854), Nortburga of Eben (27 March 1862), Convouon of Comblessac (3 May 1866), Reginald (1 October 1868), Conan (27 April 1871), Maxima (13 June 1872), Eugene III (3 October 1872).

Leon XIII (1878–1903): Benedict Joseph Labre, Claire of the Cross of Montefalco, John Baptist Rossi, Lawrence of Brindisi (8 December 1881), Alphonsus Rodríguez, John Berchmans, Peter Claver, the seven founders of the order of Servites (15 January 1888), Anthony Mary Zaccaria, Peter Fourier (27 May 1897), John Baptist de La Salle, Rita of Cascia (24 May 1900); *confirmation of cult*: Nostrien (2 May 1878), Lucida (8 January 1880), Gandulf Sachi (10 March 1881), Bertrand of Guarrigues (14 July 1881), Hilarion (10 May 1883), Severinus Beothius (20 December 1883), Eustace (18 December 1888), Germanus de Montfort (9 May 1889), Lidoine (14 March 1890), Gemma (28 April 1890), Adrian III (10 June 1891), Fauques (2 July 1893), Alferius, Leo Peter, Constable (21 December 1893), Thomas of Tolentino (23 July 1894), Sabinus (11 December 1899), Obice (23 July 1900), Nicetas (24 November 1900), Eurosia de Jaca, Eve (1 May 1902), Albert, Asicus, Carthage, and their 22 companions (19 June 1902).

Pius X (1903–14): Alessandra Maria Sauli, Gerard Majella (11 December 1904), Klemens-Maria Hofbauer, Joseph Oriol (20 May 1909); *confirmation of cult*: Justa (7 September 1903), Theobald and 16 others (December 1903), Arialdo of Cutiacum (13 July 1904), Christopher of Romandiola (12 April 1905), Placida de Sisisbert (6 December 1905), John (2 March 1906), Romede of Taur (24 July 1907), Vicald (13 February 1908), Gerard Cagnoli (12 May 1908), Bartholdus Buonpedoni (27 April 1910).

Benedict XV (1914–22): Gabriel of Our Lady of Sorrows Possenti, Margaret-Mary Alacoque (13 May 1920), Joan of Arc (16 May 1920); *confirmation of cult*: Nonius Alvares Pereira (23 January 1918).

Pius XI (1922–39): Teresa of the Child Jesus (17 May 1925), Peter Canisius (21 May 1925), Madeleine-Sophie Barat, Mary Magdelene Postel (24 June 1925), John-Baptist Marie Vianney, John Eudes (31 May 1925), Catherine Thomas of Palma, Lucy Filippini (22 June 1930), Jean de Brebeuf and his 7 companion martyrs of Canada, Robert Bellarmine, Theophilus de Corte Signori (29 June 1930), Albert the Great (bull of equipollent canonization, 16 December 1931), Andre Hubert Fournet (4 June 1933), Bernadette Soubirous (8 December 1933), Jeanne Anthilde Thouret (14 January 1934), Mary Michaela of the Holy Sacrament Desmaisieres (4 March 1934), Louise de Marillac (11 March 1934), Joseph Benedict Cottolengo, Pompée Marie Pirrotti of St. Nicholas, Teresa Margaret of the Sacred Heart of Jesus Redi (19 March 1934), John Bosco (1 April 1934), Conrade of Parzham Birndorfer (20 May 1934), John Fisher and Thomas More (19 May 1935) Andrew Bobola, John Leonardi of the Mother of God, Salvator of Horta (17 April 1938); *confirmation of cult*, Bogomile (27 May 1925), Emma of Gurk (5 January 1938).

Pius XII (1939–58): Gemma Galgani, Mary of Saint Euphrasia Pelletier (2 May 1940), Margaret of Hungary (bull of equivalent canonization, 19 November 1943), Frances Xavier Cabrini (7 July 1946), Nicholas vou Flue (15 May 1947), Bernardino Realino, John de Britto, Joseph Cafasso (22 June 1947), Jane Elisabeth Bichier of the Ages, Michael Garicoits (6 July 1947), Louis-Mary Grignion of Montfort (20 July 1947), Catherine Labouré (27 July 1947), Joan de Lestonnac (15 May 1949), Maria Josepha Rossello (12 June 1949), Mary Emily de Rodat (23 April 1950), Anthony Mary Claret (7 May 1950), Bartholomea Capitanio,

Catherine Vincentia Gerosa (18 May 1950), Joan of Valois (28 May 1950), Vincent Marie Strambi (11 June 1950), Maria Goretti (24 June 1950), Mary Agnes of Jesus de Paredes y Flores (9 July 1950), Emily de Vialar, Marie Dominic Mazzarello (24 June 1951), Anthony Mary Gianelli, Francis Marie Bianchi, Ignatius of Laconi (21 October 1951), Pius X (29 May 1954), Dominic Savio, Caspar del Bufalo, Joseph Mary Pignatelli, Maria Crucifiée di Rosa, Peter Louis Marie Chanel (12 June 1954).

John XXIII (1958–63): Charles of Sezze, Joachim of Vedruna (12 April 1959), Gregory Barbarigo (bull of equivalent canonization, 26 May 1960), John de Ribera (12 June 1960), Marie Bertilla Boscardin (11 May 1961), Martin de Porres (6 May 1962), Anthonio-Maria Pucci, Francis-Marie of Camporosso, Peter Julian Eymard (9 December 1962), Vincent Pallotti (20 January 1963); *confirmation of cult*, Joseph Hermannus (11 August 1958).

Paul VI (1963–78): Charles Lwanga, Matthias Mulumba Kalemba and their 30 companion martyrs of Uganda (18 October 1964); Brother Benildus Romancon (29 October 1967), Julie Billiart (22 June 1969), Maria Soledad Torres Acosta (25 January 1970), Leonard Murialdo (3 May 1970), Teresa Couderc (10 May 1970), John of Avila (31 March 1970), Nicholas Tavelic and his companion martyrs (21 June 1970), Cuthbert Maine and his 39 companion martyrs of England (25 October 1970), Teresa of Jesus Jornet Ibars (27 January 1974), John Baptist of the Conception García, Vincent-Marie López Vincuna (25 May 1975), Elisabeth Ann Bayley Seton (14 September 1975), John Macias (28 September 1975), Oliver Plunkett (12 October 1975), Justin de Jacobis (26 October 1975), Beatrice de Silva Meneses (3 October 1976), John Ogilvie (17 October 1976), Raphaela Marie of the Sacred Heart of Jesus Porras (23 January 1977), John Nepomucene Neumann (19 June 1977), Charbel Makhlouf (9 October 1977); *confirmation of cult*: Adelinde (27 January 1966), Berthold de Rachez (27 July 1970).

John Paul II (1978–): Crispin of Viterbo (20 June 1982), Maximilian Kolbe (10 October 1982), John of the Cross Delanoue, Marguerite Bourgeoys (31 October 1982), Leopold of Castronovo (15 October 1983) Paolo Frassinetti (11 March 1984), Andrew Kim, Paul Chong, Lawrence Imbert, Francis Simeon Berneux and their 99 companion martyrs of Korea (6 May 1984), Michael Febres Cordero (21 October 1984), Francis Anthony Fasanti (13 April 1986), Joseph Marie Tomasi (12 October 1986), Lawrence Ruiz of Manila, Dominicus Ibañez de Erquicia, James Kyushei Tomonaga and their 13 companion martyrs of Japan (18 October 1987), Joseph

Moscati (25 October 1987), Roch González, Alphonsus Rodríguez, Juan del Castillo (16 May 1988), Eustachia Calafato (11 June 1988), the 17 martyrs of Vietnam (19 June 1988), Simon de Rojas, Rose-Philippine Duchesne (3 July 1988), Dimitri Donskoi, Roublev, Maximus the Greek, Macaire, Paissy Velichkovsky, Xenia, Ignatius, Ambrose, Theophane the Recluse (10 July 1988), Magdalen of Canossa (2 October 1988), Marie Rose Molas y Vallve (11 December 1988), Clelia Barbieri (9 April 1989), Caspar Bartoni, Richard Pampuri (1 November 1989), Adam Chmielowski (12 November 1989), Mother Mutien-Marie Wiaux (30 January 1990), Juan Diego (6 May 1990), Marie-Marguerite Dufrost de Lajemmerais d'Youville (9 December 1990), Raphael Kalinowski (17 November 1991), Claude de la Colombière (31 May 1992), Ezequiel Moreno y Diaz (11 October 1992), Marie of St. Ignatius, Juana Fernandez Solar (Teresa "de los Andes") (21 March 1993), Enrique de Ossó y Cervelló (16 June 1993), Jan Sarkander, Zdislava of Lemberk (21 May 1995), Marek Krizin, Stefan Pongracz, Melichar Grodziecky, martyrs of Kosice (2 July 1995), Eugene de Mazenod (3 December 1995), Jean-Gabriel Perboyre, Juan Grande Roman, Bro. Egidio Maria of St. Joseph (2 June 1996), Queen Edviga of Poland (Hedwig) (8 June 1997), John Dukla, O.F.M. (10 June 1997), Edith Stein (11 October 1998), Marcellin Joseph Benoit Champagnat, Giovanni Calabria, Agostina Livia Pietrantonio (9 January 1999), Sr. Kunegunda Kinga (16 June 1999), Cirilo Bertran and eight companion Brothers of the Christian Schools, Inocencio de la Immaculada, St. Jaime Hilario Barbal, Benedetto Menni, Tommaso da Cori (21 November 1999), Mary Faustina Kowalska (30 April 2000), Cristóbal Magallanes and 24 companions, José Maria de Yermo y Parres, Maria de Jesús Sacramentado Venegas (21 May 2000), Josephine Bakhita, Augustine Chao and other martyrs of China, Katherine Drexel, María Josefa of the Heart of Jesus Sancho de Guerra (1 October 2000), Luigi Scrosoppi, Agostino Roscelli, Bernardo da Corleone, Teresa Eustochio Verzeri, Rebecca Pietra Ar-Rayès di Himlaya (10 June 2001), Giuseppe Marello, Paola Montal Fornés di San Giuseppe Calasanzio, Francesca Sales Aviat, Maria Crescentia Höss (25 November 2001), confirmation of cult, Agnes of Bohemia (12 November 1989). John Paul II also declared St. Cyril and St. Methodius co-patrons of Europe (apostolic letter Egregiae virtutus, 31 December 1980).

Philippe Jansen
Dominique Le Tourneau

Bibliography

Amore, A. "Culto e canonizzazione dei nell' antichità cristiana," Antonianum, 52, 1977, 38–80.

Benedict XIV (Prosper Lambertini), De servorum Dei beatificatione et beatorum canonizatione, Bologna, 1734–38.

Blaher, D. J. The Ordinary Processes in Causes of Beatification and Canonization, Washington, 1949 (The Catholic University of America, Canon Law Studies, 268).

Congregation of Rites, Index ac Status causarum beatificationis servorum Dei et canonizationis beatorum, Vatican City, 1953 (previous editions: 1890, 1895, 1901, 1909, 1931, and 1941).

Congregation of the Causes of Saints, Index ac Status causarum (editio particularis cura P. Galavotti), Vatican City, 1988. I Supplementum (1988–1989), Vatican City, 1989. II Supplementum (1989–1990), Vatican City, 1991.

De Clercq, "Les causes des serviteurs de Dieu," Revue de droit canonique, IV (1954), 76–100.

Dodds, B. Your One-Stop Guide to How Saints are Made, Ann Arbor, Mich., 2000.

Hertzling, L. "Canonisation," DS, 2, 1953, 79–81.

Jombart, E. "Canonisation," Catholicisme, II, (1949), 475–6

Low, G. "Canonizzazione," EC, III, (1949), Vatican City, 569–7.

Naz, R. "Causes de béatification et de canonisation," DDC, 3, (1942), 10–37.

Ortolan, T. "Canonisation dans l'Église romaine," DTC, 3 (1905), 1629–59.

Palazzini, P. "I processi di canonizzazione ieri e oggi," San Nicola, Tolentino, le Marche, Convengo Internazionale di Studi, Tolentino, 4–7 sett., 1985, Tolentino, 1987, 23–42.

Vauchez, A. La Sainteté en Occident aux derniers siècles du Moyen Age, Rome, 1981 (BEFAR, 241).

Woodward, K. L. Making Saints. How the Catholic Church Determines Who Becomes a Saint, Who Doesn't and Why, New York, 1990.

Zubeck, T. J. "New Legislation About the Canonization of the Servants of God," Jurist, 43 (1983), 361–75.

See also CAUSES OF CANONIZATION.

CANOSSA (FORTRESS). Only ruins remain today of this famous fortress in the Apennines, south of Reggio d'Emilia. Declared a national monument by the Italian state in 1878, Canossa derives its fame from the meeting there in 1077 of German king Henry IV with Pope GREGORY VII, to whom the king offered penitence, and to the German chancellor Otto von Bismarck's famous allusion to it in the Reichstag in 1872: "We shall not go to Canossa." The fortress, built by Count Adalbert-Atto (d. 988), is mentioned for the first time in 951, when Queen Adelaide, widow of Lothario, king of Italy, and future empress, took refuge there to escape from the new king of Italy, Beranger II of Ivrée, and put herself under the protection of Adalbert-Atto, who had to resist a siege. Canossa then became the center of a vast domain in northern Italy, over which the counts of Canossa exercised authority. Originally from Tuscany, the counts gained their power as vassals of the bishop of Reggio Emilia and, from 1032, under the marquis of Tuscany. The walls of the fortress also sheltered a convent of regular monks, confirmed by the pope in 975; it later became a Benedictine monastery and was suppressed in 1747.

The great grand-daughter of Adalbert-Atto, Countess Matilda (d. 1115), daughter of Marquis Boniface (d. 1025) and Beatrice (d. 1076), daughter of the duke of Lorraine, was the most powerful ally of the popes during the INVESTITURE CONTROVERSY and associated confrontations with Emperor Henry IV. After an unhappy marriage with Henry IV's half-brother, the Duke of Lorraine, Godefrey the Hunchback (d. 1076), Matilda offered all her possessions, including the fortress of Canossa, to the Church of Rome, subject to lifetime *usufruct*. By virtue of a testamentary clause, the inheritance of Matilda—who died childless—fell to the son of Henry IV, Emperor Henry V, and through him to the German kings and emperors or to their vassals, who where in permanent conflict with the papacy owing to the latter's primary claim to primacy over temporal powers. During the dispute about the German throne, the pretenders and, finally Frederick II, renounced claims to Matilda's property, most of which had long fallen into the hands of overlords and towns in northern Italy.

In the 12th century, the fortress became the property of a new noble family who had taken the name of Canossa. It was attacked and destroyed in 1255 by the inhabitants of Reggio on orders of the pope, who wished to punish the overlord, who had come out in favor of the GHIBELLINES. Reconstructed, the fortress was in turn the possession of Reggio, Parma, Canossa, and other captains before finally being acquired in 1449 by the Este family. The most famous captain of the fortress was unquestionably Ariosto in 1502. Following the destruction that occurred during the war between the Este of Ferrara and the Farnese of Parma (1557–8), a sumptuous reconstruction was undertaken, but the building no longer served as a permanent residence. From 1642, the Valentini of Modena, vassals of the Este who took the title of count from 1771, occupied it. Following the French Revolution, they were driven out in 1796, and the prison installed in the 18th century was stormed. Subsequently, the main part of the building was almost completely ruined by earthquakes, by the use of its rooms as stables, and by the removal of materials for new buildings in the village. The result of the reconstruction of Matilda's Castle was not to everyone's liking.

The arrival of Henry IV at Canossa constituted the climax of the investiture controversy. Condemned by Pope Gregory VII for nominating bishops in Italy, at the end of January 1076 Henry IV announced to the pope during a diet of the empire in Worms that he absolved himself

from any obedience. Furthermore, he exhorted Gregory VII to abdicate because of the complaints against him, particularly concerning his papal election. The pope's counterattack was swift. In February 1076, a Lenten synod held in Rome decreed the suspension and excommunication of the king. Incapable of reigning under these conditions, Henry had to submit to a decision adopted by an assembly of princes at Tribur (October 1076) and seek absolution before the anniversary date of the excommunication in order to forestall the election of a new king. To this end, the pope was invited to attend the diet of Augsburg on 2 February. To delay the pope—who had also rejected a suggestion that the king come to Rome—Henry left for northern Italy, crossing the Alps despite the rigors of winter. It was at Canossa that he met Gregory VII who, having reached Mantua, had put himself under the protection of Matilda.

Contemporary accounts of the event, though all by authors hostile to Henry, differ on certain points. The most important document is the pope's letter of apology to the German princes sent from Canossa itself immediately after the absolution of the king. Yet in 1077, the German annalist Lambert von Hersfeld related, certainly with some exaggeration, that the penance imposed on Henry was to remain three whole days, barefoot, in the snow and ice in front of the fortress. Matilda's biographer, Donizo da Canossa, writing in 1115, mentioned simply talks which lasted three days before the absolution of the king, who had come to present himself as a penitent. Certain evidence suggests that Henry was at that time Matilda's guest in the neighboring castle of Bianello. It is known that he sought—on his knees, as represented in a Donizo miniature—the intercession of Matilda and of Abbot Hugh of Cluny. It was not by chance that the penance began on 25 January, the day of St. Paul's conversion; this fact no doubt explains the duration of three days, in biblical allusion, attributed to the penance. The agreements recorded in the register of Gregory VII as a condition of absolution, and signed in the name of the king by the princes of his retinue and by Abbot Hugh, are dated 28 January 1077. The ceremony of absolution in the castle's chapel began with the prostration of the king, dressed as a penitent, his arms outstretched crosswise, kneeling at the feet of the pope sitting on his throne. It ended with the reception of the Eucharist. Lambert makes the scene look like the judgment of God. At the end of the ceremony, a banquet was held at the castle.

Because the German princes did not recognize the absolution of King Henry IV, the meeting at Canossa was followed by the election of an anti-king in March 1077, and Germany had a dual monarchy until 1088. After the sentence of the pope and a second excommunication in June 1080, the synod of Brixen elected an ANTIPOPE, bringing about a SCHISM that lasted until 1111. Gregory

VII, exiled with the Normans, died in 1085 at Salerno; Henry IV, crowned emperor by the antipope, died excommunicated at Liège in 1106. The investiture controversy ended in 1122 with the concordat of WORMS. By and large, Canossa thus suffered a desacralization and a consequent loss of prestige vis-à-vis royalty.

In medieval historiographers, Canossa scarcely evokes any emotion; they go as far as praising the humility of the king and condemning the severity of the pope. Only since the Reformation has attention been focused on the confrontation; this interest peaked in Bismarck's Germany during the KULTURKAMPF. Since the 16th century, the incident at Canossa has given rise to at least thirty historical depictions. North of the Alps, artists generally depict the scene of penitence in the courtyard; in the south, the absolution in the chapel of the castle is more popular. A wood cut of the history of King Henry IV, printed in 1556 at Zurich by J. Stumpf, and a scene painted in 1556 by F. Zuccari in the *Sala Regia* of the Vatican begin the series. A marble bas-relief finished in 1636 by Stefano Speranza for the epitaph of Matilda at St. Peter's and an 1862 drawing by H. Plüddemann for a tapestry in the museum of the castle at Canossa are among the best-known illustrations of that episode. A painting of H. Wislicenus, destined for the imperial palace at Goslar and finished in 1889, caused a sensation even at the start of the project. The most recent works are dated 1977, a commemorative year. Since the 18th century, more than forty stories, novels, and historical dramas have treated Canossa, which figured in the title of a work for the first time in 1839. The antagonism aroused by the personalities of the king and the pope and the role of mediator played by Matilda are the main inspirations. A poem by Heinrich Heine (1839) and a play by E. G. Kolbenheyer (1934) have also become famous. A French tragedy by Charles Cordier was performed in 1950 at Brussels. The most recent prose text at this writing is dated 1988. Bismarck's famous remark in 1872 inspired intense historical research on the audience at Canossa, and more than seventy scientific works were dedicated to the debate on this event. Interest is particularly high in Italy, but with the *Studi Matildici*, it deals with the whole epoch of Matilda.

Harald Zimmermann

Bibliography

Campanini, N. *Canossa: Guida storica illustrata*, Reggio, 1975.

Capitani, O. "Canossa: Una lezione da meditare," *Studi Matildici* (Modena), 1978, 1–23.

Fumagalli, V. *Le origini di una granda dinastia feudale*, Tübingen, 1971.

Ghirardini, L. L. *Saggio di una bibliografia dell' eta matildico-gregoriana*, Modena, 1970.

Ghirardini, L. L. *Storia critica di Matilde di Canossa*, Reggio d'Emilia, 1989.

Struve, T. "Johannes Haller und das Versohnungsmahl auf Canossa," *Historisches Jahrbuch, 110* (1990), 110–16.

Zimmermann, H. "Canossa 1077 und Venedig 1177 und Jahrhundert danach," *Im Bann des Mittelalters*, Sigmaringen, 1986, 107–32.

Zimmermann, H. *Der Canossagang von 1077*, Wiesbaden, 1975.

CAP OF THE HOLY SPIRIT. See **Blessed or Holy Hat and Sword.**

CARDINAL. Cardinals are the highest dignitaries of the Roman Church, after the pope and before patriarchs and primates. Named by the sovereign pontiff alone, they are the most eminent and closest counselors of the pope. Cardinals are divided into three orders within the SACRED COLLEGE: cardinal bishops, cardinal priests, and cardinal deacons. They alone hold the privilege of meeting collegially in CONCLAVE to elect the successor to St. Peter and of ensuring the intermediary administration of the Church during a vacancy of the Apostolic See.

Up to the Council of Trent. The origin of the word "cardinal" is disputed. Some historians believe that the adjective *cardinalis* (from *cardo*, "pivot") was first applied, in the earliest centuries of Christianity, to clerics exercising permanent administration of a given church, or to the person responsible for the principal church in a parish or diocese, and by extension to the principal dignitary of any church. Others seek the origin of the title in the verb *incardinare*, used from the time of Gregory the Great (590–604) to designate the clerics of the three major orders serving a church other than that for which they had been ordained—in particular, the bishops who had been driven from their episcopal sees by barbarian invasions and had been transferred temporarily to other cities. At Rome itself, at least from the 4th century, the pope, as bishop of the city, called on the principal dignitaries comprising the *presbyterium*, an assembly of priests and deacons in his entourage—at first, for liturgical functions and preaching—to examine important questions submitted to him by churches elsewhere. From the end of the 7th century, these priests, now designated *cardinales*, were closely associated with the administration of the universal Church. They were in charge of 25 (5th century), then 28 "titles" attached to principal parishes, which were divided into four bodies of seven each under the authority of each of the four major BASILICAS of Rome—St. Peter's, St. Paul's, St. Lawrence's, and St. Mary Major. The cardinal priests were therefore named henceforth after their titular churches. The pope was also assisted by palatine deacons for papal functions at the Lateran palace, and by regionary deacons (a disputed number, either 12 or 18) who were responsible for liturgical functions, but especially for the administration of temporal goods and the discharge of charity and public assistance in the "deacon-ries" created in Rome. Closely associated as well with the government of the Church from the 8th century on, they seem to have received the title of "cardinal," linked to their deaconry, only from the beginning of the 12th century. The dignity of cardinal bishop was applied under STEPHEN III (768–72) to the seven titular bishops of sees surrounding Rome, those later called "suburbicarian": Ostia, Velletri, Porto and St. Rufina, Albano, Tusculum (Frascati), Sabina, and Preneste (Palestrina). This pope entrusted them with the tasks of serving the Lateran basilica and of celebrating Sunday Mass on the altar of St. Peter's each in turn. Although they seem not to have played a major role before the middle of the 11th century, they nonetheless participated increasingly in the examination of questions relative to the universal Church.

From the middle of the 8th century, about 30 dioceses in Germany, England, France, and Spain obtained from the pope the creation of cardinals "according to the Roman model." With the rise of Roman cardinals, however, the term fell into disuse for other bishops; nonetheless, the designation "cardinal" (in the sense of principal cleric of a church) continued to be used until the 19th century at certain places, including Notre-Dame duets-la-Chapelle and the cathedrals of Compostela and Salerno.

The reform movement associated with GREGORY VII (1073–85) marked a crucial phase in the history of the cardinalate. Increasing recourse to the pope by the churches of Christendom on questions of reform, as well as the need for intimate counselors for the sovereign pontiff, increased the power of Roman cardinals. Their original liturgical functions diminished, but they were now entrusted with missions outside Rome and supplanted the *judices palatini* in their judicial and administrative functions. The first clear manifestation of their rise was the bull *In nomine Domini* of Pope NICHOLAS II in 1059: to end the interference of the imperial authority and of the great Roman families in the nomination of popes, he decreed that the papal election would henceforth be conducted exclusively by the Roman cardinal bishops. The other cardinals (priests and deacons), the clerics, and the people of Rome would afterward confirm their choice. The consecration of the new pope was restored to the cardinal bishops alone. The norms of this decree represented an undeniable victory for the reformists, but the vicissitudes of the fight against the empire and schisms delayed their effective application. During the confrontation between Gregory VII and Emperor Henry IV, a number of cardinal priests in 1084, rallied around the ANTIPOPE CLEMENT III (Guibert of Ravenna), obliging Gregory's successor, URBAN II (1088–99), to seek the support of the cardinal priests. The text of the 1059 bull was "rewrit-

ten"—not to say falsified—within the circle of schismatic cardinal priests in such a way that for "cardinal bishops" was substituted the generic term "cardinals." This new text soon appeared in canonical collections, and the equalization of the elective role among the three orders was henceforth the rule. Another proof of their increased powers within the administration of the universal Church, the signing by cardinals of official papal documents of major importance, appeared in the mid-11th century, but this practice became routine only from the reign of PASCHAL II (1099–18). In fact, one cannot really speak of the SACRED COLLEGE until the beginning of the 12th century, when the deacons in their turn were definitively integrated into the class of cardinals; the first papal election carried out by the three orders together was that of 1130 (INNOCENT II).

The preceding summary of the origins of the cardinalate and of the Sacred College illustrates the institutional character of the new dignity that the cardinalate *de facto* assumed in the ecclesiastical hierarchy. The great theologians did not fail to reflect on its ecclesiological elements. Opinion is divided on the doctrine of Peter Damian (1007–72), himself a cardinal bishop of Ostia. According to some, he established the cardinalate's divine origin and enhanced the participation of cardinal bishops along with the pope in the exercise of supreme power. According to others, he had a limited concept of their powers, according to which they participated by delegation in the primacy powers in accordance with the reform, and without delegation—but only *sede vacante*—in the power to judge and condemn bishops in their position as guardians of the Apostolic See.

At the beginning of the 12th century, the customary organ of consultation for important matters, the Roman synod, was eradicated to the benefit of the cardinals. Under Urban II what would soon be called the CONSISTORY took shape as an assembly called by the pope to discuss "with the counsel of our brothers, the cardinals," ecclesiastical and political-administrative matters of importance: questions relative to the faith, creation of bishoprics, nomination of bishops, granting of privileges to abbeys, essential matters of papal policy, appointment of legates, judicial affairs, management of the PAPAL STATES, and so on. Only cardinals participated in secret consistories; in public consistories reserved for the most solemn occasions, other prelates, lay princes, and ambassadors also took part. Apart from the privilege of electing the pope and of assisting him in consistories, the exclusive attribution of legations—the LEGATES *a latere* appeared under ALEXANDER II (1061–73)—the acknowledged dignity of cardinals grew. Capable of exercising great curial responsibility (as vice-chancellor, grand penitentiary, or apostolic CAMERLENGO), they also served in a judicial capacity, acting on papal commission in trials on ecclesiastical or canonical matters, assisted by a small tribunal.

One essential development of the cardinalate between the 12th and 14th centuries was the obligation of residence at the CURIA (except in cases of legation) imposed on cardinals from the time of GREGORY IX (1227–41). In fact, from the middle of the 11th century, the popes of the Gregorian reform had customarily named as cardinals the bishops or abbots of great abbeys (mainly Italian Benedictines) to ensure the close collaboration of influential reformers and to bond the great abbeys to the reform movement. The abbots continued to administer their abbeys and participated in the Sacred College only when they were at the Curia. Moreover, until the time of ALEXANDER III (1159–81), cardinals who received an episcopal see in the exterior renounced the cardinalate, which was considered a dignity inferior to the episcopate. From this pope on, however, titular cardinals of a non-Roman see administered it and resided there, participating only occasionally in the consistory. This practice, justified during the reform, was totally abandoned after INNOCENT III (1198–1216), and the cardinals' residency was thereafter obligatory.

The Sacred College is endowed with its own administrative body responsible for managing the common revenues of the cardinals: the Chamber of the Sacred College, headed by its cardinal chamberlain (later called the camerlengo) supported by a cleric and assistants. In 1289, Pope NICHOLAS IV, by the bull *Coelestis altitudo*, gave the cardinals half of the regular revenues of the Church, which was added to the amount they already received from the "common services" paid by bishops or abbots named by the pope. These sums were only part of their income; the other—and not the least—consisted of ecclesiastical benefices, annates paid by sovereigns, gifts of the popes on their accession, and other funds.

From the 13th century on, a pronounced oligarchic tendency appeared within the Sacred College: the reduction in the number of cardinals, which dropped to six, actually increased their individual power and revenues. The red hat was conferred on secular clerics by INNOCENT IV at the council of Lyons in 1245 (extended to all cardinals by GREGORY XIII in the 16th century), and the red cassock by BONIFACE VIII in 1291. Their supreme privilege, the election of the pope, was confirmed and regulated by Alexander III at the third Lateran council in 1179 (equality of the three orders; a minimum of two-thirds of the vote required to be elected). But the popes had to take measures to limit the duration of the elections and, therefore, the vacancies of the Apostolic See, during which the cardinals showed an increasing proclivity to usurp papal powers. From this need flowed the institution of the conclave by GREGORY X at the second council of Lyons in 1274.

The installation of the Curia at AVIGNON in 1309, which would last a long time, was as great an upheaval for the Sacred College as for the Church as a whole. The proportion of Italians to French was reversed within that body from the 12th century to the 14th, dropping from 80% Italian and 12% French, to 65% vs. 22% in the 13th century, and finally to 10% vs. 85% during the Avignon papacy. This reversal essentially reflects the origins of the popes themselves, but it also demonstrates the influence exerted by the sovereigns of Christendom, particularly the king of France. Nominations of what would later be called "crown cardinals," created on the initiative of a foreign sovereign, were at first exceptional but multiplied from the time of CLEMENT V (1305–14). From the 15th century on, this "right" was granted in favor of the emperor, the kings of France, Spain, Portugal, and the republic of Venice. It is at the origin of the position of "cardinal protector" of a nation within the Sacred College.

Another trend, though not begun at Avignon certainly grew there: NEPOTISM. Certain popes, such as BENEDICT XII, did not succumb to it; others, especially Clement V and JOHN XXII, could not resist. The cardinals displayed the pomp and circumstance of their dignity during sumptuous receptions offered to the pope or other sovereigns. They had at their disposal a *familia* (household) comprising some fifty persons—the popes sought in vain to limit their number—dressed in superb livery, along with the use of private palaces at Villeneuve-les-Avignon. Apart from the clerical personnel and the lay domestic staff, there were also artists and intellectuals, among them the great Petrarch as well as a throng of itinerant clients. The cardinals' courts were a scene of cultural enrichment and patronage rivaling the papal court.

The counterpoint to this princely lifestyle was the pursuit of lucrative benefices, the accumulation of multiple churches, abbeys, and priories for the cardinal and his protégés. The contest became all the fiercer as the number of cardinals was reduced to an average of about 20. Keenly aware of how to influence the pope, directly or through the intermediary of a king or a prince, they controlled a good number of cardinalate creations—theoretically the free choice of the sovereign pontiff alone—as well as the choice of legates in important political matters, and they profited from a vacancy of the Holy See to attempt to impose their dominance. At the conclave of 1352, all the cardinals signed the first capitulation (a list of their privileges), destined for a very great future, stipulating, among other things, the limit of a maximum of 20 cardinals, the establishment of the agreement of at least two-thirds of the cardinals for any new nomination or any condemnation of one of them, and the confirmation of the transfer of half the revenues of the Church to the Sacred College. Certain conclavists expressed reservations, including Etienne Aubert, who, once elected pope under the name of INNOCENT VI, declared this capitulation null and contrary to the principle of the *plenitudo potestatis* that the pope enjoys.

The demands of members of the Sacred College were coupled with canonical or theological claims considered or completed during the conflict between Philip the Fair of France and Boniface VIII, and the excommunication of the Colonna cardinals (1297). Reworking the arguments advanced in the 13th century by Pierre de la Vigne at the chancery of Emperor Frederick II, or distorting the thinking of the canonist Egidio Colonna (Giles of Rome), theoreticians of cardinalitial power such as the Augustinian Agostino Trionfo (beginning of the 14th century) did not hesitate to affirm that cardinals are the heirs to the apostles; their institution, therefore, has a divine origin, and they are thus superior to bishops; this mitigates the absence of any sacramental basis of the cardinalate. Premised on the conciliar theory that spread during the Great Schism, this doctrine aimed at reserving to the cardinals part of the *plenitudo potestatis*; the cardinal canonist Jean Le Moine (d. 1313) was one of its champions. These theses were zealously contested by contemporaries such as John of Paris, an advocate of the superiority of bishops, William of Ockham (for political reasons), and the canonist Giovanni d'Andrea, defender of papal power. The great Western schism marked both the zenith and the beginning of the decline of the power of cardinals. On the one hand, they reaped the fruits of a slow process of concentration of spiritual and temporal privileges: the reduction of their number, their growing control over nominations of their colleagues, their powerful network of influence within and outside the Curia, and finally the affirmation of their participation in the *plenitudo potestatis* of the pope all combined to create feared individuals, ready to sacrifice almost anything to maintain their positions. On the other hand, the schism caused the splitting of the Sacred College along with the division of Christianity into two obediences (and even three, after the double aborted deposition and the election of the pope at the council of Pisa, ALEXANDER V in 1409), and this greatly diminished the cardinals' revenues. The Sacred College was in the front line of attacks led by partisans of thorough Church reform. Its inability to find a solution to the schism continued to discredit it in the eyes of Christians. The choice of a council route (Pisa, 1409) restricted its claims to share power with the pope. At Pisa, the cardinals succeeded in safeguarding their elective privilege, but at Constance (1414–18) they were roundly attacked. Certain conciliary fathers even proposed the suppression of the Sacred College and its replacement by the college of bishops in the elective function. These proposals were geared toward improving the morals of the cardinals and at restricting their number to around 24, while recommending recruitment throughout the Christian world and not just in France and Italy. During the election of MARTIN V in 1417, which put an end to the schism, the cardinals had to share their elective rights with representatives of the "nations" of the council. The unity of the Sacred College was reestablished, but it emerged enfeebled from the schism.

Almost all the attempts at reform of the Sacred College during the 15th and 16th centuries remained without effect. Despite repeated requests by the councils to limit their number, successive popes increased it from around 20 to 75, especially after the reappearance of nonresident cardinals at the Curia and the modest, temporary reopening of the Sacred College to non-Italian, non-French prelates (PAUL II, 1464–71, favored Italians once again). What the cardinals gained in pomp and riches—the revenues of the Church having increased through the reconquest of the Papal States and the establishment of a financial bureaucracy–barely compensated for the loss of their collegial political power and the dwindling of their oligarchic and constitutional claims to govern the ecclesiastical institution. The papacy, suffering from instability of elective power vis-à-vis the European monarchical states, sought to compensate for the absence of a hereditary principle by practicing excessive nepotism at the Sacred College (especially from the time of SIXTUS V). Internal factional rivalries increased the pope's margin of maneuverability. Regular recourse to capitulation in the conclaves was, above all, an admission of weakness. The consistory, the cardinals' fundamental body of expression, was laid dormant on the creation of the first Roman CONGREGATIONS: in 1542, PAUL III created that of the HOLY OFFICE or the Inquisition, and in 1564, PIUS IV instituted that of the council at the close of the council of TRENT. Fifteen more would be founded by SIXTUS IV in 1588 during his great reform of the Curia. A sumptuous lifestyle (the cardinals' *familia* numbered between 150 and 550 persons), cultural and artistic patronage (a principal element in the Roman Renaissance), financial greed, ingenuity in placing relatives, and detestable lifestyles were the salient characteristics of a great majority of the members of the Sacred College at the end of the Middle Ages and the beginning of the Renaissance. A few individual theologians and religious stand out as exceptions—for example, (Pierre d'Ailly, and Nicolas of Cusa). It was necessary to wait for the council of Trent (1545–63) and its measures aimed at improving the morality of the cardinals (obligatory residence at the Curia, the same restrictive norms as for bishops, the prohibition of plural bishoprics, etc.) to see the first effects of the elevation to the purple, by Paul III (1534–49), of great reformist minds forming an influential group within the Sacred College.

Pierre Jugie

Bibliography

Alberigo, G. *Cardinalato e collegialità: Studi null'ecclesiologia tra l'XIV secolo*, Florence, 1969 (to be completed by M. Fois, "I compiti e le prerogative dei cardinali vescovi secondo Pier Damiani nel quadro della sua ecclesiologia primaziale," *AHP*, 10 [1972], 25–105).

Broderick, F. F. "The Sacred College of Cardinals: Size and Geographical Composition (1099–1986)," *AHP*, 25, 1987, 7–71.

Firpo, M. "Il Cardinale," *L'Uomo del Rinascimento*, under the dir. of E. Carin, Bari, 1988, 75–131.

Furst, C. G. *Cardinalis: Prolegomena zu einer Rechtsgeschichte des romisches Kardinalskollegiums*, Munich, 1967.

Gatz, E. "Kardinal/Kardinalskollegium," *Theologische Realenziklopädie*, 17 (1988), 628–35.

Guillemain, B. *La cour papale d'Avignon (1309–1376): Étude d'une société*, Paris, 1966, 181–276.

Hallman, B. M. *Italian Cardinals, Reform, and the Church as Property, 1492–1563*, Berkley, Calif. 1985.

Molien, A. "Cardinal," *DDC*, 2, (1937), 1310–39.

Paravicini Bagliani, A. *Cardinali di curia e "familiae" cardinalizie dal 1227 al 1254*, Padua, 1972.

Reinhard, W. "Struttura e significato del Sacro Collegio tra la fine del XV e l'ínizio del XVI secolo," *Città italiane del' 500 tra Riforma e Controriforma*, Lucca, 1988, 257–65.

After the Council of Trent. The history of cardinals and of the cardinalate after the disciplinary decrees promulgated by the council of TRENT (1545–63) naturally forms part of the history of the Holy See, whether it concerns the Roman CURIA, the SACRED COLLEGE, the CONSISTORY, or their subordinate and decentralized institutions. Until the promulgation by PIUS X of the apostolic constitution *Sapienti consilio*, (29 June 1908), the definition of the Roman Curia included the totality of its organs as well as the individuals in the pope's entourage and those assisting him, among whom the cardinals formed the most eminent group. The Curia, from the beginning of the 20th century, has been subject to a more strictly organic and functional definition, renewed by canon 242 of the *Codex iuris canonici* promulgated by BENEDICT XV in 1917; as a result, the role of the cardinals now cannot be discussed without considering the relative transparency of the Church's administrative structures.

The governmental and administrative functions transferred to the Curia should not, however, obscure the role of the papal court, which forms the pontiff's permanent entourage, a role now measured in terms of influence and no longer in terms of power. The highest category represented at the court, the palatine cardinals, observe a complex and precise etiquette based on a will to power inherited from the council of Trent and *founded* on the model of state monarchies, with a multitude of honorific functions. The constitution *Postquam verus ille*, promulgated by SIXTUS V (1585–90) on 3 December 1586, fixed the number of cardinals at 70. The qualifications required to be vested with this dignity remained those established by the Tridentine rules: at least 30 years of age, with sufficient intellectual ability and an honorable life, and with no requirement to be a cleric. At the beginning of the 17th century, CLEMENT VIII (1592–05) regularized the list of cardinalitial titles, PAUL V (1605–21) confirmed it by fixing the plenum for the Sacred College at 6 cardinal bishops, 50 cardinal priests, and 14 cardinal deacons. In 1630, URBAN VIII (1623–44) bestowed on cardinals the title of "eminence" (or "most holy eminence") in their capacity as princes of the Church, considered equals of the kings and heads of government with whom they were to establish "necessary relations" (A. Molien). This action underlines the importance given by pontiffs of the period to cardinalitial nominations as a means of enlisting the services of worthy individuals for general diplomatic functions and the maintenance of internal order. Another long-standing priority was to keep the upper levels of the hierarchy, both Italian and aristocratic by honoring members of Italy's most illustrious families. From the pontificate of PIUS V (1560–5) to that of PIUS VI (1775–99), 803 nominations divided among 182 promotions show a general correlation between the importance of a pontificate and the number of elevations to the cardinalate made during it: 78 under Urban VIII, 70 under CLEMENT XI, and 73 under Pius VI.

The tight control of cardinalitial promotions did not, however, prevent a discrepancy between rule and practice. The pontiff's freedom to use his supreme right of dispensation brought about some flagrant abuses. Among many cases related to nominations, INNOCENT IX conferred the purple on his nephew, Antonio Facchinetti, then aged 18 (1591). Paul V did the same for four members of his family, including Maurice de Savoie (age 14, in 1607), and Charles de Medicis, (age 19, 1615). This type of abuse diminished during the 18th century, particularly under the influence of BENEDICT XIV (1740–58). Moreover, profiting from a major legal void on the subject, major figures managed to accumulate—or to occupy successively—several high positions; thus Cardinal Bevilacqua was secretary of the Holy Office and prefect of the Congregation of the Index under Clement VIII, and Francesco Barberini, under the pontificate of ALEXANDER VIII (1689–91), headed the congregations of Bishops and Regulars, of Waterworks, and of the Signature of Justice.

These customs were greatly restricted by a gradual regularization in the contemporary period, but the insignia and privileges conferred on cardinals were preserved. They enjoy precedence everywhere and on all occasions, except in the presence of the pope himself. Canon 239 § 21 of the 1917 Code of Canon Law reiterates that the cardinal "should precede all prelates, even patriarchs." An instruction of the Congregation of Rites approved by PIUS XI on 2 December 1930, emphasizes yet again the dignity that should be granted to cardinals, a reflection and reminder of the dignity that is the prerogative of "the sovereign pontiff himself and the Holy See." This became all the more essential as the borders of the Catholic world extended ever farther from Rome. Symmetrically, the progressive internationalization of the cardinalate (the first American cardinal, the archbishop of New York, was promoted in 1875) from the pontificate of PIUS IX (1846–78) was based on the need to counterbalance the loss of Roman influence following the suppression of the papacy's temporal power. At the same time, the proportion of cardinals at the Curia—residing permanently at Rome—became less important relative to titulars of residential sees. Five nonresident cardinals voted in conclave during the election of PIUS VII (1800–23), 25 in 1878 for the election of LEO XIII, and 90 (from a total of 115) in 1978. Moreover, on the authorization of Vatican II, the *motu proprio Ad purpuratorum Patrum* (11 February 1965) placed patriarchs of the Eastern churches, henceforth vested with cardinalitial dignity, above cardinal priests. The 1983 Code differs from the 1917 Code, canon 231, in that it does not indicate the numerical division of cardinals in the traditional orders; this provision was in fact without individual consequences' because, since the *motu proprio Cum gravissima* (15 April 1962) all cardinals had to be consecrated as bishops. The 1991 edition of the *Annuario pontificio* counts 31 Italian cardinals out of 142 members of the Sacred College (JOHN PAUL II himself has nominated 80), as follows: 6 cardinal bishops, titulars of a *suburbicarian* church (a see serving the bishopric of Rome), 115 cardinal priests, and 20 cardinal deacons possessing a church in this same diocese. This is in conformity with the constitutional structure of the Church, for which the general authority—and that of the cardinals in particular—rests fundamentally with the Roman see. The present state of the cleavage between the universal Church and particular CHURCHES, formalized by the dispositions of the 1983 Code of Canon Law, and the valorization of other types of episcopal collegial authority from the beginning of John Paul II's pontificate have provided a partly new schema for interpreting the development of the cardinalate, now viewed as supranational and consequently as a symbol of the catholicity (in the strict sense of the term) of the ecclesiastical institution.

Francois Jankowiak

Bibliography

Fürst, C. G. *Cardinalis: Prolegomena zu einer Rechtsgeschichte des römischen Kardinalskollegium*, Munich, 1967.

Gatz, E. "Kardinal/Kardinalskollegium," *Theologische Realenzyklopädie*, XVII (1988), 628–635.

Jones, P. *Federico Borromeo and the Ambrosiana: Art Patronage and Reform in Seventeenth-Century Milan*, New York, 1993.

Martin, V. *Les Cardinaux et la Curie, Tribunaux et offices: La vacance du Siège apostolique*, Paris, 1930.

Molien, A. "Cardinal," *DDC*, II (1937), 1310–39.

Robertson, C. *"Il Gran Cardinale"*: *Alesandro Farnese, Patron of the Arts*, New Haven, Conn., 1992.

Simier, J. *La Curie romaine*: *Notes historiques et canoniques*, Paris, 1909.

Wernz, F. X. *Ius decretalium*, II, Prato, 3rd. ed., 1915.

Weber, C. *Kardinäle und Prälaten in den letzten Jahrzehnten des Kirchenstaates*, 2 vols., Stuttgart, 1978.

CARDINAL "IN PETTO." The creation of cardinals "in the breast" (Lat., *in pectore*) was of customary usage before it was ratified and confirmed by canon law. It belongs today to the regular means at the pope's discretion to nominate men for the highest responsibilities and dignities of the Church. The Roman pontiff can create a cardinal first *in petto*—that is, he can keep the name "in his heart" until he judges it opportune to make it public. An equivalent expression for the practice is *reservatio in pectore*. Notwithstanding the absence of a public announcement, the nomination has taken place and is juridically effective. The pope merely reveals the nomination at the first secret CONSISTORY. When the practice began, probably around the 14th century, the Roman pontiff nominated cardinals without such disclosure, which could pose a problem if a CONCLAVE had to meet: Was it necessary to admit the cardinal whose name had not been announced? EUGENE IV (1431–47) answered in the negative, and URBAN VIII decreed the present procedure.

The decision to nominate *in petto* is often motivated by a difficult political-religious situation faced by the Church in a certain country, ranging from serious diplomatic reservations to persecution against the Church, which makes it inadvisable to reveal the name of the new cardinal. In the CANON LAW presently in force, expressed by canon (c. 351 §3) of the 1983 Code of Canon Law, a person who is thus promoted to cardinalitial dignity is not held to any of the duties of cardinals and enjoys none of their rights. As long as the name has not been announced, the pope can still change his mind. Once the nomination has been revealed, however, the cardinal becomes a member of the college, and is subject to the common law of holders of the cardinalitial dignity, a disposition already in force under the Code of Canon Law of 1917 (c. 233 §2).

When the name is made public, the cardinal in question acquires among his colleagues the order of precedence conferred on him from the moment of the *reservatio* of his name, to be counted from the first day of his creation as a cardinal. This retroactivity is a key element of the system in that it does not penalize the newly promoted individual in any way and maintains relative equality of treatment in the college of cardinals. If the pope who made the nomination dies before having announced the cardinal *in petto*, the nomination is null and void. It does not formally bind his successor, even if the latter knows of it. The option, however, remains for the new pope to confirm a nomination made by his predecessor: thus, PIUS IX convoked a consistory on 19 December 1853 to publish the nomination of Cardinal Pecci (the future LEO XIII), made *in pectore* by GREGORY XVI at the consistory of 19 January 1846. The first cardinal reserved *in pectore* had been named by MARTIN V in 1423, and the procedure was used several times up to the contemporary era. An example of recent pontificates gives broad confirmation: JOHN XXIII never revealed the names of three cardinals whom he had created *in petto*, but PAUL VI, at the consistory of 5 March 1973, published the creation *in petto* of the Romanian Cardinal Hossu, decided on during the consistory of 28 March 1969, the individual having died on 28 May 1970. During the consistory of 28 June 1991, JOHN PAUL II made public the elevation to the cardinalitial dignity of Ignatius Gong Pinmei, bishop emeritus of Shanghai, made *in petto* under the aegis of this same pope during the consistory of 30 June 1979.

This nomination procedure is, of course, subject to the common law applicable to cardinals, in particular to the dispositions concerning the number of members of the Sacred College, which, according to article 33 of the apostolic constitution *Romano pontifice eligendo*, promulgated by Paul VI on 1 June 1975, "should not exceed a maximum of one hundred and twenty." Moreover, according to the same regulation, no cardinal older than 80 years should participate in the conclave. Within these limitations, the *in pectore* nomination procedure has given and continues to give valuable service to the Church administration, especially when dealing with certain temporary situations.

Francois Jankowiak

Bibliography

Fürst, C. G. *Cardinalis: Prolegomena zu einer Rechtsgeschichte des römischen Kardinalskollegium*, Munich, 1967.
Gatz, E. "Kardinal/Kardinalskollegiium," *Theologische Realenzyklopädie*, XVII (1988), 628–35.
Molien, A. "Cardinal," *DDC*, II (1937), 1310–39.

CARDINAL NEPHEW. From the 15th century through the 17th, it was common for the pope to name as cardinal, a son of his brother or sister or even a nephew by adoption, to assist him with government duties. This individual was also known as *cardinale padrone* because his office endowed him with great power, and he could thus make decisions and give orders in numerous areas.

The nomination of a cardinal nephew occurred from time to time during the pontificates of the second half of the 15th century and the first half of the 16th, and the role was of varying importance. However, from the reign of PAUL IV (1555–9), there existed an unbroken chain of cardinal nephews until 1691, with the sole exception of the pontificate of INNOCENT XI (1676–89). The office was conferred by a BRIEF, the terms of which were developed with extreme care, from PIUS V (1566–72) to PAUL V (1605–21). This form of brief was thereafter utilized almost without modification from reign to reign. The cardinal nephew thus became an institution with powers of command that made him a veritable prime minister, an *alter ego* of the pope for temporal matters, with the title of SUPERINTENDENT OF THE ECCLESIASTICAL STATE. This designation at the highest level illustrates the tendency of the papacy in the modern era to choose clerics to play decisive roles in the management of secular affairs under the jurisdiction of the Roman see.

Too often, however, the incumbents were interested only in the benefits accruing from the post of cardinal nephew. The most flagrant NEPOTISM occurred during the period preceding the COUNCIL OF TRENT; its advantages consisted of "subserviences," or transfers of property from the PATRIMONY OF ST. PETER. Minor nepotism was more prevalent during the following period, when the benefits were irrevocable or for life (major offices of the Curia, government of towns, abbeys, pensions, and various perquisites). In mitigation of these offenses, it must be remembered that the cardinal nephew had to assume the heavy responsibility of missions entrusted to him and his assistants.

Although political and administrative tasks constituted the central part of their responsibilities, the cardinal nephews were also inspired by the example of Renaissance popes who made the development of the arts an instrument of their policy. Patrons in their own right when their duties allowed it, they contributed greatly, with their uncles or independently, to the beautification and intellectual glory of Rome. Palaces and villas, built especially in the 17th century clan, hosted a steady stream of architects, painters, sculptors, musicians, and poets who created new modes of expression. Their model of court life was imitated throughout Europe; a great exemplar was Cardinal Francesco Barberini and the Palace of the Four Fountains, a showpiece of the Baroque lifestyle and a magnet for the most famous *virtuosi* of the time. Thanks in large part to the cardinal nephews, the capital of Christianity also became he capital of art.

Madeleine Laurain-Portemer

Bibliography

Chevailler, L. Lefebvre, C. and Metz, R. *L'Epoque moderne (1563–1789): La seconde centralisation romaine*

(Histoire du droit et des institutions de l'Église en Occident, XV, 2), Paris, 1976.

Fischer-Wollpert, R. *Lexikon der Päpste*, Regensburg, 1985.

Fürst, C. G. *Cardinalis: Prolegomena zu einer Rechtsgeschichte des römischen Kardinalskollegium*, Munich, 1967.

Hallman, B. M. *Italian Cardinals, Reform, and the Church as Property, 1492–1563*, Berkeley, Calif., 1985.

Robertson, C. *"Il Gran Cardinale": Alessandro Farnese, Patron of the Arts*, New Haven, Conn., 1992.

Williams, G. L. *Papal Geneology: The Families and Descendants of the Popes, Jefferson, N. C., 1998.*

CARDINAL PROTECTOR. This title designates a cardinal whose role was originally to defend the causes of a given institution before the Roman CURIA. Every institution—religious or lay, large (e.g., a state) or small (a church)—was interested in having a cardinal protector represent it before the pope.

The cardinal protectors of foreign states most often came from these states, but they were sometimes Italians. There were few for clerical or military orders, with the exception of the Knights of Malta. Institutions belonging to the Curia itself, such as the papal CHAPEL and the apostolic library, could also have them. The same institution could have more than one cardinal protector—up to six at once if the pope wished. Normally, up to the 19th century, cardinals who did not reside in the Papal States could not have protectorates, and certain of the latter were attached to the office that a cardinal exercised. Some cardinals preferred not to have them, and many popes kept them for themselves.

With a few exceptions authorized by the pontiff, the cardinal protector did not belong to and therefore was not a leader of the institution protected by him, apart from those of a restricted territorial nature, which he governed with full jurisdiction. For this reason, there were continuous abuses by the cardinal protectors who, not limiting themselves to counseling the superiors of the institutions on private matters, interfered excessively in their administration. Moreover, the cardinal protectors of states, particularly if they were also ministers of these states before the Holy See, often intervened prejudicially in papal elections. Nevertheless, cardinal protectors offered much beneficial influence and important advantages to many institutions, particularly women's religious congregations.

The superior of an institution desirous of having a cardinal protector sought the advice of the interested person (sometimes the role was the prerogative of a certain family), then presented the proposal to the SECRETARIAT OF STATE. In certain cases, the appointment was sought by the cardinal himself. After hearing the opinion of the congregations and of interested individuals, the Secretariat wrote up a nomination bill, which was followed by the dispatch of an apostolic BRIEF. Once the nomination was confirmed, if the institution had its own house at Rome, the cardinal officially took possession of it either in person or through a procurator. His coat of arms was then placed on the front of the building and his portrait or his bust displayed in its principal room.

The institution of the protectorate dates from antiquity in Greece as well as Rome. Known in Latin as *patrocinium*, it involved institutions (public clientele) as well as individuals (private clientele); the protector, or patron, was most often a senator. Caesar, Cicero, Pompey, Dionysius of Halicarnassus, Asconius, Apuleius, Appian, and Aulus Gellius all provide evidence of this.

Christianity reinterpreted the institution to refer to protection by saints before the Almighty. The emperor or another monarch was named protector and defender of the Church and of the faith. The Holy See itself granted apostolic protection to institutions and individuals. As a historical innovation, this protection was accompanied by an official apostolic document which gave judicial value to what had only been a public fact. For institutions, it was not necessary for the protector to be a cardinal. It was enough that he be an influential person, even a layperson, who resided at the Curia, and that his interest was commonly known.

Traditionally, it is to St. Francis and the Franciscan order that the first cardinal protector is traced: Ugolino of Segni (the future Pope GREGORY IX), whose nomination HONORIUS III accepted in 1216. This agreement was given orally, so it had a certain official standing, but it was not yet a judicial act. In fact, St. Francis had already had a cardinal protector in the person of Giovanni di San Paolo. Further, given his cordial relations with them, Cardinal Ugolino could also be considered the protector of the Camaldolites, the Cistercians, and the DOMINICANS.

In light of the extant documentation, the first legally recognized cardinal protector seems to have been Matteo Rosso Orsini, named by NICHOLAS III in 1279 for the FRANCISCANS and the Poor Clares. Cardinal protectors were later named for other religious orders, at the beginning for those that belonged to the Franciscan family.

Emboldened by papal nomination, some cardinal protectors engaged in abuses. In 1310, as a result, the council of Cologne forbade them to extort rights in kind or in money from their protégés, even in remuneration for initiatives they took in their clients' name before the Roman Curia.

In 1311, a town for the first time chose a cardinal protector—Arnaldo Pelegrua, acting for Bologna. When GREGORY XI instituted the Gregorian College of Bologna in 1372, he gave it two cardinal protectors. The following year, the same pope promulgated the bull *Cunctos Christifideles* (27 March 1373), aimed at moderating the abuses of the protectors of the Franciscan order. In fact, according to the wish of St. Francis, the cardinal was not only protector of this order but also its governor and corrector, which could easily lead to abuse of power. In 1378, URBAN VI sought to curb excessive gifts from protégés, which he deemed detrimental to the interests of the Church and to justice.

In 1424, MARTIN V disapproved of the role of protector of states and of princes; he said that cardinals should be, above all, at the service of the Church and not defend the interests of states, which might be in conflict with those of the Church. During its famous thirteenth session (25 March 1436), the council of Basel forbade the protection of individuals, which had in fact never been legally recognized. SIXTUS IV, by the bull *Sancta minorum religio* (28 January 1472), renewed the measures taken by Gregory IX against the abuses of the protectors of the Franciscans. ALEXANDER VI did the same and reiterated that it was forbidden to protect states, though this rule was not applied later. JULIUS II confirmed the limits of the protection of the Franciscans by the constitution *Exponi* (21 May 1509). In 1514, during the fifth Lateran council, LEO X formulated rules for the protectorates of princes and communities. Julius II (1503–13) had decreed that, to be promoted to bishop, religious should obtain the consent of their cardinal protector. SIXTUS V suppressed many of the functions and prerogatives of cardinal protectors of religious orders and of states when he founded the Congregation of Religious (17 May 1586) and reformed the Curia (22 January 1588).

The role of the cardinal protector was definitively clarified by a bull of INNOCENT XII, *Christifidelium* (16 February 1694). It forcefully confirmed the limits already imposed on the protectors of the Franciscans and extended them to all regular orders. Innocent XII forbade abuses and rescinded private authorizations and other contrary dispositions, reducing the protector's duty to protection before the Roman Curia and to controlling the legitimacy of internal elections and dispositions of the orders themselves. Under the pontificate of CLEMENT XI (1700–21), these dispositions were reiterated in a letter from the Secretariat of State to the Congregation of Bishops and Regulars.

In the absence of a register of cardinals protector, it is advisable to consult the series of volumes published in 1716 under the title *Notizie per l'anno...*, a title that changed several times up to the present ANNUARIO PONTIFICIO. For the period covered, all the protectorates assumed by each cardinal are found. A decision of the Congregation of Bishops and Regulars (21 July 1791) is interesting: it prohibited churches of Rome allocated to a cardinal from having, in addition, a cardinal protector. The same decision authorized resident bishops to place next to or on their own coat of arms that of the cardinal protector of an institution whose see was in their diocese.

In the contemporary era, the function and the dispositions relative to the cardinal protector were inserted in canon 499 § 2 of the 1917 CODE OF CANON LAW. A letter from the Secretariat of State to the Dean of the Sacred College (28 April 1964) suspended cardinalitial protectorates and ordered that they be effaced from the *Annuario pontificio*. The cardinals who already had this responsibility, however, maintained it until death, as was the case with cardinals König, Landazuri Ricketts, Léger, and Suenens. This letter terminated the legal and official existence of cardinal protectors, as is confirmed by the absence of reference to them in the 1983 Code of Canon Law. Nevertheless, they continue to exist in practice.

Claudio de Dominicis

Bibliography

Boni, A. "Cardinale protettore," *Dizionario degli istituti di perfezione*, II (1975) Rome, 276–80.

Cohelli, G. *Notitia cardinalatus*, Rome, 1653.

de Dominicis, C. "Protettore esslesiastiche a Roma nel secolo XVIII," *Bollettino dell'Unione Storia e Arte*, 1–2 (1985), 53–9.

Melata, B. *De cardinali protectore*, Rome, 1902.

Misserey, L. R. "Cardinal protecteur," *DDC*, II, (1937) Paris, 1339–44.

Moroni, G. "Protettore," *Dizionario di erudizione storico-ecclesiastica*, LV, Venice, 1852, 317–39.

Piatti, G. *De cardinalis dignitate et officio*, Rome, 1602.

CAREER. The term *carriere* was rejected as pejorative by the Holy See on the disappearance of the papal COURT (General Rule of the Roman Curia, 1968). Service in the Church is a vocation and not a profession whose nature assumes regular and predictable promotions. In the PAPAL STATES, where the administration (until 1870) was entrusted to clerics, "to pursue a career" implied an increase in a family's power through the granting of benefices linked to the post occupied or in the progressive acceptance of functions that honored a vocation. After an adolescent motivated by significant piety drew the interest of the bishop, he was likely to be directed to one or another institution, then recommended to a provincial COLLEGE at Rome, and thus naturally into activities within the sphere of influence of the Holy See. Training for offices, of course, has always existed. For a long time it arose from the clientage inherent in a system manipulated by the great families of the Papal States—the Medici, Boghese, and Aldobrandini. Some families produced several popes, though the Farnese produced only one, PAUL III (1533–49). The elective and lifetime character of the pontificate has long whetted appetites for accession to the seat of St. Peter, in service of which clerics have employed diverse methods of bringing pressure, inducing means favored at times by the great powers (e.g., in the election of PIUS X).

The organization of the Roman Curia still supports a tendency for certain functions to lead to the episcopate and even to the cardinalate, through such steps as secretaries of congregations or nunciatures. Since 1968, however, these positions have increasingly been at the discretion of the pope, who is not bound by any obligation to observe a set career progression. The sovereign pontiffs dispose with a freedom that renders the prospect of a career fortuitous. The desire for internationalization of the Curia has contributed to this, as well as the weight, however indirect, of public opinion.

Philippe Levillain

Bibliography

Ago, R. *Carriera e clientele nella Roma Barocca*, Bari, 1970.

Rosa, M. "La Chiesa e gli stati regionali nell'età dell'assolutismo," *Letteratura italiana*, I, Turin, 1983.

See also ADMINISTRATION, PAPAL; CARDINAL NEPHEW; NEPOTISM.

CARNIVAL. The roots of the Carnival of Christian Rome are found in the Saturnalia and Lupercalia, the egalitarian feasts of ancient Rome, whose violence and excesses the carnival retained. The magnificence of the Renaissance popes bestowed splendor on it, but the Church tried to curb its vestiges of paganism, sometimes even prohibiting it. Carnival was first limited to Holy Thursday and to the Sunday *ad carnes levandas* preceding Ash Wednesday; later it was allowed to extend to 20 days, from Sexagesima Sunday to Shrove Tuesday, excluding the two Sundays and the Friday of that period. It was eventually a high festival if its fixed date fell within this period. In contrast to the austerity of Lent, which was marked by fasting and abstinence, particularly from meat, Carnival took its name from the words of farewell to fleshly repasts, at least in the etymology given to it by some: *carne vale*. Others prefer *carne leva*, a less vivid image but with essentially the same meaning.

At the end of the Middle Ages, during which the festivities had degenerated into immoderation and immorality, and after the return of the papacy from AVIGNON, some popes—for example, EUGENE IV, NICHOLAS V, and especially PAUL II, who is viewed as the true founder of modern Carnival—welcomed the festival with benevolence and even pleasure, while controlling its violence by prohibiting the carrying of arms and suppressing the firing of firecrackers and flares to avoid accidents. Even the sites of the revelry were circumscribed to avoid problems with crowds. Subject to papal authority, Carnival could not open without a *bando*, a decree that was proclaimed and posted, setting out the festival's events and limits. Thus, in 1701 ten ritual days were authorized, and masks were permitted to women on condition that they traveled in coaches. A blind eye was turned to numerous violations, however.

Certain rigid popes used the pretext of averting scandal or catastrophe to prohibit any celebration at all, condemning the Roman Carnival to sorely felt suspensions. The disastrous 1703 earthquake was interpreted as the punishment of God, who was to be appeased by penance, and so CLEMENT XI suspended Carnival for four years. Then came war, and for the *malenconico carnevale* of 1708, it was forbidden even to travel through the town playing music. The HOLY YEARS dedicated to religious pilgrimages were also years of deprivation.

In the 16th century, St. Philip Neri tried to christianize Carnival by organizing a procession to the *sette chiese*, the seven major BASILICAS. On Holy Thursday, the devout procession joyously wound through the streets, sustained at each stage by refreshments. The "Forty Hours" adoration took place in a number of churches at the height of Carnival, with the same improving purpose. The churches rivaled one another in opulence and imagination, presenting the Blessed Sacrament in ephemeral and edifying representations, a kind of moving tableaux. Each church also took its turn to profit from the thirst for spectacle that Carnival stimulated. Sometimes fraternities of penitents traversed the Corso on their way to pray, thrusting through the crowd of masqueraders as a kind of reprobation. This type of exorcism in no way undermined the vitality of Carnival, whose duration gradually stretched from Epiphany to Lent, with revels of increasing intensity and boldness, from harmless spectacles to cathartic carousing. In 1739, the president of Brosses expressed it baldly: "You ought to see all the bacchanalian revelries of Rome, even more splendid that those of Venice; even so, only in the last eight days do they achieve their full glory."

The theater was linked to Carnival as an entertainment tolerated only in the winter months, to disappear at Lent. Its institution dates from the construction of public halls in the 17th century. Suspected of giving free rein to violent emotions and loosening morals, it was constrained by a decree of SIXTUS V, which was not rescinded until the French Revolution. Women were not permitted to appear on stage, where their roles were taken by men: eunuchs replaced them successfully at the opera; in spoken drama, the substitution was more difficult, but the curious spectators—especially foreigners—delighted in the productions unless virtuosity declined into ridicule. The president of Brosses mockingly noted that at Rome, "women are not allowed on the stage; propriety does not permit it, and only pretty little boys dressed as girls are favore . . . sometimes these camouflaged beauties are not very small. Marianini, six foot high, is playing the role of a woman at the Teatro Argentina: she is the largest princess that I'll see in my lifetime." But Goethe remarked that the portrayal engaged two levels of imitation: the actor trying to interpret life, and the man the characteristics of the woman. In this sense, Roman theater was indeed the offspring of Carnival, the mask of reality rather than revelation, but it remained somewhat marginal despite its blossoming in the 18th century. The public, limited to rare presentations, evaded the rules with private spectacles mounted by noble families in their palaces, unconcerned about dates or restrictions. This private, nocturnal entertainment, occurred on the fringe of the popular daytime festival, vibrant in the liberty of the open air.

The bells of the Capitol, the *Patarina*, used only on solemn occasions, rang out the midday Angelus to signal the start of the festivities. In the evening, they announced the end. On foot or in carriages, the maskers invaded the Corso, from then on reserved for the revelries. Over the centuries, the space allocated to Carnival varied: the Testaccio, the Capitol, the Via Lata, St. Mark's Square (where the Venetian pope PAUL II participated from his palace at key moments) the Campo di Fiori, or St. Peter's (during INNOCENT III's time). These movements bonded the authorities with the people, owing to the latter their gratitude for the success of the fete. When the Via Lata was totally urbanized, it was called Via del Corso and became the site par excellence of the spectacle. Navone had a more modest role: there performances of the *commedia dell'arte* took place on makeshift stages and in small sheds where the *burattini* (marionettes) gesticulated and recited their often satirical plays. Absurd exploits were the order of the day; in a show of strength, a man would carry an anvil on his chest, on which people were invited to break an iron bar with a sledgehammer. Another delight was the acrobats who spun on a rope stretched across the square at rooftop level—an exercise that, according to Valesio, almost ended in disaster one day in February 1701, had it not been for the skill of the young man, for which he was roundly booed by the twelve thousand spectators.

In the 16th and 17th centuries, there were races of men and of animals as part of the festival. They generated violence and exorcised fear, cruelty going hand-in-hand with frivolity. The imagination is never at a loss for inventions to incite laughter and spawn humiliation. Categories of contestants were established: children, men, old people, poor wretches who wore themselves out for a pittance. There were races of hunchbacks, who offered themselves naked to the taunts of the crowd. Though prompted by poverty, they could be considered volunteers; but the Jews participated in the festival under duress, at least after 1492, when their numbers considerably increased in Rome. Not only did the expense of the games fall entirely on the Jewish community, as a tribute to the Apostolic Camera, but they also had to place their persons in jeop-

ardy. They were obliged to exhibit themselves in ridiculous situations and in dress marked by a startling yellow. They ran burdened with stones that made them slower, or with their feet chained or even bound in bags. A decree of CLEMENT IX in 1668 abolished this form of subjugation, which was replaced by an obligation to make gifts of precious fabrics to the winners of the big competitions: somewhat of an improvement or a refinement of morality.

In the 18th century, these degrading human races disappeared from Carnival, as did the ass and buffalo races, vestiges of an agrarian society. For a long time, bullfighting was exalted for its cruel rituals. One of the high points was the pursuit of pigs, already wounded by bulls and maddened by the smell of blood running through the hills of Testaccio, which has remained the location of the abattoirs of Rome. The crowds exulted in the skill of the men who dared the perils of dragging the furious animals back to makeshift arenas filled with benches, erected temporarily in one of the higher parts of the town—the Capitol or the squares in front of the Farnese Palace or the church of the Holy Apostles. Until the 18th century, the spirit of chivalry reigned over Carnival through jousts and tournaments in which the nobility completed. An elitist sport that combined the arts of war and pageantry, it took place in a palisade constructed for this purpose, from which the general populace were excluded from enjoying the magnificent parades of knights adorned in gold, feathers, and brocades. From this past there remains only the raucous horse race that concluded each day of Carnival; foreigners marveled at this dazzling race of purebred Arabian "Barbs." The bell of the Capitol rang out the warning to prohibit carriages from entering the Corso. At the second warning, all persons immediately had to evacuate the street. Soldiers closed the exits, and the public took refuge on platforms set up on both sides, of which the best known was beside the Ruspoli palace. The nobility took their places on the tapestry-draped balconies of friends' houses. The riderless horses, adorned with plumes in the colors of the stables they represented, fretted on the Piazza del Popolo, stirred up by their grooms. At a signal, the horses dashed off, their numbers increasing until the last two days, when all ran together: this was the *mossa*, the climax of Carnival's bedlam. At the Piazza Venezia, the horses ran into a stretched cloth, stableboys captured them, and the governor of Rome proclaimed the winner. It was a contest of patrician rivalries, since each horse belonged to a great family that gained glory from the victory, but it afforded pleasure for all.

Carnival is a time of masquerade, and therefore of freedom through disguise and liberty through dissimulation. No one was unwilling to don a mask and revel in breaking down barriers. The town dwellers dressed in the embroidered peasant costumes of Latium and Ciociara. Town dwellers became farmers, intellectuals masqueraded as clowns, and women dressed as men in the padded doublers of Pierrot. Characters of the *commedia dell'arte* were the most numerous, but nationalities as well as centuries were exchanged by the choice of old French costumes that could be bought cheaply at second-hand stores. Everyone, masked in anonymity, indulged in provocative behavior, spouting invitations and jokes. People pelted each other with dried figs and candy. Eggs—banned even if their shells were blown empty—were replaced by *confetti*, small plaster discs which crumbled, scattering the Corso with an eerie white cloud. Englishmen profited from being incognito or from unnoticed chance encounters to violate the order they had received not to associate with the Stuarts or their entourage. In the 18th century people adopted humorous visiting cards; in an engraved frame, a distorted but recognizable name was handwritten, or a picture highlighting a play of words on the patronymic, such as a horseman in flight to designate "Cavaliere Fuga."

The parade of floats elevated the masquerade to the level of art. In 1515, the humanist Tommaso Inghirami of Volterra, developed for this parade a long allegorical fresco illustrating ideas, virtues, and sentiments. The tradition endured of depicting historical or satirical subjects, provided they did not offend the authorities. The artists of the Academy of France at Rome loosed their rich imaginations to offer Romans proof of their talent. In 1735, a Chinese masquerade painted by Jean-Baptiste Pierre left an indelible impression. In 1748, they depicted "the Sultan's caravan to Mecca," in which figured no fewer than 40 personages, horses, and a camel. Exoticism made a triumphant entrance, importing the Parisian fashion for chinoiserie or alluding to Oriental rituals. In the princely palaces, balls followed the daytime festivities, transforming the night; a 1701 ball at the Colonna palace featured more than three hundred lights reflected by crystals.

Such exuberance was not without risk. The *sbirro* ("police spy") kept close watch and meted out harsh punishment. To remind everyone to respect the laws of decency, the *cavaletto* ("easel") was set up the evening before Carnival. Whipping at the pillory might punish the slightest transgression. Brawling was condemned, as was the wearing of religious habits as disguise or insulting a passing cleric. Cruel people made these punishments one more source of amusement. Executions were even planned to coincide with the beginning of Carnival. The evening of Mardi Gras concluded with the game of *moccoletti*, which was played on the way home and involved the mutual snuffing out of little candles that revelers tried to keep lit.

Freedom became license in a Rome disorganized by the French occupation of the late 18th century and troubled by the importation of volatile ideas. At the Restoration, Carnival resumed its already fixed form, but it was sapped of its authenticity. It became an artificial spectacle, taken over by foreigners who came from everywhere to "enlist under the banner of lunacy, speaking a single language, Italian, having one aim, pleasure." At the same time, it took a political turn. With the movement toward Italian unity, demands for freedom became increasingly evident. Carnival survived until 1870, but the negative attitude of the papacy struck the final blow. Its religious element as an inverted form of exorcism before the penitential reflections of Lent no longer made sense.

Oliver Michel

Bibliography

Ademolo, A. *Il carnevale di Roma nel secoli XVII e XVIII*, Rome, 1883.

Boiteux, M. "Carnaval annexé: Essai de lecture d'une fête romaine," *AESC* (1977), 356–80.

Clementi, F. *Il carnevale romano nelle cronache contemporanee*, 2 vols., Città di Castello, 1899–1938.

Il teatro e la festa: Lo spettacolo a Roma tra papato e rivoluzione (exhibit catalog), Rome, 1989.

CARTHAGE. The highest authority in the African Church has always been held by the bishop of Carthage, primate of AFRICA, supported by general COUNCILS which group together the bishops of several African provinces: Proconsular, Byracian (southern Tunisia), Numidia, Mauretania, and Tripolitan. The authority of the see of Carthage over the African Church always opposed hegemonic attempts to impose papal authority, at least in the area of jurisdiction, and to hinder the right to appeal to Rome. The councils of Carthage were the final courts of appeal for priests, deacons, and minor clerics condemned by their bishops. From the beginning, however, African Christians showed great reverence toward the papacy, which proved dominant despite the bishops' real will for independence in the regulation of local problems. For St. Cyprian (bishop of Carthage, 248–58), Rome was the "womb" and the "root" of the Catholic Church; it was the "principal Church," the spring of priestly unity. The first confrontations took place in the middle of the 3rd century after the persecution of Decius (250); St. Cyprian and Pope CORNELIUS (251–3) agreed to recommend tolerance toward the faithful who lapsed during the persecution. The *lapsi* would be reintegrated after penance, and necessarily when on the point of death. The agreement broke, however, on the question of the rebaptism of heretics, which longstanding African custom recognized.

At Rome, after a period of penance, a simple laying on of hands was judged sufficient, without rebaptism. The African councils of August 255 and June 256 took a stand for the maintenance of their own custom, and St. Cyprian sent to Pope STEPHEN I, elected in 254, a letter to this effect countersigned by 71 bishops. The pope, however, held that only the Roman custom was to be observed. A new council of Carthage (1 September 256), an assembly of 87 bishops, confirmed the previous resolutions. Pope Stephen then excommunicated St. Cyprian. His successor, SIXTUS II (August 257–August 258), revived relations with the African Church. Relations between the papacy and Carthage were calm during the second half of the 3rd century. After the persecution of Diocletian, the Donatists, a group of bishops and of the faithful who wished to be exonerated of any dishonorable connection with the *traditores*—bishops who had compromised themselves during the persecution by handing over the sacred Scriptures to the pagan authorities—appealed to Rome against Cecilian (bishop of Carthage, 311/12–37/43). Pope MILTIADES (311–14) presided over a SYNOD at the Lateran on 2 October 314 and dismissed the Donatists' claims to be considered a legal Church. Thereafter, in this strictly African conflict, appeal to the emperor and civil authorities was the rule until the final contentious conference, which took place in 411 at Carthage. During the period from 387 to 407, relations between Rome and the African Church, and with Carthage in particular, were strengthened.

In 411, another question troubled Carthage: a council had condemned Caelestius, a disciple of Pelagius, who wished to become a member of the Carthaginian clergy. The Pelagian doctrine, which disparaged the notion of original sin and reduced the importance of divine grace and prayer, was judged to be erroneous by the African bishops, for whom the question of baptism was very important. In 415 at Diospolis, Palestine, Pelagius and Caelestius were cleared of all suspicion. The African bishops then demanded, after renewing their condemnation in 416 at the councils of Carthage and of Milev, the ratification of Pope INNOCENT I (401–17). The dominance of Rome in doctrinal matters had never been challenged. Pope ZOSIMUS (417–18) rehabilitated Pelagius, who had appealed. All the African bishops, in plenary council, then solemnly condemned the doctrine in May 418; they were supported by Italian bishops and individuals of the imperial court of Ravenna. This led to papal acquiescence to their views, and the final decision of Zosimus was maintained by the following popes, BONIFACE (418–22) and CELESTINE (422–32). During the plenary council of 1 May 418, appeals addressed to Rome were prohibited under pain of losing communion with the African Churches; in 419, the judicial autonomy of Africa was reaffirmed in the *Codex canonum Ecclesiae africanae*. This did not prevent appeals by Apiarius, a priest of Sicca Veneria (Le Kef), and by Antoninius of Fussala. During the final judgment of the Apiarius affair in 426, Aurelius of Carthage (391–429/30) sent a very severe synodal letter to Celestine; he harshly criticized the claims of the pope and reaffirmed Carthage's judicial authority. Africa

was soon invaded (430) by the Vandals, and relations between Rome and Carthage were interrupted. From the moment of the reconquest in 533, Justinian confirmed the autonomy and privileges of the bishops of Carthage. Unfortunately, the dogmatic controversies of the moment spread to Africa. The African bishops, including Reparatus of Carthage, supported Pope VIGILIUS in his fight against the condemnation of the Three Chapters (543–4). Justinian sought to conciliate the Monophysites, while reaffirming his adherence to the council of Chalcedon. Pope Vigilius submitted in 548 (*Judicatum*), then reverted (encyclical of 5 February 552), before capitulating (2nd constitution, February 554).

Vigilius died in June 555. The bishop of Carthage—who, at Constantinople, had supported the first opposition to the pope—was exiled in 551 to Euchaita, where he died in 563. GREGORY I the Great (590–604) established epistolary relations with Dominicus, bishop of Carthage, as well as with other African correspondents. He was preoccupied by what he took for an outbreak of Donatism. He quickly understood that the problems were mainly human, and after the council of Carthage at the end of the summer of 594, he reproached Dominicus for his too rigorous sanctions against bishops accused of flirting with HERESY. Gregory understood that appeasement was the only effective remedy for problems undoubtedly brought about by personal quarrels. He maintained a brotherly friendship with Dominicus. But from 649 onward, events interrupted their relations.

Through the correspondence between the popes and the primates of Carthage, we can follow the end of Christianity in this religious metropolis. In 975, a letter from the clergy and primate of Carthage to Pope BENEDICT VII (974–84) proposed a reduction in the number of bishops. In 1053, Pope LEO IX, writing to Bishop Thomas of Carthage, declared that only with great difficulty could five bishops be found in Africa. Finally, in 1073, Pope GREGORY VII ruled on a conflict between Bishop Cyriacus and his community: this proof of internal discord and of appeal to Rome is the last document we possess on Carthaginian Christianity.

Lilian Ennabli

Bibliography

Bevenot, M. "Cyprian von Karthago," *Theologische Realenzyklopädie*, 8 (1981), 246–54.

Ferron J. and Lapeyre, G. "Carthage chrétienne," *DHGE*, XI (1948), 1149–1233.

Marshall, W. "Karthago und Rom: Die Stellung der nordafrikanischen Kirche zum apostolischen Stuhl in Rom," *Päpste und Papsttum*, 1, Stuttgart, 1971.

Munier, C. "Un canon inédit au XXe concile de Carthage: *Ut nullus ad romanam Ecclesiam audeat appellare*," RSC Rel. 40 (1966), 113–26.

Palanque, J. R. "Les métropoles ecclésiastiques à la fin du IV siècle," Fliche-Martin, III, 437–87.

Piétri, C. "Les lettres nouvelles et leur témoignage sur l'histoire de l'Église romaine et de ses relations avec l'Afrique," *Les lettres de saint Augustin découvertes par Johannes Divjak*, colloque 20–21 Sept. (1982), 343–54.

CARTOGRAPHY. Regional and world mapmaking has been of interest to the papacy in at least two respects: the representation of papal domains and maps authorized or designed by the popes themselves. On medieval world maps, the city of Rome normally occupies a central place justified by its importance to pilgrims, but neither Rome nor AVIGNON is normally associated thereon with the papacy. Not until the end of the 15th century, in an incunabulum entitled *Rudimentum novitiorum*, dated 1475, do we find the city of Rome symbolized by the enthroned pope, dressed in the insignia of his dignity—and this is an isolated case. The absence of representations of the PAPAL STATES before the 16th century (from which we have maps of papal possessions, such as the Venaissin county, among the Vatican frescoes) should not be surprising: the representation of political boundaries is in fact usually absent from medieval maps.

The REFORMATION, in contrast, produced a decidedly original, allegorical map of the papacy: *La Mappe-monde nouvelle papistique* (The New Papist World Map), published in 1566 on the initiative of John-Baptist Trento, engraved by Peter Eskirch. Two copies of this mural map, measuring 241.2 cm by 133.5 cm, are preserved—one at Wroclaw, and the other at the British Library. It is evidence of the ideological conflict of its day: within the frame formed by a monster's jaws (Leviathan, symbol of Hell, where the usual chubby-cheeked cherubs give way to diabolical figures), the popes' world is depicted, protected by walls but besieged by European nations assisted by the great reformers, who are throwing Bibles (instead of firebrands) over the walls. The apparently absurd geographical setting does not seem to reflect the real world in any way: its disorder is assumed to represent the disorder of the papal world, but it realistically reproduces the topography of Rome in 1557. The human geography of this map refers to the institutions of the Church and to the LITURGY. The Kingdom of Good Works is divided into 19 provinces (for example, Monastery, Service of the Saints, Mass, and Penance) and six republics (among them the Jesuits). The cities are named in relation to their provinces: in the province of Penance, for example, we find Reparation and Auricular Confession. The physical geography illustrates notions of morality or immorality (Deceit, Piety, Obedience, and Poverty) and serves as a setting, realistic or otherwise, for the geography of ecclesiastical institutions. The pope himself is represented in his Vatican palace, the main building in the province of Monastery, correctly placed in the city of Rome, ringed by the valleys of Obedience and Poverty. He is sucking at the breast of Lady Fortune, while in close proximity a bishop and an abbot, assisted by the cardinal of Lorraine, are stabbing Lady Truth. The map was accompanied by a commentary, *Histoire*, by J. B. Trento (published under the pseudonym Frangidelphe Escorche-Messes), in which the intention of the author is clearly expressed: to show that the papacy has installed a "a completely carnal monarchy, full of dissipation, pleasures, and pomp," in every way comparable to the New World of America, bearer of corruption and war, contrary to law and morality. This map, important as it may be, remains nevertheless an isolated case, and it demonstrates that cartographical representation of the temporal power of the papacy was more likely to gratify its detractors than to justify it.

The popes were, however, responsible for some spectacular cartographic productions. The first known one is attributed to Pope ZACHARIAS (741–52), who—according to his 11th-century biographer, Anastasius the Librarian (LIBER PAPALIS, *Vita Zachar*, XVIII, Duchesne)—himself painted, or had painted, a map of the world accompanied by verse, in a dining room of the Lateran. He thereby conformed to the custom, well documented in antiquity and the Middle Ages, of powerful people's displaying maps of the world, or parts of it, in their residences, or offering them to communities. PIUS II donated a world map in 1463 to the cathedral of Pienza, his native city.

The two great cycles of Vatican mural maps could be taken as a mere example of a passing trend because they are so reminiscent of those in the *Guardaroba* at the Vecchio Palazzo, Florence (1563–86) and those in the "Globe Room" at the Farnese palace, Caprarola (1573–4), both of which were done by the same artists. They are more than a reflection of fashion, however. Chronologically, the older of the two Vatican cycles occupies the *Terza Loggia*, which is heavily damaged by moisture and air pollution. There were originally 34 maps, of which only 24 exist today (the original maps that have disappeared were arbitrarily replaced in the 19th century by maps taken from the Lafreri Atlas). Fortunately, however, Alessandro Taja has left us, from the early 18th century, an adequate description that gives an idea of their initial structure. This collection was done in two phases, along with the rest of the decoration: the first phase began around 1560, under Pope PIUS IV; the second in 1572, under GREGORY XIII, after an interruption of six years under the pontificate of PIUS V. The maps, often of Ptolemaic inspiration, were drawn by Stefano Francese and reproduced as a fresco by Vanosino, a specialist in mural maps to whom the Caprarola maps are also attributed. Once finished, the cartographic cycle comprised the entire world: Europe and the Near East in the west wing, and Africa, Asia, and America in the north wing.

Gregory XIII also authorized the creation, in 1580–1, of the Vatican's famous Gallery of Geographical Maps. In their original state, they were painted by Egnazio Danti, author of the *Guardaroba* maps (1630s) in the Palazzo Vecchio, Florence. In contrast to the Terza Loggia maps, which represent vast entities and cover the entire known world of the day, the Geographical Maps deal only with the provinces of Italy, arranged in the gallery in a circuit reflecting their actual positions around the Apennines, with the addition of the Venaissin. All these maps are historical as well as geographical, since they are decorated with vignettes which correspond to historical events in each place in antiquity, the Middle Ages, and the modern era.

The significance of these two map rooms, both closely associated with Gregory XIII, is considerable. They glorify the patron who affixed his name to them; they illustrate his intellectual and, consequently, spiritual and moral qualities; and at the same time, they demonstrate his power. Thus, the decorative program of the Terza Loggia, not content depicting the arms of the pope on each bay he was responsible for decorating, inscribed on the vault above the maps the acts of the pontificate of Pius V in the west wing, and those of Gregory XIII in the north wing. Between the vault and the maps, the frieze of the Gregorian wing depicts the procession that accompanied the arrival at the Vatican, in 1580, of the relics of St. Gregory Nazianzen on the initiative of his namesake, Gregory XIII. A quick reading of the maps of the gallery equally suggests the extent of the pope's temporal power.

These geographical monuments, however, possess a deeper significance, more directly linked to doctrine. To understand them, we must study them not in isolation but within their wider decorative and symbolic context. Some, like those at Caprarola, were part of a comprehensive program; this remains perceptible even in the Terza Loggia, where the superimposition of the achievements of Pius IV and of Gregory XIII somewhat obscures its intent. The ornamentation of the vaults represents the forces that govern the world, around the Primum Mobile of the Trinity (west wing) and the Heaven of the Blessed, of which the Creation is the reflection and the preparation. At the beginning and at the end of the frieze, the images of land and sea, interpreted by biblical quotations (Ps. 103,9; 104, 9; Za.9, 10), appear as the boundaries of human activities and as the image of God, and they frame the ecstasy of Gregory Nazianzen, defender of the Trinity. Finally, the maps illustrate the universality of Creation. In the Gallery of Maps, the dedicatory inscription itself leads to a comparison between the historical panels of the archways, which portray the main epochs of the history of the Church, and the maps of Italy. The significance of this parallel is clear: the Italy of the popes, now the new Holy Land, was the result of both human history and of that of the Church.

These two cartographic cycles, although realized by the same authors, contrast strongly with the secular vision of the cosmos expressed by those at Caprarola and at Florence. The palpable modernity of these two series of Vatican mural maps, though inspired by the Ptolemaic view of the earth, should not obscure the fact that they express medieval custom, showing not so much the real appearance of the world as its place in the divine economy.

Pascal Arnaud

Bibliography

Almagia, R. *Le pitture murali della Galleria delle carte geografiche* (Monumenta Cartographica Vaticana, 3), Vatican City, 1952.

Le pitture murali della Terza Loggia e di altre sale Vaticane (Monumenta Cartographica Vaticana, 4), Vatican City, 1955.

Lestringant, F. "Une cartographie iconoclaste: *La Mappemonde nouvelle papistique* of P. Eskirch and J. Trento (1566–67)," M. Pelletier (ed.). *Geographie du monde au Moyen Âge et à la Renaissance,* Paris, 1989, 99–120.

Szykula, K. "Une mappemonde pseudo-médiæevale de 1566," ibid., 93–8.

Schulz, J. "Maps as Metaphors: Mural Map Cycles of the Italian Renaissance," D. Woodward (ed.), *Art and Cartography,* Chicago, 1987, 97–122.

CASTEL GANDOLFO. See **Residences, Papal.**

CASTEL SANT'ANGELO. At first the castle was a monument that Emperor Hadrian built for himself and his dynasty in 130. It was conceived as a counterpart to the tomb of Augustus Caesar. Its location reflected this goal (the sepulchre of Augustus was on the left bank of the Tiber, to the north of the Campus Martius; that of Hadrian on the right bank opposite to the Campus Martius). So did its form (both monuments were circular, with trees planted at the upper level and the emperor's image at the summit). Hadrian's tomb thus affirmed the continuity of the imperial regime while expressing his divergence on a fundamental point: abandoning the divine designations with which the previous edifice was associated ("mausoleum of Augustus," "tumulus of the Julius"), the new dynastic tomb was known only as the *sepulchrum Hadriani* or *sepulchrum Antoninorum,* and thus demonstrated the moderate humanism of its builder.

Linked to the Campus Martius by a new bridge (the *pons Aelius*), the monument was architecturally impressive: surrounded by a brick wall 89 meters long, it had a cylinder 64 meters in diameter and 21 meters high with masonry of *caementa* (a type of very compact concrete used in Roman construction), encircled by a wall of blocks made from peperino, tuff, and travertine, covered in marble. A tower, probably circular, rose from the center of the cylinder and supported a bronze quadriga bearing an image of Hadrian. At the summit of the cylinder and around the rotunda, large quantities of arable soil had been banked for the planting of funerary shrubbery. One entered the sepulcher through a door in the center of the bridge and arrived in a room decorated with a statue of the emperor, then took a helicoidal ramp within the interior of the cylinder masonry, leading from the center of the monument to superimposed rooms used as vaults for the ashes of Hadrian, his family, and his successors. Hadrian's ashes were placed there in 139, and Caracalla was the last emperor to be buried in the tomb.

Aurelius's construction of a new wall around Rome, starting in 271, changed the function of the monument: instead of a tomb turned toward Rome, it became an advance bastion of new fortifications in the direction of the VATICAN. During the assault led by the Goth Vitiges in 537, the *sepulchrum*, converted into *castellum*, offered the defenders as projectiles the numerous bronze statues that decorated it. Ten years later, the Goth Totila, included the *castellum* in a fortification on the right bank of the Tiber (the "Burg" of Totila gave its name of "Borgo" to the entire area), again turned the monument—this time definitively—in the direction of the city.

In 590, the Plague overtook the city and gave rise to a legend, which apparently appeared between 950 and 1150: Pope GREGORY I the Great, during a procession to eradicate the disease, allegedly had a vision of St. Michael the Archangel sheathing his sword at the summit of the castle. When the legend took form, it was founded on the fact that a chapel had been dedicated at the summit of the *castellum* (in the former funerary chamber of Hadrian) at the beginning of the 7th century by BONIFACE IV: the warrior angel was evidently perceived as the patron of the fortress. This famous legend has been illustrated by the two successive images of the archangel that have been installed at the summit of the castle and turned toward the city: the marble one of Montelupo (1544), then the bronze one of Verschaffelt (1752). It is also worth noting that the representation at the summit of the edifice of a celestial being, whose wings symbolize its intermediary role between heaven and earth, is inscribed according to an ancient Roman tradition; almost all the buildings of classical antiquity (temples, basilicas, curia) were surmounted by winged Victories. During the Carolingian epoch, the region of the Vatican seemed to be sheltered from devastation in a world where only Christian powers clashed: ST. PETER'S BASILICA was the most venerated of Christian sanctuaries, and an entire neighborhood developed around it for the reception of pilgrims. In 800 Charlemagne had himself crowned in the basilica by LEO III. But danger came with the SARACENS, who, in 846, brutally attacked the Borgo area and plundered the basilica. LEO IV then undertook to protect this area by a wall linked to the Castel Sant'Angelo, thus delimiting a particularly dense zone that came to be called the "Leonine City."

This wall, inaugurated in 852, was refashioned afterwards, but today one can still see the suspended corridor constructed by NICHOLAS III in 1277 on the part of the wall linking the Vatican to the Castel Sant'Angelo, which allowed the popes, on more than one occasion, to take refuge in the fortress.

The 10th century was marked by the weakening of imperial power and the ascendance of the Roman NOBILITY vis-à-vis the popes. Of the 28 popes who succeeded each other from 896 to 999, four met their deaths in the dungeons of the Castel Sant'Angelo. The daughter of Theophylactus, Marozia, made the castle the residence from which she exercised absolute power from 928 to 932 and where she celebrated her marriage to Hugh of Provence in the presence of her illegitimate son, Pope JOHN XI (932).Then it was the turn of the house of Crescenzi to dominate the Roman scene. In 998, Crescentius shut himself up in the castle to resist attack by Otto III; however, he was beheaded on the platform of the citadel and entered into legend as a hero of Roman independence. From the 11th to the 13th centuries, during the long period of struggle between Church and Empire, Rome was covered with citadels of the nobility, and Castel Sant'Angelo became one entrenched camp among many. Here, GREGORY VII victoriously resisted the attacks of Henry IV in 1083 and was rescued by Robert Guiscard. Here, too, ANACLETUS II, of the Pierleoni family, carried the day in 1133 and again in 1137 against the army of Lothair II, successor to Henry V, who had come to support INNOCENT II in his bid to retake Rome. In the 13th century, as the struggle between Church and Empire waned, it was the Orsinis turn to dominate the city. They attacked numerous fortresses of their noble rivals (for example, Augustus's mausoleum, property of the Colonnas) and seized the Castel Sant'Angelo, which Nicholas III of the Orsini family made his official residence and which he linked, by the suspended corridor mentioned above, to the fortified palace that he had constructed in the Vatican (1277–80).

The 14th century, marked by the transfer of the papacy to Avignon, was consequently an era when the vast papal residence at the LATERAN suffered neglect and ruin. When URBAN V negotiated with the commune of Rome to secure his return to the city in 1367, he demanded that the keys to the Castel Sant'Angelo be returned to him, rather than the keys of the city. And from the spring of 1379, his successor, GREGORY XI, had to submit to repeated attacks by the Roman populace, who seized the castle and tried to destroy it. From then on, the papacy installed itself in the Vatican, and for five centuries the Castel Sant'Angelo became its best protection against the city, and the instrument of its dominance over it. From 1389, BONIFACE IX made of the half ruined *castellum* a strong fortress modernized in line with the progress made in the military arts of the 14th century, particularly the introduction of fire arms. The cylinder was isolated from the outside wall by a trench, and an elevated entrance was added and made accessible by a narrow drawbridge. The helicoidal ramp of Hadrian's time was walled in, and Nicola Lamberti, the pope's architect, audaciously hollowed out a rectilinear ramp in the interior of the masonry of the cylinder, allowing direct access to its summit and passage to beasts of burden transporting arms, food, and munitions. At the level of the former funerary chamber, large loopholes permitted the defenders of the *castellum* to hold intruders under fire. The central tower was altered on a square plan and the pope's lodgings were built on the terrace of the cylinder.

These alterations did not discourage uprisings by the Roman commune, and EUGENE IV was forced to abandon the city for ten years. Starting in 1447, NICHOLAS V, his successor, undertook to further reinforce Castel Sant'Angelo by the construction of bastions at the corners, and by two towers at the bridge entrance. The pope's architect, Leon Battista Alberti, did not, however, realize his grandiose project of constructing vast fortifications to enclose the Vatican, protected by the Castel Sant'Angelo. The pope set up apartments in various parts of the central tower by enclosing the ancient medieval structures within two symmetrical buildings, which formed, with the central tower, a single edifice oriented toward the center of the bridge, the ancient *pons Aelius*, which had become during the Middle Ages the *ponte Sant'Angelo*. The position and height of these two symmetrical edifices had the effect of containing almost the entire central tower, which now barely dominated the mass of construction on the terrace of the cylinder.

Free space in the building left by this placement allowed for the arrangement of two symmetrical courtyards ("Courtyard of the Angel" and "Courtyard of the Wells"). Through these courtyards one had access to cisterns containing reserves of water, oil, and grain for the castle. The "Courtyard of the Wells" even served as a garden during the Renaissance thanks to the arable soil placed there since the time of Hadrian. Nicholas V also reinforced the Holy Angel bridge, causing the flooding of the Tiber. Within the context of the unceasing popular rebellion against the papacy, ALEXANDER VI reinforced the fortifications between the bastions, dug a trench in front of them, and constructed a tower at the entrance to the bridge. His architect, Sangallo the Elder, completed the construction of the central tower with large consoles and crenellation, while he restored the upper half of the great cylinder with a beautiful brick section. Around the cylinder and on the tower were placed the arms of the Borgia pope to mark the completion of these works. After the brief interlude of PIUS III's reign, his successor JULIUS II, improved, from 1504, the comfort of the papal APARTMENTS left by Nicholas V, commissioning Bramante to construct an open loggia facing the Tiber, as well as a steam room, a veritable masterpiece of illusionist architecture. In 1514, his successor, LEO X, en-

trusted Michaelangelo with building a small marble façade to the chapel and papal apartments facing the "Courtyard of the Angel." But in 1527, Pope CLEMENT VII had to witness, helplessly, from the top of the fortress, the brutal sack of Rome by Charles V. The pope was able to keep up six months of resistance (from 6 May to 6 December) within the Castel Sant'Angelo before accepting the conditions of the conqueror. His successor, PAUL III, transformed the buildings constructed by his predecessors into a veritable palace: from 1544, a new loggia was opened, this time facing the Borgo, and the apartments situated at the level of Nicholas V's construction efforts were sumptuously decorated. The greatest sculptors, architects, and painters collaborated in the work (Raffaele de Montelupo, Antonio da Sangallo, the young, Perin del Vega, Domenico Zaga), and in the most ostentatious room (the "Pauline room"), two Greek inscriptions specified that "Paul III, supreme pontiff, transformed this sepulcher of holy Hadrian into a royal palace, magnificent and divine." In the second half of the 16th century, PAUL IV and PIUS IV constructed a pentagonal wall around the castle, and in 1628, when URBAN VIII destroyed all the projecting parts with which Alexander VI had encumbered it near the river, the Castel Sant'Angelo took its definitive form. During the Renaissance and the modern epoch, the castle never lost its function as a prison, and it seems that the famous prison of "San Marocco" should be identified with the antique room of funeral urns of Hadrian's sepulcher whose *arcosolia* served as dark, narrow cells (archbishop Bartolomeo de Flores died there in 1498).

In the second quarter of the 18th century, efforts were made to improve the comfort of the castle (the chatelaine's apartment was linked to the entrance by an elevator built into the cylindrical masonry). However, at the end of the century, the first French occupation (1798) brought devastation, particularly the destruction of the papal arms.

In the 19th century, the first archeological investigations were done at the castle (1823: rediscovery of the helicoidal ramp), but it continued to be used as a political prison during the pontificates of GREGORY XVI and PIUS IX. On 21 September 1870, the castle's papal flag was solemnly lowered, as the Italian army rendered military honors to the papal troops who had offered the papacy its last defense there.

Gilles Sauron

Bibliography

Borgatti, M. *Castel Sant'Angelo in Roma*, Rome, 1890, 2nd ed. augm. 1931 (Major Mariano Borgatti had been responsible, from 1870, for the restoration and design of the castle).

Castel Sant'Angelo e Borgo tra Roma e papato, Rome, 1978.

D'Onofrio, C. *Castel S. Angelo*, Rome, 1971.

Eisner, M. "Zur Typologie der Mausoleen des Augustus und des Hadrian," *Romische Mitteilungen*, 86 (1979), 319–24.

CASTRATI OF THE PAPAL CHAPEL. The subject of the employment of castrati (eunuchs) in the papal chapel seems to have been deliberately obscured, no doubt because many people were uncomfortable with the very fact that the papal court encouraged—or, at any rate, tolerated—a practice that seemed to go against Christian moral principles. In 1749, Matteo Fornari, a papal singer wrote in his *Narrazione istorica* (BAV, CS. 606) that "*Jacomo Spagnoletto*," the first papal *castrato*, was engaged on 18 May 1588 to replace the falsetto singer Jacques Brunet. However, numerous documents suggest the presence of castrati much earlier. An example is this comment in the *Sacra Visita Apostolica* (ASV, *Armadio* XI, § 92, f. 152): "*Joannes Paredes* is a *castrato* who has been hired because sopranos were needed. He does not have a very good voice, but we may keep him until other sopranos arrive from Spain." Paredes was recruited in 1571. At any rate, this document clearly indicates that it was considered normal at that time to recruit castrati from Spain to serve in the papal chapel. Francisco Soto was hired in 1562, and at the end of the 16th century; Orazio Griffi, camerlengo or treasurer of the papal chapel, makes several references to him in his papal accounts as a "eunuch." One can scarcely doubt his account: Griffi was a well-educated and cultivated man, well aware of what the word "eunuch" meant. Despite the ambiguity that surrounds this subject, it must be acknowledged that the first castrati to be heard in Italy were Spaniards recruited to serve in the papal chapel.

The real reason behind the practice of using castrati in the papal chapel also remains unclear. Antimo Liberati, writing in 1671 (document BAV, CS .679), states: "As young boys often lose their soprano voices even before they have reached a sufficient musical level, it is convenient to use adults." Although this argument was certainly valid for most of the musical chapels in Europe, it could hardly be applied to the papal chapel, which had never used young boys, at least not since the return of the popes to Rome from Avignon. Liberati concludes, "For this reason the sovereign pontiffs saw the advantage in recruiting eunuchs and castrati from Spain to serve in the papal chapel." However, he condemns the practice and complains that it has become widespread in Italy. At the time he wrote, almost all the sopranos in the Italian chapels were castrati.

Girolamo Rosini, the first Italian castrato to be hired by the papal chapel, is reported to have been castrated as a result of "an infirmity." It may have been the result of an inguinal hernia: this operation had become quite widespread in the 16th century, but the operation developed by Ambroise Paré, which avoided castration, was not known in Italy until the middle of the next century. Rosini, who came originally from Perugia, entered into service at the chapel in April 1599 by order of the pope and at the behest of Cardinal Gallo, the protector of the chapel and at that time bishop of Perugia. He was dismissed a few weeks later, only to be rehired in April 1601. The arrival of Italian castrati posed a number of problems for the papal chapel. In the first place, they were recruited by *motu proprio*, without having to undergo a competitive examination. This fact in itself provoked the jealousy of the other singers. The last castrato to be recruited as a result of a competitive process was Guidobaldo Boretti, who began singing in the chapel in 1619, and he already was an exceptional case. Furthermore, castrati were generally recruited at the age of eighteen or nineteen, whereas the other singers would have to apply several times before being admitted and were rarely hired before they had reached twenty-five or thirty.

Some castrati served as deans for several years. The first was Soto himself, then another Spaniard, Juan Santos (1572?–1652), who was hired in 1588 and succeeded Soto as dean of the college in 1619. Upon Santos's death, Domenico Tombaldini became dean until the end of 1665. Prior to his recruitment in 1609, he had been in the service of Cardinal Montalto. This was also true of Gregorio Lazzarini (1607?–86), who entered the chapel in 1619 at the request of Cardinal Scipione Borghese, the nephew of PAUL V; he served as dean for twenty years. On 10 January 1699, Cardinal Pietro Ottoboni, protector of the chapel, requested that Francesco Antonio Besci, the nephew of Pompeo Besci and a castrato at the age of just fifteen, be admitted to the papal chapel. Francesco Besci, who is also known by the nickname Finaia, died in Rome in June 1753.

The castrati entered into service in the papal chapel at the request of an important cardinal and thus felt that they enjoyed special protection. They tended to take advantage of a situation where they enjoyed almost total impunity, and one can scarcely blame them for this, given the mentality of the time. The case of Loreto Vitori (1603–70), who entered into service in 1622, is illustrative of this. In the winter of 1637, he was accused (doubtless wrongly, although he confessed to it) of having abducted a young woman in the middle of Rome, in broad daylight. Pope URBAN VIII demanded that the guilty singer be punished, but Vitori, who had taken refuge in Spoleto, nevertheless continued to receive his singer's salary, as well as the salary paid to him by Cardinal Antonio Barberini. The pope did not expel him from the chapel, and in 1642 he was elected master of the chapel without this evoking the least condemnation from Urban VIII. In the meantime, he had been ordained into the priesthood.

Some castrati of the papal chapel became famous and were in demand in almost all the churches of Rome whenever special music was required, notably for vespers and solemn masses for the feasts of patron saints, or whenever there were several choirs gathered together. The organizers of these festivities deemed it indispensable that a few papal singers be heard, and, more important, one or two castrati. Their reputation spread beyond Rome; Marcantonio Pasqualini (1614–91), who was admitted to the chapel on December 1630, went to Paris to sing Luigi Rossi's *Orfeo* in 1647. Among those in greatest demand in Rome were Domenico Palombi, who entered the chapel in 1646 and died in 1690 and was better known by the nickname Rodomonte, Domenico dal Pane (1640–1700), and his younger brother, Francesco Maria (1642?–84). Giovanni Francesco Grossi (1653–97), nicknamed Siface, was hired for the chapel in 1675 but left after two years to pursue a career in opera. All these singers were instrumentalists as well, and many were capable of writing good music. During the reign of Louis XIV, two castrati from the papal chapel arrived in Paris—Guiseppe Ceccarelli (1657–1733), who spent the entire year of 1677 "at the service of his Majesty," and Pasqualino Tiepoli, who entered chapel service in 1690 and remained in service to the duke of Orleans from 1703 to 1705. All the time of his death in 1742, he was dean of the college.

The behavior of castrati varied according to individual character. Some put on airs, but there were others like Girolano Rossini, a devout man of God who worked all his life with the congregation of Oratorians of St. Philip Neri. Another admirable person was Bonaventura Argenti, who entered into service in 1645 and died as dean in 1697. He made his fortune thanks to Canillo Pamphili, the nephew of Pope INNOCENT X, and often acted as a conciliator in the college of singers. He left his entire fortune to the Oratorians.

At least until around 1660, the castrati of the chapel were chosen from among the best musicians in Italy, and their elaborate techniques of ornamentation influenced the style of singing in the chapel for more than a century. These techniques, however, lost all spontaneity during the 18th century, when the singers merely reproduced simplified formulas. These techniques were described by Felix Mendelssohn in his correspondence during his stay in Rome (1830–1).

By the 19th century, the presence of castrati in the papal chapel was the object of rather morbid interest among visitors to Rome. Indeed, one has the impression that now their main purpose there was to sing the *Miserere* during the three days of Holy Week. Since the period of French administration in Italy under Napoleon, the castration of young boys had been strictly prohibited, so there is some mystery surrounding the presence of castrati at that time, and this served to pique the interest of tourists, curious to hear them sing. For example, Mariano

Padroni had received permission to leave Rome, but Guiseppe Baini tried to get him to come back to sing in the Holy Week festivities. Later, Domenico Mustafa (1829–12) tried to effect some order in the papal chapel. Following the conquest of Rome in 1871, the pope had become a voluntary captive at the Vatican, and these conditions had also affected the chapel. In 1903, Pope PIUS X finally prohibited the recruitment of castrati for the chapel.

We will never know how the castrati sounded when they sang Palestrina's music. The recordings made in 1902 and 1903 by Alessandro Moreschi (1858–1922) are not very helpful, since the only castrato ever recorded restricted himself to tunes that were fashionable at the time, in solo performance.

Jean Lionnet

Bibliography

Burney, C. *The Present State of Music in France and Italy*, London, 1771–3.

Celani, E. "I cantori della Capella pontificia nei secoli XVI–XVIII," *Rivista musicale italiana*, 1907, 1909.

De Angelis, A. *Domenico Mustafà, la Cappela Sistina e la società musicale romana*, Bologna, 1926.

Hucke, H. "Die Besetzung von Sopran und Alt in der sixtinischen Kapelle," *Miscelanea en homenaje a Monseñor Hignio Angeles*, Barcelona, 1958–1961, I.

Raguenet, B. F. *Parallèle des Italiens et des Français en ce qui regarde la musique*, Paris, 1702.

CATACOMBS. In antiquity the place-name "Catacombs" was applied exclusively to a site on the Appian Way, *ad catacumbas*, Greek in origin and meaning "near the ravine." It may have been derived from the deep depression situated to the west of the Appian Way, or from a subterranean *pozzolano*, or sand quarry, which was once in use in that area. At any rate, the *ad catacumbas* site is known today as St. Sebastian. Perhaps because it has always struck the imagination of pilgrims, the name was subsequently used to denote the Roman Christian necropolises that were rediscovered in later times, and this is the meaning employed in this entry. To avoid ambiguity, however, one can instead use the term "cemetery," another word of Greek origin, innovated by the early Christian community (cf. Eusebius of Caesarea, *Histoire Ecclésiastique* VII, II) that quickly gained currency.

The word "cemetery" has three advantages. First, it clearly indicates what the sites were used for. Despite the legends made popular in 19th-century novels like *Quo Vadis?* or *Fabiola*, the catacombs were used only occasionally as shelters during periods of persecution or rivalry in the Church of Rome—for example, following the disputed election of Bishop Damasus. Second, since the term "cemetery" does not refer exclusively to a subterranean burial ground, it can perfectly well be used to denote Christian necropolises in Rome, all of which included structures on the surface above the underground chambers. Finally, the word "cemetery" stresses the communal aspect of these burial grounds, since *koimeterion coemeterium* in Latin, could also be translated as "dormitory." This enty focuses on community burial grounds rather than the private hypogea (group tombs) however remarkable the latter may be—for example, the one discovered in 1955 on the Via Latina, which housed members of a rich family, some of them Christians who had been laid to rest in separate rooms, and some apparently adherents of the traditional Roman religion. It also focuses on the cemeteries of Rome rather than those of Latium, although the latter have also been well studied.

For the city of Rome, the oldest known reference to a Christian cemetery is found in the writings of Hippolytus, who reports that Bishop Zephyrinus (199–217) entrusted the administration of the cemetery to the deacon (and future pope), CALLISTUS (*Philosophoumena*, II, 12, 44). Despite the opinion of 19th-century researchers (not to mention their predecessors, who were rather inclined to ascribe greater age to their discoveries than they actually possessed), archeological investigations have not revealed older Christian cemeteries. Zephyrinus's initiative may therefore have been among the first of its kind. It responded to the needs of the pastoral Church at the beginning of the 3rd century, characterized by a new burden for the Christian Church, as well as a need for Christians to affirm their identity even in death.

It is possible to find traces of the earliest cemetery created by Callistus in Area I of the Appian Way cemetery, which was named after its founder. It is well known for the monuments found there, including the "crypt of the popes" where a number of the 3rd-century bishops of Rome were laid to rest. The tomb of St. Cecilia, especially venerated by worshippers of medieval times, is also found here. Nearby are other burial grounds created by early Christians—for example, the "Lucinus crypts" where Pope CORNELIUS (251–3) was laid to rest. However, this first necropolis is modest in size, covering around 3,000 square meters. The subterranean chambers, as well as its surface—which has been less thoroughly studied—were only gradually brought into use. However, its network is more extensive and its layout much more coherent than those of other, more ancient or contemporary structures which show that in antiquity it was a widespread practice to bury people underground. This practice is even more evident in succeeding generations. The use of community cemeteries became more exclusive in the second half of the 3rd century at the Praetextata, Priscillan, and Domitillan sites.

The cemeteries are evidence of the progress made by early Christians in spreading their religion. Economic necessity forced them to make use of the subterranean chambers. For communities that practiced inhumation, it was important that the necropolises be as large as possible. To increase their size, it was less costly and more convenient to choose land that had been previously excavated and could subsequently be used for the purpose of burial.

Sand quarries (such as the one on the *ad catacumbas* site mentioned above) and the vast underground cisterns or hydraulic galleries, which were particularly numerous on the outskirts of the city, were used for burial as well as for storing irrigation water. They soon became the basis of a network that extended rapidly to meet the growing need. This was the case at the Priscillan as well as the "Two Laurels" on the Via Labicana. These cemeteries are unusual in that they cover a wide expanse; they are unequaled in Rome except by the catacombs created by the Jewish community around the same time or somewhat later on the Nomentana, Labicana, Appia, and Portuensevie, in Monteverde.

Despite the importance given to communal burial grounds in the 3rd century, the growth of these cemeteries was also due largely to simple pragmatism. Recent research leads us to qualify the theory made popular by G. B. de Rossi, which closely linked the administration of necropolises to the deaconry. Although the deaconry was indeed charged with the responsibility of giving essential assistance to the Christian community, the particular form of assistance constituted by inhumation could come from several sources. The bishop played a role, as in the case of Callistus, but there was ample opportunity for private benefactors, many of whom gave their names to the cemeteries. Local communities no doubt also played their part, although there is not much documentation of this.

We know little about the administration of the necropolises, but we know that they were dug by specialized workers called *fossores*. They did not really belong to the clergy but were doubtless recruited from among workmen with long experience in digging the volcanic rock, or tuff, which was easy to work, yet sufficiently resistant (except in some strata) to permit large-scale excavation. From inscriptions found in the cemeteries, we have some idea of how these groups functioned. They no doubt worked in small groups, despite the considerable size of some of the largest of the necropolises. We also know that they lived off the sale of the tombs, the price of which varied considerably according to where they were situated.

The last point explains the very marked social stratification that is obvious in the cemeteries. The tombs of Roman citizens were doubtless in mausoleums built above the now buried surface, which for the most part is still unexplored. Even in the subterranean strata, however, there is a marked contrast between the tombs of rich and poor in most cemeteries, and also between entire sections of the cemetery, which are largely divided between the two groups.

The poorest were buried in tombs known in antiquity as *loculi*. A *loculus* was a recess dug in the wall of the gallery and covered with bricks, tiles, or pieces of scrap marble. The wealthier citizens could afford an *arcosolium*, a tomb topped by an arched dome carved into the rock. The tomb of the richest was called a *cubiculum*, a chamber that could be locked. In some cases, illumination was provided by an opening above. The walls were excavated to accommodate *loculi* and *arcosolia* and even, in exceptional cases, sarcophagi. Sometimes the *fossores* tried to make the *cubicula* resemble the mausoleums on the surface, adding architectural touches such as columns and capitals, and in some cases ground vaults which they carved directly out of the tuff. It is mostly in these chambers that pictorial examples of early Christian art are to be found.

In their general layout, the tombs closely reflected the typical funerary art of the times, not only in the use of the "red and green linear style," in which graceful bands of color punctuate wide walls or ceilings which have been first coated with white, but also in the figures painted on the walls. These were stylized representations of flowers and sometimes of animals, especially birds. The Christians also adopted other more ancient images, such as the orant or the shepherd—traditional symbols of *pietas* and *philanthropia*. It is only on the smaller panels, in the vault, the arcosolia, or the entrance walls, that we see more original scenes drawn from the Scriptures replacing the mythical figures common to cemeteries of the era. This is particularly evident in the private hypogeum on the Via Latina, mentioned above, where the Christian chambers are distinguished from the pagan ones only by the subjects depicted in the scenes drawn on the walls. With some exceptions, Christian art is typified by very simple sketches, or "sign-images," to borrow an expression from A. Grabar. Most depict scenes from the Old Testament (Moses striking the rock at Horeb, Jonah, Daniel, Noah in the ark); there are fewer from the New Testament, including the resurrection of Lazarus, the miracle of the loaves and fishes, the healing of the cripple, and the adoration of the Magi. Although it is true, as has often been stated, that these images reflect the faith of the early Church, they owe more to traditional Classical art than to the influence of Church authorities. Far from interpreting a well-articulated theological dogma or discourse, their strength lies in repetition. They all depict key moments in the history of Salvation and the image of Christ the miracle-worker, thus providing a guarantee of life beyond the grave.

This guarantee was not, however, sufficient for the ancients, who were accustomed to a veritable cult of the dead. One of the most important manifestations of this was the funeral banquet, or *agape*, which they regularly celebrated in memory of their dead. As a result, some catacombs—for example, in the "Two Laurels" cemetery, the cemetery of Sts. Marcellinus and Peter—contain many representations of banquet scenes. For a long time,

these were taken to depict the Eucharistic banquet. These images perpetuated practices that were far easier to carry out in the *cubicula* than in the humble *loculi* dug out in the walls of narrow galleries; indeed, the latter were often condemned to make way for the debris from further digging to extend the network. Thus, the possibility of paying homage to one's dead long after the death depended to a large degree on a family's wealth.

There is no doubt that these ceremonies took place in underground cemeteries, where specific arrangements were made for the purpose. There were small platforms on stone supports, or *mensae*, which were probably designed more for placing offerings of food than for oil lamps. There were seats carved in the tuff, these are particularly numerous in the Maius cemetery, and were perhaps meant symbolically for the deceased. There were also rooms designed for the *agape*, such as the one that has been restored in the Greek chapel at the Priscillan cemetery. But the cemeteries constructed above ground were even more appropriate for this purpose. The large basilicas constructed in necropolises from the 4th century on, often on the initiative of the emperor, were also used for funeral banquets. This is certainly true of the basilica of St. Peter, where for some particularly sumptuous banquets it was necessary to set up couches just under cover of the atrium (Paullinus of Nola, *Lettres*, 13, 11); it is no doubt also true of the basilica of the Apostles (today known as the basilica of St. Sebastian), St. Paul, St. Agnes, St. Lawrence, and even that of Sts. Peter and Marcellinus on the Via Labicana, and doubtless other establishments founded in the first half of the 4th century.

These constructions were "polyvalent" or multifunctional rooms, as one would say nowadays. They could be used to honor the dead as well as to celebrate the Eucharist, while at the same time housing a large number of rooms. Indeed, the creation of these basilicas had an effect on the cemeteries themselves. Mausoleums and other funerary structures were housed within and close to annexes, often vast, while the excavation and extension of underground cemeteries continued. Close to the tomb of the Martyrs—a coveted spot for burial, for which believers paid a high price—new installations, or *retrosanctos*, were constructed. The plans of these *retrosanctos* were adapted to the topography, and the smallest available space was put to maximal use. New tombs were dug on the floor and close to the holy crypts. These were called *formae*, and their covers often served as an ornamental pavement. The growth of the Christian community caused other regions or sections to be created, often by digging deeper layers of galleries. The largely regular layout of these new sections, and indeed their very conception, are evidence of the skill of the *fossores*. The excavation could go as deep as 18 meters beneath the surface, and some catacombs had three superimposed levels (or even more) of unequal length.

In order to understand the importance of the cemeteries in use around the 4th century, a map is indispensable, even though it cannot take full account of the new geography of the area of Rome at that time. First, a map cannot show the constant cart traffic between the city and its margins, the funeral processions, the visits by families to tombs, and the crowds of pilgrims. Furthermore, a map cannot fully reflect the hierarchy of the necropolises. Although there is not a single important road of the time without at least one Christian cemetery, the areas most notable for their concentrations of cemeteries are also those where the most important ones were built. This is particularly noticeable in two sectors, but it is not known whether this was due to mere chance, or whether these cemeteries were built because of their proximity to an area more densely populated by Christians. These sectors are in the north, on the Nomentan and the Old and New Salarian, and especially in the south, in the Appian-Ardeatine sector. There, the necropolises of Callistus and Domitilla alone cover more than sixteen hectares, all layers included. They include 15 kilometers of galleries and hundreds of *cubicula*, and each held 15,000 to 20,000 dead. A more precise estimate is impossible because much of the networks have not yet been excavated, either in the cemeteries or in the catacombs as a whole.

From the second half of the 4th century, there was a marked decline in the rate of burials, and by the beginning of the next century there is little evidence of new excavation or even burials. This trend has often been attributed to the SACK OF ROME by the troops of Alaric in A.D. 410, but this is hardly a convincing argument, even if it is difficult to envisage other, more plausible explanations. Should we posit that new cemeteries were created on the surface in this area around the city, whose mainly underground cemeteries are better known today? Or, did the practice of burying in the city begin earlier than previously believed, in churches or even in marginal sectors of the city? The second hypothesis is made more plausible by recent research, which seems to support it.

The end of burial in the catacombs would have signaled the end of their use if some of them had not housed the tombs of martyrs. This ensured a second life for them. Originally cemeteries, they now became centers of devotion, attracting growing masses of pilgrims from all of Christendom, especially from the West. Specific installations were introduced from the 4th century to facilitate pilgrimage. The venerated crypts were enlarged and monuments built; one-way traffic was introduced; staircases leading down from the surface were built. Pope DAMASUS (366–84) was particularly active in this effort. The installations were continually improved and updated, especially during the 6th and 7th centuries, which undoubtedly mark the high point of pilgrimages to Rome during the early Middle Ages. At the same time, other installations indispensable for the comfort, well-being, and spiritual needs of the pilgrims were built: hospices or *xenodochia*, baths, monasteries, and baptistries.

These institutions contributed heavily to keeping the Roman countryside active as a religious venue, long after the bishops of Rome (from the 8th century on) began massive transfer of the remains of martyrs from the countryside to the city, far from the greed of those searching for relics. The removal of the body of a saint did not immediately signal the end of the devotion to that saint, however, and even though they were now subject to pillage; the catacombs were not really abandoned until well into the early Middle Ages, probably around the year 1000.

With the exception of a few sporadic incursions, such as those of a few visitors who left their signatures (Johannes Lonck in 1432; Pomponius Leto and his friends from the *Accademia Romana* in the second half of that century), the catacombs were not really rediscovered until the end of the 16th century. On 31 May 1578, workers extending a sand quarry stumbled on the Priscillan cemetery on the Salarian way. The popular impression that the discovery was a "subterranean Rome" gained currency; it is reflected in the title of a posthumously published work by A. Bosio (1636), the man who is rightly credited with rediscovering the catacombs, owing to his systematic study of them from 1593. His account of his work is remarkable for his times owing to its serious nature, its extent, and the quality of its illustrations; he included a topographical survey of the networks explored, as well as engraved plates of the main paintings. Bosio's successors were less painstaking in their research and showed far less respect for the monuments. They viewed the cemeteries essentially as a source of relics, and people searching for the bodies of the saints did far greater damage than the men of the early Middle Ages. This situation changed in the 19th century, thanks to the efforts of Father Marchi, and of G. B. de Rossi, who launched Christian archaeology as a science with his research work on the catacombs. It is significant that he chose to use Bosio's title, *Roma sotteranea*, for his unfinished synthesis. Today it is still reference reading, and an indisputable inspiration for research. The 20th century has been marked by spectacular discoveries (at St. Sebastian and the Latin Way, for example), extensive syntheses (such as that of Styger on topography, Msgr. Wilpert on the paintings and sarcophagi, A. Silvagni and A. Ferrua on the inscriptions), and a number of serious monographs. The Christian cemeteries of ancient Rome are now much-frequented places for study and are open to researchers of all nationalities. They are the property of the Italian state, but by virtue of the concordat they are administered by the Pontifical Commission for Sacred Archaeology.

Jean Guyon

Bibliography

Bagatti, B. *Il cimitero di Commodilla*, Vatican, 1936.

Baruffa, A. *The Catacombs of St. Callixtus: History, Archaeology, Faith*, W. Purdy, trans., Vatican City, 1993.

Bosio, A. *Roma sotterranea*, Rome, 1632. "Débuts de l'art chrétien—Rome," *Dossiers de l'archéologie*, 18, 1976.

De A. d'Ossat, G. *La geologia delle catacombe romane*, Vatican, 1943.

De Rossi, G. B. *La Roma sotteranea cristiana descritta e ilustrata*, 3 vols., Rome, 1863–77.

Deckers, I. G. Seeliger, H. R. Mietke, G. *Die Katakombe "Santi Marcellino e Pietro": Repertorium der Malereien*, Vatican and Münster, 1987.

Ferrua, A. *Catacombe sconosciute—Una pinacoteca del IV secolo sotto la via Latina*, Rome, 1990.

Guyon, J. *Le Cimitiere "Aux deux Laurier,"* Vatican and Rome, 1987.

Krautheimer, R. (dir.), *Corpus basilicarum Urbis Romae*, 5 vols., Vatican, 1937–80.

Nicolai, V. F. *I cimiteri paleocristiani del Lazio—I. Etruria meridionale*, Vatican, 1988.

Reekmans, L. *La Tombe du pape Corneille et sa région cémeteriale*, Vatican, 1964; *Le Complexe cémeterial du pape Gaius dans la catacombe de Calixte*, Vatican, 1988.

Styger, P. *Die römischen Katakomben*, Berlin, 1933; *Die römischen Märtyrergrüfte*, Berlin, 1935.

Testini, P. *Le catacombe e gli antichi cimiteri cristiani in Roma*, Bologna, 1966.

Tolotti, F. *Il cimitero di Priscilla*, Vatican, 1970.

Wilpert, G. *Le pitture delle catacombe romane*, Rome, 1903; *I sarcofagi cristiani antichi*, Vatican, 1929–36.

CATACOMBS, SAINTS' BODIES IN THE. From the earliest times, Rome has always shown its devotion to martyrs. If the account of the priest Gaius is to be believed, *tropaia* were erected in honor of the Apostles Peter and Paul from the beginning of the 2nd century, at the latest. The one to Peter was located at the Vatican, while that to Paul was erected on the road to Ostia (Eusebius, *Ecclesiastical History*, II, 25, 5). It was not until the middle of the 4th century, though, that there was a list of the saints whose bodies had been laid to rest above- or below-ground in the cemeteries around Rome. This first catalog is to be found in the *Calendar* of 354, which, in the *depositio martyrum* and the *depositio episcoporum*, provides a list of bishops and saints, perhaps rested as early as A.D. 336. These texts reveal a Roman martyrology still in its embryonic stage, as it is limited to only around fifty names. They do not give any measure of evaluation for the exact number of saints, or the veneration of the faithful. This is quite clear from the epigrams that Bishop Damasus (366–84) ordered placed on the tombs of the martyrs a generation later. Not only are there the names of new saints, there are also comments indicating other tombs that should be venerated. This clearly shows that the bishop had selected names from sanctoral canon (see, for example, epigrams 16 and 32 of the Ferrua edition).

While there is no doubt that from the 4th century, there were a considerable number of recognized bodies of saints, two much later documents provide a more accurate indication of their number. Firstly, there is the *Hieronymian Martyrology*, a document that possibly dates from the 5th century but is known to us only as the result of an inventory taken at the end of the following century. More importantly, there are the *Itineraries*, intended for use by pilgrims. The oldest one dates back to the first third of the 7th century. These documents are quite remarkable for their detailed rendering of a sacred geography. They provide more precise indications than the *Martyrology* for the exact location of the bodies of the saints. They cover an extensive area, along which there are frequent collective tombs—XXX martyrs, LXX martyrs, etc. In fact, due to the presence of a group of LXXX martyrs, the Callistus catacomb alone contains more bodies of saints than do the early-4th-century *depositiones*. Nevertheless it is quite possible to hear the phrase *et multi alii* "and many others" at the end of a guided visit to the catacombs. The guides have made their own selection, often more extensive than that in the *Martyrology*, but only giving an account of saints authenticated by the Church.

The success of the *Itineraries* attests to a level of devotion that actually posed some danger to the tombs of saints, and the Romans tried as long as possible to protect them. In a famous letter by GREGORY I the Great (590–604), the pope refuses to send any relics to the Empress of Constantinople, proposing to send instead a fragment of the chains of St. Peter (*Epistulae*, 4, 30). However, the demand of the faithful for relics (and not only by eminent persons) was so great that trafficking in the bodies of saints developed. The authorities sought to remedy this by having the remains most in demand removed to the city of Rome or to the Vatican.

Apart from rare instances of exhumation and reburial in the 7th century, the first bishop to take significant action was PAUL I (757–67). His intervention followed the Lombard invasion, which was particularly devastating for the cemeteries. His successors often had to take similar action. However, none of this effectively put a stop to the traffic in relics, especially from Rome to the court of the Franks, then the Carolingians. There is ample documentation of this, for example, an account describing the theft of the relics of Marcellinus and Peter, and their arrival in Seligenstadt, Germany. In 827, this account became known throughout Europe thanks to the reputation of its author, Einhard, adviser to and biographer of Charlemagne.

The transfer of relics to the city evidently marked a gradual decline in the importance of the catacombs. But Because of the practice—periodically widespread—of placing relics beneath altars, the rediscovery of underground cemeteries starting at the end of the 16th century led to even more considerable pillage than in the past. In 1622, GREGORY XV entrusted Cardinal Pier Paolo Crescenzi with the task of searching for the holy remains. Fifty years later, the post of "Guardian of Holy Relics and Cemeteries" was created. The holder of this title headed an entire department placed under the authority of the cardinal-vicar, providing a clear indication of the importance of the job. The creation of this post was not intended to put an end to the pillaging, however, and it continued for another century or so.

The sacred remains were identified by a series of archaeological criteria that are considered quite unscientific by today's standards: the depiction of doves or palm leaves on the tomb itself. The body of St. Philomena, so dear to the Curé d'Ars, was authenticated in this way. Sometimes a relic was deemed holy on the basis of so-called signs of martyrdom, such as "urns containing blood," within the *loculi*. Debate on these signs continued within scientific circles until the 19th century. As tombs dating from the 3rd and 4th centuries often have nothing remaining in them, one may well imagine the extent of the plunder, especially since those seeking to recover bodies of saints relics have been painstaking in their research. The accounts of their activities testify to this. Since the 19th century, researchers have had to refer to these accounts to trace inscriptions, golden goblets, lamps, and so many other relics that have been irretrievably lost because of this vain quest for relics.

Jean Guyon

Bibliography

De Rossi, G. B. *Roma Sotterranea*, I, Rome, 1864, 175–83.

De Rossi, G. B., ed. *Martyrologium hieronymianum*, Brussels, 1894.

Duchesne, L. ed. LP, I, Paris, 1886.

Duchesne, L. *Acta Sanctorum*, Nov., II, I Brussels, 1890.

Ferrna, A. ed. *Epigrammata damasiana*, Vatican City, 1942.

Guiraud, J. "Le commerce des reliques au commencement du IXe siecle," *MEFRH*, 12, 1892, 73–95.

Testini, P. *Le Catacombe e gli antichi cimiteri cristiani in Roma*, Bologna, 1966.

CATECHISM, ROMAN. Since the end of the 16th century, the term "Roman Catechism" has been used only to designate the catechism promulgated by the COUNCIL OF TRENT (1566). Today, a catechism is several things: a series of lessons designed to teach Christian faith and morals, the class or group to whom this teaching is given, and the book used to impart the such teaching. The practice of teaching and the book are relatively new to Christianity, introduced in the 16th century, when Catholics and Protestants alike deemed that the faith should be taught systematically and could be verified like any other source of knowledge.

Until then, since Carolingian times, catechism had only been part of the normal ritual when the priest asked the godmother and godfather to respond with *Credo* for the child and to teach him the common prayers. The catechism was a liturgical and participatory process, more practical than intellectual. From the 13th century, however, the role of the clergy in Christian teaching grew considerably. The synod statutes following the fourth Lateran council (1215), and later the manuals for priests in charge of souls as well as the ritual of the sacraments, all gave increasingly specific instructions as to what the priest should say when administering the sacrament and during the sermon. The early origins of the Roman Catechism are to be found in this priestly responsibility.

The publication in Rome in 1566 of the *Catechismus ex decreto concilii tridentini ad parochos* marks the end of a process whereby initiation into Christianity ceased to be centered on what to say and became more oriented toward what to believe. It also marks the beginning of standardization in the transmission of the faith, with centralized control.

For any intellectual, error is the child of ignorance; and from the beginning of the 15th century, the uncovering of ignorance became the daily task of scholars. In France, Jean Gerson was one of the first university scholars to devise a pedagogy to help children avoid the errors of their parents. His treatise *De parvalis ad Christum trahendis* (1406) explicates the method, and his three opuscules in the *Opus tripartitum*, the content (commentary on the Decalogue, how to confess, the art of dying well). They would serve as a reference for a century and a half.

Luther admired Gerson. In 1529, seeking to unify his movement, he published the *Large Catechism* in German and the *Small Catechism for the Use of Less Educated Pastors*. The latter volume took the form of a dialogue in which the pastor was the holder of information. It presents the law, faith, prayer, and the sacraments. Calvin's first catechism, *Instruction and Confession of Faith as Used in the Church of Geneva* (1537), is no different. It is a commentary on the common prayers, also practiced in a less systematic manner by priests having responsibility for souls, based on formulas and rituals and such well-known opuscules as the *Great Ordinary of Christians* (1469) and those of Gerson, as well of other bishops such as Artus Fillon (d. 1526), and Guillaume Petit (d. 1536).

Priests began to ask the questions prescribed in the catechism on the occasion of conferring the sacraments.

Calvin's catechism, *Formulaire d'instruire les enfants* (1541), marks a change. Like Bucer in Strasbourg, he made the catechism obligatory, functioning outside the liturgy. It finishes with a public profession of faith and is divided into 55 lessons presenting all the dogma in the form of a dialogue, with the minister asking the questions and the child replying.

The Jesuit Emond Auger in Bearn attempted to rebut this manual with his own *Catechisme* (1563), which offers point-by-point replies to all the questions. Around the same time, writing in the context of the peace of Augsburg (1555), a Jesuit priest of Ingolstadt, Peter Canisius, composed his *Summa doctrinae cristianae* (1554), followed in 1556 by the *Catechismus minimus* and in 1557 by the *Catechismus major*. These were distributed by the Jesuit colleges and were popular until the middle of the 17th century. Christian training was no longer a mere learning of rhythmical, enumerative formulas (as had been the case at the beginning of the 16th century), but of learning simplified points of dogma.

The council of Trent set about examining the question of the catechism in February 1562. On 11 November 1563, at its 24th session, canon 7, the council decided that the bishops should translate the catechism into everyday language and have the clerics explain it to the people. A commission on this question was set up under the direction of cardinal Seripando, although—as was the case for the INDEX and the MISSAL—the pope had the final say on its actual implementation. A new commission was established, consisting of the archbishop of Zara, Muzio Calini, and three Dominicans—the Italians Leonard Marini and Egidio Foscarini, and the Portuguese Francesco Foreiro. They took up the task where the council had left off, under the leadership of Charles Borromeo. On the basis of their work, the canonist Gabriele Paleotti drafted a text in Italian, which was translated into Latin by the humanist Giulio Poggiani.

The work came off the printing press of Paolo Manutius at the end of 1566, after a final revision by Cardinal Sirleto. It was immediately approved by PIUS V (24 September 1566), who directed that it be translated into German, Polish, and French (the French translation first appeared in Bordeaux in 1567). Provincial and synodal statutes decreed that clerics were obliged to read it, (Benevento, 1567; Ravenna, 1568; Genes, 1574; Milan, 1576; Rouen, 1581; Bordeaux, 1582; Tours and Reims, 1583; Aix, 1585; Aquilea, 1586; Toulouse, 1590). Very soon in France, the new Roman Catechism replaced Gerson as the material to be read during the sermon.

This work does not constitute a sustained catechistic plan, but rather a working instrument adaptable to diverse situations. Indeed, the preface states: "As for the manner in which they will deal with these matters, they will choose the way which they deem most suitable to the people and to the times." There are 46 chapters in four unequal parts: "On the Faith and Comments on the Credo" (13 chapters); "On the Sacraments and Explanation of the Different Sacraments" (14), with particular emphasis on penance (4) and the Eucharist (3); "On the Decalogue, and Its Commentary" (9); and "On Prayer and the Explanation of the *Pater*" (8). Its extremely wide distribution is measured in the number of editions (351) and translations (58 languages).

Better than the works of Auger and Canisius, the Roman Catechism provides a synthesis of all evangelical and patristic research of the 16th century, while maintaining the essential elements of Scholastic definition, all written in an optimistic and serene tone, doing away with controversy and short-sighted moralizing. The work supplied the pastors with the elements of doctrinal, biblical, and spiritual catechetics, although its theological subtleties and its literary presentation must have posed difficulties for priests who were not well educated.

This is a great catechism; but the catechetical movement was also developing in Italy and in Spain. There began a trend to produce small catechisms, including that of Robert Bellarmin, published in 1598. This *Dottrina Christiana breve* is the fruit of several years of catechetical experience. It was approved by Pope CLEMENT VIII and quietly distributed by the Brothers of Christian Doctrine and by the Ursulines. It explains everything useful for a Christian through the words and gestures of daily prayers. However, it was Bellarmin's method rather than the content of his catechism that came to be utilized. During the 17th century, every bishop dreamed of publishing his own small catechism, even a large catechism, or to be read from the pulpit during Advent or Lent, or on feast days. However, in France at least, resistance to the organization of a catechesis outside the liturgy lasted until the end of the 17th century. It was only then that the lessons gained precedence over the sermon.

The uniformity sought by the council of Trent and St. Pius V through the publishing of the Roman Catechism was only a façade that masked a variety of interpretations in the smaller catechisms. The Roman Catechism merely provided the framework for the catechists; it is not the Roman Catechism that generations of Christians have learned by rote.

The Roman Catechism has, however, been an inspiration for the universality and unity of Catholicism. It is this symbolic heritage that it bequeaths to future generations. This is the heritage perceived by VATICAN I, which on 14 January 1870 launched a project for a universal catechism to replace that of the council of Trent. The sudden suspension of the council made it impossible to realize this plan. At the end of the 20th century, the desire to defend the unity of doctrine, threatened by the upheavals of the post-conciliar period, has given rise to nostalgia for the homogeneous teaching of doctrine.

There is also a need for a coherent summary of the faith, a need that would not have been felt had it not been for the quality of the Roman Catechism of 1566.

Nicole Lemaitre

Bibliography

Bellinger, G. *Der catechismus Romanus und die Reformation*, 1970 (Konfessionskundliche und Kontroverstheologische Studie, 27).

Benard, M. "Le catechisme au temps des réformes," *Les Quatre Fleuves*, issue no. 11, *Transmettre la foi: La catéchèse de l'Église*.

Colin, P. Germain, E. Joncheray, J. Venard, M. *Aux origines du catéchisme en France*, Paris, 1989.

d'Hotel, J. C. *Les origines du catéchisme moderne*, Paris, 1967.

Germain, E. *Langages de la foi à travers l'histoire*, Paris, 1972.

Henrivaux, O. *Les Catechismes dans la Wallonie actuelle, de 1559 à 1806*, Louvain-la Neuve, 1981.

Hezard, *Histoire du catéchisme depuis la naissance de l'Église à nos jours*, Paris, 1900.

"L'encadrement religieux des fidèles . . . jusqu'au concile de Trente," *Actes du 109 Congrès National des Sociétés Savantes*, Dijon, 1984, *Section d'histoire mediévale et de philologie*, 1, Paris, 1985.

Mangenot, E. "Catechisme," *DTC*, 2 (1932), 1895–1968.

Porter, F. *L'Instruction catéchetique au Canada: Deux siècles de formation religieuse*. 1633–1833, Montreal, 1949.

Rodriguez, P., and Lanzetti, P. *El manuscrito original del catechismo Romano. Descripción del catechismo del Concilio de trento*, Pamplona, 1987.

Rodriquez, P. ed. *Catechismus Romanus seu Catechimus ex decreto concilii tridentini ad parochos*, Pamplona, 1989.

Testore, C. "Catechismo," *ECM* 3, 1949, 1118–25.

Toscani, X. "Le scuole della dottrina cristiana come fattori di alfabetizzazione," *Società e storia*, 1984, 757–81.

"Transmettre la foi: XVI–XV siècle," *Actes du 109 e Congrès National des Sociétés Savantes*, Dijon, 1984, *Section d'histoire moderne et contemporaine*, 1, Paris 1984.

CATECHISM, ROMAN (1992). The promulgation by JOHN PAUL II of the apostolic constitution *Fidei depositum*), (11 October 1992), and subsequent publication of the *Catechism of the Catholic Church* form a high point in the experience of the religious community, and especially of the Catholic Church, since the closure of the second Vatican council (1959–65). This catechism was developed following the collective recommendation of the bishops at the second special SYNOD held in October 1985, on the occasion of the twentieth anniversary of the end of VATICAN II. They called for "A catechism or *compendium* of all of Catholic doctrine." The writing of the latest Roman Catechism follows the example of post-conciliar efforts aimed at renewing the major documents in the life of the Church, as exemplified by the new codification of canon law published in 1983.

In the long-term history of the church, however, the catechism signals a turning point. No all-embracing catechism—only versions pertaining to national Churches—had been produced since the *Catechismus ex decreto concilii tridentii ad parochos,* or *Catechism of Saint Pius V*, which was established in April 1546 and published twenty years later, the fruit and instrument of the COUNTER-REFORMATION, in reply to Martin Luther's *Greater* and *Smaller* catechisms of 1529. The national catechisms were written in everyday language and adapted to local cultures. The most recent is the *Catechism for Adults*, drawn up by the conference of bishops of France and published in May 1991. The new version of the Roman Catechism, which lays out the truths of faith and Christian morals according to the classical definition of "cathechism," is intended to be a point of reference for future diocesan catechisms, according to a tradition that reserves to bishops the preparation of pedagogical instruction and teaching tools, since they are primarily responsible for imparting this knowledge and belief.

In 1967, PAUL VI expressed the idea that all "texts of the Council will constitute the great catechism of modern times." However, the project of writing a new catechism was not in fact foreseen by Vatican II, which, in the interest of decentralization and "collegiality" was hesitant to impose its authority on the newly constituted national episcopal conferences. Nonetheless, two apostolic exhortations—*Evangelii nuntiandi* (1976) and *Catechesi tradendae* (1979)—showed concern for the need to renew the Tridentine Catechism. The latter exhortation was written by Paul VI, following confidential proposals made at a synod of bishops in 1977, but was later published by John Paul II. Finally, at the request of the bishops themselves, the pope in July 1986, announced the creation of a drafting commission made up of bishops from the various continents and of heads of DICASTERIES of the Curia, to be presided over by a doctrinal official, Cardinal Joseph Ratzinger. Cardinal Ratzinger had been prefect of the Congregation for the Doctrine of the Faith since 1982. At the end of the 1960s, he became well known for his condemnation of the *Dutch Catechism*, which he deemed too pragmatic. To this eleven-member commission was added a drafting committee consisting of seven resident bishops (including Jean Honoré, archbishop of Tours), a publishing commission presided over by Msgr. Lajolo, a group of forty consultants (theologians, exegetes, and liturgists), and a secretariat. The main force behind the secretariat was Father Christoph

Schönborn, a Dominican who taught at the faculty of theology of the University of Freiburg (Switzerland) and later became auxiliary bishop of Vienna.

Following an inaugural meeting of the committee in November 1986, the year 1987 saw the preparation of two successive outlines, culminating in December in a preliminary draft which stressed, in the words of Ratzinger, "the usefulness of a more frequent use of traditional terminology." There were mixed reactions to this. The opinions of forty consultants were sought, and the amended draft was sent *sub secreto* to the entire episcopacy and through them to Catholic academic institutions. The time period for examination of the draft was from 1 November 1989 to May 1990, with a five-month extension for those who had not finished within the time limit.

More than 24,000 amendments were submitted with a view to producing a final draft. With the help of a computer, a survey of the suggestions was made. It became clear that there was wide-ranging agreement on the need and appropriateness of a single catechistic text for the Catholic Church; 10 percent of those surveyed disagreed with the revised text, 78 percent considered it "good" or "very good," and 12 percent expressed reservations. An amended text was drafted between November 1990 and September 1991, then a "preliminary final draft," which was itself corrrected—the seventh draft version since the beginning of the process—and approved by the commission in October 1991. The draft was approved unanimously on 14 February 1992 and presented to the pope, who gave his official endorsement on 25 June. The new catechism was promulgated on 11 October and offered to "the people of God" on 8 December, during the feast of the Immaculate Conception.

An analysis of its contents reveals that the overall structure is unchanged with respect to the catechism of 1566, which consists of 46 chapters divided into four sections: Credo, Sacraments, Commandments, and Prayer. The catechism of 1992 follows the same outline (the profession of faith, celebration of the Christian mystery, life in Christ, Christian prayer), with 2,863 articles distributed into chapters, sections, and paragraphs, including summaries (headings "in brief") and numerous quotations from the Bible and from various authors, including Cardinal Newman. The layout of the material has caused some theologians to comment that the catechism consists more of an expression of faith than a moral code, since the Credo takes up more space (articles 26 to 1065) than the Decalogue (articles 2641 to 2557).

The Jesuit Paul Valadier condemned the extensive media coverage of the launching of the catechism as confusion between the "strength of the Truth" and the will for commercial power. With respect to the actual content of the work, Bishop Lucky of New Ulm, Minnesota, stated that the publishing of the catechism should not lead one to think that "all problems can be solved by a book"

and questioned the "very great stress" on faith and obedience rather than the call of Jesus and the response of the disciple. Sometimes seen as an attempt by the pope to bring church doctrine back to hand, this tendency is confirmed or denied depending on the points dealt with in the catechism, from the treatment of sexual relations with respect to procreation to relations with non-Christian religions. The Roman Catechism is a synthesis of the teachings of a Catholic Church "marching toward the third millennium," and since its publication it has been sold widely. This success is as unexpected as it is significant. It shows that people had been awaiting the new catechism, for reasons as varied as the responses it elicited.

Phillippe Levillain

Bibliography

Marle, R. "Un Catéchisme de l'Église catholique," *Études*, (Dec. 1992), 689–95.

Simon, M. *Un catéchisme universel pour l'Église catholique: Du concile de Trente à nos jours*, Louvain, 1992.

CATHERINE OF SIENA. *(b. near Siena, 1347, d. Rome, 23 April 1380). Saint.*

Catherine of Siena was made a Doctor of the Church by Pope PAUL VI in 1970. She had been canonized in 1461 by the Sienese pope PIUS II. Although she has become known to posterity as Catherine of Siena, after her birthplace, her life experiences and thought went far beyond its boundaries.

Catherine's father, Iacopo, kept a dye workshop in the Fontebranda quarter of Siena. Together with his wife, Lapa, he had a large family, of whom Catherine was the youngest. She grew up in the difficult aftermath of the Black Plague. She discovered her mystical vocation very early; at the age of six or seven, she had a vision of Christ, and chose him as her husband, the object of her love. With some difficulty, she convinced her family of her religious choice, and around the age of 17 (1364 or 1365) she was admitted as a tertiary of a Dominican order, known as the *mantellate*. These were normally pious widows of a more advanced age. Catherine thus chose to live as a virgin in her marriage with the Church through the perils of the world. She continued to live in her parents' house.

The next five to ten years were formative. Catherine received theological guidance from the monks of the monastery of San Domenico, especially from Thomas della Fonte and Thomas Caffarini, as well as from monks of other orders—for example, the Englishman William Flete, who lived in the Augustinian hermitage of Lecceto, a few kilometers from Siena. Catherine developed her own form of mysticism, based on a system of physical ascetism as a means of achieving the ideal of fusion with Christ. She also developed a practice of charity toward the poor and sick and soon gathered a spiritual family of which she was *la mamma*.

Very soon, Catherine began to feel torn between her desire to continue in the contemplation of Christ her husband, and Christ's urging her to enter into active service for the good of others and for Christendom. She could not refuse Him, and around 1370 she embarked on her "public life." Her commitment had several objectives, all interlinked and dictated by God. One was the crusade, which was at that time motivated by the obliteration of the kingdom of Jerusalem and the advance of the Turks.

The name of Catherine, like that of Bridget of Sweden, is linked first and foremost to the project of securing the return of the papacy from AVIGNON to Rome. This was essential not only to promise the crusade, but also, in the long term, to reform the Church. These undertakings implied the return of peace to Christendom, or at least to Italy. Catherine set herself to take political action, through intensive correspondence and numerous travels.

Doubts were raised about the religious nature of her life, and in 1374 she was summoned to Florence by the general chapter of the Dominican order. She emerged from this inquiry with a firm conviction as to the path she should follow, as well as with a confessor, Raymond of Capua, who followed her for the rest of her life and wrote her biography, or *Legenda Major*, completed in 1395.

Catherine then went to Pisa. There, on 1 April 1375, she received the stigmata of Christ, which, unlike those of Francis of Assisi, remained invisible and secret. Finally she traveled by sea to Avignon, where she stayed from the latter part of June to the latter part of September 1375. Her confrontation with the papal court, which she found worldly and venal, was difficult and often disappointing, but Catherine—after a new inquiry into her orthodoxy, which decided in her favor—succeeded in meeting with Pope GREGORY XI. She wrote to him, and strengthened by her closeness to Christ, she harshly upbraided him to give him the courage to leave. It is difficult, however, to assess her actual influence on Gregory's decision to transfer the Church administration back to Rome in 1377.

In the meantime, Catherine had returned to Siena. Still pursuing her goal of peace, she intervened by correspondence in the political affairs of the city and of the Italian nobility in both the territory of Siena and Florence, where she stayed for a long period in 1377–8, since she wanted at all costs to reconcile this city with the pope. But her political interventions were ill-informed and often badly received, and in Florence Catherine at one point found herself in serious difficulties. Furthermore, good Christians disapproved of this "wandering woman" (*mulier girovaga*).

In 1378, there was a setback to the success of the return of the pope to Rome. After the death of Gregory XI in March, the successive elections of URBAN VI and of CLEMENT VII led to the Great Schism. Catherine, called to Rome by Urban VI, stayed there from autumn through the next few months, entirely devoting her public life to the cause of the Roman pope and the reform of the Church. She died there in the spring of 1380 at the age of thirty-three.

The chronology of the life of Catherine, in the midst of important events affecting the Church, is not very certain. It was not the primary concern of her confessor and first biographer, Raymond of Capua. Furthermore, her stated age at death—thirty-three—has drawn criticism from Robert Fawtier because of the obvious association with the life of Christ. However, the places where Catherine spent her life may easily be traced. She invented a place of reference, her "interior cell," which served as a meeting place with Christ wherever she went. The real model for this was her childhood room, from which her parents had once even banned her in an effort to discourage her religious vocation. Until she was about twenty-three, she lived in the city of Siena, in a specific room in a specific house in the quarter close to the church of the Dominicans. However, her mental geography embraces all of Christendom, the ideal of the crusade and the realities of Avignon and Rome, where she lived under the protection of her spiritual family. In this material and psychological space, Catherine of Siena led her life of combat against her body and in favor of her love, fighting against obstacles to union of God and his Church.

The documentary work of this woman who never learned to write is considerable. The *Dialogue of the Divine Providence*, or *Book of the Divine Doctrine*, composed between 1377 and 1378, was dictated by Catherine in her moments of ecstasy. It defines, in a manner more filled with imagery and affection than with theory, her theological positions and her doctrine on the union between God and humans in Christ. The *Letters*, which are still being studied and analyzed, have not reached us in their originally dictated form, since they have been recopied and recompiled by her disciples to spread her thought and her cult.

The cult of Catherine of Siena did not spread immediately. It was promoted by the Dominican order rather than by the city of Siena. Beyond her political and religious failures, Catherine's life offered a model of feminine spirituality to the world and consecrated an incomparable mystical experience.

Odile Redon

Bibliography

Bianchi, L., and Giunta, D. *Iconografia di S. Caterina da Siena*, I, *L'immagine*, Rome, 1989.

Dupreé-Théseider, E. "Caterina da Siena," *DBI*, 22 (1970), 361–79.

Flusin, M. "Art, société et dévotion: Les dominicains et la première statue de Catherine de Sienne," *Symboles de la Renaissance*, II, Paris, 1982, 151–252.

Maffei, D., and Nardi, P., eds. *Atti del Simposio internazionale caterinaiano-bernardiano* (Siena, 1980), Siena, 1982.

CAUDATARY. The papal train-bearer (*caudatarius*, also *lembifer*) was the priest whose job it was to hold up the train or hem of the robe of a pope or cardinal (or even of a bishop when he wore a long cape or cassock with a train). The papal caudataries followed the pontiff to hold the hem of his cassock. A caudatary was appointed by the pope's major-domo immediately following the papal election and automatically became part of liturgical processions in the papal ceremonies. Upon the death of the pope, it was the caudatary who received the vase containing the *praecordia pontificis*, a crystal urn filled with 90 percent alcohol, containing the intestines, liver, heart, and spleen of the dead pope, which were extracted by the surgeons of the Apostolic Palace during the embalming process. It was placed in a wicker basket covered with a cloth embroidered with the name of the pope, and the vase was then borne by the caudatary to the church of Sts. Vincent and Anastasius, where the *praecordia* of earlier popes were kept.

The train-bearers of cardinals held the hems of their masters' robes in consistories and papal liturgies. The *cappa magna* ("great mantle") worn by cardinals of the Sacred College was conferred on them by Pope BONIFACE VIII in 1295; in 1494, Pope PAUL II determined that it should be red in color. The cardinals actually had three types of *cappa*: the first, made of red watered silk, they wore most of the time; the second, of violet watered silk, was worn in times of penitence such as Advent and Lent; and the third was made of violet wool and was worn on Good Friday, and originally only by those cardinals appointed by a deceased pope. From 1870, however, all cardinals wore the last type during the conclave. The religious cardinals, whose habit did not otherwise differ from that of the secular clergy, had to wear a *cappa* made of wool and not watered silk as a sign of poverty. Those who wore a special habit generally wore a *cappa* of the same color as the habit of their order: black for the Benedictines, Basilians, Minims, and Augustinians, white for the Trinitarians, Camaldolese, and Olivetans, blue for the Silvestrines, brown for the Capuchins, and so on. Numerous meanings have been given to this vestment: prefiguration of the immortality of the body in the Kingdom of Heaven, or the majesty and dignity of the priesthood whose permanence until the end of time was represented by the length of the train.

Originally, the *cappa* was secured on the head by the cardinal's hat and fell down the back, remaining open in the front. Later, it was placed directly on the shoulders and covered with a *cappa magna* or cape made of ermine for winter and of red silk for summer for secular cardinals, or of wool of varying colors for certain regular cardinals. This woolen cape was usually of the same color as the habit, but for Dominicans it was white, and for Cistercians black. It covered the entire body down to the feet in front but was much longer—up to seven meters—in back. In Rome, the cardinals wore the *cappa* only in the papal liturgies or in their cardinals' titles. In 1952, Pope PIUS XII abolished the use of silk and the wearing of the *cappa* in papal liturgies and consistories. He also ordered that the length be reduced by half (*motu proprio Valde solliciti*). When among themselves in the cardinals' liturgy, members of the Sacred College wore the *cappa* rolled up around the left arm; from 1953, this practice was extended to the papal liturgies. Outside Rome, though, the *cappa* was always worn.

The train-bearers were introduced into the Roman court to help the cardinals move around while wearing the *cappa*. In 1538, PAUL III created a brotherhood whose members received practical training in how to handle the *cappa*. They enjoyed such privileges as the twice-weekly use of the altar for their private Mass, or bonuses for their services to the Vatican. They ended their function with the recitation of the final prayers while the body of their master was being placed in the coffin. Their habit consisted of a cassock made of purple silk with black velvet buttons. Over this, they wore a specific garment known as a *croccia*, a light coat of purple wool opening in front with a purple silk lapel and very wide three-quarter sleeves with a high silk cuff. At about chest height, the *croccia* formed a sort of hood where the cardinal kept his breviary or documents distributed in the consistory.

At the Sistine or St. Peter's liturgies, the train-bearers were seated on the second step of the platform, at the feet of their respective cardinals. They held the red Cardinal's biretta, which was never worn in the presence of the sovereign pontiff. At the moment of rising or during the Obedience, they held it out to the cardinal, who placed his skullcap in it. Whenever the cardinal celebrated Mass himself, he removed the *cappa* to don his priestly vestments, and the train-bearer held the tail of his cassock.

The wearing of the cardinal's *cappa magna* ceased to be obligatory following the *Ut sive sollicite* instruction of the Secretariat of State (31 March 1969), which—strangely enough—prohibited it in Rome but reserved its usage outside of the city to "especially solemn occasions." The use of the *mosetta*, or ermine cape, was abolished everywhere.

Joël-Benoit D'Onorio

Bibliography

Battandier, A. "La cappa cardinalice," *Annuaire pontifical catholique*, 1899; M. Noirot, "Notes sur la prélature," *L'Ami du clergé* (Langres), 29 Jan. 1948.

CAUSES OF CANONIZATION.

Definitions. BEATIFICATION is a solemn act by which the sovereign pontiff of Rome declares that a venerable servant of God may be called "blessed" and that his or her feast may be celebrated by specific groups of the faithful, in specific places, according to the canon law. This declaration is promulgated by an apostolic letter in the form of a papal brief, *sub annulo piscatoris*, signed by the secretary of state. CANONIZATION is a solemn act wherein the pope, after having called a consistory of cardinals and prelates, declares that a blessed person is a saint, inscribes him or her in the catalog of saints, and determines that the saint may be venerated throughout the Church. This declaration is promulgated by a letter of decree in the form of a papal bull, signed by the pontiff, bishop of the Catholic Church.

Beatification and canonization are prerogatives of the Roman pontiff. However, the ceremony itself may be performed by a papal legate, as was the case during the last illness of JOHN XXIII. The infallibility of the pope is involved in the declaration of canonization; It witnesses only to the certainty that the canonized saint does in fact enjoy the Beatific Vision and not to the reality of the saint's miracles, even though the latter are first exhaustively researched and recognized with all the necessary guarantees. Infallibility consists in the tenet that the pope cannot mislead the Church by proposing for veneration, with full apostolic authority, someone who is a sinner. The aid of the Holy Spirit must preserve the Church from error in such a vital matter. The *cult* of saints is an active profession of faith, and objections raised against canonizations are always resolved (BENEDICT XIV, *Opus de Servorum Dei beatificatione et beatorum canonizatione* 1, XIV, 28).

Historical Background. From the 2nd century, martyrs have been venerated as objects of public worship; the faithful collected and honored their relics. This was the simplest and most ancient form of canonization. Among the local cults directly encouraged by Rome were those of St. Vigile, honored in the 4th century by BENEDICT IV; St. John Chrysostom, honored in the 5th century by INNOCENT I; and St. Maur, honored in the 7th century by BONIFACE III.

In the 4th century, simple confessors began to be venerated. These are Christians who were not martyred but who heroically practiced Christian virtues. In the 9th century, the worship of new saints began with the *vox populi*. The bishop was called; the life of the saint and the history of miracles performed by him were read in the bishop's presence, usually during a diocesan or provincial synod. When the cult had been approved by the bishop, the body was exhumed to give it a more fitting burial, an act called the *elevatio*. Sometimes a *translatio*, or transfer of the body close to an altar, was performed. The altar then took

the name of the saint who was henceforth venerated there. Sometimes the church would be enlarged and rededicated to the new saint.

Sometimes a pope himself made the decision for canonization, as was the case when JOHN XV decreed the translation of Ulric, bishop of Augsburg (31 January 993), in the most ancient papal bull known. It does not, however, contain the word "*canonization*," which first appears later in a letter from Uldaric, bishop of Constance, to Pope CALLISTUS II (1119–24), regarding the canonization of Bishop Conrad.

URBAN II (1088–99), Callistus II, and EUGENE III (1145–53) recommended that the examination of the virtues and miracles of candidates for sainthood be carried out only in councils, preferably general councils. Nevertheless, some pontiffs used their right to confer beatification and canonization outside of councils. This was the case in the canonizations of Emperor Henry (by EUGENE III), and Edward III of England, Thomas Becket, and Bernard of Clairvaux (by ALEXANDER III).

Alexander III (1159–81) decreed that causes of canonization and beatification should be reserved for the sovereign pontiff (*Decret.*, 1. III, tit. XLC, "*Audivimus*"). He submitted such causes to the college of cardinals. Despite this, some bishops continued to confer beatification, even after INNOCENT III (1198–1216) reiterated the view of his predecessor by canonizing Empress Kunigunde (bull *Cum Secundum*, 3 April 1200). From that time on, the act of beatification has implied at least a retrospective act of papal authority, with restrictions with respect to time, place of worship, or level of approval.

The question was finally settled by URBAN VIII (1623–44). The Congregation of the Holy Office prohibited (decree of 13 March 1625) the cults of persons who had not been beatified or canonized by the Holy See, without prejudice to the age-old cult of saints (decree of 2 October 1625). Urban VIII confirmed that bishops were no longer qualified to introduce new local cults (constitution *Caelestis Hierusalem cives*, 5 July 1634). During the period from 1181 (death of Alexander III) to 1534 (a century before the new discipline imposed by Urban VIII), the cult to the servants of God could remain in the status quo, even though formal canonization could be obtained *per viam cultus seu casis exceptis*, thus achieving an equipollent canonization—in other words, through the recognition of an *immemorial popular cult*. Bishops were instructed to continue making the preliminary inquiries (Congregation of Rites, instruction of 12 March 1631). SIXTUS V had created the Congregation of Rites and had given to them the task of examining the causes of saints (constitution *Immensa Aeterni Dei*, 22 January 1588). Urban VIII decreed the adoption of a new procedure (decretal *Servanda in canonizatione et beatificatione sanctorum*, 12 March 1642). This procedure remained in force for a long time after having been completed by

Pope Benedict XIV (1754–8). It is to be found among canons 1999–2141 of the 1917 CODE OF CANON LAW.

In 1659, a decree regarding the honor due to the "blessed who are not yet canonized" was fundamental for establishing the liturgical difference between blessed and saint. CLEMENT X ordained that the Congregation of Rites should rule on beatification without making any reference to canonization, thus clearly establishing the difference between the two. ALEXANDER VII conferred the first formal beatification, that of Francis de Sales, on 8 January 1662. The exceptional procedure for the recognition of a cult was defined by the Congregation of Rites (decree of 11 November 1912). The final outcome of this procedure was beatification or equipollent canonization. In view of the progress made in the methodology of historical criticism, PIUS XI created a historical section within the Congregation of Rites which was responsible for examining the written sources of causes (*motu proprio Già da qualche tempo*, 6 February 1930). In so doing, he made the apostolic procedure for "historical" causes superfluous (*Normae servandae in construendis processibus ordinariis super causis historicis*, 4 January 1939).

VATICAN II called for a revision of all ecclesiastical procedures, and causes of beatification and canonization were affected by this revision. The fathers of the council sought to stress the pastoral significance of canonization by proposing updated models of sainthood for the faithful—models more in keeping with contemporary sensibilities. The section relating to the Congregation of Rites was reformed by PAUL VI, with the introduction of a new method for examining and discussing causes (apostolic constitution *Regimini Ecclesiae universae*, 15 August 1967, n. 62). The preliminary phase, composed of the hearing before the diocesan courts, was updated by the same pope (*motu proprio Sanctitas clarior*, 19 March 1969). The revision provided that the bishops cooperate with the pope in the hearing of the causes. Under the new revision, there was one single hearing led by a bishop acting on his own authority and reinforced by the authority delegated by the Holy See. This replaced the previous order in which the cause was presented by a local ordinary acting on his own authority, or the apostolic case presented by virtue of the authority delegated by the Holy See. This change was the most significant innovation brought about by the revision. The *positio super introductione causae*, which was formerly drawn up by the postulator and submitted to a commission of theological consultants for study, also disappeared under the new revision.

A bishop who wished to promote a cause for beatification would submit a *supplex libellus* to the Apostolic See. The Holy See verified whether the cause had a sound basis and then gave its *nihil obstat*. On the basis of this, the bishop could then promulgate a decree introducing the cause and inform the Holy See of this. Once the cause was introduced, the candidate would receive the title "servant of God."

The case included an inquiry into the writings of the servant of God, into his or her life and virtues, or martyrdom, and into the absence of a cult. After the closure of the diocesan case, the records were sent to the Congregation of Rites, which, after examining them, could request complementary information or else proceed to make the additions it deemed necessary. A *super miro* case—an inquiry on miracles—was conducted separately, after the congregation granted this to the bishop.

With respect to courts for the hearing of causes, Paul VI introduced an innovation by ordaining that in order to a have better process for the hearing of cases, the conference of bishops, possibly at the suggestion of the assembly of bishops of a province or ecclesiastic region, might set up special courts recognized by the Holy See.

In place of the Congregation of Rites, Paul VI introduced two new dicasteries: one reponsible for the divine cult, and the other for the processing of causes (apostolic constitution *Sacra rituum congregatio*, 8 May 1969).

Current Procedures. The Code of Canon Law of 1983 limits itself to referring causes of canonization of servants of God to specific papal laws by virtue of which the provisions of universal law apply to these causes, or to norms which, by their nature, also refer to these causes (c. 1403). The specific papal law in question is the apostolic constitution *Divinus perfectionis Magister*, given by JOHN PAUL II on 25 January 1983, which abrogates the previous law on the question. To this is added the *Decretum generale de servorum Dei causis, quarum iudicium in praesens apud Sacram Congregationem pendet* (7 February 1983). The constitution is made up of three parts.

The first part describes the diocesan inquiry. The bishop, who now has the right to inquire into the candidate's life, virtues, or martyrdom, the presumed miracles, and the existence and duration of the cult, proceeds as follows:

a. An in-depth inquiry into the life of the servant of God is carried out by the postulator of the cause.
b. The candidate's published writings are examined by theologian censors.
c. If nothing is found in these writings contrary to faith and morals, the bishop orders an inquiry into the unpublished writings (letters, private journal, etc.), as well as all other documents related in any way to the cause. A report is drawn up.
d. If the bishop deems that the case may continue, he may arrange for testimony by witnesses produced by the postulator or those who have been called as a matter of course. If it is urgent that these witnesses be heard to avoid the loss of elements of proof, they will be questioned even before all the relevant documents have been gathered.

e. The inquiry into the presumed miracles takes place *separately* from that into the virtues or martyrdom of the candidate, but in strict observance of the prodigious quality of the events, so that no proof may be lost. If the bishop submits the records of this cause to the congregation before the completion of the study of the candidate's virtues, the cause concerning the presumed miracles is provisionally placed in the archives. However, it is possible to verify the formal validity of the cause on the miracle.

f. An authentic copy of all the records is sent, in duplicate, to the Sacred Congregation (now known simply as the Congregation, following the reform of the Roman Curia, John Paul II, apostolic constitution *Pastor bonus* 28 June 1988). Together with the records sent in duplicate to the congregation are copies of the writings of the servant of God, with the comments by the theologian censors who have examined them. The bishop adds a statement on the observance of the decrees of Urban VIII with respect to the absence of a cult.

The second part describes the objective and function of the Congregation for the Causes of Saints. It deals with all questions relating to canonization, helping the bishops in the hearing of the causes, carrying out exhaustive studies of them, and giving its opinions. It is also competent in matters relating to the authenticity and conservation of relics. The congregation consists of a college of reporters presided over by a reporter general. Each reporter must study, together with outside consultants, the causes for which he is responsible; he then prepares the dossiers (called *positiones*) on the virtues or martyrdom of the servant of God. He must draft the written notes requested by the consultants and participate without the right to vote in the meetings of the theologians. One of the reporters is specially charged with preparing the dossiers on the miracles; he attends meetings with the doctors and theologians. The reporter general, who chairs the meetings with the consultant historians, is helped by assistants. The congregation consists of a promoter of the faith or prelate theologian (formerly called the "Devil's advocate"), who presides over the meetings of theologians, gives his opinion, and presents a report of the meetings. He must also participate in the Congregation of Cardinals and Bishops as an expert. The Congregation for the Causes of Saints has consultants who are specialists in history and theology, especially spiritual theology, chosen from different regions of the world. For the examination of healings that have been deemed miraculous, there are medical experts.

The third section of the constitution describes the "procedure of the congregation. After ensuring that the diocesan case has been conducted according to the established norms, the cause is submitted to a reporter who, together with an outside consultant, prepares the dossier, the *positio*

super vita et virtutibus on the martyrdom according to the historical criticism observed in the hagiography. For old or recent causes where it may be required, the dossier is submitted to consultant specialists, possibly outside the group of consultants to the congregation. The dossier is submitted to the consultant theologians with the written votes of the consultant historians and, if necessary, clarifications by the reporter. The final votes of the consultant theologians are submitted with the written conclusions of the promoter of the faith to the cardinals and bishops who must make a judgment, formalized by a decree on the heroic nature of the virtues of the candidate, who thus becomes a venerable servant of God.

The presumed miracles are studied during a meeting of experts (the group of doctors, if the miracles are healings), and their votes and conclusions are included in the report. The proof of one miracle is sufficient to justify beatification, as opposed to two in the previous legislation (*Regolamento della congregazione per le Cause dei Santi*, 21 March 1983, no. 26, 1). The miracles are discussed in a plenary meeting of theologians and finally in the Congregation of Cardinals and Bishops. The outcome of this is a decree recognizing a miracle that may be attributed to the intercession of the servant of God. The names of all the consultants are secret to guarantee their independence. The congregation has created its own school for the training of postulators, delegated judges, and promoters of justice in the courts for the causes of saints (decree of 2 June 1984).

The decree of the congregation instituting the procedure of inquiry carried out by the bishops (*Normae servandae in inquisition; bus ab episcopis faciendi in causis sanctorum*, 7 February 1983) includes several stipulations. One is that, unless the congregation decides otherwise, the bishop competent for presenting the cause must be from the territory where the servant of God died. For a presumed miracle, the competent bishop is the bishop of the place where the event occurred. A cause is deemed recent if it can be proved by oral depositions by eyewitnesses. The petition, or articles of the postulator, may not be addressed to the bishop by the postulator for the opening of a cause unless at least five years have passed since the death of the servant of God. This effectively abolishes the time limit established by the Code of Canon Law of 1917 (c. 2101), which stipulated that fifty years must have passed between the death of the servant of God and the declaration of heroic virtue. A dispensation has often been applied to this rule (St. Frances Cabrini was beatified twenty-one years after her death; St. Theresa of the Child Jesus was beatified twenty years after death and canonized two and a half years after that). The petition must be accompanied by a serious biography or, failing this, a chronological account of the life and actions of the servant of God, his or her virtues or martyrdom, reputation for saintliness, or miracles, without omitting anything that may be contrary or unfavorable to the cause. There should be authentic copies of any writings published, and, for recent cases, a list of persons who may assist in establishing the authenticity of the virtues or martyrdom of the servant of God, as well as the reputation for saintliness and any miracles performed.

The bishop also publishes the position of the postulator in other dioceses to ask the faithful for useful information that they may have concerning the cause. When he introduces the cause, the bishop asks two theologian censors to state whether the published writings of the servant of God conform to faith and good morals. If they express a favorable opinion, he issues an edict to collect all unpublished writings and other useful historical documents. The experts state their opinion on the authenticity and value of the documents as well as on the personality of the servant of God as revealed by these documents. Following this, the bishop submits everything to a promoter of justice or to another expert to prepare the cross-examination. At the same time, he addresses a note to the Holy See on the life of the servant of God and the importance of the cause.

The bishop or his delegate hears the witnesses who have been summoned as a matter of course or produced by the postulator. In general, these must be eye-witnesses. A few of them need not be, but they must be reliable. First the family members or relatives by marriage are called, then friends and people with whom the servant of God has lived.

If the servant of God was a member of an institute of consecrated life, many of the witnesses must be people unconnected to that institute. Priests may not be witnesses on the basis of what they may have been told during confession. Habitual confessors and spiritual guides may not be witnesses because of confidential information they may have received outside confession; neither is the postulator allowed to be a witness. The experts who have researched documents are automatically called as witnesses. They must state under oath that they have researched and gathered all the available documentation and that they have nei-

ther falsified nor excluded information. For cases of miraculous healings, attending physicians are called as witnesses. Should they refuse to testify, they will be asked to submit a written account of the illness and its development, or at least of their medical opinion. No account will be taken of testimony that does not name its sources. Before closing the hearing, the bishop closely examines the tomb of the servant of God, the room he or she occupied or died in, and, if necessary, places where one may find signs of a cult in his or her honor. He then writes a report on the observance of the decrees issued by Urban VIII.

The authentic copy of the inquiry and its accompanying documents are sent to the Congregation for the Causes of Saints, with copies of the books of the servant of God studied by the theologian censors, together with their judgment. The bishop appends the letter regarding the credibility of the witnesses and the legitimacy of the acts.

For a presumed miracle, the bishop carries out an inquiry at the request of the postulator. This inquiry is accompanied by an account of the miracle and related documents. The witnesses are heard on the basis mentioned above. If the inquiry concerns a miraculous healing, a doctor is present at the hearing. Ceremonies or panegyrics in honor of the servant of God whose saintliness is being studied are forbidden in the church. It is not to be thought that an inquiry into the life of a servant of God automatically ensures his or her canonization. If a new miracle is acknowledged after the recognition of the one miracle necessary for beatification, the blessed person is automatically canonized, according to the procedure described above.

Statistics. The first known canonization after the creation of the Congregation of Rites took place during the papacy of CLEMENT VIII (1592–1605), who honored Hyacinthe Odrowaz on 17 April 1594. This was followed by the canonization of Raymond of Peñafort (29 April 1601). The following tables show the number of beatifications and canonizations in subsequent centuries and under individual popes of the 20th century.

	17th century	18th century	19th century
beatification	75	39	65
canonization	25	29	80
confirmation of cult	33	894	397

	Pius X (1903–14)	Benedict XV (1914–22)	Pius XI (1922–39)	Pius XII (1939–58)
beatification	72	41	533	170
canonization	4	3	34	33
confirmation of cult	45	73	18	0

	John XXIII (1958–63)	Paul VI (1963–78)	John Paul II (1978–91)	Total, 1588–1991
beatification	5	61	503	1,564
canonization	10	84	271	573
confirmation of cult	1	7	2	1,470

Dominique Le Tourneau

Bibliography

Alfonso, M. *La prova in genere e la fama di santità in specie nei processi dei santi prima e dopo il M. P. "Sanctitas clarior,"* Agnesotti, 1977; "Origine divina della fama di santità e suo valore giuridico ecclesiale sociale, *Monitor Ecclesiasticus*, 104 (1989), 474–90.

Benedict XIV, *Opus de servorum Dei beatificatione et beatonum canonizatione*, Prati, 1839–42 (1st ed., Bologna, 1734–8).

Blaher, J. D. *The Ordinary Processes in Causes of Beatification and Canonization*, Washington, 1949, 1090–6.

Cabreros, M. "El proceso juridico de beatificación y canonización," *Illustración del clero*, 45 (1952), 155–63, 263–43.

Congregazione per le Cause dei Santi, Miscellanea in Occasione del IV Centenario della Congregazione per le Cause dei Santi (1588–1988), Vatican City, 1988.

Casieri, A. *Postulatorum Vademecum*, Rome, 2nd ed., 1986.

Congregation for the Causes of Saints, *Index ac status causarum (Editio particularis cura Petri Galavotti)*, Vatican City, 1988; *II Supplementum* (1989–1990), Vatican City, 1991.

Congregation for the Causes of Saints, *Normae servandae in inquistionibus ab episcopis faciendis*, 7 Feb. 1983; *Decretum generale de servorum Dei causis, quarum indicium in praesens apud Sacram Congregationem pendet*, 7 Feb. 1983.

Crnica, A. "De canonizatione aequipollenti," *Monitor Ecclesiasticus*, 86 (1961), 258–80.

de Clercq, C. "Les causes de serviteurs de Dieu," *RDC*, IV, (1954), 76–100.

Delooz, P. *Sociologie et canonisations*, Liège, 1969.

Eszer, A. "La congregazione delle Cause dei Santi, il nuovo ordinamento della procedura," In *La Curia Romana nella cost. Ap. Pastor Bonus* (ed. by P. A. Bonet and C. Gullo), Vatican City, 1990, 309–29.

Garceau, C. *Le Role du postulateur dans les procès ordinaires de béatification*, Paris, 1954.

Gutiérrez, J. L. "La certezza morale nelle cause di canonizzazione, specialmente nella dichiarizione del martirio," *Ius Ecclesiae*, 3 (1991), 645–70.

Hertling, L. "Materiali per la storia del processo di canonizzazione," *Gregorianum*, 16 (1935), 170–95.

Indelicato, S. *Le basi giuridiche del processo de beatificazione*, Rome, 1944; *Il processo apostolico di beatificazione*, Rome, 1945.

John Paul II, apostolic constitution *Divinus perfectionis Magister*, 25 Jan. 1983.

Kemp, E. W. *Canonization and Authority in the Western Church*, Oxford, 1948.

Kuttner, S. "La reserve papale du droit de canonisation," *Revue historique de droit français et étranger*, 4th ser., XVII, 1938, 172–228.

Lauri, A., and Fornari, G. Santarelli, A. M. *Codex pro postulatoribus*, Rome, 5th ed., 1940.

Löw, G. "Beatificazione," EC, II, 1096–1100, "Canonizzaione," EC, III, 1949, 571–607.

Machejek, M., and Padacz, W. *Sprawy beatyfikacyjne na terenie diecezji*, Poznan, 1957.

Misztal, H. *Cenzuea uprzednia pism i drukow w Kosciele, studium historycznoprawne*, Lublin, 1968; "De revisione scriptorum quae servi Dei publice ediderunt, in nova procedura canonizationis," *Monitor Ecclesiasticus*, 112 (1987), 239–52.

Mittri, A. *De figura iuridica postulatoris in causis beatificationis et canonizationis*, Rome, 1982.

Molinari, P. *I santi e il loro culto*, Rome, 1962; "Observationes circa miraculorum munus in causis beatificationis et canonizationis," *Periodica de re morali, canonica, liturgica*, 63 (1974), 341–84.

Naz, R. "Causes de beatification et de canonisation," *DDC*, 3, 1942, 10–37.

Paul V, *motu proprio Sanctitas clarior*, 19 March 1969.

Piacentini, E. "Concetto teologico-giuridico di martirio nelle cause di beatificazione e canonizzazione," *Monitor Ecclesiasticus* 103 (1978), 184–247; *Il martirio nelle Cause dei Santi*, Vatican City, 1979.

Porsi, L. "Cause di canonizzazione e procedura nella Cost. Ap. *Divinus perfectionis Magister:* considerazioni e valutazioni," *Monitor Ecclesiasticus*, 110 (1985), 365–400; "Collectio Legum Ecclesiae de beatificatione et canonizatione a saeculo decimo usque ad praesens" (1985) 550–9; 111 (1986), 225–39, 345–66, 521–44; 113 (1988), 405–43.

Regolamento della congregazione per le Cause dei Santi, 21 Mar. 1983.

Rodrigo, R. *Manuale per l'istruzione dei processi di canonizzazione*, Rome, 1991.

Santarelli, A. M. *Codex pro postulatoribus causarum beatificationis et canonizationis*, Rome, 1929.

Sarno, P. J. *Diocesan Inquiries Required by the Legislator in the New Legislation for Causes of Saints*, Rome, 1988.

Schulz, W. *Das neue Selif- und Heiligsprechungsverfahren*, Paderborn, 1988.

Sefourne, P. "Saints, culte des," *DTC*, XIV, 1939, 870–978.

Spedalieri, R. *De Ecclesiae infallibilitate in canonizatione sanctorum quaestiones selectae*, Rome, 1949.

Torresani, A. "Santi fondatore calunniati," *Studi Cattolici*, 373/374 (1992), 229–33.

Veraja, F. "La canonizzazione equipollente e la questione di miracoli nelle cause di canonizzazione," *Apollinaris*, XLVIII (1975), 222–45, 475–500; *La beatificazione: Storia, problemi, prospettive*, Rome, 1983; *Commento alla nuova legislazione per le Cause dei santi: Sussidi per lo studio delle Cause di santi*, Rome, 1983.

CELESTINE I. *(d. Rome, 28 July 432). Consecrated pope on 10 September 432. Buried at St. Sylvester on the Via Salaria.*

Celestine is believed to have come from Campania; according to the *Liber pontificalis*, he was the son of a certain Priscus. He was deacon of the Roman Church under Pope ZOSIMUS (417–18), and he was known to have written a letter in the summer of 418 to Augustine of Hippo, who assured him of his regard. Celestine appears to have been elected unanimously to succeed Pope BONIFACE I, (418–22) although the *Liber pontificalis* states that the supporters of EULALIUS, who had been ousted in favor of Boniface in 419, sought to regain their advantage.

Celestine strove to continue the task of restoring papal authority, begun by his predecessor. From 425 on, he received the support of Galla Placidia and Valentinian III, who were concerned with consolidating their own power in the West, where they reestablished the privileges of the Church. In August 425, they issued an order to the prefect to prosecute all heretics who refused to communicate with the pope, and to exile them one hundred miles beyond the city.

In Italy, Celestine took action against the heretics. In Rome itself, he ordered that the churches of Novatians, who were actively spreading opposition, be taken away from them. He also rejected a request for an audience by Celestius, a disciple of Pelagius, who had been excommunicated by previous popes and banned from Rome. Celestine succeeded in expelling the heretics from Italy, but apparently without being able to put a complete stop to the spread of Pelagian ideas. He also sought to ensure respect for canonical legislation in Italy. In July 429, he severely reprimanded the bishops of Apulia and Calabria, who had ordained laypeople into the clergy, and threatened serious repercussions if they should do so again. He requested that they publish widely the pontifical letter prohibiting such practices (JK, 371).

With respect to the Churches of Gaul and Africa, Celestine carried out a policy of intervention, with mixed results. Shortly after acceding to the papacy, Celestine was informed of the case of Bishop Antoninus of Fussala (in Numidia). Antoninus had been appointed during the term of Celestine's predecessor. The pope received a letter from Augustine asking that he reject the appeal addressed to Boniface by the bishop, who had been rightly condemned for arbitrariness. It does not seem that Celestine acted on Antoninus's complaint.

However, he gave favorable consideration to the African priest Apiarius and received him in Rome. Apiarus had been excommunicated for a second time and had come to complain to the pope, ignoring the ban issued by the council of CARTHAGE in 419 against making appeals abroad. Celestine intervened in a rather clumsy manner. He sent Apiarius back to Africa accompanied by Faustinus of Potentia, the papal legate charged with following

the affair. During a previous visit to Carthage in connection with the Apiarus affair, Faustinus had alienated the Africans by his brusque attitude. It was probably in the year 425 that Apiarius appeared at the council, and Faustinus turned the African bishops against him. Apiarius admitted that he was guilty of the crimes of which he was accused, thus putting an end to the intervention by the pope. Faustinus returned to Italy carrying a letter from the council to Celestine, deploring the attitude of his legate, protesting against the interventionist policy of Rome, and notifying the pope that the council of Carthage held jurisdiction for the appeal.

In Gaul, Celestine's intervention met with success. Following the assassination of Patroclus of Arles in 426, Celestine used the death as a pretext to reduce the importance of Arles. Shortly before 429, the pope intervened for the first time, unsuccessfully. He tried to ensure that the monk Daniel be judged. He had come to Gaul from the East with serious charges pending against him. On 25 July 429, Celestine expounded on pontifical authority in a letter on more general issues addressed to the bishops of Vienne and Narbonne. In it, he solemnly reminded them of the need for ecclesiastical discipline. He attacked Hilary of Arles and the Ascetic movement of which he was the center. He denounced the extreme rigor and ostentatious piety of the Ascetics. He stressed the negligence shown in Arles over the Daniel affair and demanded that judgment be immediately passed on this monk, who had easily attained to the episcopate, as well as on Proculus of Marseille, a bishop who had been in schism since the time of Pope Zosimus, and had cordially received the murderer of Patroche of Arles. Celestine, in his letter, stressed the need to observe the ecclesiastical *cursus* and prohibited metropolitans from intervening in neighboring provinces. No particular role was recognized by the pope for Arles (JK, 368)

Celestine also took a position in a controversy that shook the south of Gaul. He favored the requests of the monks Hilary and Prosper, opponents of the Pelagians, who had come to denounce Gallic priests accused of preaching the heretical doctrine on predestination and grace, and of attacking the memory of Augustine. After August 430 the pope, taking a stance in favor of ecclesiastical discipline, addressed a letter to Venerius of Marseilles and a group of Gallic bishops under his jurisdiction. He upbraided them for having failed to maintain their authority over their clergy. He praised Augustine, who had always been in communion with Rome. Celestine justified his intervention by claiming that the pernicious doctrines had affected the entire Church. However, he did not define the true faith. The theological dossier attached to the letter was written subsequent to the pontificate of Celestine. It has been attributed to the future Pope LEO I, although the author may have been Prosper himself. At the suggestion of the deacon Palladius, Celestine decided to send a mission to Brittany to fight the Pelagians who were spreading their ideas there. Bishop Germanus of Auxerre was apparently entrusted with this mission. In 431, Celestine ordained Palladius bishop of the Scots.

In the East, the pope was asked to intervene in a dispute between Nestorius, bishop of Constantinople since April 428, and Bishop Cyril of Alexandria. It was a christological controversy, but at the same time a power struggle between the two major seats of the East. Rome took the side of Alexandria in this quarrel and unknowingly supported the ambitions and theology of Cyril.

Celestine was on his guard against Nestorius, who had received in Constantinople the Pelagians condemned in the West. Nestorius had twice requested from the pope further information on the Pelagians. Celestine was also unhappy with Nestorius's theological stance. By rejecting the title Theotokos (mother of God) attributed to Mary, Nestorius might lead people to think that he was denying the divinity of Christ. Complaints coming, undoubtedly, from Constantinople and various writings of Nestorius that caused a scandal in Rome convinced Pope Celestine to back the bishop of Alexandria. The bishop had sent him a whole dossier on the affair after June 430, accompanied by a letter from Cyril denouncing Nestorius and presenting himself as the spokesman for an orthodoxy in peril. He called on the pope to intervene. A summary of the doctrine of Nestorius, whom he accused of considering Christ an ordinary mortal man, was enclosed to support the claim. Nestorius's doctrine was also examined by a monk from Marseilles, Cassian, at the insistence of Deacon Leo, the future Pope Leo I. Cassian did not bother to take account of nuances but accused the bishop of Constantinople outright of regarding Christ as an ordinary man, of teaching a doctrine of two Sons, and of having dealings with the Pelagians.

During a council meeting in Rome on 10 August 430, Celestine uttered a condemnation. It was probably on the basis of these two dossiers that he condemned Nestorius and ordered him to retract his errors in the ten days following the notification of the sentence (JK, 374). Furthermore, he sent notification of the condemnation to the major Churches of the East and of Illyria (JK, 373, 375). Cyril of Alexandria was commanded by the pope to ensure that Nestorius subscribe publicly to the faith professed by Rome, Alexandria, and the Universal Church (JK, 372). Celestine was more concerned with pastoral questions than with theology; indeed, his Eastern bishops often referred to his *simplicitas* in matters of theology. Celestine's order to Nestorius was not accompanied by any doctrinal definitions. Cyril made use of the time lag to send to Constantinople a letter containing a profession of faith in twelve articles (the anathemas). These reflected his own Christology, to which he wanted Nestorius to subscribe. The pope was not informed of this profession of faith; its distribution, particularly in the Eastern diocese, only served to further fan the flames of controversy.

The proceedings begun by Rome against the bishop of Constantinople were unsuccessful. On 30 November 430, the ultimatums issued by Rome and Alexandria were rejected by Nestorius, who, strengthened by support from Emperor Theodosius II, managed to secure the convening of an ecumenical council at Ephesus for June 431, in order to restore unity to the Church. However, Nestorius assured the pope of his orthodoxy and sent him a letter (no doubt in the winter of 430) in which he renounced the term Theotokos and said that Cyril would be denounced before the council.

Faced with this new situation, Celestine adopted a more provident attitude, though without giving in on the substantive issues. He accepted the imperial convocation and sent three legates to the council: the Italian bishops Arcadius and Proiectus, and the Roman priest Philip of the *titulus Apostolorum*. The legates had instructions (dated 8 May 431) to ensure that the condemnation of Nestorius not be questioned by the council and that they adopt the position of Cyril of Alexandria in all matters (JK, 378); they also bore a letter for Theodosius II (JK, 380) for the future council (JK, 379), as well as for Cyril himself (JK, 377). In this letter, Celestine reponded to Cyril's question as to whether Nestorius should be admitted to the council and advised that he not be excluded. The council of Ephesus showed the extent to which Rome had become eclipsed by the Church of Alexandria. Cyril ignored the absence of the papal legates and, despite opposition from a number of bishops present, convened a council meeting on 22 June 431. There he presented himself as the emissary of the pope and secured approval of his Christology and the deposing of Nestorius. When the legates finally arrived at Ephesus on 10 July, they sat among the ranks of the Cyrillians and gave their approval to the deposing of Nestorius and the backing of Cyril's cause during the council, against Bishop John of Antioch. The latter protested against the anathemas of the Church of Alexandria and the deposing of Nestorius, of which Rome was unaware. Two of the legates, Philip and Arcadius, together with the leaders of the Cyrillians, took part in the conflicting conferences convened by Theodosius II in Chalcedon from September 431. After obtaining victory for the Cyrillians, they participated, on 25 October 431, in the appointment of a new bishop of Constantinople, Maximian, an ally of Cyril. They also had a part in the ultimate deposing of the hard-liners.

The sovereign pontiff was informed only after 17 July 431 that the council had split into two rival assemblies, and he received the news of Maximian's election only on 25 December 431. He does not appear to have expressed any reservation on the way the council was conducted. On 15 March 432, he addressed letters of congratulation to Theodosius II, to Maximian, and to the clergy and faithful of the imperial capital (JK, 38–388), to Bishop

Flavian of Philippi, and finally to the council of Ephesus (JK, 385). He demanded that Nestorius be exiled somewhere even farther than Antioch and that John of Antioch be excommunicated by the Cyrillians and not readmitted to the Church until he had submitted a written profession of faith. This demand met with no success. Despite the injunction of Theodosius II calling on John of Antioch to reconcile with Cyril and the pope, the head of the Eastern bishops refused to compromise.

Celestine restored the liturgical equipment of the churches, of St. Peter's, St. Paul's, St. Mary's of Trastevere, and the *titulus Iulii*. The *Liber pontificalis* attributes to him the introduction of the *ante sacrificium* psalmodies.

In the West, Pope Celestine was successful in affirming, if not always ensuring, that the Apostolic See prevailed over local churches. In the East, the miscalculated the influences and the issues at stake. He lost ground to the Church of Alexandria, and in the Nestorian controversy he was unable to play the role of arbiter between the two rival sees.

Celestine was more preoccupied with the danger of the spread of Pelagianism than with the Nestorian controversy. By failing in 431 to speak out in the definition of the faith, he unwittingly gave his support to the Christology and particularly to the anathemas espoused by Cyril of Alexandria. This paved the way for the Christological controversies of the 6th century.

Christiane Fraisse-Coué

Bibliography

ACO, I, 1, 7, 142–3.

ACO, I, 2, 5–12, 15–26, 98–101.

LP, I, 230–1.

PL, 50, 430–7, 528–30.

Amann, E. "L'Affaire Nestorius vue de Rome," *Revue des sciences religieuses*, 23 (1949), 5–37, 207–44; 24 (1950), 28–52, 235–65.

Bardy, G. *DHGE*, 12, 56–8.

Batiffol, P. *Le Siège aspostolique*, Paris, 1925.

Caelestinus, *Epistulae* 4–5, 21.

Collectio Veronensis, I, 5–10, 23–6.

Epistula Collectio Atheniensis 98.

Epistulae 11–14, 16–19.

Gaspar, E. *Geschichte des Papsttums*, I, Tübingen, 1930, 384–416.

Pietri, C. *Roma christiana*, Rome, 1976, 224, 1026–43, 1272–5, 1347–93.

Sermo, PL, 50, 458.

CELESTINE (II). *Theobaldus Buccapeccus (d. after 1124). Elected pope on 15–16 December 1124, forced to resign 16 December 1124.*

In the upheaval that followed the death of CALLISTUS II (13 December 1124), most of the cardinals wished to elect the cardinal-priest Saxo of Santo Stefano as a compromise candidate between the old Gregorians and the innovators led by chancellor Cardinal Aimeric. The candidature was not approved. On 16 December at St. Pancras near the Lateran, at the proposal of the cardinal-deacon Jonathas of Sts. Cosmàs and Damian, the cardinal-priest Theobaldus Buccapeccus (or Boccapecora) of Sant' Anastasia was unanimously elected, named Celestine II, and given the red papal cape. He was of advanced age, and in the college of cardinals he belonged to the oldest group, supported by the Pierleoni. During the *Te Deum*, Roberto Frangipane and his partisans burst into the church, swords unsheathed. They had previously come to an agreement with Cardinal Aimeric, who, after having voted with everyone else, was now taking part in the singing. The ceremony stopped abruptly. The newly elected pope was violently handled. Once outside, the perpetrators proclaimed the cardinal-bishop Lambert of Ostia the new pope, with the name HONORIUS II. Celestine had not yet received the episcopal consecration and had not been officially enthroned. The next day, the gravely injured Celestine II declared whether of his own will or not, that he would step down, while his supporters argued among themselves. After intensive negotiations in which money and promises played a significant role, Honorius II was unanimously elected and enthroned on 21 December 1124.

Theobald came from a Roman family, the Boccapecconi, and had been appointed cardinal-deacon of Santa Maria Nuova around 1103, by PASCAL II. In 1123, Callistus II named him cardinal-priest Sant' Anastasia. The election of Celestine was canonical, so it is a mistake to associate him with the antipopes. After the election of 1124, there is no further record of him. Wounded and tried by these events, he probably died soon afterward.

George Schwaiger

Bibliography

LP, 327 ff., 379; III, 136 ff., 170 ff.

Hüls, R. *Kardinäle, Klerus, und Kirchen Roms 1049–1130*, Tübingen, 1977, 149, 235 ff., *DHGE, XII*, 58 ff.

March, J. P. *Liber pontificalis completus ex codice Dertuensi*, Barcelona, 1925, 204 ff.; JL, 1, 822, 824.

CELESTINE II. *Guido di Città de Castello (b. Umbria, d. Rome, 8 March 1144). Elected pope on 26 September 1143, consecrated October 3. Buried in Rome in the Lateran cemetery.*

This pope took his pontifical name in remembrance of CELESTINE I, considered a model and exalted in legends and by canonical tradition. Celestine II was a student and friend of Peter Abelard (Bernard of Clairvaux, in letter 192, warned him not to follow his master into error). He acquired a reputation for great theological erudition and bore the title of *magister*.

Guido was at first canon of the cathedral chapter of Città di Castello, then was promoted by HONORIUS II to be cardinal-deacon of Santa Maria in the Via Lata. He was related to Cardinal Aimeric. At the time of the double election of 1130, he was one of a group of cardinals, generally younger and favorable to change, who sided with INNOCENT II against ANACLETUS II. He journeyed with Innocent II to France and, in October 1131, took part in the council at Reims. At the end of 1131 and in 1132, he was sent as a papal legate to Germany, where he met Emperor Lothar III at Cologne, to negotiate the first part of his journey to Italy. Guido also attended the royal assembly at Aix-la-Chapelle. From 1132, he was an almost constant member of the entourage of Innocent II. In December 1133, he was elevated to the post of cardinal-priest of the titular church of San Marco.

In 1137, Guido participated with Cardinal Gerard of Santa Croce and with Cardinal Aimeri in a delegation to Emperor Lothar III, to demand the direct submission of Montecassino to the Roman Church. That abbey was required to cease its support of the antipope of Anacletus. That same year, together with Gerard, Aimeric, and Bernard of Clairvaux, Guido took part in Salerno in negotiations with Roger II of Sicily, protector of Anacleus, in an attempt to lessen the schism. Roger listened for four days to the viewpoints of Anacletus's supporters but made no decision. It had been arranged that Guido should represent the interests of Innocent II at a synod which had been planned for Christmas 1137, at Palermo, but it never took place. Instead he went as a papal legate to Lombardy and France. He supported Empress Matilda when, probably in the same year, she asked Innocent II to recognize her right to the English throne and to deny the right of Stephen of Blois. However, the pope deferred his decision. No doubt the empress played a part in the election of Guido to succeed Innocent II. As proof of this, Guido as Pope Celestine II would subsequently prohibit Theobald of Canterbury from making any modification whatever to the succession to the throne of England, thus effectively preventing Stephen Blois from having his son crowned king.

Innocent II had proposed five candidates, including Guido, for election as his successor. The situation in Rome in 1143 was particularly explosive owing to the threats of the Roman Commune against the Curia. Guido was chosen because of his extensive political experience and because it was believed that he would stand up to the rebels. Furthermore, to limit the ambitions of Roger II, it was necessary to take firm action with Sicily. Celestine II refused to ratify the treaty of Mignago, concluded by his predecessor with the Norman king, and in so doing refused to recognized his right to the throne. When Roger's troops plundered the papal possessions of Benevento, Ce-

lestine II sent two parliamentarians to Palermo at Christmas of 1143–4. Negotiations with Roger II were not concluded by the time of the pope's death. In France, Celestine II removed the INTERDICT placed by Innocent II following the contested election at the archiepiscopal seat of Bourges, after King Louis VII had submitted to the demands of the Church. In December 1143, the pope appointed nine cardinals, an unusually high number for the 12th century, which obviously changed the whole face of the Sacred College. Abelard's student, Hyacinthus Bobone—the future Pope CELESTINE III—was one of the new cardinals. Little is known of the intellectual stance of the others.

During his pontificate, Celestine II never left Rome. It has often been thought that, granted the time, he would have tenaciously pursued ecclesiastical reform; however, there is no trace of a single new initiative taken during the five years of his brief reign. The majority of his decisions were simply confirmations of privileges. For his contemporaries, Celestine II embodied the harmony of a noble heritage. They praised both his piety and his erudition. His correspondence with Peter the Venerable, abbot of Cluny, Bernard of Clairvaux, and Gerhoh Reichersberg bears testimony to his areas of intellectual interest. Gerhoh of Reichersberg dedicated to him the *Libellus de ordine donorum Sancti Spiritus*. In his will, the pope bequeathed fifty-six books to the cathedral of the Città di Castello.

Karl Schnith

Bibliography

JL, 2, 1–7.

LP, 2, 385.

PL, 179, 761–820.

Girgensohn, D. "Celestino II," *DBI*, 23 (1979), 388–92.

Maleczek, W. "Das Kardinalskollegium unter Innocenz II. und Anaklet II.," *AHP*, 19 (1981), 27–78; "Coelestin II," *LexMA*, 3 (1984–6), 4.

Mols, R. "Célestin II," *DHGE*, 12 (1953), 59–62.

Watterich, 2, 276–7.

Wilmart, A. "Les livres légués par Célestin II a Città di Castello," *RB*, 35 (1923), 98–102.

Zenker, B. *Die Mitglieder des Kardenalcollegiums von 1130 bis 1159*, Diss., Wurzburg, 1964.

CELESTINE III. *Giacinto/Hyacinthus Bobone (b. Rome, ca. 1105–6, d. Rome, 8 January 1198). Elected pope March or April 1191, consecrated 13–14 April. Buried at St. John Lateran.*

Hyacinthus was the son of Pietro Bobone, a member of an influential family of the Roman NOBILITY from the Arenula district. He was elected pope in the period between 20 March and 11 April 1191, but most probably on 21 March, according to numerous sources. When he was elected, the new pope was only a DEACON, so he had to be ordained a priest, probably on 20 March; his consecration took place very late, on Easter Sunday, 14 April. At that time, Henry VI was near Rome, where he expected to be crowned emperor. One is therefore tempted to link the political significance of this ceremony with the late date of the consecration, since the pope had to be consecrated before crowning the emperor. If that was the case, this move revealed the political skill of the pontiff, who was then almost ninety years old. He also had a great ability to use legal arguments to serve political considerations, born of his long experience as a papal legate. He had embarked on an ecclesiastical career early in life, and by 1126 he had been appointed *prior subdiaconorum sacrae basilicae* at St. John Lateran, and then, in 1138, *prior subdiaconorum sacri palatii*. At the end of the 1130s, he studied dialectics and theology under Peter Abelard in Paris. In 1140, at the council of Sens, he and his fellow student Arnold of Brescia defended Abelard against the attacks of Bernard of Clairvaux.

Bobone did not suffer for having defended Abelard's teaching, since he had links within important circles of the CURIA from which CELESTINE II came. His predecessor promoted him to cardinal-deacon of Santa Maria in Cosmedin in 1144. He held this title for almost forty-seven years, without ascending to the priesthood.

It may be noted that Hyacinthus belonged to a family which, like the Frangipani and Pierleoni, sought to set up a sort of dynasty within the SACRED COLLEGE—a dynasty that went by the name of Bobo (or Bobone). Cardinal Bobone of Sant'Angelo (later of Sant'Anastasia and di Porto, Cardinal 1182–9) and Cardinal Bobone of San Giorgio were members of this family, as was Gregory of Sant'Angelo (Cardinal 1190–1202), a nephew of Hyacinthus who, like his uncle, became a legate in the Iberian Peninsula. Celestine III himself made one of his Bobone nephews cardinal-deacon of San Teodoro (1193–9), which later caused him to be accused, rightly, of nepotism. The Curia soon recognized the diplomatic skills of Cardinal Hyacinthus Bobone and entrusted him with difficult legations in the Iberian Peninsula in the years 1154/5 and 1172/4. During these missions, which took him to Aragon-Catalonia, Castille-León, and Portugal, he attended the provincial councils of Valladolid and Lerida, as well as that of Narbonne (1155), on his way back to Rome.

Bobone had a decisive influence on the reorganization of the Church of Spain. He conducted delicate negotiations on the primateship of the see of Toledo and the metropolitan organization of the rival ecclesiastic provinces of Braga and St. James of Compostela. Thus, he became an invaluable specialist on the ecclesiastical and political situation of the peninsula. His thorough knowledge would also become evident during his reign as pontiff. He was a powerful supporter of the CRUSADE, strengthening the trend toward unification in Spain against the centers

of Moorish power. His actions seemed to spring from a personal commitment: not only did he personally head the whole undertaking, he also bore the cross. His success in Spain served to increase his political skills, so that people appealed to him to intervene in other problems. Thus, he was gradually made the intermediary between the pontifical Curia, the German emperor, and the king of France. After the Besançon affair in June 1158, the cardinal legate in Augsburg maintained a conciliatory attitude toward the imperial side, despite temporary imprisonment. Subsequently, though, Bobone adopted a harder stance; in 1162, together with Cardinal Bernard di Porto, he arranged a meeting between the king of France and Pope ALEXANDER III at Souvigny. Negotiations with the emperor remained at a stalemate.

His participation in these missions, which after the truce of Venice were intended to restore normalcy in central Italy, evidences the role he played in important decisions. It also reveals his thorough knowledge of political matters and the questions at stake in negotiations between the Curia and the emperor. As a cardinal, he had a vast network of friends. These relationships had been formed on legations which, apart from Spain and the empire, had taken him to France (1162 and 1165), to Genoa (1165), and to northern Italy (1177, 1181, 1187). Furthermore, he was the oldest member of the Sacred College and head of the Roman faction within the college. In the delicate situation in the spring of 1191, he seemed the ideal choice to ascend the pontifical throne in order to avoid the risk of a schism.

The particular circumstances of the crowning of the pontiff prove that, following the death of the pope, convinced of the political supremacy of the Church and imbued with the idea of *plenitudo potestatis* with its innate right to depose the emperor, was particularly concerned with relations with the empire. He feared the foreseeable encircling of the Patrimony of St. Peter, which indeed became a reality in 1194, when Henry VI accumulated power in his own hands over the empire and the kingdom of Sicily. If historical sources are to be believed, Celestine III made his prerogatives known to the emperor as soon as he was crowned. He insisted particularly on the ceremony of investiture, though without seeking to submit the empire to the papacy, as has sometimes been claimed. After crowning Henry VI, he induced him to drive out the inhabitants of Tusculum, hated rivals of the Romans. During his papacy, he obtained restoration of the PATRIMONY OF ST. PETER and financial benefits. Celestine III also won several cases of litigation, in particular the restoration of the rights of Duke Henry the Lion. But his most important victory came with the Sicilian question. With the concordat of Gravina, reached in June 1192, the pope finally recognized Tancred of Lecce, to whom he had gradually become closer, as king of Sicily in exchange for a fee of homage.

This concordat assured, for the time being, the suzerainty of the Church over lower Italy and Sicily. Henry VI had always refused the suzerainty of the Church over this region because he claimed feudally independent possessions by virtue of an *antiquum jus* of the empire. Celestine III also considerably improved the conditions of the treaty of Benevento (June 1156) by extending the rights of the Church. But Tancred's sudden death on 20 February 1194 put an end to this string of successes. Imperial troops occupied the Norman kingdom, encountering little or no resistance. Apart from this, Henry VI had a male heir to the throne. The Curia could henceforth expect the long-term presence of the Hohenstaufens in the south of Italy. It also feared that, in the long run, it would lose suzerainty over Sicily and the right to direct the Church there. Nor was the papacy in a favorable position with respect to other countries in Christendom, whose leaders had participated in the Third Crusade. The king of England was seeking to impose his own interests by force in Normandy and in Flanders, to the detriment of the French king's security.

Philip Augustus, for his part, was illegally annexing the continental possessions of Richard the Lionhearted. Despite imposing severe ecclesiastical sanctions—even an INTERDICT—Celestine III did not manage to break the alliance between the Hohenstaufens and the Capetians before 1192. Adding to the anxiety of the Curia were the murder of the bishop of Liège, Albert de Brabant, attributed to supporters of Henry VI; the ensuing establishment of a nobility in opposition in the lower Rhine region; and the role played by the Hohenstaufens in the imprisonment of the king of England by Leopold of Austria. By recognizing the suzerainty of Henry VI over his kingdom, Richard the Lionhearted had strengthened the emperor's position, despite opposition from the GUELPHS, all the more since Philip Augustus was embarrassed by the matter of his divorce.

The rapprochement between the opponents of Henry VI and the Palatinate did not weaken the emperor's position. He was able to undertake the task of transforming an elective empire into a hereditary monarchy. However, he did not manage to gain the consent of Celestine III, even though the latter had indicated his readiness to lead a second crusade and to pursue negotiations on the occupation of central Italy, a stance that demonstrated his political acuity. The pope saw clearly that the regime would seriously hamper his freedom to choose an emperor.

The mysterious "great offer" made by Henry VI to the Curia—he may have promised long-term financial security if the Curia renounced its claim on the state of the Church and the inheritance of Mathilde of Canossa—could not convince the pope to give ground on the main questions. It was only the unexpected death of the emperor (28 September 1197) that defused the situation and allowed the pope to regain much of the ground he had lost.

With respect to the internal life of the Church, Celestine III from the beginning encouraged a structural reform aimed at strengthening and radically centralizing the administration of the Curia. The *Liber censuum*, written between 1192 and 1195, testifies to the efforts made in fiscal and financial administration. At a time when the question of property and rights was leading to great conflict with the Emperor, the Curia, with an eye to the future, was making legal claims and seeking to obtain the taxes and quotas due to it. At the same time, its central administrative services were gaining importance. There was a marked trend toward strengthening the legal machinery of the Curia, manifested in the legislation on DECRETALS. This tendency would come to full flower during the papacy of INNOCENT III. In parallel with these new developments, the pope transformed the Sacred College into the personal instrument of his policy of increased centralization. This he did by appointing new cardinals loyal to him. The changes he introduced were made despite—or perhaps because of—the many sources of opposition. At the end of 1197—shortly after the death of Henry VI, whose actions had threatened to lead the empire into chaos, and had rendered the pope's fears groundless—Celestine III stated his intention of abdicating in favor of his favorite cardinal, Giovanni of Santa Prisca. This shows how obsessed he had become with his rivalry with the empire. However, he did not succeed in his aim. The opposition within the Sacred College frustrated his plan and, on the very day of the pope's death, managed to secure the election of Lothar of Segni as his successor, Innocent III.

Ludwig Vones

Bibliography

JL, 577–644, 727, 771–2.

LP, 2 451.

PL, 206, 864–1304.

"Analekten zur Geschichte Papst Coelestins III.," *Historisches Jahrbuch*, 109 (1989), 191–205.

Baaken, K. "Zur Wahl, Weihe und Krönung Papst Coelestins III," *Deutsches Archiv*, 41 (1985), 203–11.

"Der Vorgänger: Das Wirken Coelestins III., aus der sicht von Innocenz II.," *ZRGKA*, 60 (1974), 121–67.

"Die Innere Verwaltung der Kirche unter Papst Coelestin III.," *Archiv für Diplomatik*, 18 (1972), 343–98.

Friedberg, E. *Quinque compilationes antiquae* (1882), 66, 104.

Laurent, V. "Rome et Byzance sous le Pontificat de Célestin III," *Echos d'Orient*, 39 (1940), 26–58.

Leineweber, J. *Studien zur Geschichte Cölestins II.*, diss., Jena, 1905.

Malekzek, W. *Papst und Kardinalskolleg von 1191 bis 1216: Die Kardinäle unter Coelestins III. und Innocenz III.*, Rome and Vienna, 1984.

Molls, R. "Célestin III," *DHGE*, 12 (1953), 62–77.

Pfaff, V. "Célestin III," *LexMa*, 3 (1948–6), 4–7 (with bibliography).

Pfaff, V. "Feststellungen zu den den Urkunden und dem Itinerar Papst Coelestins III.," *Historisches Jahrbuch*, 78 (1959), 110–39.

Pflugk-Harttung, J. *Acta pontificum Romanorum*, 1, 352–83, 2, 396–402.

Reisinger, C. *Tankred von Lecce*, Cologne-Weimar-Vienna, 1992, 246 ff.

Thielepape, O. *Das Verhältnis Papst Coelestins III. zu den Klostern*, diss., Greifswald, 1913.

Watterish, 2, 708–84.

CELESTINE IV. *Goffredo da Castiglione (b. before 1323, d. Anagni, 10 November 1241). Elected pope on 25 October 1241, probably not consecrated. Buried at St. Peter's, Rome.*

This pontificate of seventeen days is one of the shortest in papal history. Nothing was sent out from the CHANCERY. All that is known of Celestine IV concerns his family and his legation in Tuscany and Lombardy. Goffredo da Castiglione was a member of a noble Milanese family named after its principal fief, the fortress of Castiglione Olona near Seprio. Reliable documentation of the genealogy of the family begins with Guido, the father of Corrado III, who died around 1180. In accordance with a family tradition, the pope's father, Giovanni, *armorum dux* (leader of a military band), married Cassandra Crivelli, sister of the archbishop of Milan who became Pope URBAN III (1185–7). Thanks to the protection of his uncle, Goffredo is believed to have rapidly ascended the stages of his ecclesiastical career, reaching the chancery of the archbishop of Mlan in 1223. No documentation is available to confirm this genealogical interpretation; however, several documents make unmistakable reference to his nephews, Alberto, Passaguado, and Guido, and to the family's links with Castelseprio. We also know that he was linked through the marriage of his sister to the Longhi family of Bergamo. His name appears in 1226, in the *explicit* of the *Rettorica antica* of Boncompagno da Signa, with the note *theologus*. Along with comments in a chronicle written by Rolandino of Padua, this is the only available indication of Goffredo's ecclesiastical training. He attended a public lecture on the work of Boncompagno da Signa on 31 March 1226, with Bishop Giordano of Padua and the papal LEGATE Alatrino.

Goffredo was among the first group of cardinals appointed by GREGORY IX; he took the presbyteral title of St. Mark, as attested by his first signature as cardinal on 23 September 1227. Shortly afterward, Gregory IX sent him as legate to Tuscany and Lombardy. His mission in Tuscany was to ensure that the commune of Pisa return to the bishop of Lucca the seven occupied fortresses in the valley of Era. Following a bilateral agreement and a suit against Pisa, neither of which had any effect, Goffredo placed an INTERDICT on Pisa on 17 October 1228. In Lombardy Gregory IX sought to intensify the struggle against those towns faithful to Frederick II. The presence of the legate was designed to strengthen links with the papacy, reestablish internal peace, fight against heresy, and reform the clergy.

Goffredo got the League of Lombardy to send troops to the pontifical state and attempted to convince Padua and Treviso to sign a truce. However, he did not manage to establish peace between the rival factions sharing the town of Bergamo. The podestà (mayor) whom he had installed was driven out and replaced by another podestà chosen by the rival party, which freed the heretics who had been imprisoned. The legate again imposed an interdict on the town and forced the rebels to submit. In Milan, all plans were put in place in Januray 1228 to get the commercial authority to cooperate with the court of the Inquisition against the heretics. He finally held a provincial synod in Lodi (May 1229) which laid the basis for a drastic reform of the clergy. Perhaps the results of Goffredo's legation were considered unsatisfactory by the pope, because he was not granted further diplomatic missions. From that time on, he devoted himself to legal activities within the Curia. In view of this, it is difficult to explain his promotion to bishop of Sabina in 1238.

Upon the death of Gregory IX, Senator Matteo Rosso Orsini submitted the cardinals to very rigorous and uncomfortable conditions, akin to imprisonment to ensure the quick choice of a pope. From the beginning of the CONCLAVE, Cardinal Goffredo obtained the most votes, but he fell short of the required two-thirds majority. The first election yielded the name of the Dominican general, Humbert of the Romans. However, Matteo Rosso forced an internal election within the Sacred College. It is under these conditions that Goffredo da Castiglione was chosen pope, after sixty days of confinement and deliberation. Two days later, he fell gravely ill. The cardinals took refuge in Anagni, where Celestine IV died a few days after the All Saints' Day celebration.

Therese Boespflug

Bibliography

Paravicini Bagliani, A. "Celestino IV," *DBI*, 23 (1979), 398–402; "Coelestin IV," *LexMA* 3 (1984–6), 7.

CELESTINE V. *Pietro del Morrone (b. Molise, probably in Saint' Angelo de Mimosano, 1209/10, d. Castel Fumone, 19 May 1296). Elected pope in Perugia on 5 July 1294, consecrated 29 August 1294, abdicated 13 December 1294. Buried at Santa Maria di Collemaggio, Aquila.*

Pietro del Morrone (the surname is from a mountain east of Sulmona) was born to a family of peasants, the second-to-last child of Angelerio and his wife, Maria. At the urging of his mother, he entered the small Benedictine convent of Santa Maria di Faifula (at Montagano, close to his presumed birthplace). Around 1231, he decided to lead the life of a hermit, in keeping with the original rule of St. Benedict; he spent several years on Mount Porrara in the southern part of the Maiella range. Around 1233 or 1234, he was ordained into the priesthood in Rome. He had received a very rudimentary education. Between 1235 and 1240, he lived on Mount Morrone, where he later founded (1259) the church of Santa Maria di Morrone (or da Sulmona). The name was later changed to the church of the Holy Spirit. From that time, Pietro had a reputation for saintliness. Between 1240 and 1245, when a large number of pilgrims began to visit, he withdrew to the most inaccessible section of the Maiella mountains. The hermitage, Santo Spirito di Maiella (near Roccamorice), subsequently became the center for the brotherhood which he founded.

In 1264, an act of the bishop of Chieti, approved by URBAN IV and definitively confirmed in 1275 by a bull of GREGORY X, incorporated the hermitical brotherhood into the Benedictine order. From that period, Pietro was in contact with the Franciscans and their radical wing, the Spirituals—without, however, subscribing to their ideal of poverty. Since 1252, he had perhaps received numerous donations to his congregation, which was confirmed by Gregory X in 1275 at his request during a visit to the Curia in Lyons. He also received donations for Rome, for the church of San Pietro in Montorio, and, from 1289, the title of St. Eusebius. Most of the property, however, was in the region of Morrone and Maiella. There were also churches at Isernea, Ferentino, Sgurgola, Anagni, and, after 1287, Santa Maria di Collemaggio in L'Aquila. Although the Celestines closely imitated the mode of dress and way of life of the Franciscans, their organization more closely resembled that of the Cistercians. After Pietro's return from Lyons in 1275, annual general chapters were held at Santo Spirito di Maiella, where the prior carried out the function of prior general from around 1287, and then that of father abbot (*abbas pater*). However, the latter was elected for only three years, as opposed to the abbot general of the Cistercians, who was elected for life. Pietro himself served as father abbot several times.

In 1276, Pietro became abbot of the monastery of Santa Maria di Faifula. At that time he came into closer contact with Charles I of Anjou, king of Sicily. In 1279, he was made abbot of the monastery of San Giovanni in Piano, in the diocese of Lucera, which he restored to material prosperity. Within the strict confines of his congregation, Pietro was a skilled organizer, capable of achieving economic success. Following his journey to Lyons, his general horizon had widened. In 1280–81, he visited Tuscany and Rome. At an advanced age, he had ceased to be the simple hermit of the Abruzzi as he is so often represented, despite his predilection for the solitary existence to which he returned after every period of great activity. During this period, he acquired still more property: the monastery of San Pietro di Vallebona near Manopello in 1285, and Santa Maria di Collemaggio at L'Aquila in 1287.

Pietro's reputation for saintliness drew many pilgrims and sick people to visit him in Maiella, and the *Vitae* refers to many instances of miraculous healing. In 1293, he retired once more to his region of origin, the Morrone, where the abbey of Santo Spirito had been enlarged. The grotto of S. Onofrio where he preferred to stay, halfway up the mountain from the abbey, contains a fresco bearing the oldest portrait of him.

At that time, the pontifical throne had been vacant for a year following the death of NICHOLAS IV (4 April 1292). Family rivalries divided the Sacred College between the Colonna (Giacomo and Pietro) and the Orsini (Matteo Rosso, Napoleone, and Latino Malabranca). Pietro Boccamazza, from the Roman family of the Savelli, favored the Colonna, whereas Matteo d' Acquasparta favored the Orsini. Benedetto Caetani, the future Boniface VIII, was isolated and at that time had no chance of being elected pope. Gerardo Bianchi of Parma, bishop of Sabina, was also independent, while the Milanese Pietro Peregrosso leaned more toward the Orsini. Representing French interests and the Angevins, the two French cardinals, Hugues Aycelin and Jean Cholet (who died in August 1297) had no chance of election. Political motives did not play a large role in this schism, since in the conflict that began during the Sicilian Vespers, none of the cardinals favored the secession of Sicily to the Aragonese. Indeed, they all supported Charles II of Anjou, though not unconditionally, and at the same time supported GUELPH interests in Italy. Adrian V had abrogated the rules for the organization of CONCLAVES developed by Gregory X, so the cardinals met in Rome in the Savelli Palace on the Aventine and at the monastery of Santa Maria sopra Minerva. They were not confined to either place. For months, the cardinals could reach no agreement by the necessary two-thirds majority, even after the Perugia meeting in October 1293. On his return from Provence at the end of March 1294, King Charles II of Anjou stopped in Rome. He was anxious that a pope be elected quickly; certain provisions of the La Junquera peace treaty, designed to put an end to the Sicilian war that had been dragging on for several years, had to be confirmed by the pope. The king proposed a number of names to the cardinals (the names are unknown to us), but they rejected this attempt to meddle in their affairs. On the way back to Naples, the king visited the hermit Pietro del Morrone at St. Onofrio, whom he had already supported when Pietro was organizing his congregation. Charles II suggested that Pietro write a letter to the Sacred College, reproaching the cardinals for their reprehensible attitude.

In so doing, it is fair to say that the king was involving Pietro as a possible candidate, but it would be false to see in his move an intrigue based on selfish motives.

The name of the pious hermit was already known to Latino Malabranca, who favored the hermitical Spiritual movement, as well as to the Orsinis. From the arrival of Pietro's letter in Perugia, Latino began to consider him as a possible candidate. In view of the danger of upheaval in Rome and the threat this posed to the Church, the offensive led by the Orvieto commune in the valley of Lago (Bolsena), and the shock caused by the sudden death of a young brother of Napoleone Orsini, Pietro del Morrone was elected pope on 5 July 1294. Thus, the proposal of Latino Malabranca was adopted. It was certainly determined, in the final analysis, by tactical considerations. A delegation arrived in St. Onofrio to bring the elderly Pietro news of his election. After the first moments of reticence, he accepted the result of the vote. Charles II visited him immediately in Sulmona to bring pressure to bear. As a result, his consecration and coronation did not take place in Perugia as the cardinals might have wished, but on 29 August at Santa Maria di Collemaggio in L'Aquila, the southernmost town of the states of Charles II.

The accession of Pietro del Morrone to the papal throne was the result of a conjunction of spiritual motives and political calculation, since his advanced age made a quick re-election more than likely. But in essence, it was an irresponsible act. Although he had proved himself a capable organizer in his congregation, he completely lacked the necessary experience. He had no knowledge of canon law, the complex machinery of the Curia, or the numerous ecclesiastical and political problems that a pope had to face. Furthermore, he had limited general knowledge and education—he barely understood Latin—and he was already elderly. During his lifetime, he appears to have viewed himself in the light of the eschatological speculations of the disciples of Joachim of Flora, probably grasping the real essence of that doctrine. This may be seen in the numerous inscriptions to the Holy Spirit to be found on monasteries founded by him; this bore no relation to the order of Santo Spirito in Sassia of Rome.

Celestine V entered L'Aquila seated on the back of an ass, in imitation of Christ's entry into Jerusalem; he appointed twelve cardinals (a certain reference to the twelve apostles), among them several monks. It is possible that he saw in the monks of his congregation the monastic order of the end of the time prophesied by Joachim of Flora. But political reality was different. From the time of his consecration and coronation in L'Aquila, Celestine V—the name he chose for himself at the inspiration of celestial powers—was under the control of Charles, who prevented the new pope from going to Rome and forced him to set up residence in Naples, the principal city of his kingdom. The pontifical chancery was immediately reorganized in L'Aquila. The archbishop of Benevento, Giovanni di Castrocoeli, who had been called into question during the papacy of Nicholas IV, replaced the canonist Jean Lemoine as vice chancellor, while the latter was elevated to the role of cardinal.

Charles II's chief chancellor, Bartolomeo of Capua, controlled the pontifical chancery. Benefits and indulgences were given out at random, subsequently to be revoked by BONIFACE VIII. Cardinals like Hugues Aycelin and Giacomo Colonna took advantage of the old pope's naiveté. The APOSTOLIC CHAMBER also seems to have been partially reorganized under Pietro di Sora and again later, under Teodorico. The pope was surrounded by men loyal to Charles II. Rainaldo di Lecto was appointed marshal of the court. With respect to the administration of the states of the Church, Oderisio da Aversa was made rector of the Romagna, and Gentile di Sangro rector of the March of Ancona. Tommaso di Sanseverino, confidant of Charles II of Anjou, was appointed a senator of Rome and subsequently replaced, by special authorization from the pope, by the king himself (13 December 1294). On 18 September, Celestine V appointed twelve new cardinals in L'Aquila, including two members of his congregation (Thomas de Ocra and Francesco Ronci di Atri, who died on 13 October of the same year). There were also two further monks, Robert, abbot of Citeaux, and Simon, prior of the Cluniae monastery of La Charité-sur-Loire. There were other Frenchmen; Simon de Beaulieu, archbishop of Bourges, Bernard de Goth, Bishop Jean Lemoine (who had been ousted from Lyons), Guillaume Ferrier the provost of the Marseilles chapter, and Nicolas Nonancour, chancellor of the University of Paris. There were also the Italians Pietro del L'Aquila, the bishop-elect of Valva, Landolfo Brancaccio of Naples, a relative of Charles II, and Guglielmo Longhi of Bergamo. The substantial increase in the membership of the Sacred College was clearly intended to decrease the influence of the Roman nobility. To facilitate a future pontifical election, Celestine V reorganized the conclave according to the order of Gregory X (10 December 1294). These rules were also to prevail in the event of the abdication of the pope. He granted many indulgences and graces to his congregation of Celestines. The Franciscan Spirituals Pietro di Fossombrone (Angelo Clareno) and Pietro di Macerata (Liberato), who had returned from Armenia, also came to L'Aquila. The Celestines shared similar beliefs with the Spirituals on living as a hermit, but they nevertheless belonged to the Benedictine order, and unlike the Spirituals, they allowed the possession of property. The Spirituals therefore could not be admitted to the congregation, but Celestine nonetheless offered them his protection as poor hermits and his brothers. He placed the institute under the protection of Napoleone Orsini. After the abdication of Celestine V, the Spirituals were once more persecuted and fled to Greece.

As far as international policy was concerned, Celestine V was entirely at the mercy of such skilled advisors as cardinals Matteo Rosso Orsini, Gerardo Bianchi of Parma, and Benedetto Caetani. He confirmed the treaty of La Junquera (1 October 1294) and sent ambassadors to the courts of Philip IV of France and of Edward I of England to mediate in the conflict between those countries. On 6 October 1294, the pope and King Charles II left L'Aquila for Naples. On the way there, Celestine installed a Celestine abbot of the old Benedictine abbey of St. Vincent on Mount Volturno. He did the same in Montecassino, but the monks resisted this move, and some went into exile. Actions such as these revealed the pope's injustice and senile obstinacy.

The elevation of the ambitious Giovanni di Castrocoeli to the rank of cardinal was another mistake. On 5 November 1294, Celestine V arrived in Naples and arranged that a wooden cell be prepared for him at Castel Nuovo. Faced with growing criticism, he began to contemplate abdication, as he did not feel that he was equal to the responsibility of being pope. He took counsel with such canonists as Gerardo di Parma, Jean Lemoine, and Benedetto Caetani, who explained that pontifical abdication was legal from a canonical standpoint. In 1190, in the presence of a council of the Sacred College, Hugoccio of Pisa had contemplated abdication under similar circumstances. Since that time, other canonists had declared it legal, even without the intervention of the cardinals.

Celestine made the decision to abdicate in the presence of the cardinals. Despite expressions of support from his supporters, he expressed in simple terms, on 9–10 December, his reasons for abdicating. Foremost among these were illness, his lack of knowledge and experience, and his desire to retire to his hermitage. Shortly afterward, he promulgated a constitution on pontifical abdication that has not been preserved but whose content may be known from similar provisions of Boniface VIII (*Sextus* 1,7,1). On 13 December, he announced his abdication in moving terms before the Sacred College at Castel Nuovo, lay down his papal insignia and habit, and donned the gray robe of a hermit. On 24 December 1294, Benedetto Caetani was elected pope, taking the name Boniface VIII.

Given the exceptional nature of the abdication of Pietro del Morrone, as he was once more called, the new pope wanted to keep an eye on him. Pietro himself and the monks of his congregation had never doubted the legitimacy of his abdication, but some of the Spirituals, as well as opponents of Boniface VIII such as the Colonna, had their doubts. While returning to Rome from the Curia, Pietro took refuge in his cell at St. Onofrio, and from there he went on to his monastery of San Giovanni in Piano before setting off by boat to Greece, as the Spirituals had done before him. However, he ended up in Viesti at Gargano, whence he was transferred to Anagni by

order of Boniface VIII (1295). The new pope, furious, had Pietro locked up in the Castle of Fumone, where he died of natural causes on 12 May 1295, aged eighty-four.

Pietro was first buried at his church of St. Onofrio in Ferentino; later his body was transferred to Santa Maria di Collemaggio at L'Aquila, where the guild of drapers had a sumptuous monument built in his honor in the style of the Lombard Renaissance, in stark contrast to the hermit's life he had lived.

The dispute surrounding the legality of Pietro's abdication and the election of Boniface VIII began in earnest after his death. Even though such Spirituals as Peter John Olivi (Pierre Olin) and especially Aegidius Romanus (Giles of Rome) proved that the election of Boniface VIII had been perfectly regular from the canonical and theological standpoints, others were not quite so sure. Numerous people maintained that Caetani had secured the abdication of the elderly pope by less than legitimate means. The Colonna, several members of the University of Paris, and supporters of the French king, Philip the Fair, used these arguments to throw doubt on the legitimacy of the abdication. At the same time, eschatological speculation around the former pope was growing among the Spirituals. Around 1295–6, Robert d' Uzès identified him with the figure of an angelic and eschatological pope, a somewhat secondary figure for Joachim of Flora but likened to that of the emperor of the end of time popularized especially by Pseudo-Methodius. Pietro-Celestine played a special role in the fifteen pontifical *Vaticinia* which refer to the sixteen imperial Byzantine prophecies translated into Latin by Liberato and Angelo Clareno. This work was distributed in Italy on their return from Greece in 1304–5 and is generally attributed to Joachim of Flora. The eight of the *Vaticinia*, which draws very closely on the prophecies of the emperor of the end of time, bring forward the figure of the angelic, eschatological pope and relates it to Pietro-Celestine. Around 1500, these *Vaticinia* ceased to be applied to specific popes and were replaced by the Pseudo-Malachi, 111 brief maxims concerning the popes from the time of Celestine II (1143–4) to the end of time. Thus, Pietro-Celestine lived on in eschatological speculations from the Middle Ages to the beginning of the modern era. Criticism of his abdication was rare, through mentioned by Dante (*Inferno*, III, 58 ff.).

The king of France, Philip the Fair, campaigned in 1305–6 for the canonization of Pietro-Celestine. At the same time, there was a growing campaign of slander and a trial against Boniface VIII. The figure of Celestine appeared as luminous as that of the beleaguered Caetani appeared dark. Clement V encouraged this, naturally with the wholehearted support of the Celestines and some of the Spirituals, with a view to delaying Boniface's trial. Examination of witnesses for the canonization process began in 1306 in Pietro's birthplace and ended only in

1313. At the end of April 1313, the cardinals met in a secret consistory and approved a number of miracles. On 5 May, Clement V canonized Pietro del Morrone (not Celestine V) in the cathedral at Avignon. On that occasion, the legitimacy of the abdication was once more emphasized. The saint's day (19 May), was incorporated into the calendar of the universal Church in 1669, but it was dropped during the reform of the calendar in 1969, because the cult was not practiced everywhere.

Pietro is now once more viewed with favor, not only in the popular piety of the Abruzzi, but also as a result of historical conferences held in L'Aquila. He has also become the emblematic figure of the "alternative pope" offered in oppostion to the official Church by such polemicists as Giovanni Papini and Karl Joseph Kuschel, among others. The socialist writer Angelo Silone dedicated a play to Pietro (*L'avventura d'un povero cristiano*, 1968). This type of rereading hardly stands up to historical criticism. The visit of PAUL VI to Fumone on 7 September 1966 fed speculation about the possible abdication of the pope. The pontificate of Celestine V lasted only five months and did not in any way present a real alternative to the church of his time; however, his decision to abdicate reveals the elderly pope's sense of responsibility, since it spared the Church additional damage.

Peter Herde

Bibliography

Convegni Celestiniani, I, Indulgenza nel Medioevo e perdonanza di papa Celestino, L'Aquila, 1987; II, *Celestino papa angelico*, L'Aquila, 1988; III, *San Pietro del Morrone, Celestino V nel medioevo monastico*, L'Aquila, 1989; IV, *Celestino V e I suoi tempi: Realtà spirituale e realtà politica*, L'Aquila, 1990.

Herde, P. "Celestino V," *DBI*, 23 (1979), 402–15; *Celestin V, (1294), Peter von Morrone, der Engelpapst*, Stuttgart, 1981; "Coelestin V." *LexMA*, 4 (1984–6), 7–9.

CENSURE, CANONICAL.

CENSURE, CANONICAL. CANON LAW, within the general framework of penal regulation, has traditionally distinguished several types of censure in accordance with the object of the sanction and the seriousness of the punishment. The terminological ambiguity of the word "censure" (*censura*) springs from its general nature, which derives from Roman imperial law. It was not known to ecclesiastical legislation until the development and popularity of the DECRETALS. Censure, in the broad sense of the word, may be defined as a judgment exempt of indulgence and consisting, in a given case, more of a moral assessment than of a strict material application of a judicial norm, since it applies to faith or morals.

In doctrinal and theological matters, censure and its consequences derive from the recognized infallibility of the pope and that of the ecumenical council, and from the recourse to this infallibility to impose sincere religious adherence on the faithful. This exceeds the simple submission of faith. The term "judiciary censures" is sometimes used in the plural to signal its solemnity, and these types of sentences differ from the fifty "scientific" sentences as used by theologians. This distinction, which springs from the degree of authority of the source emitting the censure, does not nullify the punishment to be meted out to the object of censure concerning the speculative order, such as heresy or error. Disciplinary censure (regarding practice) is different from the systems regulating the so-called "economic" censures, delivered with regard to a doctrine or a proposal of a purely preventive nature. The history of the latter is generally merged with that of ecclesiastical punishment in general, without intruding on the specific domain of the censorship of books (taken in the broad sense of "published writings" by canon 1384 of the Code of Canon Law of 1917). This censure—or censorship—was formally exercised in a nonrepressive manner for the deliverance (or possible refusal) of *imprimatur*.

Contemporary canonic penal legislation, apart from several specific modifications, recalls (canon 1312 of the Code of Canon Law, 1983) the marked difference between expiatory punishment, which accentuates the dissuasive and retributive aspects of punishments—or censures—which stress the improvement of the guilty person. In this regard, canonic censure appears to relate to law of a disciplinary nature rather than penal law in the strict sense of the term.

François Jankowiak

Bibliography

Borras, A. *L'Excommunication dans le nouveau Code de droit canonique*, Paris, 1987.

Jombart, E. "Censure des livres," *DDC*, III (1942), 157–69.

Quilleit, H. "Censures doctrinales," *DTC*, II/2 (1949), 2101–13.

Vermeersch, A. *Epitome iuris canonici*, II, Malines, 5th ed., 1934.

CEREMONIAL, PAPAL.

CEREMONIAL, PAPAL. Liturgy and papal ceremonies have been known from their origins until the present day, and may be divided into several main periods.

The Early Centuries. One may note the *Didache* and Apostolic Tradition (HIPPOLYTUS), then the cult of the papal churches of Rome until the time of Charlemagne. It presents the liturgy of the three basilicas of the Lateran, of St. Mary Major, and of St. Peter and establishes a relationship between the liturgy and the development of the architecture of the basilicas. It relates closely to the *Liber pontificalis*, from which the most objective inventories of instruments of worship can be gleaned. The *Liber pontificalis* can, in turn, be compared with the first texts edited by Mohlberg and with the early *Ordines Romani*.

The Middle Ages. The same kind of book was used until the 13th century. The ancient *Ordines* were used until the *Ordinary* of INNOCENT III. In 1298, while the future Innocent III was a young cardinal, he authored a treatise on the papal mass in which he gave the religious meaning of the Roman ceremonies, as passed on to the Christian mystics. Other books may be consulted on this including the *Micrologus* of ecclesiastical observances; the *Gemma animae* of Honorius of Autun; and a book published in St. Petersburg by an anonymous writer. The *Ordinary* of Pope Innocent III refers to liturgical tradition of the 12th Roman century. Its annexes list the rules, especially those on the papal mass, which were passed down to all of Christendom, brought to life through Franciscan tradition since Maymo of Faversham in 1243, and which would last until the SECOND VATICAN COUNCIL. Around 1273, Pope GREGORY X published the ceremonial of the Roman Curia. This does not refer as much to the court as to worship that occured in the presence of the Vicar of Christ. The texts that follow provide the ceremonial of the bishops (modeled after that of the popes), and those of the cardinals, namely the text of the bishop of Ostia Latino Malabranca, a nephew of Pope NICHOLAS III and elector of Saint CELESTINE V. It is useful to compare their rubrics to those of the pontiff.

Cardinal Giacomo Caetani Stefaneschi, a grandnephew of Nicholas III, revised the rubrics and ceremonials more extensively. He worked in Rome on his ceremonial around the year 1300 and finished it in Avignon in the year of his death (1341). He discusses the accession of popes (election, coronation, and consecration), the liturgy of the cardinals and the pope, and the liturgy of Christmas, Pentecost, and papal masses. There are also details of sermons, anniversaries, consistories of the council, imperial and royal coronation, canonization, creation of cardinals, transfers, nuncios, and legates. The Avignon texts succeeded this essentially Roman ritual and reveal the practices of the French popes until GREGORY XI. The Patriarch Pierre Arneil continued the text following the election of URBAN VI. The texts were once more taken to the eternal city following the consecration of Oddo Colonna (MARTIN V) in Constance in 1417. The medieval "Masters of Ceremonies" are well known: the Swiss Jean de Sion, under BENEDICT XII; François de Conzie of Savoy, who worked as CHAMBERLAIN of the Holy See under the Aragonese "antipope" BENEDICT XIII, who transcribed the traditions of the Curia and the cardinals; Guido di Busco was master of ceremonies at the council of Constance and also during the papacy of EUGENE IV; Aeneas Silvios Piccolomini (the future PIUS II) was himself, before becoming a priest, cleric of ceremonies at the conclave that elected FELIX V at Basel in 1439. Records also exist for a half dozen lesser-known clerics.

The Renaissance Onward. The pontifical ceremonial would be codified once more, this time by the humanist bishop of Pienza. He was the friend and secretary of Pius II. Agostino Patrizi Piccolomini had left a large manuscript for use in the papal chapel, a copy of which fell into the hands of a Venetian. The archbishop of Corfu, Christopher Marcello, decided to edit Patrizi's excellent book in his own fashion and without asking for advice from the office of ceremonies, and had it printed in 1516. The master of ceremonies, Paris de Grassi, complained about this to LEO X, but the pope dropped the matter. The book remained in use by the Curia on an almost official basis. An edition more faithfully reflecting the 25 manuscripts of Patrizi as well as the role of Johannes Burckard has been published for use today. Johannes Burckard was the first of the diarists to be published. The diaries of Antoine Rebiol and Agostino Patrizi himself (15th century) have been lost. Those written by Burckard do exist and have been published twice, once by Louis Thuasne in three volumes with annexes that are still of great value (Paris, 1886), and by Enrico Celani in the 20th century, on the basis of more judiciously chosen manuscripts; Celani's edition is, generally speaking, the better one. The index, however, is unfinished.

The text of Haselach, the Alsatian, is the work of a skilled writer, although it is unfortunately full of indecent anecdotes which have no historical value and which people such as Leibniz and Turmel wanted to have completely removed. His chronicles of the Curia, however, are still indispensable, and the liturgical work remains valid. He added an *Ordo missae* that came into active use beginning in 1496, at the time of the Roman Pontifical. He collaborated with Patrizi for the first edition in 1485. Haselach, who was a man of ambition, was made bishop of Orte and Città Castellana and assistant to the pontifical throne under JULIUS II. He was received as citizen of Strasbourg and died in 1506 at his Roman home under the Argentina Tour. Paris de Grassi succeeded him.

Grassi had received his surplice of "master of ceremonies" in 1504, and he kept it until his death in Rome in 1528. He was canon of Bologna and San Lorenzo in Damaso and enjoyed other benefices such as the parish of Madonna della Strada in Rome, before the Jesuits. Nominated archpriest of Saint-Celsus by Julius II in 1509, he became bishop of Pesaro in the Marches at the beginning of the reign of Leo X. He owned a villa situated to the North of the Vatican and a silver works, which subsequently became the property of the Chamber. He was somewhat of a humanist and authored more than ten liturgical or curialist works including:

1. Commentary on the Ceremonial de Patrizi (practices of the Curia, the liturgical year, ceremonies of cardinals)
2. The consecration of bishops

3. La chevauchée papale de Jules II (The papal caval-cade of Julius II)
4. La création des cardinaux (The creation of cardinals)
5. Treatise on intonations (the original manuscript and a more complete copy are to be found at ms. Vat. Lat. 5634 t.2, ff66v-90r.)
6. The papal liturgies or summary of the ceremonial of popes, presented to Cardinal Guillaume Briconnet in 1507, and published by Martene as *Ordo Romanus*. A manuscript has the same text dedicated to Riario in 1510. It figures in a private collection. The Ms. Vat. Lat 5634.t.2 already had several chapters with variants in 1505.
7. The ceremonial of cardinals of Bologna (printed for all bishops in 1565)
8. The treatise on funerals (1506–11)
9. The treatise on Ambassadors (*De oratoribus Romanae Curiae*).
10. The fifth Lateran Council
11. The treatise on papal ceremonies (1506–25)

Paris' first successor was Biaggio Martinelli of Cesena, who kept diaries that were enriched in various ways by his nomination from 1518 to 1540. He died in 1544 at the age of 80. He is known for the revenge taken on him by Michelangelo after he objected to the nudes in the Sistine Chapel. There is a portrait of the elderly Martinelli painted with the ears of an ass above the present entrance door of the choir. The face is finely rendered. His diaries, kept during the pontificates of Leo X, ADRIAN VI, CLEMENT VII, and PAUL III show that he led a very active life. The main manuscripts are to be found in the Vatican Archives, Borghese IV 64 and in the Vatican Library Barberini lat. 2799 (omitted in Salmon) and Vat. Lat. 12377. His texts of Barberini lat. 2801 recount the coronation of Charles V in Bologna in 1529, his second stay since 1532 in Bologna with Clement VII; the journey to Nice in 1533; to Perugia in 1535; and again to Nice for Francis I in 1538. These episodes were edited in 1753 by Gattico on the basis of tome 2 of a lost manuscript. Blaise's colleague from 1529 was Gianfranco Fermano of Macerata. Fermano's diary contains very interesting manuscripts, despite numerous gaps, and covers the pontificates of Clement VII to PIUS IV. His two nephews, Luigi and Cornelio, masters of ceremonies from 1548 and 1565, respectively, also left manuscripts. Luigi was the owner of ms. Vat. Lat. 5636 (original manuscript by Grassi), which was erroneously attributed to him. However, on the Council of Trent, he left notes that are comparable to those of Massarelli. Cornelio continued in service during the pontificate of St. PIUS V.

Francesco Mucante, and afterward his brother Gianpaolo, took up where Luigi and Cornelio left off. They were the grandsons of Biaggio Martinelli, and their manuscripts recount the reigns of successive popes until PAUL V.

Paolo Alaleone, a nephew of the last Fermano, had the privilege of writing his diaries in his own hand for 56 years. His accounts take us up to the reign of URBAN VIII in 1638. Leone Caetani, duke of Sermoneta and a reputed orientalist, has left a study of Alaleone with an inventory of the manuscripts of his seven predecessors. They have been kept throughout all of Europe. Salmon has made an inventory of almost all of the manuscripts in the Vatican. There were however, other clerics of ceremonies. Pierluigi Galletti, the Benedictine, made a handwritten list of ceremonial clerics from Burckard up to the year 1715. Gattico, in his foreword of 1753, named those he knew of up until that date. The Archives of the Vatican prefects of ceremonies reveal other masters and other diairies. The catalog of their manuscripts, which has been attributed to Giovanni Fornici and Gregorio Palmieri, lists them with other sources to be compared with the manuscripts of the Vatican Library. The names of masters of ceremonies may also be found in the *ANNUARIO PONTIFICIO* or its predecessors and especially in the *Ruoli* of the Vatican Library.

Following the Second Vatican Council. Even before the council, the Prefect of the College of Masters of pontifical ceremonies was the future cardinal, Enrico Dante. His successor was Virgilio Noè, followed by John Maggee and Piero Marini. Marini's title is master of pontifical liturgical ceremonies. All liturgical works of the council and commissions, which preceded and followed it, should be recalled here.

National languages took the place of Latin and many of the rites were shortened. A new liturgy was in the making.

Marc Dykmans

Bibliography

Amalarius, *Opera liturgica*, Hanssens, J. M. ed., 3 vol., Vatican City, 1948–50, repr. 1967.

Amohlberg, L. C., et al., *Sacramentarium Veronense*, Rome 1956; *Sacramentarium Gelasianum*, Rome 1960.

Andrieu, M. *Les Ordines Romani du haut Moyen Age*, 5 vols., Louvain, 1931–61.

Andrieu, M. *Le pontifical romain au Moyen Âge*, 4 vol., Vatican City, 1938–41.

Antonelli, F. et al., *Costituzione conciliare sulla sacra liturgia*, Rome, 1964.

Bishop, E. *Liturgica historica*, Oxford, 1918, repr. 1962.

Bogel, C., and Elze, R., ed. *Pour le Moyen Âge le Pontifical romano germanique du dixieme siècle*, 3 vol., Vatican City, 1963–72.

Botte, B. ed., *Hippolyte de Rome La Tradition apostolique*, Paris, 1968.

Bugnini, A. *La riforma liturgica*, Rome, 1983.

Burchard, J., ed. *Ordo Misse*, Rome, 1496 (cf. T. Accurti, *Editiones Saeculi XV . . .*, Florence, 1936, 125, n° 8).

Burckard, J. *Diarium sive rerum urbanarum commentairii 1483–1506*, L. Thuasne, ed., 3 vols., Paris 1883–5; *Liber notarum ab anno 1483 ad 1506*, E. Celano, ed., 2 vols., *Citta di Castello*, 1906–43.

Caetani, L. "Vita e diario di Paolo Aleone de Branca . . . 1582–1538," *Archivio della Soc. Rom. di storia patria*, 16 (1893), 1–39.

Celier, L. "Sur quelques opuscules de Francois de Conzie," *MAH*, 26 (1906), 91–108.

Cholodniak, M., ed. *Honorius dit d'Autun, Gemma animae, PL*, 172, 541–758, *Aurea Gemma*, St. Petersburg, 1898 (cf. ms. Vat. lat. 1150).

Constant, G. "Les maítres des cerémonies au XVI siécle," *MAH*, 23 (1903), 161–229, 343–53.

De Blaauw, S. L. *Cultus et Décor. Liturgie en architectuur in laataniek en middleeuws rome*, Delft, 1987.

De Lucci, J. and Gurchard, J., ed., *Liber Pontificalis*, Rome 1497.

de Pamele, J., ed. *Micrologus de ecclesiasticis observationibus*, Anvers, 1565, and *PL*, 151, 973–1022.

Deshusses, J. *Le Sacrametaire grégorien*, 3 vols., Fribourg, 1972–82.

Diener, H. "Enea Silvio Piccolomini Weg von Basel nach Rom," *Adel und Kirche*, 1968, 516–33; "Camera Papagalli im Palast des Papstes," *Archiv fur Kultergeschichte*, 49 (1967), 43–97.

Duchense, L. and Vogel, C. ed., *Liber pontificalis*, 3 vol., Paris, 1955–7.

Dykmans, M. "L' Ordinaire d'Innocent II," *Gregorianum*, 59 (1978), 191–203.

Dykmans, M. "Paris de Grassi," *Ephemerides liturgicae*, 96 (1982), 407–82; 99 (1985), 383–417; 100 (1986), 270–333; and *DHGE*, 21, 1986, 1217 sq.

Dykmans, M., and Minnich, N. H. ed. "Le cinquieme concile du Latran," *Archivum historiae conciliorum*, 24 (1982), 271–460.

Dykmans, M. *Le Cérémonial Papal du la fin die Moyen Áge a la Renaissance*, Brussels, 1. *Le Cérémonial papal du XII siecle*, 1977; 2. *De Rome en Avignon ou le Ceremonial de Jacques Stefaneschi*, 1981; 3. *Les textes avignonnais jusqu' à la fin du Grand Schisme d' Occident*, 1983; *Le Retour à Rome ou le Cérémonial du Patriarche Pierre Ameil*, 1985; *Le plus ancien manuscrit du Cérémonial de Grégoire X, AHP*, 11 (1973), 85–112; "Un nouveau manuscrit du Cérémonial papal de vers 1300," *Ephemrides liturgicae*, 92 (1978), 472–6; "La troisieme élection du pape Urbain VI," *AHP*, 15 1977, 217–64.

Dykmans, M., ed. *Paris de Grassi, Ceremonial de Jules II et de Leon X*, (épreuves typographiquer inédites déposées à la biliothèque vaticane).

Dykmans, M. "Mabillon et les interpolations de son Ordo Romanus XIV," *Gregorianum*, 47 (1966), 316–342.

Fabre, P. and Duchense, L. ed., *Le liber censuum de l'Église romaine*, 3 vols., Paris, 1910–52.

Gattico, J. B. *Acta selecta caeremonalia sanctae Romanae Ecclesiae*, 2 vols., Rome, 1753.

Hanssens, J. M. *La Liturgie d'Hippolyte. . .*, Rome 1959, repr. 1965.

Hesbert, R. J. *Corpus antiphonarum officii*, 6 vol., Rome, 1963–86.

La liturgie apres Vatican II, Paris, 1967.

Lettre à Leon X sur l'edition Marcello du Ceremonial de Patrizi, dans Mabillon, *Museum Italicum*, 2, 1689, 587–602.

"Liturgie d'aujord'hui," *Catholicisme*, 7, 1975, 889–93.

Mabillon, J. *Museum Italicum*, 2 vol., Paris 1689.

Martimort, A. G., et al., *L'Eglise en prière*, 4 vols., Paris, 1983–9.

Merkle, S. *Concilium Tridentinum*, 2, 1911, CVIII–CXXII, and index, 918, sur les Fiemano.

Palmieri, G. "De Archivo sacrae congregationis caeromialis," *Analecta ecclesiastica, Revue romaine. . .*, 1 (1893), 413–30 et tirage a part de 47 p., Rome 1893.

Patrizi, A., and Burchard, A. J., ed., *Pontificale romanum*, Rome, 1485.

Rordorf, R. and Tuilier, A. ed., *La Doctrine des Douze Apótres (Didache)*, Paris, 178.

Schimmelpfennig, B. *Die Zeremonienbücher der romischen Kurie im Mittelalter*, Tübingen, 1973.

Sources of the Modern Roman Liturgy. The Ordinals by Haymo of Faversham and Related Documents (1243–1307), 2 vol., Leiden, 1063.

Van Dijk, J. P. *The Ordinal of the Papal Court from Innocent III to Boniface VIII and Related Documents*, Fribourg, 1975.

"Vatican II et la reforme liturgique"; "liturgie et vie chrétienne," *DE*, 9 1976, 911 sq., 923–39.

Vogel, C. *Medieval Liturgy: An Introduction to the Sources*, Washington, D.C., 1996.

Wasner, F. "Eine unbekannte Ms. des diariums Buckardi," *Historiches Jahrbuch*, 83 (1964), 300–31.

Wasner, F. "Beiträge zum papistlichen Zeremonienwesen," *AHP*, 4 (1966), 74–104; 6 (1968), 113–62.

THE CHAIR OF ST. PETER. The Chair of St. Peter is located at the rear of the apse of the Basilica of St. Peter in Rome. It is a monumental structure erected by Bernini at the request of ALEXANDER VII (1657–67) and is one of the most explicit symbols of pontifical magisetrium in the basilica. The exercise of *magisterium* conferred upon the Vicar of Christ is a response to apostolic succession as symbolized by the KEYS. Between the two, the papal altar, covered by a canopy at the nave and transept crossing, attests to the fact that Rome is the center of Christendom. Therefore, the Chair of St. Peter, with its basrelief in wood is the legacy of a long tradition. It is constructed of diverse materials, notably in ivory (between the 5th and 9th centuries, or perhaps later) and was placed by Bernini at the center of a bronze construction, which closes the transept (crossing), supported by two lateral pilasters. In the Constantinian basilica, the seat reputed to be the Chair of St. Peter, has been placed in numerous positions: near the baptistery in the time of St. Damasus (366–84), in the chapel of Adrian 1st (772–95), near the crucifix in the 9th century, and once again near the baptistery during the pontificate of URBAN VIII (1623–44).

Bernini's work lasted ten years and cost 82,000 écus (crowns). A number of models were made, and the final ones may be seen in the museums of the VATICAN. Bernini's work diverted interest from the controversy over the authenticity of the seat included in the monument. In fact, the controversy has never been resolved and is still the subject of debate: Is this the chair from the early centuries of Christianity, or was this a throne bequeathed to the papacy by Charles the Bald in the 9th century? The monument is most famous for the light coming from the oculus overlooking the chair, which has, in its center, a mystical dove symbolizing the Holy Spirit. At the back of the chair, two cherubim hold the keys of ST. PETER and the TIARA. The chair is flanked by colossal statues around five meters high representing four doctors of the Church: St. Ambrose and St. Augustine in front, representing the Latin Church, and St. Athansius and St. John Chrysostom representing the Greek Church at the back. These four figures symbolize the will to regain unity of faith between the Western and Eastern Churches, which was broken in 1054. They also recall the formula of Saint Augustine, *Roma locuta est*, which was accepted by the council of Chalcedon (451). The figures also represent the principle by which Fathers and doctors of the Church assist the sovereign pontiffs, whose authority supercedes their own.

On each side of the Chair of St. Peter are the tomb of PAUL III (1534–48), who convoked the Council of Trent (to the left), and the tomb of Urban VIII (1623–44) on the right.

Philippe Levillain.

Bibliography

Battaglia, R. *La cattedra berniniana di S. Pietro*, Rome, 1943, 271 *sq.*

Cascioli, G. "Fusione della Cattedra di Bronzo del Bernini in S. Pietro," *Boll. Assoc. Archeol. Romana*, Rome, June 1925.

De Rossi, G. B. "La cattedra di S. Pietro nel Vaticano e quella del cimitero adriano," *Boll. Archeol. Crist.*, 1867.

Mariani, V. "Bernini e la "Cattedra" di S. Pietro," *Boll. Arte*, 1931, 161–72.

Rich, A. *The Legend of Saint Peter's Chair*, London, 1851.

Saccheri, G. P. *Della cattedra del Principe degli Apostoli conservata in Roma*, Rome, 1879, 29.

Schiavo, A. "La cattedra di S. Pietro," *Emporium*, 1941, 157–62.

Tapié, V. L. *Baroque et classicisme*, Paris, 1957.

von Einem, H. "Bemerkungen zur Cathedra Petri des Lorenzo Bernini," *Nachrichten A. K. Göttingen*, 1955, 93–114.

Zanelli, D. *La Cattedra di S. Pietro in Roma*, s.l.n.d., 12 *sq.*

CHAMBERLAIN. Historians of the medieval papacy use the term "chamberlain" to translate *camerarius*, the officer known as the CAMERLENGO in the modern era. In modern usage, the "chamberlains" of the pope are those who, in the medieval context, are called "chamber servants" (Latin *camerari*, especially the *cubiculari* and *cambreri*). Originally, the *cubiculum*—"bedroom," as distinct from the *camera*, a financial chamber which appeared later—was one of the offices in the Lateran; the designation, if not the exact concept, was also present in the palace of the Byzantine emperor. Under Pope GREGORY I, the *cubiculari* were all clerics and monks. Servants of the pope, they were sometimes entrusted with confidential missions, but it was not until the 14th century that they were promoted to the Curia. This is explained by the fact that by this time they served a less accessible pope and were entrusted to deliver summons to prelates calling them to CONSISTORIES and ceremonies, as well as seeing to the smooth running of the pope's daily life. They might also be given more sensitive missions—for example, acting in the APOSTOLIC CAMERA or delivering secret letters. These clerics numbered two at the end of the 13th century but grew to six under CLEMENT V (1305–14), the traditional number despite additions at certain times. Discreet and sometimes powerful collaborators, they arrived with a pope and left their duties on his death, sometimes to take up thereafter a less directly political curial responsibility.

On the transfer of the papal see from Avignon to Rome under the pontificate of GREGORY XI (1377), the chamberlains (*cubicularii*) of the papal household continued to fulfill a relatively simple function of assistance and service to the person of the pope, material or honorific according to the circumstances. Although the duties confided to these clerics (or, from 1573 or 1592, depending on the source, to laymen with the title of privy chamberlains of sword and cloak, *ab ense et lacerna*), chosen for their loyalty and their competence, scarcely changed, the return to Rome favored a distinction accrued from prerogatives and titles, dividing the chamberlains into several categories. In particular, the papacy renewed relations with the Roman NOBILITY that had been interrupted sixty-eight years before. The first group, enjoying precedence over all the rest, was the "participant" privy chamberlains, so called, supposedly, because they formerly participated in the distributions in kind handed out by the apostolic palace. They were all ecclesiastics and fulfilled the role of cupbearer (*pincera*), giving the pontiff drink at ceremonial dinners of the secretary of the embassy (*nuntius*), carrying solemnly blessed objects such as the palms or the *Agnus Dei*, and acting as *vestiarius* (Italian *guardaroba*) or ceremonial dresser to sovereigns and other persons of royal blood, as well as putting on the hat of new cardinals created in public consistory. To these specialized duties, which demanded a fixed incumbent, was added the general and common mission of assisting the master of the papal chamber, present in the privy antechamber when cardinals and authorized persons were admitted into the presence of the pope in private AUDIENCE. Numbering eight under SIXTUS V (1585–90), this group grew to twenty under CLEMENT X (1670–6), dropping to eleven under PIUS VI (1775–99), then to four under PIUS VII (1800–23), and stabilizing at around five members. Remaining at the disposition of the pontiff outside of audiences and solemn ceremonies, the participant privy chamberlains sometimes became, at the whim of papal practice and styles of government, the private chaplains of the pope, his librarians, or—as was the case in the pontificate of PIUS XI (1922–39)—his private secretaries. In exceptional cases, this could also apply to laymen: PIUS XII (1933–58) appointed on 30 June 1948 a participant privy chamberlain of sword and cape, conferring on him the role of secretary of the embassy, while the ecclesiastic *nuntius* retained the same title.

The majority of chamberlains, though members of the papal FAMILY, did not have access to the privilege of actual service. One of these categories included supernumerary privy chamberlains or *di mantellone*, from the name of the quilted overcoat of wool or purple silk (winter or spring dress), a garment distinguishing the lower prelature. They had the right to neither ring nor candleholder during the celebration of the mass, but their title constituted a desirable honor, the first step in a prelatial career toward the cardinalate and even, as was the case for INNOCENT XIII (1721–4), to the pontificate. Receiving remuneration in silver (abolished by Pius VI) and benefiting from distributions in kind (*parate di palazzo*), the supernumerary chamberlains went from nine, documented under ALEXANDER VII (1655–67), to sixty under GREGORY XVI (1831–46).

It is uncertain when honorary chamberlains—bearing the title of monsignor and restricted to remaining in the antechamber of honor (throne room)—were first named, but certainly their office is recent. In 1741, at the beginning of the pontificate of BENEDICT XIV (1740–58), they numbered thirty-two. There were ninety-two in 1757, proof both of inflation and of the extreme complexity of etiquette at the papal court. Pius VI distinguished honorary chamberlains in purple dress (*paonazzo*), officiating at Rome, from their counterparts *extra urbem*, who did not have the right to enter any of the antechambers but were responsible for chamberlain duties when the pope traveled to the countries where they resided. As with all chamberlains, their duties ceased *de jure* on the death of the pope and could not be renewed without the express agreement of the new pontiff, who often preferred to surround himself with personnel who had served him before his accession to the throne. Symmetrically, the chamberlains drawn from the laity were divided into three distinct classes of long-standing tradition, but the incumbents are known only from their roles in the palace of PAUL IV (1555–9). The participant privy chamberlains, numbering five, fulfilled the following functions: master of the Holy Hospice; major quartermaster of the Sacred Palaces (the statutory prerogatives of which were defined by Gregory XVI in 1832); grand cavalier of His Holiness (successor to the *prior stabuli*, documented from 590); bearer of the Golden Rose to sovereigns; and superintendent general of the papal postal services. Born into the Roman nobility and robed in habits of black cloth bordered with gold olive leaves, they were assisted directly in their duties by the so-called *de numero* chamberlains, and indirectly by the supernumerary chamberlains, whose numbers reached several hundred in the modern era. Some honorary chamberlains were belatedly appointed in order to allow persons not of noble extraction but judged worthy to approach the sovereign pontiff. The four oldest of this group were nominated for life.

PAUL VI (1963–8) instituted an important reorganization of services attached to the person of the pope with his *motu proprio Papalis Domus* of 28 March 1968, in an attempt to give efficiency and rationality precedence over "what is only nominal, decorative and exterior." He eliminated the honorary and *extra urbem* chamberlains in purple habits, as well as the responsibilities and titles held by the participant sword and cape chamberlains. Paul VI created by this same act the GENTLEMEN OF HIS HOLINESS, a group that accommodated the privy and honorary sword and cape chamberlains, while the supernumeraries took the title of honorary prelates. The contemporary configuration of this section of the papal household, thus reduced and simplified, has not since undergone substantial modification, and it closely resembles in its entirety the model that prevailed before the Avignon stage of the papacy.

Oliver Guyotjean
Françnois Jankowiak

Bibliography

Annuario pontificio per l'anno 1993, Vatican City, 1993.
Felici, G. *La Camera apostolica*, Rome, 1940.
Frezza di San Felice, Ph. *Dei cameri segreti e d'onore del sommo pontefice, Memorie storiche*, Rome, 1884.

Goller, E. "Die Kubikulare im Dienste der Päpstlichen Hofverwaltung vom 12. Bis 15. Jahrhundert," *Papstum und Kaisertum: Forschungen . . . Paul Kehr dargebracht*, Munich, 1926, 621–47.

Guillemain, B. *La cour papale d'Avignon 1309–1376*, Paris, 1966, 373–6.

Raffalli, J. "Chamberlain," *DDC, II*, (1937), 1273–5.

Redig de Campos, D. *I Palazzi vaticani*, Bologna, 1967.

CHANCELLORS AND VICE CHANCELLORS.

Following is a list of the chancellors and vice chancellors from the beginning of the 14th century onward:

Pietro Testore (1319–25)

Pierre Depres (1325–61)

Pierre De Monteruc (1361–80)

Rainulfe De Gorze De Monteruc (1381–82)

Francesco Moricotti Prignano (1382–94)

Angelo Acciaiuoli (1394–1408)

Jean De Brogny (1409–26)

Giovanni Di Rupescissa (1436–37)

Francesco Condulmaro (1437–53)

Rodrigo Borgia (Alexandre VI) (1457–92)

Ascanio Sorza (1492–1505)

Galeotto Della Rovere (1505–07)

Sisto Della Rovere (1507–17)

Giulio De Medici (Clement VII) (1517–23)

Pompeo Colonna (1524–26)

Ippolito De Medici (1532–35)

Alessandro Farnese (1535–89)

Alessandro Peretti (1589–1623)

Ludovico Ludovisi (1623–32)

Francesco Barberini (1632–79)

Pietro Ottoboni (1689–1740)

Tommaso Ruffo (1740–53)

Girolamo Colonna (1753–56)

Alberico Archinto(1756–58)

Carlo Rezzonico (1758–63)

Henry Stuart (1763–1807)

Francesco Carafa Di Trajetto (1807–18)

Giulio Maria Della Somaglia (1818–30)

Tommaso Arezzo (1830–33)

Carlo Odescalchi (1833–34)

Carlo Maria Pedicini (1834–43)

Tommaso Bernetti (1843–52)

Luigi Amat Di S. Filippo E Sorso (1852–78)

Antonino De Luca (1878–83)

Teodolfo Mertel (1884–99)

Lucido Maria Parocchi (1899–1903)

Antonio Agliardi (1903–15)

Ottavio Cagiano De Azevedo (1915–27)

Andrea Fruhwirth (1927–33)

Tommaso Pio Boggiani (1933–42)

Celso Costantini (1954–57)

Giacomo Luigi Copello (1959–67)

Luigi Traglia (1968–73)

Joel-Benoit d'Onorio

Bibliography

Baumgarten, P. M. *Von der Apostolischen Kanzlei*, Cologne, 1908.

See also CHANCERY, PAPAL.

CHANCERY, PAPAL.

The use of the word *cancellaria* to describe the office responsible for drawing up and issuing pontifical documents appeared for the first time in three letters of ALEXANDER III (JL 11,356; 14,139; 14,142) between 1160 and 1170. Prior to this, the office had been called *scrinium*, modeled after similar institutions of the old imperial court. From earliest times, the popes have needed qualified individuals to help prepare and draft the documents necessary to govern the Universal Church and administer the heritage of the Church of Rome. Let us look at the development of the chancery over time.

Until the 11th Century. From the beginning to the 11th century, we have very few original pontifical records, perhaps 20 in all. This is mainly due to the fact that papyrus, a fragile material, was used. Although parchment also came into use after A.D. 1000, papyrus would still be used until after the middle of the 11th century. From ancient times, popes wrote letters of consolation and admonition, answered questions of theology and discipline, and took the measures necessary to administer the PATRIMONY OF ST. PETER and manage the affairs of the Universal Church. The pontifical records and letters emulated the form of the ancient epistles and the official letters of the Roman Empire.

Under PASCHAL I (817–24) a particular form of privilege appeared. The phrase *in perpetuum* was substituted for the salutation and the phrase *Scriptum per manum* directly linked to the body text was introduced into the eschatology. The new phrase included the name and title of the scribe as well as an indication of the month and year *indictio*. This was followed by the *Bene valete* of the pontiff and the *grand date*, included by the person responsible for issuing the document. These additions make it possible for us to know the persons who were responsible for the preparation and issuance of pontifical acts. The actual work was done by the *notarii sanctae Romanae Ecclesiae*, some of whom were called *notarii regionarii*, already known in the 3rd and 4th centuries.

The notaries were organized into *schola*, led by the *primicerius* and his deputy the *secundicerius notariorum*. Since the office to which they belonged was called the *scrinium*, the expression *scriniarii sanctae Romanae*

Ecclesiae was used. Their names occur most often in the dating of privileges, where one also finds the names of high dignitaries in the papal court: *primus defensorum, arcarius, saccellarius, nomenculator.* These six dignitaries, to which group the *protoscuriarius* was added in the 9th century, made up the powerful *judices de clero,* also called *judices palatini.* In the 9th century a new post was created, that of *bibliothecarius sanctae sedis apostolicae,* or librarian. The librarian was a bishop, (with the exception of Anastasius *bibliothecarius* (d. 879) who was an abbot), and was more willing to submit to the authority of the pope. The *judices de clero,* on the other hand, were tonsured clerics or belonged to the minor orders, and maintained links with the principal families of Rome. Toward the end of the 9th century, the librarian completely replaced the *judices de clero,* in the dating of privileges. The notary scriveners also had close links with the notaries in Rome, so much so that the Roman curial also became adopted as the writing for the acts drafted by the Roman lawyers. Around A.D. 1000 the post of *cancellarius* was created within the chancery. Although the *cancellarius* was initially subordinate to the *bibliothecarius,* as of 1037, the positions were merged under the title of *bibliothecarius.* The chief of the Chancery became known as the *bibliothecarius,* or *bibliothecarius et cancellarius.* During the 11th century, this task sometimes fell to the Archbishops of Cologne (1024–26 to Pilgrim II, *bibliothecarius, apostolicale sedis*; 1057–67 to Herman II and to Annon II, *archicancellarius*). From the middle of the 11th century, the actual head of the Chancery was usually a *cardinal-deacon* or a *cardinal-priest,* who, if for any reason could not fulfill his duty was replaced by a subordinate.

There were also changes at the beginning of the 9th century that affected officials of lesser rank. Notaries from among the clerics close to the pope, the *notarii sacri palatii,* were used more and more often for dispatching letters. The importance of the notaries increased under LEO IX, the traveling pope. During the pontiff's absences from Rome, the notaries wrote the privileges. The use of the notary-scriveners became more and more rare and ceased altogether in 1123.

Under Leo IX a new formal style of privilege came into use. In the space between the body text and the *grand date* the *rota* and the monogram *Bene valete* were added. Toward the end of the 11th century the stamps of the pope (in the center) and of the three orders of cardinals (in three columns) were added.

The 11th to 13th Centuries. From the 11th century onward, there was a change in the management of the Curia. The system of paternalistic preferences was discarded in favor of a more modern approach, which may be described as bureaucratic. It was during this period that the Sacred College, the Apostolic Chamber, and the group of pontifical chaplains refined their focus. The general outlines of a real chancery, with a cardinal at its head, became more precise. Chancellors Giovanni di Gaeta (1088–1118) and Aimeric (1123–41) contributed decisively to the development of the institution. During the pontificates of GREGORY VIII and his successor CLEMENT III (1187–91), no cardinal chancellor was appointed. Moyse, canon of Lateran, was entrusted with heading that important office as *cancellarii vicem agens.* CELESTINE III (1191–98), reestablished the previous order, which was once more interrupted for some years in the time of INNOCENT III.

From 1216 onward, no one was appointed to the post of chancellor. The group of notaries appointed to the chancery were then nominated to the administration of the chancery. Their coordinator was the *vicecancellarius,* one of the notaries of the pope or an ecclesiastical dignitary of lesser rank, who was an expert jurist or man of letters (for example, 1226–27: Sinibaldo Fiesche, later pope INNOCENT IV; 1244–51, Marino Filomauni; in 1296–1300; Ricardo Petronius of Siena). The notaries, called *notarius papae, notarius domini nostri,* according to the old tradition of regional notaries, usually numbered about six or seven. They were men of learning and experts in the law. They enjoyed special privileges and were often entrusted with important missions. Each one worked in his *camera,* assisted by *breviatores,* or ABBREVIATORS *notariorum,* who were employed on a private basis by the notary. In the 13th century the directorate of the chancery was largely collegial. This may be seen in the communal life led by the vice chancellor and the notaries. Toward the end of the century the authority of the vice chancellor had begun to prevail, especially with respect to the final inspection and delivery of documents free of charge. The vice chancellor called upon the most qualified *abbreviators* to assist him in that task. The rapid increase in the number of documents required led to more efficient deligation of work and more precise specification of the work to be done within the chancery. There were numerous requests for the pope's intervention on questions of justice, as well as requests for funds for ecclesiastical benefices. Previously the notaries themselves had seen to the copying of documents to be sent, but at the end of the 12th century a body of *scriptores litterarum apostolicaram,* or *scriptores papae,* was established to do this work. The members were appointed by the pope and numbered up to 100. In the 13th century the *scriptores,* like the notaries, were almost all Italian. It was only under CLEMENT V that Frenchmen began to be hired and gained majority in Avignon under CLEMENT VI.

The *scriptores* were organized in colleges and designated some of their number for the appointment by the vice chancellor and notaries of a *distributor notarum grossandarum.* There were also the posts of *rescriben-*

darius (for the more equitable distribution of letters to be rewritten), *computator*, (to ensure that the amount of the tax was correct), and *auscultatores et lectores*, (to supervise the transcription done in the chancery). There were also posts in the *audientia publica*, assistant to the *audito litterarum, contradictarum*, and the *corrector litterarum apostolicarum*. Innocent III also introduced two offices, which were intended to ensure the security of documents coming from the chancery. One of these was the post of *auditor litterarum contradictarum*, who was responsible for resolving differences arising between the parties when certain documents, intended to be made into BULLS, were being read publicly. He also had to deal with the procurators who had to act in accordance with instructions from their clients. The other post was the *corrector litterarum apostolicarum*, who had to verify that documents being validated conformed with the law and prevailing provisions. The two *bullatores (plumbatores)*, assisted by the *magistri plumbi* or *taxatores in bullaria*, were responsible for affixing the leaden bull or *bulla*. The *bullatores* were generally lay Cistercian monks from Fossanova, (under the Avignon papacy, from Fontfroide). Traditionally, they did not know Latin. For better management of the affairs of the Curia, the plaintiffs could get the advice of experts, called *procuratores*. Each *procurator* had to present to the *auditor litterarum contradictarum* the power of attorney giving him the *ad agendum* power to follow on behalf of his client, the trials at the Curia tribunals, and *ad impetrandum* power to ensure, on behalf of his client, that the required documents were obtained and sent. From the 13th century, the name and stamp of the *procurator* was found at the back of the parchment in the middle of the upper margin.

The staff of the chancery was paid in part by the Apostolic Chamber and in part by the collection of taxes on the documents requested. The letters sent out at the request of the petitions bore, from the papacy of ALEXANDER IV (1254–64), the amount of the tax written on the original, under the fold to the left. The distributor (or the *rescribendarius* or *taxator* of the college of writers was responsible for determining the tax. The tax (in *grossi turonenses*) was generally paid: (a) to the writers; (b) as required to the notaries and abbreviators; (c) to the *bullaria*; (d) to the registry office. The first two taxes paid the respective categories of persons, while the last two went to the Apostolic Chamber. Almost all chancery employees were clerics (more often than not, of minor orders). They could easily obtain ecclesiastical benefices in different countries of Europe.

The *de gratia* and *de justitia* letters were added to the privileges under Innocent IV (1243–54). Another very formal and solemn kind of letter (*litterae sollemnes*), recognizable by the omission of the address (*inscriptio*), and the substitution of the salutation with the phrase "*ad perpetuam (futuram) rei memoriam*," was added. A number

of the letters sent were *de curia* or, in other words, sent in the interest of the pope, cardinals, or the Curia administration. The vast majority of letters sent implied some action to be taken by the interested party. In the 13th century a written petition was required, whereas prior to that time it had been done verbally. The petitioner or his representative (procurator), drew up the PETITION in the style of the Curia and presented it to one of the notaries, who in turn received the petitions at fixed hours and on particular days (*data communis*). The requests, collected and examined by the notaries, were presented to the pope who, in the 13th century, verbally expressed his decision. The notary (or his assistants), who had dealt with the petition, drew up the minutes which were passed on to writers after the notary's approval. The *distributor notarum grossandarum* gave it to one of the notaries to make the original copy. The writer copied it by his own hand, and from the time of pope Innocent III, placed his signature to the right of the fold. Initially, it was in the form of initials, but by the end of the 13th century the entire name appeared.

Beginning in the 12th century, there were precise rules for the graphic form of the *cum serico* letters, that is, sealed with silk threads. The initials of the pope had to be enlarged; spaces were placed between the letters and a floral design (*cum spatiis et floribus*) was included. The *cum filo canapis* letters had the initial written completely in black ink (*sine floribus et divisione*). In the *litt.c.ser.*, the other letters of the pope's name were highlighted by adopting the *elongata* of upper-case form. In the *litt.c.f. canapis*, the name of the pope, after the initial, was written in normal lower-case writing. The highlighted upper-case letters were used in the *litt.c.ser.* for different first initials of the first word of sentences.

The final copy was the duty of the *distributor* or the *rescribendarius*, who together with the *computator*, set the tax and collected the money. From the time of Alexander IV, the payment of this tax was verified by the signatures of the *distributor* (or the *rescribendarius*) and the *computator* under the amount of the tax. The control of the original copy began with a comparison between the minutes and the copy to verify the accuracy of the transcription (*prima visio*). In the 13th century, the notaries and their assistants (*abbreviatores notariorum*) made this comparison. The second tax was paid to them. The final approval of the document followed. Before the 13th century it was read before the pope (*litterae legendae*) or a summary revision (made at the chancery) was delivered to the interested party (*litterae dandae*). From the time of Innocent III, it was the *corrector literarium apotolicarum*, assisted by the *auscultatores*, who monitored the document for style and content. Letters concerning the justice system, which could affect the interest of third parties, were read during the *audientia publica* at which the vice chancellor was present, along with notaries, the *lectores audientiae*, and representatives of the parties. The approving party, if its rights had been infringed, could introduce an alternative (*contradicere*). At that time, the auditor *litterarum contradictarum* dealt with the case. Following the necessary discussion about the alternative, he either dismissed it, or invalidated the document, and produced a supplementary explanatory one in his own name and bearing his seal, called a *litterae audientiae: cautio*. The bull was then affixed and the third tax was paid. The affixing of the bull was done by the *bullatores (plumbatores)*. Based on whether the pope's initial was in black ornaments or had white spaces and floral designs, they knew whether to use the hempen or silken string for the seal. The document was subsequently transcribed in the register, and the fourth tax was paid. The registration could also take place at another time, for example at the end of the pontifical year. In that case, the minutes, which had been collected over time, were used. The registration of documents allowed the Curia to monitor its activities, but it was also a guarantee for the addressee in case the original was lost.

From the 13th century, separate notebooks or volumes were reserved for the registration of the *litterae de curia*, which separated them from the mass of *litterae communes*. Only 20 percent of the correspondence from the chancery was registered in the first three-quarters of the 13th century, whereas in the last quarter, 60 percent of the documents were registered. The letters read during the *audientia* and, in general, the *litterae minoris iustitiae* were not registered. It was still customary in the 13th century to write a large "R" on the back of the page of the original version. This was sometimes accompanied by the note *script* (the meaning of which is unclear), and later by the annotation of the volume and entry number (*capitulum*) on the register.

The 14th and 15th Centuries. During the Avignon period, the activity of the chancery increased even more. Due to the very large number of benefices, letters concerning funds were introduced. These were a formal style used for the important decisions made during the consistory. In their opening and text, they resemble other letters (*litterae gratiosae, litterae sollemnes*), however, on the last leaf, they display some elements of the privileges. There was the rota and the signature of the pope and the cardinals (the monogram *Bene valete*, and the phrase *Dat per manum* are missing). The *litterae consistoriales* were very rare, but they still exist to this day and are called *litterae decretales* (for canonizations, convocations of a council, etc.). JOHN XXII, through the *Paterfamilias* constitution (1331), changed the procedure for issuance of the documents of the chancery. Letters concerning the granting of pardons were drafted by the vice chancellor with his abbreviators, while the notaries and their abbreviators prepared letters concerning judicial acts. Certain

activities in the production of documents, which had, until then, been effected in the chancery, were carried out by other offices. Thus the entire preparatory stage; the acceptance of petitions and their approval (*signatura*), became, from the time of BONIFACE VIII (1294–1303), the responsibility of those who answered directly to the pope. The subsequent development of this new office led, at the end of the 15th century, to the creation of the *Signatura Apostolica*. This office, which affixed the leaden seal (*bullaria*), as well as the registration bureau, passed in the 14th century from the purview of the vice chancellor to that of the cardinal camerlengo. For documents for which authorization to affix the seal during the final control had been refused, an *expeditio per cameram* could be requested. In such a case, the final stage of the issuance including intervention by the secretary for the authorization of the pope, payment of the *taxa quinta*, affixing of the seal, and registration, took place in the Apostolic Chamber. At the end of the 14th century and during the 15th, a large number of political documents were produced by this process. The secretaries and, consequently, the Apostolic Chamber, were responsible for the preparation and issuance of de curia letters, the *litterae secretae*, and the briefs (the last being the sole responsibility of the secretaries). It is evident that the chancellery, which was traditionally important especially for matters of benefices, gradually became a purely technical service for the concession of pardons and everyday dispositions in matters of justice. It ceased to exert influence on general policy and the conduct of the affairs of the Curia and chancery itself. The great SCHISM from 1378 on, had fewer repercussions on the activities of the Avignon chancellery, where the previous vice chancellor and a large number of the former staff remained. This was not the case for Rome, where almost the entire chancellery had to be renewed, even though it was fashioned according to the traditional models.

In the Curia in Rome, a new form of pontifical act, the BRIEF was created. The Curia of MARTIN V (after 1417) had to absorb the employees of at least two obediences. This is why for some time, efforts were made to reduce the extra staff by not naming a successor to a vacant post and by having recourse to the system of participants. In the second half of the 15th century, many offices of the Curia, including those of the chancellery, became venal as a result of fiscal policy. Others were created to quickly obtain large sums of money in times of pressing need (such as the fight against the Turks and others). This was how the college of abbreviators was created, along with the *collectores taxae plumbi* and *sollicitatores litterarum apostolicarum* (or "janissaries") in Curia jargon.

Although the makeup of the staff of the chancellery was essentially the same as it had been in the 13th century, certain tasks became more important, and others, less. From 1320 the head of the chancellery was always a cardinal, but he continued to bear the title *vicecancellarius* (until 1908). He had a substitute called the *regens cancellarium*, usually a bishop. In the 15th century, there was also a *notarius cancellariae* different from the notaries of the pope, and called PROTONOTARIES. The *abbreviatores litterarum apostolicarum* from the chancellery, rapidly gained in number and importance from the beginning of the 15th century. EUGENE IV, through the *Sicut Prudens* Constitution (1445), organized the activities of the *scriptore litterarum apostolicarum*. The final approval (*iudicatura*) of documents ready to receive a bull or seal was better organized, and the coordinator of this work, and intermediary between the vice chancellor and the staff of the chancellery, [called *custos (seneschallus) cancellariae*], gained importance. To improve the procedure for granting and issuing acts, especially with respect to benefices, the popes, from the time of John XXII, published the *Regulae Cancellariae*.

As stated above, the procedure for issuance of acts differed according to whether they were letters of pardon or letters containing juridical acts. The vice chancellor, together with the notaries and a few chosen abbreviators, were responsible for letters of pardon. The final control of judicial acts was the responsibility of the *corrector litterarum apostolicarum* and only part of these were read in *audientia pubblica*, then dealt with (possibly) by the auditor *litterarum contradictarum*. It was not uncommon to have a document not completely in conformity with the rules and customs and, therefore, refused by the chancellery, issued and approved *per Cameram Apostolicam*. Letters on the nomination of apostolic notaries, portable altars, permits for celebrations before dawn, choice of confessors, and indulgences were reserved for the pope's secretaries, who received a tax payable to the abbreviators. The pope's secretaries were also responsible for the *per Cameram* issuance of documents they prepared themselves (*litterae secretae*). In such cases, the secretary in question signed the original under the text, to the right.

At Avignon, the registration was done on paper registers, (today known as *Reg. Aven.* de l'Arch Vat.). Clement VI ordered that they be recopied on parchment paper (fonds *Reg. Var. de l' of AV*). Since 1378 the registers of documents issued by the chancery in Rome have been merged into a homogenous whole, a series presently known as *fonds Reg. Lat de l'AV*. This series was also called the *Registrum Commune*, as it contained the *litterae communes*, or *communes*, and *de curia*.

From the 16th Century to the Present. The decline of the chancery, which began in the 15th century, continued steadily in the following centuries. Repeated calls for reform "*in capite et in membris*," and the Protestant Refor-

mation also brought about changes and reorganization in the chancery itself. The concession of EXPECTATIVES had fallen into disuse, as was the practice of creating officers only to collect taxes. The whole system of benefices underwent a profound change, as did the collection of annates. The number of documents issued by the chancery was drastically reduced. The head of the chancery was called the *vice-chancellarius* until 1908, when the title became *cancellarius*. He was assisted by the *regens cancellariam* and six *protonotarii participantes*. The college of abbreviators, which had been reduced to just a few members, was abolished in 1908, and the college of apostolic protonotaries, *participantes de numero*, assumed its functions. The college of apostolic writers continued to exist in a very reduced form even after the suppression of the *vacataires* in 1814, but died out completely during the 19th century, when substitutes for the abbreviators assumed their duties. In 1569, PIUS V transferred the chancery writers from the Penitentiary to work as *scriptores minoris gratiae*, who, like other apostolic writers, soon saw that their posts had been abolished. The *Regulae cancellariae* was renewed by each new pope at the start of his pontificate and contained the provision for granting benefices (Göller, *Die Kommentatoren*). The last renewal of the *Regulae* dates back to 1910, after which it was partially abolished, and in part absorbed by the code of Canon Law in 1917.

From the middle of the 16th century, the writing of documents containing a bull, (that is, almost all documents issued by the chancery), was transformed into BOLLATICA. During the reform of the Curia by SIXTUS V in 1588, responsibilities of different offices were reorganized. This was a consequence of the powers conferred on the congregations of cardinals. By the 18th century all traces of the original process for issuing documents were gone. Only the *audientia litterarum contradictarum* survived until the reform of PIUS X in the person of a "substitute of contradictions," associated with the chancery. In the 19th century, the documents were taxed by two general depositaries who, at the end of the bureaucratic process, collected the whole tax. From the pontificate of LEO XIII (1978), the bull was only used for acts concerning consistorial provisions and other important questions. In all other cases a red inked stamp was used. For briefs, stamps had been in use since 1842.

With the constitution *Sapienti Consilio*, Pius X limited the chancery to documents to be issued *sub plumbo*. This applied particularly to the most important letters concerning the provision of benefices (consistorial letters), the setting up of diocese and their chapters, and other important acts (AAS, 1, 1909, 16). In 1909 the chancery consisted of the chancellor, the *regens cancellarium*, five protonotaries, the *adjutor studii*, a "notary secretary and archivist," and four writers (Ibid., 132). The apostolic datary, on the other hand, was empowered with the right to draft acts for the granting of minor benefices (Ibid., 16). The reform of the Curia by PAUL VI reserved certain functions for the chancery with the constitution *Regimini Ecclesiae Universae*. These included the issuing of the consistorial letters, (*litterae decretales*), constitutions (*constitutiones apostolicae*), and the most important letters in forma *bullae vel brevis*. The State Secretariat issued briefs of lesser importance (AAS, 59, 1967, 923). Finally, on 27 February 1973, Paul VI abolished the chancery and transferred its duties to the secretariat of state, within which he established a section called *cancellaria litterarum apostolicarum*. The function of chancellor was abolished, and in the recent editions of the *Annuario pontificio*, there is no mention of the chancery.

Paulius Rabikauskas

Bibliography

Barbiche, B. "Le personnel de la chancellerie pontificale aux XIII et XIV siècles," *Prosopographie et genèse de l'État moderne*, Paris, 1986, 117–30.

Cheney, C. R. *The Study of the Medieval Papal Chancery*, Glasgow, 1966.

Claeys-Bouaert, F. "Chancellerie," *DDC*, 3 (1942), 464–71.

Del Re, N. *La Curia Romana. Lineamenti storico-giuridici*, Rome, 3e éd., 1970.

Frenz, S. T. *Die Kanzlei der Päpste der Hochrenaissance 1471–1527*, Tübingen, 1986.

Frenz, T. *Papsturkunden des Mittelalters und der Neuzeit*, Stuttgart, 1986; trad. ital.: *I documenti pontifici nel medioevo e nell'età moderna*, Cité du Vatican, 1989 (bibliographie, 99–129).

Herde, P. *Beiträge zur päpstlichen Kanzlei- und Urkundenwesen im 13. Jahrhundert*, Kallmünz, 2e éd., 1967; *Audientia litterarum contradictarum*, 2 vols., Tübingen, 1970.

Leclercq, H. "Chancellerie apostolique," *DACL*, 3/2 (1913), 175–207.

Meyer, A. *Arme Kleriker auf Pfründensuche ("Litterae in forma pauperum")*, Cologne-Vienne, 1990.

Nüske, G. F. "Untersuchungen über das Personal der päpstlichen Kanzlei 1254–1304," *Archiv für Diplomatik . . .*, 20 (1974), 39–240; 21 (1975), 249–431.

Poole, R. L. *Lectures on the History of the Papal Chancery down to the Time of Innocent III*, Cambridge, 1915.

Rabikauskas, P. R. *Diplomatica pontificia*, Rome 5e éd., 1993.

Schwarz, B. *Die Organisation kurialer Schreiberkollegien von ihrer Entstehung bis zur Mitte des 15. Jahrhunderts*, Tübingen, 1972.

Tangl, M. *Die päpstlichen Kanzleiordnungen 1200–1500*, Innsbrück, 1894.

CHAPEL, PAPAL.

Historical. In the ROMAN CURIA, the expression "papal chapel" generally designated the mass sung in the Sistine Chapel of the Vatican. The pope participated on his throne. The CARDINALS lined up around him with all the members of the CURIA arranged according to hierarchy. The ambassadors of states in communion with the Holy See were also present, along with the rare invited prince or two.

From a 1578 engraving illustrating Patrizi Piccolomini's *Ceremonial* one can see that the participants have remained the same since the 15th century. The celebrant at the altar is either a cardinal or a prelate designated by the Master of Ceremonies, the sacristan, or the master of the chapel. Around 1495 a summary of the 26 annual papal masses was published. It appears as an appendix to Patrizi's work. In Paris de Grassi's *Ceremonial papale*, published by Martene, it is reproduced in a more complete form. An unedited 1510 manuscript dedicated to cardinal camerlengo Raphael Riario and currently part of a private collection includes a description of these masses, which totaled 35 at this point because they included the three celebrated each year by JULIUS II himself (at Christmas, Easter, and on the feast of St. Peter and St. Paul) as well as those of the cardinals, bishops, or priests designated according to the feasts of the liturgical year. Sermons were also scheduled. General procurators of religious orders, then the most renowned Roman preachers, were assigned particular days. The text would be received in advance by the master of the Sacred Palace. As a recent work has established, their piety and orthodoxy did not preclude philosophy or humanism.

The term "papal chapel" can also be viewed in a more general sense. Gaetano Moroni, the scholarly chamber valet of GREGORY XVI, devotes to this subject a volume of more than 400 pages, published in Venice in 1841, and also appearing in his *Dizionario di erudizione storico-ecclesiastica*, a work of more than 100 volumes. He discusses, in succession, papal chapels, cardinalitial or prelatial, and the private chapels of the popes. In the first book on the papal chapels, ten chapters are devoted to the following topics: their origins, Vatican chapels, the Sistine, the Pauline, and the Quirinal; the revival, under the Restoration, of the ancient papal custom of celebrating the liturgy in different churches in Rome; ministers, servants, and cantors; vespers, matins, masses, and pontifical rites where the pope participates; processions and other liturgical functions; movable or extraordinary chapels; personalities and their roles; the rights of sovereigns; the required procedures for admission; the escorts and retinues of popes and cardinals en route; preliminaries for assistants; speeches and sermons to be heard; the announcements of papal couriers; and, finally, the calendar of these ceremonies. And that is not all. Seventy other articles referred to Stations, Processions, Cardinalitial Titles, *Presbiterium*, Collect, Avignon Apostolic Palace, Other Palaces, Tiara (*Triregno*), Throne, Conclave, Sacristy (*Sagrista*), Canon (*Canonico*), Rota, Signatura of Justice, Clerics of the Camera, Church Song, Chaplains, Bells, Brotherhood, Filippini, Anniversary of the Election of the Pope, *Dies irae*, Adoration of the Pope, Greeks, Profession of Faith, Death of the Pope (*Cadaveri, Precordii, Traslatione, Esequie, Orazioni funebri*), Clerk of the Sacred College, Cavalries (*Calvalcate*), Canonization, Baptism, Confirmation (*Cresima*), Anointment of Bishops, Dedication of Churches, Ordinations, Nuptials (*Sposalizio*), Imperial Coronation, Consistories, Benedictions, Pontifical Chants, Prefect of Rome, Gospel, Papal Cloak, Washing of the Hands, Voyages and Vacations, Castel Gandolfo, Silver Mass, Sermons (*Prediche*), Obedience (*Ubidienza*), Candle Holders (*Bugia*), Papal Scribes (*Scrittori apostolici*), Altarist, Ashes (*Ceneri*), Golden Rose, *Corpus Domini, Sepolcro*, Ambassadors, Senator of Rome, Footwear (*Calze*), *Sancta Sanctorum*, etc. The authors cited by Moroni—Ducange, Mabillon, Martene, and Petau—are highly regarded, but he also includes more on the ancient works of the Roman and Italian scholars. Moroni never saw a manuscript source (he sometimes cites the MS Vat. Lat. 4736, but that is taken from Gattico). He uses fifty works, such as those of Adami, Ameil, Ammannati, Azevedo, Bernini, Bonanni, Borgia, Burckard, Camarda, Camuccini, Cancellieri, Casimiro, Cenni, Ceo, Chacon, Chattard, Ciampini, Condivi, Fantoni, Fracco, Galletti, Gallicciolli, Gattico, Gavanti, Garampi, Giorgi, Grassi, Guattani, Infessura, Landucci, Marangoni, Mazzinelli, Moretti, Novaes, Oldoini, Pagi, Panigarola, Panvinio, Patrizi, Piazza, Pistolesi, Platina, Ratti, Richa, Rocca, Sarnelli, Sestini, Suarz, Taia, Ugonio, Vasari, Zaccaria, and a few others, all cited in this single article and all in relation to the chapel.

Another meaning of "papal chapel" is a building reserved for papal occasions. The best known is the SISTINE CHAPEL commissioned by SIXTUS IV in 1483. Within the Vatican, Angelico painted the small private chapel dedicated to St Nicholas. The *sacellum palatii*, or pre-Sistine chapel preceeded the Sistine. A third chapel no longer exists. The so-called common chapel within the Sistine was allocated to the chaplains and cantors for their daily mass. Papal elections sometimes took place there. The space occupied by this common chapel, 20 meters deep, still exists within a staircase of the papal sacristan's apartment.

Marc Dykmans

Bibliography

Ehrle, F. and Egger, H. *Gli Affreschi del Pinturicchio ...*, Rome, 1897, 21–2; *Der Vatikanische Palast ...*, Rome, 1935, pl. V.

Moroni, G. *Dizionario di erudizione storico-ecclesiastica*, "Capelle pontificie o papali," 8, 114–320; 9, 1–122; "Capelle cardinalizie," 122–47; "Capelle prelatizie," 147–52; "Capelle secrete del Papa," 152–68.

Noirot, M. and Lesage, R. *Catholicisme*, 2 (1951), 935–38.

O'Malley, J. W. *Praise and Blame in Renaissance Rome*, Durham, N.C., 1979.

Patrizi Piccolomini, A. *Le Ceremonial papal de la premiere Renaissance*, ed. M. Dykmans, 2 vols., Rome, 1980–82.

Rasmussen, N. K. *Maiestas pontificia, Analecta Romana Instituti Danici*, 12 (1983), 109–48.

Redig De Campos, D. *I Palazzi Vaticani*, Rocca San Casciano, 1967.

Shearman, J. *Raphael's Cartoons ...*, London, 1972.

Steinmann, E. *Die Sixtinische Kapelle*, 4 vols., Munich, 1901–05.

Music. The papal chapel is the only musical institution directly linked to the sovereign pontiff. Comprised of a group of chaplain singers, its role is to provide the daily liturgical service (recitation of the office and celebration of the mass) in the palace where the pope resides. Traditionally, the papal chapel sings without any musical accompaniment, not even the organ, in order to provide a terrestrial version of a group of angels surrounding the throne of God to sing His praises. When the pope celebrates or participates at a solemn function, it is said that he is "holding chapel." These ceremonies, whether they are for Vespers or mass, have an official character and take place on regular dates.

The pope holds chapel at mass every Sunday of Advent and of Lent, as well as for a selected series of major feasts: the Christmas Triduum, Circumcision, Epiphany, Chair of ST. PETER, Annunciation, Easter and Easter Monday, Ascension, Pentecost, Holy Trinity, Corpus Christi, St. Peter, Assumption, All Saints, and All Souls. From the reign of ALEXANDER VIII on, the Nativity of the Holy Virgin also became an occasion for papal chapel. Papal chapels at Vespers are less frequent and always take place at First Vespers, the vigil of a particular feast. There are nine during the year: All Saints, Christmas, Circumcision, Epiphany, Ascension, Pentecost, Holy Trinity, Corpus Cristi, and St. Peter. Three anniversaries are also the occasions of a papal chapel: the death of the previous pope and the election and coronation of a new pontiff.

The chapel service is held in the chapel of the papal palace; if the pope is living in the Vatican, it is held in the Sistine Chapel, the premier chapel. From PAUL V on, the popes most often reside in the QUIRINAL PALACE, where an exact copy of the Sistine Chapel was built. Nevertheless, during the course of the 17th and 18th centuries, the sovereign pontiffs always returned to the Vatican for the Christmas feast and the Easter season, if not for the entire Lenten season. On days when the pope solemnly participated in a procession, the papal mass that preceded it was only a Low Mass. This was always the case on the morning of the feast of Corpus Cristi, and every time the pope decided to celebrate a jubilee, which included two or three processions in the city. During papal low masses, the papal chapel sung a motet for the offertory and another for the elevation. Apart from these purely liturgical performances, the papal chapel was invited to sing three motets at public consistories when the hat was conferred on new cardinals. For this extra service the singers received a gratuity from the new cardinals. The pope also invited his chapel to sing motets for him at lunch four times a year. It was an opportunity for the singers to have a private audience with the sovereign pontiff for whom, on the following afternoon, they sang Vespers in his private chambers. These "private Vespers" became the rule starting from the reign of CLEMENT VIII. Some cardinals obtained the pope's authorization to use the chapel for feasts other than papal feasts, and thus were conceived certain "cardinalitial chapels" such as those for St. Thomas Aquinas at the Church of Minerva or for St. Bonaventure at the Holy Apostles' Church. The college of papal cantors sang at the funerals of all cardinals who died in Rome. For all these services, which had nothing to do with the sovereign pontiff, the singers received a gratuity.

Documents from the congregation of the Sacra Visita Apostolica dating back to the 16th century speak repeatedly of an ideal number of twelve singers, which would have been the number of the chapel from MARTIN V to PAUL II because "*multitudo vocum melodiam tollit et confundit auditum.*" But the document in which this statement appears contradicts itself a little further on when it says that the chapel of PIUS II, who preceded Paul II, had eighteen singers. In fact, the number of chaplain-singers varied, continually increasing. Some popes tried to restrain this tendency without great success. Under LEO X, there were thirty-six singers, with the number dropping to twenty-four under CLEMENT VII. When SIXTUS V reformed the chapel in 1586, he again fixed the number at twenty-four. The number would continue to increase regularly, and URBAN VIII would fix it at thirty-two but leave open the possibility of hiring additional singers on condition that they were not paid. The numbers would continue to rise until the revolutionary period. From its creation, the papal chapel was placed under the control of a prelate called the Master of the Chapel who exercised his authority over the musical personnel—the singers, the copyist(s), and the keeper of the music books. The musical direction was the responsibility of the dean of the college, who was assisted by the most senior singers.

In addition to the dean, the college had two other officers elected by their colleagues—the camerlengo and the pointer. The former had the responsibility of collecting the chapel wages at the end of each month, as well as any other gratuities accruing to the singers, of distributing them among his comrades, and of keeping an accounts ledger related to these activities. The latter was responsible for noting lapses in discipline (absences, lateness, errors in singing), which were liable to fines that were subsequently shared among those who did not commit any infractions. The post of secretary of the college was never official and would often be merged with that of pointer. It disappeared definitively at the end of the 16th century.

In 1586, Pope Sixtus V reorganized the chapel. He decided that instead of having a master prelate of the chapel, each year the singers would elect their own master of the chapel from among their colleagues who had at least fifteen years of seniority. In addition, the college would have a CARDINAL PROTECTOR, who would guarantee the privileges of the college, as well as evaluating its performance. During the course of the following centuries, intervention by cardinal protectors would become more frequent and incisive.

In order to increase the salary of the singers and to ensure the financial autonomy of the college, Sixtus V combined three existing ecclesiastical benefices—an abbey near Mantua, another near Taranto, and a priory near Perugia—and allocated their revenues to the college. The administration of these benefices caused such difficulties (in particular, the long absences by singers sent to these places), that Pope GREGORY XIV annulled this provision in 1591 and fixed the salaries of chaplain-singers at 200 ecus per year, to be paid monthly by the treasurer of the Apostolic Camera.

New singers were hired only when a place became vacant through death or because a singer obtained authorization to retire: Posts at the papal chapel were granted *ad vitam* and one could not leave without authorization. If there was a vacancy, a competitive examination was announced by edict, and candidates were put through a series of tests, after which the singers of the college met as a quorum and voted for those who seemed to demonstrate the necessary qualifications. The vote was secret; to be admitted, a candidate must have obtained two-thirds of the vote plus one. In the event no candidate was elected, the college left it up to the cardinal protector to admit the one who obtained the most votes or to hold the competitive examination again. Singers who had at least twenty-five years service had the right to retirement, that is they continued to receive their full salary but were not required to serve. They were still welcome at offices but were not subject to the point system.

This system remained in place until 1793, when the Roman republic under the protection of the French army was installed. From that time the pope was apparently able to hire anyone he pleased, without holding the competitive examinations that had been frequent throughout the 17th century. CASTRATI, in particular, were recruited in this fashion, with very few exceptions. This recruitment by *motu proprio*, even when used only for extra singers, was one cause of the expansion in the number of chapel singers. As a singer could not be retained for a very long time as a supernumerary, that is, with no salary, the cardinal protectors instituted the practice of dividing one salary between two singers. The phenomenon became so important that in the second half of the 18th century, it was decided to give the supernumeraries a small salary so that the regular singers could have a full salary. In 1747, for example, there were sixteen salaried singers out of a total of thirty-two active singers; of the 16 retired singers, 9 were castrati. As the latter were hired without a competitive examination, they generally become members of the chapel at a much younger age than the other singers, who had to prove themselves in other Roman chapels before being able to take part in the competitive examination and therefore were rarely hired before the age of twenty-five or thirty.

Before the reform of Sixtus V, the election of new officers took place during the first days of January. In the last years of the 16th century, the custom emerged of organizing the elections on 28 December, which allowed the outgoing master of the chapel to present his successor to the pope during the audience held on 1 January. During the 17th century, election to the posts of master of the chapel and pointer progressively became a mere formality, and appointment to these two important offices was transformed into a right acquired by seniority (ten years for the pointer and fifteen for the master of the chapel). By the end of the century it would become so customary that only one candidate was presented for each post, the one whose turn it was! Under GREGORY XIII, the college gained the right to be divided into two groups, which alternated for the daily service, except for Sundays, when everyone had to be present. By the beginning of the 17th century, this system was thoroughly established, and each vocal part was divided into two sections, each of which performed every other day at the daily service, which was practically the only time for practice, since the regulations of the chapel did not provide for rehearsal. During the century, these daily services diminished in number, while vacation days increased.

The popes of the 15th and 16th centuries were almost all concerned about the prestige of their chapel and attracted musicians of great talent, most often by promising personal benefices. Until the beginning of the 16th century, there was, therefore, a preponderance of musicians of the Franco-Flemish school. The first important composer of this group is Guillaume Dufay (1400?–1474), who joined the papal chapel in 1428, left in 1433, and returned for a brief period between 1435 and 1437.

Josquin des Prez (1440?–1521), after a sojourn in Milan, joined the chapel in October 1468 and stayed for about a dozen years. Elzear Genet, called Carpentras (1470?–1548), ariving in Rome for the first time, joined the papal chapel from 1508 to 1510 and once again became a member in 1514–21 and 1524–26. His *Lamentations pour la Semaine sainte* (Lamentations for Holy Week) were regularly sung up to the time of Sixtus V. Jacques Arcadelt (1505?–1568?) was the last French composer to work for the pope, for a dozen years starting from 1540.

A group of Spanish musicians were gradually integrated into the chapel from the 15th century on and became one of its most important elements. Among them must be mentioned Francisco de Penalosa (1470?–1528), who was in the service of Pope Leo X from 1517 and returned to Spain only in 1521. Cristobal de Morales (1500?–1553) was in the papal chapel from 1535 to 1548. Francisco Soto de Langa (1534–1619) was recruited in 1562 and died at Rome, dean of the chapel. All of these composers, except Soto, wrote for the chapel.

The first Italian musician who left a significant impression on the chapel's repertoire was Costanzo Festa (1490?–1545), who joined in 1517 and remained until his death. JULIUS III admitted Giovanni Pierluigi da Palestrina (1525–94) to the chapel in January 1555. A cardinalitial commission, which reformed the papal chapel at the request of PAUL IV, expelled him in September of the same year because he was married and did not have a very good voice. At the end of his life, when he was master of the chapel of St. Peter's Basilica, Pope Clement VIII reintegrated him into the papal chapel, which was obliged to pay him the pension that Paul IV had granted him in compensation for his expulsion. On the death of Palestrina, Cardinal Aldobrandini, nephew of Clement VIII, named Felice Anerio as his replacement. The latter had the right to full salary as composer of the chapel. Based on Anerio's appointment, Giuseppe Baini, Palestrina's first biographer, claimed that the latter had also been the official composer of the chapel. Upon the death of Anerio in 1614, the college of papal singers petitioned its cardinal protector to replace him with a singer and to hire no more composers for the papal chapel.

In fact, since the beginning of the 16th century, the college had had within its ranks a number of very talented composers. Apart from those already noted, there was Annibale Zoilo (1537?–92), who was recruited in 1570 and asked to retire in 1577, probably because he wished to marry. He was replaced by Giovanni Maria Nanino (1543?–1607), another important composer of the Roman school. In 1614, besides Soto, Arcangelo Crivelli (1546–1617), and Orazio Griffi (1565–1624), who represented the old school, we find Ruggiero Giovannelli (1560?–1625), Teofilo Gargari (?–1648), and Vincenzo De Grandis (1577–1646), who all left behind compositions in the chapel's collection. It was, therefore, not really necessary to have a composer specially attached to the chapel, particularly since he displaced a singer.

During the reign of PAUL V, the papal chapel was truly one of the best musical ensembles in Europe. During the 17th century, the chapel was especially renowned for the vocal talents of its members, and of the castrati in particular. Nevertheless, singers who were also excellent composers continued to be recruited. In 1629, Stefano Landi (1586?–1639) was engaged; Marco Marazzoli (1602?–62) joined in 1637, Gregorio Allegri (1582–1652) in 1639, and Mario Savioni (1608–85) in 1642. This first group corresponded to the reign of Urban VIII, who understood and loved music. ALEXANDER VII also made an effort to recruit excellent musicians, and his reign saw the arrival of Antonio Cesti (1623–69), who remained barely two years starting from the end of 1659; Antonio Liberati (1617–92) who was engaged in 1661; and Matteo Simonelli (1619?–96), admitted in December 1662. After Simonelli, there were no longer special slots for composers.

Several factors can explain this disaffection with a career that still had real material advantages. Beginning during the reign of Paul V, the musical repertoire became fixed as tastes took a very conservative turn, and "modern" composers obviously realized that their works would not enter the repertoire of the papal chapels. The second factor is related to the obligation to take at least minor orders to join the chapel, which excluded a priori all married musicians. This restriction had not been of great importance during the preceding centuries, when the profession of church musician was practiced mainly by clerics. However, the importance of secular music in society as well as the growing spectrum of professional employment led more and more laymen (and thus married men) to enter the profession. In the 18th and 19th centuries, the few composers who wrote for the papal chapel wrote for it exclusively, and in the style of Palestrina and Allegri. They included Giovanni Biordi (1691–1748), who joined the chapel in 1717; his student Pasquale Pisari (1725?–78), admitted in 1752; and Giuseppe Baini (1775–1844), who was recruited in 1795 and became the architect of the Restoration after the French hiatus. Although his volume on Palestrina is still used as a reference, his music is completely forgotten today, except within the present Cappella Sistina.

The papal chapel ceased its activities with the exile of PIUS VI. What remained of the college of papal singers upon the advent of PIUS VII was placed by the French

under the administrative responsibility of the Cappella Giulia, the musical chapel of St. Peter's Basilica. This institution had been founded by Pope JULIUS II and was a dependency of the chapter of the basilica. At the Restoration, Baini became camerlengo of the papal chapel, a post he would keep until his death, and also assumed its musical direction. His ultraconservative attitude within the papal chapel, and his very opinionated stance vis-à-vis the congregation of St Cecilia, did not facilitate the reorganization of the world of Roman music.

During the 19th century, the papal singers became one of the tourist attractions of the city of Rome. People flocked to hear them, especially during Holy Week, and the legend of Allegri's *Miserere* that Charles Burney gave rise to in the preceding century grew. This interest was also rooted in the presence of the castrati, whom the chapel continued to recruit even though castration of young boys had been forbidden since the French occupation of Rome.

The papal chapel was above all a liturgical institution, and the majority of what was sung was, therefore, based on the traditional Gregorian repertoire, often embellished by the use of fauxbourdon for the psalms and improvised counterpoint for the introits and graduals, for certain hymns, and for the vesper antiphons. Polyphonic music, especially at the beginning of the mass, followed suit: thus was sung the music of Dufay, Josquin, Arcadelt, Carpentras, Festa, Morales, and Palestrina, but also that of other composers who were never part of the chapel, such as Tomás Luis de Victoria.

At the beginning of the 17th century, the musical repertoire of the papal chapels at mass (mass and the motet for the Offertory) began to be fixed, with a clear preference for the music of Palestrina. The repertoire for Vespers, was established a little later and favored two or three of Morales's magnificats, one of Marenzio's (1553?–99)—although this composer was never a member of the college of papal singers, and a series of psalms by Crivelli, Nanino, Giovannelli, Anerio, De Grandis, Gargari, and others. Urban VIII's reform of the breviary brought about a revision of the pieces, particularly of the Vesper hymns. Certain compositions of Gregorio Allegri, including his *Miserere*, entered the repertoire at the end of his life. The trend toward reduction was one of the characteristics of this repertoire, from the middle of the 17th century on. In 1616, twenty-three of Palestrina's masses were included in the program of the papal chapels; in 1695–96, there were no more than a dozen. In addition, there was practically no change in the repertoire, and no works by such great 17th-century composers as Stefano Landi, Marco Marazzoli, and Mario Savioni. The only opportunities for these composers to provide contemporary music for the papal chapel was during private Vespers, which were always accompanied by the organ from Paul V on, but the chapel has not preserved any of these scores.

During the 15th and 16th centuries, the popes maintained a small group of wind instruments—horns and trombones that the Romans called *i trombetti di Castello* because they were under the authority of the governor of the CASTEL SANT'ANGELO. At the beginning of the 17th century, this ensemble came under the authority of the Roman Senate and became *i trombetti di Campidoglio*.

Pope Leo X formed a group of musicians hired for the fetes of the papal court: a vocal ensemble with one or two lute players, and an instrumental ensemble for dances. The ensemble did not survive his pontificate. In the 17th century, popes traditionally made two trips to the Frascati region every year, and some of them were accompanied by a small group of three to five singers chosen from among the members of the college. Among these popes were Paul V, Urban VIII, and Alexander VII. There was always at least one composer among these singers, brought along to entertain the pope's guests or to enhance his private devotions with music.

At least from the reign of GREGORY XIII, the pope customarily invited the cardinals to dinner on Christmas Eve. After assisting at the Vespers of the vigil, they also stayed for the Matins and the midnight Mass. The Christmas Cantata for the apostolic palace sprang from this custom. The banquet was the responsibility of the CARDINAL NEPHEW. A meal without music was unthinkable, and this one did not depart from the rule. Only from 1676 was the organization of this dinner with music entrusted to the majordomo of the pope, and the musical arrangements for the cantata to the master of the papal chapel. The majordomo chose the composer and the author of the text, and the master of the chapel was responsible for the performance and the selection of the singers. Pope BENEDICT XIV abolished this custom in 1741. The majority of written scores for this occasion have not been preserved, while practically all the texts survive because they were printed and distributed to the guests and the singers. Some of the composers mentioned in these booklets are obscure; however, the name of Alessandro Scarlatti is cited four times between 1695 and 1707.

During the course of the 18th century, the brass band of noble guards sometimes accompanied official processions. Charles Gounod wrote the *Marche pontificale* ("Papal March") in 1869 for the anniversary of the coronation of PIUS IX, and it enjoyed a great deal of success. In 1950, Antonio Allegra set the words "*Roma Immortale di martiri et di santi . . ,*" from the anthem adopted by PIUS XII, to this march. This music is played quite regularly by the small brass band of the Swiss guards.

Jean Lionnet

Bibliography

Adami, A. *Observazioni per ben regolare il coro della Cappella Pontificia*, Rome, 1711.

Baini, G. *Memorie storico-critiche della vita e delle opere di Giovanni Pierluigi da Palestrina*, Rome, 1828.

Celani, E. "I cantori della Cappella Pontificia nei secoli XVL-XVIII," *Rivista musicale italiana*, XIV, (1907) and XVI (1909).

Celler, L. *La Semaine sainte au Vatican, étude musicale . . .*, Paris, 1867.

Collectif, "Studien zur Geschichte der papstlischen Kapelle, Tagungbericht, Heidelberg, 1989, herausgegeben von B. Janz," in *Capellae Apostolicae Sixtinaeque Collectanea Acta Monumenta*, Vatican City, 1993.

Frey, H. W. "Die Gesange der Sixtinisschen Kapelle an den Sonntagen und . . .," *Mélanges Eugene Tisserant*, VI, I, Vatican City, 1964.

Gianturco, C. "*Cantate spirituali e morali* with a Description of the Papal Sacred Cantata Tradition for Christmas," *Music and Letters*, 73, (February 1992).

Haberl, F. X. *Die Romische "Schola cantorum" und die papstlischen Kappellsanger bis zur Mitte des 16. Jahrhunderts*, Leipzig, 1888.

"L'évolution du repertoire de la chapelle pontificale au cours du XVIIe siecle," *Atti del XIV congresso della Societa Internazionale di Musicologia 1987*, Turin, 1990.

Lionnet, J. "La Cappella Pontificia e il Regno di Napoli nel Seicento," *Atti del convengo,* Napoli 1985, Rome, 1987.

Lionnet, J. "Performance Practice in the Papal Chapel During the 17th Century," *Early Music*, XV, I (February 1987).

Lorens, J. M. *Cappellae Sixtinae codices musicis notis instructi*, Vatican City, Apostolic Vatican Library, 1960.

Mendelssohn, F. *Voyage de jeunesse, lettres européennes* (1830–1832), Paris, 1980.

Moroni, G. *Histoire des chapelles papales . . . , suivie d'un exposé sommaire des chapelles que tiennent a Rome pendant l'année les cardinaux et prelats,* translated from the Italian by A. Mananvit, Paris, 1846.

"Palestrina e la Cappella Pontificia," *Atti del Convengo di Studi Palestriniani*, Palestrina, 1991.

Roth, A. "Studien zum fruhen Repertoire der papstlischen Kapelle unter dem Pontificat Sixtus IV (1471–1484)," *Cappellae Apostolicae Sixtinaeque Collectanea Acta Monumenta*, Vatican City, 1991.

Schelle, E. *Die sixtinische Kapelle*, Vienna, 1872.

Sherr, R. "Performance Practice in the Papal Chapel in the 16th Century," *Early Music* XV, 4 (November 1987).

Sherr, R. *The Papal Chapel c. 1492–1513 and its Polyphonic Sources*, Ph.D. diss., Princeton University, 1975.

Sherr, R. "The Singers of the Papal Chapel and Liturgical Ceremonies in the Early 16th Century," *Rome in the Renaissance, the City and the Myth*, ed. P. A. Ramsey.

Sherr, R. "The Spanish Nation in the Papal Chapel, 1492–1521," *Early Music*, XX, 4 (November 1992).

Starr, P. *Music and Musical Patronage at the Papal Court*, 1447–1464, Ph.D. diss., Yale University, 1987.

For manuscript sources see the nearly complete collection of "Diari Sistini," which are the books of the chapel pointers (BAV - CS Diari), and the books of the camerlengo (BAV - CS Camerlingo).

CHAPLAIN, PAPAL.

Middle Ages. The history of the medieval papal chaplains (*capellani domini pape*) is inseparable from that of the complex institution to which they belonged, the papal chapel. The latter first appeared at the turn of the year 1000 during the papal reform of the Lateran Palace that was based on the palatine model of the Roman kings and emperors, but it was only organized in the second half of the 12th century, when it acquired particular characteristics within the papal *familia*. Although the first-known chaplain already carried this title, it was not until the 12th century that chaplains appeared in significant numbers. The popes after CLEMENT II, the majority of whom had themselves been participants in the papal chapel, transferred to Rome the model of the Salians Palace, naming former chaplains of their own *familia* as papal chaplains. Growing increasingly numerous in the 12th century, they were designated papal subdeacons with certain privileges (the right to be consecrated by the pope; exemption from the jurisdiction of the ordinary). Starting with CELESTINE II (1191–98), they were given the title "subdeacon and papal chaplain." To their original liturgical functions (assisting the pope at Christmas, Easter, the feast of St. Paul, the exaltation of the Cross) were added judicial and diplomatic missions, legations, and nunciatures and instruction on the simplest canonical procedures. Close ties also existed between the chapel and the chancery, and many notaries were papal chaplains. The recruitment of a great number of cardinals from the ranks of the papal chaplains (thirty in the 12th century) illustrates the importance of this post.

INNOCENT III (1198–1216) included them in his reform of the CURIA. He assigned part of the reform of the LITURGY to them and had a chaplaincy built as a complement to the existing one in the Lateran, and gave them a substantial role in the reformed chancery (the three cardinal chancellors and five vice chancellors of his pontificate came from their ranks). In the 13th century, they filled key posts. When the court for causes of the Apostolic Palace (the ROTA) was inaugurated, the chaplains played a judicial role even greater than that of the cardinals, who, busy with the consistory and the legations, ceded some part of their judicial functions to the chaplains. Under INNOCENT IV (1243–54), the judges of causes were henceforth designated as "papal chaplain and judge for causes of the Sacred Palace." At the Penitentiary, others are at the service of minor penitentiaries from HONORIUS III on (1216–27). Within the church government they had two particular responsibilities: verifying the canonical validity of an episcopal election and conferring the pallium on a metropolitan.

Starting with Innocent IV their function changed radically. Their number quadrupled, rising from 50 under Innocent III and his immediate successors to 200, and the recipiendaries were recruited increasingly from outside the Curia. The pope thus availed himself of the services of a network of increasingly zealous confidants in the temporal courts as well. By the end of the century, a split had gradually developed between the commensal chaplains (those taking meals at the pontiff's table) and those who would be confined to the category of "honorary chaplains" beginning with the reign of CLEMENT VI. The latter, nominated for life by the pope, had to be sworn in by the chamberlain or one of his assistants, like any other member of the Curia. Papal chaplains, in lieu of a designated income, enjoyed highly sought-after privileges. They were legally answerable solely to the pope; if they were monks, they were no longer obliged to reside in their convents; if they were at the Curia, they had the right to collect from the "spices" and to eat at the pope's table at Christmas and Easter. They derived additional advantages from their position, which helped them acquire material goods and numerous benefices. Ultimately the popes were forced to curb these privileges due to the abuses that occurred. The introduction of "honorary apostolic protonotaries" by MARTIN V broke their monopoly.

Under the AVIGNON popes, the role of commensal chaplains was redefined as well. JOHN XXII (1316–34) noted that the chaplains lacked liturgical functions but provided no remedy. BENEDICT XII (1334–42), an austere theologian, undertook a major reform of the Curia, including the chapel, immediately after his election. He created a college of twelve "chaplains of the chapel" responsible for chanting the Hours, who had to live in a palace dormitory and eat at the pope's table, at the expense of the papal kitchens. They received a salary like all other members of the Curia, in spite of the pope's objections. In 1336, their number rose to thirteen. Then from 1341 a "master of the chapel," then the evocative title of "cantors of the chapel," made their appearance. The "chaplains of the chapel" ultimately took over the liturgical functions of the simple commensal chaplains and the *Schola cantorum*. Beginning under Clement VI (1342–52) and INNOCENT VI (1352–62), a supplementary distinction emerged: from 1345, the chaplains of the chapel were also called "chaplains of the intrinsic chapel" (the private chapel of the pope) to differentiate them from the chaplains of the "great chapel," who officiated for all members of the Curia. Under URBAN V cantors gradually replaced the chaplains. Under GREGORY XI (1370–78), a priest—rather than the chaplains of the chapel—was responsible for saying mass with the pope in his private chapel, while a subdeacon and two acolytes were taken from the college of commensal chaplains to perform liturgical functions for the Curia. This structure, maintained by the Avignon popes during the Great Western Schism, restored by the councils of Pisa and Constance, and perfected by the successors of Martin V, experienced few modifications until the end of the Middle Ages.

Pierre Jugie

Bibliography

Burns, C. "Vatican sources and the honorary papal chaplains of the fourteenth century," *Romische Kurle... Studien zu Ehren von H. Hoberg*, I, Rome, 1979, 665–95.

Elze, R. "Die papstliche Kapelle im 12. Und 13. Jahrh," *ZRGKA*, 36 (1950), 145–204.

Guillemain, B. "Les chapelains d'honneur des papes d'Avignon," *MAH*, 64 (1952) 217–38.

Haider, S. "Zu den Anfangen der papstlichen Kapelle," *Miteillungen des Instituts dur osterreichische Geschichtsforschung*, 87 (1979), 38–70.

Haider, S. "Kapelle, papstliche," *LexMA*, 5 (1990), 932–34.

Roth, A. "Zur "Reform" der päpstlichen Kapelle unter dem Pontifikat Sixtus V." *Zusammenhänge, Einflüsse, Wirkungen, Kongressakten zum I. Symposium des Mediävistenverbun (Tubingen, 1984)* Tubingen, 1986.

Schimmelpfenning, B. "Die Organization der papstlichen Kapelle in Avignon," *QFIAB*, 50 (1971) 80–111.

16th Century Onward. Once the chaplains (*cappellani*) attached to the service of the pope definitively became part of PAPAL FAMILY toward the end of the 12th century, the situation of the papal chaplains evolved considerably both in terms of numbers as well as in the division into categories. In this sense, the chaplains underwent an evolution similar to that of the PAPAL HOUSEHOLD in the modern epoch (post-tridentine), characterized by an increasingly complex etiquette specifically attuned to the composition of the clientele and driven by the search for prestige, on the part of the central authority of the Church.

Under the designation of *cappellani*, the judges of the ROTA could be discerned, recognized as permanent chaplains of the pope, and, exercising their functions during solemn manifestations, celebrated by the pope or those he honored by attending. Generally, the body of chaplains was divided between secret (private) and ordinary (common) chaplains. The first undertook confidential duties, assisting the pontiff during the celebration of mass in his private chapel. One of them presided immediately afterward at the thanksgiving there. At public ceremonies, the first private chaplain had the privilege of carrying the papal train; the second—the crucifer—walked before the pope with the cross. These chaplains, still called titular (*di numero*), enjoyed precedence over all other levels in the hierarchy. In addition, they scrutinized papal correspondence, drafted summary notes for the pope, recited the breviary and the rosary with him, and often accompanied him on his walks, sometimes rising to the rank of confidants. The special category of honorary private chaplain with the rank of monsignor was instituted on the initiative of CLEMENT XII (1730–40). These chaplains substituted in the event of an absence by one of the official private chaplains, who numbered about one hundred at the end of the 18th century. PIUS VII (1800–23) included in their ranks honorary chaplains *extra urbem*, who theoretically carried out their functions when the pope traveled to their country of residence. However, they did not enjoy these honors within the walls of the capital of Christianity.

Common chaplains (*communes*) were not distinguished from private chaplains until the pontificate of CLEMENT VII (1523–34). ALEXANDER VII (1655–67) brought them together in a college (along the lines of a canonical chapter) and granted them the responsibility of serving as acolytes and candle bearers in the papal chapels. He bestowed on them the right to wear a surplice (*cotta*) over the violet soutane (*paonazzo*), a distinctive sign of the lower prelature, whether they were titular (*di numero*) or supernumerary chaplains. They served the common chapel and enjoyed an appointment for life, effected by a BRIEF, and the guarantee of retaining their posts during any vacancy in the Apostolic See (a decision made by Alexander VII on 10 June 1657). These privileges were confirmed many times, particularly by an apostolic letter of Clement XII dated 18 May 1731, before PIUS IX conferred the title of monsignor on the chaplain.

PAUL VI (1963–1978), in the *motu proprio Pontificalis Domus* (28 March 1968), abolished the titles and responsibilities of the private and honorary private chaplains (*in urbe* and *extra urbem*), as well as those of the common chaplains. The designation "Chaplain of His Holiness" was thereafter reserved for the closely related corps of supernumerary privy CHAMBERLAINS. In accord with a policy promulgated by VATICAN II, underscored by a desire to simplify and rationalize the composition and structure of the papal household, the above structure has not since undergone any substantial modifications.

Francois Jankowiak

Bibliography

Annuario pontificio per l'anno 1993, Vatican City, 1993.

Bourgin, G. *La famiglia pontificia sotto Eugenio IV*, Rome, 1904.

Cancellieri, F. *Descrizione delle Cappelle Pontificie e Cardinalizie di tutto il mondo e dei Concistori pubblici e segreti*, Rome, 1790.

Chevailier, L. Lefebvre, C. and Pacaut, M. *L'Epoque moderne (1563–1789). Les sources du droit et la seconde centralisation romaine (Histoire du droit et des Institutions de l'Eglise en Occident*, XV), Paris, 1976.

Felici, G. *La Camera apostolica*, Rome, 1940.

Meyer, *La Curie romaine moderne, ses fonctionnaires et leurs attributions*, Leipzig, 1847.

CHEF, POPE'S. The pope's chefs were as little known as their counterparts who served temporal princes. However, many traces of their presence may be found in documents dating from the late Middle Ages and the Renaissance, the point at which they emerged from anonymity and became known as authors of books on cookery.

The papal chef practiced his art in an environment similar to that of an aristocratic house of the same period. During the Avignon papacy, the kitchen, together with the bakery, the cellar, and the blacksmith's workshop, was one of the four most important centers of the household. In the time of CLEMENT V, some twenty people worked in the kitchen. They did so under the strict control of a master chef (*magister coquinae*). Other personnel included a buyer, who ensured that the kitchen was stocked, and a keeper of supplies. In addition, the chef directed an entire brigade of kitchen boys (*brodarii*), aides, and valets.

The chefs and their staff worked in what amounted to two separate kitchens. There was the private kitchen that prepared food for the pope and the common kitchen that cooked for the *Curia*, whose membership was continually on the increase. This duality was especially marked in the AVIGNON palace. The private kitchen was adjacent to the small dining room where the pope normally took his meals, while the chefs who prepared the rations for prelates and officers of the palace, or banquets to be held in the large dining room, worked in the kitchen tower. On certain special occasions, however, such as the marriage of the pope's grandniece, chefs were also called in from outside. Apart from the kitchens used by the pope and other members of his staff, there was also the Pinhote, which provided soup and cheese for the sick and the poor. But while some French chefs like Taillevent served several generations of kings, their colleagues in Avignon and Rome were obliged to leave their posts upon the death of the pontiff. The election of a new pope almost automatically implied a complete turnover of the kitchen staff. With a new pope—whose tastes were not necessarily like those of his predecessor—a complete new "family," a pressure group with strong regional loyalties, would come to power and distribute jobs. It was rare for a chef to climb the internal ranks of the kitchen staff to accede to his post. More often than not, they were imposed from outside. The

career of Jean Postel, who served at least four popes—from CLEMENT VI to GREGORY XI—therefore shines as a brilliant exception. The chefs, who were constantly in contact with blood, were generally laypeople. The wages they received at the beginning of the Avignon period placed them on the same footing with the chief wine bearer or master bread maker. Within a short period of time, they were paid as much as the chefs and the provisioner. This indicates the great interest shown in their art. This interest and respect may also be seen in the title of "master chef" (*magister coques*), which was conferred upon the best among them.

The papal table, was, in fact, a major site of political power. Like the great princes of the times, the pope showed his power by organizing succulent and sumptuous feasts. There were many occasions to justify such banquets: the weddings of relatives or knightly feasts of the pope's family members, the promotion of new cardinals, and, of course the crowning of a new pope. For the celebratory banquet following the crowning of Clement VI, fifty thousand tarts were made, requiring tens of thousands of eggs and cheeses.

Such banquets were of necessity magnificent. Beginning in the 14th century, they inaugurated a tradition that would be followed in the court of Europe for two centuries. The guests were plied with desserts that were veritable edifices, a delight to the eye as well as the palate, and for which special cooks and artists were required. Judging from the lists of supplies, the papal table in the Avignon period rivaled that of the king of France in variety, and in the range of spices that were used. It reflected some characteristics of Mediterranean cuisine, such as the habit of cooking with pine nuts, dried dates, and raisins, as well as orange and lemon flavors. Some Italian culinary habits may also have been introduced in France—after URBAN V returned from Italy, lasagna made its first appearance on the papal menu.

The two cookery books that came out of the papal kitchens have provided the best information on the fare prepared there. The first was written between 1431 and 1435—a century after cookery books first appeared in the West—by Jean de Bockenheim, "former cook to Our Holy Father Martin V." His *registre de cuisine* shows originality. Bockenheim, who was a German cleric when he was recruited during the COUNCIL of Constance, combined German-inspired recipes with Italian techniques for an extensive and varied social circle. His *Registre de Cuisine* specified exactly the social category or nationality for which each dish was intended, a feature not seen in any other cookery book of medieval times. Most dishes were geared toward the palates of Germans and Italians—the two nationalities most frequent in the Curia of MARTIN V. Bockenheim also lists notaries, prelates, and even mercenaries, and—more curiously—procurers and their protégés, who also cooked the common meals.

Bockenheim's very slim *Registre* was limited in scope, in stark contrast to the *Opera*, by Bartolomeo Scappi. Comprising nine hundred pages and more than seven hundred recipes, his was a real encyclopedia of the Italian cuisine of the Renaissance. It was continually reprinted from 1570 to 1643 and marked a new turning point in culinary literature, beginning with the end of the 15th century. Bartolomeo bore the honored title of *cuoco secreto*—secret cook—to Pope PIUS V, and his book openly flaunted his role, from the frontpiece engraving that pictures show him surrounded by his utensils, to the warning to the reader, reminiscent of an advertising prospectus. The recipes are divided into chapters (with an entire one devoted to pasta), and a table is provided for convenient consultation. The recipes themselves are interspersed with standard menus for all the months of the year. In the classic dialogue between master and disciple that opens the book, as well as the images that illustrate it, Scappi undertakes to reveal to his readers all the elements of cooking, from kitchen utensils to table settings. The book is a viable commercial product suitable for a housewife as well as the master chef of a noble house, and fully in keeping with the literary canon of its time. There is even a section on "how to serve at the conclave." His treatise is proof of the fascination with which the public viewed the papal cooks and their kitchens.

Bruno Laurioux

Bibliography

Benporat, C. "Bartolomeo Scappi: Ipotesi per una biografia," *Appunti di gastronomia*, 1, 1989, 5–15.

Guillemain, B. *La Cour pontificale d'Avignon (1309–76)*, Paris, 1962, 392–408.

Laurioux, B. "Le Registre de cuisine de Jean de Bockenheim, cuisinier du pape Martin V," *MEFRM*, 100, 1988/2, 709–60.

Muratori, L. A., ed. "Avvisamenta pro Regimine et dispositione Officiariorum in Palatio Domini Nostri Panae" (1409), *Rerum Italicarum Scriptores*, III/2, Milan, 1734, col. 810–24.

Schafer, K. H. *Die Ausgaben der Apostolischen Kammer . . .* (1316–75), Paderborn, 3 vols., 1911–34.

Tramezzino, M. *Opera di M. Bartolomeo Scappi, Cuoco Secreto di Papa Pio Quito divisa in sei libri*, Venice, 1570.

CHINEA. The chinea, or palfrey, was a white mare offered to the pope during a solemn ceremony. It carried in an urn, attached to the saddle, that was the tribute of the kingdom of Naples. Charles of Anjou in 1265 was the first ruler, who upon investiture, was obliged by CLEMENT IV to pay the tribute, and Alphonse V of Aragon, heir of Jeanne II of Anjou Durazzo, agreed, only in 1456, to de-

liver it during an impressive ceremony in Rome. Ferdinand the Catholic, who in 1503 transformed the kingdom of Naples into a Spanish vice royalty, continued to pay this homage. The fête of the chinea took place regularly, in spite of the objections of some who did not like to see this feudal dependence on the Holy See displayed in such a spectacular fashion. Difficulties arose during the succession of Spain in 1700, when Naples passed from Spanish to German control. The Bourbons of Spain paid the tribute "privately" in 1701 and 1702. Then there was a long interruption, followed by its official resumption by the Empire from 1722 to 1733. In 1734, the successive conquests of the kingdom of Naples by Don Carlos de Bourbon, and then by the duke of Parma (later Charles VII of Naples, the future Charles III of Spain) threw the chinea into crisis, as each of the two adversaries wished to pay the tribute as proof of his legitimacy. The outcome of the war being uncertain, the pope, in 1735, decided in favor of the Empire, but afterwards waited for the investiture of the new dynasty, which resumed the rite in 1738.

Following further incidents, the king of Naples, in 1775, reduced the political aspect of the chinea by making the tribute an homage to the prince of the apostles rather than a debt to the sovereign pontiff. The suppression of the ceremony in 1788 elicited a solemn protest from the pope that was repeated annually until 1855. PIUS IX and Ferdinand II came to an agreement on the chinea. The tribute was abolished in exchange for 10,000 écus offered by the king for the erection of a column in the Piazza di Spogna in honor of the Immaculate Conception, whose dogma had just been proclaimed (1854).

Normally, the ceremony took place on the eve of the feast of St. Peter and St. Paul. A long procession wended its way to the Vatican or, very rarely, to the QUIRINAL (or to Santa Maria del Popolo under exceptional circumstances for example, when the festivities were postponed to 8 September because of the *sede vacante*). In the 17th century it set out from the Spanish palace, and during the "imperial" years from the Holy Apostles square, the residence of the greatest feudatory of the kingdom of Naples, the High Constable Colonna, accredited both by Spain and the Empire as ambassador extraordinary. But in the year 1734, the prince of Santacroce claimed this honor and left from the town square of San Carlo ai Catinari, where he lived. Still later, the king of Naples insisted on the Farnese palace, the seat of his legation, until, relenting in 1775, he allowed Prince Colonna to resume the former tradition. After the drums of the Roman populace, the trumpets of the ambassador, and the light calvary, came the nobility of the kingdom of Naples, followed by their pages and livery. In 1691, the grandees of Spain present in Rome received the official order to join the cavalcade. They preceded the chinea, which was accompanied by the ambassador and his equerry, surrounded by the

SWISS GUARD. (In 1535 PAUL III, had substituted them for Spanish soldiers, who were deemed too numerous and menacing in a city that was sometimes hostile to them). An anonymous engraving of 1746, in which the Farnese Palace, the Castel Sant'Angelo, and St. Peter's basilica all appear, depicts the spectacle in miniature. On arrival, the palfrey, properly trained, knelt before the pope, who waited in the basilica or in the Sala Regia. He received the tribute from the hands of the ambassador—most often in the form of a letter of exchange—and the mare was entrusted to the care of grooms, after an exchange of speeches that sometimes slyly elaborated the claims of both states. The ceremony ended with a fête in front of the ambassadors' palaces featuring wine fountains, cantatas, and fireworks. Two similarly constructed pyrotechnic "machines" presented two different displays, one each evening, for the fête extended over two days. It was an expensive opportunity for sovereigns to seize the imagination and rouse admiration. The preparations engaged the most diverse body of workers: carpenters, painters, and stucco workers labored for two months or more in the rooms of the Spanish, Colonna, or Farnese palace.

A number of engravings have preserved the memory of the 18th-century "machines" and about a dozen of their builders. They worked in harmony with designers, who could also be the inventors of the composition. Their names include those of many FOREIGN ARTISTS, including, particularly from 1738 to 1750, the residents of the Academy of France at Rome: Charles Bellicard, Francois Hutin, Louis Le Lorrain, Pierre-Ignace Parrocel, and Edmond Petitot. Their presence shows the close links between the Bourbons of France and those of Naples, as well as the dearth of available Neapolitan artists that the king filled by drawing from the local pool of Frenchmen.

From 1750 on, the role of architect fell to Paolo Posi and that of engraver to Giuseppe Vasi. The "machines" played diverse roles. True architectural laboratories, they often seemed to be fanciful embodiments of recent or future happenings. They paralleled new structures built in Spain and Naples: ports, aqueducts, fountains, bridges, and other generally utilitarian efforts. This is symbolic aspect expressed *exempla virtutis*, but also political allusions—the "Temple of Peace" of 1749 alluded to the treaty of Aix-la-Chapelle that had just been signed. These "machines" did not escape the destiny of ephemeral constructions. A source of enchantment, they were also a form of instruction and propaganda.

Olivier Michel

Bibliography

Frigola, Montserrat Moli, "Efimeras maquinas de fuego artificiales napolitanos en Roma, 1700–37," *I Borbone di Napoli e i Borbone di Spagna*, II, Naples, 1985, 459–94.

Le Palais Farnese, Rome, 1980

CHRISTIAN DEMOCRACY. Christian Democracy (CD) is unique in the history of political ideas and instruction in terms of its fundamental ties to religion and to Christianity in particular—and, more precisely, to Catholicism. Its emergence in the 19th century was, in part, the result of an intransigent response to the challenges brought on by the FRENCH REVOLUTION, which had shaken up the immutable order of things, and the Industrial Revolution, which had brought about the upheaval of the social order. Christian Democracy was a descendant of the parties of religious defense created to preserve the interests and the rights of the Church against anticlericalism and laicism, but it also incorporated liberal Catholicism.

The fate of the Christian-Democratic synthesis appears to be strongly linked to papal attitudes. In fact, history shows that no party claiming association with the Christian faith had been able to develop or survive without the more or less explicit support of the Holy See. The relationship between the sovereign pontiff and parties inspired by Christianity, therefore, lies at the heart of Christian Democracy's history. Successive popes have not been able to deny this potentially useful if, sometimes cumbersome, relationship with the Christian Democratic party. In their eyes, the party has, at times, acted in an impetuous or clumsy manner, upsetting the political hierarchy, and at other times, acted in total communion with this hierarchy. This delicate and contrasting relationship, often characterized by papal distrust, constitutes a complex story that begins with the meeting of two different views. One was that held by the popes at the head of a structured Church with a centralized hierarchy, where obedience was raised to the level of dogma, and where the clergy was by definition given a special role that placed it far above the lay population. During the second half of the 19th century and throughout the 20th, these popes, aided by their great popularity in the Catholic world, were occupied in preserving Catholic unity, which might be disturbed by the Christian-Democratic current, long a very minor movement within the rather conservative world of Catholicism. Their distrust of an active political party, their desire to control it, to muzzle it, and use it for their own purpose, is not surprising. The perspective of the popes met that of the Christian-Democratic laity, generally practicing Catholics tied to the Church by their faith, as well as through their instruction in Catholic activist organizations, or by strong familial, intellectual, or spiritual personal relationships, but careful to ensure the existence of nonconfessional parties independent of the Church hierarchy. They drew their inspiration from Holy Scripture and the papal magisterium.

The complexity of relations between the popes and Christian Democracy also came from the fundamental ambiguity between theory and practice in political movements and the parties. Should CD begin on the political level, including the electoral meaning of the term, with a party, which is an independent nonconfessional organization, or should it remain tied to the actions of the Church, to become a Church movement reduced to a subordinate role of that of apologist? The question became even more important beginning in 1878, when LEO XIII opened the way for the Church to take society in hand once again, encouraging the priests to leave their sacristies and go out among the people in order to "*instaurare omnia in Christo*," according to the expression of PIUS X. This ambiguity seemed to disappear right after WORLD WAR I when BENEDICT XV allowed the formation of the Italian People's Party, but it continued to be an issue at least until WORLD WAR II. The confusion over whether CD was a party or a movement was fed by the Church's obvious distrust of democracy. It took the catastrophe of World War II, the fruit of totalitarianism and the "exaggerated nationalism," denounced by PIUS XI, for the pontifical magisterium to give up its traditional position of neutrality regarding the form of the State and propose democracy to the people as a government capable of putting Christian social principles into practice (radio messages by PIUS XII on Christmas 1942 and Christmas 1944). Until then, the teaching of the Church had barely shown any concern about authoritarian regimes. The nostalgic dream of a Christian monarchy, the papal speeches about authority and respect for the ruling power, the trauma of the French Revolution, and the identification of democracy—primarily through the French and Italian experiences with it—as a Godless State based on aggressive anticlericalism all promoted opposition to a form of government accepted as only one solution among many others. Although Leo XIII had opened the way in 1888 with the ENCYCLICAL *Libertas praestantissimum* and invited French Catholics to rally to the Republic (in the encyclical *Au milieu des solicitudes*, 1892), defiance toward democracy remained strong, with Catholics often feeling more strongly drawn to a political environment like those of Monsignor Seipel or of Dollfuss in Austria, or of Salazar in Portugal—the *Estado novo*, a corporatist authoritarian regime with a religious basis, appeared to be an ideal system. When totalitarian systems were in place in Italy and in Germany, Catholics attempted to compromise with them, and in each case the party allied with Catholicism—the Italian People's Party and the Zentrum—disappeared.

Encyclicals condemning totalitarian practices (*Non abbiamo bisogno* in 1931, *Mit brennender Sorge* and *Divini Redemptoris* in 1937) served as reminders of Christian principles, especially the respect due to any human being, but they did not contain any references to democracy. There also were none in *Summi pontificatus*, the first encyclical of Pius XII, promulgated on 20 October 1939. His radio message on Christmas 1942 on "the order of

nations" brought forth for the first time the fundamental elements for a Christian reconstruction of society based upon democracy. These would later be confirmed and expanded by the radio message on Christmas 1944, which offers, in the words of Guido Verucci, a "solemn consecration of democratic government by the Church." Democracy, organized according to social principles and Christian morals, was presented as the best system for the common good. The pope clearly affirmed its ethical and political superiority over any other type of government, confirming this view in later speeches, in particular on 2 October 1945, when he addressed the tribunal of the ROTA. He appeared totally opposed to placing any obstacles in the path of people moving toward democracy and, indeed, convinced of his duty to guide them there.

This viewpoint aided in the emergence and the Church's lasting affirmation of Christian Democratic parties in several countries. Long held back or even sacrificed due to the Church's distrust of them, they were able to gather strength as groups of Catholics—sometimes even in an interdenominational framework as in Germany—outside the authority of the Church hierarchy and far from any clericalism. Their reconstitution, in secret at the end of the war, or publically after the Liberation, took place outside the Church and without any approval at all, while still benefiting from the increased papal approval.

The development of Christian Democracy may be traced chronologically with reference to certain milestones. An initial period includes the years from the middle of the 19th century to 1942–4, which was characterized by the total dependence of the Christian Democratic party on the Church, if only for its survival. Then, with the end of World War II, a period of development and strengthening began, marked by accession to power and management of business in a number of countries in Western Europe and South America, as the Church was changed by the SECOND VATICAN COUNCIL, and a consumer society developed. Relations with St. Peter's successors, each imprinting his own style, were visibly modified as time passed. A third phase may be discerned, beginning at a certain point in the late 1970s. The year 1978 seems particularly important, with secularization clearly on the rise, brought on by a serious crisis, the assassination of Aldo Moro, the president of Italy's Christian Democratic party, and the election of JOHN PAUL II, a pope from a part of Europe still under Soviet control, who was quite unfamiliar with the Christian Democrats.

Origin of the Party to World War II. From the early days of CD in the 19th century, the popes showed considerable resistance toward initiatives of 1830 and 1848, which smelled of the sulfur of the revolution and liberalism. The expression "Christian democracy" was, in fact, not used in 1830. Still, the ideas developed by Lamennais in *L'Avenir* were harbingers of CD. Although they owed much to counterrevolutionary thought, they owed as much to authority in the name of freedom and democracy, with, as a result, a call for universal suffrage. The motto "God and Freedom" worried Pope GREGORY XVI sufficiently that he took a knife to it on 15 August 1832, with the encyclical *Mirari vos*. The events of 1848, which saw the emergence of a political, parliamentary priesthood in France, Prussia, Belgium, and Austria, allowed the development of the Christian democratic current, represented in France by the daily paper *L'Ere nouvelle*. The paper was founded by the abbé Maret who would cry out: "Christian democracy is the future," giving the term a political meaning and using his vows to make a democracy inspired by Christianity. The future of CD was soon restricted by PIUS IX, and obstructed by the encyclical *Quanta cura* and the SYLLABUS of 8 December 1854. Directed mostly against LIBERALISM and liberal Catholics, these texts still dashed all hope of reconciling Catholicism with the modern world of the time, and condemned democracy at the same time by rejecting certain freedoms. For a long time the *Syllabus* was the manifesto of antidemocratic Christians. Yet its severe condemnation of economic liberalism would actually encourage social Catholicism, leading to the appearance of a second wave of Christian democracy.

With Leo XIII came the will to create a new Christian society, thanks to a project whose theological foundation is found in the return to St. Thomas represented in the encyclical *Aeterni Patris* (4 August 1879). The social question became the major battlefield in this new campaign to promote a society that conformed to the principles of Christian morality. The teaching of Leo XIII brought the engagement of laymen around whom a true program to reform society appeared and *Rerum novarum* (15 May 1891) soon became a real social charter for the Christian Democrats. Certainly, social Catholicism was not identified with them alone: the intransigent, traditional, liberal, paternalistic, and later, progressivists all shared a common attachment to this encyclical. Nonetheless, by freeing political energies, recognizing a significant role for the state, and opening the way for labor unions, *Rerum novarum* strongly encouraged Christian democrats to adopt concrete initiatives, for which Leo XIII did not hide his sympathy, and to interpret, deepen, expand, sustain, and popularize the papal message. Examples of these initiatives are found in the activities of Father Leon Dehon, the Belgian abbé Antoine Pottier, and democratic abbés like Abbé Lemire.

The expression of Christian democracy was remarkably successful in a political sense, as seen in the magazine *La Démocratie chrétienne*, founded in Lille in 1894 by the abbés Six and Vanneufville. The birth of a movement, with regional meetings in 1895 and early 1896, led

to the creation of a Christian Democratic party and then to national meetings in Reims and Lyon in 1896 and December 1897. The creation of an organization led to a politicization of social Catholicism in a democratic sense. A similar phenomenon could be seen throughout the rest of Europe: "The encyclical *Rerum novarum* has given an impetus to the social Catholic movement and brought about the birth of Christian democracy," wrote Jean-Marie Mayeur. In Italy, Romolo Murri sought to give the encyclical a political thrust. In Belgium, Georges Helleputte created the Belgian Democratic League, slightly before the appearance of *Rerum novarum*, with the help of the Pottier.

Just as in 1885, Albert de Mun's attempt to found a Catholic party ran up against divisions in French Catholicism and the hostility of Rome, and Christian democracy's turn toward politics exacerbated these divisions in France, where the People's Action of Jacques Piou, which was quite removed from CD, received the support of the largest part of the episcopate. The situation was similar in Belgium, where the bishops applied pressure to preserve the unity of the Catholic party, and in Italy, where the unity of the lay organization was threatened by the controversy surrounding the Roman question and the *Non expedit*, which forbade Catholics from participating in political elections. Several documents made public by the Holy See then emerged to head off any trends judged to be dangerous during the transition from Leo XIII's reign to that of Pius X: these were the *Graves de communi* of 18 January 1901; the *Instructions on Christian People's Action or Christian Democracy in Italy*, made public by the Congregation for Special Ecclesiastical Affairs (27 January 1902); and the *motu proprio* of Pius X on the Christian People's Action on 18 December 1903.

CD regained the status of a movement—as opposed to that of a party—with a social rather than a political mission, repeating the pattern that had occurred before. By defining CD as *benefica in populum actio christiana*, Leo XIII was returning to his initial ideal of Christianizing society and ending the politico-religious ambiguity that was aggravated by the fact that many of those responsible for the Christian democratic political organization were churchmen who modeled their behavior on that of France's "democratic abbés." "It would be wrong," said Leo XIII, "to change the term 'Christian Democrat' from its earlier meaning to a political one. According to the etymology of the word and the way philosophers use it, democracy probably indicates rule by the people; but, in actual circumstances, it should not be used without removing all of its political connotations and any meaning other than that of a beneficial Christian action on behalf of the people." Some time earlier, reflecting on this question at the pope's request, Giuseppe Toniolo had come up with a definition similar to that of CD as a defender of the interests of the people, in the *Rivista Internazionale di Scienze Sociali*: the social question was not political, but only social and religious, and it was necessary to stop the exacerbation of tensions within Catholicism and preserve the *unanimitas christiana*, even if it was only a myth. In Italy in 1901, Leo XIII was most concerned with maintaining unity in the *Opera dei Congressi*. At the congress held in Tarento in September 1901, he issued a BRIEF reviewing his interest in seeing the Christian Democrats integrated into a larger movement, defining them as "a group of young people with fresh strength and sharpened will." The dispositions of 1901 were confirmed in February 1902 in the *Instructions* that called upon all Italian Christian Democrats to reject any political action, denying them any autonomy within the Opera.

While Leo XIII had some sympathy for the Christian Democrats, (evident in the article he published in the *Osservatore Romano* on 24 December 1902, where "Christian Democratic action" was labeled as "a fact of no small importance"), a much harsher position would be taken by Pius X, who made the battle against MODERNISM the major issue of his reign, and who was preoccupied by anything that might resemble a dangerous deviation. The *motu proprio* on the Christian People's Action of 18 December 18 1903, following the example set by Leo XIII, cautioned that CD should not be "mixed up in politics" and insisted strongly on the essential unity of Catholics, reproaching CD implicitly for introducing the turmoil by fomenting a scandalous division. This stance explains a certain sympathy for the Belgian Democratic League, a Christian Democratic group, but one integrated into the Catholic party: an area of agreement with the conservatives had been found. In Italy on the other hand, Christian Democratic tendencies encountered Pius's resolute hostility, despite a tendency to apply the *Non expedit* with less rigor, to the point of accepting with a pact called *di Gentiloni* in 1913, permitting the election of Catholics to the Chamber of Deputies and consolidating the moderate clerical line. This policy gained support after the dissolution of the *Opera dei Congressi* in July 1904, and upon the organization of Catholic Action, firmly controlled by the church hierarchy (encyclical *Il fermo proposito*, 11 June 1905), and considered the sole group capable of restoring everything to Christ, as a way to prepare Catholics for political life "prudently." Romolo Murri truly found himself swimming against the current when he founded his National Democratic League in November 1905. Proposing to reform society, as well as the Church, it was not able to take control in the long run, a victim of its own excesses and its condemnation by the pope: on 28 July 1906, the encyclical *Pieni l'animo* forbade clerics to join. Murri was suspended in 1907 and excommunicated in 1909, and Modernism was condemned by the encyclical *Pascendi dominici gregis* on 8 September 1907.

In France, where a Christian democratic party had been damaged by internal divisiveness and the Dreyfus affair, social Catholicism gave birth to the Sillon, an initially apolitical youth movement that eventually tended toward political instruction and action under the charismatic leadership of Marc Sangnier. Its evolution incurred condemnation in the encyclical *Notre charge apostolique* (25 August 1910), which began by recalling the "good days of the Sillon" only to bemoan the hopes that the pope had placed in this movement and how they had been dashed. Pius X condemned "the pretense that the Sillon can escape ecclesiastical authority. . . . The winds of Revolution did this, and we can conclude that while the social doctrines of the Sillon may merely be in error, its essence is dangerous and its education harmful." Marc Sangnier submitted to this censure and was able to found a party, the Young Republic, in 1912, but the CD current remained embryonic in France. It would take a long time to recover from the setback of August 25. Pius X reproached this movement, whose sole intention had been to enthusiastically endorse democracy, with mingling politics and religion while placing itself outside the hierarchy, and of extending its hand to non-Catholics. Georges Jarlot reports the enlightening comment the pope made in 1907 to the bishop of Bayonne: "These young people are following a dangerous path. . . . I don't like priests to enter this association; they seem to be led and advised by laymen, not clerics. As a result, these young people are following a political ideal and nothing else, while placing themselves outside Catholic control. Priests should not get involved in this movement." Yet the pope had not yet decided on condemnation, because he recommended that the bishop be "good to these young people who are sincere and generous." This document, published in the *Bulletin religieux du diocèse de Bayonne*, clearly reveals what was expected from such an organization of laymen, even those under Christian Democratic influence: action according to the magisterium, with no autonomy or original initiative.

This negative attention seemed to abate somewhat during the pontificate of Benedict XV, which was marked by the tragedy of war, upheaval in Europe, and the problems of reconstruction. The Christian Democrats were allowed greater liberty, and the pope, who received Marc Sangnier with sympathy, let them take some initiatives. This hands-off policy was bolstered by the personal confidence Benedict XV had in Luigi Sturzo (named a member of the national leadership of Catholic Action, whose secretary he became), as well as the loss of influence over consistency under the new pontificate, and the abandonment of the *Non expedit* in Italy. Although its influence had already been limited by Pius X, its elimination provided a new sense of freedom. Participation by Catholics in the political life of Italy would soon take shape, and under the leadership of Luigi Sturzo, it would go in a Christian Democratic direction. The Italian People's Party (PPI) was founded on 16–17 December 1918. Proclaiming itself non-denominational, with no official references to Catholicism, it was the result of an initiative by Sturzo and his companions, who didn't ask for the explicit support of the Holy See but took the precaution of keeping the pope completely informed, with statutes submitted for his approval. Benedict XV allowed things to take their own course, and the secretary of State, Cardinal Gaspari, was content to give a bit of advice and let Sturzo act "at his own risk and peril." Personally, he was sorry that a priest was at the head of the party and did not show much enthusiasm. His relationship with Sturzo remained quite cold and later, in a letter to Count Carlo Santucci on 1 August 1928, he said that, for him, the PPI was only *il meno peggio di tutti*. Despite Gaspari's reticence, whereas Sturzo had a great degree freedom to act as well as implied approval, in Germany the Zentrum saw its relations with ecclesiastical authorities suspended, and it became a more autonomous structure in relation to the hierarchy. The PPI had a remarkable electoral success in 1919, benefiting from the support of a tightly knit group of Italian Catholic organizations and associations of all types (unions, charitable organizations, rural cooperatives and banks, Catholic Action, and the diocesan and parish network). With a party that numbered more than 250,000 members by the end of 1919, won 20.6% of the votes cast at elections, and had 100 parliamentary representatives, the Christian Democrats, experienced political autonomy for the first time. But this autonomy bore internal contradictions: the leader of a party built on a nondenominational foundation was a priest, its electoral success was due largely to the support of the Church apparatus throughout Italy, and the party whose aim was to reunite Catholics was itself crisscrossed by varied and contradictory currents that undermined its unity. However, the advent of a new pope on 6 February 1922, and of fascism on 30 October 1922, was going to change things.

Achille Ratti, Pope PIUS XI, saw the engagement of laymen in this group as a way to bring about the reign of Christ, if he could make it an obedient instrument of the Church. This viewpoint was expressed during the first year of his pontificate both by the letter that Cardinal Gasparri addressed to the bishops of Italy on 2 October 1922 (the Holy See, he said, "has always been and intends to remain totally separate from the People's Party as well as from any other political group") and by the first encyclical of his reign, *Ubi arcano Dei* on 23 December 1922, which expressed the pope's intention to support a reorganized Catholic Action, conceived as an army with a battle to fight. The letter of the sovereign pontiff to the episcopacy of Lithuania on 24 June 1928, *Peculiari quadam*, confirmed this view while revealing a great distrust of any political party that claimed to be Catholic, as Pius XI was trying to avoid confusion between religious activity and political activity. If the condemnation of the Action Française in 1926 was seen by contemporaries as

a revenge for that of the Sillon in 1910, it was certainly not a gesture in favor of Christian democracy. This condemnation demonstrates the rejection of any attachment between the religious and the political, and, in France as well as in Belgium, where the movement of intellectual young people was taken seriously by Rome, the refusal to see Catholics engaged in a movement led by agnostics and a rejection of the "politics first" formula. This condemnation, accompanied by a policy of episcopal nominations to key posts, made it possible to reduce the ties between the Catholics and Maurrassism. The Christian Democrats in France, a divided minority party, were not accepted in Rome unless they promised they would not compromise the position of the Church or oppose Catholic Action or the conservative political positions, that were associated in particular with the National Catholic Federation of General de Castelnau. Despite the submission of 1910, they were still suspect, even in the eyes of many bishops.

In Italy, the Italian People's Party (PPI), Luigi Sturzo's party, fell victim to both the policies Mussolini used to gain respectability by allying himself with Catholicism and the Church (at least officially) and the determination of Pius XI to settle the Roman question. Divided over fascism the party soon lost its main political significance (and justification), that of returning Catholics to Italian public life as the defenders of the rights of the Church. Many Catholics rallied to support the regime in response to multiple gestures by il Duce, who broke with the anticlericalism of the liberal regime that arose from the Risorgimento (for example, his decision to place crucifixes in classrooms and courtrooms had a remarkable psychological impact). Within the PPI the so-called clerico-fascist group became very influential and was very active regarding the CURIA, which had been extremely alienated by the contacts between the PPI and the socialist party in July 1922.

The Holy See set a high priority on finding common ground with the regime in order to settle the thorny Roman question, assure the Church's freedom of apostolate, and pursue, its objectives for Catholic dominance of the State and Society even though it had no illusions as to the true nature of fascism. Thus, the party that hindered these steps was condemned. In July 1923, Luigi Sturzo was forced to resign as secretary of his party, and in October Italian Catholic Action (AC) was reorganized according to the pope's wishes, "*sicut acies ordinata*," with a centralized structure controlled by the hierarchy. The party disappeared—it went into its final throes in 1924 and was dissolved in November 1926. The AC would be the instrument that would allow the Church to maintain its position during the years of dictatorship. Unlike Germany, where the disappearance of the Zentrum was not directly linked to the concordat signed with the Nazi regime in July 1933 but was part of the evolution of the party itself, in Italy the search for an agreement with the dictatorship illustrates the priority given to Catholic Action and the works they believed would thus be protected.

The papacy of Pius XI, framed by two world wars and confronted by totalitarianism, was certainly not favorable to Christian democracy. However, its effect was not wholly negative, if one takes into account the fact that CD was sustained by papal teaching and by the Holy See's policies. Its reinforcement by the pontificate on the ideological level can be seen in two areas. One is the beginning of social teaching with the publication on 15 May 1931, of the *Quadragesimo anno*, which gave the Christian Democrats a powerful impetus. The second has to do with international diplomatic positions: the condemnation of exaggerated nationalism, the defense of peace, the support given to the policies of Aristide Briand. These are the areas where the Christian democracy overlapped with the teaching of Pius XI and drew a certain legitimization from it despite the distrust the pope harbored toward them.

World War II and Aftermath. The papacy of Pius XII marked a major turning point in two ways. On one hand, the part of his reign that occurred after 1945 saw the spectacular growth of Christian democracy with the emergence of powerful governing parties whose leaders rose to power in many countries. On the other hand, the new pope's speeches on this subject displayed a noticeable alteration. In his Christmas radio messages of 1942 and 1944, Pius XII closed the period opened by *Graves de communi* by his definition of "true and healthy democracy." From then on, democracy was accepted, as both Christian—meaning inspired by evangelical principles—and popular in the Sturzian sense of the word: based upon the responsibility and participation of the citizens. For Pius XII, Catholic Action remained an essential element in the plan to conquer society for Christ through democratic groups; it also defined the needed to train an elite capable of assuming responsibilities in society and to prepare citizens to be aware of their civic duties and their rights.

This new orientation could not completely explain the renewal of Christian democracy after the war, but it certainly helped. First, Christian references could be made obvious. If some remained faithful to the reference to popularism, as in France with the Mouvement Républicain Populaire, or in Austria with the Österreichische Volkspartei, clear references were displayed—the Democrazia Cristiana Italiana, the Christian Social Party in Belgium, the Christlich-Demokratische Union in Germany, with a tendency to generalize this type of denomination, as we can see in 1970 with the transformation of the conservative Swiss People's Party into the Christian Democratic People's Party (Christlich-Demokratische Volkspartei). When compared to the period after the First World War, this revolution can be interpreted as freedom from Roman power. Expanded in secret, without ties to the Holy See, matured in the battles of the Resistance and the Liberation, supported in some cases by extra-ecclesiastical ideological reflection in the years before the war, they struck the pope as a fait accompli and were able to profit from the new Church discourse while displaying considerable autonomy.

In this way interdenominationalism occurred in Germany. In Italy, where the electoral successes of the Democrazia cristiana owed more to mobilization by the church apparatus, Alcide De Gasperi forced a governmental openness to "lay" parties and refused the compromising electoral alliances desired by Pius XII and some of his entourage for the municipal elections of Rome in 1952. The Vatican had wanted an alliance between the Christian Democrats and the neo-fascists of the MSI to oppose the Marxist parties; faithful to his beliefs, De Gasperi refused what would have been for him a compromise. The episode cost him papal esteem and confidence, but it showed that the pope was not in any way able to impose his choices on the Christian Democrats. Thus the papacy of Pius XII marked yet another turning point: CD parties had developed and taken over in certain countries by taking advantage of the political environment of postwar reconstruction, functioning as an anti-Communist bulwark, and benefiting from the Vatican's openness and the support they received at the highest level of the hierarchy in order to unite all Catholics. But at the same time, these parties had become indisputably indispensable, for the Vatican, except in France where the MRP never united Catholics. From now on they could no longer be used by the Vatican. Even if the pope gladly received their leaders, they would no longer be simply a corridor of transmission that could eventually be cut off: the time of the PPI had come again. Vatican pressures continued to be felt, and papal ties, especially in Italy, remained tight, but the Christian democracies had acquired a fundamental autonomy. Through their political success, they escaped clericalism. This was a major victory for them, the result of the philosophies of Luigi Sturzo and Jacques Maritain in particular, the political strategies of Konrad Adenauer and Alcide De Gasperi, and the policies of Pius XII, for whom the primary imperative was to defend Christian civilization against communism.

In Italy, an area still indispensable for any assessment of the relationship between the pope and Christian democracy, increased autonomy, which did not exclude intervention by bishops or by officials of the Curia, was accepted and reinforced by the policies of the immediate successors to Pius XII. JOHN XXIII wanted to "enlarge the Tiber," he said in 1961, meaning to distance himself from Italian politics. Placing his confidence in laymen and their political involvement, he refused to support cardinals Siri and Ottaviani in their offensive against Aldo Moro and his policy of openness to the left. On the contrary, the encyclicals *Mater et Magistra* (15 May 1961) and *Pacem in terris* (11 April 1963) encouraged the Christian Democrats to abandon conservative positions and unreservedly apply the social doctrine of the Church, and to extend themselves to work for the common national and international good, with non-Catholics or even "men who lived outside any Christian faith but who, guided by the light of reason, are faithful to natural morality" (*Pacem in terris*, no. 157). The Second Vatican Council would move in this direction as well. The importance of *Gaudium et spes* (7 December 1965) would be emphasized, particularly paragraph 76 devoted to "the political community and the Church": the restoration of the Catholic State was no longer an objective for the Church. From a "beacon of civilization" under Pius XII, it was becoming an "expert in humanity" under Paul VI, which naturally brought with it a modification of its relationship with parties inspired by Catholicism.

PAUL VI, during whose papacy *Gaudium et spes* was promulgated, confirmed this tendency. He appeared to be the pope most attached to Christian Democracy, linked to it by intermingled intellectual and familial ties and those of friendship. Coming from a background rooted in Lombard Catholic tradition (more precisely Brescian, that of liberal Catholic sentiments) the young Giovanni Battista Montini had seen his father join with Luigi Sturzo and participate in the grand undertaking of launching the people's party. To the lesson of Luigi Sturzo, (in whom, as a young priest, he recognized himself) was added that of Jacques Maritain, whose *Trois réformateurs* he translated in 1928, introducing the Italian edition with an important preface. He brought French philosophy into Italian Catholicism, establishing a first fruitful contact with it. Maritain would be a teacher for this future pope (he even called him "my master"). Although Paul VI knew how to freely make his own synthesis, we must see, says, Philippe Chenaux, Maritain's role "in the genesis of the great Montinian design of reconciling the Church with the modern world." The friendship between the two men was born during the ambassadorship of the philosopher to the Holy See (1945–8), when Montini was the substitute SECRETARY OF STATE. The men believed in the same principles. Maritain found Montini a strong defender against attacks from certain elements in the Curia, expressed in a biting article in LA CIVILTÀ CATTOLICA in 1956. Paul VI wanted to associate him with the council after that, and it was to him that he handed the message "to men of thought" on 8 December 1965 on the steps of St. Peter's: "The Church is grateful to you for your life's work," he said to him.

Montini knew the men of the Christian Democrats well, the "popular men" of his father's generation, his companions like Alcide De Gasperi, and especially the generation of young leaders of the party during the years from 1950 to 1960, whom he knew under fascism when he was the national almoner of the University Federation of Italian Catholics (FUCI) from 1925 to 1933. During that period he formed close ties with many of the young men who, like Aldo Moro or Giulio Andreotti, would hold prominent positions in republican Italy. He became, says Andrea Riccardi, "the point of reference for the Italian ruling class." When he was substitute for the Secretary of State, Montini, whose brother Lodovico had been elected a CD deputy in 1946, worked hard and successfully, (against the advice of large sectors of the Curia) to have the party of De Gasperi recognized as the only party uniting the Catholics, thus helping to block any right-wing tendency in Italian Catholicism, such as that seen in the 1920s. His relations with the men of the CD were often friendly and warm, and not only with the Italians, but also with figures such as the Chilean Eduardo Frei and the Venezuelan Rafael Caldera. In an audience on 29 November 1975 Montini received the participants in the World Conference organized in Rome, with the parties and Christian Democratic movements from sixty-five countries, which gave him a chance to meet many of the leaders of Europe and the Americas. "What could be, in a way, more interesting, more prestigious, than a spiritual, historical, social, and political movement like the one that you have?" he asked the leaders of the International Union of Young Christian Democrats he received in an audience on 31 January 1964.

It is evident that Paul VI was deeply attached to CD, with which he shared a basic concept of man as the subject, foundation, and end point of democracy. But as a disciple of Sturzo and Maritain, he believed in the autonomy of the political sphere from the religious. As pope, he maintained a need for reserve and separation from Italian affairs: Giulio Andreotti mentioned his "great respect for our autonomy," which did not exclude great attention to the evolution of CD and the problems of Italy. The torment of Aldo Moro; kidnapped by a commando of the Red Brigade on 16 March 1978 and assassinated on 9 May, was his own torment, an intensely felt trial. On 2 April he sent out a heartrending appeal for Moro's life to be spared, and on the 22 April he sent a signed letter to the kidnappers, in vain. He insisted on being personally present at the funeral ceremony organized on 13 May 1978, at St. John LATERAN in memory of the statesman, a highly symbolic gesture, a homage to a martyred friend, and a gesture of support for Italian democracy, more than for Christian democracy, which had been unable to either prevent the kidnapping or save its leader. An era appeared to end here, affected by the introduction in 1978 and the following years of new elements that noticeably modified the relationship between the pope and Christian Democrats.

1978 Onward. In the first place, there was the election of a non-Italian, Polish pope in 1978, only a few months after the drama Aldo Moro, and after the brief Vatican tenure of JOHN PAUL I, who was also, like Paul VI, from an area with a long-standing, solid background in the Catholic movement: Venice, where the CDI was especially strong in elections, and where he had climbed the ranks from priest to bishop of Vittorio Veneto, and then patriarch of Venice. In contrast, John Paul II was not familiar with the Christian Democratic situation, being foreign to this tradition. However, he was not hostile to it. He gave a speech, which he repeated over and over, and which the CD recognized, on the rights of man, on the social question, and on democracy: "During this century that separates us from *Rerum novarum*, the tie between democracy and Christianity has deepened. The Church holds that the State by law and democratic methods of solution of conflict by the means of negotiation, dialogue and the participation of all, are the important elements for safeguarding and exercising the rights of man in the world today," he declared on 23 November 1991, on the occasion of the International Forum of Christian Democratic Parties on the Social Magisterium of the Church.

Supporting the engagement of Christians in politics on many occasions (especially in the speech given at Loreto on 11 April 1985), he recognized the usefulness of Christian democratic parties and advocated Catholic unity. Where they existed, it was necessary to preserve them. This was the case in Italy, where the president of the Italian episcopal conference (who in Italy is named by the pope), Cardinal Camillo Ruini, who was also vicar of Rome, multiplied his appeals on this topic. Opening the deliberations of the conference's permanent council in Rome on 23 September 1991, he made a long, forceful, highly political speech, on the theme of the union of Catholics in favor of common, essential values. This intervention in politics provoked lively polemics in Italy with the socialist party railing against what looked very much like support for the CDI. However, on 29 September the pope gave the CDI his support, affirming that he "greatly appreciated the social actions of Italian bishops." At the same time, the priority given to "the new evangelization" diverted the pope's attention from parties to lay movements more capable of spreading the Church's message in increasingly secular societies. The non-Italian pope knew, perhaps better than his predecessors, how to distinguish the specific features of Italian political life from those of other European countries, especially those of the communist bloc, and those of the world throughout which he traveled unceasingly.

Although the pope's speech on the rights of man was in accord with the beliefs of the Christian Democrats, on other issues he found himself in disagreement. Europe furnishes the most interesting case, because there was a quasi-superposition of concepts between Pius XII to Paul VI: the Europe of the popes was the Europe of the Christian Democrats, communitarian and federal. John Paul II reflected on the other Europe, and if the formation of the European Community was a given for him, he spoke willingly of the Europe of nations, since he thought, as did Benedict XV, that "the nations are not dying" and he defined "the right to be a nation" (speech at UNESCO, 2 June 1980).

The pope also took notice of the accelerated secularization of society. Christian Democracy knew how to fight against communism, but how could one fight against a society that has lost sight of God? The very concept of a party of Christian inspiration was called into question. Certainly the process of secularization did not imply that the pope had to renounce all hope of acting in society. However, he believed that the situation required a new type of papal presence. He was especially conscious of this since, as a non-Italian, his thoughts were not circumscribed by Christian Democratic schemas. Moreover, the crumbling of communism allowed the easing of a political situation that had been rigid for more than a half a century, a situation unknown to his predecessors.

At the same time, a new ingredient interfered: the crisis of the Christian Democrats, sparked by the sudden fragmentation of the political scenario, the emergence of new and often uncontrollable social forces, and the diversification of Catholic political alliances, an ancient reality in France, but one that was now spreading throughout Europe. In Italy, Cardinal Ruini gave speeches to no avail. Diversification became a fact with the appearance of a new party, the Rete, which put an emphasis on the moral question and the fight against the Mafia, with several secessions within the CDI, and with the engagement of Catholics in the leagues, especially the Lombard League, which showed remarkable electoral results in the northern Catholic fiefs, despite the repeated warnings of the bishops. The fall of communism deprived the CD of a handy adversary against whom the discourse of unity had been effective, whereas in the countries liberated from Soviet control a very unstable political situation was emerging: Nationalist-populist political currents enjoyed substantial influence and parties of Christian inspiration had difficulty taking hold.

The pope also had to take into account the factors in a triple moral and political crisis of CD: questions about the honesty of political personnel sometimes implicated in scandals whose revelation was even more shocking because of their connection to ecclesiastical authority; a crisis of efficiency, casting doubt on the party's capacity to face the problems of the time (problems of the Italian State, difficulties linked to the reunification of Germany, the rise of intolerance and violence, economic difficulties, etc.); and the crisis of faith—faithlessness to the evangelic message and the seductiveness of liberal socioeconomic ideas.

By the 1990s CD had become part of the Church environment with no further risk of condemnation by the Holy See. Since then it has exercised a unique role in assuring the Catholic presence in society. CD has been an important link for the Church and papal politics even if it has not been their instrument, having acquired its autonomy from the ecclesiastical apparatus. The Church could get by without CD, yet the party's ability to adapt to new situations was an open question. On this issue, the evolution of the Italian situation explains the degree of attention given by the episcopal conference and by the pope himself to the reformation of the party aimed at restoring its original spirit of faithfulness. This is ardently wished for in Rome. Its success would have encouraged the Christian Democrats, and its failure might have brought about a thorough restructuring of papal politics, already presaged by the pope's attention to popular movements and the care he has taken to speak directly to Christians.

Jean-Dominique Durand

Bibliography

This listing does not include studies done on various CD parties, even those that discuss the parties' relationships with the Holy See.

Acerbi, A. *Chiesa e democrazia. Da Leone XIII al Vaticano II*, Milan, 1990.

Acerbi, A. *La Chiesa nel tempo. Sguardi sui progetti di relationi tra Chiesa e società civile negli ultimi cento anni*, Milan, 1979.

Alberigo, G. Riccardi A., eds. *Chiesa e papato nel mondo contemporaneo*, Bari, 1990.

Calvez, J. Y. and Tincq, H. *L'Église pour la démocratie*, Paris, 1992.

Chenaux, P. *Une Europe vaticain? Entre le plan Marshall et les traités de Rome*, Brussels, 1990; "Paul VI et Maritain," *Jacques Maritain et ses contemporains*, Paris, 1991, 323–42.

De Rosa, G., *Luigi Sturzo e la democrazia europea*, Bari, 1990.

Durand, J. D. *L'Église catholique dans la crise de l'Italie (1943–48)*, Rome, 1991.

Giovagnoli, A. *La cultura democristiana*, Bari, 1991.

Jarlot, G. *Doctrine pontificale et histoire. L'enseignement pontifical de Léon XIII, Pie X et Benoît XV vu dans son ambiance historique (1878–1922)*, Rome, 1964.

Maier, H. *Revolution und Kirche (Zur Frühgeschichte der christlichen Demokratie)*, Friburg, 1988, French transl. *L'Église et la démocratie. Une histoire del 'Europe politique*, Paris, 1992.

Mayeur, J. M. *Catholicisme social et démocratie chrétienne, Principes romains, expériences françaises*, Paris, 1986.

Mayeur, J. M. *Des partis catholiques à la démocratie chrétienne*, Paris, 1980.

Poulat, É. *Église contre bourgeoisie. Introduction au devenir du catholicisme actuel*, Tournai, 1977.

Prélot, M. M. "Catholicisme social et démocratie chrétienne selon Pie XII," *Mélanges André Latreille*, Lyon, 1972.

Riccardi, A. *Il "partito romano" nel secondo dopoguerra (1945–54)*, Brescia, 1983; *Il potere del Papa. Da Pio XII a Paolo VI*, Bari, 1988.

Schwalm, B. "Démocratie," *DTC*, 271–321.

Scoppola, P. *La proposita politica di De Gasperi*, Bologna, 1977; *La repubblica dei partiti. Profilo storico della democrazia in Italia (1945–90)*, Bologna, 1991; *La "nuova cristianità" perduta*, Rome, 1985.

Verucci, G. *La Chiesa nella società contemporanea*, Bari, 1988.

Zoppi, S. *Dalla Rerum Novarum alla Democrazia cristiana di Murri*, Bologna, 1991.

The review *Concilium* devoted its issue No. 213 (1987) to *The Church and the Christian Democrats*.

[CHRISTOPHER]. *Antipope (?–d. under Sergius III). Elected in September 903, deposed in January 904. Buried at St. Peter's in Rome.*

Christopher, cardinal priest of the titular church of San Lorenzo in Damaso and a native of Rome, assumed pontifical responsibilities around September 903, after having imprisoned Pope LEO V. *Usurpator* or *invasor* are the names by which he is generally designated. He is also often counted among the antipopes. Since, like Leo V, he seems to have belonged to the Formosan faction, a schism among the supporters of Formosus could have been the origin of his "usurpation." But it is also possible that his deep roots within the Roman clergy were a determining factor in his opposition to Leo V. From his pontificate, only one bull establishing the monastery of Corbie survives. Between the middle and end of January 904, FRANKS and Romans hired by SERGIUS III imprisoned Christopher. Many sources mention a DEPOSITION, followed by imprisonment in a monastery. His death—criminal or natural, the debate continues—must be placed under the pontificate of Sergius III. Christopher was probably buried in St. Peter's.

Klaus Herbers

CHURCH-STATE CONFLICT (SARCERDOTIUM/IMPERIUM 1125–1356). The Church reform during the time of the quarrel over INVESTITURES had grave consequences for the Empire. Not only was the emperor rejected from the sacred arena, he also lost any prerogatives he had had in Rome when he was there. The only function that was still allowed him was the acknowledgment of the Roman Church, and thus a mission in the

Church. The Roman CORONATION being the only rite of accession to the Empire, the pope appeared to be the creator of the Empire and the imperial office, but GREGORY VII imposed a condition on the coronation by withdrawing his approval of the election of the candidate for the Empire (since 962 it had been the elected king in Germany, called the King of the Romans). Following the CONCORDAT OF WORMS Lothair of Supplinburg (1125–37) and Konrad III of Hohenstaufen (1137–53) were elected through the influence of the court in Rome. The former asked for and obtained the approval of Pope HONORIUS II; Konrad was consecrated king of the Romans by a pontifical LEGATE. It was against this sort of guardianship of the Empire that the sovereigns Hohenstaufen and first the successor of Konrad, his nephew Frederick I (Barbarossa) reacted with force. For him and his counselors, the Roman Empire was not reduced to a job in the Church conferred by Roman coronation. It predated to the latter and was made up of three kingdoms, Germany, Italy, and Burgundy. This entity, the territorial Empire, was absolutely independent of the pope. As Frederick would say in a famous declaration in 1156, the Empire belonged to God alone through the election of princes. A century later (1252), several electors meeting in Brunswick would proclaim that as soon as he was elected, the King of the Romans was able to immediately exercise his imperial rights; he was therefore an emperor in fact and deed.

In the very beginning of the period, the events centered around the kingdom of Sicily were created by Count Roger and recognized by the ANTIPOPE ANACLETUS II (1130). Pope INNOCENT II mobilized the emperor Lothair against this new state, but the expedition attempted in 1127 met with no success. The same fate awaited Frederick I, who came to Rome in 1155 to receive the imperial crown from the hands of HADRIAN IV, who expected him to lead a campaign against the Sicilian kingdom. This time, lack of sufficient forces and opposition by Frederick's army would stop the project from being completed. Another obstacle was the fact that Frederick's defense of the honor of the Empire included the restoration of imperial rights everywhere they had been lost, particularly in Italy. In 1158 the emperor held a famous diet in Roncaglia where the rights of public sovereignty were defined: known as the *regalia* (Regalian rights), they were sometimes conceded, but more often usurped by the nobles, the bishops, and especially the cities: these rights were to be restored to the emperor. The enforcement of the Roncaglia decrees triggered opposition from a large number of cities, joined by Pope Hadrian when the recovery of the *regalia* was extended to ST. PETER's Patrimony.

The latent conflict between church and state resurfaced after the death of Hadrian IV in 1159. Frederick wanted a flexible pope on his side, one who would cooperate with his political policies. He got his chance when a dual elec-

tion followed the death of Hadrian IV under very questionable conditions: the majority of the cardinals elected Chancellor Roland Bandinelli (Alexander III), a remarkable canonist and ardent defender of Church freedom, whereas the choice of the minority fell upon Victor IV, a moderate cardinal who favored rapprochement between Church and Empire. The emperor called a general COUNCIL at Pavia to designate the true pope (1160). It was actually a Germano-Italian council that chose VICTOR IV, whereas Alexander, who had taken refuge in France, was obtaining the support of the kings of France, England, and soon, almost all the Christian world. In the spirit of the council of Pavia, Frederick tried then to help Victor IV's cause through diplomacy. Having failed to accomplish this with Louis VII (1162), he had better luck with Henry II, who promised in 1164 to force his clergy to obey PASCAL III, who had just taken over from Victor IV. Strengthened by this success, the emperor did not hesitate to require the German princes and the bishops present at the diet of Wurzburg to swear an oath never to recognize "Roland" or his successors.

All that remained was to get Pascal to Rome. At the head of a large army, Frederick was able to take the city, enthrone the antipope in St. Peter's, and crown Pascal a second time himself (1167). But a deadly epidemic forced the imperial army to retreat, while, on its heels, sixteen cities in northern Italy were forming the Lombard league, whose members swore to remain united both in war and in peace. These facts convinced Frederick that he needed a more flexible policy. The SCHISM was prolonged by the election of CALIXTUS III in 1168, whose obedience declined steadily. The emperor first negotiated with the Lombards, but when the negotiations failed, he fell back on a military solution. Inferior in numbers, however, he was defeated by the Milanese militia at Legnano in 1176. The Lombards remained intractable, so the emperor turned to Alexander III, who also desired peace. A treaty was concluded in Venice in 1177: Frederick would abandon the antipope and recognize Alexander without reservation, and the Roman Church would get back its *regalia* and all the possessions belonging to St. Peter that it had had before the conflict began. Six years later, in the peace treaty of Constance, the emperor promised not to enforce the decrees of Roncaglia and recognized the *regalia* of Lombard cities, while reserving few elements of sovereignty for himself in each situation. In the following years, he consolidated his domination over central Italy and achieved the greatest success of his reign: the marriage of his son Henry VI, already elected king of the Romans, to Constance of Sicily, who would inherit the kingdom if Frederick's nephew King William should die without a son.

The danger of being surrounded was clearly seen by Pope URBAN IV (1185–87), who hurried to make contact with the German opposition incited by the rival Staufen lineage, the GUELPHS, whose leader Henry the Lion had just been stripped of his two duchies of Bavaria and Saxony. A coalition against Frederick was formed, directed by the archbishop of Cologne, Philip of Heinsberg, and supported by Richard the Lionhearted. To counter them, the emperor concluded an alliance with Philip Augustus, who was interested in finding an ally in the battle he was waging against the Plantagenets. From the beginning of his reign, Henry VI, son and successor to Frederick—who died on the way to Jerusalem—saw his rights to the kingdom of Sicily contested after the premature death of King William II in October 1189 by a national party that arose and enthroned Tancred da Lecce, the son of an illegitimate son of Roger II. Detained in Germany, Henry wasn't able to get to Italy until 1191. Crowned emperor by Pope CELESTINE III, he pressed forward to the South right away, but was unable to take Naples. Military operations were not renewed until 1194, this time with success: on December 25, Henry was crowned king of Sicily at Palermo. In possession of a hereditary kingdom, he began working to secure the title of "King of the Romans" as a hereditary title for his family. Since this plan was rejected by the German princes, Henry presented it to Pope Celestine, who wanted nothing to do with it: he knew perfectly well that making this title hereditary would have devalued the imperial coronation and deprived his successors of a way of intervening in German affairs.

Thwarted, Henry returned to the German princes but had to be content with the election of Frederick, born in 1194, as King of the Romans (1196). But this royal position was almost immediately jeopardized by the premature death of Henry on 28 September 1197, as he prepared to leave for the East, and by the crisis due to the dual election. The circumstances allowed Celestine's successor, INNOCENT III, to play a very important role, revealing both a man of action who could impose his will, without clumsiness or errors, and a diplomat who knew how to be evasive and to pull out just in time from a bad situation. Profiting from the fact that the Empire had no unanimously recognized King of the Romans, Innocent III took possession of the duchy of Spoleto and the March of Ancona. He justified his actions on privileges from Louis the Pious and Otto the Great, which had actually been more theoretical than real. Besides these "recoveries" (Innocent's expression), the pope was able to turn the situation regarding the kingdom of Sicily to the Church's benefit. At his instigation, the regent Constance had her infant son Frederick crowned and, in the official documents, crossed out his title of King of the Romans. After her death, Innocent himself was, through the worst difficulties, the guardian of Frederick, whose kingdom, theoretically at least, seemed separate from the Empire.

In Germany Innocent was caught up in a game with serious consequences. Although elected King of the Romans, Frederick, by reason of his age, was set aside by the princes. On 8 March 1198 a group of them brought the younger brother of Henry VI, Duke Philip of Swabia, to the *imperatura regii solii*, or the imperial throne, to administer an Empire made up of three kingdoms. One year later (May 1199) these princes notified Innocent of this election and, without asking for his approval, announced that they would not further delay coming to Rome to crown their elected emperor. Meanwhile, in July 1198 the princes of the Guelph party had elected Otto of Brunswick, the son of Henry the Lion and nephew of John Lackland, and they respectfully asked for Innocent's approval and an imperial coronation for their choice. Caught between two sides, Innocent made his decision known in his *Deliberation in consistory* (late 1200–1). As expected, it went in favor of Otto, who, before being recognized, had to make certain precise promises before the papal legate. He did so on 8 June 1201, at Neuss, recognizing the pontifical "recoveries" and assuring the pope of his support in the defense of the kingdom of Sicily. In return for this and additional promises, the papal legate proclaimed his kingship in the cathedral of Cologne, in the pope's name, on 3 July 1201. In the civil war that then began in Germany, Otto, supported mostly by English money, enjoyed the early advantage. But in 1204 circumstances began to change in a manner that ultimately led Innocent himself to promise the imperial crown to Philip. But Philip was assassinated, a victim of private vengeance, in 1208, and everyone rallied around Otto. Reelected unanimously, he renewed his promises to the pope in 1201. The following years still held one of the most painful ordeals of Innocent's pontificate. Otto had scarcely been crowned emperor (October 1209) when he underwent a complete transformation and took over the Staufen policy in Italy. He invaded the kingdom of Sicily, pushing as far as Calabria. The pope excommunicated him in late 1210 and, probably on the advice of Philip Augustus, proposed Frederick II as a candidate for king of Germany, who was soon elected by princes after deposing Otto in September 1211. The latter returned to Germany and took up residence in the north. Frederick II consented to the separation of Sicily from the Empire as the pope requested, having his young son Henry crowned king at Palermo. After an eventful voyage, he arrived in Germany, where he rapidly gained many supporters. In 1212 he concluded an alliance at Vaucouleurs with Prince Louis, the eldest son of the king of France, against Otto and John Lackland. Two years later, the victory at Bouvines assured his own victory in Germany. Otto IV died four years later, almost forgotten.

The first act of Frederick II's reign was his royal consecration in 1215 at Aix-la-Chapelle, where he took the cross. His initial relations with the papacy were made easier by the personality of Innocent's successor: HONO-

RIUS III (1216–27) was completely open to conciliation. He allowed the election of Frederick's son Henry as King of the Romans. Recalled to Germany, he crowned Frederick emperor in 1220 and tolerated at least tacitly, his control of the government of the kingdom of Sicily. The union of the two monarchies was going to become the major permanent cause of conflict, to which was added the continuous pressure from the emperor on the "Papal State," whose expansion by Innocent III he had never recognized. Other issues would poison the relationship between the pope and the emperor. An example was the CRUSADE for which Frederick finally departed one year after the final deadline set by Honorius. His successor GREGORY IX, who was impulsive, violent, and deeply distrustful of Frederick, excommunicated him. In Frederick's absence (1228), Gregory allied himself with the Lombards and had the kingdom of Sicily invaded. With difficulty, peace was reestablished between the pope and the emperor (in 1229, with the treaty of San Germano). The pope also criticized the Church's forced subjection to a State transformed into an absolute monarchy by the imperial Constitutions of Melfi (1231). Finally, the restoration of the Empire in northern Italy increased the tensions as well. The Lombard league had been reunited, Frederick refused to recognize the peace treaty of Constance, and Gregory, secretly allied with the Lombards, was proposing arbitration without success. The situation was exacerbated when King Henry, rebelling against his father, allied himself with the Lombard cities. Frederick cruelly punished his son, replacing him in Germany with his second son Conrad IV, whom he had elected king in 1236. Then he declared war on the Lombard league and crushed their troops at Cortenuova (1237) but compromised his victory by the conditions he set down for a return to peace. Certain cities, including Brescia, continued the battle, always encouraged by Gregory. When the emperor married one of his natural sons, Enzio, to the heiress to half of Sardinia, an area that the papacy had designs on, Gregory found a pretext to definitively break off relations with Frederick, whom he excommunicated a second time in 1239.

The last phase of the conflict began. Despite ferocious battles between the Empire (backed by the GHIBELLINES) and the Church (supported by the Guelphs), Frederick continued his administrative reorganization of royal Italy by incorporating Innocent III's "recovered" territories into it. Moreover, he sent the Christian rulers fiery circulars inviting them to join him in a *corpus saecularium principum*, a secular Christianity, in defending their kingdom against the encroachments of the Church. In 1240, to resolve the situation, Gregory IX convened a general council to be held on Easter 1241. But this council was not able to convene because the Genoese ships transporting the prelates were intercepted by a Pisan fleet in the employ of the emperor; several bishops and two cardinals were surrendered to him.

In the interim, Gregory IX died, and his successor was not elected until 23 June 1243, after a vacancy of more than two years. He was the Genoese Sinibaldo Fieschi, INNOCENT IV, who retired to Lyon, where he convoked the council for 1245. An eminent canonist and a dispassionate and clear-sighted politician, he easily obtained the assent of an assembly that few attended, whose members he had consulted individually before the final session: on 17 July 1245, he officially removed Frederick II from the throne, releasing his subjects from their oath of loyalty and inviting the German people to elect a new king. This invitation was extended by the three archbishops from the Rhine region who, with no participation by a lay prince, elected Henry Raspe, the landgrave of Thuringia in 1246. Dead after only one year's reign, he was replaced in 1248 under similar circumstances (but this time with the cooperation of a layperson, the Duke of Brabant) by Count William of Holland, to whom two other princes, the duke of Saxony and the margrave of Brandenburg also rallied. The royal election was proclaimed at Brunswick. In Italy, Frederick II fought with indomitable energy until his death on 13 December 1250, winning some cities, losing others, and betrayed by top Sicilian officials. Innocent then became preoccupied with trying to keep the Hohenstaufen family out of Italy and Sicily. Death quickly eliminated Conrad IV, who had entered Italy to enforce his rights in 1254. But Manfred, one of Frederick's illegitimate sons, succeeded in getting himself crowned king of Sicily in 1258 and in making himself the head of the Italian Ghibellines. The second successor of Innocent IV, Urban IV, took up the challenge by making the Sicilian kingdom a feudal subject of the brother of St. Louis, the Count of Provence, Charles d'Anjou, who defeated Manfred at the battle of Benevento in 1266. Two years later, the young son of Conrad IV, Corradino, as the Italians called him, tried in turn to claim his Sicilian inheritance. Beaten at Tagliacozzo in 1268, he was decapitated by order of King Charles, who until the Sicilian Vespers in 1282 would demonstrate his power in Italy as leader of the Guelph party.

Germany continued its progress toward territorialization. The weak interest shown by the princes toward the kingdom and the Empire explains how, toward the middle of the century, royal election became the monopoly of a college of seven privileged electors: the archbishops of Mainz, Cologne, and Trier, the king of Bohemia, the palatine count of the Rhine, the duke of Saxony, and the margrave of Brandenburg. The college was created in 1257, but that same year it split into two groups, who simultaneously elected two foreigners to the throne: Richard of Cornwall, brother of Edward I, the king of England and Alfonso X, the king of Castille. Both were related to the Hohenstaufen dynasty. The former made several visits to Germany, the latter never traveled there. This period (1257 to 1273) was known as the "Great Interregnum." It ended in large part due to the influence of Pope GREGORY X (1271–76), who wanted to balance the Angevin power in Italy with a sufficiently powerful Empire: his appeal was heard by the electors, who agreed on Count Rudolph of Habsburg on 1 October 1273. He obtained Gregory's approval without difficulty, and the promise of an imperial crown, but he never received it despite his devotion to the Church and the ceding of Romagna to the pontifical State, due to the differing political orientations of Gregory X's successors. The first emperor to be crowned since 1250 was Henry VII of Luxembourg (1312), who proposed himself as arbitrator and peacemaker between the rival Italian parties, but his goal was never achieved due to opposition from a strong Guelph coalition composed of King Robert of Naples, Pope CLEMENT V, and Philip the Fair.

The final conflict between the Church and the Empire pitted Popes JOHN XXII and BENEDICT XII against the king of the Romans, Louis of Bavaria. Elected amid discord in 1314, the latter had not asked for approval and still bore the royal title. John XXII waited several years before declaring himself, but in 1323, he accused Louis of having usurped the rights of the Empire, and commanded him, under pain of excommunication, to abdicate within the next three months. After having appealed and defended his position, the Bavarian, pressured by all of John's enemies (Italian Ghibellines, Franciscans in revolt, theoreticians such as Marsilius of Padua, who favored popular sovereignty), traveled to Italy and received the imperial crown at the Capitol from the hands of a representative of the Roman commune, Sciarra Colonna. This unorthodox coronation was doomed from the start. Under the pressure of public opinion, the emperor retreated, adopting more moderate and efficient modes of opposition. First he, and later the electors who met at Rhens in 1338, proclaimed the independence of the elected king and his power to immediately exercise imperial rights without needing papal approval first. This doctrine had matured sufficiently since the 12th century that it was no longer necessary for approval of the election of the King of the Romans in the Empire's constitution, the Golden Bull enacted in 1356 by Emperor Charles IV. Thus ended the battle between the Church and the Empire, which was essentially a conflict of ideas.

Robert Fols

Bibliography

Kempf, F. *Papsttum und Kaisertum bei Innocenze III*, Rome, 1952 (MHP, 19).

Schneider, F. *Kaiser Heinrich VII*, Leipzig, 1924–8, 3 vols. (*Quellen und Forschungen zur Verfassungsgeschichte des deutschen Reiches*, 6–1).

Stengel, E. E. *Avignon und Rhens*, Weimar, 1930.

Ullman, W. *The Growth of Papal Government in the Middle Ages*, London, 1955.

CHURCHES, NATIONAL, IN ROME. In Rome, national churches are houses of worship founded and maintained by the members of different "nations." The meaning of the word "nation" has undergone a gradual evolution since the Middle Ages: first defined by linguistic faculties inside UNIVERSITIES, it was later used by the council of Constance to designate English, Spanish, French, German, and Italian "nations." These categorizations survived in the Roman Curia of the 15th century, although a common language effected a horizontal regrouping that was imposed over the collegial interests of the Curia's different groups of superior officers. On the other hand, the vogue of PILGRIMAGES to Rome, encouraged by the declaration of a jubilee year (1300), as well as the impossibility of travel to the Holy Land, caused a multitude of the faithful to swarm to the city, giving birth to the permanent presence of beggars and welfare assistance to the most indigent. In the period between the mid-14th century and the end of the 15th, shelters were established for pilgrims of different nations. They generally consisted of a hospice, a church, and a cemetery. Pontifical documents sanctioned these institutions and communities, in some cases using the title of "parish church" instead of "churches of cult."

Fragmentation of the "great nations" occurred soon afterward: the region of Flanders, on rather poor terms their German brothers, obtained its own foundation during the pontificate of EUGENE IV; the Bretons, who claimed an ancient tradition in Rome, established a permanent presence in Rome under MARTIN V; the Portuguese, whose relationship with the Spanish had always been a difficult one, reunited in the middle of the 15th century to form a unique coalition composed of small older institutions. Also, in the middle of the 17th century, the pope's Swiss Guard, whose members wanted to be autonomous in their relationship with their German peers, organized their own "national" church. All these groups, whose prosperity depended strictly on the importance of each individual community in Rome, were tenacious about acquiring property to obtain income for the cult (yearly masses) and for charity (alms to pilgrims, dowries, etc.) with the surplus used at the discretion of the members of the brotherhood. Through their embassies in Rome, the European monarchies were soon involved.

Since the 15th century, the brothers solicited the patronage of their sovereigns, who accorded it willingly but did not bother to get involved in management of the institutions. From the beginning of the 16th century the monarchies gradually began to take a more active role in the confraternities' sphere of activity without any resistance from the popes. It is interesting to note that very often the monarch, or rather his ambassador, used the situation existing in another foreign confraternity as a pretext to justify its own attempts at appropriation. The Portuguese ambassador had managed that nation's confraternity since 1539. In 1593, after the union between Portugal and the crown of Spain, the representative of Philip II took over. In 1699, the Count of Martinitz, representing Leopold I, brought the Germans' church and hospice of Santa Maria dell'Anima under imperial control. The French, strangely enough, took longer to submit to the pressures of their ambassador: it was not until the beginning of 1730 that he took control of the confraternity of St. Louis. When the great political upheavals occurred at the end of the century, every sovereign took active interest in the property of the national confraternities. The French, under the Empire, even appropriated the goods of the confraternity St. Julien-des-Flamands by invoking the fact that the ancient Austrians of the Low Countries had been annexed by France. When the upheaval of Revolution had passed, the restored sovereigns took back control of the national churches and imposed new regulations on them.

The Italian government, after being installed in Rome, abstained from imposing laws concerning pious works on the foreign brotherhoods. On 1 December 1870, article 8 of a royal decree stated that "there are no innovations regarding charity and welfare institutions designed for the social benefit of foreigners." This meant admitting their existence permanently the way it had appeared on 20 September 1870. These measures were carried out mostly to appease the "catholic" powers (Austria, Belgium, Spain, France, and Portugal), who had the greatest interest in maintaining the status quo. The confraternities formed by refugees from the cities and provinces of Italy (Lombardy, Florence, Picenum, Sicily, etc.) benefited from similar measures (article 11 of the 20 July 1890 act), but once the anti-clerical vogue passed, they were absorbed into the framework of lay religious associations regulated by the law.

In fact only the Campo Santo Teutonico and the Italian Groups maintained the traditional structure of a confraternity. The Spanish and Portuguese associations were managed directly by their respective embassies at the Holy See. The French ones, reorganized by PIUS VI in 1793, were run, beginning in 1803, by the French ambassador to the Holy See, assisted, from 1817 on, by a congregation of members named after him.

The Holy See rarely interfered in the internal life of the organizations. Nevertheless, it remained morally accountable to the Italian state for their existence, and it was always to the Holy See that they turned at difficult moments. Thus, in 1915, when Italy entered the war against Austria, Santa Maria dell'Anima was transformed into an ecclesiastical institute of the Holy See to avoid sequestration of its property. The existence of national foundations did require a certain degree of prudence. It is for this reason that Pius XI modified the text of the Lateran agreement at the last minute, confining the borders

of Vatican City to exclude the Campo Santo Teutonico for fear that a German-speaking country might one day claim some rights to it. This fear turned into a self-fulfilling prophecy in 1941, when under the pretext that Lorraine had been annexed to the Reich, the German Embassy in Rome made a request—left unfulfilled—to the Italian government asking to be granted possession of the Church Saint Nicolas des Lorrains.

Francois-Charles Uginet

Bibliography

De Almeida Palme, M. *Santo Antonio do Portugueses em Roma*, 2 vol. Lisbonne, 1951–2.

Fernandez Alonso, J. "Las iglesias nacionales de Espana en Roma. Sus origenes," *Anthologica annua*, 4 (1956) 9–96.

Fiorani, L. "Discussioni e ricerche sulle confraternita' romane negli ultimi cento anni," *Ricerche per la storia religiosa di Roma*, 6 (1985) 11–105.

Les fondations nationales dans la Rome pontificale, Rome, 1981 (CEFR, 52).

Tencajoli, O. F. *Le chiese nazionali italiani in Roma*, Rome, 1928.

CHURCHES OF THE ORIENT (ANTIQUITY AND MIDDLE AGES). The story of the relationship between the papacy and the Eastern Churches should be seen not only in light of their conflicts, but also keeping in mind periods of normalization and peace. Furthermore, it cannot be characterized solely by the progressive estrangement that began as early as late antiquity with a rift over the churches' christological theories, prior to the ecumenical COUNCIL of Chalcedon (451).

In accord with the principle of accommodation between the ecclesiastical hierarchy and the civil administration of the Roman Empire, the founding of Constantinople as a second capital (324–30) called for the swift promotion of its bishop. Since his city was known as the "New Rome," the third canon of the council of Constantinople of 381 recognized his honorary primacy after the bishop of Rome. This decision was confirmed by the twenty-eighth canon of Chalcedon, which sanctioned the formation of a patriarchate of Constantinople. Even though the canon was not aimed against the Roman See, which kept its preeminent status in the church hierarchy, Pope LEO I refused to approve it although he accepted the doctrinal definition of the council. According to a recent interpretation (A. de Halleux), the pope's refusal can be explained by his previous hostility toward both the honorary presence and legitimate privileges accorded the see of the new capital. By establishing a patriarchal jurisdiction based on a political primacy, Leo argued, the council's decision was hurting the Petrine concept of the papacy. The fact remains that Leo opposed the authority of apostolic tradition against the principle of accommodation between the Church and the Empire as equal seats as set down by the canon. This attitude resulted from the evolution of the Roman doctrine on primacy since the second half of the 4th century. It might also be due to concern about associating the pope's authority with a divided Empire, the western part of which had experienced a sharp decline.

The views of the Eastern Church with regard to papal primacy during the first millennium were certainly not limited to recognizing that its preeminence was founded on council decisions and on the fact that Rome had been the first capital of the Roman Empire before BYZANTIUM. Certain texts provide evidence of a broader but less well-defined concept. The see of Rome appears as a center of church communion, enjoying superior authority and even a special jurisdiction sometimes linked to the apostle Peter. The statements of Theodore the Studite at the beginning of the 9th century are among the most explicit on this matter (PG99, 1017–29, 1152–56). But the greater number of these declarations came from individuals or groups seeking support from the papacy or expressing satisfaction at seeing it defend a position similar to their own. They did not accept Rome's "monopolizing" of Peter's prerogatives. The basis of the universal church and often of their deference to the pope was solely his honorary primacy, the only one that was unanimously accepted. In any case, they never considered accepting any inherent sovereign or universal authority on his part. It was the councils that judged whether papal decisions conformed to the doctrine transmitted by scripture, by the Church Fathers, and by tradition. Likewise indispensable was unanimous agreement by the five patriarchates (Rome, Constantinople, ALEXANDRIA, Antioch, and Jerusalem) formed in the 4th and 5th centuries, whose cooperation expressed the unity of the Church. The East remained in fact deeply attached to the principle of COLLEGIALITY, and the patriarchs were eager to keep their internal autonomy.

The See of Rome usually accepted this autonomy by not interfering except when Church unity was threatened. From the Byzantine conquest of Italy in the 6th century to the birth of the "pontifical state" in the 8th century, it truly constituted a patriarchate of the Empire. It adapted to the situation, tried to be more integrated in Church collegiality, and kept close watch over the Emperor's role in the domain of religion. Nevertheless Roman doctrine took a dim view of the concept that declared the Emperor the human image of God and his representative on earth, as well as the person most responsible for Church unity. From the 4th century on, the authority of the sovereign and that of the pope came into conflict at various times, provoking a series of rifts between Rome and the Church of Constantinople, which was more dependent on imperial power.

After the Arabian conquest of Egypt, Syria, and Palestine in the 7th century, Constantinople, the only patriarchate of the Orient remaining in the Empire, found itself de facto at the head of Eastern orthodoxy. The Byzantines continued nevertheless to emphasize the necessity of agreement among the five patriarchates with regard to Church government (the idea of the "pentarchy"). Rome soon had no more than sporadic contact with the seats at Alexandria, Antioch, and Jerusalem, whose importance had diminished considerably. In return, its relationship with Constantinople remained characterized by alternate periods of tension and harmony, a succession of ruptures and reconciliations that, as before, often depended on the religious politics of the Byzantine emperor. In addition to doctrinal quarrels, there were disagreements over matters of practice, and above all some conflicts of interest. The rivalry for influence centered around Illyrium (a major part of the Balkans). Growing out of a situation that dated back to the 4th century, this rivalry flared during an epoch of iconoclastic clashes, when, in 730 or 740, the emperor Leo III transferred the bishops of Illyrium from the patriarchate of Rome to that of Constantinople and also transferred those of Calabria and Sicily (which returned to the Roman seat only after the Norman conquest of southern Italy and Sicily, after the 11th century). In terms of institutional implications, the transfers placed these bishoprics within the cultural orbit of the Greek Church. Following the political detachment of Rome, which occurred soon afterward, the ecclesiastical domain of Constantinople came to coincide with that of the Empire. This was resented in Byzantium as treason and created conflicts sorrounding the imperial coronation of Charlemagne in 800. The estrangement of the two Churches intensified.

In the 860s a conflict, mostly around the conversion of Bulgaria, set Pope NICHOLAS I against the patriarch of Constantinople, Photios. His ruthlessness revealed the extent of ill will and antagonism between the two seats. The Roman Church did not succeed in imposing her authority in Bulgaria, and the rupture was once more temporary. Yet the polemic left its traces. It was then that the papacy was first criticized for inserting the words Filioque into the Credo. Any relationship that still existed between the two Churches weakened during the 10th century, particularly due to the effacement of the papacy during that period. The situation had almost reached a "state of mutual indifference" when, in the middle of the 11th century, the Norman invasion of southern Italy made a political rapprochement between Rome and Byzantium advantageous. The patriarch of Constantinople, Michel Cerularius, saw a threat to his jurisdiction over the Italian bishops, which the Church of Rome, who by then accepted the idea of reformation, reclaimed with new vigor. Polemics flared up once more. In 1054, Roman delegates who had come from Constantinople and the city's patriarch mutually excommunicated each other.

Although 1054 is often considered the date of the beginning of the "SCHISM," contemporaries of that epoch in fact gave very little importance to this new predicament of the two estranged churches. The existence of the separation did not hinder various contacts in an epoch when relations between East and West were intensifying. Still, negotiations aimed at unity failed. The monarchic character of Rome's primacy, which had increased considerably since the Gregorian reformation, was opposed by Byzantine views on collegiality among bishops and by the emperor's supreme power in an empire that identified itself strongly with Orthodox Christianity (even though the patriarchate of Constantinople had been expanding beyond the established frontiers of the Byzantine State since the 9th and 10th centuries). Furthermore, Western expansion in the Orient increasingly created a climate of hostility, which the events of 1204 intensified. The conquest of Constantinople after the Fourth CRUSADE, the establishment of a Latin patriarchate, and the plunder of the Byzantine Church finalized the split.

The Byzantine emperors, "in exile" in Nicaea and after returning to Constantinople (1261), made several attempts to negotiate with the Church of Rome even though the latter held to the position that there was no salvation "for the schismatic" and "heretic" Greeks. One segment of the Byzantine high clergy more or less adapted to a policy aimed above all at preventing aggression from the West, and later at obtaining military assistance against the TURKS. On the other hand, a certain number of high-ranking clerics and lay intellectuals sincerely aspired to a reconciliation between the two Churches. Still, a majority of the Greek population, including monks and lower clergy, was hostile to them. The unity proclaimed in 1274 at the Council of Lyon and in 1439 at the Council of Florence met with fierce resistance. Its opponents triumphed: the unity of Lyon was abandoned after the death of Emperor Michael VIII Paleologue in 1282, and that of Florence did not survive the fall of Constantinople to the Turks in 1453.

Among the Eastern Churches whom the crusades had put in contact with the West, only the small Maronite patriarchate of Lebanon concluded a lasting union with Rome by accepting its primacy. The long process of Catholic integration of the Maronites, which had begun in the 12th century, nevertheless provoked various conflicts between partisans and adversaries of the union.

Jean-Marie Sansterre

Bibliography

Apanasieff, N. et al., *La Primauté de Pierre dans l'Eglise orthodoxe*, Neuchatel-Paris, 1960.

Beck, H. G. *Geschichte der orthodoxen Kirche im byzantinischen Reich*, Gottingen, 1980.

Brehier, L. *Le Schisme oriental du Xime siecle*, Paris, 1899; "Avant la séparation du XIme siècle. Les relations normales entre Rome et les Eglises d'Orient." *La documentation catholique*, 415 (1928), 387–404; repr. Istina, 6 (1959) 352–72).

Congar, Y. M. J. "Neuf cent ans apres. Notes sur le 'Schisme Oriental,' 1054–1954." *L'Eglise et les Eglises*, Chevetogne, 1954, I, 3-95.

Congar, Y. M. J. *L'écclésiologie du haut Moyen Age. De sant Gregoire le Grand a' ladesunion entre Byzance et Rome*, Paris, 1968.

Conte, P. *Chiesa e primato nelle lettere dei papi del secolo VII*, Milan, 1971.

De Halleux, A. "Le decret chalcedonien sur les prerogatives de la Nouvelle Rome," *Ephemerides theologicae Lovaniensis*, 64 (1988) 288–323.

De Vries, W. *Rom und die Patriarchate des Ostens*, Fribourg-Munich, 1963.

De Vries, W. *Orient et Occident. Les structures ecclesiales vues dans l'histoire des sept premiers conciles oecumeniques*, Paris, 1974.

Ducellier, A. *L'Eglise byzantine. Entre Pouvoir et Esprit (313–1204)*, Paris, 1990.

Dvornik, F. *Le Schismes de Photius*. Histoire et Legende, Paris, 1950.

Dvornik, F. *Byzance et la primauté romaine*, Paris, 1964.

Fedalto, G. *Le Chiese d'Oriente da Giustiniano alla caduta di Constantinopoli*, Milan, 1983.

Gill, J. *Byzantium and the Papacy, 1198–1400*, New Brunswick, 1979; *Church Union, Rome and Byzantium* 1204–1453, London, 1979.

Gouillard, J. "L'Eglise d'Orient et la primauté romaine au temps de l'iconoclasme," *Istina*, 21 (1976), 25–54; repr. *La Vie religieuse a Byzance*, London, 1981, V.

Herrin, J. *The Formation of Christendom*, Princeton, 1987.

Hussey, J. M. *The Orthodox Church in the Byzantine Empire*, Oxford, 1986.

Jugie, M. *Le Schisme byzantin*, Paris, 1941.

Lemerle, P. "L'orthodoxie byzantine et l'oecumenisme medieval: les origines du schisme des Eglises," *Bulletin de l'Association G. Budé*, 4 serie, 2 (1965) 228–46; repr. *Essais sur le monde byzantin*, London, 1980, VIII.

Maccarone, M. ed., *Il primato del vescovo di Roma nel primo Millennio*, Vatican, 1991.

Magi, L. *La sede romana nella corrispondenza degli imperatori e patriarchi bizantini (VI–VII sec.)*, Rome Louvain, 1972.

Meyeendorff, J. *Imperial unity and Christian Divisions: The Church 450–680 AD*, Crestwood, 1989.

Michel, A. *Humbert und Kerullarios*, 2 vols. Paderborn, 1924–30.

Norden, W. *Das Papstum und Byzabz*, Berlin, 1903.

Peri, V. "La pentarchia: istituzione ecclesiale (VI–VII sec.) e teoria canonico-teologica," *Bisanzio, Roma e l'Italia nell'alto medioevo*, Spoleto, 1988 (Settimane1/4, XXXIV), 209–311.

Runciman, S. *The Eastern Schism*, Oxford, 1955.

Setton, K. M. *The Papacy and the Levant*, 1204–1571, 4 vols., 1076–1984.

Spiteris, J. *La critica bizantina del primato romano nel secolo XII*, Rome, 1979.

Wojtowytsch, M. *Papsttum und Konzils von den Anfaengen bis zu Leo I. (440–61)*, Stuttgart, l981.

CINEMA, POPES AND. Papal interest in film was not precocious, and early on it was about the same as what most contemporaries experienced when they witnessed the Lumière brothers' invention. Thus, as patriarch of Venice, when PIUS X attended the projection of the inaugural ceremony for the new belltower in St. Mark's, he was amazed to recognize familiar faces and places, and commented on every scene with no concealment of his emotion. He was like any other spectator of the day: what stood out most—what fascinated him most—was the movement, the "truth" of what was shown. It was really not until films began to acquire irrefutable international popularity that the Church in general, and the pope in particular, became aware of its significance as a means of social, cultural, and political communication. The first tangible traces of Catholic concern about this new medium did not appear until the second half of the 1920s—some thirty years after its creation. At the time there were some 50,000 movie theaters throughout the world.

It was the lower echelons of the church hierarchy rather than the Vatican who first to showed a serious interest in moving pictures. A number of committees were formed in Western Europe after 1920; in France there were masses called *messes du cinéma*, with film professionals in attendance. A number of Church figures had a clear appreciation of the spectacle and wanted these professionals to be conscious of their role, which was necessarily pedagogical.

Concerns about cinema gradually made their way up the hierarchy: in November 1928, the first Congrès Catholic du Cinéma took place. The archbishop of Paris, Cardinal Dubois, gave weight to the assembly by his very presence. In the first months of 1929, on the occasion of the meeting of the Union Internationale des Ligues Féminines Catholiques, PIUS XI proposed an international conference on film; this is not to say that he was actually endorsing the creation of the International Catholic Office of Film, which held its first convention that same year in Munich.

It was not until seven years later, in 1936, that the pope got involved with the subject of film. Even then it was not through his own doing that Pius XI promulgated the ENCYCLICAL *Vigilanti Cura* (29 June), but in response to the requests of officers from the Legion of Decency, founded in the United States two years earlier. The American Catholic association was fighting against the "moral depravity" hanging over the film industry, and working for a code of censorship (the famous Hayes Code) over which it would have strict control. The Legion of Decency, with the backing of a number of Catholic associations, with access to the press and radio, and with an increasingly significant influence over film distributors, asked the pope to support it by blessing the legitimacy of its actions; such support came in *Vigilanti Cura*. Although the encyclical was primarily addressed to those involved in the Legion of Decency and to the American bishops, it carried weight with the rest of the Catholic world.

It was not ANATHEMA that developed, but the film industry's desire to adhere: "It is both necessary and truly urgent to act so that throughout the ages all innovation in human undertakings, including the technical and industrial arts obtained through divine favor, serve effectively to enhance the glory of God, the salvation of souls, and the spread of the kingdom of Jesus Christ. . . . The seduction of the moving image, easy access to showings, even for the general populace, and all of the circumstances surrounding this mode of recreation make it impossible today to discover another influence capable of producing a greater effect on people." And Pius XI continued: "Movie theaters are veritable schools where lessons are given regarding things that can lead the majority of men toward either good or evil much more readily than abstract reasoning. The film industry thus needs to promote the salutary demands of the Christian conscience and repudiate all that might be of a nature to wound or corrupt good morals." This text bears witness to an unfailing conviction of the influence, and indeed even the tyranny, that moving pictures work on the spectator: it supercedes words and imposes itself upon the individual despite his or her convictions, and perhaps even helps the individual forget those convictions. This image is credited with a persuasive omnipotence that may make it dangerous, in the eyes of the sovereign pontiff, for weaker spirits, especially those of young people. This idea has lost credence today, but it was commonly accepted at the time.

More justly appreciated, without a doubt, was the overall nature of the cinematic spectacle, although even here its power was overestimated: "Film is not aimed at . . . the individual; in a way, it is aimed at the community, through circumstances of time, of material, and of place that are singularly apt to inflame souls, to evil as well as to good. And we all know from experience in what a deplorable direction this collective enthusiasm can be led."

Such considerations were still applied only to the contents of a film, and the effort for which the pope was calling concerned the production of the image much more than how it was interpreted by the spectator: the spectator should be provided with a film that was in accord with Catholic morals rather than expected to learn how to discern the film's meaning properly.

This attitude was confirmed with the passage of time: receiving personalities from both film and theater on 26 August 1945, PIUS XII addressed only the professional producers—in the larger sense of the word—of film, not the consumers. Similarly, in June and October 1955 in his speech to the world of film regarding the "ideal film," the pope again spoke about replacing meaningless or "perverted" spectacles with beautiful and noble images.

Changes in the papal stance on the cinema were not actually seen until 1957, with the encyclical *Miranda Prorsus* on film, radio, and television. This document was undoubtedly influenced by the work of the Papal Commission on Film, which has been the Vatican's official body for the study of the multiple relationships between faith, morals, and film since the time of its creation in the spring of 1952.

Miranda Prorsus naturally reaffirmed the need for Christian inspiration in audiovisual productions, but this reaffirmation was conditional: "Would it not be . . . the highest vocation of media techniques to make the teachings of God and His Son Jesus Christ known to all?" And Pius XII called for an educational, formative effort to prepare both adults and young people to make better use of the cinematic spectacle. "We must," he wrote, "teach [people] to choose programs that conform to the moral and religious teachings of the Church, according to the information offered by important offices of the Church."

This shift is interesting, and undoubtedly reveals an admission of failure: the profession was no longer being called upon to produce good films, but rather the spectator was being encouraged not to go see the bad ones. A second noticeable shift was that the film industry lost its specificity. It was now no more than one "media technique" among others, such as radio, and especially television, which at the time was only beginning to expand.

This evolution found definite confirmation a few years later, at the time of the second VATICAN COUNCIL, where it was evidently impossible not to bring up the subject of modern means of communication: on 4 December 1963, PAUL VI promulgated the decree on the media of social communication, which once and for all refuted the exclusively recreational nature of the audiovisual arts. They were above all bearers of moral and cultural values, and it was in this capacity that the decree concerned itself with them, and urged Catholics to take an interest in them: "It is unacceptable for the sons of the Church to accept passively that the word of salvation be chained up and forbidden by the (albeit considerable) problems of technique and money inherent in these means of communication.

The Holy Synod also reminds Catholics of their duty to support and assist Catholic newspapers, periodicals, cinematic enterprises, broadcasting stations, and radio and television programs whose primary goal is defending the truth and providing for the Christian education of human society."

In addition to creating national offices for the press, film, radio, and television, the decree called for the "fundamental right" of the Church to use these media for SOCIAL COMMUNICATIONS, to such an extent that they seemed to have become indispensable for the propagation of Christian teachings. Today, this assertion applies only indirectly to film, for television has usurped its place in the public eye, and has thus become the Church's primary concern.

Popes on the Screen. Even though the Vatican II decree formulated the Church's right to use audiovisual techniques, no pope either prior or subsequent to the decree has sought recourse to this medium. In general, moreover, the pope has rarely appeared on the screen despite the substantial quantity of film that has retraced the history of Christianity. The exploits of the earliest Christians have supplied the central theme for over a hundred films from a variety of countries and time periods: films that in almost all cases feature the classical scene of martyrs thrown to the lions, to the great pleasure of the cruel Romans. And though Peter does appear in all the Passions filmed since 1895, it is naturally in his capacity as apostle rather than as the first pope, with the exception of *Chemin de Damas* (Max Glass, 1952), where the apostle was played by Jacques Dufilho.

The first case of a pope appearing on the screen, cited here for the record, goes back to the earliest days of film; it was filmed not by Lumière but by the American William K. L. Dickson, using his Mutograph, in Rome during the summer of 1898. In this first and quite brief strip of film, LEO XIII's silhouette could be seen in the half light, dominating the inside of the Vatican. Emerging into the light, the smiling pontiff walked toward the camera. After the apostolic blessing, a different shot showed him in his carriage surrounded by the Vatican guard. Later, in 1900, Leo, who showed a real and undeniable curiosity about the new invention, gave his permission for Giuseppe Filippini to project, inside the SISTINE CHAPEL, a second film in which he appeared.

Given that film has since taken a turn toward fiction, these early works hold little interest for posterity. The pope obviously cannot be a fictional character, and his appearance on the screen is thus reduced to only two scenarios, and two film genres: carefully done, more or less faithful historical reconstructions, and authorized biography, occasionally including the rare genre of feature-length documentaries. There is one film that forms the exception to this statement, and deserves recognition here: *Shoes of the Fisherman*, adapted in 1968 by

Michael Anderson from the historical novel of the same name by Morris West. Anthony Quinn quite credibly played the role of a fictional Russian pope, Cyril I, who worked to safeguard world peace, at the time threatened by China and its Communist president Peng. At the end of the film the pope lays down his TIARA and proclaims the Church's renunciation of all goods and riches that come at the expense of the poor. Cyril I puts an end to Vatican luxury, condemns the Church as a social and political system, and returns to the source of the Gospels' message. The film is, of course, fiction.

Among films of a historical nature, the pope is almost always relegated to a walk-on role, a foil at most. And even though Ermete Zacconi did briefly play the role of CLEMENT VII in his troubles with the king of England, Henry VIII (*Les Perles de la Couronne*, by Sacha Guitry) in 1937, it must be noted that between 1950 and 1970 such appearances were rare. The Napoleonic saga, with which French film has dealt on numerous occasions, usually reserves one appearance for PIUS VII, an appearance that tends to be downplayed to the maximum: in the credits for *Napoleon* (Sacha Guitry, 1954), Gino Antonini, who plays Pius VII, appears thirty-sixth in the credits, far behind Jean-Pierre Aumont, Pierre Brasseur, Danielle Darrieux, Jean Gabin, Orson Welles, Michelle Morgan, and Jean Marais. Vittorio de Sica had a better role in Abel Gance's *Austerlitz* (1959), but even in this case he was relegated to staying in the shadow of Napoleon, played by Pierre Mondy. Four years later, in 1963, while GREGORY X was sending Marco Polo to China (*La Fabuleuse Aventure de Marco Polo*, Denys de La Patellière and Noel Howard), an equally insignificant role was being played by Paolo Stoppa as ALEXANDER III in *Becket*, adapted by Peter Glenville from Jean Anouilh's play *Becket ou l'honneur de Dieu*. Alexander III, saddled with a quite improbable Cardinal Zambelli, played by Gino Cervi, was reduced to the role of distant advisor to King Henry II, in whose mannerisms Peter O'Toole could be recognized. It is interesting to point out that Jean Anouilh's play, which premiered in Paris in February 1960, with Bruno Cremer and Daniel Ivernel in the lead roles, had been produced in New York in 1961 by Peter Glenville, with Laurence Olivier and Anthony Quinn in the main roles. Rex Harrison's role as JULIUS II in Carol Reed's *The Agony and the Ecstasy* (1965) was, albeit more developed, hardly different in spirit. The British actor was second in the credits, as a miserly and quarrelsome pope who commissioned a fresco for the ceiling of the Sistine Chapel. But the main role was of course reserved for the artist Michelangelo, a role to which a bearded and passionate Charlton Heston lent his talents.

The niche filled by biographies and documentaries on the papacy is smaller than that of fictionalized historical representations, but it is also more interesting, often con-

sisting of official films. The first case in point is the 1942 film *Pastor Angelicus*, produced by the Centro Cattolico Cinematografico. This frank panegyric about Pius XII begins with a quick review of Eugenio Pacelli's career, from its beginnings to the point where Pius XI appoints him to the papal diplomacy service, sends him as a nuncio to Berlin, and makes him secretary of state. After Pius XII's election, the work details the Vatican's actions during WORLD WAR II. emphasizing the humanitarian aspects of his actions: his relations with the Red Cross, visits to prisoners' camps, and so forth. It includes a day in the life of the pope: his early rising, mass, his visit to the QUIRINAL, a walk in the VATICAN GARDENS, his private, official, and public audiences, and of course a solemn high mass in ST. PETER's. As a whole it is somewhat confusing, and certainly lacking in unity. *Pastor Angelicus* is nevertheless of considerable historical importance: Gian Piero Brunetta sees in it the first conscious attempt to replace the waning Mussolini myth with the image of a pope capable of rallying Italians together and overcoming the trials of the war. It is, in any case, a full-length film used in a deliberate way: cleverly released throughout the country after the war, it certainly played a great role in the mobilization of Catholics at the time of the April 1948 elections. And last but not least, *Pastor Angelicus* is clearly the only film of its kind that did not suffer commercial failure.

The attempts that follow cannot fairly be said to have achieved success in this genre; some were even blatant failures. Such was the case for a film by Umberto Scarpelli, *Gli uomini non guardano il cielo* (1953), a biography of PIUS X that went almost completely unnoticed when it came out. The film opens in the month of June 1914, and details the pope's attempts to forestall the impending conflict. When his efforts meet with no success, he resorts to prayer, and then a flashback takes the spectator through the important events of his life. The work concludes with the declaration of war and the pope's death. Although it was received by the Italian public with complete indifference, this biography of the adversary of MODERNISM nevertheless did play outside of Italy: *Gli uomini non guardano il cielo* opened in Paris on 9 June 1954, just a few days after Pius X's BEATIFICATION. The film was met with the same indifference as in Italy; the magazine *Radio-Cinéma-Télévision*, never accused of anticlerical activism, deplored the film's heavy dullness.

Four years later, in France, a full-length wide-screen color documentary, *Tu es Pierre*, directed by Philippe Agostini, attempted to outline the history of the papacy on the screen for the first time. Working for Les Films du Parvis, Agostini had already directed three religious films before undertaking *Tu es Pierre: La Nuit des Pâques, Ordinations*, and *Semaine sainte*. At the time of its filming, the film "benefitted" from a twist of fate: the death of Pius XII. Planning for the film, and its script, were inevitably affected: the work was enriched by a long appendix dedicated to the new pope's election. "The death of Pius XII," Agostini stated when the film opened, "his funeral, the CONCLAVE, the election of John XXIII, and his coronation, added great dramatic and documentary interest. They provided a concrete demonstration of the idea of continuity and succession that is central to the subject at hand." But they did not guarantee commercial success, even though this kind of film sought more than just commercial distribution networks. Despite the best of efforts, such films often meet with failure: a papal biography is a risky subject.

Ermanno Olmi was undoubtedly aware of this fact when he undertook *E venne un uomo* in 1965. The film was an authorized biography of JOHN XXIII, inspired by his *Journal of a Soul*, but it was not a traditional biography. Rod Steiger did not play the role of John XXIII, rather he portrayed the *idea* of John XXIII. Bearing a vague resemblance to the pope, the actor trod before Olmi's camera in places where the deceased pope had lived or stayed. Steiger never donned a cassock: his only purpose was to evoke thoughts through his presence. Even if the film's poor reception can be attributed to the performance of an actor literally fitted to his role rather than to the originality of the form, it nevertheless illustrates the powerlessness of film to deal with such subjects. This is not the last papal biography to provide support for this assertion: *D'un pays lointain* (Krzysztof Zanussi, 1981), dealing with the life of JOHN PAUL II and poorly received at the Cannes Film Festival, never reached movie theaters.

A few minor appearances by popes in films should also be mentioned. Among the most recent was the scene—bearing the stamp of antiestablishment inspiration—in which the devil was at work on Rosemary as television was rebroadcasting PAUL VI's speech in New York's Yankee Stadium (*Rosemary's Baby*, Roman Polanski, 1968). More than his spiritual power, it was the temporal power of the Church and the structure of this power that were at issue in *The Audience* (*L'Udienza*, Marco Polanski, 1971), a film in which a young Catholic man attempts desperately to meet the pope and dies without attaining his goal, the victim of the closed hierarchy of the Vatican. In this case, Paul VI, who pays the cost for the conflict, appears only in a photo, but it is his absence, or we should perhaps say, his latent presence, that underlies the entire film.

A similar inspiration is seen in *Brother Son, Sister Moon* (Franco Zefirelli, 1972), which sets a kind of "hippy" Francis of Assisi up against a frankly conservative—although convinced *in extremis*—INNOCENT III. And it is impossible to forget Federico Fellini's *Roma* (1972), in which the ecclesiastical fashion parade comes to a close with the hallucinatory shot of a pseudo-pope bathed in unbearable light, a sickly old man drowning in fabrics and precious stones: proof, if need be, that film is not art for hire, and that Fellini is not Michelangelo.

Selected Filmography.
Pastor Angelicus, 1942, Italy. Dir. Romolo Marcellini. Prod. Centro Cattolico Cinematografico. 80 min.
Gli uomini non guardano il cielo, 1953, Italy. Dir. Umberto Scarpelli. Prod. Cinelia. 87 min. Screenplay and adapt. G. Mori, E. Bacchion, Margadonna, Duse, F. Scarpelli. Starring Enrico Vidon (Pius X), Tullio Carminati, Isa Miranda.
Tu es Pierre, 1958, France. Dir. Philippe Agostini. Prod. Les Films du Parvis. 88 min. Screenplay Jean-Pierre Chartier. Commentary: Daniel-Rops.
E venne un uomo (this film had two titles in English: *The Intermediary* and *And There Came a Man*), 1965, Italy-USA. Dir. Ermanno Olmi. Prod. Harry Salzman. Screenplay Vicenzo Labella. Starring Rod Steiger, Adolfo Celli.
The Agony and the Ecstasy, 1965, Italy-USA. Dir. Carol Reed. Prod. Carol Reed. 139 min. Screenplay Philip Dunne, from the novel by Irving Stone. Starring Charlton Heston, Rex Harrison (Julius II), Harry Andrews.
Shoes of the Fisherman, 1968, USA. Dir. Michael Anderson. Prod. George Endglund. 162 min. Screenplay John Patrick and James Kennaway, from the novel by Morris West. Starring Anthony Quinn (Cyril I), Laurence Olivier, Oskar Werner, Vittorio de Sica, John Gielgud.
Brother Sun, Sister Moon, 1973, England-USA. Dir. Franco Zefirelli. Prod. Paramount. 121 min. Screenplay S. Cecchi d'Amico, K. Ross, L. Wertmuller, F. Zefirelli. Starring Graham Falkner, Judi Bowker, Leigh Lawson, Alec Guinness (Innocent III).
From a Far Country, 1981, Italy-USA-Poland. Dir. Krzysztof Zanussi. Prod. Films RAI, Transword Film, ITV. 135 min. Screenplay J. Szczepanski, Andrzej Kijowski and Krzysztof Zanussi. Starring Sam Neill, Lisa Harrow, Christopher Cazenove, Maurice Denham.

Frédéric Delmuelle

Bibliography

Gritti, J. *Eglise, cinéma et télévision. Choix de textes des papes et des évêques*, Paris, 1966.

CITIZENSHIP, VATICAN. The principle of Vatican citizenship is based on article 9 of the LATERAN agreements of 11 February 1929, which resolved the Roman question by creating the VATICAN CITY STATE. A Vatican City law promulgated by PIUS XI on 7 June 1929—the date of the treaty went into effect—precisely sets out the regulations.

Vatican citizenship has nothing to do with nationality in the usual sense of the term. The phrasing of article 9 of the treaty, which speaks of persons "subject to the sovereignty of the Holy See," implies that it is an acquired status with characteristics of allegiance to a sovereign. Vatican citizenship is strictly linked to stable residence in Vatican City, which implies a dwelling from which one is at liberty to come and go. Citizenship is, therefore, not bestowed by birth, and it is precarious since it is lost as soon as the Vatican citizen loses his resident status by losing his qualification as a subject of the Holy See. "Nationality of function" has been mentioned. But it is possible that some persons can have Vatican citizenship without exercising any function, and some persons reside in the Vatican without holding citizenship. By simple logic, it is evident that it can neither constitute a nationality per se nor replace one's nationality of origin, since in that case a Vatican citizen who loses his citizenship would become stateless.

There is a special regulation for CARDINALS, who become Vatican citizens as soon as they take up residence in Rome, even outside of Vatican City. The texts do not address the case of the sovereign pontiff, who, when the Lateran agreements were signed, had ordinarily been an Italian over the last five centuries. Obviously the pope is a Vatican citizen, since he lives there and he is its sovereign. But if a pope were to resign, two scenarios could result. If he took up residence in Rome, he would maintain his citizenship, like a cardinal of the CURIA or of a diocese who retires; if he went to VITERBO or AVIGNON or elsewhere outside of Rome, he would lose his Vatican citizenship.

Under article 2 of the 7 June 1929 law, Vatican citizenship is extended to family members of a Vatican citizen who effectively live under his roof in the City. But it is not granted by right: it depends on an authorization that is not transferable by marriage or consanguinity, because it is *de gratia* for a non-separated wife, sons less than twenty-five years old or incapable of working, and unmarried daughters. In the same way, it can be extended to parents, brothers less than twenty-five years old or incapable of working, and to unmarried sisters on condition that these persons are the responsibility of the citizen.

Philippe Levillain

Bibliography

Bachelet, V. "L'organisation administrative du Saint-Siège et de la Cité du Vatican," *Revue internationale des sciences administratives*, 1955, 2–21.

Zielewicz, Z. *La Situation internationale du Saint-Siège*, Lausanne, 1917.

CIVILTÀ CATTOLICA. Bimonthly magazine published by the Italian JESUITS. *La Civiltà Cattolica* holds a special place in the cultural panorama of Italy, based on the intellectual quality of the articles, the diversity of the themes treated, the functioning of the editorial team, and the publication's close and continuous ties with the popes. Its prestige is attested to by its wide circulation in dioceses, seminaries, and Catholic associations, but also beyond Catholic milieus: reading it is, in Italy, quasi de rigueur for any leader, political or not, Catholic or "lay." Its beginnings go back to 1850. The first issue, which appeared in Naples on 6 April, sprang from the problems of Pope PIUS IX and the desire of a few clergymen to create an instrument for the defense of the Catholic religion. The idea of a regular publication in Italian, aimed at a wide audience, first took shape among the JESUITS in 1846, when the provincial, Father Pasquale Cambi, consulted prominent members of the Society of Jesus, such as Matteo Liberatore, Antonio Bresciani, and Luigi Taparelli d'Azeglio. This initial project came up against the mistrust of the General of the Jesuits, Father Roothaan, who feared political manipulation of the publication, as well as involvement in polemics and departure from a spiritual orientation. But the project did not disappear. After the storms of 1848, which led to the dispersal of the Society of Jesus and the retreat of the pope to Gaeta, the project was reactivated by Father Carlo Maria Curci (1810–91) after his return to Naples, from exile in Malta at the end of 1849. He was able to interest the secretary of state, Cardinal Giacomo Antonelli, in the project to present the project to Pius IX. The role of the exiled pope was decisive. It was he who understood the importance of what was at stake, overrode the still vigorous objections of Father Roothaan, and made the decision during an audience granted to Curci on 9 January 1850. From that time on, things moved very quickly. Curci formed a group of collaborators: Luigi Taparelli d'Azeglio, Antonio Bresciani, Giovanni Battista Pianciani, Matteo Liberatore, Giuseppe Oreglia, Francesco Pellico, and Carlo Piccirillo. A few weeks later, after further decisive intervention by the pope to smooth over financial difficulties, the magazine appeared in Naples, where it set up shop until September, when it moved to Rome. Its directors believed it best, after the capture of Rome, to transfer it to Florence, where it remained until 1887. On its return to the capital of the popes, it was housed for many years at 246 via Ripetta, before moving to via di Porta Pinciana in 1952.

The initial success of *La Civiltà Cattolica* was rapid and consistent: 6,307 copies of the first issue were distributed, and a few months later the magazine had close to 12,000 subscribers throughout the Italian peninsula. In 1946 it reached a high point in circulation—18,000. In 1968 the print run was 15,220, in 1978 it was 15,848. The magazine continued on an upward track, with

16,275 copies in 1989 and 16,731 in 1991. From the beginning, it found its quasi permanent form at: publication every two weeks in a small booklet of about a hundred pages. It was divided among in-depth articles on every kind of subject (theology, piety, archaeology, politics, economics, history, social problems, sciences, literature, pedagogy, sociology, contemporary news reports, commentary on current developments within and outside of Italy, reviews of the press, and bibliographic reviews (introduced in 1856). In the beginning, novels, such as *L'Ebreo di Verona* by Father Antonio Bresciani, were published in serial form and contributed to the success of the endeavor. Very soon a publishing house was set up to put out works by regular contributors to the magazine, and articles were collected in volumes on particular themes. The Edizioni La Civiltà Cattolica was organized in its present form in 1948. Its publications are numerous; since 1980 editorials have been collected each year in a special publication.

La Civiltà Cattolica was developed and met with unquestioned success at a time when the press became a fundamental outlet for defending or attacking the Church: it was defined by Carlo Maria Curci as "a veritable remedy" against evil and a means of bringing society back to its Christian origins, as the title of the magazine clearly indicated. The prestige of *La Civiltà Cattolica*, which has remained constant from the time of its creation until today, is derived from two principal sources: a modus operandi that guarantees the quality and coherence of the publication, and its close relations with the pope.

Pius IX instituted *perpetuamente* the college of editors of *La Civiltà Cattolica* by the BRIEF of 12 February 1866, confirmed by LEO XIII in the CONSTITUTION *Sapienti consilio* of 8 July 1889. The editors thus constitute a veritable community dependent not on the Jesuit province, but on the Father General of the Society of Jesus. The magazine became an autonomous institution within the latter. This privilege, which is without precedent, is proof of the importance that is given to it and of the central role it is called upon to play. The editors, all Jesuits, are engaged exclusively in writing and research. Their number has varied over time: normally around nine, they currently number twelve. The superior general designates them, as well as the magazine's director, after requesting the *placet* of the Holy See. Since 1852, there have been nineteen directors: Carlo Maria Curci served as director until 1854, followed by Giuseppe Calvetti from 1854 to 1855. After the premature death of the latter, Carlo Maria Curci reassumed his former position (1855–64). Next came Giuseppe Oreglia (1864–5), Matteo Liberatore (1865–8), and Carlo Maria Curci once again (1868–72), but he lived outside the community headed by Valeriano Cardella. During these years Curci was planning to follow a different path, separate from that of the magazine. The direc-

tors who followed were Valentino Steccanella (1872–81); Giuseppe Fantoni (1881–5); Giovanni Cornoldi (1885–8); Francisco Berardinelli (1888–92); Ruggero Freddi (1892); Alessandro Gallerani (1892–06); Salvatore Brandi (1906–13); Giuseppe Chiaudano (1913–5); Enrico Rosa (1915–32); Felice Rinaldi (1932–9); Giacomo Martegani (1939–55); Calogero Gliozzo (1955–9); Roberto Tucci (1959–73), Bartolomeo Sorge (1973–84), and Gian Paolo Salvini from 1984. The editors have always had a solid university education; each is a specialist in a particular field, but each article is the fruit of collective reflection. After a first reading by the director, the text is submitted to two specialists on the subject dealt with. The author then integrates the proposed corrections. All proposed articles are then submitted to the entire college of editors, which meets every fifteen days, while a few examples are sent to the Vatican. Collegiality, despite the specialization of the different authors, and rigid discipline constitute the major principles of the magazine's operations. They guarantee the editorial consistency of the writings.

Submission to the pope is automatic. From its installation at Rome in September 1850, the Holy See has reviewed each issue. From then on the Jesuit magazine founded at the pope's behest became an unofficial voice of the papacy—the "courier of papal will" (liberal Catholic historian Arturo Carlo Jemolo), "barometer of the Church" (politician and historian Giovanni Spadolini), "laboratory of the pope" (Francesco Dante, historian on the origins of *La Civiltà Cattolica*). These terms express its close dependence on the pope. The magazine, prepared by a college of editors, is not an official mouthpiece of the Holy See, but since its creation, it has been its instrument. Through the pontificate of Pius XII, popes personally reviewed the proposed articles. For this purpose, the director was received in audience every fifteen days. This tradition remained in full force under Pius XII, when the director was Father Martegani. It was interrupted by the illness of the pope, and the SUBSTITUTE, Angelo Dell'Acqua, then worked with the director until the end of the 1950s. John XXIII did not revive the tradition, leaving to the secretary of state, Msgr. Tardini, the responsibility of examining the work of the editors. Under Paul VI, Cardinal Villot maintained the new custom. In 1978 John Paul I advised Father Sorge of his intention of resuming the bimonthly papal audience, but John Paul II has maintained the orientation of John XXIII and Paul VI, personal control being impossible because of his many apostolic trips. Even though the direct link with the pope has been broken in the last decades, the bimonthly meeting of the director of *La Civiltà Cattolica* with the Holy See is a continuing tradition. It is an unofficial magazine whose articles can nevertheless be considered "authorized." From Pius IX on, it has remained faithful to the perspective of each pontiff.

The intrinsic quality of the articles and their official character explain the interest with which the opinions, positions, and polemics of *La Civiltà Cattolica* are followed, as well as its prestige and influence. It exercises, says Father Sorge, "a function of doctrinal and pastoral orientation." For the priests and bishops of Italy, it often constitutes a trustworthy source for the substance of their directives, and a guarantor of orthodoxy.

The Jesuit magazine is closely linked to the life of the Church and of Italy. An analysis of articles in *La Civiltà Cattolica* is an obligatory route for any historian of religious events and of contemporary Italy. The magazine accompanied the popes in all their decisions: the proclamation of the dogma of the Immaculate Conception, the VATICAN I Council and papal infallibility, the condemnation of AMERICANISM, of MODERNISM, of the French nationalist and royalist group, of social ENCYCLICALS. The restoration of Thomistic philosophy was a major battle waged by the magazine, the editors basing all their analyses, in whatever domain, on the doctrine of St. Thomas Aquinas. Rosmini, Teilhard de Chardin, Maritain, and others were, for a variety of reasons, the subjects of scathing articles reflecting the church's official position. The history of Italy is also intensely evident: the failure of neo-Guelphism, the realization of Italian unity to the detriment of the popes' temporal power, the status of Catholics in Italian society, the populist party and Don Luigi Sturzo, fascism and conciliation, the world wars, Christian democracy and Alcide De Gasperi, the democratic reconstruction of Italy after World War II, the serious problems of society, the question of the Mezzogiorno and more recently, the moral question and that of the reform of the Christian Democratic party.

The great moments of history are represented in the magazine; all religious, social, and political problems are analyzed according to papal doctrine.

Jean-Dominique Durand

Bibliography

Aubert, R. *Le pontificat de Pius IX*, Paris, 1952.

Cestaro, A. "Rome capitale ne 'La Civiltà Cattolica,' *Un secolo da Porta Pia*, Naples, 1970, 219–47.

"'La Civiltà Cattolica' e il problema della scuola nel secondo dopoguerra (1945–1965)," *Pedagogia e Vita*, 4, 1983–1984, 415–34.

Da De Gasperi a Fanfari. "La Civiltà Cattolica" e il mondo cattolico italiano nel secondo dopoguerra (1945–1962), Brescia, 1986.

Dalpane, L. "Il socialismo e le questioni sociali nella prima annata della 'Civiltà Cattolica,'" *Studi in onore di G. Luzzatto*, Milan, 1950.

Dante, F. *Storia della "Civiltà" (1850–1891). Il laboratorio del Papa*, Rome, 1990.

De Rosa, G., ed. *La Civiltà Cattolica 1850–1945. Antologia*, 4 vols., Rome, 1971–2.

De Rosa, G. in *Rassengna di politica e storia*: "'La Civiltà Cattolica' e la sua prima organizzazione" (103, 11–18), "'La Civiltà Cattolica' e la censura napoletana" (104, 23–30), "Alle origine dello, 'La Civiltà Cattolica' (107, 7–16), "'Civiltà Cattolica' e Carlo M. Curci (108, 6-13), "'La Civiltà Cattolica' da Roma a Firenze" (109, 4–13), "Il Non Expedit e 'La Civiltà Cattolica,'" (114, 7–15).

Di Nolfo, E. "'La Civiltà Cattolica' e le scelte di fondo della politica estera italiana nel secondo dopoguerra," *Storia e Politica*, 1971, 187–239.

Dioscuri, A. "La rivoluzione italiana e 'La Civiltà Cattolica,'" *Rassengna storica del Risorgimento*, 1953, 258–66.

Droulers, P. "Question sociale, Etat, Eglise, dans 'La Civiltà Cattolica' à ses débuts," *Chiesa e Stato nell' Ottocento. Miscellanea in onore di Pietro Pirri*, Padou, 1962, 123–147.

Durand, J. D. *L'Eglise catholique dans la crise de l'Italie (1943–1948)*, Rome, 1991.

Durand, J. D. "Un exemple de l'engagement de l'Eglise dans le débat politique italien: la "Civiltà Cattolica" et les élections (1945–1948)," *Risorgimento*, 1983/3, 175–95.

Gipponi, T. *Stato e Chiesa nella "Civiltà Cattolica" dalla Liberazione all'entrata in vigore della Costituente*, Lodi, 1981.

Greco, G. "'La Civiltà Cattolica' nel decennio, 1850–1859," *Annali della Scuola Normale di Pisa*, 1976, 1051–95.

Jemolo, A. C. *L'Eglise et l'Etat en Italie, du Risorgimento à nos jours* (trad. Fr.), Paris, 1990.

Malinverni, B. "Risorgimento e unità d'Italia ne 'La Civiltà Cattolica'" (1870–1898)," *La Scuola Cattolica*, 1961, 444–61.

Martina, G. *La Chiesa in Italia negli ultimi trent'anni*, Rome, 1977.

Mucci, G. *Il primo direttore della "Civiltà Cattolica." Carlo Maria Curci tra la cultura dell'immobilismo e la cultura della storicità*, Rome, 1986; *Carlo Maria Curci. Il fondatore della "Civiltà Cattolica,"* Rome, 1988.

Prandi, A. "Una interpretazione dei rapporti Stato-Chiesa. 'La Civiltà Cattolica' negli anni 1945–1947," *Il Mulino*, 1971, 330–41.

Riccardi, A. *Il "partito romano" nel secondo dopoguerra (1945–1954)*, Brescia, 1983.

Sani, R. "Un Laboratorio politico e culturale: 'La Civiltà Cattolica,'" *Pio XII*, A. Riccardi, ed. Bari, 1985, 409–36.

Sorge, B. *Uscire dal tempio. Intervista autobiografica*, ed. P. Giuntella, Geneva, 1989.

Traniello, F. "Cattolicesimo e società moderna dal 1848 alla 'Rerum novarum,'" *Storia delle idee politiche, economiche e sociali*, a cura di L. Firpo, V, Turin, 1972.

CLEMENT I. *(d. A.D. 98 or 100. Pope during the '90s).*
Saint.

According Eusebius, the person we call Clement I led the Church of Rome from A.D. 92 or 93 to 98 or 100. These dates correspond to those proposed by modern historians, give or take two or three years. On the life of Clement, the most ancient and trustworthy account is that of Irenaeus, who knew the Roman community, having visited it around 177.

Clement enjoys great prestige in Christian antiquity because of his links with eyewitnesses of the life of Christ. In the 3rd century, Clement of Alexandria conferred on him the title of apostle. Origen sees in him the Clement whom Paul, in the Letter to the Philippians (4:3) names among his companions. The same idea appears in Eusebius, Jerome, and Rufinus, but it seems that this identification, on which Irenaeus is silent, rests merely on a possible resemblance and not on an ancient Roman tradition.

On the place of Clement in the chronology of bishops of Rome, the sources give three different versions. Irenaeus gives this list: Peter, Linus, Anacletus, and Clement. Another account, attested to by Tertulian and Jerome, says that Clement was ordained by Peter and was his immediate successor. Finally, the *Liberian Catalog* proposes this line of succession, which is found in the *LIBER PONTIFICALIS*: Peter, Linus, Clement, Cletus, Anacletus. Having used two forms of the same name, Cletus and Anacletus, for two distinct individuals, the chronicler had to place Clement before them in order to place him closer to Peter, whose disciple he was, according to certain accounts, and to the illustrious bishop within the apostolic era, for Rome's prestige.

Some tried to reconcile these divergent versions. In the 370s, Epiphanus proposed the following: Peter ordained that Clement succeed him; on the death of the apostle, Clement defers to Linus then to Cletus, whom he succeeds. According to the *Apostolic Constitutions*, composed in the east around 380, Paul allegedly ordained that Linus be first bishop, and Peter allegedly ordained that Clement be successor of Linus. Finally, in the prologue to his Latin translation of the pseudo-clementine *Recognitions*, Rufinus says that Peter, after having had Linus and Anacletus as auxiliaries, left his chair to Clement on his death. Eschewing these fanciful reconstructions, historians rely on the most ancient document, the list of Irenaeus.

The *Liber pontificalis* gives these details without any sources: It maintains that Clement was born at Rome of a father called Faustinus. As pope, it attributes to him the division of the City into seven ecclesiastical regions (which was probably the work of Fabian in the 3rd century) and the institution of NOTARIES responsible for the investigation of the history of martyrs (which ought to correspond to 6th-century custom). Catholics celebrate the feast of Clement, as "pope and martyr," on 23 November. The title of "martyr" is based on late sources: the

De adulteratione librorum Origenis of Rufinus (c. 400) and a letter of Pope Zosimus. When he enumerates the Roman bishops, Irenaeus mentions a single martyr, Telesphorus. Since he specifies that Clement had known the apostles and written to the Corinthians, he would certainly not have failed to note (if he had heard about it) the heroic death of the latter. As for the *Passion of Clement*, which circulated in Rome no doubt from the 5th century, it contains nothing historical, but was of great inspiration to artists.

If, in spite of these biographical uncertainties, Clement is the best known of the first successors of Peter, he owes it to his *Letter to the Corinthians*, which has come down to us, having been written in Greek between 95–98. After those of the New Testament, it is the oldest Christian text whose author has been identified. A letter of Bishop Dionysius of Corinth to Bishop Soter of Rome, cited by Eusebius, attests that around 170, the Corinthians read Clement's letter during the Sunday liturgy. This public reading was practiced at the time of Eusebius in many churches and again in certain places in Jerome's time. Latin, Syriac, and Coptic translations of this work were in circulation. This success explains why antiquity placed apocryphal texts under Clement's name including a *Second Letter to the Corinthians* (in reality a homily, probably written around 150); two *Letters to the Virgins* (without doubt from the 3rd century); and especially the famous *Pseudo-Clementines*, twenty *Homilies*, and 10 books of *Recognitions* (*Recognitiones*), which form a kind of novel with the apostle Peter as the hero, and seem to have been composed, based on older writings, at the end of the 4th century.

The authentic *Letter* exhorted the Christians of Corinth, some of whom had revolted against their minister of the cult, to reconciliation and obedience. Historians and theologians saw, in this struggle, the first manifestations of Roman PRIMACY. In fact, this text springs from a concern for fraternal correction, which is manifested with tact and authority, but it is true that Clement created a precedent: he gave an example of what would later be the solicitude of Peter's successors for the other Churches. Beyond this aspect of disciplinary precepts, the *Letter* constitutes a fundamental document on the doctrines of primitive Christianity: It outlines, notably, an ecclesiology in which obedience is based on the Johannine concept of sending and on submission to the leaders appears as one of the expressions of fraternal charity.

Jean-Marie Salamito

Bibliography

DHGE, 12 (1953), 1089–93.

Bardy, G. *Catholicisme*, 2 (1949), 1183–85.

Beatrice, P. F. *DECA*, Paris, 1990, 1, 503–5.

Bowe, B. E. *A Church in Crisis: Ecclesiology and Paraenesis in Clement of Rome*, Minneapolis, 1988.

Cavallera, F. *DS*, 2 (1953), 962–63.

Delahave, H. *Etudes sur le legendier romain*, Bruxelles, 1936, 96–115.

Duchesne, L. *Le Liber pontificalis*, Paris, 1955–57, 1, LXIX–LXXIII, 53 and 123–4.

Evans, R. S. "Soteriologies of Early Christianity Within the Intellectual Context of the Early Roman Empire: Barnabas and Clement of Rome as Case Studies," Ph.D. diss., University of Michigan, Ann Arbor, 1996.

The Epistles of St. Clement of Rome and St. Ignatius of Antioch, translated and annotated by J. A. Kleish (*Ancient Christian Writers*, 1), Westminster, Md., 1946.

Pietri, C. *Roma christiana*, Rome, 1976, 393–4, 1598–1603.

Salamito, J. M. *Histoire des saints et de la sainteté chrétienne*, Paris, 1987, 2, 109–13.

Siouville, A. *Les Homelies clementines*, Paris, 1991.

Thompson, D. J. *A Critical Concordance to the First Epistle of Clement to the Corinthians*, Wooster, 1996.

Treviano, R. "Clementines (Pseudo-)," *DECA*, 505–6.

Zannoni, G., and Celletti, M. C. *Bibliotheca sanctorum*, Rome, 1964, 4, 38–47.

CLEMENT II. *Suidger (b. 9 October 1047). Elected pope 24 December 1046 at Rome, enthroned 25 December 1046. Buried at Bamberg.*

Clement II is the first of a series of popes of German origin who were named by the emperor and who maintained their episcopal sees. Clement worked closely with the emperor and continued the reform begun by his predecessors. Of Saxon origin, Suidger was educated at the cathedral school of Halberstadt and became canon there. In 1032 he entered the service of Archbishop Hermann of Hamburg as chaplain, and in 1035 became chaplain at the imperial chapel. At the end of 1040, Henry III appointed him to the see of Bamberg and Archbishop Bardon of Mayence consecrated him at Christmas. Little is known of his activities as bishop, and only the foundation of the abbey of Theres sur le Main is attributed to him.

Suidger accompanied the king to Italy at the end of 1046 and participated in the synod of Sutri, at which two of the three concurrent popes were deposed: Silvester III and Gregory VI. The court moved to Rome and a new synod was held to judge Benedict IX, who was deposed in his turn (23 December). Henry III then proposed to the assembly, on 24 December, the bishop of Bamberg (Suidger) as Roman pontiff. The following day the enthronement of the new pope, who took the name of Clement II, took place. He immediately proceeded to the imperial CORONATION of the royal couple. On 5 January 1047, Clement II convened at Rome a synod during which the deposition of the preceding popes was confirmed, and measures taken against SIMONY and NICO-

LAISM. A little later, the pope accompanied the emperor to southern Italy and launched an investigation into the election of the archbishop of Salerno. On his return to Rome for the summer, he met Odilo, abbot of Cluny; Peter Damiani wrote to him asking to speed up the execution of Church reforms. He left for a pastoral visit to northern Italy and fell ill on 24 September at the abbey of St. Tommaso, near Pesaro, and died there on 9 October. His remains were taken to Bamberg where they were laid to rest in the cathedral. Later, suspicions of poisoning surfaced, which have never been completely ruled out.

Michel Parisse

Bibliography

LP, 2, 272.

PL, 142, 577–90.

Beumann, H. "Reformpapste und Reichsbischofe in der Zeit Heinrich III," *Festschrift Friedrich Hausmann*, ed. H. Erbner, Graz, 1977, 21–37.

Foreville, R. "Clement II," *DHGE*, 12 (1953), 1093–6.

Hauck, K. "Zum Tode Papst Clemens II" *Jahrbuch für frankische Landesforschung*, 19 (1959), 265–74.

Laqua, H. P. "Clemente II," *DBI*, 26 (1982), 178–81.

Muller-Christensen, S. *Das Graf des Papstes Clemens II. im Dom zu Bamberg*, Munich, 1960.

Rimmel R., and Zimmermann, G. "Bischof Suidger von Bamberg—Papst Clemens II," *Frankische Lebensbilder*, 10 (1982), 1–19.

Watterich, 1, 73–4, 77–80, 714–17; JW, 1, 525–28; 2, 709.

Wendehorst, A. "Clemens II" *LexMA*, 2 (1981–3), 2138–9.

Wittmann, P. "Bischof Suidger von Bamberg als Papst Clemens II und der Patriciat Kaiser, Heinrichs III," *Archiv für katholische Kirchengeschichte*, 51 (1884), 228–43.

[CLEMENT III]. *Guibert/Wibertus (d. Civita Castellana, 8 September 1100). Antipope named by the emperor on 25 June 1080, elected by the Romans in March 1084, enthroned in the Lateran on 24 March 1084.*

Guibert was probably a member of the Guiberti family, a side branch of the marquis of CANOSSA: who ruled in the dioceses of Reggio Emilia and of Parma. The Guibertis were once counts of the city of Parma, where they were ousted during the hard won victory of the partisans of the Gregorian reform in Emilia. This possible origin tallies with Guibert's career. In 1052 he was a cleric in the entourage of Bishop Cadalus of Parma; in 1054 he was at the imperial court and, with the support of Empress Agnes (then regent of young Henry IV), was the imperial chancellor for Italy between June 1058 and June or September 1063.

As chancellor, Guibert attended the synod of Sutri in January 1059, where Pope NICHOLAS II, with imperial support, anathematized antipope BENEDICT X, who had been elected by the Roman NOBILITY. A paragraph reserving the rights of the emperor in the decree on pontifical election, done by Nicholas II himself, is attributed to Guibert. It was also as chancellor that Guibert supported his former patron Cadalus beginning in 1061, antipope of the imperial faction under the name of HONORIUS (II). Nothing further is known of Guibert until 1073, when after, perhaps, hoping for the bishopric of Parma, he was nominated by the emperor to the archbishopric of RAVENNA. He maintained his relationship with the Roman CURIA, and Hildebrand, one of the leaders of the Reform party (and future GREGORY VII) persuaded the pope to consecrate Guibert during the Roman Lenten synod of 1073, after Guibert had given his oath of allegiance. Guibert apparently maintained good relations with the new Pope Gregory VII until a break in 1075. Though there is no proof that he took part in the Roman synod of that year, when his suffragan, Dionigi di Piacenza, was dismissed, he was suspended by the pope around the same time and excommunicated in 1076.

Guibert, devoted, because of his heritage to a vision of the Church cooperating with the emperor even without his tutelage, rejected the hard line of the Roman reformists. He refuted their ecclesiology but also its theology, at least in relation to the nonvalidity of sacraments administered by schismatic clerics or considered as such, aggressively asserted by the Gregorians. The old antagonism between Rome and Ravenna heightened tensions. Guibert was nevertheless, a reformist, in Rome as in Ravenna, and was involved in the struggle against SIMONY and NICOLAISM. He reformed the lifestyle of the clergy, instituted common life for the canons of his cathedral, defended the ecclesiastical patrimony, and administered his province with a firm hand. In Rome, he was, like the Gregorians, a promoter of the expanded role of the cardinals, for which many repaid him with their fidelity. While he was in Rome he established links with BYZANTIUM, with the Eastern Church, and even with the metropolitan of Kiev, with the hope that they would join the Latin Church. In short, Guibert, in the absence of all opportunity, had all the required qualities: He was noble and learned, rigorously moral, and eloquent, "adept at Greek rhetoric," *graecis facetiis affluentem*, which is not meant to imply that he knew Greek, though he might have; he was also involved at a high level in the imperial administration.

He, therefore, became the ideal candidate when Emperor Henry IV decided to raise up a new antipope against Gregory VII, which became a fait accompli in June 1080 at Brixen. The two decades of his antipontificate reproduced, in reverse, the failures and successes of the Gregorian popes. When Henry IV seized Rome, Guibert arrived in the wake of the emperor, and had himself "elected" with due ceremony by the Romans, before being consecrated pope. Guibert, who since 1080 considered himself a simple *electus* (he insisted on consecration along with Gregory VII), took the pontifical name of Clement (III). Was this a subtle allusion to the German pope, Clement II, victorious over the vile Gregory VI, or a mark of respect to St. Clement I, and proof that the ideal of returning to the apostolic era was not the monopoly of the Gregorian party? Clement (III) crowned Henry IV emperor at ST. PETER'S, on Easter Sunday, 31 March 1084, almost under the nose of Gregory VII, besieged in Castel Sant'Angelo, then moved, with the emperor, into the Lateran palace. Two months later Robert Guiscard, with a Norman army, forced the imperialists to withdraw. A series of reversals ensued, which strained the meager resources of both camps. The city constantly changed hands and a large part of the surrounding area was held by the imperialists. After the flight and semi-captivity of Gregory VII in the South, Clement (III) regained the advantage, but Victor III managed to be consecrated at St. Peter's on 9 May 1087. Nevertheless the antipope officiated (from 30 June) in a basilica retaken by his rival the following day. The latter retreated to Monte Cassino, the faction of Clement (III) retook the city, which Urban II took over in June 1088 before abandoning it to him. In 1089 Clement (III) held a "reformist" synod there, to which Urban II responded with a semblance of a council on the island of the Tiber. Although the antipope, with imperial assistance, consolidated his Roman positions in 1090–92, while the pope consolidated his recognition in Europe, his position weakened, even though in 1093 he still held the Lateran, which Urban II, back in Rome that same year, seized in 1094.

The antipope also spent long periods of time at Ravenna, of which he remained archbishop. It is documented that he was there from May 1083 to January 1084, Christmas 1085, Lent 1086, April 1088, April 1090, spring 1093, August 1093 or 1094, Easter 1098, and June 1099. The city became, under his influence and that of writers such as his suffragan Bishop Guy of Ferrare (author of *De scismate Hildeerbrandi*), an active center of anti-Gregorian propaganda, but he became the favorite target of Gregorian propaganda, in a theoretical manner as in the *Liber contra Wibertum* of Anselm of Lucca, or via polemics as in the verses of the following pro-Gregorian poem:

Tres contra dominum conjuravere potentes,
Rex et Wigbertus et Roma, Deum reprobentes:
Rex, diademate quod Wigbertus eum decoraret.
[Three powers have conjured against the Lord,
The king and Guibert and Rome, in contempt of God

The king, by his diadem which Guibert decorated.
MGH, Libelli de lite, III, Hanover, 1879, 703.]

Thus Clement (III) remained, several decades after his death, the prototype of the imperial antipope; a neologism, *wipertizare* was concocted from his name *Wibertus*, as expressed in an epigram composed in France:

Papa wipertizas, regem heinrizare videmus;
Nec te pro papa nec eum pro rege tenemus.

[Pope, you are doing a Guibert; the king under your nose is doing a Henry;
But for us you are not a pope, nor is he a king.
(A. Wilmart, "Le florilege de Saint-Gatien," *RB*, 48 (1936), 29.)]

But even while staying in Ravenna, Guibert labored to maintain, in his obedience, a province undermined, especially in its western half, by the Gregorians. In Rome his situation worsened, though Urban II was not apprehensive about leaving for a long tour of France. In 1098 Castel Sant'Angelo, still held by the partisans of the antipope, fell into the hands of the Pierleoni, supporters of the Gregorian party. On the death of Urban II, Guibert launched into a new campaign to take Rome. Paschal II, with the help of Norman intermediaries, expelled him from Albano and the antipope died some time after, without having abandoned the struggle, allowing the emperor to engage in a semblance of reconciliation with the new pope.

Olivier Guyotjeannin

Bibliography

JW, 5314–41, 649–655.

Dolcini, C. "Clemente III," *DBI*, 26 (1982), 181–8 (for polemic literature).

Heidrich, I. *Ravenna unter Erzbischof Wibert (1073–1100)*, Sigmaringen, 1984 (*Vortrage und Forschungen*, 3).

Struve, T. "Clemens (III)," *LexMA*, 2 (1981–3), 2139–40.

Ziesse, J. *Wibert von Ravenna: der Gegenpapst Clemens III (1084–1100)*, Stuttgart, 1982 (*Päpste und Papsttum*, 20).

CLEMENT III. *Paolo Scolari (b. Rome, ?, d. Rome, end of March 1191). Elected pope at Pisa on 19 December 1187, crowned on 20 December. Buried at St. John Lateran.*

Son of Giovanni Scolari and his wife Maria, Paolo was of a highborn family, though not part of the Roman NOBILITY. There is little information on his life and career. He was brought up at ST. MARY MAJOR by the Benedictines, but did not belong to the order. In 1176 he became its subdeacon and a little later, its archpriest. On 21 September 1179, Pope Alexander III appointed him cardinal DEACON of SS. Sergius and Bacchus, then cardinal priest of St. Pudenziana and, finally, in December 1180, cardinal bishop of Palestrina (his signature is noted for the first time on 4 January 1181.)

The Roman consul, Leone de Monumento, was a confidant of Frederick Barbarossa, who had been invested in 1186, within the city and the county of Sutri, before mediating to ensure the coronation of Emperor Henry VI at Rome, and played a decisive role in the election of Clement III. The cardinal bishop, already of an advanced age, belonged to the "Roman party" in the SACRED COLLEGE and appeared to be the ideal candidate for the supreme ecclesiastical position, capable of reestablishing the necessary balance between the CURIA, the SENATE, and the Roman people. At the beginning, the imperial hopes were not disappointed. After his triumphal entry into Rome (beginning of February 1188), the pope succeeded in concluding with the Senate, a *concordia pacis*, based on reciprocal compromises, that was destined to become the founding act of relations between the Curia and the Roman commune. The agreement, ratified on 31 May 1188, restored the pope's sovereignty over the city as well as his urban and suburban tributes and possessions. In addition, the Senate recognized the rights of the public powers, a guarantee against encroachment of the Hohenstaufen, and undertook to swear a yearly oath of allegiance and peace to the pope, as well as to ensure the security of the Curia and its visitors. Clement III guaranteed communal autonomy and agreed to pay, apart from a series of personal indemnities, the customary annual financial contributions (*donativa*) of the senators and officials of the commune, and to destroy the ramparts of Tusculum. However, he did not succeed in conquering it during his pontificate. The pressing need to mount a new CRUSADE, which permitted him to compensate for the role played by the imperial party in the papal election, hastened the settlement of questions pending for years between the Curia and the Empire. During the negotiations, which took place at Strasbourg in the spring of 1189, the papacy formally promised the coronation of Henry VI before the death of his father. In exchange, Frederick Barbarossa, who had solemnly taken the cross from 27 March 1188 along with numerous representatives of the imperial nobility, left for the crusade. He also guaranteed the restitution of all the territories of the patrimony of St. Peter, occupied in 1186 by Henry VI, with the exception of the inheritance of Matilda of Canossa and of other contested possessions. The Empire maintained its rights over the Italian patrimony and territories, which favored the concessions granted by the imperial party. A compromise was reached, which saved face for both parties, on the matter of the bishopric of Trier. The two claimants were dispossessed. Rudolphe of Wied was forced to resign, and Volkmar, who had refused to appear before the

Curia, was also dismissed. A new election was held in accordance with the dispositions of the CONCORDAT OF WORMS. The dispute was, in fact, resolved in favor of the imperial party, since the person nominated, John of Trier, was chancellor of the Empire.

In 1189, the death (in November) of William II of Sicily, the Norman, threatened to disturb the fragile equilibrium and revived the question, pending since 1184, of the Sicilian succession. Foreseeing these complications, Clement III had, since the summer of 1188, forced the king of Sicily to reaffirm the vassalage of *regnum Sicilie* to the Holy See by a new oath of allegiance, taking care to broaden the oath to include the phase *et heredibus meis*, so that the heirs of William II were also obliged to be invested by the pope. Despite Clement's efforts, Henry VI immediately staked his claim, without planning to renew his homage, particularly as that would have implied an oath of allegiance to the pope, which he refused to give as king of the Romans and future emperor. Clement III promptly withdrew recognition of Henry VI as king of Sicily. Considering himself absolved of any responsibilities with respect to the heirs of William II, he supported the accession to the throne of Tancred of Lecce, member of a collateral branch of the Norman house of Hauteville, and sought to legitimize his sovereignty by arguing against the choice of the nobility. Having promised before his coronation (18 January 1190) to recognize the suzerainty of the Holy See and the rights of the Roman church over his kingdom, Tancred obtained the pope's agreement.

These complex political decisions relegated strictly ecclesiastical interests to the background, but the pope had a few successes in this field as well. Under his pontificate, during which Cardinal Albinus began to register all the taxes payable to the Roman church by kingdoms, domains, and institutions, centralization made rapid progress at the Curia. The desire to enlarge and unify canonical legislation through the DECRETALS goes hand in hand with the effort to ensure a solid base for papal jurisdiction and FINANCES. Although it is recognized today that many of the decretals formerly attributed to Clement III are, in fact, the work of his successor, Celestine III, their sheer number attests to the activity of the pope in the field of matrimonial legislation, sworn agreements, the fight against SIMONY and against the abuse of concessions of privileges, and sanctions promulgated by clerics in relation to the laity. He made the bishopric of Kammin, (erected by the Baltic mission) directly subject to the Holy See, while the bishoprics of Lubeck, Schwerin, Ratzebourg, and Uxkull in Lituania (Ykeshola) were incorporated, as suffragans, into the ecclesiastical province of Hamburg-Bremen. The Scottish Church was released from its dependence on the metropolitan of York. He intervened decisively, for the future, in the diocesan structure of the Iberian Peninsula (erection of the bishopric of Plasencia). Clement III carried out four CANONIZATIONS:

the Irish archbishop Malachy O'Margair (1190), the Dane Kjeld (Ketil) of Viborg (1188), Etienne of Muret, founder of the order of Grammont (1890), as well as Bishop Otto I of Bamberg (1189). He examined the controversial works of the Cistercians Joachim of Flora and Ralph Niger—whom he held in great esteem—in 1188 and 1191, respectively. In addition, he was engaged in the political preparation and organization of the third crusade, which began in 1189. This focus on the crusade explains the pacification measures taken in relation to Pisa and Genoa, and of Parma and Piacenza and their allies. The kings of France and of England, Philip Augustus and Richard the Lionhearted, decided only with difficulty to participate in the crusade; despite the efforts of cardinal legates Henry of Albano and Jean de Saint Marc, they did not decide until July 1190, after long negotiations. Deep divisions among the principal European sovereigns were already visible, which must have weighed heavily on the curial policies of the 1190s, and which were certainly due, in part, to the diplomatic inadequacy of Clement III.

Ludwig Vones

Bibliography

JL, 535–76, 727, 770.

LP, 2, 451.

PL, 204, 1273–1506.

Csendes, P. "Die Anfänge der Kanzlei Heinrich VI und die Verhandlungen mit der Kurie 1188/89," *MIOG*, 82 (1974), 403–11.

Fliche-Martin, IX-2 (1953), 198–215.

Foreville, R. "Clement III," *DHGE*, 12 (1953), 1096–1109.

Geyer, J. *Papst Klemens III (1187–91)*, Bonn, 1914.

Haller, J. "Heinrich VI, und die römische Kurie," *MIOG*, 35 (1914), 385–454, 545–669, reprinted, Darmstadt, 1962.

Hoffmann, H. "Petrus Diaconus, die Herren von Tusculum und der Sturz Oderisius II von Montecassino," *Deutsches Archiv.* 27 (1971), 1–109.

Holtzmann, W. "Die Benutzung Gratians in der päpstlichen Kanzlei im 12. Jahrhundert," *Studia Gratiana*, 1 (1953), 323–49.

Houben, H. *QFIAB*, 68 (1988), 65–73.

"La Collectio Seguntina et les decretales de Clement III et de Celestin III," *RHE*, 50 (1955), 400–53.

Maleczek, W. "Clemens III," *LexMA*, 2 (1981–3), 2140–1.

Petersohn, J. "Clement III," *DBI*, 26 (1982), 188–92.

Petersohn, J. "Der Vertrag des römischen Senats mit Papst Clemens III. 1188 und das Pactum Friedrich Barbarossas mit den Römern 1167," *MIOG*, 82 (1974), 289–337.

Pfaff, V. "Papst Clemens III," *ZRGKA*, 66 (1980), 261–316.

Reisinger, C. *Tankred von Lecce*, Cologne-Weimar-Vienne, 1992.

Watterich, 2, 693–707.

Zerbi, P. *Papato, Impero e "respublica christiana" dal 1187 al 1198*, Milan, 1980, 2, 9–62.

CLEMENT IV. *Gui Foucois (b. Saint-Gilles-du-Gard ca. 1200, d. Viterbo, 29 November 1268). Elected pope on 5 February 1265, crowned 15 or 22 February. Buried at San Francesco of Viterbo in 1870.*

Eminent jurist during the establishment of the Capetian dynasty in the South of France and second of the three "French" popes of his century, Clement IV witnessed the first COUNCIL of Lyons, and, divided between the ideal of the reconquest of the Holy Land which makes him close to St. Louis, and the political realities of a divided and changing world, was the victim of ambitious scheming on the part of Charles I of Anjou.

Son of a chancellor-judge of the county of Toulouse, he pursued his studies at the University of Paris and returned to work as a legal consultant in the provostry of Uzes around 1234. From the service of Count Raimond VII (d. 27 September 1249) he joined that of Alphonse de Poitiers and accompanied him on a trip through his domain, excised invalid clauses from the will of Raimond VII (May 1251), arbitrated conflicts between the viscount and the archbishop of Narbonne, and between the seneschal of Venaissin and the bishop of Vaison, then drew up the county land register for Venaissin ("Red book") in 1253 to 1254. For King Louis IX, he was involved in the drafting of the great ordinance of December 1254 on the reform of the administration and the government of the kingdom. Sole jurist among the five investigators in the estates of Carcassonne and Beaucaire, the council of Beziers allowed him to publish the new royal statutes for them and for the province of Narbonne. He chose new inquisitors from among the DOMINICANS and finished his 15 legal opinions on the functions of the inquisitor a few years later. On becoming a widower, he was ordained priest around 1256. As archdeacon of Puy, the king named him bishop in 1257, but the Holy See delayed his consecration, as it did later for the see of Narbonne. As a member of Parliament and councilor of the king, he could live in his bishopric, but in the matter of the royal prerogative, he enacted regulations that were rather favorable to his clergy. As archbishop of Narbonne (1259), he promoted the reconstruction of the cathedral, took strict measures in relation to the Jews (wearing of the "roundel," struggle against usury), but he gained their respect by defending them against royal officers.

He accompanied James I of Aragon to Montpellier for a reconciliation with his subjects and the bishop, and arbitrated between the bishop and the citizens of Lodeve.

Made cardinal, against his will, by Urban IV (24 December 1261), he was delayed by the marriage of Philip of France and Isabel of Aragon, which he celebrated at Clermont-Ferrand, then by negotiations on the neutrality of James I in the conflict between Manfred, king of Sicily, and the Church, and later in consultation with Cardinal Henri of Suse, by the regulation of the rights of Queen Marguerite over Provence, violated by Count Charles of Anjou. As Bishop of Sabina, he arrived at the Curia in November 1262, and succeeded the Dominican, Cardinal Hugues of Saint-Cher, as PENITENTIARY. In the company of legate Simon of Brie, he pushed the court of France to have Charles accept Sicily. Charged by the pope to effect a reconciliation between the English barons and Henry III, he did not obtain the safe passage necessary to accomplish his mission (November 1263 to October 1264).

Absent from Perugia, he was elected pope "by compromise." The SACRED COLLEGE, without its full complement (less than 20 members), had been improved by Urban IV, who was careful to maintain parity between the French and Italians. Clement IV did not create a single cardinal and he relied on Giovanni Gaetano Orsini (the future Nicholas III) and Simon of Brie (the future Martin IV). The activities of the LEGATE in England, Ottobono Fieschi, concluded with the pacification and the reform of the Church (1265–8). The pope's policy was concentrated on the mission to adopt a policy followed by Urban IV with respect to Charles of Anjou, in order to break the Sicilo-Ghibelline encirclement. Clement IV hastened to annul the investiture of the kingdom of Sicily (1255) on the son of the king of England (25 February 1265), to confer it on Charles (28 June), and to have him crowned (6 January 1266). The financial situation was very difficult: at the end of 1265, the pope had at his disposal 100,000 pounds and had to petition bankers, particularly Florentine bankers, Louis IX, and Alphonse. He increased the tax on local churches, which evoked major discontent, and even involved the real estate of the Roman churches.

Once Manfred, illegitimate son of Frederick II, was killed at Benevento (26 February 1266), the pope was forced to defend the rights of the churches of Sicily through the legate Ridolfo Crosparmi, and to moderate the ambitions of the new king, who accumulated magistrates and interventions in Tuscany, by limiting the senatory of Rome to three years. The rallying of Siena and Pisa around Conradin, grandson of Frederick II, the treason of senator Henry of Castile debarking in Sicily, the revolt of the SARACENS of Lucera, and the triumphal entry of Conradin into Rome (24 July 1268), may have made the pope fear the worst in the absence of Charles. Finally, Charles, using skillful strategy, is victorious at Tagliacozzo (23 August 1268). He was rewarded afterward with the title of senator for life.

The frequent troubles in Rome caused Clement IV, after spending 13 months at Perugia, to take up permanent residence at VITERBO and to build a palace, which has been partially preserved. The crusade to the Holy Land became secondary to the reconciliation of the Christian sovereigns; Clement IV favoring the crusade against Manfred, began by checking the ardor of St. Louis and Alphonse and finally has the crusade preached in France; the king and his sons set out. Secret agreements were made with Charles I (May 1267) to allow the Latin emperor, Baldwin II, to recover Constantinople. The doubling of scholarships to the University of Paris for theologians who speak Arabic and other eastern languages was explained by the desire to train missionaries. The crusade was simultaneously preached against the Tartars (1265) in Hungary, Poland, Bohemia, Austria, Styria, Carinthia, and Brandenburg. Relations with Central Europe were intense: a double marriage of the children of Charles, arranged by the pope, was aimed at forging an alliance between the houses of Anjou and Hungary; Hedwig of Poland is canonized (1267). Cardinal Guy of Burgundy was active as legate in the provinces of Bremen, Magdebourg, and Gnesen, as well as in Sweden and Denmark. Envisaging a crusade against Prussia and Lithuania, the pope supports the king of Bohemia, Ottokar II Presysl, in Bavaria. This prelate, former abbot of Citeaux, who became cardinal protector of his order, develops the constitution *Parvus fons* (6 June 1265) to appease the abbot of Clairvaux, who was enamored of reform. The constitution reinforced the authority of the general chapter. Clément IV expressed a certain mysticism in his provençal poem *Les Sept Joies de la Vierge*; he protected the Franciscan savant and philosopher Roger Bacon and rejected nepotism as well as the plurality of benefices. History has maintained an image of him as a hard and courageous man who legalized the papal custom of exercising the right of reservation on all vacant churches and dignities (constitution *Licet ecclesiarum*, 27 August 1265). The realism of the representation of his corpse on his tomb at Viterbo is innovative.

Michel Hayez

Bibliography

Aubert, R. "Guy de Bourgogne," *DHGE*, 22 (1988), 1257–62.

Carena, C. *Tractatus de officio S. Inquisitionis et modo procedendi in causis fidei*, Lyon, 1669, 365-91.

D'Achille, A. M. "Sulla datazione del monumento funebre di Clemente IV a Viterbo: un riezame delle fonti," *Arte medievale*, 1989, 85–91.

"Die Hedwigspredigt des Papstes Klemans IV," ed. J. Gottschalk, *Archiv für Schlesische Kirchengeschichte*, 15 (1957), 17–35.

Dossat, Y. "Gui Foucois, enquêteur-reformateur, archevêque et pape," *Cahiers de Fanjeaux*, 7 (1972), 23–57, 437–45.

Forey, A. J. "The Military Orders and Holy War Against Christians in the Thirteeth Century," *English Historical Review*, 104 (1989), 1–24.

Hayez, M. "Clemens IV," *LexMA*, 2 (1981–3), 2141–2.

Heidemann, J. *Papst Clemens IV. Eine Monographie. I, Das Vorleben des Papstes und sein Legationsregister* (only one published), Münster, 1903.

Kamp, N. "Clemente IV," *DBI*, 26 (1982), 192–202.

Kolmer, L. "Papst Clemens IV beim Wahrsager," *Deutsches Archiv für Erforschung des Mittelalters*, 38 (1982), 141–65.

Les Registres de Clement IV, ed. E. Jordan, Paris, 1893–1945 (BEFAR).

"Les Sept Joies de la Vierge," ed. C. Fabre, *Mem. Soc., scient. et agricole de la Haute-Loire*, 16 (1909–10), 257–455.

Martene, E., and Durand, U. *Thesaurus novus anecdotorum*, II, Paris, 1717, 16–636.

Mollat, G. "Clement IV," *DHGE*, 12 (1953), 1109–15.

Mueller, W. "L'Aquila zwischen Staufern und den Anjou: Ein neu aufgefundener Brief Papst Clemens IV von 1268," *Deutsches Archiv fur Erforschung des Mittelalters*, 44 (1998), 186–94.

Nicolas, C. *Un pape saint-gillois, Clement IV dans le monde et dans l'Eglise (1195–1268)*, Nimes, 1910.

Ollendier, H. *Die Papstlichen Legaten. . .*, Fribourg, 1976 (*Historische Schriften des Universitat Fr., 3*).

Paravincini Bagliani, A. *Cardinali di curia e "familia" dal 1227 al 1254*, Padua, 1972, 2 vols.

Richard, J. *Croises, missionnaires et voyageurs*, London, Variorum reprints, 1983, esp. XV and XVIII.

Schaller, H. M. "Ein Originalmandat Papst Clemens IV. gegen Konradin," *Deutsches Archiv für Erforschung des Mittelalters*, 44 (1988), 181–5.

CLEMENT V. *Bertrand de Got (b. Villandraut, Gironde, middle 13th century, d. Roquemaure, Gard, 20 April 1314). Elected pope 5 June 1305 at Perugia, crowned 14 November at Lyons. Buried at Uzeste (Gironde).*

Clement V was pope during the time of the Templars. Some historians have portrayed him as an evil pope, and he has generally been seen as a pope subject to the king of France, Philip IV the Fair. But, Clement V was able to protect the best interests of the Church throughout his pontificate.

Bertrand was born in Guyenne, a French fiefdom of the kings of England, and was the third of eleven children of Beraud de Got, lord of Villandraut, and of Ida de Blanquefort. He began his studies at the Deffez priory (near Agen), then studied law at Orleans and Bologna. Little is known of the beginning of his career, because he

333

is often confused with an uncle of the same name. The uncle, Bertrand de Got, was archdeacon then bishop of Agen (1292); Bertrand, the pope, was canon of Bordeaux and of Agen until 1295. He owes his career, however, not to his uncle, but to his brother, Beraud, archdeacon of Montaut (Agenais), who became archbishop of Lyons in 1289 and called him to his side as vicar general. In 1294 Pope Celestine V elevated Beraud to the cardinalate and made Bertrand his chaplain, a post in which he was confirmed by Boniface VIII before being named as bishop of Comminges in March 1295. The favor of two such dissimilar popes can only be explained by the political context of the end of the 13th century. Concurrent with their ecclesiastical careers, the two brothers, like their uncle, were in the service of the king of England and were given various missions, as clerics of the king; the future Clement V, from 1285, was also the procurator of Edward I at the parliament of Paris.

Celestine V and Boniface VIII sought to prevent, then to stop, the conflict that placed France and England in opposition in 1294; the Got brothers seemed to be the most qualified, if not the most efficient, mediators. Bertrand's career advanced, and with the support of Edward I, he became archbishop of Bordeaux (December 1299). Edward I could only have rejoiced at his ascension to the pontificate. Although a French pope had been elected, it was not a pope subservient to the king of France. He had participated in the Estates General of Paris, then at the SYNOD convoked by Boniface VIII at Rome (1302).

The CONCLAVE of Perugia was lengthy (July 1304 to June 1305). There was no majority candidate within the SACRED COLLEGE, and it chose the archbishop of Bordeaux, who enjoyed the support of the adversaries of the "Bonaficians" without being objectionable to them. Clement V did not owe his election to Philip the Fair; their meeting at Saint-Jean-d'Angely is only a fabrication of the Florentine Villani (hardly credible for this period). The pressures began after the election and continued during practically the entire pontificate. Thus, Clement V decided to be crowned at Lyons where royal influence had just triumphed. He did not go to Rome, torn apart by the struggles of the various factions, but instead installed himself at Poitiers before going to the banks of the Rhone in 1309, to settle not at AVIGNON but in the county of Comtat, which belonged to the papacy.

Two urgent matters awaited the new pontiff. First, peace between the western states, a precondition of any crusade, was advanced in Flanders and in Franco-English relations; in the Empire, the pope only half-heartedly supported the brother of the king of France, Charles of Valois, and hastened to approve the election of Henry VII. Second, matters between the French monarchy and the papacy became more contentious. Philip the Fair insisted on total absolution for his actions and those of his councilors involved in the Anagni assault, and the posthu-

mous condemnation of Boniface VIII. To avoid this, Clement V confirmed the absolution given by his predecessor Benedict XI, but still excluded Nogaret, the leader of the assault. At the end of 1305 he granted a bevy of French CARDINALS to the king. Philip the Fair wanted more, and in the affair of the Templars, found a new way of putting pressure on Clement V, while unintentionally offering him a bargaining tool.

The king affirmed his desire to organize a crusade and imposed a condition: the suppression of the international military ORDERS accused of having failed, and the institution of a new order under his authority (the ideas of the Catalan, Raymond Lull). All the military orders were, consequently, suspect. In 1310 the pope resolved to open an inquiry on the behavior of the Teutonics, but the libelous denunciations raised against the Templars in France beginning in 1305 gave the king an opportunity to act, mandating the arrest of all the Templars in the kingdom (13 October 1307). Clement V protested, but the first confessions impressed him, and in an effort to retake the initiative, he ordered the arrest of all Templars throughout the world. At Poitiers, in June and July 1308, pressured by Philip and threatened by his officials, who linked the process against Boniface VIII to the Templars, the pope postponed the inevitable by rapidly initiating two procedures. Clement V succeeded in avoiding the posthumous condemnation of Boniface VIII by issuing the bull *Rex gloriae virtutem* (1311), which credits Philip the Fair with praiseworthy intentions, and the BULL of canonization of Celestine V (1313), which does not condemn Boniface. To accomplish this, the pope sacrificed the Templars. Provincial councils judged individuals, but it was the responsibility of a general council to judge the order. The council, assembled in Vienne (France) beginning in October 1311, was reluctant to condemn the Templars. To force the decision, after secret negotiations with the king of France, Clement V decided on his own, by the bull *Vox in excelso* (22 March 1312), to suppress the order without judging or condemning it, and to give Templar property to the order of Hospitallers.

Two factors help in understanding the attitude of Clement V during these five years: his desire to save the memory of Boniface VIII at any cost and his will to mount a crusade. It seemed impossible to mount a crusade without the help of the king of France, but this could only be secured if Franco-pontifical relations were extricated from the impasse in which the Anagni affair had placed them, and it was, therefore, necessary to be conciliatory. Philip the Fair spoke a great deal about the crusade, but did nothing to make it a reality, and Clement V found it necessary to narrow his objectives and explore other options. He relied on the forces involved in the eastern Mediterranean, Little Armenia, Cyprus, Greece, and Rhodes. The "special crossing" of 1309 through 1310, which was to precede a "general crossing" led by the king of France, was reduced to a combined operation of the papacy and the Knights Hospitallers, which reinforced the latter's seizure of Rhodes. The deliverance of Jerusalem was postponed, particularly because the Iberian sovereigns were pressuring the pope to grant the status of a crusade to the war being waged at the same time against the kingdom of Granada, which weakened the crusade in the east. Clement V also preached a crusade to defend the interests of the papacy in Italy. The activities of rectors, placed at the head of provinces of the PAPAL STATE (Gascons for the most part), were not effective. When Venice was taken over by Ferrara in October 1308, a crusade began, which Cardinal Arnaud of Pellegrue, an ally of the pope, led with great success. Although Clement V used the crusade on all battlefields where it could be applied—Jerusalem, *Reconquista*, defense of the Church—he also developed the peace mission alongside, and not in place of, the crusade. Toward this end, he created chairs of oriental languages at the great UNIVERSITIES, and established ecclesiastical structures in China that supported missionary activity.

The ecclesial policy followed by Clement V in the west earned him bitter criticism, which was fully justified. Although he did not invent papal taxation or the apostolic reserve system, he gave them such impetus that this centralization policy remains associated, through him, with the Avignon papacy. Naturally, the profits of this policy had to be shared with the lay powers, and at the council of Vienne, Philip the Fair obtained eleven annual tithes levied on the clergy! Clement V was criticized for his policy on benefices in particular: of the 10,500 bulls collected in the REGISTERS of Clement V, half refer to France and one-quarter to the Aquitanian south of France. The pope was generous to the churches and convents of his native region: He was able to satisfy several humble Gascon clerics by granting them minor benefices; the major benefices were mainly distributed to the relatives and friends of the pope; several received the cardinalate itself. Of the five sons of his sister Marquise, one became a cardinal, two became bishops of Agen, and the last, bishop of Albi. His nepotism, more than anything else, contributed to his bad reputation. Although he was not insensitive to the abuses that tarnished the image of the Church, and was not closed to the idea of reform, making changes in this direction without jeopardizing papal centralization which, rightly or wrongly, Clement V considered to be the only way of responding to the challenges of his time, proved difficult. He left a juridical compilation, the *Clementines*, which forms part of the *Decretals* collection.

Clement V suffered, during his entire pontificate, from a painful illness that may have been cancer of the stomach or of the intestines, and which was the cause of his death on his return to Bordeaux. This, no doubt, affected his style of government.

Clement was both weak and tenacious. It is wrong to say that he submitted in everything to Philip the Fair, and in fact he preserved the memory of Boniface VIII. It was quickly claimed that he had succeeded on the essential issue, but at what price? A thin line separates skillful compromise from dubious surrender, and some denounced the alliance between the new Herod and the new Pilate.

Alain Demurger

Bibliography

Conciliorum *Oecumenicorum Decreta*, Rome, 1962 (decrets du concile de Vienne).

Denton, J. M. "Pope Clement V's early career as a royal clerk," *EHR*, 83 (1968), 303–14.

Finke, H. *Papsttum und Untergang des Templerordens*, Munster, 1907.

Fornasari, G. "Il conclave perugino del 1304–1305," *RSCI*, 10 (1956), 321–44.

Guillemain, B. *Les Recettes et les dépenses de la Chambre apostolique pour la quatrième année du pontificat de Clement V* (1308–9), Rome, 1978 (*CFR*, 39).

Housley, N. "Pope Clement V and the crusades of 1309–1310," *Journal of Medieval History*, 8 (1982), 29–43.

Iernard, J. "Le nepotisme de Clement V et ses complaisances pour la Gascogne," *Annales du Midi*, 61 (1949), 369–411.

Lanhers, Y., and Fawtier, R. *Table des Registres*, Paris, 1948–57.

Lizerand, G. *Clement V et Philippe le Bel*, Paris, 1910.

Menache, S. *Clement V*, Cambridge, 1998.

Menache, S. "Clement V et le royaume de France. Un nouveau regard," *RHEF*, 74 (1988), 23–38.

Mollat, G. "Clement V," *DHGE*, 12 (1953), 1115–29.

Mollat, G. *Vitae Paparum Avenionensium*, I, Paris, 1916 (comprises six lives of Clement V).

Muller, E. *Das Konzil von Vienne*, Munster, 1934.

Paravicini Bagliani, A. "Clement V," *DBI*, 26 (1980), 202–15.

Regestum Clementis Papae V, Rome, 1884–94, 8 vol.

Schmidt, T. "Clement V," *LexMa*, 2 (1983), 2142–3.

Soranzo, G. *La guerra fra Venezia e la Santa Sede per il dominio di Ferrara, 1308–1313*, Citta di Castello, 1905.

The Avignon Papacy and the Crusades, 1305–1378, Oxford, 1986.

Their, L. *Kreuzzugsbemuhungen unter Papst Clemens V (1305–1314)*, Werl, 1973.

CLEMENT VI. *Pierre Roger (b. Maumont, Correze, 1290/1291, d. Avignon, 6 December 1352). Elected pope 7 May 1342, crowned 19 May. Buried, in April 1353, at the abbey of La Chaise-Dieu (Haute-Loire).*

Clement VI has long been seen as the emblematic figure of the AVIGNON papacy, with its excesses and unbridled nepotism. A victim of the contradictions of his time, he deserves a more balanced portrayal.

Pierre Roger was born between May 1290 and May 1291 at Maumont (Correze) of Guillaume Roger, a squire, and Guillemette de Mestre, both of the Limousin gentry. In 1301 he was placed in the Benedictine abbey of La Chaise-Dieu (Haute-Loire) where he made his profession. In 1307 his abbot and the bishop of Puy sent him to study at the UNIVERSITY of Paris. Accepted at the Narbonne college, he did advanced theological studies and was trained in CANON LAW. He seems to have taught at some time in Paris, and his income was guaranteed by the small Limousin priory of Saint-Pantaleon de Lapleau (1316), then of Savigny in the diocese of Lyons (1323), and of Saint-Baudil in the diocese of Nimes (1324). He quickly distinguished himself as a theologian and orator; certain characteristics of his personality, more traditional than original, are well known. Between 1318 and 1321 he took part in the virulent attacks against Jean de Pouilli, his advice having been sought by the pope. He brilliantly defended the Thomist doctrine of the indivisibility of the Trinity against the Scotist positions of the Franciscan master, Francois de Meyronnes (1320–1321). Finally, as a canonist, he gave his support to John XXII on the issue of the poverty of Christ and his apostles, maintaining his absolute right to define matters of doctrine. That earned him the conferment by the pope of the Master of Theology on the intercession of the king of France, Charles IV, then, in 1326, the collation of the rich Norman abbey of Fecamp. He rose rapidly in his career and enjoyed royal favor as well as papal grace and entered the CURIA, under the protection of CARDINAL Pierre de Mortemart. As bishop of Arras on 3 December 1328, he was named archbishop of Sens on 24 November 1329 and, eventually of Rouen, the richest see in the kingdom, on 14 December 1330. The latter was a reward for his efficient and clever defense against Philip VI's lawyer, Pierre de Cugnieres (assembly of Vincennes, 1329), regarding the superiority of the rights of ecclesiastical jurisdiction over those of the temporal courts. Sitting in Parliament (1328), president of the Financial Chamber (1330), competently defending the rights of the king against English claims and the interests (political and financial) of the Valois during the planning of the 1333 crusade, but also those of his archbishopric, he still played an expanding role in the Curia, as theologian and diplomat. Anticipated since 1335, he was the sole promotion to cardinal made by Benedict XII on 18 December 1338, and received the presbyterial title of Santi Nereo e Achilleo on 5 May 1339. The most visible cardinal at the Curia, he was unanimously elected at the CONCLAVE following the death of Benedict XII. Elected on 7 May 1342, he chose the name of Clement, emphasizing the omnipotence of the one who dispenses clemency, and was crowned on the following 19 May.

The entire pontificate of Clement VI was based on a central idea, illustrated by his oratory as well as by his politics: A master of scholastic discourse, he continually sought to defend papal sovereignty and infallibility against the frontal and indirect attacks of partisans of political Aristotelianism and Ockhamist theories. The exaltation of the *majestas* attached to his function was nurtured by the deportment of the king of the Romans, Charles IV, in a position subordinate to him, as well as by his doctrinal intransigence vis-à-vis Greek and Armenian schismatics, in addition to the ostentatious splendor of his lifestyle, the imposing construction of the Palais-Neuf of Avignon, and his generous artistic and literary patronage.

To carry out his mission successfully, Clement VI exploited, more than any other Avignon pope, increases in financial and tax revenues and the extension of control of the ecclesiastical hierarchy. Profiting from the severe economic policies of his predecessor, he guaranteed to the Apostolic Camera funds accrued through the systemization of collection from the benefices (even minor ones), the methodical application of the right of SPOIL (a quarter of the cases registered during the entire 14th century, sad record of the Black Death), and stricter control of payments. However, one should guard against attributing this general development, which, like the growth of the administrative machine, characterizes not only the pope, but the totality of contemporary royal and princely courts.

With respect to personnel, the pope adopted recruitment and promotion practices that were very prevalent at the time—NEPOTISM. It is the excessive numbers that earned him so much criticism from his contemporaries. Although he allowed his lay relations to profit from his fortune, to which they owed, in large part, their riches, it is particularly to ecclesiastics of his family that he ensured brilliant careers. Of the 25 cardinals he created, 19 came from the South of France, among them 11 Limousins (the others were 2 French from the North, one Castilian, and 3 Italians). Among them were his own brother Hugues and five cousins, including Pierre Roger de Beaufort, the future Gregory XI. He peopled the Curia with Limousins, especially in key posts. The nomination of a second Limousin pope in the person of Etienne Aubert only highlighted this issue after his death.

Clement VI had difficult relations with the cardinals. Heir to a situation of conflict with the SACRED COLLEGE, a legacy of Benedict XII, he failed to maintain a balance between his own autocratic behavior, undermining the oligarchic claims of the cardinals, and his propensity to increase their powers and property to allow them to benefit more from their share in the administration of the universal Church. This lead his councilors to better define their own claims and, by "modern" ideas of political Aristotelianism, to slowly abandon a reasonable attitude.

They rebelled during the conclave of 1352, drawing up the first "capitulation" in the history of the conclave.

To maintain his status, Clement VI kept a magnificent court, imitated by a large number of cardinals (thus, Annibaldo Caeani di Ceccena and Pedro Gomez at Gentilly and Montfavet offered receptions for the pope in 1343). Some historians regarded him as a humanist pope. It would appear that, in the final analysis (Wood, 1989), this man of traditional intellectual preoccupations, in spite of a certain sensibility about pre-humanist ideas, was more sponsor than humanist, his essential role consisting of developing the crucial position of Avignon as a foyer of exchange between the north and Italy in the field of painting and music. The accusations of debauchery made against him by Petrarch, Matteo Villani, and partisans of Louis of Bavaria, do not stand up to review of the sources [Mollat (1953) and especially Wrigley, *AHP*, 3 (1965), 127–38].

Certain important events stand out in this highly active pontificate. One would have expected, from a pope so steeped in theology, great concern with respect to doctrinal and ecclesiastical matters. Yet, caught in the whirl of diplomatic negotiations, he paid little attention to them. He never intended to return the papacy to Rome—in fact, he anchored it a little more at Avignon by purchasing the city for 80,000 florins from Joanna I of Naples in 1348—consequently, he was called upon to reaffirm the strength of the ties between the pope and the see of Rome. He was criticized by those who denied his right to possess his own see, and urged to exalt the position of the Roman see as the center of the Christian world. He did promulgate the jubilee of 1350, an expedient maneuver in response to the demand to return to Rome by the Roman delegation of 1343 and the definition of the doctrine of indulgences (constitution *Unigenitus Dei filius*, 27 January 1343). In his relations with the world outside the Church (heretics, schismatics, and infidels), he defended the plenitude of papal power with an increasing intransigence which, in light of the devious unwillingness of his negotiators and the very unfavorable political conditions, led to the failure of efforts to reunite the Greek schismatics (1343 and 1350) and those of Little and Greater Armenia (1341–42, 1344–6). He also restored or created archdioceses in Anazarbe, Mamistra, and Seleucie (1345), and in Hierapolis and Bossra (1346), to give more authority to the mendicant missionaries. In addition to Armenia, he instituted, in 1349, the caucasian province of Matrega (Taman). The ultimate failure of the crusade, despite small military successes (seizure of Smyrna in 1344), revealed the inability of the western Christian kingdoms to unite under the papal banner. While he abandoned, vis-à-vis the infidels, his initial tolerance for a policy of conversion by force, he firmly defended the Jews (scapegoats of the Black Death in 1348), and he had complex intellectual relations with the Jewish religious community. Confronted on the other hand with the flagellants, he con-demned their heterodox excesses without reserve (*Inter sollicitudines*, 29 October 1349).

Diplomacy remained his principal concern. He had, in spite of his reputation for great political skill, fewer successes than failures, or rather qualified setbacks. Papal authority was seriously challenged even in the PAPAL STATES, and in Italy. The famous and short-lived takeover of Rome by the notary-tribune, Cola di Rienzo (May to December 1347) was, in the end, less serious than the hegemonic designs of the prefect of Rome, Giovanni di Vico, and of the new GHIBELLINE party against the patrimony of ST. PETER. The truces only prolonged the threat during the entire pontificate. In the north of Italy, the pope could not, any more than Benedict XII, restrain the expansionism of the Pepoli, especially with respect to the terrible archbishop of Milan, Giovanni Visconti, whom he invested, under duress, vicar of Bologna for the Church against an annual tax of 12,000 florins (28 July 1352). In the south he had to reckon with the incredible complexity of the Angevin problems at Naples: the feudal tutelage over the covetous heir to the kingdom, Joanna I (1343–82), the protection and investigations followed by her schemes after the murder of her husband, Andre of Hungary (18 September 1345), and a temporization policy vis-à-vis the threats of King Louis of Hungary, allowed the Holy See to maintain its authority over this vassal state.

Faced with the imperial question, he adopted the "route of compromise" (Wood), carefully handling papal interests by choosing the confirmation-nomination of Charles of Monrovia, his former disciple at Paris, as king of the Romans. Charles was elected 11 July 1346, after patient diplomatic preparation by Clement VI, which included the definitive condemnation of Louis of Bavaria in 1343, and an oath taken by Charles to staunchly defend the Church. Amid subtle theoretical jousting opposing the pope (whom the imperial electors elected as individuals) and the electors themselves (claiming to act as *universitas* with the right to invest the individual chosen with the power to administrate the Empire), loomed the imperial decision of Charles IV on the Golden Bull.

Although he may not have succeeded in preventing the forced annexation of the kingdom of Majorca (Roussilon, Cerdagne, and Baleares) to Avignon to the detriment of Jaume II (1342–4), or to truly lessen the tensions between Bohemia and Poland, the impossibility of ending the Anglo-French war was his most profound disappointment. Papal diplomacy was unsuited to the very nature of the conflict. Once elected, the pope could not break his staunch attachment to France and to his king, who reciprocated by honoring his family, particularly his brother Guillaume, with special favors. Clement VI gave immense sums to the royal treasury as loans or indirectly as tithes theoretically levied for the crusade. This partiality rendered all the efforts of mediation of the pontiff and of his LEGATES ineffective (truce of Malestroit, 29 January 1343; conferences of Avignon of 1344; truce of 28 September 1347 after the French disaster at Crécy and Calais). Among the serious consequences of this situation were the installation in England, in reaction to the systematic papal reserve, of a regime of state seizure of church property in the kingdom (by among others, the statute of provisors, 9 February 1351) and the threats proffered by Edward III of recourse to a general council.

In fragile health, he suffered from kidney stones for more than one year before he succumbed to an internal hemorrhage on 6 December 1352, having just celebrated his 60th birthday. His funeral took place in Avignon, but it was at the abbey of La Chaise-Dieu, where he had been ordained a Benedictine monk, that he was buried, in April 1353, in an impressive tomb built by Jean de Soignolles (De Sanholis) and Jean David, under the orders of Pierre Boye. Clement had seen it finished in 1351. A cortege of 44 people surrounded his recumbent figure (still preserved in situ), most of whom belonged to his close family.

Pierre Jugie

Bibliography

His Work: Pierre Roger left about 120 sermons or speeches given during political events or on return from a legation as cardinal, *quaestiones* on the 4th book of *Sentences*, advice on the decretal of John XXII *Quia quorumdam mentes* on the poverty of Christ and his apostles, as well as notes and handwritten philosophical and theological *reportationes* from his youth. He also wrote a mass for salvation from the plague in 1348.

Baluze, E. *Vitae paparum Avenionensium*, ed. G. Mollat, I, Paris, 1914, 241–308 [text of six lives] and II, Paris, 1927, 335–453 [notes].

"Clemens VI," *DBI*, 26 (1982), 215–22 [sources and bibliography].

Guillenmain, B. *La cour pontificale d'Avignon, 1309–1376: Etude d'une societe*, Paris, 1966, Index.

Lettres closes, patentes and curiales interessant les pays autres que la France, ed. E. Deprez, and G. Mollat, Paris, 1960–1 [to be completed and corrected by C. I. Kyer, "A misplaced quarternion of letters of Benedict XII," *AHP*, 16 (1978) 337–40].

Lettres closes, patentes and curiales se rapportant a la France, ed. E. Deprez, J. Glenisson, and G. Mollat, Paris, 1909–61.

Maier, A. "Der litterarische Nachlaas des Petrus Rogerii (Clemens VI) in der Borghesiana," *Recherches de theologie ancienne et medievale*, 15 (1948), 332–56 and 16 (1948), 72–98, reprinted A. Maier, *Ausgehen des Mittelalter Gesammelte Aufsatze zur Geistesgeschichte des 14 Jahrhunderts*, II, Rome, 1967 (*Storia e literatura*, 105), 255–315, with *Addenda*, 503–17.

Mollat, G. "Clement VI," *DHGE*, 12 (1953), 1129–62 [sources and bibliography].

Mollat, G. *The Popes of Avignon*, transl. Janet Love, New York, 1963.

Mollat, G. "L'oeuvre oratoire de Clement VI," *Archives d'histoire doctrinale et littéraire du Moyen Age*, 3 (1928), 239–74.

Viard, J. "La messe pour la peste," *Bibliotheque de l'Ecole des chartes*, 61 (1900), 344–48.

Wood, D. *Clement VI. The Pontificate and Ideas of an Avignon Pope*, Cambridge, 1989 (*Cambridge studies in medieval life and thought*, 4th series, 13) [sources and bibliography, 216–43.]

Wood, D. "*Maximus Sermocinator verbi Dei*: The Sermon Literature of Pope Clement VI," *Studies in Church History*, 11 (1975), 163–72.

Wrigley, J. E. "Clement VI before his pontificate: The early life of Pierre Roger (1290/91–1342)," *The Catholic Historical Review*, 56 (1970–1), 433–73.

[CLEMENT VII]. *Robert of Geneva (b. Annecy, 1342, d. Avignon, 16 September 1394). Elected in the Avignon obedience on 20 September 1378, crowned on 31 October. Buried at Notre Dame d'Avignon, and afterwards Les Celestins de Villeneuve-les-Avignon.*

Robert, the fifth son of the Count of Geneva, Amadeus III, and of Mahaut of Bologna, daughter of Robert, Count of Auvergne, was born at Annecy castle in 1342. He was related to the German imperial family, to the French royal family, and to the nobility of the Rhone valley. Destined for holy orders, he was, at the age of seven, already part of the retinue of Guy of Bologna, his uncle and the cardinal bishop of Porto, head of one of the most important factions of the SACRED COLLEGE, then at the height of its importance. Franciscan, canon of Paris where he attended the UNIVERSITY, chancellor of the Amiens church, cleric, then apostolic PROTONOTARY, and an intimate of INNOCENT VI, he became bishop of Therouanne on 3 November 1364, then archbishop of Cambrai (11 October 1368), but he did not reside in his dioceses. On 30 May 1371, he became cardinal priest of the Twelve Apostles basilica, called in the texts, *Cardinalis Gebennensis*. He was responsible for various diplomatic missions concerning, in particular, the league against Bernardo Visconti and the peace between Savoy and Saluces (1374), princes to whom he was related. He lived at Avignon and had a "livery" at Villeneuve des Avignon. He inherited some lands in the county of Geneva from his father (who died in 1367).

In 1376, he was sent as papal LEGATE to Romania and Lombardy to put down a fairly widespread revolt of the PAPAL STATES. He left Avignon on 24 May 1376 with a large army composed of Breton mercenaries hired by Gregory XI. Robert of Geneva entered Lombardy and signed the peace with Duke Gian Galeozzo Visconti. He recovered many towns in Romania but failed in Bologna. In a riot in Cesena he had many losses, was incarcerated in the citadel, and forced to appeal to *condottiere* John Hawkwood. The massacre of the Breton and English mercenaries was bloody, for which Robert of Geneva was bitterly reproached. His influence over the "crooks," infuriated by the killing of their colleagues, must have been quite limited. After the pacification of Romania, the Marchers of Ancona, and the capitulation of Bologna, the cardinal returned to Rome on 12 March 1378.

Evaluations of the reasons for the Great Schism are most often conditioned by the education and origins of the authors and the subsequent development of the papacy. There are two opposing theories: one based on orthodoxy, whose authors are very critical toward the cardinals vis-à-vis what they considered a scandal, and the other whose authors consider the pontificate an institution susceptible to dysfunction and who are sensitive to the realities of the 14th century. The first add to their judicial criticisms an analysis of the lifestyle of the Sacred College, which they consider shocking, forgetting that not all cardinals were wealthy. Robert of Geneva and his friend Jean de Murol, for instance, were of more modest origins, as opposed to a Jean de la Grange. The second note that Avignon is one of the better organized of the sovereign courts, and recognize the desire of the cardinals to share the administration of the Church with the pope and to fully assume it *sede vacante*. Vincent Ferrer gives a good definition: *Romana ecclesia, id est collegium apostolicum, scilicet papa et cardinales*. This concept is closely allied to that of the nobility of Christian states, France, England, Castile, Naples, and the HOLY ROMAN EMPIRE.

Although limited in number, the cardinals formed factions whose composition and leaders varied according to the circumstances and the times. In 1378 the two competing parties were the "Limousin" party and the "French" party; there was also an ill-defined faction composed of four Italian cardinals and one Spaniard. It was even suggested that there was a plot by Guy de Boulogne's party in 1378, though he had died five years before. If these observations on the cardinalitial families shed light on certain aspects of the political alliances within the Sacred College, we believe that the demise of one of its high-ranking cardinals, such as Guy de Boulogne, very quickly reactivated competition. It certainly was not Robert of Geneva who succeeded his uncle at the head of the French party in comparison to a Jean de la Grange, but he was perhaps the spokesman. It is true that succession in an elective monarchy will always result in a few intrigues, and that of Gregory XI was no exception, even if the consequences were serious.

The election of URBAN VI (Bartolomeo Prignano) occurred in an atmosphere of violence and riot on 8 April 1378, which made it unique, but regardless of their feelings, the cardinals made the best of it and notified the Christian world.

During the summer of 1378, however, Urban VI's tactlessness in his relations with the Sacred College and the CURIA, as well as with foreign princes, and his blundering desire to reform everything while satisfying his relatives, gave the picture of a well-intentioned prelate who had been influenced by power and who squabbled with his entourage at both the theological and juridical levels. Relations between the newly elected pope and the cardinals became strained, and the cardinals eventually regretted the April election. While recognizing the growing influence that the council of princes claim to exercise at the end of the 14th century, the role of Cardinal de la Grange and of CAMERLENGO Pierre de Cros, who had been accused by Urban VI of embezzlement, can be discerned. The role of the king of France has sometimes been questioned, but he cannot be held responsible because his intervention always followed the actions taken by the Sacred College.

The cardinals, however, had many other reasons to dread the continuation of this pontificate, including Church reform and its encroachment on their privileges; the repercussions of Urban VI's pontificate would prove them right. Concerned, they suggested an honorable abdication to the pope. On his refusal, a coadjutor was envisaged. From the beginning of the conflict, the Italians propose a council, but the majority of the Sacred College reject this solution, suggested by Urban, perhaps because the council could only be convoked by the pope, which would render its deliberations suspect. Other milieu, like the University of Paris, had long clamored for it. Some cardinals perhaps regretted the provencal compassion. On 20 July they denounced the validity of the election.

It has not been possible to determine exactly when the candidature of Robert of Geneva was proposed. If the DEPOSITION of Urban was the consensus of the majority of cardinals, it did not appear in July 1378 that the aim was to substitute Cardinal Robert of Geneva. Urban VI's refusal to accept the verdict of the Sacred College forced the electors to find a candidate who would ensure them the support of the princes. Robert of Geneva was the only one from a princely family of the Holy Roman Empire, related to the emperor and to the king of France, and these relationships compensated for his youth. These hopes would be partially betrayed because half of the Christian world would not recognize him. At the conclave at Fondi, on 20 September 1378, the cardinals elected Robert of Geneva on the first ballot, by twelve votes to one with three abstentions, the three Italians. Immediately, the Curia rallies en masse to the new pope, who takes the name Clement VII. The coronation takes place at Fondi on 31 October. From the outset, apart from notification of the election, the new pope initiates action against his rival and his partisans, who had already dismissed the rebel cardinals and had constituted another Sacred College, composed mostly of Italians.

Clement VII was in no hurry to return to Avignon and, strongly supported by the Breton mercenaries, the Count of Fondi, the queen of Naples, and his other partisans, he stayed in Italy until 22 May 1379. He arrived in Avignon on 30 June, and left only to visit places in the region.

By September 1378 the Schism can no longer be denied and the Christian world needed to choose between the two rival popes. Clement VII could, from the outset, count on almost the entire Curia, those who accompanied Gregory XI to Italy as well as those who stayed in Avignon; very few curialists chose Urban VI. This is borne out by the records, which show a remarkable continuity in every department from Gregory XI to Benedict XIII, and throughout Clement's entire pontificate. The main religious orders were his: Cluny and three of its "daughters," Citeaux and its four "daughters," Prémontré, the Chartres, Saint-Antoine-de-Viennois, the majority of the DOMINICANS and Franciscans, and the Hospitallers and other military orders (with the exception of the Teutonic knights). If St. Catherine of Siena firmly supported Urban VI, St. Vincent Ferrer and St. Peter of Luxembourg would also.

Success was less evident at the diplomatic level. In Italy, Clement VII, on Church lands, could count on the Count of Fondi, rector of the Campania, on the Caetani, on Viterbo and a few localities, and on the kingdom of Naples, the Piedmont, and the Montferat. Central and southern Italy remained Urbanist, with scattered Clementine seigniories. Milan under the Visconti, Ravenna and the Da Polenta, and Bologna vacillated between the two obediences. With Florence, the war of the Otto Santi was ended by the peace of Tivoli in July 1378, signed by Urban VI. The Florentine Cardinal Piero Corsini rapidly turned away from the Roman pontiff, and leaving Fondi, finished by rallying to Avignon in 1381. However, the republic oscillating between "indifference" and the Roman obedience never rallies to Clement VII, in spite of his efforts, without also supporting his rivals in a policy of shrewd and crafty bargaining. The kingdom of France supported him as well as the minor princes on whom he exerted his influence. In Germany, he never secured the support of Emperor Charles IV, to whom he was related, and he was able to count only on a few princes in the western part of the Holy Empire, such as the dukes of Lorraine, Bar, Juliers, the counts of Cleves, La Marck, Montbeliard, and especially Leopold III of Habsburg. There were Clementine scattered pockets, notably in Prague and Breslau. Erfurt obtained the foundation of its university from Clement VII in 1379. Clement could naturally count on the counties of Geneva and Savoy, and here and there he had other support including the kingdom of Scotland and the bishoprics of Ireland, which

broke away from England. After a period of "indifference," the Spanish kingdoms rejoined Clement's camp, Castile in 1380, Aragon in 1387, and Navarre in 1390. Portugal passed from one camp to another, finally opting for Urban VI in 1385.

Clement VII was not disinterested in the fight against Islam nor in the Christian east. The king of Cyprus and the Latin east sided with him, but not without him having to fight against the Genoese and the Venetians who were Urbanist. He sent Aymon Sechaux, provost of Grand-Saint Bernard, promoted to patriarch of Jerusalem, on a mission to the east, but as he did not have the military and financial means, the mission was quite ineffective.

Such unprecedented action did not fail to provoke a large quantity of contradictory evidence, none of it published. The jurists were divided between the two camps to justify their choice. Gilles Bellemere, Boniface, and Ammanati, for example, took the part of Clement. Secret letters concerning the changes in the membership of the two parties and the unstable geography of the obediences have disappeared, but these issues are evident in Clement VII's common letters, which have been conserved.

Although the princes sometimes organized veritable inquiries and their decisions always involved canonical reasons, it appears their choices were made for political reasons. This can be seen particularly in the situation at the frontiers of the obediences; a good example has been described for the territory of present-day Switzerland. The support of the king of France had been especially highlighted, but Clement also removed from Avignon, the princes hostile to Capetian, whether from England or Hungary, rival of the ANGEVINS for Naples. In the contested regions, there were sometimes two clergy disputing the same church or benefice. The low clergy was incapable to choose its camp, much less its people; the princes determined their choice. The principle of *Cujus regio ejus religio* was very clear during the time of Clement VII, but some clerics who opted for one pontiff were forced into exile.

The ecclesiastical censures of the two pontiffs did not ensure the success of their causes, and they turned to action, seeking to end the schism by military force. Clement VII considered encircling central Italy and the lands of the Church, a permanent concern of the popes because of the frequent conflicts between two vassal kingdoms, Naples (Sicily in the texts of the times, created in 1265, where Queen Joanna I reigned, who was faithful to him), and a kingdom of Adria, which he granted to Louis of Anjou, brother of King Charles V of France, but which the Angevin prince first had to reconquer. The two vassal kingdoms did not have the right either to fight or to be united under one hand (17 April 1379). This attempt is foiled and Clement VII, who later disavows the plan, turns to another solution: the adoption of Louis of Anjou by Joanna I of Naples, who has no children.

In the summer of 1381, Charles of Durazzo, cousin of Joanna, who also claimed the kingdom of Naples, entered the service of Urban VI, conquered Naples, and took the queen prisoner, who he savagely strangled the following summer. Louis I of Anjou, heavily subsidized by Avignon, descended on Italy to deliver Naples in the summer of 1382. He conquered Pouilles, but the Angevin expedition stopped abruptly on the death of Louis I (1384). Charles of Durazzo remained master of Naples, but battled with Urban VI, who wished to take part of his territory for his nephew Francisco Prignano. Urban VI, saved by the Angevin barons (still, however, partisans of Clement), cruelly castigates his cardinals, who were opposed to his policies and planned to impose a coadjutor on him. Two manage to flee to Clement VII who generously welcomed them (1387). The death of Charles of Durazzo again called the issue into question and the last husband of Joanna, Otto of Brunswick, entered Naples (1387). Louis II of Anjou, son of Louis I, was proclaimed king and for the fourth time the Avignon party triumphed (1389).

When Urban VI died on 15 October 1389 it was believed that the schism would come to an honorable conclusion, Clement VII having proved that he would confirm the Urbanist cardinals. With a haste that precluded discussion, 14 Urbanist cardinals elected BONIFACE IX on 2 November; the court at Avignon had only learned of the death of the Roman pontiff at the beginning of November. With this, the schism ceased to be a juridical accident caused by a confused double election, to become a veritable break between two Christian parties, which the equally rapid election of Benedict XIII later confirmed. On 27 November 1389, Clement has no recourse but to start action against his new rival and forbid the jubilee pilgrimage to Rome, which Urban VI had reduced to 33 years. More skillful than his predecessor, Boniface IX recouped Roman factions in Italy and in Germany, which slowly eroded, and benefited from the financial fruits of the 1390 jubilee.

Fifteen years of sterile struggle demonstrated the failure of strong-arm tactics and the "route of knighthood," to resolve the crisis. An indecisive struggle then begins where land gained by one camp is balanced against land lost elsewhere. The cost of this fight, which was disproportionate, plunged both popes into great financial crisis and multiplied the tax exigencies and expedients in both obediences, and this in a generally depressive economic climate. Clement VII, having become the last count of Geneva in 1392, was reduced to using his patrimonial fortune to plug the holes in the papal coffers. Indifference—a refusal to choose one pontiff over his rival—gained ground among a disillusioned clergy and the princes. Public opinion had tired of the quarrel without

solution, and ideas emerged that threatened the traditional structure of the Church (Wycliffe's, for example), but the majority was still persuaded that the Church would be regenerated. The way of cession, that is, simultaneous abdication of the two popes, gained in popularity, an idea that each pope dreaded. Clement VII, however, clung to the hope of a new expedition, which he had been negotiating since 1391 with the French court, and which King Charles VI was to lead in Italy in 1392, but this plan, about which some had reservations, was postponed. The University of Paris wrote to the Avignon pope on 17 July 1394 demanding his abdication in order to resolve the schism. Clement VII had regained some hope when he was struck down by an attack of apoplexy and died on the morning of Wednesday, 16 September 1394. He was buried on 18 September in the cathedral of Avignon, then transferred on 8 September 1401 to the church of the Celestine convent, which he had built at Villeneuve-les-Avignon to house the tomb of Pierre of Luxembourg. At Clement VII's death, the two obediences counterbalanced each other. Rome was a little larger, but Avignon had better resources.

Clement VII made 12 promotions to cardinal during his pontificate, and thus maintained the traditional number of the Sacred College. In spite of the nomination of two distant relatives and three close friends, who had all been named for having supported him for years in the administration of the Church, it cannot be said that he peopled the college through NEPOTISM. It seems that he got on well with his cardinals, who generally supported him, and several in their wills resolutely emphasized his legitimacy and their affection.

Along with most of the Curia, Clement VII was not very innovative and did not interfere with the complex machinery the papal administration had become in the 14th century. In 1390 he defined the rules of the court and the offices of the palace. Like all pontiffs, he designated a certain number of family and ordinary functionaries of his country, generally as vacancies arose. The Genevans will eventually number around fifty of the 500 to 600 curialists of the court, but his compatriots will never constitute more than a minority in the entourage of Clement VII.

As the only way of financing such a large papal administration, the policy of benefices continued to be that of his predecessors, bringing in its wake abuses which have been denounced time and again. Clement VII was able to institute only minor corrections. He clearly excluded the parish churches from the benefices touched by his reserves, but entered into direct conflict with the diocesan clergy who practiced the same policy of distribution of sinecures and canonries, and especially with the University of Paris, where the pope sought, by his benefices, to allow the provincials to study in the schools he had attended.

Accusations of cupidity have been made against this pontiff, as they were against his rival. In fact, Clement VII had the better tax organization, but the English and the Germans were the ones to complain most bitterly about papal taxation. As it seems that he had at his disposal the equivalent of what Innocent VI collected, about 180,000 florins, increased pressure from the Apostolic Camera was reasonable, particularly because only one-third of the sums levied in his name came from Avignon. The greatest expense was the cost of military campaigns in Italy and for the defense of the county against Raymond of Turenne, lord of Baux.

Although the personnel of the Church administration was somewhat numerous, there were only 23 servants for the palace service, while there were more than 100 scribes. An official record exists.

His pontificate has often been presented as an Indian summer for the papacy in Avignon. This image masks the reality. When Cardinal Bertrand Lagier notes that nowhere in the Scripture is Rome mentioned as the obligatory see of the vicar of Christ, and that only Jerusalem, where the Redemption was accomplished, could be, more than another place, the see of the Vicar, he obviously reflected an opinion shared by many other prelates. If the Avignonese did not derive the benefits they expected from this return, the general economic situation was more likely the reason. The population had declined. The failure of the Urbanists to return and the conflict with Florence under Gregory XI have been blamed, but the absent were replaced and the confiscations affected only about 20 Florentines, to which must be added two dozen of Urban's partisans, while the Apostolic Camera took possession of 24 buildings, for various legal reasons, during the pontificate. In addition, Clement VII lifted the sentences against Florence. From 23 December 1383 to 19 August 1392, in imitation of his predecessors, he retained the revenues of the episcopal income. He might have wished to bring to the court the brilliance he witnessed as a child under the pontificate of Clement VI, but the almost constant neediness, which was his lot, did not permit it. His patronage, therefore, was not very considerable. He constructed Saint Martial College and began the Celestine convent to hold the tomb of Pierre of Luxembourg (and where his remains would be transferred in 1401). The artistic and intellectual influence of the city of the Rhone was maintained under his pontificate. The university remains prosperous.

The pontificate of Clement VII was born of the 1378 crisis. The subsequent destiny of the papal institution should not mask the fact that this crisis must be placed within the context of the troubles and uncertainties that affected all the States at this, a time of transition from a medieval to a modern world. Struck by the parallelism of the attitudes of the two cardinalitial colleges with respect to Urban VI, we cannot blame the schism principally on the vested egotism of Gregory XI's cardinals, in view of the proliferation of ideas on the Church at the time, which will continue until the 16th century. We must not forget that almost all the reports come from clerics interested in the issue for more than one reason, and the effect of the troubling spirit of the times must be seen in its proper perspective. Urban's character and the beginnings of his pontificate brought the administration of the Church to the forefront, budding nationalism contributed to the hardening of positions, the dismal economy gave an often bitter tone to the criticisms of the clergy, but nothing of this created, *ex nihilo*, the problem of 1378 through 1449. The cardinals of 1378 were, for the most part, jurists and not theologians, and their argumentation was constantly a matter of law. From this perspective, the rivalry of the two pontiffs perhaps deviated from the fundamental question to a problem of personalities, turning it into a dispute about the granting of the same benefice to two clerics, without questioning the nature of the benefice, or the magisterium. Having become a full State, but with competencies and responsibilities sometimes spread throughout the world, the main resources of the Holy See are derived from territories over which it has no political control. Unable to provide it with a regular and secure income, the popes multiplied the sources and pretexts, while developing their administrations. The policy of benefices was one of the available means of remuneration, but it hurt many interests. The political crisis of the schism brought with it a clear abuse of the granting of benefices from which the princes, the king of France in particular, profited. In this sense, the crisis would also be the harbinger of the REFORM.

During his enthronement Clement VII found this situation seriously aggravated by the existence of a double administration. He continued in the Avignon tradition and was in no way a reformist. In administrative matters, he was not an innovator, not even in correcting the right of SPOIL so contested. Instead, he contented himself with the fiscal policy of fully using the available possibilities to fulfill his material needs, which were increased by the schism. His faith was sincere, but he was not a theologian. He did not, however, lack good qualities. Of advantageous presence, intelligent, generous to a fault, polyglot, a courageous and skillful diplomat, the man had charm. The abuses for which he has been criticized may be wide-ranging, but where the pope had a policy of benefices, the clerics also knew how to utilize it to advance their own careers. He seems to have risen to the expectations of the cardinals who elected him, and the administrative team he nominated maintained throughout the entire schism and beyond the council of Constance, the central structure of the Church, in the gravest crisis of its existence in the Middle Ages.

Roger-Charles Logoz

Bibliography

Baluze, E. *Vitae paparum Avenionensium*, ed. G. Mollat, Paris, 1916–28, I, 469–542, II [notes] and IV, 169–417 [documents].

Dykmans, M. "Clement VII," *DBI*, 26 (1982), 222–37.

Favier, J. *Les Finances pontificales a l'epoque du Grand Schisme d'Occident*, Paris, 1966 (*BEFAR*, 211).

Genèse et début du Grand Schisme d'Occident (1362–1394), Colloque, Avignon, 1978, Paris, 1980.

Goller, E. *Repertorium Germanicum . . . I. Band: Clemens VII, von Avignon, 1378–1394*, Berlin, 1916.

Hanquet, K. *Documents relatifs au Grand Schisme*, 2 vol., Bruxelles-Paris, 1924, 1930 [Texts and analyses].

Lenzenweger, J. "Das Kardinals-Kollegium und die Papstwahlen 1378," *Theologisch praktische Quartalschrift*, 126 Bd 4, Linz, 1378, 316–25.

Logoz, R. C. *Clement VII (Robert de Geneve), sa chancellerie et le clergé roman au debut du Grand Schisme (1378–1394)*, Lausanne, 1974.

Mollat, G. "Clement VI," *DHGE*, 12 (1953), 1162–75.

Muntz, E. "L'antipape Clement VII. Essai sur l'histoire des arts en Avignon vers la fin du XIVe siècle," *Revue archeologique*, 11 (1888), 8–118, 163–83.

Nelis, N. *Documents relatifs au Grand Schisme*, III, Rome, 1934.

Rinaldi, O. *Annales ecclesiastici ab Anno quo desinit card. Caesar Baronius MCXCVIII usque ad Annum, MDXXXIV continuati . . .*, Cologne, 1691–1727, XVI and XVIII [documents].

Sauerland, H. V. "Itinerar Klemens VII," *Historisches Jahrbuch*, 13 (1892), 192 *sq*.

Seidlmayer, M. *Die Anfange des grossen abendlandischen Schismas*, Münster, 1940 (*Spanische Forschungen der Görresgesellschaft*, S. II, 5), 199–262.

Stelling-Michaud, S. "Genevois à la Curie d'Avignon au XIVe siècle," *Bulletin de la Société d'histoire et d'archeologie de Genève*, 9 (1950), 272–323.

Swanson, R. N. "Obedience and Disobedience in the Great Schism," *Archivum Historiae Pontificiae*, Rome, 1984, 307–87.

Swanson, R. N. "The Problem of the Cardinalate in the Great Schism," *Authority and Power: Studies on Medieval Law and Government*, Cambridge, 1980, 225–35.

Valois, N. *La France et le Grand Schisme d'Occident*, Paris, 1896.

CLEMENT VII. *Giulio de' Medici (b. Florence, 26 May 1478, d. Rome, 25 September 1534). Elected pope November 1523, crowned 26 November. Buried at Santa Maria sopra Minerva.*

Clement VII was crowned amidst great acclaim and died ten years later, beset by terrible physical suffering. The reign of Clement VII represents one of the most somber episodes in the history of the papacy. His indecisive, clumsy leadership was the most prominent characteristic of a reign that began disappointingly and ended tragically. During his papacy, the Holy See relived the darkest periods of the Avignon exile, from which great pontiffs like MARTIN V, ALEXANDER VI, and JULIUS II had saved it with such difficulty. The Holy See now became weakened and discredited, a mere toy—even less than a pawn—in the hands of the three princes who ruled Europe at the time: Charles V, Francis I, and Henry VIII. Clement VII's pontificate saw the sacking of ROME, the defeat of Pavia, which brought about a dangerous imbalance in alliances, and the excommunication of the king of England as a consequence of his divorce. This was the prelude to the Protestant SCHISM. While Clement VII, the last Medici pope, cannot be held responsible for all the catastrophes that occurred during his reign, it is nonetheless true that he did nothing to avoid them and was incapable of learning from them. And yet the pope had two important advantages. First, he had real intelligence, which was unfortunately given over to false calculations and underhanded dealings. A second and very important advantage was that his cousin was the king of an extravagantly wealthy neighboring state. Clement VII's career had been characterized by political intrigue, and he had no real ecclesiastical vocation to offset this. His innate cowardice prevented him from rising to the challenges confronting him, not only in the realm of spiritual leadership but also in the management of the temporal affairs of the Church. Throughout his reign, he continued to behave in much the same petty and narrow manner he had learned as a cardinal, with no notion of long-term consequences. He lacked any psychological astuteness. Neither did he have any of the dogmatic convictions that would have allowed him to oppose or support a given group or cause with any firmness or commitment.

He was the illegitimate son of Giuliano de' Medici. Nevertheless he had been raised on an equal footing with the sons of his uncle Lorenzo the Magnificent, with Ambrogio di Sangallo as godfather and Bernardo Michelezzo as his tutor. Living in the shadow of his cousin Giovanni, who had been made cardinal, Giulio de' Medici suffered from the fall of the Medici regime in 1494 and from a long exile, which took him to Flanders, Bavaria, and England. For ten years he maneuvered to bring about the return of the Medicis to Florence. He acted as clandestine ambassador to Julius II, conspired against the Soderinis, and brokered a marriage and consequently a rapprochement with the Strozzi family—ten years of intrigue with one sole aim in view, an objective finally achieved in 1512 with the return to favor of the Medicis and the election of his cousin Giovanni to the throne of St. Peter in 1513. That same year, Giulio was elected archbishop of Florence, with the title cardinal-deacon of Santa Maria in Domnica; he also received a plethora of benefices. The difficulties he had so tenaciously overcome had all been due to his name, as was the rest of his dazzling career. He had learned from his travels during years of exile and had no trouble being accepted as CARDINAL PROTECTOR of England by Henry VIII when Thomas Wolsey was elected cardinal. Francis I also accepted him as cardinal protector of France.

Giulio's diocese of Florence was still shaken by the preaching of the disciples of Savonarola, and also beset by serious problems. These he resolved by convening a provincial council and defending with equal passion the interests of the Medicis and those of the Holy See. Indeed, the interests of both sides were very closely linked.

From his cousin, LEO X, the future Clement VII learned the art of hedging and evading, of trying to maintain an even balance between France, which could on no account become subservient to the wishes of Milan and Naples, and the Swiss, who served the interests of the Duke of Milan. The future pope was LEGATE of the papal ARMY and suffered the consequences of the Battle of Marignano. However, he also benefited from the changes and reforms undertaken by Leo X, and from the latter's increased authority over the states of the Church. The year 1519, and the death of his cousin Lorenzo, marked a turning point in the life of the future Clement VII. Previously he had been a vice-chancellor of the Church, and as legate in Tuscany he was responsible for governing Florence, which was still in a state of upheaval following the despotic rule of the Duke of Urbino. He learned of the death of his cousin Leo X on 1 December 1521 and suddenly found himself in line for the papal tiara. However, the opposition of Cardinals Colonna and Soderini, as well as the bad memories left by the papacy of another member of the Medici family, led to the election of Adrian Florensz, bishop of Utrecht. He was to be the last non-Italian pope until John Paul II in 1978, and was known as Hadrian VI. However, his pontificate lasted a mere two years. During that time, Giulio de' Medici stifled a fresh revolt in Florence, begun at the instigation of the Soderinis. He also managed to regain the good graces of the previous pope, following attempts to discredit him in the eyes of the pontiff. The latter favored Charles V, whom he had tutored, and set about upsetting alliances. This would ultimately prove costly for the future Clement VII, but at the time it smoothed the way for his election by neutralizing Cardinal Colonna, who would remain the only opponent to the Medicis, but also head of the pro-imperial faction. Following a tight contest, lasting a month and a half, with the help of Cardinal Farnese, the future Paul III, Cardinal Medici was elected pope on 19 November 1523. As a gesture of reconciliation, he took the name of Clement.

The reign of Clement VII thus began under favorable auspices. Alphonso d'Este laid down arms and swore an oath of obedience for Parma and Reggio, and Charles V openly hailed the election of the new pope, an election in which he had a large financial stake. Direct contacts were established with the French court and Venice, with a view to carrying out a crusade, and Florence was finally reassured by the presence of another Medici pope. Unfortunately, Luther's diatribes were becoming increasingly violent and had begun to gain a following. As a result of this, Charles V thought it necessary to convene another Council, but the pope was opposed. TRENT was eventually chosen as the venue for the Council. In an effort to stall for time, Clement VII announced a reform of the CURIA and angrily issued a bull condemning the amassing of benefices and decreeing that auditors would be sent out to visit churches and convents. Other measures were taken to ensure that Rome would be kept reliably supplied and assure proper administration of the patrimony of ST. PETER, whose finances had been seriously depleted by the extravagant spending of Leo X. These measures included creation of a loan fund, nicknamed the "Monte della Fede," to redress the burden of debt. However these measures displeased Roman feudal lords such as the Colonnas, Orsinis, Savellis, and Massimos, as well as the Baglionis in Perugia and the Fuggers of Augsburg, from whom the right to stamp coins had been withdrawn.

The pope was being pressured by the Emperor and was isolated within Rome. He saw with horror the rising threat of a French military campaign in northern Italy and the specter of another Marignano. When asked to mediate in the question of the possession of Milan, Clement VII committed the fatal error of taking sides rather than allowing the opposing parties to iron out their own differences. Moreover, he chose to defend the wrong side, reneging on his moral commitment to Charles, who had brought him to the papal throne, and downplaying the problem of rising Protestantism, which would have such grave consequences for the future of Christendom. Once again, temporal considerations and caution had risen above spiritual questions, which would have required courage and determination. The catastrophic results are all too well known: the defeat of the French at Pavia on 25 February 1525 brought about the seizure of Florence by Charles V. The Holy See was forced to pay an enormous tribute, and Louise of Savoy came up with the idea of an alliance between Venice and Milan, which ultimately proved ineffective but was consolidated the following year and given the name "League of Cognac." With this final development, Clement VII was completely discredited. The Emperor was furious and repeated to Baldassare Castiglione, the ambassador of the Holy See, his express wish to convene a council. He refused any suggestion of a compromise and did nothing to oppose the Colonnas when they ransacked the Vatican Palace in September 1526.

Clement VII found himself deprived of any real support from the French, at loggerheads with the Emperor, and accused by the Colonnas of having been elected as a result of simony, or the sale of benefices. Despite all this, and the threat of being deposed, Clement VII did not contemplate changing his policies. Rather, he chose to take revenge on the powerful Roman family by sending what remained of his troops to fight against their fiefdoms. Retaliation came swiftly. The troops of Marshal Lannoy, the viceroy of Naples, made a pact with the mercenaries of the Constable of Bourbon, who had passed over to the service of Charles V and the bands recruited by the Colonnas. On May 6, Spanish and German soldiers entered Rome and held the pope prisoner in the Castel Sant'Angelo, effecting the total breakdown of the policy, so cleverly pursued in the era of Leo X, that had been known as "Freedom of Italy." The pope was forced to grant immediate amnesty to the Colonnas, pay out four hundred thousand ducats, give up Parma, Piacenza, Modena, Civitavecchia, and Ostia, melt down the papal treasure, and free a large number of hostages. In the meantime, Florence had rebelled. The sole, bitter consolation remaining for the pontiff was the knowledge that the ambitious Cardinal Wolsey was seeking to rally opposition among the cardinals who remained outside of Rome. This he sought to achieve by annulling the marriage of Henry VIII to Catherine of Aragon.

Rome was sacked for the third time in September, and Clement managed to escape only in December, heavily disguised. He took refuge in Orvieto, then in Viterbo. The pope refused to follow the advice of those who urged him to side with the League of Cognac. Instead, he stubbornly continued to demand that Venice return Cervia and Ravenna to the Duke of Ferrara, Reggio and Modena. He also demanded that the Medicis be allowed to reestablish themselves in Florence. In an attempt to pacify and soothe hurt feelings, he had included two Florentines among the first set of cardinals promoted during his reign—Nicolo Gaddi and Benedetto Accotti. (The others included the Genoese Agostino Spinola, Marino Grimani from Venice, and Ercole Gonzaga.) Seven months later, on 21 November 1527, he appointed eight more cardinals. They were Antonio Sanseverino, Giovanni Carafa, Andrea Matteo Palmieri for Naples, and Antoine Du Prat for France. Eruco Cardona was the Spaniard chosen with Girolamo Grimaldi, Pineo Gonazaga, and Sigismondo Pappacorda. Francisco de Quinones was chosen on December 7 and Francesco Conaro on December 20. Meanwhile, the pope stood by his demands while at the same time proposing peace to Charles V. He had not abandoned the old dream of hegemony for the Medici family. To further this, he placed his illegitimate son at the head of the council of the city-state of Florence after hastily marrying him off to the Florentine Emperor's illegitimate daughter, Margaret of Austria. Meanwhile his nephew, Ippolito, was made cardinal at the same time as Girolamo Doria, on 10 January 1529. Everyone had grown weary of the succession of dramatic events and allowed him to have his way. The king of France had signed the Treaty of Madrid with Charles V, and the primary concern of Henry VIII was to have his marriage annulled. The Emperor wanted at all costs to have a Council convened. He was also getting ready to assume the Iron Crown in Bologna, which he did on 22 February 1530.

Out of sheer, relentless determination, the pope had managed to gain some material advantage from a disastrous situation, although his moral authority lay in ruins. His primary interest was Florence, followed by Bologna, Modena, and Milan. In 1532, by bribing Baglioni, he finally managed to make Alessandro de Medici duke of Florence. This he did after having neutralized France and Spain by appointing a series of cardinals in March and June 1530: François de Tournon, Gabriel de Gramont, Louis de Challant, Juan Garcia de Loyasa, Iñigo de Luniga, Alonso de Manrigiez, and Jian de Tavera. Another meeting with the Emperor was arranged in Bologna. Once more the pope managed to put off convening a Council, on the pretext of the threat of a schism, as a result of the actions of Henry VIII. He also used the hostility of Francis I as an excuse. However, in the CONSISTORY of December 20 he did consent to appoint a commission of cardinals to study the practical and theological advantages of holding a council, but only after prior reconciliation with the princes of Christendom. In the meantime, the archbishop of Canterbury declared that the marriage of Henry VIII to Anne Boleyn was valid. An order of excommunication was pronounced against the king, but without immediate effect. The pope wanted first of all to settle the matter of the marriage of his niece Catherine to the son of the king of France. He accompanied Catherine to Marseilles, after having appointed a group of new cardinals, all of them French (Jean Le Veneur, Claude de Givry, Odet de Coligny, and Philippe de la Chambre). Once the deal had been concluded, the pope once more rallied to the cause of Charles V, the nephew of the repudiated queen. The definitive excommunication of Henry VIII was announced in the consistory of 24 March 1534. This marked the culmination of a break that had in fact begun six years before. Clement VII had only a few more months to live, weighed down by the increasingly virulent rivalry between his son and his nephew Ippolito. He died on 25 September, after a long, drawn-out period of suffering. His death marked the definitive break in the link that had been established over more than twenty years between Florence and the Holy See.

François Fossier

Bibliography

Castiglione, B. *Le Lettere*, ed. G. La Rocca, 1 (1467–1521), Milan, 1978.

CLEMENT VIII

Chastel, A. *The Sack of Rome*, Princton, 1983.

Guicciardini, F. *La Storia d'Italia . . .* , ed. C. Paganica, Bari, 1967.

Hook, J. *The Sack of Rome*, London, 1972; "Clement VII, the Colonna and Charles V; A Study of Political Instability of Italy in the Second and Third Decades of the Sixteenth Century," *European Studies Review*, 2 (1972), 281–99.

Jedin, H. *Storia del concilio di Trento*, I, Brecia, 1949.

Mols, R. "Clement VII," *DHGE*, 5 (1958), 1241–44.

Monaco, M. "Le Finanze pontificie al tempo di Clement VII," *Studi romani*, 6 (1958), 278–96; "Considerazioni sul pontificato di Clement VII," *Archivi*, ser 2, 27 (1960), 184–223.

Muller, G. *Die romische Kurie und die Reformation 1523–1534. Kirche und Politik wahrend des Pontifikates Clemens' VII*. Heidelberg, 1969.

Prosperi, A. "Clemente VII," *DBI*, 26 (1982), 237–59.

Sanuto, M. I *Diarii*, Venice, 1878–1903.

Stephens, F. N. "Pope Clement VII, a Florentine Debtor," *Bull. of the Inst. of Historical Research*, 49 (1976), 138–41.

Wilkie, W. E. *The Cardinal Protectors of England. Rome and the Tudors before the Reformation*, Cambridge, 1974.

CLEMENT VIII. *Ippolito Aldobrandini (Fano, province of Pesaro and Urbino, 24 February 1536—died in Rome, 5 March 1605). Elected pope 30 January 1592, ordained bishop 3 February, crowned 9 February. Buried at St. Mary Major.*

Ippolito Aldobrandini, the son of Silvestro and Lisa Deti, was born into a patrician family from Florence. His father was a renowned jurisconsult who was exiled in 1531 for political reasons. Ippolito entered into service in the pontifical administration. In 1548, he became a CONSISTORIAL ADVOCATE through the sponsorship of Cardinal Alexander Farnese. It was probably also through the patronage of Cardinal Farnese that the young Ippolito pursued university studies at Padua, Perugia, and Bologna. His exemplary life and unimpeachable morals attracted the attention of PIUS V from the very beginning of the latter's pontificate. He was first appointed consistorial advocate, then in 1568, auditor to the cardinal CAMERLENGO, and in 1569, auditor of the Rota, replacing his brother Giovanni, who became bishop of Imola and later a cardinal. In 1571, he was a member of the entourage of Michaele Bonelli, the pope's nephew and Alexandrine cardinal, who was sent as *a latere* legate to Spain, Portugal, and France (June 1571–April 1572). In 1572 Ippolito's brilliant career was suddenly interrupted by the death of Pius V. During the pontificate of GREGORY XIII, the young auditor of the Rota remained in the background, confined to his judiciary functions. In 1580 he decided to

take sacred orders, perhaps at the instigation of St. Philip Neri, of whom he was the penitent. He was ordained a priest by the cardinal of Florence and future pope LEO XI on 31 December 1580, and on 1 January 1581, he celebrated his first mass. From then on, his links to the Oratory continued to grow stronger, and he chose his confessors from among the fathers of that congregation: Giovanni Paolo Bordini and then Cesare Baronio.

Upon the accession of SIXTUS V, who became his new protector, Ippolito's career accelerated once more. Sixtus V put him in charge of the datary on 15 May 1585, and on the following December 18 made him a cardinal. This sudden promotion was all the more surprising since up until then Aldobrandini was little known outside the CURIA. His appointment to the office of GRAND PENITENTIARY, on 12 June 1586, came as further confirmation that he enjoyed the favor of Sixtus V. Even more so was his appointment in 1588 as legate *a latere* in Poland. The choice of Aldobrandini was due not only to his personal qualities, but also to the fact that he was independent of the factions within the SACRED COLLEGE. The mission of the legate consisted of bringing peace to a country that had been bitterly divided by the rivalry of two competitors to the throne of King Etienne Bathory. The armed conflict had ended in 1587 with the victory of the crown prince of Sweden, Sigismond Vasa, over Archduke Maximilian of Habsburg, whom he had taken prisoner. Following difficult negotiations, a peace agreement was concluded on 9 March 1589, and the legate returned to Rome at the end of May. His diplomatic triumph had given him an aura of prestige and success, and he now became one of the most prominent members of the Sacred College.

Following the death of Sixtus V (27 August 1590), three popes succeeded each other to the pontifical throne in the space of a year and a half—URBAN VII, GREGORY XIV, and INNOCENT IX. They had all been elected with the support of the king of Spain, a support that was indispensable at that time. Phillip II had not favored the choice of Aldobrandini during the first conclave following the death of Urban VII. He subsequently included his name in the list of candidates he supported, without, however, placing it at the top of the list. Aldobrandini was finally unanimously elected on 30 January 1592, after twenty days of discussions and rounds of voting during which none of the candidates favored by Phillip II got a clear majority vote. Clement VIII was 56 years old. He was an indefatigable worker and a scrupulous person. He was also an anxious man, which explains his difficulty in making decisions. But his most outstanding character trait was his profound and very genuine piety. He celebrated mass every morning and confessed every evening. During the day, he liked to meditate in the chapel. He observed strict fasts, especially on Friday. He was seen to follow barefoot behind processions in the streets of Rome. During his pontificate, he visited the seven Churches more than a hundred and sixty times. During the HOLY YEAR of 1600, he visited the four major BASILICAS some sixty times to gain the INDULGENCE of the Jubilee.

While his own personal needs were simple and modest, he displayed great prodigality as far as his family was concerned. According to a practice established during the papacy of Paul IV, he entrusted the direction of the STATE SECRETARIAT to his nephews Pietro Aldobrandini (son of his brother Pietro) and Cinzio Passeri Aldobrandini (son of his sister Giulia). They were also charged with the administration of the Ecclesiastical State, and Clement VIII divided their responsibilities according to geographical considerations. He then elevated both of them to the dignity of cardinal on 17 September 1593. After a few years Pietro gained the upper hand over his cousin and concentrated all of the traditional powers of the CARDINAL NEPHEW in his own hands. However, he had no real autonomous power to make decisions, as the pope personally took an interest in all matters relating to work, reading all dispatches and noting them by hand.

His election as pope on 30 January 1592 had made Clement VIII the temporal sovereign of the Ecclesiastical State, the head of Christendom (i.e. the Catholic Church), and the supreme pastor of the Universal Church. He was an authoritarian leader who pursued and expanded on the efforts of Sixtus V toward greater administrative centralization. An example is the creation on 30 October 1592, of the CONGREGATION of Buon Governo. In 1598, Clement included the duchy of Ferrara, a vassal of the Holy See, among the territories he administered. Following the death of Alfonso II d'Este, there had been no legitimate heir to take over the throne of the duchy. Clement VIII was also responsible for several urbanization projects in Rome on the occasion of the jubilee year 1600.

From the time of his accession to the papacy Clement VIII had to deal with a major problem: during that period France was torn by a serious crisis in its political and religious succession. By virtue of Salic law, Bourbon, king of Navarre, had succeeded his cousin Henri III as the last Valois king, on 2 August 1589. He was a Huguenot, condemned by Sixtus V in 1585 and declared unsuitable to succeed to the French throne. Despite this, a large section of Catholic opinion had recognized Henry IV as king. However, the Leaguers, radical Catholics backed by the king of Spain and hispanophile popes, remained resolutely hostile to him, and the throne-to-be still vacant. Henri realized that only his conversion could put an end to division in the kingdom, and in 1592 he decided to become a Catholic. He converted in St. Denis on 25 July 1593 and was crowned on 27 February 1594. During this period, he sent several emissaries to Clement VIII to ask that the censures pronounced against him by Sixtus V be lifted. The emissaries were Cardinal Gondi and the Marquess of Pisano, in October 1592, and the Duke of Nevers in October 1593. Clement VIII had long been reticent about granting absolution and feared a Gallic SCHISM. However, he gave in to the arguments of Jacques Davy du Perron, the appointed bishop of Evreux and Arnaud d'Ossat, both future cardinals. On 17 September 1595 he solemnly pronounced the absolution of Henri IV at ST. PETER'S in Rome. The king was represented by his two legal stand-ins or "procureurs."

Clement VIII sought to seal the reconciliation between France and the Holy See and reestablish the diplomatic relations broken off in 1588. He sent the cardinal of Florence as *a latere* legate to France. His mission was to secure Henry IV's ratification of the act of absolution, to reorganize the church of France in the wake of previous difficulties, and to mediate between the kings of Spain and France, at war since 1595, on behalf of the pope. The absolution of Henry IV by Clement VIII and the lengthy legation by the cardinal of Florence (1596–98) had incalculable consequences on both the religious and political fronts. By accepting Henry IV back into the fold of Roman Catholicism and recognizing his legitimate right to be king, the pope made it possible to secure the acceptance of the most reticent Leaguers, allowing for the full flowering of Tridentine reforms. Indeed, these had already begun in the 1580s but had been hampered by the civil war. Soon a number of former Leaguers could once more be found among the dévot.

Through his actions the pope was restoring the independence of the Holy See, and becoming the arbiter of Christendom. The cardinal of Florence took part in the peace negotiations between France and Spain, which culminated in the treaty of Vervins on 2 May 1598. Two years later another *a latere* legate, Cardinal Aldobrandini, the pope's nephew, presided over the signing of the treaty of Lyon between Henry IV and the Duke of Savoy, on 17 January 1601. Clement VIII had succeeded in achieving peace between the Catholic powers, an objective that had been sought by all the sixteenth-century popes but had eluded most of them. During the rest of his reign, he tried successfully to maintain the fragile peace between France and Spain, notably during the diplomatic crisis of 1601 and the tariff war of 1604. He was less successful in uniting the Catholic princes in a league against the TURKS, who were threatening the expansion of Christendom to the East. However, he spared no effort in mobilizing opposition against the Turks. He deployed an intensive diplomatic campaign, paid enormous subsidies to support the Emperor's war effort, and finally, sponsored papal expeditionary forces in 1595, 1598, and 1601. (It was in this last campaign that Gian Francesco Aldobrandini, the pope's nephew, met his death at Varadin on 17 September 1601.)

As head of the Catholic Church, Clement VIII was profoundly influenced by the spirit of the Council of Trent, and was a firm believer in CATHOLIC REFORM. He undertook to implement its program of reform everywhere, beginning with his diocese in Rome. He personally made the pastoral visit from 1592 to 1600 and again in 1602–1603. An uncompromising guardian of the faith who participated in the proceedings of the congregation of the INQUISITION on a weekly basis, Clement took various steps to strengthen existing regulations. Between 1595 and 1605, more than thirty people were condemned to death for the crime of HERESY. The most famous execution was that of Giordano Bruno, in 1600. A new *Index Librorum prohibitorum* was published in 1596. The papacy of Clement VIII was also marked by great activity in the publishing of Biblical and liturgical material. The first official edition of the Vulgate appeared in 1592, followed by the Roman Pontifical in 1596, the Bishop's Ceremonial in 1600, the BREVIARY in 1602, and the Roman MISSAL in 1604. The pope intervened in the theological controversy on the relationship between grace and free choice that pitted DOMINICANS against JESUITS, and Augustinians against Molinists. Following the publication in 1588 of the *Concordia liberi arbitrii*, by the Jesuit Luis de Molina, the dispute had acquired a new dimension. In 1595, Clement VIII deliberated over the matter but was hesitant to pronounce a condemnation. He appointed a commission of cardinals to study the question at great length. They were called the congregation *de auxiliis*. From 20 March 1602, Clement himself presided over their deliberations. The discussions had been practically completed, and the decision of the pope was deemed imminent when on 3 March 1605, he died from an attack of apoplexy. His successors chose not to issue a decision on the matter.

Finally, Clement VIII infused the Church with a vigorous missionary spirit. In 1599, he instituted the congregation *super negotiis sanctae fidei et religionis catholicae*, or *propaganda fide*. It had only a brief existence in this preliminary form, but was definitively reestablished by GREGORY XV in 1622. The efforts of Pope Clement took place on three fronts: Protestant Christianity, Orthodox Christianity, and non-Christians. Unable to prevent the promulgation of the Edict of Nantes in France, he decided to make the best of things by demanding the implementation of the clauses ordering the reestablishment of Catholicism in those regions where it no longer existed. In two other countries, he tried in vain to profit from the accession of new leaders to obtain advantages for the Church. In Sweden, following the death of Jean III Vasa (1593), the crown went to Sigismond III Vasa, king of Poland, and a Catholic. However, the latter was unable to restore Catholicism in his new kingdom. In England the king of Scotland, James VI Stuart, succeeded Elizabeth, who had died in 1603. He assumed the name of James I. The pope thought he discerned favorable intentions on the part of the new king, and even the possibility of a conversion. Here again, though, he was disappointed.

He was more successful in his attempts to rally the EASTERN CHURCHES, separated from the see of Rome. In March 1592, he sent a nuncio to the Coptic patriarch of Alexandria, Gabriel. This mission was completely successful, since the act of obedience of the Coptic Church to the Roman Church, proclaimed on 25 January 1595, was solemnly ratified on 25 June 1597. However, this union did not survive its two participants. On the other hand, the union with the Ruthenian Church (known today as the Ukrainian Church), decided on by the Synod of Brest-Litovsk and solemnly proclaimed in Rome on 25 December 1595, was a lasting one.

Clement VIII also sought to develop MISSIONS in far-flung countries. He took particular interest in the evangelization of Latin America (Chile, Peru, and Mexico) and the Far East. In 1595, he was responsible for founding the ecclesiastical province of Manila in the Philippines. In 1600, he extended to the mendicant orders the privilege of Gregory XIII, which had reserved the evangelization of Japan and China for the Jesuits. He also sent the first Catholic missionaries to Persia.

Pope Clement was an unyielding and uncompromising defender of Christian dogma, but he can also be seen as the father of the prodigal son (in his relationship with Henri IV), and as the good shepherd concerned with ensuring the unity of the Church. He was also an accomplished diplomat, quick to seize any opportunity for conciliation. His legates and nuncios, who were sent as far as Moscow and Persia, were indefatigable agents working for the higher interest of religion, the spread of the Gospel, and the fight against heretics and infidels. In taking stock of the papacy of Clement VIII, there are great contrasts and great successes and failures. Yet Aldobrandini remains one of the great figures of Catholicism in the post-Tridentine period.

Bernard Barbiche

Bibliography

Borromeo, A. "Clemente VIII," *DBI*, 26 (1982), 259–82.

Jaitner, K. *Die Hauptinstruktionen Clemens' VIII. für die Nuntien und Legaten an den europaischen Fürstenhofen, 1592–1605*, Tübingen, 1984, 2 vols. (*Instructiones pontificum Romanorum*); "Il nepotismo di papa Clemente VIII (1592–1605); il dramma del cardinale Cinzio Aldobrandini," *Archivio storico italiano*, 146 (1988), 57–93.

Mols, R. "Clement VIII," *DHGE*, 12 (1953), 1249–97.

Pastor, 23 and 24.

Wojtyska, H. D. *Acta nuntiatura poloniae*, I Rome, 1990, 232–3.

CLEMENT IX. *Giulio Rospigliosi (b. Pistoia, 27 January 1600, d. Rome, 6 December 1669). Elected pope 20 June 1667, crowned 26 June 1667. Buried at St. Peter's in Rome, transferred in 1680 to St. Mary Major.*

After pursuing classical studies at the ROMAN COLLEGE, Giulio Rospigliosi enrolled at the University of Pisa. He became a Doctor of Philosophy and Theology (1624) and made a career in the Roman CURIA, and became closely associated with the Barberini family. In 1631 he was appointed secretary of the congregation of rites, then referendary at the Tribunal of the Two Signatures (1632), consultor of the apostolic PENITENTIARY (1641), vicar of the chapter of St. Mary Major (1643), and *Sigillatore* of the penitentiary (1643). In 1644 he was appointed archbishop of Tarsus and apostolic nuncio in Spain (1644–53). He received the episcopate on March 29. Giulio was governor of Rome during the vacancy of the Holy See (1655), and was chosen by ALEXANDER VII to be secretary of state. On 9 April 1657 he was made Cardinal of the Title of Saint-Sixtus. On the death of Alexander in 1667, Giulio was elected pope as the result of a rare convergence of French and Spanish interests. He received support from a group that was under the influence of Cardinal Azzolini, for whom the new pope had worked as secretary of state.

As a prelate, Giulio Rospigliosi was a lover of poetry and drama. He was the author of plays that have been put to music by Landi (*San Alessio*, 1631), and Rossi (*Il Palazzo incantato d'Atlante*, 1642). Clement was considered an affable and moderate man, and his sense of moderation was made evident by the papal name he chose and by his motto "*Aliis non sibi clemens.*" He was undoubtedly a conciliator, but always kept the objective of a reformist papacy in view: the strengthening of the common front for a Catholic Europe.

This concern may be seen in Clement's support of efforts to achieve reconciliation between Spain and France. The papal nuncio Franciotti presided over the preparatory conferences for the treaty of Aix-la-Chapelle in 1668. The pope's conciliatory attitude may be seen in the cautious approach of the Holy See over the annulling of the marriage of Marie of Savoy to Alphonso VI, King of Portugal. The annulment granted her the dispensation necessary to allow her to marry his brother, Pedro, in December 1668. Clement's approach was even more apparent in the manner in which the Jansenist affair was resolved. To ease the tensions created in France by the resistance of four bishops to the anti-Jansenist stance of the bull *Regiminis Apostolici* (1665), Clement agreed to a negotiated compromise. He gave his agreement at the request of Louis XIV. The negotiations led to the decision by Rome to accept the submission of the prelates, despite certain doubts.

As early as the time of his mission in Spain, Giulio Rospigliosi showed great interest in halting the advance of the Ottomans in the Mediterranean. Despite all the efforts to defend the besieged citadel of Candia in Crete, an international expedition failed to prevent the fall of the town on 6 September 1669. The brief pontificate of Clement IX was characterized by a striving for continuity. The pope chose to abide by the basic principles of the Curia, and was moderate in showing favor to the members of his own family. He generously used the patrimony of the church in the works done in St. Mary Major and the Sant'Angelo bridge. The congregation of religious was reorganized and a new dicastery created: the Congregation of Indulgences and RELICS (*Motu proprio: In ipsis pontificatus nostri primordiis*, July 1669). Clement IX held three consistories, canonized Pedro of Alcantara and Maria Maddelena dei of Pazzi (1669), and beatified Rosa of Lima (1668).

Jacques Gres-Gayer

Bibliography

DBI, XXVI, 282–93.

DHE, XII, 1297–1313.

LTK, II, 1227.

Brezzi, "La personalità e l'opera di Giulio Rospigliosi," *Bolletino storico pistoiese*, LXIX (1966), 3–17.

Bullarium Romanum Taur., XVII, 512–839.

Cauchies, A. "La paix de Clement IX (1668–1669)," *Revue d'histoire et de Littèrature religieuses*, 3 (1898), 481–501.

Cristofori, R. "Le opere Teatrali di Giulio Rospigliosi," *Studi romani*, XXVII (1979) 302–16.

Darricau, R. "Une heure mèamorable dans les rapports entre la France et le Saint Siège: le pontificat de Clement IX," *Bolletino storico pistoiese*, LXXI (1969), 73–98.

Dieudonne, P. "Fragilité de la Paix de l'église," *Chroniques de Port-Royal*, 29 (1980), 17–33.

Ferrali, S. "Giulio Rospigliosi sacerdote," *Bolletino storico pistoiese*, LXXI (1969), 73–98.

Hierarchia catholica, V, 3–5.

"La diplomatie pontificale et la paix d'Aix-la-Chapelle de 1668, d'après les archives secretes du Saint Siège," *Bulletin de l'institut historique belge de Rome*, XXVII (1952), 249–68.

Pastor, 31.

Petrocchi, M. La politica della Santa Sede di fronte alla invasione ottoman, Naples, 1955.

Sanesi, I. *Poesie musichale di Giulio Rospigliosi*, Pistoia, 1894.

Terlinden, C. *Le pape Clement IX et la Guerre de Candie*, Louvain-Paris, 1904.

CLEMENT X. *Emilio Altieri (b. Rome, 12 July 1590, d. Rome, 22 July 1676). Elected pope 29 April 1670, crowned 11 May. Buried at St. Peter's, Rome.*

Emilio was the son of Lorenzo and Vittoria Delfino, members of an old Roman family. He studied at the Roman college, and then at university. He was a doctor in civil and canon law and in 1611 started work as a lawyer in the service of Giambattista Pamfili, later known as Pope INNOCENT X, but at that time auditor of the Rota. Following in the footsteps of his older brother Giambattista, bishop of Camerino in 1624 and future cardinal (1589–1645), Emilio embarked upon an ecclesiastical career. He entered the priesthood on 6 April 1624 and was the auditor of Giambattista Lancellotti during his nunciature in Poland from 1622 to 1627. On 29 November 1627, his brother Giambattista relinquished the bishopric of Camerino to him, and Emilio kept it until 1666. He then looked after his diocese and carried out a number of functions within the papal State under URBAN VIII, including the posts of governor of Loreto and of the Marches. His brother's promotion to cardinal in 1643, and even more importantly, the election of Pope Innocent X, opened the door to an even more brilliant career. He was appointed nuncio of Naples at the end of 1644, where the situation (Naples was striving to free itself from Spanish domination) was particularly delicate. Apparently Altieri did not cope very well with the demands of the viceroy of Spain, the intrigues of the Neapolitan nobles, or the popular uprising of Masaniello in 1647. He was almost recalled at the beginning of 1648, but stayed in Naples until 1652. He had fallen out of favor with Innocent X and withdrew to his bishopric.

The election of Alexander VII in 1655 provided a new boost to his career. He was appointed secretary of the Congregation of Bishops and regulars in 1657, consultor of the HOLY OFFICE, and was appreciated by Giulio Rospigliosi, then secretary of state. When Rospigliosi was elected pope in 1667 under the name of Clement IX, he chose Altieri as his CHAMBERLAIN. This was, of course, a domestic position, but one from which one could hope to be promoted to cardinal. Indeed, Clement IX did make him a cardinal on 29 November 1669, a few days before his death. The new cardinal was almost 80 years old when he entered the conclave that began 20 December 1669, without yet having received the cardinal's hat. None could have foreseen that Emilio Altieri would leave the conclave as the new pope. But the different factions within the Sacred College could not agree on a viable candidate who was not the exclusive favorite of the ambassadors of France and Spain, who attempted to influence the conclave. The conclave was dragging on, without an end in view. Finally, it was Flavio Chigi, head of the faction of cardinals of ALEXANDER VII, who pushed the candidacy of Altieri. Chigi's faction was the largest within the college, and perhaps they harbored the secret hope that soon, another election would have to be held.

The new pope took the name of Clement X in honor of his predecessor and benefactor. During his long career, he had gained experience in affairs, but lacked the knowledge that comes from occupying important political or diplomatic posts. His piety was widely acknowledged. He led an exemplary private life, and he had a well-developed sense of economy. However, despite his robust constitution, the pope's advanced age led observers to expect his imminent death and a certain lack of energy. In view of this, the pope could not avoid resorting to NEPOTISM help him discharge his duties as head of the Church. However, none of his many brothers and sisters had had any children, and on 30 April 1670 Clement X adopted Cardinal Paluzzi, the uncle of the husband of Laura Caterina, the daughter of one of his cousins. Paluzzo Paluzzi degli Albertoni (1623–98) would, from then on, be known as Cardinal Altieri. He was made *cardinale padrone* or prime minister, an all-powerful figure who was indispensable to the elderly pope. While Paluzzi-Altieri was not lacking in abilities, he did not neglect his personal enrichment. While he was prime minister, the cardinals' secretaries of state Federigo Borromeo (d. 1673), then Francesco Nerli (1636–1708), and the cardinal *prodataire* Gaspare Carpegna (1625–1714), merely carried out his orders. The pope chose as his chamberlains the Romans Camillo Massimo (d. 1677), and Alessandro Crescenzio (d. 1688), whom he later promoted to cardinal, then the Neapolitan Antonio Pignatelli, the future INNOCENT XII.

A loan fund for small traders working in the food sector was one of the achievements of the government of the ecclesiastical state. Clement X sought to develop and protect locally produced goods by increasing duties on silks and woolen articles imported into the Papal States. However, an edict of 11 September 1674, which imposed a new tax expressly on foreign ambassadors (like the tax imposed on the cardinals and the apostolic palace), caused a long, drawn-out conflict with Cardinal Altieri. The ambassadors, of the emperor and of France, Spain, and Venice, albeit representing countries at war among themselves, joined together to defend their privileges of financial exemption and claim reparation for the measure. The conflict, which became known as the "affair of the ambassadors," became so acrimonious that Altieri soon found himself in a very difficult situation. The pope was harassed by the ambassadors, and tired and exasperated by a situation that he could not resolve. The ambassadors felt he could be prevailed upon to sacrifice his prime minister, especially because the ambassadors' noisy protests against Altieri had unleashed a violent campaign in Rome. The sovereigns—especially Louis XIV—supported their ambassadors' conduct. Indeed, the French court hoped that in exchange for reconciliation with Altieri, two of its candidates would be appointed as cardinals. The crisis came to a head during the audience of 21 May 1675. The French ambassador, the duke of Estrées, was a man of violent temper and was exasperated by the pope's procrastination and contradictory statements with regard to the appointment of the cardinals. He grew so angry that the pontiff warned him that he could be excommunicated. Clement X, highly indignant, named six cardinals of his own choosing on 27 May, following the audience. This decisive action by the pope served to reconcile Altieri with the other ambassadors, who were deeply relieved that France had not won appointment for her candidates for cardinal through the revocation of the ill-considered edict, but diplomatic relations with Louis XIV were effectively broken off until the end of the pontificate of Clement X.

Under the guidance of architects Bernini and Carlo Rainaldi, Clement X carried out several projects to beautify the city of Rome. The tomb of Clement IX at St. Mary Major, the magnificent stairway which enclosed the apse of the basilica, and the completion of the statues on the Sant'Angelo bridge were all completed during his pontificate. The construction of a fountain in St. Peter's Square, matching the one built by Maderno for Paul V, are further achievements of Clement's papacy.

Among the saints canonized by him were Gaetano of Thiene, founder of the Theatine movement, Francis Borgia the Jesuit general, and Rose of Lima, the first South American saint. He beatified Pope PIUS V and John of the Cross, the reformer of the Carmelites. By a decree of 1672, Clement X issued regulations concerning the veneration of relics discovered in the CATACOMBS. The year 1675 was celebrated as a HOLY YEAR in Rome. The pope performed some of the usual ceremonies and made several visits to the seven churches, despite frequent attacks of gout.

Missionary work during Clement X's papacy included the establishment of the archbishopric of Quebec, the first diocese in North America, on 30 April 1674. He placed Francois de Laval de Montigny at its head. It marked the culmination of more than 15 years of negotiations with the intervention of the Congregation of Propaganda and of Louis XIV. Doctrinal disputes had abated, and there was relative calm. The official silence imposed in 1669 was respected, even though the writings of the Jansenists still provoked controversy. The papal Bull *Superna magni patrisfamilias*, issued at the beginning of the pope's pontificate on 21 June 1670, definitively settled the question of relations between bishops and the regulars of the diocese, after decades of stormy incidents.

Although the pontiff had the exclusive right to appoint cardinals, Clement X was constantly besieged by demands from the emperor, from the Spanish court, and especially from France, to promote their own national candidates alternately with those candidates submitted by the pope. Clement X made an effort to promote members of the Curia or his relations by adoption. In 1672 Louis XIV, through the use of pressure and negotiation, secured the appointment to cardinal of the bishop of Laon, Cesar

d'Estrées, and the Archbishop of Toulouse, Pierre de Bonzy. The emperor used the same methods to ensure the appointment of the abbot of Fulda, Bade-Durlach, and the queen regent of Spain obtained that of Nithard, her Ambassador to Rome. From 1674, Louis XIV lobbied hard to ensure that Toussaint de Forbin-Fanson, bishop of Marseilles and his emissary in Poland, be promoted to cardinal as a candidate of the new king of Poland, Sobieski. We have seen how the French court tried to use the Affair of the Ambassadors to achieve its own ends, and how Clement X put a stop to this by appointing five people of his own choosing. They were nuncios or curialists and an English Dominican, Howard of Norfolk, and all were appointed on 27 May 1675. It was the last set of promotions of his pontificate.

On the diplomatic front, difficulties arose beginning in 1672. From the month of April, Louis XIV of France led the war, dubbed the War of Holland, against the United Provinces. At the beginning of the conflict, Clement X had hoped that Catholicism would be restored in the heretical lands. However, he soon became concerned that the troubles would spread to the main Catholic powers, the empire and Spain, which were allies against France. The situation became even more complicated when the TURKS took advantage of the weakness of Poland to attack it and seize the strategic fortress of Kamenets-Podolski in August 1672. Clement X was acutely conscious of the risks to Christendom, and anxious to secure unity among the Catholic kingdoms in a crusade against the infidels. He offered his services as a mediator in 1673, but suffered numerous setbacks. The first congress, which opened in Cologne in June 1673, was a failure, the emperor having ordered the removal of Prince William of Fürstenberg, a plenipotentiary representative and one of the principal agents of Louis XIV in Germany. Whereas the emperor had immediately accepted the pope's offer of mediation, France and Spain did not give a positive reply until the end of 1674. Furthermore, the three powers chose a heretical city, Nejmegen, for the resumption of peace talks, without regard for the mediation of Clement X. From the spring of 1675, papal diplomatic efforts were aimed at ensuring that the talks resume in a Catholic city, and that Prince William of Furstenberg be reinstated as a member of the papal guard.

Despite this, Clement X resolved in October 1675 to send papal nuncios to Vienna, Paris, Madrid, and Nejmegen to conduct peace talks. He died, however, before the start of the congress. Clement X was more successful in Poland. The former auditor of the nunciature sent generous subsidies and an energetic nuncio, Buonvisi, who managed to bring about a successful offensive against the Turks, under the command of Sobieski. Meanwhile, the weak-willed king, Michel Wisnoiviecki, died on 10 November 1673. Poland was plunged into the intrigues of the interregnum, intrigues in which the emperor and the French were involved.

Clement X proclaimed strict neutrality with respect to the candidates who were Catholic and in a position to bear arms, but welcomed the election of Sobieski, giving financial support to Poland's war effort against the infidels until his death. Sobieski, however, presented Forbin-Janson, one of the people responsible for his election, as a candidate to be cardinal, thus placing the pope in a delicate position.

Relations with France were problematic for the entire papacy of Clement X. In December 1672, Louis XIV issued an edict whereby several orders and other groups would be linked to the military and hospital orders of Our Lady of Mount Carmel and Saint Lazarus of Jerusalem. He wished to make them into commanderies for the benefit of his officers. Similarly, an edict of March 1673 automatically transformed the charges of the bankers who were forwarding agents into titles. These bankers were used by the papal court for forwarding to private persons. While Louis XIV and his ministers saw this move as a purely financial expedient, the pope saw the measure as a usurpation of papal authority by the lay powers. Despite protests from Rome, Louis XIV insisted on implementing the edict.

Relations with Spain were no better. There was conflict in Milan and Naples over the question of the right to asylum, beginning in July 1674; a fresh revolt by Messina against the Spaniards gave rise to some tension. In the summer of 1670 the pontifical government had renewed diplomatic relations with Portugal, following the break caused by the war of independence against Spain in 1670.

Clement X died after a short illness. Although his pontificate had not been beset by any major crises, it nevertheless illustrated the weakness of a government presided over by an elderly man and his adopted nephew. He was not, however, as lacking in energy as has often been claimed, and he did demonstrate a certain awareness of the higher interest of Christendom.

Sigolene de Dainville-Barbiche

Bibliography

De Dainville-Barbiche, S. "Clement X," *Dictionnaire du Grand Siècle*, Paris, 1990, 334–5.

De Dainville-Barbiche, S. *Correspondance du nonce en France Fabrizio Spada (1674–75)*, Rome, 1982.

Mols, R. "Clement X," *DHGE*, 12 (1953), 1313–26.

O'Connor, J. T. "French relations with the papacy during the Dutch war," *Proceedings of the Annual Meeting of the Western Society for French History*, 13 (1986), 51–9.

Osbat, L. "Clemente X," *DBI*, 26 (1982), 293–302.

Pastor, 31.

CLEMENT XI. *Giovanni Francesco Albani (b. Urbino, 3 July 1649, d. Rome, 19 March 1721). Elected pope on 23 November 1700. Buried at St. Peter's, Rome.*

Giovanni Francesco Albani was born into a distinguished family belonging to the nobility of the small duchy of Urbino. His family had close links to the HOLY SEE and Roman ecclesiastical circles. His grandfather, Orazio, had been a Roman senator, his father, Carlo, was the chamberlain of Cardinal Francesco Barberini. In 1660, Giovanni went to Rome to study with the Jesuits at the Roman COLLEGE, where he showed great interest in the teachings of the Byzantinist Poussines. Under his direction, Giovanni dedicated himself to researching the Oriental manuscripts of Grottaferrata and translating from Greek. He obtained his degree at Urbino in 1668. Back in Rome, Giovanni frequented academic and intellectual circles and libraries and was an assiduous visitor of the ruins and artifacts of antiquity in the city. With the protection of the powerful Cardinal Barberini, he quickly moved up through the ranks of the Curia bureaucracy. He was referendary of the two Signatures, governor of Rieti, Sabina, and Orvieto, and finally secretary of briefs (3 October 1687). Meanwhile, he had obtained benefices for two canonries (St. Peter of the Vatican and St. Lawrence in Damaso). Pope ALEXANDER VIII made him a cardinal on 13 February 1690. He was an enlightened ecclesiastic with great competence in jurisdictional and administrative matters. This made him an appreciated member of several Roman congregations and a protector of religious orders (among others, the Minims, the Carthusians, and the Knights of St. George). Several pontiffs trusted his judgment on matters of particular importance. Alexander VIII, when he was dying, asked Cardinal Albani to read the papal bull canceling the decisions of the general assembly of the French clergy in 1682. Pope Innocent entrusted to him the drafting of the text condemning NEPOTISM.

Cardinal Albani's pro-French stance was soon apparent, though it is still unclear whether he played a role in the decision made by the king of Spain, Charles II, to choose Philip of Anjou as his successor. During the CONCLAVE, which began on 27 September 1700 and ended on 9 October, there were differences among the various groups of voters. These differences were fed by fears of Cardinal Albani's pro-French leanings. Thirty-eight cardinals were present, later joined by twenty others, out of a total of sixty-six. Finally Cardinal Albani, with strong support from the *zelanti* (cardinals who wanted a non-political pope with the Church's interests at heart), received the votes of all the cardinals, who were convinced that he would defend the independence of the Church. They were also sure that, within the Church itself, he would effectively fight against the nepotism of his predecessor. He left the conclave as the new pope on 23 November 1700 and was consecrated a bishop on the 30th and crowned on 8 December.

The beginning of Clement XI's pontificate coincided with that of a long war of succession for the Spanish throne between Philip of Anjou and Charles of Habsburg. Clement XI was inclined to side with the French, for reasons of political expediency, but made an effort to be neutral and work in favor of peace. He feared that the opposing armies would invade Italian territory; however, Louis XIV invaded Milan and northern Italy. In retaliation, the imperial troops occupied Parma, a fief of the Holy See. The pope had hoped to keep the Italian princes apart from military operations but saw these hopes frustrated. Relations with Emperor Leopold I and his successor, Joseph I, became increasingly difficult. Toward the middle of 1706, all the pope's hopes ended in bitter disappointment. Not only were the French beaten in Ramillies (24 May), losing a large part of Flanders, but Archduke Charles was proclaimed king of Spain in June of the same year. He established his seat provisionally in Barcelona because Philip V had occupied Madrid. To further compound matters and add to the pope's disappointment, a large part of northern Italy had fallen to the imperial forces. During these operations, the enemy armies were crossing back and forth across papal territory. The royal *exequatur* was imposed everywhere, and fiscal exemptions favoring the clergy were revoked. On 24 May 1708, Comacchio, an important fishing and salt-trading center on the Ferraro coast, was invaded. The pope made several protests, but to no avail. Clement XI began to feel the full measure of the imperial power. It almost frightened him, but he was a realist. At the same time, he was becoming aware of the decline of French hegemony. He was therefore forced to soften his stance vis-à-vis the Habsburgs, and this new attitude immediately bore fruit: their troops withdrew from the occupied territories, and war expenses were reimbursed. As could be expected, Philip V suffered a setback as a result of this change in papal diplomacy, which was unfavorable to him.

The clearest sign of the disagreement between Clement XI and the king of Spain was the recognition by the pope of the sovereignty of Charles of Habsburg (14 October 1709). Diplomatic relations with Madrid were also broken off, another clear indication of discord. The pope sought to compensate for this by creating a nunciature in Barcelona. A state Church was created in Spain, and Clement XI did not hesitate to show his opposition, condemning the appointment of new bishops and unilaterally abrogating decrees which, he claimed adversely affected pontifical prerogatives.

The first policy measures taken by Joseph I, who succeeded Leopold following the latter's premature death on 17 April 1711, revealed a clear antipapal orientation. Rome's representatives were received with extreme reserve and suspicion during meetings or high-level diets,

when they defended the rights of the Holy See. The legate Domenico Passionei was excluded in the most blatant fashion from the peace talks at Utrecht. He obtained, after much negotiation, an agreement to the wishes of the pope, who, among other things, sought ratification for article 4 of the treaty of Ryswick (1697). This provision introduced guarantees for Catholics in the territories handed over to Protestant princes after 1702. In the final phase, the emperor and Louis XIV dealt directly with the problems and shamelessly promoted their own interests. The treaty of Rastatt (1714) did take into account the wishes of Clement XI with respect to the treaty of Ryswick. It was, however, counterbalanced by other compromise measures harmful to the interests of the Holy See. These included the granting of Sicily to the Duke of Savoy, and, even more important, legitimization of the succession of Lutheran princes on Catholic territory. There was noisy protest against a speech made during the CONSISTORY of 21 January 1715, but it also showed the intrinsic weakness and failures of pontifical diplomacy.

In the same speech, however, Clement XI, after detailing the results of the peace treaties, stated his intention of responding to another request to help Venice in the face of the Turkish threat. War had been declared on 8 December 1714, and the pope had managed to secure the help of the German Catholic princes as well as of the kings of Poland and Portugal in the war effort. In Vienna, though, the authorities were concerned at the improvement of relations between the Holy See and Philip V. For his part, Louis XIV, who would die shortly, had no intention of giving up his friendship with the Ottomans. The Turks won the Peloponnesus, and Corfu was in danger of falling to them. Finally, the emperor decided to enter the fray. He was satisfied by the large sums of money deducted from the ecclesiastical tithes, and he had received assurance that Spain would not invade the Vatican's Italian possessions. On 13 April 1716, he concluded an alliance with Venice which immediately yielded results: victory for Prince Eugene at Patravardin in Hungary, and the eviction of the Turks from Corfu.

At that point, Giulio Alberoni, representing the duke of Parma and supporters of the policies of the Farnese, intervened to convince Philip V to enter the war on the side of the European powers and against the Turks. Alberoni's controversial action and its real objective soon became evident: he was far more interested in furthering the purpose of the Farnese in Italy than in furthering the purpose of the Holy See. In fact, while the Spanish fleet was setting sail to fight against the Turkish enemy, Philip V was directing his ships to Sardinia, which he ordered his troops to occupy to the detriment of the emperor. The pope was extremely embarrassed, and the reaction from Vienna was swift in coming. The emperor demanded that some of his candidates be promoted to cardinal and that the pontiff break off relations with Spain. The CONCORDAT signed on 26 August 1717 bound the pope to review his policy toward the Spaniards. In fact, Clement XI found himself in an awkward position. He was badly served by his ministers and upset by the lack of scruples shown by Philip V. He therefore did not hesitate to adopt extreme measures, such as revoking the ecclesiastical privileges that had been granted to Spain. This marked the beginning of a long series of reprisals, starting with the confiscation of ecclesiastical property in Malaga and Seville, the dissolving of the tribunal of the nunciature in Madrid, and finally, the occupation of Sicily. The empire, France, England, and the United Provinces reacted by signing a new alliance and declaring war against Philip V. The Spanish fleet was wiped out by the English. Unexpectedly, Philip decided to join the Quadruple Alliance. He withdrew his troops from Sardinia and abruptly dismissed Alberoni, who was brought to trial, and the empire gained Sicily. Even while the two sides continued to pursue state interests, there was a gradual normalization in relations between Rome and Madrid. Clement XI placed his stamp of approval on this by signing an agreement on 11 March 1721, a few days before his death.

This intense activity on the European political and diplomatic scene did not prevent the pope from dealing with matters directly related to religion and faith. Indeed, the revival of JANSENISM, which now gave rise to more than mere moral concern, was the pope's main worry. Almost at the start of his pontificate, Clement XI was called on to take a stance on two questions of great importance. The first was the canonical trial of the apostolic vicar of the Netherlands, Pietro Codde, who was accused of allowing the spread of Jansenism in the territory. Despite the protest of the Dutch States General, Codde was dismissed, but Clement XI could not get the clergy to accept his successor, Teodoro de Cock. The second matter was a difficult and drawn-out affair. It arose from a case of conscience raised by a Normandy priest (in fact, a religious from Clermont-Ferrand). He had asked a number of theologians and members of the ecclesiastical authority if it was acceptable to grant absolution to a penitent. The point was that the penitent, a woman, claimed to subscribe to the anti-Jansenist formula of Alexander VII while at the same time maintaining a silent refusal with respect to some passages that were deemed unacceptable, such as those that attributed the five condemned proposals to the *Augustinus* of Jansenius. The case had been discussed at the Sorbonne in the summer of 1701, and a group of theologians had replied in the affirmative, greatly outnumbering those who judged that absolution should not be granted. The bishop of Paris, Cardinal de Noailles, had taken a tolerant stance. Clement XI intervened first with a brief (12 February 1703), then with the papal bull *Vineam Domini* (16 July 1705). In the latter,

the formal and trenchant condemnation of the theory of respectful silence was totally in keeping with the rule expressed by his predecessors, and it did not take into account the protests of Louis XIV and members of his court. The decisions of Pope Clement were the subject of learned and subtle discussions by the clergy and the French bishops, as well as the sovereign himself. It was only after fresh intervention by the pope and his legates that the decisions were accepted by the bishops, with only a few exceptions. The nuns of Port-Royal, however, were increasingly opposed to the bull and were reticent about giving their outright support to it. Louis XIV was concerned about the situation developing even further and requested that the pope intervene once more. Clement XI decreed that the abbey be closed (11 July 1709). It was at this point that Cardinal de Noailles stepped in and, with the agreement of the king, ordered the transfer of the nuns to other monasteries, without taking into account their health and advanced age.

An even more unpleasant situation arose following the condemnation of the ideas expressed by Quesnel in his writings, which basically opened a new phase in the long Jansenist controversy. The two texts at issue were the *Abrégé dé la Morale*, and the *Nouveau Testament français, avec des réflexions morales sur chaque verset*. They had been widely distributed in religious and intellectual circles between 1693 and 1699. However, they had been sharply criticized because of their doctrine on grace, and because they had adopted the French text of the Bible formerly condemned by Clement IX. All indications were that the situation was steadily heading toward a final condemnation by the pope. First, there appeared the brief *Universi dominici gregis* (13 July 1708). But the protests did not die down, and the king himself entered the quarrel on the side of some members of the episcopate who thought the document should be more restrictive and far-reaching. Clement XI ordered that the question be studied afresh, even while he sought to avoid the controversy becoming even more bitter. On 8 September 1713, the bull *Unigenitus* was issued. It condemned all 101 proposals contained in Quesnel's works. Contrary to the pope's expectations, a majority of the clergy contested the bull. Cardinal de Noailles sided resolutely with the bishops who opposed it, arguing that the papal document was too vague. He even managed to dissuade his clergy form granting it full credence, and joined calls for a national council. In two new interventions, the pope managed to get Cardinal de Noailles to back off, by threatening to withdraw his cardinal's rank. The negotiations continued, but to no avail. After several attempts by the regent, Louis XIV's successor, as well as other government representatives, to arrive at a compromise, Clement XI broke off the talks. He harshly stigmatized the position of the appellants (consistory of 27 June 1716). The way was now open for excommunications, which came with the bull *Pastoralis officii* (28 August 1718), and a subsequent decree of the Inquisition (19 December 1718). Cardinal de Noailles, with the support of some twenty bishops, reacted harshly by lodging a new appeal to a council. But things took a new twist with the death of Quesnel on 2 December 1719 and the formation of a majority of bishops now favorable to the pope's position. The archbishop of Paris finally signed the formulation of the body of the doctrine, although the pope tried to get him to subscribe to an act of real submission. The controversy ended only with the death of Clement XI.

On the ecumenical and missionary front, Clement XI gave new momentum to the evangelization of the Protestant world of northern Europe—the Balkans, Poland, and Russia—as well as the Middle East. This he achieved by increasing the activity of the Congregation of the Propagation of the Faith. However, it was during his pontificate that a long dispute that had simmered for more than half a century finally came to a head. It opposed the Roman ecclesiastic authorities and the superiors of religious orders regarding the religious rites of the Chinese people. Once again, the problem centered on the degree of compatibility of the religion of Rome with the indigenous culture and customs of any given civilization that embraced Catholicism. The question concerned not only the conversion of the local people but also the possibility for the missionaries themselves to adopt some local rites. The matter had been resolved with the idea that Christianity, which was a universal religion, could adopt at least some of the gestures and signs of other religions. The polemic was reopened with Clement XI, whose position was contrary to that of the Society of Jesus, which had authorized its missionaries in China to adopt the funeral rites and certain religious expressions in honor of Confucius. Clement XI was not convinced by the oft-repeated professions of faith by the Jesuits and clarifications as to the purely legal and juridical nature of their actions. The pope issued a series of interdicts in 1704, 1710, and 1715. The Chinese emperor was indignant at the disdain shown to the traditions of his people and their ancient civilization. He expelled the missionaries and had the Catholic churches destroyed. The new papal legate to China, Ambrogio Mezzabarba, tried to win back the emperor with a concession authorizing ceremonies at the altars of the ancestors and rites in honor of Confucius; these efforts, however, bore no results.

Thus, the pontificate of Clement XI is clearly characterized by some moments of great openness and by others where extreme and humiliating caution won out over courage and a far-sighted vision of the future. His pontificate quite faithfully reflects the theological questions and the complex nature of the affairs into which he was drawn, without revealing any real consciousness on his part of their complexity. One need not mention the diffi-

culties experienced by the Church in acting in coherence with its traditions and spiritual role, in a society increasingly inclined to be guided by political expediency. The conflict was further deepened by a culture characterized by jurisdictional and secular intrigues on the one hand, and, on the other, principles of tolerance and religious pluralism.

Luigi Fiorani

Bibliography

Aldobrandini, A. *La guerra di successione di Spagna negli stati dell'Alta Italia dal 1702 al 1705 e la politica di Clement XI*, Rome, 1931.

Andretta, *DBI*, 26, 302–20.

Baudrillart, A. *Philippe V et la Cour de France*, Paris, 1890.

Bignami-Odier, J. "Clement XI amateur des livres et des manuscrits," *Miscellanea A. Campana*, 1, Padua, 1981, 101–23.

Buder, *Leben und Taten des klugen und berühmten Papstes Clements der Elften*, 3 vols., Frankfurt, 1720.

Ceyssens, L. "Autor de l'Unigenitus: Le pape Clement XI," *BIHR*, 53–4 (1983–84), 253–304.

de Lafiteau, P. F. *Vie de Clement XI*, 2 vols., Padua, 1752.

Gres-Gayer, J. M. "The Unigenitus of Clement XI: A Fresh Look at the Issues," *Theological Studies*, 49 (1988), 259–82.

Hanotaux, G. *Recueil des instructions données aux ambassadeurs et ministres de France depuis les traités de Westphalie jusqu'à la Revolution française*, XVII, Rome, II.

Johns, C. M. S. *Papal Art and Cultural Politics: Rome in the Age of Clement XI*, Cambridge, 1993.

Just, L. *Klement XI und der Code Leopold (1701–1710)*, Frankfurt, 1935.

Le Roy, A. *La France et Rome de 1700 à 1715: Histoire diplomatique de la bulle Unigenitus jusqu'à la mort de Louis XIV*, Paris, 1892.

Mols, R. *DHGE*, XII, 1326–61.

Nina, L. *Le finanze pontificie sotto Clemente XI*, Milan, 1928.

Pastor, 33.

Peret, P. "Une négociation secrète entre Louis XV et Clement XI en 1715," *Revue des questions historiques*, 85 (1909), 108–45.

Pometti, F. "Studi sul pontificato di Clemente XI (1700–1721)," *ASR*, 21 (1898), 279–457; 22 (1899), 109–79; 23 (1900), 239–76, 449–515.

Thomas, A. *Histoire de la mission de Pekin*, Paris, 1923, 135–304.

Thuillier, V. *Rome et la France: La seconde phase du jansénisme*, Paris-Lyon, 1901.

Weaver, E. F. "Scripture and Liturgy for the Laity: The Jansenist Case for Translation," *Worship*, 59 (1985), 510–21.

Wright, A. D. *The Early Modern Papacy: From the Council of Trent to the French Revolution, 1564–1789,* New York, 2000.

CLEMENT XII. *Lorenzo Corsini (b. Florence, 7 April 1652, d. Rome, 6 February 1740). Elected pope 12 July 1730, crowned July 16. Buried at the Basilica of St. John Lateran.*

Lorenzo Corsini came from a family that had settled in Florence in the second half of the 13th century and had immediately become integrated into the political class. The Corsinis were merchants and bankers, and in the 16th century extended their activities from England to Sicily. Following the acquisition by his uncle of fiefs in Umbria around 1610, Filippo Corsini, grandfather of the future pope, settled in Rome around 1620. A few years later he was followed by one of his nephews, Andrea. His family was closely linked to that of Pope URBAN VIII, the Barberinis, who were originally from Florence. The pope had made the Corsinis' lands in Umbria into a marquisate. From then on, and over two centuries, the Corsinis developed a family tradition whereby the eldest owned the land and the youngest son became a cardinal. Filippo together with the Medicis, managed one of the richest banks in Europe located in Rome. He was the last son to be directly involved in business. While the Corsini family still maintained industrial and commercial investments in Florence in the first decades of the 18th century, they were first and foremost very powerful landowners. They owned property in Tuscany, but also in the pontifical States and in the kingdom of Naples. On becoming a cleric of the APOSTOLIC CAMERA in 1620, Ottavio (1588–1641), younger brother of Filippo and great uncle of the pope, was renewing an ancient family tradition. Andrea had been bishop of Fiesole, a cardinal in the 14th century, and Pope Urban VIII canonized him. Ottavio began a tradition whereby members of the family served as prelate of the Curia, starting as cleric in the Apostolic Camera, and subsequently holding administrative and diplomatic posts before becoming cardinal. Neri (1624–79); Lorenzo Neri (1685–1770), and Andrea (1735–95) all followed the same path.

Lorenzo was the youngest son of Bartolomeo Corsini (1622–85) and Elisabetta Strozzi (d. 1682). After studies in Florence (doubtless with the Jesuits), he went to Rome in 1667 to study at the ROMAN COLLEGE. He lived with his uncle Neri, who was then a cardinal and who intended to obtain a *chiericato* for him in a few years, thus placing him well on the way to becoming a cardinal. When in 1672 his uncle was appointed bishop of Arezzo, Lorenzo left Rome for Pisa where he earned a doctorate in *utroque iure* in 1675. Following the death of his uncle in 1677, he stayed in Florence until his father died, in 1685. At that time he settled permanently in Rome and embarked on the ecclesiastic career typical of a prelate of the Curia.

He obtained, for 30,000 ecus, the post of Regent of the Chancellery, and then at the end of 1689 or the beginning of 1690, that of cleric of the Apostolic Camera, a post he purchased for 80,000 ecus. On 18 February 1690 Alexander VIII appointed him prefect of the Signature of Grace. On 10 April he was named Archbishop of Nicomedia, with a special dispensation as he had not yet been made a priest. He received the major orders in May and was consecrated as bishop on June 18. He was designated an apostolic NUNCIO to Vienna on 1 July, but his appointment was met with a refusal from the imperial court, so he remained in Rome. He then became treasurer and collector general of the Apostolic Camera (6 December 1695), a post in which his uncle had served under Alexander VII. He was general commissioner of the sea and prefect of the Castel Sant'Angelo (9 December 1690). Apart from a short mission to Ferrara as commissioner in the summer of 1704 (to settle a dispute with the Empire), he remained in Rome in charge of the financial administration until his resignation in 1707. During his tenure he adopted an openly mercantilist approach.

He was appointed cardinal at the consistory of 17 May 1706, with the title of cardinal-priest of Saint-Susanna (June 25), then of S. Pietro in Vincoli (16 November 1720). On 19 November 1725, Lorenzo was appointed cardinal-bishop of Frascati. In September 1709 he had refused the post of papal LEGATE of Ferrara, electing instead to remain in Rome, where he was named camerlengo of the SACRED COLLEGE (19 February 1710), and later prefect of the signature of Justice (22 November 1726).

During his years as cardinal, Lorenzo served as a member of ten ordinary congregations. He sat also as a member of two extraordinary congregations: for the war in Hungary against the Turks (1716), and the trial of Cardinal Alberoni in 1720. He was also a protector of several religious orders and charitable institutions.

As one writer stated, Lorenzo Corsini was, as a cardinal, "the most magnificent nobleman in all of Rome, and owned the largest estate of anyone in the Sacred College." He was an unrivaled player of chess, and "one of the best violinists in Italy." He soon became known as a protector and patron of the arts. He was the founder of the famous Corsini library, which was set up with funds inherited from his uncles, at that time still a modest amount. The library was placed at the disposal of men of letters and located in the family palace on Piazza Fiametta. It was relocated in 1713 to the Pamphili palace on Piazza Navona. In 1728 Lorenzo added the library of Cardinal Gualtieri, doubtless at the urging of his librarian, Dom Joseph-Dominique d'Inguimbert. He acted as protector for several academies, including the ones operated by the Quirinis, and amassed an extraordinary collection of antiques.

In the two papal conclaves of 1721 and 1724, Lorenzo Corsini was well placed among the *papabili*. The new conclave held following the death of BENEDICT XIII lasted from 5 March to 12 July. From 15 April Lorenzo's candidacy was supported by the *zelanti* and a few others. After a preliminary rejection, his candidacy was finally accepted by the emperor, thanks to intensive lobbying by Neri Corsini, the cardinal's nephew and secretary, among others. With the French having backed down, Lorenzo was unanimously elected from among the 52 cardinals present, on 12 July 1730. He took the name Clement in honor of Clement XI, who had made him a cardinal.

The pope's activity was more centered on matters of a temporal rather than a religious nature. Indeed, his actions in the religious sphere were rather transitory. Furthermore, he was hampered by his infirmities. Although he was struck by blindness in 1732 and showed a stubborn will to continue working, he became progressively weaker and from 1737 suffered from memory loss. He became almost permanently bedridden in the autumn of 1739. His nephew Neri, who had been made cardinal on 14 August 1730, started to play an increasingly important role from 1731 onward.

Clement XII ordered an inquiry into the financial scandals of the previous pontificate and the person who had profited most from them, Cardinal Coscia. Clement needed to try to redress finances overburdened with a public debt of 60 million ecus. He first had recourse to such measures as the famous reintroduction of the *lotto* (December 1731), or the issuing of bills by the *Banco di S. Spirito* and the *Monte di Pietà*. He tried to secure payments from such restive Catholic nations as Naples, Spain, and Portugal. Since austerity and monetary measures were not proving sufficient, the pope developed a protectionist policy and tried to boost production and exports in line with the principles of mercantilism. Ancona was given the status of a free port on 14 February 1732.

At the international level, the papacy of the 1730s was in a position of weakness. It sometimes lacked clarity in the conduct of its affairs and was often forced to make difficult and embarrassing compromises. The death of the Duke of Parma, Antonio Farnese, in January 1731, led the pope to decree the return of the duchies of Parma and Piacenza to the administration of the Holy See, but the duchies were occupied first by the troops of Carlos of Bourbon then handed over to Austria in 1735. Their fate was decided by the European powers over the protests of the pope.

Clement XII continued to pursue a policy of restricting Spain's power in Italy. The Bourbons had reestablished themselves in Naples, following a brief military campaign in 1734. This made relations between the pope and Spain more difficult, despite the political savvy of Don Carlos, who had appointed the pope's nephew Bartolomeo as viceroy of Sicily. The regalist pretensions of the court of Madrid led to a break in relations. Following the resumption of negotiations, a new CONCORDAT was signed with Spain in September 1737, and ratified by the pope on 12 November. The power of the nuncios had diminished and the Spanish clergy was obliged to pay a yearly tax of 150,000 ducats. Ecclesiastical discipline was reinforced, but the king gave up patronage of the Spanish episcopate, a clause that was not actually applied. Don Carlos of Bourbon finally received papal investiture in May 1738. However, relations with him remained tense, especially in view of the resolutely anti-Roman policies of one of his ministers, Tanucci.

Clement XII had to deal with the first advances of JURISDICTIONALISM. He maintained the position of the Church against the Jansenists, thought to be heretic, in his *In eminenti* constitution of 28 April 1738. In January he prohibited his subjects from becoming members of lodges and forced them to renounce masonic meetings. As a cardinal, Lorenzo had been a patron of the arts. As pope he undertook projects of construction and decoration, but he added to existing structures more often than he built from scratch. Apart from the churches of Bambino Gesu, Santi Celso, and Giulino, the new palace of la Consulta, and the Trevi fountain, which remained unfinished after his death, he redecorated the portico of St. Mary Major the façade of S. Giovanni dei Fiorentini, and that of St. John Lateran. This latter had been designed by the Florentine architect Alessandro Galilei. The family chapel in the Basilica of St. John Lateran was also redone (1731–33).

Clement XII was passionately interested in archaeology and an extremely erudite man. He developed the Vatican Library, under the direction of Cardinal Angelo Maria Quirini. The statuary museum of the Capitol, run by Alessandro Capponi, was the first museum of European antique objects. He also opened the collections of antiques from the curator's museum for public viewing.

Jean Boutier

Bibliography

Ago, R. *Carriere e clientele nella Roma barocca*, Rome-Bari, 1990.

Caffiero, M. "Corsini, Neri," *DBI*, XXIX, (1983), 651–7.

Caracciolo, A. "Clemente XII," *DBI*, XXVI (1982), 320–8.

Corsini, V., *Corsini*, Rome, Istituto di Studi Romani, "Le Grandi Famiglie Romane," XII, 1960.

Fabroni, A. *De vita et rebus gestis Clementis XII P.M. comentarius*, Rome, 1760.

Mols, R. "Clement XII," *DHGE*, XII, (1953), 1361–81.

Moroni, A. "Il patrimoio dei Corsini fra Granducato e Italia unita: Politica familiare e investimenti," *Bolletino storico pisano*, LIV (1985), 79–106; "Le ricchezze dei Corsini. Struttura patrimoniale e vicende familiari tra Sette e Ottocento," *Societe e Storia*, IX, 32 (1986), 255–91.

Orzi Smeiglio, P. "I Corsini a Roma e le orgini della Biblioteca corsiniana," *Atti della Accademia nazionale dei Lincei*, s VIII, Memorie, Classe di Scienze moral, storiche e filologiche, VIII, 1959, 293–331.

Passerini, L. *Genealogia e Storia della famiglia Corsini*, Florence, 1858.

Pastor, 34.

CLEMENT XIII. *Carlo Rezzonico (b. Venice, 7 March 1693, d. Rome, 2 February 1769). Elected pope 6 July 1758, crowned 16 July. Buried at St. Peter's, Rome.*

Aut sint ut sunt aut non sint. "Let them be what they are, or let them cease to be." This saying, which has been attributed to Clement XIII in defense of the Society of Jesus, could well serve as a motto for his pontificate. The papacy of Clement XIII signaled the start of the intransigent, and in many ways powerless, reaction of the Church in the face of the affirmation of state and secular logic, during the Age of Lights. The Church also faced enlightened despotism.

Carlo Rezzonico was born in 1693, in the Republic of Venice. His father, Gian Batista, originally came from Como, and settled in Venice in 1640. His family had grown very rich through trade, but joined the ranks of the Venetian nobility (1687), of which his mother, Vittoria Barbarigo, was a member. Between the ages of 10 and 18, he attended a Jesuit college, St. Francis Xavier in Bologna. He went on to study law at the University of Padua, then at the Academy of Ecclesiastic Noblemen in Rome. He entered the prelacy in 1716 and was successively governor of Rieti in Umbria (1716–21), then of Fano in the Marches (1721–23). He served in the Consulta (1723–28) and was auditor of the Rota tribunal for Venice (1728–37). At the age of 44, Carlo was made a cardinal by CLEMENT XII, on 20 December 1737. Six years later on 19 March 1734, BENEDICT XIV, then bishop of Padua, consecrated him. For 15 years Carlo served as bishop in Venice, under the double patronage of Carlo Borromeo and his elderly relative, Gregorio Barbarigo, whom he beatified in 1761. Carlo's episcopacy provides insight into the orientation and priorities of his papacy. He attached great importance to religious life, ecclesiastic discipline, and morals. He turned his attention to reorganizing the diocesan seminary and then providing intellectual training for members of the clergy. Carlo had great concern for the well-being of the poor and an interest in public and private charity. Benedict XIV saw him as "our most worthy prelate in Italy."

Benedict XIV died on 3 May 1758, after serving for 18 years. His papacy had been characterized by a policy of reconciliation and openness to the century's changes.

During the conclave, which began a few days following his death on 15 May, the intransigent Cardinal Rezzonico sided with the *zelanti*. The latter group was anxious to restore the authority of the Church on all fronts, and opposed those who supported "the Crowns," and favored a policy of entente with the princes. This group was actively supported by the ambassadors of the "family pact," consisting of the Bourbons of France, Spain, and Naples. Following failure to agree on several candidates (Spinelli, Mosca, Archinto, Crescenzi), and the debarment by France of *zelante* cardinal Cavalchini on 22 June, Austria and the *zelantis* agreed on the candidacy of Rezzonico, the Venetian. After a conclave lasting 52 days, he was elected by 31 votes out of 44, and took the name Clement, in memory of Clement XII.

The immediate challenge before the new pope was the union of the Catholic princes and their ministers (Pombal in Lisbon, Aranda in Spain, Tanucci in Naples, and du Tillot in Parma). They were opposed to the supranational character of the Catholic Church, as well as its legal and fiscal privileges. Austria, led by Maria-Theresa, was the only one to observe cautious neutrality and keep her distance from this group. Pope Clement XIII was also called upon to fight the convergence of a whole series of doctrines originating in the State (GALLICANISM, Regalism, JURISDICTIONALISM), or in ecclesiastic circles (conciliarism, Episcopalism, Richerism). They advocated separating civil power from the religious, the authority of a prince over the clergy in his kingdom and his competence to reform the Church. They also deemed that the council had a greater authority than the pope and believed in the divine election of bishops and even of priests. In 1763 the coadjutor of the archbishop of Treves, von Hontheim, writing under the pseudonym Febronius, set down these theories from a Regalian and episcopalist standpoint in his treatise *De Statu Ecclesiae*. It caused a great sensation. These theories were part of a vast movement of protest within and outside Catholicism. It consisted of a composite of the Jansenist current of theological, moral, ecclesiological thought and the radical rethinking of the philosophy and thinking of the Century of Lights.

The Society of Jesus was the institution that condensed the various currents of the opposition to Clement XIII's pontificate. The Jesuits had a special vow of obedience to the pope and a pyramidal hierarchy. They were well organized internationally and over two centuries had acquired considerable influence in the Roman Catholic Church. This influence extended to the religious, missionary, scholarly, social, and political spheres. In the second half of the 18th century, all of the hostility of the opposition—the courts and the policies, the Jansenists and Philosophes—was concentrated and directed against the Jesuits. Clement XIII had studied with the Jesuits and had picked, as his secretary of state, the authoritarian Cardinal Torrigiani, who had close links to them. He also had a high regard for their general, Father Ricci, and he had no intention of damaging the great order of Catholic Reform by making concessions or giving ground on behalf of the Church of Rome. In his first papal encyclical, *A quo die*, of 14 September 1758, he cautioned his bishops: "let us be careful lest like the dumb dogs of the Scriptures, we stand silently whilst fierce creatures attack our sheep. Let nothing deter us from confronting the greatest perils for the glory of God and the salvation of souls." The pope was rigidly committed to the tradition of the Church, its discipline and privileges, as well as an ecclesiology straight out of the COUNCIL OF TRENT. He was an extremely pious man, with a lasting commitment to the pastoral mission of the Church. His rigid, and at times narrow, affirmation of pontifical authority inevitably led Clement XIII to a head-on confrontation with the powers—and in the short term, failure.

The members of the Society of Jesus were expelled gradually from the main Catholic States throughout the pontificate of Clement XIII. Portugal made the first move. The Jesuits were accused of plotting against the State and the monarch himself and expelled from the kingdom and its colonies on 5 October 1759. Three of their number were executed on 21 September 1761. The NUNCIO Acciaiuoli was, in his turn, expelled from Lisbon on 15 June 1760. In France, the scandal caused by the sensational failure of Father Lavalette in the French-owned West Indies was the starting point for a general offensive against the order. The Gallicans, the Jansenists, and the Philosophes led this offensive.

On 17 April 1761 the Parlement of Paris undertook to examine the constitutions of the Society, to see whether they were in conformity with the fundamental laws of the kingdom. Father Ricci, with the agreement of the pope, refused to give up his authority over the province of France, or to change the constitutions. On 6 August 1762 a writ of the Parliament of Paris deprived the Society of Jesus of its legal existence. This move was quickly imitated in the rest of France. In Spain and in the kingdom of the Two-Sicilies, the *Exposition of Christian Doctrine* was condemned in a brief of 14 June 1761. The Jesuit Mesenguy had written the document, and Charles III had distributed the brief in all of the States and even to his family. This gave rise to the first conflict on papal jurisdiction, a conflict that was stifled with great difficulty. Six years later, the Jesuits were accused of plotting against the State and expelled from Spain and its possessions (including the Indian territory in Paraguay). They were expelled from Spain on 2 April and from Naples on 31 October 1767. Finally, on 23 April 1768, Malta issued an order for the expulsion of the Jesuits. Clement XIII had, at that time, retaliated with the BULL *Apostolicum Pascendi* of 7 January 1765, in which he solemnly reconfirmed the constitutions of the Society. The events in

Parma, which was also ruled by the Bourbons, led to the final offensive. Clement XIII protested against the Regalian ecclesiastic policies of Minister du Tillot, and on the basis of the bull *In Coena Domini*, and in a monitory of 30 January 1768, canceled all the measures taken by the duchy of Parma. Du Tillot expelled the Jesuits during the night of 7 February, and the Bourbon Triplice (R. Mols) threatened the pope by mounting a concerted action on 15 and 16 April; Benevento and Pontecorvo were occupied by Naples and Avignon and le Comtat by France on 11 June. Finally, from 16 to 24 January 1769, the three Ambassadors of Spain, Naples, and France demanded that the pope do away with the Society, once and for all. Clement XIII was preparing to put up a resistance, but died on the night of 2 February.

The dramatic conclusion of the conflict left the future of the society hanging in the balance. It shows the extraordinary determination of its adversaries. On one hand, there were secular governments determined to break through an order conceived as the spearhead of the privileges of the Roman Church, in order to do away with all theocratic influence. On the other hand, there was a pope who was weakened but determined to do everything necessary to protect the heritage and prerogatives of the HOLY SEE. One should not forget that the pontiff was also a ruler. He was the last defender of the body of political doctrine of the medieval papacy (he was the last pope in the history of the Church to order the reading every Good Friday of the bull *In Coena Domini*).

Clement XIII was also a secular prince interested in how his States were governed. For example, he dipped heavily into the treasures left by SIXTUS V in the Castel Sant'Angelo in order to come to the aid of his subjects in the horrible famine of 1764. In 1766 he appointed Giovangelo Braschi, the future PIUS VI, to the post of treasurer general, so that he could implement a far-reaching program of financial and economic modernization and beautification of Rome. In 1762 the remodeling of the Trevi fountain was completed. In 1763 the pope appointed Winckelmann as head of the antique museum of Rome. He also ordered that the nudes in the SISTINE CHAPEL be modestly covered. The latter-day and unfortunate "Eighteenth-century pope Gregory" consistently reaffirmed, by his words and actions and despite the trends of his century, the legitimacy of the union of spiritual and temporal power in the hands of a sovereign pontiff.

The religious orientation of Clement XIII was inspired by the same intransigent reaction. The fight against the Lights was the first axis of the break begun in 1758. There was a resumption of the activity of the CONGREGATION OF THE INDEX, which in 1759 condemned Helvetius' *De l'Esprit*, the *Encyclopedie* of Diderot and d'Alembert, and Rousseau's *Emile*. In 1764 the *De Statu Ecclesiae* by Febronius was condemned.

However, the decrees of the Index did not carry the force of law in most Catholic states. The encyclical *Christianae reipublicae salus* of 25 November 1766 condemns, in a general way, the lack of religious belief in the philosophies of the Enlightenment. It was the first extensive text of intransigent Catholic dogma. The pope, as a professor at la Sapienza, appointed the Jesuit Francantonio Zaccaria (1714–95), who had been expelled from Modena in 1767 for fighting against Febronius. He was at the origin of a renewal of Roman apologetics in the last part of the 18th century.

It was, however, the renewal of piety that was the pope's most enduring legacy. The development of the cult of the Sacred Heart, with its concern for atonement, its symbolism, and even its iconography, was profoundly repugnant to the Jansenists, not to mention the Philosophes. It will always be linked to Clement XIII. By the decree of 26 January 1765, approved by the pope on February 6, the Congregation of Rites granted the feast day of the Sacred Heart to Poland and the Roman congregation of Saints Theodore. It had its own mass and liturgical hours. Clement XIII placed Spain and its possessions under the patronage of the Immaculate Conception on 8 November 1760. On 16 August 1767 the Congregation of Rites canonized six saints who were instrumental in the reform of the Catholic Church including Jeanne de Chantal, founder of the Visitation and José Calasanz. It approved the cult of the founder of the Ursulines, Angela Merici, on 30 April 1763. The papacy of Clement XIII signaled a decisive turning point in the strict reaffirmation of the authority and discipline of the Church. This may be seen in the spiritual and devotional orientation of the pope, as well as in his desperate attempts to protect the Jesuits in the face of the political determination of the princes. The Church was weakened and more uncertain of its future as it stood on the threshold of an age of revolution, but it was more secure in its convictions and hopes.

Philippe Boutry

Bibliography

XVI, 1 (trad. ital.: XVI, 1, 465–1053).

Baum, W. "Luigi Maria Torrigiani (1697–1777) Kardinalstaatssekretar Papst Klemens XIII," *Zeitschrift für katholische Theologie*, 94, 1972, 46–78.

Bellinati, C. *Attivita pastorale del card. Carlo Rezzonico vescovo di Padova poi Clemente XIII (1743–58)*, Padua, 1969.

Cajani, L., and Foa, A. "Clemente XIII papa," *DBI*, 26, 328–43.

de Ravignan, X. *Clement XIII et Clement XIV*, Paris 1854.

Lukowski, J. F. "The Papacy, Poland, Russia and Religious Reform, 1764–8," *Journal of Ecclesiastical History*, 39 (1988), 66–94.

Mols, R. "Clement XIII," *DHGE*, 12 (1953), 1381–1410.

Van Kley, D. *The Jansenists and the Expulsion of the Jesuits from France (1757–1765)*, New Haven-London, 1975.

CLEMENT XIV. *Giovanni Vincenzo Antonio (in religion, Lorenzo) Ganganelli (b. Sant'Arcangelo di Romagna, near Forlì, 31 October 1705, d. Rome, 22 September 1774). Elected pope 18 May 1769, crowned 4 June. Buried at St. Peter's, Rome.*

Should Clement XIV go down in history only as the pope who accepted and sanctioned the banning of the Jesuits? A comprehensive and less controversial view of this pope has gradually become more accepted. It leads to an examination of the global context prevailing on the eve of the French Revolution, at a time when the Catholic monarchies had imposed restrictions on the Church.

Giovanni Vincenzo Antonio Ganganelli was born in 1705 in the little town of Sant'Arcangelo di Romagna, near Forlì. His father Lorenzo belonged to the patriciate of Sant'Angelo in Vado, near Urbino, in the Marches. Lorenzo worked as a doctor from 1699 to 1708. His son, Giovanni is, therefore, the first pope in the history of the church to have come from the liberal bourgeoisie of the Papal States. He was raised in modest establishments in Verichio and Rimini. On 15 May 1723, when he was not yet 18 years old, he took the habit of the conventual Franciscans and adopted the religious name of Lorenzo. He served as novice for one year at Urbino and took final vows on 18 May 1724. For many years, his life did not differ from that of other friars. Lorenzo completed his theological training in the tradition of Duns Scotus at the monasteries of Pesaro, Recanati, and Fano, and then from 1728 to 1731, at the St. Bonaventure College in Rome, where he was taught by Antonio Lucci, the future bishop of Bovino. He was promoted to doctor of theology, and taught, from 1730 to 1740, in the monasteries of his congregation at Ascoli Piceno, Bologna, Milan, and again in Bologna.

In 1740, in the early days of the pontificate of BENEDICT XIV, he was called to Rome to serve as regent of the St. Bonaventure College. There his knowledge of theology earned him the respect of several cardinals, including Andrea Negroni, a relative of the pope. It is doubtless true that Lorenzo owed his appointment in 1746 as advisor of the Holy Office to Negroni. In his new post he participated in the condemnations of the philosophy of Montesquieu and Voltaire. At the same time, he showed a special interest in the men and their ideas. In 1759, shortly before his accession to the Sacred College, he submitted a report to his congregation on the accusation of ritual crimes brought against the Jews. The subject had again gained interest as a result of bloody events in Poland at that time. The report was written in a spirit of charity and was later approved by CLEMENT XIII. It called into question the traditional prejudices against the Jews, and explicitly reproved the actions of the Polish bishops. The future pope's concern at the injustices committed against Jews by Christian society (Ganganelli's report would only become known and published in 1888), was later borne out by his actions. Upon his accession to the papacy, Clement XIV replaced the Saint Office, established in 1581 as the supervisor of dogma for the Jewish community, and placed them instead under the ordinary jurisdiction of the cardinal vicar.

He was made cardinal by Clement XIII on 24 September 1749 and for the next ten years took no prominent or controversial positions. In 1761 he approved the condemnation of the *Exposition de la doctrine chretienne*, by the Jesuit Mesenguy. Beginning in 1764, his position moved toward that of the Spanish Court, partly out of his hostility to Secretary of State Torrigiani. Upon the death of Clement XIII on 2 February 1769, the future pope entered the conclave, which opened on 15 February. He did not openly favor any one side, neither the pro-Jesuit faction faithful to the traditions of Clement XIII and led by Cardinal Torrigiani, nor the moderate *zelanti* side led by Cardinal Albani, nor did he show open allegiance to the powerful faction of the crowns, led by the Frenchman Bernis and the Spaniards De Solis and La Cerda. They were supported by the Bourbon ambassadors of Spain, France, and Naples, who blatantly violated the code of secrecy of the deliberations and directly influenced the choice of candidate. They were determined to extract from any future pope a commitment to abolish the Jesuits. One hundred eighty-five voting sessions and more than three months of bargaining, pressure, and scheming would be necessary before there was a clear vote for Ganganelli, the only religious within the Sacred College. He was elected on 18 May 1769 by 46 votes out of 47 (he himself had voted for Cardinal Rezzonico, the nephew of the dead pope) and took the name of Clement XIV in memory of his predecessor. He was consecrated bishop on 28 May and crowned pope on 4 June.

Had the future pope promised during the conclave to abolish the Jesuits, as he was subsequently accused of doing? There is no formal proof that this was the case, but it seems improbable that he would have been approved by the crowns faction without a commitment on his part. Indeed, he had written shortly before his election that "the religious orders are like auxiliary troops and only the Supreme Pastor may determine when they are useful and when they no longer are." Whatever the case may be, the pope waited four years before making his position known. He was less inclined than has been thought to break with the intransigent line of Clement XIII and, for the first months of his papacy, quietly tried to adopt the conciliatory appoach of Benedict XIV.

The intransigent Cardinal Torrigiani was replaced by Cardinal Pallavini, former nuncio to Madrid, as secretary of state. The pope favored his personal advisors over counsel from the Sacred College, from which he gradually distanced himself. He also strove to establish direct personal relations with the sovereigns by multiplying letters of praise, obliging gestures, and gracious concessions. He offered to go to Madrid to visit Charles III and to Versailles to see Louis XV. In July 1772 he even sent the nuncio Caprara to London. In his first encyclical, *Cum summi apostolatus* (12 December 1769), he exhorted the princes to "love the Church as their mother, and defend its rights." Without explicitly disavowing the monitory of his predecessor concerning the ecclesiastic policies of the duchy of Parma, he ignored the demands contained in it. Similarly, he did not protest in 1769 against the abolition of the right to asylum in Tuscany. Among the first set of cardinals appointed by Clement XIV was the brother of the Portuguese minister Pombal. He agreed to extend the provisions of the 1516 concordat to Corsica (1770), which had recently been acquired by France. The benefits of this policy of appeasement soon became evident. Beginning in June 1769, King Charles III of Spain withdrew the sanctions that limited the freedom of the Holy See. A nuncio was appointed to Lisbon in November 1769 (relations with Portugal had broken off in 1760). Although relations with France and Naples warmed, the pope was unable to secure withdrawal from papal possessions Pontecorvo and Benevento, Avignon and le Comtat, occupied since 1768.

The crowns, especially Spain, were still determined that the Jesuits be entirely abolished. For Rome, the years 1770 and 1771 were characterized by a clever policy of stalling for time. The pope held consultations prior to the drafting of a brief abolishing the Jesuits, and took a few limited measures against them (secularization of the Frascati seminary and the Irish College). He also paid an apostolic visit to the Roman College. He entertained hopes for an opportunity from the fall of Choiseul in France (1770) and a softening of Spain's position. However, international events went against his expectations, and under the influence of Joseph II (co-regent of Austria since 1765) and his sister Maria-Carolina (queen of Naples since 1768), Austria, joined the sovereigns' camp. Until then Austria under Maria Theresa, had maintained a neutral stance. The first partition out of Poland weakened the position of the Society of Jesus even further. Paradoxically, only Protestant Prussia, ruled by Frederick II, and the orthodox Russia of Catherine II supported them. In March 1772 José Monino, the future count of Floridabianca, was named as Spain's ambassador to Russia. He, of all the advisors of Charles III, was the most hard-line representative of the Regalian faction. His appointment hastened the final solution. Clement XIV gave in to further pressure from the courts of Spain, Naples, and France and on 16 August 1773, published the brief *Dominus ac Redemptor* (dated 21 July), officially doing away with the Jesuits. The brief reaffirmed the Holy See's right to suppress orders that had become "sterile," such as the Templars or the Jesuits. It further listed the numerous "abuses" and "troubles" within the Jesuits, and ordered that it be disbanded: "We hereby abolish and suppress all their offices, ministries and administrations. We divest them of their houses, schools, colleges, hospitals, farms and any other property in any province or dominion where they may exist." The Gesù and the German, Greek, and English colleges of Rome were closed and the Jesuit general, Ricci, and his chief advisors were imprisoned in the Castel Sant'Angelo. The fathers were secularized and on 1 September deprived of the right to exercise all pastoral duties in the Papal State. Finally, a congregation of cardinals was formed on 8 June and entrusted with the liquidation of all the property belonging to the Jesuits. The brief was applied all over Europe, with the exception of Prussia (until 1780), and Russia, which was anxious to maintain Jesuit schools. This caused concern and some prophetic upheaval in the Church as well as in Italy and France. However, on 14 January 1774, Clement XIV was able to announce to the Sacred College that the "proof" of Catholic power would soon be returned to the Church. On 23 March the sovereignty of the pope was indeed reestablished over Benevento and Pontecorvo, and on 25 April over Avignon and le Comtat.

Clement XIV died five months later on 22 September 1774. Rumors that he had been poisoned, and that near death (*in articulo mortis*), he had changed his mind about the brief *Dominus ac Redemptor*, seem to be based on nothing more than the climate of rancor and suspicion prevailing in the last year of his pontificate. The condemnation of the Jesuits has eclipsed any assessment of the pontiff himself in contemporary opinion. Clement XIV was, like his predecessors, concerned with combating the anti-Christian thinking that characterized the ENLIGHTENMENT. The work of La Mettue and the *Systeme de la Nature* by Holback were condemned by the Index in 1770; the *Historie Philosophique* by Raynal and the treatise *De l'Homme* by Helvetius were condemned in 1774.

Despite these problems, Clement XIV was the pastor who facilitated the spread of the cult of Mary and celebrated the entry of Madame Louise, the daughter of Louis XV, into the Carmelite Order of Saint-Denis in 1772. He was also the temporal sovereign, who under the stewardship of his general treasurer Braschi (the future Pope PIUS VI), began taking timid measures for financial reform. He also laid the foundations of the Museo Clementino. Clement XIV hoped that the suppression of the Jesuits would be viewed as part of the tradition of apostolic authority and the enlightened defense of the interests of the Church. His diplomacy, when viewed as a whole, with its spirit of conciliation and attempts to achieve harmony between the crowns and the Church, did not differ greatly from that of Benedict XIV, but times had changed. The brief *Dominus ac Redemptor* was rescinded by PIUS VII in 1814, and the Jesuits were reestablished in Rome and in the Church. However, the brief unambiguously demonstrates that beyond the polemics of the Jesuit question, the papacy itself had gradually weakened in the face of state and national logic in an age of enlightened despotism.

Philippe Boutry

Bibliography

Berra, L. "Il diario del conclave di Clement XIV del card. Filippo Maria Pirelli," *ASR*, XVI–XVII, 1962–63, 25–97, and 98–319.

Cretineau-Joly, *Clement XIV et les Jesuites*, Paris, 1847.

Dammig, E. Il *movimento giansenista a Roma nella seconda metà del secolo XVIII*, Cite du Vatican, 1945.

Pastor, 39 and 40.

Preclin, E. "Clement XIV," *DHGE*, XII (1953), col. 1411–23.

Rosa, M. "Clemente XIV papa," *DBI*, XXVI (1982), 343–62.

Theiner, A. *Histoire du pontificat de Clement XIV*, Paris, 1854, Pastor, XVI, 2 (trad. ital.: XVI, 465–1053).

Venturi, F. *Settecento riformatore. La chiesa e la republica dentro i loro limiti*, 1758–74, Turin, 1976, 326–42.

von Reumont, A. *Ganganelli, Papst Clements XIV*, Berlin, 1847.

CODE OF CANON LAW (1917). *Codex Iuris Canonici*, promulgated in 1917, is the result of the first contemporary codification of the law of the Roman Catholic Church. It set the normative framework for the life of the Church until 1983, when the new Code governing the present law of the Church entered into force. The Code of 1917 contains 2,414 canons divided into five books, which form the almost exclusive foundation for legislation applicable to Christendom. (The Code establishes a provision for EASTERN CHURCHES with Catholic rite, and for liturgical law as well as for bilateral agreements made with secular powers—canons 1 to 3.) It was drafted from 1904 to 1917. During these years, which also signaled the birth of the contemporary world, it occupied a central place in the history and activities of the Church.

Motu proprio, Arduum sane munus, a decree issued by Pope PIUS X on 19 March 1904, launched the effort to codify the law of the Church. There were several reasons behind Pope Pius's initiative. Many canonists and members of the clergy, who applied the ecclesiastical norms and standards on a daily basis, had frequently encountered difficulties in implementing them. Directives were dispersed throughout different collections and compendiums of laws whose legal status varied. They had also been published at different times and often gave rise to serious internal contradictions. The canon laws still in force at the beginning of the 20th century were essentially based on the already outdated *Corpus Iuris Canonici*. They had been written on the initiative of PIUS V and drafted by a commission of cardinals called *correctores romani*. There were great disparities in the texts of the official reference edition, dated 1580, and laws applying to the public and private domains were mixed indiscriminately. The "private" laws were also contained in the *Corpus*, from the *Decret de Gratien* (around 1140) up to the *Extravagantes Communes*, containing 74 decretals by popes who had occupied the throne of St. Peter from 1294 to 1484. This set of laws was referred to as the *Ius novissimum*, to distinguish it from the ancient laws, which dated back to before the COUNCIL OF TRENT. The *Liber Septimus Decretalium* by Pierre Mathieu (1590) was a set of private laws that complemented the preceding ones. The *Liber* consisted of five books containing texts promulgated by successive popes from Sixtus IV to Sixtus V (that is, from 1471 to 1590). Annexed to these were excerpts of Council decisions and some older DECRETALS not published in the *Corpus*. The collection was praised at first for its usefulness and republished on several occasions after 1591. However, jurists, who deemed that it took great liberties in the distribution of material, subsequently criticized it. It was listed in the INDEX from 1623 on, but this did not prevent the participants in the drafting of the 1917 Code from making extensive use of it as reference material. The only other previous canonical work had been the *Bullarium* of BENEDICT XIV. It was a collection of 146 apostolic constitutions and legal acts drawn up by this pontiff between 1740 and 1746. Only the first volume had had official status.

There was, therefore, no coherent source law covering the intervening periods, and canonists had been obliged to operate in a vacuum. This was hardly reassuring, especially with regard to legal acts arising from canon law, and the absence of laws posed an obstacle to many aspects of religious life. At the same time, the legislative activity of the church had continued steadily, with periods of great normative activity. Apart from acts directly related to the papacy, there were more and more decrees issued by the Roman CONGREGATIONS. These were an indication of the considerable influence exerted by the Roman CURIA on the government of the Church during the 19th century.

Prior to the *sine die* adjournment of their deliberations, the fathers meeting at the First Vatican Council on 20 October 1870, had decided to speak out about the inconsistency and incoherence of the laws. As early as 1864, a commission of cardinals from the Curia had been set up to consider a reform of Church law. Cardinal De Reisach headed this commission. A special commission continued the study in 1867 and submitted four drafts of laws to the council. Although all four drafts were adopted, they constituted a rather disappointing result. The episcopates of Belgium, France, Germany, Central Italy, and the provinces of Naples submitted several *postulata*, through which they signaled their wish to have a more comprehensive set of laws. Riario Sforza, archbishop of Naples, stressed the "imperative need to put an end to this disorder." Eleven French bishops suggested that a special congregation be established to "reject what needs to be rejected, add what should be added, and modify whatever should be modified" since "there are enough laws to crush us all" (*obruimur legibus*). On a lighter note, a group of twenty-seven Neapolitan ecclesiastics expressed the view that there were enough laws to weigh down "a whole caravan of camels." An anonymous request submitted by thirty-three members of the Council advocated the grouping together of all the canons to form a new and effective Code, which could be used to govern "Christian life, morals and institutions." They solemnly called upon PIUS IX to gather together the most eminent canonists and theologians to draft a new Code. Apart from its goal of standardization, the Code would be an indication of the pope's continued authority in the world. The fathers, in conclusion, stated that this was "a very difficult task" (*opus sane arduum*). Pope Pius X was to echo those words thirty-four years later, in the midst of an even more difficult situation for the Church.

Historians have supplied three conflicting accounts of how the decision to codify canon law was made. The first version stated that Pius X had put Felix von Hartmann, archbishop of Cologne, in charge of the codification. On the night of 4–5 August 1903, following his election to the papacy, Pius X had been unable to sleep and was "assailed by all sorts of thoughts." The second version refers to a conversation between Cardinal Gennari, an eminent canonist and founder of the review *Il Monitore Ecclesiastico* and the new pope. During the conversation, which is said to have taken place on 11 January 1904, the pope expressed his wish to see the work of codification begun. It was not until 1934 that Pietro Gasparri, the true architect and mainstay of the codification project, recounted his conversation with the pope to delegates at the international congress on canon law. He stated that in the first audience accorded him as secretary of the congregation on ecclesiastical affairs, Pope Pius asked him, "What do you think needs to be done at this time?" (*Che cose Vi sarebbe da fare ora qui?*). Gasparri replied, "The drafting of a code of canon law." All three accounts are mutually compatible on several points, and all three acknowledge that Pope Pius X took the initiative and, very importantly, made the final decision in favor of codification. This decision was made concrete by the *motu proprio* promulgated 19 March 1904, on the feast of St. Joseph, the pope's patron saint.

The text is remarkable for its clarity and its deliberately concise and pithy style. It seems to be the work of Pietro Gasparri, who had formerly been a professor at the College of Propaganda in Rome. He went on to teach at the Catholic University in Paris, founded in 1875, where he occupied the canon law chair from 1880 to 1898. There he had impressed his listeners with his clarity of thought and the practical style of his writings. The Church's desire for a new compilation of canon law was no different in 1904. Rome wanted clear, precise, and concise texts, like the articles of the various codes that modern nations had enjoyed since the previous century.

The French civil code of 1804 served as the archetype. Nevertheless, it was important for a code of canon law to follow its own logic and be assigned a system appropriate for it. The Holy See seemed to favor the drafting of a real code, which would revamp the style and in large measure the content of previous material. This was apparently deemed preferable to the drafting of a new *Corpus*, or a collection of laws that, although updated, would have been conceived along the lines of the old and outdated compilations. The expression used in the *motu proprio* to describe the new code was "a drafting in one single code of all of the laws of the church."

Another initial decision concerned the way in which the process of codification should be approached. The two known main drafts of the *motu proprio* differ significantly on this point. The final text recognizes the Apostolic See as the sole directing body, as opposed to the ecumenical COUNCIL, which is also mentioned in the first version. Rome therefore was exclusively responsible for guiding the codification effort (or, as Ulrich Stutz ironically puts it, the responsibility was exclusively "papal").

It was therefore decided that a specific commission should be established, consisting at the outset of 15 cardinals. They all had to be members of the Curia and reside permanently in Rome, which guaranteed effective follow-up and monitoring of the work. A preliminary list of prelates followed the pope's *motu proprio*, a clear indication of the urgency of the task in the eyes of Pius X. In his list, he mentioned those persons with the greatest competence in matters of canon law. They were Cardinals Seraphin Vannutelli, Antonio Agliardi, Vincenzo Vannutelli, and Mariano Rampolla del Tindora (former secretary of state to LEO XIII, from 1887 to 1903). Others included Francesco Satolli, Girolamo Gotti, Domenico Ferrata (an advocate before the Roman Congregations, nuncio in Paris in 1891, and later prefect of the Congregation of Bishops and Regulars). Francesco Cassetta, F. Mathieu, Casimiro Gennaric, Beniamino Cavicchioni (doctor in *Utroque*), and Raphael Merry del Val (secretary of state under Pius X from 12 November 1903) were

also members of the group. The last three members of the commission were Francesco Legna, Joseph Vives y Tuto, and Felice Cavagnis, professor of canon law at the Apollinare and prelate referendary of the Signature. The pope was, in principle, president of the commission and in his absence—as was always the case—the dean of the cardinals present. The commission of cardinals formed a council (*consulta*) with a secretary (*ponens*) who was not a cardinal but had the main task of coordinating the working sessions and setting the agenda for the meetings. Pietro Gasparri assumed this responsibility from the very outset. He became the craftsman of the new code, assuming the chairmanship of a second commission. It was called the *consulta* of the advisors, who were chosen from among members of the cardinals' commission and from the episcopates of the different nations of Christendom.

Less than a week after the *motu proprio* was promulgated, on 25 March 1904, the cardinal secretary of state, Merry del Val, addressed a circular letter to all metropolitan archbishops of Latin Christendom. The circular letter (*Per gratum mihi*) authorized the bishops of each country to collectively (and not on an individual basis) appoint one or two specialists to represent them in Rome. These specialists would work together with the consultants appointed by the cardinals. The Holy See also required the participation of all the dioceses, which were asked to submit their observations. After consultation with the bishops and all other competent persons, these observations were collected and sent to Rome within a period of four months following receipt of the letter.

Several figures emerged from this selection process. Canon A. Pillet, a professor of canon law at the University of Lille, was a resident prelate at the Curia and author, in 1890, of the widely acknowledged *Juscanonicum distributum in articulos*. In his work, canonical material was, for the first time, distributed in short articles. Alexis Lepicier was a professor of theology at the College of Propaganda, and Father Franz-Xavier Wernz was a professor of canon law at the Gregorian University, and General Superior of the Society of Jesus. Gaetano de Lai was a future cardinal.

Simultaneously, Pietro Gasparri addressed a letter entitled *Per legisti iam certe litteras* and dated April 6, to the Catholic UNIVERSITIES. He sought their help in distributing ecclesiastical law into articles or canons "in accordance with the most recent styles" and classifying those sources that might be of juridical interest to the contemporary Church. From the indications provided by Gasparri and supported by evidence from the archives, it was agreed that the laws would be divided into five books. This decision probably had the approval of Pius X. A set of rules of procedure governing the commissioning of consultants was published on April 11. It bound the members of the commission to absolute pontifical secrecy with respect to their work and its progress, on pain of excommunication *latae sententiae*. They swore an oath of secrecy six days later. Many observers were astonished at the strict observance of this oath over 13 years, especially since almost five thousand people were more or less directly involved in the work of codification.

After the structures had been put into place, the rate of concrete progress was undeniably steady. However, on May 3, the commission of cardinals split, to form a special five-member commission that would work more quickly and effectively. The five-member commission would examine those points that did not present serious difficulty or represent any modification of existing laws. The more important issues were reserved for the plenary sessions of the commission, whose membership had swelled from 17 to 42. Among the new appointees was one lay member, Count Balthazar Caprogrossi, dean of advocates of the Consistorial. A balance between the two commissions was achieved rather late thanks to Pietro Gasparri, who acted as a link between the two. Eugenio Pacelli (the future Pope Pius XII) assisted him within the *consulta* of advisors. As indicated in the rules of procedure, the latter did not have the right to vote but was responsible for noting the main points of the discussion and submitting the minutes to the cardinals. His modest rank should not obscure the key role he played in providing regular information to Gasparri, who was, necessarily, somewhat further removed from the day-to-day discussions. The creation in May 1905 of a second "special" commission of consultants complicated somewhat the structural configuration of the codification process. It also consisted of five members, and their task was to examine specific headings and chapters of the future code. There were now two meetings per week set by the consultants: one Thursday morning at eleven, and another at one o'clock on Sunday afternoon. As many as four consultants would work on the same subject without prior consultation among themselves, with the subjects being distributed in advance. After examining the canons drafted by the consultants and hearing the observations of the various members, Pietro Gasparri summarized these in the form of a *compte-rendu* that was immediately printed on the Vatican printing press, which had been mobilized for this purpose. This document was then distributed to the consultants for final examination in plenary sessions. Apparently it was not always easy to achieve the unanimous agreement needed for the adoption of a given draft. Certain points had to be resubmitted to plenary sessions as many as twelve times. The commission pragmatically chose to adopt the draft approved by the majority. If there was dissent concerning the adoption of a certain change, they decided to maintain the status quo.

The comments and preferences of almost all the Church dignitaries throughout the world were dispatched to Rome—a major step in the history of the codification of law. The remarks were all drafted in Latin according to the requirements. One consultant, Father Bernard Klumper, was responsible for compiling them into a single volume of 283 pages and classifying them according to the general framework decided for the code. Out of a total of 2,958 observations recorded as a result of the consultations of 1905 and 1908, almost 60 percent are concentrated in Book III of the Code (*De rebus*), especially under heading VII on matrimonial law. This subject is mentioned 538 times, attesting to a degree of complexity and confusion not unlike that found in the secular world.

There were requests for comments on other subjects, such as modes of acquisition and administration of, and allocation of, ecclesiastical property, and fasting and abstinence (these last were part of ecclesiastical discipline, in the traditional sense of the words). There were also remarks on matters such as the powers of bishops and questions relating to parishes. By the number of responses elicited, it was clear that these subjects were all deeply intertwined with the reality of ecclesiastical life.

Based on the attention given to these remarks by Rome, one could be justified in comparing these consultations with the bishops to a veritable "ecumenical council by correspondence" (Attilio Giacobbi). This was the level of integration that Rome had always desired in accord with the Church's perception of itself at the time as a sort of *societas perfecta*, due to the influence of a resurgent Thomism and a certain juridical positivism borrowed from secular society. Within the Church, canon law enjoyed the authority of a sacred science. It logically depended on, and acted as a vehicle for, the concepts and ideas of the pope. Some academics, mainly from Germanic countries, criticized the codification process as an anachronistic attempt to restore the papacy of the 19th century. However, these criticisms grew out of the same logic.

The first complete draft of the Code appeared in 1912. All the schemata of the code were submitted to the bishops for their opinions, despite the reticence of some cardinals. This step was initiated by Pietro Gasparri, who had become a cardinal in 1907 and, in the interval, chairman of the commission of cardinals. As a result of this preliminary consultation, the first few canons were entirely redrafted, as they were deemed too dogmatic. It was also decided to drop the profession of faith (*formula professionis fidei*), which had already been omitted in the body of liturgical law, in the preface of official editions of the Code. This undoubtedly gave the Code a more modern character, but it also introduced an element of generalized abstraction and *ordinatio rationis*, by which the technique of codification was perfected, but the concrete realities of the Church as a community of faith were passed over.

The First World War barely interrupted the pace of work on the Code. Pope Pius died on 20 August 1914, and BENEDICT XV was elected. It was a critical moment, since the subject of canon law had become of secondary importance, not for the authorities in Rome, but for most of the European episcopate. Giacomo Della Chiesa, on his election to the papacy, chose the name Benedict XV; it was noted that Prospero Lambertini (Benedict XIV) had been known as a legislator. The new pope immediately set about continuing work on the project, despite the appointment on 13 October 1914 of Cardinal Gasparri as secretary of state. Because of the war, his job was a particularly demanding one. Nevertheless, all indications are that the Code was ready for printing and publication toward the end of 1916, and Benedict XV announced its official completion during the secret consistory of 4 December. The Code was promulgated on the day of Pentecost 1917 (Apostolic constitution *Providentissima Mater Ecclesia*, 27 May 1918) and entered into force a year later. Benedict XV, on receiving a copy of the Code on 28 June 1917, had announced his intention of closing his ears to "all derogation, whatever they may be" with respect to the implementation of the new laws. By his *motu proprio, cum iuris canonici* Codice (15 September 1917), he created a commission charged with the "authentic" interpretation of the Code, of which it was to be a vigilant guardian.

The Code was generally well received in ecclesiastical circles. The fact that the Church had not disturbed previous concordat laws was especially appreciated. The undertaking had been a typically Roman one, down to its method of consulting those on the periphery. The codification of canon law was an attempt to restore the papacy as *Mater et Magistra* (J. Gaudemet) following the loss of its temporal states. The task of codification was more than a mere legislative *aggiornamento*. It was also an attempt by the Church to define its modernity, and the Code was the instrument used to signal this change.

François Jankowiak

Note: In 1985, the *Codex Iuris Canonici* of the Vatican archives was opened to the public, thus making it possible to have an in-depth understanding of the entire genesis of the Code of Canon Law. The collection consists of some 15,000 documents, grouped in ninety-seven file boxes. It is an irreplaceable source for the study of the first contemporary codification of the law of the Catholic Church.

Bibliography

Epp, R., Lefebre, C., and Metz, R. *Le Droit et les institutions de l'Eglise catholique latine de la fin du XVIII siècle à 1978, Sources et institutions*, Paris, 1981.

Gasparri, P. (cardinal), "Storia della codificazione dei diritto canonico per la Chiesa latina" *Acta congressus iuridici internationali VII saeculo a Decretalibus Gregorii IX a XIV a Codice iustitatio promulgatis*, IV, Rome, 1937, 4–10.

Guademet, J. "Collections canoniques et codifications," *RDC*, XXXIII (1983), 81–109.

Naz, R. "Codex Iuris Canonici," *DDC*, III (1942), 909–40.

Stutz, U. "Der Geist des Codex iuris canonici. Eine Einführung in das auf Geheib Papst Pius X. und von Papst Benedikt XV. erlassene Gesetzbuch der Katholischen Kirche," *Kirchenrechtiliche Abhandlungen*, 92 and 93, Stuttgart, 1918.

CODE OF CANON LAW (1983). The Code of Canon Law promulgated by JOHN PAUL II on 25 January 1983, (APOSTOLIC CONSTITUTION *Sacrae disciplinae leges*) is the major repository of the law of the Roman Catholic Church. It is the outcome of a process that developed over more than half a century and was constantly compared to two essential points of reference. The first is the CODE OF CANON LAW (1917), the fruit of the first effort to codify Church law in contemporary times. The other is the Second Ecumenical Vatican Council (VATICAN II), the deliberations and decisions of which considerably influenced, among other things, the conception of power within the Church. The 1983 Code, which provides the substance of present-day canon law, has joined these two influences. JOHN XXIII (1958–1963) publicly announced on 25 January 1959, that the Church's canon law would be renewed. The announcement was made in a room adjoining the Basilica of St. Paul's Outside the Walls, with the apostolic constitution *Humanae salutis* which thus established its link with other momentous occasions in the life of the Church, such as the convocation of Vatican II and the celebration of the Roman SYNOD.

The Code of 1917 had helped develop a rich process of critical reflection lasting over forty years. It had provided the science of canon law with a normative body of laws that were exhaustive at the time and based on a sound foundation. However, it has been noted that the codification exercise that ended in 1983 did not sufficiently distance itself from a body of laws that were not as clear-cut as could be desired, despite an impressive body of laws that had been built up over the years 1918–1959. The 1917 Code, for its part, had been based on the updating of legislation since the Council of Trent. There was also uncertainty about the model of the Church to be institutionalized. A majority believed that the Church model should be based on the order of the *communio* rather than that of the *institutio*.

The Council's answer to this was not long in coming. While there were few changes to the 1917 Code between 1962 and 1963, the pace of change and renewal subsequently increased, in the form of derogations, abrogations, reinforcement, and improvement. There were eleven conciliar commissions in all, including the central commission and two secretariats. Their work officially began on 14 November 1960, and ended 20 June 1962. The commissions drafted some seventy-five *schemata*— soon reduced to seventy—which were to be examined by the fathers of the Council. Some of the documents were veritable treatises on canon law, touching on the status of parishes and ecclesiastical benefices, the sacraments, and especially matrimonial law. There was another, more drastic phase of reducing the number of schemata under discussion (from seventy to seventeen) at the beginning of the second session and at the initiative of PAUL VI (1963–1978), who had just been elected. Among the documents sacrificed in this second selection process were texts with a certain legal scope. Before the end of the first session on 5 December 1962, John XXIII had set up a co-ordination commission with an explicit mandate: "All matters relating to the revision of the Code of Canon Law will be the responsibility of a competent commission." The Council, therefore, was content to establish a general direction for the Code, leaving the technical details up to a special commission.

However, this mechanism of delegating responsibility should not be seen as a sign of relinquishment on the part of the papacy or, even less, by the council. John XXIII, in his first ENCYCLICAL (*Ad Petri cathedram*, 26 June 1959), stated his intention of adapting the New Code to the needs of the times. Paul VI, on 22 June 1963, the day following his election, mentioned the revision of the Church law in his first message to the world. As he saw it, the laws should "accommodate the needs of God's people." The importance of this goal would be confirmed by his two successors. JOHN PAUL I (1978) referred to it specifically on 27 August 1978, the day after his election, and JOHN PAUL II also did so in the same circumstances, on 17 October 1978. He stated that he would do his utmost "to promote the implementation of the standards and positions of the Council."

An ad hoc commission was officially established on 28 March 1963, during the first intersession, allowing the fathers to prepare remarks and suggestions on the codification. Cardinal Pietro Ciriaci was appointed president of the commission and Msgr. Violardo secretary. The latter was shortly afterwards appointed to the Congregation for the discipline of the sacraments and replaced by Father Bigador, who was in turn replaced in 1975 by Msgr. Castillo Lara. There were major changes in the membership of the commission. Twelve more cardinals were appointed in November 1963, adding to the thirty CARDINALS initially named. The number of members was therefore brought to forty-four, evenly divided between twenty-one cardinals from the Curia and twenty-one titulars of residential sees. These latter were expected to bring their practical experience of canon law to the

process of codification. On 17 April 1964, Paul VI added to this committee of cardinals a body of seventy consultants, one of whom was a layman, Professor P. Ciprotti. Other appointments followed, including that of eighteen more cardinals and three patriarchs of the Eastern Catholic Churches. The group of consultants numbered as many as 125 in 1969. Among them were eight laymen, professors of canon law for the most part, such as Jean Gaudemet from France and Stephan Kutter from the United States.

A first informal meeting of the commission of cardinals was held in December 1963, and the decision was made to postpone work until the end of the Council sessions. In June 1965, after a preliminary exchange of views, the consultants produced a document containing the *Quaestiones fundamentales* for review by the commission. On November 1965, at the official opening of the Codification process, Paul VI spoke in favor of a "readaptation" (*recognoscere*) of canon law, which would imply going beyond a simple updating of the Code of 1917. In a circular letter of 15 January 1966, Cardinal Ciriaci appealed to all the bishops of Christendom, requesting that they send to Rome their suggestions as well as the names of canonists who might be added to the list of consultants. This procedure was reminiscent of the method employed in 1904.

At the end of January 1966, the consultants divided into ten groups; later on, there would be fourteen. Each group had to study a specific subject dealt with in the old Code. Another group of coordinators put together a number of guiding principles that were submitted to the SYNOD of bishops in Rome in October 1967 at the request of Paul VI. The document was voted on by the 120 bishops present and approved by a two-thirds majority. Work continued on the basis of this approval. As Cardinal Felici said in 1969, it was a question of "reviewing, changing, and reworking, like Penelope's cloth."

In his speech of 20 November 1965, the pope had also raised the idea of a fundamental law (*Lex fundamentalis*), which would contain the provisions of a constitutional law for the Church. The first elements were to be reflected in conciliar documents, outlining the legal consequences of new pastoral positions. In fact, the council had made important changes to the normative order inherited from the 1917 Code. Some principles were highlighted, for example that of the authority of the Episcopal College (constitution 22, *Lumen Gentium*), the principle of Episcopal conferences (decree 28, *Christus Dominus*), and the new codification process (for example, the constitution governing the liturgy, *Sacrosanctum Concilium*, 128; *Christus Dominus*, 44).

The commission of cardinals expressed its approval of the drafting of a "fundamental Code" for the Church (plenary meeting of 25 November 1965). They proposed a few successive drafts, the fourth of which was sent out to the bishops in 1970. Opinion among the bishops was divided as to the appropriateness of having a body of laws recognizing the fundamental rights of the faithful. Some observers noted that the Church already had a fundamental law—the Gospel. The difficulties inherent in this project led to the disbanding of the commission in 1981. The main difficulty, as noted above, was the lack of sufficient distance from a body of laws which were not very clearly defined.

In 1980, in view of the many requests for information and explanation from the synod of bishops, the commission had decided to include thirty-six canons of the draft of the fundamental law in the future Code. Technically, the legislation made concessions on the possible formalization of the law and the changes in the hierarchy of canonical norms. However, the abandonment of the project in the autumn of 1981 provided normal legal protection only for those rights deemed essential by the same legislator. The dissolution of the commission meant that the Church may have missed the opportunity to create a normative platform that could be used by both the Latin and Eastern Churches.

The codification of Eastern law had been a pending question for some time. John XXIII had refused, during an audience with Cardinal Agagianian on 12 December 1958, to promulgate a fifth section of the Code, the drafting of which had begun in 1927. The refusal by the pope meant that the question would be deferred until after the Council. Cardinal Agagianian was president of the commission for the drafting of the Eastern code of canon law.

In 1967 Paul VI issued an official reminder (*motu propio Episcopalis potestatis*) that the four parts already promulgated were still in force, with a reservation with respect to modifications made to the canonical *ordinamento* by the Council. After the death of Cardinal Agagianian in 1971, a new commission was formed and the code of canons of the Eastern Churches was promulgated in 1991. However, no juridic link was established with the Latin Church Code of 1983 despite the apparent unanimity of views seen in the decisions of the Council.

The groups that were formed concentrated their efforts on the *schema novissimum*, which resulted from the revision of 1981. John Paul II committed himself to studying it in detail with the assistance of five experts, and then with the help of a special commission made up of Cardinal Casaroli, secretary of state, and Cardinal Ratzinger, N. Jubani Arnau, and V. Fagiolo. In the meantime several drafts of the code, intended to provide the general body of legislation, had been produced by the commission (1977, 1980, and 1982). Cardinal Felici, who had replaced P. Ciriaci following the death of the latter in 1967, was the president. Upon his death on 22 March 1982, he was in turn replaced by Msgr. Castillo Lara, secretary of the commission since 1975. The material was divided into seven books (rather than five for the Code of 1917). This was in accordance with a decision taken at the time of the very first draft. The themes broke with the traditional conception of the Church as a perfect society by placing emphasis on the Church as communion (*communio Ecclesiarum*), in a model described in detail in books III and IV of the Code. In these books teaching and sanctification were more closely associated with service and with function in the Church than with power in the traditional sense. This in no way challenged the authority of the sovereign pontiff, and it recognized his right to intervene directly to settle any question in his role as universal pastor. The Church was therefore to remain a "hierarchical communion" (J. B. d' Onorio), *cum et sub Pietro*.

Other trends and influences appeared quite early in the codification process. The concept of the particular Church gained ground. The Church in this case was conceived of as a living community of the faithful and was defined in and of itself and by its own activity, rather than simply by its relationship to the discipline of the universal Church.

Successive outlines of the code employed the technique of subsidiarity as expressed by PIUS XI (1922–1939) in his 1931 encyclical *Quadragesimo anno*. It advised that groups of lower rank within the Church should not be deprived of the opportunity to perform functions and duties of which they were capable in favor of groups with greater powers and authority. More flexibility could be achieved if one paid greater attention to specific circumstances. Furthermore, the recognition of customs that sometimes went against the law (canons 23 to 28) made the Code a document rich in pastoral sensitivity and allowed for a reduction of the number of norms by 30 percent compared with the Code of 1917 (1,752 canons versus 2,414).

Work continued on the drafting of the Code, with a sort of "shuttle diplomacy" among the commissions. Some people guessed that the final version of the Code would be ready for the year 1980 or 1981. The announcer of VATICAN RADIO even declared on October 21, 1980, "E pronto il nuovo Codice!" However the last passages and revisions took longer than expected, and after some 5,561 hours of collegial work, over 154 plenary sessions, and 58 mixed sessions or small groups of consultants working, the final draft was placed in the hands of John Paul II on 22 April 1982. Prior to this, 90 percent of the bishops had had the opportunity to air their views on the successive stages of the Code over seven general consultations. The date chosen for its promulgation had a special symbolic significance: the drafting of the Code had taken twenty-four years to the day—from 25 January 1959, to 25 January 1983. In keeping with the conditions governing periods of transition between two legal systems, it entered into force on 27 November 1983.

The Code was indeed like the "disciplinary crowning" (J. Herranz) of Vatican II. John Paul II himself described it as the "Code of the Council" (l'OSSERVATORE ROMANO of 21–22 November 1983). In his speech presenting the

Code, on 3 February 1983, the pope explained the expression "Code of the council" and described his conception of a norm or law within the Church. In his view, the Church has a pyramidal structure, with Scripture at the head and beneath it, side by side, the acts of Vatican II and the Code. Before him, Paul VI, "the theologian of ecclesial law," had adopted the adage *ubi Ecclesia, ibi jus* ("as is the Church, so is its law")—different in principle from any civil or human law. It was conceived of as a "law of the spirit" (speech of 8 February 1973) that avoided establishing an undesirable separation between the institution and the spirit, between theology and law. Beyond the strictly legal domain, the Code of 1983 should be more of an *ordo* than a code, since it identifies so closely with pastoral concerns and the conciliar notion of "the people of God." In fact, this title is used in Book II of the Code.

Based on reactions to the Code over the past ten years, it would seem that one essential aspect has received the most attention: the translation into legal terms of the Council's opinions. For example, one Chilean priest expressed regret that the Code had made the law "rigid." He believed that much remained to be done before canon law could free itself of the charge of "legalism." Many observers were disappointed that the Code offered such insignificant changes in areas like the organization of parishes, the situation of women in the Church, and the ordination of married men. Observers have also criticized the fact that the Code distances itself from some of the bold steps of the Council (such as the pastoral council or the opening up of functions to lay persons). It has also been noted that there is a more authoritarian approach and a greater tendency toward centralization from Rome. Most of the criticism from non-Catholic churches was directed at this last point. Protestants expressed disagreement with canon 331 of the Code, which describes the pope as the "Vicar of Christ." At the time the new Code was published, an American association reopened the controversy surrounding the dropping of fundamental Law. They published a draft charter that sought to guarantee to all Catholics the "fundamental rights inherited from their baptism": freedom of worship, the right to choose the leaders of the Church, and the right to abortion. Therefore, despite the many efforts made and despite a definite new tone, the Code was received with mixed responses but never with indifference. Certainly the new Code seems to be guided less by the search for a rational perception of the canonical order than by the wish to develop the contents of the faith into a legal framework. The fact that many would have liked theological principles to prevail over juridical considerations in the Code has led to the mixed reactions of some who have read it. For the ecclesial society, the Code represents an instrument of transition in the search for new directions within a modern society. It is not the perfect expression of the Church as a model of society.

François Jankowiak

Bibliography

Documentation from the codification process of 1983 has been turned over to the Vatican Archives, but they are still not open to researchers. Therefore, one may only consult periodicals that have recorded the stages of the process such as *La Civiltà Cattolica* in Italy, *La Documentation catholique* in France, or the *Herder Korrespondenz* in Germany. In response to a wish expressed by participants in the International Congress on Canon Law in Rome, 20–25 May 1968, the Holy See requested that the commission make available information on its activities. This was published in several volumes in the form of two annual volumes entitled *Communicationes*. They remain the most valuable source of information available today.

Castillo Lara, R. J. "Le livre I du CIC de 1983. Histoire et principes," *L'année Canonique*, XXXI (1988), 17–54.

Corecco, E. *Théologie et droit canon. Ecrits pour une nouvelle théorie générale du droit canon*, Fribourg, 1990.

d'Onorio, J. B. *Le Pape et le gouvernement de l'Eglise*, Paris, 1992.

D'Ostilio, F. *La storia del nuovo Codice di diritto canonico*. Revisione, promulgazione, presentazione, Cité du Vatican, 1983.

Epp, R., Lefebvre, C. and Metz, R. *Le Droit et les institutions de l'Eglise catholique latine de la fin du XVIII siècle à 1978. Sources et institutions* [Histoire du droit et des Institutions de l'Eglise en Occident, XVI], Paris, 1981; *La nuova legislazione canonica, corso sul Nuovo Codice di Diritto Canonico*, Rome, 1983.

Erdo, P. *Introductio in historiam scientiae canonicae, Praenotanda ad Codicem*, Rome, 1990.

Fox, F. "A general Synthesis of the work of the Pontifical Commission for the Revision of the Code of Canon Law," *The Jurist*, XLVIII (1988), 800–40.

Gaudemet, J. "Le Droit canonique au milieu du XX siècle. Du Code de 1917 à l'avenement de Jean XXIII," *Les quatre fleuves*, 18 (1983), 35–42.

Grocholewski, Z. "Die Canones über den Papst und das ökumenische Konzil in dem neuen Kodex des kanonischen Rechts," in *Kanon-Jahrbuch der Gesellschaft für das Recht der Ostkirchen*, IX (1989), 51–81.

Morrisey, F. G. "Recent Ecclesiastical Legislation and the Code of Canon Law," *Studia canonica*, 6 (1972), 3–77.

Potz, R. "L'idée de droit et le développement juridique d'après le CIC de 1983," *Concilium CCV* (1986), 31–41.

Schouppe, J. P. *Le Droit canonique. Introduction générale et droit matrimonial*, Malines, 1990.

Schulz, W. "Problemi della recezione del nuovo Codice nella Germania Federale," *Il diritto ecclesiastico* (1987), 1010–20.

Viladrich, P. J. *Teoria de los derechos fundamentlales e los fieles. Presupuestos criticos*, Pamplona, 1969; *El Proyecto de Ley fundamental de la Iglesia, texto y analisis critico*, Pamplona, 1971.

CODE OF CANONS OF THE EASTERN CHURCHES. PIUS IX was the first pope to express the wish to collect the canons of the Eastern Churches together in one code (constitution *Romani Pontifices*, 6 January 1862). VATICAN I recognized the need to provide the Eastern Churches with a complete code that would be common to them all. LEO XIII shared the same concern and approved the canons of several Eastern synods: the Syrian synod of 1888, the Ruthenian synod of 1891, the synods of Alba Iulia (Romania) in 1882 and 1900, and the Coptic synod of 1898. PIUS X approved the canons of the Armenian synod of 1911. All of these canons, together with those of the 1736 Maronite synod of Mount Lebanon, which was specifically approved by BENEDICT XIV (brief *Singularis Romanorum*, 1 September 1741), and the Greek Melchite synod of 1835, make up the disciplinary heritage of all Eastern Churches.

The CODE OF CANON LAW (1917) deals with the Roman Church only. On 3 August 1927, PIUS XI, in an audience granted to Cardinal Luigi Sincero, decided that the law of the Eastern Churches would be codified. Work on the code was carried out in three stages. The preparatory phase began on 25 July 1927, when the cardinals of the Congregation for the Eastern Churches voted on the timeliness of codifying Eastern canon law. On 23 November 1929, PIUS XI created the commission of cardinals, *Pro Studiis Praeparatoriis Codificationis Orientalis*, under the chairmanship of Cardinal Pietro Gasparri, the secretary of state. The pope was opposed to the idea of a single code governing the Latin and Eastern churches (audience of 1 March 1930). Delegates of the Eastern Churches met for the first time on 7 March 1930 and decided to use the 1917 Code of Canon Law as the basis for their work. The preparation of the *Schema ad episcopos* lasted from 1930 to 1935, ending with the establishment in 1935 of a papal drafting committee. The chairman was Cardinal Luigi Sincero, who upon his death was replaced by Cardinal Massimo Massimi (17 February 1936). His successor, Cardinal Agagianian, Peter XV, would serve until 6 May 1971.

The drafting phase lasted from 1935 to 1948. A preliminary draft sent to the printer in 1942 was completed in 1945 under the title *Codex Iuris canonici Orientalis*. The writing phase ended on 13 March 1948, following approval by PIUS XII of final corrections.

Then began the phase of promulgation. The code, however, was not published in its entirety, but in parts: matrimonial law (motu proprio *Crebrae allatae sunt*, 22 February 1949); law on procedure (motu proprio *Sollicitudinem nostram*, 6 January 1950); law governing monks and nuns and patrimonial law, as well as definition of the terms used in Eastern law (motu proprio *Postquam apostolicis litteris*, 2 February 1952), oriental rites, and the rights of persons (motu proprio *Cleri sanctitati*, 2 June 1957). All of these comprised 1,590 canons out of a proposed total of 2,666.

The codification exercise was interrupted by several events. On 9 October 1958, Pius XII died; then, on 25 January 1959, JOHN XXIII announced the convening of VATICAN II. An ecumenical dialogue was opened with those Eastern Churches that had separated from the Roman Catholic Church. Codification did not resume after Vatican II had concluded, because the code no longer represented the council's orientation. The committee, however, continued to publish its sources, as it had begun to do in 1931, and gave the official interpretation of those parts of the code that had already been published.

Work started again at the initiative of PAUL VI. On 10 June 1972, he appointed a new papal commission to prepare a new code of Eastern canon law based on the guiding principles of Vatican II, the *Pontificia commissio Codici Iuris canonici Orientalis recognoscendo* (PCCICOR).

The commission carried out preparatory work between June 1972 and January 1974, and began work on the drafts after the plenary assembly opened by Paul VI on 18 March 1974. The pope expressed the wish that the members of the Eastern Churches themselves draft the code. The commission also approved guiding principles for the revision of the code. The text was divided into eight outlines, which were dispatched from June 1980, to be read and approved.

On 17 November 1986, the complete *Schema Codicis Iuris canonici Orientalis* was sent to the members of the commission, chaired by Cardinal Joseph Parecattil, who died on 20 February 1987 and was not replaced. The deputy chairman, Msgr. Emile Eid, presented the *Schema novissimum*, with incorporated amendments, to the Roman pontiff on 28 January 1989.

John Paul II promulgated the Code of Canons of the Eastern Churches (apostolic constitution *Sacri canones*, 18 October 1990). The first codification of the law of the Eastern Churches, it is common to the twenty-one Eastern Churches in full communion with the Apostolic See: the Coptic and Ethiopian (Alexandrian rite); Malankarese, Maronite, and Syrian (Antiochian rite), Albanian, Belarussian, Bulgarian, Greek, Hungarian, Italo-Albanian, Melchite, Romanian, Russian, Ruthenian, Slovakian, Ukrainian and Yugoslavian (rite of Constantinople); Armenian (Armenian rite); and Chaldean and Malabaran (Chaldean rite).

This concluded the updating of the laws of the entire discipline of the Catholic Church, which had begun with the Vatican II council.

Together with the Code of Canon Law of the Roman Church and the apostolic constitution *Pastor bonus* (28 June 1988) reforming the Curia, the Code of Canons of the Eastern Churches is a unique *ius canonicum* (John Paul II, speech presenting the code, 25 October 1990).

Simplified Outline of the Code of Canons of the Eastern Churches. The code is divided into thirty titles, which are in turn divided into chapters, themselves further broken down into articles and numbers. The norms deal successively with the Christian faithful, their rights and obligations (title I); the *sui iuris* and ritual churches (title II); the supreme authority of the Church, in other words, the Roman pontiff and the College of Bishops (title III); the patriarchal churches, i.e., the election, rights, and obligations of patriarchs, the synod of bishops of the patriarchal Churches, the patriarchal Curia, the vacant or impeded see, the metropolitan of the patriarchal church, the patriarchal assembly, the territory of the patriarchal church and the power of the patriarch and synod outside of this territory (title IV); the major archiepiscopal churches (title V); the metropolitan and other *sui iuris* churches (title VI); the eparchs and bishops (title VII); the exarchates and exarchs (title VIII); meetings of exarchs of several *sui iuris* churches (title IX); the clerics, i.e., the training of clerics, the joining of clerics to an eparchy, the rights and obligations of clerics, and the loss of clerical status (title X); laymen (title XI); monks and members of religious orders, as well as other members of institutions of consecrated life, including monks and other religious, communal life societies *ad instar* of members of religious orders, secular institutes, other forms of consecrated life and societies of apostolic life (title XII); associations of the faithful (title XIII); evangelization of people (title XIV); the ecclesiastical magisterium, subdivided into the teaching role of the Church in general, the ministry of the Word of God, Catholic education, and instruments of social communication and books in particular (title XV); divine worship, especially the sacraments (title XVI); baptized non-Catholics who come to full communion with the Catholic Church (title XVII); ecumenism and the promotion of Christian unity (title XVIII); juridic acts and persons (title XIX); offices (title XX); the power of governance (title XXI); recourse against administrative acts (title XXII); temporal goods of the Church (title XXIII); procedure in general (title XXIV); contentious procedures (title XXV); some special procedures, i.e. matrimonial procedures, nullity of sacred orders, and proceedings for the removal and transfer of priests (title XXVI); penal sanctions within the Church (title XXVII); procedure for inflicting punishment, i.e., penal proceedings and the infliction of punishment by extrajudicial decree (title XXVIII); administrative law, customs, and acts (title XXIX); prescription and the calculation of time (title XXX). The text of the apostolic constitution *Pastor bonus* appears as an annex.

Dominique Le Tourneau

Bibliography

Badii, C. "Intorno alla codificazione canonica orientale," *Il diritto ecclesiastico* 44 (1933), 3–15.

Cicognani, A. G. "De codificazione canonica orientale," *Apollinaris*, 5 (1932), 86–95.

Congregation for the Orient Churches, *Servizio Informazioni Chiese Orientali* (SICO).

Les Eglises catholiques orientales, Paris, 1970.

Faltin, D. "La codificazione del diritto canonico orientale," *La sacra Congregazione per le Chiese orientali nel cinquantesimo delle fondazione (1917–1967)*, Rome, 1969, 121–37.

Fonti della codificazione orientali (since 1931).

Giannini, A. "Sulla codificazione del diritto canonico orientale," *Il diritto ecclesiastico* 58 (1947), 193–204.

Metz, R. "La premiere tentative de codifier le droit des Eglises orientales catholiques au XX siècle. Latinisation ou identité orientale?," *L'Année Canonique*, 23 (1979), 289–309; "La premiere codification du droit des Eglises orientales catholiques (1927–1958)," R. Epp, C. Lefebvre, and R. Metz, *Histoire du droit . . . , de la fin du XVIII siècle à 1978. Sources et institutions*, Paris, 1981, 272–81; "La seconde codification du droit des Eglises orientales catholiques a partir de 1972," ibid., 343–52; "La nouvelle codification du droit l'Eglise (1959–1983)," *Revue de Droit Canonique*, XXXIII (1983), 110–68; "Quel est le droit pour les Eglises orientales unies à Rome?," *L'Année Canonique*, 30 (1987), 393–409.

Nuntia (since 1973), *organe de la commission pour la révision du Code de droit canonique oriental.*

"Pontificia Commissione per la revisione del Codice di diritto canonico orientale."

COINS, PAPAL. The minting of coins is one of the basic expressions of sovereignty; papal coins are therefore the coins of the Church in the role of a temporal power. However, questions remain about whether the Church can properly be viewed as a state. Any state that puts its mark on a piece of money is claiming legitimacy and credibility. Can the Church of Rome, a spiritual power, have the confidence in its temporal power needed to assert itself in the realm of material goods by issuing coins? "My kingdom is not of this world" and "Render unto Caesar that which is Caesar's" are difficult formulas to reconcile for anyone who inspects the marvelous monuments in gold and silver that are the papal coins. But in fact, the inscriptions and denominations show the desire to honor the triumphant post-Tridentine Church through characteristics that include artistic beauty. So, *a* *posteriori*, given the temporal politics of the papacy, the governing organ of the Church felt itself justified in minting coins by reason and right. In economic terms, however, the rationalization was not as certain.

Early Papal Coins. On the basis of the PATRIMONY OF ST. PETER, granted by imperial Byzantine power, the Roman Church found itself, little by little, associated with money of Byzantine origin at the end of the 7th century: some quarters of silver silica (0.35 g) are engraved with the initials of Pope SERGIUS I (687–695). The situation changed in 731, when the papacy condemned iconoclasm; in 732 Emperor Leo III reacted and confiscated the Patrimony of St. Peter in Sicily and Sardinia. This led the papacy to distance itself from him. GREGORY III (731–741) and ZACHARIAS (741–752) are known to have issued the same small coins as their predecessor, but their initials occupy more space. Due to material circumstances surrounding the alloy used in these coins, their value diminished rapidly, and their area of circulation was limited to Latium. It is therefore generally accepted that papal coins did not truly exist until the moment when the papacy was recognized as a state apart from any other exterior political power, including the Frankish royalty and the Carolingian empire. Details about the workings of the Roman mint, which struck the first coins for HADRIAN I (772–795) and LEO III (795–816) are not known, but the coins themselves allow us to follow the political evolution that shaped them.

The first type of coin had a front, or right side, bearing a bust of the pope in full view, together with his name, "HADRIANVSP(A)P(A)"; on the back was a cross in brackets laid across two steps, with the inscription "VICTORIA D(omi)N(I)" and the name of the workshop, "R(o)M(a)," in the background. The legends and types were still inspired by the Romano-Byzantine type, but the pope, by affixing his name, showed his desire for independence from BYZANTIUM. The second type, already moving away from figured motifs, illustrated the growing influence of the FRANKISH powers. However, the name of the pontiff, as well as that of the first designated pastor, St. Peter, clearly define the Church's authority. The coronation of Charlemagne in 800 symbolically put the Patrimony in the Carolingian geopolitical sphere: the coins thereafter reproduce the Carolingian epigraphic type. The monogram of the pope is on the front, and the legends make reference to a political entity (the domain of St. Peter) and to a temporal authority (emperor, king of Italy, or sometimes the Roman nobles during periods of weakened imperial power). This formal simplification allowed the use of dies to create legends and types, a technique easier to master than engraving directly on the coins. Typological innovations are rare and have only a brief existence: the blessing hand (for Benedict IV, 900–903); palm leaves and rosettes (JOHN XI, 931–935); the "realis-

tic" façade of the porch of a basilica (BENEDICT VII, 974–983); and, more often, a bust of St. Peter (JOHN VIII, 872–882; JOHN IX, 898–900; SERGIUS III, 904–911; BENEDICT VII, 974–983).

From the 9th century until the end of the 10th (about 980), the Roman workshop made the denier—a silver coin adapted from the Carolingian monetary system (in theory, 1.7 g, but variations go from 1.6 g to 1 g according to the era)—in the name of various popes. We have only one record of the administrative operations of this workshop: in 936 an Andreas is mentioned, a moneymaker and son of a moneymaker (Johannes), who belonged to the well-to-do elite of Rome—the City—where the papacy supported the minting of money through fees paid to the Church. Some of these revenues came from the commercialization of property in landed domains throughout Latium, thanks to the influx of foreign money during PILGRIMAGES to Rome, and finally, thanks to the St. Peter's pence (Romscott) paid by the Anglo-Saxon principalities. Papal coins during this time were an expression of a sovereign power wishing to confirm the principle of the succession to St. Peter's throne. Furthermore, during the time when the power of the papacy was not being questioned, and when the circulation of abundant, strong, and stable coins (the deniers of the imperial workshops at Pavia and then Lucca, finally replaced around 1160 by the "international" denier from Provins) answered the needs of commerce and of the papal treasury, there was a prolonged interruption in the production of papal coins (from around 980—Benedict VII—until 1180—ALEXANDER III).

Stages in the Restoration of Papal Coins. A slow evolution occurred during the course of the 12th century, reflecting new political and economic pressures. In order to restore the freedom of action and speech that had been lost during the 11th and 12th centuries, the papacy undertook the restoration of its material patrimony—territorial and fiscal—and therefore interested itself once again in monetary issues.

Beginning at the end of the 11th century, papal power was wielded through a central governmental organ: the SACRED COLLEGE, heading a collection of administrative structures among which was the CHAMBER (*Camera*), charged with all financial management of Church possessions and revenues. From this point on, the latter, through the intermediary of the cardinal CHAMBERLAIN, was able to establish an economic policy, both financial and monetary.

Although it was still legally under the control of the papacy, the Roman commune had obtained the right to coin its own money during the course of the 1170s, issuing a small coin with a low value, called a provinois. In 1188, CLEMENT III reaffirmed his authority through an agreement signed with the commune, under the terms of which he conceded a third of the profits from coining money to the commune. Then, in 1208, INNOCENT III set the rate for money-changing between the Champagne region provinois and the Roman provinois: 12 Champagne coins equaled 16 Roman ones, a rate that provoked, in the short term, the hoarding and recasting of the Champagne coins. Still, incessant confrontations between the great Roman families led the Romans to appeal to Brancaleone degli Andalo, a foreign podestà (magistrate) who lived in the city, in 1252. Degli Andalo and his successors coined money without being concerned about the papacy—money adapted to the new needs of the Italian economy, whose effects were being felt in Rome. These were the first silver gros (3.5 g), placed under the sole authority of the podesta and the Roman SENATE. Tensions between the pope and the City, and between the pope and the senators, led the pontiff to desert Rome and to live in an itinerant fashion in the Papal States. Finally, in 1309, growing insecurity led him to move to AVIGNON, where he was able to resume his own monetary operations. The workshops of Pont-sur-sorgues and Avignon were directly administered by the Chamber and from then on minted coins only in the name of the ruling pontiffs.

CLEMENT V (1305–1314) first issued a silver gros inspired directly by the French gros tournois, the standard currency of Europe. On the front was the mitered bust of the sovereign pontiff in the act of performing a blessing; on the back, a footed cross, surrounded by a ring on which the name of the principality was inscribed. Next, JOHN XXII (1316–1334) created a gold coin to be used for major transactions, modeled on the florentine of Florence. It can be distinguished from the latter by the words "SANT PETRI." A second type had, on the front, the sovereign enthroned, and on the back, a leafy cross, motifs probably taken directly from royal French coins. John also issued a silver coin copied from the Neapolitan gillat—the carlin—on the face of which was the same motif. By putting viable, stable coins into the marketplace, John XXII seems to have wished to clean up the mass of coins coming into his treasury and to meet the needs of regional commerce. Ultimately, however, the Avignon papacy—under pressure from moneymakers worried about profiting from their activity, and at the same time faced with growing expenses—allowed some repeated manipulations of the title and weight of the billon coins, with the weight of a gold florin. The 1370s also saw GREGORY XI put out lighter florins adorned on the front with three linked crowns (an expression of the triple authority of the pope) and, on the back, with two crossed keys.

Several technical documents show us the organization of the workshop. The papacy hired local men and signed a contract (in general for a three-year period) with a banker ("moneyer") to mint the amounts the papacy needed. At first, these were mostly Florentine bankers. Similarly, another agreement was signed with a master engraver to get the tools ready, recruit the technical personnel, and manage the workshop. At the end of the minting of a series, a sampling of the coins, taken at intervals during the minting, was examined in the presence of representatives of the pope. Then the money was released into the market by the moneyers and the merchants. The return of the popes to Rome in 1378 might be expected to have corresponded to a renewal of pontifical prerogatives. Urban V, during his brief stay in Rome in 1367, had had a silver gros minted that showed him seated and performing a blessing on the front, and, on the back, had two crossed keys and the words "FACTA IN ROMA." In fact, the beginnings of the Great SCHISM and the power of the rival aristocratic families of Rome rendered the papacy powerless, and the pope had to come to terms with the Roman SENATE. From 1350 until 1432 the latter had been minting a gold ducat that copied a Venetian prototype: Christ was depicted on the front, and, on the back, St. Peter handing a banner to a kneeling senator. It was only with EUGENE IV that this senatorial usurpation was symbolically ended, a process that occurred in two stages. Around 1437, he had a ducat minted according to the senatorial type, but his arms placed in the exergue bore witness to the decisive restoration of papal power. Made of fine gold, this ducat weighed 3.52 g (96 to the livre). Then Eugene completely eliminated all references to the Senate. From then on, the front was adorned with the pope's arms topped by the keys and the tiara, and including his name and number in the order of popes: "EUGENIUS P.P. QUARTUS"; while the back showed St. Peter and the words "ROMA CAPUT MUNDI" and "S. PETRUS ALMA ROMA."

In the second half of the 15th century, papal power was restored in Italy. Nicolas V reconquered lost territories and attached the local potentates to himself; his legates controlled activity in the moneymaking centers of Ancona, Macerata, Perugia, Camerino, and even Bologna. A ducat was adorned with St. Peter as the fisher of souls. The end of the Great Schism also allowed him to celebrate the recent reunification for the jubilee of 1450, the occasion for the minting of a triple ducat and the beautification of Rome. But by 1453, the fall of Constantinople and the subsequent CRUSADE were the major preoccupation of the papacy, which had also let itself be drawn into the Franco-Aragonese quarrel over the throne of Naples. In 1461, the discovery of veins of ALUM at Tolfa brought in large amounts of money regularly for the papacy, which decided to dedicate them to the crusade effort. Although coin types had gradually diversified, they remained traditionally inspired until PAUL II created an innovative ducat on the back of which was an image of Veronica. Whether an allusion to the relic that the pilgrims of the jubilee of 1475 could appreciate, or a statement of the pope's theological opposition to the Hussite heresy, the motif referred to current realities. In addition, the Roman capital tended to be displayed in the words on the coins, and the numbering of the years of the pontificate appeared. Paul's successor, SIXTUS IV, continued the modernization of papal coins. Emulating the rulers of northern Italy, he had his first portrait put on a double gros made of silver. Probably at the time of the 1475 jubilee, he created the first true florin from the Chamber to facilitate the collection of taxes. It was conceived along the lines of the "stretto" florin of Florence and sized so that there were 100 per livre (3.39 g).

Although its effect was limited, a final innovation was seen during the pontificate of INNOCENT VIII, with the minting of a divisionary coin of pure copper that was entirely fiduciary: the *quattrino*.

Renaissance and Reforms. A consistent territorial base, significant economic resources, and active contact with the cultural centers of the Italian Renaissance led the papacy to pursue independence and prestige. Papal coins were one of the factors in this pursuit, if only to recruit mercenaries for the defense and extension of the PAPAL STATES. Gold and silver coins of the time were routinely decorated with the bust of the reigning pontiff. At the same time, the papacy was trying to set up a stable monetary system worthy of its ambitions. While continuing to mint the florin of the Chamber in Italy and the papal ducat and its multiples, Julius II first experimented in Avignon with a papal coin that could compete with other European coins. He created the *scudo d'oro* weighing 3.39 g, with a standard of 96.3%. Then CLEMENT VII made it Italian by having it coined at the workshop in Bologna. Finally, the former treasurer of the Church, PAUL III, brought it to Rome but pragmatically modified the conditions of its production. Heavier and of a better alloy than foreign coins, the papal money was regularly exported and recast, a movement of capital strongly detrimental to the papacy. Therefore, Paul III made his *scudo* conform to the prevalent European model: a standard 91.6% and with 100 per livre (3.39 g); the value was then set at 10 "julius," or 100 *baiocchi*.

In 1504, the constant depreciation of the *grosso papale* had prompted JULIUS II to create a new standard for currency: the "julius" (*giulio* or *paolo* according to the name of the pope). Standardized at 91.6% and with 106 per livre (about 3.2 g), it was worth 9 and later 10 *baiocchi*. Beginning with Leo X, the large coins multiplied and diversified: a teston worth 3 giuli (about 9.6 g), ducat, quarter ducat . . . Finally, under SIXTUS V (1585–1590) the piaster appeared, worth first 10, then 10.5 *giuli* (in 1643) and weighing about 30 g. Thus, while technically not related to the smaller coins (made from alloys), gold and silver found stability—relative stability, at any rate, for silver coins were becoming more and more abundant in Europe and therefore were depreciating in value.

However, the newfound stability did not extend to coins for daily use: the *baiocco* and its component coins of lesser value (down to the *quattrino*), made of billon (a silver-based alloy). During a period of economic and financial crisis, it was the most vulnerable coin, for rulers tended to release more of these, thereby weakening their value. It was also the favored coin of counterfeiters who, by billonage (extraction of the silver), hastened its depreciation. Under CLEMENT VIII (1592–1605), the flood of counterfeit billon was such that he decided to mint the *quattrino*, and also the multiples of it, up to the *half-baiocco*, out of pure copper in order to stop this process.

In effect, the financial needs of the papacy were always greater than the available resources. Actively participating in the Italian wars, opposing protestantism and the Turkish peril, and dedicated to the patronage of art, the ruling pontiffs had difficulty balancing their budget. In order to build the new ST. PETER'S, Julius II and Leo X sold INDULGENCES, positions, and cardinalates, which supplied ammunition for Protestant attacks. Moreover, to put pressure on the papacy in wartime, in order to control the national churches, Christian rulers did not hesitate to forbid the transfer of funds to Rome. The most extreme case was the sack of ROME. In 1527, the Imperials plundered the city and held Clement VII captive; the pope had to pay a ransom of 400,000 ducats. The papal treasures were then melted down under the watchful eye of the bombardier B. Cellini, and Angelo Schauer, a chargé d'affaires of the Fuggers who remained in Rome, minting coins as was necessary: silver ducats and their divisions (the half- and quarter-ducat), decorated simply with the arms and busts of Peter and Paul, and the appropriate denomination: "DVCATO, QVART."

Paul III fought against the loss of gold, PIUS IV tried to restore the economy of his states, Pius V cut back on the court's luxurious lifestyle and forbade any secession from the Papal States: all unfortunately unsuccessful efforts because, at the same time, the spendthrift practices of Leo X emptied the coffers, and ill-conceived measures by Pius V (the internment of Jewish communities, creation of the commission of the INDEX) weakened several economic sectors, while the political interventionism of Gregory XIII brought about an uncontrolled increase in fiscal pressures, even causing some serious social disorder.

Sixtus V offered a crude correction of the situation. Banditry was stopped, and economic and financial measures were taken (price-fixing, customs protection, subsidies for agriculture and artisans). But he focused especially on accumulating a war treasury destined for a crusade. More than four million *scudi* were piled up in CASTEL SANT'ANGELO. From GREGORY XIV (1590–1591) to GREGORY XV (1621–1623), this extravagant sum and others were swallowed up by the needs of the multifaceted battle against the Protestants (the creation of the Roman COLLEGES, subsidies paid to the League, a pension paid to Queen Christina when she converted, etc.).

Historical developments and coin circulation had a definite and immediate impact on monetary art, as new techniques for minting and controlling money developed. Beginning in the 1520s, certain dates of issuance appeared (in both Roman and Arabic numerals) in some workshops in the Papal States, a practice that spread to Rome after 1555, along with the numbering of the year of the current pope's reign. Workmen regularly signed coins issued under their aegis, and under PAUL V, in 1617, the appearance of copper coins with fiduciary value explains the appearance of the name of a coin as a monetary type: "MEZZO BAIOCCO."

By the early 1600s there was an extraordinary degree of artistic flowering in papal coins. The quarter ducat (29 mm in diameter), the teston (30 mm), and especially the piaster (43 mm) offered engravers all the latitude necessary for creating portraits and "tableaus." Of the remarkable gallery of portraits done By by V. Belli, Caradosso, and others, the best of all is the one of CLEMENT VII, bearded (in deference to a vow made during captivity), done by Benvenuto Cellini around 1529. Coins also became an important chronicle of papal history. Three formats stand out in particular. The first is a thematic series based upon events, either realistic and descriptive (views of St. Peter's façade under Leo X and Sixtus V) or allegorical: allusions to the Calvary of Clement VII (B. Cellini made a double ducat with Christ in chains and the words "ECCE HOMO"); a double carlin with Christ fishing Peter from the water, and the words "QUARE DUBITASTI"; a julius with the Angel releasing Peter from prison, an allusion to the (repressive) justice of Sixtus V and to the perils threatening the papacy (a teston for Clement VIII showing Peter at the keel of a boat tossed by the winds and the waves). The second format is an illustration of a Biblical text: the miracle of Moses, the baptism of Christ (Gregory XIII), the three Magi (Leo X), Jesus among the scholars (Paul III), Paul struck down on the road to Damascus (Paul V). The final one consists of witness accounts, taking religious positions: Clement VII asked Valerio Belli in 1525 to show a liturgical act for the very firs time—the pope "opening the door" for the holy year on the back of a multiple of five ducats (on the front was a manger scene); PAUL IV reaffirmed papal authority on a teston where we see Peter holding out the keys to a kneeling pope near a ship's wheel, and the legend "SUMMA POTESTAS RERUM TIBI"; Sixtus V proposed an example, also for the first time, of a saint from modern times: Francis of Assisi receiving the stigmata (a piaster done by Guglielmo Troncio of Pisa); Gregory XIII made a reference to post-Tridentine piety by a representation of the Sacred Heart on a *quattrino*. No other state, on its own, could show this much originality, directly taken from the numismatic tradition of antiquity.

The Time of Crisis, from Urban VIII to Innocent XIII. The second third of the 17th century saw the economic and financial situation of the papacy and its states continue to worsen. Though he tried to remain neutral in all the conflicts between Christian princes, the pope often became involved despite himself, and his states paid an economic price on several occasions, despite costly fortifications and artillery. Under URBAN VIII, the states were devastated by an alliance including Venice, Tuscany, and Modena; under Alexander VII, the attack on the French embassy in Rome provoked a response from Louis XIV; Avignon and the Venaissin region were occupied and the Italian possessions were threatened; in 1688, and from 1707 to 1709, the papacy hired large armies at great expense in an unsuccessful attempt to stop the troops of Emperor Joseph I, who pillaged the Papal States.

Another heavy financial burden came from the ideological obligations of the papacy. One of its constant projects was to organize and support crusades by Christians against the infidels. In 1668–1669, the "European" campaign to reconquer Crete failed, and the papacy was handed all the debt incurred in the undertaking. In 1673, the pope financially supported Jan Sobieski, who crushed the TURKS. Similarly, in 1683, Leopold I, John III, Sobieski, and the rulers of Venice, supported by Innocent XI, chased them from Hungary and Belgrade. In 1714, Clement XI came to the aid of Venice, but the Turks succeeded in taking the Peloponnese, while a fleet armed by the pope was used by the EMPIRE for its own ambitions. It was a controversial crusade effort, to which the costs of the MISSIONS to evangelize the Far East were added. The ideal of supporting this defense and expansion of Christendom may be found on a coin from Innocent "XI: MELIUS EST DARE QUAM ACCIPERE." Nevertheless, the coffers were empty. Besides, the fortune hoarded by Sixtus V had already had the effect of blocking future productive investments in the Papal States. In the 17th and the early 18th centuries the papal economic crisis grew in proportion to the lifestyle led by the court. At the same time, the court was the only financial force helping Rome survive, as the city's situation became increasingly stagnant, requiring increasing assistance from the authorities. In order to maintain its sociopolitical prestige, the court demanded that coins be worthy of pontifical rank (e.g., of greater weights and better alloys). The "beautiful and good coin" of the pope then traveled across the border to be melted down and recast for profit by other countries, thus contributing to the existing imbalance of payments.

Technical measures failed to curb the growing debt: from Urban VIII to Alexander VII, the workshop was permanently moved to a Vatican property, saving upkeep costs for separate buildings. Under ALEXANDER VII, the development of a machine press driven by the water of the Aqua Paola brought technological advances in the minting of coins. Similarly, starting in 1646 under INNOCENT X, small denominations of copper coins (*quattrino, mezzo baiocco*) were minted exclusively in the workshop of Gubbio to combat the circulation of counterfeit coins of billon, rationalize production, and control costs. As for INNOCENT XI, though he suspended the issuing of the problematical piaster and reduced the weight of the teston in 1683–1684, he also modified the relationship that had been set up between gold and silver for more than a century and returned the monetary system to its former state of instability.

To a certain extent, these problems overshadow the gallery of portraits and types of backs inspired by the baroque esthetic and created by engravers such as G. Mola, Hier, Lucenti, P. P. Borner, and F. de Saint-Urbain. Foremost among them were the Hamerani, a veritable dynasty: the hands of Giovanni, Hermenegilde, and Otto signed many coins from INNOCENT XI (1676–1689) to PIUS VI (1775–1799). Their work includes busts of Innocent XI, Alexander VIII, Clement XI, Clement XII, and Benedict XIV, as well as a St. Peter enthroned in the clouds and a St. Matthew writing under the inspiration of an angel—numismatic scenes whose bodily foreshortening and movements of draped clothing show exceptional virtuosity.

On another level, the "beautiful coin" expected by the sociopolitical hierarchy of the pontifical court allowed the artist to cover the large space on the backs of gold quadruple coins, piasters, and silver testons with complex designs. These served to illustrate artitistic expressions of the papacy (the façade of St. Peter's, the fountain and square of the Pantheon [by Clement XI], the palace at Urbino); the guiding principles of papal politics: the battle against the Turks (St. Michael putting down Lucifer and, in 1690, the allegory of the Church holding a legionary banner), allusions to Innocent XII's efforts to lessen the tensions between the Christian princes (1694–1697) (such as the pelican feeding its children with its own flesh, 1693: NON SIBI SED ALIIS), aid for agriculture, and relaxation of taxes (1690), public works (the bridge of Castellana, the ports of Civitavecchia and Anzio); the pope's desire to promote the ideals of the council of TRENT: the Immaculate Conception (whose feast day was set in 1708), the cult of the saints, including Frances of Rome. It was also in this period, during the vacancy of the Holy See in 1655, that the symbol of the dove was set into the "glory" symbol of the Holy Spirit inspiring the cardinals meeting in CONCLAVE to elect the new pontiff; the first legend illustrates this idea: IN-FUNDE AMOREM CORDIBUS! But a rapid election was not what all the speakers wanted. While the papal throne remained vacant, the pontifical workshop issued coins under the direction of the CAMERLENGO, who benefited from the situation.

Pressing Reforms and External Crises. Due to the growing difficulties posed by conflicts with Christian rulers who threatened the Papal States, and the somewhat chaotic management resulting from the appointment of corrupt political favorites, such as Niccolo Coscia under Benedict XIII, the papacy was obliged to concentrate its efforts on the financial rather than the aesthetic aspects of coin production. Beginning with Innocent XIII (1721–1724), this trend grew stronger despite the development of several extremely popular and long-lived typological creations (allegories of the Church, and STS. PETER AND PAUL); coin designs were mostly limited to a portrait or the arms of the reigning pope, pious or political sayings, or even just the simple denomination of the coin.

In 1729, BENEDICT XIII replaced the existing gold coins with a new one: the *zecchino romano*, decorated with a rose. Its size was rapidly brought into conformity with the European standard (99 to the pound) in order to cut short the exportation of precious metals that followed the initial conditions of its release (97 to the pound). Also, the cut edge of the coin was patterned with a twisted design to counteract the shaving practiced by the counterfeiters. Clement XII tried to restore the economy of the Papal States by encouraging commerce and industry, creating a free port at Ancona, and even issuing paper money. He had the last rare piasters minted. In 1734 he reformed the julius and the silver gros: their weights were brought back, respectively, from 3.055 to 2.802 g and from 1.498 to 1.401 g, and their edges were also twisted.

In addition, the workshop in Rome was once again minting small copper coins. Nevertheless, Clement's efforts were negated by the ravages of invasion by Spanish troops, as well as by the decision to mint the billon again, a growing factor in monetary instability.

Benedict XIV tried to implement reforms, especially on silver coins by creating the *scudo romano* and its smaller denominations to replace the piaster; all had their edges marked with fleurons, the same as the billon coins. However, it was a sign of the times that the papacy had to restructure its workshop in 1749 so that it was directly managed by the state, and no longer managed through intermediaries, the gold to silver ratio being too unstable to guarantee sufficient profits to pay their debts. From then on, its operations were supported by two public banking institutions: the Montidi Pietà and the Bank of the Santo Spiritu. However, little by little, they acquired real autonomy because the directors, from 1759 to 1870, were members of a single family: in succession, Giacomo, Francesco and Giuseppe Mazio.

The pontificate of Pius VI (1775–1799) saw the introduction of the *doppia romana*, a denomination of the *zecchino* that rapidly became the currency standard—until the papal coinage system was swept away in the Napoleonic whirlwind. Caused primarily by the gifts the pope made to his family, as well as by a foolhardy plan to improve the Marais Pontins, the impoverishment of papal finances was aggravated by the involvement of the Papal States in the confrontation between the Austrians and Italian republicans supported by the troops of the French republic. In order to finance troops and, after their defeat, take care of repayments demanded by the French in the treaty of Tolentino, the papacy added to the already large amount of bad billon and copper coinage as well as paper money (*cedole*) already in circulation. Based on nonexistent metals (the remelting of holy vases was only symbolic), these *cedole* would have represented, in 1797, the sum of 21 million *scudi*. The material ruin of the Papal States was completed by the ROMAN REPUBLIC, thanks to 10 million extra *scudi* labeled as *cedole* and then as scrips payable in papal real estate. By 1815 Pius VII was installed in the Vatican, but it wasn't until March 1818 that the previous monetary system could be partially restored, the economy having remained anemic for a long period. After reestablising order in the Papal States with the help of Austrian troops, Gregory XVI (1831–1846) tried to mop up in the wake of the crisis. Taking note of previous monetary upheavals, he undertook a new reform. In January 1835, he inaugurated a two-metal system with one gold coin (the *scudo* and its multiples— 2.5, 5, and 10 *scudi*) and one silver coin (the 10-*baiocchi* piece (or "*paolo*") and its multiples (20, 30, and 50 *baiocchi* and a *scudo* of 100 *baiocchi*). Based on the French decimal system, this coinage was minted only in the workshops of Rome (R) and Bologna (B).

The coin dies were reduced to the simplest designs: the effigy of the pope, an emblem (a dove in the "glory"), a graphic ornament, and characters indicating the value of the coin. In the first half of the century, the brothers G. and N. Cerbara tried to renew the aura of the Church's spiritual power with a design of allegory enthroned upon clouds, but their esthetic quest gave way most often to mannerist insipidity, and then academic conventionality.

The Decisive Reform of Pius IX (1846–1878). At first open to Italian nationalistic ideals, Pius IX later opposed the nationalists' constitutional aspirations and was overthrown in 1849. Restored to St. Peter's throne by French troops in 1850, he was not able to stop the annexation of a large part of his territory in 1860 by the new kingdom of Italy. He was more or less forced to return the pontifical coins to the dominant monetary system in 1866. He created the lira, modeled on the coins of the kingdom of Italy and based on the decimal system (one lira = one hundred *centesimi*). Then, in February 1867, he rallied the Latin Monetary Union, including France, Belgium, Switzerland, and Italy. In this embryonic economic union, all coins, whether gold (valued at 100, 50, 20, 10) or silver (valued 5, 2.5, 2, and 1), and with various names (lira, franc, *centesimo*, centime), were equivalent to each other, their minting conditions having been uniformly defined. A specific value, weight, and form was assigned to each of them, and the level of purity was fixed at 90%. The quantity of lesser denominations released was determined, so that, with the five-franc/lira piece, there would be the equivalent of 6 francs/lira per inhabitant in circulation. Harmonization of the monetary systems was helped along by new technical equipment in the workshops in Rome (1851) and Bologna (1857): rolling mills, cutters, Hulhorn presses, etc. The appearance of the words: "STATO PONTIFICIO" on these coins should be noted: they put the accent on the permanence of the institution. In the same manner, the formal rigor and the classicism of his engraved portrait by C. F. Voigt had already attempted to magnify his papal dignity, placing him above human weaknesses. Despite these symbols, in September 1870 the Italian army entered Rome, abolishing the temporal power of the pope and ending all issuance of papal coins. The papacy was not fully restored to its sovereign prerogatives until 1930, since that year saw the reissuance of coins agreed upon in the LATERAN PACTS. These institutional transformations were reflected in the revised motto: "STATO DELLA CITTÀ DEL VATICANO." This state now issues every denomination of the Italian monetary system, based upon the lira; entirely fiduciary, it uses nonprecious metals such as nickel and steel. The papacy has renewed its tradition of using various decorative motifs to adorn the reverse sides of its coins; they most often illustrate the ideals of the ruling popes, but in a less anecdotal manner than before.

Jean-Luc Desnier

Bibliography

Balbi De Caro, S. *Le monete dello Stato Pontificio, Roma—Museo della Zecca*, Rome, 1984 (*Bolletino di Numismatica*, special series, 1).

Balbi De Caro, S. and Londei L., *Moneta Pontificia, da Innocenzo XII a Gregorio XVI*, Rome, 1984.

Bompaire, M. "La monnaie de Pont de Sorgues dans la première moitié du XIVe siècle," *Revue numismatique*, 25 (1983), 139–76.

Cipolla, C. M. *Le avventure della lira*, Milan, 1958.

Clain-Stefanelli, E. E. *Italian Coin Engravers since 1800*, Washington, D.C., 1965 (*Contributions from the Museum of History and Technology*, 33), 17–30.

Delumeau, J. *Rome au XVIe siècle*, Paris, 1975.

Giuntella, V. E. "La Giacobina Republica Romana (1798–1799)," *ASR*, 73, (1950), 1–213 (VII–VIII, 37–68).

Muntoni, F. *Le monete dei Papi e degli Stati Pontefici*, I–IV, Rome, 1972–1973.

Traina, M. "Benvenuto Cellini e i ducatoni di Castel S. Angelo," *Rivista Italiana di Numismatica*, 76 (1974), 277–89.

Travaini, L. "Le monete a Roma nel Medioevo," *Studi Romani*, 37 (1989), 38–49.

COLLECTORS. Collectors were temporary local agents of the papal tax system. They could be chosen from among the local clergy (from the end of the 11th century, in Spain, prelates worked as collectors). They were also recruited from outside the local clergy and sent to work in a kingdom (in England and Poland, the majority of collectors were Italians). They generally kept their status as commissaries. During the period of the AVIGNON papacy, they were affected by a powerful trend whereby their jobs became increasingly permanent and their duties legally fixed.

The phenomenon began in England and spread during the first half of the 14th century, with the expansion of papal taxation of benefices. The collector was the head of the collectorate, which for the most part included several dioceses and even ecclesiastic provinces. There were already collectorates in the 13th century, but these were strictly temporary, as they were set up for the collection of specific contributions. In 1274, for example, there were 26 collectorates established for the collection of the tithe. These were subsequently made into permanent collectorates although their constituencies were often redivided. Between 1353 and 1354, there were 31 collectorates (15 in France, 6 in central and northern Europe, 4 in Italy, 3 in the Iberian Peninsula, 2 in the British Isles, and 1 in Cyprus).

The collector was assisted by a receiver and deputy collectors, with all the staff members belonging to the hierarchy of the Apostolic Camera and subjected to a series of binding oaths and strict monitoring procedures. Apart from the ordinary taxes, the collector was responsible for the various taxes arising from benefices. The usual title of the letters of commission was *fructuum, jurium et proventorum Camere apostolice debitorum et debendorum collector et receptor generalis*.

The collector was not only a papal fiscal agent; he was also a manager. In the event of seizure by the papal authorities of the goods and chattels of a deceased prelate, the collector would take possession of them, create an inventory, and make arrangements for the inheritance. The inventories and accounts available in the Camera are some of the best sources of information on the economic history of Church property. The inventories of books, which often went to swell the number of volumes in the papal library are also a precious source of information on cultural history.

It was also the collector's responsibility to administer all temporal matters relating to vacant benefices on which there was a papal reservation. He paid the expenses with the earnings from this exercise and dispatched the receipt to the CURIA. After checking the account of his assistant collectors, a general statement of accounts was dispatched to the Camera, where it was painstakingly examined.

The collectors were officers of the ecclesiastical treasury. During the time of the great SCHISM, their role was especially important. The Avignon obedience was deprived of the papal state and could only count on meager earnings, insufficient with respect to the real needs of the papacy. The collection of the greater part of papal earnings was, therefore, the responsibility of the collectors. This accounted for the fact that the collectors and collectorate constituency remained stable and unchanged for the most part. The collectors of the Roman obedience, on the other hand, rapidly succeeded each other. The responsibility of the collectorates also varied a great deal, and there was a marked trend toward fragmentation (there were over 20 collectorates in Italy, for example).

In the 15th century, the role of the collectors underwent a change in two ways. First, they increasingly came to be regarded as permanent papal agents to the sovereigns, and their credentials increasingly reflected this. This was even more striking in England, where collectors during the pontificate of MARTIN V were charged with conducting actual negotiations with the court of England on matters relating to the Holy Roman Church. Under EUGENE IV, the collector Piero da Monte defended the pope against the accusations of the council of Basel. At the end of his mission to England, he was almost immediately appointed ambassador to the court of the king of France. The second change concerned the reduction in the burden of papal taxation as a result of the various CONCORDATS. The schisms had also spread (England, Germany, and the East), and together these factors progressively reduced the importance of the work of the collectors. By the middle of the 16th century, no new collectors were appointed, and subsequently, taxes on the collation of benefices made up the bulk of strictly ecclesiastical earnings. These were paid directly to the Curia through the bankers.

Olivier Guyotjeannin
François-Charles Uginet

Bibliography

Blet, P. *Histoire de la representation diplomatique du Saint Siege*, Vatican City, 1982, 142–50, 158–91.

Favier, J. Les Finances pontificales a l'époque du Grand Schisme d'Occident (1378–1409), Paris, 1966, ad indicem; "Les finances pontificales aux lendemains du concile de Pise," *Annali della fondazione italiana per la storia amministrativa*, 1967, 75–113.

COLLEGES OF ROME. From the earliest days of the Church, a high priority was given to the training and instruction of those whose mission it was to preach the gospel. Jesus himself taught his twelve Apostles and seventy-two disciples before sending them out to teach his Word (Mt 10:5; Lk 10:1).

The Didaskleion of St. Justin (ca. 100–ca. 165) was the first school established in Rome to teach Christian doctrine. It opened its doors during the 2nd century through the personal initiative of converted laymen, who had received no explicit instructions from the ecclesiastical authorities. Soon the education and training of clerics became the sole responsibility of the religious hierarchy. By the 6th century, a center of study for young men from the farthest regions of Western Europe was already in operation in the Patriarchium Lateranense. This school would remain in operation for almost a thousand years. It was reformed during the papacy of GREGORY I (590–604), and the famous *Schola cantorum* became affiliated with it. Its influence spread throughout the entire Latin Church, and between the 7th and 8th centuries several popes received their scriptural, patristic, and theological training in this institution.

During his stay in Lyon, INNOCENT IV (1243–54) founded the *Studium Romanae Curiae*, around 1244–5. This was intended to provide training to future clerics in theology as well as canon and civil law. The school was under the direct patronage of the popes and followed the papal court everywhere, as had formerly been the case with the Palatine school of Charlemagne. CLEMENT V (1303–14) conferred on it the rank of *Universitas Sacri Palatii*, which placed it on an equal footing with the UNIVERSITIES of Paris, Bologna, Salamanca, and Oxford. It remained in operation until the beginning of the 16th century.

It was BONIFACE VIII (1294–1303) who in 1303 founded the University of Rome—the Studium Urbis, better known as the Sapienza. Despite many ups and downs, the University exists to this day. Theology as well as canon and civil law were the main subjects taught there.

During the Middle Ages, the monasteries of Rome as well as Monte Cassino were the main seats of intellectual and religious learning. The 13th century saw the establishment of new centers for the instruction of friars, such as the Aracoli for the Franciscans or the St. Sabina (directed by Thomas Aquinas himself in 1265–7) for the Dominicans. Similarly, the Augustinians and the Carmelites ensured that their younger members received orthodox training in church doctrine.

In the 15th century, Cardinal Capranica was a pioneer in recognizing the need for constant renewal within the Church. In 1457 he founded a college for training young clerics. The upheaval caused by the Reformation and the great challenge of evangelizing the New World made it increasingly urgent to train young people, who were best suited to meeting the changing needs of the Church. Ignatius of Loyala founded the Roman College in 1551 in answer to these new needs. Many students from the Sapienza were attracted by new schools that taught theology, philosophy, and the humanities. The Roman College soon became the "College of all nations" and a center of cardinal importance for religious studies in the Church of the Counter Reformation.

The Jesuits opened a college for German seminarians in 1552. Similar establishments were founded in rapid succession for the neophytes (1577), the Greeks (1577), and the English and Hungarians (1579). This latter institution became part of the German College a year later. There were also colleges set up for the Poles (1582–4), the Maronites (1584), and the Scots (1600). Two more establishments were founded during the pontificate of URBAN VIII (1623–44): the college of PROPAGANDA FIDE (1627) and the Irish College (1628). A little earlier, in 1565, the Roman seminary had been founded at the express request of Cardinal Borromeo, partly as a direct consequence of the excitement generated in the seminaries following the decree of the Council of Trent.

Religious were instrumental in ensuring more up-to-date intellectual and moral training for young clerics. The various orders founded colleges where young people could receive instruction. They were the St.-Bonaventure College for conventual Franciscans (1587); the St.-Isidoro college for Irish Franciscans (1625); and the College of St. Norbert for Premonstratensians, or Norbertines (1626). The College of St. Patrick was created for the Irish Augustinians (1656), the St. Clement College for Irish Dominicans (1667), the College of Enrico-Gandavense for the Servites (1669), and St. Anselmo for the Benedictines (1687).

The 19th century saw a substantial increase in the number of Roman colleges with the founding of the following institutions: The Belgian College (1844); the Convitto (student hostel) of St. Louis, by the French (1845); the College of Bede for convert priests (1852); the French seminary (1853); the Pius Latin-American (1858); the Lombard Seminary (1859); the Teutonic College of Santa Maria dell'Anima (1859); the Polish College (1866); the Armenian College (1883); the Canadian college (1888); the College of Bohemia (1890); the Maronite college (1891); the Spanish college (1892); the Ukrainian college (1897); and the Portuguese college (1900).

The trend continued during the 20th century with the following colleges established before and after VATICAN II; the Croatian College (1901); the convitto of Maria Immacolata (1902); the Ethiopian college (1919); the Russicum (1929); the Dutch college (1930); the Rumanian College (1930); the Brazilian college (1934); the college of St. Mary of the Lake (1935); the convitto of the Leonine college (1938); the Hungarian Institute (1940); the convitto of Santa Maria in Monserrato (1945); the Lithuanian college (1948); the international convitto of St. Thomas Aquinas (1948); the convitto of Santa Maria dell'Umiltà (1953); the Slovenian college (1960); the college of the Philippines (1961); the St. Charles convitto (1963); the college of St. Paul the Apostle (1965); and the John Paul II seminary (1986).

The institutions opened in Rome to attend to the needs of religious orders and congregations were just as numerous. Several Roman foundations were transformed into papal universities. Affiliated with these were institutes of higher learning offering a wide range of disciplines and areas of specialization for graduates and undergraduates. These institutes reflected the vitality so important for the secular and religious education and training of the clergy. The following colleges and institutions were transformed into universities: the Roman College became the Pontifical Gregorian University (1556); the Roman Seminary was turned into the Pontifical Lateran University (1959); the College of *Propaganda fide* became the Pontifical Urban University; the Angelicum became the Pontifical University of St. Thomas Aquinas; the Salesian Athenaeum became the Pontifical Salesian University (1973); and the Roman Athenaeum of the Holy Cross (Opus Dei) became the Pontifical University of the Holy Cross (1998).

List of Establishments.

Universities and Institutions of Higher Learning

Pontifical Gregorian University (Jesuits)
Founded 23 February 1551; became a university 17 January 1556.
Piazza della Pilotta, 4.

Pontifical Biblical Institute
Founded 7 March 1909.
Via della Pilotta, 25.

Pontifical Oriental Institute
Founded 15 October 1917.
Piazza S. Maria Maggiore, 7.

Pontifical Institute "Regina Mundi"
Founded 25 December 1970.
Lungotevere Tor di Nona, 7.

Institute of Religious Sciences
Founded 31 May 1971.
Piazza della Pilotta, 4.

Pontifical Lateran University
Founded 1 February 1565; became a university 17 May 1959.
Piazza S. Giovanni in Laterano, 4.

Higher Institute of Religious Sciences "Ecclesia Mater"
Founded 9 November 1973.
Piazza S. Giovanni in Laterano, 4.

Pontifical Urban University
Founded 1 August 1627; became a university 1 October 1962.
Via Urbano VIII, 16.

Pontifical University of St. Thomas Aquinas (Dominicans)
Founded 4 August 1577; became a university 7 March 1963.
Largo Angelicum, 1.

Higher Institute of Religious Sciences "Mater Ecclesiae"
Founded 11 May 1972.
Largo Angelicum, 1.

Pontifical Salesian University (Salesians)
Founded 3 May 1940; became a university 24 May 1973.
Piazza dell'Ateneo Salesiano, 1.

Pontifical Higher Institute of Latin
Founded 22 February 1964.
Piazza dell'Ateneo Salesiano, 1.

Higher Institute of Religious Sciences "Magisterium Vitae"
Founded 29 June 1986.
Piazza dell'Ateneo Salesiano, 1.

Pontifical Atheneum of St. Anselm (Benedictines)
Founded 4 January 1888.
Piazza dei Cavalieri di Malta, 5.

Pontifical Altheneum "Antonianum" (Friars Minor)
Founded 17 May 1933.
Via Merulana, 124.

Higher Institute of Religious Sciences "Redemptor Hominis"
Founded 31 July 1986.
Via Merulana, 124.

Pontifical University of the Holy Cross
Founded 9 January 1990; became a university 17 July 1998.
Piazza di S. Apollinare, 49.

Higher Institute of Religious Sciences "Ut unum sint"
Founded 17 September 1986.
Via Monte della Farina, 64.

Pontifical Faculty of Educational Sciences "Auxilium" (Daughters of Mary Auxiliatrix)
Founded 27 June 1970.
Via Cremolino, 141.

Higher Institute of Religious Sciences "Auxilium"
Founded 25 July 1986.
Via Cremolino, 141.

Pontifical Theological Faculty Marianum (Servites of Mary)
Founded 8 December 1955.
Viale Trenta Aprile, 6.

Pontifical Theological Faculty "San Bonaventura" (Conventuals)
Founded 24 January 1905.
Via del Serafico, 1.

Pontifical Theological Faculty "Teresianum" (Discalced Carmelites)
Founded 16 July 1935.
Piazza S. Pancrazio, 5a.

Pontifical Institute of Christian Archeology
Founded 11 December 1929.
Via Napoleone III, 1.

Pontifical Institute of Arabic and Islamic Studies (White Fathers)
Founded 19 March 1960.
Viale di Trastevere, 89.

Pontifical Institute of Sacred Music
Founded 1911.
Via di Torre Rossa, 21.

Colleges, Seminaries, and Hostels for the Secular Clergy

Pontifical Ecclesiastical Academy
Founded 1701.
Piazza della Minerva, 74.

Major Roman Seminary
Founded 1 February 1565.
Piazza S. Giovanni in Laterano, 4.

Minor Roman Seminary
Founded 29 June 1913.
Viale Vaticano, 42.

"Redemptoris Mater" Training Center for Priests
Via della Tenuta Magnianella, 88.

Pontifical North American College
Founded 8 December 1858.
Via del Gianicolo, 14.

Venerable English College
Founded 1 May 1579.
Via Monserrato, 45.

Pontifical Armenian College
Founded 1 March 1883.
Salita S. Nicola da Tolentino, 17.

Pontifical Beda College
Founded 1852.
Viale S. Paolo, 18.

Pontifical Belgian College
Founded 1844.
Via G. B. Pagano, 35.

Pontifical Bohemian College
Founded 1 January 1890.
Via Concordia, 1.

Alma Capranica College
Founded 5 January 1457.
Piazza Capranica, 98.

Pontifical Scots College
Founded 5 December 1600.
Via Cassia, 481.

Pontifical Spanish College
Founded 1 April 1892.
Via di Torre Rossa, 2.

Pontifical Ethiopian College (or Abyssinian or Coptic)
Founded 1 October 1919.
Vatican City

Pontifical German-Hungarian College
Founded 28 October 1552.
Via S. Nicola da Tolentino, 13.

Pontifical Greek College
Founded 13 January 1577.
Via del Babuino, 149.

Pontifical Irish College
Founded 1628.
Via dei SS. Quattro, 1.

Pontifical Lithuanian College of Saint Casimir
Founded 1 May 1948.
Via Casalmonferrato, 20.

Maronite College
Founded 17 June 1584.
Via di Porta Pinciana, 14.

Pontifical Mexican College
Founded 13 November 1961.
Via del Casaletto, 314.

Pontifical Philippine College
Founded 29 June 1961.
Via Aurelia, 490.

Pontifical Pius-Brazilian College (for Pius XI)
Founded 3 April 1934.
Via Aurelia, 527.

Pontifical Pius-Latin American College (for Pius IX)
Founded 21 November 1858.
Via Aurelia Antica, 408.

Pontifical Rumanian College
Founded 6 May 1937.
Passeggiata del Gianicolo, 5.

Pontifical Polish College
Founded 1582–84.
Piazza Remuria, 2a.

Pontifical Portuguese College
Founded 20 October 1900.
Via Nicolò V, 3.

Pontifical Russian College ("Russicum")
Founded 15 August 1929.
Via Carlo Cattaneo, 2.

Pontifical College of the Holy Cross (Opus Dei)
Founded 29 June 1948.
Via di Grottarossa, 1375.

Pontifical Ukrainian College of St. Josaphat
Founded 18 December 1897.
Passeggiata del Gianicolo, 7.

Pontifical Urban College of Propaganda Fide (for Urban VII)
Founded 1 August 1627.
Via Urbano VIII, 16.

John Paul II International Seminary
Founded 24 May 1989.
Via Monte della Farina, 64.

Pontifical French Seminary
Founded 2 October 1853.
Viale Vaticano, 42.

Pontifical Lombard Seminary
Founded 1859.
Piazza S. Maria Maggiore, 5.

Pontifical Canadian College
Founded 11 November 1888.
Via Appia Nuova, 884.

Teutonic College of St. Mary in Camposanto
Founded 21 November 1876.
Via della Sagrestia, 17 Vatican City.

Leonine Ecclesiastical Hostel
Founded 22 November 1938.
Via Pompeo Magno, 21.

Ecclesiastical Hostel of St. Louis of the French
Founded 1845.
Via S. Giovanna d'Arco, 5.

S. Maria in Monserrato Ecclesiastical Hostel
Founded 1945.
Via Giulia, 151.

International Hostel of St. Thomas Aquinas
Founded 1948.
Via degli Ibernesi, 20.

St. John Damascene Institute
Founded 4 December 1940.
Passeggiata del Gianicolo, 5.

Ecclesiastical Institute of Mary Immaculate
Founded 11 December 1902.
Via del Mascherone, 55.

Pontifical Hungarian Ecclesiastical Institute
Founded 16 July 1940.
Via Giulia, 1.

Pontifical Polish Ecclesiastical Institute
Founded 8 September 1958.
Via Pietro Cavallini, 38.

Pontifical Teutonic Institute of S. Maria dell'Anima
Founded 15 March 1859.
Via della Pace, 20.

Casa S. Carlo
Founded 5 October 1962.
Via del Corso, 437.

Casa S. Maria dell'Umiltà
Founded 1953.
Via dell'Umiltà, 30.

Procure St. Sulpice
Via dei Fratelli Bandiera, 17a.

Vietnamese Procure
Via della Pinetta Sacchetti, 45.

Colleges for Religious

Antonine Maronites: St. Isaias College
Founded 1959.
Via Boccea, 480.

Augustinians: St. Monica's College
Founded 1882.
Via del S. Uffizio, 25.

Irish Augustinians: St. Patrick's College
Founded 1656.
Via del Piemonte, 60.

Augustinian Recollects: St. Ildefonso College
Founded 1931.
Via Sistina, 11.

Barnabites: College of St. Anthony M. Zaccaria
Via Pietro Roselli, 6.

Basilians: College of St. Basil
Founded 1631; reestablished 1935.
Via S. Basilio, 51a.

Benedictines: College of St. Anselm
Founded 1687.
Piazza dei Cavalieri di Malta, 5.

Capuchins: College of St. Lawrence of Brindisi
Founded 1908.
Circonvallazione Occidentale, 6850.

Calced Carmelites: College of St. Albert
Founded 1484.
Via Sforza Pallavicini, 10.

Discalced Carmelites: "Teresianum" College
Founded 1902.
Piazza S. Pancrazio, 5a.

Crozier Canons Regular: College of Holy Cross
Founded 1922.
Via del Velabro, 19.

Canons Regular of the Lateran: College of St. Victor
Founded 1949.
Via delle Sette Sale, 24.

Premonstratensian Canons Regular: College of St. Norbert
Founded 1626.
Viale Giotto, 27.

Cistercians: College of St. Bernard
Founded 1927.
Piazza del Tempio di Diana, 14.

Conventuals: Seraphic College of St. Bonaventure
Founded 1587.
Via del Serafico, 1.

Dominicans: Convent of Sts. Dominic and Sixtus
Founded 1932.
Largo Angelicum, 1.

Spanish Dominicans: College of the Most Holy Trinity
Founded 1741.
Via dei Condotti, 41.

Irish Dominicans: College of St. Clement
Founded 1677.
Via Labicana, 95.

Sons of the Holy Family: College of the Sons of the Holy Family
Founded 1864.
Via Giolitti, 154.

Friars Minor: College of St. Anthony of Padua
Founded 1888.
Via Merulana, 124.

Irish Friars Minor: College of St. Isidore
Founded 1625.
Via degli Artisti, 41.

Jesuits: College of the Gesù
Founded 1968.
Piazza del Gesù, 45.

Legionaries of Christ: Center of Higher Studies
Founded 1950.
Via Aurelia, 677.

Marians: College of Clerics Regular of the Immaculate Conception
Founded 1925.
Via Corsica, 1.

Marists: International Marist College
Founded 1890.
Via Cernaia, 14b.

Mariamita Maronites of B.V.M.: Maronite College
Founded 1707.
Piazza S. Pietro in Vincoli, 8.

Minims: College of St. Francis of Paola
Founded 1961.
Viale dell'Umanesimo, 36.

Missionaries of the Precious Blood: College of the Precious Blood
Founded 1815.
Via Narni, 29.

Missionaries of the Sacred Hearts of Jesus and Mary
Founded 1933.
Via dei Falegnami, 23.

Missionaries of the Holy Spirit: International Scholasticate
Founded 4 November 1926.
Piazza S. Salvatore in Campo, 57.

Missionaries of the Holy Family: International Lyceum
Founded 1957.
Via di Villa Troili, 56.

Missionaries of Scheut: Missionary College
Founded 1930.
Via S. Francesco de Sales, 25.

Missionaries of the Sons of the Immaculate Heart of Mary: International Claretian College
Founded 1924.
Largo Lorenzo Mossa, 4.

African Missions: International College for the Society
Founded 1928.
Via della Nocetta, 111.

Foreign Missions of Maryknoll: Hostel for the Fathers
Founded 1911.
Via Sardenga, 83.

Maynooth Foreign Missions: St. Columbanus' House
Founded 1934.
Corso Trieste, 57.

Mill-Hill Foreign Missions: International College
Founded 1855.
Via Innocenzo X, 16.

Parma Foreign Missions: International College "Guido M. Conforti"
Founded 1960.
Via Aurelia, 287.

Pontifical Institute for Foreign Missions: "B. Alberico Crescitelli" International College
Founded 1960.
Via F. D. Guerazzi, 11.

Montfort Fathers: Montfort Marian Center
Founded 1899.
Colle Prenestino, 1391.

Oblates of Mary Immaculate: Scholasticate for Oblates
Founded 1881.
Via Aurelia, 290.

Pallotines: "Queen of the Apostles" College
Founded 1887.
Piazza S. Vincenzo Paolotti, 204.

Passionists: International College of Sts. John and Paul
Founded 1926.
Piazza SS. Giovanni e Paolo, 13.

White Fathers: College of Our Lady of Africa
Founded 1930.
Via Aurelia, 269.

Priests of the Sacred Heart: International College "Léon Dehon"
Via Casale S. Pio V, 20.

Redemptorists: International College of St. Alphonsus
Founded 1909.
Via Merulana, 31.

Rosminians: "Antonio Rosmini" College
Founded 1937.
Via di Porta Latina, 17.

Salesians: "B. Michel Rua" International College for Seminarians
Founded 1975.
Piazza dell'Ateneo Salesiano, 1.

Salesians: St. John Bosco International College for Priests
Founded 1956.
Piazza dell'Ateneo Salesiano, 1.

Scalabrini Fathers: Theological Institute of St. Charles Borromeo
Founded 1932.
Via Casilina, 634.

Servites of Mary: St. Alexis Falconieri College
Founded 1669.
Viale Trenta Aprile, 6.

Servites of Paraclete. International Scholasticate
Founded 1952.
Via Appia Nuova, 1468.

Somaschi: International Theological Lyceum
Piazza S. Alessio, 23.

Trappists: International College for the Monks
Founded 1892.
Viale Africa, 33.

Trinitarians: College of St. Chrysogonus
Founded 1909.
Piazza Sonnino, 44.

Society of the Divine Word: International College
Founded 1928.
Via dei Verbiti, 1.

Charles Burns

Bibliography

Annuario Pontificio, Vatican City, 2001.
"Collegi Ecclesiastici," (article by multiple contributors), *EC*, 3 (1949), 1952–63.
Da Alatri, M., and Isidoro da Villapadierna, "Gli studi dalle prime fonti ai giorni nostri," *Arte, Scienza e Cultura in Roma cristiana* (Roma Cristiana, 9), Bologna, 1971, 103–97.
Seminaria Ecclesiae Catholicae (monographs by multiple authors), Vatican City, 1963.

COLLEGIALITY. The name "collegiality" was given to the doctrine emanating from the debates and deliberations of VATICAN II on chapter 3 of the dogmatic constitution on the Church *Lumen gentium*. However, the term does not appear anywhere in the document. This chapter, on the "hierarchical constitution of the Church and especially the episcopate," discusses the formation by bishops of a college linked to the head of the Church—the pope—in the image of the college of the twelve apostles joined to St. PETER. This topic was the subject of lively discussions during sessions of the council and even afterward, that attempted to arrive at a precise understanding of the theological meaning and ecclesiological scope of the college of bishops in the leadership of Christians.

The concept of an episcopal college was not, however, an innovation after two thousand years of Church doctrine. St. Cyprian of Carthage, St. Ignatius of Antioch, and St. Denis of Corinth had already designated the community of bishops under the name *collegium*. The unity of the episcopal body was thus emphasized in the spreading of the Gospel as well as in the fight against HERESIES. While the community spirit had remained present in the traditions of the Eastern Church, it had been somewhat eclipsed in Rome, where, under the influence of prevailing constitutional usage, ecclesiastical government progressively evolved in a more individualized way that favored PAPAL PRIMACY over episcopal collegiality. Yet even at VATICAN I, which promulgated the dogma of papal infallibility, the idea of an episcopal college was not absent, since a draft text *De ecclesiastico magisterio* mentioned the dual nature of supreme power in the Church: the episcopate at one with (*una cum*) the Roman pontiff, and the Roman pontiff alone speaking *ex cathedra*. Some time afterward, LEO XIII would speak of the

"*episcoporum collegium*" in his 1896 ENCYCLICAL *Satis cognitum*.

It is on the use of the world "college" that discussions on this subject have most often bogged down. Etymologically speaking, a college designates a grouping or assembly of equals. In the Church this applies to the College of Cardinals, the college of diocesan consultants, and the college of ecclesiastical judges. That is why the bishops present at Vatican II rejected this term on the grounds that it infers a *societas aequalium*, a government of peers. The primacy of universal jurisdiction attached to the office of the pope makes him the superior of the bishops, although as a bishop himself, he is their equal in terms of sacramental power. The pontifical primate is not only an honorary primate according to the Orthodox or Anglican model, but he also plays an active role in government; he is superior to the bishops individually and collectively. Even in a council invested with the supreme power of the Church, the pope, who is by right the president, is not the equal of other bishops, since he himself holds alone the same powers exercised by them as a whole. For this reason Vatican II proclaimed the following:

"just as St. Peter and the other apostles constitute, in accordance with the Lord's decree, a unique apostolic college, so in like fashion [*pari ratione*] the Roman pontiff, successor of Peter, and the bishops, successors of the apostles, are related to and united to one another. . . . But the College, or body of bishops, only has authority if one interprets 'joined to the Roman pontiff, successor of Peter' as joined to its head and without challenging the power of the primate, which extends to all, pastors and faithful alike. In fact, the Roman pontiff, by reason of his office as Vicar of Christ and pastor of the whole Church, has a full, supreme and universal power over the Church that he can always exercise unhindered. The order of bishops is the successor to the college of the apostles in teaching authority and pastoral rule. Put another way, in the episcopal order the apostolic body is perpetuated, and together with the Roman pontiff—the head, from which it is never separated [*una cum Capite suo Romano Pontifice et nunquam sine hoc Capite*], it exercises full and supreme power over the universal Church, a power that can only be exercised, however, with the agreement of the Roman pontiff. . . . The supreme power this college possesses with regard to the universal Church is exercised through an Ecumenical COUNCIL that must be confirmed as such or at least recognized by Peter's successor" (*Lumen gentium*, no. 22). . . . "The individual bishop at the head of each particular Church exercises pastoral authority over that portion of the People of God assigned to him and not over the other Churches nor over the universal Church. But, as a member of the episcopal College and a legitimate successor of the apostles, each of them is bound, with regard to the universal Church and according to Christ's arrangement and decree, to exercise a kind of solicitude that is eminently advantageous for the universal Church, even if it is not exercised by an act of jurisdiction" (*Lumen gentium* no. 23).

To avoid any doctrinal error in the interpretation of the council's thoughts, PAUL VI added a prefatory note (*Nota explicativa praevia*) to the text, to pin down the meaning of the words according to the Catholic faith and the tradition of the Church. This note emphasized that the word *college* "is not to be taken 'in the strictly juridical sense,' of a group of equals who have delegated their power to their leader, but rather of a stable group, the structure and the authority of which should be deduced from the revelation." These statements guarantee the primacy of jurisdiction of the Roman pontiff; the word *college* is used as a synonym for less egalitarian terms that describe a hierarchy. Membership in the College of bishops is acquired both by episcopal consecration and by hierarchical communion with its head and with the other members of this college. It is, in fact, from the pope that each bishop derives his legitimacy, since, for the Latin Church, the canonical mission that empowers a bishop to exercise the powers attached to the episcopal order is the assent of the pope to the episcopal election. Finally, the fact that the college of bishops, joined to the pope, has full and supreme power in the universal Church in no way undermines the pope's own prerogatives, for the college truly exists only with the pope and has no power without him. There are not, therefore, two supreme authorities in the Church—the pope on the one hand, and the College of bishops on the other—but rather two methods of exercising supreme authority: in a primatial manner by the pope alone, or in a collegial manner by the pope with the body of bishops. In addition, it is the pope, by reason of the plenitude of his power of government, who determines "at his own discretion" (*ad placitum*) and functioning for the good of the Church (*intuitu boni Ecclesiae*) the place and time when the exercise of his supreme power is to be shared with the members of the college. In this latter case, there would be a union of authority.

These official clarifications were aimed at countering the neomodernist tendency of some conciliar experts and postconciliar commentators to view the Church government as a collegial body organized around the pope, reducing the latter to being only the executive of the College. The reality is quite different: it is not because the pope is at the head of the College of bishops that he exercises supreme power, but because the pope is at the head that the College shares in the exercise of the supreme power. And even in the latter case, the College remains hierarchical (notwithstanding the etymological antinomy of the terms), since the pope is the governing head. Personally, however, the pope "remains always in commu-

nion with the other bishops as well as with the whole Church" (canon 333 § 2), for the pope only exists through and for the Church. For its part, the episcopate should always act "*cum Petro et sub Petro*" (conciliar decree *Ad gentes* no. 38): within the "*cum Petro*" is essentially a "*sub Petro*," for the episcopal body holds its power only by respecting the integrity of the power the Petrine primate exercises over all pastors and all the faithful (*Lumen gentium*, no. 22).

In truth, collegiality springs more from the spiritual order (*collegialitas affectiva*) than from the canonical order (*collegialitas effectiva*). Its true nature is evangelical (the universal and common spread of the one Gospel) and sacramental (ecclesial communion in the holy order of the episcopate). The conciliar decree *Christus Dominus* clearly shows "the role of bishops in regard to the universal Church" because "each bishop is responsible for the Church together with the other bishops" (no. 6). Moreover, the conciliar decree *Ad gentes* emphasizes the following: "The responsibility of announcing the Gospel to the entire world is, in the first place, the business of the episcopate body" (no. 29). It is a moral co-responsibility for the good of the whole Church, a natural thing for the members of an episcopal order that does not come down to a simple juxtaposition of bishops. Accession to the episcopate implies, by its very nature, entry into the fraternal and interdependent community of bishops. Vatican II underlined the communal dimension of the episcopate with the expression *collegialis affectus*, a collegial sentiment innate to every Catholic bishop. The episcopate is, in fact, a link in a divine institution, uniting the Church and rallying the bishops around the Roman pontiff. His primacy makes and maintains episcopal collegiality; and episcopal collegiality reinforces and sustains papal primacy, in accord with the conciliar image of the head and body. Collegiality therefore has a fundamentally transjuridical nature, expressing itself in terms of communion within the same faith, the same charity, and the same apostolate. It is characterized by the exercise of power in solidarity, but still retains the defining quality of hierarchical communion aimed at safeguarding the primacy of full and supreme power uniquely given by Christ to Peter and his successors. For the pope and the bishops are equal among themselves in the sacrament but not in government. Over the last few years, certain theologians and canonists have introduced the term "synodality," which expresses better than "collegiality" the ecclesiological specificity of the communal, but unequal, relationship between the bishop of Rome and the rest of the episcopate.

Joel-Benoit D'Onorio

Bibliography

Andrieu-Guttrancourt, P. "De la théocratie à la collégialité," dans *Melanges Jean Brethe de la Gressaye*, Bordeaux, 1968.

Betti, U. *La dottrina sull'episcopato nel Vaticano II*, Rome, 1968.

Beyer, J. *Du Concile au Code de droit canonique, La mise en application de Vatican II*, Paris, 1985.

Carrasco Rouco, E. *Le Primat de l'Évêque de Rome*, Fribourg, 1990.

Colson, J. *L'Episcopat catholique: collégialité et primauté pendant les trois premiers siècles de l'Église*, Paris, 1963.

Corecco, E. *Théologie et droit canon*, Fribourg, 1990.

Dockx, S. "Essai sur l'exercise collégial du pouvoir par les membres du corps épiscopal," *La Collégialité épiscopale*, Paris, 1965.

D'Onorio, J. B. *Le pape et le gouvernement de l'Église*, Paris, 1992.

Dulac, R. *La collégialité épiscopale au IIe concile du Vatican*, Paris, 1979.

Eyt, P. *"La collégialité," Le Deuxième concile du Vatican* (1959–1965), Rome, 1989.

Hajjar, J. "La collégialité episcopale dans la tradition orientale," *L'Eglise de Vatican II*, III, Paris, 1966.

Journet, C. "De la collégialité," *La Documentation catholique*, 1546 (1969).

"La collégialité épiscopale, développement théologique," *L'Église de Vatican II*, 3, Paris, 1966.

"Ministiere de Pierre et Synodalité," *Communio*, Paris, 32 (1991).

Minnerath, R. *Le Pape, évêque universel ou premier des évêques?*, Paris, 1978.

"Primauté-collégialité: sur une imprecision conciliaire et sa correction pontificale," *La synodalité. La participation au gouvernement dans l'Eglise, Actes du VIIe congrès international de droit canonique*, Unesco, 1990, *L'Année canonique*, hors series, Paris, 1992.

Ratzinger, J. "Les implications pastorales de la doctrine de la collégialité des évêques," *Concilium*, 1 (1965).

Staffa, D. "La nature collégiale de l'épiscopat," *Revue de droit canonique*, Strasbourg, 2 (1964).

Wiltgen, R. *Le Rhin se jette dans le Tibre. Le concile inconnu*, Paris, 1975.

COLOSSEUM. This huge amphitheater was the largest in the Roman world and built by the emperors of the Flavian dynasty. Emperor Vespasian began construction in A.D. 71–2, and a spectacular dedication followed the completion of the monument during the reign of Titus, son of Vespasian, in A.D. 80. In A.D. 81, Emperor Domitian added the final touches to the amphitheater. The ancient name of the monument was *amphitheatrum flavium*, with the name "Colosseum" (*colyseum, colosseo*) appearing during the early Middle Ages. This was perhaps because HADRIAN I during his reign had had Nero's colossus moved closer to the amphitheater.

There were two reasons for the building of the amphitheater. First, the fire of A.D. 64 had destroyed the previous buildings. More importantly, it was felt that the change of dynasty should be reflected symbolically in the urban landscape. It was therefore fitting to replace Nero's *Domus Aurea*, dedicated to the megalomania of one man, with a building of public entertainment, dedicated to the people. The two most common types of show were the *munera* (combat of gladiators) and the *venationes* (the chase of wild animals). This latter spectacle was rendered particularly impressive by a system that took up the two levels of the entire basement of the arena. A series of trapdoors, arranged in lines around the floor of the arena, was linked to a number of underground elevators. Several wild animals could therefore be released at once, springing simultaneously through the trapdoors in the presence of at least fifty thousand spectators. In the mornings, before the crowds had gathered, executions took place. Those people who had been condemned to be punished *ad bestias* were delivered to the wild animals without any means of defense. Towards midday, the prisoners condemned *ad gladium* were made to fight each other to the death. However, there is no evidence available today that Christians were among those condemned to die in the Flavian amphitheater.

The monument was restored several times during the Roman Empire. At the beginning of the 5th century, A.D., HONORIUS prohibited the combat of gladiators, but Valentinian III imposed a definitive ban after A.D. 438. The *venationes* survived the fall of the Western empire and the seats of the theater still bear the names of 195 senators of the time of Odoacre (A.D. 476–83). After one final *venatio* during the reign of Theodoric, the practice was abandoned. The amphitheater was stripped of the iron hooks used to hold together its blocks of travertine, the total weight of which was estimated at 300 tons. This probably happened during the siege of Rome by the Ostrogoths and the successful resistance of Belisario (A.D. March 537–March 538). The structure still bears evidence of the systematic removal of the iron hooks in the infinite number of holes visible on the façade. Over the next few centuries the silence surrounding the Colosseum was broken only by the echo of the famous prophesy of Beda, the monk who in the 8th century stated: *Quando stat colisaeus, stat et Roma. Quando cadet colisaeus, cadet et Roma. Quando cadet Roma, cadet et mundus.* From the fire of 1084 to the beginning of the 14th century, the Colosseum formed a part of the vast system of defense of the Frangipanis.

After a brief period in the hands of the Anibaldis, the Colosseum was presented to the "Senate and people of Rome" by Emperor Henry VII in the year 1312. In 1349 an earthquake destroyed the southwestern section of the monument, which from that time until the 18th century became a stone quarry. At the beginning of the 15th century, MARTIN V gave the Colosseum to the brotherhood of Santo Salvatore, with a property right on the sale of materials. At the end of the 16th century SIXTUS V cleared the area surrounding the structure. He wanted it to be visible from one of the large avenues being built in the very confused urban network of Rome. One of these large avenues was intended to link the Colosseum to the Lateran. In the atmosphere created by the Counter Reformation, the Colosseum was considered the site of the martyrdom of the first Christians and exalted as such. Bernini was entrusted with a project to make the monument into a Christian sanctuary, but the plan was never realized. In the middle of the 18th century, however, BENEDICT XIV instituted the rite of the *via crucis* and constructed 14 small chapels around the arena, placing a cross at its center. From the end of the 18th through the first half of the 19th centuries, successive popes endeavored to consolidate the structure of the monument. This was achieved especially with the use of enormous buttresses intended to shore up the building, half of which had been destroyed by a series of earthquakes. The underground area of the arena was cleared and raised by the architect Valadier during the French occupation, but they were again filled in 1814. It was not until 1870 that they were completely restored, as the chapels constructed by Benedict XIV were destroyed. As far back as can be seen from the graphic documentation available, Benedict's cross has never left the Colosseum.

Gilles Sauron

Bibliography

Colagrossi, P. *L'Anfiteatro Flavio nei suoi venti secoli di storia*, Rome, 1913.

Cozzo, G. *Ingegneria romana*, Rome, 1928 (reprinted 1970), 203–51.

Govin, J. C. *L'amphitheatre romain, Essai sur la theorisation de sa forme et de ses fonctions*, Paris, 1988, 173–80 and passim.

COMMISSIONS, PAPAL. Papal commissions are bodies of the Roman CURIA with a small number of members, generally under the presidency of a CARDINAL, that provide consultations or perform particular and quite specialized tasks. Not all those created within the Curia received the qualification "papal." The 1988 curial charter considerably reduced their number as some of them became papal COUNCILS (Justice and Peace, Migrants Ministry, Interpretation of Laws, SOCIAL COMMUNICATIONS, Apostolate of Health Personnel), while others have been downgraded and transferred to the conference of Italian bishops (Ecclesiastical Archives of Italy, Sacred Art in Italy); yet others have disappeared (Interpretation of Decrees of Vatican II, Revision of the Eastern Code of Canon Law). Two types of papal commissions coexist:

those which are permanent and attached to a DICASTERY, and those which are temporary and autonomous.

There are three permanent papal commissions:

1. The *Papal Biblical Commission*, founded by LEO XIII (*Motu proprio Vigilantiae studiique*, 1902), was reorganized by PAUL VI (*Motu proprio Sedula cura*, 1971) to be attached to the Congregation for the Doctrine of the Faith whose president by right is the cardinal prefect. Composed of twenty members nominated for five years each, by the pope, its task is to examine in detail certain biblical studies topics submitted by the supervisory dicastery.

2. The *International Theological Commission*, created by Paul VI in 1969, received its definitive status from JOHN PAUL II (*Motu proprio Tredecim anni*, 1982). Without officially having the title of papal commission, it is considered as such because of its prestige, accrued by its attachment to the Congregation for the Doctrine of the Faith and for which, like the Biblical Commission, the cardinal prefect assumes the presidency. The thirty members, from twenty-odd nations and various theological schools, respond to doctrinal consultations requested by the Holy See.

3. The *Papal Commission for Latin America* was given responsibility by PIUS XII in 1958 for overseeing the spread of the faith in South America. In 1969 it was integrated by Paul VI into the Congregation of Bishops and it received a wider mandate from John Paul II (*Motu proprio Decessores Nostri*, 1988) to study the doctrinal and pastoral problems of the Church in Latin America and to counsel the Roman dicasteries and the Latin American dioceses in every area, including economic. It also acts as the papal interlocutor for the large ecclesiastical organizations of the sub-continent (among them the Latin American Episcopal Council and the Latin American Confederation of Religious).

There are two temporary, but autonomous, papal commissions:

1. The *Papal Commission for the Revision and Correction of the Vulgate* in 1984 succeeded the papal abbey of St. Jerome erected at Rome by PIUS XI in 1933 for the restoration of the primitive text of the Vulgate (the first Latin translation of the Bible done in the fourth century by St. Jerome).

2. The *Ecclesia Dei Papal Commission* was inaugurated by John Paul II (*Motu proprio Ecclesia Dei adflicta*, 1988) to resolve the canonical and pastoral affairs of all those (priests, religious, and laity, secular or in communities) who broke away from Marcel Lefebvre to remain in full ecclesial communion with the successor of Peter. Having received from the pope himself special faculties corresponding to a real power of government, the commission sees to the canonical erection of these communities or associations of faithful in institutions of holy life or societies of apostolic life, grants dispensa-

tions, authorizes the celebration of the sacraments according to the traditional ritual, and does its best to regulate the conflicts with the dioceses.

Three other commissions are an exception to the rule:

1. The *Papal Commission for the Cultural Property of the Church*, created along with the apostolic constitution *Pastor bonus* of 1988, was part of the Congregation for the Clergy until 1993, when the *Motu proprio Inde a pontificatus* made it autonomous while placing it in close relationship with the papal council on culture. It exercises universal trusteeship over all the ecclesiastical historical and artistic property (archives, libraries, museums, works of art). It is also its responsibility to sensitize pastors and laity to the protection and valorization of the Catholic cultural patrimony.

2. The *Papal Commission on Sacred Archaeology* is a case apart, as it is both permanent and autonomous. Established by PIUS IX in 1852 for the conservation of the sacred cemeteries, famous monuments, and basilicas of Italy, it was elevated to the rank of papal commission in 1925 before being recognized by the Lateran concordat in 1929 to exercise its trusteeship over all the Italian catacombs. The concordat, revised in 1983, reduced its jurisdiction to Christian catacombs only.

3. The *Papal Commission for the Vatican City State* is not a body of the Roman curia but more specifically of the Holy See, as the few Roman cardinals of whom it is comprised constitute the collegial government of the VATICAN CITY STATE, founded in 1929 according to the terms of the Lateran agreements between the Holy See and Italy.

The disciplinary commission of the Roman curia is not a papal commission although it is permanent. It resolves the disciplinary matters of members of the papal staff.

Joël-Benoît D'Onorio

Bibliography

D'Onorio, J. B. *Le pape et le gouvernement de l'Eglise*, Paris, 1992.

COMMITTEES, PAPAL. Papal committees are minor organizations of the Roman CURIA that are entrusted with certain very particular areas of intervention. For example, in 1973 a separate committee for the family was created. It was integrated into the papal council for the laity in 1976, then elevated to autonomous papal council in 1981. Since the curial reform in 1988, there are only two autonomous papal committees, the *Papal Committee of Historical Sciences* and the *Papal Committee for International Eucharistic Congresses*. In 1954 the former replaced a cardinal commission to represent the Holy See before the international committee for historical sciences and in institutions of cooperation on the subject. The latter dates from 1879, but only attained papal rank in 1986.

It oversees the preparation of large eucharistic congresses throughout the world.

Joël-Benoît D'Onorio

COMMON AND SMALL SERVICES. Common services are the ANNATES owed by new bishops and abbots to the pope and the Sacred College. The common services give rise, like the annate, to a prior tax. The share of the cardinals is divided among the cardinals present in the CONSISTORY during the collation. To the common services are added five minor services, paid to papal officials and the cardinals. The promoted prelate is bound to pay an obligation for services to the APOSTOLIC CAMERA, in default of which his bull of collation is not delivered to him. This obligation specifies the terms of payment, normally spread over two years. In fact, the majority of prelates only make partial payments, which justify new time limits as well as absolution for excommunication incurred. Some manage to make the payment last for several years, or rather several decades. The obligation devolves, on the death of the prelate, to his successor who is indebted for his own services and for the remainder of the services of his predecessors. In case of transfer, the prelate takes his obligation with him to which is added what he has to pay for his new benefice.

Jean Faver

Bibliography

Hoberg, H. *Taxae pro servitiis communibus ex libris obligationum ab anno 1295 usque ad annum 1455 confectis*, Vatican, (1949), (Studi e testi, 144).

See more general publications in bibliography under FINANCES, PAPAL.

COMMUNE OF ROME. See **Rome.**

CONCILIAR MOVEMENT. The word "conciliarism," born within the council of Basel (1431–49), seems to have been used for the first time by Lorenzo d'Arezzo, author of *Liber de ecclesiastic potestate*. This composite movement, which developed during the Middle Ages within the Roman church, rested on the conviction that papal power should be tempered, and that the general assembly of the Church (ECUMENICAL COUNCIL) should intervene, even and especially in the framework of a true reform of the Church itself. In its most evolved phase, from the 14th to the 15th centuries, this concept might have led to the democratization of the Church, but this movement was not democratic and never dreamed of contesting the PRIMACY of the pope. Conciliarism is not a precise and uniform doctrinal system, and an understanding of its nature must be based on its historical evolution.

Precedents of Conciliarism. It can be affirmed that for about a thousand years, it was the ecumenical council that exercised the greatest authority in the Church. Conciliar decisions, which were considered to be inspired by the Holy Spirit, were faithfully accepted as "received" by the entire Christian world. In the 11th century, the advent of GREGORY VII and the impulse that he gave to centralization marked a change. Roman councils convoked at that time became the model for general councils that took place during the 12th and 13th centuries. The concept of the reception of their decisions changed radically in meaning. All members of the Church had the obligation to conform to the decisions that were made by the pope or that were approved by him. In spite of this new climate, consciousness of the ancient tradition persisted and one can discern in the works of canonists (even those who were the closest partisans of GREGORIAN REFORM) elements of the doctrine that announce what would later be conciliar theories. In the *Decretum Gratiani* canon "Si papa" (Dist. 40 c. 6) already affirmed that "*papa . . . a nemine est judicandus nisi deprehendatur a fide devius.*" Thus for the author of decretals Uguccione da Pisa (d. 1210), a heretical pope would cease to be pope and the cardinals, or the council, would therefore be judging a simple faithful cleric guilty of heresy. A contemporary canonist, Alanus Anglicus, seems to be even more resolute: It is precisely as pope that the latter can be judged a heretic.

Conciliar theories evolved from these premises. Another canonist, Enrico da Susa, the Ostiense (d. 1271), spoke of the Church as a corporation in which the authority should be exercised not only by its head but also by its members, with the authority of the head limited for the general good. These ideas will be taken up again by Jean Quidort (d. 1306). Like the pope, the bishops receive their power directly from God. As an administrator of a corporation, the pontiff has the right to act once he is seeking the common good, but he can be judged and deposed when he no longer so acts, for his authority is the fruit of human delegation, obtained through the intermediary of the Church, represented by the cardinal electors.

Bishop Guillaume Durand the Younger (d. 1328) can be considered another father of conciliarism. Before there could be any true reform, he thought it was first necessary to reduce exorbitant papal power. He wanted the bishop to regain his former importance, and the ecumenical council to cease being an extraordinary event and be convoked every ten years, by applying the juridical principal according to which "*quod omnes tangit ab omnibus approbari debet.*" Consequently, the council was no longer just a type of court of appeal or an instrument of pressure on a negligent pope, but a real organ of control, essential for the proper functioning of the ecclesiastical government.

Conciliarism in the Great Western Schism. The double papal election of 1378, and the obvious impossibility of resolving the situation by appealing to the goodwill of the two rival popes, led theologians and canonists to again study the texts of canon law of the previous two centuries with the aim of deducing possible solutions. Two influential theologians, Conrad de Gelnhausen (d. 1390) and Heinrich of Langenstein (d. 1397), relied on these texts (and new contributions by Marsilius of Padua and William of Ockham). In 1380 Gelnhausen published *Epistola concordiae*, in which he systematically exposed, for the first time, the thesis according to which only the "*via concilii*" could resolve the current crisis. He drew on the consequences of a very precise ecclesiological criterion. The universal church being the "*universitas fidelium*," the primacy therefore returned to the general council which represented it. Sometime later, Langenstein, author of the *Epistola concilii pacis*, took up his theses. The conciliar concept was defended particularly by the theologians of the University of Paris, cradle of GALLICANISM, which drew in large part its doctrinal and political argumentation from conciliarism. In 1403 Bishop Pierre d'Ailly (d. 1420), former chancellor of the university, published a learned treatise in which he justified the usefulness of a universal council in which the vote would not be limited to bishops, but extended to theologians and canonists. The doctrinal hypotheses and concrete propositions became more and more audacious. The doctors of the University of Bologna took up the doctrine of certain canonists and recalled that the pope could also be judged based on the offense of the schism. The action of persisting in the latter could be compared to the crime of HERESY. They added that if the cardinals neglected to convoke the council, the initiative could be taken by whoever had the interests of the Church at heart.

Conciliarism at the Councils of Pisa, Constance, and Basel. In 1409 the cardinal colleges of the two "obediences" had the painful decision to convoke a council at Pisa without (and against) the will of the popes. In that assembly, which was very representative given the quantity and the quality of the participants, clear professions of conciliar faith were expressed, beginning with the inaugural speech of Petros Philargos (d. 1410), largely inspired by the writings of Gelnhausen. It concluded with the formal deposition of the two rivals and with the election of Philargos himself (who became ALEXANDER V). This council, the first stage in the application of conciliar theories in the life of the Church, opened the way for the council of Constance and the end of the schism. Its apparent failure, due to the obstinacy of the two popes in rejecting the decisions of the universal Church, did not inhibit the great majority from continuing to think that the conciliar way was the only one to follow.

Armed with this bitter experience, the theologian and chronicler Dietrich von Niem (d. 1418) wrote that the council would become an efficacious means of unification and reform if it was taken in hand by the holder of temporal power in the Christian world, the emperor. That is what occurred and unity was regained thanks to the council of Constance (1414–18), when on 6 April 1415 the decree *Haec sancta* was promulgated, which made conciliarism the official doctrine of the Church in terms that can be summed up as follows: The universal council is inspired by the Holy Spirit; its power comes directly from Christ and it represents the whole Church; consequently, everyone, even those invested with papal dignity, must conform to its decisions. This decree, therefore, represented the official sanction of conciliarism, if not exactly in a form that reduced the pope to a simple executive subordinate organ, at least in a form that attributed to the council the function of the "organ of control" of the pope. In addition, this function would not be limited to particular moments of crisis, but would be permanent. In fact, by another decree of 9 October 1417 (*Frequens*), the council fixed precise periodic intervals for the meeting of general councils. If these solemn decisions had been applied thereafter, the face of the Church would have been transformed, but the Roman CURIA carried on a subtle and persistent effort to render them fruitless. A new council opened in Basel in 1431. It marked the high point of the confrontation between the council and the pope. During its tenure, notable theologians were heard who did not allow themselves to be intimidated by this confrontation. Among them was John of Segovia (d. 1458), whose ideas on the universal Church as permanent depository of the supreme power, on the general council representing this "by the identification way," as well as on the people, the unique and true sovereign subject, made him the most interesting conciliar figure, at least from the point of view of political thought. He presaged Jean Bodin by the distinction he made between monarchy and tyranny and by his attempt to combine a monarchical constitution with consultative practice. In this sense, "on the road from Constance to 1688," could be spoken about.

Conciliarism after Basel. The papacy, however, rapidly took the situation in hand. It sought and obtained the support of the princes, thanks to concordats, especially on the question of benefices, and rendered the Curia more efficacious by making it a direct instrument of the government of the universal Church. PIUS II (formerly a conciliarist at Basel) formulated an explicit condemnation of conciliarism through the BULL *Exsecrabilis* of 18 January 1460. From then on papal condemnations followed one another, but the idea continued to circulate. A new council was convoked in his name at Pisa, in 1511. It would fail, especially because of the attitude of the king of France who, like the other sovereigns, had an interest in coming to an

understanding with the pope. Bishops, like Mattia Ugoni, sometimes even those of the Curia like Giovanni Gozzadini, made no mystery of their conciliar leanings and continued to live peacefully, thanks to a papacy that had become, from all evidence, certain of itself. However (although solidly held by the popes), the specter of conciliarism continued to hover over the COUNCIL OF TRENT. Several positions, among them the Epigons, are ultimately aimed at increasing the authority of the bishops, or even of the priests (Richerism).

Aldo Landi

Bibliography

Alberigo, G. *Chiesa conciliare*, Brescia, 1981.

Black, A. *Council and Commune. The Conciliar Movement and the XVth Century Heritage*, London, 1979.

Bliemetzrieder, F. *Das Generalkonzil im grossen abendländischen Schisma*, Paderborn, 1904.

De Vooght, P. "Les Controverses sur les pouvoirs du concile et l'autorité du pape au concile-de Constance," *Revue théologique de Louvain*, I (1970), 45–75.

Die Konzilsidee des lateinischen Mittelalters (845–1378), Paderborn, 1984.

Evans, J. H. "Primacy, conciliarity and infallibility," *Colloquium*, 20 (Oct. 1987), 31–43.

Fink, K. A. "Lo Scisma occidentale e i concili," *Storia della Chiesa*, edited by H. Jedin, Milan, V/2, 1979, 135–241.

Gill, J. "The first Session of the Council of Constance," *The Heythrop Journal*, 5, (1964), 131–43.

Henn, W. *The Honor of My Brothers: A Short History of the Relation Between the Pope and the Bishops*, New York, 2000.

Jedin, J. *A History of the Council of Trent*, I, St. Louis, 1957.

Landi, A. *Il papa deposto (Pisa 1409). L'idea conciliare nel grande scisma*, Turin, 1985.

Landi, A. *Il richerismo e i suoi precedenti storico-canonistici, Il Sinodo di Pistoia del 1786, Convegno Internaz., per il II centenario del Sinodo di Pistoia (1786–1986)*, Rome, 1991, 293–304.

Oakley, E. "On the Road from Constance to 1688: The Political Thought of John Major and George Buchanan," *Journal of British Studies*, II (1962), 1–31.

Sieben, H. *Die Konzilsidee der alten Kirche*, Paderborn, 1979.

Sieben, H. *Traktate und Theorien zum Konzil, Vom Beginn des grossen Schismas zum Vorabend der Reformation (1378–1521)*, Frankfurt on the Main, 1983.

Tierney, B. "Divided Sovereignty at Constance: A Problem of Medieval and Early Modern Political Theory," *Annuarium Historiae Conciliorum*, VII (1975), 238–56.

Tierney, B. *Foundations of the Conciliar Theory*, Cambridge, U.K., 1968.

Tierney, B. *Ackham, the Conciliar Theory, and the Colonists*, Philadelphia, 1971.

CONCLAVE.

Up to the Council of Trent. The conclave is the term used for the closed place where the SACRED COLLEGE meets to elect the pope and for the election itself. Regulated since the 13th century, it is a good indicator of the struggle for influence among the pope, the cardinals, and the political powers. The word derives from the Latin *cum clave*, locked with a key, characteristic of the strict conditions of locking up the electors starting with GREGORY X (1274).

The conclave took place in the palace where the pope died or, in the case of an exterior threat, in a city of the diocese (as was the case for the election of JOHN XXII in 1316). The conclave was placed under the protection of the civil authorities of the city. It is only from 1585 that it was confided to the marshal of the Roman church. Gregory X had provided for a very austere setting (a common room for all with a single private place). Clement VI allowed the cardinals to be separated by curtains. Gradually, appropriate locations were arranged such as the conclave wing of the palace of the Avignon popes. Beginning with EUGENE IV (1431–47), the conclave was held in Rome, first at the convent of Santa Maria sopra Minerva, then at the Vatican in the Blessed Sacrament chapel, then in the Pauline chapel, and finally in the Sistine chapel, erected by SIXTUS IV. The conclavists, apart from the cardinals, included one or two servants per cardinal and personnel at the service of the whole conclave: doctors, surgeons, barbers, confessor, sacristan, cook, carpenter, etc. All persons were required to swear an oath to respect the secrecy of the conclave. Limited contacts with the outside world were made through windows similar to those of convents. Inside, the life of the recluses was placed under the authority of a commission of three cardinals (from Pius IV on, they were replaced every three days) and of the cardinal camerlengo of the Roman church.

Once the pope's funeral was concluded (the cardinals addressed letters announcing the death to ecclesiastical and lay authorities), cardinals attended the mass of the Holy Spirit before entering into conclave, then took an oath to respect the electoral norms. Customarily, the first day was not dedicated to the collegial election, but rather to mutual visits. The election could be held by secret ballot, by compromise, or by inspiration (agreement from the beginning on a name, and election only to officially validate this choice); the cardinals deposited their vote in order and according to seniority. A two-thirds majority was required for election. Even though strict rules had been decreed, information always filtered out, evidenced especially by the accounts of ambassadors (very rare before the 15th century), which multiplied beginning in the Renaissance. These documents throw light on the secret meetings, intrigues, and dealing within the conclave: Between the rule and the practice, there was often a world of difference.

If the principle of the election of the pope did not pose any problems, its application did. After several centuries of interference by lay powers, mainly imperial, the bulls of NICHOLAS II (1059) and of ALEXANDER III (1179) gradually gave the cardinals alone the responsibility for the election, which was to involve at least a two-thirds majority of votes. This measure limited the risks of a schism, but it also encouraged the cardinals in affirming their own powers. In fact, no other moment was more suitable for extending their influence than a vacancy of the Apostolic See. After a few speedy elections without conflict, difficulties reemerged because of differences of opinion among the cardinals. In 1216, well before the rules of a conclave by Gregory X, the Perugians took the initiative of confining the cardinals to speed up the election of the successor of INNOCENT III. It was the same in 1241, when the cardinals were confined in Rome to protect them from the threats and influence of the emperor. Finally, the interminable election of the successor of CLEMENT IV, who died in 1268, resulted in the imposition of strict regulations.

The first conclave is customarily viewed to be the electoral session at VITERBO, which lasted from November 1268 to 1 September 1271, the date of the election of Gregory X. The authorities of Viterbo, after several months of fruitless waiting, confined the electors to the episcopal palace, bricked up all entrances, and reduced the cardinals to bread and water. Legend claims that the roof of the building was also removed. Only such severe measures brought an end to the indecision of the Sacred College. It should not be surprising then that the newly elected pope worked tirelessly preparing a text to put an end to such excesses. In spite of spirited opposition from the cardinals, and with the support of the bishops, the pope promulgated the constitution *Ubi majus periculum*, approved by the second council of Lyon, on 7 July 1274, the official and canonical birth of the conclave. These are the essential points: (1) the cardinals, after waiting ten days for their colleagues, meet in the palace where the pope died, in a strictly enclosed location and subject to absolute secrecy and an increasingly austere lifestyle as the election progresses; (2) not receiving any income during the conclave, they occupy themselves solely with the election, except in the case of imminent danger to the Papal States; (3) the local authorities are responsible for overseeing the proper functioning of the conclave, without worsening the situation. The margin of maneuver of the cardinals and of outside powers is therefore effectively limited.

The constitution of Gregory X was respected during the conclave following his death in 1276 for the election of INNOCENT V, then six months later of HADRIAN V. The latter orally suspended the decree, applied again after his death a few months later for JOHN XXI who, however, suspended it in writing and died without replacing the text. For a few years the election took place without any real norms and began to get longer (for example, the election of CELESTINE V lasted two years) and to suffer from foreign influence (especially that of the powerful king of Naples, Charles of Anjou). Celestine V, immediately after his succession to the throne, reenacted the Gregorian constitution in September 1294 and specified, before resigning from his dignity, that it should apply equally in cases of papal resignation. His successor, BONIFACE VIII, took the precaution of inserting *Ubi majus periculum* into the *Sextus*, a collection of decretals of which he was the promoter. In spite of that, the cardinals, emboldened by the unfinished plan of toning down the constitution of BENEDICT XI in 1304, took it upon themselves, during the conclave of CLEMENT V to diminish its harshness, clearly reaffirming their use of the *plenitudo potestatis* of the pope during a vacancy. The new pontiff canceled such initiatives and completed *Ubi majus periculum* with the constitution *Ne Romani* (published at the Council of Vienne in 1311): not only did it confirm the prohibition of Gregory X against introducing changes, except in the case of imminent danger, but it added, among other things, the right of cardinals who were excommunicated or under interdict to participate in the conclave, and the possibility of the Sacred College naming, in case of the death of the incumbent, a new CAMERLENGO and a new major penitentiary of the Roman church during the time of the conclave. Despite these dispositions, the conclave that followed lasted more than two years, severely affected by the political pressures of the king of France, which complicated the start of the reign of JOHN XXII.

These regulations governed the papal election without notable change until the Council of Trent. The AVIGNON popes only slightly modified them, CLEMENT VI softening the restrictions on food and lodging in December 1351. GREGORY XI, after returning the papacy to Rome in 1378, decreed that the cardinals at Rome did not have to wait for those who remained in Avignon. The Avignon period was the zenith of the power of the cardinals. It is not by chance that during the conclave of 1352 they determined to profit form the vacancy by collecting their corporatist claims in a capitulation signed by all the conclavists, seeking to impose in advance their control over the future pope. INNOCENT VI, once elected, hastened to annul this act (on which he had revealed his reservations) attacking the *plenitudo potestatis* of the pope.

The conclaves during the Great Western SCHISM were a reflection of the politico-ecclesiastical vicissitudes of the time, beginning with the election of URBAN VI in 1378 and the external pressures on the conclave. The structure of the rules of the conclave was not questioned, but rather the principle that the electoral privilege was reserved for the cardinals, on whom public opinion, the canonists, and theologians placed the blame for the schism and the slowness in resolving the issue. During the Council of Constance in 1417, when the question arose of electing a successor recognized by all, to the three popes simultaneously deposed by the council, the solution chosen was the sole infringement on the cardinalitial privilege: The conclave comprised 23 cardinals of the three current obediences, to which 30 electors were added, delegated by the five "nations" represented at the council. MARTIN V was thus the last pope elected outside of Rome before PIUS VII (Venice, 1800). The conclave was carried out according to the rules in force.

The evolution of the Sacred College itself during the 15th century made the application of the rules difficult. The numbers multiplied threefold, the influence of "crown cardinals" (protectors born of their country of origin) increased the fights between factions and resulted in the lengthening of the elections. More importantly, SIMONY tarnished a number of elections, bought at an exorbitant price by one or another cardinal. The election of ALEXANDER VI Borgia (1492) was the climax. JULIUS II (1503–13), although himself a beneficiary of the system, put an end to it with the bull *Cum tam divino* of 1506 (and not 1503 or 1505; it was published only in 1510 and became a conciliar constitution in 1513). It decreed null any simoniacal election, even if the elected individual had been enthroned, with the threat of loss of ecclesiastical and lay dignities of any accomplice; it rendered disobedience to a simoniacal pope licit, permitted the election of a new pope by the cardinals not implicated, and even the convocation by the latter of a general council. This bull caused great commotion because it could have led to the explosion of a schism under the pretext of simony. In spite of this risk and the criticisms of numerous canonists, it remained in force until its abrogation by PIUS X in 1904 (*Vacante sede apostolica*).

After the bull *Cum secundum* of PAUL IV in 1558 attempted inconclusively (because it did not really provide the means for application of sanctions) to limit intrigues during the lifetime of the pope, a new regulation for the conclave was promulgated by PIUS IV during the Council of Trent in 1562 (bull *In eligendis*). Faced with regular violations of the existing norms (and especially the secrecy of the deliberations flouted by the cardinals and the envoys of the princes), it reinforced the regulations in force with greater precision (acceleration of the vote, increased control of secrecy, replacement every three days of the cardinal in charge), while reminding the cardinals that they did not have, *sede vacante*, any jurisdictional, legislative, administrative, or executive power, except for limited spending authority for funeral expenses for the deceased pope or for the defense of the papal territory threatened by imminent danger.

Pierre Jugie

Bibliography

Dykmans, M. *Le Cérémonial papal de la fin du Moyen Age à la Renaissance*, II, III, and IV, Bruxelles-Rome, 1981–1985, at Index.

Dykmans, M. "Le conclave sans simonie ou la bulle de Jules II sur l'élection papale," *Miscellanea Bibliothecae Apostolicae Vaticanae*, 3 (1989), 203–56.

Dykmans, M. "Les Pouvoirs des cardinaux pendant la vacance du Saint-Siège d'après un nouveau manuscrit de Jacques Stefaneschi," *ASR*, 104 (1981), 119–145.

Girgensohn, D. "Berichte über Konklave und Papstwahl auf dem Konstanzer Konzil," *Annuarium Historiae Conciliorum*, 19 (187), 351–39.

Molien, A. "Conclave," *DDC*, 3 (1942), 1319–48.

Petrucci, E. "Il problema della vacanza papale e la costituzione 'Ubi Periculum' di Gregorio X," *Atti del convengno di studio sul VIII centenaio del 1o conclave (1268–1271)*, Viterbo, 1975, 69–96.

Spinelli, L. *La vacanza della sede apostolica dalle origini al concilio Tridentina*, Milan, 1955.

After the Council of Trent. The conclaves of the 17th century, modeled by the Tridentine institution of CONGREGATIONS, were subject to the influences of three groups of cardinals: (1) a group controlled by the princes (Spanish, French, and Imperial), (2) a group formed by the partisans of a previous pope, and (3) a group composed of younger cardinals, often elevated to the purple by the deceased pontiff and generally close to the cardinal nephew. GREGORY XV, the "compromise candidate" (A. Molien) elected in 1621, decreed definitively on the conclave with the bull *Aeterni Patris* of 15 November 1621, requiring a two-thirds majority for election, and completed these dispositions with a strict framework for the material modalities of the vote. INNOCENT XII (1691–1700) took several drastic measures aimed at combating the varied forms of NEPOTISM (bull *Romanum decet Pontificem* of 21 June 1692). CLEMENT XII (1730–40) followed, ruling on the "intercessions" of lay princes during conclaves (October 1732), manifested by the right of veto or exclusion of certain cardinals of the electoral college.

The procedure of the conclave of the modern epoch is rooted in the pontificate of PIUS VI (1775–99). In 1782, while on a trip to Vienna, the pope wrote a BRIEF dispensing with the holding of the conclave at Rome, should the pontiff die while traveling. In November 1798, following the occupation of the city by French troops, Pius VI took refuge at the Charterhouse of Florence and gave, by the bull *Quum nos superiore anno*, priority to a rapid election over "the observation of ceremonies and secondary solemnities," and the cardinals saw themselves "released from the oath to observe the previous constitutions." The text was sent to cardinals in countries not occupied by the French. In fact, on the death of Pius VI at Valence (29 August 1799), Venice welcomed the conclave for the election of PIUS VII (14 March 1800), late in starting because of Austrian interference. Another bull, promulgated by Pius VII on 2 February 1808, confirmed the directions given 20 years before (*Quae potissimum*), but the rule of not starting the election before the traditional time limit of ten days, that is, after the NOVENDIALS, remained.

The return to Rome (May 1814), the death of Pius VII (20 August 1823), and the rapid disappearance of his two successors, LEO XII in 1829 and PIUS VIII in 1830, did not prevent the resurgence of troubles at the advent of Gregory XVI (1830–46), whose election lasted two months (1 December to 2 February 1831). The Austrian powers were pressuring to obtain the installation of a pontiff favorable to the Holy Alliance. This type of political intervention disturbing the procedures of the conclave was not new, and was manifested in the past by the mechanism of the so-called right of veto or EXCLUSION, defined for the first time as such during the 1605 election of PAUL V (1605–21), formulated in the name of Philip II of Spain, then progressively controlled.

There were similar preoccupations within the papacy after the loss of the temporal possessions, including the question of ensuring the security of Roman dignitaries and the freedom of the conclave, which conditioned the freedom of the election. In a little more than ten years, five successive papal documents attempted to define the conditions of legitimacy for the election of the pope. In particular, from the summer of 1871, the bull *In hac sublimi* prescribed that during the next vacancy of the Holy See, the cardinals present at the Curia immediately decide on the location of the conclave and require a two-thirds majority, without taking account of the cardinals who, for whatever reason, were prevented from voting. From a point of view of efficacy, the text suppressed the ten-day rule in cases where the conclave would have to be held *extra Urbem* (outside Rome), and the election was declared valid once the majority of living cardinals were together.

In January 1847, a Cologne newspaper published the text of an apocryphal bull (*Apostolicae Sedis Munus*) dated 28 May 1873, in which the pope allegedly opted for a quasi instantaneous election of his successor, "the cadaver still present" (*praesente cadavere*), which at least demonstrated the interest in the "event" that constitutes the election of the successor of Peter, the latter having lost his temporal sovereignty. Four months before his death, on 10 October 1877, PIUS IX (1846–78) published the bull *Consultari ne post obitum* in which he imposed the principle of nonintervention of the secular power "of whatever degree or condition it may be." In January 1878 he added some 32 paragraphs detailing the roles and obligations of the cardinal camerlengo, the prefect of the palace, and other functionaries called to intervene during the holding of the conclaves. This document was reissued by LEO XIII as an appendix to the bull *Praedecessores Nostri* of 24 May 1882, which insisted on a "certain and rapid" (*certa et expedita*) election within nine days if necessary, in the strictest secrecy. After the conclave of 1903, PIUS X reiterated the condemnation of the exclusion under pain of excommunication, and exhorted the cardinals, more generally, not to take into account worldly considerations (apostolic constitutions *Commissum Nobis* of 20 January 1904 and *Vacante Sede Apostolica* of 25 December of the same year).

The CODE OF CANON LAW promulgated by BENEDICT XV (1914–22) on 27 May 1917 reiterated these principles inherited in fact from the last years of the pontificate of Pius IX, again emphasizing the obligation of secrecy for all those taking part in the conclave. Few changes were carried out thereafter. The physiognomy of the papal election attained a point of equilibrium and was based on a corpus of strict rules leaving little room for innovation. PIUS XI (1922–39), by the *motu proprio Cum proxime* (1 March 1922), extended, at the beginning of his pontificate, the limit for the cardinals' entry into conclave from 10 to 15 days, even leaving them the right to add two or three days, based on the experience of his own election, which was held the day when the cardinals from across the Atlantic arrived in Rome.

The constitution *Vacantis Apostolicae Sedis*, promulgated by PIUS XII (1939–58) on 8 December 1945, abrogated the dispositions adopted by Pius X and adjusted the qualified majority required to two-thirds of the votes plus one, practically eliminating the examination of the ballots aimed at verifying if one of the candidates had not voted for himself. In addition, the exigency of secrecy was reformulated, in view of the massive spread of what was called "the means of social communications," by strictly prohibiting the introduction of any telephonic, telegraphic, or cinematographic apparatus into the conclave. At the same time, the text ordained the incineration of the ballots after the election as well as the burning of any documents relevant to the conclave. JOHN XXIII (1958–63), returning to this disposition in September 1962 (constitution *Summi Pontificis electio*), entrusted the conservation of these pieces to the cardinal camerlengo, to be later deposited by him in the Vatican archives. The same constitution slightly modified the rules on the majority and reduced the personnel of the officers of the conclave and their servants.

This trend toward streamlining the numbers present was confirmed in the rules enacted by his successor, PAUL VI (1963–78). At first, after the introduction of eastern patriarchs to the Sacred College (*motu proprio Purpuratorum Patrum* of 11 February 1965), the voting rights of octogenarian cardinals were suppressed (*motu proprio Ingravescentem aetatem* of 21 November 1970). The total number of the Electoral College of the pope was limited to 120 by the constitution *Romani Pontifici eligendo* (1 October 1975), an essential disposition for the form of the election which still survives today in the positive regulations of the conclave. According to the debates that took place during the development of the 1983 CODE OF CANON LAW, several cardinals demanded the suppression of the age rule. The secretariat of the commission of codification gave a quick response to these "*animadversiones*"; the rule was expressly fixed and under a special form—a *motu proprio*—by the sovereign pontiff. The code, which today constitutes the positive law of the Latin Church, takes up the argument in the form of a renunciation of responsibility (canon 354) for cardinals who have attained the age of 75, and implicitly maintains the rule of 85 applied to the conclave.

The history of the evolution of the rules, as well as the composition of the conclave gave rise to a number of commentaries, sometimes technical, in regard to that secret place par excellence that constitutes the election to the supreme pontificate and determines, in large part, the perception of life as it unfolds in the Vatican. From every point of view, the conclave was, from the Council of Trent, a real subject of preoccupation in the literal sense of the word, and has not ceased to be to this day.

Philippe Levillain

Bibliography

Aubert, R. *Le Pontificat de Pie IX*, Paris, 1952.

Berthelet, *La elezione del papa*, Rome, 1891.

de Montault, B. *Le Conclave et le pape*, Paris, 1878.

Del Re, N. *La Curia romana*, Rome, 1970.

Ehrle, W. *Die Conclave Pläne, Beiträge zu ihrer Entwicklungsgeschichte*, Vatican City, 1933.

Eisler, A. *Das Veto der katholischen Staaten bei Papstwahl seit dem Ende des 16. Jahrhunderts*, Vienna, 1907.

Epp, R., Lefebvre, C., and Metz, R. *Le Droit et les institutions de l'Eglise catholique latine de la fin du XVIIIe siècle a 1978. Sources et institutions* (Histoire du Droit et de Institutions de l'Eglise en Occident, 16), Paris, 1981.

Giobbio, A. *L'esercizio del veto d'esclusione nel conclave*, Monza, 1897.

Goyae, G., and Lesourd, F. *Comment on elit un pape*, Paris, 1935.

Lector, L., and Guthlin, J., *Le Conclave: origines, histoire, organisation, legislation ancienne et moderne*, Paris, 1894.

Molien, A. "Conclave," *DDC*, III, (1937), col. 1328–42.

Pivano, S. *Il diritto di veto "ius exclusivae" nell'elezione del pontefice*, Turin, 1905.

Vidal, G. *Du veto d'exclusion en matière d'élection pontificale*, Toulouse, 1906, (thesis).

CONCLAVIST. Conclavists, whose presence at a CON-CLAVE is the exception since the constitution *Romano pontifici eligendo* of 1975, accompanied the cardinals into the enclosure and assisted them during the meeting, at the rate of one or two per cardinal. Clerics or laymen, they had to be trustworthy so that the electors could depend on their discretion, but could not belong to the cardinal's family or to the same congregation (when the cardinal was a religious). They could not be prelates or be in the service of a secular prince, a double safeguard against the ecclesial and civil network of influence. They had to be known for the respectability of their morals and the honesty of their faith. A commission of two cardinals established a list during the final meeting of the cardinals preceding the closing of the conclave.

The cardinals were accustomed to a lifestyle appropriate for princes of the Church, and the conclavists were devoted servants, attentive observers who sometimes kept the cardinal's journal, and suspicious intermediaries (sometimes official, sometimes unofficial). Until the installation in 1878 (at the conclave that elected LEO XIII) of common meals, the conclavists took charge of the dishes and meals prepared outside for the electors. The prelates kept watch over the "windows" to avoid any communication with the outside. It is claimed that a conclavist, considering himself a representative of public opinion, encouraged Cardinal Pecci to accept the position of CAMERLENGO, which he purportedly thought of refusing.

Philippe Levillain

CONCORDAT. The term, concordat—as well as analogous designations such as "convention," "agreement," "treaty," "*modus vivendi*," and "understanding"—designates a diplomatic agreement signed between the Holy See and a state and intended to regulate matters of religious interest concerning them both. More precisely, it is an agreement allowing the two parties to bilaterally regulate juridical issues, the existence and activities of ecclesiastical institutions, and the bodies and associations of a state. The system of relationships is referred to as "concordatory."

This system, different from separatist systems, does not customarily imply, independently of its content, a confessional character for a state. Thus, there can be, even in the absence of concordats, non-lay regimes or lay states, such as the French republic, having agreements with the Holy See for the nomination of bishops, concordatory regimes in part of a territory (Alsace-Moselle), or particular regimes for certain overseas territories. In relation to the juridical system of the Church, there are sources of particular law on which the pontiff draws according to the agreements established with civil authorities. However, these sources are in a certain sense "reinforced" if they are contrary to the universal

norms of the CODE OF CANON LAW, even in cases of opposition. This principle, sanctioned by canon 3 of the 1917 Code of Canon Law, was confirmed by the new 1983 Code which, although not modifying the preceding, introduced some significant innovations in light of the principles of VATICAN II. In particular, the code introduced "other political societies" in relation to *nationes* with which the Holy See can sign conventions, which could also be the numerous international governmental organizations with which the Vatican maintains official relations (cf. the series *Annuario Pontificio*), or states' members of a federation (for example, the German Länder or the Swiss "cantons") (canon 3). Papal LEGATES representing states according to the rules of international law, have responsibility for promoting and maintaining relations between the Holy See and state authorities and for defending the mission of the Church and the Holy See. In this capacity they must solicit the advice and suggestions from national bishops and keep them informed of the evolution of various matters (canon 365 § 2 and canon 364 § 7).

The most recent concordatory practice expressly recognizes responsibilities in the matter of national episcopal conferences, while the actions taken by the interecclesial bodies acting as liaison between the national episcopal conferences confirms the instructions of the *motu proprio Sollicitudo omnium Ecclesiarum* (24 June 1969) with respect to the new role of bishops in the "foreign" policy of the Holy See. In this regard, the new concordat with Italy must be noted (18 February 1984), which not only refers to the regulation of certain matters, resolved in principle to later "understandings" between the episcopal conference and the competent authorities of states (art. 10, 2; 11, 2; 12, 1; additional protocol, art. 5, lett. B, 1–5), but also expressly establishes that "later matters for which the need for collaboration between the Catholic church and the state is manifested, should be resolved, either through new agreements between the two parties, or by understandings between the competent authorities of the state and the Italian episcopal conference" (art. 13, 2). It is specified, in addition, that among the liaison bodies of the episcopal conferences, the commission of episcopates of the European Community (COMECE) has been deemed the interlocutor of the corresponding community organization on pastoral matters regarding the community (Statute *ad experimentum*, 1980, art. 3, 1).

These are important innovations that demonstrate the interest of the Holy See not only in matters relating to the maintenance of concordatory relations—which certain schools of thought had judged to be outdated in light of the principles of Vatican II which, in fact, does not explicitly address "concordats" in its sixteen documents—but also their evolution and enhanced value in light of transformations in the international community and of the increasing complexity of diplomatic relations. It is certainly not by chance that, during the course of the 20th century, PAUL VI and JOHN PAUL II signed a much greater number of concordatory agreements than their predecessors. The concordatory policy cannot be isolated from the context of conciliar principles on the safeguarding of peace and the construction of the community of nations, which govern the presence of the Church in the international community and the role of Christians in cooperation and in international institutions (pastoral constitution *Gaudium et spes*, 77–90), even if, obviously, it is section 76 of the said constitution that provides the fundamental instructions on the relations between the Church and the political community. In fact, it recognizes, respectively, the independence and the autonomy of the two societies and hopes for a "healthy collaboration" between them that takes into account an evolution over time and circumstances.

The concordat is a very ancient institution. The first was, without doubt, the CONCORDAT OF WORMS, signed in 1122 by Pope CALLISTUS II and Emperor Henry V to end the INVESTITURE dispute. Certainly, agreements such as the concordat of Bologna (1516), the concordat with Napoleon's France (1801), or that between PIUS IX and the emperor of Austria, Francis-Joseph (1866), were of great importance, but it is the years between the two world wars which saw the increasingly wider application of the concordatory institution. The reasons for this were both the profound political and territorial transformations resulting from World War I and the need to translate, by new written agreements, the basic principles of the Code of Canon Law promulgated for the first time in 1917. Sometimes (especially in relation to nomination to ecclesiastical offices) these principles entered into conflict with the rights of certain states or with the autonomous character of a few national Churches recognized by previous concordatory agreements. However, in certain cases, the new agreements between states and Churches—thanks to the principle cited of "resistance" to canon 3—served also to protect, in some way, the rights of national Churches against the strong Roman centralization favored by the code. Between 1922 and 1940, more than 15 concordatory agreements were signed with European (14) and Latin American (2) countries, among which are concordats of great importance with Mussolini's Italy in 1929, Dolfus' Austria and with Hitler's Germany in 1933, and Salazar's Portugal in 1940. It was under the pontificate of PIUS XII, in 1953, that the concordat with Franco's Spain was signed within the framework of diplomatic action still aimed more toward Europe and Latin America (14).

After reduced activity under JOHN XXIII (four agreements), PAUL VI signed 22 agreements, notably with an African country (*modus vivendi* of 1964 with Tunisia) and with an eastern European country (1966 protocol with Yugoslavia). JOHN PAUL II—who has signed to date

more than 10 agreements—concluded the revision of the Spanish concordat, begun after the death of Franco, by signing the four agreements of 3 January 1979, and finished the process of reform of the 1929 Italian concordat with the agreement of modifications of 18 February 1984, which came into force on 4 June 1985. This agreement was completed by law 222 of 1985 on ecclesiastical bodies and property, and on the maintenance of the clergy, prepared by a bipartisan commision of Italy and the Holy See named at the signing of the agreement and approved by the protocol of 15 November 1984.

The profound changes that have taken place in the former Soviet Union and in other Eastern European countries lead one to believe that on the basis of the likely changes in the conditions of existence of the Church in a large number of these states, new perspectives and further developments in the ecclesiastical concordat can be expected. Be that as it may, it can already be noted that the 1933 German concordat and the previous regional concordats, which have continued to be applied in the territories that constituted East Germany, have again been applied in these regions after the reunification of the German republic.

List of Concordats. Following are concordats and other agreements between the Holy See and various states.

Argentina: agreement on the jurisdiction of the chaplaincy and of religious assistance to the armed forces (28 June 1957); agreement on the juridical situation of the Church in Argentina (10 October 1966—*AAS* 59, 1967, 127–30); exchange of letters on the modernization of the agreement on the jurisdiction of the chaplaincy and religious assistance to the armed forces of 28 June 1957 (21 April 1957).

Austria: concordat (5 June 1933—*AAS* 26, 1934, 249–82); convention on the regulations for patrimonial relations (23 June 1960—*AAS* 52, 1960, 933–42); convention on the erection of the diocese of Eisenstadt (23 June 1960—*AAS* 52, 1962, 641–52); convention on the erection of the diocese of Innsbruck-Feldkirch (7 July 1964—*AAS* 56, 1964, 740–3); convention on the erection of the diocese of Feldkirch (7 October 1968—*AAS* 60, 1968, 782–5); additional agreement on the regulation of patrimonial relations (29 September 1969—*AAS* 62, 1970, 163–4); additional agreement concerning the questions relative to educational organization (8 March 1971—*AAS* 64, 1972, 478–81); protocol of an additional agreement concerning questions relative to educational organization (25 April 1972—*AAS* 64, 1972, 480–1); 2nd additional agreement concerning the regulations on patrimonial relations (9 January 1976—*AAS* 68, 1976, 411–24); 3rd additional agreement concerning the regulation of patrimonial relations (24 July 1981—*AAS* 74, 1982, 27–274); 4th additional agreement concerning the regulations of patrimonial relations (10 October 1989—*AAS* 82, 1990, 230–2).

Bolivia: convention on the missions (4 December 1957—*AAS* 50, 1958, 68–81); agreement on the institution of the vicariate for the army (29 November 1958—*AAS* 53, 1961, 299–303); agreement on religious assistance to the armed forces and the police (1 December 1986—*AAS* a, 1989, 528–30).

Brazil: agreement on religious assistance to the armed forces (23 October 1989—*AAS* 2, 1990, 126–9).

Cameroon: agreement on the creation of the Catholic Institute of Yaounde (15 July 1989).

Colombia: concordat (12 July 1973—*AAS* 67, 1973, 421–34); exchange of letters on the resolution of difficulties due to the interpretation and application of the concordat (2 July 1985).

Dominican Republic: concordat (16 June 1954—*AAS* 46, 1954, 433–57); agreement on religious assistance to the armed forces (21 January 1958); additional protocol to the agreement on the vicariate to the army (11 May 1990).

Ecuador: *modus vivendi* and additional convention (24 July 1937); agreement on religious assistance to the armed forces and the national police (3 August 1978); notes of mutual concessions (5 October 1981—27 January 1982) and exchanges of letters (19 June and 6 July 1982) to clarify some points relative to the application of the agreement.

France: concordat of 1801 between Pius VII and the French republic (15 July 1801); convention on the creation of the Faculty of Theology at the University of Strasbourg (5 December 1902); exchange of letters concerning the plan of statutes of diocesan associations (7–13 May 1923); exchange of letters confirming the convention of 5 December 1902 on the Faculty of Theology at Strasbourg (16–17 November 1923); agreement on liturgical honors in countries where the French religious protectorate operates (4 December 1926—*AAS* 19, 1927, 9–10); agreement on liturgical honors in countries where the capitulations are abrogated or not applied (4 December 1926—*AAS* 19, 1927, 10–12); amendment to the diplomatic conventions of 14 May and 8 September 1928 relative to the church and the convent of Trinità dei Monti (4 May 1974); convention relative to the autonomous center of the teaching of religious pedagogy at the University of Metz (25 May 1974).

Germany: concordat with the Third Reich (20 July 1933—*AAS* 25 (1973), 389–413).

Concordats and other agreements with the German Länder:

Baden-Wurtemberg: concordat with the republic of Baden (12 October 1932) and additional protocol (7 November 1932—*AAS* 25, 1933, 177–195).

Lower Saxony: concordat (26 February 1965—*AAS* 57, 1965, 834–56); agreement modifying some clauses of the concordat on the training of teachers and on educational matters (21 May 1973—*AAS* 65, 1973, 643–6); agreement modifying the clauses of the concordat relative to the Josephinum Gymnasium in Hildesheim (8 May 1989—*AAS* 32, 1989, 1101–2).

Bavaria: concordat (29 March 1924—*AAS* 17, 1925, 41–56); agreement on the faculty of Catholic theology at the University of Ratisbon (2 September 1966—*AAS* 58, 1966, 1135–7); agreement on the suppression of the college of philosophy and theology of Frisinga and the scientific education of students of Catholic theology at the University of Munich (2 September 1966—*AAS* 58, 1966, 1138–40); agreement on the Department of Catholic Theology of the University of Augsburg (17 September 1970—*AAS* 62, 1970, 821–5); agreement providing changes to the concordat (7 July 1978—*AAS* 70, 1978, 770–5); exchange of letters on the change of name of the ecclesiastical academic complex of Eichstatt (1–5 March 1980); agreement providing modifications and additions to the concordat on the Catholic University of Eichstatt (8 June 1988—*AAS* 80, 1988, 1271–5).

Prussia: concordat (14 June 1929—*AAS* 21, 1929, 521–43).

Rhineland-Palatinate-Westphalia: convention on the election of the diocese of Essen (19 December 1956—*AAS* 49, 1957, 201–5); exchange of letters on the creation of the Department of Catholic Theology at the University of Bochum in the Ruhr (20–29 December 1967); convention for the new regulation on the training and appointment of professors of theology and Catholic religion (26 March 1984, *AAS* 77, 1985, 294–304).

Saar: exchange of letters on the procedure for the appointment of professors of Catholic theology in Saar and on the granting of the "canonical mission" (28 March, 10 April, 31 May, 11 July, 19 September 1974); agreement on private schools managed by the Catholic Church (21 February 1975—*AAS* 67, 1975, 248–54); convention on the training of professors of the Catholic religion and the teaching of the Catholic religion in schools (12 February 1985—*AAS* 78, 221–30).

Haiti: concordat between Pius IX and the republic of Haiti (28 March 1860); convention on the development of the concordat dated 6 February and 17 June 1862; additional convention on ecclesiastical goods and church property (25 June 1940); protocol on the nomination of bishops (15 August 1966); protocol on the revision of articles 4 and 5 of the concordat (8 August 1984—*AAS* 76, 1984, 953–5).

Hungary: additional act to the protocol relative to the conversations between the representatives of the Holy See and the government of the popular republic of Hungary (15 September 1964).

Italy: LATERAN agreements (11 February 1929—*AAS* 21, 1929, 209–70); financial convention (11 February 1929—*AAS* 21, 1929, 271–4); convention relative to the veneration of the tomb of St. Anthony of Padua (23 May 1932); protocol on the privileges, immunity, and exemptions of dignitaries of the pontifical court (6 September 1932); exchange of letters on the extraterritoriality of the reconstruction of the palazzo dei Convertendi (25–30 January 1937); exchange of letters on the nationality of pontifical diplomats (23 July 1940); exchange of letters on the extraterritoriality of lands ceded in exchange for the basilica of St. Paul (16 March–16 April 1945); agreement on extraterritorial zones (31 March 1947); agreement on the extraterritoriality of pontifical cities (24 April 1948); exchange of letters on the extension of diplomatic privileges to papal dignitaries (17–21 November 1949); exchange of letters on the new status of the Italian church of Our Lady of Loretto at Lisbon (14–18 July 1951); agreement on the installations of VATICAN RADIO at Santa Maria di Galera and at Castel Romano (8 October 1951); exchange of notes relative to diplomatic privileges of Italian citizens accredited to states (terzi) representing them to the Holy See (16 December 1955); agreement on the modification of some ecclesiastical boundaries and the erection of the diocese of Bolzano-Bressanone (7 July 1964); exchange of letters relative to the alienation of the palace of The Datary (28 April 1979); exchange of notes relative to the cemetery of Albano (23 January 1981); agreement on the modifications to the Lateran accords (18 February 1984—*AAS* 77, 1985, 521–35); protocol of approval of norms relative to the discipline mentioned in article 7, note 6 of the agreement of 18 February 1984, with an additional exchange of letters (15 November 1984—*AAS* 77, 1985, 536–46); clauses on ecclesiastical bodies and property (3 June 1985—*AAS* 77, 1985, 547–78); exchange of notes relative to the execution of article 3 of the agreement of 18 February 1984 (23 December 1985); exchange of notes relative to religious feasts (23 December 1985); exchange of letters on the institution of a bipartisan commission on the implementation of the agreement of 18 February 1984 (13 February 1987); exchange of letters relative to the integration of the bipartisan commission (28 December 1988–7 January 1989); exchange of notes relative to the maintenance of Italian nationality for cardinals resident at Rome, and for persons mentioned in the first paragraph of article 9 of the Lateran agreements and of the papal foreign service (24 May 1990); exchange of letters relative to the integration of the commission (31 January 1991–12 February 1991); exchange of notes on the regulation pertaining to the *Corridoio di Borgo* (Passetto) (18 May 1991); monetary convention (3 December 1991); exchange of letters relative

to the renewal of the bipartisan commission (31 December 1992).

Libya: protocol on the safekeeping of Church property by the government (10 October 1970).

Malta: provisional agreement on the question of Church schools (27 April 1985); agreement on the incorporation of the Faculty of Theology at the University of Malta (26 September 1988); agreement on the instruction and Catholic religious education in state schools (16 November 1989); agreement on the real estate of ecclesiastical bodies (28 November 1991); agreement on Church schools (28 November 1991).

Monaco: convention on the nomination of the archbishop (25 July 1981—*AAS* 73, 1981, 651–3).

Morocco: exchange of letters between His Majesty Hussan II and the Holy Father, John Paul II on the status of the Catholic church in Morocco (30 December 1983–5 February 1984—*AAS* 77, 712–15).

Paraguay: convention on the institution of the military vicariate (26 November 1960—*AAS* 54, 1962, 22–7).

Peru: agreement on matters of common interest between the state and the Church: erection of a diocese, nomination of bishops, religious assistance to the armed forces (19 July 1980—*AAS* 72, 1980, 807–12).

Portugal: concordat (7 May 1940—*AAS* 32, 1940, 217–33); missionary agreement (7 May 1940—*AAS* 32, 1940, 235–44); agreement on episcopal sees in former Portuguese colonies (18 July 1950—*AAS* 42, 1950, 811–14); agreement on the modification of article 24 of the concordat on the celebration of Catholic marriages (15 February 1975—*AAS* 67, 1975, 435–6).

San Marino: agreement on civil recognition of feasts and religious memorials (11 July 1989); agreement on matters of common interest between the Church and state (2 April 1992—ratified on 11 December 1992).

Spain: convention on the civil recognition of nonecclesiastical science studies done at the ecclesiastical university of Spain (5 April 1962); agreement on the revision of the concordat regarding the nomination of bishops and the ecclesiastical tribunal (28 July 1976—*AAS* 68, 1976, 509–12); agreement on juridical questions (3 January 1979—*AAS* 72, 1980, 29, 36); agreement on teaching and cultural questions (3 January 1971—*AAS* 72, 1980); agreement on religious assistance to the armed forces and the military service of ecclesiastics and religious (3 January 1979—*AAS* 72, 1980,

47–55); agreement on economic matters: (3 January 1979—*AAS* 72, 1980, 56–62); complementary agreement to the agreement on economic matters: application of taxes on societies (10 October 1980).

Switzerland:

1. Convention with the Federal Council: conventions on the incorporation of Poschavio and Brusio into the diocese of Chur (23 October 1869); convention on the regular administration of the diocese of Basel (1 September 1884); convention on the separation of the apostolic administration of Tessin from the diocese of Basel and relative to its erection as a diocese (24 July 1968—*AAS* 63, 1971, 212–13); additional convention on the diocese of Basel (2 May 1978—*AAS* 70, 1978, 468–70).

2. Convention with the cantons:

Aargau and Thurgau: conventions on the incorporation of the two cantons into the diocese of Basel (2 December 1828).

Lucerne, Berne, Solothurn, and Zug: conventions on the new boundaries of the diocese of Basel (26 March 1828).

Berne: conventions on the incorporation of part of the canton into the diocese of Basel (11 July 1864).

Fribourg: exchange of notes on the nomination of the pastor and monks of St. Nicholas (26 June–25 July 1924).

St. Gall: convention on the restructuring of the diocese of St. Gall (7 November 1845); never ratified by the Holy See.

Lucerne: agreement on the privileges concerning the accumulation of ecclesiastical responsibilities and benefices (11 June 1926).

Tessin: convention on the apostolic administration of the canton of Tessin (23 September 1884).

Tunisia: *Modus vivendi* (27 June 1964—*AAS* 56, 1964, 917–24).

Venezuela: convention on the juridical situation of the Church (6 March 1964—*AAS* 56, 1964, 925–32).

Yugoslavia: protocol relative to the conversations between the representatives of the Holy See and the Federal Socialist Republic (25 June 1966).

Francesco Margiotta Broglio

Bibliography

Catalano, G. *Problematica giuridica dei concordati*, Milan, 1963.

Conci, F. *La Chiesa e i vari Stati (Rapporti-Concordati-Trattati). Per una storia del diritto concordatorio*, Naples, 1954.

De La Briere, Y. "Concordats posterieurs à la Grande Guerre," *DDC*, VII, 1935, 1431–71.

Dissard, F. "Les concordats de Pie XI," *Revue des sciences politique*, LVIII (1935), 554–76.

Föhr, E. *Geschichte des Badisches Konkordats*, Fribourg, 1958.

Giannini, A. *I concordati postbellici*, 2 vols. Milan, 1929–36.

Golombeck, D. *Die politische Vorgeschichte des Preussenkonkordats (1929)*, Mayence, 1970.

Hilling, N. *Die Konkordate*, Dusseldorf, 1932.

Kupper, A. *Staatliche Akten uber die Reichskonkordatsverhandlungen 1933*, Mayence, 1969.

Lajolo, G. *I concordati moderni. Natura giuridica internazionale dei concordati alla luce di recente prassi diplomatica*, Brescia, 1968.

Minnerath, R. *L'Église et les Etats concordataires (1846–1981)*, Paris, 1983.

Mirbt, K. *Das Konkordatsproblem der Gegenwart*, Berlin, 1927.

Piola, A. *Introduzione al diritto concordatorio comparato*, Milan, 1937.

Pluck, S. *Das Badische Konkordat vom 12 Oktober 1932*, Mayence, 1984.

Ruze, R. "À propos des trois derniers concordats de Pius XI avec la Lettonie, la Bavière et la Pologne," *Revue de droit international et de législation comparée* (1926),1–56.

Scharnagl, A. "Das Reichskonkordat und die Länderkonkordate als Konkordatssystem," *Historisches Jahrbuch*, 74 (1955), 584–706.

Stutz, U. *Konkordat und Codex*, Berlin, 1930.

Van Hove, A. "Le concordat entre le Saint-Siège et le Reich allemand," *Nouvelle Revue Théologique*, 61 (1934), 158–85.

Volk, L. *Kirchliche Akten uber die Reichskonkordatsverhandlungen 1933*, Mayence, 1969.

Wagnon, H. *Concordats et droit international*, Gembloux, 1935.

Weinzierl, E. "Austria e Santa Sede," *Nuova antologia*, 1095 (1975), 91–106.

Winter, J. "La dottrina del diritto ecclesiastico statuale nella Germania del Terzo Reich," *Storia contemporaneo* (1981), 623–65.

CONCORDAT OF WORMS. See **Worms, Concordat of**.

CONFERENCE OF BISHOPS. The conference of bishops is largely a 19th-century development, although an antecedent can be seen in the informal meetings of bishops which took place—notably in France between 1561 and 1788—after a number of restrictions were placed on the particular councils by the civil authorities. The bishops of Belgium began to meet from 1830 on. In Italy, the bishops of Umbria gave the signal in 1849 for this type of assembly throughout the peninsula. Those of the ecclesiastical province of Cologne held a meeting at Surzburg on 10

May 1848. Those of the province of Salzburg met on 14 September, imitated on 17 December of the same year by those of the province of Gorz, while at the invitation of the Austrian government, meetings of bishops became regular between 1849 and 1856. The bishops of Ireland met in Dublin on 19 May 1854. PIUS IX gave his endorsement to the bishops of Bavaria who decided to meet each year (letter *Maximae*, 18 August 1864). In the United States, the bishops of the province of Baltimore held their first assembly on 5 July 1860; regular meetings of archbishops were held after the third plenary council of Baltimore in 1884.

Rome soon fixed the conditions of procedure for these conferences (Congregation of Bishops, circular, 24 August 1889). LEO XIII approved the holding of conferences. In this sense, he encouraged the bishops of Spain (encyclical *Cum multa*, 8 December 1892), of Austria (encyclical *In ipso supremi Pontificatus*, 3 March 1891), of Italy (Congregation of Bishops and Regulars, circular, 24 August 1889), of Switzerland (letter, 30 July 1889), of Portugal (encyclical *Pastoralis vigilantiae*, 25 June 1891; letter *Non mediocri*, 5 April 1892), of Brazil (letter *Litteras a vobis*, 2 July 1894), of Hungary (encyclical *Constanti Hungarorum*, 11 September 1893), of Peru (encyclical *Inter graves*, 1 May 1894), and of Australia.

This rapid development led the Congregation of Bishops and Regulars to regulate the modalities (instruction, 22 June 1898); the aim of the conferences was to develop anything that could promote the good of religion in the dioceses. The following year, the plenary council of Latin America decided to hold provincial episcopal conferences every three years.

PIUS X followed the policy of his predecessor and encouraged more frequent meetings of the different episcopates. It is, therefore, not surprising to find in the questionnaire that the bishops had to fill out on the state of their church (decree *A remotisima antiquitate*, 31 December 1909) a question on the holding of meetings of episcopal conferences. The 1917 CODE OF CANON LAW prescribed meetings at least every five years of ordinaries of the place at the metropolitan or at another bishop of the province (c. 292 § 1). These meetings had no juridical power. The consistorial congregation (circular, 24 March 1919) divided Italy (outside the north) into fifteen regions whose bishops were required to meet every year. In other countries (France and Belgium, for example) the practice of yearly meetings was soon instituted.

This section of the Code, however, addressed provincial meetings (which could be confused with the nation in small countries such as Belgium or the Netherlands). The course of events influenced the evolution, more specifically in France, where the apostolic see authorized the episcopate to meet three times at the national level in 1906 and 1907 to study the attitude after the separation of church and state. More stable was BENEDICT XV's creation of the assembly of cardinals and archbishops of France, which initially met twice a year. Because of the dispute over the free school, the assembly obtained the authorization of the HOLY SEE to convene all the bishops of France. Such a meeting was to be repeated every three years.

The bishops of Ireland met from 1854; Rome approved their assembly on 24 August 1882. Those of Germany met regularly at Fulda from 1867. Benedict XV instigated meetings of the episcopate in mission countries (encyclical *Maximus Illud*, 22 April 1919). PIUS XI recognized the American episcopal conference (4 July 1922). Nevertheless, although national conferences were encouraged, the Church feared a decrease in its central power as well as a reduction of the power of each bishop. That is why the Holy See began to recognize the conferences of bishops one by one. Successively, the following conferences were approved: Spain (15 June 1947), Austria (18 March 1950), Philippines (28 June 1952), Italy (1 August 1954), Canada (23 January 1955), Mexico (15 June 1955), Bolivia (9 May 1956), Peru (31 July 1957), Ecuador (2 September 1957), Colombia (23 October 1957), Chile (14 November 1957), Antilles (10 December 1957), Paraguay (30 March 1958), Brazil (30 March 1959), Argentina (25 April 1959), El Salvador (2 January 1960), Guatemala (21 May 1960), Switzerland (22 May 1961), Japan (18 January 1962), Dominican Republic (22 September 1962).

The same trend carried over to the mission countries: the permanent committee of ordinaries of the Belgian Congo and of Ruanda-Urundi, episcopal conferences of French West Africa, of Cameroon, of Congo-Brazzaville, and of Madagascar. Movement was made toward a continental conference of the Latin American episcopate convoked by PIUS XII (apostolic letter *Ad Ecclesiam Christi*, 29 June 1955), a prelude to CELAM and the conference of bishops of the Far East (December 1958).

Vatican II. VATICAN II treated conferences of bishops in the decree on the pastoral responsibility of bishops in the chapter entitled "Cooperation of Bishops for the Common Good of Many Churches" and in the one titled "Bishops of the Universal Church," thus distinguishing it from the episcopal college. Recognizing the difficulty of bishops to suitably fulfill their responsibilities, the council considered "it would be in the highest degree helpful if in all places of the world the bishops of each country or region would meet regularly . . . to share their wisdom and their experience. Thus from the meeting of ideas will emerge a holy union of energies in the service of the common good of the Church" (decree *Christus Dominus*, 28 October 1965, no. 37).

The council fathers define the conference of bishops as an "assembly in which the prelates of a nation or of a territory jointly exercise [*coniunctim*] their pastoral office, in order to enhance the Church's beneficial influence to all men especially by forms of apostolate and apostolic methods suitably adapted to the circumstances of the times"

(*Christus Dominus,* no. 38). The use of the adverb *coniunctim* showed that the conferences were not a restricted form of episcopal collegiality, but a mode of local collaboration of different particular churches. The doctrine on this question has been debated. No one denied that the conferences of bishops were based on the principle of collegiality, but some saw in them an expression of collegiality, in a non-strict, but wide and real sense. The 1985 SYNOD OF BISHOPS noted on this point that "they cannot be directly deduced from the theological principle of collegiality; *sed iure ecclesiastico reguntur*" (*Relatio finalis,* II, C, 4). This latter position was justified by the fact that the synod could not establish a collegial act, an act that was specific to the college of bishops as such, that is the *ordo episcoporum* with the Roman pontiff at their head. The synod inscribed its action within the framework of *affectus collegialis* which the council spoke about in regard to the relations existing within the college of bishops: Collegial unity is manifested in the mutual relations of each bishop with the particular churches and with the universal Church. In addition the conferences of bishops "can, today, contribute in manifold and fruitful ways to what the collegial sentiment realizes concretely" (dogmatic constitution *Lumen gentium,* no. 23).

Decree 23 of *Christus Dominus* established the principles of procedure of the conference: members, statutes, decision-making, relations between conferences, and synods of the eastern churches. PAUL VI made the creation of conferences of bishops obligatory wherever they did not yet exist (*Motu proprio Ecclesiae Sanctae,* I, no. 41 § 1). He specified the geographic framework of the conferences and the objectives to be pursued in the cooperation between conferences, and prescribed the revision of the statutes. The extraordinary synod of bishops of 1969 passed six recommendations aimed at reinforcing the union between the conferences of bishops and the apostolic see, and five recommendations on closer relations between the conferences themselves (27 October, in *La Documentation catholique,* LXVI [1969], pp. 1033–35.

The 1983 Code of Canon Law. The 1983 CODE OF CANON LAW defined the conferences of bishops as a permanent institution, a collegial body of ecclesiastical institution, reuniting the "bishops of one nation or of a given territory, exercising together [*coniunctim*] certain pastoral offices [but no longer their pastoral responsibility, as the decree *Christus Dominus* and the *Motu proprio Ecclesiae Sanctae* said] for the faithful of that territory." These quasi pastoral offices were, in addition, not determined by the Code. The conferences carry out, in accordance with the law, a specific pastoral purpose: "To promote the greater good that the Church offers to all people through forms and means of apostolate suitably adapted to the circumstances of time and place" (c. 447).

In general, each conference coincides with a country and therefore includes, by right, all the diocesan bishops of the territory and all those who are assimilated by right, as well as coadjutor bishops, with a deliberative vote, as well as auxiliary bishops and other titular bishops in the same territory assigned to a particular function by the apostolic see or by the conference, with a deliberative or consultative vote according to the dispositions of the statutes. The ordinaries of another rite may be invited and given a consultative vote, unless there is a contrary provision in the statutes. It is stipulated that the other titular bishops are not members by law of the conference, not even the papal LEGATE.

It is in the exclusive competence of the supreme authority of the Church, after hearing the bishops concerned, to establish, suppress, or alter the conferences. It can establish a conference that regroups only the bishops of certain particular churches constituted in a given country or, on the other hand, that includes bishops of several nations.

An auxiliary bishop cannot be president or vice president of a conference of bishops (Papal Commission for the Authentic Interpretation of the Code of Canon Law, answer, 19 January 1988). The reason is that the function of the conference is essentially pastoral and that the power "ordinary, specific, and immediate" in a particular church belongs to the diocesan bishop assisted in his duty by the auxiliary bishop who, as such, has no autonomous pastoral responsibility in the diocese. As the president of the papal commission has stipulated, "the reason for membership in the conference of bishops derives less from its episcopal character than from the condition of the pastor of a local church."

The conference, which enjoys legal personality, draws up the statutes, which must arrange particularly for the holding of the plenary assembly, provide for the permanent council, the general secretariat, and other functions and commissions necessary for the conference to better achieve its objectives. The statutes must be "recognized" by the Holy See (c. 451).

The plenary assembly meets at least once a year and any time that circumstances require it, in conformity with the statutes. The president or the vice president of the conference chairs the meetings as well as the permanent council. All members must actively participate in the proceedings. They must also accept any responsibilities confided to them by the council. The conference of bishops can only make general decrees on matters for which the universal law provides or which the apostolic see determines (c. 455 § 1). The competencies of conferences are more restricted than was the case previously, without doubt to better protect the autonomy of each particular church.

The Secretariat of State has stipulated (circular letter to presidents of episcopal conferences, 8 November 1987) that the conference must publish particular complementary norms, if the norms already established are contrary to the Code, to determine, among other things, the age and qualities required for the candidates for the ministries of reader and acolyte; the training of aspirants to the permanent diaconate; to prepare the study plan for priests; to fix the hours of liturgical offices that the permanent deacons must recite; the ecclesiastical habit; the statutes of presbyteral councils; the income of retired priests; the presentation of Christian doctrine on radio and television; the participation of clerics and religious in radio and television programs; the statute of the catechumenate; the ritual of initiation of adults; the inscription for the baptism of adopted children; the place for confessions; the regulations for engagements; the interrogation of future spouses and the publication of banns; the method of making declarations and engagements before mixed marriages; the financial contribution of the faithful; the administration of any benefices still existing; the determination of acts of extraordinary administration; the fixing of maximum and minimum sums for the alienation of ecclesiastical property and the norms for the location of the property.

The conferences may publish norms of particular law, notably on the decision to confide the duties of the college of consultants to the cathedral chapter; admit the nomination of priests for a determined period; prescribe particular parochial registers; establish practical norms for ecumenism; admit the laity to preaching (outside of the homily); organize Catholic religious education in schools; enact norms on the administration of sacraments to non-Catholic Christians; the method of administering baptism; the age of confirmation and the parochial register of confirmations; establish a more advanced age to receive the presbyteriat and the permanent diaconate, as well as for the legal celebration of marriage; draw up a proper rite of marriage; dispense from the form in mixed marriages; decide the materials for the construction of fixed altars; suppress or transfer certain feast days to Sunday; determine the matter of abstinence and the way of observing fast and abstinence; establish norms for collection; permit the laity to be instituted as judges; establish the norms for transaction, compromise, or arbitrage; decide the constitution of a diocesan office to avoid legal proceedings.

In their action, the conferences of bishops must consider the good of the Church, that is, to serve the unity and the responsibility of each bishop toward the universal Church and his particular church. The decrees of the conference only enter into force (c. 455 § 2) when they have been legitimately promulgated, after their recognition by the Holy See (to which they must be transmitted, along with the acts of the plenary assembly). The mode of promulgation and the date of entry into force are determined by the conference. Even if he has not approved a decision of the conference that does not have force of law, a bishop has a certain moral obligation to "make them his own, in a spirit of unity and charity for his brothers in the min-

istry, unless there are grave reasons which he will assess himself before God" (Congregation of Bishops, *Directorium de pastorali ministerio Episcoporum*, 22 February 1973, no. 212). However, the freedom of particular churches is protected since, to be valid, the decisions that are obligatorily juridical must be passed with a two-thirds majority of the members of the conference, whether or not they are present, a greater majority than that required for the most important collegial deliberations relative to the universal Church (c. 455 § 2).

Given the relative innovation of the structure of the conference of bishops, questions remained about its juridical nature and, primarily, about its foundation: some would have liked it to have a foundation of divine law, while others considered the conferences to be ecclesiastical law, but with a basis in divine law. Yet others denied any theological basis to the conferences of bishops.

At the end of the twentieth century debate continued about whether the authority of the conferences also extended to the function of MAGISTERIUM that is customarily attributed to it, within certain limits, or if their powers were proper or substitute, ordinary or delegated, or if there might be a reserve of matters within the competence of bishops in their diocese done in favor of the apostolic see, which, by virtue of either common law or a special mandate, delegated it to the conference of bishops.

Given the problems mentioned, the suggestion approved by the extraordinary synod of bishops is understandable: "Since the conferences of bishops are particularly useful, if not necessary, in the actual pastoral work of the Church, it is desirable that their theological status be studied, so that, in particular, the question of their doctrinal authority is more clearly and more profoundly explained in light of the conciliar decree *Christus Dominus* 38 and the Code of Canon law, c. 447 and 753" (final report, 7 December 1985).

It is the responsibility of the conference to convoke the plenary council, with the approval of the apostolic see, to fix the place within the framework of its circumscription, to elect the president, to fix the beginning and the duration of the meetings, and the agenda for them, to decide to prolong or to close it, or if need be to transfer it (c. 441). But the conference of bishops cannot rescind the decrees of the plenary council of its territory, or derogate or modify them because a) the competencies of the two institutions are different and the matters treated by the plenary council cannot be made part of the competencies of the conference; b) the deliberations of the plenary council must receive recognition which supposes participation of the apostolic see in the creation of the particular law; and c) the plenary council is the council of the particular churches belonging to the same conference of bishops, but the bishops participate in them in greater number than in the conference (c. 443 § 1–2, c. 454).

It should be noted that late-20th-century CONCORDATS take the conferences of bishops more into consideration. In Spain, the state recognizes the civil personality of the conference of bishops in accordance with the statutes approved by the Holy See (agreement on juridical questions between the Holy See and the Spanish state, 3 January 1979, articles 1, 3). In Italy, certain matters can be resolved through an understanding between the competent educational authorities and the conference of bishops of Italy (agreement between the Holy See and the Italian republic, additional protocol, 18 February 1984, no. 5). The concordat signed on 28 July 1993 between the Holy See and Poland, apart from implicitly recognizing the juridical personality of the conference of bishops (article 4.2), made express mention of excluding a bishop, who was a member, from belonging to another conference of bishops (article 6.4), provided that a non-Polish person could be a member (article 6.5), to help determine the criteria, form, and method of ensuring pedagogical preparation for teachers of religion (article 12.3), regulated the juridical status of advanced schools (article 15.2), regulated access to cultural goods and property of the Church (article 25.2), and provided for resolution of new problems that might arise (article 27).

Existing Conferences of Bishops. At the end of the 20th century, there were (*Annuario Pontificio* 1991) 101 conferences of bishops (the date of the approval of the statutes is given in parentheses): South Africa (6 May 1981); North Africa (23 February 1983); Germany (24 November 1990); Angola and St. Tomé (20 October 1981); Antilles (24 April 1975); Argentina (3 January 1987); Australia (10 March 1979); Austria (12 May 1979); Bangladesh (18 October 1978); Belgium (3 March 1984); Benin (not specified); Bolivia (19 August 1972); Brazil (16 May 1986); Bulgaria (not specified); Burkina-Faso and Niger (29 March 1978); Burundi (6 June 1980); Cameroon (19 May 1989); Canada (24 May 1986); Central Africa (9 October 1982); Chile (13 May 1989); China (21 January 1978); Colombia (2 June 1990); Congo (not specified); Korea (3 August 1973); Ivory Coast (1 August 1973); Costa Rica (15 January 1977); Cuba (28 May 1983); El Salvador (23 March 1982); Ecuador (21 June 1985); Spain (5 June 1977); United States (20 March 1981); Ethiopia (15 December 1966); France (29 September 1975); Gabon (19 August 1989); Gambia, Liberia, and Sierra Leone (31 May 1983); Ghana (5 January 1980); Great Britain: England and Wales (10 October 1987); Scotland (11 January 1986); Greece (17 April 1967); Guatemala (28 April 1973); Guinea (not specified); Equatorial Guinea (2 April 1984); Haiti (20 June 1987); Honduras (6 July 1987); Hungary (6 August 1990); India (21 April 1976); Indonesia (2 August 1973); Ireland (2 August 1979); Italy (25 March 1985); Japan (2 August 1973); Kenya (7 December 1976); Laos and Cambodia (23 April 1971); Lesotho (14 October 1980); Latvia (not specified); Lithuania (not specified); Madagascar (18 June 1969); Malawi (1 October 1969); Malaysia, Singapore, and Brunei (17 April 1980); Mali (15 June 1973); Malta (3 July 1971); Mexico (30 March 1979); Mozambique (11 October 1982); Myanmar (Burma; 2 September 1982); Nicaragua (14 February 1987); Nigeria (6 May 1976); New Zealand (14 September 1974); Indian Ocean (9 November 1990); Pacific (29 January 1974); Pakistan (6 May 1976); Panama (13 December 1986); Papua New Guinea and Solomon Islands (31 May 1983); Paraguay (21 January 1984); Arab countries (23 August 1986); Netherlands (23 August 1986); Peru (10 October 1987); Philippines (23 January 1988); Poland (26 October 1987); Puerto Rico (27 September 1986); Portugal (18 January 1985); Dominican Republic (1 April 1985); Romania (March 1991); Rwanda (6 June 1980); Scandinavia (29 January 1985); Senegal, Mauritania, and Cape Verde (14 April 1973); Sudan (15 July 1971); Sri Lanka (27 May 1989); Switzerland (20 September 1975); Tanzania (8 January 1980); Chad (25 September 1989); Czechoslovakia (17 March 1990); Thailand (28 March 1969); Togo (8 May 1979); Turkey (1 February 1978); Uganda (8 September 1974); Uruguay (7 April 1990); Venezuela (6 July 1985); Vietnam (6 July 1980); Yugoslavia (28 May 1983); Zaire (2 February 1981); Zambia (2 April 1984); Zimbabwe (25 March 1981).

Added to these are the thirteen conferences of bishops of the eastern rite: Coptic patriarchal synod; Catholic Greek-Malachite patriarchal synod; Syrian patriarchal synod; Maronite patriarchal synod; Chaldian patriarchal synod; Armenian patriarchal synod; synod of the Catholic hierarchy of the Ukraine; assembly of the Catholic hierarchy of Egypt (AHCE, 5 December 1983); assembly of the Catholic patriarchs and bishops of Libya; assembly of the ordinaries of the Arab republic of Syria, inter-ritual meeting of the bishops of Iraq; Syro-Malabar conference of bishops (4 June 1970); conference of bishops of Iran (11 August 1977).

The Code invites neighboring conferences to consult with each other, with the object of promoting and ensuring the greater good. In the case where conferences address international questions, however, they should first seek the advice of the Holy See. Bilateral relations exist between conferences (for example, invitations are extended to members of other conferences to attend the plenary assembly). About twelve continental episcopal organizations have been created: in Central Africa, the Association of Episcopal Conferences of Central Africa (ACEAC, 24 May 1985) and the Association of Episcopal Conferences of the Region of Central Africa (ACERAC, 18 November 1989); for Africa and Madagascar, the Symposium of Episcopal Conferences of Africa and Madagascar (SCREAM); for southern Africa, the Inter-Regional Meeting of Bishops of Southern Africa (IMBISA, 2 April 1979); for West Africa, the Regional Episcopal Conference of Francophone West Africa (CERAO) and the Association of the Episcopal Conferences of Anglophone West Africa (AECAWA); for East Africa, the Association of Member Episcopal Conferences in Eastern Africa (AMECEA, 4 June 1983); for Asia, the Federation of Asian Bishops' Conferences (FABC, 6 December 1972); for Europe, the Concilium Conferentiarum Episcopalium Europae (CCEE, 19 December 1981); for Latin America, the Consejo Episcopal Latinoamericano (CELAM, 9 November 1974); for Central America and Panama, the Secretarioado Episcopal de America Central y Panama (SEDAC, 26 September 1970); for the European Community, the Commissio Episcopatuum Communitatis Europae (COMECE, 3 March 1980).

Dominique Le Tourneau

Bibliography

Anton, A. *Conferencias Episcopales ¿instancias intermedias?*, Salamanca, 1989.

Arrieta, J. I. "Conferenze episcopali e vincolo di comunione," *Ius Ecclesiae*, I (1989), 3–22.

Astorri, R. *Gli statuti delle conferenze episcopali. I. Europa*, Padua, 1987.

Aymars, W. "Wesensverständnis und Zuständigkeiten der Bischofskonferenz im Codex Iuris Canonici von 1983," *Archiv für katholisches Kirchenrecht*, 52 (1983), 46–75.

Bézac, R. "Les conférences épiscopales nationales," *Revue de Droit Canonique*, 15 (1965), 305–17.

Canon, S. "Episcopal Conferences in the Code of Canon Law," *Questioni canoniche*, 23, 1984, 137–65.

Carli, L. *Le conferenze episcopali nazionali*, Rovigo, 1968.

Costalunga, M. "De conferentiis episcoporum," *Periodica de re morali, canonica, liturgica*, 57 (1968), 217–80.

Diego-Lora, C. de "Competencias normativas de las Conferencias episcopales," *Ius canonicum*, 48 (1984), 257–570.

D'Onorio, J. B. *Le Pape et le gouvernement de l'Église*, Paris, 1992, 229–83.

Fagiolo, V. "'Potestas' del vescovo e conferenza episcopale," *Ius Ecclesiae*, I (1989), 47–67.

Feliciani, G. *Le Conferenze episcopali*, Bologna, 1974.

Franck, B. "La conférence épiscopale et les autre institutions de collégialité intermédiaire," *L'Année Canonique*, 27 (1983), 67–119.

Ghirlanda, G. "De episcoporum conferentiis," *Periodica de re morali, canonica, liturgica*, 79 (1990), 625–661.

Goralsko, W. "Wladza ustawodawcza Konferencji Episkopatu wedlug Kodeksu Prawa Kanonicznego z 1983 r," *Prawo Kanoniczne* XXII (1989), 45–57.

Gouyon, P. "Les relations entre le diocèse et la conférence épiscopale," *L'Année Canonique*, 22 (1978), 1–23.

Guillemette, F. "Les conférences épiscopales sont-elles une institution de la collégialité épiscopale?" *Studia Canonica* 25 (1991), 39–76.

Gutierrez, J. L. "La conferenza episcopale come organo sopradiocesano nella struttura ecclesiale," *Ius Ecclesiae*, I (1989), 69–91.

Ibán, I. C. *Gli statuti delle conferenze episcopali. II. America*, Padua, 1989.

Jubany, N. "Las conferencias episcopales y el Concilio Vaticano II," *Ius Canonicum* 5 (1965), 343–63.

Kramer, P. "Bischofskonferenz und Apostolischer Stuhl," *Archiv für katholisches Kirchenrecht*, 156 (1987), 127–39.

Kuttner, R. W. *The Develpoment, Structure and Competence of the Episcopal Conference*, Washington, D.C., 1972.

Legrand, H., Manzanares, J., and García y García, A. *Les Conférences épiscopales. Théologie, statut canonique, avenir*, Paris, 1988.

Manzanares, J. "Las confencias episcopales hoy. Configuracíon jurídica y fundamentos doctrinales," *Revista española de Derecho Canónico*, 25 (1969), 325–72.

Miras, J. "Naturaleza jurídica de la potestad normativa de las Conferencias episcopales según el CIC 83," *Iglesia universal e Iglesias particulares*, Pamplona, 1989, 677–92.

Morrisey, G. "Decisions of Episcopal Conferences in Implementing the New Law," *Studia Canonica*, 20 (1986), 105–22.

Müller, H., and Pottmeyer, H. J. (eds.) *Die Bischofskonferenz. Theologischer und juridischer Status*, Düsseldorf, 1989.

Seraceni, G. "Conferenze episcopali e realtà politica (Tentativo d'una impostazione)," *Monitor Ecclesiasticus*, 104 (1979), 228–48.

Tomás Martin de Agar, J. *Legislazione delle conferenze episcopali complementare al CIC*, Milan, 1990.

Uccela, F. *Le Conferenze episcopali in diritto Canonico*, Naples, 1973.

CONFRATERNITIES, ROMAN. See **Roman Confraternities**.

CONGREGATION OF THE INDEX. See **Index, Congregation of the**.

CONGREGATION, PLENARY (CONGREGATIO PLENARIA). This is the supreme body of a DICASTERY. It comprises all member CARDINALS and all diocesan bishops of the dicastery and deals with questions related to general principles or those of a normative nature. Except under special circumstances (RGCR, art. 110), it sits only once per year, at a date fixed in advance. It has the privilege of asking the sovereign pontiff for permission to submit important problems involving the life of the Church to the SYNOD of bishops.

Philippe Levillain

CONGREGATIONS, ROMAN. The Roman congregations are the great ministries of the Holy See. Their name derives from the specialized assemblies of cardinals held during the 16th century, which were convened by the pope to seek the advice of the cardinals on questions arising in Rome. The Roman Congregations replaced the general consistories, which in their turn had replaced the calling of the Roman *presbyterium* of the 11th century.

The first of the Roman congregations was the Congregation of the Holy Roman Universal Inquisition convened for the first time on 21 July 1542. Almost half a century later, SIXTUS V made the fifteen congregations he had created into the essential components of his pontifical government. To this day, the congregations are the basic element of pontifical government, although now they are complemented by the pontifical COUNCILS, the APOSTOLIC TRIBUNALS, and the offices of the Roman CURIA. The congregations are decision-making bodies with ordinary power of governance and legal authority to exercise their competence. However, this power is simply a vicarial authority as it is exercised only on behalf of the pope, who is the true holder of supreme power within the Church. The Roman congregations may only exercise executive power because legislative power is reserved for the supreme pontiff, except in specific derogations (art. 18 no. 2 of the apostolic constitution *Pastor bonus*, 1988). In the past these legislative derogations were numerous, despite the ban imposed by BENEDICT XV in his *motu proprio Cum juris canonici* of 15 September 1917. In recent times they have become more restrictive in order to differentiate between powers within the Curia because judicial power belongs to the apostolic tribunals. Each congregation is presided over by a cardinal prefect (or an archbishop pro-prefect awaiting promotion to cardinal). The head of the congregation is seconded by a secretary archbishop and one or several undersecretary prelates. All are appointed by the pope for a renewable five-year term.

Since the Roman congregations were reorganized in 1988 their number has been reduced to nine. The adjective *sacred*, traditionally used to describe them, has also been dropped.

The Congregation for the Doctrine of the Faith. In 1965 Pope PAUL VI abolished the use of the word *supreme* to describe this congregation. However, it is the oldest of them all and occurs first in listings of congregations in two documents: the apostolic constitution *Regimini Ecclesiae universae* of 1967 and the apostolic constitution *Pastor Bonus* of 1988. The Congregation for the Doctrine of the Faith was the first to be singled out for modernizing, even before the end of the second Vatican Council. In the *motu proprio Integrae servandae* of 7 August 1965, Paul VI recognized that the "most important matters of the Curia" fall to this dicastery. It was an heir of the Roman tribunal, the INQUISITION and, since its creation in the middle of the 16th century, was called upon to defend the integrity of the Catholic faith in the Universal Church. With the spread of heresies, the congregation constantly had to intervene in more and more diverse activities. In the 16th century it was responsible for the censure of books (Index), while in the 19th it canonized saints and examined candidates to the episcopacy (outside of the mission countries and concordat States). In the beginning of the 20th century, the Congregation for the Doctrine of the Faith granted indulgences and Pauline privileges.

The position of prefect of the congregation was the reserve of the pope, assisted by a cardinal-secretary, who after the reform of 1967 became known as the pro-prefect. After the reform the congregation was renamed, and the words "Holy-Office" replaced by "The Doctrine of the Faith." Indeed, the term Holy Office had been introduced following the curial reform of 1908.

Paul VI also wished to see renewed cooperation between this congregation and the diocesan bishops (BENEDICT XIV, 1753, already reflected this within his apostolic constitution *Sollicita ac provida*). Pope Paul wanted to modernize the procedure for examining doctrines that had been challenged, and this was specified in a regulation dated 15 January 1971. Criticisms aired at the council had been especially directed to this point. The critics objected to the fact that condemnations were issued by the Holy Office without any possibility for the interested parties to defend themselves. In reality, it was indeed possible to defend oneself in these processes (either in person or with the help of an advocate) for crimes falling within the purview of the dicastery (which was exercising judiciary power). However, such defense was not possible in cases regarding publications. In such cases it was the written word that was being considered, as it was presented to the faithful; it was not the person who was being condemned. Any subsequent explanation or justification by the author was deemed superfluous because it would be unknown to the readers. By the end of his pontificate, however, PIUS XII had prepared a draft for liberalizing this system.

In 1967 the newly redesigned Congregation for the Doctrine of the Faith was part of the general remodeling of the Curia. The pope, however, aligned this dicastery along the model of common law by leaving the post of prefect open to a cardinal. The 1988 charter builds on the foundation laid in 1967, and confers on this body a more positive role in the protection and promotion of faith and morals. It shows greater sensitivity to the role of faith with respect to developments in culture and the sciences. The congregation has universal competence, examines new doctrines, refutes errors, and may even condemn some publications, but strictly in conjunction with local ecclesiastical authorities. In any case, the authors whose works are in question are invited to explain themselves to the dicastery and hold discussions with its officials.

The congregations also play the role of judiciary bodies and may impose sanctions with respect to crimes against the faith or morals and infractions in the celebration of the sacraments. They also oversee judgments on the privilege of the faith in marriage law. However, on 1 March 1989, the Congregation of Divine Worship and Discipline of the Sacraments assumed responsibility for examining dispensations from ecclesiastical celibacy.

Two PONTIFICAL COMMISSIONS are governed by the dicastery of the Doctrine of the Faith: the Pontifical Biblical Commission and the International Theological Commission. The following is a list of the cardinal secretaries, pro-prefects, and prefects who have presided over the dicastery: Camillo Borghese (PAUL V), 1602–5; Pompeo Arrigoni, 1605–16; Giovanni Garzia Millini, 1616–29; Antonio Barberini, 1629–33; Francesco Barberini, 1633–79; Cesare Fachinetti, 1679–83; Alderano Cibo, 1683–1700; Galeazzo Marescotti, 1700–16; Fabrizio Spada, 1716–17; Niccolò Acciaioli, 1717–19; Francesco Giudice, 1719–25; Fabrizio Paolucci, 1725–6; Pietro Ottoboni, 1726–40; Tommaso Ruffo, 1740–53; Neri Maria Corsini, 1753–70; Giovanni Francesco Stoppani, 1771–4; Luigi Maria Torrigiani, 1775–7; Carlo Rezzonico, 1777–99; Leonardo Antonelli, 1800–11; Giulio Maria Della Somaglia, 1814–30; Bartolomeo Pacca, 1830–44; Vincenzo Macchi, 1844–60; Costantino Patrizi, 1860–76; Prospero Caterini, 1876–81; Antonio Maria Panebianco, 1882–3; Luigi Bilio, 1883–4; Raffaele Monaco La Valletta, 1884–96; Lucido Maria Parocchi, 1896–1903; Serafino Vannutelli, 1903–08; Mariano Ranpolla Del Tindaro, 1908–13; Domenico Ferrata, 1914; Rafael Merry Del Val, 1914–30; Donato Sbarretti, 1930–9; Francesco Marchetti Selvaggiani, 1939–51; Giuseppe Pizzardo, 1951–9; Alfredo Ottaviani, pro-secretary 1953–9, and later pro-prefect, 1959–68; Franjo Seper, 1968–81; Joseph Ratzinger, since 1981.

The Congregation for the Eastern Churches. GREGORY XIII created this dicastery in 1573 under the name *Congregatio de rebus Graecorum*. Its role was to attend to the needs of Catholics who observed Byzantine rites and to secure the return to the Catholic Church of the churches of the eastern schism. In 1599 the dicastery was absorbed by the *Congregatio super negotiis fidei et*

religionis catholicae, created by CLEMENT VIII and later to become the Sacred Congregation *Propaganda Fide*. In 1862 PIUS IX once more granted its autonomy over eastern matters, with the Sacred Congregation *de Propaganda fide pro negotiis ritus orientalis*. In 1908 PIUS X once more made it a part of the congregation for the Propagation of the Faith. BENEDICT XV, however, changed it once again to the Sacred Congregation for the Eastern Church (1917), with the pope as its prefect (*motu proprio Dei providentis*). In a move that was confirmed by Pope JOHN PAUL II, Paul VI simply pluralized the title of this dicastery to reflect the great diversity of eastern rites that fall under its jurisdiction. They are the following: Alexandrian; Antiochian or Syro-Western; Byzantine or from Constantinople; Chaldean or Syro-Eastern; and Armenian. Its territorial jurisdiction covers the following areas: southern Albania to Afghanistan, through Bulgaria, Greece, Cyprus, Turkey, Egypt, Northern Ethiopia, Lebanon, Iraq, Iran, Syria and Palestine. Respecting the traditional autonomy of Eastern Catholics which was concretized in the 1990 Code of Canons of the Eastern Churches, this congregation oversees all matters pertaining to the subjects and territories governed by it. It accumulates the attributions given to the congregations for the Latin church, for example, the congregation for the bishops, for the clergy, and in part for the Institutes of Consecrated Life, and societies of apostolic life, divine worship, and Catholic education. The Congregations of the Doctrine of the Faith and the Causes of the Saints, as well as the Congregation of Divine Worship were the only two dicasteries to retain their full responsibility in the eastern countries. The latter congregation oversaw dispensations for unconsummated marriage as well as diaconal and presbyterial obligations. The three Roman TRIBUNALS installed since the reform of 1867, remained. The reform had caused the withdrawal of judiciary competence granted to the Eastern dicastery by Pius XII in 1957 (*motu proprio Cleri sanctitati*, can. 195 & 2).

The SECRETARIAT OF STATE naturally remained the interlocutor with the eastern political authorities. Furthermore, the Congregation for the Eastern Churches has to work closely with the pontifical council for Christian unity in order to promote ecumenical relations with the Orthodox. It also has to cooperate with the council for inter-religious dialogue for relations with Muslims.

Together with the other dicasteries, the congregation attends to the pastoral needs of the faithful of the Eastern Churches in territories where Latin rites are practiced. It also oversees the Latin patriarchate of Jerusalem. The following is a list of cardinal secretaries and prefects: Niccolo Marini, 1917–36; Eugène Tisserant, 1936–59; Amleto Giovanni Cicognani, 1959–61; Gabriele Acacio Coussa, 1961–62; Gustavo Testa, 1962–68; Maximilien De Furstenberg, 1968–73; Pierre-Paul Philippe,

1973–80; Wladislaw Rubin, 1980–85; Simon Lourdusamy, 1985–91; Achille Silvestrini, since 1991.

The Congregation for Divine Worship and the Discipline of the Sacraments. Successive popes from Sixtus V to Paul VI had always given this dicastery the responsibility for regulating liturgical worship as well as the causes of saints (beatifications and canonizations). Although the situation was not changed by the curial reform of 1967, a change was introduced in 1969. The Sacred Congregation for Divine Worship and the Sacred Congregation for the Causes of Saints were divided (*motu proprio Sacra Congregatio*). In 1975 Paul VI made yet another change, joining Divine Worship to the Discipline of the Sacraments.

Since the papacy of Pius X, this latter congregation had formed an autonomous dicastery (*motu proprio Constans Nobis*). In 1984 JOHN PAUL II realized that the two domains formed two separate and distinct sections within the same congregation and made them two separate entities presided over by the same cardinal prefect. (Chirograph *Quoniam in celeri rerum*). In 1988 they were again merged into one congregation (apostolic constitution *Pastor bonus*).

This dicastery is responsible for all questions relating to sacred liturgy and the administration of sacraments in the Latin Catholic Church. These matters include the validity and appropriateness of celebrations (notably eucharistic celebrations), liturgical texts and calendars, the monitoring of translated texts and adaptations of liturgical books by the conferences of bishops, the promotion of sacred music, singing, and art. It also has jurisdiction over all the Latin rites: Roman; Ambrosian (diocese of Milan), Lyonnais; Wisigothic or Hispanomozarabic (Toledo and Salamanca); and Slavo-Latin rites (Zagreb and Gorizia). The traditional rites of some religious institutes also come under the supervision of the dicastery such as the Benedictine, Cistercian, Carthusian, Dominican, Carmelite, and Franciscan rites. In 1988 a Zairian rite was introduced.

The congregation follows a judiciary procedure when dealing with dispensations for the non-consummation of marriage of which there are about 1,000 cases per year. There are also dispensations from obligations of the diaconate or the presbyterate, as well as cases of invalidity of holy orders. Cardinal prefects: Domenico Ferrata, 1908–14; Filippo Giustini, 1914–20; Michele Lega, 1920–35; Domenico Jorio, 1935–54; Benedetto Aloisi Masella, pro-prefect, 1947–54; prefect, 1954–68; Francis Brennan, 1968; Antonio Samore, 1968–76; James Robert Knox, 1974–81; Giuseppe Casoria, 1981–85; Paul-Augustin Mayer, 1985–88; Eduardo Martinez Somalo, 1988–92; Antonio Maria Javierre Ortas, 1992–98; Jorge Arturo Medina Estévez, since 1998.

The Congregation for the Causes of the Saints. This dicastery was created as a result of the division of the Congregation of Rites. The brief, *Coelestis Jerusalem*, issued by URBAN VIII on 5 July 1634, confers upon the Apostolic See the right to authorize the veneration of servants of God. The beatification and canonization of saints are the main responsibilities of this dicastery since the beginning of the papacy of Pope John Paul II. In the first decade of his pontificate, John Paul II conferred 299 beatifications and canonized 254 servants of God. (From 1588 and 1900, the number of saints canonized had amounted to a mere 31.)

The dicastery operates in much the same manner as a tribunal. Cases for beatification are conducted in accordance with the new norms established in the apostolic constitution *Divinus perfectionis magister*. This latter appears as an annex to the CODE of CANON LAW of 1983.

In order to carry out its work the dicastery has an office of history and hagiography (created by PIUS XI in 1930), its own chancellery, a body of advocates, procurators, and medical experts. There is also a training school for postulators of the causes and for magistrates of local tribunals for the causes of saints. This latter school was established after the diocesan decentralization of procedures in 1984.

The Congregation for the Causes of Saints confers the title "Doctor of the Church" on a saint, as well as rules on the authenticity of sacred relics. Cardinal prefects: Paolo Bertoli, 1969–73; Luigi Raimondi, 1973–6; Corrado Bafile, 1976–80; Pietro Palazzini, 1980–88; Angelo Felici, 1988–98; José Saraiva Martins, since 1998.

The Congregation for Bishops. Sixtus V created this dicastery in 1588 with the papal Bull *Immensa aeterni Dei*. Originally named Sacred Congregation for the Establishment of Churches and Consistorial Provisions, the functions of this dicastery have varied under successive popes. In 1592 CLEMENT VIII removed the requirement involving testing the theological knowledge of candidates to the episcopacy to the then newly established Congregation for the Examination of Bishops. In 1601, however, the same pope extended its authority to cover the diocesan clergy. It was also renamed Sacred Congregation in Charge of the Affairs and Consultations of Bishops and Regulars, shortened shortly afterwards to Sacred Congregation of Bishops and Regulars. In 1634 Pope Urban VIII lessened the burden of work on this dicastery. The implementation of the provisions of the Council of Trent, with regard to the presence of prelates in their respective dioceses, was no longer its responsibility. This was conferred instead on the Sacred Congregation for the Residence of Bishops. In 1908 Pope Pius X named the dicastery the Sacred Consistorial Congregation, reserving for himself the role of prefect, a role that was relinquished by

Pope Paul VI in 1967. It was also at that time that the dicastery received its present name of Congregation for Bishops.

Its responsibilities extend to all Churches that do not fall under the Congregation for Eastern Churches (eastern rites), or the Congregation for the Evangelization of Peoples (so-called mission countries). It covers the dioceses and their establishment, unification, division, and suppression, as well as ecclesiastical provinces and conferences of bishops. It governs military functions of diocesan bishops (military ordinariates), personal and territorial prelatures, and local and plenary councils. It also prepares, on behalf of the pope, appointments for bishops (diocesans, coadjutors, auxiliary, and other titular bishops). With respect to this latter function, the dicastery has to work with the Secretariat of State (section pertaining to relations with States), whenever state authorities must be consulted per the terms of some diplomatic agreements.

It naturally falls to the Congregation for Bishops to organize the *ad limina* visits that every diocesan bishop must make to Rome every five years. In his apostolic constitution *Pastor bonus*, John Paul II stressed the significance of hierarchical communion among the bishops and the successor of St. Peter (cf. directory of 29 June 1988, on the *ad limina* visit). At this time, each bishop must submit answers to a detailed questionnaire on the state of his diocese. A specialized office of the congregation organizes his stay in Rome which includes a private audience with the pope, liturgical celebrations, meetings with heads of dicasteries, and a collective papal audience with other bishops from the same province or ecclesiastical region.

The Congregation for Bishops is also the legitimate authority for granting canonical approval ("*recognitio*" of canons 446 and 455) of the juridic acts of local episcopal assemblies. These are assemblies of particular councils and conferences of bishops. Canonical approval is granted after the congregation has requested that the relevant dicasteries review the juridic acts and obtain technical advice from the Pontifical Council on the Interpretation of Legislative Texts. Since the reform of 1988 the Congregation for Bishops no longer oversees the former pontifical commission for the pastoral care of migration and tourism (which has now become an autonomous pontifical council). However, it has retained jurisdiction over the pontifical commission for Latin America. Cardinal secretaries and prefects of the Congregation for Bishops: Gaetano de Lai, 1908–28; Carlo Perosi, 1928–30; Raffaello Rossi, 1930–48; Adeodato Giovanni Piazza, 1948–57; Marcello Mimmi, 1957–61; Carlo Confalonieri, 1966–73; Sebastiano Baggio, 1973–84; Bernardin Ganitin, 1984–98; Lucas Mareira Neves, since 1998.

Congregation for the Evangelization of Peoples. This dicastery was first established by Clement VIII in 1599 as the missionary dicastery of *Propaganda Fide*, but it ceased operation the following year despite, or perhaps because of, its vast jurisdiction. It went from northern Europe to the farthest limits of Africa, from the West Indies to Japan. It was replaced by a number of specialized congregations created in 1573, 1591, and 1595 dealing with Greek, Abyssinian, and Italo-Greek affairs, respectively. Clement VIII, however, continued to maintain certain links with the general secretariat of missions, which was established in 1604. It was GREGORY XV, who in his apostolic constitution *Inscrutabili divinae Providentiae* of 22 January 1622 laid the basis for the congregation of the *Propaganda Fide*. He conferred on it full powers for the preaching of the Gospel in the vast territories under its jurisdiction. In 1967 Paul VI gave the congregation its present name, which was used in conjunction with the old name until John Paul II dropped the latter in 1988.

GREGORY XV also gave financial autonomy to the dicastery by authorizing it to receive gifts and legacies that had been made exempt from duties. It also received a tax of 500 gold ecus from every new cardinal, paid upon receipt of his pastoral ring (constitutions *Romanum decet* and *Cum inter multiplices* 1622).

In 1817 PIUS VII granted the dicastery the revenue from the *Camera spoliorum*, or Chamber of Spoils and Goods. Until the Curial Reform of Pius X this latter chamber had been responsible for managing the goods belonging to the Holy See, which were held in abeyance.

URBAN VIII had, in 1622, established the Congregation of the Economy for administering real estate and moveable property belonging to the dicastery of the Propagation of the Faith. This congregation would also be abolished by Pius X. To this day, the Congregation for the Evangelization of Peoples retains its financial prerogatives, which are administered by a pro-secretary of the economy (a post created by Paul VI in 1967). It is outside the jurisdiction of the Administration of the Patrimony of the Apostolic See. Instead, it falls under the prefecture for Economic Affairs of the Holy See. The congregation has its own budget, which is fed by real estate earnings from donations or legacies (palace of the Piazza di Spagna, farms around Rome, which were bequeathed by popes, etc.). The congregation is therefore in a position to pay its own staff. It also collects funds from all the dioceses throughout the world through the Supreme Council of pontifical missionary works. These cover the Missionary Union of the clergy, the Organization of the Propagation of the Faith, and the organizations of St. Peter the Apostle and the Holy Childhood. The Supreme Council sees to it that the collected funds are sent to their destination, without the need to send them to Rome.

The jurisdiction of the congregation covers a vast geographical area. There are more than 900 ecclesiastical territories for approximately 110 million faithful. This covers almost all of Africa and Asia, Oceania with the exception of Australia, some parts of Latin America and southeastern Europe (with the obvious exception of those areas where eastern rites are practiced). There are 50,000 priests, two-thirds of whom are originally from the regions, more than 100,000 nuns (80% of whom come from the regions themselves), 13,000 religious men who are not priests, 3,000 lay missionaries, 5,600 clinical institutions, 46,000 schools for 15 million pupils, and 87 universities for 135,000 students worldwide.

After Pius X carried out reductions in 1908, other congregations, such as the Congregations of the Doctrine of the Faith, Divine Worship, Evangelization of the Peoples, and the Discipline of Sacraments began to compete with the congregation for the evangelization of peoples with respect to its area of responsibility. The powers of the Congregation for the Causes of Saints for example, now extended to cover the mission dioceses, as was the case for the Roman Rota tribunal. The Congregation for the Evangelization of Peoples accumulated in its territory the powers and competence elsewhere granted to the Congregations for Bishops and for the clergy.

Within the dicastery there are several commissions that deal specifically with questions of theology, missionary spirituality and formation, pastoral care and missionary cooperation, catechesis and catechists, as well as with the conferences of bishops of these countries.

The congregation has long had an office of statistics, which distributes about a dozen publications in several languages. Furthermore, it is responsible for the large Pontifical University, The Urbanianan, and the Pontifical Urban College, whose imposing buildings dominate St. Peter's Square from the Janiculum. Cardinal prefects: Antonio Maria Sauli, 1622; Ludovico Ludovisi, 1622–32; Antonio Barberini, 1632–71; Luigi Capponi, vice-prefect, 1645–53; Paluzzo Altieri, 1671–98, Carlo Barberini, 1698–1704; Giuseppe Sacripanti, 1704–27; Vincenzo Petra, 1727–47, Silvio Valenti Gonzaga, 1747–56; Giuseppe Spinelli, 1756–63; Giuseppe Maria Castelli, 1763–80; Leonardo Antonelli, 1780–95; Sigismond Gerdil, 1795–1802; Stefano Borgia, pro-prefect, 1798–1800, prefect, 1802–04, Antonio Dugnani, 1804–05; Michele Di Pietro, 1805–14; Lorenzo Litta, 1814–18; Francesco Luigi Fontana, 1818–22; Ercole Consalvi, 1822–24; Giulio Maria Della Somaglia, 1824–26; Mauro Cappellari (Gregory XVI), 1826–31; Carlo Maria Pedicini, 1831–34; Filippo Fransoni, 1834–56; Alessandro Barnabo 1856–74; Alessandro Franchi, 1874–78; Giovanni Simeoni, 1878–92; Miecislaw Ledochowski, 1892–02; Girolamo Maria Gotti, 1902–16; Domenico Serafini, 1916–18; Wilhelm Van Rossum, 1918–32; Pietro Fumasoni Biondi, 1933–60;

Alfons Samuel Stritch, pro-prefect, 1958–60; prefect, 1960–70; Agnello Rossi, 1970–84; Archbishop Dermott Ryan, pro-prefect, 1984–85; Joseph Tomko, since 1985.

Congregation for the Clergy. This congregation was created in 1564 to implement the reforms of the Council of Trent. The number of cardinals assigned to operate it grew from 8 to 12. Its original title had been Congregation for the Implementation and Observance of the Sacred Council of Trent and Other Reforms, but in 1588 its area of responsibility was considerably increased when Sixtus V put it in charge of all matters concerning the clergy and of worship outside the area of dogma. While by the beginning of the 20th century other new bodies and successive dicasteral changes had come to infringe on the work of this congregation, Paul VI and then John Paul II did restore some of its prestige. The dicastery is responsible for all matters affecting secular priests and deacons of the Latin rite, except those from the mission territories, who are still under the Congregation for the Evangelization of Peoples.

The Congregation for the Clergy is responsible for the life, sanctification, discipline, ongoing formation and preaching of the clergy, the geographical distribution of its members, and their rights and obligations. In collaboration with the bishops and their conferences, it supervises pastoral and presbyterial councils of dioceses and their colleges of consultors, chapters of canons, parishes, churches, sanctuaries, and clerical associations. Social security for the clergy and the management of diocesan ecclesiastical property also fall within the purview of this dicastery. After the Curia was reorganized in 1988, the congregation continued to have responsibility for catechesis and especially for the monitoring of catechisms. It would approve the latter after prior consultation with the Congregation of the Doctrine of the Faith. Cardinal prefects: Carlo Borromeo, 1564–5; Francesco Alciati, 1565–80; Filippo Boncompagni, 1580–6; Antonio Carafa, 1586–91; Girolamo Mattei, 1591–1603; Paolo Emilio Zacchia, 1604–5; Francesco Maria Bourbon Del Monte, 1605–16; Orazio Lancellotti, 1616–20; Roberto Ubaldini, 1621–3; Cosmo de Torres, 1623–6; Bonifacio Bevilacqua, 1626–7; Fabrizio Verospi, 1627–39; Giovanni Battista Pamfili (INNOCENT X), 1639–44; Francesco Cennini, 1644–5; Pier Luigi Carafa, 1645–55; Francesco Paolucci, 1657–61; Giulio Sacchetti, 1661–3; Angelo Celsi, 1664–71; Paluzzo Altieri, 1671–72; Vincenzo Maria Orsini (BENEDICT XIII), 1673–5; Federico Baldeschi (Ubaldi) Colonna, 1675–91; Galeazzo Marescotti, 1692–5; Giuseppe Sacripanti, 1696–1700; Bandino Pianciatici, 1700–18; Pietro Marcellino Corradini, 1718–21; Curzio Origo, 1721–37; Antonio Saverio Gentili, 1737–53; Mario Millini, 1753–6; Gian Giacomo Millo, 1756–57;

Clement Argenvilliers, 1757–8; Ferdinando Maria De Rossi, 1759–75; Carlo Vittorio Amedeo Delle Lanze, 1775–84; Guglielmo Pallotta, 1785–95; Tommaso Antici, 1795–98; Filippo Garandini, 1800–10; Giulio Gabrielli, 1814–20; Emanuele De Gregorio, 1820–34; Vincenzo Macchi, 1824–41; Paolo Polidori, 1841–7; Pietro Ostini, 1847–9; Angelo Mai, 1851–3; Anton Maria Cagiano de Azevedo, 1853–60; Prospero Caterini, 1860–81; Lorenzo Nina, 1881–5; Luigi Serafini, 1885–93; Angelo Di Pietro, 1893–1902; Vincenzo Vannutelli, 1902–8; Casimiro Gennari, 1908–14; Francesco di Paola Cassetta, 1914–19; Donato Sbarretti, 1919–30; Giulio Serafini, 1930–8; Luigi Maglione, 1938–9; Francesco Marmaggi, 1939–49; Giuseppe Bruno, 1949–54; Pietro Ciriaci, 1954–66; Jean Villot, 1967–9; John Wright, 1969–79; Silvio Oddi, 1979–85; Antonio Innocenti, 1985–91; Jose T. Sanchez, 1991–98; Darío Castrillón Hoyos, since 1998.

Congregation for Institutes of Consecrated Life and Societies for Apostolic Life.

This congregation was created in the 16th century by Pope Sixtus V (brief *Romanus Pontifex*, 1586). It was subsequently joined to the Congregation for Bishops. It then worked in tandem with the Congregations of the State of Regulars (1649), of the Discipline of Regulars (1698), and the State of Regular Orders (1846), respectively. After merging the congregations for bishops and religious life in 1906, Pius X separated them definitively in 1908. In 1967 Paul VI added the secular institutes established under Pius XII to the number of entities falling under the purview of this dicastery. In 1988 John Paul II changed the name of the congregation to reflect the terminology of the new Code of Canon Law of 1983.

The congregation is responsible for promoting religious life and apostolic activity by establishing or suppressing institutes of consecrated life and societies of apostolic life. It also authorizes or dissolves unions and federations between and among them and interprets their statutes and monitors their activities, the management of property, methods of recruitment and formation of members, and ensures that the spirit of the founders and healthy traditions that form the basis of these bodies are followed. The dicastery also determines rights and duties of members of institutes, decides on dispensations to be granted them, and their expulsion if required.

There is also a certain amount of sharing of competencies. While the congregation has jurisdiction only over subjects of Latin rite, the institutes of consecrated life in mission countries only consult their Roman Congregation on matters of the internal form, as their missionary activity falls within the scope of the Congregation for the Evangelization of Peoples. On the other hand, the latter congregation has full responsibility for those societies of apostolic life that carry out missionary activity. The Congregation for Divine Worship and the Discipline of the Sacraments governs the annulment of sacred ordination of religious and the rite of religious profession, while the Congregation for the Clergy oversees the reduction of religious to lay status. Finally, academic formation programs for young religious are determined by the Congregation for Catholic Education. Cardinal prefects: José Calasanz Vives Y Tuto, 1908–13; Ottavio Cagiano De Azevedo, 1913–15; Domenico Serafini, 1916; Diomede Falconio, 1916–17; Giulio Tonti, 1917–18; Raffaele Scapinelli Di Leguigno, 1918–20; Teodoro Valvrè Di Bonzo, 1920–2; Camillo Laurenti, 1922–8; Henri-Alexis Lepicier, 1928–35; Vincenzo La Puma, 1935–43; Luigi Lavitrano, 1945–50; Clemente Micara, 1950–1; Valerio Valeri, 1953–63; Ildebrado Antoniutti, 1963–74; Arturo Tabera Araoz, 1974–6; Eduardo Pironio, 1976–84; Jerôme Hamer, 1984–92; Eduardo Martinez Somalo, since 1992.

The Congregation for Catholic Education.

Sixtus V established this dicastery primarily to serve the needs of the University of the City of Rome, hence its name *Congregatio pro universitate Studii romani*. The congregation was abolished a century later, during the papacy of CLEMENT X, only to reappear in 1824 under LEO XII, under the name Congregation for Studies. It was granted responsibility for education in the entire Papal States. The only change brought by Pius X was the extension of its functions to cover all the Catholic universities and ecclesiastical faculties throughout the world. Benedict XV added seminaries to the institutions covered by this congregation (*motu proprio Seminaria clericorum*, 1915). The sacred Congregation of Seminaries and Universities was formed in 1967 and subsequently became the Congregation for Catholic Education, as it governed the training of clerics as well as lay persons. In 1988 John Paul II at first restored the old title of Congregation of Seminaries and Institutes of Studies. This, however, was again changed in 1989 when it was used as the subtitle to the former name Congregation for Catholic Education.

This dicastery assists the bishops in fostering religious vocations in seminaries, providing "a sound training in human, spiritual, as well as doctrinal and pastoral matters" (apostolic constitution *Pastor bonus*, art. 113 § 1). It therefore establishes and approves the statutes of interdiocesan seminaries, sets the basic standards for Catholic schools at all levels, and oversees the erection of universities and ecclesiastical institutes of higher learning. It approves their statutes and provides high-level guidance by monitoring the integrity of the faith that is taught in these institutions. Over the last few years a number of guidelines have been published in keeping with these goals.

In 1990 the jurisdiction of the Congregation for Catholic Education covered some 85,000 seminarians attending 1,000 seminaries, 40 million pupils registered in

150,000 schools, and 1,500,000 students in 600 tertiary-level Catholic institutions. Cardinal prefects: Francesco Bertazzoli, 1824–30; Placido Zurla, 1830–34; Luigi Lambruschini, 1834–45; Giuseppe Mezzofanti, 1845–9; Carlo Vizzardelli, 1849–51; Raffaele Fornari, 1851–4; Giovanni Brunelli, 1854–6; Vicenzo Santucci, 1856–61; Karl von Reisach, 1861–9; Annibale Capalti, 1870–7; Lorenzo Nina, 1877–8; Antonino De Luca, 1878–83; Giuseppe Pecci, 1884–7; Tommazo Zigliara, 1887–93; Camillo Mazzella, 1893–7; Francesco Satolli, 1897–1910; Beniamino Cavicchioni, 1910–11; Francesco di Paola Cassetta, 1911–14; Benedetto Lorenzelli, 1914–15; Gaetano Bisleti, 1915–37 (Raffaelle Carlo Rossi, secretary, 1937–9); Guiseppe Pizzardo, 1939–68; Gabriel Garrone, pro-prefect, 1966–8; prefect, 1968–80; William Wakefield Baum, 1980–90; Pio Laghi, 1990–99; Zenon Grocholewski, since 1999.

Joel Benoit d'Onorio

Bibliography

Bonnet, P. A., Gullo C. (under the direction of), *La Curia romana nella Cos. ap. Pastor bonus*, Rome, 1990.

Bouix, D. *Tractatus de Curia romana*, Paris, 1880.

Del Re, N. *La Curia romana. Lineamenti storico-giuridici*, 3rd ed., Rome, 1970.

Delgago, G. *La Curia romana, El gobierno central de la Iglesia, EUNSA*, Pamplona, 1973.

D'Onorio, J. B. *La nomination des évêques. Procédures canoniques et conventions diplomatiques*, Paris, 1986.

D'Onorio, J. B. *Le Pape et le gouvernement de l'Église*, Paris, 1992.

Grimaldi, F. *Les Congrégations romaines. Guide historique et pratique*, Sienne, 1890.

Jacqueline, B. "L'organisation interne du dicastère missionnaire après 350 ans d'histoire," *L'Année canonique*, XIX, Paris, 1975.

Le Bras, G., and Gaudemet, J. *Histoire du droit et des institutions de l'Église en Occident*, 19 vols., Paris, 1955–70, 1971–90.

Marin, V. *Les Congrégations romaines*, Paris, 1930.

Naz, R. "Congrégations romaines," *DDC*, IV, Paris, 1949, col. 206–25.

Pichon, C. *Le Vatican, hier et aujourd'hui*, 3rd ed., Paris, 1968.

Poupard, P. *Connaissance du Vatican*, Paris, 1967.

Poupard, P. *Le Pape*, Paris, 1980; *Le Vatican*, Paris, 1981.

CONON. *(b. Thrace?, d. Rome, 21 September 687). Consecrated pope on 21 October 686. Buried at St. Peter's, Rome.*

During the pontificate of Conon, the growing autonomy of Rome from the Eastern Empire and its effects on Roman socio-political life were becoming apparent. Conon was the son of a Thracian but was brought up and educated in Sicily. Several other popes of the period were also natives of Sicily; this is understandable, because the region was Rome's major source of revenue and wheat.

Conon therefore had good knowledge of Greek and of the East when he began his career in the Roman Church. Although the exact title of his post there is not known, he was a priest and was third in the hierarchy after Pope JOHN V. The clergy and the army—or rather, the army officers and high civil officials—were at loggerheads. The clergy supported the first person in the hierarchy behind the pope, whereas the army officers backed the second. The dispute clearly shows the influence that the clergy exerted over the papacy, since the heads of the Church were the only ones who could claim decisive influence. It also explains the continuity of policies in Rome despite the rapid succession of popes. After lengthy negotiations, Conon, the third in line, was chosen.

The new pope sought to favor a DEACON of the Syracuse Church, no doubt a friend, by appointing him rector of the Sicilian patrimony. This post, which would make him the personal representative of the pope and head of the entire Roman administration on the island, was normally reserved for a Roman cleric. Reaction to the appointment was immediate. The local nobility and members of the patrimony revolted against the rector and sent him to be tried in Constantinople. A weak pope, lacking the authority of GREGORY I the Great, Conon could do little against the ecclesiastical administration of the city of Rome, despite his acts of generosity. In fact, he paid out to the clergy, monasteries, diaconate, and officials in charge of church property the same amount of money as had BENEDICT II.

Conon's relations with the emperor were good. Justinian II (685–95, 705–11) reappointed the Monothelite Theodore as patriarch of Constantinople, but in a letter to Conon he stated that all officials should recognize the faith defined by the Council of Constantinople (680–1). Furthermore, to ensure the pope's support in the midst of his troubles, the emperor reduced by 200 units (*annonocapita*) the tax levied on the papal patrimonies of Lucania and Bruttium. He thus freed taxpayers living in these patrimonies who had been imprisoned by the army as a precaution while awaiting the payment of their tax arrears.

Jean Durliat

Bibliography

JW, 1, 243.

LP, 1, 368–70.

Bertolini, O. *Roma di fronte a Bisanzio e ai Longobardi*, Bologna, 1971, 296–401.

Bertolini, P. "Conone," *DBI*, 28 (1983), 21–5.

CONSISTORIAL ADVOCATE. Consistorial advocates form the upper rank of lawyers authorized to intervene in matters submitted to CONGREGATIONS and Roman TRIBUNALS. Their origin dates back to antiquity. In the Church, there were always *defensores ecclesiarum*. Justinian's *Novels* (56–59) mention *defensores clericorum*, and INNOCENT I (402–17) established seven *defensores urbis* in Rome who were responsible for presenting cases before the CONSISTORIAL Congregation. Gregory the Great (590–604) instituted seven regional defenders in 598. BENEDICT XII (1334–42) was no doubt referring to these historic origins when, in the constitution *Decens et necessarium* (1340), he established seven consistorial attorneys and implied that the office had been in existence for a long time (Cherubini, *Magnum Bullarium*, vol. 1, Lyons, 1673). Their role was to handle civil and criminal matters before the Consistory. SIXTUS IV (1471–84), in the first year of his pontificate, increased their number from seven to twelve. However, after the institution of the Roman congregations, when cases were no longer handled by the Consistory but instead in the congregations, and the *auditorum sacri palatii* succeeded the Roman ROTA, consistorial advocates became, *jure proprio et nativo*, lawyers of the Rota. From their past function, they retained the exclusive right to ask for an archbishop's *pallium* in a secret consistory and the right to "postulate" publicly in cases of BEATIFICATION and CANONIZATION in public consistory. During this time, the pope entrusted their college with the rectorship of the University of La Sapienza in Rome.

Much later, BENEDICT XIV (1740–58)—who in his youth had been appointed by CLEMENT XI (1700–21) to the college of consistorial advocates—instituted the charter that would rule the college until modern times. Through the bull *Inter conspicuus* of 29 August 1744, he confirmed their privileges and codified the legislation concerning them. He kept the number of consistorial advocates at twelve, but he specified that one of them had to be from Bologna, another from Ferrara, another from Naples, and a fourth selected from the graduates of Milan. All the others had to be Roman or to belong to the Church states; they were to be selected by the pope from a list of three names made up by the college each time a vacancy occurred. They were declared the "pope's familiars" and maintained their rectorship at La Sapienza, where they were authorized to confer the degree of doctor *in utroque jure* in Rome. In addition to these functions, in Rome the attorney for the poor was a consistorial advocate expressly acting in defense of the indigent imprisoned or at court, in any cause.

Since PIUS X's reforms (1903–14), these lawyers are attorneys *proprii et nativi* of the Rota and the Apostolic Tribunals. Moreover, their college constitutes a disciplinary council for other lawyers, who in case of grave professional fault can be the object of sanctions by the college of the judges of the Rota, on the advice of the college of consistorial advocates, especially in matters of excluding someone from the list of accredited attorneys.

Bernard de Lanversin

Bibliography

Enciclopedia del diritto, "Avvocato," Rome, 1962.

Lacroix, P. *Les Institutions de la France à Rome*, 1892.

Raffali, J. "Avocats consistoriaux," *DDC*, 1 (1935), 1533–6.

CONSISTORY.

Until the Council of Trent. The consistory was the regular assembly where the pope discussed the major ecclesiastical, theological, judiciary, and political issues facing the Roman Catholic Church. It was attended either exclusively by the cardinals or by cardinals and other ecclesiastical or lay dignitaries. The term should not be confused with the Protestant or Jewish consistories, which are assemblies of ministers of the faith or secular representatives elected to administer the affairs of the Protestant or Jewish religious communities.

In the early days of the Church, the pope habitually met with the Roman deacons and priests to take their counsel on matters pertaining to the city of Rome as well as to the Universal Church. This assembly was known as the *presbyterium*. It is the early ancestor of the consistory, whose name derives from *consistorium*, the place where the imperial council met from the time of Diocletian; this also denotes the council itself. The tradition of the consistory began little by little, with twice-weekly meetings of the cardinal-priests during the papacy of LEO IV (847–55), and developed as the power of the cardinals increased and the functions of the former Roman SYNOD were extended. The consistory gradually took the place of the latter assembly. From the end of the 11th century, during the Gregorian REFORM and even before the Sacred College had fully come into being, the consistory became known as the ideal forum to discuss the serious questions facing the Church. Pope URBAN II (1088–99) was the first to place before a consistory of cardinals the question of the excommunication of emperors, kings, and bishops, without referring the matter to the Roman synod.

The consistory saw the peak of its influence between the 12th century and the beginning of the GREAT SCHISM OF THE WEST in 1378. It is difficult to determine the exact limits of its competence during this period because its powers increased in tandem with the centralization of pontifical administration. As an increasing number of questions and causes were placed before the central body of the administration, it became necessary to set up specialized subsidiary organs. Because of the regular affirmation of the power of the pope, an increasing number of causes were submitted to him from all corners of Christendom, in his role of supreme arbiter. Petitions, mostly of a legal nature, were referred by the pope's chancellor or vice-chancellor, who selected the most important for submission to the consistory. Apart from matters of excommunication, Urban II also entrusted this body with the task of creating new dioceses, settling conflicts arising from episcopal elections, and issuing exemptions from the power of the ordinary. Urban II's successor, PASCHAL II (1099–1118), added the trial of bishops to the list of duties of the consistory, taking away from the Roman synod one of its essential areas of competence. Most important, from the year 1111, the consistory was entrusted with the serious political and religious questions of relations between the emperor and the secular powers and the consequent recourse to the services of cardinal legates. A CAUSE OF CANONIZATION was referred to the consistory for the first time during the pontificate of INNOCENT II (1130–43). The trial of Peter Abelard in 1140 raised for the first time in the consistory a question pertaining to the Catholic faith. His condemnation by the synod of bishops of Sens was confirmed not by the Roman synod but by the consistory of cardinals. A few years later, during the theological clashes between St. Bernard and Gilbert de la Porrée, bishop of Poiters, the cardinals questioned the validity of the decisions taken by the synod of bishops, which had met at Reims in 1148 and condemned Gilbert. The cardinals called the judgment into question because they deemed that such a case fell under the exclusive mandate of the consistory.

From the time of EUGENE III (1145–53), plans to appoint new cardinals were discussed in secret consistory, with each cardinal giving his views to the pope on the appropriateness of the choice and the candidate proposed. Although the competence and powers of the consistory were not specified in any statutes, they included all causes of major importance. The following are some of the questions examined by the consistory: decisions on matters of faith, ecclesiastical discipline, and causes of canonization; canonical and ecclesiastical jurisdiction (creation and delimitation of dioceses, and conflicts arising from their delimitation). Other questions concerned the granting of the *pallium*, trials arising from the election of a bishop, abbot, or grand abbot, trials relating to ecclesiastical and parish property, right of burial, delimitation of ecclesiastical jurisdiction, subordination of monasteries to monastic orders, and rejection of excessive appeals to the Curia. Other matters dealt with covered political, administrative, and diplomatic questions, including relations with the Western and Eastern emperors or with kings and territorial princes, the excommunication of powerful persons, the granting of dispensations for marriages in powerful and influential families, the ap-

pointment of legates and the examination of their decisions prior to confirmation by the pope, and preparation of a crusade. The consistory also deliberated on financial and economic questions such as management of the property of the Roman Church, enfeoffments, and the appointment of rectors of the Papal States.

Consistorial procedure was still ill-defined in the 12th century, but by the following century it had become firmly established. A cardinal could not take part in the discussions of the consistory or enjoy any of the privileges of the cardinalate without having first participated in the *aperitio oris*, the rather picturesque name given to the investment ceremony (literally, "opening of the mouth"). There were three types of consistories: the secret, or ordinary consistory, between the pope and the cardinals; the semi-public consistory, where, for causes of canonization, the pope and the cardinals were joined by bishops and other prelates; and the formal public or extraordinary consistory, to which ecclesiastical and lay dignitaries (princes, ambassadors, etc.) were invited. The number of days when the sovereign pontiff could hold a consistory was strictly limited by the abundance of religious holidays (in the 14th century, there were more than seventy-eight days when other activities were prohibited: the list may be found in Dykmans, *La Cérémonial Papal*, II, 412–22). The rhythm of meetings was also hampered by the fact that the Curia moved from place to place, especially during the 12th and 13th centuries. The meetings, formerly monthly, increased to three times a week (Monday, Wednesday, and Friday) under Innocent III.

The cardinal-bishops sat immediately to the right of the pope, with the cardinal-priests a little farther away. To the left of the pope sat the cardinal-deacons, beginning with the prior of deacons, who was head of the order. Persons within each order were seated according to seniority, and it was always in accordance with that strict hierarchy that they were called on by the pope to express their views after hearing the report of the cardinal commissioners to the assembly.

Public consistories followed a precise ceremonial pattern, depending on the event. If it were the final phase of a canonization case, there would be a proclamation of the decision following first a secret, then a semi-public consistory, then the elevation of the saint to the altar. The ceremony was different for a welcoming speech to a cardinal who had returned from legation (this was an oratorical genre made popular by the great preacher CLEMENT IV), or for the solemn reception of a prince or of ambassadors. The cardinal vice-chancellor was the *ex officio* secretary-notary of the consistory. Assemblies of cardinals held while the Apostolic See was vacant and outside of the conclave itself were still referred to as consistories, since the pope to be elected was represented by the empty throne.

The increasing number of tasks before the consistory led a number of popes, beginning with Paschal II, to entrust the investigation of legal cases to commissions of cardinals. These commissions, which generally consisted of three cardinals, submitted only the results of their deliberations to the consistory. The pope made the final decision on the cases. The cases examined pertained to inquisitorial, civil, criminal, and jurisdictional matters, as well as cases arising from benefices. To lighten the cardinals' workload, the pope charged pontifical chaplains (*capellani pape*) with the task of examining minor cases. These chaplains were known as "auditors" of the cases, and from the time of INNOCENT III they were empowered with the right to hand down sentences, with the pope reserving the right to confirm them (1212). These hearings by chaplains were the early origins of the hearing of cases in the sacred palace, which later came to be commonly referred to as the Rota.

It is easy to see how the consistory fell victim to its own hypertrophy. Many criticisms were leveled against it; its procedures were extremely lengthy and laborious, and this incurred enormous expense to the people being tried. Furthermore, it had become, after the CONCLAVE, a privileged forum for the cardinals to air their oligarchic ambitions. They did not hesitate to voice their open criticism of the pope and his policies, especially during the AVIGNON papacy. The meetings were sometimes quite stormy—for example, during the consistories convened by JOHN XXII (1316–34) on the controversy of the poverty of Christ and the apostles, or on the policy with respect to Louis of Bavaria in 1322–3. In some ways, the consistory was a sort of closed combat arena where the pope and the cardinals observed each other and faced off in a subtle interplay of pressure and concession.

The Great Western Schism (1378–1417) and the corresponding reduction of the powers of the Sacred College heralded the end of the consistory's dominance as well as a decline in its role as the hub of Church administration. Council meetings in Pisa, Basel, and Constance to end the consistory's dominance lauded the role of the episcopal college, to the detriment of the cardinals. The popes of the Rennaissance moved to restore their powers at the expense of the college of cardinals and, by extension, of the consistory. They gradually deprived it of its original responsibilities, first by creating a large number of simple temporary commissions of cardinals and other prelates, meeting independently of the consistory. By the end of the 15th century, many provisions of major benefices— bishoprics and abbeys—which were *ipso facto* the field of competence of the consistory (the legal acts pertaining to benefices being known as the "consistorial schedule"), would only give rise to a meeting of "secret congregations." These consisted of a few cardinals meeting with the pope as chairman. The consistory meetings on such matters were rarely held, sometimes owing to the illness

of the pope, but more often because of the heavy schedule and inflexibility of the consistory, which met only three times a week (Monday, Wednesday, and Friday).

From the middle of the 16th century, the body that for almost four centuries had dominated the central administration of the Church was supplanted in the space of some thirty years. The new structures taking its place were the Roman CONGREGATIONS, which functioned far more efficiently. PAUL III created the first congregation on the advice of Cardinal Gian Pietro Carafa on 21 July 1542, with the bull *Licet ab initio*. This was the first permanent congregation, that of the Holy Office or Inquisition. After the Council of Trent had concluded, PIUS IV founded the Congregation of the Council on 2 August 1564 (bull *Alias nos nonnullas*). This was soon followed by the Congregations of the Index (1571) and of Bishops (1572), the latter established at the initiative of PIUS V. The generalization of the system by SIXTUS V in 1588 (fifteen congregations were created as a result of the bull *Immensa Dei*) finally deprived the consistory of all its deliberative powers. From then on, it was reserved only the task of solemnizing the most important papal decisions. The consistory also survived in the Congregation for the Establishment of Churches and in the Consistorial Provisions, responsible for preparing the questions to be dealt with in the consistory.

Pierre Jugie

Bibliography

del Ré, N. *La Curia Romana: Lineamenti storico-giuridici*, 3rd ed., rev. and augm., Rome, 1970.

Dykmans, M. *Le Cérémonial papal de la fin du Moyen Âge à la Renaissance*, II, III, IV, Brussels and Rome, 1981–5.

Fokcinski, H. "Le relazioni concistoriali nel Cinquecento," *AHP*, 18 (1980), 211–61.

Mollat, G. "Contribution à l'histoire du Sacré Collège de Clément V à Eugène IV," *RHE*, 46 (1951), 80–112.

Pastor, L. "Le cedole concistoriali," *AHP*, 11 (1973), 209–68.

Sydow, J. "Untersuchungen zur kurialen Verwaltungsgeschichte im Zeitalter des Reformpapstums," *Deutsches Archiv für Erforschung des Mittelalters*, 11 (1954), 18–73; "Il consistorium dopo la schisma del 1130," *RSCI*, 9 (1955), 165–76.

After the Council of Trent. From the 16th century on, the pivotal role of the consistory as a body of government of the Church began visibly to wane. Following a trend that had gradually gained ground since the beginning of the 13th century, the scope of action of the consistory had been continually extended. It decided on all questions pertaining to the faith and discipline as well as the general and private policies of the Holy See. The wide range of issues covered by the consistory made it necessary to hold more secret meetings, with these reaching a frequency of three meetings a week. The first half of the 16th century marked the peak of the consistory's development as well as the start of its decline. The cardinals no longer worked exclusively for the diocese of Rome; the same system governed the whole of the Catholic world. However, this extreme centralization made it necessary to have greater specialization in tasks and in subject matter, shared out among permanent commissions. PAUL III (1534–49) established the Congregation of the Holy Office (constitution *Licet ab initio*, 21 July 1542), and the Council of Trent was created in 1564 at the initiative of PIUS IV (1560–5). Their establishment marked a turning point. The consistory, at the very peak of its power as a body for making decisions and supplying information, had had the power indirectly to overshadow the authority of the pontiff. Its influence was now splintered among the cardinals who headed the various DICASTERIES. From then on, the history of the dicasteries would be closely linked to that of the Roman CURIA.

The consistory, now stripped of many of its responsibilities, gradually became a formal and symbolic institution, effective on occasions of great solemnity such as the appointment of new cardinals and procedures of beatification and canonization. Most of the reflection and groundwork behind actual decisions was done within the Congregation of the Consistorial, founded in 1587 and sometimes presided over by the pope himself. But because of its link to the consistory, this congregation played only a very modest role at the beginning of the contemporary era. The consistory often served simply as a sounding board for the projects submitted for its consideration, such as decisions to set up new dioceses or to modify the territorial limits of ecclesiastical areas.

The CODE OF CANON LAW of 1917 (c. 30) stressed the role of the cardinals who collectively made up the "senate of the Roman pontiff," for whom they worked as advisors and aides (*adiutores*). The consistory, therefore, did not play a major role in this organizational structure as an expression of collegiality.

There were several types of consistories: secret, semipublic, and public, according to the degree of confidentiality or solemnity of the questions under consideration, from promotions to cardinalships to the establishment of new dioceses. The pontificate of John Paul II changed this situation to some extent. In November 1979, after avoiding the holding of a consistory, John Paul II convened a general assembly of the cardinals, seeking their advice on the finances and restructuring of the Curia. A general assembly or plenary meeting of the Sacred College took place again in December 1982, in place of a session of the consistory. As a sign of renewed interest in collegial activity, so in consonance with the spirit of VATICAN II, the code promulgated on 25 January 1983 renewed the provisions regarding the consistory, with more details.

There are ordinary consistories convened by the pope to discuss matters which are "serious, but which arise quite frequently" (c. 353 § 2). There are also extraordinary consistories, which meet when specific needs arise within the Church, or to deliberate matters of great importance. In principle, both types are conducted in secret, although the press and certain dignitaries may be invited to some of the ordinary sessions. Among these are sessions dealing with canonization, the presentation of the *pallium*, or the public celebrations following the appointment of new cardinals (c. 353 § 4).

During the consistory of 25 May 1985, the pope stated that it was "in the very nature of the office of [a] cardinal to adhere firmly to the Apostolic See and to the one who had the supreme duty of governing the Universal Church. However, this link becomes more manifest when the Church Senate meets in a visible manner." The recent increase in the number of plenary meetings of the Sacred College has come to challenge the activities of the consistory, which nevertheless has the same powers in its extraordinary session. This places the consistory at the risk of becoming, once more, a purely symbolic body. This is undoubtedly the reason why it has fallen into disuse today.

François Jankowiak

Bibliography

Abate, A. "La Sacra Gerarchia alla luce del nuovo Codice," *La nuova legislazione canonica* (Studia Urbaniana no. 19), Rome, 1983, 181–242.

Coriden, J. A., Green, T. J., and Heintschel, D. D. *The Code of Canon Law: A Text and Commentary*, New York, 1985.

Stein, A. "Der neue Codex des kanonisches Rechtes Papst Johannes Paul II. und das einführende römisch-katholische Schriftum," *Theologische Literaturzeitung*, CIX (1984), 785–95.

Valdrini, P. (ed)., *Droit canonique*, Paris, 1989.

[CONSTANTINE]. *Antipope elected 28 June and consecrated 5 July 767; deposed 6 August 768.*

Since the year 756, the political power of the pope had increased considerably. From that time, the members of the Roman aristocracy who occupied the public, civil, and military posts depended almost exclusively on the pope. Pope PAUL I had wielded power with an iron hand, and the lay aristocracy felt disadvantaged with respect to the Lateran clerics. They were awaiting an opportunity to turn the situation around by electing a pope of their own choosing. When Pope Paul fell ill, four brothers, members of an aristocratic family from Nepi near Viterbo, saw their chance to take action. They were Duke

Toto (or Theodore), Constantine, Passivus, and Pascal. They arranged for armed contingents to enter Rome; upon the death of the pope, they entered the Lateran, where they proclaimed the eldest brother, Constantine, the new pope. Since Constantine was a layperson, he had to be ordained successively into all orders before being consecrated pope. This was an unusual procedure not approved by canon law, but at that time there had been similar cases that had elicited no scandal. Constantine informed Pepin of his election but received no reply, perhaps because the latter was busy conducting a campaign in Aquitaine. At any rate, Pepin took no action against Constantine.

The only open opponent of the new pope was one of the senior officials of the clergy, Christopher, who, as chief notary, had enjoyed great influence during the pontificates of STEPHEN II and Paul I. He had fled to St. Peter's with his son, Sergius, and managed to take refuge in a monastery at Rieti in the duchy of Spoleto. Eventually, they reached Pavia, where Didier, the LOMBARD king, promised his help. Christopher and Sergius returned to Rome accompanied by an envoy, the priest Waldipert, and a troop of Lombards from Spoleto. Their supporters, some of whom were members of the pope's entourage, opened for them the St. Pancras door to the Janiculum. In the ensuing skirmish, Toto was killed; Constantine was arrested at the Lateran on 30 July 768. Christopher and his supporters exacted cruel revenge. Constantine was paraded through the streets of Rome on the back of an ass. On 6 August 768, an ecclesiastical tribunal meeting at the Lateran declared the pope's election illegal because he had been a layperson. Constantine's eyes were gouged out, and many of his supporters were massacred. The following year, a council formally pronounced his condemnation and declared his ordination invalid. He was imprisoned in a monastery.

Jean-Charles Picard

Bibliography

JW, I, 283–4.
MGH, *Epist.*, 3, 649–53.
Bardy, G. "Constantin II," *DHGE*, 13 (1956), 591–3.
Bertolini, O. *Roma e i Longobardi*, Rome, 1972.
Duchesne, L. *Les Premiers temps de l'Etat pontifical*, Paris, 1911.
Miller, D. "Constantino II," *DBI*, 30 (1984), 314–20.
Noble, T. F. *The Republic of Peter*, Philadelphia, 1984.
Schwaiger, G. "Constantinus II," *LexMA*, 3 (1984–6), 170–17.

CONSTANTINE. The first Christian emperor was born in Naissus (present-day Niš, in Yugoslavia) on A.D. 27 February 272. His father was an officer, Flavius Valentinus Constantius Chlorus; his mother, Helena, appears to have been of humble origin.

In 293, Emperor Diocletian, who had reorganized the imperial government by introducing a tetrarchic system, appointed Constantius Chlorus as Caesar. Two Augustuses and two Caesars would share the task of ruling the empire; the two Caesars would become Augustuses if the other two were to abdicate simultaneously. When this happened in 305, Constantius assumed the office of Augustus at the same time as did the Caesar Galerius. It therefore became necessary to find two Caesars to replace them. Severus and Maximin Daia were chosen, since the sons of the two former Augustuses, Constantine and Maxentius, were not allowed to accede to the office. However, on the death of his father, whom he had joined in Brittany, Constantine was proclaimed Augustus by the troops at York in 306. He managed to secure the support of Severus and Galerius. In the space of six years, most of those aspiring to the tetrarchy were eliminated.

There were four Augustuses still in the running, and they divided up the empire among themselves; Maximin Daia in the East, Licinius in the Balkans, and Maxentius and Constantine in the rest of the West. Licinius and Constantine then became allies and eliminated the other two Augustuses. In October 312, Constantine defeated Maxentius in the battle of the Milvian Bridge (a few kilometers north of Rome), and Licinius defeated Maximin Daia in 313. Constantine thus became the sole ruler of the West. The senate recognized the title Maximus Augustus, which he now assumed, thus preparing for the second stage of his rise to power: the eviction of Licinius (324) and the consolidation of his power as sole rule over the whole empire. He died in 337, after having been baptized by Eusebius of Nicomedia. His son Constans placed his body in the mausoleum he had prepared for himself at the apostoléion of Constantinople.

In February 313, Licinius and Constantine cosigned in Milan a text that became known to posterity as the "Edict of Milan." History acknowledges it as the first official recognition of Christianity. In fact, it was a rescript addressed to the East to prescribe measures of tolerance. Some of these measures had, in 311, been contemplated in an edict of Galerius, and the Edict of Milan sought to expand on them, if possible. Furthermore, Diocletian's persecution, which had begun in 303 and 304, was by 305 being carried out in the West. The fact remains that Constantine has traditionally been credited with the "conversion" of the empire. It is true that he practiced Christian policies; however, one must remember that, in the 4th century, the literary sources of information on the reigns of Constantine and Theodosius were Christian historians and hagiographers who were on the side of the victor. Notable among these were Lactantius and Eusebius of Caesarea. Furthermore, the accounts tend to magnify the importance of the steps taken by Constantine with respect to Christianity and the Church. They are interpreted as the providential establishment of Christ's reign on earth. When Christianity became the official religion of the empire in 391, historians also tried, in retrospect, to suggest, a "Constantinian Church" along the lines of the Theodosian Church.

The exact date, sincerity, and real depth of Constantine's conversion to Christianity have been the subject of continued speculation. From a historical standpoint, this is a futile exercise. What is true, however, is that the development of the traditional Roman religion and the concept of imperial power no doubt helped to foster Constantine's interest in Christianity. From the 3rd century, the idea of imperial power tended more and more toward a form of monotheism whereby the earthly sovereign shared the divinity of the ruler of the cosmos, and this influenced Constantine, a follower of the idea of *Sol invictus*. It is unlikely that the emperor indeed saw the monogram of Christ on the eve of the battle of Milvian Bridge, even though the monogram was stamped on coins from 315 on, without replacing the traditional pagan symbols of power. Constantine, however, very soon took steps that revealed his interest in the Christians and in the affairs of the Church. This was even more apparent after Licinius was eliminated and doubtless reflected political interests as well as personal ones, since most of Constantine's opponents were pagans.

With respect to the concrete measures that Constantine adopted in favor of the Church, we will focus on those that concern the Church of Rome. They must, however, be seen within the context of the general measures taken. The restoration of property (both private and ecclesiastical) confiscated during the persecutions would lead to the development of ownership of ecclesiastical property. This implies the de facto recognition of the *corpus christianorum* as a legal entity. Fiscal exemptions and immunities were granted to the clerics, placing them on the same footing as the pagan clergy. These measures had a direct impact on ecclesiastical careers and the recruitment of clerics. They were also an implicit acknowledgment of the Church as a new *ordo*, with a specific legal status within the empire and with specific roles, notably that of giving assistance to the poor. In Rome, important donations from the imperial family ensured the material establishment of the Christian community and helped to organize it both within the city itself (basilicas for the Eucharistic synaxis), and outside it, for the commemoration of martyrs. These donations, numerous before the year 324, subsequently diminished in number as Constantine or his mother became more interested in the holy places of the East and in sites for the founding of Constantinople in 330.

Some building programs were carried out at the initiative of the emperor himself and were intended first and foremost for himself and his family, even though they were assigned to the bishop. Others were episcopal constructions (from Sylvester to Julius) which benefited from imperial donations. In both cases, the churches were fitted with liturgical furnishings and endowed with patrimonies to ensure their maintenance. Some of the earnings from real estate were intended to help the poor. Among the churches of the first group was the episcopal church of Rome, with its baptistry (St. John Lateran) built on the site of the military barracks dismantled following the defeat of Maxentius. Another was the chapel of Helena's imperial residence. This latter property (Holy Cross of Jerusalem) was doubtless not granted directly to the bishop. Of the great *martyria*, St. Paul's Outside the Walls on the Via Ostiense is probably the first apostolic *memoria*, and one of the first imperial foundations. Sts. Peter and Marcellinus, on the Via Labicana, is in some ways the counterpart of St. John Lateran, since the basilica is situated in the necropolis for the troops mentioned above. It also has a mausoleum (Torre Pignattara), originally intended for Constantine, where Helena was buried. St. Lawrence, on the Tiburtine, is built above the CATACOMB that houses the tomb of Lawrence, the Roman martyr deacon, in a burial ground which had already been the property of the Church. St. Sebastian (*basilica apostolorum*), on the Via Appia, is built on the site known as *ad catacumbas*, where, from the third century at least, the memory of Peter and Paul has been celebrated. It would seem that the church of St. Agnes on the Via Nomentana was built at the initiative of Emperor Constantine's daughter, Constantina. She is buried in the adjoining mausoleum, St. Constance. (This mausoleum is one of the rare vestiges of Constantinian architecture that has remained intact; a section of its mosaic decoration has also been preserved.) Finally, St. Peter's on the Via Cornelia, on the *Mons Vaticanus*, was built above the tomb or the first commemorative monument to the apostle. Construction began on the church during the second half of Constantine's reign but was not completed until after his death (during the pontificate of Liberius, 352–66). Five of the churches had a cruciform or even ambulatory layout, which seems to have been a characteristic of Constantinian architecture in Rome and is rarely seen elsewhere. The exceptionally Western influence of the church of St. Peter's would subsequently be of great significance when the Carolingians, for ideological reasons, looked to Rome for inspiration in their liturgical and architectural reform. Three churches linked to the papal tradition benefited from the emperor's liberality: the *titulus Silvestri* (S. Martino ai Monti), S. Marco, a *basilica Iulia* near the Trajan forum, and the *basilica trans Tiberim* (Saint Mary's in Trastevere).

Finally, mention must be made of Constantine's intervention in the internal affairs of the Church with respect to ecclesiastical discipline or the definition of the faith, whether this intervention was made in the councils or in his legal actions. But can one really use the term "caesaropapism" to describe Constantine's reign? The term hardly seems appropriate here. It was invented in the 19th century, based on a situation that cannot be compared to the one prevailing in the 4th century. Furthermore, it reflects a specific interpretation of events on the basis of very partial accounts: Eusebius of Caesarea's *Ecclesiastical History*, and the *Vita Constantini* (there are marked differences from one account to the next). There were others who perpetuated these accounts, in addition to the subsequent Constantinian legends. The events surrounding the Donatist schism and the Arian dispute are the best sources to help measure the nature and extent of the prince's intervention in the affairs of the Church.

In the Donatist SCHISM, the parties to the dispute at CARTHAGE were the first to inform the emperor of the situation. This was around 311/312, at a time when the Augustus was not yet known to have converted to Christianity. He was asked to arbitrate in the quarrel and to ensure that ecclesiastical decisions would prevail. At first, he merely delegated his legal authority to the tribunal of bishops (Roman synod of 313, when the sentence was pronounced by Miltiades, bishop of Rome; Council of Arles, 314). When ecclesiastical arbitration failed to resolve the dispute, Constantine personally intervened in 316, pronouncing a sentence absolving Caecilianus, the Catholic bishop of Carthage. This sentence was relayed to the vicar of Africa. It was only in 317 that coercive civil laws were passed against the Donatists; these would be repealed in 321.

Constantine's actions, therefore, were limited to ensuring the implementation of ecclesiastical decisions in a quarrel which, at the outset, concerned matters of ecclesiastical discipline, not of dogma. This approach was in keeping with a precedent set in 271–2. The council that had judged the case of Paul of Samosata, bishop of Antioch, had appealed to Aurelius to apply the sentence. The emperor had decided in accordance with the opinions of the bishop of Rome and the Italian bishops. Similarly, when Constantine made the "Catholic" Church the sole beneficiary of the measure taken in 313, he was merely going along with the decisions of the African councils. Constantine did not at any point make a judgment on the substance of the disputes, especially when they took a theological turn, like the question of the validity of sacraments administered by lapsed Christians and heretics. One may observe the same approach in the schism of Meletius, which started in 328.

In the Arian affair, Constantine was called on to intervene during public unrest in Alexandria. His intervention was all the more important because the emperor had recently regained control of the East from Licinius. As he did in the Donatist schism, Constantine delegated Ossius, bishop of Cordoba, to carry out an inquiry in his position as "supreme justice of the peace." Following the investigation, both parties to the dispute—Arius and the bishop of Alexandria—decided to bring their case to the prince. Arius was sentenced in 324 during a synod held at Antioch to decide on the succession to the apostolic see. However, the ecclesiastical ruling did not suffice to put an end to the conflict. Constantine decided to convene an ecumenical council (actually, it was mostly an Eastern council), which opened in Nicaea on 20 May 325. The letter of convocation, the descriptions of Constantine's attitude, and his inaugural address all prove that, once again, he was more concerned with ensuring that the ecclesiastical ruling be respected. In this, he was more interested in securing unity and peace within the empire than in pronouncing on substantive issues (especially the orthodox christological and Trinitarian formula, as well as the adoption of a single date for the celebration of Easter throughout the empire).

The emperor's letters accompanying the council's synodals lay emphasis on the wisdom of the rulings and their political necessity, as well as the valuable judgment of Ossius of Cordoba, the ecclesiastical advisor. It is true that Constantine's reversal in 328, when he decided to reinstate Arius and some of his supporters, may seem to have been the result of theological reflection: To what extent did the choice of Arius's Christology over the beliefs prevailing in Nicaea respond to the prince's personal theological and political beliefs? One must not forget the undeniable influence of the prelates, who at that time constituted a sort of permanent synod around the emperor and could greatly influence his decisions. His actions in that case would not necessarily arise from a real personal doctrinal conviction. In the case of Athanasius as in that of Donatus, the emperor's council appears only as an appeals body which confirms or invalidates the conciliar decisions.

If Constantine intervened in the affairs of the Church, it was in matters he deemed to be questions of ecclesiastical discipline, although, at a certain stage of the disputes, discipline and dogma became inseparable. He was moved to do so by a conviction that religious unity was indispensable for political unity and peace within the empire. Furthermore, there was as yet no tradition within the empire of separating spiritual and temporal matters; that would come later. In his day, the Church was part of the *ius publicum*, and the prince had authority *in sacris, in sacerdotalibus, in magistratibus*. Therefore, as *pontifex maximus*—a title he chose to keep—Constantine had supreme competence in religious matters. At that time there was no central Church authority higher than the metropolitans or the patriarchs, no authority that, in the Christian order, would correspond to that of *pontifex maximus*. Constantine had therefore to assume, to some extent, the preeminent role that would later belong to the pope. It was in this sense that he described himself as the "common bishop" (*koinos episkopos*).

One cannot, therefore, assert that Constantine practiced caesaropapism. Moreover, the emperor's move to Constantinople set the stage for the differentiation in medieval times between the imperial and pontifical authorities. Hence the almost monarchical autonomy of the Roman see was consolidated, at least from the reign of Pope Gregory the Great. However, it is true that subsequent developments in relations between Church and State and between spiritual and temporal powers would lead to a retrospective reinterpretation of Constantine's policies as a basic model of Church and State relations.

Françoise Monfrin

Bibliography

de Decker, D., and Dupuy-Masay, J. G. "'L'episcopat' de l'empereur Constantin," *Byzantion*, 50 (1980), 118–57.

Hall, S. G. "Konstantin I, der Grosse," *Theologische Realenzyklopädie*, 19 (1989), 489–501.

Pietri, C. "La politique de Constance II: Un premier 'césaro-papisme,' ou *l'imitatio Constantini?*," *L'Église et l'Empire au IVe Siècle*, Vandoeuvres and Geneva, 1989, 113–78 (Fondation Hardt, Entretiens sur l'Antiquité classique, XXXIV).

Piganiol, A. *L'Empereur Constantin*, Paris, 1932.

Sansterre, J. M. "Eusebius of Caesarea and the birth of the caesaropapist theory," *Byzantion*, 42 (1972), 131–95, 532–94.

Vogt, J. "Constantinus der Grosse," *Realenzyklopädie für Antike und Christentum*, 3 (1957), 306–79.

CONSTANTINE I. *(b. Syria?, d. Rome, 9 April 715). Consecrated pope on 25 March 708. Buried at St. Peter's, Rome.*

Constantine was of Syrian origin and for a long time before his election had been integrated into Roman society. He was the last pope to consider himself a lifelong subject of the empire of Constantinople and to accept the authority of the emperor. After his time, the influence of the Western patriarchy would continue to spread.

Constantine was the son of a certain John who came from Syria, as did the father of his predecessor, Pope SISINNIUS. The new pontiff could not be considered a foreigner, though: prior to his election, he had had a long ecclesiastical career. In his capacity as archdeacon, he was a member of the Roman delegation to the third council of Constantinople (680–1), and he later served as apocrisary (papal representative, at the Imperial Court of Constantinople) to Pope LEO II (682–3). That gave him an excellent knowledge of the court and explains the skill with which he acted when the emperor ordered him to journey to Constantinople, where he was from 5 October 710 to 24 October 711. The names and titles of those who accompanied him testify to the great strides made in papal administration by that time; equally striking is the large number of persons with Greek names. The chief negotiator was the deacon Gregory, later Pope GREGORY II. In Naples, the delegation met troops sent by the emperor under the command of the exarch Rizokopos. They had been awaiting the departure of the pope to avenge the slight suffered by Zacharias under the pontificate of SERGIUS I. The three interim administrators of Rome were executed, without time for the city to react, or with the pope in a position to make any changes to a journey under close surveillance. The biography of Constantine lays emphasis on the royal reception reserved for him wherever he went, as Justinian II had required that Constantine be given the same honors that would normally have been reserved for himself. For this reason, Constantine's biography—written under the papacy of Gregory II—sought to downplay the extent of the slight to Zacharias.

The emperor and the pope met at Nicomedia, and Justinian prostrated himself before Constantine and kissed his feet. The emperor's attitude was surprising, to say the least; never before had a sovereign considered one of the patriarchs within his empire superior to him. One can only suppose that after his acts of terror, Justinian was now resorting to flattery to weaken Constantine, who might still refuse his demands. The negotiators allowed the pope no concessions on the essential issues, while obtaining permission to return to Rome. In fact, the emperor got the pope to recognize the canons of the Quinisext Council (692), which had been convened by Justinian II to reform ecclesiastical discipline. However, the pope managed not to concede more than oral recognition exclusively for those ritual canons that did not run "counter to upright faith and good morals"—in other words, to Roman customs. Thus, the pope was able to return to Rome at his leisure. Most of the clergy and the Roman nobility came to meet him at Gaeta. Three months after Constantine's arrival in Rome came the news of Justinian's assassination. His successor, Philippicus (711–13), wanted to force the pope to recognize Monothelitism, but he met a refusal against which he could do nothing, despite the bloody intervention of the exarch. Constantine intervened without giving ground. Anastasius II (713–15), the successor of Philippicus, assured the pope that he would recognize the decisions of the third council of Constantinople. The situation remained unchanged, but the bloodshed and accumulated hatred help account for the violent nature of the clashes under the papacy of Gregory II.

In Italy, Constantine consolidated his position. Felix, the new archbishop of RAVENNA (709–23), refused to swear the required oath of obedience on the grounds that his see had formerly enjoyed autonomy from Rome. However, following his return from the exile imposed by Justinian II (712), Felix offered the required tokens of submission. Similarly, the metropolitan of Milan reminded the pope, to no avail, that before the Lombard invasion he had consecrated the bishops of Pavia. Now that the city of Milan was the capital of the kingdom, the pope reserved this right for himself. He was unquestionably the supreme chief of all the churches of Italy.

The arrival in Rome of Cenred, king of Mercia, and of Offa, king of East Anglia, who became monks, testifies to the growing prestige of the papacy. Shortly afterward, the Frankish kingdom, situated between Britain and the city of Rome, perceived all the advantages to be gained from a rapprochement with the pope.

Jean Durliat

Bibliography

JW, 1, 247–9, 2–700.

LP, 1, 389–95.

Bede, *Historia ecclesiastica*, 5, 19.

Bertolini, O. *Roma di fronte a Bizanzio e ai Longobardi*, Bologna, 1971, 417–23.

Guillou, A. *Régionalisme et independance dans l'empire byzantin au VIIe siècle: L'exemple de l'Exarchat et de la Pentapole d'Italie*, Rome, 1969, 212–16.

Miller, D. "Constantino I," *DBI*, 30 (1984), 308–14.

Sansterre, J. M. "*Le Pape Constantin Ier (708–715) et la politique religieuse des empereurs Justinien II et Philippikos*," *AHP*, 22 (1984), 7–29.

CONSTANTINOPLE. See Byzantium and the Papacy.

CONSTITUTION, APOSTOLIC. The apostolic constitution (*constitutio apostolica*) is a term derived from Roman law, where it served to describe the general prescriptions of imperial authority. Together with the *epistulae* and the *litterae*, the apostolic constitution is one of the major legal acts enacted by the sovereign pontiff. The explanation of the apostolic constitution *Rex Pacificus*, by which Pope GREGORY IX (1227–41) promulgated the decretals which bear his name (5 November 1234), stressed the personal nature of this type of text, defining it as *Quam princeps fecit proprio motu*.

The apostolic constitutions were drafted either directly by the pope or within the organs of the Curia and covered a diverse range of subjects. There were no theoretical limits imposed on their field of application. They also had a fixed terminology, which made them easily identifiable with respect to many of the texts produced by the Holy See, which had rather ambiguous names. With usage over time, the apostolic constitution became used as a general or specific law which could cover dogma, faith and morals, liturgy, sacramentary discipline, or extreme unction to the sick. PIUS XII (1939–58) defined the dogma of the Assumption of the Virgin in an apostolic constitution of 1 November 1950. In the category of liturgy, examples may be found in the constitutions of Pius XI (*Divini Cultus*, 20 December 1928; *Deus scientarum dominus*, 24 May 1931), as well as the constitution *Christus Dominus*, promulgated by Pius XII on 16 January 1953. For the discipline of the sacraments, note the constitution *auctorem fidei*, by Pius VI (1775–9), dated 23 August 1794, or the regulations on extreme unction (constitution of 30 November 1972).

Other apostolic constitutions regulate some question of an administrative nature. Some of these concern specific churches—for example, the elevation by PAUL VI (1963–78) of an apostolic prefecture to the level of an apostolic vicariate (16 December 1970). In some cases, a new bishopric is created (13 December 1972). Some apostolic constitutions have a bearing on the organization of the Universal Church, notably the CONCLAVE (constitution *Aeterne Patris*, promulgated by GREGORY XV [1621–3] on 15 November 1621; constitution *Praedecessores nostri* of 24 May 1882, published by LEO XIII and the Roman CURIA; constitution *Regimini Ecclesiae Universae* of Paul VI, dated 1967, and *Pastor bonus*, of JOHN PAUL II, 28 June 1988).

A statistical evaluation of the period 1909–1976 yields a total of 1,681 promulgated apostolic constitutions, indicating that this type of legal act has been used frequently. Only the *litterae apostolicae* were used more frequently in the same period, with 2,067 units, and both categories far outnumber ENCYCLICALS, which amounted to 78 in the same period. BENEDICT XV (1914–22) enacted 38 apostolic constitutions; PIUS XI (1922–39), 352; PIUS XII (1939–58), 570; JOHN XXIII (1958–63), 249; and PAUL VI (1963–78), 464 up to the year 1976.

Although they were not subject to any specific, formal limitations, the constitutions were all drafted in Latin and more often than not issued in the form of *sub plumbo* bulls, at least when they concerned administrative matters. They bore at their head the name of the pope, sometimes followed by the order number, the title *episcopus*, and the expression used since the pontificate of GREGORY I (590–604), *servus servorum Dei*. The pope's signature appeared at the end of the text only when there was a definition of dogma, above the signatures of the cardinals present at the promulgation. The signatures most frequently seen were those of the cardinal prefect of the congregation covering the subject mentioned in the text of the constitution.

The method of dating the constitutions also deserves some mention. Before PIUS X, all constitutions bore a mention of the year of Incarnation, starting therefore from 25 March. The days were named according to the Roman system of calends, nones and ides. The apostolic constitution *Sapienti consilio*, promulgated by Pius X on 29 June 1908, recommended that the ordinary method of dating be used, with the cycle beginning on 1 January.

However, the old method continued in use for the next five years, until its abrogation by the constitution *In praecipuis* of 29 June 1913. Far more important than the rules and format of the constitutions, however, were their content, their general scope, and their degree of solemnity. This was reinforced by a tradition that stressed the significance of corresponding dates. For example, the constitution *In praecipuis* was promulgated exactly five years after the constitution *Sapienti consilio*, and *Pastor bonus* was published on the anniversary of the 80th anniversary of *Sapienti consilio*. These factors help make the constitution an essential normative instrument for the sovereign pontiff.

François Jankowiak

CONSTITUTION, DOGMATIC. The dogmatic constitution is, by its scope and authority, one of the main legal acts of the Church and its government. The expression is used in its most restricted sense—referring explicitly to a text of conciliar origin and initiative. This distinguishes it from the APOSTOLIC CONSTITUTIONS or the ENCYCLICAL, which, in order to have executory force, must have the prior confirmation and approval of the pope. This was firmly established by VATICAN I (1869–70) by the *Constitutio prima de ecclesia Christi* (4th session, canon 3), before being confirmed in the strict legal order by Canon 227 of the CODE OF CANON LAW OF 1917. The affirmation of pontifical authority was the outcome of a global rejection of conciliary theory, widely discussed during the whole 15th century and which was more or less suspected of Gallican tendencies. However, in viewing conciliary decrees as a whole, the question becomes not only the need for the decrees to have a "definitive" binding force, as canonic doctrine assumes that this binding force is latent and not merely conditional. It appears from a reading of the constitution on Church dogma *Lumen gentium*, promulgated by PAUL VI (1963–1978), on 21 November 1964, as well as from Canons 338 § I, and 341 of the CODE OF CANON LAW OF 1983, that the ecumenical council possessed supreme power, due to the fact that the pope chaired and took part in it. The council has ordinary jurisdiction to establish infallible definitions of dogma and universal disciplinary laws. With respect to the constitution, the binding force and the authority of the council come from the pope, who inspired decisions on dogma with papal INFALLIBILITY. The apostolic constitutions are considered dogma by virtue of their power of decision and are, in principle, used in reference to matters of faith (two were adopted by Vatican I, four by VATICAN II). Decrees, declarations, and messages govern other areas and sectors of ecclesiastical life.

François Jankowiak

Bibliography

Coriden, J. A., Green, T. J., and Heintschel, D. D. *The Code of Canon Law. A Text and Commentary*, New York, 1985.

Grocholewski, Z. "Die Canones uber den Papstünd das okumenische Konzil in dem nueun Kodex des kanonischen Rechts." *Kanon-Jahrbuch der Gesellschaft für das Recht der Ostkirchen*, IX (1989), 51–81.

Naz, R. *Traité de droit canonique*, I, Paris, 1946.

Ourliac, P., and Gilles, H. *La Période post-classique (1378–1500). 1. La problematique l'époque. Les sources.* (Histoire du droit et des institutions de l'Eglise en Occident, XIII), Paris, 1971.

CORNELIUS. *(d. 253).*

Cornelius succeeded FABIAN, who was martyred during the persecution of Decius (20 January 250), but he assumed office only a year later, as the persecution was then relentless. Decius "would rather have endured and accepted that a rival prince rise up against him than see a bishop of God established in Rome" (Cyprian, *Epistles*, 55). It was only when the persecution slackened that the Church of Rome could finally meet and elect a new bishop. We do not know the exact date of Cornelius' ordination; it may have been 6 or 13 March 251 (Liberian Catalogue MGH, AA, 9/1, 75).

According to a statement by Cyprian of Carthage to one of his colleagues, Cornelius had completed all the stages of the ministry: "He has accomplished all the functions of the Church, he has served the Lord faithfully in all the tasks entrusted to him, in such a way that he reached the pinnacle of priesthood only by passing through all the ecclesiastical stages" (Cyprian, *Epistles*, 55).

The election unleashed a serious crisis. Part of the community refused to recognize Cornelius, appointing NOVATIAN in his place. During the vacancy of the Roman See, Novatian had played a prominent role. The schism was fueled by the controversy over lapsed Christians, those who had given up during the persecution. Cornelius, for his part, accepted that those who recognized their mistake and did penance could be readmitted to the Church. Novatian was intransigent in his attitude and encouraged in Rome the rigorist trend that had already been manifest on a number of occasions, and which affected other communities at the same time. Indeed, from Rome, the schism spread not only throughout Italy, but throughout Christendom as well, including Africa, Gaul, and the East, where dissident churches, each headed by its own bishops, emerged.

Cornelius was supported by Cyprian of Carthage. Two letters from the latter's correspondence (Epistles 59 and 60), show, among others, the extent of the assistance given by the great African bishop. Cyprian, who had already written *Treatise on Lapsed Christians*, drafted *Treatise on the Unity of the Church (De Catholicae ecclesiae Unitate)*. In its first version, this treatise underscores the importance of the Roman See within the Universal Church. For Cyprian, the schism that shook the Roman community was extremely serious, as the See of Rome, the seat of St. Peter (*Cathedra Petri*) and principal Church (*Ecclesia Principalis*), was the first church from which all others were genealogically derived. Its role was fundamental, as the unity of the bishops also derives from it (*Epistles* 59, 14: *Unde unitas sacerdotalis exorta est*).

In the autumn of 251 Cornelius convened a SYNOD. According to Eusebius of Caesarea, "there were 60 bishops, and an even greater number of priests and deacons" (Eusebius, *Historia Eccleslastica*, VI, 43). Novatian was excommunicated. Then a letter, whose essence has been transmitted to us by the same author, helped Cornelius to convince Fabius, bishop of Antioch, who had been swayed momentarily by the schismatics. This occurred shortly before a council restored the East to Catholic unity thanks to the actions of Denis of Alexandria.

The letter from Cornelius to Fabius of Antioch provides us with precious information on the organization of life within the church of Rome. "Did Novatian not know that there should be only one bishop in a Catholic Church? He would know that in the Church . . . there are 46 priests, 7 deacons, 7 subdeacons, 42 acolytes, 52 exorcists, readers and porters, more than 1,500 widows and indigent persons, all fed through the grace and goodness of the Almighty" (Eusebius, *H.E.*, VI, 43). The organization of the clergy is attributed to Pope Fabian. The charitable institutions, which were comparable in number to those in Carthage (Cyprian, *Epistles*, 76), or in Antioch (Eusebius, *H.E.*, VII, 30), must have had significant resources at their disposal. It has been deduced from this information that the Christian population in Rome amounted to some 30,000.

While the Novatian schism had subsided without disappearing completely, a new wave of persecution broke out under the emperor Trebonianus Gallus (251–3), the successor of Decius. At that time, the Roman Empire was shaken by a serious external crisis. In addition to the threat from the Goths, who had killed Decius on the battlefield, there was also a threat from the Sassanites, from the East, who were on the verge of invading Syria and Antioch. To make matters worse, several regions of the Roman world were in the grip of the plague. Cyprian of Carthage himself, worried by the accumulation of apocalyptic signs, expected the end of the world. At the outset of the persecution, Cornelius was arrested and exiled to Centum cellae (Civitavecchia), where he died, probably in June 253 (cf. Liberian Catalogue, MGH, AA, 9/1, 75). Shortly afterward his body was transferred to Rome, to the crypt of Lucena, near the catacomb of Callistus, on the Appian Way (LP, I, 152=MGH, GPR, I, 31). It was an old Christian cemetery, made from two catacombs that were joined together when the body of Cornelius was transferred to Rome. An inscription in Latin testifies to the burial (ICUR, IV, 9367).

The *Liber Pontificalis* (LP, I, 152=MGH, GPR, I, 29) asserts that it was during Cornelius' tenure as bishop that the remains of Paul were transferred from the catacombs to the Ostian Way, and Peter's body transferred from the Appian Way to the Vatican. These assertions are fantasies arising from the worship of the founders of the Roman community, around the middle of the 4th century.

Michel Christol

Bibliography

Danielou, J., and Marrou, H. *"Des origines à Grégoire le Grand" (Nouvelle Histoire de l'Eglise*, I, under the direction of L. Rogier, R. Aubert, and M. D. Knowles), Paris, 1963, 229–37.

Frend, W. H. C. *Martyrdom and Persecution in the Early Church*, London, 1965, 408–22.

Lebreton, J., and Zeiller, J. *De la fin du IIe siècle à la paix constantinienne* (Fliche-Martin, 2), Paris, 1943, 150–1, 193–5, 409–13.

Munier, C. *L'Eglise dans l'Empire Romain. Eglise et cité (Histoire du droit et des Institutions de l'Eglise en Occident*, under the direction of G. Le Bras and J. Gaudemet, II, 3), Paris, 1979, 249–52.

Pietri, C. *Roma Christiana. Recherches sur l'Eglise de Rome, son organisation, sa politique, son idéologie de Miltiade à Sixte III* (311–440), Rome, 1976, I, 129–41, 298–310.

Reekmans, L. *La Tombe du Pape Corneille et sa région cémétériale*, Vatican City, 1964.

CORONATION, IMPERIAL. According to the traditional view of historians, an imperial coronation brought together the two supreme authorities of Christendom: the pope and the Holy Roman emperor. However, this idea excludes a number of other "emperors"—not only the African sovereigns, but also the emperors of antiquity, the rightful heirs to Byzantium, the czars of the Bulgarians and the Russians, the "emperor" of England or Spain as well as the German emperors after 1871. If it is asserted that both pope and emperor must play an active role in the coronation, it would be necessary to exclude Napoleon, because during his imperial coronation in 1804, PIUS VII merely served as part of the ceremonial decor. For the same reason, the coronations of the emperors of the Holy Roman Empire after 1556 must be excluded, as well as those of their Austrian successors, for no pope played an active part in their coronation. We will therefore limit our observation to the period dating from the coronation of Charlemagne (800) to that of Charles V (1530). We will give a brief account of the historical development before describing the ceremony itself.

It was undoubtedly at the initiative of LEO III that it was decided to crown Charlemagne on Christmas Day, 800. The pope wished to have in Rome a legitimate judge of crimes of lèse-majesté. Charlemagne had no choice but to consent to the coronation, which legitimized him as the successor of Constantine the Great. For both protagonists, Byzantium was at once a model to emulate and a rival example to be rejected. To lessen the pope's influence on the coronation, in 813 Charlemagne had observed a Byzantine custom by crowning his son Louis coemperor at Aix-la-Chapelle. This amounted to a formal self-coronation. In 817 Louis did the same with his eldest son Lothair. However, the pope had no intention of being excluded from the coronation process. Louis had himself recrowned in 816 by STEPHEN IV, at Reims. In 823 Lothair was, in his turn, crowned again by PASCHAL I. After the crowning of Lothair's son as Louis II in 850, coronation became the exclusive domain of the pope.

Following the death of Louis II in 875, the rite lost some of its importance, as the candidates chosen by the popes all had great difficulty in imposing their rule on Italy. The situation changed only in 962 when Otto I was crowned, making him the most powerful Christian sovereign in Europe. For the next century, a succession of strong emperors faced a number of relatively weak popes. But the coronation of 962 had an even greater significance: from then until 1530, only a Germanic king had the right to be crowned emperor by the pope. Every German king through Frederick II (1220)—with the exception of the antikings—received the imperial crown. Only Conrad III, who died in 1152, failed to make the expected journey to Rome.

At this time several changes came about. The INVESTITURES CONTROVERSY had increased papal authority. Certain popes sought to impose limits on imperial power, as they felt they had the authority to confer that power. INNOCENT III, and later his successors, sought to have a say in the choice of the Germanic king, which would also determine the heir to the imperial throne.

Another change took place in Germany. From 1155, date of the coronation of Frederick I Barbarossa, one of the obligations of the vassals of the king was to take part in the journey to Rome for the imperial coronation. For the sovereign, this represented the possibility of ensuring his Italian policy by military means, even before the coronation. However, after the coronation, the vassals could effectively restrain the long-term ambitions of the sovereign, as was the case with Frederick I and Henry VII (1312).

After the persecution of the Hohenstaufens (1250–1268) died down, imperial coronations became rarer and

gradually lost their importance. Even the coronation of Louis IV in 1328, carried out against the wishes of the pope by the representatives of the "Roman people," aroused little more than passing interest. Maximilian I called himself "emperor" with the pope's approval but without ever being crowned. In 1530 his grandson, Charles V, who was locked in struggles against both Luther and the Turks, deemed it important once again to be crowned by the pope. However, the pope had no role to play whatsoever in the coronation of his brother, Ferdinand I, who became emperor in 1558.

It is difficult to describe the coronation ceremony itself. No ordo (liturgical instruction) survives from the Carolingian era, and accounts of the actual event are sketchy. Most of the ordines transmitted after 960 were never applied. Furthermore, the supposed accuracy of many historical accounts is questionable. In fact authors rarely described what they had actually seen, referring instead to the ordo which they happened to have at hand. As a result there is no reliable account of the details of any imperial coronation. Charlemagne was crowned in accordance with prevailing Byzantine customs, after which he was acclaimed by the Romans. We do not know, however, whether he was anointed; the principal act was probably the acclamation. In the 9th century this rather spare ceremony was fleshed out a little: as well as the crown, the emperor was also presented with a sword and scepter. From the 12th century, he received the imperial orb, and the laudes replaced the acclamation. An important detail is that from 816, we have exact information on the anointing of the emperor. From that time, also, before his coronation the candidate would confirm to the pope the domain where the latter could exercise his temporal power. Until 1014, and with the exception of Otto III in 996, the promise of these privileges was an integral part of the coronation. From the rule of Otto IV (1209), the imperial coronation was governed by new constitutions, no doubt resulting from the oaths of coronation mentioned in the ordines.

From the very beginning the ordines established a parallel with the papal coronation. As was customary when a pope was crowned, the cardinal bishops of Albano, Porto, and Ostia said important prayers; the cardinal bishop of Ostia anointed the new emperor and the insignia of office were presented by the pope himself. This clearly demonstrated that they were components of the whole ceremony. Except for the years 1133 and 1530, St. Peter's was always the setting for the imperial coronation, and for a long time the only subjects of discussion were the altars and the ceremonies to be celebrated there. In 1200 it was established that the ceremony of anointing should take place before the altar of St. Maurice, while the presentation of the insignia should be in front of the high altar. After that period, a coronation banquet was only rarely held at the papal palace of the Lateran. The new emperor was usually in a hurry to leave Rome and withdraw to his army camp on Monte Mario. In short, the imperial coronation became an event of little importance. It could happen that an Imperator Romanorum did not even know Rome.

Bernhard Schimmelpfennig

BIBLIOGRAPHY

Bouman, C. A. *Sacring and Crowning*, Groningen-Djakarta, 1957.

Classen, P. *Karl der Grosse, das Papsttum und Byzanz. Die Begrundung des Karolingischen Kaisertums*, Sigmaringen, 1985.

Eichmann, E. *Die Kaiserkrönung im Abendland*, 2 vols., Wurzburg, 1942.

Elze, R. *Eine kaiserkrönung um 1200, Adel und Kirche. Festschrift Gerd Tellenbach*, Freiburg-Basel, 1968, 365–373.

Elze, R. *Le consacrazioni regie, Segni e riti nella chiesa altomedievale occidentale*, Spoleto, 1987 (Settimane di studio del Centro di studi sull'alto medioevo, 33), 41–61.

Elze, R. ed. *Ordines coronationis imperialis*, Hanover, 1960 (MGH, Font. jur. Germ. ant., 9).

Folz, R. *Le Couronnement impérial de Charlemagne*, Paris, 1964.

CORONATION, PAPAL. Since about 1300, the word "coronation" has been used to describe the liturgical acts accompanying the installation of a newly elected pope. It also signaled the growing importance of the papal crown, the tiara, for the papacy as an institution. Prior to 1300, different terms had been used and more importance given to other acts of investiture. We must therefore note the prevailing differences of the various eras and establish clear differences with respect to how each pope assumed his new office.

From the end of the 2nd century, once the monarchic episcopate had been established in Rome, it became necessary to decide how the investiture of the bishop should take place. Originally, the pope was elected on a Sunday, when the community had gathered to celebrate the Eucharist. The custom was that the choice be made by the faithful, members of the clergy and laity alike. After that, several bishops from the regions around Rome would consecrate him by the laying on of hands, and imploring God's protection. We are not sure where the election and consecration took place, as at the time there was no episcopal title in Rome.

From about 400 all acts of investiture took place at the Lateran, in the basilica of the Redeemer, built by the emperor Constantine, except when a schism required the use of other churches, such as ST. PETER'S, for example. From that time onward, the election and consecration took place at separate times. Generally, the election of a new pope took place as soon as possible following the death of the last one, while the consecration took place on a Sunday, as had been the custom from the beginning. The bishop of Ostia, assisted by two other bishops from the ecclesiastical province of Rome, had a prominent role to play in the consecration of the pope. The fundamental part of the ceremony of consecration remained the laying on of hands. However, in the course of the ceremony at that time, the New Testament was placed on the head of the candidate and the pallium was given to him as a sign of the dignity of his new office. After this, it may be assumed that he took his place on the throne of the basilica of the Lateran, to receive the homage of the clergy.

After the wars against the Goths (535–53), each pope had to be confirmed by the emperor or by the exarch of Ravenna after his election but before he could receive consecration. The election therefore assumed greater importance, whereas the act of consecration played a diminished role. After the election, the new pope, seated on the throne in the apse of the Lateran basilica (where the election also took place), received the homage of those who had chosen him. Following this, he took possession of the Lateran palace where he hosted a solemn meal. Finally, he was acclaimed by the people. The new pope was consecrated at St. Peter's in accordance with ancient tradition, which custom is observed today. Before the "Gloria" of the consecration mass, the bishops of Albano, Porto, and Ostia intoned the prayers of consecration and held the New Testament above the head of the pontiff. Then the archdeacon placed the pallium around his shoulders. Homage was again paid to the new pope, before or after the "Gloria." It is useful to note that the ceremonies in St. Peter's showed the pope as the guide of all Christendom, whereas those at the Lateran symbolized the handing over of the DIOCESE OF ROME. Over the next few centuries, as the papacy became more important for the entire church, the ceremonies held at the Lateran gradually gave way to those celebrated at St. Peter's.

Ever since the time that the temporal sovereignty of the pope was acknowledged in the 8th century, the palace of the Lateran had gained importance. The taking of possession (POSSESSO) by the pope was one of the most important first acts of a new pontiff, while the Lateran basilica still played no role. After the election, the new pope received the papal robes in the palace and took his place on the throne, perhaps the triclinium throne with the three conches of LEO III. The most important clerics and laypersons then came to pay their respects by kissing his feet and pledging an oath of fidelity. The consecration took place at St. Peter's on a Sunday or on a feast day. In keeping with tradition, the cardinal bishops of Albano, Porto, and Ostia said the three prayers of consecration and raised the New Testament above his head.

Then the archdeacon attached the pallium to his chasuble and together with another archdeacon, led him to the throne in the apse that is considered the CHAIR OF ST. PETER. Here again, people came to kiss the pope, who intoned the "Gloria." After mass, he changed his robes and walked toward the steps of the church, where he was acclaimed by the people who wished him a long life (*polychronia*). Finally he was crowned with Constantine the Great's tiara. From then on the coronation ceremony, which gave rise to the many acts marking the temporal sovereignty of the pope, began to gain importance. Wearing his tiara, the pope went on horseback to the Lateran palace.

From the time of MARINUS I (882), but especially under emperors Otto I and Henry III, the popes elected in Rome were former bishops, who therefore did not need to be consecrated. This was against established legal practice of that time. From the reign of Otto I (962), the popes more and more frequently received investiture from the emperors. These two changes had repercussions on the liturgy of elevation to the pontificate. It is curious that no mention is made of the Lateran palace in this liturgy, despite the great importance that it had assumed for papal government by the tenth century. In fact, based on available information, all important events were concentrated at St. Peter's. Whenever a new pope had been chosen by "the clergy and the people," the elite of Roman society came to his residence to greet and acclaim him. On the other hand, if he had been invested by the emperor, the latter would give him the papal insignia. Apart from the traditional pallium, there was the FERULA (a stick decorated with a cross), and in the eleventh century, a purple pluviale (mantle). If the new pope was not a bishop, he was consecrated at St. Peter's before the "Gloria," in accordance with established tradition. If he was already a bishop, he was simply blessed by three cardinal bishops. The solemn enthronement by the bishops at St. Peter's was then the most essential stage of the ceremony. After 955 the changing of the name of the onomastic pope was added to the list of rituals. The *inthronizatio* referred to all stages of the ceremony as well as the actual assumption of office. There is no mention anywhere of a procession following the coronation.

After the INVESTITURE CONTROVERSY, many elections were conducted outside Rome, and those acts of investiture which could be held only in Rome had to be postponed or canceled altogether. The enthronement therefore lost importance. The most significant acts, apart from the election itself, were now the *immantatio* of the pluviale and the handing over of the pallium, as well as the consecration or benediction. If the pope was elected in Rome, the *possesso* of the Lateran regained importance. After the conciliary decrees of 1179 and 1274, the election became, from a legal standpoint, the most important act of the elevation to the pontificate. Furthermore,

the accompanying liturgical acts were reduced to ceremonies which were often as meaningless as they were pompous. If the pope had been elected in Rome, the traditional ceremonies took place, but often in a different order. First, the pope received the consecration or benediction as well as the pallium at St. Peter's, after which he was enthroned in the chair of St. Peter in the apse. Following a mass on the steps of St. Peter's, he returned to the Lateran, wearing his tiara and passing through the street. As he went by, the Jews acclaimed him as their new master, the lay people and clerics from the different churches raised arches in his honor and made gifts of money. The solemn entry into the Lateran basilica marked the end of the ceremony. In the church, the canons paid tribute to him, and in the palace, the members of the court paid their respects.

From the papacy of INNOCENT III (1198–1216) an important change was made in the order of precedence of the coronation procession. Up until then, and in keeping with tradition, the pope was followed first by the Palatine clergy, but now this place would belong instead to the cardinals and external prelates. This was meant to show participants and spectators that from then on, the pope was less the bishop of Rome and more the head of the Universal Church. As most of the popes had been bishops before their election, the benediction did not have the value of a sacramental act, and the coronation continued to increase in pomp and magnificence, until it began to overshadow all the other acts of the ceremony. The change in emphasis was again reinforced during the AVIGNON papacy. By that time, the rite of enthronement had disappeared altogether. The practices that had gained tenancy during the Avignon papacy continued even after the GREAT SCHISM had ended, but the rite of enthronement was soon practically obsolete in Rome. The *immantatio* had also fallen into disuse. The coronation, on the other hand became grander, with a three-pointed tiara being used. Since Avignon an innovation had also been introduced. Before the benediction, during the procession to the high altar, a cleric burned some tow and reminded the pope of the ephemeral nature of his office by proclaiming *"Pater sante, sic transit gloria mundi."*

After about 1500, the coronation on the steps of St. Peter's completely overshadowed the *possesso*, which had become only an accessory act, so much so that it could be performed a few days after the coronation, as was the case for the election of JULIUS II (1503). From the 13th century, the debate was open as to whether a newly elected pope could from the time of his election perform such functions as the solemn mass or the provision of consistorial prebends, or perform them only after his coronation. There has been little research on the coronation ceremony during the modern and contemporary eras. After the Vatican was chosen as the place of residence, the *possesso* of the Lateran became an increasingly irrelevant detail, and after the end of the PAPAL STATES, disappeared altogether from both the coronation ceremony and procession. PAUL VI gave up the tradition of the tiara, thus rendering the coronation obsolete. Following the decree of 1975, the papal election is the only act that installs a new pope in his office. The liturgy surrounding the election is merely a formal ceremony, during which the pope receives the pallium, the miter, and more recently, a sort of ugly baton that is a combination of a bishop's crozier and the ancient ferula. During the first solemn benediction in St. Peter's Square, the people acclaim their new pope. *Sic transit gloria liturgiae.*

Bernhard Schimmelpfennig

Bibliography

Cancellieri, F. *Storia de' solenni possessi de' Sommi Pontefici*, Rome, 1802.

Dykmans, M. *L'Œuvre de Patrizi Piccolomini ou le cérémonial papal de la première Renaissance*, 2 vols., Vatican City, 1980–2.

Eichmann, E. *Weihe und Krönung des Papstes im Mittelalter*, Munich, 1951.

Fürst, C. G. "Statim ordinetur episcopus," *Ex Æquo et Bono. Willibald M. Plöchl zum 70. Geburtstag*, Innsbruck, 1977, 45–65.

Gussone, N. *Thron und Inthronisation des Papstes von den Anfängen bis zum 12. Jahrhundert*, Bonn. 1978.

Klewitz, H. W. "Die Krönung des Papstes," *ZRGKA*, 30 (1941), 96–130.

Richter, K. *Die Ordination des Bischofs von Rom. Eine Untersuchung zur Weiheliturgie*, Münster, 1976.

Schimmelpfennig, B. "Die Krönung des Papstes im Mittelalter, dargestellt am Beispiel der Krönung Pius' II. (3.9.1458)," *QFIAB*, 54 (1974), 192–270.

Schimmelpfennig, B. "Papal Coronations in Avignon," *Coronations. Medieval and Early Modern Monarchic Ritual*," ed. J. M. Bak, Berkeley, 1990, 179–96.

Wasner, F. "De consecratione, inthronizatione, coronatione Summi Pontificis," *Apollinaris*, 8 (1935), 86–125, 249–81, 428–39.

COUNCILS, ECUMENICAL. The ancient ecclesiastical authors, canonists, and historians, used the terms "concilium" and "synodus" more or less interchangeably, to designate a meeting or a deliberative assembly. Sometimes, the ordinary place of these meetings called this, then, by extension, it came to mean the buildings (churches and temples) where the faithful assembled to follow the liturgy of the mass. Thus, the LIBER PONTIFICALIS praised DAMASUS I for composing some verses to adorn the *sanctorum concilia*. Afterward, as attested to in Spain from the end of the seventh century, these terms were only applied to meetings attended by bishops and were the occasions of decision-making related to religious questions. At first they were mixed, attended by both ecclesiastical and secular authorities (*concilia mixta*). Frequently in France in particular, "council" soon designated only those ecclesiastical meetings that had the sole and specific purpose of legislating in the religious domain.

Immediately after the apostolic period ("Where two or three meet in my name, I shall be there with them," Matt. 18:20), councils were held in the East from the second century. At the height of the persecutions, conciliar meetings united bishops of several provinces, at Carthage around 220, at Synnada and Iconium around 230, at Antioch from 264 to 269. The peace of the church, achieved at the beginning of the 4th century, facilitated the development of these institutions. The fathers of the first council of Nicaea (325) spoke of these conciliar assemblies as a matter of custom.

A distinction was naturally made between particular councils and universal councils. Particular councils are subdivided into diocesan (now called diocesan synods), provincial (bishops of an ecclesiastical province meeting under the authority of the metropolitan), and national councils. Universal councils were ecumenical councils; these are still sometimes called general or plenary. The ecumenical council is a solemn assembly of world bishops, canonically organized at the request of the reigning pope, and is held under his presidency. In the official doctrine of the church, an assembly of this type can only be considered ecumenical by the presence of bishops of all the ecclesiastical provinces; however, it also requires the presence of the pope who can, particularly in cases of disagreement, rule on and guarantee the absolute and universal authority of the decisions.

Ecumenicity is supposed to derive as much from the convocation (that all the archbishops, patriarchs, and primates have received the call) and the celebration (freedom and regularity of debates), as from the plenitude of power, thus constituting a field of application of PAPAL PRIMACY. Canon 28 of the ecumenical council of Chalcedon (451), which gave the patriarch of Constantinople primacy of place after Rome, will remain null and void because it was passed against the wishes of the LEGATES of LEO I, who refused to ratify the disposition. The question of the ecumenical character, or lack thereof, of a council has been raised on several occasions. Ecumenicity can be established without consultation, by the means of an authentic and infallible notice through the person of the pope, ruling on a question of dogmatic fact.

Up to the 6th Century. The First Council of Nicaea was assembled in 325 by CONSTANTINE (closure on 19 June), under the pontificate of SILVESTER I, who was represented at the council by two legates, Vitus and Vincentius, and was attended by 318 bishops. It condemned Arianism by defining the consubstantial (*homoousion*) character of the Word, defended in particular by bishops Eustachius of Antioch and Marcel of Ankara, as well as by deacon Thanase of Alexandria, adopting the first version of the prayer of the "Credo" or "symbol of Nicaea." Twenty canons were promulgated, among them canon 6 which maintained the ancient custom of recognizing the bishop of Alexandria as the authority over Egypt, Libya, and the Pentapolis, and granted the bishop of Aelia (the Roman name for Jerusalem since 136) a "primacy of honor."

The First Council of Constantinople was convoked at the end of 380 or at the beginning of 381. About 150 eastern bishops (Damasus I was not officially represented) gathered in the great hall of the imperial palace. Presided over by Meletius of Antioch, it dealt with the definition of the divine character of the Holy Spirit (defended by Athanasius of Alexandria and Gregory Nazianzen against the "Pneumatomachians"). It completed the "Credo" by adding the divine nature of the Holy Spirit. The bishop of Constantinople received the primacy of honor over that of Rome, "for this city is the new Rome." The council promulgated in addition four canons dealing with discipline in the Church.

The Council of Ephesus opened on 21 June 431. It condemned the theses of the patriarch of Constantinople, Nestorius, who thought that the word "*Theotokos*," meaning the Mother of God, should not be applied to the Virgin Mary, as had been the custom among ecclesiastical authors since Origen. CELESTINE I was represented by two bishops and a presbyter.

The Council of Chalcedon was convened in 451 (Today the city of Kadiköy, on the Bosphorus, opposite Istanbul.) More than 350 bishops, all Hellenophones, attended, as well as two bishops and two presbyters who represented Leo I. Opened on 8 October in the basilica of St. Euphemia the Martyr, the council condemned the troubles at Ephesus which had occurred some time before and the person supposedly responsible, Bishop Dioscorus of Alexandria. Pope Leo imposed his doctrine of the dual human and divine nature of Christ. The council promulgated twenty-seven canons which the pope confirmed on 21 March 453, close to eighteen months after the date of the closure of the council, and only those on matters of faith (*in sola fidei causa*).

The Second Council of Constantinople opened on 5 May 553 in the *sacrarium* of the St. Sophia basilica, and counted among its ranks a large majority of eastern bishops and patriarchs (150 against 25). Pope VIGILIUS, although he was present in Constantinople, refused to attend. Without being explicitly excommunicated, he was struck from the diptychs and was no longer mentioned in the Eucharistic prayer. In its eighth and final session (2 June 553), the council gave a dogmatic definition in **fourteen** anathematisms. Vigilius was constrained to accept the decrees of the council, first by a letter to Eutychius, then patriarch of Constantinople (8 December 553), then by a new Constitution, on 22 February 554.

7th Through 13th Centuries. Until 870 all ecumenical councils convoked by the emperor (later called the Byzantine emperor) took place in the East and were comprised of an overwhelming or exclusive majority of eastern prelates. After a long interruption, the first Lateran council of 1123 sanctioned the break with the ancient tradition and with the eastern Churches and suffered the consequences of the Gregorian reform, which had reserved to the Roman pope the convocation of councils. In the century and a half between the First Lateran Council and the Second Council of Lyon, the juridical construction of a "catholic and hierarchical" Western Church was defined.

The Third Council of Constantinople was held in the imperial palace, from 7 November 680 to 16 September 681. The assembly (174 bishops at the last session, among them only three Westerners) was presided over by Emperor Constantine IV; the pope was represented by four Roman clerics. It was convoked to deal with monothelitism. The Orthodox Church accepts as part of this council the council held at Constantinople in 692. Held in the trullo (dome) of the imperial palace, from which came its name Trullan Synod, it was convoked by Emperor Justinian II. It is sometimes called the Quinisext synod, for it completes the legislation of the 5th and 6th ecumenical councils. However, Pope SERGIUS refused to give it his approval. At it the patriarch of Constantinople was affirmed as primate of the entire East.

The Second Council of Nicaea took place between 4 September and 23 October 787. The assembly of 252 to 365 bishops, exclusively eastern except for the papal legates, was presided over by the patriarch of Constantinople. It refuted iconoclasm. The council was accepted by the pope, but contested by the Frankish court which rejected a poor translation of the Greek canons in the *Capitulary on Images*, also known as the *Libri Carolini*.

The Fourth Council of Constantinople was held in St. Sophia from 5 October 869 to 28 February 870. The assembly (102 bishops at the last session, exclusively eastern) was presided over by three legates who represented the pope, then by Emperor Basil. It condemned the Patriarch Photius, who wished to place the see of Constantinople above that of Rome.

The First Lateran Council was held in St. John Lateran from 18 to 27 March 1123. The assembly of about two hundred bishops was convoked and presided over by CALLISTUS II. It ratified the CONCORDAT OF WORMS, Gregorian ecclesiastical legislation, and authorized the organization of a CRUSADE.

The Second Lateran Council was held in St. John Lateran from 3 to 8 April 1139. The assembly of about five hundred bishops was convoked and presided over by INNOCENT II. It ratified Gregorian ecclesiastical legislation and condemned antisacramentary HERESIES and NICOLAISM.

The Third Lateran Council was held in St. John Lateran from 5 to 19 March 1179. The assembly of about three hundred bishops and other prelates was convened by and presided over by ALEXANDER III. It regulated the papal election and episcopal schools, and organized the fight against heresy.

LATERAN IV was held in St John Lateran from 11 to 30 November 1215. The assembly of about twelve hundred clergy was convoked and presided over by INNOCENT III. It promulgated additions to ecclesiastical regulation and to the antiheretic fight, enacted measures against Jews, and authorized the organization of a crusade.

The First Council of Lyon was held from 28 June to 17 July 1245. The assembly of about 150 clergy, among them three patriarchs from the east, was first convoked at Rome in 1241 by GREGORY IX then postponed following the attack of Emperor Frederick II. It was reunited and presided over by INNOCENT IV in a safer city. The emperor was deposed and ecclesiastical regulations enacted.

The Second Council of Lyon was held from 7 May to 17 July 1274. The assembly of about 1,020 clergy, among them 220 bishops, was convoked and presided over by GREGORY X. The eastern emperor was represented by a delegation which arrived on 24 June. There was union with the Greek Church, reforms of ecclesiastical discipline, and the authorization of the organization of a crusade.

14th Through 20th Centuries. The Council of Vienne (1311–2) was convened under CLEMENT V. It decided to suppress the order of the Templars, condemn the Dulcinian sect, and stress the necessity and urgency of a new expedition against the Turks.

The Council of Constance (1414–8) was considered an ecumenical council in its final sessions (42nd to 45th), after the election of MARTIN V (1418). He wished to end the GREAT SCHISM by proclaiming the impossibility of its dissolution before the reform of the Church "in its head and its members," giving birth to the so-called "conciliarist" theory. Its decrees, adopted during the 3rd, 4th, and 5th sessions, were never, however, approved by the popes or recognized by the Church.

The Council of Florence (1438–45) was convoked by EUGENE IV, and in reality sat at Rome from 1443. It was preceded by several aborted conciliary attempts at Basel in 1431 then at Ferrara in 1438. It decided on a reform of the Church, and new reconciliation with the Greeks, which was practiced progressively from 1439 (the return of the Armenians to the Catholic bosom) until 1445 (the return of the Maronites of Cyprus).

The Fifth Lateran Council (1512–17) was convoked by JULIUS II and closed by his successor LEO X. It initiated the reform of the clergy and the faithful, ruled on certain fiscal matters (abuse of exemptions, payment of taxes), and fixed the conditions for nomination to ecclesiastical offices.

The Council of TRENT (1545–7, 1551–2, 1562–3) was convoked under the pontificate of PAUL III, was transferred to Bologna (1547), was interrupted again under JULIUS II in 1552, and started again under PIUS IV in 1562. At the doctrinal level, in response to Protestant theses, it asserted the authority of the biblical text, declaring the Vulgate authentic. It also defined the doctrine and justification of original sin, against the teachings of the Pelagians and more directly against Erasmus, on the one hand (original sin is not only the imitation of the sin of Adam but also its hereditary consequence), and against Martin Luther on the other (man cannot be saved by his works alone but must contribute by putting himself with the help of God in a condition to receive initial grace). The council maintained, against Luther, the list of seven sacraments, declared efficacious in themselves (*ex opere operato*), and the transubstantiation of the bread and wine during the celebration of the Eucharist. It defended the doctrine of purgatory, the cult of the SAINTS, of images, and of relics. At the disciplinary level, the decree *Cum adulescentium aetas* created diocesan SEMINARIES for the education of the clergy. The canonical rules for marriage were fixed by the decree *Tametsi* (against clandestine marriages). There was a global reorientation of the ecclesiastical institution according to a pastoral spirit, in the service of the faithful for the health of their souls, to the detriment of the regular clergy and religious orders, which were submitted to the jurisdiction of the ordinaries (bishops in the general case).

VATICAN I (8 December 1869–20 October 1870) was opened by PIUS IX and held four sessions. The APOSTOLIC CONSTITUTION *Dei Filius* (24 April 1870) solemnly condemned the attacks of modern thought and civilization on the faith and revelation. The constitution *Pastor aeternus* (13 July 1870) affirmed the primacy of the pope as heir to the power divinely conferred by Christ on Peter, as well as the personal INFALLIBILITY of the popes when they teach EX CATHEDRA. The day after the vote, the Franco-Prussian war broke out and Italian troops occupied Rome on 20 September. Unfinished, the council was suspended on 20 October and has never been reconvened.

VATICAN II (11 October 1962 – 7 December 1965) was opened by JOHN XXIII and closed by PAUL VI; it had four sessions: 11 October–8 December 1962, 29 September–4 December 1963, 14 September–21 November 1964, and 14 September–8 December 1965. Sixteen conciliar documents were promulgated, among them four constitutions. The two most famous are the ones on the renovation of the liturgy (*Sacrosanctum concilium*) and on the Church in the modern world (*Gaudium et spes*). On the occasion of Vatican II, a mixed working group was created with the World Council of the Churches (February 1965) and the reciprocal anathemas between the Catholic and Orthodox Churches were lifted (7 December 1965).

Olivier Guyotjeannin
Philippe Levillain

Bibliography

Alberigo, G. *Les Conciles oecumeniques*, 3 vols., Paris, 1994.

Camelot, P. T. *et al*, *Les Conciles oecumeniques*, 2 vols., Paris, 1988 (Bibliotheque d'histoire du christianisme, 15–16).

Christophe, P. *L'Eglise dans l'histoire des hommes*, I, Paris, 1982.

Jannen, N. *The Councils of the Church*, New York, 2001.

COUNCILS, PARTICULAR OR LOCAL. The historian EUSEBIUS mentions the existence of councils or synods from the end of the 2nd century in Asia Minor (*Histoire ecclesiastique*, V, 16) which dealt with the montanist crisis, or fixing the date of Easter (on the initiative of Pope VICTOR I). It is therefore a very ancient practice in the Church.

Particular councils can be plenary (also called national until the second half of the 19th century, or general) or provincial. The latter have dealt especially with disciplinary and judicial questions for the territory of an ECCLESIASTICAL PROVINCE. Plenary councils—sometimes mixed with the participation of political individuals (in Spain, Constantinople, and especially in France)—consider doctrinal, liturgical, and even temporal matters affecting the superior interests of a church or of a particular political community. Such a division of functions established a council of CARTHAGE (13 June 407) in the African Church and the Fourth Council of Toledo (633) in the Visigoth Church.

The provincial council has as a canonical precedent the meetings of bishops of the same civil province (on which was based ecclesiastical organization) who wanted to come together to consult on serious problems that surpassed local scope. In the beginning, it had the capacity to intervene in the legislative, judicial, and administrative spheres. However, the most important councils such as ecumenical councils have the capacity to treat the same matters, which allows them to limit the competence of provincial councils, even before the law of DECRETALS was imposed as an alternative law. Ultimately, LATERAN IV (1215) assigned as their principal task the application of the general law of the reigning pontiff as well as of the

councils. SIXTUS V (1585–90) was the first to affirm the necessity of having approval (*recognitio*) by the HOLY SEE of the decrees of provincial councils (BULL *Immensa aeterni*, 22 January 1588). This was a necessary condition for the validity of their promulgation by the metropolitan archbishop, but was also a source of a greater authority for these decrees and, consequently, of the increased power of the bishops to fight against the absolutism of modern states. The Holy See was also able to stop synodal activity in Europe or across the Atlantic when it was necessary to contain conciliar or nationalist tendencies (as was the case for GALLICANISM in the 17th century), or to stimulate it in order to preserve the autonomy of the Church vis-à-vis the state (for example, to obtain a consensus of bishops on the bull *Unigenitus* of 1713, condemning Jansenist-inspired Gallicanism).

The legislation of particular councils was handled by councils of lesser importance: the patriarchal synod in the East, the plenary council in North Africa, the primatial council in southern Gaul, the national or general council in the Germanic or Roman kingdoms, or a general council convoked by the Roman pontiff and presided over by his LEGATES.

The most ancient provincial councils are those of Carthage (around 220), of Synnada and Iconium (around 230), of Antioch (from 264 to 269), of Elvira (between 300 and 306), of Arles and Ancyra (Ankara; 314), of Alexandria (320), and of Sardinia (343). In addition, including provincial and other more important synods, there were thirty-seven African councils between 390 and 427, thirty-eight Spanish councils between 306 and the beginning of the 8th century (12th Council of Toledo), sixty-two Merovingian councils, and sixty-five Carolingian councils between 742 and 842.

Canon 5 of the ECUMENICAL COUNCIL of Nicaea (325) decreed that the provincial council must be convened twice a year. This norm was reiterated in canon 17 of the Council of Chalcedon (451). The Council of Agde (506) restored the frequency to once a year, under pain, however, of excommunication of those bishops who failed to convene the council. In fact, the time fluctuated, without ever being truly observed. The Council of Constance (1414–8) adopted the decree of holding one every three years, which was reiterated by the COUNCIL OF TRENT (twenty-fourth session, *de reformatione*, c. 2). This remained the norm until the 1917 CODE OF CANON LAW fixed the convocation of the provincial council at every twenty years (c. 283). The 1983 Code did not give a precise instruction. In the late 20th century conciliar meetings were rare.

According to available data, there are forty-seven Latin councils listed between 906 and 1054. A revival begins with the Cluny movement, with 750 provincial councils listed between the death of LEO IX (1054) and the Avignon exile (1305), an average of three a year for the entire Latin Church. During the two and a half centuries preceding the Council of Trent, only about a hundred provincial councils were convened, more often in the Germanic countries and England than in the Latin countries. After the Council of Trent, two periods are discernible: the fifty years that follow the council (notably activity in France and in Italy, as well as in the province of Tarragona) and the years after the liberal revolution of 1848 (regular activity in Ireland and thirty-four provincial and plenary councils in the United States between 1829 and 1891). After the promulgation of the 1917 Code of Canon Law, there was a resumption of activity particularly in Italy (twenty councils, including seventeen plenary, of a total of fifty-one in the Church). But the councils already suffered competition from meetings of the CONFERENCES OF BISHOPS that increased steadily after 1848.

VATICAN II greatly desired that the "venerable institution of synods and councils," provincial and plenary, "experience a new vigor, to provide for, according to the circumstances and in a more suitable and efficacious manner, the progress of the faith and the maintenance of discipline in the various Churches" (decree *Christus Dominus*, no. 36), an end that is reaffirmed in the 1983 Code of Canon Law (c. 445). Particular councils, while not infallible (this is specific to ecumenical councils), are "authentic instructors and teachers of the faith" (c. 753) and should see to the preservation of the integrity of faith and of morals (c. 823 § 2). For that, particular councils have a legislative power that, while safeguarding the universal law, allows them to accomplish their mission.

The Plenary Council. The plenary council became an official institution only with the 1917 Code. Before, only the Roman pontiff could authorize its convocation. The first plenary council, from a canonical point of view, was that of Pressburg (1822) convened at the initiative of the primate of Hungary. After refusing the convention of such a council by the French and German episcopates, the Holy See authorized one in Ireland to be held in 1850. From 1850 to 1917 there were sixteen plenary councils (three in Ireland, three in Baltimore, two in the English, Dutch, and Danish colonies in the West Indies, two in Albania, three in Australia, one in Scotland, one in Rome for Latin American bishops, and one in Peru) convened essentially in countries where a Catholic hierarchy was not yet entrenched and which came under the jurisdiction of the Congregation for the Propagation of the Faith. Between 1917 (the date of the first code of canon law) and 1962 (the date of the opening of Vatican II), there were ten plenary councils, not including the nine convened in Italy. After Vatican II, very few countries (Holland, Switzerland, the German Democratic Republic, Austria, and the United Kingdom) convened a synod or council at the national level. A true plenary council took place in the Philippines in 1991.

According to legislation in effect at the beginning of the twenty-first century, a plenary council unites all the particular churches of the same conference of bishops (c. 439 § 1). It is convened in accordance with c. 455 § 2, whenever, with the approval of the Holy See, it is considered necessary or advantageous.

It chooses the location of the meeting in its territory, elects the president from among the diocesan bishops, who must be approved by the Apostolic See (c. 179), thus prolonging the canonical tradition of a papal legate holding the presidency of plenary councils (1917 Code, c. 281), and establishes the order of business, the opening and the duration of the council, the transfer, the extension, and its closing (c. 441).

The Provincial Council. The provincial council assembles the churches of the same ecclesiastical province (c. 440 § 1). It is convoked by the metropolitan, with the consent of the majority of suffragan bishops, whenever it appears advisable, but never in the case of a vacancy of the metropolitan see. It is the metropolitan's responsibility to choose the location in his territory, establish the agenda, fix the beginning and duration of the council, preside over it, and decide on transfer, extension, or termination of the council (c. 442 § 1). In the case of a legitimate impediment of the metropolitan (for example, his see becoming vacant or his unavoidable absence), the provincial council pursues its business under the presidency of a suffragan bishop elected by the other suffragans. The Code expressly gives the provincial council the task of determining by decree the fee for mass offerings (c. 952 § 1).

Prior approval of the Apostolic See is required as well for holding a provincial council of an ecclesiastical province, the borders of which coincide with the territory of a country (c. 439 § 2), as in the case of Belgium, Haiti, Honduras, Malta, Panama, and the Netherlands, for example.

Between the end of the Council of Trent (1563) and the 1917 Code, about 250 provincial councils are recorded, as opposed to the approximately 10,500 which should have been convoked during that period in the ninety existing ecclesiastical regions. From 1789 to 1917 there were 110, as follows: twenty-nine in the United States, twenty-one in France, eleven in Asia, ten in Latin America, ten in Canada, eight in Italy, six in Ireland, four in Spain, three in England, two in Australia, and six in central Europe. But the "golden age" was from 1848 to 1869, with sixty-four of these councils. According to the available dates, there should have been sixteen provincial councils from 1918 to 1959, plus five more in the Italian provinces that were not grouped into conciliar regions. After Vatican II no provincial councils were convened: the institution entered a profound crisis, especially given the prominence of the conferences of bishops and the holding of plenary councils.

Sequence of Particular Councils. The following participate in particular councils and have a deliberative vote: diocesan bishops, coadjutors, auxiliary and coequal bishops (including the diocesan administrator of a vacant see, c. 427 § 1), the other titular bishops who hold a particular responsibility in the relevant territory, and finally any other titular bishops, even those who have retired, residing in the territory. The following are also members by right, but have only a consultative vote: all the vicars general and episcopal vicars of the territory, the major superiors of religious institutions and societies of apostolic life defined by the conference of bishops or by the bishops of the province and elected by all the major superiors of the institutes and societies having their seat in the territory, the rectors of ecclesiastical and Catholic universities, deans of faculties of theology and canon law located in the territory, some rectors of major seminaries elected by the rectors of seminaries situated in the territory, priests and other faithful in a number that should not be more than half the members indicated above, without their mode of selection being specified, and other persons as observers (c. 443 § 1–4 and 6). Also invited to provincial councils are two members of the cathedral chapters as well as of the presbyterial and pastoral councils of each particular church, collegially designated by them (c. 443 § 5). All those convoked must attend the council. In case of a just impediment, however, members with voting rights can be represented by proxy, but it becomes only a consultative vote. All must make the PROFESSION OF FAITH (c. 833 § 1).

Once passed, the acts of the particular council are sent by its president to the Apostolic See, which must recognize them in order for them to be promulgated according to the form and within the limits of enforcement determined by the council itself (c. 446). If the law does not fix a time limit, they are considered in force one month after their promulgation (c. 8 § 2). However, the *recognitio* of the Holy See does not confer particular juridical force on the decrees, which remain acts of particular law. The faithful are bound to adhere to the authentic MAGISTERIUM of particular councils with "religious submission of mind" (c. 753).

The ordinary of the place can dispense with laws made by plenary and provincial councils any time he deems it necessary for the good of the faithful (c. 88), not just in particular cases for a just cause as was the case in the previous code (c. 291 § 2).

Italy Represents a Particular Case. Because of the smallness of some of its ecclesiastical provinces, Italy has been divided into nineteen conciliar regions (Consistorial congregation, decree *Pro celebratione conciliorum et appellationibus in regionibus Italiae*, 15 February 1919, circular letters of 22 March 1919 and 29 September 1933), in each of which plenary regional councils, which are true provincial councils, must be held, with the exception of the provinces of Liguria (Genoa), Lombardy (Milan), Piedmont (Turin and Vercelli), and Veneto (Venice). The data show nine plenary councils in Italy between 1917 and 1962.

Particular Councils and Conferences of Bishops. The problem is posed of the relationship between particular councils and the conference of bishops. The conference of bishops has first of all a wider function than the particular councils, which is "to further promote the good that the Church offers to men, in particular by the forms and methods of apostolate suitably adapted to current circumstances" (decree *Christus Dominus*, no. 38). It is a permanent institution which must meet at least once a year and any time that particular circumstances warrant it (c. 453) (while particular councils are convoked any time that it appears opportune), it is an assembly of bishops (participation in particular councils is wider), it possesses competencies voluntarily limited by the legislator in the pastoral sphere (as we have seen, provincial councils dealt with disciplinary and judicial matters and plenary councils treated doctrinal, liturgical, and even temporal questions), and it has as its only limit the universal law of the Church (c. 445). Finally by the recognition of the Holy See, the acts of each institution acquire the force of law (c. 7), while remaining either acts of the conference of bishops or of the particular council; however, the conference of bishops is not able to modify afterward decisions of a plenary council because the composition of members with a deliberative vote in the two assemblies is not the same (c. 443 and 454), as well as the fact that the competence of the conference of bishops is materially limited (canon 455, section 1) and cannot include matters on which the particular council has legislated.

Roman Councils. Roman councils are worthy of special mention. They are most often convened by the pope and presided over by him. Composed of a wider membership than the presbyterium of Rome, they can have up to 120 members (Roman council of 487). The council of 313, under Pope MILTIADES, resolved the Donatist affair. That of 341 under JULIUS I decided on the affair of Athanasius. At the council of 449 LEO I condemned the brigandage of Ephesus. That of 13 March 487, under FELIX II, attacked the question of the lapsed Christians. Pope GELASIUS I submitted, in 494, the definition of the authentic books of the Holy Scripture, ecclesiastical authors, and apocryphal or erroneous books. Monothelitism was condemned at the instigation of MARTIN I in 649 and of AGATHO in 680. Roman councils of the 11th century decreed disciplinary measures against the Germanic emperor, Henry IV, and of ecclesiastical personalities during the INVESTITURE CONTROVERSY.

Dominique Le Tourneau

Bibliography

Aymans, W. "Synode 1972: Strukturprobleme eines Regionalkonzils," *Archiv für katholisches Kirchenrecht*, 138 (1969), 363–88.

Bonicelli, S. C. *I concili particolari da Graziano al Concilio di Trento: studio sulla evoluzione del diritto della Chiesa latina*, Brescia, 1971.

Bouix, M. D. *De Concilio Provinciali*, Paris, 2nd ed, 1862.

Clément, O. "The Pope, the council and the emperor during the period of the seven ecumenical councils," trans. B. Ruffey, *Sourozh*, 42 (Nov. 1990), 1–15.

Collectio lacensis: Acta et decreta sacrorum conciliorum recentiorum, Freiburg im Breisgau, 1873–82.

Corecco, E. "Sinodalita," *Nuovo Dizionario di Teologia* (under the editorship of O. Arbaglio and S. Dianich), Rome, 1973, 1466–95.

Fessler, J. *Über die Provinzial-Concilien und Diozesan-Synod*, Innsbruck, 1849.

Fornes, J. "Naturaleza sinodal de los Concilios particulares y de las Conferencias episcopales," *La synodalité*, 305–48.

Garcia y Garcia, A. "Conciles particuliers du 11e millenaire et conferences episcopales," *Les Conferences episcopales*, 85–97.

Ghirlanda, G. "Munus regendi et munus docendi dei concili particolari e delle conferenze dei vescovi," *La synodalité*, 349–88.

Goralski, W. "Instytusja Synoda w Kodeksie Prawa Kanonicznego Jana Pawla II," *Prawo Kanoniczne* XXXI (3/4 1988), 35–44.

Goralski, W. "Synody prowincjonalne w Dekrecie Gracjana," *Prawo Kanoniczne* XXVI (3/4 1983), 163–79.

Guyot, J. *La Somme des conciles généraux et particuliers*, 2 vols. Paris, 1868.

Hefele, C. J. *Histoire des Conciles*, Paris, I, 1907, 1–97.

Hinschius, P. *System des katholischen Kirchenrechts*, Graz, 1959.

Jedin, H. *Ecumenical Councils of the Catholic Church*, trans. E. Graf, New York, 2000.

Mansi, G. D. *Sacrorum conciliorum nova et amplissima collectio*, Paris, 1911–23.

Murphy, F. J. *Legislative Powers of the Provincial Council. A Historical Synopsis and a Commentary*, Washington, D.C., 1947.

Orlandis, J. "Funcion historica y eclesiologica de los concilios particulares," *La synodalité. La participation au gouvernement de l'Eglise. Actes du VIIe congrès international de Droit canonique, Paris, 21–8 septembre 1990*, Paris, 1992, I, 289–304.

Palazzini, P., ed., *Dizionario dei concili*, Rome, 6 vols., 1963–7.

Pesendorfer, M. *Partikulares Gesetz und partikularer Gesetzgeber im System des geltenden lateinischen Kirchenrechts*, Vienna, 1975.

Poblete, E. *The Plenary Council: A Historical Synopsis and Commentary*, Washington, D.C., 1958.

Provost, H. "Particular Councils," *Le Nouveau Code de droit canonique. Actes du Ve Congrès international de droit canonique, Ottawa 1984*, Ottawa, 1986, 537–61.

Sawicki, J. T. *Bibliographia synodorum particularium*, Vatican, 1967.

Sieben, H. J. "Les synodes particuliers vus par eux-mêmes et vus par Rome. Quelques aperçus sur le 1er millenaire," *Les Conférences épiscopales. Théologie, statut canonique, avenir* (under the editorship of H. Legrand, J. Manzanares, and A. Garcia y Garcia), Paris, 1988, 53–84.

Tanner, N. P. *The Councils of the Church: A Short History*, New York, 2001.

COUNCILS, PONTIFICAL. The pontifical councils were first established in the years following the SECOND VATICAN Council. They were intended to lighten the task of the Roman congregations in specialized areas where promotion, guidance, and reflection were considered more necessary than management and supervision. The pontifical councils go beyond the sectoral divisions of the traditional congregations, embracing instead a more global vision (including culture, interfaith relations, justice and peace, interpretation of laws, and the media.

Their activities, more often than not, reach beyond the limits of the Catholic ecclesiastical community. Although they have been declared to be on an equal juridic footing with the congregations, the pontifical councils lack the power of government usually attributed to the former, although they have an autonomous administration.

The documents of the councils are guidelines and elements for reflection. The pontifical council for the laity is the only exception to this rule, since it has real power of government over its subjects. Each council is headed by a president (a cardinal or archbishop), a secretary or vice president of (episcopal rank, or not, as the case may be), and an undersecretary (cleric or layperson). Pope JOHN PAUL II, in the apostolic constitution *Pastor bonus* of 1988, mentioned 12 pontifical councils. The number was reduced to 11 in the *motu proprio Inde a pontificatus* of 1993. However, in both documents the pope fuses the titles of the secretariats and the commissions, which were formerly created within the Roman CURIA.

The Pontifical Council for the Laity. At the end of the last ecumenical council, a *Consilium de Laicis* was created (*motu proprio Catholicam Christi Ecclesiam*, 1967). This first *consilium* was intended to relay the provisions of the ecumenical council to the apostolate of the laity, which both PIUS XI and PIUS XII had sought to promote well before Vatican II. After an experimental period of 10 years, the council was confirmed by PAUL VI (*motu proprio Apostolatus peragendi*, 1976). Pope Paul VI turned it into the Pontifical Council for the Laity. It is modeled on the Roman congregations, and, therefore, has responsibility for all matters pertaining to the power of orders and the power of jurisdiction. Pope John Paul II has kept the attributions of the council unchanged (i.e., its competence to promote and coordinate the apostolate of the laity in all its forms: individual, associative, spiritual, and temporal). International movements of laypersons are under its authority. Many laymen and women of diverse geographical and professional backgrounds are members of this council. Presidents: Cardinals Maurice Roy, 1967–76; Opilio Rossi, 1976–84; Edward Pironio, 1984–96; James Francis Stafford, since 1996.

The Pontifical Council for the Promotion of Christian Unity. This is the oldest of all the pontifical councils, dating from the beginning of the papacy of JOHN XXIII, when the secretariat for Christian unity was created (*motu proprio Superno Dei nutu*, 1960). The secretariat continued in existence during the papacy of Paul VI and was confirmed by John Paul II in 1988, despite some hesitation on the degree of autonomy that should be granted to the council. The old Secretariat became the Pontifical Council for the Promotion of Unity Among Christians. Its documents and statements must be drawn up in close cooperation with the Congregation for the Doctrine of the Faith, and with the Congregation for the Eastern Churches in matters of reconciliation with the Orthodox Churches.

The objective of the council is, in effect, the development and deepening of ecumenism, that is, religious relations among non-Catholic Christians (Orthodox, Anglican, and Protestant). A commission governing relations with Judaism also operates under its aegis, despite the fact that Jews are not Christians, but rather the heirs to a people of the Ancient Convenant in which Christians have their spiritual origins. Presidents: Cardinals Augustin Bea 1960–68; Johannes Willebrands, 1969–89; Edward Idris Cassidy, 1989–.

The Pontifical Council for the Family. This succeeded the Committee of the Family established by Paul VI in 1973. It was subsequently rejoined to the Pontifical Council for the Laity in 1976. The Pontifical Council for the Family was created by John Paul II in 1981 (*motu proprio Familia a Deo*), to defend the dignity and the natural and social rights of the family in the contemporary world. Its main task is to ensure respect for human life in the womb, and responsible procreation. There are some 40 members within the Pontifical Council for the Family,

made up of 20 Catholic couples from all over the world. Their goal is to achieve a deeper spirituality and understanding of the pastoral issues concerning marriage through study and exchanges. Presidents: Cardinals James Robert Knox, 1981–3; Edouard Gagnon, 1983–90; Alfonso Lopez Trujillo, since 1990.

The Pontifical Council for Justice and Peace. For 22 years this council bore the title of Pontifical Commission *Iustitia et pax* and was created by Paul VI (*motu proprio Catholicam Christi Ecclesiam*, 1967). The functions of the new pontifical council of 1988 are to promote justice and peace in accordance with the Gospel and the social doctrine of the Church, with respect to social relations, the development of peoples, human rights, trade in weapons, and disarmament. This dicastery lacks any competence in canonical matters, and its functions are confined to documentation, reflection, information, and training on the above-mentioned subjects. It carries out these functions in collaboration with the conferences of bishops and international Catholic and non-Catholic associations. The national commissions for justice and peace in some countries are not splinter groups of the Roman body, as they were created independently of it.

The council must obtain endorsement from the Secretariat of State before making any statement or producing publications on international political affairs. Presidents: Cardinals Maurice Roy, 1967–76; Bernardin Gantin, 1976–84; Roger Etchegaray, 1984–1998; François Xavier Nguyen Van Thuan, since 1998.

The Pontifical Council "Cor unum." Paul VI took the initiative to entrust this council with the task of demonstrating through concrete actions, the concern of the Church for the underprivileged (*Amoris officio* letter, 1971). To this end, this dicastery encourages the faithful to perform acts of evangelical charity, coordinate charitable acts, and contribute to the fairer distribution of aid to the needy throughout the world. The funds to be disbursed are given to the various dioceses, which earmark them for the most pressing needs. The pontifical council also makes timely donations in the event of natural disasters and cataclysms. It works in close coordination with the major Catholic charitable organizations (Caritas internationalis, Papal Missionary Works, French Catholic Aid, etc.). On the structural level it now shares the same president as the Pontifical Council for Justice and Peace. Presidents: Cardinals Jean Villot, 1971–79; Bernardin Gantin, 1979–84; Roger Etchegaray, 1984–96; Paul Joseph Cordes, since 1996.

The Pontifical Council of the Pastoral Care of Migrants and Itinerants. The former Pontifical Council for the Pastoral Care of Migration and Tourism, founded by Pope Paul VI (*motu proprio Apostolicae Caritatis*,

1970), was changed in 1988 by John Paul II and given its present name. Its early forerunner was the Office of Spiritual Aid to Immigrants, created by PIUS X in 1912, within the consistorial congregation. It absorbed the two higher councils for immigration and for the apostolate of the sea and sky, created by Pius XII in 1952. It also absorbed the secretariat for the apostolate of nomads, which was established by Paul VI in 1965. After a long affiliation with the Congregation for Bishops, this body achieved full autonomy as a dicastery in 1988. Its functions are to provide spiritual assistance to refugees, the exiled, immigrants, nomads, and stateless persons as well as circus performers, aliens, aviators, and sailors, and in general terms, to all persons who have to move from place to place. This has become an increasingly important phenomenon in modern society. Pro-Presidents: Emmanuele Clarizio, 1970–87; Giovanni Cheli, 1987–98; Stephen Fumio Hamao, since 1998.

The Pontifical Council of the Apostolate for Health Workers. This council was preceded by a papal commission created by John Paul II (*motu proprio dolentium Hominum*, 1985) and joined to the dicastery for laity. This new pontifical council was given the task of ministering to the sick through all the people entrusted with their care. Its tasks include the teaching of the doctrine of the Church concerning the spiritual and moral aspects of illness and the meaning of suffering, thereby contributing to better training of health care workers. To this end, the pontifical council follows with great attention all scientific discoveries and the subsequent legislative initiatives, in order to ensure that these guarantee respect for the dignity of the human being. President: Cardinal Fiorenzo Angelini, 1985–96; Javier Lozano Barragan, since 1996.

The Pontifical Council for the Interpretation of Legislative Texts. This important dicastery dates back to BENEDICT XV, who in 1917 set up the Pontifical Commission for the Authentic Interpretation of the Code of CANON LAW, which had just been promulgated. In 1963 John XXIII replaced this with another pontifical commission—the Pontifical Commission for the Revision of the Code of Canon Law. This commission functioned in harmony with the reforms approved by the Vatican II Council. Following the publication of the new codification of the Law of the Church in 1983, John Paul II renamed it the Pontifical Commission for the Authentic Interpretation of the Code of Canon Law (*motu proprio recognito iuris canonici*; 1984). He then raised it to the rank of pontifical council, with its present name, during the curial restructuring of 1988.

This council is charged with ensuring the unity and coherence of the universal ecclesiastical legislation by setting forth the authentic interpretation confirmed by papal authority. The laws understood here are those of the Latin Church as well as those contained in the new Code of Canons of the Eastern Churches (1990). The council also offers legal counsel to the Roman Curia for administrative acts (general executory decrees and instructions) that arise from it. These acts must be submitted to the council for verification of their compliance with positive law and their correct juridical formulation. The dicasteries must consult the council concerning legal doubts about the universal law. The sphere of activity of this pontifical council extends beyond Rome and covers juridic acts (general legislative or executive decrees) of the conferences of bishops and special councils by granting pontifical canonical recognition. The intervention by the council in this case is of a technical nature. It ensures that the documents produced in meetings are in conformity with the norms of law. Finally, lower-level legislators may inform the pontifical council on the conformity of their particular laws or general decrees with the universal laws of the supreme legislator. Presidents: Cardinal Rosalio José Castillo Lara, 1983–9; Archbishop Vincenzo Fagiolo, 1990–6; Julian Herranz, since 1996.

The Pontifical Council for Inter-religious Dialogue. This dicastery continues the work of the secretariat for non-Christians established by Paul VI in 1964 (*Progrediente Concilio* brief). It is intended for all believers who are not disciples of Christ. The council organizes studies, meetings, and exchanges with non-Christians to achieve mutual understanding and respect. This body has an internal commission that deals with relations with Muslims. As with ecumenical questions, the council is answerable to the Congregation of the Doctrine for the Faith, and may collaborate, when necessary, with the dicasteries for the Eastern Churches or the Evangelization of Peoples. Presidents: Cardinals Paolo Marella, 1964–73; Sergio Pignedoli, 1973–80; Archbishop Jean Jadot, 1980–4; Cardinal Francis Arinze, since 1984.

The Pontifical Council for Culture. This dicastery was established in 1982 at the wish of Pope John Paul II. It is the practical manifestation of the traditional interest of the Church in intercultural relations, an area of privileged importance ever since the beginnings of the Christian faith. This council maintains a very active, high-level presence in most international organizations and contemporary cultural forums. In 1993 it absorbed the Pontifical Council for Dialogue with Non-Believers (*motu proprio inde a pontificatus*), and is now comprised of two sections: 1) faith and culture, and 2) dialogue with the cultures. President: Cardinal Paul Poupard, since 1982.

The Pontifical Council for Social Communication. This council reflects the spirit of the conciliar decree *Inter mirifica* (1963) on the instruments of SOCIAL COMMUNICATION. It has taken on the attributions of the pontifical commission for didactic and religious cinematography, created by Pope Pius XII in 1948. In 1954 the sector for radio and television was placed under the aegis of the commission.

The council promotes spreading of the Christian message and the progress of civilization and morals by means of the media. It encourages the faithful and Church institutions to infuse the contents of newspapers, periodicals, films, radio, and television programs with the spirit of Christianity. To this end, it carefully monitors religious information circulated by the Catholic media to ensure that it faithfully reflects the majesty and doctrine of the Church. The council is the body in charge of the Vatican Filmotheque (a collection of news documentaries on the Holy See compiled since the beginnings of cinema). The council also gives authorization for filming or recording within the Vatican. While the council does not depend directly on the Secretariat of State, it must nevertheless work in close collaboration with it. Presidents: Archbishop Martin John O'Connor, 1964–73; Archbishop Andrzej Maria Deskur, 1973–84; Archbishop John Patrick Foley, since 1984.

Joel-Benoit d'Onorio

Bibliography

Coppa, G. "Riflessioni sulla fisionomia dei Pontifici Consigli," *L'Osservatore Romano*, 27 October 1988.

d'Onorio, J. B. *Le Pape et le gouvernement de l'Eglise*, Paris, 1992.

Mauro, T. "I Consigli: finalità, organizzazione e natura," *La Curia Romana nella Cost. Ap. Pastor bonus.* Vatican, 1990.

COUNTER REFORMATION. See Reform, Catholic.

COURT, PAPAL. The word "court" in the history of the papacy has been understood in various ways, depending on the era. The Latin expression, "Curia Romana," which from the 13th century denoted all the services available to the pope for his spiritual and temporal administration, was translated very early as "Court of Rome." This expression remained in use until the 18th century, by which time it had acquired a negative connotation, due to the influence of a number of publications, notably those inspired by the Jansenists, who were hostile to Roman authority. The Jansenists insisted there be a clear distinction between the temporal and ecclesiastical courts, and they asserted that the temporal court—which they called the Court of Rome (traditionally all papal power was covered by the expression)—should in no way be confused with the principle of spiritual authority that attached to the person of the successor of St. Peter.

By the 19th century, "Court of Rome" was no longer in use; instead, "Roman Curia" was used to describe all the people and services that helped the pope carry out his spiritual ministry. Due in part to the pressure of events, but also in part to the reforms of PIUS IX, including his efforts to clarify a few terms, it became possible to distinguish between the Curia and the government of the PAPAL STATES. These were represented as two separate entities in the Roman budget. As a result, in 1870 the Italian government, which had deprived the pope of his states, and consequently of his source of income for maintaining the Curia and the APOSTOLIC PALACE, had no difficulty in evaluating the annual amount of the subsidy that it intended to give the Holy See under the so-called Law of Guarantees. This amount was allocated solely to the Holy See in accordance with its spiritual role.

Yet the word "court" had not entirely disappeared from use. From the 16th century, the expression "papal court" (*corte pontificia*) had been used to designate the pope's entourage when he appeared at public events. In practice, the words PAPAL FAMILY and court were often used interchangeably, with the only difference being that the word "court" described the members of the pope's closest circle. From 1716 the expression "*camera secreta*" began to appear in some public documents. This term meant secret chamber or antechamber, and described the ordinary train of people who accompanied the pope when he moved about within Rome. Over time, the word "court" came to be associated with the word "antechamber," especially following the pontificate of Pius IX, when the rules of the antechamber became firmly established. At the time of the last reform of the papal family (28 March 1968), the antechamber still included the majordomo, the chamberlain, the secret chaplain, the pope's auditor, the participating secret chamberlains (cupbearer, embassy secretary, master of the wardrobe), the participating secret chamberlains of the cape and the sword (master of the Sacred Hospice, quartermaster, grand equerry, postmaster general, the exempt of the noble guard, colonel of the SWISS GUARD), and a whole series of attachés and court ushers whose titles and names have now become quite picturesque. Apart from the specific functions of each of its members (although some of these functions had become obsolete), the members of the antechamber stationed themselves in the successive rooms that led to the one in which the pope was seated. This was done according to a scrupulously observed order of precedence. Under the supervision of the majordomo and the chamberlain, the court provided an ordinary daily service as well as a special service for state visits, presentation of credentials, official visits, etc. The *Motu proprio Pontificalis domus* (28 March 1968) put an end to this, relacing it with a very scaled-down ordinary service, consisting of two prelates (who succeeded the participating secret chamberlains) and the ushers, known as the *addetti* of the antechamber. For official audiences the prefect of the pontifical house, the GENTLEMEN OF HIS HOLINESS, and the Swiss Guard also participated.

François-Charles Uginet

Bibliography

Moroni, G. *Dizionario di erudizione storico-ecclesiastica,* vol. VII, Venice, 1841, 18–20; vol. XVII, Venice, 1842, 296–8; vol. XXIII, Venice, 1844, 59–126.

CROSS, PROCESSIONAL, PAPAL. From the early Middle Ages, a cross preceded the Roman pontiff on his way to celebrate mass in the basilicas or in churches customarily designated as stations. In the ninth century, Charlemagne sent a cross to LEO III, which was decorated with hyacinths and carried during papal processions. The cross of PASCHAL I, with its enameled decorations, is on display at the VATICAN MUSEUM. INNOCENT III ordered that crosses be placed on altars. From 1215, the cross given to the *a latere* legates was carried in front of them to denote their papal mission. Patriarchs and archbishops enjoyed the same privilege; the patriarchs were given a cross with two crosspieces, similar to those which may still be found in some armories. Today, at St. Peter's in Rome, the cross still precedes the papal procession, with the figure of Christ turned toward the pontiff, as required by the rite.

Marc Dykmans

Bibliography

Andrieu, M. *Ordines Romani,* III, 1951, 70–1, 241–143 (under "croix stationale et papale").

Battandier, A. "La Croix papale," *Annuaire pontifical catholique,* 11 (1908), 78–83.

Ciampini, I. *Investigatio . . . de cruce stationali,* Rome, 1694. Opera II, 1747, 38–49.

"Croce," *EC,* 4, 1950, 951–81.

"Croce," in G. Moroni, *Dizionario di erudizione storico-ecclesiastica,* 18; 1843; 226–66.

"Croix," *DACL,* 3, 2, 1914, 3045–131.

"Croix papale," (M. Noirot), "croix pectorale" (R. Lesage), *Catholicisme,* 3, 1952, 335–6.

"Croix pectorale et processionnelle," *DDC,* 4, 1949, 841–5.

"Cross," *Encyclopedia of Religion,* 4, 1986, 155–66.

"Cross," *NCE,* 4, 1966, 473–9.

Fivizzani, *De ritu crucis Romano pontifici praeferendae,* Rome, 1592.

Heim, B. B. *Coutumes et droit héraldiques,* Paris, 1949, (*Heraldry in the Catholic Church,* 1981).

"Kreuz," *LTK,* 6, 1961, 605–17.

Lexikon der Christlichen Ikonographie, 2, 1970, 562, 677–95.

Wasner, F. "XVth Century Texts . . . of the Papal 'Legatus a latere,' *Traditio,* 14 (1958), 295 ff.

CRUSADES. URBAN II was the one who, at the end of the Council of Clermont, established the first link between the tradition of a PILGRIMAGE to the holy places of Syria and Palestine and the practice of a holy war, from which the idea of the crusades originated. However, there were other initiatives prior to the papacy of Urban II that prepared the ground for the declaration of 1095. In 1063 ALEXANDER II granted Christian warriors fighting the Moors in Spain remission from the temporal punishment they incurred for their sins. With the advent of GREGORY VII and the definition of *militia christi,* the holy war became a central theme of papal policy. After the disaster suffered by the Byzantines at Manzikert (1071), the pope promised eternal reward to those who would give their life to free their eastern brothers and defend the Christian faith. Finally, in 1089 Urban II offered those willing to rebuild the church of Tarragona, destroyed by the Moors, the same indulgence as that granted to people going on pilgrimage to Jerusalem.

Urban II's message of November 1095 summarized the prevailing ideas and practices of his time. He defined the planned Crusade as the "way of God" (Via Dei)—a military undertaking justified by the need to free the Eastern Churches from oppression and to rescue the city of Jerusalem, which had fallen into servitude. At the Council of Clermont (27 November 1095), the pope advocated the Crusade, comparing it to a pilgrimage. The objective was Jerusalem, the center of the world and patrimony of Christ. He introduced the idea of the vow of a crusade, which could be satisfied only by arrival in the Holy Land. He extended the protection of the Church to the property of those making the journey and advised them to carry a cross, a sign of unity and a very important theme in the devotion of the time. To those participating in the Crusade as well as those fighting the Moors in Spain he granted remission from earthly punishments imposed by the Church on sinners. This appeal by Urban II was for the most part a traditional one, but there were also some innovative aspects. For the first time, a pope, in the name of Christ, declared a holy war. The message was addressed especially to the French knights, whose aspirations were well known to the pope. Monks and popular preachers (such as Peter the Hermit), who ensured a much wider audience than the pope could expect, relayed his appeal to the public. The pope placed the Holy See at the very heart of the process of organizing the Crusade. He himself defined the spiritual and material advantages to participants; his LEGATE accompanied the troops and established the objectives in accordance with the pontiff. The theological rewriting of the themes of the crusade by monastic chroniclers who were influenced by the often traumatic experiences of the crusaders came afterward.

During the 12th century, the papacy, with the help of St. Bernard, would try to give a solid theological and legal basis to the Crusade. The BULL, *Quantum praedecessores*, of 1 December 1145 became, in its form and content, the model of future crusade bulls. In it, EUGENE III exhorted Western Christendom to avenge the capture of Edessa. The pope claimed the exclusive right to lead the expedition, in the name of the tradition of the Church and on behalf of the initiatives of the predecessors. The fall of Edessa was a punishment for the sins of Christians. The sovereigns and the great were called upon to fight for the Church in the East. For the first time, "crusade privileges" were offered to participants. On the material level, the Church protected the families and property of crusaders, ordered deferment of the repayment of debt, and canceled payment of interest during the Crusade. On a spiritual level, Eugene III implemented the new doctrine of the "treasure of merits," and promised the remission of temporal punishment for sins. Anyone who enrolled in the army of the Crusade and showed sincere contrition was exempt from the punishment inflicted by the Church on sinners. However, at the same time, under the influence of St. Bernard, the Crusade became an enterprise for the salvation of souls. The main objective of the Holy Land became secondary to an intensive spiritual preparation, which restored the sinner to divine grace. In this way, the Crusade became exposed to possible deviations from the main purpose, since to gain greater effectiveness, the participation of warriors and sovereigns was encouraged more than that of ordinary people.

The Hattin disaster of 14 July 1187, and the capture of Jerusalem by Saladin (2 October 1187), forced the pope to take the initiative once more. On 29 October 1187, the newly elected GREGORY VIII angrily issued a bull, *Audita tremendi*, which attributed the failure of the Franks in the Holy Land to the collective sins of the Christian world. He called upon the latter to repent, and observe a strict fast, while promising all those who would take up the cross the usual spiritual and material privileges. To encourage the Crusade, he called for a seven-year truce among the various European powers, an appeal that was rather unrealistic. He entrusted the task of preaching the Crusade north of the Alps to the archbishop of Tyre and the cardinal legate, Henry of Albano. He also requested that they secure the participation of the kings of France and England in the expedition. Finally he decreed that a 10 percent tax be imposed on all income and property (the Saladine tithe), from which only future participants in the Crusade would be exempt. However, neither Gregory VIII nor his successor, CLEMENT III, could intervene directly in leading the 3rd Crusade, which was entirely led by three sovereigns—Frederick I Barbarossa, Philip Augustus, and Richard the Lion-Hearted. National and

monarchic concerns took precedence over the general interests of Christianity as defined by the popes.

INNOCENT III reacted against this trend from the time of his election in January 1198. He felt that he was invested with a power higher than that of the secular leaders: to lead a crusade and rebuild the kingdom of Jerusalem destroyed in 1187. However, he forgot that the cooperation of the sovereigns was necessary for financing and conducting the Crusade. In 1198 the pope launched a new crusade, with a special request for help from the Italian maritime republics and the French nobility, to whom he sent Pietro di Capua, the cardinal legate. He threw his support behind the preaching of a country priest, Foulques of Neuilly, who exhorted penitence, attacked lust and usury, and built up a Crusade treasury with the guarantee of the religious authorities. In 1199 despite vigorous resistance from the Cistercians, the pope introduced a crusade tax of one-fortieth of ecclesiastical income.

Innocent III does not appear to have intervened in the negotiations between the French barons and the Venetians for the organization of the sea passage of the Crusaders. On the other hand, his stance on the diversion toward Constantinople was ambiguous. He excommunicated the crusaders who had taken control of the Christian town of Zara. He then lifted the excommunication ban in favor of the Franks and Germans, without forbidding them from collaborating with the Venetians. Even though he was aware of the intentions of the young Byzantine prince Alexis IV, he did not denounce the agreement made by the latter with the crusaders to help him recover his throne. After the capture of Constantinople by the Latins, he accepted the fait accompli. Even while he deplored the horrors committed by the Westerners, he welcomed the newly reestablished Christian unity. The pope does not appear to have taken the full measure of the divisions which the pillage of Constantinople would cause to eastern Christendom, nor the deleterious effect on the spirit of the crusade, which no longer strove for the liberation of the Holy Land.

In March 1208, the pope for the first time called for a crusade against heretics, the Cathars and their protector, the count of Toulouse, Raymond VI. The actions of Simon de Montfort and the barons of northern France, who were avid to seize the property of the heretics, overcame him. In the council of LATERAN IV (1215), he was obliged to accept the relinquishment of the count of Toulouse to the benefit of the leader of the Crusade.

In spite of the failures and this last distortion of the objectives of the crusade, Innocent III did not give up his efforts to mobilize all of Christendom. In 1213 in his bull *Quia major*, he launched a campaign for a new crusade, a sort of mass movement of Christians saying this should be an ideal occasion for sacrifice and martyrdom, in imitation of Jesus Christ. The legate, Robert de Courgon, called for fasting, for the giving of alms, and contrition. The fourth Lateran Council, which met in November 1215, established the details of the project in the constitution *Ad liberandam*, a veritable synthesis of the papal doctrine on the crusade, before the canonist Hostiensis gave a complete analysis of it in the *Summa aurea*, around 1250. The policy of Innocent III was based on three series of measures. The pope, by making the vow to undertake a crusade a binding one, guaranteed the spiritual advantages offered to the crusaders. He granted a plenary INDULGENCE to all who would go on the next crusade at their own expense, at the expense of third parties, or as their substitutes. The indulgence was also extended to anyone contributing materially to the expedition, by giving a sum of money accompanied by the wish to take up the cross. Those who furnished ships to transport crusaders, or participated in their construction also benefited from the indulgence. This wide-ranging extension of the plenary indulgence, however, posed the risk of undermining the effective recruitment of volunteers. It also risked turning monetary contributions into the equivalent of personal services, which up until then had been necessary for obtaining the indulgence of the crusade. The Lateran Council was concerned also by the material advantages offered to the crusaders: subsidies, privileges, protection, and immunity. The Roman CURIA made a contribution of thirty thousand silver livres and for three years imposed a tax of one-twentieth on all ecclesiastical revenues and one-tenth of that of the pope and the cardinals. All crusaders were exempted from paying taxes and protected by the Holy See until their return, especially against the extortion of usurers. Also, the papacy sought to remove obstacles that could undermine the success of the expedition. It banned the holding of tournaments for three years, imposed a general peace of four years on the nobility, and prohibited on pain of excommunication all maritime traffic with the Saracens. Pirates were threatened with severe penalties. While the conciliary constitution fixed the date of the assembling of the army for June 1217 in the ports of southern Italy, it is evasive about its destination and the command which would be given to it.

The council of 1215 therefore established a veritable code for the crusade, which would be reflected in the conciliary decrees of 1245 and 1274. The text contained in embryonic form all subsequent papal policies, some of which would be dangerously distorted. First, by extending the indulgence, the pope offered the crusaders maximum advantages for minimum effort. The commutation and dispensation from crusade vows opened the door to all sorts of abuses for the financial administration of the Curia and the Church. Second, by placing the Saracens and the Western heretics on the same footing, and by claiming that the enemies of the pope were also enemies of the Church, the pope lost sight of the original objective of the crusade, thus justifying in advance any deviations from the undertaking.

Innocent III did everything in his power to spread the call of the crusade and to erase the memory of previous failures. He hoped for a general mobilization of Christian Europe, which had been spiritually prepared by prayer and processions. He died in July 1216, while preparations for a crusade were under way. His successor, HONORIUS III, pursued the same policies as Innocent III. Troops were led to Acre in autumn 1217 and undertook the conquest of Egypt. In 1218 the arrival of the papal legate, the Spanish cardinal Pelagius, stirred up trouble among the crusaders. Pelagius claimed the right to the military command of the army and opposed any agreement with the sultan Malik al-Kamil. The capitulation of the crusaders in 1221 reflected negatively on the pope and his legate, who were accused of being irresponsible. For the pope, the only hope seemed to lie with the emperor Fredrick II, who had taken up the cross in 1215. Honorius III appealed to him for help in 1222. The preparations were so slow that GREGORY IX, who had been elected in 1227, got impatient and excommunicated Frederick. It was therefore an excommunicated emperor who in June 1228 undertook the Crusade and concluded the treaty of Jaffa with the sultan, which returned Jerusalem to the Christians without a drop of blood being spilled. The pope could not forgive this diplomatic success by an emperor who had broken relations with the Church. The papacy would now use the crusade as a weapon to strengthen its political authority and protect the PAPAL STATES.

Innocent III was the first pope to grant the indulgence of the crusade to those who fought against an enemy of the papacy. More specifically, it was granted for fighting against Markward d'Anweiler, a seneschal of the empire, who in 1199 occupied vast territories of the Kingdom of Sicily. Repeatedly in the course of the 13th century, the papacy ordered a crusade to preserve its security and independence, which implied direct control over central Italy and suzerainty over the Kingdom of Sicily. Taxes on the income of the clergy ensured the financing of the armies that were called up on those occasions. The theory of ecclesiastical forfeiture allowed the pope to incite a prince faithful to the church to seize territory from another prince who was an enemy of Rome and who had been denounced as a heretic.

The struggle of the papacy against Frederick II and the Hohenstaufens therefore became a crusade promoted by the pontiffs. For the first time, in 1240, when the emperor threatened Rome, Gregory IX promised the faithful the same indulgences as those granted to the defenders of the Holy Land. His successor INNOCENT IV, who had Frederick II deposed at the Council of Lyon (1245), turned the war against the emperor into a real crusade in Germany and the Papal States. His call to crusade gained him enough money to pay the troops. But the protests of the Germanic clergy and the competition from the crusade of Louis IX, encouraged but not directed by the Holy See, forced the pope to moderate his stance.

After Frederick II died in 1250, the struggle continued against his heirs. Innocent IV called for a crusade against Manfred and concerned himself with finding a successor in the Kingdom of Sicily, which had been offered to the English princes. Finally, URBAN IV (1261–4) turned toward the Capetian kingdom and treated the settlement of the Sicilian question like an overseas crusade. He proposed that Charles of Anjou, the brother of Louis IX, head an expedition against Manfred. He would thus benefit from all the crusade privileges, be eligible to receive a tenth of the income of the French clergy for three years, and obtain the financial aid of Tuscan bankers. A conquered Sicily would become a vassal state of the Holy See. The agreement was secured by CLEMENT IV in April 1265. Charles of Anjou set out, strengthened by the spiritual and financial support of the pope, and defeated Manfred's troops at Benevento in February 1266. In August 1268 he defeated the army of the last of the Hohenstaufens, Conradin, at Tagliacozzo.

The "political" crusades quickly gained ground and extended beyond Italy. The expansionism of Charles of Anjou toward the Balkans and the Byzantine Empire was, in part, supported by the papacy. The Tunisian crusade and the policy for the union of the Church by GREGORY X and NICHOLAS III (Second Council of Lyon, 1274) had put a brake on Charles of Anjou's expansionist plans. However, in 1281 he received the unqualified support of the Holy See. MARTIN IV, a French pope, decreed a crusade against the infidel Michael VIII Palaeologus, who had gone into hiding after the complete union of the Churches had been achieved. The *basileus* was saved by the insurrection known as the Sicilian Vespers, on 30 March 1282, no doubt with the help of Manfred's son-in-law, Peter III of Aragon, and Byzantine gold. In the aftermath of the Sicilian affair, Martin IV excommunicated the king of Aragon, took away his kingdom, and offered it as a fiefdom to Charles of Valois, the second son of Philip III of France. A crusade was organized against Aragon, but the Capetian armies were unsuccessful in their efforts.

At that time, the papacy was moved to take new action, due to the distress prevailing in the Holy Land. Gregory X, who had been elected in 1271, made plans for a new crusade. The texts criticized the practice of granting indulgences and the misuse of the crusade taxes. The Second Council of Lyon (1274), through its *Constitutiones pro zelo fidei*, stressed that all believers had an obligation to come to the aid of the Holy Land. It listed a whole series of financial measures designed to facilitate the undertaking. But the impact of the conciliar constitutions diminished as civil society became increasingly hostile to the supremacy of the papacy. It no longer considered the crusade an appropriate response to the problems of the states of Syria and Palestine, but rather thought of it as a simple political expedient serving the interests of the papacy.

Papal intervention in the crusade did not cease in 1291, with the taking of Acre by the Mamluks, a move that dealt a fatal blow to the Eastern Christian states. In the course of the 14th century, crusade plans were elaborated by people closely associated with the papacy, which lent its support to a number of expeditions against the Muslim states in the Near East. The idea of collaboration with the Mongols also formed the basis of the external policy of the Holy See. Fidenzio of Padua, adviser to NICHOLAS IV (1288–92), argued in favor of a blockade of the Mamluk empire in his *Liber recuperationis Terrae Sanctae*. Marino Sanudo Torcello dedicated his *Liber Secretorum fidelium crucis* to CLEMENT V. In it, he suggested that a general ban be placed on trade with the Saracens. In the first half of the fourteenth century, the papacy did try to implement it, with the canonic sanctions. The advance of the Ottomans led the Holy See to encourage the formation of leagues among the Christian forces and to give its support to expeditions against the TURKS. In 1343 CLEMENT VI joined forces with Venice, the king of Cyprus, and the Hospitalers in an Aegean crusade ending in Smyrna, which remained in Christian hands until 1402. The "Crusades" of the dauphin Humbert II of Viennois to the Aegean Sea (1346), of Peter I, king of Cyprus against Alexandria (1365), and of Amadeus VI of Savoy who went to the aid of his cousin the *basileus* John V Palaeologus (1366), were all carried out with the blessings of the papacy. Other expeditions included that of Louis II of Bourbon against the king of Tunisia (1390) and the French and Burgundian knights against Bayazid I (Nicopolis, 1396). All these crusades received moral support with plenary indulgence granted to participants by the papacy.

After the Union Council of Florence, Eugene IV received financial donations and volunteers to prepare a crusade to go to the aid of Constantinople.

The papal legate Giuliano Cesarini was one of the victims of the rout inflicted on the crusading army by the Turks at Varna, in 1444. After Constantinople fell in 1453, PIUS II, in a final attempt, decided in 1463 to personally lead a crusade against the Turks. He was assured of the help of Venice and Hungary. However, his death in Ancona the following year ended the project. Despite the efforts of some committed pontiffs and their propagandists, the crusade had long ceased to be a "general stepping stone" used by Christendom to reconquer the holy places. Now crusaders were reduced to limited expeditions to halt the expansion of the Ottoman Empire, and served only to increase the bitterness of the Greeks toward the West, which was incapable of saving their empire.

By turning away from the real objectives of the crusades and by developing the practice of indulgences and the release of vows for fiscal purposes, the papacy caused the crusades to lose all credibility. For several decades prior to that, they had succeeded in achieving the unity of Christendom under the aegis of the Holy See.

Michel Balard

Bibliography

Alphandery, P., and Dupront, A. *La Chrétienté et l'idée de croisade*, Paris, 1954–9, 2 vols.

Atiya, A. S. *The Crusade in the Later Middle Ages*, London, 1938.

Balard, M. *Les Croisades*, Paris, 1988.

Becker, A. *Papst Urban II (1088–1099), II, Der Papst, die griechische Christenheit und der Kreuzzug*, Stuttgart, 1988.

Brundage, J. A. *Medieval Canon Law and the Crusader*, Madison-Milwaukee, Wis., 1969.

Cole, P. J. *The Preaching of the Crusades to the Holy Land, 1095–1270*, Cambridge, Mass., 1991.

Cowdrey, H. E. J. *Popes, monks, and crusaders*, London, 1984.

Forey, A. J. "The military orders and holy war against Christians in the thirteenth century," *English Historical Review*, 104 (Jan 1989), 1–24.

Gill, J. "Innocent III and the Greeks: Agressor or Apostle?," in *Relations between East and West in the Middle Ages*, ed. D. Baker, Edinburgh, 1973, 95–108.

Housley, N. *The Italian Crusades. The Papal-Angevin Alliance and the Crusades Against Christian Lay Powers, 1254–1343*, Oxford, 1982.

Housley, N. *The Avignon Papacy and the Crusades, 1305–1378*, Oxford, 1986.

Housley, N. "Pope Clement V and the Crusades of 1309–10," *Journal of Medieval History*, 8 (1982), 29–43.

Kedar, B. Z. *Crusade and Mission. European Approaches Toward the Muslims*, Princeton, N.J., 1984.

Mayer, H. E. *The Crusades*, Oxford, 1988.

Powell, J. M. *Anatomy of a Crusade, 1213–1221*, Philadelphia, 1986.

Purcell, M. *Papal Crusading Policy 1244–1291*, Leiden, 1975.

Queller, D. E. *The Fourth Crusade. The Conquest of Constantinople 1201–1204*, Philadelphia, 1977.

Richard, J. *L'Esprit de la croisade*, Paris, 1969.

Richard, J. *La Papauté et les missions d'Orient au Moyen Age (XIIIe–XVes.)*, Rome, 1977.

Riley-Smith, L. and J. *The Crusaders: Idea and Reality, 1095–1274*, London, 1981.

Riley-Smith, J. *The First Crusade and the Idea of Crusading*, London, 1986.

Rousset, P. *Histoire d'une idéologie. La croisade*, Lausanne, 1983.

Russell, F. H. *The Just War in the Middle Ages*, Cambridge, 1975.

Schein, S. *Fideles Crucis: Europe, the Papacy and the Crusades, 1274–1314*, Oxford, 1990.

Setton, K. M., ed. *A History of the Crusades*, Madison, Wis., 1955–89, 6 vols.

Setton, K. M. *The Papacy and the Levant (1204–1571)*, 2 vols., Philadelphia, 1976–8.

Siberry, E. *Criticism of Crusading, 1095–1274*, Oxford, 1985.

Villey, M. *La Croisade, Essai sur la formation d'une théorie juridique*, Paris, 1942.

CULTS, EASTERN. In the Mediterranean, which from the third century B.C. became increasingly unified under the aegis of Rome, traces of the two fundamental cultures of the region—Greek and Latin—have always remained. From the time of Constantine these two cultures were forcefully reaffirmed in the *pars Orientalis* (Constantinople) and the *pars Occidentis* (Rome). Military campaigns and trading relations placed the Romans in contact with the eastern religions, and brought the Anatolian, Syrian, Egyptian, and Persian cults to Rome, Italy, and all the western provinces. To varying degrees these left their mark on the religious life of the West.

The earliest cult officially introduced into Italy was that of Cybele, the Great Mother of gods, which had come from Pessinus (Phrygia) during the second Punic war. The presence of the Carthaginian armies in Italy, the defeats of their legions, and the dangers that threatened their city, led the Romans to believe that their gods had abandoned them. They therefore turned toward Cybele, who, from her sanctuary on Mount Ida, reigned over Troy, from where their ancestor Aeneas, had come. The *boetylus* or sacred stone of Cybele was brought to Rome in April 204 B.C., and since the goddess had been naturalized a Roman, the stone was placed in the Palatine, the cradle of the *Urbs*. However, the clergy of the cult of Cybele—Gallic eunuchs, and a priest and priestess from Phrygia—were confined to the sanctuary, which they left once a year, at the end of March, to perform the washing of the idol and other sacred objects in the Almo, a tributary of the Tiber. The washing was followed in April by a colorful and noisy procession in the streets of Rome, the Megalensia.

Under the empire, the cult of Cybele, which had been reformed by Claudius and Antoninus, was placed at the service of the sovereign. From then on the taurobolium, the bloody sacrifice of a bull, was performed for the salvation of the emperor and the imperial family. The oldest known taurobolium was held in A.D. 160 in Lyon, where there was an eastern community. It is unclear whether or not there is a link between the Mithraic cult and the persecution of 177. From the reign of Antoninus Pius (138–161), the taurobolium, which had previously taken place in the port of Ostia, was performed in a sanctuary (*phrygianum*) established in front of the site on which St. Peter's church now stands. From then on, the sanctuary became the most sacred place of the cult. The Great Mother, described as *salutaris*, was a sort of Our Lady of Salvation. The person for whom the taurobolium was performed was believed to be reborn to a new life, regenerated for another twenty years. The cult of Cybele and young Attis, who is said to have lost his virility as a result of his exclusive attachment to the goddess, and who was later the prototype of her priests, the Galli—spread rapidly between the second and third centuries A.D. The cult became especially popular in port cities, for example, Leptis Magna, in Tripolitana, from 72. In Gaul the cult was well entrenched in Lyon, Lectoure, and Die. It was popular in Carthage in the fourth century when St. Augustine (in his *City of God*, VII, 26) described the eunuchs during the Megalensia: "You could still see them yesterday, their hair damp with perfume with their painted faces and languid limbs, wandering around the squares and streets of Carthage with their effeminate walk, asking the passersby for money to pay for their shameful lifestyle."

During the same period, at Autun, a statue of Cybele was carried aloft during a springtime procession. This tribute to the regeneration of nature and mankind became in the fourth century one of the symbols of pagan reaction. The emperor Julian wrote a discourse on the Mother of the Gods, which he called *Virgin*. The pagan aristocracy gave many testimonies of their attachment to the goddess. Cybele was called the all-powerful sovereign (*omnipotens*) while Attis was referred to as "saint." In 394 Theodosius I banned public worship of Cybele, but it survived in different forms.

The cult of Isis was no less widespread. From Alexandria, where she was venerated along with Serapis and the sun-god Horus (Harpocrates), she had known great popularity in the Hellenic world, especially in the port cities. From the end of the Republican period, Isis and Serapis were worshiped at Pozzuoli (and before A.D. 105 at Pompei, then at Ostia). Isis was the protectress of sea trade, and reigned over the sea. She was Pelagia, Our Lady of the Waves. In Rome, the altars and private chapels built during the middle of the first century A.D. attest to her worship. She was officially worshiped on the Campus Martius (Plain of Mars) where in 43 B.C. the triumvir of Antony, Octavian, and Lepidus dedicated a sanctuary to her. The sanctuary, the *Iseum*, was destroyed under Tiberius but rebuilt by Caligula, who had a great interest in Egyptian cults, as did Nero, who worshiped the sun god (Ra). From the time of the Flavians—in A.D. 69 Vespasian received a sort of official consecration from Serapis in Alexandria—the cult of Isis spread everywhere in the West. This wide dissemination was achieved with the help of some emperors, such as Hadrian and Caracalla. Isis was honored in litanies as the mistress of heaven and earth, the inventor of writing, the teacher of laws, and mistress of the elements. She was however, first and foremost, mistress of the sea. Special homage was paid to her in the spring, when the Mediterranean was opened for navigation on March 5 (*Navigiuim Isisdis*), and again in the autumn, for the "discovery of Osiris" (*Inventio Osiris*), the god of the Nile who made the seedlings grow. This latter celebration took place on November 3. In *Metamorphoses* Apuleius of Madaura described the procession that accompanied the goddess to the sea, and threw some light on the preliminary initiation rites. He praised the powers of Isis who is equated with all the great goddesses of antiquity. It is because of her great power that she was called "Myrionyme," or goddess of a thousand names.

One of the characteristics of the cult of Isis was its preoccupation with physical and moral purity. There were many purification sites, and there was a form of public confession of sins and penitence. These preceded initiation rites and were also a part of daily services, which, together with the songs and psalmodies, included cleaning and contemplation of the statue representing the goddess. Abstinence was required from the candidates to initiation.

In the 4th century, despite imperial antipagan laws, the Alexandrian cults remained popular. Julian publicly proclaimed his preference for Serapis, Helios, the great and very holy god, and even swore by the great Serapis. While the followers of Isis and Serapis were persecuted in Egypt, and the Serapeum of Alexandria, the center of the serapist faith, was destroyed at the end of the 4th century, there were still worshippers of Isis in scholarly circles at the end of the 5th century. In Thebais, Rome, and its surrounding regions, the cult of Isis survived in the 6th century. In 417 the Hilaries of Osiris were still being celebrated at Faleri (Civita Castellana). And does not the image of Isis feeding the infant Horus survive in the iconography of the Virgin and Child?

Juvenal, in his *Satires*, III, 62, stated, "The Oront of Syria has flowed into the Tiber." This symbolized the importation into Rome of many cults that had come from Syria with the intensive development of trade (often in the hand of Syrians), and the constant movement of legions and auxiliary troops. Among these cults was Dea Syria, the goddess Atargatis of Hierapolis, the "sacred city," where she was venerated together with Hadad as goddess of water and fertility in a sumptuous temple described by Lucian in *Of the Syrian Goddess*. In the West, she had a following only among the eastern population. Her priests were also Gallos. As a mothergoddess, she formed part of the Baalbek (Heliopolis) triad, consisting of Jupiter Heliopolitan (Hadad), who had priority, Venus Heliopolitan (Dea Syria), and a son-god who was a protector of children. The father-god was depicted standing upright, wearing a sheathlike garment decorated with planetary symbols. The mother-goddess was depicted enthroned between sphinxes or bulls. The sun, moon, and planetary symbols were important features in the decor. The temple at Baalbek was one of the largest and most luxurious in the world, containing idols that were carried in procession. In 579 these gods still had a local following.

The cult of Jupiter Dolichenus came to the West from Doliche in Commagene. The god was always represented wearing a breastplate and brandishing a double axe and thunderbolt, standing on a bull, while his Dolichenian Juno stood on a doe. Jupiter Dolichenus, the god of lightning, was especially the god of Syrian soldiers. There was a temple dedicated to the Dolichenian gods (Dolecheneum) in Rome, on the Aventine.

From Tyre came the god Melquart, who had been introduced into the Boarium forum in Rome by Phoenician merchants. He was venerated under the name Hercules at the Ara maxima. He was especially popular at Gades (Cádiz), where pilgrims, including the emperor Trajan, visited his temple. Also Baal of Damas was venerated at Pozzuoli, and Baal of Gaza at Ostia. The Palmyrenian gods were the best represented among the local Baalim: Iarhibaal (sun), Aglibaal (moon), and Malakbel (angel of Bek). Baal-shamin, god of sky and thunder, sometimes preceded them. The Palmyrenian soldiers in the border armies honored them. Finally mention must be made of the god of Emesa (Homs), who was worshipped at the top of a mountain. Elah-Gabal was the god of the mountain and the high priests of this cult came from a local family (Julia Domna, the wife of Septimius Severus, also came from this family). Bassianus, the grandnephew of Julia Domna, became emperor under the name Elagabalus. Upon his arrival in Rome in 218, he had an *Elagabalium* constructed on the Palatine, on the site where the church of St. Sebastian stands today.

A mysterious sanctuary was constructed on the Janiculum. It was called the Syrian sanctuary but was actually made up of elements of different cults, perhaps built for the followers of a very syncretic paganism.

Mithra, a god of Iranian origin, deserves a special mention here. Iran was a country deeply influenced by Zoroastrian dualism, which opposed Good (represented by the god Ahuramazda) and Evil (represented by Ahriman). It was later influenced by Chaldean astrology, and Mithra became the represenative of the sun (*Sol invictus*) and the hero of the following myth: At the end of a hunt, he captured a bull, which was at once the symbol of evil and of reproductive power. He killed it and thus fertilized the earth. After partaking of a meal with Sol, with whom he made a commitment of faith (by the *dexioses* or *dextrarum iunctio*), he was taken into the sky by Sol.

The cult to Mithra was well established on the southwest coast of Asia Minor, and was introduced into Italy by Cilician pirates who had been defeated by Pompey and taken prisoner. However, the presence of the cult was not recorded in Rome until the end of the first century A.D. and did not really spread until the 2nd and 3rd centuries. There were about one hundred *mithraea* in Rome and some thirty in Ostia. It was a religion that worshipped a young god, reputed to be invincible (as the sun), and a guarantor of oaths and of sworn faith, of contracts and of friendship. Mithraism was transformed from a religion of men, whose communities were blessed by Mithra, to a religion of soldiers, and as such spread in the garrison towns and the border regions. It subsequently reached civilians, who were attracted by its doctrine, its strict morals, and its liturgy full of symbolism. It spread everywhere in the western provinces. There were normally twenty to forty initiates living within a Mithraic community, under the guidance of a pater. There were seven initiates who wore clothing reflecting their varying degrees of initiation, and who participated in sacrifices and common meals among "brothers" (*fratres*). The meals and ceremonies took place in vaulted grottos or underground crypts (*spelaea*), which were sometimes painted sky blue and decorated with stars. These *mithraea* had bench-beds that were also used for communal meals. In the background, a bas-relief depicted the taurochtony of Mithra. This scene was often flanked by busts of the sun and moon, as well as by two persons dressed as Persians, one holding up a torch (Cautès) and the other lowering it (Cautopatès); they symbolized the light of the day and night.

According to Joseph-Ernest Renan, this religion of oath and fraternal cooperation offered some competition to Christianity. There may possibly have been some liturgical borrowings. However, there were great differences between Mithraism and Christianity. The former was a religion of creation and incarnation. (Mithra was depicted as being born from a stone—*petrogenitus*.) It was not, as is Christianity, a religion of resurrection and salvation. The salvation of the Mithraists was temporal and governed by a code of good conduct.

The fact remains that eastern cults did have an influence on the development of religious sentiment. More than the coldly ritualistic Greco-Roman religion, they attracted followers with their more sensual liturgy and communal practices, their cosmology, and the answers which they strove to provide concerning the origin of the world and the destiny of humanity. Their clerics were powerful, well-organized, and sometimes learned men. Some of them maintained in their followers the good hope of happiness—as the high priest of Isis said to Lucius, "You have now reached the port of Repose" (Apuleius, *Metamorphoses*, XI, 15, 1).

The eastern cults were all centered around a sovereign divinity, which was cosmic and omnipotent. They represented a henotheism in opposition to the old polytheism, and might have helped pave the way for Christian monotheism, but ultimately they undoubtedly constituted an obstacle. This helps explain the virulence of the opponents to the Christian empire, which was revealed with such force in the second half of the 4th century.

Marcel Le Glay

Bibliography

Cumont, F. *Les Religions orientales dans le paganisme romain*, Paris, 1906, 4th ed., 1929.

Turcan, R. *Les Cultes orientaux dans le monde Romain*, Paris, 1989.

CURIA.

Origin to Gregory the Great. The Roman Curia is comprised of the advisory, administrative, and governing bodies that assist the pope in his twofold role of pastor of souls and wielder of temporal power. These governmental bodies of the Church are joined together in the Curia.

It is difficult to specify the precise moment of the Curia's birth. Its beginnings were insignificant, as befitted the bishop of Rome, whose authority did not really extend past the borders of his province. For the first four centuries, recourse to Rome in questions of faith or discipline was exceptional. But in the late 4th century, particularly beginning with DAMASUS I (366–84), and especially after success in converting aristocrats and the Roman mission's progress, an episcopal government was organized. The heads of the Western dioceses became accustomed to consulting with the pope on matters of everyday administration and discipline (for example, conditions for ordaining clergy, ECCLESIASTICAL PENALTIES, problems concerning marriage). In 416 INNOCENT I spoke of "countless questions that poured in from provinces everywhere; we reply to them after faithful, albeit summary, examination of each" (*PL* 20, 589, cited by V. Martin, c. 1879). There is also a letter from LEO I (440–1) addressed to the bishops of the province of Vienne, affirming that the bishops of Gaul went constantly to the HOLY SEE for the most diverse reasons (*PL* 54, 630, ibid.). While Roman primacy was asserting itself as a principle of universal government, and while centralization was losing its earliest appearances of spontaneity, archival services were developing in Rome in the hands of stable, specialized personnel, and methods for working and specific diplomatic procedures were guiding the composition of acts and coordinating, often from far away, the economic and political power of the Church.

Two salient characteristics dominated the first centuries of the Curia. In the beginning, the pope did not have procedures at his disposal that were any different from those of any other bishop: The staff that assisted him was originally convened for the material administration and spiritual formation of a limited local community.

But the different branches of this staff underwent a process of constant expansion that spread their sphere of influence to the limits of Christianity. The second characteristic trait is that the Holy See was aware of a prestigious predecessor, in the remarkable ability to expand. The imperial court, with its memories of Rome and its accomplishments in Constantinople, offered a powerful and smooth-running model with its advisory bodies, legates, and hierarchical administration with skills that were both proven and rich in a plurisecular tradition. The Apostolic See took its inspiration from governmental practices. The Roman Curia, relatively speaking, repeated in a number of ways the central offices and ministries of Rome and Constantinople.

Given the duty to support the pope, two kinds (organizational structures and duties) of service could be noted. First of all, the Roman clergy, which at the time was essentially an Italian clergy, brought the pope advice and assistance by means of the assemblies that he convoked and over which he presided. Secondly, specialized offices with technically educated personnel concentrated the tasks of a permanent administration. These two branches together made up the Roman Curia.

The *presbyterium*: Like any bishop, the bishop of Rome was surrounded by a council composed of the priests and deacons of his church. The role of this council, or synod, was to assist the bishop in his liturgical tasks, in pastoral education, in the administration of the sacraments, in managing material goods, and in governing. In addition to reflecting the movement of a local mission into a universal government, two activities best represent the inexorable extension of this council in which the equivalent of the senate can be seen: governmental and diplomatic activity. When SIRICIUS (384–99) wanted to condemn Jovinian, he called his clergy together, and it was with his clergy that he rendered his judgment; the matter passed beyond the purely local circle. A century and a half earlier, CORNELIUS (251–3) had intervened in the Novatian affair, giving remission of their penalties and reestablishing the condemned, both bishops and priests, in their sees. He was undoubtedly judging as bishops did, that is, surrounded by his *presbyterium*. The expansion of the local council's area of jurisdiction brought about changes in the *presbyterium*'s structure and the regulation of its sessions. All priests (a total of forty-six at the time of Cornelius) participated in meetings during the third century, while MARCELLUS I (308–10) convened only the priests of the *tituli*, the twenty-five main churches of Rome, accompanied by the regional deacons (those placed at the head of the seven regions introduced into Rome by FABIAN [236–50]). By the sixth century these priests, the habitual advisers to the popes, would be given the title of cardinal priests.

Additional rigor was similarly introduced into assemblies. During public sessions, evidence was presented and witnesses were heard, but one principle remained: The *presbyterium* provided only counsel and with its vote gave but a consultative opinion. The final decision always belonged to the pontiff, whose judgment was thereafter submitted for acclamation. There was no set location for meetings; churches (the basilica of St. Clement was one), private residences, and, after the fourth century, the Lateran palace were typical settings.

Diplomatic activities complemented deliberative responsibilities. Beginning in the 4th century, the pope drew on his clergy for priests in whom he had confidence. These individuals would represent him as LEGATES at the great councils (Arles, 314: two priests; Nicaea, 325: two priests, one of whom was Vincentius, later promoted to the see of Capua); they would also be entrusted with delicate missions—as was the case for the priest Philip, sent to Africa to resolve a dispute and impose a ruling—or they (for example, the priest Pancratius and the deacon Hilarius) would accompany a bishop to assist him (cf. C. Pietri, I, 143–44). Entrusted to apostolic vicars or *apocrisiarii*, missions in some cases became permanent, as happened in Thessalonica, Arles, Constantinople, and RAVENNA.

Roman councils assisted with the task of consulting, an activity that developed during the entire first millennium—these were not ecumenical or provincial (that is, limited to the province of Rome) councils. In addition to his priests and deacons, the pope called the bishops of all Italy to these councils, and sometimes even those of Gaul, or foreign bishops who were passing through Rome, or others who were called for specific reasons. These trusted individuals were invited to disentangle delicate questions that in some cases were submitted to a hundred bishops (under SYMMACHUS, 498–514), or, at the time of the third council of Rome (487), to thirty-eight bishops, sixty-six priests, and six deacons. Administrative personnel, who answered to the regular officers of the Curia, assisted the bishops, acted as secretaries during sessions, sought out and read documents, and introduced those appearing before the assembled body. The purview of the councils was limited strictly to papal jurisdiction, which had been affirmed in the matter of ecclesiastical discipline, faith, and any HERESY that threatened unity. However, whether it was a question of faith or of morals, and regardless of the canonical punishments handed down, the pope remained the supreme judge and the council played only an advisory role. In the trial against Athanasius, JULIUS I (337–52) pronounced the sentence himself after hearing the bishops, of which there were some fifty, all from Italy.

Tasks in the central administration were apparently more modest, and also more technical. In reality, given that they were every bit as essential, and given the stability and training of personnel, they covered both aspects of the Apostolic See's power: its power to order, expressed with the help of acts the CHANCERY prepared, edited, and preserved; and its economic, or material, power, which was manifestly visible in St. Peter's patrimony, which the administration managed and protected.

Clearly, the work of preservation is essential in a government founded on respect for tradition. It is quite probable that the first office or bureau, the *scrinium*, which was the prototype for the entire central administration, was specifically charged with archiving documents, thus constituting the Apostolic See's "memory." The oldest mention of an archival service comes from an inscription from Damasus I mentioning the generosity of his father, thanks to whom a new building (St. Damasus) was constructed for the archives. Similarly, Jerome sent those who disagreed with him regarding the authenticity of a letter to the archives of the Church of Rome (to the *chartarium ecclesiae Romanae*; Hier., *adv. Rufinum* 3, 20). Consequently, there are numerous references *ex scrinio*, or *de scrinio nostro*, that either confirm privileges granted by the pope or publish a council's acts. The popes' political correspondence and their decrees, as well as the acts of the martyrs, were likewise preserved from the earliest times: three letters from LIBERIUS (352–66), five from Damasus I, six from Siricius, thirty-one from INNOCENT I (401–17). There is also evidence of the existence of papal registers from the time of ZOSIMUS (417–8) and CELESTINE I (422–32), that serve as collections of pontifical letters for the canonists of the Middle Ages; but no papacy reached the level of activity of that of GREGORY I the Great (590–604), from whose time 850 letters are extant. In 544, the poet Arator offered his *De actibus Apostolorum* to VIGILIUS (537–55), who passed the codex to the *primicerius notariorum*.

The archives and the library (housed in the Lateran before 650) were entrusted to the care of *scriniarii*, who are often confused with *notarii*, as the same employees were responsible for preserving and composing acts. They were both archivists and drafters of documents.

The drafting of papal acts, later expanded to the drafting of the deliberations of synods—where the *notarii* also played the role of secretaries in meetings of the *presbyterium* and Roman councils—was an essential activity. These papal functionaries shaped diplomacy and outlined the proper style for papal legislation (letters, mandates, DECRETALS), without breaking with imperial tradition in any way. It would clearly be of great interest to know who these notaries were, how they were trained, and what their contacts were with the imperial administration; but on these matters we are still in the dark.

What we do know is that, from the time of Julius I, the *notarii* had considerable status; from 422, they had the title of "notaries of the Apostolic See," and their office, in imitation of the *auditorium* of the Eastern emperors, was reorganized by Gregory the Great. The pontiff organized the notaries (their number is not known) into a body; among them were seven regional notaries, for the seven regions of the city. According to the *Schola notariorum* (letter of 598), they were presided over by the *primicerius notariorum*, who was assisted by the *secundicerius notariorum*. These titles are explained by the place (first and second row) that the names of these individuals held on the wax tablets containing the list, in rank order, of the staff of the central administration, unless these tablets contained something other than authenticated acts. The earliest *primicerius* known is Laurentius, to whom Augustine's *Enchiridion ad Laurentium* was dedicated. The existence of a *secundicerius* is seen as early as 525.

The head notary—who was also the head of the papal archives and head of the chancery—was the highest dignitary in the court; he was a member of the papal family. And on him, along with the archpriest and archdeacon, lay responsibility for Church government in times of vacancy of the See.

The *notarii* did not come from the clergy, but were laymen, who generally entered the minor orders at the time of their recruitment. There was a certain tendency toward hereditary duties that was still present in the 9th century.

It was probably during the time of GELASIUS I (492–6) that a special section, the one in charge of the administration and revenues of the Church, broke off from the *scrinium* of chancery notaries. Gelasius had a register drawn up in which the revenues of all the lands belonging to the Church were consigned. A revenue office then had to be set up for management of the land, in cooperation with agencies that, on location, oversaw these properties and distributed the revenues into four parts, according to a prescription with a long-range impact: the bishop, the clergy, the poor, and the upkeep of churches.

Gregory the Great continued Gelasius's work, complementing the statement of receipts with a register of expenses (alms, allocations, and salaries). An enormous roll, kept in the Lateran, listed all the beneficiaries of pontifical generosity. At the time there were two officers, whose (perhaps earlier) naming also owed much to the imperial model. The *arcarius*, who was the precursor to a real minister of finance, deposited incoming tributes; Gregory said that he, himself, was in charge of this duty, which is evidence either of the scarcity or the low level of competence among the personnel at his disposal. The *saccellarius*, the general paymaster, disbursed salaries to the troops and distributed alms, among other duties.

In 598 Gregory organized the duties of *defensores ecclesiae Romanae*; this duty was clearly inspired by the *defensores civitatis*, responsible for overseeing the patrimony of the Church (in the role of lawyers general for the Church) as well as defenders of the poor (food distribution). Seven *defensores* (one for each region) were grouped into a college (*schola*) under the authority of a *primicerius defensorum*. As was the case for all the organs of the nascent Curia, they would see their areas of responsibility expand. Beginning with the modest, and certainly limited, tasks of reporting encroachments and pursuing usurpations, they would end up being associated with the establishment of the primacy of the Apostolic See, by applying measures condemning heresy and SCHISM.

Étienne Humbert

Bibliography

Bresslau, H. *Handbuch der Urkundenlehre für, Deutschland und Italien*, I, Leipzig, 1889.

Casper, E. *Geschichte des Papsttums*, I–II, Tübingen, 1930–2.

Del Re, N. *La Curia romana, lineamenti storico-giuridici*, Rome, 1952.

Halphen, L. *Études sur l'administration de Rome au Moyen Âge*, Paris, 1907.

Jordan, K. "Die Entstehung der römischen Kurie," *ZRGKA*, 59 (1939).

Liber Pontificalis, ed. L. Duchesne, Paris, 1877, CLIII–CLIV.

Martin, V. "Pape, Progrès de la centralisation," *DTC* (1932).

Michand, M. "Chambre apostolique," *DTC* (1942).

Pietri, C. *Roma christiana*, I–II, Rome, Paris, 1976.

Plöchl, W. *Geschichte des Kirchenrechts*, I, Vienna, 1952.

Torquebian, P. "Curie romaine," *DTC* (1949).

6th to 10th Centuries. The pope's activities entailed the need for offices for the preparation, wording, and implementation of decisions. In the 6th century, these services were solely carried out by the Roman patriarchy, and accounted for both early traditions (for example the existence of the seven regional deacons managing, since at least the 3rd century, the seven ecclesiastical regions of the city) and the general constraints defined by the ecumenical councils that were convened at the emperor's orders; the emperor then proclaimed the council decisions as civil laws affecting both Rome and elsewhere. The popes managed the affairs of the diocese and the regions for which they were metropolitans, and intervened in matters concerning other churches with the approval of the king. Constantinople's distance, close ties with the Carolingians, and the advantages that devolved from their decline in the 9th century, and, beginning in the 10th century, increasingly intense relations not only with the empires of both East and West, but also with the states (royal, county, and others), as well as direct relations with their bishops and abbots, stimulated an imperceptible expansion of each service and a more systematic organization of the offices.

But it is important to distinguish between the pope's religious activities, which are the only ones relevant to the Curia, and his civil activities. Through the Pragmatic Sanction of 552, Justinian imposed a number of responsibilities on the bishop of Rome, particularly in relation to supplying provisions for and defending the city. Civil responsibilities and religious responsibilities were not always clearly separated, not least because revenues of the same patrimony were allocated simultaneously for operations pertaining to both budgets: their rectors and defenders had two responsibilities. It is just as difficult to distinguish between the two kinds of duties in the PAPAL STATES as they were formed beginning at the time of the break with Constantinople and were affirmed after Pepin the Short's recognition of the false DONATION OF CONSTANTINE.

The area of responsibility for each office was easily described because, despite the small number of sources, once they were defined specifically, they remained relatively stable for the entire period. Whatever their importance was relative to one another, there was always a council to prepare decisions; a CHANCERY to shape and transmit them, and to receive letters and send the respective replies (particularly to exemptions and other privileges for permanent or temporary diplomats); a tribunal for local trials or for judgments of appeals when plaintiffs from the patriarchy asked the pope to decide; and an office of management for the local clergy of the city and churches dependent on the Roman metropolitan; a "house of the pope" (the episcopium); a guild (the FABRIC) for urban buildings; charity offices (long under the purview of the diaconate); and financial services whose duty it was to manage revenues and expenses. The fact that imperial laws applied to the administration of a diocese, even a patriarchal diocese, until the 7th century explains the absence of a real government. Each service was directly dependent on the pope, who, with the assistance of his close collaborators, made decisions in areas of conflicting responsibilities. The latter had an influence out of proportion to their actual duties.

How the Curia functioned in reality depended on a few individuals who were sometimes outsiders, or whose influence greatly exceeded their official roles. GREGORY the Great governed with monks whom he placed in key positions, in particular the *apocrisiarius*, the permanent LEGATE to Constantinople. The secular clergy slowly regained all its prerogatives, but needed to share the important choices, particularly that of who was to be pope, with the notables and the military leaders of the city. Under Charlemagne, it was the royal, and then the imperial court that exerted pressure, such that the pope was even forced to justify himself before the civil tribunal regarding accusations relating to his management. In the 10th century, pressure came less from the emperor, who was too far away, than from the extremely powerful Theophylactus family, who sometimes combined military duties, as *magistri militum*, with religious duties, as those dealing with papal finances. The conditions governing how the popes were "elected" reflected this succession of different influences.

The contrast between the many decision-making centers and the slow evolution of the services and their organization, which did not fundamentally change, can be seen through a brief comparison of the situation at the beginning of this period, when there were a number of sources available, and the end, when they again became abundant.

In the sixth century, little is heard about the council. Gregory the Great's correspondence and the careers of some of his successors show the influence of the three clerics in charge of administration between papacies: the archpriest, the archdeacon, and the head notary. To these should be added at least the first of the defenders. Around the year 1000, it comprised the seven cardinal bishops, those from the outskirts of Rome, the twenty-five cardinal priests, and the seven deacons who were also called cardinals. Clearly larger and better organized, it reflected the growing importance of the questions that needed to be dealt with, as well as the rank of chief of state, which had fallen upon the pope.

The notaries (*notarii*) and the *scrinarii* always made up the offices of the chancery, under the management of a *primicerius* and a *secundicerius*. However, in the seventh century, the growing importance of the archives (*scrinium*) explains the institution of a librarian, who was a bishop starting in 829 and was ranked above his two colleagues.

Among the diplomats, the *apocrisiarius* residing permanently in the court of Constantinople kept the first rank and the other missions were entrusted to different individuals (vicars or legates), depending on the circumstances; St. Boniface established regular relations with the court of Frankish mayors of the Palace, who became kings and then emperors. The Roman court, led by a *nomenclator*, grew in importance, as it organized the reception for bishops, who were arriving in ever-increasing numbers to receive the pallium, and of state emissaries, who were likewise concerned about their relations with the papacy. There was still no strict protocol; everything depended on diplomatic relations at the time. Moreover, the pope did not legislate during this period as an undisputed source of authority. He most often answered questions that were submitted through rescripts and not through laws. One of the most important activities was that of granting or confirming privileges.

All services had judicial powers to the extent of their area of purview, but civil proceedings were most often placed in the hands of defenders (*defensores*), who were under the authority of a *primicerius*, during the entire period in question here. This is all the easier to understand since the *defensores* held quite diverse positions in the general administration of ecclesiastical affairs. Moreover, they were supposed to defend the interests of the papacy against the usurpations of the powerful, regardless of their nature; from the time of Charles the Bald they were called *rapinae*, and they were quickly held to be "plunderings" perpetrated by feudal landowners—who were treated as pirates—against the personal "goods" of the "poor" (farmers), conveniently forgetting that all "goods"—real property or property seized by eminent domain—of the Church had always been defined as the "goods of the poor."

Responsibility for the clergy always fell upon the archpriest and the archdeacon, the former being in charge of parish clergy, among whom the priests from titular churches (*tituli*) were not included; the second was in charge of deacons, who were individuals with considerable power, as they managed the primary administrative services, especially that of FINANCES. Among them, the seven deacons who were regional representatives were responsible for an increasing variety of duties, and duties that were increasingly distant from what they had previously been: administrative responsibility for the seven religious districts of Rome. The Fabric, the service in charge of maintaining religious buildings, had always been in the hands of the *mansionarii*, who had a sizable budget for this purpose. On the other hand, the organization of charity went through considerable evolution. The service of the diaconate helped the local poor and received foreigners (who had come for religious reasons, primarily PILGRIMAGES) in the city, organizing soup lines, free bathing, and distributions of various kinds, as well as reception centers and hospices for the old, the infirm, children, and other Romans who were incapable of providing for their own needs. In the 8th century the task was divided among diaconates that had a church, hostelries, hospices, and other installations. At the head of these was a "father" (*pater*), who often came from the high ROMAN NOBILITY and was close to the pope; he enjoyed considerable prestige, since he contributed to the expenses for the decoration of buildings and made occasional gifts in addition to the sums allocated by the papal budget. He supervised the population of one section of Rome and participated in holding urban society together; this was all the more true since, on the great feast days, the pope, followed by a long procession, visited the deaconries, and was received by the pater in all of them. The pater had a dispensator under him, who was in charge of dispensing aid to the extent possible, given the resources made available to him. Deacons, undoubtedly assisted by personnel that are not mentioned in extant sources, assured the functioning of the different institutions.

Between the 6th and 10th centuries we see both a continuation of these great services, including the primary duties, and the effects on the Roman Curia of the papacy's gradual emancipation. In the year 1000 the Curia remained essentially a service to the local interests of the pope, although it did intervene throughout the West, and the means at its disposal allowed for a wide range of activity.

Jean Durliat

Bibliography

LP, I, 285–521; II, I–264.

Foerster, H., ed. *Liber diurnus romanorum pontificum*, Berne, 1958.

Jordan, K. *Die Entstehung der römischen Kurie*, Darmstadt, 1962.

Lohrmann, D. *Das Register Papst Johannes' VIII., 872–882*, Tübingen, 1968.

Pitz, E. *Papstreskripte im frühen Mittelalter. Diplomatische und rechtsgeschichtliche Studien zum Brief-Corpus Gregors des Grossen*, Sigmaringen, 1990.

Pöchl, W. M. *Geschichte des Kirchenrechts, 1, Das Recht des ersten christlichen Jahrhunderts von der Urkirche bis zum grossen Schisma*, 2nd ed., Vienna, 1959, 305–25.

Richards, J. *The Popes and the Papacy in the Early Middle Ages, 467–752*, London and Boston, Henley, 1979.

11th to 13th Centuries. It was at the end of the 11th century that the new organization of the Church's central government was given the name "Roman Curia." The Latin word "curia" became increasingly current in the 11th century in reference to the king's or the emperor's court in both its personnel (the entourage) and its institutional aspects (chapel, tribunal, diet). The Western royal and imperial courts had borrowed both the word and the concept from ancient Rome. In Rome the word "curia" referred above all to a group of important families, and then to the place where they met, and finally to where the senate met, as well as to the body of senators itself.

Beginning in the 11th century in Rome, coincidental with what was happening among kings and emperors, the old terms (especially *palatium*) which had been used for centuries in reference to the court, fell into disuse, to be replaced by curia.

This radical change was largely influenced by the reformational papacy's program in the 11th century. Starting with LEO IX (1049–54), the popes began to struggle systematically against the alienation of Church properties and revenues for the profit of lay lords, considered to be one of the primary causes of the impoverishment of religious institutions and of the decline of discipline and morale. A papacy so firmly set on spreading its program of reform was obligated to put into place, within the central government of the Church, a program of administrative reform aimed at ensuring the proper resources. This was all the more true since revenues in Rome itself had been monopolized during the 9th and 10th centuries by the Roman barons, particularly by the counts of Tusculum. The members of the great Roman families, little touched by the ideals of reform, continued to occupy key positions in the Roman administration, the nucleus of which was traditionally composed of the *sacrum palatium Lateranense*. The Palatine judges were dependent on it, according to their different functions: *acarius, saccellarius, primus defensor, adminiculator, vestariarius, vicedominus*. At the beginning of the eleventh century, the holders of the old offices were all relatives of the count of Tusculum, the real master of the papacy. The emperor Henry II (1014–24) freed the papacy from the domination of the counts of Tusculum, but had not taken from them the lucrative offices of the Apostolic See.

The decision by Leo IX to name Hildebrand, the future GREGORY VII (1073–85), treasurer and cardinal subdeacon marked a break with the tradition of the ROMAN NOBILITY and an innovation with respect to the title. The choice was a good one. Under his administration, the papal revenues increased considerably, or at least that is what we are led to believe by the fact that shortly after his election, NICHOLAS II (1059–61) entrusted Hildebrand with responsibility for Rome's temporal holdings, by naming him archdeacon of the Roman Church, an important position, which itself had been held previously by members of the Roman aristocracy. It certainly is not a coincidence that the first list of the properties and revenues of the Roman Church goes back to the papacy of Gregory VII. Under his papacy, important progress was made in the reorganization of the Roman Church: Control of its temporal interests was centralized and the holding of regular accounts was introduced. The properties of the Roman Church were now defended by the beginnings of penal legislation. On the whole, the administration remained under the authority of the archdeacon.

With lay and French models as references, especially Cluny, URBAN II (1088–99) modified the structure of the papal administration even more radically by laying the foundations for a "curial" organization that was destined to have a long future. It was under his papacy that the word "curia" is seen to have been used for the first time, and that the Camera and the Chapel became concretely understandable administrative realities. A Frenchman, formerly from Cluny, Urban II borrowed not only a new word from Cluny for the financial body of the Apostolic See, but he also appears to have used the Clunisian camera for receiving and transferring rents, revenues, and donations. And it was to Cluny that pope Urban II went to seek the Apostolic See's first chamberlain (*camerarius*), whose name was Peter. Under PASCHAL II (1099–1118), the Clunian camera was still in close collaboration with the Roman financial administration. Under CALLISTUS II (1119–24), it even had a "branch" in Cluny. It was only

after Callistus II's departure for Italy that ties between the APOSTOLIC CAMERA and Cluny ceased to exist, and the Camera acted as an autonomous institution.

The introduction of new forms of organization did not necessarily mean a complete break with the past. In a manner that was often unexpected, old bodies, like the Roman subdeacons, found their way into the papal chapel. Transformations that were radical were made gradually. A college of PAPAL CHAPLAINS was not seen until Urban II's papacy. The importance of the chapel, the organization of which was certainly of Germanic origin, grew considerably under Paschal II. Urban II chose a great number of chaplains who had previously had important duties within the CHANCERY, such as the roles of Palatine *scriptores* and *notarii*, and made them cardinals. The rise of the chapel was closely linked to the decline in the institution of the former *scrinarii*. Urban II also reorganized the chancery, introducing important innovations: the former Roman curial hall was abandoned, to be replaced by the quite small chancery; a new time period to calculate indiction was adopted, as was a new date for the beginning of the year. The illustrious deacon John of Gaeta, a monk from Monte Cassino and the future pope GELASIUS II, was entrusted with its leadership.

The cornerstone of the post-Gregorian Roman Curia was undoubtedly the CONSISTORY, the institution within which the pope discussed with the cardinals the most important of the problems concerning the government of the Roman Church. The term "consistory," which originally denoted the place where the emperors' advisers held their deliberations, and then the imperial council itself, came into use long after the institution's effective birth. Affirmation of the consistory's importance, which had been given considerable impetus by Urban II—in his reserving for the consistory questions regarding the excommunication of the emperor, kings, or bishops, litigious episcopal elections, problems regarding EXEMPTIONS or diocesan organizations which had been dealt with in the Roman synod, even under Gregory VII's papacy—went hand in hand with the gradual strengthening of the college of cardinals as members of the senate of the church and exclusive collaborators with the pope in matters of the administration of justice. This evolution likewise encompassed the former Roman synod, which left its relatively provincial role and became the nucleus for the great ecumenical councils of the twelfth and thirteenth centuries. It certainly was not by chance that, with regard to papal privileges, using subscriptions for cardinals became more frequent from the time of Urban II's papacy. These subscriptions, which at the beginning had only the pope's signature (they became the rule under the papacies of HONORIUS II and INNOCENT II), reflected the active participation of the cardinals in the government of the universal Church. Since 1059 the authority of the cardinals had increased; this movement even accelerated after the CONCORDAT OF WORMS. Between 1123 and 1153, cardinals' duties developed considerably. Under Callistus II, the cardinals had become privileged collaborators with the pope in the area of administration of justice. In general, the cardinals' role of mediation within an increasingly centralized Church could only grow. The consistory met regularly beginning with Innocent II's papacy. It permanently replaced the old synod of the Roman clergy. At the time of the double election in 1130, the old question of ranks within the college of cardinals had not been raised. Equality of rights among different orders of cardinals concerning papal elections was respected. The prestige of the rank of cardinal came out of this all the stronger. Moreover, it cannot be ruled out that for a certain number of cardinals the schism of 1130 increased feelings of responsibility for matters of faith. This would explain the role of arbitrator in the area of doctrine that the pope and the consistory assumed under EUGENE III's papacy (1145–53). Reactions were quick to come. During the consistory of Reims (1131), the French bishops and Bernard of Clairvaux made no secret of their concerns. It is true that within a period of a few years the cardinals had become conscious of their new prerogatives, to such an extent that when Eugene III—in this same consistory, which was supposed to be examining the teachings of Gilbert de La Porrée—was leaning toward the abbot of Clairvaux's position, the cardinals reminded him that no negotiation could take place definitively without their authorization: They were the points (*cardines*) around whom the axis of the universal Church turned, and it was they who had made him, a private individual, its universal father.

By the time of the victory of the GREGORIAN REFORM and the end of the schism of 1130, the Roman Church had become a veritable high court of justice toward which APPEALS of all kinds flowed with increasing frequency. The Roman prerogatives in the judicial domain found a natural extension at the level of doctrine. Even though the initiative never came from Rome, appeals from outside encouraged the Roman Curia to assume the role of arbitrator. Later, in the 13th century, other stages were reached in a development that lead the papacy not only to play the role of arbitrator, but also to see that the value of its decisions was fully recognized. The role of arbitrator that the Roman Curia was able to play in the area of doctrine was fully appreciated by Abelard at the opening of the synod of Sens (1140). When Bernard of Clairvaux publicly read the list of theses called into question, Abelard immediately appealed to Rome and set out for the papal court. The bishops of the provinces of Reims and Sens likewise sent Innocent II a summary of their arguments. For his part, Bernard immediately admonished him no longer to delay his decision. Six weeks after the synod of Sens, Innocent II condemned all of Abelard's doctrinal theses and forced the theologian into perpetual

silence and monastic reclusion, and ordered him to burn his books. It bears noting that the pope based his decision solely on the bishops' report, ignoring Bernard of Clairvaux's interventions and his list of Abelard's "errors." In the case of accusations against Gilbert de La Porrée, the Roman Curia also played a central role. The two archdeacons of Poitiers, Arnold of Brescia and Kalo, in disagreement with the dilatory decisions made by the diocesan synod of 1146, appealed to Rome. They met Eugene III in Siena or Viterbo while on their way to France. The accusation procedure remained in the hands of the pope, who heard Gilbert at the time of the consistories of Paris (21–22 April 1147) before closing the debate of the synod of Reims (21 March 1148). Appeals to Rome in the area of doctrine show that in the world of the 12th century the highest authorities of the Roman Church had assimilated the great intellectual transformations of their time, founded on a new method (early scholasticism) in the study of theology and law. This was the result of a slow evolution. Beginning in the first decades of the 12th century, the *litteratura*, that is, the acquired knowledge of the great formational centers of the West (first Cluny, and later Paris and Bologna), had become one of the most important criteria for the recruitment of cardinals and members of the Curia. The influx of judiciary appeals of all kinds to Rome required new areas of expertise. The recruitment of cardinals suffered from it. The first half of the twelfth century showed an increasing presence of *magistri* among the cardinals as well as eminent jurists (for example, Peter of Pisa) and theologians (for example, Robert Pulleyn). Pulleyn was no more than the first in a long series of great English intellectuals, like Hilarius, Boson, John of Salisbury, and Nicholas Breakspear, who was to become HADRIAN IV (1154–9), coming into the service of the Roman Curia under Eugene III.

The protection Abelard was accorded by eminent prelates in the Roman Curia devolves from a wider phenomenon, which had important consequences for the composition of the personnel of the Curia, as well as for the intellectual evolution of circles tied to the central Church government. Since the beginning of the 12th century, countless bonds had formed in terms of personnel between the most important monastic and religious institutions in France and the Roman Curia. Even though the two candidates to St. Peter's throne in 1130 were Roman by birth, ANACLETUS II had begun his career in Cluny; in Innocent II's camp, the primary personality was a Frenchman, Aimeric. For nearly a century, since the time of Urban II and up to ALEXANDER III, the popes sought refuge in France to resolve problems tied to the papal election. Eugene III had been a monk in Clairvaux, Hadrian IV had drafted the congregation of canons regular of St. Ruf in Avignon before entering the college of cardinals. Since the papacy of Eugene III, and thanks also to the impetus of the chancellor Rolando Bandinelli, the future Alexander III, a growing number of Romans went to Paris to complete their literary and theological educations. The great Roman aristocratic families (Saso, Pierleoni, Boboni, Capocci, and Frangipani) had long since acquired the habit of sending their children first to Cluny, then to St. Victor, in Paris. They understood perfectly well that time spent in the finest schools of the Latin West could assure a career at the highest levels of the Curia.

The end of the 12th century and the beginning of the 13th were marked by several important events. The growth of curial affairs and the need to be able to rely on a fully available cardinalate encouraged the papacy to no longer allow cardinals to reside in their respective dioceses after their accession to the rank. The phenomenon of becoming a nonresident cardinal was interrupted under the papacy of HONORIUS III. Between 1198 and 1276, eighty-one cardinals were named, of whom only three were "exterior," that is, not residents of the Curia. Eighty percent of the cardinals were natives of two countries: Italy and France (forty-six and eighteen, respectively). After Honorius III's papacy and during the entire 13th century, the German lands of the empire no longer sent a single national to the college of cardinals. INNOCENT IV's creation of the first Hungarian cardinal (Stephen, the former chancellor of the kingdom) in 1244 was perhaps related to problems with the Tartars. The Iberian peninsula, and the kingdom of Aragon in particular, was almost always represented by at least one cardinal, with even more constancy than the kingdom of England. The great number of cardinals born in Rome and Latium and created by INNOCENT III, of which there were thirteen, is partially related to his politics of (re)foundation of the Papal State. Only four Roman cardinals were named after 1216, and two of them were Orsinis. The other great rival Roman family, the Colonnas, was no longer represented by a cardinal after the death of Giovanni (ca. 1245). The Roman pope Honorius III named no new cardinals from Rome or central Italy. A brilliant career in the Curia—belonging to the papal chapel under Innocent III, and later, especially, duties as vice chancellor, notary of the pope, or curia judge *auditor litterarum contradictarum*—favored accession to the cardinalate. In the 13th century, even more than a career in the Curia, a university education acquired in Paris or Bologna constituted a considerable advantage. Only two of the ten cardinals created by GREGORY IX— the Cistercian Giocomo Pecorara and the Roman Riciardo Annibaldi—are known to not have had the title *magister*. A certain number of cardinals of the time even held positions as professors (in Paris, Bolgona, or Naples: for example, Stephen Langton, Geoffrey of Trani, Hubert of Pirovano, Hugues of St. Cher, John of Abbeville, Peter of Bar, Robert of Courson, Sinibaldo Fieschi) or ecclesiastical responsibilities that made them responsible for a

studium (in Paris, the chancellor Eudes of Châteauroux; in Bologna, archdeacon Ottaviano Ubaldini). The fact that eminent jurists like Geoffrey of Trani, and especially Henry of Suse, called Hostiensis, became cardinals, confirms the extraordinary role that law was beginning to play in the institutional, doctrinal, and pastoral development of the Roman Church. A number of bishops also made their way into the college of cardinals. It is significant that GREGORY I, who was elected pope when he was patriarch of Jerusalem, promoted no cardinal who had a career in the Curia during his time, but, on the contrary, four members of the episcopacy. Belonging to the entourage (or *familia*) of a powerful cardinal, or being his relative, might facilitate entrance into the college of cardinals. This phenomenon concerned not just popes who were natives of Rome (most notably Innocent III) or Roman families (for example, the Colonnas or the Orsinis). The Genoan Fieschis, certainly the most important of the non-Roman Curial families in the 13th century were almost uninterruptedly present in the Curia for a century, beginning in 1227, with five cardinals, two of whom became popes (Innocent IV and HADRIAN V).

When Innocent III became pope in 1198, the chancery and the Camera had been, since 1194, under the authority of only one cardinal, Cencio Savelli, the future pope Honorius III. This was nothing more than an interlude. Innocent III returned to the previous situation and even Honorius III made no attempt to join these two traditionally distinct bodies.

As in the lay sovereign courts, the personnel of the chancery were closely related to the pope's CHAPEL. Innocent III's three chancellor cardinals and his five vice chancellors came from the chapel, as was also the case for the *scriptores*. Since the time of Honorius III (1216–1227) and during the entire 13th century, the chancery was managed by a vice chancellor; he, in turn, was assisted by notaries, ABBREVIATORS, correctors, distributors, and "rescribendaries," as well as by clerks in charge of the REGISTERS. Vice chancellors and notaries were generally men of experience, trained in the great new schools of law, like Bologna and Paris. They had often begun their careers in the Curia by being admitted into the college of papal chaplains. The notaries were directly under the pope's jurisdiction, which strengthened their position in the Curia. Like the old *notarii regionarii* they were limited to seven in number. Under Gregory IX (1227–41) even this number does not appear to have been reached. A number of them were entrusted with important diplomatic missions. Like the cardinals, the professional activity and the daily life of the vice chancellor and the notaries took place within the framework of the *familiae*, bringing clerks and servants into it. At the beginning of the 13th century, probably under pressure from tasks that demanded increasing levels of professionalism, the *scriptores* were relieved of their liturgical duties and devoted their time specifically to the implementation of acts. The *scriptores*, who really should not be considered true administrators, constituted a body (or a college) the first traces of which can be seen in the papacy of Innocent III. A number of Innocent III's reforms were aimed specifically at controlling more systematically the work of the papal chancery, and at the same time at avoiding abuses in the collection of taxes. It was only during Innocent III's papacy that the *scriptores* began placing their signatures (or acronyms thereof) on the covers (*plica*) of documents, upon which their fees were based. In general, those circles connected to the papal chancery in the 13th century played a quite important role in the development of the *ars dictaminis*, collections of forms and letters, or treatises that would end up enjoying unquestionable prestige; added to this was the importance and the prestige of the *stilus curiae*, which was in continual evolution during the 13th century. The continual series of registers of the letters produced by the papal chancery began with the papacy of Innocent III.

The *cursores* (couriers) carried out a number of important tasks. It was they who were supposed to convene the cardinals and the prelates, to take dossiers for trials to the auditors in charge of hearing them, and to protect the palace when the pope was away. In this regard, they replaced the *schola majorentum*, which was still functioning in the 12th century. The couriers were also expected to take letters from the pope to their destinations in the different lands of Christianity. The work was difficult and often subject to certain pressure. Although couriers had been in existence since the time of Honorius II, it is difficult to estimate how many there were. In May 1278 thirty-one were known to exist. By the end of the century, the couriers had united into a college.

By the beginning of the 13th century, at the height of its political power, the papacy had also become a powerful financial center. The duty of *camerarius* had basically been taken out of the hands of the Romans. Up to the end of the 13th century, very few cardinals led the Camera. The CAMERLENGO was constantly in close contact with the pope. A new pope assigned the duty to someone in whom he had confidence. It is significant that the *camerarius* was also called the *domini pape* and not *sancte Romane Ecclesie*, as was the case for other members of the Curia. His importance continued to grow. The head of the Camera probably became the most powerful member of the Curia during the 13th century. The way had been prepared in the 12th century by individuals like Boson and Cencio Savelli. Toward the end of the century, his jurisdiction also appeared to be established during times of vacancy in the Apostolic See. The office of chamberlain was by that time no longer connected exclusively to the person of the pope. The council of Vienne (1311) would decide that in cases of the pope's death, the cardinals should name a new chamberlain for the duration of the vacancy in the Apostolic See. The chamberlain resided in the Lateran, near the pope. When Innocent III constructed a new palace in the Vatican, the Camera got a new headquarters and its head received an apartment. Such was also the case when Nicholas III restructured the Vatican palace. His duties were several: He was responsible for the revenues of the Roman Church; he presided over the distribution of the *presbyteria*; he was administrator for the papal palaces and those churches that were dependent on the papacy; at least until the middle of the 13th century, the library, archives, and papal treasury were placed under his immediate responsibility; he was also in charge of the administration of the patrimony consisting of the lands belonging to the Papal States, and was therefore supposed to supervise and manage the activity of the rectors of the different provinces of the state. As was the case for the vice chancellor and the papal notaries, the camerlengo's entourage was organized according to the principles of the *familia*.

Beginning in Innocent IV's papacy, the pope's treasure, which included the library, archives, jewels, silver and gold table service, furniture, carpets, and liturgical objects and vestments, was placed under the responsibility, of first one (Paul of Garfagnana), and later two treasurers, who generally belonged to the college of the pope's chaplains.

The first traces of the presence of bankers residing officiallly in the Roman Curia go back to Cencio Savelli's *ordo*, which speaks of *officiales camerarii* and mentions a *cambiator*. The title *campsor camerae* (Chamber money changer) appears under Gregory IX. It belonged to two individuals from Siena. Under URBAN IV the title *mercatores camerae*, or *mercatores domini pape* appeared. For a long time the Sienese, especially the company of Buonsignori, had a monopoly on the position. GREGORY X brought bankers, the Scotti, to the Curia from his native city of Piacenza. Toward the end of the century (NICHOLAS IV's papacy), six companies of bankers were active in the Curia. The most important of these were the Mozzi, Spini, and Chiarenti, the only companies attested under BONIFACE VIII. These bankers were responsible for seeing to all the Camera's payments, even those going to the members of the Curia; they were also in charge of the financial administration concerning the provinces of the Papal States, and they kept a close eye on the financial relations between the Curia and the different parts of the Christian world.

The arrival of Innocent III marked a significant innovation in the life of the chancery. In the *audientia publica* (public audience), in the course of which letters sent by the chancery were read, those in disagreement were allowed to contest the contents of a papal letter: Arguments could be presented, by the parties or by prosecutors during a session before the curia judge (*auditor lit-*

terarum contradictarum), who had the power to demand that the necessary corrections be made. The institution of these audiences, which are seen for the first time in 1205–1206, constituted undeniable progress from an administrative and judiciary point of view, with everyone having, at least theoretically, the possibility of having his rights heard, even more so than was the case in the preceding judicial climate. Innocent III had understood that the old administrative organisms of the Roman Church's central government, especially those of the chancery, whose procedures were archaic, needed to adapt to the growth of the Curia's affairs. Since the papacies of Eugene III and Alexander III, the number of papal interventions (rescripts) had grown, primarily because of the increasing number of petitions seeking arbitration by the pope. The importance that this new body of the Curia acquired, especially in the areas of jurisprudence and administration of justice, was made manifest by the fact that during the 13th century, the position of curia judge was generally occupied by a canonist of renown (Sinibaldo Fieschi, the future Innocent IV, Geoffrey of Trani, Guido da Baisio) who had become one of the most important ordinary judges in the Curia. Through this new body, the Roman Curia was endowed with further possibilities for intervention in the administration and jurisprudence of local churches. The enormous increase in petitions addressed to Rome from everywhere indirectly reinforced this decision-making power of the Roman Church in the judicial and administrative domains. Old theoretical claims, forcefully advanced by the reformational papacy of the 11th century, could now be realized because of effective judicial and administrative practices that encompassed all Christendom.

The growing complexity of judicial and administrative procedures in the Roman Curia had made the presence of procurators in Rome indispensable; for the most part these were Italian jurists with specified areas of responsibility and access to a network of personal relations within the Curia that only a long sojourn *apud Sedem apostolicam* could offer. The work of the procurators was controlled by the *audientia litterarum contradictarum*, whose primary characteristic was that of being a kind of tribunal for the procurators.

The number of cases brought before the Roman Curia increased so substantially beginning in the 12th century that it had become impossible to judge them directly in Rome, especially as a long and expensive trip to the city could not always be demanded. Thus it happened that since the beginning of the 12th century a new figure appeared in a number of dioceses in the Christian world— the ecclesiastical judge, who was responsible for presiding over trials on papal delegation. The importance of the jurisprudence produced by these JUDGES DELEGATE was considerable, since it was the primary channel through which canon law of the Roman type was able to make its

way into practice throughout the different diocesan courts of Latin Christianity. The principles promulgated in the DECRETALS were adapted to thousands of individual and specific situations. The first examples go back to the papacies of Paschal II and Honorius II. Under Innocent II, the number of delegations rapidly increased, but it was ultimately Alexander III and Innocent III who would systematically take advantage of this new Roman judicial instrument. Gregory IX contributed to its refinement, as we see by the chapters *"De officio et potestate judicis delegati"* and *"De rescriptis"* in the *Liber Extra*.

The incessant growth of the number of cases submitted for papal arbitration, both initially and on appeal, also had important consequences for the reorganization of the Roman Curia's judicial and administrative procedures. Throughout the first half of the thirteenth century a new kind of judicial personnel appeared, composed primarily of the pope's chaplains, called to replace cardinals, who up to that time were his only collaborators in matters of administration of justice. The innovation was once again attributed to Innocent III, who sought effective solutions within the existing institutions of the Curia. Innocent's actions in this regard were decisive. On the one hand, as he enjoyed their trust, he used the members of his chapel as auditors much more systematically than had been the case in the past. On the other, starting in 1202, their function in this regard was completely analogous to that of the cardinals. Under Innocent IV, the judicial body within the Roman Curia underwent further transformation. Within the relatively vast group of the pope's chaplains, the names of a few *auditores (generales) sacri palatii* stood out. This specialized judicial body gradually separated the other papal chaplains who resided within the Roman Curia from the administration of justice. At the same time, the role played by the cardinals in the matter changed: not only did their activity diminish quantitatively, especially after Gregory X's papacy, but the most important trials also began to be reserved for them: those involving bishoprics, abbeys, highly placed Church dignitaries, or questions of ecclesiastical jurisdiction; the chaplains presided over appeal cases brought before the Apostolic See and those cases involving benefices.

In the final decades of the 12th century the first signs of centralization in the area of penitence appeared, still provoked by a continual flood toward the Roman Church of reqeusts for dispensations and absolutions, which would lead to a gradual concentration of these rights in the hands of the pope. This concentration was based on the principle according to which the power of dispensation lay in the hands of the legislator, that is, the pope. An important step in this direction had been taken in the 11th century, when personal dispensations appeared for the first time. This was a significant innovation. According to traditional canonical ideas, dispensations previously had a general value. Effectively supported by the development of the decretals, one consequence of the phenomenon would be to limit further the right of dispensation belonging to bishops. The number of sins whose absolution was reserved explicitly for the pope further increased after the 12th century. One of the main causes was undoubtedly to be found in the inability of local churches to satisfy within their own confines an issue of casuistry which had been made more complex by the rapid development of judicial thought. The PENITENTIARY was put into place in the early thirteenth century. The only body within the Curia that had purely spiritual tasks, other than the chaplaincy, it was also the only body in the 13th century to be presided over by a cardinal. The first evidence of a cardinal from the Curia specifically responsible for following the affairs of the Penitentiary coincides with Innocent III's papacy. The Roman cardinal John of St. Paul was named by Giraud of Cambrai to be the *cardinalis, qui confessiones pro papa tunc recipiebat.* Beginning in 1246, the penitentiary cardinal had the title *penitentiarius summus,* and he was seconded by specialized personnel, the minor penitentiaries, whose functions also came into existence during Innocent III's papacy. Recruited almost exclusively from the two main mendicant orders (the DOMINICANS and the FRANCISCANS), the penitentiaries had the power to give absolution and to mandate ordinary bishops to give dispensations. The traveling done by the papal court made the presence of penitentiaries necessary in the principal Roman basilicas (ST. PETER'S in the Vatican, ST. JOHN LATERAN, and ST. MARY MAJOR). The penitentiaries minor were thus divided into two distinct bodies, those that traveled with the papal court and those that remained in Rome.

Under Innocent III, the official distribution of alms by the pope and the Roman Curia appeared to be a well-established tradition. Although its specific origins are unknown, a distinct body was created in the 13th century: the chaplaincy. The poor gathered every day, generally in the refectory of the basilica of Theodore, to receive food, money, and clothing. When the pope was traveling, all the poor who followed him received two denarii. The chaplains were responsible for keeping the oil for extreme unction, the candles for the Holy Saturday liturgical offices, and the wax for making *Agnus Dei.* When a pope died, they were to wash the body, dress it in papal vestments, and then entrust it to the penitentiaries. Because of this, they had the right to the bed upon which the pope had died. The chaplaincy had several sources of finance: the buildings in the Lateran and around it; ten percent of the oblations offered at St. Peter's basilica, as was traditional; all the offerings that were placed at the feet of the pope. Beginning with the papacy of Nicholas III, the chaplaincy also received the revenues from the VATICAN GARDENS recently constructed around the new papal palace. From this period on, it was the chaplaincy that

took responsibility for the palace administration, and of distributions in the Vatican, in the Lateran, at St. Peter's, and in a few other churches in Rome. The chaplaincy was also responsible for the annual procession from St. Peter's to Santo Spirito hospital. This hospital was another important charitable institution dependent on the Roman Curia. It was founded (ca. 1201) by Innocent III, on a public road along the Tiber, in front of St. Peter's and near the church of Santa Maria in Sassia, the former national church of the Saxons. From the beginning, it had been dedicated not only to receiving pilgrims and the infirm, but also to the care of popes and cardinals. Its administration was entrusted to the founder of the Hospital of Montpellier, Brother Guido. Four clerics of the new order were supposed to pray in it for the intention of the pope and the members of the college of cardinals, and to administer the sacraments to them. Guido died shortly after the hospital's foundation. Honorius III suspended the connection between the hospital and the Hospitaller order of Montpellier. Nicholas III would place the hospital in the hands of a cardinal. Beginning with Innocent IV, a second hospital was at the Roman Curia's disposition, which was entrusted to the order of the Antonins (from Vienne, in Dauphiné). It was built especially for the members of the Curia and individuals residing in the Curia. It was endowed with a portable hosptial, very useful during the numerous movements of the Roman Curia in the thirteenth century. The Antonians not only cared for the ill in the Curia, they were also responsible for burial.

Agostino Paravicini Bagliani

Bibliography

Cheney, C. R. *The Study of the Medieval Papal Chancery,* Glasgow, 1966.

Classen, P. "Die römische Kurie und die Schulen," *Studium und Gesellschaft im Mittelalter,* ed. J. Fried, Stuttgart, 1983.

Elze, R. "Die päpstliche Kapelle im 12. und 13. Jahrhundert," *ZSSR, kan. Abt.,* 36, 1950, 157, 171–5.

Herde, P. *Beiträge zum päpstlichen Kanzlei- und Urkundenwesen im dreizehnten Jahrhundert,* Kallmünz, 1967.

"Il 'concistorium' dopo lo scisma del 1130," *RSCI,* 9 (1955), 165–76.

Jordan, K. "Die päpstliche Verwaltung im Zeitalter Gregors VIII.," *Studi Gregoriani,* 1 (1947), 137–68.

Miethke, J. "Theologenprozesse in der ersten Phase ihrer institutionellen Ausbildung: die Verfahren gegen Peter Abaelard und Gilbert von Poitiers," *Viator,* 6 (1975), 111.

Nüske, G. F. "Untersuchungen über das Personal der päpstlichen Kanzlei, 1254–1304," *Archiv für Diplomatik,* 20, 1974, 39–240; 21, 1975, 249–431.

Paravicini Bagliani, A. *Cardinali di Curia e 'familiae' cardinalizie dal 1227 al 1254*, 2 vols., Padua, 1972.

Paravicini Bagliani, A. "Il 'Registrum causarum' di Ottaviano Ubaldini e l'amministrazione della giustizia alla Curia romana nel secolo XIII," *Römische Kurie. Kirchliche Finanzen, Vatikanisches Archiv. Studien zu Ehren von Hermann Hoberg*, II, Rome, 1979, 635 ff.

Rusch, B. *Die Behörden und Hofbeamten der päpstlichen Kurie des 13. Jahrhunderts*, Königsberg, 1936.

Sayers, J. "Canterbury Proctors at the Court of 'Audientia litterarum contradictarum,'" *Traditio*, 22, 1966, 311–45.

Sydow, J. "Cluny und die Anfänge der Apostolichen Kammer. Studien zur Geschichte der päpstlichen Finanzverwaltung im 11. und 12. Jahrhundert," *Studien und Mitteilungen zur Geschichte des Benediktiner-Ordens und seiner Zweige*, 63 (1951), 45–66.

Von Heckel, R. "Das Aufkommen der ständigen Prokuratoren an der päpstlichen Kurie im 13. Jahrhundert," *Miscellanea Francesco Eherle*, II, Vatican City, 1924, 290–321.

14th and 15th Centuries. If it is logical to include in the Roman Curia all those who surround the pope and assist in the fulfillment of his mission, then it should be recognized that in the 14th and 15th centuries, it was under a *familia* that the Curia appeared, composed of the PAPAL FAMILY, which included servants and guards as much as it did bureaucrats. One document that must have been composed early in CLEMENT V's reign, when the Curia was still dallying in the kingdom of France and its new members were running the risk of not knowing the old customs, described the duties of the family members, set the food rations (*vivandae*) and forage (*prebendae*) they were to receive, and determined which were to be lodged by the APOSTOLIC CAMERA and receive clothing. One part of the administrative personnel did not have a right to this statute: these were the scribes, who shared in the "pie" of their bosses, while stablemen, sergeants, and couriers were housed and fed. The domestic nature of the papal Curia is the result of its origins: private service and public service were not differentiated in it, as the same individuals were responsible for both.

Nevertheless, the Curia evolved over the period of two centuries: remuneration with silver replaced distribution of goods; the organization of administrative services was perfected and better separated from the pope's "hostel," or house; income increased. The distinction of being a *familiar*, which signified attachment to the pope, continued to be appreciated, and to be sought: The scribes of the CHANCERY and the PENITENTIARY acquired it, theoretically, in 1347, although it appears as though it was gradually given out individually; on the other hand, the honorary chaplains—nominations for which passed from a hundred under JOHN XXII (1316–34), to nearly nine hundred under GREGORY XI (1370–8)—who did not reside with the pope but were rather dispersed throughout Christendom, were admitted into the family, which was even opened to a few individuals that the head of the Church wished to honor.

The replacement of *vivandae* and *prebendae* with a monetary allocation was not practiced until at least the end of the 13th century, when the court moved; when this occurred only the *parva* or *stricta familia* followed the pope. Besides the clerics of the Camera, who dealt with daily expenses, and the bull writers who sealed the acts that were continually being composed, this permanent entourage was composed only of cooks, bread makers, stablemen, chaplains, sergeants at arms, and notaries of the domestic offices. Beginning in the time of John XXII, the system of salaries was extended to all the personnel who had a right to the delivery of goods; it continued to be modeled after him, since it was applicable only to those who spent the night in the court after a day of work; those who were forced to leave got a special indemnity. Some members of the Curia even received a lesser sum on days of abstinence. Beginning in 1319, salaries, the value of which varied on a scale from one to nine, were paid on Saturdays every eight weeks. It was necessary to keep an attendance register in order to make a precise calculation of the *vadia ordinaria familiarium papae*, which had a special heading in the accounts. During the AVIGNON period, the mean sum was close to thirty thousand florins per year. To this was added the product of taxes paid by the beneficiaries of apostolic graces, most notably what was called "lesser services" (*servitia minuta*), determined relative to "common services" that those who held major benefices paid; they were divided into five sections such that, according to their classification in each of them, the officers received unequal parts.

Beginning in 1309, the distribution of clothing, before winter and before summer, was replaced with a lump allocation that varied from two to twelve florins, depending on the rank of the officer. However, the master doorkeeper knights, the squires, and chamberlains continued to receive sheets of wool, the color of which was not always the same, until the end of 1347; then the chamberlains were the only ones whose clothing was provided. Lodging was similarly replaced by a lump sum; if the officer accepted a higher rent, he paid the difference with his own money. A few privileged individuals lived in the palace, or in houses rented by the Camera.

Numbers increased after the end of the 13th century, and then stabilized. But there is some disparity in statistics, and they can be compared only with great care. A list from 1278 that goes back to the papacy of NICHOLAS III enumerates more than two hundred members of the Curia, but this does not take into account the lesser members who did not belong to the family, which included perhaps a hundred individuals. Under BONIFACE VIII (1299–1303), the number goes up to 350 by including the squires, stablemen, knights who had been enlisted, and the scribes. It grew further with Clement V, who recruited sergeants and valets in Gascony, until the point where he employed more than 150 individuals. CLEMENT VI (1342–52) had an even larger court. For the Avignon period the average figure was some five hundred. Relative to the time of Nicholas III, the increase was in the order of 40 percent. The personnel was divided nearly equally between administrative services and the domestic entourage; it included approximately three clerics for every two laymen. A document from 1409, composed in Pisa the day after ALEXANDER V's election and reflecting a previous situation, draws a distinction between members of the Curia whose office did not cease when the pope died and who, when such was the case, did not dress in mourning (these were the *officia perpetua*), and those who no longer retained their positions when their superior passed away, and whom the Camera dressed in *vestibus lugubris*.

The growing importance of the administration and the onset of the payment of wages and pecuniary indemnities were contemporaneous with the establishment of a furnished, permanent residence for the Curia. Rome, the undisputed spiritual capital, which justified the authority of Peter's successor over the Church as a whole, had not always been the administrative capital. Boniface VIII traveled throughout the PATRIMONY, BENEDICT XI died in Perugia, and Clement V, who was pulled between meetings with the king of France (Philip the Fair) that had taken place in Poitiers, a council held in Vienne, and the illusion of regaining his health by breathing the air of his native Gascony, did not take up permanent residence anywhere. It was John XXII, the former bishop of Avignon, who decided to have his court stop in the city. He enlarged and remodeled the old episcopal palace, he used the spacious convent of the Dominicans, he had blocks of houses allocated for his cardinals, and some relatively cramped quarters for the members of the Curia. His successors BENEDICT XII and Clement VI wanted to correct the precariousness of the original structure; they ordered the construction of a castle on the episcopal palace's location. The entirety of the Curia was certainly never housed there: the domestic help took their shifts around the pope, the primary host, and his guards took their turn on watch, while his judges held session; only the chamberlain and the treasurer, who administered his finances, lived in his castle with their indispensable collaborators. The chancery scribes, who composed an enormous series of letters, worked outside, in residences allocated for the vice chancellor or NOTARIES. But even though there was not a methodical distribution of locations, the Curia was established in Avignon; it had a fortress to protect it, chapels where the papal liturgy took place, and rooms where princes and their ambassadors were received; the pope's stays in the nearby Comtat Venaissin did not incur an exodus of the administrative apparatus which, complex and powerful as it had become, needed stability in order to work.

A great number of documents shed light on the Curia's organization and personnel; these include liturgical books, rules for administrative and judicial services, registers for the officials who taxed lodgings, and expense registers for both provisions for domestic offices and payment for the members of the Curia. There were important publications during the time when the legitimate popes were in Avignon. Correspondence and other writings from the period shed light on the small world of the Curia, a world which they show, occasionally with vehemence, to be devoid of neither love for money nor the refinement of intrigues. Sources of the same nature, although less regularly preserved, exist for the long period of the GREAT SCHISM and for the 15th century. But these are still awaiting researchers and editors in the VATICAN ARCHIVES; since light has been shed on only a few sections of the total picture, we have a less than clear view after 1378.

No description of the Curia is complete without mention of the cardinals: they are the pope's electors, the advisers he convenes in CONSISTORIES, the heads of his administrative services, his delegates for judging cases, and his legates to Christendom; they accompany him, they assist him, and they participate in ceremonial pomp, where a place is reserved for them in the first row. This is not the place to examine their recruitment, their influence, or their actions. It suffices to say that, from 1305 to 1375, 134 cardinals were created in twenty-three promotions, that their college barely went beyond twenty members, but each had right to a livery composed of buildings that were requisitioned and partially transformed into a true palace, and that they maintained a court. The Great Schism forced rival popes to fill out their respective colleges in order to maintain better affiliation with the kingdoms and churches that recognized them: seventy-three cardinals reinforced the Roman obedience in nine promotions, forty-nine cardinals of Avignon, in eighteen promotions, and eighteen cardinals that of Pisa, in five promotions. When unity was reestablished, 149 cardinals were created up to 1484. The choices of the popes were guided by their NEPOTISM, by the desire to reward good servants, and by their wish to indulge temporal sovereigns. Under the Avignon popes, who were natives of France, four-fifths of the cardinals were French, with a net preponderance of men from the Languedoc-speaking south. In the 15th century, under Italian popes, half the cardinals were drawn from Italy. The simple mention of recruitment shows the point to which the cardinals were involved in a Curial society the composition of which reflected the needs and preferences of its head.

The personal nature of the Roman Curia suggests that its description should begin with the domestics who were attached directly to the service of the pope. It was even to this part of the Curia that the 1409 notice was restricted. The notice paid considerable attention to the pope's "housekeeper" (*magister hospitii pape*) who came from the nobility and was present at the pope's meals; he kept the keys to his residence, rang the bell that marked the pace of work and indicated when doors were to be shut, and oversaw each day's expenses. This duty was performed under the reign of Clement VI; it does not appear to have had the importance at the time that it would hold in the 15th century; it was perhaps honorific. The salon master (*magister aulae*), who appears after 1362, was primarily in charge of setting tables, placing guests after they had washed their hands, and seeing to the smooth running of banquets; he was an assistant to the housekeeper, and often his replacement.

The chamberlains (*cubicularii* or *camerarii* or *cambrerii*) were responsible for such intimate duties that the pope recruited them from the same milieu as that from which he had come: members of the great families of the Quercy, under John XXII, Cistercian or Benedictine monks under Benedict XII and URBAN V. They were constant companions: some were there when the pope went to bed at night, and when he arose in the morning; they recited the hours with him and surrounded him during his mass and divine offices, but they also played the role of private secretary, receiving requests and presenting them, and then sending them off once they were signed; others even slept in the same room as the pope. In 1409 chamberlains had their own responsibilities: one took charge of private letters, another the jewels, another the woolen garments, another the linens, another still was in charge of the pope's sweets, his spices, and his medicines. Their numbers grew, from three to at least six. They were so closely related to the pope that a few prelates were made honorary chamberlains in an attempt to show high esteem. Forty-four doctors (*physici*) were consulted by the legitimate popes of Avignon; obligatorily, there were one or two in the Curia. But it was quite frequent that a famous doctor was called in; twelve came from Italy, namely Bologna, but there were others from Montpellier. Several doctors (for example, John of Tournemire) cared for two or three popes in succession. A chaplain's office, and occasionally a bishopric, rewarded care that was especially appreciated. After 1340 we see evidence of surgeons (*surgici*); at the time, they were increasing in status. Some barbers and apothecaries filled the ranks of this personnel; these were laymen who were placed on the same level as sergeants at arms.

Continual prayer around Peter's successor made the presence of a body of chaplains (*capellani pape*) indispensable. Nicholas III set their numbers at twenty-five. It might be wondered, however, if the regularity of this essential service was correctly assured during the first third of the 14th century, where we see Clement V and John XXII name the holders of the most diverse offices to the chaplaincy. John XXII began to react when he instituted the chaplains of honor, for whose selection there were no rules, and whose role in the Curia was carried out only by their presence. It was Benedict XII who clarified the situation. The commensal chaplains (*capellani commensales*), who played roles in papal ceremonies and received a salary and other gifts, allowed the pope to incorporate into his particularly estimable company clerics whom he intended to favor or who were recommended to him—there were from ten to more than twenty of them, and their presence in Avignon's accounting records was quite noticeable. But the singing of daily and nightly hours, starting in 1335, was entrusted to twelve private chaplains (*capellani intrinseci* or *capellani capelle*) who lived in community under the direction of a master of the chapel (*magister capelle*); they would soon be referred to only as cantors (*cantores*). With Clement VI, the private chapel was filled primarily with clerics who were natives of the north of France, where the ars nova, with its introduction of polyphony, renewed church singing; how this novelty passed into the daily liturgy of the Avignon court is unknown. The list in 1409 mentions only the master and twelve cantors; the other chaplains had disappeared.

One would be on less than certain ground in asserting that the office of papal confessor, which appeared in 1343 for the Limousine Carmelite Pierre de Besse, corresponded to this title. The successive "confessors" called to take responsibility for the library, the holy vessels, and the pope's ornaments, were automatically raised to the episcopacy. When the pope traveled, the "confessor," mounted on a mule, carried the blessed sacrament.

The doctrinal authority held by the head of the Church was connected to the master of the Sacred Palace (*magister sacri palatii*), a name given, starting in 1343, to the professor of theology in the Curial school, which had been created in the mid-13th century. This was a *studium generale*, which conferred the degree of *licentia ubique docendi*. The master's pedagogical role is unknown. He was almost always chosen from the order of preaching friars and the honor of a bishopric awaited the end of his career in the Curia.

The four domestic offices that traditionally saw to the Curia's daily needs continued to figure first in the accounts, even though the offices' expenses, once the Curia was established in Avignon, represented only a small fraction of the Camera's disbursements (from 3 to 7 percent, except under the reign of Clement VI when it was 14 percent). These included the kitchen (*coquina*), bread bakeries (*panetaria*), bottle shops (*buticularia*), and the blacksmith shop (*marestella*).

The kitchen was managed by an administrator who purchased food and a scribe who kept tallies and kept the provisions (whence the name *custos cibariorum*, which began to be applied in 1367). A kitchen master, which we see under Clement VI, oversaw the assistants. The distinction was maintained between a small or private kitchen, which served the pope's table, and a large or common kitchen, which took care of the guests and the distribution of supplies. The two bread bakeries supplied the city's bakers with grain, purchased through the almonry according to a contract that stipulated the number of loaves to make from each measure of grain. They obtained salt and cheese, and kept the dishes. Two bottle makers, at least, a scribe, and some servants kept the wine and what was needed for making wine, and furnished what was necessary for both tables. During the Avignon period, the bottle shop purchased the fruit that previously, and then again in the 15th century, was acquired by the bread makers.

The utility of the blacksmith's shop varied, depending on whether a pope was sedentary or fond of traveling. In Avignon, two masters of the smith and a notary, and from eight to sixteen grooms and a few valets sufficed. The former purchased harnesses and other gear, and the latter cared for the ANIMALS—two palfreys for the pope, seventeen horses, five mules or asses, and three packhorses, according to a document from 1 March 1372. But, when traveling, Urban V was accompanied by 121 horses and mules on the Montefiascome road in 1368; 315 animals boarded ship for Gregory XI's return to Rome in 1376.

The regular personnel for the four offices did not exceed fifty men. To this were added the commander for supplying water (*aquarius pape* in 1342, later *magister aquae*), the master of the light (*magister cire*), who had torches and candles lit in the chapel and the rooms of the palace, and set out the candelabra; the quartermaster (*furrerius*), who became the keeper of the furniture, bedding, and draperies (*custos paramentorum*), the guardian of the dishes (*custos vaxellae*), a tailor, a furrier, and the laundryman. Some were responsible for the upkeep of the residence and, if need be, changed the interior decor, and watched over the pope's wardrobe; they had a few employees working under them. The cleanliness of the buildings was the responsibility of a *scobator*, who supervised the sweepers. There were gardeners for the orchard; they also oversaw the fishpond and the poultry; at one point a guardian was named to care for the deer and other animals that had been given to the pope.

The length of the description dedicated to the tasks of the two brother almoners in the early 14th century attests to the importance attached to the charitable work of the Curia; the rations provided were sufficient to feed a hundred of the poor each day, while by virtue of a calendar with fifty-nine liturgical feast days provisions were made for meals for an additional number of indigents; this number reached three hundred on the feast day of St. Benedict (21 March) and St. Thomas Becket (29 December), four hundred for the Assumption, and even a thousand for Holy Thursday, according to a decision attributed to Boniface VIII; sergeants assisted the almoners in distributing coins during trips. The diversity of responsibilities that people were in the habit of attributing to members of the Curia was such that the almoners were responsible for preparing the chrism and the holy oils for Holy Saturday, and for washing the pope's body when he died.

With the residence in Avignon, the almonry, traditionally called the Pignotte, continued its work, and even expanded it. Each year it spent from twelve to twenty-five gold florins, and even went through some fifty thousand florins from 1346 to 1348. The two aspects of its activity were separate: the private almonry distributed gifts to convents, churches, and individuals; the almonry of the poor (*elemosina pauperum*) gave out food, wine, and clothing. An administrator (*administrator domus elemosine Pinhote*) managed the service, the two former brothers almoner, chosen from among the lay brothers of the Cistercian monastery of Fontfroide, ordered the meals that were prepared by three cooks and a butler; two ushers supervised the throngs that crowded around the distribution sites; scribes kept accounts; valets did the work of distributing the stores of food. This subordinate personnel was supervised only by an administrator, and was supported by the Pignotte, which had a storehouse. This office referred to as the almonry was part of the Curia, as was also the case for those in armed service, who provided security and prestige.

The companies, formed by laymen, were clearly identified in the early 14th century: doorkeepers guarded entrances to the papal residence and apartments, knights and squires escorted the head of the Church, sergeants were ready to do whatever was commanded of them. Their rations, and later, their wages, varied depending on their level of responsibility. Then tasks became more similar, and even mixed up, even though the difference between groups and hierarchies of soldiers were preserved. Enrollment never was stable. Missions to the exterior spread out the individuals involved, such that registers showed only the presence of those that were within the Curia. Among the doorkeepers, a distinction could be made between the majors (*hostiarii majores*), who kept guard around the pope's living quarters and of which there were fifteen, on the average, and the minors (*hostiarii minores*), who were spread out among the entrances to the palace and who were responsible, if need be, for preparing the rooms for a consistory or a reception. The number of sergeants at arms (*servientes armorum seu massarii*) fluctuated considerably: set at forty-five in 1278, it fell to twenty-five in 1316, and was finally held at about sixty. They constituted the court guard, surrounding the pope, assuring that the palace was policed; they arrested delinquents and kept guard at the prison. They were freed from the duty of setting up churches where the pope was going to be officiating; they no longer had to take orders from the heads of the blacksmith's shop; they no longer had to share the old cloaks or the used saddles that had belonged to a deceased pope. Their promotion rivaled that of the knights, squires, and equerries (*miles, domicelli, scutiferi*), of whom there had been some seventy under Clement V and John XXII, although after that time they declined dramatically; the office remained, although it had no further utility. Doorkeepers and sergeants alone had a small administration; they formed two companies.

The Curia's lay personnel, for all matters concerning it, was under the marshal of justice, although the latter's supervision also extended to those who frequented the court, who were called *cortisani*. This was a heavy responsibility. The high officer was assisted by an ordinary judge and a criminal judge; there were more than thirty sergeants under his command. Serious complaints were lodged against them, to such an extent that in 1340 a number of them were hung and the marshal committed suicide.

These numbers were very similar to those of what might be called the pope's "house" (his entourage, his domestic offices, and his military corps), found in the administrative services, with the exception that the scribes of apostolic letters and those of the Penitentiary did not have the possibility of being considered "members of the family," that is, members of the Curia, until 1347; it was only in 1390–1391 that BONIFACE IX confirmed this title upon all the scribes of the chancery. *Officiales*, but not necessarily *familiares*, in the earliest days, these scribes—whose labor was essential to the administration's work—were not admitted into the Curia, the very nature of which was that of a family.

What made the Apostolic Camera important was precisely that it was the body without which the Curia could not have existed. It provided the financial means; there was no distinction between the funds of the pope and the members of his *family* and the receipts and expenses of the Church's central government. The chamberlain (*camerarius*) ended up being, also, the closest official to the pope; he lodged near the pope, and followed him wherever he went. It was the need for absolute trust in this individual that explains why, beginning in 1301, the chamberlain was no longer chosen from among the cardinals who, through their connection with a prestigious college, might be tempted to oppose the pontiff. On the other hand, the chamberlain's area of responsibility and his knowledge of affairs justified the fact that a number of popes retained the same individual in the position: Gasbert of Laval, from 1319 to 1347; Stephen Cambarou, from 1347 to 1361; Arnold Aubert, from 1361 to 1371;

Peter of Cros (a tenacious opponent to URBAN VI from the moment of his election), from 1371 to 1383; and Francis of Conzie, from 1383 to his death in 1432, who became so identified with his duties, and so indispensable to them, that he served, successively, the popes of three different obediences. All these individuals held an episcopal, or archepiscopal, see in the south of France, often the see of Arles. The treasurers kept the treasury of the Roman Church. There was only one treasurer in the mid-14th century; as he kept track of receipts and expenses, his importance increased. Like the chamberlain, he, too, lived in the palace. The Camera's clerics, of which there were usually four, sent instructions to all the financial agents throughout Christendom, and then checked their accounts. The high administration officials had at their disposition notaries and scribes (*servitores camerae*) who were answerable only to them, and thanks to whom the financial records and those of the Camera's letters have been preserved.

The problems that relations between the Camera and taxpayers tended to raise fell under the jurisdiction of the Camera auditor, who was assisted by procurators and fiscal lawyers, the latter of whom were experts in law, and were almost all Italians. The auditor had the power to incarcerate. All those found guilty by the administrative jurisdictions, the most important sector of which was that of the Camera auditor, were detained in the *soldanus*, the prison reserved for financial infractions, while the marshal of justice's prison took members of the Curia and those courtiers found guilty of other infractions.

The Camera was not only a financial institution; it became the pope's political intermediary in the sense that it was completely under his control. Notaries and men trained with the pen could be chosen to compose his most private correspondence. *Scriptores papae* were soon drawn from the Camera's personnel. Beginning in 1341, from three to six secretaries (*secretarii*) were selected; having made an oath to the chamberlain, it was they who wrote the most important letters. These men were capable of exerting some influence, and even of becoming agents of papal diplomacy. There were as many Italians as Frenchmen in their ranks. Urban V, dreaming of his return to Rome, engaged Niccolo de Romani d'Osimo and the already famous Florentine Francesco Bruni. The private letters were recorded elsewhere.

The Camera still had control of the couriers (*cursores*); even though they carried a number of letters or citations, they also made certain purchases, made arrests, and accompanied the pope, holding the baldachin over him during entrances into cities and protecting him from the jostling of the crowd. There was not much difference between them and the sergeants. The number of couriers was kept at fifty to sixty, although it fell to about twenty before the time of the Great Schism. The 1409 notice attributed to them only the role of palace servants, where six of them, who were named by a master, were to be available at all times.

The chancery's primary sender of letters that were called "common letters," the volume of which increased with papal centralization, was much more an administrative body than an element of the Curia. Until the mid-fourteenth century, only the vice chancellor (who was a cardinal), six notaries, a corrector, an auditor of letters of contestation, and two drafters of bulls were considered members of the pope's family. Scribes were private employees of the notaries. John XXII announced specific rules on 16 November 1331. A vice chancellor's term of office could in some cases be quite long; Pierre des Près held the position from 1325 to 1361, and Pierre de Monteruc did so from 1361 to 1385. The notaries, whose control over "chambers" of editors appears to have been outmoded, were divided between the chancery and the Camera; their duties, which appear to have been less than extensive, were for the most part honorary. On the other hand, the corrector (who remained in his role for a considerable length of time, with the duty of checking the conformity of acts), the two bull drafters, Cistercian *conversi* who resided in a private house and who held the seal, still carried out their traditional duties, as did, also, the auditor of letters of contestation, an eminent jurist who would be elevated to the rank of bishop or cardinal.

The most important work was done in the chancery by the *referendarius* and the scribes of apostolic letters. The *referendarius*, a title that did not appear until 1358, read requests to the pope, but his office was not recognized in the 14th century, and it was a notary or auditor who filled this role, unless it was an abbot from Montmajour, like Pierro de Banhac (1362–68). In actuality, the pope named whomever he wished. And there were some hundred clerks who were referred to as *scriptores litterae apostolicarum*. Their importance continued to grow to the point where the drafters of papal briefs, of which there were twenty-four, constituted their own college, and requested to be considered as scribes, even though the latters' duty was to put into form, and engross, the minutes drawn up by the *scriptores apostolicarum*. Recruitment of Italians never ceased. But in addition to the specialists, the group of scribes took in individuals who had no real responsibility in their area of expertise. This is because scribes became members of the family after 1347. The drafters of papal BRIEFS had assistants about whom the Curia had no knowledge. It is probable that the hundred scribes were not all present in Avignon. Many probably worked outside the palace, in notaries' offices or in the houses of the vice chancellor's "livery." Like the registrars, of which there was one for the private letters written by members of the Camera and two for the letters of the Curia and common letters, they coordinated the work of several copyists. With Clement VI, the petitions granted were also recorded.

Cases which the pope reserved for himself to examine, in matters such as those of granting absolutions, or removing excommunications or interdicts, were submitted to the Penetentiary: this included the "major penitentiary" cardinal, and sixteen to eighteen members of religious orders who were approved to hear confessions in the main languages spoken in the Christian world. These men were carefully recruited from among theologians and experts in canon law; since Rome continued to be the mystical seat of the papacy, some of the penitentiaries remained there, near the Lateran basilica and St. Peter's. The pope gave great consideration to his minor penitentiaries (*penitentiarii minores*), whom he treated like his chaplains. But the scribes of the Penitentiary, of whom there were from twelve to eighteen, constituted a college that was overseen only by the great penitentiary.

By the mid-13th century so many cases were sent that they could not all be judged by the pope and his cardinals. Chaplains began to examine them; trials regarding benefices gradually increased, and a company of judges was formed, receiving its constitutions in 1331 and 1340. It was called the TRIBUNAL OF THE ROTA. These auditors of the sacred palace, of which there were twelve divided into three degrees (*gradus*), were professors or doctors of civil law or CANON LAW whose esteem by the pope virtually assured them of various missions and then a bishop's miter, if not a cardinal's hat; under the Avignon papacies, thirty-six became bishops and another ten cardinals. Each of the Rota's auditors was assisted by four notaries.

The picture of the Curia seems clear, and its members' duties appear to have been well distributed. In Avignon the popes published constitutions, and they replaced fringe allocations with wages or allowances. But being both the house of the pope and a governmental administration, the Curia fundamentally remained the papal family. Each member, regardless of his apparent specialty, did as the pope commanded. There was considerable mobility from one office to another. Some individuals held titles, even though they did not always perform the duties associated with that title. Being a scribe of apostolic letters was sought by chapel masters, doctors, and almoners. There were even cases where purveyors, bankers, or goldsmiths were accepted as squires or sergeants at arms. Elevation to these honorary titles became a means of government: beginning with John XXII, the names of new honorary chaplains were published in batches.

The popes during the Great Schism retained this organization for the Curia, drawing their men from their respective groups of followers. Antipope FELIX V did exactly the same thing in 1439. The councils, in calling for the reform of the "head," were naturally thinking of the Curia. In its fortieth session, the Council of Constance included this reform in the measures it was demanding of the pope it would elect. The effort was in vain. With the Curias of GREGORY XII and John XXII divided up, MARTIN V built his court on the old model. The fathers at the twenty-third session of the Council of Basel (24 March 1436) held to calling for a maximum of twenty-four cardinals, a reduction in papal interventions in matters involving benefices, and a reduction in the taxes levied by the Apostolic Camera. The papal government's procedures raised more criticism and rancor than did the importance of the court. It is not surprising that its development, which had begun during the Avignon period, continued.

The PETITIONS received and the different kinds of correspondence sent out required reorganization. Petitions were gathered into the *data communis* and, after approval, they were given a date that specified at what point the concession began. This arbitrary procedure set up a hierarchy in the flow of responses. In the early 15th century, an officer, the *datator* or *datarius*, was assigned to this task (1420). His position grew in importance. Under INNOCENT VIII (1484–92), he oversaw the petitions going to the pope, checked their contents, and kept a record of favors granted. He had his own staff and space in the new Vatican palace, and he collected some taxes. In 1497 protests were raised against the Datary, which had taken some of the chancery's prerogatives away from it. Nevertheless, the drafters of papal briefs, who were supposed to be assisted in the preparation of minutes, evolved into a college of seventy members, divided into three categories, under PIUS II.

Diplomatic mail was already written by secretaries. Martin V grouped his secretaries into a private chamber (*camera secreta*), which was later to become the Apostolic SECRETARIAT, with twenty-four scribes in 1487.

Even though the number of Rota auditors remained stable—it reached twelve in 1472—and although the rise in the dignity of sergeants was marked by their recruitment from the nobility, by their status in 1436, and by their limitation to twenty, the staff tended to increase, as if attachment to the Curia were a means of earning consideration and rising in the hierarchy. Thenceforth, *referendarii* were prelates whose knowledge and probity were praised, since EUGENE IV allowed them to review certain petitions; there were seventy-five under Martin V! Pius II kept only eight. The chamberlain, now chosen from among the cardinals, was assisted by a vice chamberlain. Regulations were written, in 1438, for the Camera clerks, of which there were seven. One of the Camera's councils convened not only the officers of finance, but also jurists and bishops. For the Italian clergy, which made up a great majority of the body in the 15th century, passing through the Curia was the best way to access the papacy. Members of the laity were not to be outdone: the squires were all honorary squires; some even had a role in the palace; most of them managed to be able to appear at some time

or other, and to have the privilege of carrying a dish to the pope's table. The members of the Curia who effectively were employees or supernumeraries became members of the court (*cortisani, cotegiani*) in the modern sense of the word. The secretaries, whose *Facetiae* the Florentine Poggio has recounted, delighted in ridiculing the ignoramus cardinals and spreading malicious gossip. Ever coveted and prestigious in name, the Curia's decline opened the door for the critics.

Bernard Guillemain

Bibliography

"Curie romaine," *DDC*, 4, 971–1008.

"Cour romaine," *DTC*, 3–2, 1931–83.

Baix, F. "Notes sur les clercs de la Chambre apostolique (XIIIe–XIVe s.)," *BIHR*, 27 (1952), 17–52.

Bourgin, E. "La *familia* pontificia sotto Eugenio IV," *ASR* (1904), 203–24.

Celier, L. *Les Dataires du XVe siècle et les origines de la Daterie apostolique*, Paris, 1910 (*BEFAR*, 103).

Genèse et débuts du Grand Schisme d'Occident, Paris, 1980 (Colloques internationaux du CNRS, 586).

Guillemain, B. *Histoire d'Avignon*, Aix-en-Provence, 1979.

Guillemain, B. *La Cour pontificale d'Avignon. 1309–1376. Étude d'une société*, Paris, 1962 (*BEFAR*, 201).

Haller, J. "Zwei Aufzeichungen über die Beamten der Curie im XIII. und XIV. Jahrhundert," *QFIAB*, 1 (1898), 1–38.

Katterbach, B. *Referendarii utriusque signaturae supplicationum a Martino V al Leonem XIII*, Vatican, 1913.

Mollat, G. *The Popes of Avignon*, trans. James Love, New York, 1963.

Muratori, *Rerum italicarum scriptores*. III, 2, 810–24 (notice of 1409).

Partner, P. *The Pope's Men: The Papal Civil Service in the Renaissance*, Oxford, 1990.

Schaefer, K. H. *Die Ausgaben der apostolischen Kammer*, 3 vols., Paderborn, 1911, 1914, 1937 (*Vatikanische Quellen*, II, III, VI).

Schuchard, C. *Die Deutschen an der päpstlichen Kurie im späten Mittelalter (1378–1447)*, Tübingen, 1987.

Schwarz, B. *Die Organisation kurialer Schreiberkollegien von ihrer Entstehung bis zur Mitte des 15. Jahrhunderts*, Tübingen, 1972.

Tangl, M. *Die päpstlichen Kanzlei-Ordnungen von 1200–1500*, Innsbrück, 1894 (Aalen, 1959).

Uginet, F. C. *Le Liber officialium de Martin V*, Rome, 1975 (Pubblicazioni degli Archivi di Stato. Fonti e Sussidi, 7).

Von Hoffmann, W. *Forschungen zur Geschichte der kurialen Behörden vom Schisma bis zur Reformation*, 2 vols., Rome, 1914.

15th Century. Beginning with MARTIN V, the papacy started to turn toward a kind of pontifical monarchy more appropriate to the times, a reinterpretation of the theocracy of an earlier age. It was in this context that two of the phenomena most characteristic of the Roman Curia of the period can be placed: the reorganization of the powers of the SACRED COLLEGE and the expansion of the court of Rome, along with the systematic creation of new bodies in the Curia and the impressive development of the papal family, and of the cardinals and high dignitaries who constituted it.

During the 15th century, the CONSISTORY declined as the center of decision making for important matters concerning the papacy, and its responsibilities tended to be limited to approving particularly important political and administrative acts (such as declarations of war or the naming of a cardinal) which, nevertheless, were decided elsewhere, and for which the pope was unable to forgo the canonical approval of the *consilio fratrum cardinalium*. Meeting, on the average, every seven to ten days, the consistory's primary task was providing the main benefices, a question of paramount importance because of the revenues that the cardinals drew from them, through sharing the *servitium commune* with the pope and the connections it created between the cardinals and secular sovereigns. The need for a cardinal as liaison for a candidate for a bishopric or abbey would even favor the birth of the "CARDINAL PROTECTOR" of a state, which was legitimized by JULIUS II in the early sixteenth century, on the basis of an already well-established practice analogous to the cardinal protector of the religious orders.

For questions, the popes preferred to follow personal methods of government. A fairly tight core of cardinals, who were habitually the pope's nephews and confidants, resided within the Apostolic palace (whence the name *cardinales palatini*), and were able to see him daily. Other than these, only the pope's *secretarius domesticus*, a few occasional advisers (his banker, for example), and a small number of high officials in the Curia (the *datarius*, the treasurer, the *referendarii*)—none of whom was eligible to be elected a cardinal—had access to the pontiff's private life. In practice, then, the constitutional importance of the Sacred College was neglected; its importance depended solely on the personal prestige of some of its members who succeeded in exercising influence on the pope in occasional, specific instances.

While the actual political importance of the body of cardinals (especially as this body related to secular sovereigns) was increasingly limited to the CONCLAVE, its duties as a consultative body were expressed in the 15th and 16th centuries through the custom of forming special congregations of cardinals within the consistory: ad hoc commissions charged with examining a specific problem or engaging in deliberations, the results of which were later to be referred to the consistory. It was to these temporary

congregations to which, in the period preceding the COUNCIL OF TRENT, projects for the reform of the Roman Curia, like those of ALEXANDER VI and LEO X, would be entrusted. This was an indispensable precondition for the reform *in capite*. The fact that these plans would not be carried out proves the dramatic inability for self-reformation shown by those in the Curia up to the time just before the Council of Trent, underscoring the role played by cardinals in resolving or not resolving difficult situations, which in a number of aspects takes the Roman Curia out of the complete control of the pope himself.

From an institutional point of view, the long-term phenomena characteristic of the Roman Curia between AVIGNON and Trent are the loss of influence of the CHANCERY in the papal system of government as a whole and, within it or superimposed upon it, the birth of new bodies more closely tied to the pope himself and his *plenitudo potestatis*. Well into the 15th century, the vice chancellor appeared to be stripped of practically all his decision-making power. The position was thenceforth reserved for a cardinal and, usually, it was the prerogative of one of the pontiff's nephews or favorites, given the increased revenues attached to the position and the prestige conferred upon the second-highest rank in the Roman Church, after the pope. Even though the chancery's offices had no physical location to call their own until well into the 16th century (before this time they were located in the cardinal vice chancellor's private palace), their duties as the official office for composing apostolic letters appears to have been well defined. They were given substantial autonomy as a body—an autonomy that would increase with the expansion of the venality of duties—and endowed with proper automatic functioning in the production of documents whose contents were decided elsewhere. Approval of a petition, presented to the pope by a *referendarius* or a datarius, took place via a *signatura*. The offices of the *referendarii*, which were regrouped into a college presided over by one or two *referendarii domestici*, who were endowed with broad discretionary powers, were later divided by Julius II into the *signatura gratiae* and the *signatura justitiae*, in reference to the different content of the requests contained in the petitions. When the matter at hand was a judicial case, it was passed to the TRIBUNAL OF THE ROTA, which was reorganized by SIXTUS IV in 1472 and composed of twelve *auditores Sacri Palatii*.

Petitions were to be transcribed in the appropriate wording for the Roman Curia, and recopied on a parchment which would be sealed by a leaden *bulla*, so that, for all practical purposes, it could be considered an Apostolic letter with prescriptive force. The transformation of a petition entailed from five to nine operations, which in their totality were referred to as an *expeditio*. At each step, payment of a tax to the office in question was expected; on the whole, the procedure was long and expensive, which made room for a widely tolerated form of corruption, one justified by the fact that it could expedite the matter in question. Attempts to reform the system under Leo X paradoxically led to an increase in taxes, which was primarily dictated by pressures from *officiales* to bring a quick return on their investments.

Beginning with the papacy of Sixtus IV, the phenomenon of the venality of duties in the Roman Curia actually underwent an impressive impetus, and ended up definitively becoming a method of financing the papal treasury, with the help of a long-term investment. It created a broad class of shareholders in the papal public debt, in the form of officials of the Curia's bureaucracy, who could count on an annual revenue equal to approximately 10 percent of the purchase price of a charge.

In just a few years, from 1479 to 1483, under pressure from the costs of war and following the example of a long used practice in the bureaucracies of secular governments of the time, Sixtus IV created or reorganized some of the primary services of the Curia in the form of a college, selling the positions thus created and guaranteeing their holders a fixed income, which came from the resources of the service and income from the PAPAL STATES. The already extant college of *scriptores* is an example. Colleges of the seventy-two drafters of papal briefs and the seventy-two notaries of the Roman Curia were instituted, while sending bureaucratic matters relating to the composition of bulls on behalf of those interested became the monopoly of a special body of lawyers and procurators, the *sollicitatores litterarum apostolicarum*, who were regrouped into a college with one hundred members called janissaries.

The sale of duties was entrusted to the datarius, an important individual in the pope's family who, under Sixtus IV, was placed at the head of a specialized service (the Datary) with financial connections to the *camera secreta* and controlled by the datarius himself. The datarius was also responsible for determining the *compositiones*, that is, the sums due to the pope for the concession of graces and special dispensations, which he decided on the basis of his tremendous discretionary powers.

The creation of new colleges, which, among other things, allowed a number of responsibilities to be accumulated by a single individual, continued under Sixtus IV. In 1487 INNOCENT VIII created the college of 30 secretaries; in 1497 Alexander VI created the college of 104 *collectores taxae plumbi*; Julius II, from 1507 to 1509, created that of the 101 *scriptores archivii* and the 141 administrators of the port of Ripa, on the Tiber. Beginning with Leo X, the institution of new venal responsibilities was no longer confined within the framework of the chancery, but also concerned the pope's *familia* (the 60 chamberlains and the 140 equerries) and the fiscal administration of the city of Rome (the 612 sections of entrances into the port of Ripa). It also entailed the creation

of new orders of chivalry (the knights of St. Peter, instituted by Leo X; the knights of St. Paul, instituted by PAUL III; and the knights of Pius, instituted by PIUS IV), which responded as much to the demand for sure investments as it did to the need for new ways of entry into the nobility appropriate for European society at the dawn of the modern age.

The number of venal charges in the Roman court thus grew impressively from the 15th to the 16th century: from 300 to 625 under Sixtus IV, to 936 under Julius II, and to 2,232 on the eve of the SACK OF ROME. The Roman court became a theater for careers which, in order to be open to all talents, needed to be sustained by wealth. The primary backer for funds and the beneficiary of this process was the Italian patrician and noble class, with which the pope would end up creating a bond in a more or less privileged fashion, by inaugurating a long-term osmosis between the aristocracies of the peninsula and the high spheres of the Roman Curia.

Transformation of the chancery into an autonomous bureaucratic apparatus structured into internal corporations provided the model that served as an inspiration for other dicasteries in the Curia. First of all, the PENITENTIARY was presided over by the cardinal penitentiary (generally a nephew of the pope) and composed of minor penitentiaries, of clerics in service to the Roman basilicas, as well as of a body of *scriptores* and *correctores* assigned to the delivery of special BULLS. But within the papal palace the popes created a reservoir of venal charges to auction off. Besides the chamberlains and the squires, the secretaries were also structured into a college. An important group within the *familia*, their duties were shown to be necessary just at the time when the pope had ceased to find in the chancery a body that could respond to the demands of immediate government. These duties were taken on in an increasingly clear fashion during the 15th century by a corps of secretaries, which was detached from the chancery early on, and, with one or two *secretarii domestici* at their head, became the nucleus for what later became the SECRETARIAT OF STATE. In close contact with the pope and the cardinal nephew, the domestic secretaries coordinated the dispatching of diplomatic affairs, which were usually entrusted to members of the secretary's office sent out as *nuntii* or *commissarii*. In the second half of the fifteenth century, their missions still had a semipermanent nature and were habitually connected to the duty of collecting tithes, but it is interesting to note that this practice, which gave birth to the system of permanent nunciatures in the sixteenth century, was modeled on the diplomacy of the potentates of the Italian Renaissance and autocratic governmental techniques developed by their chanceries. The brief (*littera brevis*) was a document that was specific to the papal secretariat. It owes its name to the succinct nature of the ideas it contains. The office assigned to draw up briefs, which was organized under Julius II and Leo X in the form of the *secretaria brevium*, was sought after by humanists and *litterateurs*.

During the course of the 15th century the APOSTOLIC CAMERA evolved into a dicastery responsible primarily for managing the temporal revenues of both the papacy and the government of the Papal State. This occurred after the change that took place in the composition of the financial resources the Holy See had at its disposal. Spiritual receipts, already greatly diminished with the GREAT SCHISM following the concordats signed by Martin V with the princes—and which were destined to be reduced even further because of the Protestant crisis—already represented no more than a third of the papacy's income under Sixtus IV. Besides tax collections, which at this time were also diminishing in quantity from the level they had reached during the Avignon period as a source of profits for the papal court, the only spiritual receipts remaining from what the Camera controlled were the annates and the services paid for the apostolic provision of benefices. In this context, the Camera increased its role as treasury and administrative tribunal of the Papal State, which the papacy increasingly depended on to finance its governmental apparatus and its initiatives. The Camera's staff was supposed to divide its activities between its own bureaucratic responsibilities and responsibility for the administrative offices in the Papal State.

Service to the papacy thus gathered in the court of Rome an international society of high prelates, nobles, financiers, and men of letters who, in committing themselves to a career with a questionable future, both adopted rules of behavior appropriate for members of the ecclesiastical court and perpetuated the ideology peculiar to Renaissance Rome, according to which the mission of universal government taken on by the city, *civitas sacerdotalis et regia*, did not disappear as the pagan age gave way to Christianity. It just evolved and took on a sacred connotation. In the culture that developed in the 15th century Curia, the humanistic idea of continuity between antiquity and the present exalted the concept already contained in the DONATION OF CONSTANTINE of *translatio Imperii* of emperors and pontiffs. From this point of view, the way the government of the Roman papacy functioned in Christianity was based on a primacy that was not only of a divine, but also of a historical and cultural nature, since it claimed responsibility for the role Rome had played in civilizing the West through the construction of a papal monarchy founded on the concentration of the system of benefices, the judicial system, and the fiscal system. But the contradictions of this process, which took for granted a juridical and cultural prestige for the Roman Church as guaranteed by the consensus necessary for the system to work, became evident when the Protestant Reform exploded.

Marco Pellegrini

Bibliography

Celier, L. *Des Dataires du XVe siècle et les origines de la daterie apostolique*, Paris, 1910.

D'Amico, J. F. *Renaissance Humanism in Papal Rome*, Baltimore, 1983.

Frenz, T. *Die Kanzlei der Päpste in der Hochrenaissance (1471–1527)*, Tübingen, 1986.

Gottlob, A. *Aus der Camera apostolica des 15. Jahrhunderts*, Innsbruck, 1889.

McClung Hallman, B. *Italian Cardinals. Reform and the Church as Property, 1492–1563*, Los Angeles, 1985.

Partner P. *The Pope's Men. The Papal Civil Service in the Renaissance*, Oxford, 1990.

Stinger, C. L. *The Renaissance in Rome*, Bloomington, Ind., 1985.

Von Hofmann, W. *Forschungen zur Geschichte der Kurialen Behörden vom Schisma bis zur Reformation*, I–II, Rome, 1914.

16th to 18th Centuries. The need to reform the Curia became increasingly urgent under HADRIAN VI, most notably because of Luther's break with the Church. Nevertheless, Hadrian VI's short papacy permitted no more than a decrease in the number of referendaries in the *signatura* and a few timid adjustments in the structure of the PENITENTIARY. The obstacles encountered by various attempts at reform were due especially to the Datary, and the last isolated measures taken by the pontiff that struck at the resources of various services and the revenues of the knights of St. Peter, stirred up protests from a number of cardinals and gave rise to the ironic *Capitolo di Papa Adriano*, "O poor, wretched courtiers," written by Francesco Berni, who, at least in intention, gave evidence that the page was now being turned on a way of life and on the plethora of *litterateurs* in existence under LEO X. In the absence of any concrete intervention regarding the structure of the Curia during the papacy of CLEMENT VII, upon whose shoulders the SACK OF ROME in 1527 certainly weighed, a period of partial measures follow under PAUL III. In particular, the bull of 1535 tied reform of the Curia to a wider agreement among the groups concerned with Church reform. A commission, presided over by Cardinal Gasparo Contarini, was created to develop the famous *Consilium de emendanda Ecclesia* (1537). Once again, the Datary was the major obstacle to reform, because of disagreements within the commission on the subject of abolishing the *compositiones*. However, some important areas of progress were possible, with the institution of the first permanent congregation, that of the Holy Office of the INQUISITION (1542), to combat HERESY, and with other interventions concerning the CHANCERY and especially, due to the energy of Gian Pietro Carafa, the Apostolic Penitentiary. It was precisely under the steadfast Carafa, once he became PAUL IV, that the reform of the Curia got a definitive impulse.

By the pope's design, reformation of the Curia was inserted into a much more complex and broader plan of concentrating powers and strengthening the authority of the pope. Besides the pontiff's essential decision to create for his nephew Cardinal Carlo Carafa the superintendency of the PAPAL STATES for the government of temporal affairs, it is also significant that in 1557 a large number of responsibilities that had previously fallen under the jurisdiction of the Penitentiary, the chancery, or other tribunals of the Curia, were given to the Congregation of the Inquisition—of which Paul IV had been a quite influential member when he was a cardinal. This pope's line of conduct would be pursued with determination, albeit with less rigor, by his successor PIUS IV and by the cardinal nephew Charles Borromeo. The decisive sessions of the COUNCIL OF TRENT, with their disciplinary deliberations, created a climate in which are situated the reforms of the ROTA (1561), the Penitentiary (1562), and the APOSTOLIC CAMERA (1564), as well as the institution of the Congregation of the Council (1564) for the interpretation and execution of the measures voted into being at Trent. At the same time, measures were taken against the staff of the papal palace and the *familia* of the pope himself, the size of which was greatly reduced, while a new state of mind began to develop that would allow more important developments to take place under the papacy of PIUS V. In fact, in 1566–7, in addition to more rigorous asceticism, Pius V attempted to impress upon a partially "reformed" court and Curia a stern and conventual character that conformed to the aspirations of the old Dominican that he was. It was not completely by chance that Pius V's attention was drawn more specifically toward a general reform of the Penitentiary (1569), in so doing following Cardinal Borromeo's suggestions, and toward the institution of two new congregations, those of the INDEX (1571), which worked along with the Inquisition (where Pius V had long worked before becoming pope), and the Congregation for Bishops (1571–72), after the institution of the Congregation of the Council, for forms of intervention that were more in line with a centralizing and Curial mind-set regarding the peripheral Church hierarchy.

In the last thirty years of the 16th century, the mountain of issues, the political and religious interests in both the Italian and the international arenas, the very broadening of spheres of intervention, and the general climate that set in following the Council of Trent, made the forms the Curia had taken during the first decades of the century look increasingly outmoded. The consistory still remained a collegial body that gathered the pontiff and his cardinals in the most important moments of the life of the Church state and the Catholic Church. It was also useful in allocating the principal benefices (bishoprics and large abbeys), but it gradually delegated its responsibilities to

ordinary and extraordinary congregations. These answered to the pope alone, especially under GREGORY XIII (1572–85), while through the network of nunciatures, the organization of the great Roman colleges, and the missions in Europe, in the New World, and in Asia, the Curia became the active center for the Counter-Reformation, an early characteristic of a process that came to a climax under SIXTUS V. Besides the activity so energetically unfurled against the centrifugal forces within the state, such as the struggle against banditry and the Roman barons, and the politics of urbanization and constructions glorifying a militant and triumphal Church, what is interesting to underscore regarding Sixtus V's papacy is the exceptional procedures for centralization he was able to bring about in the Roman Curia. The Congregation of the Council had more power given to it over the activities of all bishops, through the reestablishment of the program of "AD LIMINA" VISITS *Apostolorum*, previously carried out in Rome by prelates only by custom, and through the generalized obligation of the "reports" on the state of each diocese.

For their part, on the model of Pius V, the Inquisition and the Congregation of the Index would see their domains of intervention expanded. But where Sixtus V's activity was most coherent and incisive was in the area of reform of the college of cardinals and, consequently, the radical reorganization of the Curia through the system of congregations. The bull *Postquam verus* (1586) set the number of cardinals at seventy, in memory of the seventy Elders of the Bible called to Moses' side, while a second bull, in 1587, subsequently defined formally the characteristics of the SACRED COLLEGE and the status of cardinal titles. This was a first, but essential, step, after a series of papal interventions, more numerous since the time of Paul III, aimed at a definitive transformation of the Curia's system of government, which had been based, despite the gradual concentration of power in the pope himself, on the dialectic relationship between the pontiff and the college of cardinals during the consistory's weekly meetings. A second step was taken by the bull *Immensa Dei* (1588), which was passed with opposition, especially on the part of the cardinals Santa Croce, Madruzzo, and Paleotti. This bull totally abolished the old consistorial system, which was replaced by a complex mechanism of fifteen permanent congregations (some, like those of the Inquisition, the Index, and the Council, were already in existence). Nine of them were designed to deal with the Church's spiritual questions, and six with the temporal matters of the state. The Curia's center of gravity thus passed from the consistory to the congregations, for which the model of the Inquisition was adopted and made general. The congregations were presided over by a cardinal (while the pope continued to preside over the Inquisition), with areas of competence that were specified during meetings which, like those of the consistory, were weekly, but worked under a polycentric and polysynodal system. If, on the one hand, these measures took any remaining real powers away from the college of cardinals, albeit without reducing the individual weight of "political" cardinals (members of reigning families or influential protectors of religious orders), on the other they permitted a new balance of forces to assert itself through a gradually refined bureaucratic mechanism. Even though it reflected the many different orientations in existence in the body of the Church, and though, at the level of the Curia, it sometimes did not preclude the possibility of divisive choices and confrontations (as had been the case for JANSENISM, QUIETISM, laxism, rigorism, and Jesuitism), this balance did allow, without any real break for the continuation of the management style of a varied and heterogeneous group in power. In fact, the 16th century did not see a real administrative reform of the Curia, but it did see the institutionalization of a new structure of government. Although the individuals and the groups within the structure changed, the ways of governing did not, as the old, unstable ecclesiastical oligarchy dating from Avignon and the time of the Renaissance was finally replaced by a broader oligarchy that was stable, or at least tending toward stability, due to the purchase of duties and to different forms of cooptation. As in the past, this system was characterized by a number of aristocratic and financial overlappings.

Even though Sixtus V's strong personality had in a way relegated to the background both his closest collaborators and his quite young nephew, Cardinal Alessandro Montalto, with CLEMENT VIII papal nepotism developed at the highest levels of Curial power, to reach its apogee with the Borghese family, but especially with the Barberinis. Beyond the rigorist and political accusations he had to face later, during the course of this period in history he responded to the specific need to strengthen the authority of the pope. At the time—this was the period during which the polyvalent system of congregations was born—the pontiff was more than ever in need, in the government of the Church and of the state, of a means for coordination and reference, that is, of one or more men in whom he had absolute confidence (or even men "of his own blood," as Paul IV had said in legitimizing the rise of his nephew Carlo Carafa). But in a broader sense nepotism most often resulted from favoritism or from family intrigues, which were so much a part of aristocratic society that they were both practiced and demanded to an increasing extent. Besides pontifical grace, political interventions, and the support of orders and regular congregations, nepotism had become one criterion for selection in the lower and higher cadres of the Curia and in the very development of careers in the court of Rome. This different, but not really new, period of an actual Roman Curia was described in the memoirs of Cardinal Guido Bentivoglio. It is similarly evoked in countless descriptions and "forewords" concerning the court of Rome. Despite the possible drawback of an uncertain future and the vain hope of enjoying protection, these forewords attracted to the capital city of Catholicism those with ambitions of climbing to the echelons of the *cursus honorum*, especially if they were from the lower or middle nobility of provincial Italy. After Sixtus V, this new stage in the Curia would find a fulcrum in the politics of the Aldobrandini family.

In the context of more prudent political mediation after Sixtus V's intransigence, and with a view toward strengthening the institution of the papacy not so much in the framework of the state but as an institution above the state, the Curia began to look more and more like the central motivator of international games and missionary zeal. In this "great theater of the world" as it was called, the Counter-Reformation's social disciplining, perfervid diplomacy, artistic and literary masterpieces, and piety, and the Inquisition could coexist and confront one another. This phase, beginning in the late 16th century, was characteristic of at least the entire first half of the 17th. It witnessed two distinct (although connected in a number of aspects) phenomena in the life of the Curia and that of the Church. On the one hand, although the temporal revenues of the Church state had greatly increased, the draining off of the "spiritual" revenues in the Curia took on increasing importance. These revenues originated from local ecclesiastical institutions and, even though they continued to be much lower than the general levels of the early 16th century, they did increase in the Apostolic Camera with the recuperation of the right to spoils and the collection of ordinary and extraordinary papal tithes, due to the reorganization of the tax collection system, especially in Spain, Portugal, and Naples. They increased likewise in the DATARY, not so much by means of the old game of playing with ecclesiastical benefices as through "new" resources, like marriage annulments. These increased according to a meticulous casuistry after the practice, which was imposed following the Council of Trent, had defined the forbidden degrees and the exceptions allowed concerning the sacrament of marriage, while pensions (imposed with increasing frequency on episcopal revenues or major benefices) also increased. Their easy transfer from one holder to another allowed the formation of a clientele at the middle and lower levels and integration of revenues at the middle and high levels, including the revenues of cardinals. This drain, which gave rise to protests on the part of local churches, and later, in the 17th and 18th centuries, to individual states opposing it, was commensurate with the growing weight of the Roman and peripheral (e.g., nunciatures) Curial bureaucracy and at the cost of the papal *familia*, which under Clement VIII and URBAN VIII would return to levels (in both numbers and finances) that were far from those of Pius V. But with growing rivalry for recognition, the drain nevertheless responded to demands for sponsorship by the pope, the cardinals, and members of the Curia of baroque Rome just as much as it did at the (henceforth princely) level of papal nepotism. On the other hand, the importance of political and religious interests and an increasingly strong involvement in the European theater in the 16th and 17th centuries subordinated the Curia's task of building and reorganizing the Papal States (the last coherent attempt at this had been by Sixtus V) to the demands of centralization, certainly, but also of universal politics. Even though Clement VIII had created the Congregation for Good Government (1592) in order to ensure better control over the communities of the state and reattached the duchy of Ferrara to the Holy See, and even though Urban VIII had gotten involved in the Castro war for small territorial interests, from that time, at the level of the Curia, the gap would grow between the state's system of government—which would be increasingly ecclesiastical and would distance itself from a "modern" kind of structural development—and the universalist ideology that was then receiving substantial doctrinal and ecclesiological support from the works of Robert Bellarmine and Cesare Baronio.

The consequences of these directions were seen throughout PAUL V's long papacy (1605–21), not only through a more accentuated nepotism and the strengthening of the pope's authority, but especially with an increasingly ecclesiastical power, with an increasingly generalized Church rationale (as opposed to reasons of state), that would lead to the INTERDICT of Venice, that is, to an assertion of the political power wished for by the Roman Curia regarding ecclesiastical immunities. This had never happened previously with Venice or other states, despite numerous jurisdictional conflicts. The Interdict affair reinforced an attitude of defensiveness and enclosure in the Curia. On the one hand this attitude led to reflections on the historical memory of the Church in the area of its rights and institutional privileges, of which the first systemic development of the Vatican ARCHIVES (1611–4) is tangible evidence and, on the other, it led to the development of strategic lines of a jealous defense of ecclesiastical privileges, as was seen, after GREGORY XIV's bull *Cum alias* (1591), with the institution of a special congregation for ecclesiastical immunity (1626) under Urban VIII. The short papacy of GREGORY XV (1621–3) produced two bulls on the reform of papal electoral procedures within the conclave and on the institution of the Congregation for the Propagation of the Faith (1622) for the centralized and unified control of missions. It was, however, with the longest papacy of the century, that of URBAN VIII (1623–44), that this process and development was completed, although not without some failures. The most sumptuous and extravagant nepotism would have as a true counterpoint the

exaltation of the pope's power, which definitively reduced the cardinals to the role of grand assistants to the central administration of the Church, with no effective authority. Designated by the title "eminence," they were enriched by considerable revenue and accompanied by sumptuous ceremony, as apparent compensation for lost prerogatives. During these years, an ecclesiastical rationale appears to have generally dominated the Curia, which was unshakable in the face of the upheavals taking place in Europe. These politics met with bitter failure with the treaties of Westphalia and the pope's isolation from the international scene, but they also weighed heavily in the area of discipline, to follow the work begun more than sixty years earlier of regrouping ecclesiastical institutions around the Holy See, to intervene sternly against the new scientific culture through the second trial of Galileo (1633), and to begin the battle, with the bull *In eminenti* (1642), against Jansenism that would last for a century and a half.

The serious humiliation that the treaties of Westphalia imposed upon Urban VIII's successor, INNOCENT XI (1644–55), marked a certain change of climate that could be seen in the reaction against the Barberinis, that was especially visible in nepotism's initial crisis. After the brief presence of cardinal nephew Camillo Pamphili, the pope named Cardinal Fabio Chigi (later ALEXANDER VII) to the position of secretary of state, a position that was at the time evolving from the institutional haziness of its role. Chigi would be the first in a long line of secretaries of state coming from the ranks of the nunciature. Nepotism was again seen in the Curia under Alexander VII (1655–67) with his nephews Chigi and Bichi, despite the presence of Secretary of State Giulio Rospigliosi (later CLEMENT IX). But against even this less blatant nepotism the first important restrictive measures began to be taken with a bull in 1656 that took away from the pontiff's family and relatives the revenues that had come from the sale of offices in the Curia. There is no question about the fact that, later, there was greater largesse on the part of the pontiff for his "own blood" and that Alexander VII's sponsorship—as had already been the case with Urban VIII's sponsorship—required substantial sums. There is no doubt that a certain moral rigor, which had begun to take root in some sectors of the Curia and the Church after the terrible financial situation of the Papal States due to Barberini family politics and the Thirty Years' War, began to contribute to a different climate. Sponsorship in the arts appears to have been a response to other idealistic and practical demands, resulting in movement away from the construction of monuments (like the colonnade at St. Peter's) and urban restructuring and toward concerns that were more directly tied to the organization of culture and studies. The VATICAN LIBRARY and the Alexandrine Library were enriched and the Roman university La Sapienza was expanded.

This latter measure was in line with the plan of reform that the pontiff intended to pursue regarding the administrative ranks of the Curia and the state. Alexander VII was well aware of the both central and peripheral structure of the Curia. He reshaped it radically, and took similar measures regarding diplomatic careers in nunciatures. Even though the secular appeal that had characterized, and continued to characterize, the cosmopolitanism of the ranks in the Curia continued to exist, a constitution in 1659 formally established the conditions and qualities required for entrance into the prelature by admission of candidates to the level of *referendarius* in the two Signaturas (*Gratiae* and *Justitiae*), the first level within the bureaucratic apparatus. The new procedure, as with the abolition of the venality of duties under INNOCENT XII, introduced a kind of selection, but did not change what was (and would continue to be until late in the 18th century) a well-anchored practice, strengthened by custom and imposed by the existence of extensive literature of advice from the Curia. This underscores the importance of blood relations (even through women), the affinities of interests, and the reciprocity of possible exchanges of favors between a candidate (including the family that invested its resources and expectations for the future prestige of the family name on its younger son) and a notable member of the Curia, an older relative, or a protector willing to pave the way for a protégé—especially if he was Roman or Florentine, although the same could be true for someone from Milan, Genoa, Lucca, or Naples—wanting to cast his fate into the labyrinths of a career in the Curia.

The negative evolution of nepotism, which continued under Clement IX (1667–9), whose cardinal nephew Giacomo Rospigliosi had a position that was clearly subordinate to the secretary of state Decio Azzolini, would be overturned under his successor, CLEMENT X (1670–6). With Clement X, an octogenarian at the time of his election, we witness the peculiar creation of a false cardinal nephew, as described by the libertine and critical pen of Gregorio Leti. The pontiff adopted Cardinal Paluzzi, uncle of Gaspare Paluzzi, who had married his only niece. The position of cardinal nephew already had as its historical raison d'etre in the last thirty years of the 17th century a kind of *valido* or *privado* dressed in a cardinal's red, a position that the very evolution of the Curia, with its gradual bureaucratic strengthening, was endangering, but which the Curia could not yet manage to eliminate totally. Other evidences of this were the reforms of Innocent XI (1676–89), whose antinepotism would lead to protests from ambassadors and other high-ranking individuals whom the absence of a cardinal nephew deprived of an access to the pope. And even though for Innocent XI, at a time of what would be called the turning point between the dreaded Turkish problem and the conflict with Louis XIV's France, it was not too difficult to do away with the commander general of the Church and other offices with members of the pontiff's family sitting in them, it also was not possible for him to publish a formal bull against nepotism, as he had intended. The document's composition took an entire decade (1677–86), and ran into strong opposition from a few influential cardinals (Barberini, Chigi, and Ottoboni) and even caused considerable perplexity among some sectors of the Curia that were more concerned about the timeliness of the measure, which was contested outside the Curia by political powers as weighty as Spain. Despite everything, there had been glimpses of new aspirations and new behaviors in the Curia. And it was an Italian Curia that was beginning to be described and celebrated at the end of the 17th century, a Curia in which the pontiff would reward with red members of religious orders who had become eminent for their morals or their culture, as well as, and especially, those who, in the congregations and nunciatures, would distinguish themselves in the service of the Holy See, as one of the most prestigious members of the Curia, G. B. De Luca, would outline in *Il cardinale della Santa Romana Chiesa pratico* (1680).

An exceptional renaissance of nepotism was seen under ALEXANDER VIII (1689–91) in the person of his young grand-nephew Pietro Ottoboni, who received responsibilities and prebends and who, in his residence in the chancery palace among his musicians and collections of manuscripts and silver objects, was, in a Rome at the end of the baroque period, an example of magnificence worthy of the Renaissance. But this was actually only a brief period between the time of the austere Innocent XI and that of Alexander's successor, the equally austere Innocent XII. A diffuse rigorism and a subsequent need for rationalization of the bureaucratic structure would characterize Innocent XII's reforms and his plan for reorganization of the judicial sector governing the different levels of decision making, since procedures had been simplified to a certain extent and the different magistracies had been gathered together in Innocent's Curia, the present palace of Montecitorio. But, most importantly, the bull against nepotism *Romanum decet Pontificem*, was completed and finally published (1692). To finish this series of reforms, steps were taken in 1694 to abolish the venality of offices through a costly financial system of reimbursing their holders and through a series of interventions aimed at compensating the losses of the Apostolic Camera. This was the last of a number of attempts and initiatives that had characterized the second half of the 17th century. Nevertheless, there were scarcely any changes in the secular relationships, bonds, and interests that defined the reality of the Curia. Likewise, the general view had not changed regarding politics and religion which, in the final decades of the century, had increasingly pitted itself against Jansenism, GALLICANISM, and Louis XIV's authoritarianism. It was with this weighty heritage that the Curia, henceforth a bureaucratic and political instrument of Roman Catholicism, prepared itself to face the difficult 18th century.

In effect, with the new century, with the Spanish war of succession and its consequences in the international arena, the Curia would need, under the long papacy of CLEMENT XI (1700–21), to confront unforeseen situations in the face of which it would appear to be almost without precise orientations. It was during these years of extensive political and territorial developments, with the replacement of the pale Spanish hegemony by the active presence in Italy of the Austrian Habsburgs, that the anti-Curial and anti-Roman line, which had never completely disappeared in Italian and European culture, acquired new strength, adding to the former reasons of state an anti-Jesuit, Jansenistic attitude that was reinforced by the subsequent condemnation of Jansenism in the bull *Unigenitus* (1713). This political and religious current opposed to the Curia found particular expression in Italy in the dispute over Comacchio, the occupation of which by the Empire to the detriment of the Church provoked one of the most heated political and diplomatic polemics of the time. It also came up again in Sicily under the House of Savoy, and later under Austria, in the debates over the Sicilian monarchy, regarding prerogatives enjoyed by the sovereign in ecclesiastical matters by virtue of being the pontiff's legate; and in the Austrian vice-kingdom of Naples—considered the vassal of the Holy See—where the Habsburgs intended to put relations between the state and the church on a new basis. Since immunities and juridical and economic ecclesiastical privileges were being discussed, and since the Curia was in a state of weakness and decline, BENEDICT XIII (1724–30), quite realistically, even though he was in the midst of difficulties and preoccupations of a religious nature, managed to establish a climate of entente with the political powers. While confirming the broad lines of Gregory XIV's constitution on ecclesiastical immunity, the pontiff found a compromise to resolve the old problem of the Sicilian monarchy (1278), after signing a concordat—one quite favorable to the state—with the kingdom of Sardinia. In this case a new event in relations between the pope and the Curia deserves mention. Up to the end, talks concerning the concordat took place on the Roman side within the pope's close entourage, short-circuiting the traditional bodies of the Curia and the college of cardinals in a procedure that BENEDICT XIV would later regularly adopt in his political negotiations. The fact that this was a period of transition and that the Curia was following a policy of alternating party alliance is confirmed by the papacy of CLEMENT XII (1730–40) which, because of the pope's advanced age and blindness, saw a reappearance of an aulic kind of nepotism in the person of Cardinal Nephew Neri Corsini. While power tended to split depending on the thought that prevailed in each of the groups in the Curia, the salient na-

ture of the Curia throughout these years was one of action through the intermediary of extraordinary congregations, four of which were created immediately after the pope's election, so that Benedict XIII's policies could be radically revised. Since Cardinal Niccolò Coscia, his closest confidant, had been condemned for his speculations and embezzlement, and since a number of the pontiff's measures were annulled, the harshest reaction from the Curia concerned the concordat with the court of Turin, which was invalidated in 1731 because there had been no consultation with, or approval from, the cardinals. Even to the end of Clement XIII's papacy, the intransigence and the grand gestures from the most traditional of the Curia's structures nevertheless did not prevent the search for a new entente with Turin, nor did it prevent attempts being made for agreements with Naples and Spain, although these were not concluded until the time of Benedict XIV. Moreover, besides the private sponsorship of the Corsini family in the palace of Lungara, the Curia was at the time playing a more specific role in the area of artistic and archaeological collections, with the foundation of the Capitoline Museum and plans for a lapidary gallery in the Vatican, thus ushering in the great period of ancient Roman culture in the 18th century that extended from Benedict XIV to PIUS VI.

The contradictions in the Curia's orientations and the tensions between the different groups appear to have disappeared with the election of Benedict XIV (1740–58). A skillful member of the Curia, and one enriched by his direct pastoral experience from being a bishop, the new pope would, to the extent of his capabilities, blow a breath of fresh air into the central structures of the Church, in doses that were balanced between a respect for tradition emanating from the Council of Trent and a spirit of renewal, by welcoming reforms whose time had come and which had forced themselves into broad sectors of Catholicism. He was fortunate to have been able to choose an entourage of high-caliber collaborators, from Secretary of State Valenti Gonzaga to Prodatarius Aldrovandi. He reduced the weight of the Sacred College and found ways to circumvent the delays and often the forms of passive resistance from the principal congregations of the Curia. Consequently, even though much is owed to the personality of the pontiff and less to the effective reality of the Curia, the new orientation of entente would inevitably have repercussions for the climate around the Curia as would be the case, with the Spanish concordat of 1753, which allowed a later draconian reform of the Datary. Though the Congregation of the Index was given new and more open rules (1753)—more than the stable congregations, which would nevertheless be stimulated, like the Congregation of the Council and the Congregation for Bishops, in accord with the pope's pastoral concerns and his concerns about Church discipline—it would be the specific and extraordinary congregations that would set a particular, and constructive, tone for the entire period: the Congregation for the Revision of the Roman Breviary and the Congregation for Liturgical Books, the Economic Commission, which would (to a limited degree) instigate freedom of commerce in the state (1748), and those more restricted commissions that would support the pontiff in composing his encyclicals, which were used by Benedict XIV in their modern form.

Although the pope's mediations and efforts succeeded in opening gaps in the tightly closed Curial system, and in renewing around Rome and in the Curia a political and religious consensus that seemed to have disappeared, they nevertheless were unsuccessful in erasing the past and the network of relationships and beliefs that solidly tied the Curia to the society of the old regime. The forces in the Curia that were hostile to Benedict XIV's most open tendencies, though partially set aside, had been neither undone nor replaced, and they made a strong reappearance during the 1760s, under the papacy of CLEMENT XIII (1758–69), in the face of the spread of the ecclesiastical politics of enlightened despotism. They used as their rallying point the 18th century Catholic Church problem of the Jesuits. It was at this time that the Roman Curia, in its most intransigent sectors, personified by Secretary of State Luigi Torrigiano and a group of cardinals, rejected any possibility of dialogue, as begun by Benedict XIV, and imposed a renewed Church rationale against the ENLIGHTENMENT and the process of secularization. On the one hand, suffering the blows of reform on institutional structures, and on the other, weaving over a long period the threads of a deeper work of recovery, positions were being lost on other fronts, in the obedience and loyalty of the clergy and the faithful in regard to the Roman pontiff. The short papacy of CLEMENT XIV (1769–74), despite the decision to disband the Society of Jesus (1773), was not able to bring about in real terms the possible alternative, even though it was both wise and prudent, that had been outlined by Benedict XIV, or to displace the political-religious axis upon which the papacy and the Curia had been so solidly set.

From the apex of the century of the ENLIGHTENMENT to the French Revolution, under Pius VI (1775–99) the Curia underwent a singular period in which, as in the last act of a dramatic work, all the protagonists met. A short period of political pragmatism overseen by honest executors like secretaries of state Pallavicini, Buoncampagna, and Zelada (although there were unforeseen points like the pontiff's famous trip to Vienna), were set in opposition to a nepotism greatly encouraged by the benevolent pontiff, in truth the last flame of a Curial and courtly society that was preparing for the tragedy at the end of the century. If Pius VI and the Curia's "Jesuitism" found its sanction in the last condemnation of Jansenism with *Auctorem fidei* (1794) and in the confirmation of the unity of Catholicism

in the face of any anti-hierarchical, episcopalist, and parishonist tendency, regardless whether it was Febronian or Jansenist, the events of the French Revolution would be much more serious for the Curia. As the civil constitution of the clergy had been condemned (1791), all later initiatives, from the pontiff, the Curia, or a specific congregation, were viewed through the lens of an older logic. Neither enlightened reformism nor the Revolution succeeded in creating new correspondences in a structure connected largely with the first modern age and integrated into the reality approriate to the old regime in a process of dissolution. It is not surprising that when the Papal States were invaded by Napoleon's armies, with the peace of Tolentino (1797) and the deportation of Pius VI (1798), the structure momentarily melted like snow in the sun. But Pius VI's last measures before his death were aimed at regulating the election of the pope in the difficult circumstances that were present. This would help insure the continuity of the Roman Curia in the new postrevolutionary, Napoleonic climate.

Mario Rosa

Bibliography

Ago, R. *Carriere e clientele nella Roma barocca*, Bari, 1990.

Broderick, J. F. "The Sacred College of Cardinals: Size and Geographical Composition (1099–1986)," *AHP*, 25 (1987), 7–71.

Del Re, N. *La Curia romana. Lineamenti storico-giuridici*, 3rd ed., Rome, 1970.

Felici, G. *La reverenda Camera Apostolica. Studio storico-giuridico*, Vatican City, 1940.

Kraus, A. *Das päpstliches Staatssekretariat unter Urban VIII., 1623–1644*, Rome-Freiburg-Vienna, 1964.

Laurain-Portemer, M. "Absolutisme et népotisme. La surintendance de l'État ecclésiastique," *Bibliothèque de l'École des chartes*, CXXXI (1973), 487–568.

Litva, F. "L'attività finanziaria della Dataria durante il periodo tridentino," *AHP*, 5 (1967), 79–174.

Partner, P. "Papal Financial Policy in the Renaissance and Counter-Reformation," *Past and Present*, 88, 1980, 17–62.

Pasztor, L. "L'histoire de la Curie romaine: Problème d'histoire de l'Église," *Revue d'histoire ecclésiastique*, LXIV (1969), 353–66.

Piola Caselli, F. "Aspetti del debito pubblico nello Stato pontificio: gli uffici vacabili," *Annali della Facoltà di Scienze politiche dell'Università di Perugia*, 1970–72, 98–170.

Pitz, E. "Die römische Kurie als Thema der vergleichenden Socialgeschichte," *QFIAB*, 58 (1978), 216–359.

Prodi, P. *The Papal Prince: One Body and Two Souls: The Papal Monarchy in Early Modern Europe*, New York, 1987.

Reinhard, W. "Ämterlaufbahn und Familienstatus. Der Aufstieg des Hauses Borghese 1537–1621," *QFIAB*, 54 (1974), 328–427; "Nepotismus. Der Funktionswandel einer papstgeschichtlichen Konstante," *ZKG*, 86 (1975), 145–85.

Reinhard, W. *Freunde und Kreaturen. "Verflechtung" als Konzept zur Erforschung historischer Führungsgrippen Römishe Oligarchie im 1600*, Munich, 1979.

Reinhard, W. *Papstfinanz und Nepotismus unter Paul V (1605–1621)*, Stuttgart, 1974, 2 vols.

Reinhardt, V. *Kardinal Scipione Borghese (1605–1633)*, Tübingen, 1984.

Rosa, M. "Curia romana e pensioni ecclesiastiche: fiscalità pontificia nel Mezzogiorno (secoli XVI–XVIII)," *Quaderni storici*, 42, 1979, 1015–55.

Rosa, M. "La scarsella di Nostro Signore: aspetti della fiscalità spirituale pontificia nell'età moderna," *Società e Storia*, 38, 1987, 817–45.

Contemporary Era. Since the beginning of the 20th century, the Roman Curia has included the totality of the administrative bodies of the HOLY SEE used by the pope to govern the universal Church. Such was not always the case. Under the Roman Empire, the Curia was where the SENATE met. This civil curia coexisted with an ecclesiastical curia in service to the Roman pontiff. It was not until 1089 that we find the word "curia" in a papal document, under the reign of URBAN II.

As papal duties grew, the Roman Curia expanded from the *presbyterium*, including, until the 11th century, the heads of the great parishes of the city (*presbyteri titulorum*, beginning in the 6th century, had become *presbyteri cardinales*), in the CONSISTORY that would gather around the Roman pontiff from the 11th to the 16th centuries to deal with the important affairs of the Church, be these religious or political. Gradually, administrative bureaus of the Curia were created within the papal court: notaries, archivists, lawyers (both clerics and laymen) for the poor and for the Church patrimony, accountants and tax inspectors, guardians of the treasury and papal ornaments. In a parallel fashion, bodies grew as needs dictated: the apostolic CHANCERY for composing papal letters, the apostolic DATARY for dating them, the private Camera for sending them out, the PENITENTIARY for judging matters of the internal forum, the Roman ROTA for judging matters of the external forum, the Apostolic Signatura for dealing with administrative and contentious cases. After covering the entire papal court and papal services, the words "Roman Curia" would be applied (beginning in the 12th century) to the Church of Rome of which the pope was bishop. Using the expression in such a manner would not be without certain terminological difficulties when the papacy moved to AVIGNON in the early 14th century, or when it set up residence for a short period in Ferrara, in the late 16th century. In such cases the term was perhaps inappropriate, or at least incorrectly used, as it was applicable only to papal services that had remained in the Eternal City. CLEMENT VIII nullified these doubts with the BRIEF *Cum ob nonnullas* (10 April 1598), confirming the unity of the Curia and initiating the now traditional adage *ubi Papa, ibi Roma*. The decline of consistories brought the emergence of ROMAN CONGREGATIONS, specialized commissions of cardinals convoked by the supreme pontiff to examine certain cases. The first of these was created by PAUL III on 21 July 1542 with the bull *Licet ab initio*, which instituted the Congregation of the Holy, Roman, and Universal INQUISITION (the future HOLY OFFICE). The second was the Congregation of the Council, to which PIUS IV entrusted application of the measures from the COUNCIL OF TRENT (constitution *Alias nos nonnullas*, 1564). In so doing, these two popes established a precedent: In 1572 PIUS V set up the CONGREGATION OF THE INDEX to censure books deleterious to faith or morals, and the Congregation for the Examination of Recourse Against Bishops. His immediate successor, GREGORY XIII, had at his disposal a great number of Roman congregations that were involved with spiritual affairs as well as issues of temporal jurisdiction: the archbishopric of Toledo, the anti-Turk league, Germanic affairs, reform of CANON LAW, CEREMONIALS, jubilees, the new edition of the Holy Scriptures, finances, issues with France, Poland, Spain, the City of Rome, and roads and waterways in the PAPAL STATE.

After aborted attempts at general reform by PIUS II, SIXTUS IV, ALEXANDER VI, Paul IV, and Pius V, it was SIXTUS V's plan that met with success in 1588. With the constitution *Immensa aeterni Dei* (22 January 1588), he promulgated the first great charter for the Roman Curia (for which there have been only four up to the end of the 20th century). Fifteen congregations of cardinals were created, ten with universal jurisdiction in spiritual matters (the Holy Inquisition, the *Signatura Gratiae*, Construction of Churches and Consistorial Provisions, Rites and Ceremonies, the Index of Forbidden Books, Implementation and Interpretation of the Council of Trent, the University of Rome, Regulars, Bishops and other Prelates, and the Vatican Printing Office) and five with temporal jurisdiction over the Papal States (Provisions, the Defense Fleet, State Responsibilities, Streets, Bridges and Waterways, and Consultations on Matters of State). Each congregation was composed of a small group of three to five cardinals assisted by secretaries, and dealt collegially with matters in an area of responsibility over which it enjoyed delegated authority. Each was to refer the most important decisions directly to the pope. It was at this time that the Roman Curia acquired a general configuration that lasted for centuries, and it still has the same configuration at the beginning of the 21st century. This does not mean that it remained unchanged or immobile in its structures, which were modified depending on the needs of the time. Numerous popes made minor modifications to the Sistine organization, either by creating new congregations or by reforming those already in existence.

It was not until the 20th century that a new general reorganization was put into effect by PIUS X (1908). Until that time, the Roman Curia included all the ecclesiastical and lay personnel that gravitated around the sovereign pontiff. This concerned different categories, such as cardinals, archbishops, bishops in the Curia, the prelature (the auditor of the APOSTOLIC CAMERA, the governor of Rome, the treasurer of the Roman Church, the substitute for the cardinal vicar of Rome, the majordomo of the Apostolic palace), the staff members of the congregations and the palace, the magistrates and auxiliaries of the Church justice system, the papal chapel comprising the liturgical retinue for papal solemnities (cardinals, patriarchs, archbishops, bishops, and princes who are assistants to the throne, His Holiness's majordomo, the college of protonotaries—both participants and nonparticipants—prelate auditors of the Rota or voters in the Signatura, etc.), and the papal family that makes up the reigning pontiff's court (the palatine cardinals: the datarius, the secretary of state, the secretary of memorials, and the secretary of briefs; the Palatine prelates; the master of the chamber; the master of the Sacred Palace; the master of ceremonies; the sacristan; private domestic prelates; the PALATINE GUARD, etc.). In places where time had added functions or titles, which for the most part had become obsolete because of the end of the popes' temporal powers, Pius X simplified, modernized, and generally put things in order. Thenceforth the Roman Curia would be reduced to eleven congregations (the Holy Office, the Consistory, the Discipline of Sacraments, the Council, Religious Orders, Propagation of the Faith, the Index, Rites, Ceremonial, Extraordinary Ecclesiastical Affairs, and Studies), three tribunals (the Apostolic Penetentiary, the Roman Rota, and the Apostolic Signatura), and five offices (the Apostolic Chancery, the Apostolic Datary, the Apostolic Camera, the Secretary of State, and the SECRETARIATS OF BRIEFS TO PRINCES and Latin Letters). The administration of the DIOCESE OF ROME and the papal court were split, and all surviving structures from the time of temporal power were abrogated.

Before including this new structure in the CODE OF CANON LAW of 1917, BENEDICT XV added a few corrections: the Congregation of Studies became the Congregation for Seminaries and Institutes of Study, the Index was annexed to the Holy Office, Oriental matters were detached from the Propagation of the Faith, giving birth to the Congregation for the Oriental Churches. This system would last until the reign of PAUL VI who, in accord with the wish of VATICAN II (num. 9 of the 1965 decree *Christus Dominus*), threw himself into a new updating of the Curia with the apostolic constitution *Regimini Ecclesiae*

Universae (15 August 1967): four old DICASTERIES were disbanded and absorbed by others (the Ceremonial Congregation, the Apostolic Datary, and the Secretariats of Briefs to Princes and of Latin Letters), and from them three new, more modern dicasteries were created (the two prefectures of Economic Affairs and the Apostolic Palace, and the Office of Statistics); within the Curia, juridical integration of the three recently created secretariats (Unity of Christians, Non-Christians, and Nonbelievers) took place, as was also the case for the Council of the Laity and the Papal Commission *Iustitia et Pax*, which had resulted from the Council's concerns. But especially, all the bodies of the Curia, most of which saw their names changed to something more explicit, were placed under the supervision of the SECRETARIAT OF STATE which—formerly a simple office—was given the highest place in the new Curia. The Curia was thus composed of the Secretary of State of His Holiness and the Council for Public Affairs of the Church, nine congregations (Doctrine of the Faith, Oriental Churches, Discipline of the Sacraments, Clergy, Institutes of Consecrated Life and Societies of Apostolic Life, Evangelization of Peoples, Doctrine of the Faith, Divine Worship, and Catholic Education), three tribunals (Apostolic Penitentiary, Roman Rota, and Supreme Tribunal of the Apostolic Signatura), three secretariats (Unity of Christians, Non-Christians, and Nonbelievers), the Council for Laity, the papal commission *Iustitia et Pax*, and the six offices (Apostolic Chancery, Apostolic Camera, Prefecture for Economic Affairs, Administration of the Patrimony of the Apostolic See, Prefecture of the Apostolic Palace, and the Central Statistics Office). To this was added a series of commissions and committees (Biblical Studies, Revision and Emendation of the Vulgate, Revision of the Latin and Eastern Codes of Canon Law, Latin America, Social Communication, Sacred Archaeology, Historical Sciences). The Reverend FABRIC of ST. PETER'S (in charge of the Vatican basilica), the Private VATICAN LIBRARY and ARCHIVES, and the Vatican Bookstore and Printing Office were unchanged, and the old apostolic almonry changed only its name to the Holy Father's assistance service (for alms distributed personally by the pope).

The fourth fundamental charter of the Roman Curia would be the apostolic constitution *Pastor bonus*, signed by JOHN PAUL II on 28 June 1988. It preserves the 1967 model, but with several modifications. It results in a more restrictive definition of the Curial institution, since it is comprised of twenty-seven dicasteries: the Secretary of State's office, nine congregations (Doctrine of the Faith, Oriental Churches, Divine Worship and Discipline of Sacraments, Causes of Saints, Bishops, Evangelization of Peoples, Clergy, Institutes of Consecrated Life and Societies of Apostolic Life, and Seminaries and Institutes of Studies, also called Catholic Education), three tribunals (Apostolic Penitentiary, Roman Rota, and Supreme Tribunal of the Apostolic Signatura), twelve papal councils (Laity, Promoting Christian Unity, Family, Justice and Peace, *Cor unum*, Pastoral Care of Migrants and Itinerant Peoples, Pastoral Assistance to Health Care Workers, Interpretation of Legislative Texts, Interreligious Dialogue, Dialogue with Nonbelievers, Culture, and Social Communications), three offices (Apostolic Camera, Administration of the Patrimony of the Apostolic See, and Prefecture for Economic Affairs). Three other bodies are included in the Curia, although they are not considered to be dicasteries: the Prefecture of the Papal House, the Office of Liturgical Celebrations of the Sovereign Pontiff, and the Office of the Work of the Apostolic See. On the other hand, a few traditional institutions were excluded from the Curia, although they either preserve their autonomy in the papal system (the Vatican Archives and Library, the Academy of Sciences, and the Fabric of Saint Peter's), or they are attached to a dicastery (the Vatican Bookstore and Printing Office, OSSERVATORE ROMANO, VATICAN RADIO, and the Vatican Television Center). Finally, the apostolic almonry was placed under the direct supervision of the pope, as beforehand. The three previous secretariats were transformed into papal councils and the permanent papal commissions were annexed by different dicasteries; only the temporary commissions remained autonomous. The papal commission for the State and the City of the Vatican and its administrative services were excluded from the Roman Curia, as was the vicariate of the Diocese of Rome, where the pope is the bishop. In its new look, the Roman Curia was also desacralized, since the word "sacred" has been abolished for all papal institutions.

The present Roman Curia works in accord with principles announced in the apostolic constitution *Pastor bonus* (28 June 1988) and in the General Norms of the Roman Curia (4 February 1992).

Under the authority of the Cardinal Secretary of State, the nine congregations and the tribunal of the Apostolic Signatura are managed by a cardinal prefect (or proprefect, in the case of an archbishop waiting to be named cardinal at the next series of cardinal nominations); the twelve papal councils and the administration of the patrimony and the Prefecture of Economic Affairs are headed by a president (a cardinal or archbishop); the Apostolic Penitentiary is under the leadership of the cardinal penitentiary (or major penitentiary); the Roman Rota is under that of a dean; and the Apostolic Camera is entrusted to the cardinal camerlengo of the Holy Roman Church. The heads of the dicasteries meet the pope and the secretary of state approximately once every two or three months. They also have individual audiences with the Holy Father whenever needed, occasionally with their main collaborators. Each prefect or president is assisted by a secretary (an archbishop, in the case of congregations; a bishop, a

prelate who is not a bishop, or a simple member of a religious order in councils where the secretary can bear the title of vice president), and by one or more undersecretaries (prelates who are not bishops, members of religious orders, or even laypeople in certain papal councils). Most of the dicasteries are composed of three categories of individuals who tend to be internationally recognized: members, officers, and consultants. The members, who make up the dicastery's high council, are primarily cardinals, or Roman or diocesan bishops; they may also be simply priests or laypeople in the case of papal councils. The officers (clerics, members of religious orders, or laypeople—both men and women) make up the administrative staff of the dicastery: department heads, editors (*minutanti*), attachés, archivists, copyists, etc. They are assisted by their staffs. Consultants, whose introduction into the Curia goes back to Sixtus V, are recruited from throughout the world regardless of their status (clerics, members of religious orders, or laity), but because of their competence to provide their dicastery with needed information. Prefects and presidents, secretaries and undersecretaries, members and consultants are all named by the pope himself for a period of five years (which is occasionally renewable); the only individual not subject to this limit is the cardinal secretary of state, whose position is at the discretion of the sovereign pontiff. For their part, the officers are subject to a more stable status as stated in the general regulations of 1992 which, in essence, is a restatement of those of 1968: The heads of departments are named by the secretary of state after being proposed by the head of the dicastery, and the other officers are named by the heads of their dicasteries, after being authorized by the secretary of state's office and approved by the administration of the patrimony, the paying authority. The age of retirement is set at eighty for all members, seventy-five for prefects, presidents, and secretaries, seventy for undersecretaries and officers who are priests or members of religious orders, and sixty-five for lay officers. In the case of the pontiff's death, the secretary of state and all prefects, presidents, and members of dicasteries cease their duties immediately (except two cardinals: the major penitentiary and the camerlengo); the secretaries expedite current matters, but need to be confirmed by the new pope within three months. In practice, this rule, which was introduced by Paul VI in 1967, has not entailed great mobility in Curial duties; the newly elected pope has tended to keep people in their respective positions, at least to finish the five-year mandate in progress.

Administrative decisions in the Roman dicasteries are made by three kinds of internal bodies: Current affairs are settled and filed by the conference that gathers the permanent staff of the dicastery (the prefect or president, the secretary, the undersecretary, the department heads, and interested collaborators); the most important cases are studied by the ordinary assembly (called the ordinary congregation prior to 1988), which is often convoked (in weekly or bimonthly sessions) as it is composed of the cardinals and members of the dicastery who are either residents of, or present in, Rome; the most important matters fall under the jurisdiction of the plenary assembly (formerly the plenary congregation, or *plenaria*), a supreme dicasterial authority in which all members participate, usually once a year. Major decisions are to be submitted for the pope's prior approval (except in the case of special rights or the sentences of the tribunals of the Rota or the Signatura). Actually, the Roman Curia has no administrative power except in the name of and in the place of the pope, as it has no authority and no power outside that it receives from the Supreme Pastor (apostolic constitution *Pastor bonus*, preamble, sect. 7). Coordination of the Curia—which was a great concern in John Paul II's reform—was assured as much by meetings of all the heads of dicasteries with the pope as by permanent or ad hoc interdicasterial commissions. Moreover, the Congregation of the Doctrine of the Faith is in charge of the doctrinal coordination of the Curia as, prior to their publication, all documents from the other dicasteries relating to questions of faith or morals need to get its approval; the works of the papal councils for Promoting Christian Unity and for Interreligious Dialogue also fall under its doctrinal supervision. Coordination of the canonical acts of the Holy See is the responsibility of the Papal Council for the Interpretation of Legislative Texts.

Joël-Benoît D'Onorio

Bibliography

Bouix, D. *Tractatus de Curia Romana, seu De cardinalibus, romanis congregationibus, legatis, nuntiis, vicariis et protonotariis apostolicis.* . . . Paris, 1859.

Del Re, N. *La Curia romana*, Rome, 1970.

D'Onorio, J. B. *Le Pape et le gouvernement de l'Église*, Paris, 1992.

Martin, V. *Les Cardinaux et la Curie romaine; tribunaux et offices. La vacance du Siège apostolique*, Paris, 1930.

Pichon, C. *Le Vatican hier et aujourd'hui*, 3rd ed., Paris, 1968.

Poupard, P. *Connaissance du Vatican*, Paris, 1967.

Torquebiau, P. "Curie romaine," *DDC*, IV, 1949, 971–1008.

Style and Praxis. The CODE OF CANON LAW of 1917 referred to the style and praxis of the Roman Curia as two canonical institutions, quite similar to one another, that served as norms in the case of a lacuna in the law and are brought to bear after those laws that applied to similar cases were considered and general legal principles were applied with canonical equity, and before the common and constant opinion of the doctors (c. 20) was considered. Foreseeing the same sources of supplementary law, canon 19 of the CODE OF CANON LAW of 1983 preferred the term "jurisprudence" to that of the "style" of the Roman Curia, that is, central bodies of the Church in direct service to the Roman pontiff. Given the knowledge, the experience of judges, and their authority as the pope's judges, they are expected to offer the best guarantees. Jurisprudence, primarily that of the Roman ROTA and the Apostolic Signatura, should take precedence over practice. The jurisprudence of the Rota "has acquired in the history of the Church, relative to the evolution of norms, a growing, not only moral, but also juridical, authority" (JOHN PAUL II, allocution to the Roman Rota, 26 February 1983). For example, the tribunalis jurisprudence added a number of details concerning natural law in the matter of matrimonial consent at the time of the formulation of the Code of Canon Law of 1983 (John Paul II, allocution to the Roman Rota, 26 January 1984).

In order to appeal to the style and the praxis of the Curia, there must be an absence of legal norms for the case in question, thus making recourse to subsidiary norms indispensable, and this recourse must be licit. In fact, canon 19 (as was the case for canon 20 in the Code of 1917) explicitly excludes penal cases from them.

Style is a constant and specific way of acting in the Church's judiciary and administrative central offices. The style of the Curia is thus the constant fashion in which a dicastery regulates the affairs falling under its purview. The style of the tribunals is called jurisprudence and praxis.

The ensemble of procedures habitually observed in expediting a matter is called formal style. These should be observed by those who act when delegated by the HOLY SEE. Material style is the decision or resolution brought to a class of matters or juridical acts. Material style is the praxis commonly followed in resolving an issue. It is to be distinguished from formal style, which is why "style" and "praxis" are both spoken of: style relating to the formalities or procedure followed (material style), and praxis to the decision made or the custom of judging in the same manner (formal style). Both can be of fact, meaning such that no obligation results from them, or of law, and, thus, obligatory, since they are established by the law or confirmed by a legitimate custom or some other obligatory norm. Style can be judiciary as well, being taken from the authority of the things judged in the same fashion (*auctoritas rerum similiter iudicatarum*), or extrajudiciary, meaning that which is followed by the bodies of the Roman Curia.

The Curial style or jurisprudence that serves as a source of auxiliary law, in cases that fall outside the area of general law, could be formal style as easily as general style, or judiciary style as much as extrajudiciary style.

Contrary to the style of fact, the style of law that has an obligatory nature is a true auxiliary law; judiciary sentences and administrative acts (for example, decrees and decisions), although they cannot produce a general right, can furnish norms by which particular cases can be resolved in the absence of legal measures, and thus impose themselves.

Style can become popular usage or a custom of law that is legitimately prescribed or approved by agreement of a competent superior, *transit in ius consuetudinarium*. Even the isolated decisions of the Roman Curia, which do not constitute a style in themselves, can acquire a high indicative value when they have been applied authentically. The insertion of a sentence in the *Acta Apostolicae Sedis* clearly confers a specific authority upon it.

When it becomes necessary to remediate the silence of a specifc law, appeal may be made to the jurisprudence or the praxis of other curias, particularly the most important.

Dominique Le Tourneau

See also CURIA.

Bibliography

Ercolani, F. "Stilus et praxis curiae," *EC*, XI, 1953, 1341–2.

Fransen, G. "La valeur de la jurisprudence en droit canonique," *La norma en el Derecho Canónico. Actas del III Congreso Internacional de Derecho Canónico*, Pamplona, 10–15 de octubre de 1976, Pamplona, 1979, I, 198–212.

Holböck, C. *Tractatus de iurisprudentia Sacrae Romanae Rotae*, Gratz-Vienna-Cologne, 1957.

Lefebvre, C. "Style et pratique de la curie romaine," *DDC*, 1965, VII, 1092–4.

Le Tourneau, D. "Discursos del Papa Juan Pablo II a la Rota Romana y comentario," *Ius Canonicum*, XXVIII (1988), 541–618.

López Alarcón, M. "La posición de la jurisprudencia en el sistema de fuentes de Derecho Canónico," *La norma en el Derecho Canónico*, Pamplona, 1979, I, 1105–12.

CURSOR, APOSTOLIC. The office of apostolic *cursor* (courier) in the papacy's service appears to have existed from the earliest centuries of Christianity: the pope's *cursor*—referred to as *cursor*, or *viator apostolicus*—was the pontiff's messenger, responsible for making his wishes known regarding the public affairs of the Church. Known to exist in their modern form since the 13th century, apostolic *cursores* accompanied the pope on horseback by forming a cortege, most notably at the time that solemn possession (POSSESSO) was being taken of the BASILICA OF ST. JOHN LATERAN: *apparitores* and *viatores* were cited among GREGORY IX's retinue in 1227; the rolls of the papal FAMILY showed thirty *cursores* in CLEMENT V's service in 1305, and fifty in the service of GREGORY XII in 1406;

twelve *cursores Papae* accompanied INNOCENT VIII to the Lateran in 1484, carrying red banners; in 1513, LEO X was surrounded by banners raised by twelve *cursores, vexilla XII cursorum*; in 1644, INNOCENT X was preceded by twenty *cursores* from the apostolic college, *cum collegii apostolici cursoribus XX*; the *cursores Papae* that formed CLEMENT X's cortege in 1670 were all carrying silver KEYS; and even though BENEDICT XIV, out of his concern for austerity and economy, reduced their number from eighteen to twelve by a chirographic document of 18 August 1748, the last pontifical cavalcade in the streets of Rome, during PIUS VI's *possesso* in 1775, still saw the *cursores* mixed among the pontiff's following among the different bodies of papal guards, *lancie spezzate*, SWISS GUARDS, *cavalleggieri* and *mazzieri*. In 1826, finally, LEO XII reorganized the college of the twelve apostolic couriers, whom he transformed into salaried employees of the papal palaces.

The college of apostolic *cursores*, presided over by a master of *cursores*, thus constitutes a specific group within the papal family. Invested in their offices (which were *vacabile*, i.e., acquired by money, until the early 19th century) by the pope, and in early times paid by those to whom pontifical messages were dispatched, the couriers took an oath and were placed under the authority of the majordomo and the prefect of the papal palaces. With a CARDINAL PROTECTOR until the early 18th century, they participated as a group in the Roman archbrotherhood of the Holy Sacrament and the Five Wounds. Dressed in black and carrying a silver club and a wand of brambles (*lo spino*) in the manner of the old lictors (for, as the learned Moroni said, "brambles symbolize the obedience all Christians owe to the head of the Church, just as inobservance of the prince's laws and commandments renders all things difficult and 'thorny'"), to cardinals, prelates, the clergy, and the faithful, they declare the orders of the sovereign pontiff, they call members of the SACRED COLLEGE to the pontifical liturgies, they intervene in the course of all solemnities in the papal court (cavalcades and processions, beatifications and canonizations, openings and closings of holy years, the sepulture of a pope or the principle cardinals), and they assist the majordomo during the CONCLAVE. At the speed of their dashing steeds, thus, the college of pontifical *cursores* has, for centuries, projected the power and prestige of the papacy in the immediate surroundings of pontifical Rome and its outskirts.

Philippe Boutry

Bibliography

Moroni, G. "Cursori apostolici o pontifici," *Dizionario di erudizione storico-ecclesiastica*, XIX (1843), 49–62.

CUSTOM. The words "custom" and "tradition" should not be confused, as they have often been, for the convenience of language. "Custom is a set of practices of a legal nature, which have acquired binding force in a given sociopolitical group through the repetition of peaceful public acts over a relatively long period of time" (J. Gilissen).

Custom is generally not written. From the days of antiquity, jurists have given much thought to the idea of custom in societies where it prevailed over law as a binding force. These reflections on customs are summarized in the *Etymologiae* (5, 3, 2) of Isidore of Seville (ca. 560–636). The chapter on normative sources was included in the CANONICAL COLLECTIONS up to Gratian. From the end of the eleventh century, canonists also had direct knowledge of the passages from the compilations by Justinian which deal with custom, and they presented the definitions reflected there. The popes of the GREGORIAN REFORM were very hostile to the idea and condemned "bad customs." However, some of these were not customs in the legal sense of the word, but rather dues, which were often improperly demanded. The word "*consuetudo*" had acquired this derived meaning by the end of antiquity. The popes of the Gregorian reform criticized any custom that was contrary to the truth ("Christ did not say, 'I am the custom,' but 'I am the truth'"; Gregory VII), to usefulness, and of course, to divine or natural law. The doctrine establishes a clear difference between custom that is against the law (*contra legem*), and that outside the law (*praeter legem*) and brings in the notions like the relative antiquity of the custom and the tacit or express consent of the legislator, who in the final analysis, has the determining word. So despite the DECRETAL *cum tanto* by Gregory IX (X, 1, 4: *On custom*, 11), which admits that custom may depart from positive law provided it is reasonable, custom is very clearly subordinated to the law in medieval CANON LAW. Neither the popes nor the doctrine of the ensuing centuries have been more favorable to it. The few canons of the CODE OF CANON LAW of 1917 (c. 25–30) and of 1983 (c. 23–8), even though they repeat the favorable assessment of custom by Ulpien in the *Digest* of Justinian—"custom is the best interpreter of the law"—still give it second place. This is more favorable, though, than that given to it in French civil code, which ignores the matter altogether.

Gerard Giordanego

Bibliography

Gaudemet, J. "La coutume en droit canonique," *La Coutume. Europe occidentale médiévale et moderne*, Bruxelles, 1990, 41–61 (*Recueils de la societé J. Bodin*, 52; issues 51 to 54 of this journal are dedicated to custom).

Gilissen, J. *La Coutume*, Turnhout, 1982 (*Typologie des sources du Moyen Age occidental*, 41).

Gouron, A. "Nondixit: Ego sum consuetudo," *ZRGKA*, 105 (1988), 133–40.

Liesching, P. "Consuetudo und ratio im Dekret und der Panormia des Bischofs Ivo von Chartres," *ZRGKA*, 105 (1988), 535–42.

Sériaux, A. "Réflexions sur le pouvoir normatif de la coutume en droit canonique," *Droits, Revue française de théórie juridique* 3 (1986) 63–73.

Van Hove, A. "Coutume," *DDC*, 4 (1949), 731–55.

Vidal, H. "Grégoire VII, Urbain II et la coutume," *Recueil . . . de droit écrit*, 14 (1988), 255–61.

CYCLE. See **Calendar.**

D

DAMASUS I. *(d. 11 December 384). Consecrated 1 October 366.*

The pontificate of Damasus is one of the longest of the 4th century. The personality of the bishop, as well as the evolution of the political situation of the Empire, contributed to its importance as a key stage in the affirmation of the primacy of the see of Rome. Moreover, the relative abundance and diversity of sources allow us to grasp, for the first time, the intellectual personality of a Roman bishop.

Jerome tells us that Damasus died "almost an octogenarian, during the reign of Emperor Theodosius" (*De viris ill.*, 103) on 11 December 384, according to the *Hieronymian Martyrology* (p. 152, and *LP*, I, 213), and we can place his birth around A.D. 305. Although the *LIBER PONTIFICALIS* says he came from a Spanish family background, (*LP*, I, 212), he was most probably Italian, perhaps even Roman. In fact, his entire family served the Church of that city: His father (named Antonius, according to *LP*, I, 212) was a NOTARY, a lector, and then a deacon before being made a bishop, perhaps in the suburbs of Rome, and he had a house that his son made into a *titulus* (San Lorenzo in Damaso: *Epigramm.* 57; *LP*, I, 212–14). (Damasus was a patrimony of Italian lands located in the neighborhood of Ferentino and Cassino.) His mother Laurentia belonged to an order of widows for 60 years before dying a nonagenarian (*Epigramm.* 10), and his sister Irene made the vow of virginity (*Epigramm.* 11).

Of Damasus' career before his episcopal election we only know that, as a deacon of Liberius, he followed his bishop into exile. However, the vicissitudes of his rise to the episcopate are fairly well known, even if the information comes mostly from his adversaries (*Gesta Liberii*, a chronicle published in 368 by the partisans of Ursinus, designed to sway the Italian episcopate to the Ursinian party: *Coll. Avellana*, I, *CSEL*, 35, ed. Guenther, p. 1–4; documents relating to the suit filed by Isaac; *Libellus Precum*, a pamphlet published around 380 by the two Lu-

ciferian priests Marcellinus and Faustinus, and presented at the same time as the *Gesta* to Theodosius in Constantinople, probably in 384: *Coll. Avellana, Ep.* II, 121 *ff. CSEL* 35).

The difficulties surrounding the election of Damasus, which would trouble his pontificate, were a direct consequence of the division of the Roman community caused by the meddling of Constantius II in Church affairs, and by his policy favoring the Arians. At the time of Liberius' death on 24 September 366, several priests and three deacons, presenting themselves as his followers, met in the *basilica Iulii* in the Trastevere and elected Ursinus, who was soon consecrated by Bishop Paul of Tivoli. A larger group met in the *titulus Lucinae* (San Lorenzo in Lucina) and elected Damasus, but the Ursinians accused Damasus of having supported the antipope Felix, placed in office by Emperor Constantius in 355 (Felix seems to have been orthodox, but he must have violated the Roman clergy's desire not to replace Liberius). Supported, according to his adversaries, by the populace—the circus people and the grave diggers (which proves he was supported by an organized group from the Christian community)—Damasus attacked the basilica of Julius and then occupied St. John's of the Lateran, where he was consecrated by the bishop of Ostia, according to Roman custom, on 1 October 366.

It is probably the regularity of his consecration and the fact that he held the official *episcopium* that legitimized Damasus, to some extent, in the eyes of the civil authorities, called in to bring peace. On the orders of Viventius, the prefect of the city, Ursinus was exiled with his deacons Amantius and Lupus. His followers pulled back to the *basilica Liberii* (perhaps a significant choice for those representing themselves as faithful of the previous pope; this would become the future church of St. Mary Major), which Damasus once more assaulted: the end result seems to have been about 100 dead Ursinians (*Gesta Liberii* and Ammianus Marcellinus, *Res Ges-*

tae, XXVIII, 11–13). One year later, Valentinian I granted amnesty to the exiles, who returned to Rome on 15 September 367 and again tried to occupy the basilica of Liberius. Pretextat, the prefect of the city (a pagan), expelled the schismatics, while Damasus took further action with Valentinian to regain the church. An imperial order forbidding any schismatic meetings within 20 miles of the city put the final touches on the civil actions by the authorities in favor of Damasus, the legitimate pope (proclamation *Ea nobis* on 12 November 368, *Coll. Avellana*, 7, 49). The Ursinians turned back toward northern Italy where they probably allied themselves with the Arians (the see of Milan was occupied by the Homean bishop Auxentius). After several years of calm they began agitating again in 374 in favor of a relaxation of the sanctions against them. They took advantage of the criminal charges made against Damasus by a converted Jew named Isaac. The sources available do not allow us to clearly reconstruct the issue, but according to *LP*, I, 212, Damasus was suspected of being mixed up in a matter of morals and is once again implicated in the massacres of the Esquiline. Whatever the accusation, Damasus was acquitted by his Italian colleagues, and Ursinus was exiled to Cologne, Isaac to Spain, and their followers expelled from Rome. In the 380s Ursinus tried one last time, unsuccessfully, to take the offensive (cf. the Council of Aquileia in 381). After Damasus' death, he again tried for the see of Rome, but it was SIRICIUS who was successful.

Paradoxically, this troubled and even bloody accession to the see of Rome reinforced Damasus' authority—and with it, that of the see of Rome—by the fact that civil authorities intervened on his behalf. More than just a position taken during a religious conflict, this choice was based on a need to keep public order: faced with a small, schismatic, and heretical group, Damasus appeared to represent the majority, and it was therefore necessary to support him in order to keep peace in the State. His victory can also be seen as the attainment of the "accord" between the Church and the Empire to which the synod of 378 had aspired (where the Ambrosian conception of the relationship between the Church and the State may be perceived). Nevertheless, after the accusation by Isaac, Damasus—as the successor to St. Peter—did have one setback. He was unable to brush aside the actions of the prefect of the city and gain control of the tribunal, which the council of 378 had claimed on behalf of the Apostolic See (an expression found beginning in Liberius' pontificate, but which became common and specific in Rome during Damasus' pontificate). During a criminal trial, the bishop had to submit to ordinary judicial procedure (under the jurisdiction of the prefect) whereas he claimed he could be tried only by the emperor's council (synod of 378: *PL*, 13, 575–84 and in response the proclamation of Gratian, *Ordinariorum: Coll. Avellana*, 13, 3, 55; Ambrosius, *Epist.* 21, 5; Rufin, *Ecclesiastical History*, 2, 20;

Socrates, *Ecclesiastical History*, 4, 19). Despite, or because of, these difficulties, Damasus made it his priority to develop the structures of the Roman community, as much on the level of material and liturgical organization as on that of the administrative and legal organization of the local government. In the Damasian concept of the exemplary role of the Roman see, and of the unity of the Church realized through the communion with it, the effort toward local organization became the basis for the establishment of Roman primacy, not only as a matter of faith, but also as a matter of jurisdiction. His pontificate therefore is a decisive step in this regard.

Within the city, three new foundations of *tituli* (titulary churches provided with priests assuring liturgical services in that quarter of town, taking the place of the bishop, but not autonomous), which allowed small centers of cathechesis and pastoral activities to be established (*titulus Anastasiae*, at the foot of the Palatine [Saint Anastasia]; *titulus S. Laurentii in Damaso*; *titulus Fasciolae*, near the baths of Caracalla). It was probably also during his pontificate that the construction of San Clemente began, after the decommission of the *mithraeum*, and also that of Santa Pudentiana (finished under Siricius). For episcopal rites he established a BAPTISTRY at St. Peter's, but it was especially in the organization of the commemoration of martyrs and the cult of the saints that Damasus placed his greatest effort. The real and holy topography that he drew around Rome was a way to promote, and, at the same time, control popular devotion, and watch for little heretical groups that tended to hold meetings in the *suburbium* (at the same time, Ambrosius followed a similar policy of channeling Christian fervor in Milan). In most of the great cemeteries of the city, he built tombs of martyrs of the Roman ferial of 336 and promoted new cults (for example, the underground basilica of Saints Nereus and Achilleus, the tombs of Saints Peter and Marcellinus in the catacomb of the same name; the crypt of the popes at Calixtus). He also intervened in numerous churches and six or seven new basilicas *ad corpus* were built during his pontificate. Perhaps it was he who began the project of building ST. PAUL'S OUTSIDE THE WALLS, whose construction would not, however, begin until the pontificate of Siricius. Most of these works are known through inscriptions of verses written by Damasus himself that were engraved in large, elegant letters by the calligrapher Furius Dionysius Filocalus (see for example *Epigramm.* 6, 7, 10–12, 15–21, 32, 34, 35, and 49); some have been found, and others are known through copies preserved in ancient collections. These inscriptions were, for the bishops, a way of officially proving the recognition of a cult. Sometimes they only served to authenticate the saint whose memory was venerated, but they were also often an occasion for developing the themes of Church unity based on St. Peter's tradition (*Epigramm.* 4, with a reference to *Eph.*

4, 5), and of the triumphal reign of the new founders of Rome who were the martyrs, especially apostles Peter and Paul (*Epigramm.* 20). They were, therefore, included in the elaboration of a Roman theology of the *renovatio Urbis*, which was going to be one of the strongest arguments for the affirmation of Roman primacy (see Leo). Today, these inscriptions constitute important records of the development of Roman hagiography in the 4th century, as well as the Christianization of one of the main forms of communication in the Roman civilization, the *monumentum* (J. Fontaine). This material commemoration, probably financed through an episcopal BENEFACTION (private or communal, depending on the case) that would continue the imperial monetary support during the first half of the century, corresponds to an effort to organize the liturgical year, punctuated by commemorations of saints inserted between the great observances (Easter, Christmas, Lent).

Damasus dedicated himself to developing a means of episcopal government, taking the civil government as his model. He established a juridical service, organized a pontifical chancellery, developed the synodal institution, and elaborated protocol of procedures and argumentation. He thus founded the basis for Church law. If certain previous functions were reinforced, such as those of notaries, new ones were created, such as that of the *defensor ecclesiae*, a lay person in charge of defending the rights of the Church in public cases and seeing that the law was applied to the benefit of the bishop against heretics and schismatics (first known intervention: the petition of 367 to the prince to obtain the restitution of the basilica of Liberius, *Coll. Avellana*, 6, 2). In delicate situations, Damasus also used "experts" (*periti*, a position established, among others, by Jerome at the time of the synod of 382). Church archives (*scrinium, chartarium*) were organized with the collation of conciliar documentation and Roman decisions, which were at the origin of future canonical collections. Among the documents put into the first canonical collection was the decretal *Ad Gallos*. This was, first of all, a response to the episcopate of Gaul requesting a ruling on the relationships between church communities and the ecclesiastical *cursus*, a definition of the moral and spiritual obligations of the priesthood, of the discipline of marriage, etc. Damasus developed themes that transformed this circumstantial response into a fundamental document for the establishment not only of spiritual primacy, but also the jurisdiction of the see of St. Peter: a shining example of the Roman faith, based upon apostolic tradition; respect for any similar ecclesiastical discipline, considered as an instrument for Church unity (see, for example, c. 3: "Since the law is one, the tradition must be one also. If there is only one tradition, the Churches must also have only one discipline"). This, the first known pontifical decretal, organized like an imperial decree, which used a scriptural argument imitating

that of Roman jurists, is therefore the formal church model for future pontifical interventions in the West. The fact that the episcopate of Gaul asked the bishop of Rome to settle its disciplinary problems, which could have been decided through a regional council, shows implicitly the recognition of the preeminence of the Roman model.

In the same way, the battle Damasus fought against his adversaries, even in Rome itself (strict partisans of Lucifer of Cagliari, Montanists, Donatists, Arians, etc.), helped by allowing him to gain imperial authority for himself and to rally the Italian episcopate around him, reestablishing Roman orthodoxy, especially until the 380s. The synod of Rome (between 368 and 372), which repeated its condemnation of the Arian bishop Auxentius of Milan, served as an occasion to spread the confession of Roman faith in the Trinity (*una deitas, una virtus, una figura*; see *Clavis*, 1633) throughout Illyricum and the East (it was communicated to Athanasius of Alexandria by the deacon Sabinus of Milan), and to affirm the responsibility of St. Peter's see for the entire Church. The emergence of a powerful new personality in northern Italy, Ambrosius of Milan, somewhat limited Rome's influence toward the end of the 370s (Damasus was absent from the council of Aquileia of 381), but a series of imperial measures taken by Gratian confirmed the strength of Roman interventions in Italy.

As a countermeasure against the pro-Arian policy of Valens and to put an end to the divisions created, among others, by the schism of Antioch, the eastern churchmen also turned to Rome. In 377 Damasus called a synod to attempt to settle the conflicts of the East (the condemnation of Apollinarius of Laodicea and of Timothy of Beirut as well as of Marcellus of Ancyra, recognition of the legitimacy of Paulinus of Antioch). He took this opportunity to publish a real syllabus—to use the expression of C. Pietri—the *Tomus Damasi*. Attaching 24 anathemas against the Sabellians, the Arians, the supporters of Eunomus and Photius, the Apollinarists and the Pneumatomachs to the Nicene Creed, the Tome became, in a way, the Western formulation of Nicean orthodoxy, insisting particularly on the unity of power, will, and action of God. The association of the Tome of Damasus to the Nicene Creed, in a number of canonical collections, is proof of the authority of Roman theology during this time, marked by the influence of Hilarius of Poitiers and of Eusebius of Vercelli.

It was, however, the edict of Thessalonica, addressed to the people of Constantinople that, on 27 February 380 (*Cth* XVI, 1, 2; *CJ* 1, 1, 1, 1), recognized officially, for the first time (and in the East) the exemplary value of Roman communion and Roman primacy, justified by apostolic tradition (already recognized by the council of Antioch of 379, which subscribed to the Tome of Damasus). It indeed defined orthodoxy as communion with

Damasus ("We want all people . . . to live in the religion that the divine apostle Peter transmitted to the Romans . . . that Pope Damasus is obviously following . . ."), and imposed civil sanctions (applying to heretics punishments of infamy that were aimed at the Manichaeans by Valentinian in 372) on those who would refuse it. It was probably as much the worry of reestablishing public peace in the part of the Empire that he governed as theological involvement that inspired Theodosius to issue this edict, made before his illness and his baptism, and not after (as stated in the chronology of Sozomenes, *Ecclesiastical History*, 7, 5). Also, we must not exaggerate its effect, as there is sometimes a tendency to do. It was a circumstantial action mostly concerning Constantinople, and not a program destined to be applied throughout the Empire. However, given the dogmatic and disciplinary division in the eastern episcopate at the time, only communion with the sees of ALEXANDRIA and Rome could be taken as a criterion of orthodoxy; therefore, the reference to Roman communion does not necessarily reveal the direct influence of Damasus on Theodosius (to justify the authority of the see of Rome, the text does not furnish any new argument with regard to those that the bishop advanced in his synodal of 377).

This edict marks the *acmè*, and also the limit of the reach of the Apostolic See, again restricted by the evolution of the East. The reconstitution of an orthodox episcopate made it less necessary to turn to Rome; the putting into place of a religious geography which adopted the limits of political geography favored the imperial residence, Constantinople; finally, the more and more marked political division between the two parts of the Empire turned the East away from Rome. In 381 the Second Ecumenical Council of Constantinople was called without the see of Peter being informed, and one of its canons (c. 3) would incite a hostile reaction from Damasus. In fact, though it recognized more formally than ever before in the East the primacy of Rome in the Church (and reiterated the tenor of the edict of Thessalonica, which accorded the right of defining conditions of ecclesiastical communion first to the bishop of Rome), the council gave a second primacy of honor to the bishop of Constantinople, "because it is a new Rome." Damasus immediately perceived the threat this political justification of primacy held for Rome (for the expression *nea Romè* had first a political meaning, and it was in this sense that most of the contemporary pagan writers like Libanios used it). By implicitly excluding the jurisdictional responsibilities of Rome in the East, canon 3 of the Council of Constantinople in fact heralded canon 28 of the Council of Chalcedon which would mark, seventy years later, the failure in the East of Roman pretensions on matters of discipline, containing within it the seed of many conflicts between the see of Rome and Byzantium.

However, the council that met in 382 in the West to pass judgment on the events in the East (the successions of Constantinople and Antioch) allowed Damasus to affirm once again Rome's primacy, placed at the head of the hierarchy of churches by virtue of apostolic tradition (and not by political criteria), with, for the first time in this context, a reference to Mt 16: 17 (a small treatise of ecclesiology preserved in the *Decretum de libris recipiendis et non recipiendis*). The knowledge acquired during Damasus' pontificate was felt most strongly in the West, but by developing the structures of the Church of Rome and trying to extend its prerogatives regarding faith and discipline to the entire Church (to impose its model), the bishop had nonetheless laid the groundwork for the future development of the papacy.

Françoise Monfrin

Bibliography

"Damase," *Dictionnaire encyclopédique du christianisme ancien*, 1, 621–3.

Ferrua, A. *Epigrammata Damasiana*, Vatican City, 1942.

Février, P. A. "Un plaidoyer pour Damase. Les inscriptions des nécropoles romaines," *Institutions, société et vie politique dans l'Empire romain au IVe s. apr. J.-C., Actes de la Table Ronde autour de l'oeuvre d'A. Chastagnol* (Paris, 20–21 January 1989), ed. by M. Christol, S. Demougin, Y. Duval, C. Lepelley, and L. Pietri (*Collection de l'EFR*, 159), Rome, 1992, 497–506.

Fontaine, J. *Naissance de la poésie dans l'Occident chrétien (Études augustiniennes)*, Paris, 1981, 11–125.

Pietri, C. "Damase et Théodore. Communion orthodoxe et géographie politique," *Epektasis. Mélanges patristiques offerts au cardinal Jean Daniélou*, published by J. Fontaine and C. Kannengiesser, Paris, 1972, 627–34.

Pietri, C. *Roma Christiana*, I, especially VI–X.

Saecularia Damasiana, Atti del Convegno internazionale per il XVI Centenario della morte del Papa Damaso I (11-12-384–10/12-12-1984) promosso dal Pontificio Istituto di Archeologia Cristiana, Vatican City, 1986.

Shepherd, H. M. "The Liturgical Reform of Damasus I," in Granfield, P., and Jungman, J. A., eds. *Kyriakon: Festschrift Johannes Quasten* 2 (Munich, 1970), 847–63.

Van Roey, A. "Damase," *DGHE*, 14, 1960, 48–54.

DAMASUS II. *Poppon (b.?, d. Palestrina, 9 August 1048). Named pope Christmas 1047, enthroned on 17 July 1048. Buried at San-Lorenzo-fuori-le-Mura.*

This very short pontificate (20 days) took place during troubled times. After the death of CLEMENT II (9 October 1047), a Roman ambassador was sent to the emperor to ask for a new pope. On Christmas day, Henry III, in his palace at Pöhlde, south of Harz, designated Poppon, the bishop of Brixen, who had accompanied him on his visit to Italy in 1046 and 1047, and who had attended various SYNODS. Informed of his choice, Poppon went to Ulm to the sovereign's court (25 January 1048); Henry asked the Marquis Boniface of Tuscany to accompany the new pontiff to Rome. Boniface refused to do this because he supported the return to power of BENEDICT IX, the pope deposed on 23 December 1046, who had returned to Rome. Poppon returned to Germany. Henri III strongly renewed his injunctions and threatened Boniface, who deposed Benedict IX through his representative, and then accompanied Poppon to Rome, where he was accepted and enthroned under the name of Damasus II on 17 July. His rapid death left him no time to undertake any action whatsoever.

Michel Parisse

Bibliography

LP, 2, 274.

JW, 1, 525–9.

Anton, H. H. "Bonifaz von Canossa, Markgraf von Tuszien, und die Italienpolitik der frühen Salier," *Historische Zeitschrift*, 214, 1972, 552 *sq*.

Bertolini, P. "Damase II," *DBI*, 32, 1986, 289–92.

Schieffer, R. "Damasus II," *LexMA*, 3, 1984–6, 470.

Van Roey, A. "Damase II," *DHGE*, 14, 1960, 53.

Watterich, 1, 74; 78–80; 716.

DANTE. In *The Divine Comedy*, Dante did not spare the members of the Church. In it, we see his time reflected: the anticlerical vehemence was, in the Middle Ages, the reverse of a nostalgic attachment to the evangelical virtues of poverty and humility. On the last judgments that adorned the walls of Romanesque churches, clerics and mitered churchmen are seen being thrown into the mouth of Hell. Among the ecclesiastical personalities most mistreated by Dante are the popes, because he believed they had substituted a temporal patrimony that led them to political mismanagement and financial bargaining for the spiritual patrimony inherited from St. Peter. To this denunciation, common to men of the Middle Ages, was added, in Dante's case, the resentment due to having been personally betrayed by BONIFACE VIII, as well as the violence of his poetic temperament.

During the PILGRIMAGE that leads him through the three sections of the next world, Dante first meets five popes spread among different circles of Hell: CELESTINE V, ANASTASIUS II, NICHOLAS III, CLEMENT V, and Boniface VIII. In Canto II he meets two others among the souls in Purgatory: HADRIAN V and MARTIN IV. As for popes named in the third Canto, the one portraying Paradise, they are not there for their own deeds, but rather for having been St. Peter's immediate successors [Linus and Cletus (III, 27, 41–43); SIXTUS I and PIUS I (III, 27, 44)]; or the contemporaries of the great saint of poverty, Saint Francis of Assisi [INNOCENT III (III, 11, 85–93) and HONORIUS III (III, 11, 94–99)]. The last pope named in Paradise, JOHN XXII (III, 27, 55–60), accused of having handed out excommunications in order to collect money for their annulment, could be added to the list of popes in Hell.

Popes in Hell.

1. The hypothesis about Celestine V (I, 3, 58–60). Most of the critics of Dante's work agree in attributing the sin of the "great refusal" (*che fece il gran rifiuto*) to Celestine V, though he was not specifically named among the sinners of cowardice located at the entrance to Hell. Celestine V actually abdicated barely five months after having been elected on 5 July 1294, feeling unworthy. This hypothesis had been refuted with judicial arguments by Auguste Valentée, among which the most persuasive is the canonization of the same Celestine V in 1313, a date at which Dante had not yet finished *The Divine Comedy*. Also, A. Valensin proposes substituting the name of Pilate, which seems to be a more exact reference regarding the "refusal" (*op. cit.*, p. 100–5).

2. Anastasius II (I, 11, 4–9), pope from 496 to 498. He is expiating the sin of heresy, lying in a tomb on which is inscribed: "I hold Pope Anastasius / whom Photinus caused to turn from the straight path."

3. Nicolas III (I, 19, 64–84), pope from 1277 to 1280. Head plunged down in a hole and with his feet burned by flames, he is expiating the sin of simony.

4. Clement V (I, 19, 82–7), elected pope 3 June 1305, transferred the pontifical see to Avignon. It was this decision that caused Dante's vehement "A pastor without laws."

5. Boniface VIII (I, 19, 52–7 and 79–82), elected pope in 1294, was still alive when Dante prepared a place in Hell for him. This audacity is proportionate to the heavy sins said to be his: SIMONY, avarice, nepotism, duplicity, and impiety. The main reason for Dante's vindictiveness is personal: the pope had betrayed the white GUELPH party, his own, for that of the black Guelphs, and Dante held him personally responsible for his exile far from Florence.

Popes in Purgatory.

1. Hadrian V (II, 19, 88–145) only reigned for 40 days during the year 1276. He is punished for his avarice but the noble speech of repentance he makes to Dante shows that he is on the path to conversion. "Make no mistake: I am a serf with you / and those of a single power."

2. Martin IV (II, 24, 20–4), pope from 1281 to 1285. For his legendary gluttony, Dante placed him among gluttons forced to learn temperance.

Contemporary popes have known how to intelligently draw the lesson from the attacks made by Dante on certain ones among them. Leo XIII, who purportedly knew *The Divine Comedy* by heart, considered the poet "an illustrious glory of Christianity . . . who never wavered from Christian truth." Benedict XV paid homage to Dante in his encyclical *In preclara summorum copia hominum* (20 April 1921): "Who could deny that, at that time, there were not among the clergy things to chastise, capable of totally disgusting any soul as devoted to the Church as that of Dante?"

Henriette Levillain

Bibliography

Dante, *La Divina Commedia* (Italian edition) ed. N. Sapegno, 3 vols., La Nuova Italia editrice, Florence, 1977.

Dante, *La Divine Comédie* (bilingual ed.) trans., introd. and notes by J. Risset, 3 vols., "L'Enfer" (1985), "Le Purgatoire" (1988), "Le Paradis" (1992), Flammarion, Paris.

Guardini, R. *Dante visionnaire de l'éternité*, Paris, 1962.

Valensin, A. *Le Christianisme de Dante*, Paris, 1954.

DATARY, APOSTOLIC. For seven centuries the apostolic datary was one of the most important DICASTERIES of the Holy See, until its termination by PAUL VI during the general reform of the Roman CURIA of 1967 (apostolic document *Regimini Ecclesiae universae*). Its function was to receive, examine, and accord favors. As its name indicates, the decisive moment of the procedure occurred when the document granting the favor was dated, making it official.

In the beginning, a member of the apostolic chancellery filled this position, but after the increase in the number of petitions beginning in the 14th century, a distinction began to be made between their reading, given to a specialized section of the chancellery, and their execution, done by this office until, during the 15th century, the datary became autonomous. For a long time there was no titled worker to do this. Under antipope BENEDICT XIII they spoke simply of the *datum ponens* or the one *qui datam ponit* to designate the functionary who occasionally performed this task (ruling on 14 December 1406), but soon afterward, under antipope JOHN XXIII, the *datator* appeared (ruling on 18 May 1410). With Pope MARTIN V, this duty was called *dataria* and its performer took the name of *supplicationum apostolicarum datarius* (rulings of 1 September 1418, 15 September 1420, and 15 October 1421). The list of dataries, beginning with Jo-

hannes de Feys, began during this pontificate as well. This person takes on considerable importance when, from the middle of the same 15th century, CALLISTUS III decided that the dataries would receive episcopal consecration. After the middle of the 17th century, they were honored with the rank of cardinal; they would then take the title of *prodatary* to exercise a function normally given to a prelate of episcopal rank.

Constantly enlarged, the job of apostolic datary was strongly affirmed by SIXTUS V in his great curial charter *Immensa aeterni Dei* in 1588. In the early days, the datary attended the signing of concessions by the pope, after which he dated them. Under Sixtine organization, he would go back to the apostolic datary to confer nonconsistorial (that is to say, not episcopal) benefices from the Holy See, to grant "letters of expectance" (promises to grant a benefice upon the death of its current holder), to accord matrimonial dispensations or pensions from ecclesiastical possessions, etc. The petitions that arrived at Rome were studied by the Curia who then summarized the contents on two slips of paper: the first for the list of grounds for granting it, the second for the terms and eventual conditions of this favor. At the bottom of the first paper, the pope would write the words *Fiat ut petitur* (may it be done according to what is asked), followed by the initial of his baptismal name (or his denomination if he belonged to a religious order); on the second slip, there would only be the word *Fiat* accompanied by the same type of signature. Due to the great number of these, matrimonial dispensations were signed by a CARDINAL after approval by the pope, with the note "*Concessum ut petitur in praesentia D. (omini) N. (ostri) Papae*" (accorded as requested in the presence of our Lord the pope), followed by his name and his title. If the favor accorded had any restrictions, the pope replaced the *Fiat ut petitur* by the word *Placet*.

The distribution of favors by the datary was a source of great revenue for the pontifical treasury: the *componendes* were payments made by the beneficiaries of the exemptions or privileges. The collection of petitions that arrived at the court of Rome from the reign of Martin V to PIUS VII fill about seven thousand volumes! The venal sale of certain offices in the Roman Curia also brought considerable resources to the apostolic datary: the "officials" (*vacabilia officia*) were jobs given to some "vacabilists" within the pontifical government upon the payment of a certain sum to the datary, whereas others were given free of charge by the APOSTOLIC CAMERA. The need for a system of offices corresponded to the great financial needs of the papacy for the functioning of the Universal Church and the PAPAL STATES. The latter brought in little to the Roman treasury due to the low rate of taxation the subjects of the pope would tolerate and their communal freedoms. Therefore, it became necessary for the Curia to tax legal documents it issued and to establish venal charges in the ecclesiastical government, similar to those in contemporary States. Byzantium had already set the example. The great organizer of offices was Sixtus V, who proceeded to set the monetary tariffs for 3,898 ecclesiastical or lay posts, representing a sum of about 5 million gold crowns. Among these jobs we find the CAMERLENGO of the holy Roman Church, the auditor, the steward and the general treasurer of the Apostolic Camera, the 101 apostolic writers, the 108 registrars of apostolic letters, the 140 chamberlains and the 140 squires, the 752 presidents and providers of Ripa for the provisioning of Rome, the 401 knights of St. Paul's, 260 knights of Our Lady of Loreto and 350 knights of the lily, the 88 solicitors of apostolic letters, 143 men who sealed the BULLS with lead, the collectors of lead, and others. The occupation of Rome by Napoleon put a number of these officials out of work and Pius VII took advantage of this to reduce their number even further, until LEO XIII decreed their complete abolishment in 1901. The signature of certain CONCORDATS had already reduced the revenues of the datary because ecclesiastical benefices were then directly assigned by the temporal sovereigns, as in Spain with the concordat of 1753 between BENEDICT XIV and Ferdinand VI. The latter still paid the Holy See a large sum (1,143,000 crowns, called the *Compenso di Spagna*), of which part was spent on the *Palazzo Madama* (which has become, in our day, the seat of the senate of the Italian Republic). Benedict XIV also reduced the powers of the datary, especially regarding the possessions of the Church (constitution *Gravissimum Ecclesiae*, 1745). In 1872 PIUS IX gave it complete authority to interpret, in his name, the requirements for the giving of ecclesiastical benefices, but Leo XIII saw things otherwise, first ordering a reduction in office staff (1878) and in the personnel of the datary (1897), and then the elimination of 700 official jobs still in existence (1898–1901). This pope, however, provided the datary with a new structure divided into three sections: the recording of benefices, matrimonial dispensations, and administration. A secretary and a council of theologians were added to the datary. In his general reform of the Roman Curia (the apostolic document *Sapienti consilio*, 1908), PIUS X continued the reductions of this dicastery begun by his predecessors: Matrimonial dispensations were taken away from its duties, and the monopoly on awarding favors (*privilegium exclusivae*) was removed from the *apostolici ministri expeditorum* who, after having numbered more than 100, had been reduced to only 35 under Leo XIII. The duties of the datary of 1908 were sanctioned by canon 261 of the CODE OF CANON LAW of 1917: judgment of the capacity of the candidates for non-consistorial benefices reserved for the Holy See, sending out letters on these assignments, granting dispensations on this matter, and fixing charges and pensions pertaining

to them. Rules published on 11 November 1930 and an instruction from 1942 outlined the rules for petitions.

The reform by Pius X also had the effect of making the head of the datary a datary cardinal, and not just a pro-datary. By reason of his proximity to the reigning pontiff, this cardinal was called *oculus papae*, or *organum mentis et vocis papae*—eye, mind, and voice of the pope, reflecting the enviable place he held: He followed the pope wherever he went. After living in the Lateran palace, he moved to AVIGNON, then to the Vatican, and finally to the datary palace built by PAUL V below the QUIRINAL. The popes left a datary with their vice legate in Avignon from 1378 to 1768, with jurisdiction over the southern provinces of France. Even the ANTIPOPES had their own datary in Avignon during the Great Schism, and in Geneva with Amadeus of Savoy, who became the antipope FELIX V. The tenure of the datary ended with the death of the pope who had named him, and the petitions extant at that time were then given, in a sealed box, to the Holy College to be given to the new pope upon his election.

The first of the Palatine cardinals, the datary was logically received first in the morning AUDIENCE of the sovereign pontiff (at first every day, then twice a week, on Tuesdays and Fridays), the pope wishing to begin his workday by granting several favors. The cardinal datary was accompanied to this audience by the vice datary, who carried a velvet purse (red or violet according to the calendar of the pontifical court), which held the petitions for marriage to give the sovereign pontiff. The subdatary prelate was the director of the following personnel of the apostolic datary: the prefect of the service *per obitum* (of death); the legal counselor of the dicastery, who would take care of all vacancies of benefices through natural or civil death of their holders; the prefect *per concessum*, who handled ordinary matrimonial dispensations; the prefect or administrator of the *componendes* (a post of papal confidence occupied by the cardinal nephew, predecessor of the SECRETARY OF STATE), who set the taxes and oversaw the fruits of the sale of vacant positions; the prefect of the dates, who stamped the smaller date (for the arrival of the petition) as separate from the larger date, which the datary himself placed on it at the time of the final signature; the auditor of matrimony, in charge of examining the dispensations for marriage; the first and second auditor, respectively charged with petitions relating to benefices and pensions; the officer *de missis*, who sent the files to be registered with a note of the amount due; the officer of letters, who kept minutes; the auditor of accounts, for the accounting books; the writer of bulls *in via secreta*; and the custodian of petitions in charge of filing them and preserving them. These directors of the dicastery were assisted by a large number of employees attached to the datary, but this personnel had been considerably reduced during the course of centuries, so that just before its elimination, on 1 January 1968, the apostolic datary, then directed by Cardinal Paolo Giobbe, the last datary, included only a dozen people: a vice datary, three officers, an archivist, a cashier, two writers of bulls, and three theologians (one DOMINICAN, one FRANCISCAN, and one JESUIT).

Joël-Benoît D'Onorio

Bibliography

Del Re, N. *La Curia romana. Lineamenti storico-giuridici*, Rome, 1970.

Celier, L. *Les Dataires du Xve siècle et les origines de la daterie apostolique*, Paris, 1910.

"Les vacables de la daterie," *Annuaire pontifical catholique*, Paris, 1902.

Nez, R. "Daterie apostolique," *DDC* (1949), 1034–41.

Storti, N. *La storia e il diritto della Dataria apostolica, dalle origini ai nostri giorni*, Naples, 1969.

DEACONS. Deacons, who rank in Christian ministers below presbyters, are not the same as the "Seven" described in Acts 6 of the Bible, although this was believed to be true some time later (Ireneus, *adv. haer.* 1, 2-, 3; *Cyp. Ep.* 3, 3; *Council of New Caesarea*, 314, c.15). The term "deacon" refers to a function or a service. It is not a title. The New Testament texts refer to their service (ministry). Ignatius of Antioch (martyred in Rome around 107) places deacons in the third level of the hierarchy, after bishops and priests. According to the "Apostolic Tradition," which explained the organization of the Christian community in the early 3rd century, deacons are not ordained for ministry, but rather to serve the bishop (the same statement is in the *Statua Ecclesiae Antiqua*, c. 4). Cyprian (*Ep.*, 3.1) calls them "ministers of the bishop and the Church." The Didascalia, composed around 230 in the patriarchate of Antioch (II, 34) holds that they are "the ear and the mouth, heart and soul" of the bishop, as the *APOSTOLIC CONSTITUTIONS* repeat (II, 44, 4). Their numbers vary according to the importance of the community (sometimes only a single deacon or two, *CA*, III, 19, 1; II, 57, 13 and 15). In principle there should not be more than seven (council of Neo-Caesarea, c. 15), but in Constantinople in the 5th century, we find about 100, and Emperor Heraclius (610–41) would increase that number to 150. In Rome at the end of the 6th century, a deaconal college had a dozen deacons and just as many subdeacons, with an archdeacon as their head. A deacon's career is different than that of a priest. It often begins in pontifical administration as a NOTARY. The Roman pontiff's representative to the emperor of Constantinople was a deacon (an apocrisary).

Their duties are many, but essentially involve assisting the bishop in his liturgical, public service, and administrative duties. Close to the bishops, they had more influence over them than the priests. In Rome, several popes of the 4th and 5th centuries had been deacons (LIBERIUS, FELIX, DAMASUS, URSINUS, SIRICIUS, BONIFACE, LEO I, HILARUS, FELIX III). The *Apostolic Constitutions*, compiled in Syria (Antioch) probably in 380, described their role by recopying the instructions about them from the Didascalia with no major changes. They added several reminders of their duties of obedience to the bishop (II, 30–2; VIII, 46, 16–17), because they do not perform the sacraments but are in the bishop's service (VIII, 28, 4; 46, 10–11). This is what c. 18 says from the Council of Nicaea. In the liturgical assembly, deacons welcome and oversee the laymen and are responsible for keeping order (II, 57, 4, 11–13; 58, 1, 4–6; VIII, 11, 10). They introduce the common prayer (VIII, 10, 2; 11, 7–9; 13, 9) and take care of the altar service (VIII, 12, 3). They receive the offerings, distribute material aid, visit the sick and the poor, and help those who are in need. They have a role in the administration of penitence (II, 16, 1), judicial service (II, 42, 1; 47, 1), and baptism (II, 16, 2–4), and attend ordinations (VIII, 4, 6; 16, 2; 17, 2; 19, 2).

The importance of their duties explains the care taken in their recruitment (minimum age of 25 or 30, according to location), the reminder of their duties, the specifics of their listed duties: They are not authorized to baptize or offer communion (council of Arles of 314, c. 15) nor to preach. They can distribute communion. As needed, they are allowed to read the Gospel at mass, baptize under certain conditions (Gelasius, Ep. 14, 7 and 8. Thiel, Epist. 366). In Rome (early 2nd and 3rd centuries), the seven deacons, assisted by seven subdeacons, collected donations and distributed them as needed to the sick, captive, and poor, each having a region to cover (Hipp., *Trad. Apost.*, 8, 26; Amb., *de off.* 1, 41, 204; Prudence, *Per.* 2, 156). In the middle of the 3rd century, Pope FABIAN confirms this territorial division for the purpose of assistance: *Hic regiones divisit diaconibus* (Catal. Liberianus, *LP, Lib. Pont.*, 5). A similar partitioning into regions existed in CARTHAGE, but the number of regions is unknown.

The Ambrosiaster (*Quaest novi et vet.* Test. 101, 4; *CSEL*, 50, 195), Jerome (Ep. 146, 2), denounced the pretensions of Roman deacons. The restrictions of the college, the importance of the duties of the deacons, and perhaps a "transfer" of the pride of Roman aristocracy (Gaspar) may explain certain of these abuses.

Jean Gaudemet

Bibliography

Faivre, A. *Naissance d'une hiérarchie*, Paris, 1979.

Grossi, V., and Di Berardino, A. *La chiesa antica*, Rome, 1984, 103–5.

Klauser, T. "Diakon," *Reallexikon für Antike und Christentum*, 1957, 890–903.

LeClercq, H. "Diacre," *DACL*, IV, 738–46.

Pietri, C. "Clercs et laïcs romains . . . ," *Grégoire le Grand*, 1988, 110–13.

Prat, F. "Les prétentions des diacres romains au IVe siècle," *Rech. sc. rel*, III, 1912, 463 *ff*.

DEATH OF THE POPE, MIDDLE AGES. The most
ancient allusions to a funerary ritual reserved for a pope
go back to the beginning of the 12th century. The *Vita* of
URBAN II (1088–99) in the *Liber pontificalis* tells us that
his remains were entombed "with honor," according to
tradition, in St. Peter's basilica (*LP*, II, 294); the *Vita* of
PASCAL II (1099–1118) states that the dead pope had
been dressed in sacred garments according to the instructions of the *ordo* (*LP*, II, 305); the *Vita* of HONORIUS II
(1124–39) adds that the Roman *ordo*, outlining the honors of the burial of popes, was ancient (J. M. Watterich,
Pontificum Romanorum qui fuerunt Vitae, II, Lipsiae
1862, 189). For the kings of France, also, the sources
speak about "royal funerary traditions" for the first time
at the beginning of the 12th century (1129: A. Erlande-
Brandeburg, *Le roi est mort*, Geneva-Paris, 1975, 14). In
England, the funeral of King Henry II (1154–89) was the
first to have been celebrated, according to sources, *more
regio* (ibid., 16). If, in Rome the existence of an *ordo* was
verified as early as the death of Pascal II (d. 1118), it was
not until the final decades of the 14th century that the first
complete ceremonial relative to a pope's funeral was
known. Its author is Pierre Ameilh (ed. Dykmans, *Le
Cérémonial papal*, IV, 216–27), whose Curial career extended from the pontificate of URBAN V (1362–76) until
his death (Rome, 4 May 1401; ibid., 13–24).

Administrative and ritual responsibilities were given
to three main participants: the CAMERLENGO (chamberlain), the PENITENTIARIES, and the CARDINALS. According
to this ritual, the pope spent the final instants of his life
in the *camera*. Two or three days before he "would lose
the power of speech," the camerlengo had to call in the
cardinals so that the dying pope could dictate his testament in their presence and choose the place of his burial. After having pronounced his profession of faith, the
pope must "recommend the Church" to the cardinals,
called to choose a new pastor in peace and tranquility.
To the cardinals, he gave all his possessions as well as
the treasures and jewels belonging to the Church. The
preparation of the body was entrusted to the individuals
in charge of formulating the pontifical BULLS (The
Brothers of the Bull). The camerlengo and the sacristan
gave them the balm used to anoint the body. Dressed in
religious vestments, "as if the dead man was going to
celebrate mass," the pope would first be displayed in the
chapel, and then in the church before the official funeral. The *feretrum* was decorated with the coat of arms
of the deceased pope and those of the Roman Church.
The entire ritual took place over a period of nine days
(*novena*). By the way, this was the first time this word is
found in a pontifical ceremony.

The second ceremony related to the pope's death was
the work of François de Conzié, who was camerlengo
for 48 years under popes CLEMENT VII, BENEDICT XIII,
ALEXANDER V, JOHN XXIII, and MARTIN V (1383–1431).
The role of the camerlengo was not changed. He was always the one who closed the palace doors and assured its
protection. As for the vice chancellor, the ceremonial describes a new role, destined to last until modern times.
The vice chancellor, whose role does not end with the
death of the pope, used a hammer to break the seal of the
bull that bore the engraved name of the deceased; the
seal that bore the images of apostles Peter and Paul had
to be preserved by the camerlengo *integra et illesa* until
the election of the new pope. For analogous reasons the
ring allowing the pope to use his seal, called the FISHER-
MAN'S RING (*anulus* or *sigillum piscatoris*), was given to
the college of the cardinals. The most ancient record of
the existence of such a ring dates back to CLEMENT IV.
During the trial of CLEMENT V's nephews, the cardinal of
Santa Maria Nuova made sure that the *sigillum piscatoris* was given to the cardinals after the pope's death.

At the end of the 15th century, the papal funerary ritual was rewritten as ordered by INNOCENT VIII
(1484–94) by the master of ceremonies, Agostino Patrizi
Piccolomini. The novena appears there, completely distinct from the entombment of the dead pope; a fiction
would even be necessary in order to simulate the presence of the remains during the funeral: two grooms,
dressed in black, at the foot of the two sides of the *castrum doloris* would "continually and placidly" wave
black fans, decorated with the pope's arms, as if they
were chasing off flies. The most ancient record of this
custom comes to us from Enea Silvio Piccolomini, eye-
witness to the death of EUGENE IV (23 February 1447).
The fly-chasing was also incorporated into the funerary
ritual of cardinals. Even before the pope was dead, a
commission of three cardinals, representing each of the
three orders, had to preside, together with the camerlengo, at the creation of the inventory of all the possessions in the palace (the inventories of decorations and
other objects found after their deaths in the *camera* of
CALLISTUS III and PIUS II were published by E. Müntz,
*Les Arts à la cour des papes pendant le XVe et le XVIe
siècle. Recueil de documents inédits tirés des archives et
des bibliothèques romaines*, Paris, 1878, 213–19;
323–9). By informing the princes and prelates of the
Christian world of the popes's death, the cardinals were
supposed to use the "apostolic style," "as if the sender of
the letter were the pope."

The record of the final moments of Pope BENEDICT XI
confirms the information about these rituals. The pope
confessed and received absolution in the presence of the
cardinals. The profession of faith served to certify the orthodoxy of the papal action. The dying pope exhorted the
cardinals to come to agreement and chose his place of

burial (the Dominican convent at Perugia). The relative stipulations for the *familia* and the goods possessed by the dying man when he was still a cardinal correspond to the stipulations of testaments. The indications of P. Ameilh about the dressing of the pope's remains are also found in the descriptions of the openings of the tombs of GREGORY VII and of BONIFACE VIII. The gold broaches adorned with precious sapphires found in the tomb of Boniface VIII are also seen on the funerary statues of HONORIUS IV and Boniface VIII himself. The arms of the dead pope are visible on the funerary monument of Honorius IV. On the sarcophagus of Boniface VIII, completed by Arnolfo di Cambio around 1296 (today partially preserved in the Grottos of the Vatican), we see the arms of the Caetani family. The most dominant piece of the funerary ritual described by Pierre Ameilh is the novena. Not documented with certainty until the middle of the 14th century (at the time of Clement VI's death in 1352), the novena would not have been possible without the decree *Ubi periculum*, a real "constitutional charter of the conclave," which forced the cardinals to wait ten days before beginning the process of electing a new pope. By requiring such a delay, GREGORY X was, in fact, creating a new ritual time, permitting the celebration of funerary rites for nine days. This was a real innovation. The ancient canons prescribed that the election of the pope had to begin the third day after the death of his predecessor. The dead pope was generally buried the day he died. During the 13th century, the interval between the death and burial grew longer. Popes INNOCENT III (d. 1216), HONORIUS III (d. 1227), and INNOCENT IV (d. 1254) were buried the day after their deaths, but JOHN XXI (d. 1277) was buried six days after his death, NICOLAS III (d. 1280) three days after, and MARTIN IV (d. 1285) four to five days after his death. This suggests that the introduction of the novena was related to the famous decree *Ubi periculum*. Promulgated on 1 November 1274, it was applied during the three vacancies of 1276, but was then suspended and perhaps revoked. CELESTINE V reestablished shortly after his election. His successor, Boniface VIII, was the first pope to have been elected after a vacancy of ten days. According to the testimony of Tolomée de Lucques, his funeral was still celebrated *more vetusto*, which could mean that the new rite of the novena was not respected (for reasons we do not know).

The hypothesis that this ceremony, destined to last until today, was modeled upon that of the imperial Byzantine court possible. After all, during the funeral of Emperor Andronikos II (1328), the funerary ceremony lasted nine days (*Nicephori Gregorae byzantina historia*, IX, 4, ed. L. Schopen, I, Bonn, 1829, 463). In BYZANTIUM, the emperor's relatives wore mourning clothes for nine days after the death of a wife, a brother, or a child (O. Treitinger, *Die oströmische Kaiser und Reichsidee nach ihrer Gestaltung im höfischen Zeremoniell*, Jean, 1938, 156 no. 57). It is certain in any case that the novena

lengthened, by guaranteeing what is the most demonstrably important innovation recorded since the first decades of the 13th century: the public display of the pope's remains. Innocent III was shown in the cathedral of Perugia, where he was robbed of the precious adornments with which he should have been buried; his cadaver was abandoned naked in the church, in a state of advanced decomposition. Entering the cathedral, Jacques de Vitry said he had seen with his own eyes how "brief and vain the false splendor of this world is" (*Letters of Jacques de Vitry*, ed. R. B. C. Huygens, Leide, 1960, 73). That J. de Vitry would use the rhetoric of *sic transit gloria mundi* reminds us that the public display of the remains was a form of glorification of the dead man and an element of the imitation of Roman antiquity. In Byzantium also, the emperor's body was displayed, dressed in his coronation clothing (Constantine VII Porphyrogenetus, *Le Livre des cérémonies*, II, Paris, 1939, I, 69).

In order to be able to display the pope's body to the public, embalming procedures were refined. The *Vita* of Pascal II (d. 1118) tells us that the pope's body was "prepared" with balm. For at least two centuries, however, no other source allows us to see if and how the bodies of the deceased popes were embalmed. At the beginning of the 14th century, information becomes more accessible and comes from the best surgeons and anatomists of the time: Henri de Mondeville (who knew Guillaume of Brescia, doctor for Popes Boniface VIII, Benedict XI, and Clement V) confirms that the remains of the ruling pontiffs (as well as those of kings, queens, and prelates) were "prepared" in order to be displayed with "face uncovered" (J.-L. Pagel, *Die Chirurgie des Heinrich von Mondeville*, Berlin, 1892, tract. III, doctr. I, cap. 7, 390). Guy de Chauliac, personal physician of Clement VI (1342–52), was said to have learned from the "apothecary Jacques who had embalmed several Roman pontiffs" how to preserve the *corpora mortuorum* by opening the abdomen and pulling out the internal organs (*Cyrurgia magna*, tract. I, doct. I, cap. VIII, 274). Pierre Argellata, professor of medicine and anatomy at the University of Bologna, embalmed Pope Alexander V (who died in that town on 3 May 1410) in such a way as to be able to display it for eight days. The author of the only description of the embalming of a pope that we have before modern times stipulates that the face, hands, and feet were left bare, so that "the hands and the feet, as well as the face, might be seen." The pope's death had to be publicly authenticated and his remains had to be displayed for devout people to see.

The fact that the sources talk about rituals relating to the death of popes only at the very end of the 11th century and the beginning of the 12th is not due to chance. As early as LEO IX's pontificate (1049–54), the reforming papacy of the 11th century took note of the necessity of basing the continuation of the Roman Church on new institutional foundations. In the 9th century, popes like

STEPHEN VI (885) opposed the pillaging of the palaces of the pope perpetrated by the people of Rome after the death of the ruling pontiff (*LP*, II, 192). Under Leo IX, however, the battle fought by the Roman Church against these abuses was based on an argument that explicitly distinguished between the physical condition of the pope and the perenniality of the Church (*Die Briefe des Petrus Damiani*, ed. K. Reindel, I, Munich, 1983, 336–9, no. 35). The pope's life is "brief" (Pierre Damien), and his power is transitory. Dying, the pope loses his *potestas*, whereas the Church is eternal: *dignitas non moritur.*

The pillaging of the palace is not documented when the pope did not die in Rome, which was very often the case in the 13th century because of the great mobility of the Roman Curia, and during the long stay of the papacy in Avignon. This was also why such pillages are no longer seen after the death of Gregory IX (1227). The pillaging and disorders that the pope's death unleashed during the course of the 15th and 16th centuries were not directed against the palaces as such. According to funerary rituals of the 14th and 15th centuries, the protection of the palace against the outside world no longer seems to have been a problem.

The custom that the pope's regular visitors could take goods belonging to him has lasted into modern times. These appropriations were a ritual-type reaction to the breaking of the oath of fidelity brought about by the pope's death, the system of papal government of the early Middle Ages, based essentially on nepotism, not favoring the interpersonal institutional relationships typical of modern bureaucracies. To this idea, all the attempts of the Roman Church, whose funerary ceremonies take this into account, were doomed to failure.

The divergence between rituals and reality was a constant in the history of the death of the pope that we cannot ignore. Even though they were not always respected, the funerary rituals of the papacy are nevertheless the reflection of important ecclesiastic thought that accompanied the institutional evolution of the papacy between Gregorian reform and the return of the popes to Rome in the 15th century. As such, they exerted a lasting influence on the ceremonial organization of the vacancy of the Apostolic See until our time. Born to handle institutional problems involved in the death of the pope, these rituals ended in the 14th century with the transformation of the funerary rituals of the cardinals: since the 15th century the novena has been a funerary rite reserved exclusively for the Roman hierarchy.

Agostino Paravicini Bagliani

See also PRIVATE LIVES, POPES'.

Bibliography

Cancelliere, F. *Notizie sopra l'origine e l'uso dell'annello piscatorio e degli altri anelli ecclesiastici*, Rome, 1823.

Dykmans, M. *L'Œuvre de Patrizi Piccolomini ou le cérémonial papal de la première Renaissance*, 2 vol, Vatican City, 1980–2; *Le Cérémonial papal de la fin du Moyen Âge à la Renaissance*, 4 vol., Brussels-Rome, 1977–85.

Ehrle, F. "Der Nachlaß Clemens V. und der in Betreff desselben von Johann XXII. (1318–1321) geführte Process," *Archiv für Litteratur und Kirchengeschichte des Mittelalter*, 1889.

Elze, R. " 'Sic transit gloria mundi': la morte del papa nel medioevo," *Annali dell' Istituto storico italo-germanico in Trento*, 3, 1977, 23–41.

"Giacomo Grimaldis Bericht über die Öffnung des Grabes Papst Bonifaz VIII. (1605)," *Römische Quartalschrift*, 61, 1966.

Herklotz, I. *"Sepulchra" e "monumenta" del Medioevo*, Rome, 1985; "Paris de Grassi Tractatus de funeribus et exequiis und die Bestattungsfeiern von Päpsten und Kardinälen in Spätmittelalter und Renaissance," *Skulptur und Grabmal des Spätmittelalters in Rom und Italien*, Vienna, 1990, 217–48.

Il Duomo di Salerne, ed. A. Capone, I. Salerno, 1927.

Paravicini Bagliani, A. *I testamenti dei Cardinali del Duecento*, Rome, 1980.

Paravicini Bagliani, A. *Le Corps du pape*, 1994.

Petrucci, E. "Il problema della vacanza papale e la costituzione Ubi Periculum di Gregorio X," *Atti del Convegno di studio per il VIII Centenario del I° Conclave (1268–1271)*, Viterbo, 1975.

Schimmelpfennig, B. *Die Zeremonienbücher der römischen Kurie im Mittelalter*, Tübingen, 1973.

Schimmelpfennig, B. "Päpst- und Bischofswahlen seit dem 12. Jahrhundert," *Wahlen und Wählen im Mittelalter*, Sigmaringen, 1990, 173–96.

Wolkan, R. *Der Briefwechsel des Eneas Silvius Piccolomini*, II, Vienna, 1912.

Zoepffel, R. *Die Papstwahlen und die mit ihnen im nächsten Zusammenhänge stehenden Ceremonien in ihrer Entwicklung vom 11. bis zum 14. Jahrhundert*, Göttingen, 1871.

DECORATIONS. The Holy See gives honorary distinctions whose divisions and hierarchy go back to the ancient orders of knights without having an actual link with them. There are actually five of these honorary awards, which are, in order of precedence: the Supreme Order of Christ, the Order of the Golden Spur or the Golden Host, the Order of Pius IX, the Order of Saint Gregory the Great, and the Order of Saint Sylvester. Their history is complex. Some, like the Order of the Golden Spur and the Order of Christ, have their origins in medieval times, but the others were created during the 19th century. This matter is actually regulated by a series of BRIEFS *Multum ad exercendos* given by PIUS X on 7 February 1905. In them, the orders are defined as they exist today. The last adjustment was made by PAUL VI who, in 1966, limited the rank of Knight of the Collar, by order of Pius IX, to chiefs of state. By the 19th century Pope GREGORY XVI had prohibited pontifical orders from conferring personal or hereditary nobility. PIUS IX reexamined this rule when making sure that the order he founded, the Order of Pius IX, would confer hereditary nobility to the Knights of the Holy Cross and personal nobility to the commanders. This privilege, maintained during the reform by Pius X, was abolished in a brief by PIUS XII on 11 November 1939.

The pontifical orders were designed to recognize the merits that men fulfilling public functions or ordinary persons could acquire from the Holy See. They are awarded directly by the pope (*motu proprio*) or indirectly, that is, after a demand addressed to the SECRETARIAT OF STATE. A large number of these decorations are awarded in an almost automatic way during official visits by sovereigns or politicians, or at the end of diplomatic missions to the Holy See, but the crosses are also used to reward lay workers of the CURIA and Vatican City as well as all those who are brought to the attention of the Secretariat of State by bishops throughout the world. Other than the Order of Christ and that of the Golden Host, the orders may be awarded even to non-Christians, but clerics and nuns cannot receive them. They are often given instead the cross *Pro ecclesia et pontifice* ("For the Church and the Pope"), an honorary distinction created especially by LEO XIII in 1888 that became permanent in 1898.

The Secretariat of State and within it, the Commission for Decorations (*Commissione per le onorificenze*) has the job of examining the dossiers of the candidates. Until the pontificate of Paul VI, the annual awards received a certain amount of press through the publication of lists in the *Attività della Santa Sede*, a semiofficial annual chronicle of the events at the court of Rome. The names of those who receive titles of nobility are no longer published, and the lists of awards only appear in the *Acta apostolicae Sedis*, an official publication difficult to find and plagued by long delays. Does the Holy See feel a bit ill at ease in bestowing honorary distinctions beyond Rome, or is it a sign of disinterest on the part of the Christian world? In France, the number of bishops who would admit to having proposed the name of their diocesans for a papal award can be counted on the fingers of one hand. This is why some laypersons responsible for associations or important institutions, and who want to signal to the rest of the world, by some exterior sign, the Holy See's kind view toward them will obtain decorations through direct contact with certain members of the Curia. The Holy See recognizes the religious military orders whose statutes it approves but whose members it does not select. This is the case with the Order Hospitaller of Saint John of Jerusalem (called the Knights of Malta) and the Order of the Holy Sepulchre and the Teutonic Order.

Philippe Levillain

Bibliography

Cardinale, H. E. *The Orders of Knighthood, Awards and the Holy See*, Gerrards Cross, 1983.

DECRETALS. The vague term "decretal" (*epistola decretalis, litterae decretales*) designates, among papal documents, letters by means of which the pope reveals a ruling, whether of universal applicability or specific, on a matter of discipline or CANON LAW, in answer to a request. By extending this definition, the commissions given to JUDGES-DELEGATE have been considered decretals, because they contribute toward enlightening points of law or procedure. From 1160–70, Étienne of Tournai defined a decretal as a "rewriting [decision following a request] addressed to a bishop or to an ecclesiastical judge on a point in doubt (*super aliqua causa dubitante*) or to resolve a problem of procedure." From the time when the different types of papal documents were defined, decretals, by definition, took the form of letters sealed with hemp thread, as opposed to privileges (documents confirming possessions or rights) and letters of perpetual deed, sealed with a silk thread; they differed also from other letters (letters granting pardons, administrative correspondence, political and diplomatic letters). Even when sent for temporary use and for a pressing affair, they had, especially at the time of their apogee during the 12th and 13th centuries, an important jurisprudential value in the formation of classic canon law. Their texts, carefully researched by canonists or preserved by the popes themselves, have made their contents predominant in CANONICAL COLLECTIONS, next to the canons of COUNCILS and what are properly called papal decrees (decisions of general import made by the pope under his own initiative), which were much less numerous.

Olivier Guyotjeannin

Bibliography

Duggan, C. "Decretals," NCE, 4 (1967), 707–9.
Fransen, G. *Les Décrétales et les collections de décrétales*, Turnhout, 1972 (*Typologie des sources du Moyen Âge occidental*, 2).

DECRETUM OF GRATIAN. (ca. 1140) The biography of the canonist Gratian, author of a *Decretum* that, until the codification of 1917, was one of the most important keys to the construction of church law, only contains, after actual research, a few elements not subject to caution (R. Metz). The *Chronicle* by Martin of Troppau assures us that Gratian (whose first name might have been John) was born in Chiusi in Tuscany; a second source places his birth in the hamlet of Carraria, near Orvieto, in Umbria. According to Robert de Torigny, the man who was known everywhere by the unique name of "Master" became the bishop of Chiusi, but other chroniclers said he had been the adviser of INNOCENT II (1130–43), a legate for EUGENE III (1145–53), or even a cardinal. Legend made Gratian the brother, through adultery, of Peter Lombard, the author of the *Sentences*, and of Peter the Eater (*Comestor*), author of the *Historia ecclesiastica*. The death of Gratian is shrouded in this same uncertainty and obscurity. It must have taken place before the Third LATERAN COUNCIL (1179), since some sources mention Gratian as no longer being in this world; Roland Bandinelli, a disciple of Gratian, became pope under the name of ALEXANDER III, in 1159 (d. 1181), leaving no doubt that his master was still alive. The only information still considered probable is that Gratian was Italian, that he became a Camaldolese monk at the convent of Saints Nabor and Felix in Bologna, and that he taught law there.

Compiled sometime in the 1140s, the *Decretum* contained more than 3,800 texts comprising the entire diverse tradition remaining of ancient law: canons said to have come from the apostles, canons from the general and individual councils from the beginning of the 4th century to the Second Lateran Council, DECRETALS from Saint DAMASUS (366–84) to INNOCENT II, augmented by fakes from the pseudo-Isidorian tradition, penitentials, liturgical books, episcopal statutes, as well as Roman and Frankish laws. Gratian dredged up most of these texts with a sure hand from previous large collections, especially those put together by Yves of Chartres at the end of the 11th century and early 12th-century Italian collections inspired by the Gregorian reform.

The work is divided into three unequal parts. The first part contains 101 *Distinctiones*, making up a treatise on the sources of Church law (D. 1 to 20), listing a hierarchy of ministers (D. 21 to 24), and a long treatise on ordination (D. 25 to 101). The second part is made up of thirty-six *Causae* examining the greatest questions concerning CANON LAW (administration and management of church properties, marriage law, prescriptions for penitence, and so forth). The final part is the *De consecratione*, the shortest of the three sections, divided into five *Distinctiones*. Despite several overlaps (*paleae*) and some associations of ideas that are rather vague, one of the major strengths of this manual often designated, perhaps by Gratian himself, as the *Concordia discordantium canonum*, was to set up definitively canon law as a discipline of knowledge. It introduced rules of reflection and comparison of texts that recognized the diverse authorities and respective values of the sources of law included therein. Established as the basic text for any teaching, Gratian's work was commented upon and *dicta* were added, but it was never replaced. Although it was never "approved" by the Church, the book was a starting point for the "new law" of the decretal letters, used more and more frequently by popes from Alexander III on to inter-

pret and develop the law with the weight of papal authority. The *Decretum* was universally recognized as an essential Church resource for nearly eight centuries.

Summary of Gratian's Decretum.

First part. [Divided into 101 distinctions.]:

Definitions: divine, natural, positive and customary law

Sources: written law, canons of councils, papal decretals, Roman law.

Clerics: offices, rights and duties, conditions of access.

Episcopate: conditions, qualities, hindrances and irregularities, election, powers of the order.

Ordination of clerics: clerical titles, letters of dismissal, degrees and delays in the hierarchy of ecclesiastical orders.

Qualities of a bishop; revenues of clerics; liturgical songs; aid for the poor, widows, those persecuted.

Relationships between religious and civil powers.

Second part. [Divided into thirty-six cases, subdivided into questions.]:

Simony: procedure, accusation and appeal, parties and witnesses, the order of the trial procedures.

The bishop: accusation and judgment; conflict between two candidates for the same see; succession; excommunication of the bishop; episcopal power outside the diocese, temporalities for the bishopric.

Tribunals for clerics.

Temporalities and revenues of clerics: buildings, tithes, and funerals.

Clerics and justice: actions and witnessing; usury; procedure.

The rights of religious orders: the vow, abbots, passage from a regular order to a secular one, leaving a monastery or changing.

Secular clerics.

Oaths and perjuries.

Repressive power: War, the right to kill.

Heresy and excommunication.

Privileges.

Divinatory practices, superstitions.

Marriage: engagements, hindrances, separation, annulment.

Penitence.

Third part: Consecration. [Divided into 5 distinctions.]:

Consecration of churches; celebration of mass; the eucharist; feasts; baptism; confirmation; fasting.

Later Concordances: Outline of the *Decretals* by Gregory IX (1234).

Book I. Jurisdiction and ecclesiastical hierarchies.

The Trinity and Catholic faith.

Normative sources.

Constitutions: rescripts, customary law.

Bishops.

Postulation; translation; the pallium; renunciation; negligences; ordination; scrutiny; clerics ordained by the bishop who renounces his office.

Clerics.

Age; unctions; nonreiteration of sacraments; the sons of priests; the ordination of serfs, clerics handling money, corporal defects; bigamy; pilgrims.

Ecclesiastical offices.

Archdeacon, archpriest, dean, sacristan, guardian, vicar.

Legates, judge delegates, judges.

War and peace.

Contracts and representation.

Synods.

Flaws in contracts.

Fraudulent alienation for judicial reasons.

Arbitration.

Book II. Canonical procedure.

Judgments, the competence of the judge.

The steps of the trial.

Lawsuits in court.

Confession and proof.

Methods of recourse.

Book III. Rights and duties of clerics and religious orders; ecclesiastical possessions.

Behavior of clerics.

Relationships with women; married clerics.

Dignities and prebends.

Administration of possessions.

Contracts and agrarian contracts.

Precarium, loans, sales, exchanges, fiefs, debts and securities, payments, donations, estates and testaments.

Parishes.

Tombs, prayer books, tithes, and rents.

Regulars.

Charters, for religious orders: relations with the bishop, chapels.

Conversion of the infidels.

Vows.

The right of patronage.

Census and procurations levied by the bishops.

Consecration of altars.

Mass and eucharistic sacrifice.

Baptism.

Nonbaptized priests.

Eucharistic reserve and preservation of the oils.

Veneration of relics.

Purification after giving birth to a child.

Construction and maintenance of churches.

Immunity of churches, cemeteries and their possessions.

Forbidding clerics and religious orders to dabble in profane business.

Book IV. Marriage.

Engagements and marriage.

Marriage of those under the age of puberty.

Clandestine marriages.

Bigamy.

Clauses in marriage contracts.

Marriage permitted to certain clerics.

Marriage of adulterers, lepers, serfs.

Condition of children born to a free woman.

Spiritual and legal relationships.

Consanguinity and affinity.

Impotence.

Marriage despite prohibition by ecclesiastical authorities.

Legitimacy of children.

Who can bring a case to trial against a marriage.

Separation of spouses.

Second marriages.

Book V. Criminal procedures and punishments.

Accusation, inquiry, denunciation.

Calumny.

Simony.

Prohibiting prelates from rendering their services for payment.

University teaching masters, granting of a license to teach.

Jews, Saracens and their slaves.

Heretics.

Schismatics and people controlled by them.

Apostates and clerics who have repeated baptism.

Infanticide, and the exposure of infants and sick people.

Voluntary or involuntary homicide.

Tourneys, and the use of the bow and crossbow.

Clerics fighting duels.

Adultery and rape.

Theft, fire-setters and profaners of churches.

Theft, usury, falsification, spells.

Agreement of the parties in a criminal case.

Crimes of children.

Clerics hunting.

Clerics hitting people.

Insults and blasphemies.

An excommunicated, deposed, or banned cleric who continues to officiate.

A promoted cleric who skips several degrees up the ladder of the hierarchy.

A cleric entering an order in secret.

Excesses of prelates and their subjects.

Denunciation of new works.

Privileges and abuses by those privileged.

Canonical and vulgar purgatory oath.

Insults and damages.

Punishments.

Penitence and remission.

Excommunication.

Several definitions of words.

Several rules of law.

The outlines of the contents of the codes of 1917 and 1983 suggest the influence of the *Decretum*.

Outline of the *Codex Juris Canonici* (1917).

Book I. General rules.

Ecclesiastical laws.

Custom.

Computation of time.

Revisions.

Privileges.

Dispensations.

Book II. Persons.

Generalities (physical people, minority, majority, home, relationships. Moral persons).

I. Clerics

Generalities.

Enrollment in a diocese.

Rights and privileges of clerics.

Obligations of clerics.

Ecclesiastical offices. Provision: collation, election, postulation. Loss.

Power of ordinary or delegated jurisdiction.

Power of order.

Reduction to the lay state.

Different categories of clerics.

Territorial division: provinces, dioceses, parishes.

The supreme power of the Church: the pope, ecumenical council, cardinals, Roman Curia (congregations, tribunal, offices), legates, patriarchs, primates, metropolitans, plenary councils and provincial councils, vicars and apostolic prefects, apostolic administrators, inferior prelatures.

The episcopal power and its auxiliaries: the bishop, coadjutators and auxiliary bishops, the diocesan synod and curia (vicar general. . .), cathedral chapter, consultants. Vacancy of the see and capitulary vicar. Country vicars (deans, archpriests), parishes, parish vicars, curates.

II. The religious orders

Generalities.

Establishment and suppression (congregation, province, house).

Government and administration.

Entry into religion. Studies.

Obligation and privileges.

Changing congregations.

Demotion to lay status.

Congregations without vows.

III. The lay members

Associations of laymen: third orders, confraternities.

Book III. Things.

I. The sacraments.

Baptism, confirmation.

Eucharist.

Penitence.

Extreme unction.

Order.

Marriage.

Sacraments.

II. Sacred places and times.

Churches, oratories, altars, tombs.

Holidays. Fasts.

III. Divine worship.

Communion (preservation, worship).

The cult of saints.

Processions.

Liturgical objects and clothing.

Vows and oaths.

IV. Ecclesiastical magisterium.

Cathechism.

Preaching.

Missions.

Seminaries.

Schools.

Censure and index.

Professions of faith.

V. Ecclesiastical benefices.

Definition.

Constitution.

Union, translation, suppression.

Collation.

The right of patronage.

Rights and obligations of benefices.

Hospitals and foundations.

Book IV. Trials and procedures.

I. Trials

Jurisdictions and judiciary organization.

How a suit takes place. Fees and judiciary assistance.

Transactions and arbitration. Criminal trials. Matrimonial cases. Procedure for ordination.

II. Procedures for cases of beatification and canonization.

III. Special procedures (against curates and clerics).

Book V. Crimes and punishments.

I. Crimes: natural, imputability, tentative.

II. Punishments.

Notion, classification, application.

Curative punishments or censure: excommunication, banishing, suspension.

Vindictive punishments: degradation, deposition, withdrawal from office or benefice.

III. Punishments applicable to certain crimes.

Outline of the *Codex Juris Canonici* (1983).

Book I. General norms.

Laws. Customs, decretals, and instructions. Administrative actions. Statutes and rulings.

Physical and moral persons.

Juridical Acts.

Power of government.

Ecclesiastical offices (obtainment, loss).

Prescription and computation.

Book II. The People of God.

I. The followers of Christ.

Obligations and rights of all the faithful, the laity.

The sacred ministers and clerics.

The personal prelatures.

The associations of the faithful.

II. The hierarchical organization of the Church.

    The Roman pontiff. The episcopal college.

    The synod of bishops. The cardinals.

    The Roman Curia. The legates.

    The particular churches.

    Bishops. Provinces and ecclesiastical regions.

    Metropolitans.

    Particular councils and episcopal conferences.

    Diocesan organization: synod, diocesan curia, presbyterial council, cathedral chapter, pastoral council, parishes.

III. The institutions of consecrated life and societies of apostolic life.

    General norms.

    Religious institutions. Establishment and suppression of houses. Hierarchy and advice.

    Temporalities and administration. Admission and profession of nuns and monks. Training.

    Transfer, leaving, abandonment.

    Secular institutions.

    The societies of apostolic life.

Book III. The teaching profession.

Ministry of the Word: preaching, catechism.

Missions.

Catholic education: schools and universities.

Means of social communication.

Profession of faith.

Book IV. The function of sanctification.

I. The sacraments.

    Baptism, confirmation, communion, penitence, unction for the sick, order, marriage.

II. Other actions of divine worship.

    Sacramentals, liturgical hours; funerals; the veneration of saints, images and relics; vows and oaths.

III. Sacred places and times.

Book V. Temporal possessions.

Acquisition, administration.

Contracts (in particular, breaking them).

Pious foundations.

I. Crimes and punishments in general.

II. Punishments for specific crimes.

    Against religion or Church unity. Against ecclesiastical authorities or the freedom of the Church.

    Usurpation of ecclesiastical charges. Falsification. Crimes against life and human freedom.

Book VI. Trials.

I. Generalities.

    Competence, organization, and judiciary administration; parties, actions, and exceptions.

II. Trial procedures.

III. Special procedures.

    Matrimonial cases. Cases of nullification of ordination. Oral procedures.

IV. Penal procedure.

V. Adminstrative procedure. Revocation or transfer of curates.

François Jankowiak

Bibliography

Kuttner, S. "Gratien," *DHGE*, XXI (1986), col. 1235–9.

Le Bras, G. Lefebvre, C., and Rambaud, J., *L'Âge classique (1140–1378)—Sources et théorie du droit (Histoire du Droit et des Institutions de l'Église en Occident*, VII), Paris, 1965.

Metz, R. "Regard critique sur la personne de Gratien, auteur du Décret (1130–1140), d'après les résultats des dernières recherches," *Revue des sciences religieuses*, LVIII (1984), 64–76.

Noonan, J. T. "Gratian Slept Here: The Changing Identity of the Father of the Systematic Study of Canon Law," *Traditio*, XXXV (1979), 145–72.

Reuter, I. and Silagi, G. *Wortkonkordanz zum Decretum Gratiani*, Munich, 1990.

Vetulani, A. *On Gratian and the Decretals*, London, 1990.

Wintroth, A. *The Making of Gratian's Decretum*, Cambridge, 2000.

DEPOSITION OF A POPE. This article could be considered meaningless since all popes who, in the Middle Ages, "made the great refusal" (Dante, *Inferno*, 3, 60) by abandoning their pontifical appointment, did so either at the moment of their election, by renunciation, or later by abdication. Those who have been deposed have almost all been declared antipopes, which simplifies the problem canonically but does not fully satisfy historians. For the popes of the GREAT SCHISM, "judgement is impossible for critics and historians" (A. Amanieu), and we remember the doubts expressed in 1958 at the time of the election of JOHN XXIII on the pertinence of the number (XXIII or XXIV). More realistically, the former canonists had foreseen, in vague terms, the deposition of a heretic pope, and Nicholas II (1059–61) had foreseen that of the simoniac pope at the COUNCIL of Rome of 1059; these texts have been handed down in the great canonical collections, Anselm of Lucca, Adeodatus, Yves of Chartres, and through the DECRETAL OF GRATIAN. The later official collections were no longer interested in questions such as the hypotheticals used in schools, though the issue could have been raised for JOHN XXII (1316–34), whose opinions on beatific vision were somewhat unorthodox. JULIUS II nullified the simoniac character of the election by the constitution *Cum tam divino* 14 January 1505, so there was no deposition, but PIUS X revoked it on 25 December 1904 (constitution *Vacante Sede Apostolica*; the methods of the Holy Spirit can be strange!). In view of the proclamation of INFALLIBILITY and considering the ways one can prolong the life of very old men who are no longer in control of their minds or bodies, and without even thinking of these extreme situations, the question of heresy still deserves to be seriously reexamined, even though the Codes of Canon Law of 1917 and 1983 make no allusion to it. Even if contemporary canonists affirm that, theologically speaking, the pope cannot be a heretic (although we know that canonists are poor theologians), certain integral currents made the "HERESY of Paul VI" an argument against his liturgical reform and for the decretals of the Second Vatican Council.

Depositions of Popes (590–1294).

This list, prepared by Olivier Guyotjeannin, does not include the antipopes.

Martin I. After having refused to ask for imperial approval of his consecration and condemning monothelitism, the pope was captured on 17 June 653 by the exarch of Ravenna in the name of Constans II. For the latter, it was not a matter of a deposition, exactly, for the *basileus* believed him a vulgar usurper. Condemned at Byzantium, banished to Chersonesus, he died there on 16 September 655.

Leo V. September or October 903 (died in prison).

John X. May or June 928 (died in prison).

John XII. 4 December 963 (died on 14 May 964).

Leo VIII. 26 February 964.

Benedict V. 23 January 964.

John XIV. April 984.

John XVIII. 1009; a doubtful case.

Silvester III. Deposed by Emperor Henry III on 20 December 1046.

Gregory VI. Deposed by Emperor Henry III on 20 December 1046.

Benedict IX. After having renounced the papacy, but not his ambitions, Benedict IX was, like his rival Silvester III and his successor Gregory VI, deposed by Emperor Henry III: The sentence was pronounced in his absence on 24 December 1046. The death of the pope named by the emperor, Clement II, allowed Benedict IX to briefly return to power. On the emperor's orders, he was deposed on 16 July 1048 in favor of Damasus II.

Gérard Giordanengo

Bibliography

Aimone, P. V. "Prima sedes a nemine judicatur: si papa a fide devius," *Trabajos en homenaje a F. Valls i Taberner*, Barcelona, 14 (1989), 4145–62.

Décret by Gratien, d. 40, c. 6; c. 2, q. 7, c. 12; d. 79, c. 9.

Vacandard, E. "Déposition et dégradation des clercs," *DTC*, 4 (1439), 451–521.

Claeys-Bouaert, F. "Déposition," DDC, 4, 1949, 1153–60.

Zimmerman, H. *Papstabsetzunger des Mittelalters*, Graz-Vienna-Cologne, 1968.

THE DEPUTY. A play by Rolf Hochhuth (originally entitled *Der Stellvertreter*), produced 20 February 1963 at the Free People's Theater of West Berlin by Erwin Piscator. The action, developed in five acts, essentially takes place in October 1943, when Rome is occupied by German troops and the persecution of the Jews is being carried out. The play depicts some historic characters, including PIUS XII, while others are fictitious.

The young Jesuit Riccardo Fontana, overwhelmed by the accounts of extermination of Jews told to him by the S.S. commandant, Karl Gerstein, wants the pope to issue a condemnation of Nazism and break off the concordat signed between the Holy See and the Third Reich in

March 1933. Seeing Pius XII's inflexibility, he considers assassinating him and making the S.S. accountable for his murder. Seized with remorse, he confronts the pope again, but Pius XII confines himself to the possibility of making an appeal in general terms. Father Fontana joins a convoy of Roman Jews who are being deported, and later dies at Auschwitz.

The play created a sensation. Before its staging in 1962, Erwin Piscator had added an accusatory foreword (6 November 1962), backed by a documentary appendix. Following the production and the debates it aroused, the publication of the text, which Hochhuth reworked between November 1962 and January 1963, underwent multiple and successive changes, particularly in the presentation of the foreward and enclosures.

PAUL VI reacted to the controversy by deciding, in 1963, to open the archives of the *Archivio Segreto Vaticano* (the Secret Vatican Archive) covering the period of the Second World War. An international commission of Jesuit historians was established, including Fathers Pierre Blet (France), Angelo Martini (Italy), Burckhart Schneider (Germany) and Robert Graham (United States).

Eleven volumes of documents were published regularly from 1966 to 1981 by the *Libreria editrice Vaticana* (Vatican Publishing House), nine of them during the pontificate of Paul VI (1963–78). The *Acta and documents of the Holy See relating to World War II* opened the way for a great deal of research which has gradually brought about a refashioning of the image of Pius XII who, since *The Deputy*, had become the most criticized pope of the 20th century.

Basing its argument on the 1929 concordat, the Roman Prefecture (in 1965) prohibited an Italian-language production of the play directed by the actor Gian Maria Volonte. The prohibition was the pretext for a bomb explosion near the Vatican (Borgo Pio) and aroused huge protests on the part of the Italian left.

Philippe Levillain

Bibliography

Hochhuth, R. *Der Stellvertreter*, Berlin, 1963; Eng. trans. *The Deputy*, Baltimore, 1997.
Nobécourt, J. "*Le Vicaire et l'Histoire*," Paris, 1964.

DEUSDEDIT. See Adeodatus I.

DEVOTION TO THE POPE. We may be astonished at the use of the word "devotion" regarding the pope. It does not involve worship, though there is a religious movement where a deep Catholic conviction is expressed. This is also an expression of devotedness, a movement toward an important and significant man. In fact, what is called "devotion to the pope" dates from the 19th century, more precisely from the pontificate of PIUS IX. A look back into history can help us better understand the definition.

Medieval Period. Authors talk about the pope and the Church in many places. Saint Anselm (1033–1109), in his letters to URBAN II (1088–99) and to PASCHAL II (1099–1118), constantly gives evidence of respect, humble submission, and a filial and confident affection. Saint Bernard (1091–1153), in the *De consideratione*, addressed to EUGENE III (1134–53), former monk of Clairvaux, reflects on the authority of the pope. However, neither spoke of devotion that must be accorded him. Also, in the Middle Ages the theocratic doctrines were formulated by GREGORY VII (1073–85) or by BONIFACE VIII (1294–1303) affirming, for example, that Christ had to have made St. Peter and his successors participants in his rights over the temporalities of kings and even over the property of private individuals. These theses would be resumed in part by extremists in the 19th century at the time when PIUS IX was losing his States. Saint Thomas Aquinas did not speak of devotion to the pope, but of devotion to the saints, "devotion that does not stop with them but which rises up to God; for it is God we venerate in His servants" (II, IIae, Q. 92, arr. 2 *Ad tertium*). This sentence formed the theological foundation for the contemporary definition of devotion to the pope.

Modern Era. During the modern era, the COUNCIL OF TRENT (1543–63) had the essential problem of defining the power of order in the sacrament of the Eucharist: the place and role of the pope was be evoked, but it is certain that the conduct and good outcome of this council, despite so many obstacles, restored the credibility of the papacy in the eyes of Catholics. The best proof of this evolution of mind-sets is undoubtedly the canonization of PIUS V at the beginning of the 17th century by PAUL V (1605–21). It would still need to be proved that this canonization had, among other goals, that of stimulating devotion to the pope among the faithful.

Contemporary Period. Most theologians are in agreement that the term "devotion to the pope" is an original idea belonging to the 19th century.
Before Pius IX.

In France the first movements of devotion to the pope surfaced regarding PIUS VI (1775–99) and PIUS VII (1800–23). Exiled to France after the proclamation of the Roman Republic, Pius VI died in Valence in 1799. Many rejoiced at what they believed was the end of the papacy: "Pius the Sixth and last." Others compared the pope's calamities to the martyrdom of Louis XVI and the royal family. Engravings from this period associate their destinies to the same sacrifice. When Napoleon had the exiled Pius VII taken from Fontainebleau to Rome in 1814, the new martyr pope was received in triumph.

496

Under Pius IX.

Devotion to the pope took on its modern meaning under Pius IX (1846–78). The devotion shown to Pius IX had, as its major theme, the tribulations of the pope linked to the Roman question. The ultramontanists never stopped publicizing the image of a mistreated pope, betrayed, unhappy, and suffering.

Even if the medieval time period said nothing on this topic, it was still the thought of Saint Thomas Aquinas in the framework of the Thomist renewal that justifies the need for a devotion to the pope. Wishing to devote themselves to God, the faithful should devote themselves to their Church; wishing to devote themselves to the Church, they should devote themselves to the one who governs them for the benefit of God. The faithful cannot devote themselves to Jesus Christ and his Church without devoting themselves to the pope. This devotion must not be for the personal saintliness of the pope, but for that of his mission regarding Jesus Christ; the pope is father, pontiff, and king on both the temporal and spiritual level. The duties that devotion to the pope places on the faithful can be summarized in three principles: to defend (ZOUAVES), to pray, and to pay (St. Peter's Pence). Unfortunately, deviations quickly appeared. At a time when Pope Pius IX's mission was changing, theologians rallied to defend the person of the pope to the point of identifying the pope with the Church.

After Pius IX.

Devotion to the pope was maintained. Manuals of piety reminded the faithful that they owed the sovereign pontiff not only veneration and respect, submission and faith, but also a tender and filial love. The pontificate of PIUS XII (1939–58), especially at its end, was a moment of real renewal of devotion to the pope. The prestige he had acquired certainly contributed to this, though he had little of the personal charm of Pius IX. He contributed, by his authority, a depiction of a pyramidal image of the Church which recentered her in Rome with the pope at its apex. JOHN XXIII (1958–63) quickly announced a council. Voice was going to be given to the Church. His prestige was no less than that of Pius XII, but it was of a different nature. It was not centered on his power, but on an openness to mankind coupled with a disposition to love all. The pope appeared like a possible universal father.

Paul VI (1963–78) and the council insisted on co-responsibility and communication: The pope was not alone, presiding over a passive people from atop a pyramid. The episcopate formed a body over which the bishop of Rome was the head, with the privileges of a leader, but whose members are all totally active.

John Paul II.

We want to see the pope. During his pastoral travels, hundreds of thousands of the faithful sometimes travel great distances to do so. They applaud him without it necessarily being a full spiritual adhesion to his teachings. According to the situation, John Paul II is a vector of hope. He speaks for dignity and human rights, for freedom, for the poor and the dispossessed. Devotion to the pope touches deeply upon the ecclesiastic function of the bishop of Rome. This duty is to be the guardian of Catholic communion in faith, love, mutual exchanges, and relationships. His mission, like any mission, includes a task to perform and the necessary means (charisms, powers). What people come to look for in the pope is a living icon of Catholic unity. He has an unequalled symbolic value. He is the concrete representation of Catholic unity professed through faith. To write to the pope, or better, to see him, expands one's consciousness of faith of universal dimensions. Such is the nature of devotion to the pope.

Bruno Horaist

Bibliography

"Dévotion au pape?" *La Vie spirituelle*, 676, 1987, 390–468.

Dumax, V. A. *Nos devoirs envers le pape dans les circonstances actuelles*, Paris, 1860.

Faber, F. W. *De la dévotion au pape*, Paris, 1860; *Dévotion du pape*, Strasbourg, 1868.

Gaucheron, M. "Dévotions," *Catholicisme*, Paris, 1952, III, 714–15.

LaJeunie, E. "Nos Devoirs envers l'Église et le pape," *La Vie spirituelle*, special issue, April 1928, 85–129.

DIACONIA. The Latin word "diaconia" (pl. *diaconiae*) was only a rewording of the Greek word διακονια, which designates a service, and in Christian terms, especially the assistance of the poor independently of any particular legal or material support. The term is used already with this meaning in Acts 6:1, in 2 Corinthians 9:12, and in Revelation 2:19. But the *diaconia* would also become the Christian institution in charge of this service, with its own rules, legal status, personnel, establishments, resources, and duties. Such a *diaconia* was usually linked to a place of worship, served by monks.

Panvinio in *Le sette chiese Romane* (Rome, 1570) confused the *diaconiae* with the regional diaconates of the seven regions of Rome, which were designated in the third century. Duchesne was the first to dispute this misinterpretation (*LP*, I, 364, 7; II, 253, 7 and *MAH*, VII, 1887 = *Scripta minora*, Rome, 1973, 36–43), and his demonstration has never been contested. Rome was not the first to have a *diaconia*. The *diaconia* began in the mid-4th century, with the Cenobites of Upper Egypt, then in Thebaide around 522, in Alexandria in 527, a little later in Palestine (Gerasa, 565) and in Constantinople (571).

In Italy *diaconiae* are mentioned in the correspondence of GREGORY I the Great, for Pesaro (V, 25; 594–95), Naples (X, 8; April 600), and Ravenna (XI, 17, December 600). Perhaps these were only references to charitable activities run by the local church, thanks to re-sources of public origin (*annonae et consuetudines*, says the pope in X, 8) or private donations. In Naples some "true *diaconiae*," located near a church in the center of town and at crowded crossroads, are mentioned at the end of the 7th or the early 8th century. Thus the *diaconia* that the East had since the 4th century are not found in Italy until after the Justinian reconquest (535–55), which would make them a Byzantine import (H.-I Marrou). In Rome *diaconiae* are not mentioned until later. The *Liber pontificalis* mentions some *monasteria diaconiae* at the end of the 7th and 8th centuries regarding some donations that they received (I, 363, 367, 369, and 410). There were sixteen in 772, in the early days of Pope HADRIAN (LP, I, 504) who raised their number to eighteen by creating the *diaconiae* of Hadrian and Sts. Cosmas and Damian (ibid. 509). These were establishments for public assistance, run by monks. Benefiting from the generosity of individuals, but also from contributions from the public powers, they took care of the distribution of food to the poor, thus filling in the void left by the former distributions made by the Roman administration. The *diaconiae* were sometimes also asylums, hospitals, and hospices that welcomed pilgrims. They included a place of worship, a church or a chapel. Several texts also mention a "lusma." This term has sometimes intrigued historians. It is a Latin transposition of the Greek λουσμα, meaning bath. If the *diaconia* did not have a place to bathe, the guests would go to nearby baths.

Only three of the Roman *diaconiae* were located outside the city, in the Borgo (Santa Maria in Caput Portici; Santa Maria in Adriano, and San Silvestro). Most were in the center of Rome, between the embankments of the Tiber, where wheat arrived, and the zone of the Forums. Others were strung out along the main roads, where they were accessible by most forms of transportation (Santa Maria in via Lata, Santa Maria in Aquiro, Santa Agatha, Santi Silvestro e Martino, etc.). Sixteen of the eighteen *diaconiae* were set up in buildings dating from pagan Rome, half ruins or ancient broken-down temples, sometimes in buildings that had previously belonged to the provisioning services of imperial Rome.

This locating of *diaconiae* in the center of town and on the main routes for traffic, which corresponded to their need for the transport of food and the needs of the parts of town that most required assistance, may be found in other cities with *diaconiae*, especially Naples.

The organization of the Roman *diaconiae*, the generosity of those who provided for them, the motives that guided the donors (*pro remedio omnium peccatorum, pro remedio animae suae, pro sua sempiterna memoria*, etc.), the beneficiaries of this assistance—the poor, the sick, pilgrims, foreigners—are known only by documents written after the time of their existence (in particular the *Liber Diurnus*, 88, 95, 98).

At the time of LEO III (795–816), there were the following *diaconiae* in Rome (LP, II, 18): St. Hadrian, St. Agatha, St. Archangel, St. Boniface, Saints Cosmas and Damian, St. Eustace, St. George of Velabro, Santa Lucia in Orphe, Santa Lucia *in septem vias*, Santa Maria Antiqua, Santa Maria in Ciro (in Aquiro), Santa Maria in Cosmedin, Santa Maria in Dominica, Santa Maria *in via lata*, Sts. Nereus and Achilles, Sts. Sergius and Bacchus, Sts. Silvester and Martin, St. Theodore, St. Vitus; in the Borgo: Santa Maria in caput portici, Santa Maria in Adriano, Saint Silvester (cf. Vhr. Hülsen, *Le chiese di Roma nel medioevo*, Florence, 1927).

Jean Gaudemet

See also DEACONS.

Bibliography

Bertolini, O. "Per la storia delle diaconie romane nell'alto medioevo fino alla fine del secolo VII," *ASR*, 52 (1947), 1–145.
Duchesne, *Notes sur la topographie de Rome au Moyen Âge*, 2, "Les titres presbytéraux et les diaconie," *MAH*, 7 (1887) = *Scripta Minora*, Rome, 36–43.
Frutaz, A. P. "Diaconia," *EC*, 4 (1950), 1521–35.
Kalsbach, A. "Diakonie," *RLAC*, 3 (1957), 9093–917.
Leclercq, H. "Rome, Particularités, 4, Diaconies," *DACL*, (1920), 735–38.
Lestoquoy, I. "Administration de Rome et diaconie du VIIe au IXe siècles," *Riv. A.C.*, VII, 1930, 261–98.
Marrou, H. I. "L'origine orientale des diaconies romaines," *MAH*, 57 (1940), 95–142, reprinted with comments and update in *Patristique et Humanisme*, Paris, 1976, 81–117.
Veillard, R. *Recherches sur les origines de la Rome chrétienne*, Mâcon, 1941, 110–22, with a map showing the locations of the Roman *diaconiae*.

DICASTERY. The generic term "dicastery" (from the Latin *dicasterium*, meaning ministry) designates the organs that make up the Roman CURIA, which are: the SECRETARIAT OF STATE, the CONGREGATIONS, the TRIBUNALS, the pontifical COUNCILS, and the offices. Other institutions included in the Curia (VATICAN SECRET ARCHIVES, Apostolic Library, Pontifical Academy of Sciences, Polyglot Typology, Vatican Bookstore *L'Osservatore Romano*, VATICAN RADIO, VATICAN TELEVISION, St. Peter's Vestry, and the apostolic chaplaincy) are directly attached to the Holy See (prefecture of the Papal RESIDENCE and the office of liturgical celebrations by the holy pontiff, office for the work of the Apostolic See, and autonomous COMMISSIONS and COMMITTEES) are not actually dicasteries.

All the dicasteries are legally equal, although they have different powers. Each has its own internal management, approved by the secretary of state, and its own functional quinquennial organizational structure (*tabella organica*) approved by the pope upon presentation by the secretary of state in consultation with the administration of the Apostolic See's patrimony, which pays all the salaries of the personnel of the Holy See.

Joël-Benoît D'Onorio

Bibliography

D'Onorio, J. B. *Le Pape et le Gouvernement de l'Église*, Paris, 1992.

DICTATUS PAPAE. The *Dictatus papae* are a collection of twenty-seven lapidary propositions, affirming the independence and extent of papal power, transcribed into the REGISTER of GREGORY VII, between two letters from 3 and 4 March 1075, which allows us to date them approximately. The title of *Dictatus papae*, also given to several other pieces of writing in the register, indicates only that these propositions were written personally by the pope (*dictare* means to compose a text by dictating it). Though their date and attribution are obvious, their exact meaning is not as clear and has elicited several hypotheses. On the superiority of the Roman Church (§ 26: "he who is not with the Roman Church must not be considered as Catholic") the text designated only one source: the Church's foundation by Christ (§ 1). From it derives the universal and unique power of the pope, with anti-Byzantine implications (§ 2, 10, 11, 26), his INFALLIBILITY (§ 22), his sanctification (§ 23), and his authority over the episcopate, including deposition, absolution, and transfer of bishops (§ 3, 25, 13), and his authority for the creation and union of dioceses (§ 7). The pope also has the power to change a collegiate church into an abbey (§ 7) and can directly consecrate clerics (§ 14, 15). APPEAL TO THE POPE is suspensive (§ 20); the pope judges all major cases for the Churches (§ 24); he can judge anyone without being judged by anyone (§ 19, 18); he is the foundation of CANON LAW (§ 7, 17). We find in this text the entire panoply of the weapons of the Gregorian REFORM: the meeting of general synods (§ 16) and councils where those absent may be deposed (§ 5), excommunication (§ 6, 26), the possibility of direct accusation before the pope (§ 24), and extraordinary powers of the LEGATES (§ 4). The propositions are no less radical regarding temporal power: the pope can use all the imperial insignia for his own use (§ 8) and the Eastern rite of kissing his feet (§ 9: "the pope is the only man whose feet all princes kiss"); only his name (excluding therefore that of the sovereign) is cited at mass (§ 10); he can depose emperors and release subjects from their oath of fidelity (§ 12, 27).

Many of these ideas are found in Gregory VII's correspondence as well as in the writings of his predecessors, especially GELASIUS I, GREGORY I, and NICHOLAS I, and in CANONICAL sources, particularly in what are called the pseudo-Isidorian DECRETALS. The originality of the text lies mostly in the peremptory affirmation and in the coherent presentation—although still somewhat disordered—of these various propositions, as well as the ability to draw practical consequences from them on the disciplinary and political level. For some, this document is a simple memorandum. For others, it is an outline for a speech made by the pope to the Roman synod in February and March 1075, in the framework of a hardening of papal politics. A more persuasive argument sees the *Dictatus* as a preliminary step in the composition of a canonical collection; the propositions are a sort of table of contents or the titles of chapters, which the citations would then be used to elaborate. We know how much the need for collections of this sort was being felt then in Roman reforming circles. It is true that a parallel text has been preserved, the *Proprie auctoritates apostolice sedis*, transcribed into a manuscript from Avranches (where it gets its name "the *Dictatus* of Avranches"). For a long time it was believed that it was a reworking of the first *Dictatus* by Norman canonists of the 12th century; the discovery of other manuscripts and collected studies has recently allowed us to see the Avranches manuscript as a new text published in Italy at the beginning of the 12th century, perhaps during the time of VICTOR III or CALLISTUS II. These are minor uncertainties. The *Dictatus* are still among the most striking formulations of medieval THEOCRACY and one of the best examples of the roots and structure of the great themes of Gregorian reform.

Olivier Guyotjeannin

Bibliography

Borino, G. B. "Un'ipotesi sul 'Dictatus Papae' di Gregorio VII," *ASR*, 67 (1944), 237–52.

Das Register Gregors VII., II., 55a, ed. E. Caspar, Berlin, 1920 (*MGH, Ep. sel.*, 2), I, 201–08.

Fuhrmann, H. "Randnotizien zum Dictatus Papae," *Festschrift für Helmut Beumann*, Sigmaringen, 1977, 263–87.

Hofmann, K. *Der 'Dictatus Papae' Gregors VII. Eine Rechtsgeschichtliche Erklärung*, Paderborn, 1933.

Woitowytsch, M. "*Proprie auctoritates apostolici Sedis*: Bemerkungen zu einer bisher unbeachteten Überlieferung," *Deutsches Archiv*, 40 (1984), 612–21.

DIOCESE OF ROME. A diocese is an ecclesiastical region placed under the jurisdiction of a bishop or an archbishop. Though this dictionary definition says what a diocese is today, it is obvious that it does not cover all the shades of meaning, both civil and Christian, for this word during ancient times. Diocese is a word in the administrative language of ancient Rome, and Cicero, proconsul in Cilicia, wrote that he was going to hold his court sessions in the three dioceses assigned to him. It was especially under Diocletian that this word took on another meaning, when this emperor reorganized the Empire and regrouped the provinces into dioceses whose number varied according to events. These dioceses were then very vast entities that could include more than ten provinces. It was this meaning of the word diocese that entered the ecclesiastical domain. It also meant either the territory given to a bishop (which is the current meaning), or simply the territory that would today be called a parish. In Rome, we find it with the limited meaning of a parish, seemingly for the first time, in the LIBER PONTIFICALIS, in the biography of Pope MARCELLUS (308–9): *titulos in urbe Roma constituit quasi diocesis propter baptismum et penitentiam*. Although this biography was written after the death of Marcellus, it still shows us that in Rome, during the 6th century, *diocesis* and *parrochia* could be synonymous.

Several years later, Silvester (314–15) seems to use the term diocese with the meaning it has today: *concilium a nobis congregatum in diocesi nostra* (PL, VIII, c. 824), because this council only included several bishops from near Rome. However, if we talk about the diocese of Rome during the 4th and 5th centuries, despite the two examples above, it is with the meaning of the vast territory placed under the immediate jurisdiction of the bishop of Rome. This is confirmed by the many councils or synods where the bishops of the same diocese are invited to participate. What was the territorial extent of the diocese of Rome? It is obvious that it has changed over the course of centuries, but it seems likely that, beginning in the 3rd century, this diocese (in its ecclesiastical aspect) extended over the entire Italian peninsula, as far as the Alps. In 378, Parma was still under the direct authority of the bishop of Rome, because the Roman council of this time alluded to the deposition of Urban of Parma, which Damasus wanted. Around this date (378) a diocese of Milan was created (thanks to the influence of Ambrosius?), which would infringe, in the north, on the diocese of Rome. The latter, from Tuscany to Sicily, included the seven provinces of the mainland and the three large islands, Corsica, Sardinia, and Sicily. This vast territory also included a large number of bishoprics, probably about 200 during the 5th century. As in all the other dioceses of this time, the bishops of the diocese of Rome had practically no autonomy. They depended entirely upon the bishop of the city. If he wasn't the one who chose them, he had to approve and confirm their election, and Pelagius (555–60) would make the candidate proposed by the city of Syracuse wait more than a year. What's more, the newly elected bishop had to come to Rome for his ordination. This explains, if we are to believe the *Liber pontificalis*, the impressive number of episcopal ordinations performed by the bishops of Rome: 62 by DAMASUS (366–84), and 32 by SIRICIUS (384–99). These Roman *Ordines* also show us the rites of these ordinations. They speak extensively on the interrogation that precedes the ordination itself. They

also tell us especially about the fact that the bishop of Rome, when ordaining another bishop, does not need to be assisted, but does this ordination himself, contrary to the general rule that episcopal ordinations must be done by at least three bishops.

Even without taking into consideration the word diocese as a synonym for "parish," it is obvious that between the meaning Silvester gave it and the one we see used in practice, it is difficult to define what the diocese of Rome was in ancient Roman times. Only little by little will we find Rome, as in all other cases, to be a diocese with the restricted meaning of this word as we know it today. Traces of the primitive territory of the diocese of Rome will long be found in the PAPAL STATES.

Patrick Saint-Roch

Bibliography

LP, under the names of the popes cited.
Fourneret, P. "Diocèse," *DTC*, 4 (1920), 1362–3.

DIOCESES "IN PARTIBUS." The first bishops *in partibus* or *in partibus infidelium* were presiding bishops chased from their see as a result of the annexation of their diocese by non-Christians, "infidels," most often Moslems. Welcomed in Christian lands, they became auxiliaries of other bishops.

Upon their deaths, successors were consecrated to replace them. These bishops thus became bishops *in partibus* according to the actual meaning of the expression: keeping a legal tie with the historical diocese, essentially of Asia Minor or North Africa, whose title they bore (from which came the name of titular bishops), and which, in our time, has often disappeared or has not developed, but has remained a village. This practice was confirmed and organized by the COUNCIL of Vienna of 1311 (c. 5 in Clem. I, 3) and by the Council of Trent (sess. XIV, c. 2, *de reformatione*).

We see in this the will of the Church to preserve its jurisdiction over these dioceses, which had belonged to her and over the people for whom she felt spiritually responsible. The Catholics who stayed in any of the *in partibus* dioceses were, in fact, under the care of the bishop of a larger diocese depending on the CONGREGATION for the eastern Churches or the congregation for the evangelization of the people.

The origin of titular bishops goes back to the 4th century. At that time, the bishops who had subscribed to the NOVATIAN heresy and who converted could keep the title and honors of the episcopate, but not the office of bishop (council of Nicaea, canon 8). The oldest mention of bishops *in partibus infidelium* is found in c. 37 of the council *in Trullo* (a. 692). This denomination became traditional from the 7th century. Indeed, the bishops were expelled in great numbers by the Saracens (as much in the East as in Africa and Spain). There were still more expulsions in the 13th century under the pressure of the pagans of Livonia and the Turks, after the definitive fall of Jerusalem in 1244 and of St. John of Acre, the last Christian bastion in the Holy Land, which fell on 18 May 1291.

The name of bishop *in partibus infidelium* was rescinded by the Congregation of Propaganda (decree of 27 February 1882) and by LEO XIII (apostolic letter *In suprema*, 10 June 1882). The reason for this was the expansion of the faith that brought about the return of certain territories to the Catholic Church (for example, Elvas in Portugal, included in the actual archdiocese of Evora), and the protests of countries like Greece, which refused to be assimilated to the infidels of Africa or Asia, strangers to the Catholic faith handed down by the apostles.

The titular bishop has no jurisdiction over the location of his titular Church (GREGORY XV, decree *Inscrutabilis*, 5 February 1622). The CODE OF CANON LAW of 1983 only recognizes the diocesan bishop and the titular bishop (c. 376).

An archaic title is usually given to bishops fulfilling duties concerning the entire Church, with the understanding that it should be someone who has the rank of bishop, and whose duties should not be carried out along with the administration of a diocese. This is the case with papal LEGATES or secretaries of Roman DICASTERIES, brought by their position to deal with governments and episcopates.

Titular bishops may also be bishops emeritus or a diocesan bishop who has retired and been transferred to a new see *in partibus*. These include the bishop in service of a particular Church, whether he is a coadjutor (with the right to succession; c. 403 § 3); an auxiliary, named by reason of pastoral necessities; or by reason of more serious circumstances, with special powers (c. 403 § 1 and 2); the apostolic vicar in charge of one group of God's people not yet organized into a diocese (c. 371 § 1); the apostolic exarch placed at the head of eastern Catholics living in countries following the Latin rite; the apostolic administrator in charge of a group of faithful not established as a diocese "for special and serious reasons" (c. 371 § 2); a personal prelate, if he is raised to the episcopate (c. 295); or a bishop for the military.

Dominique Le Tourneau

Bibliography

Bézac, R. "Évêques coadjuteurs et auxiliaires," *La Charge pastorale des évêques*, Paris, 1969.
Villar, J. R. "La capitalidad de las estructuras jerárquicas en la Iglesia," *Scripta Theologica*, 23 (1991), 961–82.

DIOCESES, SUBURBICARIAN. A little while after Diocletian's administrative reform, the provinces of Italy were regrouped into two dioceses, with one having the city of Rome at its center, sometimes called suburbicarian Italy. This administrative diocese included the provinces from Tuscany to Sicily, plus the large islands of the Mediterranean, and was established along the lines of church administration to form the "DIOCESE OF ROME," but it does not appear that any of the episcopal sees of this huge territory were called suburbicarian dioceses. In fact, this term arose relatively late, going back no farther than STEPHEN III (768–72). It has a much more specific meaning, applying only to a small number of dioceses, those closest to Rome. It is difficult to say with certainty which dioceses these were in the beginning. During the time of Stephen III, there were seven, certainly those of Ostia, Porto, Albano, and Palestrina, to which we would probably add those of Sabina, San Rufino, and Tusculum. By their proximity to the see of Rome, it was obvious that the bishops of these seven dioceses had special ties with the bishop of the City, since they were his "suffragans." The *LIBER PONTIFICALIS* mentions them in the biography of Stephen III, showing that they were in the direct service of the bishop of Rome, who decided (in 769) that each of these seven bishops, in turn, would be responsible for Sunday mass at the Lateran on St. Peter's altar. Closely tied to the bishops of Rome, the titular bishops of these suburbicarian dioceses also had to serve as vicars when necessary. There were also, traditionally, three of this group who ordained the new bishop of Rome, the bishops of Ostia, Porto, and Albano. It was curious that if one of these three needed to be replaced, the bishop of Velletri was called, although Velletri is not on the list of suburbicarian dioceses that we know, at least during the time of Stephen III. The explanation lies perhaps in the fact that we do not know much about these dioceses and that their number had to have varied often. This is why, for example, CALLISTUS II had to get rid of the diocese of San Rufino to combine it with that of Porto in 1119.

Patrick Saint-Roch

Bibliography

Noirot, M. "Diocèses suburbicaires," 3 (1952), 848–51.

DIONYSIUS. *(d. Rome, 26 December 268). Elected on 22 July 259 or 260.*

Dionysius did not succeed SIXTUS II until at least one year had passed, for, as under Decius, persecution raged and kept the Christian community of Rome from leading anything close to a normal life. During this period Christian Rome was led by the council of priests, as is mentioned in the *Liberian Catalogue* (MGH,AA, 9/1, 75), whose text was reconstructed thanks to the *LIBER PONTIFICALIS* ("and the priests took care of leadership since the consulate of Tuscus and Bassus [which means since 258] until the twelfth day before the Calends of August [21 July 259] during the consulate of Aemilianus and Bassus").

The date of his ordination is questioned between 22 July 259 (Duchesne) and 22 July 260 (Turner). The first solution is more in line with other known chronological facts. Therefore, it is not useful to tie the election of Pope Dionysius to the capture of Valerian and the promulgation of tolerance by Gallienus. His episcopate began as the persecution began to lose its intensity. In 260, Valerian was captured on the eastern front by King Sapor. Gallienus, his son, whom he had designated to assume his power from the beginning, immediately suspended the edicts of persecution. Then, by rescripts addressed to bishops, he gave the places of worship back to the Church (Eusebius, *HE*, VII, 13). This began a period of calm that is called the "little peace of the Church," favorable to the development of all the communities.

The episcopate of Dionysius shows, once again, how the Church of Rome was recognized as an authority in matters of faith. The event is even more significant because it concerns the church of ALEXANDRIA, the first community in the Roman east, a great theological center rendered illustrious by Clement and then Origene, and whose see was held by another Dionysius beginning in 247. The latter opposed the development of the Sabellian heresy in the Pentapolis of Libya. By 257, he had shared his misgivings with Sixtus and described the doctrinal deviation he fought in this way: it was "an impious doctrine and greatly blasphemous on the subject of Almighty God, father of Our Lord Jesus Christ, a doctrine incredulous on the subject of his only son, the first born of all creatures, the Word made flesh, a doctrine ignorant of the Holy Spirit" (Eusebius, *HE*, VII, 6). However, in order to defend the distinction of persons within the Trinity, he had, according to some, lost sight of the unity of their substance. His adversaries accused him of separating the Son from the Father, of denying his eternity and his consubstantiality with the Father, and representing him as a creature and not as the true Son of God. Dionysius of Rome, recognized as the supreme doctrinal authority, received their request and met with his council of Italian bishops, which condemned the teaching of the bishop of Alexandria on this point. Then the bishop of Rome, at the same time he was writing to his colleague, addressed a long letter to the Alexandrian Church to establish the doctrine. A long fragment, preserved by Athanasius, is the most important text on the dogma of the Trinity in the pre-Nicaean period.

The inspiration for this document was drawn from Roman doctrinal tradition on divine unity. It also affirmed that the authority of the magisterium of the Church was in Rome, for the letter contained a sovereign and categorical decision on the definition of faith. Recourse to Rome and its consequences are important from the point of view of the history of Roman primacy in doctrinal matters. Dionysius of Alexandria responded to explain, clarify, and defend his thought, not to oppose the judgment from Rome.

Dionysius died on 26 December 268, a little after Emperor Gallienus, during the reign of Claudius the Goth, when the Empire was undergoing the most serious crisis of the third century. His body was placed in the catacomb of Callistus, on the Appian Way (*LP*, 1, 159; *MGH*, *GPR*, 1, 36; *MGH*, AA 9/1, 70 and 75).

Michel Christol

Bibliography

Daniélou, J., and Marrou, H. *Des origines à Grégoire le Grand (Nouvelle Histoire de l'Église)*, I, L. J. Rogier, R. Aubert, M. D. Knowles, Paris, 1963, 238–54.
Duchesne, L. *Étude sur le Liber pontificalis*, Paris, 1877.
Lebreton, J., and Zeiller, J. *De la fin du IIe siècle à la paix constantinienne* (Fliche-Martin, II, 1943, 327–30, 417–18).
Turner, C. H. "The Papal Chronology of the Third Century," *JThS*, 17, 1916, 343–5.

DIOSCORUS. (*d. 14 October 530*). *Elected pope on 22 September 530.*

Dioscorus' short papacy was marked by the SCHISM, with his rival BONIFACE II opposing him. He was a legitimate pope, as the title that was given to him in 553 at the council of Constantinople proves: "*papa Romanae ecclesiae.*"

This DEACON of the Church of Alexandria, driven from the East, took refuge in Rome where he was prominent on two occasions. During the Lawrentian schism he took sides in favor of Pope SYMMACHUS against his rival Lawrence: in 506–7, he took King Theodoric at Ravenna a *PETITIO* from Symmachus and argued the pope's case so well that King Theodoric ordered the patrician Festus to return the churches of Rome to Symmachus and to stop aggressions. Ennodius of Pavia gave him the job of obtaining repayments of money lent to Symmachus by Bishop Lorenzo of Milan. Then, between December 518 and March 519, he was sent, a Roman deacon, as a legate to Constantinople by Pope Hormisdas, with the bishops Germanus of Capua and Johannes, the clerics Blandus and Felix, and the notary Petrus, to put an end to the Acacian schism. He sent a personal report to the pope in April 519 on the success of his mission. He received a *libellus fidei* from the Scythian monk John Maxentius; an unwavering partisan of Chalcedon, he refused the phrase "*Unus de Trinitate crucifixus est.*" Then he played a role at the top level: the pope's letter on 3 December 519, presented Dioscorus to all the Churches of Italy as the main person responsible for reestablishing religious peace. The pope would have liked him to be named to the episcopal see of ALEXANDRIA, while the emperor wanted to place him at Antioch. This plan was not followed through because Dioscorus returned to Rome, no later than 17 September 520, where he appeared as "the emperor's man," and where he had many supporters. He canvassed for the episcopal see beginning perhaps in 526, if he can be identified as the *summota persona* who had to be put away when Felix IV was elected. In any case, this time with the support of 60 priests and many senators, he was elected and consecrated on 22 September 530 in the Constantinian basilica (a choice that could only displease the court at Ravenna), whereas his rival the archdeacon Boniface was elected in the *basilica Julii*. Dioscorus' death on 14 October 530 put an end to the schism. Peace was obtained at the expense of the memory of Dioscorus, who was anathematized. He was rehabilitated under Pope AGAPITUS in 535, who had the *libellus* of anathema burned.

Janine Desmulliez

Bibliography

LP, I, 4, 100–103, 281–7.
LTK, 3, 410.
Cassiodorous, *Variae*, 8, 15, *CC*, 96, 319.
Coll. Avellana. CSEL, 35, 2, 589–694.
Ennodius, *Ep.* 6, 33; 7, 28; 9, 16; *MGHAA*, 12, 229, 259, 304.
Justinian, *Confessio rectae fidei*, *PL*, 69, 226; *Ep. adu. Theodorum Mopsuet. PG*, 86, 1094.
Marot, M. "Dioscore," *DHGE*, 14 (1960), 507–8.
Schwartz, E. *ACO*, IV, 1, 104; *ACO*, IV, 2, 47, 51–4, 97, 98.

DIPLOMATIC CORPS ACCREDITED TO THE HOLY SEE. With the LATERAN PACTS, Italy recognized the right of the Holy See to passive and active legation (art. XII). It confirmed that envoys of foreign governments to the Holy See should enjoy the prerogatives and immunities granted to diplomats under international law. This recognition was general; in other words, the States did not necessarily have to have diplomatic relations with Italy for them, or their residences, to benefit from this immunity. In reality, this article simply codified a de facto situation and removed any problem or embarrassment that Italy could have caused the papacy since the annexation of Rome. Indeed, such problems had been scrupulously avoided. It might be said that up until WORLD WAR I, Italy showed greater consideration to than it received from the Holy See. The conclave of 1903, at which PIUS X (1903–14) was chosen, was held without any difficulty, as was that of August 1914. The AD LIMINA visits by the bishops took place regularly. Communication between the Holy See and the rest of the world, as well as the regular supply of goods to the Vatican, were always guaranteed. The Holy See, however, did not tolerate a head of state visiting the King of Italy before or after being received by the pope. Like many other countries, France kept its ambassador to the Holy See after Rome had been annexed, but also set up an embassy to the government of Italy after 1870. From 1874, the embassy was housed in the Farnese Palace. In the crisis of 1904, which led to the separation of the Church and the State a year later, France broke off diplomatic relations with the Holy See. They were reestablished in 1921, but France did not go back on its stance with respect to the separation of Church and State. This is a fairly good example of the nature of diplomatic relations that many States have with the Holy See. They are relations with a sovereign entity—the Holy See—which is a moral entity and a subject of international law. Its representative is the sovereign pontiff. The loss of Rome and the Papal States, that is, the loss of temporal power, did not justify an absence of diplomatic relations. The State of Vatican City merely simplified them. Diplomats are, therefore, accredited to the Holy See and not to the State of Vatican City. During the 20th century, the number of diplomatic representatives has continued to increase and now there are more than 120. In fact, the settlement of the Roman question has not affected the rule in place since 1870 by which no country can have the same common diplomatic representation to the State of Italy and the Holy See.

The People's Republic of China does not have diplomatic relations with the Holy See, as was the case with the Soviet Union from its creation until 1990. Prior to the fall of the Berlin Wall, no diplomatic relations existed with the communist bloc in general. The *ANNUARIO PONTIFICIO* lists, with a line followed by three dots, all the Central European or Balkan States with which the Holy See had diplomatic relations until just after WORLD WAR II. Yugoslavia, however, sent an ambassador, and Poland had a permanent head of delegation. One of the acts of resistance that the Holy See could show against the violent geopolitical realities of the time was the maintenance of diplomatic representation with Lithuania through a first secretary. The fact that the Cuban ambassador was, for a long time, dean of the diplomatic corps was a source of Roman humor. With respect to Israel, up until December 1993, the idea of a de facto recognition of Tel Aviv was circulated in the Vatican. Great Britain did not send an officially accredited ambassador until 1982, and the United States followed suit in 1984. After 1989 there was a definite change in diplomatic relations. The Holy See officially renewed diplomatic ties with Poland (17 July 1989), Hungary, Czechoslovakia, and Rumania (1990), Albania (7 September 1991), then Mongolia, Armenia, Azerbaijan, Georgia, Moldova, Bosnia-Herzegovina, Kyrgyzstan, Kazakhstan, Uzbekistan, and Mexico in 1992.

It sometimes happens that a country has no diplomatic representative to the Holy See, in which case a diplomat from the embassy to the Quirinal may be asked to deal officially with those questions relating to the Holy See and to establish useful unofficial contacts. Such was the case with the United States until 1984, when President Reagan appointed a personal representative; such is still the case with Israel. Some embassies manifest a magnificence in the tradition of a history linked to that of the Church despite their many vicissitudes: Austria, Spain, France, and Italy. Other embassies have rather more modest facades. At any rate, the post of ambassador to the Holy See is considered an important one, and in Europe it is thought to be a prestigious post, one which, in some countries, is usually reserved for an ambassador at the end of his career.

An embassy to the Holy See has fewer staff members than others; there are no trade officers, military attaches, or cultural services. In the latter case, France has been an exception. However, the embassy to the Holy See often includes a member of the clergy on its staff.

There is no mystery surrounding the work of an ambassador to the Holy See. His job focuses on the relations between the Church and the State in a given country, and in Rome on the activities of the Holy See, the center of the Catholic Church. When Rome was the capital of the States of Europe, the mission of the ambassador to the pope was twofold. He represented his country's government and authority to the point of inspiring fear, and tried to obtain assurances from the pope, in ecclesiastical matters, that his country's sovereign would be treated with the utmost deference. The ambassador dealt directly with the pope and established contacts within the Curia, which could help further his influence. He had a lifestyle reserved for members of the nobility, a lifestyle further enhanced by the dignity of his office and thus participated in the extraordinary splendor of Roman life. Nowadays, an ambassador is granted a private audience with the pope only on exceptional occasions, to discuss matters of political and religious importance. The large number of ambassadors to the Holy See is the obvious explanation for this. Today, an ambassador's privileged interlocutor is the SUBSTITUTE, formerly the secretary of the council for the public affairs of the Church. That office has now become the second section of the SECRETARIAT OF STATE. The substitute receives visitors on a fixed day, usually Thursday. The diplomats meet in the antechamber and talk as "in a hairdressing salon," (an expression often used to describe such meetings). Meetings with individual diplomats are more rare and are requested for specific reasons.

The Holy See must make the distinction between indispensable meetings with the pontiff and others, which could result in an overwhelming routine of visits for the pope. Representatives of powerful and influential nations may have direct and renewed access to the pope, while others may be received only when they present credentials and take their leave. Access may also be determined by circumstances.

The duties of the diplomatic representation and the social obligations of an embassy, on the other hand, are unchanged from the days when there were no telephones or mass media. Information is spread through personal contact and the ease of relations that only an experienced ambassador can achieve. It is for this reason that, while some States may be tempted to send to the Holy See representatives without diplomatic experience but well known in the Church, it is more appropriate to send seasoned diplomats or eminent experts on the Roman Catholic Church.

Philippe Levillain

Bibliography

The *Annuario Pontificio* provides a list of the representatives accredited to the Holy See.

Cardinale, I. *Le Saint Siège et la Diplomatie*, Paris, 1962.

Jemolo, A. C. *Premesse ai rapporti tra Chiesa a stato*, Milan, 1965.

DISPENSATION.

Until the 15th Century. Suspension of the application of law in a special case, dispensation accompanied a slow evolution of the papal powers over the Church. Even its definition was not set down by canonists until the 12th century, which went from Yves of Chartres (*mitigatio ad tempus rigoris juris ob necessitatem temporum vel utilitatem Ecclesiae*, which tells a lot about its timely and, it may be said, opportunistic character), to Rufinus (*canonici rigoris casualis facta derogatio*). For a long time, in effect, papal dispensations suffered a double limitation: their province was limited, and the pope did not intervene except with the agreement of the bishops or particular COUNCILS. During the 12th century, when the Gregorian REFORM and the *DICTATUS PAPAE* were launched, Gratian linked the dispensation and papal *plenitudo potestatis* over the universal Church (his commentators will sometimes argue by presenting the pope as the successor of the emperor of Rome, supreme legislator); bishops were able only to dispense laws enacted at the diocesan level.

With the pope equated to a monarch, the dispensation from ecclesiastical legislation, as produced by human law, was fully justified. Then the problem arose of the limits of papal dispensation regarding natural or divine law, for example, whether the pope was able to dispense impediments to marriage like those stated in the Scriptures (as in Lev. 18). A fundamental question arose, in juridical doctrine, about contemporary marriage. The answers were particularly varied, but a progressive evolution emerged, which mirrored that of the pontifical appointment and glosses on the power of the pope as vicar of Christ. ALEXANDER III was the first pope to dispense a vow (for a vow of chastity and then a vow of PIL-GRIMAGE), although from St. Augustine to Gratian this dispensation had been considered impossible. INNOCENT III, who strongly declared he was not able to dispense cases of close blood relationships forbidden by divine law, still gave such dispensations in a DECRETAL at the same time that he was insisting on the exclusive ability of the Holy See to dispense vows of pilgrimage to the Holy Land. INNOCENT IV extended the pope's capability to dispense matters of vows of chastity and religion. The pope also intervened for dispensations for marriage, when the marriage, though valid, was not consummated; the procedure was codified by BENEDICT XIV (constitution *Dei miseratione* of 1741). Exceptionally, the dispensation was still presented as a judicial measure, taking certain matters into consideration, detailed in the papal document: public utility, the merits of the plaintiff, etc. (just as, in the area of finances, the popes of the 13th and 14th centuries never systematically claimed the SPOILS of prelates but seized them still). The enlargement of the domain of dispensations accompanied their quantitative growth. Of the 1,904 common letters registered by the apostolic chancellery from August 1311 to April 1314, 700 are dispensations; 89 were for laymen, including 65 for consanguinity; 611 were for clerics, with the majority concerning the detention of benefices: dispensations of canonical impediments due to lack of sufficient age, legitimate birth, or the conferring of orders (there is even one for poor eyesight), dispensations for residence, visits, etc. The canonical legitimatization followed. In the 14th century, Baldo degli Ubaldi wrote that in certain dispensations, the pope did not act as a man but as God (*non facit papa tanquam homo sed tanquam Deus*), and since Thomas Aquinas, from the 13th through the 16th centuries, theologians put into place a coherent doctrine of infallibility of papal dispensation. In the 16th century, Sanchez also showed that the pope could directly dispense a vow. Criticized by the CONCILIAR MOVEMENT as well as by GALLICANISM, the theory was nevertheless firmly set in canon law, by which the pope could grant dispensations not only from any ecclesiastical laws or local ones owed to himself or his inferiors but also from those that his predecessors or the apostles had handed down.

Olivier Guyotjeannin

Bibliography

Coache, L. "Vicaire (pouvoir)," *DDC*, 7 (1958), 1434–78.
Gaignard, R. "Le gouvernment pontifical au travail [1311–1314]," *Annales du Midi*, 1960, 169–214.
Gilles, H. "Mariages de princes et dispense pontificale," *Mélanges Louis Falletti* (= *Annales de la faculté de droit et des sciences économiques de Lyon 1971-II*), 295–308.
Naz, R. "Dispense," *DDC*, 4 (1949), 1284–96.

Since the 16th Century. The traditional definition of canonical dispensation, established since the 12th century in Gratian's *DECRETUM* (especially *Dict. post.* c.16, C. XXV) and then commented by the decretalists, like Rufinus, imposed the legislative use of the term of *dispensator* as the person or the entity having the authority to assess obligations and duties within a given group. From there, and following a technique of classical juridical analysis, it was supposed *a contrario* that in case of an impossibility or an impediment, progressively defined, exceptions would be made for the application of this or that law; the decision to exempt was based in principle on this same authority, with exceptions made for possible delegations of power. The capability to dispense and its theory, linked to a very strict hierarchy of norms—from divine laws to diocesan legislative measures—were naturally strongly influenced by the various conceptions of ecclesiastical power in general, and of papal power in particular. Among the decretalists of the modern time, especially Sanchez and de Soto, the idea prevailed that bishops, by virtue of their appointment, were intrinsically imbued with the power of dispensation, even in penal matters, except when they were expressly prohibited from exercising authority. The episcopal authority, by analogy, would therefore have the same powers within the limits of the diocese as those of the pope over the entire Church, unless the sovereign pontiff decided to reserve it exclusively for himself. The great canonist Barbosa thus recognized that "the customary law can make it so that a dispensation was valid, which otherwise would be seen as invalid" (*De officio et potestate episcopi, Compendium*, 1724). Against a pure and simple centralization, the Gallicans took hold of this doctrine to assure that of the superiority of the council, declaring that the pope was incompetent to dispense conciliar legislative decisions, as well as privileges and customs of the Gallican Church. In the 18th century, Febronius and, after him, the Febronianists used the theoretical mechanism of dispensation to assert the rights of bishops against what they called "the abuses of secular power of Rome" and affirm them by referring to the command of Christ that "*posuit episcopos regere Ecclesiam.*" Professed with vigor—and probably with some excess—at the council of Pistoia in 1786, this interpretation was condemned without equivocation by PIUS VI on 28 August 1794.

By a broad movement rearranging the relationships of powers within the Church, BENEDICT XV in canon 80 of the revised CODE OF CANON LAW (1917) returned to the general principle according to which dispensations could be given only by the legislator himself or his successor, or by the supreme authority. In strict logic, since all Church laws were promulgated by the pope in his position as legislator, the ordinaries subordinate to the pope had no power to dispense any general rules of the Church on the spot unless that power was specifically accorded to them: the juridical geometry of the dispensation therefore was exactly inverse to that pronounced by the decretalists. There still remained cases in which recourse to the Holy See would have been difficult, or when serious damage was feared, or finally when it was a dispensation that was customary for the Holy See to grant (canon 81, § 2), which left a margin of interpretation open that canonical practice and jurisprudence hurried to limit. Nevertheless, the case of exceptional circumstances, seen during the years of war, had determined that in urgent cases the bishops could give dispensations to deacons and subdeacons by authorizing them according to this canon. A note from the pontifical COMMISSION for authentic interpretation of CANON LAW, dated 26 June 1947, definitively imposed this narrow interpretation, forbidding the qualification of "difficult situations" since the local ecclesiastical authority could speak to the papal NUNCIO.

The VATICAN II Council basically renewed the basis for canonical dispensation: except for a special reservation on the part of the reigning pontiff, bishops could dispense general ecclesiastical laws "each time that in his judgment the dispensation would benefit the spiritual welfare of the faithful" (decretal on the pastoral duty of bishops in the Church *Christus Dominus* on 28 October 1965, § 8b). The *motu proprio De Episcoporum Muneribus* (15 June 1966) put into effect the conciliar decree that specified that this rule "departed from canon 81," before setting up the list of cases reserved for the Holy See, among which were the obligation of celibacy required of deacons and priests. The Code of Canon Law of 1983 (Book I, title IV, c. V, canons 85 to 93) made important innovations in the matter of dispensations, forming the positive law of the Latin Catholic Church.

François Jankowiak

Bibliography

Couly, A. "Les dispenses en droit canonique," *Revue catholique des institutions et du droit*, LXXI (1932), 174–84.

Naz, R. "Dispense," *DDC*, IV (1949), col. 1284–96.

Rietmeijer, J. "Essai de réflexion théologique et canonique sur le pouvoir de dispense de l'évêque," *Concilium* 48 (1969), 91–102.

Stiegler, M. A. *Dispensation, Dispensationswesen und Dispensationsrecht im Kirchenrecht geschichtlich dargestellt*, Mainz, 1907.

Van Hove, A. *De privilegiis. De dispensationibus*, Malines, 1939.

DOMINICANS.

13th Century. The close relationship of the Dominicans with the pope began with St. Dominic. His chapter of the diocese of Osma belonged to the restored province of Toledo, where the popes intended to establish model dioceses, headed by clerics of the common life. In 1199 the bishop, the primate of Toledo, and INNOCENT III established a status under rule for the chapter. Dominic, a subprior, collaborated with Diego, the prior, and then the bishop (1201). In 1205 Diego and Dominic, who aspired to convert the heathens, were unable to persuade Innocent to relieve them of their appointments to Osma; but, soon after, they were officially involved in the Cistercian mission of Narbonensis directed by the pope for the spreading of the faith. Diego led the preachers to adopt evangelical poverty, which Innocent approved. Diego had planned to firmly establish this "holy preaching" with the pope's aid. After his death, Dominic took it to Lauraguais, and then to Toulouse, as the leading example of the diocesan preacher that the council of Avignon, on the pope's orders, had instituted in 1209 and that the Lateran council wanted to generalize. In January 1215, when the council of Montpellier, presided over by Innocent's LEGATE (*a latere*) decided to renew this "holy preaching" at Toulouse, he confided it to Dominic and wanted to make it permanent. Assuming this ministry in the spring of 1215, Dominic established it immediately in a community he was setting up in Toulouse. He asked the pope for "confirmation of an order that would be established and would be called an order of preachers," to "go out in evangelic poverty, on foot, religiously, to preach the word of evangelical truth." The pope promised confirmation as long as the order would adhere to regular tradition. The position of the preachers regarding the papacy was defined by the actions of its founder: the order was in strict contact with the pope, who confirmed its goal, its institutions, and its essential missions; but it reserved for the community alone the choice of its leaders, its laws, and the management of its friars.

From the beginning, the action of the pope was expressed through numerous BULLS. Three of them (1216, 1217, 1219) confirmed Dominic's requests of 1215. In 1217, when Dominic decided to expand the preaching in Toulouse to a worldwide order, he obtained a bull of approval from HONORIUS III accrediting the order everywhere. Others ensured the diffusion of the order, the collaboration of prelates, and the unity and authority of the order over its members. They also conferred several privileges for their ministry, such as the missions, beginning in 1225. The bull *Nimis iniqua* was issued in 1254 to protect the Dominicans from their adversaries. Beginning in 1261, the bull *Virtute conspicuos*, called *Mare magnum*, periodically published the list of their privileges. Apart from a problem before the death of Innocent IV, their growth was not limited until 1296 when BONIFACE VIII made it necessary to obtain the pope's authorization for the establishment of any new foundation. In 1300, his bull *Super Cathedram* increased the control of bishops over the preaching of the friars, whom it forced to share bequests and burial fees ("Bonifacian fourth") with the parish priests. These decisions only stopped the forward motion of the order for a short time.

Beginning in 1207, at Prouille, Dominic had founded a group of cloistered nuns whose support he found indispensable to his preaching. At St. Sixtus' in Rome in 1221, at Honorius' request, he completed the plan of INNOCENT III to join together all the nuns of the city in a model convent. The rule that he wrote would from then on be used by the Holy See with respect to the nuns. The general chapters of the friars feared the responsibility of caring for a growing number of nuns, and in 1252, decided to reject them. The inclusion of the sisters and of most of the masters general, supported by the actions of the popes, restored the previous situation in 1259, when the order issued its rule for nuns, based upon that of St. Sixtus. In 1267, all the monasteries founded by the order were incorporated into it. There were 56 in 1277, and 154 in 1303.

Preaching in all its forms, popular, learned, or missionary, and study and sacred teaching are the main objects of the attention and privileges of the popes. Numerous acts concern the Dominicans in the universities, especially in Paris. There, in 1229 and 1231, GREGORY IX obtained two chairs on the faculty of Theology for the order, which alone confers the precious *jus ubique docendi*, the keystone of the educational system of the order. This collaboration of the Dominicans with the universal pastorate of the popes was accomplished on three levels; action; institutions through the spreading of the educational system of the Dominican preachers; and instruments—the considerable activity of theological and pastoral publishing by the order. For Church law, the composition by St. Raymond of Penyafort of the five books of the DECRETALS (1230–4) at the request of Gregory IX, became the foremost official collection of CANON LAW for the next seven centuries.

The collaboration between the popes and the Dominicans created a series of new offices. Beginning in 1257 the order had a permanent procurator on the CURIA, however, it was not until 1376 that a CARDINAL PROTECTOR appeared. The job of master of the Sacred Palace, begun in 1244 for the *studium* of the Curia, was soon reserved for the Dominicans, but the papacy drew so many penitentiaries, CHAPLAINS, commissioners, and legates from the order that INNOCENT IV compared it, in 1254, to the "public workhorse" of Christianity. The church took a number of bishops from it as well. Dominic was totally opposed to this, believing that the order's preaching should only rely on its evangelic practice and not on a Church position. The papacy ignored his feelings beginning in 1230: until the 15th century, the Church took 450 bishops from the order; between 1244 and 1327, 14 cardinals, and finally two popes, INNOCENT V (1276) and BENEDICT XI (1303–4). On the other hand, when GREGORY IX instituted the Office of the INQUISITION (1231), he gave it to the Dominicans in France and in the Languedoc (1233) before assigning it to the Friars Minor.

In 1252–6 and again in 1265, 1274, and 1281–4, the popes protected the Dominicans during dangerous conflicts with urban priests, secular teachers, and several bishops and prelates who attacked their ministry and even their existence. The crisis, which arose from the founding of the order in the cities where it conflicted with established rights, was aggravated by a disagreement over the jurisdiction given to the preachers by a general delegation from the pope, that seemed to deviate from the monopoly of the bishops and priests recognized by the canons of the Lateran on penitence and preaching. It was temporarily solved in *Super Cathedram* by BONIFACE VIII, but we see from the beginning a strong divergence from the idea of the Church that, for many priests, teachers, and prelates, was similar to that of the future Gallicans, whereas the order defended the complete and immediate jurisdiction of the pope. This was, in the 13th century, the ultimate reason for the tight collaboration between the Dominicans and the pope.

Marie-Humbert Vicaire

Bibliography

Bullarium ordinis Fr. Praedicatorum, ed. A. Bremond, 1–2, Rome, 1729.

Congar, Y. "Aspects ecclésiologiques de la querelle entre mendiants et séculiers dans la second moitié du XIIIe siècle et le début du XIVe," *AHDLMA*, 28, 1961, 35–161.

Duval, A. "Les soeurs dominicaines," Ibid., 1410–15.

Koudelka, V. J. "Notes sur le cartulaire de saint Dominique; 3: Bulles de recommandation," *AFP*, 34 (1964), 5–44.

Mandonnet, P. *St. Dominic and His Works*, St. Louis, 1944.

Mirus, J. A. "On the Deposition of the Pope for Heresy," *Archivum Historiae Pontificiae*, 13 (1975), 231–48.

Monumenta diplomatica S. Dominici, ed. V. J. Koudelka, Rome, 1966 (*MOPH* 25).

"Saint Dominique chanoine d'Osma," *AFP*, 63 (1993).

Vicaire, M. H. "Frères prêcheurs [ordre des]," *DHGE*, 18 (1979), 1372–88 and 1391–4.

Vicaire, M. H. *Saint Dominic and His Friars*, New York, 1964.

14th and 15th Centuries. The day after his coronation, celebrated in the Dominican convent church at AVIGNON on 19 May 1342, CLEMENT VI declared that he no longer wanted to have any relationship whatsoever with the Dominicans, guilty, according to him, of having shortened the lives of his two predecessors by their doctrinal disputes and their institutional quarrels. It is true that the confrontation was fierce between JOHN XXII and a raft of Dominican theologians over some hazardous theses of the old pontiff in the 1330s, and between BENEDICT XII and the entire order, arrayed behind its master, Hugues of Vaucemain, when it stood up to the interventionist attacks of the Cistercian, who had become pope, between 1338 and 1342. Regardless, after his coronation in the Dominican church in Avignon (8 January 1335) Benedict praised the sons of St. Dominic as models for all Christianity because of their theological knowledge and their apostolic zeal.

The role played by the Dominicans in the Roman CURIA in residence in Avignon was significant. CLEMENT V, in the first days, chose their convent as his residence. It was in their church that Benedict XII and Clement VI were crowned. This is more than symbolic. Nicolas Alberti of Prato took the initiative, right after the installation at the papal service in Avignon, to create, within the Curia itself, a school of theology whose master of theology came from the Dominican order. The job of master of the Sacred Palace has, since then, traditionally been held by a member of the order.

The Avignon popes showed their confidence in the Dominicans by promoting several cardinals: eight in all. In the uproar of speculative polemics born of the Nominalist upsurge, the doctrines of Thomas Aquinas served as ammunition for the defenders of the rights of the papacy, and JOHN XXII hastened to canonize him in a particularly solemn manner on 18 July 1323. Such a favor did not, however, stop the conflicts. It was during the reign of John XXII that two famous trials were held before the tribunals of the Curia, bringing Dominican brothers up on charges for their opinions, specifically the German Master Eckhardt, in 1327 and Thomas Walleys (the Welsh), in 1333. Under Benedict XII it was the Italian preacher Venturin of Bergamo's turn to feel the papal thunder in 1335. In each of these three cases, the Dominican convent of Avignon intervened to provide the accused friars with protection. The first three popes at Avignon were at the origin of an extremely active missionary movement. Especially important was the Society of Roving Friars for Christ, created in 1305, which received its definitive statute in 1312. In 1318 the vicar general of the society, Franco of Perugia, was named archbishop of Sulthanyeh in Persia by John XXII, with six suffragan bishops, who settled in Turkey. In 1375 GREGORY XI further endorsed the group by establishing the Latin hierarchy in Armenia, and sending in a team of Dominican missionaries, who spoke the language. The trials of the Black Plague, in 1348, were borne in a catastrophic fashion by all the orders, whose ranks were literally decimated. The long and pathetic letter from Clement VI to the whole order dated 1 June 1348, during the worst of the pestilence, represents a moving and solemn homage to the services it rendered to Christian Europe. The consequence was to elicit a reform move-

ment. Simon of Langres, the superior of the order and crafter of this renewal, had unwavering support during the 1360s from INNOCENT VI and URBAN V, pontiffs with whom he collaborated, especially in the conflict between France and England. Gregory XI wanted to intervene, in a rather disputable way, by keeping the order from holding its traditional annual meeting of the general chapters, which, from 1372, only met every two years, and by granting it a cardinal protector in 1376.

Thirty years after the plague, Latin Europe found itself confronting another scourge—no less fearsome—that of the schism or quarrel of obediences between Avignon and Rome, unleashed after the conclave of 1378. The Dominicans chose sides according to their geographic or ideological situations, and found themselves on one side or the other. Supporting BENEDICT XIII, we find, in the front ranks of his advisors, a Spanish Dominican, Saint Vincent Ferrer, dead at Vannes at age 69 on 5 April 1419. On the opposite side, under the Urbanist banner (Roman side), we see CATHERINE OF SIENA, dead in Rome at age 33 on 9 April 1380.

On the eve of the famous conclave of 1378, responsible for the schism, the Dominican order had just placed at its head Elie Raimon of Toulouse, the 22nd superior of the order. He would remain in this position until his death at Avignon on 31 December 1389. From URBAN V, Raimon obtained permission to transfer the relics of Thomas Aquinas, then at the abbey of Fossanova, to the Jacobins of Toulouse on 28 June 1369.

At the turning point between the 14th and 15th centuries, it was, in Church history, time for the conciliar period. The Dominicans were very much present during this time, with John Dominici at their head, the author of the *Lucula noctis*. Created a cardinal in 1408 by Gregory XII, whose advisor he was, it was with this title in 1415 that he was received at the Council of Constance, where he became plenipotentiary. Later, with unity once more achieved, Martin V sent him as a legate to Bohemia-Hungary, where he died on 10 June 1419. By his side, it must be pointed out, was the determining presence of Andrew, a Greek and a Dominican who had become archbishop of Rhodes in 1413, a specialist on questions of the union with the Greeks. Leonardo Dati, the ambassador for the city of Florence and master of the order, was also a council father and a remarkably active one.

The successor to Leonardo Dati at the head of the order was a Provençal born at Draguignan, Barthelemy Texier, who would reign from 1426 to 1449. He was among the main contributors to the council of union opened at Florence by Pope EUGENE IV on 26 February 1439. Among the auditors was an attentive Dominican, Antonino Pierozzi, originally from Florence, a direct disciple of John Dominici, who, within his native city, had just opened a new convent, San Marco. Eugene IV would remember him and give him the responsibility for the diocese of Florence on 9 January 1449, at the head of which he would remain until his death (10 May 1459). He was the spiritual father of Marsilio Ficino and a friend of Fra Angelico (d. 1455), to whom Eugene IV, as well as his successor NICHOLAS V, appealed to decorate the walls of the apostolic palace at the Vatican.

In the Quattrocento, the city of Florence took its place as a central city with which the bishops of Rome, from EUGENE IV to ALEXANDER VI, had to contend. The existence of the convent of Santa Maria Novella, together with that of San Marco, as well as the presence of Saint Antonino at the head of the diocese, assured the Dominicans of a privileged place within the City of the Lily. In July 1491, a prior of particular notoriety was elected to head the convent of San Marco, Savonarola. Between Alexander VI, crowned pope on 11 August 1492, and the fiery Dominican, who had become the political leader of Florence, things quickly heated up. It ended with a trial, accompanied by torture, held before a Florentine tribunal at the request of the pope, which decided that the three friars of the San Marco community were guilty. Girolamo Savonarola, Domenico of Pescia, and Silvestro Maruffi were hanged, and their bodies burned on Wednesday, 23 May 1498.

Paul Amargier

Bibliography

Amargier, P. *Études sur l'Ordre dominicain*, Marseille, 1986.

Hinnebusch, W. A. *Brève histoire de l'Ordre dominicain*, adapted by G. Bedouelle, Paris, 1990.

Vicaire, M. H. "Frères prêcheurs [ordre des]," *DHGE*, 18 (1979), 1369–1426.

16th Through 18th Centuries. To confront the vicissitudes that shook it during the first half of the 16th century, the papacy found a rather faithful, if not always effective, support from the Dominicans. The Dominican reform that took place beginning at the end of the 14th century had not spread throughout the entire order, but was already producing solid results in the provinces where the congregations were Observant: Lombardy, Tuscany, Spain, and Holland. The latter was neutralized by the Protestant Reformation, but the three others furnished the Apostolic See with precious human, spiritual, and doctrinal assistance.

Defeated by Louis XII and threatened in his power at the council of Pisa (1511), JULIUS II found the superior of the order, Cajetan, to be a very staunch defender of the primacy of the pope over the COUNCIL. In his *De auctori-*

tate papae et concilii utraque invicem comparata, he reaffirmed the traditional doctrine of the Dominicans defended by J. de Torquemada at Basel and Florence. Against the Sorbonne, which was trying to have his theses condemned, he clarified the definitive foundations of modern papal primacy. The following year, his theological influence succeeded in having this doctrine recognized officially by the Fifth Lateran Council (1512). In exchange for this support, LEO X defended the mendicant orders against the charges of numerous bishops and dissuaded the council from revoking their privileges.

Leo X was looking for money to build ST. PETER'S BASILICA. The Saxon Dominican Tetzel took charge of preaching INDULGENCES across Germany (1516–17). His clumsy enthusiasm and his oratorical exaggeration furnished a pretext for Luther to post his 95 theses at Wittenberg.

Unaware of the looming danger, Leo X sent Cajetan to Germany to collect the funds destined for the CRUSADES. The cardinal immediately had to face Luther, whom he met at the diet of Augsburg. He had no influence over him. Back in Rome, he presided over the commission in charge of trying his case. Very conscious of the new challenges advanced against Catholic faith and theology, he started to compose Biblical commentaries as well as several treatises against the Lutheran positions.

CLEMENT VII planned to use the Dominicans in the front line of the apostolic and doctrinal battle. At the first elective general chapter held in Rome in 1525, he addressed an exceptional letter to the members, outlining the portrait and program of the future superior of the order. His candidate was elected: Sylvester of Ferrara, eminent theologian and commentator on Saint Thomas. Under his leadership and that of his successors, among them Ghislieri (future PIUS V), inquisitor at Côme and Bergamo, and Catharinas and Radini, authors of anti-Lutheran treatises, the Dominicans were able through verbal and written commentary, to contain the protestant tide in northern Italy. Badia, head of the Sacred Palace from 1523 to 1542, participated in the first commission charged with reforming the Church in 1536; in 1541 PAUL III sent him to Germany as cardinal LEGATE to have discussions with the Lutheran doctors. The creation of the HOLY OFFICE by Paul III in 1542 removed the INQUISITION from the direct jurisdiction of the superior of the order, but not from under Dominican influence, for many occupied the highest positions in it, in particular that of commissioner general, first assigned to Tropea and then to Ghislieri.

Incapable of containing the loss for the Roman Church of entire regions of Europe, the Dominicans played a considerable role in the evangelization of the Americas. Their presence there with the Indians (Las Casas and Minaya) and the reflection of the Spanish doctors on the conditions of conquest (Vitoria) prepared the condemnation of slavery by Paul III and that of the excesses of colonization (the bull *Sublimis Deus* of 1537).

The pontificate of Pius V (1566–72), the third Dominican pope, demonstrated the highest Dominican influence in Catholic reform. Very attached to his order, the pope proclaimed Thomas Aquinas a doctor of the Church and undertook the publication of his *Opera omnia (Editio piana)*; he promoted in the Church the devotion of the rosary and established Dominican penitentiaries at St. Mary Major. While some bishops had requested and obtained from the council the reduction of privileges for the mendicant orders, especially regarding preaching, he gave these decretals a very liberal interpretation, retaining for the Dominicans their essential right to speak. He put three Dominicans in charge of accomplishing important tasks the council had assigned to the Holy See: Marinis, Foscherari (already named) and Foreiro (a Portuguese theologian) edited the *Catechism of the Council of Trent* published in 1566, as well as the *Missal* and the *Roman Breviary* published in 1568.

At the same time the order was working to support the papacy in its renewal efforts, it felt its influence on its own inner life. The growing centralization within the Church resulted in more and more frequent interventions by the pope in the governing of the order, contrary to its own rules. It became customary for the convocation of general elective chapters to be done in Rome by the pope, instead of by the vicar general at the place decided upon by the chapter. When Sylvester de Ferrara died in 1528, CLEMENT VII named himself the vicar general, when another had been chosen according to the constitutions of the order; he began again in 1532. With the chapter and the vicar general on his side, the pope was tempted to impose his own candidate. In 1539, Paul III went even further: he gave the presidency of the elective chapter to the cardinal protector of the order, Carafa, a secular, and not to the vicar general whom he had himself appointed. In 1589 SIXTUS V called a general elective chapter while the superior of the order, Fabri, was in charge; he deposed the latter, who intended to govern the order as an absolute leader, because of Fabri's hatred of the cardinal protector Bonelli.

This increased control was still progressing in the direction of Observance. The popes encouraged Dominican reform as much as they could. Almost all the candidates they supported belonged to reformed provinces or congregations, so that most of the superior generals of the 16th and 17th centuries were fervently Observant. Papal interventions were often direct, going over the head of the superior of the order. In 1530–1, Clement VII transferred the name and rights of the Roman province to the unreformed San Marco congregation and those of the former Lombard provinces to the congregation of Lombardy. In 1569 Pius V himself participated in the general chapter

that he had transferred from Anvers to Rome; he enforced strict measures against the convent's members, as well as the establishment of a reformed congregation of France in the province of Occitania.

The absolutism that would envelop Europe during the 17th century doubly affected the order's relationship with the papacy. The papal authority at the head of the order could not lose its control. While Gregory XV, in 1622, promulgated a bull suppressing the last privileges of the mendicants—a bull rescinded by URBAN VIII after his election in 1625—his successors preferred to make the superior of the order a great papal clerk, and very closely supervised his election. The 14 general elective chapters of the 17th and 18th centuries took place at Rome, almost all presided over by the cardinal protector or an appointed vicar general. After the death of Beccaria in 1600, the elective chapter was to have been held at Toulouse and presided over by the local provincial. Clement VIII transferred it to Rome and put Cardinal Baronius in charge, who secured the election of the candidate the pope preferred, the Spaniard Xavierre. After the refusal of authorization from the popes, the general nonelective chapters (triennial, according to the constitutions) became more and more rare after 1620. Ridolfi (1629–44) was not able to preside over any chapter except that of his election; Urban VIII canceled the one he had called at Seville for 1632. J.-B. De Marinis (1650–69) only presided over a single nonelective chapter in Rome in 1656; INNOCENT X and ALEXANDER VII refused to let him hold any chapter celebration outside Italy. The workings of representative government within the order were annulled by an ever-increasing centralism.

However, through a simultaneous evolution, papal control over the order was severely reduced by the growing national absolutisms. A significant event, the brutal deposition of Ridolfi by Urban VIII in 1644, may be explained as much by the unhappiness of Richelieu and then of Mazarin (whose brother Michel was trying to control the government of the order) with his ties with the court of Spain, as by the Roman intrigues of the pope's family, the Barberini clan. In 1686, Innocent XI was unable to oppose Louis XIV's pressure in favor of A. Cloche, the first Frenchman placed as the head of the order in 150 years.

Although popes continued to encourage Dominican Observance—a bull by Innocent X in 1652 required, although in vain, the closing of small convents—the sources of renewal in the 17th century relied mostly on the civil authorities. It was through the direct intervention of Henri IV, in 1608, that Michaëlis was able to establish the reformed congregation of Occitania. When the latter found itself threatened with suppression in Rome in 1629, its vicar general, Girardel, ran to Louis XIII for help: the congregation was officially placed under the personal protection of the king of France and took the name of the Congrégation Saint-Louis. In 1668 Louis XIV forced the superior of the order and the pope to establish it as a province with full rights. The more and more stringent control by national states on the life in the provinces considerably reduced the effective authority of the Roman power. A sign of the times, the general chapter of 1650 had to take steps against individual recourse of priests to the civil powers. The provinces governed themselves with increased autonomy. In France, papal bulls could not be applied without royal patents, nor were the ordinances of the superior of the order in effect until approval by parlement. The French Dominicans, under Louis XIV, aligned themselves staunchly with Gallican doctrines. Despite the theological tradition of the order, none of them defended the Roman point of view during the quarrel over the *regalia* (1682)—the right of the king to administer vacant sees. In fact, the opposite was true: the historian Noël Alexandre, director of studies at the Saint-Jacques convent of Paris adopted the Gallican positions of the Sorbonne in his ample *Histoire ecclésiastique* [History of the Church]. Neither the pressure from the superiors of the order nor Innocent XI's placement of them on the Index (1684) were able to change this point of view, despite his submission on principle. This doctrinal Gallicanism led several French Dominicans (including Alexandre) to be found among the "supplicants" to the council, in opposition to the bull *Unigenitus* (1713). They rallied less for Jansenism than for Thomism, which they believed the bull betrayed; they supported their position with Gallican liberties and the non-infallibility of the pope.

During the 18th century, the ties between the order and the papacy continued to grow stronger again. The popes kept order, more through good will than authority. Some came to preside over the election of the superior general (BENEDICT XIV in 1756 and PIUS VI in 1777). BENEDICT XIII, the fourth Dominican pope (1724–30), showered the order with benefits and prerogatives that were partially withdrawn by his successor CLEMENT XII. Benedict XIV and Pius VI grew friendlier toward the Dominicans as their other supporters disappeared. The superior general enjoyed a lot of prestige and influence in Rome. No serious crisis put the order in opposition to the papal Curia and two members became cardinals (Augustin Pipia in 1724 and Jean-Thomas de Boxadors in 1775). The Roman See; however, found itself totally powerless to defend the rights of the order against trampling by political powers. The Gallican spirit spread from Spain to Naples. German Febronism and Austrian JOSEPHISM took over northern Italy and Poland. The superior generals found themselves deprived of any effective control over the direction the order was taking. They could neither travel nor legislate, but only send unenforceable circulars. In France, when the commission of regulars called a na-

tional Dominican chapter to draw up new constitutions (1771), Boxadors refused to ratify them, but he had no papal authority to influence the course of things. In Austria, many convents were closed and the novitiates arbitrarily limited; neither the order nor the pope had any recourse. A sign of this common weakness was that the general elective chapter of 1777, although presided over by Pius VI and then by the Cardinal de Boxadors, was completely silent on these civil interventions, which were ruining the entire order. From 1765 to 1790, vocations almost completely ceased and global manpower diminished by one third. The revolutionary turmoil rendered the order as weak as the papacy.

Henry Donneaud

Bibliography

Amargier, P. *Études sur l'Ordre dominicain*, Marseille, 1986.

Archivum Fratrum Praedicatorum, Rome, one vol. annually since 1930 (cf. in particular the articles by A. Duval and B. Montagnes).

Hinnebusch, W. A. *Brève histoire de l'Ordre dominicain*, adapted by G. Bedouelle, Paris, 1990.

Mortier, A. *Histoire des maîtres généraux de l'Ordre des frères prêcheurs*, 7 vol. and index, Paris, 1903–20.

Vicaire, M. H. and Duval, A. "Frères prêcheurs [ordre des]," *DHGE*, XVIII, Paris, 1977, col. 1369–1426.

Vicaire, M. H. *Histoire de saint Dominique*, 2 vol., Paris, 1982.

19th and 20th Centuries. In the 19th century, the renewal of the Dominican order depended largely on the papacy. During the following century, in the name of different conceptions of Church service, certain conflicts appeared, but did not destroy their mutual confidence.

Henri-Dominique Lacordaire (1802–61), by deciding to reestablish the order of Preachers in France in 1839, recognized the role that the papacy had played in its beginnings. This joined with his own ultramontanism and was strengthened by his years of collaboration with Lamennais. The real attachment of the author of *La Lettre sur le Saint-Siège* (1836) to the chair of St. Peter was expressed in his *Mémoire* of 1838 on the reestablishment of the Dominicans, addressed to the French public, and in *Life of Saint Dominic* (1840), which had several passages on Poland that upset the Roman censors. In these two works, the roles that INNOCENT III and HONORIUS III played are fully displayed, giving Lacordaire's works their historic value.

Less than ten years after the foundation of the first French convent at Nancy in 1843, the Holy See gave its endorsement to Lacordaire's enterprise when PIUS IX named Father Vincent Jandel (1810–72) vicar general on 17 December 1855. This encouraged the work to restore observance that Jandel had begun, especially in Italy where he reminded the friars involved in the Italian cause of their obedience to the pope. In 1865 Pius IX supported sending Dominicans to the Equator of Garcia Moreno. While in 1804 Pius VII reduced the generalship from a life term to only six years, Pius IX set it at twelve years in 1862, with elections normally held in Rome. That same year, the general chapter elected Father Jandel, who governed the order until his death, in all, 22 years. Lacordaire intervened publicly in 1861, several months before his death, on the Roman question. In his essay *De la liberté de l'Italie et de l'Église* he suggested that Italian unity had everything to gain from preserving the pope's temporal sovereignty.

Father Jandel sat in the VATICAN I COUNCIL. Just as he had been a partisan of the *SYLLABUS*, he upheld the principle of papal INFALLIBILITY without taking part in the extremist current. He did not have the opportunity to explain his position to the council. Of all the Dominican bishops present, only the Irish P. J. Leahy belonged to the minority. Filippo Guidi (1815–79), a former professor of theology in Rome and then in Vienna, was made a cardinal and then, in 1863, archbishop of Bologna, without being able to take possession of his see. On 18 June 1870, in a desire to rally the minority, he proposed removal of the notion of personal infallibility of the pope by mentioning the collaboration of the episcopate and conformity to tradition in the council's definition. Pius IX had announced the famous phrase: "I am the tradition," that very night during the course of a stormy interview with Guidi, who nonetheless voted *placet* at the final session.

Before his death, Jandel was able to see the abrogation of the bull *Inter graviores*, issued by Pius VII in 1804, who removed the Spanish domains from the superior general's jurisdiction: on 12 July 1872, Pius IX thus reestablished unity. This decision had been prepared, in particular, by Father J. M. Larroca (1813–91) who was elected general in 1879.

Father A. Frühwirth (1845–1933), elected in 1891, was selected by LEO XIII to promote devotion to the ROSARY and renew Thomism. It was with this title that he accepted, on behalf of the order, the task of continuing the edition of the works of Saint Thomas called the Leonine edition. The ENCYCLICAL *Aeterni Patris* on the study of Saint Thomas, was based on the works of numerous Dominicans like Cardinal Th. Zigliara (1833–93). At the new university of Fribourg-en-Suisse, professors like A. M. Weiss and J. Berthier participated in the work on the Union of Fribourg, which contributed to the elaboration of ideas in *Rerum novarum*. While Father Frühwirth was named NUNCIO to Munich by PIUS X in 1907, and then archbishop and cardinal by BENEDICT XV, it was Father H. Cormier (1832–1916) who had to confront the modernist crisis. He was elected in 1904 at age 72 when he was known to have the total confidence of Pius X. Cormier supported his priests with loyalty and moderation against the antimodernist attacks, whether from Fri-

bourg or Jerusalem, at the new L'Ecole Biblique with M. J. Lagrange. The latter, in disfavor due to his *Méthode historique* in 1902, wrote a letter of obedience to Pius X in 1912. When Father Lagrange was taken prisoner by the Turks, the intervention of the Holy See secured his release. Father L. Theissling (1856–1925), from the province of Holland, was elected in 1916. When Benedict XV suggested his peace plan in 1917, which did not include the reintegration of Alsace and Lorraine into France, D. Sertillanges, in a sermon at the Madeleine church in Paris on 10 December, with the endorsement of Cardinal Amette, made himself the vehement mouthpiece of French opinion against the papal propositions. Secretary of State Gasparri immediately placed sanctions on them.

Of the pontificate of PIUS XI, we should mention the generalship of Father B. Garcia de Parédès, elected in 1926; the long mandate of Father M. Gillet, which lasted from 1929 to 1946; and the condemnation of *L'Action française* in 1926. The French Dominicans had varying attitudes: while the famous preacher of Notre Dame, M. A. Janvier, submitted, T. Pègues wrote an open letter to Pius XI and encouraged resistance to authority. M. V. Bernadot, together with E. Lajeunie, released a collective work with Jacques Maritain: *Pourquoi Rome a parlé*, followed by *Clairvoyance de Rome*. Pius XI intervened so that Lajeunie and Bernadot might found *La Vie intellectuelle*, but the review *Sept*, judged too adventurous, was suspended in 1937. Relations of the Dominican order with PIUS XII were marked by the crisis of the worker-priests in France. With the pope, having ordered the end of this experiment, and the French Dominicans who had participated in it being reluctant to agree, Father E. Suarez, elected in 1946, thought it his duty, in 1954, to preempt the eventual Roman sanctions by deposing the three provincials of France. Some theologians of the order, like Y. Congar or M. D. Chenu, were then reduced to silence.

More than 50 Dominicans participated in the VATICAN II COUNCIL in one way or another. The encyclical of Pope PAUL VI, *Populorum progressio* of 1968, owed much to the experience and thought of Father J. Lebret, the founder of *Économie et humanisme*, who represented the Holy See at certain international conferences. This widely known example only illustrates the work often behind the scenes, sometimes anonymous, of so many Dominicans in the service of the papacy, beginning with the masters of the Sacred Palace (who had become theologians of the papal household), and who traditionally belonged to the order of Preachers.

Guy Bedouelle

Bibliography

Bedouelle, G. *Lacordaire, son pays, ses amis et la liberté des ordres religieux en France*, Paris, 1991.

Duval, A. "Lacordaire et Monseigneur de Quelen, 1836–1838. *La lettre sur le Saint-Siège* et la vocation dominicains," *AFP*, 56 (1986), 380–428 and 57 (1987), 291–340.

Horst, U. "Kardinalerzbischof Filippo Maria Guidi und das I. Vatikanische Konzil," *AFP*, 49 (1979), 429–511.

Laudouze, A. *Dominicains français et Action française, 1899–1940*, Paris, 1989.

Leprieur, F. *Quand Rome condamne, dominicains et prêtres-ouvriers*, Paris, 1989.

Montagnes, B. *Exégèse et obéissance, Correspondance Cormier-Lagrange*, Paris, 1986.

DONATION OF CONSTANTINE. "*Ahi, Constantin, di quanto mal fu matre, / non la tua conversion, ma quella dote/che da te prese il primo ricco patre!*" (Dante, *The Inferno*, XIX, 115–17): the object of polemics beginning in the 13th century when the heretics of the "Apostolic life" made it the starting point of a new era in the history of a Church that had become rich, the "Donation of Constantine" (*Constitutum Constantini*) is the most famous forgery in the history of the papacy. The story has a lot of appeal: The mystery of a police inquest that has never really ended, for we still have difficulties pinpointing the exact circumstances of its birth; it is also of interest to historians because the richest story of the forgery is less that of its manufacture than, for more than ten centuries, its circulation and its reception.

The document, attributed to Emperor CONSTANTINE and addressed to Pope SILVESTER I during the fourth consulate of Constantine (315) and that of Gallicanus (317), is very eloquent and is divided into two distinct parts, called by modern critics the *confessio* and the *donatio*. In the first, the emperor acknowledges the faith that Pope Silvester has taught him, as well as relates the long tale of his being cured of leprosy, brought about before his conversion by the pope (a fable told again in the *Actus Silvestri* during the 5th century). In the *donatio*, Constantine gives, indiscriminately, the following to the successor of St. Peter: primacy over all Eastern churches (Antioch, Alexandria, Constantinople, and Jerusalem); the churches of the LATERAN, ST. PETER'S and SAINT-PAUL'S-OUTSIDE-THE-WALLS, with properties in various other provinces (Judea, Greece, Asia, Thrace, AFRICA, Italy, and some islands); his palace of the Lateran; the imperial insignia; to clerics of the pope's entourage he accords the privileges and badges of senators; to the pope, again, the exclusive privilege of raising senators to the clerical state and all power (*potestas, ditio*) over the Lateran, the city of Rome, Italy, and the western regions. He then declares he will retire to the eastern portion of the Empire, to which he limits his terrestrial power. The dissemination of this text was clandestine, for there is no sure witness of the text's diffusion before the mid-9th century. Even in Rome it does not seem to have appeared much earlier: it

is not cited explicitly until a pontifical document in 979 (but trace references may be found, perhaps in the correspondence of Nicholas I) and in 1053 it became, under the pen of Cardinal Humbert de Silva Candida, a central argument of Gregorians in favor of papal primacy; it is then integrated into Roman canonical collections and the *Decretum* of Gratian (canon 14, D. 96). However, from the middle of the 9th century, it is known and cited in Carolingian Gaul: Its real success dates, in fact, from its incorporation in the collection of DECRETALS called pseudo-Isidorian, and in 869 the bishop of Paris wrote, not without exaggeration, that the text could be found in almost every church in Gaul. This reality (together with the fact that a version interpolated by Cardinal John was rejected by Emperor Otto III in 1001) caused several to advance the hypothesis that the document had been forged in the Carolingian kingdom. If it is true that the Frankish kings and then emperors were pleased with the position taken by the new Constantine (a compliment made by the pope to Charlemagne), and if it is also true that the phantom of the donation is found, more or less, in the great documents of protection and confirmation or restitution given to the sovereign pontiff (the promise of Quercy by Pepin, a document perhaps interpolated by Charlemagne and analyzed in the *LIBER PONTIFICALIS*, the *Ludovicianum* of Louis the Pious in 817, the *Ottanianum* of Otto I in 962, the acts of Henry II in 1020, Henry V in 1111, Otto IV in 1201, Henry VII in 1310, and Sigismond in 1433), the tone, the vocabulary, the background, and the planned profit lead us, not to Gaul, but to a papacy that, after the middle of the 8th century, freed itself from the Byzantine emperor and worked to get its preeminence over Italy recognized. More precisely perhaps, we are led to the years between 750 and 770 when the break with the East was finalized, when the pope felt a universal spiritual primacy and a temporal primacy over the West within his grasp, where the *basileus* was no longer interferring and where papal leadership could perhaps be imposed on the half-barbarians without too much difficulty. Whatever may be, it was the reception into the canonical collections, pseudo-Isidorian and the Gregorian, that dates the career of the fake, which then became a deed of gift, or rather of "restitution," and a guarantee of "freedom" in the Gregorian sense of the word, in short, a fundamental legal privilege.

The donation leaves itself open to criticism. This was quickly expressed, but with polemic intentions, the obvious incoherencies of the text being bypassed or emphasized according to whether persons wished to defend or attack the Roman primacy. By the 12th century, Arnold of Brescia saw the donation as a document of the Antichrist, an expression that Luther would adopt. In the 14th century the propagandists of imperial power again attacked the document: Marsilius of Padua, dealing with the question of authenticity, uses the text's own words to attack it; if the emperor granted temporal powers, they were those he had before the pope; William of Ockham recalls the doubts about the authenticity of the document. An in-depth philological critique, displaying a better knowledge of the language and classic Latin institutions, comes from the 15th century humanists, but always with heavy political consequences, in the context of the crisis of conciliarism. Nicolas of Cusa, in 1433, criticized the form more than the content. Lorenzo Valla issued a long imprecation in 1440, although his manuscript text was not printed until 1506 and was not really disseminated until the editions of 1518–19 done by Ulrich von Hutten. Baronius, a century later, admitted the falseness of the form, but not of the content, still leaving some leeway for protestant polemics. The falsity of the document was not officially admitted by the Church, or for the pseudo-Isidorian decretals, until the mid-19th century.

Errors in method have perhaps led us, until now, to misleading conjectures about its origins and character. Dom Huyghebaert pointed out how the "falsifier" was clumsy in composing it; more exactly, how much the donation, listed as a "decree" since its incorporation in canonical collections, had rather been composed as a long narration. He linked these findings to the heavy insistence placed in it on the Lateran: the palace (the favorite palace of the emperor, given to the pope, is named five times and is presented as the center of both Rome and Italy), the admirable basilica (where the author portrays the scene of the emperor laying the foundations of the basilica of the Vatican according to the *Actus Silvestri*, which he plagiarized), the devotion to the patron of the basilica the Savior, without forgetting the geographical lists that could correspond to the maps painted at the Lateran. He was thus able to propose an extremely persuasive trail of events: the document was not forged at that moment, as are many historical fakes, to obtain confirmation of contemporary authority. This was, rather, a hagiographic legend, a "foundation legend," not acquiring legal status until much later: a work as clumsy as it was rich in ideas, by a cleric in the basilica at the Lateran, with little historical knowledge and who was trying to exalt his basilica more than he was the papacy. That the document had been composed as a "travel narrative" of the basilica for pilgrims, and that the author had shown them in the form of an inscription, remains pure conjecture, but this new critical look takes the context of the birth of such a text more into account, as well as its spreading more rapidly through Gaul than to Rome, and its very late transformation into a legal resource.

Olivier Guyotjeannin

Bibliography

Fäschungen im Mittelalter, II, Hanover, 1988 (*MGH Schriften*, 33-2), 413–90 and 509–44 (articles by W. Pohlkamp, K. Zeillinger, and J. Quillet).

Das Constitutum Constantini, Fuhrmann, H., ed. Hanover, 1968 (*MGH, Fontes juris*, 10).

Fuhrmann, H. "Constitutum Constantini," *Theologische Realenzyklopädie*, 8 (1981), 196–202.

Huyghebaert, N. "Une légende de fondation: le Constitutum Constantini," *Le Moyen Âge*, 85 (1979), 177–209.

Valla, L. *De falso credita et ementita Constantini donatione*, W. Setz, ed., Weimer, 1976 (*MGH, Quellen zur Geistesgeschichte des Mittelalters,* 10).

DONUS. *(b. Rome, ?, d. Rome, 11 April 678). Consecrated pope 2 November 676. Buried in St. Peter's in Rome.*

During this brief and fairly obscure pontificate, the papacy increased its autonomy vis-à-vis the emperor as well as its power over Rome and Italy. The son of a Maurice and born in Rome, Donus probably had an ecclesiastical career, but we have no information about it. Once elected, he was attentive to the needs of the city. He paved the atrium in front of ST. PETER'S with marble slabs and restored two churches. The clergy received several honors. An investigation revealed that the Syrian monks of the monastery called "Boetian" were in fact Nestorians. He dispersed them to other monasteries in the hope that they would convert, and he put other priests in their place. More than the facts themselves, the care with which the *LIBER PONTIFICALIS* reports them shows that local administration is considered an essential aspect of pontifical activity after this time. In Italy, Donus temporarily reestablished his authority over the see of RAVENNA. In 666, Constans II had given this metropolitan autocephalous status, which removed it from papal control, but archbishop Reparatus reached an agreement with Donus that his successors would present themselves in the week following their election in order to be consecrated by the pope. Although Theodore, the successor of Reparatus, had been consecrated by his suffragans and by the pope, the principle of a definite reconciliation was established. We see behind this accord the hand of the emperor who, wishing to get closer to Rome, no longer retained his pretensions regarding Ravenna.

In fact, the systematic opposition of Rome, whose popes always rejected the synodic letters of the patriarchs of Constantinople, created religious and political tensions in the entire Empire. The patriarchs—especially Theodore (677–9)—were partisans in the rupture because they were especially anxious to extend their power. Constantine IV (668–85), on the other hand, saw that he could not require Rome to obey and that he had to compromise. He thus forced Theodore to send a cordial letter to the pope making no mention of his Christological opinions and sending another on his own, also cordial, on 12 August 678, that invited Donus to send envoys to his court for discussions. As always when the emperor called for a meeting of clerics, the exarch would put boats at the disposal of the papal representatives and would pay all the costs. The pope, however, was dead when the messages arrived.

Jean Durliat

Bibliography

MANSI, XI, 1, 238.
1, 348–9.
Bertolini, O. *Roma di fronte a Bisanzio e ai Longobardi*, Bologna, 1971, 196–201, 365–7.
Schieffer, R. "Donus," *LexMA*, 3 (1984–6), 1253.

E

EASTER-DATE CONTROVERSIES. This term covers the various controversies over the question of how to set the date of Easter. The vehement disputes that raged from the 2nd century to the 8th reflected a fundamental problem of autonomy on the part of Christianity vis-à-vis Jewish usage and, later, the problem of relations among the Christian Churches. The first controversy, which took place in the 2nd century, was mainly liturgical. The Quartodeciman rite, observed in the East, insisted that Christian Easter be celebrated on the 14th day of the month Nisan, the day of the full moon of the first month of the Jewish year, whatever day of the week it fell on. Dominical ritual, by contrast, prescribed celebrating Easter on the Sunday after that day. In mid-2nd century, Polycarp, bishop of Smyrna, and Pope ANICETUS debated the matter inconclusively yet peaceably. The controversy flared up over the ensuing decades, coming to a climax in the years 180–90, when Pope VICTOR I considered excommunicating anyone observing the Quartodeciman ritual.

Quartodecimanism declined of its own accord, until in the 5th century it was practiced by only a few isolated Eastern Churches. Another problem had reared its head, however: once the Dominical observance was allowed, the Christian Churches were eager to separate themselves from Jewish practice and settle the date of Easter in their own way. The second Paschal controversy therefore consisted of a number of astronomical and chronological disputes over the means of calculating and foretelling, without the help of a synagogue, the concordance of the Jewish lunar CALENDAR with the civil solar calendar. Some Churches, as in Gaul, chose a time to celebrate the anniversary of Easter on a fixed date, 25 March (a tradition that lingered on vestigially in the Western medieval calendar, when 27 March was a feast day under the name Resurrectio Domini). But most Churches agreed to keep Easter as a movable feast, linked to the moon. The problem, then, was to find a cycle of years of the solar calendar at the end of which the synodic months, and therefore Easter, would return in the same order, on the same calendar days.

Secondary questions confused the issue: Which fixed date should be assigned to the equinox—21 or 25 March? Could Easter precede the equinox, and could it be celebrated on the Sunday after the full moon? At first, Rome adopted a 16-year cycle drawn up by St. Hippolytus. This was soon found to be imperfect and, at the end of the 3rd century, it was replaced by an 84-year cycle (the cycle of Augustalis), which was amended in the next century. The Alexandrian Church, for its part, opted for a far more accurate 19-year cycle. To be conciliatory, Alexandria sometimes adopted Rome's method of dating, as Rome did Alexandria's. The Church of Gaul often used Rome's method, the schismatic Quartodecimans followed their own practice, and other Churches relied on the Jewish reckoning.

These divergences were more and more regarded as scandalous. In 325, the council of Nicaea consecrated the break with Jewish computation by stating its wish for a single date on which to celebrate Easter, one that came after the equinox and was based on the Roman and Alexandrian methods. However, although tradition says otherwise, it did not prescribe the adoption of the 19-year cycle. From the 460s, the cycle proposed by Victorius of Aquitaine—one of 532 years, a multiple of the 19-year cycle—was adopted fairly widely in the West. But Pope SYMMACHUS, in his struggle against the antipope LAWRENCE, reverted in 501–2 to the 84-year cycle. In the end, the 19-year cycle was accepted in Rome and elsewhere in Italy in the course of the 6th century by the adoption of the Paschal Tables. These were drawn up by Dionysius Exiguus, who had followed Cyril of Alexandria's tables for the years 532–626, at the same time introducing the idea of the Christian Era.

Alexandrian practice also penetrated the Iberian Peninsula, though it was far from exclusive there. Unity was thus reestablished little by little, with Rome helping to spread the calculation it had at first opposed. At this point, the third series of Paschal controversies began when, in the West, the Roman-Alexandrian method came up against the archaic Roman calculations adopted in the earliest stages of Christianization. Under the influence of missionaries sent by Rome in the late 6th century, the Roman custom coexisted with ancient Celtic practice, faithful to the 84-year cycle. In 664, for instance, Oswy, king of Northumberland, who had formerly celebrated Easter the same day that his wife was celebrating Palm Sunday, opted for the new method. In the 8th century, the Venerable Bede popularized the Paschal Tables and succeeded in eradicating the Celtic practices, which had been reintroduced to a limited extent on the continent by St. Boniface and by missionaries from Ireland and the British Isles. Not until Charlemagne's time would the Frankish kingdom definitively adopt the Roman computation. From that time on, Western Christianity uniformly celebrated Easter on the Sunday following the full moon after 21 March, a Sunday that, depending on the year, could fall on any date from 22 March to 25 April.

The gradual adoption of the Gregorian calendar again brought confusion, as did the diffusion in the 18th century of the "Rodolphian Tables" of the astronomer Kepler, proposing yet another cycle. Thus, in 1704 Easter was celebrated in different places on 23 March or 20 April. Switzerland and Germany did not join the common practice until 1775. The Orthodox Churches, however, continue to celebrate Easter on a different date.

Olivier Guyotjeannin

Bibliography

Fritz, G. "Pâques," *DTC*, 11–2 (1932), 1948–70.
Leclerc, M. "Pâques," *DACL*, 13–2 (1938), 1521–74.
Strobel, A. *Ursprung und Geschichte des frühchristlichen Osterkalenders*, Berlin, 1977 (*Texte und Untersuchungen zur Geschichte des altchristlichen Literatur*, 121); *Texte zur Geschichte des frühchristlichen Osterkalenders*, Münster, 1984 (*Liturgiewissenschaftliche Quellen und Forschungen*, 64).

ECUMENISM.

Unionism vs. Ecumenism. On 6 January 1928, in his ENCYCLICAL *Mortalium animos*, Pope PIUS XI reminded Catholics of the official position of the Roman Church concerning ecumenism: "It is not permissible [. . .] to bring about the union of Christians otherwise than by encouraging the return of dissidents to the one true Church of Christ from which they unfortunately were separated in times past." The general tone of the encyclical is all rather strict in that "dangerous illusions" were threatening Catholics attracted by the ecumenical movement.

The movement arose in the 19th century. First the Universal Evangelical Alliance (1846) and then the World Alliance of Christian Unions (1855) aimed at establishing steady, regular relations among the members of the diverse Churches that had grown out of the REFORMATION. At the beginning of the 20th century, after the Edinburgh Missionary Conference (1910), the movement took shape with the creation of Life and Action (Stockholm, 1925) and Faith and Constitution (Lausanne, 1927). Under the influence of personalities like the Episcopalian bishop Charles Brent and the Lutheran archbishop of Uppsala Nathan Söderblom, ecumenism ventured beyond the boundaries of Protestantism and ANGLICANISM. Contacts were set up with the Orthodox Church and the Roman Catholic Church. But whereas the Orthodox leadership, faced with revolution in Turkey and the Soviet Union, became progressively more involved in ecumenical structures, the Vatican forbade its faithful to participate in the conferences at Stockholm and Lausanne. Pius XI reaffirmed a unionist strategy already defined by LEO XIII in the encyclicals *Orientalium dignitas* (1894), *Praeclara gratulationis* (1894), and *Satis cognitum* (1896), and by the very Leonine BENEDICT XV when the promoters of Faith and Order had asked to meet him. In 1914, he replied to them through his secretary of state, Gasparri, that the pope was the sole "source" and "cause" of unity. In 1919, he received them in paternal fashion; he told them he was praying that the participants in the coming conference would decide to reunite with the visible Head of the Church; if so, he assured them, they would be welcomed with open arms.

In contrast to ecumenism, conceived as a convergence of Churches through reflection on doctrine and through common action, unionism defines Christian unity as a reconciliation of the separated Churches with the one Church of Christ, whose seat is in Rome. Reconciliation is subordinated to two requirements: that the dissident Churches confess the fault committed by their founders in separating, and that they return to the truth represented by the Catholic Church, the fullness of truth of individual and also of social salvation. On this basis, accommodations concerning liturgy and discipline could be negotiated.

From the uncompromising perspective of a humanity reconciled and at peace through Christ's restoration of the social order, Pius XI recapitulated his predecessors' declarations from the beginning of his pontificate. His first encyclical, *Ubi arcano Dei* (1922), calls Christians to "the unity intended by Christ" but recalls that the pope alone "holds the place" of this "eternal Pastor." This echoes Leo XIII, who in 1894 wrote in *Praeclara gratulationis*, "We hold here the place of God." The encyclical *Mortalium animos*, therefore, differs from previous papal documents only in the urgency of the new situation, in which a dynamic and structured ecumenism was in danger of attracting Catholics with hope of unity. In 1914, Benedict XV had responded to the overtures of Charles Brent and his friends with a polite and courteously worded refusal. In 1929, Pius XI adopted a firmer tone. The response was no longer a polite refusal but a prohibition: "Catholics are not permitted at any price to adhere to such enterprises or to contribute to them; if they did so, they would give authority to a false Christian religion, one completely foreign to the one Church of Christ."

An Urgent Unionism. Pius XI was convinced that the modern world, founded on the exclusion of God from society, was rushing to catastrophe. In an attempt to prevent it, he developed Catholic Action and invited the separated brethren to rejoin the Roman Church in its effort to reestablish the sovereignty of Christ. In practice, he put the dissidents in some form of hierarchical order. With the Anglicans and Protestants, his policy was laissez-faire rather than action. At the beginning of his reign, he permitted the Malines Conversations between Catholics and Anglicans (1921–5), but on condition that they remain strictly private. At the end of his pontificate, he allowed Cardinal Gerlier, archbishop of Lyon, to support Fr. Couturier in his effort to develop the Octave of Prayer for Christian Unity, an all-embracing enterprise in which the Anglicans nevertheless played a privileged role. Paul Couturier acted on his own, without a mandate, and it would be dangerous to attribute to any Roman influence the ecumenical tendency of the Octave, which became known as a Week of Prayer in 1939, after Couturier had engaged in a real but discreet dialogue with the Protestants at the heart of the "Dombes Group."

Pius XI had the Eastern Christians especially in mind when he revived the unionist strategy. In the encyclicals *Ecclesiam Dei* (1923) and *Sancta Dei Ecclesia* (1938), he reminded them that their return would not compromise their customs or particular rituals. In the encyclical *Rerum orientalium* (1928), he encouraged the development of two institutions created by Benedict XV in 1917: the CONGREGATION for the Oriental Church, detached from Propagation of the Faith, and the Pontifical Oriental Institute, devoted to training specialists for a better understanding of Eastern affairs. In 1926, the Benedictine Dom Lambert Beauduin, acting on the authority of the BRIEF *Equidem verba*, which urged the monastic order to work toward the return of Russia, founded the unionist priory of Amay-sur-Meuse. In 1939, the journal started by Beauduin, *Irenikon*, wrote that Pius XI had always been its "father and protector." There was a pious omission here: caught up like Couturier in the ecumenical vision, Dom Lambert in 1928 was relieved of his duties as prior and had to leave Amay. In 1937, Fr. Congar's publication, in the Dominican series *Unam Sanctam*, of *Chrétiens désunis. Principes d'un "oecuménisme" catholique* had repercussions in high places. The work was all but condemned and the series almost suppressed. The pope was opening his arms to his separated children, but remained all the more intransigent in his determination to develop a

Catholic Action that would save humankind from disaster while restoring a peaceful order according to the SOCIAL TEACHING of the Church.

Disaster struck, and urgency gave way to agony. In his encyclical *Mystici Corporis Christi* (29 June 1943), PIUS XII adjured non-Catholics to "leave their condition, in which they cannot be sure of their eternal salvation." Indeed, "even if their desires and their unconscious wishes orient them toward the mystical Body of Christ, they are nonetheless deprived of all the gifts and divine help that can be enjoyed only in the Catholic Church." While the Red Army's successes seemed to presage an expansion of communism, the Vatican gave more and more attention to the unionist strategy. On 9 April 1944, on the occasion of the fifteenth centennial of the death of St. Cyril of Alexandria, Pius XII solemnly addressed the Eastern Church in the encyclical *Orientalis Ecclesiae*. According to the pontiff, the Orthodox Church must return to the bosom of the Catholic Church in order for a "common front" to be presented to atheism.

It seemed at the time to non-Catholics, and also to the Catholic fringe that had embraced the ecumenical vision of unity, that Roman unionism was turning into isolationism. While the ecumenical movement was taking final shape with the official founding of the World Council of Churches (Amsterdam, 1948), Pius XII was maintaining Pius XI's position: there were no Catholic observers at the Amsterdam conference. Yet the WCC included not only the majority of Protestant Churches but also eminent representatives of the Orthodox Church. One of its six vice presidents was the ecumenical patriarch Germanos of Constantinople. And among the thirteen members of the executive committee were two who were Orthodox. Pastor Visser't Hooft, secretary general of the WCC, deplored the fact that "all ecumenism with Rome [is] impossible because of the intransigent attitude of the Catholic Church." An exasperated Karl Barth exclaimed at the Amsterdam conference, "I am sorry you don't hate the pope."

Two years later, it looked as though Roman unionism was breaking all ties with organized ecumenism. In his Christmas radio message of 1949, Pius XII renewed his appeal for Christian unity and announced the beginning of the HOLY YEAR, the jubilee year that occurs every twenty-five years and, among other spititual benefits, allows pilgrims to obtain a plenary INDULGENCE if they make the rounds of the principal basilicas of the Eternal City. In 1950, the mobilization of the mass of Catholic faithful (more than 2.5 million pilgrims went to Rome) was solemnized by the definition of the dogma of the ASSUMPTION OF THE VIRGIN MARY. Non-Catholics reacted with a mixture of disappointment and hostility. Protestants, Anglicans, and Orthodox came together to denounce this exercise of papal INFALLIBILITY, which had been defined by the VATICAN I council in 1870. According to the Orthodox, the dogma had been "proclaimed irregularly by the pope." For the Anglican archbishop of

Canterbury, the Catholic Church had "deliberately" aggravated the dogmatic differences "that separate Christianity and had thereby gravely compromised the agreement based on the fundamental truths which Christians hold in common." Finally, one of the co-presidents of the WCC, Pastor Marc Boegner, judged that all possibility of unity with the Catholic Church was henceforward out of the question.

The John XXIII Effect. When the patriarch of Venice succeeded Pius XII on 28 October 1958, no one expected that a new period was beginning in the history of relations betweeen the papacy and non-Catholics. And indeed, in his Christmas radio message of that year, Angelo Roncalli expressed the wish, as his predecessors had done, for a "return to the house of the common Lord" on the part of all those "separated" from the Apostolic See.

So the surprise was all the greater when JOHN XXIII announced quite unexpectedly the meeting of a council to which non-Catholic Christian observers were invited. This perhaps did not mean the end of unionism; but to the observers, it was official approval given by the head of the Roman Church to a Catholic ecumenism that Pius XI and Pius XII had marginalized or repressed. The pioneers were enthusiastic; Fr. Congar, for example, exclaimed a few days after the announcement of VATICAN II, "Either the pope has gone mad, or this is the Holy Spirit!" L'OSSERVATORE ROMANO adopted a middle-of-the-road position by recalling that John XXIII knew the East well, having spent more than ten years there (from 1925 to 1937) as apostolic visitor to Bulgaria and then as apostolic delegate in Turkey and Greece. If a few stones had been hurled at him by way of criticism, still he knew how to win the liking and respect of those with whom he dealt. And in fact the new pope inspired confidence in the ecumenical patriarch of Constantinople, Athenagoras I, who reacted quickly. He hoped that actions would follow words and that the Orthodox Church would be able to cooperate "with the venerable Church of the West." Another emblematic figure of Christian unity, Pastor Roger Schutz, founder of the ecumenical community of Taizé, was instantly won over and saluted the "spirit of openness" animating the new pontiff.

For John XXIII, openness meant first of all a change of language. The first part of the encyclical *Ad Petri Cathedram* (26 June 1959) was devoted to the separated Christians. They were no longer simply invited to rejoin the one and only fold: the pope was now encouraging them to "seek and renew," with their Catholic brothers, the unity desired by Christ. This was a repetition of Fr. Couturier's basic formula. Openness meant, next, the institution of a curial body to coordinate dialogue, that is, bilateral conversation, between Rome and the separated Churches. On 5 June 1960, John XXIII created the Secretariat for Promoting Christian Unity, entrusting it to Cardinal Bea, the former rector of the Biblical Institute of

Rome. Finally, there was the concrete step taken in the establishment of personal links with non-Catholics. In November 1960, the pope welcomed the primate of the Church of England: this was the first official contact between Rome and Canterbury since Henry VIII, the first meeting between the Roman pontiff and the highest authority of a separated church. He also received leading proponents of basic ecumenism, beginning with Pastor Roger Schutz, and it was in evoking his ties with him that the pope spoke of the "springtime of the Church." So that the overture should truly herald a spring and not lose itself in short-lived effusions or soulless institutions, John XXIII judged that it should be accompanied by an *aggiornamento*, an updating of the Roman system and modes of discourse. The majority of the council fathers had no trouble understanding him; he was telling them loud and clear what the pioneers of Catholic ecumenism had been suggesting for some thirty years. After Pope John's death, they voted, on 21 November 1964, the decree *Unitatis Redintegratio*, which unmistakably stated that movement toward unity would not take place without a "renewal" of the Church. The non-Catholic observers were not content merely to observe. Cardinal Bea testified that "they played a decisive role in the establishment of the decree on ecumenism. Their presence at the council, their participation in prayer and study, the very varied contacts, and their proposals brought the ecumenical problem profoundly to life for the bishops."

The observers knew quite well that John XXIII had not invented ecumenism, not even Catholic ecumenism. But, in the words of Roger Schutz, "he was the first one to rid our hearts of their anxieties [. . .]. When he died, it was as though the earth had crumbled. It took me several days to console myself." By announcing, right after his election, that the council would resume its work, Giovanni Battista Montini signaled his intention of carrying on his predecessor's work. At the beginning of the second session (November 1963), in the name of the Catholic Church and as its first pastor, PAUL VI called for repentance for past and present sins committed by Rome against unity. Addressing his separated brethren, he evoked his predecessors' responsibility for the various SCHISMS and asked forgiveness for the injustices of which the papacy had been guilty over the centuries. Along with the renewal of discourse came a renewal of the system. Paul VI revived the notion of COLLEGIALITY, whereas at least since Vatican I the bishops had been regarded by the CURIA as executors of Rome's decisions. This positive reevaluation fostered dialogue with the Orthodox Church, especially as Paul VI was making gestures whose reach "surpasses the most opportune colloquies between theologians." On 4 January 1964, he went on a PILGRIMAGE to Jerusalem, where he gave the kiss of peace to Patriarch Athenagoras. The following year, on 7 December 1965, Paul VI and Athenagoras I lifted the

ANATHEMAS between Rome and Constantinople. These had been imposed nine centuries earlier, in 1054. Rapprochement with the Anglicans also gained momentum with the opening, in 1966, of a theological dialogue between representatives appointed by both Churches. On that occasion, Paul VI, who had a feeling for the symbolic gesture, slipped the ring of the bishop of Rome onto the finger of the archbishop of Canterbury. Thus was born the idea of "sister Churches," at least in the sense of a "possible future," to use the expression coined by Dom Emmanuel Lanne, a disciple of Dom Lambert Beauduin.

"Non Possumus." Paul VI was not, however, calling into question his apostolic authority. At the beginning of the third session of the council, he recalled the primacy of the bishop of Rome. Vatican II did not annul any previous council but was in keeping with the growth of a Church founded on Scripture and Tradition. That is why, when Paul VI made the first visit ever by a supreme pontiff to an ecumenical conference, in Geneva (1969), his first words were "My name is PETER." He thus set the limits of the dialogue between Roman ecumenism and the organized ecumenism, established in the 20th century by the reformed Churches. The Church was one, and the bishop of Rome the visible symbol of its unity. This unity could be manifested only around the successor of Peter, the servant of the communion of "particular CHURCHES within the universal Church."

Fifteen years after the first papal visit to the WCC, John Paul II also went to Geneva (June 1984). In his address, he explained that his coming was evidence of his desire for unity; the Catholic Church was engaged in the ecumenical movement in an "irreversible" way. But if the pope saw the rapprochement of the Churches as remaining a "pastoral priority" for him, like Paul VI, and using the same language as his predecessors, he reaffirmed Catholic specificity in ecclesiastical matters: "In spite of the moral miseries that have marked the life of her members and even of her heads in the course of her history, [the Catholic Church] is convinced that in the ministry of the Bishop of Rome she has maintained, in all fidelity to the apostolic tradition and to the faith of the Fathers, the visible pole and guarantor of unity." The Church could not, therefore, adhere to the WCC, and refused to take part in the world assembly at Canberra, to which the central committee of the WCC had invited her in January 1987.

If the papacy did not call into question its ecclesiastical PRIMACY, it was eager to develop doctrinal dialogue. Bilateral or trilateral commissions multiplied: the Joint Lutheran-Catholic Study Commission (1965); the Joint Working Group between the Catholic Church and the World Council of Churches (1965); the Anglican Roman Catholic International Commission (ARCIC, 1966); the Joint Commission between the Roman Catholic Church and the World Methodist Council (1966); Theological Conversations between Representatives of the Russian Orthodox Church and the Roman Catholic Church (1967); the Joint International Commission between the Catholic Church and the Coptic Orthodox Church (1974); the Commission for International Dialogue between the Ecumenical Advisory Council of the Disciples of Christ and the Roman Catholic Church (1977); the Joint International Commission for Theological Dialogue between the Roman Catholic Church and the Orthodox Church (1979); the International Conversations between the World Baptist Alliance and Roman Catholics (1984); and so on. Thus, from 1968 on, the papacy committed itself to a global dialogue within organized ecumenism. That year, in fact, nine Catholic theologians officially joined the Faith and Constitution commission of the WCC. The first three documents prepared by this enlarged commission concerned baptism, Eucharist, and ministry; they were published in 1974 by Les Presses de Taizé. The problem lay in getting the results of theological reflection to touch the lives of individuals and communities. The documents issued by the numerous national and international commissions had to be truly "received," or else they would remain so many dead letters. And the feeling grew, in the 1970s, that this reception had failed. At the heart of the Churches, cleavages became apparent that had nothing to do with traditional doctrinal differences. In spite of the papal declaration of June 1984 of the Catholic Church's irreversible commitment to the ecumenical movement, was the movement about to die?

Ecumenism Between Prophetism and the New Evangelization. While the theologians were working in the background on furthering unity, the papacy was taking prophetic initiatives. The United Nations had proclaimed 1986 an International Year of Peace, and JOHN PAUL II addressed all believers on 25 January, urging them to organize a day of prayer for peace at Assisi. The interreligious outlook behind his appeal became concrete in March, when he visited the Great Synagogue in Rome, the first visit ever made by a pope to a synagogue. Despite "the fear that the papal initiative might eclipse other religious manifestations scheduled on the occasion of the year of peace," the WCC called on member Churches to participate in the meeting at Assisi. On 27 October, close to two hundred representatives of a dozen religions responded to John Paul II's invitation. After listening to a papal address on the theme of peace, each group withdrew to a different place to pray, and then assembled in front of the upper basilica of St. Francis and took part in a ceremony in which sixty-three religious leaders, from some thirty countries and representing nearly three billion people, all covened together, one in intention.

The Assisi meeting did not signal that Roman ecumenism had dissolved into an interreligious dialogue.

Rather, it seemed to have reinforced the moral authority of the papacy in the Christian world, with the notable exception of certain Catholic circles that affirmed their identity only by the systematic rejection of everything John Paul II might say or do. Recognizing that only the Bishop of Rome was able to bring about an event like Assisi, Dr. Runcie, archbishop of Canterbury and primate of the Anglican communion, expressed his hope that the pope would place his ministry at the service of all Christians. Dr. Runcie was received at the Vatican in the autumn of 1989. Twenty-five years after *Unitatis Redintegratio*, John Paul II seized the opportunity to say once again that he considered ecumenical engagement not only a priority but an obligation, incumbent on him particularly by virtue of his pastoral responsibility. In his travels, he never fails to meet the leaders of the various Christian communities and to take part in interconfessional celebrations. But given new impetus by prophetism, Roman ecumenism increasingly finds itself clashing with competing plans for the new EVANGELIZATION of EUROPE.

Before the collapse of the Berlin Wall, it was not clear that the two projects might be in competition, much less in opposition. During his trip to Scandinavia, in 1989, the first Slavic pope associated the unification of Europe with a new evangelization still in keeping with an ecumenical perspective: it was a question of rediscovering together "the faith transmitted to the saints once and for all." In Oslo, John Paul II declared, for instance: "Protestants and Catholics in Norway possess a common heritage. The Gospel was brought here centuries ago, long before the events of the 16th century." According to the pope, the rediscovery of a common heritage that existed before the schism was a challenge not only for Anglicans and Protestants, but also for Catholics. To take up the challenge was to proceed together to a rereading of history, or, as John Paul II wrote on the occasion of the fifth centenary of the birth of Luther, a "clarification of history," which "must go hand in hand with the dialogue we are undertaking today, in the quest for unity." Similarly, in the presence of Dr. Runcie and with his approval, he invited Catholics and Anglicans to rediscover together the faith preached by St. Augustine—at the risk of having to redefine the ecclesial primacy of the bishop of Rome, which was certainly not understood in the 6th century in the way it was in the 20th, even after Vatican II.

Then came the collapse of the Soviet Empire. By suddenly opening up an unexpected field of action to the Catholic communities of Central Europe, Lithuania, Belarus, and Ukraine, this extraordinary event gave the project for a new evangelization a meaning far different from the one John Paul II had proposed to the Scandinavians and Anglicans before the sudden disappearance of the German Democratic Republic. In March 1990, the meeting of the central committee of the WCC showed that ecumenism was, to adopt Jean Bourdarias's phrase, "a victim of the upheavals in the East." While one of the co-presidents of the WCC, Marga Buhrig, was indignant that the Catholic Church did not recognize "the diversity of theological currents," the Orthodox bishop of Poland, Jeremiah, was disturbed by the confrontations between Orthodox and Catholics of the Greek rite in western Ukraine, as well as the "massive missionary offensive" of the Catholic Church in Eastern Europe.

In 1991, John Paul II sent out more and more messages in an attempt to ease tensions. On 5 June, for example, he informed the Orthodox of his "very profound compassion on the occasion of the painful trials that the Orthodox Church has recently suffered in Poland. I think with sorrow of the criminal fire that destroyed the Orthodox sanctuary of the Transfiguration of the Lord on Mt. Grabarka, and of the robbery committed in the monastery of St. Onuphrius at Jableczna. These acts of sacrilege provoke a profound grief in my heart and the heart of Catholics. Everything that disturbs the fraternal life of Christians comes from the Evil One." Instead of a common clarification of history, a whole forgotten world was violently reemerging.

The pope's messages in no way appeased tensions, especially since in April 1991 the Holy See appointed two Latin bishops in Russia, two in Belarus, and one in Kazakhstan. The Holy Synod of the Russian Orthodox Church saw this not as a restoration of former sees but as a creation of new dioceses. It denounced what it considered "attempts [. . .] to establish parallel ecclesiastical structures on our canonical territory." It declared "with bitterness" that in these conditions the Russian Orthodox Church could not take part in the Special Assembly for Europe of the SYNOD OF BISHOPS, to which John Paul II had invited all the Eastern communities. Out of solidarity, the Orthodox Churches of Bulgaria, Greece, Romania, and Serbia likewise refused to send delegates.

In December 1991, the Catholic bishops of all Europe met for the first time without restrictions of any kind: no longer was there a "Church of silence." And for the first time in the history of the Roman synod, Orthodox, Armenian, and Protestant delegates took part in the discussions. Yet what could have been a grand moment of ecumenism was disturbed by a charge leveled by the representative of the patriarch of Constantinople. Bishop Papagheorgiou deplored, en bloc, the "violences" (the occupation of places of Orthodox worship by Catholics of the Greek rite in Ukraine and Romania), the creation of Latin dioceses in Russia, John Paul II's positions in favor of Croatia, the accusations of compromise with the communist regimes made by VATICAN RADIO against the Orthodox hierarchies of Sofia and Bucharest, etc. Immediately after him, Jean Fisher, general secretary of the Conference of Christian Churches (an umbrella group of the European Protestant and Orthodox churches), attacked the "rush to the East," the "competition" and "proselytism" in which not only the Catholics but also, as Fisher emphasized, the Baptists, the Methodists, and other Protestant communities were engaging. According to Henri Tincq, on that occasion ecumenism had "one of its most serious crises since the Vatican II council."

Ecumenism is no longer threatened by indifference, as in the 1970s, nor by nostalgia for Lenin or Salazar, as in the 1980s, but rather by a massive tendency on the part of resurgent nationalistic movements to "reclaim the sacred," in the words of the then bishop of LeMans, Georges Gilson. More than ever before, the non-Orthodox are virtual strangers in countries like Russia, Greece, and Serbia, while Poland, Slovakia, and Croatia are known simply as "Catholic nations." From there to defining the war between Serbia and Croatia as a religious war is merely a step, which some have no hesitation in taking.

Ecumenism Without Unity. In these circumstances, is it right to speak of the failure of ecumenism? The patriarch of Moscow, Alexis II, does not think so. In the declaration in which he refused to send delegates to the synod of Rome, he insists on explaining: "We have traveled a long road together, loyally. The progress in our theological dialogues is evident. There are many other promising signs of mutual understanding. A great number of our hierarchs, clergy, and lay members have set up good personal contacts. That is why we do not want this declaration to be considered a rupture." In its reply, the Holy See gave the assurance that "the reorganization of Church structures and the appointment of apostolic administrators for certain territories of the Soviet Union did not carry with it the slightest intention of proselytism. The Holy See has great esteem and a great respect for the Russian Orthodox Church."

But in this same reply Rome declared that "the 'missionary' activity of the Catholic Church and the demands of a 'new evangelization,' considered imperative at the dawn of the third millennium, do not disregard ecumenism, but rather intend to promote it. This is clearly stated in the recent encyclical of John Paul II, *Redemptoris missio*, concerning the permanent validity of the missionary mandate." This time, the new evangelization is identified with the Catholic Church's missionary activity in Europe. And when the Holy See declares that the mission will be able to promote ecumenism, one may legitimately ask if it uses the term in the same sense as Patriarch Alexis or the WCC.

Well before the revolution of 1989, people knew that Christian division was not a matter only of doctrinal misunderstanding or moral reaction. Perhaps the time has come to recognize, like Émile Poulat, that "the concept of unity, that simple word, has not, and cannot have, the same meaning for the Roman Church, in the Protestant Churches, and in the Orthodox tradition [. . .] If ecumenism is our daily portion, unity remains an eschatological promise."

Marie-Christine Devedeux
Régis Ladous

Bibliography

Aubert, R. *Le Saint-Siège et l'union des Églises*, Paris, 1947.

Barot, M. *Le mouvement oecuménique*, Paris, 1967.

de Lubac, H. *Églises particulières dans l'Église universelle*, 1971.

Desseaux, J. *Dialogues théologiques et accords oecuméniques*, Paris, 1982.

Fouilloux, E. *Les Catholiques et l'unité chrétienne du XIXe au XXe siècle*, 1982.

Frost, F. "Oecuménisme," *Catholicisme*, 9 (1982), 1501–35 and 10 (1985), 1–21 [bibliography].

Mayeur, J. M., ed. *Histoire du christianisme*, XII, Paris, 1990.

Villain, M. *Introduction à l'oecuménisme*, Paris, 1964.

ELECTIONS, PAPAL. See **Conclave.**

ELEUTHERIUS. *(d. 189).*

The end of the pontificate of this twelfth successor of Peter has been recorded by Eusebius of Caesarea as having occurred during the tenth year of the reign of Emperor Commodius (189), a date which has very generally been accepted. According to the *Liber pontificalis* his episcopate lasted for fifteen years, three months, and two days, and even if Eusebius did not give him more than thirteen years, the general chronology of the popes confirmed his pontificate from 175 to 189.

Eleutherius was probably of Greek origin, from Nicopolis, in Epirus. According to Hegesippus, quoted by Eusebius, he may have been a DEACON of Pope ANICETUS. As a successor of Pope SOTER, he had to intervene in numerous areas of interest to the internal life of the Church. Following Soter, he confirmed the plan of placing Easter on the Sunday after the fourteenth day of Nisan. His attitude in regard to the Montanists was little known at a moment when that doctrine troubled Asia and spread to the West even into the Christian community in Rome. It was in reference to this severe problem that in 177 he received the priest Irenaeus who had come with letters from Christians and martyrs of Lyon. Irenaeus asked him to put an end to the latent conflict that was tearing apart the communities and damaged the unity of the Church. We have no record of the attitude of Eleutherius. In one of his polemic writings, Tertullian attacked a bishop who appears to have been at a certain time in favor of Montanism but it is not clear whether it was Eleutherius. Probably, Eleutherius was arguing for an institutional hierarchy rather than for charismatic prophets. A decree was attributed to him that was directed against the Gnostics and against the Marcionites, according to which Christians should not despise any kind of food. It was merely a restatement of a precept that for a long time had eliminated any distinction in the area of food. A confusion about the tradition had put him in touch with a certain Lucius, king of the Bretons supposed to have been sent by missionaries. With Eleutherius the list of bishops of Rome supplied by Irenaeus came to an end. His feast is celebrated on 26 April. He is believed to be buried in the Vatican, near St. Peter. There is, however, no proof of this.

Jean Pierre Martin

Bibliography

Bardy, G. *Catholicisme hier, aujourd'hui, demain*, Paris, 1956, IV, 1–2.
Botte, *DHGE*, 1963, XV, 147–8.
Clerval, *DTC*, 1924, IV, 2, 2319–2320.
Eusebius, *HE*, IV, 22, 2; V, 3, 4; 5, 9; 6, 4; 22.
Irenaeus, *Adv. haeres*, III. 3.3.
Weltin, E. G. *NCE*, V, 265.

ENCYCLICAL. The common translation of the expression *litterae encyclicae* means, according to the Greek etymology, circular letters. Originally the term referred to correspondence between archbishops and bishops or between them and members of their administration. In its present use, the term refers exclusively to a form of expression of the pontifical MAGISTERIUM. The letters sent by bishops to their diocesan clergy have come to be called pastoral letters. The encyclical is a particular category of apostolic letter. The major characteristic of *litterae encyclicae* is that they are generally addressed "to patriarchs, primates, archbishops, bishops, and other ordinaries at peace and in communion with the Apostolic See." They can be directed specifically to the bishops and the faithful of a particular country and published in the national language. This was the case under the pontificate of LEO XIII for the "Ralliement" (*Au milieu des sollicitudes*, [In the midst of concern], 20 February 1892), and under that of PIUS XI concerning Fascism in Italy (*Non abbiamo bisogno* [We have no need], 29 June 1931) and Nazism in Germany (*Mit brennender Sorge*, [With searing anxiety], 21 March 1937). It is worth noting that in some cases the pope supplies the main text or portions of the encyclical himself, but *litterae encyclicae* are usually composed in Latin (until 1967, it was under the responsibility of the Secretariat of Latin Letters and the SECRETARIAT OF BRIEFS TO PRINCES), which more and more often has been doubled with an Italian version from which the text is gradually put into its final form. At times, an initial Latin draft followed by drafts of some sections in Italian resulted in the official version in Latin. That is how the encyclical *Rerum novarum* (15 May 1891) was written. Like the BULLS and other apostolic letters, *litterae encyclicae* are named after their first two or three words and so pass on to posterity under the form of an *incipit*.

Litterae encyclicae do not promulgate new definitions. Proclamation of the dogma of the Immaculate Conception was made after the publication by Pius IX of the encyclical *Ubi primum* (2 February 1849). But *litterae encyclicae* condemn errors globally, remind or reveal to Catholics the truths of sound doctrine, offer remedies and analyses, and exalt model figures like the Virgin Mary.

The first *litterae encyclicae*, in the sense in which we understand them today, date from the time of BENEDICT XIV (1740–58). The number of encyclicals began to grow beginning with the pontificate of Leo XIII, as did the number of those to whom they were addressed. The encyclical *Veritatis splendor* (The splendor of truth), published by JOHN PAUL II on 5 October 1993, was addressed to the whole world. Since Leo XIII, it has been customary for a recently elected pope to publish *litterae encyclicae* during the year following his election. The date of their publication usually coincides with a liturgical commemoration that clarifies their purpose. Thus, the encyclical *Rerum novarum* (*De condicione opificum*) was published on the feast of St. Joseph, whom PAUL VI proclaimed patron saint of workers in 1964. Commemoration of the encyclical *Rerum novarum* by the successors of Leo XIII, from Pius XI to John Paul II, has almost always taken place on 15 May, with the first words marking the years passed since 1891 (*Quadragesimo anno; Mater et magistra; Ottogesima adveniens*). *Centesimus annus* was published on 1 May 1991.

Encyclicals do not have the weight of EX CATHEDRA pronouncements. But they do indicate a direction binding on all Catholics. The privilege of INFALLIBILITY can be attached to them, even though they belong to the ordinary magisterium.

List of Principal Encyclicals.

BENEDICT XIV (1749–1758)
Inter Omnigenas
    February 2, 1744: baptism
Vix pervenit
    November 1, 1745: usury
LEO XII (1823–1829)
Ubi primum
    May 5, 1824: indifference
PIUS VIII (1829–1830)
Traditi humilitati nostrae
    May 24, 1829: against secret societies
GREGORY XVI (1831–1846)
Mirari vos
    August 15, 1832: indifferentism and rationalism
Singulari vos
    June 25, 1834: condemnation of Lamennais
Commissum divinitus
    May 17, 1835: the impediments to marriage

Dum acerbissimas
   September 26, 1835: against hermesianism
Inter praecipuas
   May 6, 1844: translations (versions) of Holy Scripture
Probe nostis
   September 18, 1844: Holy Scripture
PIUS IX (1846–1878)
Qui pluribus
   November 9, 1846: rationalism and INFALLIBILITY
In suprema Petri sede
   January 6, 1848: the Orthodox and Church unity
Ubi primum
   February 2, 1849: the Immaculate Conception
Inter multiplices
   March 21, 1853: the liturgy—imposition of the Roman missal
Amantissimus
   April 8, 1862: Catholicism of the East
Quanto conficiamur
   August 10, 1863: indifferentism
Quanta cura
   December 8, 1864: socialism—the Church's independence from the State
Ubi nos
   May 15, 1871: the Church's temporary possessions
Vix dum a nobis
   March 7, 1874: papal infallibility and the Church of Austria
Quod nunquam
   February 5, 1875: against the KULTURKAMPF (anticlerical laws)
LEO XIII (1878–1903)
Quod apostolici muneris
   December 28, 1878: the rights of men in society
Aeterni Patris
   August 4, 1879: philosophy—recalling the authority of Thomas Aquinas
Arcanum divinae
   February 10, 1880: Christian marriage
Grande munus
   September 30, 1880: the cult of Saints Cyril and Methodius
Diuturnum illud
   June 29, 1881: civil society
Nobilissima Gallorum gens
   1884: French Catholics and politics
Humanum genus
   April 20, 1884: secret societies
Immortale Dei
   November 1, 1885: the aims of civil society—definition of the Church as the perfect society (*societas perfecta*)
Libertas praestantissimum
   June 20, 1888: natural law and the relationship between freedom of religion and human dignity

Quamquam pluries
   August 15, 1889: Saint Joseph
Sapientiae christianae
   January 10, 1890: the relationship between the Church and the political parties
Rerum novarum
   May 15, 1891: the conditions of labor—presentation of social doctrine
Octobri mense
   September 22, 1891: Virgin Mary, our mediator
Au milieux des sollicitudes (In the midst of cares)
   1892: a suggestion of solidarity to the Republic to French Catholics
Providentissimus Deus
   November 18, 1893: interpretation of the Bible
Satis cognitum
   June 29, 1896: Church unity
Apostolicae curae
   September 13, 1896: Anglican ordinations
Fidentem piumque
   September 20, 1896: meditation of Mary
Divinum illud
   May 9, 1897: the Holy Trinity and the Holy Spirit
Annum sacrum
   May 25, 1899: Christ the King and devotion to the Sacred Heart
Graves de communi
   January 18, 1901: Christian Democracy
Mirae caritatis
   May 28, 1902: the Eucharist
PIUS X (1903–1914)
Ad diem illud
   February 2, 1904: the meditation of the Virgin Mary
Il fermo proposito
   June 11, 1905: Christians and politics
Vehementer nos
   February 11, 1906: a condemnation of the separation (in France) between the church and the state
Pieni l'anima
   1906: the formation of the clergy and the place of St. Thomas Aquinas
Gravissimo officio
   August 10, 1906: the prohibition of associations of worship established by the French government
Pascendi dominici
   September 8, 1907: modernism and the method of religious science
Jamdudum
   May 24, 1911: against the separation of church and state in Portugal
BENEDICT XV (1914–1922)
Ad beatissimi Apostolorum
   November 1, 1914: the progress of theology
Maximum illud
   November 30, 1919: the missions

Pacem Dei munus
May 23, 1920: diplomatic relations
Spiritus Paraclitus
September 15, 1920: Holy Scripture
PIUS XI (1922–1939)
Ubi arcano
December 23, 1922: the peace of Christ in the kingdom of Christ
Studiorum ducem
June 29, 1923: Thomism
Ecclesiam Dei
November 12, 1923: St. Josaphat and the Christian East
Maximam gravissimamque
January 18, 1924: French diocesan associations
Quas primas
December 11, 1925: exaltation of Christ the King
Rerum Ecclesiae
February 28, 1926: the missions
Iniquis afflictisque
1926: the situation in Mexico
Mortalium animos
June 1, 1928: Christian unity
Rerum orientalium
September 8, 1928: promotion of studies of Eastern Christianity
Rappresentati in terra
December 23, 1929: the Christian education of the young
Divini illius Magistri
December 31, 1929: the education of the family
Casti connubii
December 31, 1930: marriage
Quadragesimo anno
May 15, 1931: commemoration of the 40th anniversary of the encyclical *Rerum novarum* (May 15, 1891)
Non abbiamo bisogno
June 29, 1931: the dangers of fascism
Ad catholici sacerdotii
December 20, 1935: holy orders and the priesthood
Divini redemptoris
March 19, 1937: social justice
Mit brennender Sorge
March 21, 1937; dangers of Nazism
Firmissimam constantiam
March 28, 1937: against abuse of power
PIUS XII (1939–1958)
Summi pontificatus
October 20, 1939: the relationship between natural law and human rights
Mystici Corporis
June 29, 1943: the Church of Christ

Divino afflante Spiritu
September 30, 1943: Holy Scripture and its interpretation
Orientalis Ecclesiae decus
April 9, 1944: the Churches of the East
Mediator Dei
November 20, 1947: the liturgy and the priesthood
Humani generis
August 12, 1950: the relationship between philosophy and theology
Evangelii praecones
1951: the missions and indigenous Churches
Mediator Dei
March 20, 1951: the liturgy
Sempiternus Rex
September 8, 1951: The Council of Chalcedon
Orientales Ecclesias
December 15, 1952: the Eastern Churches
Fulgens corona
September 8, 1953: Centenary of the definition of the Immaculate Conception
Sacra Virginitas
March 25, 1954: marriage and virginity
Ad Sinarum Gentem
October 7, 1954: the Church in China
Ad caeli Reginam
October 11, 1954: the dignity of the Virgin Mary
Musicae sacrae
December 25, 1955: the liturgy and sacred music
Haurietis aquas
May 15, 1956: the cult of the Sacred Heart and the mediation of the Virgin Mary
Fidei donum
1957: the diocesan bishops and the missions
JOHN XXIII (1958–1963)
Ad Petri cathedram
June 29, 1959: truth, unity, and peace
Sacerdotii nostri primordia
July 31, 1959: the Curé of Ars
Grata recordatio
September 26, 1959: the Rosary
Princeps pastorum
November 28, 1959: the missions
Mater et magistra
May 15, 1961: for the 70th anniversary of *Rerum Novarum*
Aeterna Dei sapientia
November 11, 1961: Leo the Great and the unity of the Church
Paenitentian agere
July 1, 1962: the preparation to the council by doing penance
Pacem in terris
April 11, 1963: peace

PAUL VI (1963–1978)

Ecclesiam suam

August 6, 1964: the Church in dialogue with the world

Mense maio

April 29, 1965: for the council and peace

Mysterium fidei

September 3, 1965: the Eucharist

Christi matri

September 15, 1966: peace, particularly in Vietnam

Populorum progressio

February 26, 1967: development of peoples

Sacerdotalis coelibatus

June 24, 1967: the priests' celibacy

Humanae vitae

July 25, 1968: birth control

JOHN PAUL II (1978–   )

Redemptor hominis

March 4, 1979: redemption and human dignity

Dives in misericordia

November 30, 1980: the mercy of God

Laborem exercens

September 14, 1981: labor

Slavorum apostoli

June 2, 1985: Saints Cyril and Methodius

Dominum et vivificantem

May 18, 1986: the Holy Spirit

Redemptoris Mater

March 25, 1987: the Virgin Mary

Sollicitudo rei socialis

December 30, 1987: social doctrine

Redemptoris missio

December 7, 1990: the missions

Centesimus annus

May 1, 1991: commentary on the centennial of *Rerum novarum*

Veritatis splendor

October 9, 1993: morality

Evangelium Vitae

March 25, 1995: the value of human life

Philippe Levillain

Bibliography

Carlen, C., ed. *The Papal Encyclicals 1740–1981*, 5 vols., Raleigh, N.C., 1981.

Denzinger, H. *Enchiridion symbolorum, definitionum et declarationum de rebus fidei et morum*, 32nd ed., annotated by A. Schönmetzer, Barcelona–Freiburg im Breisgau, 1964.

La documentation catholique. Tables générales, 4 fasc., 1960–90.

Epp, R., Lefebvre, C., and Metz, R. *Le Droit et les institutions de l'Église catholique latine de la fin du XVIIIe siècle à 1978. Sources et institutions*, Paris, 1981.

Hinschius, P. *Das Kirchenrecht der Katholiken und Protestanten in Deutschland. System des katholischen Kirchenrechts*, 3, Berlin, 1883.

Lijdsmam, B. *Introductio in ius canonicum*, 2 vols., Hilversum, 1924–9.

Martini, V. *Les Cardinaux et la Curie. Tribunaux et offices, la vacance du Siège apostolique*, Paris, 1930.

Moersdorf, K. *Lehrbuch des Kirchenrechts auf Grund des Codex iuris canonici*, Munich-Vienna, 1964.

Pesendorfer, M. *Partikulares Gesetz und partikularer Gesetzgeber im geltenden lateinischen Kirchenrecht*, Vienna, 1975.

Raulx, *Recueil des allocutions consistoriales, encycliques et autres lettres apostoliques des souverains pontifes Clément XII, Benoît XIV, Pie VI, Pie VII, Léon XII, Grégoire XVI et Pie IX, citées dans l'encyclique et le Syllabus du 8 décembre 1864*, Paris, 1865.

ENLIGHTENMENT. "The Enlightenment," a translation of the German term *Aufklärung*, describes a massive European movement of ideas as diversified as the social and religious contexts in which it flourished in the 18th century. While the term has been linked with anti-Catholic assaults upon the Church's authority and tradition, as found in the satirical blasts of Denis Diderot (1713–84), Voltaire (1694–1778) and other French *philosophes*, it also describes the maturation of educational and religious reform that originated in an earlier age. Recent historical studies support the view that the 18th century witnessed a true Catholic Enlightenment, marked by enthusiastic commitment to critical and free scientific inquiry. This extended at times to the doctrinal and scriptural arenas, and brought its adherents into conflict with ecclesiastical authorities, including some of the eight popes of the period. However, many of its supporters were able to reconcile their faith with "enlightened" ideas and avoid major confrontations with Church officials.

The battles for religious ideas and ideals throughout the 18th century were drawn up on theological and political fronts that occasionally became indistinguishable from each other. These conflicts preoccupied the papacy throughout the period. Many papal skirmishes were centered on quarrels with Jansenists, who were ardent supporters of the popes when it came to a Catholic political alliance against Protestantism; however, Jansenist theological teaching had come under censure and had been condemned in 1653 by INNOCENT X (1574–1655). Originating in 17th-century France as a religious reform movement centered on Augustinian theories of grace, JANSENISM had contributed much to political and cultural debate in the changing intellectual geography of 18th-century Europe. United in their antagonism toward JESUITS, whom they accused of laxity in moral and sacramental teaching, the Jansenists represented spiritual athleticism, theological pessimism, and moral rigorism. Their leaders engaged in various political disputes, becoming in effect a "Jansenist party" that included some of the most eminent and edifying clergy, monks, and religious women in France. The condemnation of Jansenism by CLEMENT XI in 1713 with the bull *Unigenitus* ushered in an era of spiritual and temporal confrontations between popes and rulers that would culminate in a universal suppression of the Society of Jesus by the FRANCISCAN pope, CLEMENT XIV, in 1774.

Catholic proponents of the Enlightenment, most of them intellectuals, displayed common interests and attitudes despite diversified backgrounds. Like their Protestant counterparts, they advocated the use of reason, observation, and experiment as methods of intellectual research. They were equally concerned with placing this knowledge at the service of their humanitarian ideals of justice, equality, and tolerance. This tolerance did not, however, extend to the Society of Jesus, to which they were largely inimical, and whose members were perceived as too traditional in their pedagogical methods. It was thought that the Jesuit monopoly on higher education prevented the dissemination of fresh ideas. However, to paint all Jesuits with the brush of obscurantism would be an oversimplification. Because of their contacts at the university level, many Jesuits were forward-looking and played a major role in promoting the Catholic Enlightenment, especially in areas of penal reform, the arts, mathematics, and natural sciences.

Open-minded in matters of academic inquiry, Catholic Enlightenment leaders endorsed freedom in the use of the best scholarly texts available, even if such writings were of Jansenist or Protestant origin. Toward the end of the century, for example, German Catholic UNIVERSITIES and colleges affected by the suppression of the Jesuits were revising their syllabi and teaching methods based on methods and programs used in Protestant centers of higher education that they had visited.

The Catholic "enlightened" scholars displayed a new historical consciousness based on acclaimed critical studies such as those of the Italian theologian Lodovico Muratori (1672–1750), and the French Maurist scholar Jean Mabillon (1631–1707). As a result, they sought to establish courses in church history at the colleges. Their reforming educational ideals found allies among Italian and French Jansenists, who shared their eagerness to make biblical and liturgical texts available in the vernacular. Like the Jansenists, they mistrusted affective piety based on dubious historical tradition. By purifying breviaries and prayerbooks of "superstitious" accretions, they endeavored to recreate a more authentic, "rational" Christian devotion.

As a European intellectual movement, the Enlightenment peaked in the latter half of the 18th century. Among Protestants, it became more stridently anti-Catholic, attacking the obscurantism and dogmas of the Church of Rome, as well as assailing the institutions of monastic life and the discipline of clerical celibacy. Among Catholics, it resulted in a growing antipathy toward Jesuits, papal temporal power, and church institutions that seemed "useless," such as monasticism. Likewise, it allowed for a transforming modernization of the Austrian church by the Emperor Joseph II, whose edict of toleration in 1781 became a model for similar statements by French and German rulers at the end of the century.

Reform was the order of the day, and it came to rest on the old privileges of the Church, like the right of sanctuary or exemptions of ecclesiastics from taxes, military service or secular court trials. In an age when absolute monarchs were tottering on the brink of fiscal calamity and being confronted with new republican movements, it was in the interest of reform that the "most Catholic" powers in Europe shored up their own prestige by diminishing and limiting papal authority in temporal affairs. Thus, the anti-papal Gallican Articles, approved in 1682 by the French Assembly of the Clergy, a meeting mobilized by an angry Louis XIV (1638–1715) in the wake of a dispute with INNOCENT XI over the latter's refusal to enter a "Holy League" against the Turks. These four articles paid lip service to papal primacy in spiritual matters but denied the Pope temporal authority and subordinated his role to that of a general council. By the beginning of the 18th century, the papacy's influence was greatly weakened. Popes of this period publicly professed political neutrality, but they often found themselves bobbing between warring powers whose Catholic loyalties to Rome shifted with the changing political tides of rulers and prime ministers. As one scholar has noted, the popes of the Enlightenment were "humane, comfortable, paternal, considerate" (Chadwick), and generally ineffectual. They projected an image of general good humor and benevolence in sharp contrast to the fiery Jansenist polemicists calling for their conversion, and the arrogant heads-of-state demanding their compliance.

The profile of the 18th-century popes reveals anything but a uniform picture. While all were Italians, not one was a Roman. Two pontiffs, BENEDICT XIII (1724–30) and Clement XIV (1769–74), were friar-monks at the time of their election. The cardinal-deacon candidate who became CLEMENT XI was ordained a priest just prior to the papal conclave, and the last pope of the period, PIUS VI (1775–9), had to be consecrated a bishop before he could assume the Chair of Peter. With the exception of Clement XI, who was fifty-one when elected—among the youngest in papal history—all the pontiffs were old men, with an average age of sixty-four at the time of their election, ensuring fairly short pontificates.

The average length of conclaves in the 18th century was just under three months; the shortest, electing INNO-

CENT XIII (1721–4), went a few days over five weeks, while the longest took six months and 255 ballots to produce its compromise candidate, BENEDICT XIV (1740–58), whose long rule would reflect wise and "enlightened" leadership.

All the popes of this period were devout men, but that does not mean they were good popes. In fact, the holiest among them stands out as the worst pope of the century. Benedict XIII, the stern and ascetic Dominican friar, proved to be a compassionate, able pastor to the people of Rome. He was the first modern pontiff to place spiritual matters over temporal. That meant his papacy was administered by a secretary-chancellor from his former diocese who turned out to be unscrupulous and disreputable and brought down upon Benedict the ire of the cardinals and the Roman people. Finally, the pontiffs of the Enlightenment overcame the nefarious presence of nepotism and the role of the "cardinal-nephew," or scurrilous advisor, in favor of the services of a SECRETARY OF STATE to handle pontifical political affairs. These generally managed the growing influence of Catholic governments over the papacy and national churches in an upright, honest fashion. All in all, this was an age of papal concordats, condemnations, and ENCYCLICALS.

CLEMENT XI (G. Albani, 1649–1721) had a long and largely ineffective pontificate, undermined by his role in the Jansenist and Chinese rites controversies, as well as his humiliating military surrender to the Austrians in the War of Spanish succession (1701–13). Pressured by Louis XIV, in 1708 Clement condemned a book of moral reflections on the Gospels by a French Jansenist, the Oratorian Pasquier Quesnel (1634–1719). Five years later he followed up with a condemnation of Jansenist propositions in the famous bull, *Unigenitus Dei Filius*, and ignored the entreaties of the movement's leaders to be heard. By 1718, Clement had excommunicated several of the Jansenists, who ignored the condemnation.

While he was committed to promoting the missionary expansion of Catholicism, Clement was forced to deal with the matter of Jesuit adaptation and integration of Chinese customs in their preaching and liturgies, a problem that had created many disputes among friars and theologians. The missionary methods of the Jesuits proved more successful in China, since they were seeking to promote a fully Chinese Christianity rather than a European import. The controversy had become widely known when Jesuits were attacked as promoting idolatry in one of the *Provincial Letters* of the Jansenist Blaise Pascal (1623–62), and the whole rites controversy was caught up the wider religious battle for "true Catholicism." In 1704, under mounting pressure from DOMINICANS and others, not wanting the missions to be labeled as superstitious, Clement condemned much of the Jesuit practice in the Chinese rites, inaugurating a revolution in the missions. The anticipated resistance to the decree's implementa-

tion, followed by the persecution and expulsion of missionaries on the part of the Chinese government, were only the beginning. Distraught missioners witnessed the destruction of a century's labors and the banning of Christianity from Chinese soil. Clement's action would be reversed only in 1939, by PIUS XII (1939–58).

Innocent XIII (Conti, 1655–1724) had a brief and unproductive rule, during which he reaffirmed Clement's condemnations of Jansenism. Educated by Jesuits, he nevertheless forbade them from accepting novices until he was certain they had accepted the papal ban on the use of Chinese rites. He was followed by the pious, politically-inexperienced Dominican, Benedict XIII (Orsini, 1649–1730), whose six-year reign was disastrous. Against the protests of many cardinals, Benedict retained his episcopal see at Benevento and brought into the papal household his former chancellor and secretary, Niccolò Coscia, who isolated the pope from the cardinals while he grew rich on bribes and the sale of church benefices. Under Benedict, the financial affairs of the Papal States were neglected and brought to the verge of collapse. He attended instead to a Tridentine, Borromean reform of clerical mores and church discipline, canonizing several saints, and pastoral concerns. Despite this, he was unpopular with the Roman people.

The ten-year pontificate of CLEMENT XII (Corsini, 1652–1740) was generally a failure. Elected at the age of seventy-eight, Clement was often bedridden, and became totally blind from the second year of his pontificate, after which he relied on a cardinal-nephew to oversee pontifical business. On the plus side, Clement brought the "evil genius" of BENEDICT XIII, Coscia, to trial and imprisonment for abuses of power. Thanks to his family wealth, he was the patron of many beautification projects throughout Rome, including the famous Trevi Fountain. He also enlarged the collections of the Vatican Library.

With the election of Benedict XIV (Lambertini, 1675–1758), a true man of the Enlightenment was chosen for the See of Peter, a man in whom the changing nature of the papacy came to light. While the two Benedicts of this period shared common episcopal experiences, Lambertini was poles apart from his predecessor in style and practice. A genial personality, an able and attractive diplomat who was also a gifted theologian, lawyer, and administrator, Benedict XIV was known for his wit, almost clownish and sometimes crude behavior, and self-deprecating sense of humor. As the interminable conclave prior to his election brought the cardinals to the point of exhaustion, he is said to have remarked, "Do you wish to have a saint? Take Gatti. A politician? Take Aldovrandi. But if you wish a good man, take me!" The electors could have done far worse than elect the man who up until the last ballot had not received a single vote! Conciliatory yet politically realistic and moderate, Benedict surrounded himself with wise advisors, and approached international affairs by signing many concordats containing concessions that mollified Catholic sovereigns. He reduced the number of Church feast days, updated and streamlined the Index of prohibited books (1758), and ended a ban on writings defending Copernican astronomy. He mandated the reform of the Breviary to rid it of legends, supported the rights of indigenous peoples in Latin America, and exempted "mixed" marriages (between Catholics and non-Catholics) from the Tridentine canonical form.

In an attempt to promote clerical and episcopal formation, he wrote what is considered to be the first encyclical. *Ubi primum* (1740) was a circular addressed to bishops worldwide, dealing with their episcopal duties and responsibilities. Theologically and spiritually, Benedict's policies followed those of his predecessors, but many Protestant and agnostic scholars admired his breadth of intelligence and academic interests. Voltaire dedicated one his tragedies, *Mahomet*, to Benedict, whom he respected. This pontiff's lengthy treatment of beatifications and canonizations (1738–48) remained the classic treatment on this topic for many years. For all his tact, geniality, and conciliatory political moves, Benedict was unable to hold back the tide rising in what one writer has called "the shark pool of eighteenth-century power politics" (Duffy).

What to do with the Jesuits became a central concern as the century wore on. A month before his death in 1758, Benedict initiated an investigation of the Portuguese Jesuits because he had received many complaints about their laxity and commercial enterprises. When CLEMENT XIII (Rezzonico, 1693–1769) came to the throne, he took up the investigation of charges against the Society, which had now become a campaign offensive of the Bourbons in France, Spain, Naples, and Parma. When an unscrupulous Portuguese minister confiscated Jesuit properties and assets, then imprisoned and deported over 1,000 of its members, Clement protested the action and defended the accomplishments of the Society, to no avail. In spite of the pope's invocation of bulls of excommunication condemning the efforts of secular rulers to control the Church, the Bourbons proceeded with the destruction of the Jesuit order.

CLEMENT XIV (Ganganelli, 1705–74), first pope to be born in this Enligtenment century, was a Franciscan friar who had been friendly to Jesuits prior to his election, but his place in history has been secured for his universal suppression of the order in 1774. During a contentious conclave in which the Catholic powers threatened to veto any candidate who favored the Jesuits, Ganganelli gave the impression that he thought a suppression was canonically feasible and would not oppose it. On the eve of his election, a cardinal-observer wrote in his diary, "No one is more capable of doing more good in these times. No one is more capable of ruining the see of Rome" (Chadwick).

Once elected, Clement distanced himself from the Society while temporizing with the monarchs in hopes that the situation would resolve itself. Renewed calls from rulers for suppression of the Society of Jesus were countered with resistance on the part of curial officers and other cardinals. By 1773, the monarchs declared they would break diplomatic relations with Rome if their wishes were not heeded. On July 21, Clement issued the bull *Dominus ac Redemptor noster*, dissolving the Society of Jesus in the Catholic world and imprisoning the Jesuit superior general, Lorenzo Ricci (1703–75) for questioning the validity of the decision. The reasons that the bull offered for such a radical move were that Jesuits had incurred enemies and were responsible for controversies that divided Catholicism. A year later, depressed and frightened of possible assassination attempts, Clement XIV died, bringing the prestige of the papacy to one of its lowest levels in centuries.

When Pius VI (Braschi, 1717–99) came to the papal throne, he became notorious for lavish expenditures and for resistance to the Enlightenment ideas that seemed to be coursing through Catholic nations like Austria and Germany. In 1786, these ideas had spread to Italy and Tuscany, as witnessed by the decisions of the Synod of Pistoia, which adopted the four Gallican Articles and exempted the bishops from papal interference. In 1794, Pius issued a formal condemnation of most of the decisions at Pistoia, but the event that would cast the longest and darkest shadow over this last pontificate of the "enlightened" century was the French Revolution. The failure of Pius to act quickly on the question of church reorganization by the Civil Constitution of the Clergy (1790), and his belated denunciations of oaths to the new regime, resulted in a decade of schism in French Catholicism. His support of the royalist cause and refusal to withdraw his condemnations of the Revolution led to Napoleon's invasion of the Papal States in 1796. During the Roman occupation in the ensuing years, Pius was deposed as head of state and imprisoned in Valence, where he died. Many were of the opinion that with the passing of Pius VI the papacy itself had come to an end, but this "last pope" was more likely perceived as a symbol of the triumph of Enlightenment thought over outmoded Catholic structures. In a future era, other ideas and movements would shape another style of papal power, one that confronted modernity with spiritual weaponry that triumphed for a time, until at last the popes of the 20th century endorsed and even embraced the very ideas their predecessors in the 18th century had condemned.

Janice Farnham

Bibliography

Bangert, W. J. *A History of the Society of Jesus*, chaps. 5 and 6, St. Louis, 1986.

Bantle, F. X. *Unfehlbarkeit der Kirche in Aufklärung und Romantik*, Freiburg-Basel, 1976.

Callahan, W. J., and Higgs, D., eds. *Church and Society in Catholic Europe of the Eighteenth Century*, Cambridge, 1979.

Chadwick, O. *The Popes and European Revolution*, Oxford, 1981.

Châtellier, L., ed. *Religions en transition dans la seconde moitié du XVIIIe siècle*, Oxford, 2000.

Dudon, P. "De la suppression de la Compagnie de Jésus," *Revue des questions historiques*, 132 (1938), 75–107.

Duffy, E. *Saints and Sinners. A History of the Popes*, New Haven, 1997.

Grès-Gayer, J. "The *Unigenitus* of Clement XI: A Fresh Look at the Issues," *Theological Studies* 49 (1988), 259–82.

Gross, H. *Rome in the Age of Enlightenment. The Post-Tridentine Syndrome and the Ancien Regime*, Cambridge, 1990.

Hanotaux, G. and J., eds. *Recueil des instructions [. . .] Rome*, Paris, 1888–1936.

Heer, R. *The Eighteenth-Century Revolution in Spain*, Princeton, 1958.

Heyer, F. *The Catholic Church from 1648 to 1870*, D. W. D. Shaw, trans., London, 1969.

Johns, C. M. S. *Papal Art and Cultural Politics: Rome in the Age of Clement XI*, Cambridge, 1993.

Kovàcs, E., ed. *Katholische Aufklärung und Josephinismus*, Vienna, 1979.

Kraus, F. X., ed. *Briefe Benedicts XIV, an de Canonicus Francesco Peggi in Bologna [1727–1758]. Nebst Benedicts diarium des conclaves von 1740*, Freiburg-Tubingen, 1888.

Morelli, E., ed. *Le lettere di Benedetto XIV al cardinale de Tencin, III, 1753–1758*, Rome, 1984.

Pastor, L. *History of the Popes from the Close of the Middle Ages,* 40 vols., London, 1912–1952.

Plongeron, B. *Théologie et politique au siècle des lumières, 1770–1820*, Geneva, 1973.

Sedgwick, A. *Jansenism in Seventeenth-Century France*, Charlottesville, 1977.

van Kley, D. *The Jansenists and the Expulsion of the Society of Jesus from France, 1757–1765*, New Haven, 1975.

Venturi, F. "Elementi e tentative di riforme nello stato pontificio del Settecento," *Rivista Storica Italiana* (1963), 778–817.

Venturi, F. *Settecento Riformatore*, Turin, 1969.

Wright, A. D. *The Early Modern Papacy. From the Council of Trent to the French Revolution, 1564–1789*, Harlow, England, 2000.

EUGENE I. *(Rome, ?, d. Rome, 2 June 657). Elected pope on 10 August 654. Buried at St. Peter's in Rome. Saint (added to the Roman Martyrology by Baronius).*

The actions of this elderly priest, elected on the order of the emperor and renowned for his gentleness, are a good reflection of the contradictory forces at work on the Roman see. After the arrest and deportation of MARTIN I (17 June 653), the clergy resisted imperial pressure for almost a year but finally gave in by electing a new pope, even though his predecessor was still alive. Eugene, whom his biographer presents as gentle and affable with everyone, was ready to seek a compromise, which would have been all the easier to arrive at since the patriarch Pyrrhus had died on 1 June 654. He sent envoys, who arrived in Constantinople on 15 May 655. They visited Maximus the Confessor in his prison shortly before his trial, but, overstepping the pope's formal orders, they entered into communion with the new patriarch, Peter, at Pentecost. Peter thought he could affirm that the unity of the Church had been restored around the emperor. But he was not counting on Maximus's friends, who were still active in Rome. When the envoys returned to the pope with the synodal letter in which Peter informed him of his election and defined his theological position, the clergy refused to allow the pope to celebrate mass in the church of ST. MARY MAJOR until he had condemned such an obscure text, one principally designed to please everyone at the cost of being rife with contradictions. Maximus's two trials and the death of Martin contributed to a hardening of positions, whereby was set up a situation analogous to the one after the LATERAN COUNCIL (649). Moreover, Constans II promised to use force to constrain the pope as soon as he had finished with his enemies in the East. But he never had the opportunity to carry out his threats, since Eugene died before Constans could intervene.

Besides, violent action would have had no chance of success, since the pope was increasingly the man of his City. Born in the first *rione*, of a Roman father named Rufinianus, he had passed his entire career in the Church. The clergy, whose members belonged to the Roman NOBILITY, not only influenced his behavior vis-à-vis the emperor, but also obtained the regular payment of their salaries and the guarantee that those would not be interrupted during the vacancy of the see after the pope's death. Likewise, the poor would receive alms. Information concerning these measures in favor of clerics and the poor subsequently became standard in the *LIBER PONTIFICALIS*. Constantinople's power had managed to stop Martin I. From Eugene's time on, that would no longer be possible.

Jean Durliat

Bibliography

JW, 1, 234; 2, 699, 740.

LP, 1, 341–2.

Bertolini, O. *Roma di fronte a Bisanzio e ai Longobardi*, Bologna, 1971, 351–5.

Mallardo, D. *Papa S. Eugenio I*, Naples, 1943.

Marot, H. "Eugène Ier," *DHGE*, 15 (1963), 1346–7.

Scheffer, R. "Eugen I," *LexMA*, 4 (1987–9), 77–8.

EUGENE II. (*b. ?, d. August 827*). *Elected pope in May or June 824*.

It is generally thought that his pontificate was pro-Frankish and pro-aristocracy, which clearly distinguishes it from that of his predecessor, PASCHAL I. In reality, this image undoubtedly depends partly on the sources consulted. Most sources are of Frankish origin, since Eugene II's biography in the *LIBER PONTIFICALIS* is far from complete and, what is left of it, poorly written. Little is known of his formation, except that he was *presbyter* of Sta Sabina at the time of his election. According to Eginardo's *Annals*, his appointment came about owing to pressure from the Roman nobility, but above all owing to the mediation of Lothair's adviser, Wala, who happened to be in Rome at the time of the death of Paschal I.

The events that followed were shaped by Lothair's direct intervention in Rome, although it is difficult to say what Eugene II's contribution was to the measures we are about to discuss concerning the first year, at least, of his short pontificate. Lothair actually came to Rome to complete the inquiry into the murders and persecutions that had taken place during the last year of Paschal I's pontificate. When his work was finished, a *constitutio* was decreed in which Lothair imposed on the city a specific set of regulations as to the form of government in ROME. It defined the relationship with the empire, including the latter's responsibility for maintaining order. The papal administrators were to come before Lothair to undergo an examination of their ability to carry out their offices. The Romans were granted the right to choose whether they wanted to live, and, should the case arise, be judged, according to the Roman, the Salic, or the Lombard law. The pope's judiciary power was thus limited, and potentially arbitrary acts on his part prevented. A final court of appeal was also created. It was made up of two *missi*—one nominated by the emperor and the other by the pope—who were to keep the emperor apprised of the working of the administration; any problems would be resolved by the emperor as a last resort. Moreover, it was established that papal elections should be the concern of Romans alone, and that the elected pope should take an oath before the Roman people and the imperial *missus* before his ordination.

All this was subordinate to the preamble that individuals under the protection of the pope and the emperor were to be considered inviolable. This was tantamount to protecting, against abuses from the pope, those who, enjoying the trust of the emperor, controlled the Roman situation on his behalf. It is important to notice the essential difference between these arrangements and those Paschal I had persuaded Louis I to ratify in 818. In a way, Eugene II needed to reestablish internal cohesion in the Roman political scene, which was undoubtedly possible only with the support of an authority like that of the emperor, capable of "dictating rules" that would be accepted by all, either voluntarily or out of fear. And it is probably through this lens that Eugene II's "pro-imperial" stance can most fairly be examined.

Federico Marazzi

Bibliography

LP, 2, 69–70.

MGH, SS In usum scholar, 6, 164–6.—*MGH, Cap.*, 1, 322–4.

PL, 105, 639–46.

Bertolini, O. "Osservazioni sulla *Constitutio Romana . . . del 824*," *Scritti scelti di storia medievale*, ed. O. Banti, II, Livorno, 1968, 705–38.

Brezzi, P. *Roma e l'Impero medievale*, Bologna, 1947.

Duchesne, L. *Les Premiers Temps de l'État pontifical*, Paris, 1898.

Llewellyn, P. *Rome in the Dark Ages*, London, 1971.

Schieffer, R. "Eugen II," *LexMA*, 4 (1987–9), 78.

EUGENE III. *Bernardo Paganelli de Montemagno (b. near Pisa, d. Tivoli, 8 July 1153). Elected pope on 15 February 1145, ordained in Farfa. Buried at St. Peter's in Rome. Venerated as a saint (feast day on 8 July, cult officially recognized in 1872 by PIUS IX).*

His pontifical name can perhaps be accounted for as an allusion to the word *Evangelium*. Bernardo is attested as canon and *vicedominus* (an administrator of the possessions of the Church) at Pisa; he was probably also a monk and prior at the Camaldolese monastery of S. Zeno. Under the influence of Bernard of Clairvaux, he became a Cistercian. He entered the monastery of Clairvaux in 1138 and became abbot of S. Anastasio (S. Anastasio of the Salvian Waters, near Rome) in 1141. Immediately after the death of LUCIUS II, he became pope during a process that was expedited by troubles in Rome. He was the first Cistercian to occupy the throne of Peter. It is possible that he did not belong to the SACRED COLLEGE.

Early on, Eugene III was unable to take possession of the Lateran. Unwilling to recognize the commune of Rome, he was forced to flee the city. He established his residence in VITERBO, whence he was able to block the flow of provisions to Rome. In December 1145, the Roman SENATE was forced to sacrifice its prefect Giordano Pierleone and to reach a provisional peace. At the time of the Sutri accords, the pope managed to have the pontifical prefect reestablished, and the senators pay homage to him after their election. Eugene III was then able to return to Rome.

Bernard of Clairvaux had reproached the cardinals for having drawn Bernardo out of the solitude of the cloister and placed him above princes and bishops, even though he recognized the hand of God in the event. Were Eugene III's decisions dependent on Bernard of Clairvaux's opinion? John of Salisbury, a well-informed observer, reported that, between Bernard's opinions and those of the cardinals, the pope managed to have his voice heard only with great difficulty. In any case, he refused to budge on the issue of decentralization in Church government called for by the abbot of Clairvaux in his *De consideratione*, a kind of portrait of the ideal pope.

The CURIA became the court of final appeal in Western Christianity, even encroaching upon "national" interests. Word spread concerning the fall of Edessa into the hands of the infidels; some Armenian bishops appealed to the pope to arbitrate on the differences of rite between them and the Greeks: Eugene III then preached a crusade, one purpose of which was to help reunite the Eastern Churches with the Western Church. On 1 December 1145, he addressed a bull to the king of France, Louis VII, inviting him to undertake a second CRUSADE, and shortly thereafter he made an appeal to the Italians. He reiterated his call to the French on 1 March 1146. Charged with preaching the crusade, Bernard of Clairvaux managed also to win the participation of the king of the German lands, Conrad III, but the pope was not in favor of this, since he had hoped for the speedy assistance of the Hohenstaufen against the Romans. Afterwards, Eugene III confirmed the privileges that Bernard had taken it upon himself to promise to Germans willing to take up the cross against the infidels. Before the crusading armies set out, the pope made his way to France, in early 1147, where he engaged in intense activity. He was received by Louis VII at Dijon. In Paris, he held a synod to examine the teachings of Gilbert de la Porée. He handed the banner of the crusade over to Louis VII in St-Denis. He was present in Cîteaux when the monasteries of the congregation of Savigny were affiliated with the Cistercian order. During a long stay in Trier (winter 1147–8), Eugene approved Hildegard of Bingen's *Liber Scivias*.

In March 1148, he held an important synod in Reims that condemned the itinerant preacher Eon de l'Étoile as a heretic. The cardinals opposed the condemnation of Gilbert de la Porée, promoted by Bernard of Clairvaux, since they feared for the primacy of the Roman Church. The disciplinary decisions made at the council of Reims essentially reiterated the canons of the Lateran synod of 1139. Eugene III thought of excommunicating the king of England, Stephen, who had forbidden his bishops to at-

tend the Reims meeting, but he did not carry out his project. In the struggle for the throne of England, the pope nevertheless supported, against Stephen, the soon-to-be-victorious party of Empress Matilda. Ties between the Curia and the Northeast were for the most part strengthened. In 1147, Eugene III intervened in the problem of the archdiocese of York: he refused to recognize Archbishop William Fitzherbert, who had occupied the bishop's see for four years, and installed the Cistercian Henry Murdac in his place. In 1152, during the synod of Kells, Cardinal John Paparo organized the Irish Church into four archdioceses, defining their relationship with Rome. Scandinavia also came into the pope's horizon. In 1152, the LEGATE Nicholas Breakspear, the future HADRIAN IV, placed the ecclesiastical organization in Sweden and Norway on a proper footing.

When the news arrived of the total failure of the crusade in 1148, both Bernard of Clairvaux and Eugene III became the object of bitter criticism. Moreover, the situation deteriorated in Rome; the canon regular Arnold of Brescia, who had long been fighting against temporal intrusion by the Church, gave the rise of the commune a religious dimension. In 1146, the pope had attempted a reconciliation with Arnold, but Arnold persisted in his scheming. Upon his return to Italy, Eugene III excommunicated him, since Arnold was encouraging the Romans to rebel against the cardinals and the pope. But the Senate took responsibility for Arnold's reforms.

In April 1149, the papal court installed itself in Albano. It was then necessary to gather troops against the Romans. Roger II of Sicily dispatched reinforcements in exchange for the papal promise to send legates to the Norman kingdom only with his authorization. The king sought support from the Curia against Conrad III and the Byzantine emperor Manuel I, who were planning an expedition against Sicily. The attack of the papal troops against Rome met with failure. Eugene III nevertheless succeeded in drawing up an accord with the Senate toward the end of 1149, which permitted him to return to the city for at least a few months. In July 1150, in Ceprano, he negotiated an agreement with Roger II allowing Roger to have free election of bishops in his kingdom, but denying Roger full recognition of his royalty.

Eugene III did not want to fall into a state of subordination to Sicily; that is why he refused to suscribe to the Franco-Norman alliance sought by Roger II, who needed to thwart the German-Byzantine coalition. The pope had maintained a certain relationship with the German court. Conrad III was waiting to be crowned emperor by Eugene III. In the summer of 1151, the pope sent two legates to the German lands, inviting Conrad to come to Rome. Henceforth, the supreme pontiff counted on German support against the Romans. Conrad III attempted to play the role of mediator between Eugene III and the Senate, but the expedition against Rome never took place, prevented by Conrad's death in February 1152. Shortly thereafter, Frederick Barbarossa ascended the throne. He announced his election to the pope, promising both his protection and the fulfillment of Conrad III's promises. Eugene III gave an approval for which he had not been asked, and held out the prospect of crowning Frederick emperor. It seemed a short time later that Frederick had little concern for the pope or the rights of the Church: for example, Eugene III raised a protest in the case of the archbishop of Magdeburg, but, given the precarious situation in which he found himself, he was not in a position to go so far as to sever ties. Barbarossa sent ambassadors to Rome in order to prepare an Italian expedition; the ambassadors entered into negotiations with a number of cardinals in December 1152. They may also have participated in the settlement that took place between Eugene III and the Romans, which allowed the pope to return to Rome toward the end of 1152.

Arnold of Brescia was authorized to remain in the city. The principal result of the negotiations between the German lands and the Curia was a bilateral treaty, to which Frederick Barbarossa subscribed in Constance in March 1153. The emperor agreed, among other things, to sign no peace accords with either the Romans or the Normans without the approval of the pope, to keep the Romans under control, to defend against all comers the *honor papatus*, and to grant no concessions of Italian territory to Byzantium. For his part, the pope promised, among other things, to crown Frederick Barbarossa emperor, to contribute to the defense and increase of the *honor imperii*, and to concede no Italian territory to Byzantium. These were declarations of intent that satisfied the interests of both parties. For Eugene III, it was important to ensure the Curia's position with regard to its political adversaries. The pope was opposed to Frederick Barbarossa in a number of respects, but he agreed to annul his marriage. A conflict nevertheless arose between the legates and the pope over the question of Magdeburg. Thus, forced collaboration on matters between Church and Empire in Italy coexisted with real tensions between the two powers. Eugene III was not able to harvest the fruits of his policies; he died outside Rome in June 1153.

The people quickly began to venerate him as a saint. Subsequently, he was sometimes seen as a weak representative of Christ, so poorly fitted for his work that a number of his tasks fell on the shoulders of those around him. It certainly was not easy for him to acquit himself equitably in the tasks of everyday politics within the framework of a Cistercian ideal of life. But it was precisely because of the way he conceived of his responsibility that the pope enjoyed such great prestige. Gerhoh of Reichersberg pointed out that he accepted no gifts from those who came to him for justice. Others praised his benevolence and the uprightness of his judgment. The fact that he commissioned Burgundio of Pisa to translate

John Chrysostom's homilies on Matthew (*Homiliae in Matthaeum*) shows that theological texts were important to him. Eugene III was able to spend only an eighth of his pontificate in Rome, and was confronted by a number of difficult situations. But he nevertheless demonstrated firmness toward the Romans and the NORMANS. He strengthened papal sovereignty in the PATRIMONY OF ST. PETER. The large proportion of canons regular and of Cistercians among his appointments to the cardinalate reveals a spiritual dimension in his conduct. Three of these cardinals (HADRIAN IV, ALEXANDER III, and VICTOR IV) later ascended to the throne of Peter. He contributed to the future power of the papacy by extending his activity to a great part of the West. But his weaknesses cannot be overlooked. He was unable to calculate the consequences of his call for a crusade, and the essence of the activity for which he is given credit is limited to appeals and the sending of legates. More was needed.

Karl Schnith

Bibliography

JL, 2, 20–89.

LP, 2, 386–8.

PL, 180, 1013–1642.

Baker, D. "San Bernardo e l'elezione di York," *Studi su san Bernardo*, 1975, 115–80.

Dimier, M. A. "Eugène III," *DHGE*, 15 (1963), 1349–55.

Engels, O. "Zum Konstanzer Vertrag von 1153," *Deus qui mutat tempora. Festschrift A. Becker*, Sigmaringen, 1987, 235–58.

Gleber, H. *Papst Eugen III*, Jena, 1936.

Haring, N. "Das Pariser Konsistorium Eugens III. vom April 1147," *Studia Gratiana*, 11 (1967), 91–117.

Horn, H. *Studien zur Geschichte Papst Eugens III. (1145–1153)*, Frankfurt–Berne–Paris–New York, 1992 (*Europäische Hochschulschriften*, 508).

Jacqueline, B. *Papauté et épiscopat selon saint Bernard de Clairvaux*, Paris, 1963.

Jacqueline, B. "Le pape et les Romains d'après le *De consideratione* de saint Bernard," *Mélanges Pierre Andrieu-Guitrancourt*, Paris, 1973, 603–14.

Maleczek, W. "Eugen III.," *LexMA*, 4 (1987–9), 78–80.

Rassow, P. *Honor Imperii*, Munich, 2nd ed., 1961.

EUGENE IV. *Gabriele Condulmaro (b. Venice, ca. 1383, d. Rome, 23 February 1447). Elected pope on 3 March 1431 and crowned on the following 11 March. Buried at S. Salvatore in Lauro (Rome).*

His mother was GREGORY XII's sister. Committed to an ecclesiastical career while still quite young, he is considered, along with his cousin Antonio Correr and other pious Venetians, one of the founders of the congregation of canons of S. Giorgio in Alga (1404). Nevertheless, his experience of religious life, which probably oriented his character for the rest of his days, was not of long duration. In 1407, his uncle the pope made him bishop of Siena, exempting him from the canonical age requirement, and on 9 May 1408 he was made cardinal priest of the title of S. Clemente, despite the opposition of the SACRED COLLEGE, which was opposed to an increase in its membership just when it was felt that reunion with the obedience of Avignon would bring an end to the schism. Gabriele Condulmaro was thenceforth known as the cardinal of Siena, and he was close to his cousin Antonio Correr, who was named cardinal at the same time as he. He replaced him for a while (1409) at the head of the APOSTOLIC CAMERA, when Gregory XII was residing in Rimini. After Gregory renounced the pontificate, the two cousins once again joined the council, which was meeting in Constance. There they so vehemently supported the king of the Romans, Sigismund, in his opposition to the cardinals, that for a short time they were asked to abstain from attending the meetings of the college of cardinals. Active partisans of the former obedience of Gregory XII, they tried in vain to force the conclave to admit his official representatives, rather than the elected representatives of the nations in which Gregory had no partisans. During the pontificate of MARTIN V, Gabriele especially distinguished himself by an important legation to Ancona and in the Marches, where he worked quite energetically to reestablish papal authority (1420).

The CONCLAVE that met in Sta Maria sopra Minerva after the death of Martin V forced upon its members (thirteen cardinals of the twenty-two who made up the Sacred College) a capitulation which returned control of the government of the Church and part of its revenues to the cardinals. This capitulation was ratified by Gabriele Condulmaro almost immediately after his election as pope. The whole situation was clearly most difficult for him: Martin V's harshness toward the cardinals and the favors lavished upon his relations called for a settling of scores; the work of Constance was not finished, and a new council was about to be opened in Basel, with all the risks it entailed for affirming papal authority; the Hussite question, to which Jan Hus's death sentence had not put an end, had given rise to a merciless war in Bohemia; after the defeat of Thessalonica in 1430, the plan for union with the Roman Church proposed by the Greeks was hastening preparations for a crusade against the Turks; the Papal State, taken charge of once again by Martin V and the Colonna, was newly threatened by the designs of the duke of Milan, who lent a hand in all initiatives opposing at least the formal recognition of the pope's sovereign authority. Eugene IV faced all these challenges with inflexibility, and despite the firmness of his principles, he seems to have suffered through rather than directed events.

As soon as he took possession of his office, he found himself confronted, in Rome, by the Colonna family's control over the Curia and the local government. His desire to hold the Colonna family to account for all they had gained from Martin V and his harsh summonses of old friends of the deceased pope brought things to a head: the entire Colonna clan took up arms, while their partisans' palaces in Rome were pillaged. The Colonna hatched a plot—or so it was thought—to take over CASTEL SANT'ANGELO. Some of the guilty were apprehended, but the pope preferred to make peace with the prince of Salerno and his brother, Cardinal Prospero Colonna.

Shortly after his election, Eugene IV conferred upon Cardinal Cesarini the mission of LEGATE to the council convened in Basel by Martin V. Sessions formally opened on 23 July 1431, presided over by Cardinal John de Palomar, representing Cesarini, who was on the CRUSADE and did not reach Basel until the following 9 September. In response to a darkly painted report of the atmosphere of the council, made in November by an ambassador of the council fathers and the legate, the pope sent Cesarini full power to dissolve the council and announce another, in Bologna, for the summer of 1433, in which the Greeks would be able to take part and over which the pope would preside. Not content with this first step, Eugene IV pronounced the dissolution of the COUNCIL of Basel in a BULL of 18 December 1431, although Cesarini had scarcely assembled it and had celebrated its first session the previous 14 December. The reform, which all Christendom was demanding, seemed to be compromised by the papal decision. Reactions were strong, especially among the council fathers, who recalled (15 February 1432) the teachings of Constance on the primacy of the council with respect to the pope. Facing the threat of a schism and under pressure from part of his entourage, Eugene IV yielded in stages, each of which became the object of bitter arguments between the council fathers and the papal representatives. The pope's position was weakened, though not fatally, by the difficulties of the political situation in Rome. He then attempted to find support in the Romans' king, Sigismund, whom he crowned emperor in Rome on 31 May 1433. Imperial mediation could not diminish the demands of the fathers, who sent the pope an ultimatum that either he present himself at the council or they would begin proceedings against him. The emperor headed off the proceedings, but the pope, abandoned by the majority of his cardinals, withdrew the bull for the dissolution of the council (15 February 1433).

For a number of months, the Papal States had been overrun by the duke of Milan, Filippo Maria Visconti, and by the *condottiere* Francesco Sforza. The incessant pillaging in Rome and in Latium occasioned by the military actions of feudal clans encouraged in their resistance to the pontifical authority had long wearied the population and particularly the Romans, many of whom, with interests in the surrounding countryside, brought their complaints to the pope. Eugene IV sent them to the camerlengo, his nephew, Cardinal Francesco Condulmaro, whose disdainful reception of them caused an uprising. The rebels chased the magistrates appointed by the pope from the Capitol, and the camerlengo was taken hostage. Anxious about his own fate, the pope took refuge in the palace adjacent to Sta Maria in Trastevere, from which he fled, not completely unscathed, to Florence, where he arrived on 23 June. The confusion that reigned in Rome after Eugene IV's departure allowed Giovanni Vitteleschi, bishop of Recanati but, more important, the pope's chief deputy in the city government, to get the situation under control before the end of the year. Nevertheless, the pope would not return to Rome for a number of years. The bishop of Recanati was given full authority to take back by force all the positions the pope had lost. The prelate clamped down harshly but effectively; it was on his orders that Palestrina, the feudal estate of the Colonna, was razed (1434).

Encouraged by its victory over the pope, the council in Basel continued its work by abolishing nearly all papal taxes throughout Christendom (9 June 1435). In the face of this last attack, Eugene addressed a solemn protest to the Christian princes. But the split between the pope and the council was consummated by the possibility of union with the Greeks. As a place of entente, the council fathers offered Avignon or an unspecified city in Savoy, excluding Florence and Modena, which had been proposed by the pope, and even Ancona, which the Greeks would have preferred. The Greek delegation, which had come to Basel, ended up opting for Eugene IV's choice, and joined the pope in Bologna (24 May 1437). This success put an end to the scruples of the council fathers, who summoned the pope to their court. Eugene IV riposted by threatening (18 September 1437) to relocate the council to Ferrara, which he did on 30 December. The council opened in Ferrara on 8 January 1438. The assembly in Basel suspended Eugene IV on 24 January 1438 and proclaimed his deposition on 25 June the following year. Amadeus VIII of Savoy was elected in his place, taking the name FELIX V (5 November 1439). The assembly in Basel retained the support of prelates who were subjects of the king of France and, when an assembly of clergy meeting in Bourges had come to an end, some of his decrees were integrated into the Pragmatic Sanction promulgated officially by Charles VII as a law of the kingdom (7 July 1438). After Sigismund's death (9 July 1438), the princes in the German lands declared their neutrality. But thenceforth the scale was tipped in Eugene IV's favor. On 5 July 1439, in Florence, to which the council had been transferred— perhaps because the plague had broken out in Ferrara,

but undoubtedly also for financial reasons—he signed the decree of unity with the Greeks. The act, signed also by Emperor John VIII Palaeologus, who was under the threat of an imminent Turkish invasion, was in force for only a very short time, but in the West it reinforced the authority of Eugene IV. It was followed by similar accords with other Churches that felt threatened: the Armenians (1439), the Copts or Jacobites of Egypt (1443), and dissident groups of Nestorians in Mesopotamia (1444) and Cyprus (1445). The logical consequence of all these alliances was the organization of a crusade financed by the pope (1443), which ended tragically in Varna, Bulgaria, where the pope's legate, Cardinal Cesarini, was found among the victims (10 November 1444). This failure in no way jeopardized the advantages Eugene IV had gained against the Basel assembly. Frederick III, the new emperor, strengthened his ties with him. In 1443, Alfonso of Aragon, who had more or less openly supported Felix V, drew up a treaty with Eugene IV. The same year, Scotland unconditionally returned to the Roman pope. The council of Basel, which had lain in slumber since 1440, held its final solemn session on 16 May 1443. Eugene IV did not manage to get the Pragmatic Sanction in France abolished. He was happier in the German lands, where, thanks to the efforts of Enea Silvio Piccolomini, the former secretary to Felix V, he was able to come to terms with the princes. Thanks to mutual concessions that formerly had been vigorously refused, an agreement was concluded on 5 and 7 February 1447. Eugene IV confirmed the accord on his deathbed, being careful to reserve the rights of the Holy See.

Rome having been retaken by Giovanni Vitteleschi in October 1434, the pope still spent considerable time in Florence, which he left on 18 April 1436 to make his way to Bologna; he remained in Bologna until January 1438 before returning to the council meeting in Ferrara. After a return to Florence a year later, he finally left the city on 7 March 1443, and on the following 19 September he returned to Rome for good. In the Papal State, Vitteleschi pursued his work of reestablishing the authority of the pope, from Civitavecchia to the confines of the kingdom of Naples. The brutal force of the *condottiere* bishop was so successful that he was rewarded by being named cardinal in 1437. His arrest and death at Castel Sant'Angelo (2 August 1440) in mysterious circumstances that raised questions about Eugene IV's authority left the field for a "Venetian," Ludovico Scarampi, who was just as energetic as Vitteleschi and who governed Rome until the death of the pope.

During his pontificate, Eugene IV named twenty-seven cardinals, seventeen of them at the promotion of 18 December 1439. He did not forget his relations, one of whom, Pietro Barbo, named cardinal in 1440, would become Pope PAUL II. The Roman NOBILITY was kept from promotion. On the other hand, Eugene IV brought in two illustrious deserters from the Greek Church, Bessarion and Archbishop Isidore. The presence in Florence of seasoned participants in the theological discussions also brought to Eugene IV's attention Tommaso Parentucelli, who succeeded him as NICHOLAS V. By naming cardinal (1444) Alfonso de Borja, who had been the architect of the rapprochement between Alfonso of Aragon and the pope, Eugene IV was putting the foot of the future CALLISTUS III in the stirrup and, through him, the Italian destiny of the Borgia family.

For a long time, the conflict between Alfonso of Aragon and René of Anjou for possession of the kingdom of Naples had seen the two sovereigns begrudging the support of their respective clergies for Eugene IV. But when Alfonso had established himself as master of Naples (12 June 1442), the pope had him recognized as the legitimate successor of Joan II (14 June 1443). He thus assured himself both of the allegiance of the bishops who were subjects of the king of Aragon and, at the same time, of support against Francesco Sforza, who had held the Marches of Ancona for some years and would not be driven therefrom for good, with the exception of Iesi, until a few days before the pope's death. The duke of Milan made an alliance with Rome the same day as Alfonso of Aragon, and the pope was able to return to Rome.

The conduct of Eugene IV's personal life was invariably modest: he ate almost nothing but fruit and vegetables and drank almost no wine. This moderate asceticism went well with a complete dissociation from the humanist movement, of which, however, there were very many representatives in his entourage, and which he had been able to see in action in Florence. And yet, at the beginning of his pontificate (1431), he devoted himself to restoring the University of Rome, though this initiative was cut short by his sudden departure in 1434 and not brought to completion until later. His role as a patron of the arts, though limited by his financial means, was not negligiable. In Florence, where he had gone to consecrate Sta Maria del Fiore, he commissioned Ghiberti to fashion an extraordinary tiara, which he wore at the time of the signing of the accord with the Greeks. But beginning in 1433, he called Filarete to Rome to decorate the doors of St. Peter's basilica. The execution of the project, little appreciated by the critics but made famous by the reputation of the sanctuary, took twelve years (1433–45), and over the course of its completion it was enriched by the description of events contemporary to the pontificate of which Filarete was an eyewitness. At St. John Lateran, Eugene IV had Vittore Pisanello continue the frescoes on the life of John the Baptist that Gentile da Fabriano had begun under the pontificate of Martin V. At the Pantheon, he cleared the portico of the monument by having the hovels that blocked it knocked down. Some have seen in this a renewed interest in the monuments of antiquity,

even though the Pantheon had always had a claim to special attention because it sheltered a church.

His efforts for the reform of the Church in its head and in its members were limited, held back as he was by the outbidding tactics of the council of Basel and by the material impossibility of forcing economic and administrative reforms on a CURIA upon which he was greatly dependent. His attention was directed especially to a local reform of clerical life, limited to the places of papal residence. In Rome, he attempted to replace the secular canons of St. John Lateran with canons regular. The measure, highly unpopular among the Romans, who saw themselves as being deprived thereby of a certain number of canonical offices, was withdrawn by Eugene IV's successors but reintroduced provisionally under the pontificate of his nephew, Paul II. Eugene IV's charitable initiatives met with fewer difficulties. He was very active in the reconstruction of the hospital of S. Spirito in Sassia, giving it increased revenues and restoring the buildings that were in poor condition. Most of all, by his own example he encouraged the cardinals to enroll in the Confraternity of the Holy Spirit, thus ensuring that the hospital would have a regular and substantial supply of alms. For the consolation of prisoners, he inaugurated the *visita graziosa*, a mandatory bimonthly visit to the incarcerated, especially insolvent debtors, by magistrates and those who administered the goods of the poor.

After Eugene IV's death, his nephew, Cardinal Pietro Barbo (the future Paul II), had a monument built for him, erected first in the chapel of Sts. Peter and Paul in St. Peter's basilica. A few years later, the monument was transferred to S. Salvatore in Lauro by Cardinal Latino Orsini. The transfer was approved after an explicit request by the canons of S. Giorgio in Alga, who had recently moved into the convent of the church founded for them by Cardinal Orsini. First placed in the cloister, the monument was installed in the 19th century in what had been the canons' refectory, where it is still located today. The work in its entirety is attributed at present to Isaia da Pisa, despite doubts raised formerly about the hand that wrought the recumbent effigy.

Francois-Charles Uginet

Bibliography

Gill, J. *Eugenius IV, Pope of Christian Union*, Westminster, Md., 1951.

Gill, J. *The Council of Florence*, Cambridge, Eng., 1959.

Gill, J. *Eugenius IV: Pope of Christian Union*, Westminster, 1961.

Helmrath, J. "Eugen IV.," *LexMA*, 4 (1989), 80–2.

Miglio, M. *Storiografia pontificia del Quattrocento*, Bologna, 1975, and review by R. Fubini, "Papato e storiografia nel Quattrocento," *Studi medievali*, 18 (1977), 321–51.

Monfrin, J. "A propos de la bibliothèque d'Eugène IV," *MEFRM*, 99 (1987), 101–21.

Müller, H. *Die Franzosen, Frankreich und das Basler Konzil (1431–1439)*, Paderborn, 1990.

Ourliac, P. "Eugène IV (1383–1447)," *Études d'histoire du droit médiéval*, Paris, 1974.

Paschini, P. *Roma nel Rinascimento*, Rome, 1940, 120–65.

Stieber, J. W. *Pope Eugenius IV, the Council of Basel and Secular and Ecclesiastical Authorities in the Empire*, Leiden, 1978.

EULALIUS. *(d. 423). Antipope, elected on 27 December 418, ordained on 29 December, deposed on 3 April 419.*

Of unknown origin, Eulalius was archdeacon of the Roman Church when Pope ZOSIMUS died on 26 December 418, after a pontificate that was contested even within the Roman clergy and that therefore presaged a difficult succession. With his partisans—a few priests, the deacons, and a sizeable crowd—Eulalius hurriedly barricaded himself in the church of the Lateran on 27 December, where he was elected pope the same day and remained entrenched so that he could be consecrated on the Sunday. His opponent was the Roman priest BONIFACE, the former representative of Pope INNOCENT I to the East, who was supported by the great majority of the Roman priests and part of the populace, and who was elected in his turn in the basilica of Theodora on Saturday, 28 December. Eulalius, disregarding the step taken by the opposing party of imploring him not to continue, was ordained on Sunday, 29 December, by the bishop of Ostia, while his rival was ordained the same day at the church of St. Marcello. Emperor Honorius, on the basis of a report from the prefect of the city, Symmachus, who favored Eulalius, first confirmed him (3 January) as regularly elected, and demanded that Boniface be expelled from Rome. On 5 January, Eulalius celebrated Epiphany at ST. PETER'S in the Vatican, while his adversary moved to the outskirts of Rome.

But after a complaint from the partisans of Boniface, who protested Eulalius's bid for power and Symmachus's partiality, Honorius convened a council in RAVENNA (8 February 419) to decide between the two rivals; the debates having failed to lead to a decision, on 15 March the emperor decided to convene a larger council to meet on Pentecost at Spoleto; he had Eulalius and Boniface withdraw from Rome, where riots were on the increase, and entrusted Bishop Achilleus of Spoleto, who was partial to neither of the contestants, to celebrate the Easter feasts. But on 18 March, Eulalius returned to Rome, where violent confrontations took place; on 26 March, the emperor ordered his expulsion and decreed heavy sanctions against his partisans. Eulalius countered by taking control of the Lateran church on Holy Saturday (29 March), from which he was dislodged with great difficulty by the local authorities. He was put under house arrest outside Rome, while some of his partisans were imprisoned. By an imperial letter of 3 April 419 (received in Rome on 8 April), he was declared expelled from the city; his adversary was authorized to return to Rome, and recognized as the legitimate bishop of Rome. With no further reason for meeting, the council planned for Spoleto was cancelled.

According to the *LIBER PONTIFICALIS*, Eulalius subsequently received a diocese in the provinces, in Campagna or Tuscany; he is even said to have been invited by the clergy and the people of Rome to return to the city after the death of his rival in 422.

Christiane Fraisse-Coué

Bibliography

LP, 1, 227–9.

Collection Auellana, 14–36; *CSEL*, 35, 1, 59–84.

Gaspar, E. *Geschichte des Papsttums*, I, Tübingen, 1930, 361–4.

Piétri, C. *Roma christiana*, II (*BEFAR*, 224), Rome, 1976, 948–9.

EUROPE.

A European Church? Contemporary Europe remains an important center for the variety of Christian confessions found on all the continents. Despite the profound evolution of relationships between Europe and the contemporary world, especially with the emergence of North America and decolonization, the role of Europe in the life of the Churches has not been challenged. In fact, it is in Europe that the principal points of reference of the universally diffused Christian Churches are located: the world's believers have their eyes turned to places like Rome for the Catholic Church, Constantinople (and Moscow) for the Orthodox Church, Geneva for the World Council of Churches, and Canterbury for the Anglican Communion. The considerable human and material resources necessary for the universal work of the Churches still come from Europe.

For Catholics, moreover, the relationship to Rome, to its bishop, and to its Church takes on a special value. Since VATICAN II, despite the great debate regarding Eurocentrism, Rome has strengthened its role, becoming a meeting place for Catholics, certainly, but also for Christians in an ecumenical context, as well as for non-Christians. Historically, the Church of Rome has always had a privileged relationship with Europe, and especially with Italy. The pope is the bishop of Rome, metropolitan of the Roman ecclesiastical province, and primate of Italy. The ties among the Church of Rome, Italy, and Europe are deeply rooted in the history of Western Christianity. It should be further noted that for centuries the Catholic Church was essentially a European Church, at least until 1492.

From that period on, and despite the rifts within Western Christianity in Europe, Catholicism has been a world religion, expanding first to Latin America, then to Africa, and finally to Asia, where its penetration has nevertheless been limited. Missionary zeal, with its culmination in the 19th and 20th centuries, confirms this still decisive role for Europe, under the backing of Rome and with the help of both European missionary congregations and the mobilization of European resources. Although it represents a community that is less and less exclusively European, the Church of today continues to look upon the old continent as the privileged place of reference. The Church of Rome, through the many seasons of Europe's history and in different ways depending on the age, has always thought of the continent as a whole. In the Europe of the 19th-century nations, the Catholic Church reflected and progressively modified its discourse. Europe seemed to be freeing itself from a Christian dispensation and turning toward strong national identities that were often characterized by their secularity. At the same time, however, the Catholic Church was showing tremendous missionary zeal, finding most of its energy in Europe.

Secular Europe and the Papacy. Given a secular Europe made up of nations, Catholic culture was in need of rethinking the history of the European Middle Ages and bringing to light the fundamental role played by the Church in the founding of civil society and the birth of communication among the diverse entities taking shape as states. This new reflection began to be integrated into the papal magisterium. In the encyclical *Immortale Dei* (1885), Leo XIII spoke of Europe by referring to the lessons of the past: the spirit of Christianity had accomplished a work of great civilization on the continent, but it would not have been possible without harmony between the spiritual power and the temporal power. The Middle Ages, from the starting point of a clearly very singular rereading of history, once again became the model for the modern age. In Rome, Christianity was once again proposed as offering the most certain path to harmony among the nations of Europe.

The thread of this reflection was taken up by the successors of LEO XIII in the framework of a Europe marked by secularity and nationalism. The First WORLD WAR, as is witnessed by the initiatives and the magisterium of BENEDICT XV, gave rise to a new meditation on the nations of Europe. "Nostalgia" for the Catholic states and for European Christianity was slowly but surely vanishing from the papal magisterium. The plurisecular history of both Europe and Christianity, conceived in their close relationship, became the focus of the new reflections. But it was above all the crisis of the Second WORLD WAR that renewed examination of the relationship between the Catholic Church and modern Europe. The most recent popes have emphasized the theme of Europe's Christian roots, as a remembrance of the past and a project for the future. It is not by chance that this reading has developed precisely in step with the deep division of the continent wrought by the Cold War. After the Second World War, the international role of Europe was profoundly recast, but for the Roman Church Europe remained the decisive continent. The popes, from PIUS XII to JOHN PAUL II, have given great attention to the problems, the history, and the diverse realities of the continent, and have even gone so far as to develop an organic dialogue on Europe. From 1939 to 1978, there were 137 pontifical interventions on the theme: Pius XII addressed the issue 36 times, JOHN XXIII, 7 times, and PAUL VI, 94 times. The interventions of John Paul II have been even more numerous. Until 1948, Pius XII referred only in a general way to the problems of a continent ravaged by war and divided by the Yalta accords. In the programmatic encyclical of his pontificate, *Summi pontificatus* (1939), the pope clung to his predecessors' interpretation in addressing the role of Christianity in Europe: "There was a time when this doctrine gave spiritual cohesion to Europe, which, educated, ennobled, and civilized by the Cross, reached such a level of civil progress that it could educate other peoples and other continents." The moral crisis, which reached its climax with the war, was born of "the abandonment of Christ, for whom Peter's throne is both teacher and trustee."

Pius XII: Europe United and Christian. The problem for Europe thenceforth was one of returning to its Christian roots and to a full adherence to the teachings of the Church of Rome. The exaltation of Rome as a "beacon of civilization" represented for Pius XII a way of reading the reconstruction of the world after the ravages of the war. From the heart of Europe, from Rome, came a teaching of Christian civilization that was indispensable for conceiving a future of peace. The proposal for a return to a profound union with the magisterium of the Church of Rome was accompanied by acts as symbolic as Pope Pius XII's proclaiming St. Benedict of Nursia "Father of Europe" in 1947. On the occasion of the fourteenth centenary of the birth of the saint, who is considered the founder of Benedictine monasticism, the pope proclaimed in his message the deep interpenetration of Roman civilization and the Gospel, which alone can "powerfully unite the peoples of Europe under the colors and the authority of Christ and can easily create a Christian regime."

Pius XII progressively clarified his thoughts on Europe. His concern that the Christian roots of the continent should be remembered did not lead him to withhold his support for initiatives in favor of European unity: the pope encouraged "generous spirits" and affirmed the interest of all Catholics in their initiatives. Europe was at the heart of the Holy See's concerns after the Second World War. The leaders of the principal Catholic parties worked in this direction, and were often at the origin of the first attempts at a common construction of Western Europe. This is what sometimes led the project for a united Europe to be criticized as the expression of a "Vatican Europe." In actual fact, the Holy See encouraged and supported the beginnings of the process of European integration without going into the particulars of political choices, the responsibility for which belonged to the ruling classes of the "Europe of the Six."

In 1953, Pius XII made an appeal for "continental union" among the European nations, without surrender of the individual identity of any one of them. According to him, the time had come to "pass from idea to action." Between 1955 and 1957, papal interventions intensified on the issue of European integration. The 1957 treaties of Rome were an occasion for the pope to express his staunch support for the development of the new Europe. On 27 March 1957, L'OSSERVATORE ROMANO presented the signing of the accords as one of the most significant events in the modern history of Rome. The Vatican daily saw Pius XII as continuing in a coherent fashion the plurisecular commitment of the papacy to European solidarity, in the direct line of INNOCENT XI and the Note addressed by Benedict XV to the warring powers in 1917. The pope himself intervened more than once in European questions, testifying to his interest in a supranational federalism that could promote the liberty both of local communities and of individuals. The Church of Rome felt committed to the spiritual foundation of European unity "for the defense of the freedom of the Europe that was still free," in the words of Pius XII, "and for the liberation of that part of Europe that had lost its freedom."

The Popes and a Divided Europe. On a number of occasions, Pius XII drew the attention of public opinion to the plight of the countries of Eastern Europe. The Catholic Church refused to limit itself to being the Western religious institution that the press and the propaganda of socialist regimes described; it claimed its roots in Eastern Europe. The pope's intention was to keep alive the West's interest in the East and to favor greater union among Western countries in the face of communist governments. New reflections concerning European history led him to this conclusion: when Europe needs to confront a common enemy (he was referring here to Islam in the past and communism in the present), division among the nations of Europe greatly weakens the continent's ability to resist. Innocent XI, beatified by Pius XII, came freshly to mind as a pontiff eager to move beyond the internal conflicts in Christendom in the face of the TURKS. In 1956, the lively protest made by the pope against events in Hungary was counterbalanced by bitter awareness of the division in Europe and the West vis-à-vis Soviet aggressiveness.

With the thaw in international relations, the pontificate of John XXIII was characterized by his ability to conceive of Europe, both East and West, as a unified whole, without

disregarding the process of Western integration that was under way. It is in this more relaxed context that the initiatives of the mayor of Florence, Giorgio La Pira, took place. They had begun in the preceding years and were directed at making spiritual values a rallying point among the countries of Eastern and Western Europe, as well as among the Mediterranean countries. The mayor of Florence was an interpreter of the pope's vision and enjoyed his support. In 1959, La Pira made a trip to Moscow, while the Soviet Union showed its interest in defining new relations with the Holy See. John XXIII intervened to favor contacts between the Holy See and the bishops of the East, and above all to secure their presence at the council of Vatican II. In order to have his plan succeed, the pope engaged in noteworthy diplomatic efforts with the Soviets. Even if the results of this activity were quantitatively modest, their consequences were of considerable importance. Within the meetings of the council there was a common meeting of the entire episcopate of Europe, after nearly twenty years of division on the continent. The Polish bishops especially, almost all of whom were at the council, developed deep and serious contacts with other Western European bishops and made known the singular situation of the socialist world. Relationships within the Church, broken off immediately after the war, began to be reestablished. These were the significant first fruits of a unitary conception of Europe.

Paul VI: Europe Small and Large. After Vatican II, the Holy See's commitment to Europe followed in the furrow already plowed. Ever since his time as prosecretary of state, Giovanni Battista Montini had followed with great attention the activities of Catholic politicians in favor of Europe. Like his predecessors, Paul VI emphasized not only the political and economic character of European unification, but also, and above all, its religious, moral, and spiritual character. The 1964 proclamation of St. Benedict as "Patron of Europe" was one more sign of this commitment: the message of the saint was interpreted as one aiming to teach faith and unity to the peoples of Europe. The tenth anniversary of the treaties of Rome offered the pope the opportunity to underscore the still lively interest of the Church in the unity of Europe despite results that were not always satisfying. For Paul VI, European unification was the fruit of a cultural process and of a change in attitudes: within this process, the role of the Catholic tradition seemed fundamental. Paul VI declared that Europe would cease to be itself if it repudiated its Christian heritage.

For the pope, while the 19th century had been the century of the awakening of national identities, the 20th ought to become evident as the time for states to draw together in fraternal unity. On a number of occasions, Paul VI made the observation that his vision of Europe was perfectly in line with that of his predecessors who had encouraged European unity. The pope knew full well that the foundations for a united Europe were many, but he gave consideration to the great importance, among those foundations, of the Catholic Church's contribution and of the Christian heritage. Europe, for which the Roman Church was working, did not coincide with Christendom even if it did maintain a vital relationship with the Christian tradition. The integration of Europe had the unequivocal support of the Holy See; but it was not forgotten that Europe went beyond the ensemble of nations delimited by structures shared in common. The Church of Rome did not accept the mutilation of Eastern Europe.

Diplomacy and Pastoral Work. Through the will of Paul VI, the Holy See participated in the Conference for Security and Cooperation in Europe up to the time of the HELSINKI Accord. The direct involvement of the Holy See met with a number of difficulties: the traditional reserve imposed upon those involved in multilateral negotiations, its will to remain outside "temporal rivalries" (article 24 of the Lateran pacts), the danger of being crushed between the two blocs, and the prudence always necessary when confronted with the risk of being reduced to a political power. Paul VI made this innovative choice in order to contribute to the creation of a wider Europe: "The Conference," we read in a letter sent by the pope to Cardinal Casaroli on the eve of the signing of the agreements, "by consolidating peace, will contribute to a tremendous increase in the exchanges of values that form the spiritual strength of Europe." If the Holy See's immediate interest was to see religious liberty recognized by the socialist regimes, even greater was its desire for the creation of a European platform common to the Eastern countries, within the framework of a Europe that would not be limited to the West. That is why on a number of occasions (and even under the pontificate of John Paul II, an ardent defender of the Helsinki principles) the Holy See has referred to these fundamental liberties accepted by all the countries that participated in the conference. The Europe of Helsinki corresponded to the aspirations of the Holy See, marking the end of the geopolitical divisions inherited from the Second World War. This interest prompted the Vatican to commit itself actively to a multilateral international political process despite the Holy See's traditional, almost prescribed reserve. The Helsinki principles were the preamble to a wider European integration and could support the efforts pursued by the Holy See for religious freedom and communication among the diverse European Churches.

During the pontificate of Paul VI, a greater integration among the continent's conferences of bishops began to develop. Nevertheless, the Council of Episcopal Conferences of Europe (CCEE), founded officially in 1971, was not created on the initiative of Rome, as was CELAM in Latin America. It was due to the initiative of Bishop R. Etchegarray, then secretary of the French bishops, who in 1965 worked out a *Note sur la collaboration entre les conférences épiscopales d'Europe* (Note on Collaboration among Episcopal Conferences of Europe). The text points out the need for unified reflection on the part of the bishops on the common problems of the continent in order to allow for a more concerted effort in their pastoral ministry. Etchegarray's initiative gave birth to the Episcopal Liaison Committee, which organized two symposia before the official founding of the Council of Episcopal Conferences of Europe. In the first elections, Etchegarray was chosen as president, flanked by a Western bishop and one from the East—the archbishop of Wrocław, Poland—as vice presidents. The CCEE became the privileged partner in the dialogue with the Conference of European Churches (KEK), which drew together both Orthodox and Protestants. A number of interventions on the part of the CCEE and the dioceses of Europe focused on the European theme; in 1976, the second symposium of the European bishops prepared a text significantly entitled *Reinvigorating Europe*, while the Belgian bishops concentrated on *The Vocation of Europe*.

The European Utopia of John Paul II. From the beginning of his pontificate, John Paul II has raised the theme of Europe: "Throughout the last two millennia," he declared in December 1978, "Europe has become the bed of a great river in which Christianity has flowed, fertilizing the earth and the spiritual life of the peoples and nations of this continent." The history of Europe obliges the Church to renew the role it assumes in the life of the continent, as he declared to the bishops of his country during his visit to Poland, the first one made by a pope to an Eastern socialist State: "Christianity must commit itself anew to the formation of the spiritual unity of Europe." However, this project stumbled over the reality of a Europe divided into two different "worlds," characterized by opposing systems. Despite the activity of the Holy See, which multiplied its contacts with socialist governments and committed itself to the Helsinki agreements, neither religious liberty nor full communication among the European Churches was reestablished. The pope openly intervened for the defense of human rights and especially for religious liberty. John Paul II strongly emphasized the need to consider Europe as a unified whole, beyond divisions. In a Europe still dominated by the political logic of Yalta, despite all the changes it had gone through, that idea was seen as utopian. In addition to Benedict, the "European saint," the first Slavic pope proclaimed Cyril and Methodius, the two saints who evangelized the Slavs, patron saints of Europe. In his encyclical *Slavorum apostoli* (1985), written in a still divided Europe, the pope outlined his plan for a common European consciousness, and this despite the diversity in its religious and cultural traditions. With a zeal that was new by comparison with that of his predecessors, John

Paul II underscored the existence of the "other lung," the Greek and Slavic, of Christian Europe: "In fact, Europe, as a geographic whole, is what might be called the fruit of two currents of Christian tradition, to which are added two forms of culture that are different and at the same time profoundly complementary." For the pontiff, rediscovery of the Christian roots of Europe seemed the essential condition for thinking of the continent in terms broad enough to transcend the divisions of the present: "Show Europe her soul and her identity," he stated to the 1982 Symposium of the European bishops, "and you offer Europe the keys for interpreting her vocation."

The European problem at the center of John Paul II's pontificate has been that of "a more intense communication between East and West," as he told the European bishops in 1985. He was referring here to an ecumenical problem between the Western and the Orthodox Churches, but also to the difficult situation of Christianity in Eastern Europe. In the East, the Church had to face the challenges of secularism in a way different from that in the West; besides, as Cardinal Wojtyła had pointed out regarding the conciliar documents, the Church had to use different approaches in confronting the problem of atheism and religious liberty in the two "worlds" of the same continent. To the pope, Europe seems a land in which enormous efforts have been made to "eradicate Christian convictions from the minds of Europeans," through both secularism and militant atheism. Thus he wishes fervently for a renewal of the coordinated initiatives among the Churches of Europe for EVANGELIZATION, a condition for their becoming viable parties in the different European societies. Throughout his TRAVELS in the diverse countries of Europe, John Paul II has aimed at laying out the "vocation" of the different nations in *The Papacy and the "European House" of Nations*. Reflection on European history (the pope gave a series of short speeches, for example, on the occasion of the fortieth anniversary of the end of the Second World War and of the fiftieth anniversary of its beginning), with its long pageant of losses and sorrows, has allowed him to point out the path the continent must find for its new mission in the world: "Europe exported war; today it must become the artisan of peace." In this spirit, Karol Wojtyła, attentive to all discourses favorable to a unitary idea of the continent, has given them his support; such was the case for Gorbachev's speech on the "common European house," which the supreme pontiff echoed in his own speeches. The great changes of 1989 were prepared for and followed with great attention by the Holy See. John Paul II himself proposed a reconstruction of the events in the encyclical *Centesimus annus*: "It seemed that only a new war could shake up the European order born of the Yalta accords. It is on the contrary, through a general commitment to nonviolence that they have been bypassed. According to

the pope, that was the beginning of a new season for the European continent: ". . . it is now, in a sense, that the real postwar is beginning."

After the fall of the socialist regimes, it became necessary to sketch out a new plan for the European Churches. In this regard, European Catholicism needed to try its best to renew its approach toward evangelization: that is why, in 1991, the pope convened the Special Assembly for Europe of the Synod of Bishops, in order to develop the main features of a European pastoral ministry. The political evolution of Eastern Europe put the Church back in contact with different national identities, which, given the politics of Eastern European regimes, were often held in contempt. The Holy See showed itself favorable to the development of these national identities in the Baltic countries and in the former Yugoslavia. However, this process of national rebirth led to conflicts, such as that of the Balkans, which also brought questions of religious identity into play. John Paul II wished to avoid the transformation of these conflicts into wars of religion, as had been the case in the Gulf War, and on a number of occasions he recalled the role of Christianity as a means of transcending contradictions through understanding. The various problems linked to European situations, in the former Yugoslavia or in Ukraine, to name but two, engendered ecumenical difficulties between Catholics and Orthodox. Under the pontificate of John Paul II, the Europe of the post–Second World War came to an end, the Europe in which the papacy had struggled to avoid being marginalized as a Western institution far from the East. One great problem did remain: that of bringing into harmony the courses on which different nations within Europe had set out, something for which Rome sensed that the spiritual contribution of its own tradition would be decisive, as would also be that of the Orthodox and Protestant traditions. During these last few years, as throughout the 20th century, the Roman Church has considered European unity an important coming together, to which she must bring the benefit of her tradition and spirituality.

Andrea Riccardi

Bibliography

Chenaux, P. *Une Europe vaticane?*, Brussels, 1990.

Conseil des conférences épiscopales d'Europe, *I vescovi d'Europa e la nuova evangelizzazione*, introduction by H. Legrand, Milan, 1991.

John Paul II, *Europa, un magistero tra storia e profezia*, ed. M. Spezzobottiani, Milan, 1991.

Riccardi, A. *Il potere del papa da Pio XII a Paolo VI*, Rome-Bari, 1988.

Spezzobottiani, M. "Il magistero europeistico dei Papi da Pio XII a Giovanni Paolo II," *La Scuola cattolica*, (1985), 113, 143–70.

EUSEBIUS. *(d. Sicily, August–September 309 or 310).* *Elected on 18 April (?) 309 or 310. Buried in the cemetery of Callistus on the Via Appia. Saint.*

After the deposition, or perhaps after the death, of MARCELLUS, Eusebius was elected to succeed him, as is attested by Eusebius of Caesarea, and later Optatus of Milevis and Augustine of Hippo, as well as the *Liberian Catalogue*. If the date of 18 April provided by the *Liberian Catalogue* for his accession to the episcopacy is generally accepted, the length given for his term as bishop varies from four months (from 18 April to 17 August), according to the *Liberian Catalogue*, to six months, according to Eusebius of Caesarea. The testimony of the *LIBER PONTIFICALIS* should not be relied on, as it wrongly considers his term as bishop to have lasted six years.

Eusebius was of Greek origin, the son of a doctor or a doctor himself, according to the note in the *Liber pontificalis*; the remaining biographical data cannot be accepted as accurate since they are the product of later revisions. Like his predecessor Marcellus, he found himself embroiled in the quarrel that divided the Roman community regarding the *lapsi*, apostates who sought to reenter the Church. Heraclius rose up against him, and disturbances and violence within the Church ensued (*scinditur partes populus*). While Heraclius, in his intransigence, "contested the right to repent of those who had fallen," Eusebius "taught that these poor souls had the right to lament for their crimes." Emperor Maxentius reacted, as he already had in the case of Eusebius's predecessor, but this time he banished both adversaries (*ex templo pariter pulsi feritate tyranni*). Eusebius was sent into exile in Sicily (*litore tinacrio*), where he died. The events of Eusebius's pontificate are known from a metrical inscription the first fragments of which were found in 1852 by G. B. De Rossi in the cemetery of Callistus in Rome. In this eight-line poem composed by Pope Damasus and engraved by Furius Dionysius Filolocalus, Eusebius is described as a "bishop and martyr." If the *Liberian Catalogue* mentions 17 August as the date of his death, the *Depositio episcoporum* and the *Martyrologium hieronymianum* give 26 September; the latter mentions also 2 October and 8 December; these variations could be accounted for as the result of confusion between the date of Eusebius's death and that of the *translatio* of his body to Rome.

Élisabeth Paoli

Bibliography

AASS, Sept., VII, 245–50.

BHL, I, 411.

Augustine, *Ep.* 53, 3, *CSEL*, 34, 2, 153–4.

Bardy, G. *Catholicisme*, 4 (1956), 697–8.

Carini, I. *I lapsi e la deportazione in Sicilia del Papa S. Eusebio*, Rome, 1886, 3ff.

Carini, I. *Le Catacombe di S. Giovanni in Siracusa e la memoria del papa Eusebio*, Rome, 1890, 1–52.

Caspar, E. *Geschichte des Papsttums*, I, Tübingen, 1930, 99–101.

Daniele, I. *Bibl. Sanct.*, 5 (1965), 246–8.

de Rossi, G. B. *Roma sotterranea*, II, 1867, 191–210.

Depositio episcoporum, MGH, AA, 9, 70.

Duchesne, L. *Histoire de l'Église ancienne*, II, Paris, 1911, 95ff.

Epigrammata Damasiana, ed. Ferrua, Vatican City, 1942, 129–36.

Eusebius of Caesarea, *Chron.*, II, *PG*, 19, 583 (= *PL*, 27, 493).

Falconi, C. *Storia dei Papi*, Rome-Milan, 1967, I, 330.

Marcora, C. *Storia dei Papi*, Milan, 1961, 123.

Marot, H. *DHGE*, 15 (1963), 1143.

Martyr. Hieron., AASS, Nov., II, *p. post.*, 527, 537, 639.

Marucchi, O. *Le catacombe romane*, Rome, 1933, 215–17.

Optatus of Milevis, *De schismate don.*, II, 3, *CSEL*, 26, 37.

Rottges, E. H. "Marcellinus-Marcellus, zur Papstgesch. der diokletian. Verfolgungszeit," *Zeitschrift für katholische Theologie*, 78 (1956), 385ff.

Schwaiger, G. *LTK*, 3 (1959), 1198–9.

EUTYCHIAN. Eutychian followed FELIX as pope at the end of Aurelian's reign. Early sources vary on the length of his pontificate. Eusebius states that he did not last a whole ten months (*Ecclesiastical History* VII, 32). But the *Liberian Catalogue* (*MGH*, AA, 9/1, 75) assigns to him eight years, eleven months, and three days, from 4 January 275 to 7 December 283. The *Liber pontificalis* gives roughly the same information, adding that he was of Etrurian origin (*LP* I, 159 = *MGH*, *GPR*, I, 38).

Although it was long, little is known of his pontificate, which covers the end of the reign of Aurelian and the reigns of Tacitus, Florian, Probus, and Carus—a period of peace for the Church. Toward the end of Aurelian's rule as prince, a renewal of persecutions could have been in the offing, but the sovereign's death kept him from carrying out his plans.

The *Liber pontificalis* wrongly states that he suffered martyrdom. Eutychian was buried in the catacomb of Callistus on the Via Appia (*MGH*, AA, 9/1, 70; *LP* I, 159 = *MGH*, *GPR*, I, 38), where his epitaph was found (*ICUR* IV, 10616).

Michel Christol

EVANGELIZATION.

The Kerygma or Proclamation of the Good News. Starting with the first generation of Christians, spreading the "good news" (the Greek meaning of "evangelium") contained in the life and teachings of Jesus constituted a burning obligation, and this missionary perspective was never abandoned, even though the forms it took have evolved greatly over the centuries.

Jesus himself seems to have considered that his mission should be addressed first and foremost to his fellow Jews: "I have been sent but to the lost sheep of the House of Israel."

According to the evangelist Matthew, this was the answer Jesus gave to a pagan Syro-Phoenician woman who appealed to him for help (Matt. 15:24). However, the woman finally obtained satisfaction, just as did the centurion from Capernaum (Luke 7:1–10). Sending the Twelve out on their mission, Jesus instructed them, in the words of Matthew (10:5–6): "Go nowhere among the Gentiles and do not enter any Samaritan city; rather go to the lost sheep of the House of Israel." Nevertheless, the three synoptic Gospels end with a universal mission: "Go throughout the world, proclaiming the good news ["evangelium"] to all creatures" (Mark 16:15). The broad outlines of evangelization were drawn in the earliest days of the Church, as is apparent, for example, in Peter's great speech following the outpouring of the Spirit at Pentecost (Acts 2:14–41). The "good news" was that Jesus was the Messiah announced by the Prophets, raised from the dead by God. But this proclamation calls for an appropriate response from man: conversion, a turning inward that normally leads to baptism, the guarantee of salvation. There could be no proclamation of the gospel without a call to enter the Church.

The Progressive Split with Judaism. Did the salvation brought by Jesus Christ concern only Jews, or was it for pagans, also? This preliminary question was quite rapidly decided in favor of the universalist option, as is seen in two key episodes from the Acts of the Apostles: the conversion of the Ethiopian eunuch (Acts 8:26–40) and, especially, that of the centurion Cornelius (Acts 10), which was confirmed by God himself. One subsidiary question remained: Were pagans who converted obligated to follow Jewish law? Following stormy debates and sometimes violent confrontations in which Paul played a leading role, the answer was no: pagans could be baptized without being forced into practices as distasteful to a Greek or a Roman as circumcision or dietary prohibitions. This decision left the doors of Christianity wide open to the Roman world. However, the first targets of evangelization were the Jewish populations of Palestine and the diaspora (Antioch, present-day Turkey, Greece, Alexandria, Rome). Throughout his travels, Paul approached the Jews, teaching first in synagogues. Even as late as the year 49, despite the intensity of the quarrels between Jews and Christians, the Roman powers saw no real difference between the two, since, according to Suetonius (*Lives of the Twelve Caesars, Claudius*, 25), they "chased from Rome the Jews who, under the influence of a certain Chrestus [Christ], were continually getting rest-

less." The definitive split came at the time of the Jewish War that brought about the destruction of the Temple of Jerusalem in 70, when the Christians refused to join with the insurgents, for which they were not to be forgiven. A group of Judeo-Christians was to persist for a number of centuries, attempting to reconcile Jewish law with faith in the risen Jesus. However, they were rejected by the Jews and marginalized by the massive numbers of Christians who had been converted from paganism, and their mission sank into meaninglessness, eventually becoming incomprehensible.

Installation in the Roman World. Thenceforth, it was toward the pagan world that evangelization efforts turned. The Christian writers of the 2nd and early 3rd centuries—those whom we call the apologists—expended considerable effort on articulating the Christian message within the intellectual framework of the Greco-Roman world, and on working out a Christian morality that would be responsive to the concrete questions posed by daily life within this civilization. Despite their best efforts, these spokesmen of a new, exotic, exclusive religion were disquieting both to the authorities and to their own neighbors: the 2nd and 3rd centuries were an era of persecutions, which counted more and more victims as Christians grew in number. The conversion movement seemed in no way discouraged. Expansion, made easier by the existence of a huge empire favorable to the spread of information, was spectacular, and as early as the 2nd century Christians boasted of being represented throughout the entire world (Tertullian, Irenaeus of Lyon, Origen). In fact, although there was a sizable Christian population in what is now Turkey, in the Near East—even beyond the borders of the Roman world—and in Egypt, their presence elsewhere was still limited to the large commercial cities that harbored sizable colonies of Easterners (Rome, Carthage, Lyon, Corinth, etc.). Moreover, this religion that exalted the humble repelled the exceptional, and the pagan Celsius railed: "They only want, and only know how to win over, the stupid, souls as vile as they are idiotic, slaves, poor women, and children [. . .]. Their teachers seek out and find as disciples only men who are thick headed and lacking in intelligence [. . .], wool carders, cobblers, cloth fullers, people who are utterly ignorant and completely devoid of education" (Origen, *Against Celsius*, III, 44 and 55).

In the 3rd century, evangelization widened and deepened in scope: a council convened 71 African bishops in CARTHAGE in 216, and another 60 bishops in Rome toward the middle of the century. There were a dozen episcopal sees in Spain, mostly in the south. In the Persian Empire, there were already more than 20 bishoprics in the year 224 (*Chronicle of Arbelius*) as well as, apparently, a number of other Christian communities. Moreover, all social classes were infiltrated. Throughout this whole period, Rome, which at the end of the first century prided itself on possessing the relics of the apostles Peter and Paul (Clement of Rome, *First Epistle*), played no privileged role in the work of evangelization. The Christianization of Italy did not happen particularly early. Northern Italy counted only five or six bishoprics in 300. Christian communities sprang up here and there, the fruits of the spontaneous missionary activities of Christians who had come from elsewhere, and then, when a community became sufficiently large, it would ask for a bishop from an already organized Church, but how the process worked seems to have escaped documentation. We can only at best imagine it from the somewhat idealized picture painted by Eusebius of Caesarea (*Ecclesiastical History*, III, 37, 2–3) in the 4th century: "In those days, many Christians felt their souls stirred by the Divine Word with a violent love for perfection. They began carrying out the Savior's advice by distributing their worldly goods to the poor; then, leaving their lands with the desire to preach the faith and transmit the books of the Divine Gospels, they carried out the work of the evangelists among those who had not yet heard of it. They only laid the foundations of the faith in foreign places; then they set up other pastors, entrusting them with the care of cultivating those whom they had brought into the faith. Then they left again for new lands and other nations with the grace and help of God, for the many and marvellous powers of the Divine Spirit were acting through them."

Christianity, a State Religion. The beginning of the 4th century saw a major event: the conversion of the emperor himself, in the person of Constantine. Spreading of the word henceforth met no institutional obstacles, even though the somewhat meddlesome intervention of emperors in theological disputes did create other problems, and eventually persecutions of another sort, directed against the heretics of the day. Christianity now gained favor with the elite, who no longer had to make the wrenching choice between faithfulness to Christ and fidelity to Rome. It succeeded in rooting itself solidly in all the provinces of the Empire, especially in the West. Only the world of the countryside—or, in other words, the great majority of the population—still resisted, for the most part, and a number of centuries would pass before they were Christianized. The Church organized itself based on the administrative structure of the state: in the 5th century an episcopal see was established in most of the larger municipal administrative centers.

Christianity, which in the 2nd century had looked to most people like a dangerous cancer within the Roman world, was, by the end of the 4th, becoming such an integral part of that world that some people made no distinction between the struggle against the Barbarians and the defense of the faith. Christianity was already present among the Barbarians, however. Armenia, along with its king, Tiridatus, was converted at the end of the 3rd century by one of the country's noblemen, Gregory the Illuminator, who was baptized in Caesarea during his exile from Cappadocia. While Christianity had difficulty surviving the terrible persecutions of King Shapuhr II (309–379) in Persia, Georgia was evangelized around 330 by the female Christian prisoner Nino. In Ethiopia, two young Roman travellers who had fallen into slavery won favor with the sovereigns and used it to spread Christianity. Wulfila, a descendant of Roman captives who was ordained bishop in 341, evangelized the Goths (under the form of Arianism) and translated the Bible into their language. From there, Christianity spread to most of the Germanic peoples. Similarly, the Breton Patrick, between 432 and 461, returned to evangelize Ireland, where he had earlier been held captive. In all these cases, evangelization took place via personal initiatives.

The Role of the Papacy. The first Roman evangelical mission did not appear until 596, when Pope Gregory the Great sent a group of monks to Great Britain armed with a clear directive: to convert the Anglo-Saxons. What explains the prolonged absence of the papacy from missionary work? At least one hypothesis can be suggested: during the early period, Rome's influence collided with that of the other great episcopal sees: ALEXANDRIA, CARTHAGE, ANTIOCH, and, shortly thereafter, Constantinople and MILAN. Much of the popes' energy thus was expended trying to get the other churches to recognize the primacy of the Roman see (see, for example, the article on Innocent I), and attention was thus focused on maintaining internal organization and discipline within existing communities, rather than on winning over new populations. Moreover, with theological quarrels adding fuel to personal rivalries, the Church was being split into rival sects that divided the community. In the 4th century, with the vicissitudes of the Arian crisis, a large part, if not all, of the Eastern Church was tending toward separation from Rome, a foreshadowing of the definitive break in the 11th century. Consolidation of Roman primacy had as its counterpart the progressive loss of all influence over those churches that refused to align themselves with its positions. As the 7th century approached, the popes were in a position to play a key role in missionary work, although their authority was limited to Western Europe (the dynamic African Church had been snuffed out by the invasion of the Vandals, followed thereafter by the Arabs). Inaugurating a policy destined for great future success, the popes thenceforth leaned on the most active branches of MONASTICISM, which had evangelized the Angles and the Saxons, as well as the countries on the other side of the Rhine. Boniface (673–754) worked for the conversion of the Germans, in close collaboration with the pope, who had named him his legate. A trend that was to take definitive shape in the 13th century was slowly starting the institution of missionary work entrusted to specialized corps by the pope.

Nancy Gauthier

See also MISSIONS.

Bibliography

Bardy, G. *La Conversion au cristianisme durant les trois premiers siècles*, Paris, 1949.

Chaumont, M. L. *La Christianisation de l'Empire romain, des origines aux grandes persécutions du IVe siècle*, CSCO, Subsidia, Louvain, 1988.

Danielou, J., and Marrou, H. I. *Nouvelle Histoire de l'Église*, I, Paris, 1963.

"Évangélisation" and "Mission," *Catholicisme, hier, aujourd'hui, demain*, Paris, 1982.

Jedin, H., Latourette, H., and Martin, J. *Atlas zur Kirchengeschichte*, Fribourgen-Br., 1970.

Latourette, K. S. *A History of the Expansion of Christianity*, I, *The First Five Centuries*, New York, 1937.

Siniscalco, P. "Évangélisation," *Dictionnaire encyclopédique du christianisme ancien*, Paris, 1990, I, 933–36.

Van der Meer, F., and Mohrmann, C. *Atlas de l'antiquité chrétienne*, German ed., Gütersloh, 1959; English ed. London, 1959; French trans., Paris-Brussels, 1960.

Von Harnack, A. *Die Mission und Ausbreitung des Christentums in den ersten drei Jahrhunderten*, 2 vol., Leipzig, 1924.

EVARISTUS. An early list of the bishops of Rome, drawn up under Eleutherius and cited by Irenaeus of Lyon (*Against Heresies*, III, 3, 3), attests that Peter's fourth successor was called Evaristus. According to Eusebius of Caesarea (*Ecclesiastical History*, III, 34; IV, 1; *Chronique*, ed. Helm, 193), his papacy lasted from 99 to 107. Modern historians suggest conjectural dates that are very similar to these. The details proffered by the *LIBER PONTIFICALIS* (Jewish father who was a native of Bethlehem, martyrdom, sepulchre near that of the apostle Peter) belong to the realm of legend. Thus, in its suggestion that Evaristus divided the Roman churches up among the different priests of the city, the work is projecting the Church's organization as it was in the 6th century onto the past. Some apocryphal texts (two letters, which Pseudo-Isidorus used in the 9th century, and fragments of two decretals) have long circulated under Evaristus's name.

Jean-Marie Salamito

Bibliography

Bardy, G. *Catholicisme*, 13 (1956), 772.
Botte, B. *DHGE*, 16 (1967), 111.
Duchesne, L. *LP*, 2nd ed., Paris, 1955–1957, 1, 126.
Pietri, C. *Roma christiana*, Rome, 1976, 1, 625.

EX CATHEDRA. A term denoting a solemn, absolute, and immutable declaration through which the Roman pontiff, by virtue of the powers conferred upon him by his magisterium, decides that a certain truth should be believed by all as something revealed by God himself. The pronouncement is therefore infallible in that it comes from a prerogative conferred upon the person of the pontiff of Rome: "Whenever he expresses himself *ex cathedra* [that is, from the chair of ST. PETER]—or when he is carrying out his duties as pastor and doctor of the Christian Community as a whole—he is announcing by virtue of his supreme apostolic authority that a doctrine on faith or on its manifestations must be respected by the entire Church, and that, through the divine assistance reserved for him in St. Peter, he enjoys this INFALLIBILITY with which the Divine Redeemer wanted his Church to be invested when she affirms a doctrine on faith and its manifestations; it follows that those affirmations as they emanate from the Roman pontiff are immutable in themselves and do not depend on the consensus of the Church" (constitution *Pastor Aeternus*, 18 July 1870, chapter IV).

Philippe Levillain

Bibliography

Del Rè, N. "Ex cathedra," *Dizionario ecclesiastico*, I (1953), 1046.

EXARCHATE OF RAVENNA. The word Exarchate (*exarchatus*) did not appear until after 751, when it referred to the *provincia Ravennantium*, formerly subject to the direct authority of the exarch. However, scholars have been in the habit of applying a wider meaning to the word, using it to denote the Byzantine province of Italy headed by the exarch. In that sense, around the year 600, the Exarchate comprised the *provincia Ravennantium* (upon which Calabria was dependent), and also the military governments of Istria, Venetia, Pentapolis, Rome, Naples (with the *Bruttium*), and Liguria, ruled by dukes or *magistri militum*. A century later, after the loss of Liguria, it included the *provincia Ravennantium*, Istria, the duchies of Ferrara, Venice, Pentapolis, Perugia, Rome, Naples, and Calabria. The exarch responsible for this entity, first mentioned in 584, undoubtedly owed his installation to the need to resist LOMBARD pressure. He was really a vice-emperor, with all civil and military powers at his disposal; he intervened in matters of finance and justice, he governed local diplomacy, and around 681 he received from Emperor Constantine IV the right to confirm the election of the pope. In the 8th century, the Exarchate broke up, to the benefit of other powers: starting in the 720s, the politics of Pope GREGORY II and his successors became more and more independent of the emperor, while the Lombard Liutprand moved forward at the expense of BYZANTIUM and occupied RAVENNA in 732–734. In 751, Ravenna was again in the hands of the Lombards, who were threatening Rome. Pope STEPHEN II called upon the king of the FRANKS, Pepin, who promised to "restore" the annexed lands to the *respublica Romanorum*. Pepin intervened in Italy in 755–756, which allowed the pope to obtain the Exarchate (that is, the *provincia Ravennantium*), Pentapolis, and Perugia, but Rome was confronted by Ravennese individualism. At the time of his coronation in 962, Otto I once again promised the restitution of the Exarchate and the Pentapolis, but their integration into the PAPAL STATES would be infinitely slow.

Jean Pierre Brunterc'h

Bibliography

Brown, T. S. *Gentlemen and Officers, Imperial Administration and Aristocratic Power in Byzantine Italy A.D. 554–800*, Rome, 1984.

Diehl, C. *Études sur l'administration byzantine dans l'exarchat de Ravenne (568–751)*, Paris, 1888 (BEFAR, 53).

Ferluga, J. "L'esarcato," *Storia di Ravenna*, II-1, Ravenna, 1991, 351–377.

Guillou, A. *Regionalisme et indépendance dans l'Empire byzantin au VIIe siècle, l'exemple de l'Exarchat et de la Pentapole d'Italie*, Rome, 1969 (Istituto storico italiano per il Medio Evo, Studi storici, 75–76).

Hartmann, L. M. *Untersuchungen zur Geschichte der byzantinischen Verwaltung in Italien (540–750)*, Leipzig, 1889.

Simonini, A. *Autocefalia ed Esarcato in Italia*, Ravenna, 1969.

Uhlirz, M. "Die Restitution des Exarchages Ravenna durch di Ottonen," *MIÖG*, 50 (1936), 1–34.

EXCAVATIONS IN ST. PETER'S. From 1940 to 1949 during the construction of PIUS XI's tomb in the "Vatican grottoes," archaeological excavations were undertaken under the main altar of St. Peter's basilica in the Vatican, for the purpose of researching evidence linked to the Apostle. Other explorations followed in 1952. On this occasion a necropolis was discovered, although the existence of part of it was already known, since elements had been found during the time of GREGORY I the Great (7th century), and later during the building of Bernini's canopy in the modern basilica (17th century).

The necropolis bordered a lane, probably a branch from one of the three arteries that run through the *ager Vaticanus* (the Aurelian, the Cornelian, and the Triumphal), whose trajectories are yet to be defined precisely. The depression in which the Vatican is located—borderd by the right bank of the Tiber and by the *montes Vaticani*—because of its argillaceous geographical nature was somewhat unhealthy. Since antiquity it supplied much of the material for potters' ovens. In early imperial times, texts referred to an imperial residence there, the circus of Caligula and Nero (called *Gaianum*), the *Naumachia* (perhaps located north of the present CASTEL SANT'ANGELO), the *templum Apollinis*, Nero's *Therebinthus*, the *Meta romuli* (a sepulchral structure), and the *Phrygianum*, the temple of Cybele, known in the 4th century. A large part of the area was for funeral purposes: scattered concentrations of sepulchers and mausolea have been found in the area located below the Vatican's automobile parking structure.

The necropolis that has been excavated under St. Peter's basilica is thus but a small part of something much more extensive. The mausolea are set at the foot of the hill in two parallel lines running from east to west. They were built with a highly crafted brick technique and are adorned with priceless decorations in marble, stucco, and mosaic. The niches on the internal walls of different mausolea were built to hold urns and vases containing cremated remains, which allows us to date the sepulchers to the 2d century, at the latest. During the 3d century, the rite of cremation gradually gave way to that of inhumation. At the time, the mausolea were probably already in existence, with pagan tombs and, in rare cases, with the presence of Christians: in mausolea F (the *Caetenni*), H-H1 (the *Valerii*), and M (the *Julii*). This latter mausoleum, which was pagan at the time of its foundation, still has mosaic decorations inspired by Christian subjects (the fisherman, the Good Shepherd, Jonas, Christ-Helios with his head surrounded by rays of light). At the eastern end of the excavations, under the apse of St. Peter's basilica, an open space presented a system of sepulchers in the open earth covered with a layer of MOSAICS, of areas covered with vaults, and of tombs separated by ridge tiles. Access to the open area was via a *clivus* that ran along the slope of the Vatican hill, and was entered by a stairway. During the same period, there was a conduit to take away water, which can be dated from the middle of the 2d century thanks to a mark impressed into one of the tiles used for its construction. The mausolea converge toward a covered rectangular area called *campo P*.

The excavations have shown a deteriorated sepulcher oriented from southwest to northeast, filled with shapeless remains and closed with the inscription *Elius Isidorus* already encountered, and perhaps picked up from, the nearby mausoleum of the *Aelii*. Other sepulchers that form the borders of a precise area have been found in the open earth all around this tomb. The oldest of these tombs are graves closed by a covering of ridge tiles that date back to the end of the first century A.D. One of the tombs has a stamp on a brick from the time of Vespasian. Another slightly later tomb is dated from the first half of the 2d century. *Campo P* appears to have had early improvements made about this time. To the east, a brick wall was constructed and covered on its western side by a red coating (whence the name *muro rosso*). Three sepulchers for inhumation are also dated to this same period, as is the construction of a buried recess, which nevertheless left the older inhumation sepulcher intact, this latter being attributed to the Apostle. The sides of the recess have overlapping reinforcements, separated by a horizontal travertine paving stone; it is protected by two small walls covered with marble and filler; this area is also paved with mosaics. This is probably Peter's "trophy" mentioned with that of Paul by the priest Gaius in the 2d century, as opposed to the tomb of the deacon Philip of the East, from the time of the Montanist controversy (Eusebius, *Historia ecclesiastica*, XXV, 6–77).

When Constantine decided to construct a basilica dedicated to St. Peter during the papacy of SILVESTER (314–35), the necropolis was still in use: the tombs covered with marble around that of St. Peter appear to date from this period. The natural slope of the soil and the presence of the necropolis made one preliminary arrangement necessary: the hill was leveled. The private mausolea located on the basilica's location were partially buried, and strong masonry structures for the basilica's foundation and support, which are still visible today, were built. The building was constructed parallel to the north side of Nero's circus, and not on the perimetral structures, as was thought before the excavations. The elevated sections are in brick and the foundations in *opus lisatum* (alternate rows of small blocks of bricks and tuff). The monument's body, in the shape of a Latin cross (64 × 90 m.), was divided into five naves separated by a series of twenty-two columns topped with architraves or arcades and ending with a continual transept with lateral appendices divided by columns. The *presbyterium*, raised .36 meter relative to the 2d century level and .11 meter relative to the basilica's pavement, had an arrangement in the center that encompassed the trophy of *Gaius*. Around the two recesses referred to above, a rectangular structure was constructed, bordered by the red wall and other walls that were, likewise, covered with marble. The kiosk would have been accessible by the front section, for worship, and this part was perhaps closed by a double door and protected by a canopy that rested on four of the six twisting columns, a gift from the emperor (*LP* I, 120). Two more of these columns were located on the corners of the apse's half-dome. The area was bordered by an enclosure of marble tiles. The reconstruction, which was made possible because of a decoration on a box that came from Samagher, was confirmed by the excavations. During the investigation, it could be seen that in one of the bordering walls of Gaius's trophy a small *loculus* had been made (29 × 32 × 77 cm), rendered inaccessible by

one of the walls constructed during the time of Constantine when work to protect the *memoria* was done. A number of artifacts were discovered inside the *loculus*: pieces of cloth, a coin from the 11th/12th century, and some pieces of bone that analysis has shown belonged to an elderly man living during the first century A.D. A lively debate has arisen around this discovery, between those who thought they had found St. Peter's bones and those affirming, with convincing arguments, that this hypothesis was completely unfounded.

Information from the time of the apostles places Peter's crucifixion and sepulcher in Rome in the area of the *ager Vaticanus*. One of the topographical references was the *Therebinthus*, placed by some researchers in the area of the *templum Appolinis*, which Duchesne identifies with the *Phrygianum*, while Lugli, and more recently, Giordani, prefer to place the latter monument inside the circus, thus establishing a relationship between the solar symbolism of the cult of Apollo and games played in the circus. This is how the legend of Peter and his martyrdom was born (John 21: 18; *Acta Petri*, 37; *LP* I, 118; Tacitus, *Ann.*, 15, 44; Tertullian, *Scorp.*, XV, 3; Eusebius, *HE*, III, 16; IV, 92; VII, 18), and since then Peter's grave has been placed in the Vatican. Some maintain that the grave was always there (Delehaye, Guarducci), and that the bones were simply taken away so that they could be protected from the humidity of the earth. One irrefutable proof of the presence of Peter's tomb is in the abundance of devotional inscriptions on the covering of one of the walls in the recess of Gaius's trophy. These inscriptions have also given rise to debates. Other authors (Duchesne, Carletti, Ferrua), based on the *Deposition martyrum* which refers to a *memoria* of St. Peter *ad Catacumbas* in 258, considered the possibility that the body, or part of the body (only the cranium, for Testini), was transferred to the Via Appia around the middle of the 3d century. Father Ferrua sees the sign of this transfer in the land, based on marks left by the violent reopening of the tomb. Independent of these motivations, archeological investigation has confirmed a place of veneration of Sts. Peter and Paul on Via Appia, a continual PILGRIMAGE destination, as inscriptions on the walls of the *Triclia* of S. Sebastiano prove. Delehaye posited a transfer of worship, rather than of relics. Luiselli pointed out that the meaning of the verb *habitare* (to inhabit while still alive) cannot refer to a funeral *memoria*. Thus, the date of 29 June spoken of by the chronograph in 354 is probably a reference to the feast of the two Apostles, rather than to the feast of Romulus and Remus, the founders of Rome, which is celebrated the same day in the temple of the QUIRINAL.

The naves of the basilica were a kind of covered cemetery; in the area of *campo P*, a stonework tomb seems to have been built after the basilica's construction, and, in the same fashion, a number of other graves were placed below its pavement. Some sarcophagi were also buried during the latter part of the 4th century, as can be deduced from part of a metric inscription. This sarcophagus, found in 1597, is preserved in the Vatican MUSEUM.

In front of the church there was an *atrium* surrounded by a portico with a *cantharus* (a bronze pinecone from the 2d century, topped by a bronze canopy) in the center, accessible by a path (*Porticus Sancti Petri*, or *Cortina*: Procope, *Bell. Goth.*, I, 22) that went from the Tiber to the steps of the main access. Around it were mausolea of a kind known in other buildings of the Roman *suburbium*. To the south, two circular mausolea dating from the 3d century were later transformed, one in the rotunda of St. Andrew's and the other in the grave of Mary, the wife of Honorius, which was later dedicated to St. Petronilla after the transfer of her relics from the catacombs of Domitilla.

According to Tolotti, the basilica's abnormal orientation is due to these two mausolea, the *Therebinthus* and the necropolis, since its axis is slightly rotated. The basilica, begun by Constantine in the years 319–29, was completed by Constance II. Among the interventions by Roman pontiffs, that of Pope DAMASUS (366–84) deserves special mention, since, in reference to the work done to keep groundwater from the area, he is credited with the installation of a baptismal font in the right arm of the transept (*Gesta Liberii*, Epigr. 3; Prudence, *Perist.*, 12, 31–5).

Excavations have not led to the discovery of traces of these works by Damasus, since they were probably erased by the construction of the Renaissance basilica. Smith believes that sources relative to Damasus are not concerned with the Vatican, but rather with the Janiculum.

Constantine's basilica represents the first example of a martyrial basilica constructed on a grave; previously, only an occasional LITURGY had taken place on the site, liturgies connected with the principal holy days and processions. The faithful had access to the *presbyterium*, an object of pilgrimage because of the *memoria*, although during ceremonies the space was reserved for the clergy. Pope GREGORY I the Great wanted to institute a regular liturgical service and a permanent altar for St. Peter. It was at this time that the transformation of the *presbyterium* took place; it was raised 1.45 meters relative to its height at the time of Constantine and furnished with two lateral stairiways. A semi-circular corridor was dug along the curve of the apse, 1.6 m. wide and .64 m. deep, the covering for which was the pavement of the new level of the apse. In the center, a rectangular arm led to the *confessio*. A crude masonry altar made with small blocks of tuff and bricks and covered with marble (.70 × .80 × .98 m.), has a small well on top of it for relics and a *fenestrella confesionis* in the front. A split in the masonry allowed for the preservation of some ashen remains, as well

as pieces of bone and glass; these belong, perhaps, to some form of relic worship *ex contactu*. Such a device, allowing access to the place of worship, was considered to be the architectural prototype of semicircular crypts. Based on a letter by Gregory the Great (IV, 30), its construction can apparently be credited to Pope PELAGIUS II, although the altar is attributed to Gregory. Six other columns, a donation by GREGORY III (731–41), were lined up along the front of the apse, in such a way that they shield the *confessio* (*LP*, I, 312).

An object of continual pilgrimage, the sanctuary became a pole around which the city grew. Places of worship sprang up around it, as did centers of assistance and places to welcome foreign pilgrims; an urban neighborhood, properly speaking, also formed, and got Pope LEO IV (847–55) to protect both it and the basilica from Saracen incursions by means of a walled enclosure that formed the borders of the *civitas leonina* (*LP* II, 124). Transformation of the *memoria* into a recess for *pallii* dates from the 9th century; the recess was decorated with a mosaic image of Christ giving his blessing; from the base of the recess, an opening allowed access to the Apostle's tomb.

Among later interventions, the altar of CALLISTUS II (1119–24) also deserves mention; it encompasses part of the aforementioned altar, and covers it with marble. In the middle of the 15th century, Pope NICHOLAS V decided to reconstruct the severely damaged church, and he entrusted the project to Bernardo Rossellino. During the following papacies (JULIUS II and LEO X), several architects, painters, and sculptors participated in the project, from Bramante to Michelangelo and Raphael, split between a Latin cross project and a Greek cross project. The present day church is elevated relative to the Constantinian basilica, and the space between the two constructions, called the "Vatican grottoes," is where the pontiffs are buried. Nothing is visible today of the early basilica, but remains of the apse, the transept, and perimeter walls have been uncovered during excavations. Of the twelve columns, eight are in the relic loggia, and one is in the chapel of the Pietà. The flagstones around the *presbyterium* are found in the grottoes. The *confessio* has also undergone transformation: Bernini's *ciborium* crowns CLEMENT VIII's (1592–1605) altar, and the kiosk of *Gaius*, formerly the recess of the *pallii*, is accessible by the uncovered *confessio*, which has become a spacious chapel.

Rossanna Martorelli

Bibliography

Apolloni, B. M., Gretti, J., Ferrua, A., Josi, E., Kirschbaum, E. *Esplorazioni sotto da Confessione di San Pietro in Vaticano eseguite negli anni 1940–1949*, Vatican City, 1951.

Degrassi, N. "La datazione e il percorso della via Aurelia e la via Aurelia Nova nella zona del Vaticano," *Rend. Para*, LXI, 1988–89, 309–42.

Duchesne, L. "Vaticana—Notes sur la topographie de Rome au Moyen Âge," X–XIII, *Scripta minora. Études de topographie romaine et de géographie ecclésiastique*, Rome, 1973, 181–244, 253–59, 303–13; "Naumachie," "Obélisque," "Terebinthe," ibid., 315–28.

Fasola, U. M. *Pierre et Paul à Rome*, Rome, 1980.

Ferrua, A. "La tomba di San Pietro," *La Civiltà cattolica*, 141, 1, 1990, 400–07.

Ferrua, A. *Memoria dei SS. Pietro e Paolo nell'epigrafia*, in *Saecularia Petri et Pauli* (Studi d'Antichità cristiana, 28), Vatican City, 1969, 9–34.

Ferrua, A., trans. *Damaso e i martiri di Roma anno Damasi saeculari XVI*, intro. by C. Carletti, Vatican City, 1985, 30–31.

Giordani, R. ". . . in templum Appollinis . . ." A proposito de un incerto tempio d'Appollo in Vaticano menzionato nel Liber pontificalis," *Rivista di archeologia cristiana*, LXIV, 1988, 160–88.

Giuntella, A. M. "Spazio cristiano" e città altomedievale: l'esempio della civitas leoniana," *Atti del VI Congresso Nazionale di Archeologia Cristiana (Pesaro-Ancona, 19-23 settembre 1983)*, Ancona, 1985, 309–25.

Guarducci, M. *I graffiti sotto la Confessione di San Pietro in Vaticano*, Vatican City, 1958.

Guarducci, M. "I 'trofei' degli Apostoli Pietro e Paolo," *Rendiconti della Pontificia Accademia Romana di Archeologia*, LV-LVI, 1982-4, 129–36.

Guarducci, M. "Pietro in Vaticano—Commento ad una recensione del P. Antonio Ferrua," *Archeologia classica*, 36 (1984), 266–98.

Guarducci, M. "Il culto degli Apostoli Pietro e Paolo sulla via Appia: riflessioni vecchie e nuove," *MEFRA*, 98 (1986), 811–42.

Guarducci, M. "Feste pagane e feste cristiane a Roma," *Rendiconti della Pontificia Accademia Romana di Archeologia*, LIX, 1986-7, 119–25.

Guarducci, M. *La tomba di Pietro*, Rome, 1989.

Janssens, A. "I pelligrinaggi primitivi alla tomba di San Pietro," *Akten 12. Internationaler Kongress für Christliche Archäologie* (Bonn, 22–28 Sept. 1991).

Krautheimer, R., Corbett, S., Frazer, A. *Corpus Basilicarum Christianarum Romae*, V, Vatican City, 1980, 171–285.

Luiselli, B. "In margine al problema della traslazione delle ossa di Pietro e Paolo," *MEFRA* 98 (1986), 843–54.

Pietrangeli, C., ed. *La Basilica di San Pietro*, Florence, 1989.

Reekmans, L. "L'implantation monumentale chrétienne dans le paysage urbain de Rome de 300 à 850," *Actes du XIe Congrès international d'archéologie chrétienne (Lyon-Vienne-Grenoble-Genève, 21–28 septembre 1986)*, II, Vatican City, 1989, 861–915.

Russo, E. "La recinzione del presbiterio di San Pietro in Vaticano dal VI all' VIII secolo," ibid., 3–33.

Saxer, V. "Pietro apostolo," *Dizionario patristico e d'Antichità cristiana*, II, Rome, 1983, 2784–89.

Saxer, V. "L'utilisation par la liturgie de l'espace urbain et suburbain: l'exemple de Rome dans l'Antiquité et le haut Moyen Âge," ibid., 505–58.

Smith, C. "Pope Damasus' Baptistery in St. Peter's reconsidered," ibid., 257–86.

Testini, P. "Le presunte reliquie dell'Apostolo Pietro e la traslazione 'ad catacumbas,'" *Actes du Ve Congrès international d'archéologie chrétienne (Aix-en-Provence, 13–19 septembre 1954)*, Vatican City, Paris, 1957, 529–38.

Testini, P. *Archeologia cristiana*, 2d ed., Bari, 1980.

Tolotti, F. "I due mausolei rotondi esistenti nel lato meridionale del vecchio San Pietro," ibid., 287–315.

EXCLUSION. Anticipating the 1879 CONCLAVE that appeared imminent due to LEO XIII's advanced age, the French embassy defined the right of exclusion as "a privilege shared by three great powers [France, Spain, and Austria], based more on custom than on a formal act of recognition [and] consisting in the ability of each of these three governments to exclude *one* name from the list of candidates for the [papal] crown." Actually, Portugal claimed the same right. Without entering into issues of origin or legitimacy, memoranda note that Austria used the right of exclusion in 1823 against Cardinal Severoli, and Spain in 1830 against Cardinal Giustiniani. If the past were plumbed further, Spain's exclusion of Baronius in 1604 and the French ambassador's exclusion of Odescalchi in 1676 could also be cited. The archives note that in 1829 Chateaubriand had entrusted Cardinal Clermont-Tonnerre with the authority to pronounce exclusion against Cardinal Albani and, in 1830, La Tour-Maubourg, special ambassador to the conclave, entrusted Cardinal d'Isoard with the task of excluding Cardinal Macchi. The government of the Third Republic was not giving up the prerogatives of the Very Christian King. In 1878, it was Cardinal de Bonnechose, archbishop of Rouen, who had the veto; during the conclave, seeing votes going in favor of Cardinal Bilio, more in the interest of maintaining France's privilege than for fear of seeing Bilio end up with the tiara, he warned the dean of the SACRED COLLEGE that his government was opposed to the cardinal's exaltation.

When the conclave of 1903 opened, the French government was less interested in the exclusion of another candidate than in the triumph of its own, Cardinal Rampolla, the deceased pope's former secretary of state. But on the morning of 2 August, when 29 votes had been gathered in Rampolla's favor, it was Cardinal Puzyna, prince-bishop of Kraków, who resorted to exclusion against the front-runner on behalf of the Austrian emperor. The results were not long in coming: the second vote of the day brought Rampolla his thirtieth vote, but the next day he lost six of those on the first round, and an additional eight on the second. On 4 August, Giuseppe Sarto became Pope Pius X.

In his commentary on the failure of his candidate, the French ambassador noted the unhappiness caused by the Austrian veto. However, he declared, "the risky step was successful." Moreover, "as long as the right of the three great powers has not formally or juridically been abrogated, France remains entitled to make use of it [the veto] according to its interests." Cardinal Puzyna explained in his memoirs that he had asked Franz-Joseph to make use of his right of exclusion to avoid electing a "political pope." In his opinion, there was nothing that was not legitimate in the matter. But that was the last time exclusion was used. In his constitution *Commissum Nobis* on 20 January 1904, Pius X strictly forbade all cardinals, under threat of excommunication, from allowing themselves to be the bearers of a veto or of any other type of government intervention in a conclave during papal elections.

Pierre Blet

Bibliography

Blet, P. "La diplomatie française et l'élection de Pie X," *Pro fide et justitia. Festschrift für Agostino Kardinal Casaroi zum 70. Geburtstag*, Berlin, 1984, 549–62.

Dimier, A. "Exclusive," *DDC*, 5 (1953), 612–15 (extensive bibliography).

Pius X, "Commissum Nobis," *Codex Juris Canonici*, Rome, 1917, 484–85 (*Acta Apostolicae Sedis*, IX/II, 1917).

Sagmüller, "Das Recht der Exclusive in der Papstwahl," *Archiv für katholisches Kirchenrecht*. 1895, 193–256.

Vidal, G. *Du droit d'exclusive en matière d'élection pontificale*, Toulouse, 1906.

EXCOMMUNICATION. See Anathema.

EXEMPTION. "In ecclesiastical matters, the word *exemption* normally means only the privilege that shields a church, or a secular—or other—community from the jurisdiction of a bishop" (Durand de Maillane, *Dict.*, II, 406). Every Christian—everyone baptized—is spiritually and temporally subject to the authority of the sovereign pontiff and to that of the diocesan bishop, i.e. the "ordinary," for whom the power of jurisdiction is a divine institution, like the power to ordain or to command. It was thus that the first monks, either clerics or lay brothers, were subject to the local bishop, a submission that was confirmed at the time of the COUNCIL of Chalcedon in 455 (c. 4 and 8), although exceptions were soon made to it,

since the Council of Arles (455) limited the power of the bishop of Fréjus over the lay monks of Lérins. A special privilege thus permitted a monastery to be shielded from the temporal and spiritual jurisdiction of the ordinary. It is this privilege, commonly granted by the pope since the 8th century, that constitutes exemption.

Essentially, exemption concerns the clergy, although others can also benefit from it. It differs from dispensation, which is more specific. In the case of exemption, the person is always shielded from the authority of his superior, while dispensation implies the exercise of this superior's power. The pope can exempt congregations, courts of the CURIA, NUNCIOS, metropolitans, religious superiors, or pastors, from the jurisdiction of an ordinary but also from the jurisdiction of all ecclesiastical authorities with any power whatsoever. Exemption may cover individual persons, as well as places and the people in them, or legal entities such as monasteries and chapters. The exemption granted to monasteries shields the clerics, who are under the authority of an abbot, from the jurisdiction of the ordinary, but it can also be extended to the entire population included in their domain (*sacrum bannum*).

The Origins of Monastic Exemption. The principles of the Council of Chalcedon were widely applied by Western bishops, since the monks' submission to their abbot in no way excluded the authority of the bishop. In 511, the Council of Orleans decided that all churches would be subject to the local bishop, and that the bishop had the right to correct abbots (c. 17, 21). The Second Council of Carthage, in 525, reaffirmed that only the bishop of the area where a monastery was located could ordain clerics and proceed to the blessing of oratories (Mansi, VIII, 649–651), although the monastery was free from the bishop's authority in other matters. The bishop of the diocese retained his right of jurisdiction over the monastery, and certain liturgical acts were reserved for him: ordinations, consecrations, and some benedictions. Without codifying the relations between bishops and monasteries, St. Gregory, pope from 590 to 604, frequently referred to them in his correspondence. He reaffirmed that the bishop had the right and the duty to watch over monasteries in his diocese and authorize foundations, that he enjoyed the right to visit, and that he should confirm the election of an abbot and oversee his administration. Clerics becoming monks were to abandon all other charges, and monks who received ecclesiastical offices were directed to leave the monastery. Nevertheless, the bishop was not to abuse his rights, nor was he to meddle in the temporal administration of the monastery. On a number of occasions, St. Gregory called on the authority of the Holy See to guarantee agreements made between bishops or princes and monasteries: St-Cassien de Marseille, in 596; Sts. John and Stephen in Ravenna, in 598; Arles in 599; and the monasteries of Autun, in 602, even though these privileges were not, properly speaking, what canon lawyers might call exemptions.

Irish monks taking up residence on the continent accelerated the movement, coming as they did from monasteries that had jurisdiction over a specific territory, and whose abbot (sometimes a simple monk) fulfilled the role of bishop and exercised the power of ordination. St. Colombanus arrived in Gaul about 590 and founded, successively, Annegray, Luxeuil, and Fontaine, before leaving for the Alps and, in 612, founding Bobbio, where he died in 615. All these initiatives took place without much concern for ecclesiastical authority. The privilege accorded to Bobbio by Honorius I in 628 went beyond anything that had been granted up to that time, forbidding any bishop—with the exception of the pope—to exercise jurisdiction over it, or even to celebrate mass there without the abbot's invitation (Jaffé, 2017). The *Liber Diurnus Romanorum Pontificum*, in use at the PAPAL CHANCERY from the end of the 7th century until GREGORY VII's papacy, contains two formulas governing monastic privilege. Formula 77 was the one used for Bobbio; formula 32 was the one used by GREGORY II or III for two monasteries in Benevento between 715 and 741, and it was used again for privileges pope ZACHARIUS granted to Fulda (Jaffé, 2293), and in 757 by STEPHEN II, and then again in 786 by HADRIAN I at St-Denis (Jaffé, 2331 and 2454). The Carolingians reacted against this movement, and Charlemagne proclaimed that all monasteries would submit to episcopal jurisdiction, granting them only the freedom to elect their abbot and administer their daily affairs, returning to St. Gregory's principles governing the privileges of immunity, exemption from taxes, and from royal jurisdiction. With the weakening of royal power in the second half of the 9th century the monasteries, leaving behind his protection, again sought the protection of the pope. Vézelay went to Nicholas I in 863 (Jaffé, 2831), and the diploma granted by Charles the Bald in 868 was but a confirmation of the papal bull. Vézelay was given by its founder, Count Girart de Roussillon, to the holy apostles Peter and Paul, and handed over to the holy pontiff of Rome; in exchange, the monastery owed the pope, in his capacity as the apostle's vicar, an annual *servicium* of one pound of silver, a symbolic form of tribute. The Roman Church thus became the owner without usufruct of the monastery and its dependent structures. But the principle raised here was that St. Peter's lands were not liable to anyone for tax nor should there be any question of imposing any other obligations whatsoever. On the other hand, spiritual dependency was maintained, although the bishop was to refrain from exacting any type of recompense in return for his power of ordination. At stake here was the issue of immunity granted by the pope, to the detriment of the king. Belonging to the

Holy See and showing up in Lucca, Italy, at the end of the 8th century, did not automatically imply exemption. Through these means, the papacy increased the bases of support liable to back up its actions. Thus, Cluny, founded in 910 by William of Aquitaine on his estates, was given to the PATRIMONY OF ST. PETER at the time of its foundation but remained the spiritual subject of its ordinary, the bishop of Mâcon. The powers of ordination and jurisdiction were clearly separated from each other.

Exemption Reaches Its Peak. The reform movement instituted at the end of the 10th century saw in exemption an efficient way to combat the influence of bishops who were politically rather than religiously inclined. The abbot of Fleury, Abbon (988–1004), obtained an important privilege from Pope Gregory V in November 996: it was forbidden for any bishop to come to the monastery, celebrate mass or perform an ordination in it without being invited, or to claim any authority over the monks he had ordained. Only the abbot had power over the men and women dependent on the monastery, and only he could discipline the monks. He was not subject to a general interdict, and if accused, he could appeal to the Apostolic See and go to Rome whenever he thought it would be useful (Jaffé, 3872). The same pope granted a similar privilege to Cluny in 998 or 999, augmented, however, by an essential clause: for the blessing of a new abbot, the monks could turn to the bishop of their choice: *Abbates namque, qui consecrandi erunt, de ipsa congregatione cum consilio fratrum communiter eligantur, et ad eum consecrandum, quemcumque voluerit, eposcopum advocent* (Jammé, 3896; Zimmermann, *Papsturkunden*, 351). It goes without saying that the bishops voiced their opposition to such privileges and, at the council of Anse (1025), appealed to the canons of the Council of Chalcedon for support of their position. The papacy had found an effective way to assure the support of the monks, by implicating them not only in its religious but also in its political actions. The privileges of exemption spread quickly and, to name but one example, William of Volpiano extended benefits to the abbeys he reformed in Burgundy, Italy, and Normandy. A decade later, Lanfranc did likewise.

By the middle of the 11th century the papal chancery was working out a new submission clause *nulli nisi nostrae apostolicae sedi*, tightening the connections already established between monasteries and the Holy See. In the "Collection in 74 Titles," drawn up in the Roman CURIA around 1050 by Hildebrand, the future GREGORY VII, texts concerning exemption come directly after those that affirm Roman primacy.

The privilege of exemption and the concomitant independence enjoyed by monasteries was also granted to priories and to lands whose abbot, as temporal lord, had sole spiritual responsibility; these lands which were given the name "exemption," were often reintegrated into dioceses after the council of Trent. At the end of the Middle Ages, abbeys *nullius diocesis* also benefited from the privelege of exemption.

One of the consequences of the development of the privilege of exemption was the formation of the idea of religious orders, which, regardless of the geographical structure of the diocese, grouped together monasteries that were affiliated with a [mother] house under the direct purview of the pope. This is what happened with Cluny very early on, and it was not just by chance that in the 11th century the popes entrusted the Cluniacs with abbeys that they wanted to reform. If exempt abbeys were rare in England and Germany, there were many more in France and Italy, and for some monasteries affiliation with a congregation was a de facto way to benefit from exemption.

Let it be borne in mind that exemption, in contrast to apostolic protection—a distinction evoked in a decree by Alexander III (ca. 1177; Jaffé, 14037)—did not apply to monasteries alone; it could also be granted to collegial churches.

New Orders and Exemption. The new orders created in Italy and France at the end of the 11th and the beginning of the 12th centuries were searching for a way of life close to an idealized apostolic life and had little concern for exemption. The Cistercian *carto caritatis* left substantial room for actions by the bishop, who alone could authorize the founding of a monastery and consecrate its abbot, even though he did not have visitation rights. Although the Cistercians avoided the use of the word "exemption," they managed to obtain privileges that gradually removed all episcopal authority over them: in 1152, Eugene III allowed them not to observe the restrictions (Jaffé, 9600); in 1169, Alexander III excused the new Cistercian abbots from requesting consecration whenever their bishop wanted to take advantage of the situation by forcing a promise of submission upon them (Jaffé, 11632); in 1184, Lucius III forbade bishops to excommunicate Cistercians (Jaffé, 15118). In the 13th century, exemption was fully recognized.

The case was the same for the Carthusians. In 1176, Alexander III placed the order under his protection (Jaffé, 12733); in 1185, Lucius III allowed them to appeal to any bishop of their choice (Jaffé, 15344).

From the beginning, the mendicant orders were faced with the problem of exemption. The religious way of life they had chosen led them to care for souls throughout the Christian world and even beyond, and they quickly took the form of centralized orders, subordinated to a superior general. The monks were no longer tied to a house but

were *ad nutum superioris*, which entailed a certain freedom vis-à-vis the diocesan bishop. In 1231, GREGORY IX granted exemption to the Franciscan and the Dominican friars. The exemption became personal, no longer local. Exemptions granted to the mendicants increased throughout the Middle Ages, to the point where protests were raised at the council of Constance.

A similar phenomenon developed toward the end of the Middle Ages, when in order to avoid the system of abbeys *in commendam* and the system of benefices, stability in the monastery was replaced by stability in the congregation, which suppressed all ties with the local clergy. The example of the congregation of Santa Giustina, in Padua, is a case in point, since in 1504 it joined Monte Cassino, and its influence spread beyond Italy's borders. Beginning in 1434, abbots, who were no longer elected for life but rather for a set period of time, were freed from the obligation of being blessed by the bishop, and beginning in 1435, the congregation received a large exemption, later supplemented by other BULLS, which freed the monks altogether from their ties with the local church.

The Council of TRENT addressed this problem at a number of points (decrees *De Reformatione* in the fifth session [ch. 2], in the 21st session [ch. 9], in the 22nd session, and especially in its 25th session, on 3 and 4 December 1563, part of which deals in 22 chapters with the reform of the clergy, both male and female, *De Regularibus et monialibus*). Bishops were recognized as having the right to impose punishment for crimes committed by members of religious orders outside their houses if the superior was informed of the case and took no action. The rights of bishops over the convents of cloistered nuns were set. But the council did not address the question of exemption of members of religious orders in any systematic fashion.

The Congregation of Exempts. Chapter 8 of the reform for religious orders had been adopted during the 25th session of the Council of Trent. In taking up INNOCENT III's constitution *In Singulis*, which had fallen into disuse, the council stipulated that exempt monasteries should hold general chapters and have canonical visits to supervise discipline; otherwise, the monasteries would be visited by the ordinary, acting as apostolic delegate. The result of this was the effective suppression of one of the primary privileges of exemption. A number of independent monasteries took the council literally and grouped themselves together in congregations—congregations of exempts. The first to do this were the monasteries of northern France and Belgium and in 1564 they formed the congregation of exempts of Flanders or of Belgium, which disappeared in 1781 after the edicts of Joseph II. In 1628, it gave rise to another branch, the congregation of the Presentation

Notre-Dame, inspired by the St-Vanne reform, which was dissolved in 1658 in order to avoid the hold that the bishops of Cambrai and Malines had over them. In France, in 1579, the États Généraux of Blois put an end to the privilege of exemption for isolated monasteries, forcing them, too, to join congregations and hold triennial general meetings. The publication of the ordinance of 1580 gave rise to the formation of the congregation of exempts of France, a movement that began with Marmoutier and took in 55 houses in 6 provinces (Tours, Sens, Bourges, Lyon and Vienne, Aquitaine, Toulouse and Narbonne). The Société de Bretagne was formed in 1604, starting with the priory of Léhon-sur-Dinan, under the influence of Dom Noél Mars; in 1628 the society, as a block, joined the congregation of St-Maur.

In 1607 the congregation of St-Denis was created around the abbey of the same name; shortly thereafter it, too, joined the congregation of St-Maur. The main objective of these congregations was to preserve the old privileges of exemption for the monasteries that they comprised, and to fight against the *ad commendam* system and against the power of the bishops, but they lacked a real unity that would have let them evolve and avoid stagnation.

The congregation of exempts of France, which in 1768 comprised only 68 monks divided among 11 houses located in the southwest (St-Ferme, Guîtres, St-Sauveur, La Reule, Charroux, Moreaux, Nanteuil-en-Vallée, Le Mas-d'Azil, Baignes, Terrasson, Le Tasque), was disbanded by the Commission des Réguliers in 1770.

In practice, monastic exemption no longer exists today. The CODE OF CANON LAW OF 1917 posited, in principle, that regulars were exempt from the jurisdiction of the ordinary of the region, "with the exception of nuns who are not under regular superiors" (c. 615); regular abbots were, after their elections, "to receive, within a period of three months after their election, the benediction of the bishop of the diocese in which the monastery is located" (c. 625). The 1983 code, in which only one canon deals with exemption, is even more concise: "In order to better provide for the good of the institutions and the needs of the apostolate, the supreme pontiff, by reason of his primacy over the Church as a whole, and out of consideration for the common welfare, may exempt institutions of consecrated life from the authority of the local ordinary and make them subject to himself alone or to another ecclesiastical authority" (c. 591).

Jean-Loup LeMaitre

Bibliography

Croocker, R. W. "Exemption, History of," *NCE*, 5 (1967), 716–17.

Denton, J. H. *English Royal Free Chapels, 1100–1300. A Constitutional Study*, Manchester, 1970.

Dubois, J. "Esenzione monastica," *Dizionario degli Istituti di Perfezione*, 3 (1976), 1298–1306.

Fabre, P. *Étude sur le "Liber censuum" de l'Église romaine*, Paris, 1892.

Falkenstein, L. "Alexander III. und die Abtei Corbie. Ein Beitrag zum Gewohnheitsrecht exemter Kirchen in 12. Jahrhundert," *AHP*, 27 (1989), 85–195.

Fogiasso, E. "Exemption canonique," *DDC*, 5 (1953), 637–46; "Exemption des religieux," ibid., 646–65.

Goeting, H. "Die klösterliche Exemtion in Nord und Mitteldeutschland vom 8. bis zum 1514," *Archiv für Urkundenforschung*, 14 (1936), 105–87.

Hourlier, J. *L'Age classique (1140–1378). Les religieux*, Paris 1974, 442–8 (*Histoire du droit et des institutions de l'Église en Occident*, 10).

Jombart, E. "Exemption (droit canon)," *Catholicisme*, 4 (1956), 900–4.

Knowles, D. "Essay in Monastic History. The Growth of Exemption," *The Downside Review*, 50 (1932), 210–31, 396–436.

Lemarignier, J. F. *Étude sur les privilèges d'exemption et de juridiction des abbayes normandes depuis les origines jusqu'en 1140*, Paris, 1937; "L'exemption monastique et les origines de la réforme grégorienne," *A Cluny. Congrès scientifique. . . , 1949*, Dijon, 1950, 288–340.

Letonnelier, G. *L'Abbaye exempte de Cluny et le Saint-Siège*, Ligugé-Paris, 1923.

Mahn, J. B. *Ordre cistercien et son gouvernement, des origines au milieu du XIIIe siècle*, Paris, 1951.

Marié, J. and Gazeau, R. "Exempts," ibid., 505–907.

Morelle, L. "Formation et développement d'une juridiction ecclésiastique d'abbaye: les paroisses exemptes de Saint-Pierre de Corbie (XIe-XIIe siècle)," *L'Encadrement religieux desfidèles au Moyen Age et jusqu'au concile de Trente, 109e Congrès national des sociétés savantes, Dijon, 1984*, Paris, 1985, 597–620.

Pfaff, V. "Die päpstlichen Klöstersexemtionen in Italien bis zum Ende des zwölften Jahrhunderts," *ZRGKA*, 71 (1986), 76–114.

Pfurtscheller, F. *Die Privilegierung der Zisterzienserordens im Rahmen der allgemeinen Schutzund Exemtionsgeschichte, vom Anfang bis zur Bulle "Parvus Fons" (1295)*, Berne-Frankfurt, 1972.

Scheuermann, A. "Exemption," *LTK*, 3 (1959), 1295–6.

Schreiber, G. *Kurie und Kloster im 12. Jahrhundert. Studien zur Privilegierung. Verfassung und besonders zum Eigenkirchenwesen der vorfranziskanischen Orden . . . (1099–1181)*, Stuttgart, 1910.

Szaivert, W. "Die Entstehung und Entwicklung der Klösterexemtion bis zum Ausgang des XI. Jahrhunderts," *Mitteilung des Instituts für Österreichische Geschichtsforschung*, 59 (1951), 265–98.

EXPECTATIVE GRACE. Expectative grace, or simply expectative, was the promise made by the pope of a collation to come for an ecclesiastical benefice that was not yet vacant. Expectatives were abused as early as the papacy of JOHN XXII, and abuse persisted throughout the AVIGNON PAPACY, despite periodic annulments, like the one pronounced by BENEDICT XII when he became pope. The entourages of princes and individuals connected with universities were those to whom benefices were primarily granted, but potential recipients realized that the number of expectatives was greater than the number of collations possible. Collations thus were soon looked upon in the same way as counterfeit money and became the object of acerbic comments (François Villon derided them in his will).

Jean Favier

Bibliography

Tihon, A. "Les expectatives *in forma pauperum*, particulièrement au XIV siècle," *Bulletin de l'Institut historique belge de Rome*, 5 (1925), 51–118.

F

FABIAN. *(d. 20 January 250). Consecrated pope 10 January 236.*

Pope Anterus died 3 January 236 after a brief papacy during Maximinus the Thracian's persecutions, and Fabian succeeded him a few days later. The context of his election suggests that the situation was not overly dramatic for the Roman Church. Eusebius of Caesarea put a marvellous stamp on the event:

"All the brothers were gathered together for the election of the one who was to receive the bishopric; the names of a large number of famous and remarkable men came to the minds of most of them; no one was thinking of Fabian, who was present among them. However, a dove suddenly descended from the sky and landed on his head, from what we are told, much like the descent of the Holy Spirit upon the Savior in the form of a dove. At this, all those who were gathered there, as moved by a divine breath, in a single impulse and with a common soul, cried out that he was worthy, and without further delay they took hold of him and seated him upon the bishop's chair" (*Historia ecclesiastica*, VI, 29). He was ordained bishop of Rome on 10 January 236 (according to the *Liberian Catalogue, MGH, AA*, 9/1, 75).

Fabian's long papacy (236–50) took on some importance, since times were again peaceful after the end of Maximinus the Thracian's rule, and through the reigns of Gordian III (238–44) and Philip the Arab (244–49), who acquired the reputation of being favorable to Christians (Eusebius, *HE*, VI, 34). Moreover, HIPPOLYTUS'S SCHISM had been overcome and unity was reestablished in the Roman community.

A decisive reform in the administrative organization of the Church of Rome must be attributed to Fabian. In the Christian communities, the deacons, invested with a liturgical role and with the responsibility for charitable works, administered the community's goods under the control of the bishop and took care of the distribution of offerings. In Rome, as elsewhere, there were seven, corresponding to the "seven deacons" of the Church of Jerusalem. According to the *Liberian Catalogue* (*MGH, AA*, 9/1, 75), it was under Fabian that the city was divided into seven districts or diaconates (which grouped the fourteen regions of the civil administration from Augustus's time together in pairs). Around this time other reforms included the institution of subdeacons, acolytes, exorcists, and porters. Since these ministries are mentioned in 251 in a letter addressed to Fabius of Antioch by CORNELIUS of Rome, their institution can be attributed to Fabian, Cornelius's predecessor (Eusebius, *EC*, VI, 43), but some aspects of the restructuring predate him.

Fabian fell victim to the persecution of Decius (249–51). In order to respond to problems accumulating in the life of the empire (the attacks of the Goths, the aggressiveness of the Persians, material difficulties), Decius believed he had found a way out in a rigorous restoration of religion. He hoped that would unify Rome and ward off danger by appeasing the gods. He forced the inhabitants of the empire to swear an act of allegiance to the official divinities. Some Christians submitted, conformed (they were called *sacrificati*), and burned a few grains of incense on the altars (*thurificati*). Certificates of sacrifice (*libellatici*), or sometimes compliance, were issued to them. But there were also martyrs, one of whom was Fabian, 20 February 250 (*LP*, I, 148 = *MGH, GPR*, 1, 27; *Liberian Catalogue, MGH, AA*, 9/1, 75). He was buried in CALLISTUS's catacomb, where his epitaph was found (*ICUR*, 4, 10694).

Michel Christol

Bibliography

Frend, W. H. C. *Martyrdom and Persecution in the Early Church*, London, 1965, 408–22.

Jost, E. *Il cimitero di Callisto*, Rome, 1933.

Lebreton, J., and Zeiler, J. *De la fin du IIe siècle à la paix constantinienne* (Fliche-Martin, 2), Paris, 1943, 121–22, 145–51, 391–94, 409.

Meunier, C. *L'Église dans l'Empire romain. Église et cité (Histoire du droit et des institutions de l'Église en Occident*, under the dir. of Lebras, G., and Gaudemet, J. II, 3), Paris, 1979, 249–52.

Testini, P. *Archeologia cristiana*, I, Rome and New York, 1958, 208–14.

Turner, C. H. "The Papal Chronology of the Third Century," *JThS*, 17 (1916), 343–45.

Vogel, C. *LP*, III, 74.

FABRIC OF ST. PETER. The official administrative body responsible for management of St. Peter's basilica originated during the papacy of Julius II. In the constitution *Liquet Omnibus*, 11 January 1510, he conferred upon a few individuals the care of seeing to the reconstruction of the old basilica and of collecting offerings from the faithful for this purpose. The Fabric's managing body—persons in charge of the administration of funds and revenues allotted for the construction and maintenance of a church—was also granted the exclusive right to promulgate indulgences, to grant certain dispensations, and to allow compositions for the absolution of usurping legacies to be used for pious works. These earliest arrangements were strengthened and made more specific by successive popes, and on 12 December 1523, Clement VII established a commission of sixty members of the Curia of all nationalities; the commission was entrusted with overseeing the Fabric's administration. The body had not only administrative but also judicial power over all the matters that concerned it. Later advantages were granted by nearly all the popes of the 16th century. Paul III gave it river rights on the Aniene from Ponte Luciano to its confluence with the Tiber (thus freeing the Fabric from taxes due along the river for transporting construction material), and he reduced to a minimum the tariffs it had to pay to the papal tax office.

Julius III extended the sixty-member college's sphere of authority to include donations from living individuals for good works, authorizing the Fabric to take one-fifth of the value of gifts. Pius IV obliged notaries, who were already supposed to declare donations, wills, and any other act that concerned the Fabric, to open sealed wills one year after the passing of the deceased and to have an authentic copy made for the execution of charitable bequests. Pius IV, through a series of constitutions in 1568, permitted the college, among other things, to execute for the Loretto sanctuary charitable bequests that would not have been efficiently carried out, as well as all those that were not executed in the year following the death of the will's maker.

On 4 March 1589, Sixtus V placed the college under the jurisdiction of the cardinal-archpriest of Saint Peter's, and in the first years of the 18th century Clement VIII replaced the college with a congregation of cardinals, called the Congregation of the Reverend Fabric of St. Peter, which took over all the functions of the earlier college. The congregation's function was to collect offerings for the basilica, to care for the many interests of the Fabric by scrupulously overseeing the execution of bequests on its behalf, to grant reprieves and indults reserved for it, and to deal with any litigation directly concerning or relating to its staff. Its broad scope in matters of charitable bequests and the possibility of admitting to it the cases of all those that had not been executed or could not be executed, so that they could be used for work on the basilica, led the congregation to appoint delegates or commissioners in all the provinces of the Papal States and even, through special conventions, in the kingdom of Naples. Benedict XIV split the congregation into two sections, one of which he called the general congregation, composed of a number of cardinals and prelates who met twice a year to look into contentious issues, and the other, called the particular congregation, composed of the cardinal prefect (of three cardinals who were members of the general congregation), an economist, and a judge, which was in charge of the financial and administrative management of the Fabric (constitution *Quanta curarum*, 15 November 1751). This arrangement was of short duration, however, since it was no longer in effect in the papacy of Clement XIII (1758–69).

Administrative reforms in the 19th century gradually undermined the congregation's legal jurisdiction, with its power to grant dispensations and indults soon to follow. Saved by Pius VII at the time of the general reform of courts in 1816, it was made subject by Gregory XVI to the rules of procedure of the Rota and, when it made a judgment on an appeal, to those of the Signature. Under Pius IX, an edict by the secretary of state on 28 November 1863 did away with the Fabric's tribunal and provincial commissioners. Cases concerning charitable bequests went through ordinary courts, while the Congregation of the Council judged in appeals. Reduced to administration of the basilica's assets and to its conservation, the congregation still kept an inherent jurisdiction over matters of bequests and of performing celebrations of the mass, a jurisdiction that it also had the right to delegate to diocesan bishops. Through the constitution *Sapienti consilio* (26 June 1908), which reformed the Curia as a whole, Pius X deprived it of all the powers it enjoyed that competed with other congregations, and limited its activities to those that fell strictly within the administration of the basilica and its assets. The Code of Canon Law of 1917 no longer mentioned it among congregations, but it continued to appear regularly in the *Annuario Pontificio*. With Paul VI's reforms (constitution *Regimini ecclesiae*, 1 March 1968), it ceased to exist as a congregation and became a simple Palatine administration; John Paul II (constitution *Pastor Bonus*, 29 June

1989) placed it among the "administrations connected to the HOLY SEE."

The congregation played a discrete, though not insignificant, role in making the basilica's image known. In 1629, it reprinted the early basilica's floorplan, drawn in the preceding century by Tiberio Alfarano. In 1694, it financed the publication of Carlo Fontana's work dedicated to the basilica, and it is to this work that we are indebted for the book in which all the inventions of Niccola Zabaglia—who was responsible for the church's scaffolding—are described (*Castelli e ponti de Maestro Niccola Zabaglia*, Rome, 1743).

Among the employees of the Fabric, the *sampietrini* deserve special mention, for it was they who were responsible for the installation and upkeep of the basilica's temporary equipment. Up to the time of World War II, it was acrobatically talented members of the *sampietrini* who saw to St. Peter's exterior illumination by descending on ropes from the top of the cupola to light the wax torches placed along the most salient of the basilica's architectonic lines. One particular section of the Fabric is the *Studio del mosaico* (mosaic shop), created at the end of the 16th century, which has made extraordinary reproductions of paintings that decorate a number of the sanctuary's altars.

The Fabric has important archives (some 5,300 articles from the 16th to the 20th centuries) relating to the basilica's construction and the early juridical powers concerning charitable bequests.

François-Charles Uginet

Bibliography

Del Rè, N. "La Sacra Congregazione della Reverenda Fabbrica di San Pietro," *Studi romani*, XVII (1969), 229–301.

FALDA. See **Vestments, Pope's Liturgical**.

FAMILY, PAPAL, MIDDLE AGES. The papal "family"—*familia papae*, not to be confused with his relatives—was composed of the ensemble of the members of the Roman CURIA, as well as lay people connected either truly or honorarily to the personal and domestic service of the pope, or belonging to the papal administration, and whose subsistence was provided by the APOSTOLIC CAMERA.

The very existence of the papal family is inextricably tied to the idea of patriarchal community within which the entire curial society appears to have been organized as early as the 12th century, in *familiae*. From the time that the Roman Curia began to take form, in the middle of the 11th century, as it did in the royal and princely courts of the day, all lay persons or clerics who belonged to the

pope's immediate entourage were considered part of the pope's family. Belonging to the family theoretically depended only on the wishes of the pope, who kept whomever he wanted for curial duties or for his personal service. On the other hand, however, the pope's death automatically entailed the loss of familial privileges: from the beginning of the 12th century to the end of the 13th, everyone lost the privileges of "familiarity" through the decease of their master; thereafter, this obsolescence happened only to the members of the *parva* or *stricta familia*, the closest family members. These latter included everyone who dealt with daily needs, even when the court traveled: chaplains above all, but also the members of the Camera and of the bull office, domestic services (kitchen, bakers, blacksmiths, notaries for domestic offices), guards, and almoners.

The members of the family all belonged to the Curia and enjoyed subsistence rights allocated by the Camera: from the chamberlain and the vice-chancellor to subordinate workers, guards, and ushers. At the end of the Middle Ages, they could be classified as follows: the members of the pope's immediate entourage; the pope's "domestic familiars and long-term guests"; the drafters of papal briefs, the scribes of the CHANCERY and the PENITENTIARY (Pope CLEMENT VI accorded the privilege on 8 July 1347); individuals playing a political role, or having a role in defense, such as mercenaries, members of the high nobility or high clergy, suppliers to the Curia (goldsmiths, tailors, etc.), generally honored with the title of papal sergeant at arms; and the family members of the papal family. Given their duties, the group of papal CHAPLAINS formed the heart of the family (the members of the "intrinsic chapel" were not admitted until 1444). The honor of belonging to the papal family nevertheless kept a personal character, as popes attempted to control its development as much as possible.

At least after the second half of the 13th century, entry into the papal family required the ecclesiastical candidate to obtain a letter patent of familiarity in due form, as was the case for papal chaplains. Besides the allocation of daily needs, which during the 14th century was changed into ordinary wages, the members of the papal family enjoyed a certain gratuity in the issuance of bulls, and choice places, for clerics, when ecclesiastical benefices were conferred. During the time of the AVIGNON PAPACY, family members also had preferential rents in the city. All these privileges disappeared if the individual left the particular curial duty he exercised. Given the confidence that tied family members to the pope, it was upon them that he called to carry out important or delicate missions (ambassadorial missions, inquiries, etc.). Reaching the figure of some 190 individuals in 1309, the family comprised some 270 at the time of JOHN XXII (1316–34), roughly half of the curial force. At the time of the last Avignon pope, Gregory XI (1370–78), assimilation of the *officiales Sedis apostoliae* (from 500 to 600) into members of the papal family was not complete, but well on the way.

Following the example of the papal family to a certain extent, the cardinals and higher administrators of the Curia had a personal family that was quite well organized as early as the 13th century; the system's influence on the central administration of the Church grew considerably, until a certain osmosis took place between it and the papal family.

Pierre Jugie

Bibliography

Bäthgen, F. "Quellen und Untersuchungen zur Geschichte der päpstlichen Hofund Finanzverwaltung unter Bonifaz VIII," *QFIAB*, 20 (1928–29), 114–237.

Dykmans, M. *Le Cerémonial papal de la fin du Moyen Age à la Renaissance*, III, Brussels and Rome, 1983, 420–45.

Fabre, P., and Duchesne, L. *Liber censuum Romanae Ecclesiae*, I, Paris, 1889, 290–316.

Felici, G. "Famiglia pontificia," *EC*, V (1950), 999–1008.

Frutaz, A. P. "La famiglia pontificia in un documento dell'inizio del sec. XIV," *Paleografica, diplomatica et archivistica. Studi in onore di Giulio Battelli*, Rome, 1979, II, 277–323.

Guillemain, B. *La Cour pontificale d'Avignon, 1309–1376: étude d'une société*, Paris, 1966, 493–95 and index.

Paravicini Bagliani, A. "Il personale della curia romana preavignonese," *Proceedings of the Sixth International Congress of medieval Canon law*, Ser. C., *Monumenta juris canonici*, 7 (1985), 391–410.

Schimmelpfennig, B. "Familie päpstliche," *LexMA*, IV (1987), 256.

Schuchard, C. *Die Deutschen an der päpstlichen Kurie im späten Mittelalter (1378–1447)*, Tübingen, 1987, 128–1332.

Schwarz, B. "Kurie, Römische (Mittelalter)," *Theologische Realenzyklopädie*, XX (1991), 323–47.

FANON. See **Vestments, Pope's Liturgical**.

FATHERS OF THE CHURCH, GREEK. The patristic sources relating to the Church of Rome and its bishop can be analyzed historically only through a long, complex work of transposition: traditionally grouped in florilegia designed to support or refute the theses of a treatise *De primatu* and thereby subject to as many hermeneutic distortions, the sources must be painstakingly reinserted in their original context. Such a historiographical treatment is indispensable for avoiding the pitfall of interpretations whose seductive systematizing is the result of applying a filter of preestablished theological reading or else an excess of legalism, which is often one of the biases of such interpretations. Only by looking at the whole of the history of Christianity and paying close attention to the interplay of ecclesiastical discourse and practice (the *corsi e ricorsi* of the relations among the various Churches, the inner development of each Church, the relationship of the Churches to political and social change) can the historian attempt to judge the significance of the patristic testimony issuing from the Eastern Church.

Before 324. By studying the highly diffuse documentation, which is always linked to occasional writings and very rarely to theoretical thinking, one can gradually discern the features that certain Christians—or, when a tradition can be perceived as continuous, certain Eastern Churches—attributed to the Church of Rome.

At the beginning of the 2nd century, Ignatius, who ensured the unity of the Church at Antioch, sang the praises of the Church of the city to which he was journeying willingly to suffer martyrdom. He bestowed on the Church of Rome the wholly spiritual title of "The Primacy of the Community of Love" (*prokathêmêtês agapês; Ep. ad Rom.*, prologue). A half-century later Bishop Dionysius of Corinth, answering a (lost) letter from the Roman community and its head, Soter, applauded the tangible signs of the traditional solicitude of the Roman Church for his own Church (Eusebius of Caesarea, *Ecclesiastical History*, IV, 23, 9–11). Already in the last years of the 1st century, CLEMENT, following an apostolic method of maintaining ecclesiastical unity, had sent, in the name of the Roman community, a letter of brotherly correction to the Church of Corinth, exhorting it to put an end to its internal strife. The letter was carefully preserved so that it could be read in public, as it would continue to be as late as the 4th century (ibid., III, 16). DIONYSIUS also praised the charity of the Romans, who, like other communities (Cyprian, *Ep.* 62, 3–4), sent subsidies to the Churches in need. Clearly, this charitable concern captured attention: in the wake of the Decian persecution, Dionysius of Alexandria would bear witness to it (Eusebius, *EH* VII, 5, 2) and, shortly after that, the Cappadocian Christians would benefit from it (Basil of Caesarea, *Ep.*, 70).

To the natural drawing-power of the capital of the pagan Roman Empire, the Church, "on pilgrimage there," added its own brilliance and community of language to attract to itself, in the 2nd and early 3rd centuries, theologians or traveling preachers coming from the East, such as Justin from Palestine, Tatian from Syria, Valentinus from Egypt, Marcion from Pontus, Hegesippus after a stay in Corinth, Theodotus from Byzantium, Abercius from Hieropolis in Phrygia, and Origen, who came from Alexandria "to see the very ancient Church of the Romans" (Eusebius, *EH* VI, 14, 10). Irenaeus, the disciple of Polycarp of Smyrna, was probably another visitor. From his seat in the Rhône valley, in the late 2nd century, he opposed the secret traditions of the Gnostics with the apostolic teaching handed down through the regular episcopal succession. As the central example for his proof, he chose that of the Roman Church, which possessed a "stronger authority" (Irenaeus, *Adv. haer.* III, 3, 2: *propter potentiorem principalitatem*; alternative translation: "a more excellent origin"). This authority, he claimed, flowed from its importance, its antiquity, its universal renown, and its foundation and constitution "by the two most glorious apostles Peter and Paul" (ibid.) and conferred on it the responsibility of being, at the very least, a privileged center of reference for ecclesiastical unity. In actual fact, this witness held good mainly for the West, where, throughout the 3rd century, the Roman bishops—by means of the traditional exchange of letters of communion between the Churches, at the request of the pastors or the various parties—intervened in an attempt to settle conflicts and disputes, invoking an apostolic tradition which in the West only Rome could claim.

From the East, matters appeared in a different light. A number of communities had the advantage of having been founded by an apostle, for example Corinth, as Dionysius reminded SOTER (Eusebius, *EH* II, 25, 8). A few years earlier, during the debates between Polycarp of Smyrna and Bishop ANICETUS over the divergent customs of their two Churches regarding the Easter observance, both bishops had legitimized their own practice by invoking the tradition handed down by their predecessors, and although they could come to no agreement, the two parted in peace (ibid., V, 24, 16). When Bishop VICTOR of Rome (189–99), called upon by the adversaries of Polycrates, bishop of Ephesus, insisted that Polycrates follow the Roman practice of celebrating Easter on pain of rupturing the communion between the two Churches, Polycrates refused, arguing that the Eastern tradition went back to St. John the Apostle. He received the support of several bishops, among them Irenaeus of Lyon (ibid., V, 24). Similarly, when STEPHEN (254–57), citing apostolic tradition, sought to impose Roman discipline on the Asian Churches with regard to the baptism of heretics, Firmilian of Caesarea in Cappadocia, in his reply to a letter from Cyprian of Carthage, violently stigmatized the pretensions of the Roman bishop (Cyprian, *Ep.* 75; cf. Eusebius, *EH* VII, 5, 4), while Dionysius of Alexandria wrote profusely to the Roman Christians, preaching appeasement (dossier in Feltoe, 40–59).

Thus the Roman community increasingly voiced its conviction that it was witness *par excellence* to the apostolic tradition and therefore bound to exercise a particular responsibility for maintaining ecclesiastical unity, an attitude that encountered strong opposition in the East. Yet its prestige and influence in the West made Rome a much sought-after ally when conflict arose at the heart of the

Eastern communities. Origen wrote to FABIAN (236–50), among other bishops, to defend himself when accusations were brought against him (Eusebius, *EH* VI, 36, 4; Jerome, *Ep.* LXXXIV, 10). In the early 230s, his bishop, Demetrios of Alexandria, had communicated to the Church of Rome, as to other leading communities, the judgment that had been rendered, and a Roman synod had thereupon approved it (Jerome, *Ep.* XXXIII, 5). The debate initiated by Novatian in the wake of the Decian persecutions, over which attitude to adopt with regard to the *lapsi*, had repercussions throughout the whole Greek world: despite attempts at mediation by Dionysius of Alexandria, which were proof of the privileged ties between the Church of Peter and that of Mark, its interpreter, the Eastern bishops were split into partisans and opponents of the rigorist arguments, some giving their allegiance to CORNELIUS, some to his adversary; unity was restored only when a synod held in Antioch condemned Novatian and his allies (Eusebius, *EH* VI, 45 and 46; VII, 5, 1–2). In the late 250s, some Egyptian Christians denounced Dionysius of Alexandria to his namesake in Rome, accusing him of having jeopardized divine unity in a letter intended to combat the Sabellians; the Alexandrian bishop had to refine his arguments in order to preserve communion with Rome (see Feltoe, 165–98). Finally, in 268, the council of Antioch, which condemned and deposed Paul of Samosata, sent its synodal decision to Maximos of Alexandria as well as to bishops of other provinces and, in the West, to Dionysius of Rome, who approved it (Eusebius, *EH* VII, 30, 1). These first centuries of the known relations between the Eastern Churches and the Roman community ended with an exceptional intervention on the part of the emperor; faced with the stubborn refusal of Paul of Samosata, who was also engaged in local political struggles, to abandon his see, the neighboring bishops appealed to Aurelian, the pagan emperor; he decided that the episcopal residence should belong "to those who are in epistolary relation with the bishops of Italy and the bishop of the City of Rome" (ibid., VII, 30, 19).

From 324 to 536. After fifty years of silence on the part of the sources, Constantine's victory over Licinius (autumn 324), which unified the empire under the protection of an emperor who was a professed Christian, opened up a new era: the emperor now became an active partner in the ordering of ecclesiastical unity. Not only did Constantine endow certain Roman basilicas with Eastern landholdings, but he extended to the newly conquered territories the system, already instituted in the West (Arles, 314), of the "imperial council," designed to clear up the Churches' outstanding business. At the SYNOD of Nicaea I (325), the absence of the Roman bishop (who was, however, represented by two unobtrusive priests) confirmed Rome's fundamental reticence regarding this new procedure for maintaining the unity of the Church. The almost exclusively Eastern bishops, assembled at the emperor's initiative, twice passed laws by invoking Roman usage. Regarding the decision on the date of Easter, they recognized the exemplary value of the practices of Alexandria and Rome. On the other hand, in order to safeguard the traditional authority of the bishop of Alexandria over Egypt, Libya, and the Pentapolis, which was threatened by the general rules adopted by the council, in an interpolated clause they resorted to a parallel with Roman custom (canon 6). On balance, the Eastern assembly made use of reference to Rome without furthering the claims of the Roman Church.

Relations between the Eastern and Roman communities remained uneventful up to 338. This was the time when Eusebius of Nicomedia and his followers were seeking allies against Athanasius, who had been deposed at the council of Tyre (335) and had since then made a triumphal return to Alexandria from exile. Through an embassy they solicited the support of Julius, the bishop of Rome, calling for "communion for a certain Pistos," their candidate for the bishop's seat against Athanasius. When a rival embassy sent by Athanasius reached Rome, Julius, who professed to be an arbiter and conciliator, was obliged to improvise a solution to the question and proposed a council, to be held at a site chosen by the accused. Even before it took place, events moved rapidly. Constans II had Athanasius expelled from his city, and in 339 the latter took refuge in Rome, where he was joined by Marcellus of Ancyra, some Egyptian monks, and bishops from Thrace, Coelo-Syria, and Palestine. Julius, obeying ancient custom, had to decide to whom to grant communion with him, and gave it to the refugees. Then, following an unusual procedure inspired by the practice of civil tribunals, he held a council in Rome, the place chosen by Athanasius. This council, in which the Arian Eusebians, pleading threats of war and the long journey, refused to take part, concluded that the election of Athanasius's replacement was null. From the point of view of the Eastern clergy, the Roman bishop had scorned the regionalization of the ecclesiastical jurisdictions following Nicaea and set himself up as an appeal judge, over the synod's head.

In answer to Julius's arguments, put forth in a synodal letter addressed to the Eusebians, as well as to those of the Western participants in the synod of Sardica (343) legitimizing a posteriori the Roman bishop's actions, the Eastern bishops opposed "an ecclesiology of the *partitio imperii*" (C. Piétri): just as the West's judgments against Novatian's followers were respected in the East, so the Western bishops had to ratify the judgments of the great regional synods held in the East regarding Eastern affairs. Henceforth, Athanasius's enemies would ignore the bishop of Rome. In fact, Athanasius himself, even before returning to Alexandria in 346, lost no time in recovering his freedom of action. True, the Roman bishop was a valuable ally, but only an ally, and moreover one apt to fall short in the complex twists of the Arian crisis, as Athanasius would discover during the reign of Julius's successor Liberius.

To the victims of episcopal factions who were in the favor of a Christian prince more and more convinced of the solidarity between the unity of the Empire and that of the Church, the bishop of Rome no doubt seemed, in a period of *partitio imperii*, like a refuge, possibly an intermediary to help win the support of the Western emperor. In 365 or 366, without any lasting result, and then from 371–2, not without incident, Eastern clergy who were opposed to the official Arianism and who were increasingly persecuted, though always divided, especially in Antioch, tried to forge fresh links with those in the West. If Peter of Alexandria, Athanasius's successor, was forced to take refuge in Rome in 373 and remain there until 377, Basil of Caesarea attempted to negotiate the union of all anti-Arians and called for a synod. He deplored the arrogance and pretensions of Damasus, bishop of Rome, as well as the misunderstandings that arose from the diversity of languages (Basil, *Epp.* 215 and 239), and preferred to address the Western clergy generically. But only Damasus answered him as representative of all in the West, demanding adherence to a precise confession of faith. Yet in 377 or 378, a Roman synod, which Peter of Alexandria attended, clarified the relations of the Church of Rome with the various anti-Arian parties and drew up an important formula of faith, a true chart of Nicaean orthodoxy, which had immediate repercussions. The accession in the East, in 379, of a Nicaean emperor who came from the West, Theodosius, made it easier to rally Eastern anti-Arians to the Roman side. Thus, on 27 February 380, the emperor was able to publish an edict enjoining his subjects to "live in the religion which the divine PETER transmitted to the Romans (as the religion which he himself taught attests, to this day), in the religion which the pontiff DAMASUS manifestly follows, as does Bishop Peter of Alexandria" (*Theodosian Code* XVI, 1, 2). For the first time, an official text recognized the exemplary importance of the Roman communion and, above all, its reason for existence. It affirmed the "primacy which the apostolic tradition confers on Rome," a PRIMACY that "implies not jurisdiction but prerogative [. . .] the right to be the first to be questioned on faith and the first to define the conditions of ecclesial communion" (C. Piétri).

Roman influence in the East had ephemeral success. The imperial council of Constantinople (381), which brought order to the Eastern Churches after the Arian turmoil, was convened without the knowledge of the bishop of Rome and bore witness to the Eastern bishops' new-found independence. The council decreed that ecclesiastical geography be more strictly adapted to the great administrative divisions: "The bishop of Constantinople must have primacy of honor after the bishop of Rome, because Constantinople is the new ROME" (canon 3). The promotion of Constantinople to the heart of the Theodosian system, which singled out certain leading sees as privileged centers of Church unity, was in no way directed against Roman primacy, which was here reaffirmed. Yet this promotion meant that a see was consecrated on the basis of political and not apostolic criteria, in total opposition to the values of Roman ecclesiology represented at the Roman synod of 382, which claimed, to the detriment of many Eastern bishops, to settle the divisions of the Antioch community. At least until the 8th century, Roman bishops would refuse to use the expression "New Rome."

The conflict between Alexandria and Constantinople for supremacy in the East now came into the open. Next to alliance with the emperor, alliance with Rome was sought by both sides, to ensure at least the neutrality if not the support of the Western see, which always proceeded with caution. A preliminary joust in 381 saw Gregory of Nazianzus retreat before Timothy of Alexandria, Rome's favored Eastern representative. Next, the confrontation between Theophilus of Alexandria and John Chrysostom of Constantinople, which started in 403, brought into Rome a flood of exiled partisans of the bishop of Constantinople, while a friendly Christian aristocracy used all its networks of support to secure Roman commitment to ecclesiastical freedom. Communion between Rome and the great Eastern sees was interrupted for some ten years after the convening of a Roman synod, modeled on those of 340 and 382. The reestablishment of communion meant that the pattern of normal relations between these Churches would be resumed: mutual notification of episcopal successions, mention of the bishops of the other sees in the diptychs read out at mass, and, for Alexandria and Rome, search for agreement on the part of those who computed the date of Easter.

In 430, the pope of Alexandria, Cyril, succeeded in dragging his Roman colleague Celestine into the war of influence he was waging against Nestorius, bishop of Constantinople, by deploying a pious, verbal "ecclesiology of circumstances" (C. Piétri) on the Roman primate. At the imperial council of Ephesus (431), the Roman see was referred to, for one of the first times in the East, as "the Apostolic See," following a formula employed in Rome since LIBERIUS; while by the end of the 4th century, the theme of apostolic episcopacy, so dear to Roman ecclesiology, had been taken up by Epiphanius of Salamina (*Panarion* 27). The political and religious conjuncture immediately following Ephesus led the Roman LEGATES to participate in the restoration of order in the East, and even to send a bishop to Constantinople. Even if Rome was subsequently given a back seat in the pacification

brought about by the *Henoticon* of 433, the works of Church history written by Socrates, Sozomen, and Theodoret of Cyrrhus bore witness, in their rereading of the past, to the prestige of the Roman see in the East.

In 448, Eutyches, a monk in Constantinople, sent a letter to LEO of Rome as well as to the holders of other important sees—Alexandria, Jerusalem, and Thessalonica, at one time a papal vicariate serving the Church of Illyricum, a territory shared between East and West—seeking their support against his bishop, Flavian, who was accusing him of HERESY. In the resultant schism dividing the Christian world and the ruthless struggle that ensued, Leo sided with Flavian against Dioscorus of Alexandria. At first, Dioscorus triumphed, at the imperial council held at Ephesus in 449, and then he was defeated, at the council of Chalcedon (451), where the Christological *Tome* sent by "the bishop of the Apostolic See" to Flavian two years before was acclaimed and served as a basis for the elaboration of the conciliar formula of faith. This unprecedented triumph of Roman theology was tempered by the adoption, during a session attended only by Eastern bishops, of canon 28. This canon represented an attempt to legitimize the traditional *de facto* power exercised by the bishop of Constantinople over the metropolitans of the provinces of Pontus, Asia, and Thrace, by invoking the Theodosian hierarchy of the great episcopal sees and, especially, by developing its political justification: "The fathers [of Constantinople I] have with reason given the see of ancient Rome precedence, because this is the imperial city; moved by the same reasoning, [they] have granted the same precedence to the most holy see of the new Rome, considering with justice that the city honored by the presence of the emperor and the Senate and enjoying privileges equal to those of Rome, the most ancient imperial city, should have a greatness equal to hers in the affairs of the Church, and should occupy the second rank after her." Although in no way directed against Rome, these considerations could not have been more contrary to the principles of Roman ecclesiology, which were reaffirmed forcefully by Leo, who refused to subscribe to the offending canon.

The opponents of Chalcedon, most of them in Egypt and many in Palestine and Syria, anathematized "Leo the Impious," while the Nestorians appreciated the Roman bishop's intervention against the heirs of Cyril of Alexandria, whom they loathed. Meanwhile, relations between Constantinople and Rome adopted the *corsi e ricorsi* of the power struggles between the two Churches and of the emperor's attempts to ensure a peaceful settlement of the theological disputes by proposing a formula for union that Rome insisted on rejecting. The ending of imperial power in the West (476), which placed ancient Rome in barbarian hands, encouraged Acacius of Constantinople (472–89) to consider himself the first bishop of the Church of the Christian emperor. Having secured the departure into exile of John Talaia, the Chalcedonian bishop of Alexandria, who took refuge in Rome, Acacius supported Emperor Zeno's *Henoticon* (482), which led to rupture with Rome in 484. Thirty-five years of schism followed. Yet when Gelasius of Rome put forth his own arguments supporting the ecclesiology dear to the see of Peter, the only known reaction was an unusually deferential letter sent to Symmachus of Rome by certain Chalcedonian bishops who had been ousted from their sees, in which they implored Rome's help (Symmachus, *Ep.* 12). In 519, the new emperor, Justin I, and his nephew Justinian, who favored reconciliation with Rome, ordered the *Henoticon* to be abandoned, caused Acacius's name to be struck from the diptychs, and sanctioned return to the definitions of Chalcedon. The Eastern bishops were made to subscribe to the formula of faith put forward by Hormisdas, bishop of Rome, who affirmed with renewed vigor the role of guardian of orthodoxy that fell to the Roman see as well as its apostolic foundations: "One cannot pass over in silence the affirmation of Our Lord Jesus Christ, who said, 'Thou art Peter, and on this rock I shall build my Church . . .' These words are made true by the facts, for it is in the Apostolic See that the Catholic religion has remained pure . . . That is why I hope to succeed in being in communion with the Apostolic See, in which the entire and true and perfect stability of the Christian religion is to be found" (*CSEL*, XXXV/2, 520–2).

Rome's success should give rise to no illusion. While the patriarch of Constantinople, writing to his Roman colleague, strove to recall the dignity attached to the sees of both the ancient and the new Rome, the emperor praised Roman primacy the better to enlist Rome's help in reestablishing unity of empire and of the faith under his authority. Whereas the Christian East was torn among Nestorians, Monophysites, and Chalcedonians, with both Alexandria and Antioch being for the most part anti-Chalcedonian, the bishop of Rome became a key player in the emperor's reorganization of the Church and in his dream of restoring Rome's former grandeur. In 526, in Constantinople, Emperor Justin I deferentially received Pope JOHN I (the title was beginning to be used, in the West, exclusively for the bishop of Rome). On Easter Day, the pope celebrated mass in St. Sophia in place of the patriarch, and crowned the new emperor. But the first bishop of the Apostolic See to be officially welcomed by the New Rome was none other than the drafted ambassador of Theodoric, king of the Goths. In 536, Agapitus, also sent on an involuntary embassy, deposed the patriarch Anthimus after he had infringed the canon law forbidding the translation of sees, and ordained his successor Menas. The following year the Byzantine reconquest of Italy ended with the deposition of Pope SILVERIUS, accused of treason. From that time on, the bishop of Rome

was at the direct mercy of the emperor. The way appeared open to the full deployment of the "caesaropapist" system.

Michel Perrin

Bibliography

Amand De Mendieta, E. "Basile de Césarée et Damase de Rome: les causes de l'échec de leur négociation," *Biblical and Patristic Studies in Memory of R. P. Casey*, Fribourg, 1963, 122–66.

Batiffol, P. *Cathedra Petri. Études d'histoire ancienne de l'Église* (*Unam Sanctam*, 4), Paris, 1938.

Bréhier, L. "Avant le schisme du XIe siècle. Les relations normales entre Rome et les Églises d'Orient," *La Documentation catholique*, 415 (18 February 1928), 387–404 (repr. in *Istina*, 6 [1959], 352–72).

Caspar, E. *Geschichte des Papsttums*, I. *Römische Kirche und Imperium Romanum*, Tübingen, 1930; II. *Das Papsttum unter byzantinischer Herrschaft*, Tübingen, 1933.

Chadwick, H. *The Role of the Christian Bishop in Ancient Society* (*Center for Hermeneutical Studies. Protocol Series of the Colloquies*, 35), Berkeley, 1980.

Chapman, J. "Fides romana," *RB*, 12 (1895), 546–57.

Congar, Y. *L'Ecclésiologie du haut Moyen Âge. De saint Grégoire le Grand à la désunion entre Byzance et Rome*, Paris, 1968.

Dagron, G. *Naissance d'une capitale. Constantinople et ses institutions de 330 à 451* (*Bibliothèque byzantine*, 7), Paris, 1974.

Dagron, G. "Rome et l'Italie vues de Byzance (IVe–VIIe s.)," *Bisanzio, Roma e l'Italia nell'alto medioevo* (*Settimane di studio del Centro italiano di studi sull'alto medioevo*, XXXIV), Spoleto, 1988, 45–72.

Das Konzil von Chalkedon. Geschichte und Gegenwart, II, *Entscheidung um Chalkedon*, ed. A. Grillmeier and H. Bacht, 5th ed., Würzburg, 1979.

De Vries, W. *Der Kirchenbegriff der von Rom getrennten Syrer* (*Orientalia christiana Analecta*, 145), Rome, 1955, and useful synthesis in *L'Orient syrien*, 2 (1957), 111–24.

De Vries, W. *Orient et Occident. Les structures ecclésiales vues dans l'histoire des sept premiers conciles oecuméniques* (*Histoire des doctrines ecclésiologiques*, 5), Paris, 1974.

Dölger, F. J. "Rom in der Gedankenwelt der Byzantiner," *Zeitschrift für Kirchengeschichte*, 56 (1937), 1–42.

Duchesne, L. *Autonomies ecclésiastiques. Églises séparées*, Paris, 1896.

Dvornik, F. *Byzance et la primauté romaine* (*Unam Sanctam*, 49), Paris, 1964.

Dvornik, F. *The Idea of Apostolicity in Byzantium and the Legend of the Apostle Andrew* (*Dumbarton Oaks Studies*, 4), Cambridge, 1958.

Feltoe, C. Διονυσιου λειψανα. *The Letters and Other Remains of Dionysius of Alexandria*, Cambridge, 1904.

Frend, W. H. C. "Eastern Attitudes to Rome during the Acacian Schism," *Town and Country in the Early Christian Centuries* (*Variorum Reprints*, 119), London, 1980, 69–81.

Hanson, R. C. P. *Tradition in the Early Church*, London, 1962.

Horn, S. O. *Petrou Cathedra. Der Bischof von Rom und die Synoden von Ephesus (449) und Chalcedon* (*Konfessionskundliche und Kontroverstheologische Studien*, 45), Paderborn, 1982.

Il primato del vescovo di Roma nel primo millennio. Ricerche e testimonianze, ed. M. Maccarrone, Vatican City, 1991.

Jalland, T. G. *The Church and the Papacy. An Historical Study*, London, 1944.

Joannou, P. P. *Die Ostkirche und die Cathedra Petri im 4. Jhdt* (*Päpste und Papsttum*, 3), Stuttgart, 1972, reviewed by W. De Vries in *Orientalia Christiana Periodica*, 40 (1974), 114–44.

Jugie, M. *Le schisme byzantin. Aperçu historique et doctrinal*, Paris, 1941.

L'Église et l'Empire au IVe siècle (*Fondation Hardt. Entretiens*, 34), Geneva, 1989.

Maassen, F. *Der Primat des Bischofs von Rom und die alten Patriarchalkirchen. Ein Beitrag zur Geschichte der Hierarchie, insbesondere zur Erläuterung des sechsten Canons des ersten allgemeinen Concils von Nicäa*, Bonn, 1853.

Maccaronne, M. *Romana Ecclesia Cathedra Petri*, I (*Italia Sacra*, 47), Rome, 1991.

Maccarrone, M. *Apostolicità, episcopato e primato di Pietro. Ricerche e testimonianze dal II al V secolo* (*Lateranum*, n.s. XLII/2), Rome, 1976.

Magi, L. *La sede romana nella corrispondenza degli imperatori e patriarchi bizantini (VI–VII secc.)* (Bibliothèque de la Revue d'histoire ecclésiastique, 57), Louvain, 1972.

Meredith, A. *The Cappadocians*, Crestwood, 1995.

Nautin, P. *Lettres et écrivains chrétiens des IIe et IIIe siècles* (*Patristica*, 2), Paris, 1961.

Piétri, C. "Damase et Théodose. Communion orthodoxe et géographie politique," *Epektasis. Mélanges J. Daniélou*, Paris, 1972, 627–34.

Piétri, C. "La question d'Athanase vue de Rome (338–360)," *Politique et théologie chez Athanase d'Alexandrie* (*Théologie historique*, 27), Paris, 1974, 93–126.

Piétri, C. "Les origines de la mission lyonnaise: remarques critiques," *Les Martyrs de Lyon (177)* (*Colloques internationaux du CNRS*, 575), Paris, 1978, 211–31.

Piétri, C. *Roma christiana. Recherches sur l'Église de Rome, son organisation, sa politique, son idéologie de Miltiade à Sixte III (311–440)*, 2 vols. (*BEFAR*, 224), Rome, 1976.

Piétri, C. "Roma. Storia ed archeologia," *Dizionario patristico e di antichità cristiane*, Rome, 1983, II, 3009–22; "La géographie de l'Illyricum ecclésiastique et ses relations avec l'Église de Rome (Ve–VIe s.)," *Villes et peuplement de l'Illyricum protobyzantin* (C, EFR, 77), Rome, 1984, 21–59; "D'Alexandrie à Rome: Jean Talaia, émule d'Athanase au Ve s.," in Αλεξανδρινα. *Mélanges Claude Mondésert*, Paris, 1987, 277–95.

Richards, J. *The Popes and the Papacy in the Early Middle Ages (476–752)*, London, 1979.

Rimoldi, A. *L'apostolo San Pietro, fondamento della Chiesa, principe degli apostoli ed ostiario celeste nella Chiesa primitiva dalle origini al Concilio di Calcedonia* (*Analecta Gregoriana*, 96), Rome, 1958.

Scott, S. H. *The Eastern Churches and the Papacy*, London, 1928.

Sieben, H. J. *Die Konzilsidee der Alten Kirche*, Paderborn, 1979.

Sieben, H. J. *Die Partikularsynode. Studien zur Geschichte der Konzilsidee* (*Frankfurter Theologische Studien*, 37), Frankfurt, 1990.

Twomey, V. *Apostolikos Thronos. The Primacy of Rome as Reflected in the Church History of Eusebius and the Historico-Apologetic Writings of St. Athanasius the Great* (*Münsterische Beiträge zur Theologie*, 49), Münster, 1982, reviewed by A. de Haleux in *RHE*, 80 (1985), 130–4.

Ullmann, W. *Gelasius I. (492–496). Das Papsttum an der Wende der Spätantike zum Mittelalter* (*Päpste und Papsttum*, 18), Stuttgart, 1981.

von Harnack, A. "Römisch u. katholisch," *Lehrbuch der Dogmengeschichte*, 5th ed., Tübingen, 1931, 480–96.

Wojtowytsch, M. *Papsttum und Konzile von den Anfängen bis zur Leo I. (440–461). Studien zur Entstehung der Überordnung des Papstes über Konzile* (*Päpste und Papsttum*, 17), Stuttgart, 1981.

FATHERS OF THE CHURCH, LATIN. The concept of "Father of the Church" is both a modern and an ancient one. Modern, inasmuch as it was not until the 17th century that "patristic theology" (a term coined by the Lutheran J. Gerhard, author of the first *Patrologia*, published in 1653) became the part of theological education systematizing the teachings of the "Fathers." Ancient, because whereas the term "Father" was commonly used in antiquity to describe the master in relation to his pupil, it took on a specialized meaning from earliest Christian times, and became a title within a dogmatic category: the "Fathers of the Church." Soon the works of the "Fathers of the Church" were thought of as a secondary source of theology and one of the monuments of Tradition, along with the liturgy, canons, constitutions, etc. The category emerged against a twofold background: on the one hand, that of the episcopal MAGISTERIUM in general, and on the other, that of the development of Christian writings. Moreover, the terms "Father of the Church," "patristic," and "patrology" were also adopted by historians of the literature, but in a broader way that was more chronological and descriptive than dogmatic (embracing the ecclesiastical, or simply Christian, writers and literature of Christian antiquity).

Gradual Specialization of the Term: From the Episcopal Magisterium to the Fathers of the Church. "For though you might have ten thousand guardians in Christ, you do not have many fathers. Indeed, in Christ Jesus I became your father through the gospel" (1 Cor. 4:15). Already, Paul recognizes a special magisterial authority that derives from the Gospel itself and will be taken up by the apostolic tradition in later generations. If the expression "apostolic fathers" (*patres apostolici*), used to describe Barnabas, Clement of Rome, Ignatius of Antioch, Polycarp of Smyrna, and Hermas as well as the anonymous authors of the *Didachè*, goes back no farther than the 12th century, the very notion of "father," embodying the principle of tradition, can be traced from the beginning of the 2nd century. (Compare, for example, *Martyrium Polycarpi* 12, 1: the Jews and pagans called Polycarp "the master of all Asia, the father of the Christians"—*o tès Asias didaskalos, o pater tôn christianôn*; 16, 1: the Christians considered him an "apostolic and prophetic master"—*didaskalos apostolikos kai prophetikos*.)

But bishops in general were also addressed as "father" (*papa*), being heirs of Peter and the *traditio legis*. As Clement of Alexandria recalls in the *Stromates* I, 11, 3 (*SC* 30, 50–2, C. Mondésert and M. Caster), they formed a chain of living tradition that extended from generation to generation: "These masters, preserving the authentic tradition of the blessed teaching, which had issued straight from the holy apostles, Peter, James, John, and Paul, each son receiving the teaching of his father [. . .] have survived up to our era, thanks be to God, to place in us those fine seeds of their ancestors and the apostles."

From the 4th century, we see signs of a wider use of the term along with a greater specialization of the title. This dual development is the result of a number of factors, which in turn are tied in one way or another to the Peace of the Church of 313, even if the three preceding centuries were largely a preparation for what is usually known as "the golden age of the Fathers of the Church," dating from the second half of the 4th century. The organization of the Church and the eruption of the great religious controversies pointed theological thought in new directions. More and more, thinkers came to realize that faith also depended on a rationality which had to be organized in a discourse about God (*theologia*) (the development of the Arian controversy is revealing in this connec-

tion). The setting up of a universal (ecumenical) organization of the Church entailed in particular the development of the institution of the council, which would play a regulating role in matters of dogma and set the standard for the teaching of orthodox faith. Two further factors contributed to this development: the affirmation of the preponderance of certain leading episcopal sees, Rome in particular; and the social and cultural consequences of the conversion of the empire, which led the descendants of cultivated Christian families to embrace an ecclesiastical career, thereby giving rise to new generations of Christian writers (cf. for instance the career of Ambrose of Milan).

In the councils, or, for some, in their respective sees, the bishops tended to be thought of as guardians of dogma and hence to be called "Fathers of the Church." Athanasius, Basil, and Gregory of Nazianzus applied the term especially to the bishops of the council of Nicaea (325), who according to tradition numbered 318, like the servants of Abraham who delivered Lot. "That which we teach is not the result of our personal reflections, but what we have learned of the Holy Fathers": Basil (*Ep. 140, 2, PG* 32, 588) here expresses one of the criteria of what a century later would be the definition of "Father of the Church": the idea of a "shared sense" transcending personal opinion—the Church being the sole source and guarantor of the authenticity of the faith and tending to establish "magisterial" declarations. In this sense, a significant evolution took place, from the "I believe" of the first baptismal declaration to the "we believe" of the Nicene-Constantinopolitan creed officially adopted in the late 4th century, and then to the formulas of the council of Chalcedon in 452: "The holy and great ecumenical council [. . .] has defined what follows"; "[. . .] Following the holy Fathers, we believe [. . .] and we teach all with one voice to confess . . ."

For a century and a half, the trinitarian and Christological debates helped to hone this dogmatic concept of the "Fathers of the Church," considered as the authentic witnesses of orthodox doctrine. The dual use of "ecclesiastical writers" (*scriptories ecclesiastici*) and "doctors" (*doctores*) to distinguish the writers of the Church from profane writers, in Jerome's prologue to *De viris illustribus* (392/393, *PL* 23, 601–4), is ample confirmation of this: during the 4th century certain "ambassadors of the Divine Word," to cite a formula of Eusebius of Caesarea from the early 4th century, were recognized as having a peculiar referential authority. But if the use of "florilegia," that is, thematic anthologies of quotations from ecclesiastical writers, is attested as early as the synod of Constantinople of 388 (Sozomen, *Church History* VII, 12), it was chiefly in the 5th century, in the context of the Nestorian controversy, that the "patristic" argument developed, according to a method familiar to ancient philosophy and jurisprudence (the doxographies of Greek philosophy and the references of Roman jurisprudence). In this way, little by little a body of reference was built up, which collated the dogmatic formulations recognized by the Church and approved if need be by the great councils. Thus at the first session of the council of Ephesus (431), Cyril of Alexandria caused a dossier to be read against Nestor that consisted of "extracts of the books of the venerable holy fathers, bishops, and divers martyrs"—namely, quotations from Peter of Alexandria, Athanasius, Julius and Felix of Rome, Theophilus of Alexandria, Cyprian, Ambrose, Gregory of Nazianzus, Basil of Caesarea, Gregory of Nyssa, Atticus of Constantinople, and Amphilochius of Iconium (Mansi IV, 1184–96). (The quotations from Julius and Felix of Rome in fact come from false Apollinarists; moreover, the multiplicity of such false authorities was to vitiate the use of these quotations.) The opposing side followed suit in order to refute Cyril's anathema.

These "florilegia" were made up chiefly of quotations from 4th- and 5th-century texts. To take only the Latin anthologies, typical citations are those of Prosper of Aquitaine, *Liber sententiarum* (the first Augustinian florilegium), or John Cassian, *De incarnatione Domini*, which would pass into medieval theology as *sententiae patrum*.

But it was Vincent of Lérins (d. before 435 or 455) who drew up a theoretical definition of the criteria for recognizing "Fathers of the Church," in his treaty known as *Commonitorium* ("Manual" or "Aide-mémoire") (434). Its precise title, *Tractatus pro catholicae fidei antiquitate et universitate adversus profanas omnium haereticorum novitates* (*PL* 50, 630–886), reveals its principle and program. The work is a true theory of biblical and patristic proof which systematizes the work of discernment slowly carried out by the Church, providing a method that makes it possible to identify and refute new heresies: "That which has been believed everywhere, for ever and by everyone, that is what is truly Catholic" (*Comm.* I, 2, *PL* 50, 640). The three criteria presented here are thus universality (catholicity), antiquity and agreement with tradition, and unanimous consensus (cf. also I, 27, ibid., 674). In I, 4, Vincent illustrates his theory with three examples: Donatism sets itself up against universality, Arianism against tradition, and the baptism of heretics against consensus (ibid., 641–3). As the text proceeds, he describes the sources of orthodox doctrine. These are the agreed propositions of the Fathers who have remained in the communion and faith of the Catholic Church, and whose orthodoxy (inerrancy) is guaranteed by the definitions of the ecumenical councils (I, 3 and I, 27–8, ibid., 641 and 674–6).

Nevertheless, it is important to place this treatise in the context of its time, one characterized by the elaboration of dogma and in which reflection was still encountering difficulties of vocabulary and formulation. Indeed, this theological "discourse on method" had as its aim not so much to fix once and for all the quasi-providential and eternal canon of a patristic theology—which is the impression given by Catholic exegesis of the *Commonitorium*, notably from the 16th century and especially the 18th (Bellarmine, Bossuet, etc.)—as to determine norms for what the Church admits in confessions of faith and in individual theological reflection. In doing so, it proposed to provide criteria by which to distinguish between progress—consolidation and amplification of the *depositum fidei*—and innovation—its transformation or alteration (cf. I, 23, ibid., 668–9; certain formulas would be taken up by VATICAN I).

From the 5th century, the Roman character of the criterion of orthodoxy by which a writer could be numbered among the Fathers emerges in the West. Pope CELESTINE expressed it apropos of Augustine in 431 (*Ep.* 21, 1, *PL* 50, 530): "Augustine [. . .] has always been in our communion [. . .] and his knowledge is such that he was already counted among the best masters by our predecessors"—a judgment echoed by HORMISDAS a century later (*Ep.* 70, *PL*, 63, 492–3), and thereafter in one of the texts of the false decrees of GELASIUS (*Decretum gelasianum de recipiendis et non recipiendis libris*; ed. Dobschütz, "Das Decretum Gelasianum," *Texte und Untersuchungen*, 38, 4, 1–13). This 4th-century "decree" (no doubt relying on previous documents), whose author has strong Roman sympathies, sets up to some extent the official corpus on which the magisterium is based: the biblical canon, a list of recommended readings and their use, an index of proscribed authors, a list of apostolic sees, etc. The decree confirms the dogmatic conception of the title "Father of the Church" by defining the Roman character of consensus in 4, 3: "[. . .] in the same way, the works and the treatises of all the orthodox Fathers who have never deviated from accord with the Holy Roman Church, have never been separated from her faith and teaching, but, by the grace of God, have remained in communion with her until the last day of their lives, these writings we declare may be read." The author thus provides the first list of ecclesiastical writers recognized as Fathers of the Church: Cyprian, Gregory of Nazianzus, Basil of Caesarea, Athanasius, John Chrysostom, Theophilus and Cyril of Alexandria, Hilary of Poitiers, Ambrose, Augustine, Jerome, Prosper of Aquitaine, and the author of the *Tome to Flavian*. The list covers all those who took part in the great theological debates of the 3rd to the 6th century, and matches the list that can be drawn up based on quotations from the patristic disputes. However, it is neither exhaustive nor complete, lacking at least LEO the Great (by name) and GREGORY the Great.

It is customary today to think of Gregory as the last "Father of the Church"; some would add Isidore of Seville to the list. On the other hand, in the 16th century, medieval writers were still being referred to as "Father." It was Gregory who established the temporal power of the papacy and thanks to him that the patristic tradition he inherited would nourish the culture of a Europe that was no longer only that of Rome but also that of the barbarian kingdoms. Gregory, too, perhaps best embodied the four criteria finally retained by the Church for its definition of the title of "Father of the Church": orthodoxy, holiness of life, the approval of the Church, and antiquity. This definition covers not so much perfection in each of these four areas as what Yves Congar has formulated as the "typical" role of certain ecclesiastical writers, who "in some way engendered the Church" (*La Tradition et la vie de l'Église*, Paris, 1984, 110).

The Doctors of the Church. In the 13th century, BONIFACE VIII, ratifying a distinction made long before, by the Venerable Bede (672–735) (*Ep. ad Accam, PL* 92, 304), singled out four Doctors in the commonly received list of "Fathers of the Church": Ambrose, Augustine, Jerome, and GREGORY the Great. (In the 6th century, Licinian of Cartagena had already drawn up a list of four "fathers, doctors, and defenders of the Church," which omits Jerome but includes Hilary (*Ep.*, 1, 2, *PL* 72, 691.) The popes of the 18th and 19th centuries would add four more names: Peter Chrysologus (BENEDICT XIII in 1729), Leo the Great (BENEDICT XIV in 1754), Hilary of Poitiers (PIUS IX in 1851), and the Venerable Bede (LEO XIII in 1899). The criteria do not exactly match those for the definition of the "Fathers": antiquity counts for nothing, the requirements being recognition of an exceptional degree of knowledge (*eminens eruditio*) and the express approval of the Church (*expressa ecclesiae declaratio*), through the voice of the pope or the general councils. Furthermore, the Doctors make up an authority that is not only dogmatic but also liturgical (proper antiphon to the office, proper mass).

Chronology of the Fathers.

Cyprian, 258

DAMASUS of Rome, ca. 305–84

Hilary of Poitiers, ca. 315–67

Ambrose of Milan, ca. 339–97

Jerome, ca. 347–419

Augustine, 354–ca. 430

John Cassian, ca. 365–ca. 435

Peter Chrysologus, ca. 380–ca. 450

Prosper of Aquitaine, ca. 455

Leo the Great, 461

Gregory the Great, ca. 540–604

Isidore of Seville, ca. 560–636

Françoise Monfrin

Bibliography

Amann, E. "Pères de l'Église," *DTC*, 12 (1933), 1192–1215.

Bernardino, A. di, and Studer, B. *History of Theology I: The Patristic Period*, Collegeville, Minn., 1997.

De Ghellinck, J. *Patristique et Moyen Âge. Études d'histoire littéraire et doctrinale*, II: *Introduction à l'étude de la patristique*, Gembloux-Brussels-Paris, 1967.

Esler, P. E. *The Early Christian World*, 2 vols., New York, 2000.

Hadot, P. "Patristique," *Encyclopedia Universalis*, 12 (1968), 604–5.

Hanson, R. P. C. *The Search For the Christian Doctrine of God*, Edinburgh, 1998.

Mondésert, C. *Lire les Pères de l'Église*, Paris, 1988.

Studer, B. *Trinity and Incarnation in the Faith of the Early Church*, Collegeville, Minn., 1993.

Vatton, E. "Docteurs de l'Église," *DTC*, 4 (1911), 1509–10.

von Campenhausen, H. *Les Pères latins*, Paris, 1967.

See also, patristic handbooks and histories of Christian literature, as well as bibliographical notices of the writers in dictionaries.

FEASTS OF PAPAL ROME. In the city of Rome, the capital of Christianity, Catholic nations competed among themselves with a magnificence aimed at reflecting their greatness, and the pope, as spiritual and temporal sovereign, presented a brilliant image of his double power symbolic of both the truth and the power of the Church. In this world of representation, the feast day was proof made visible. It was a spectacle that continually replayed itself, and joy came less from a break from everyday life than from enchantment. Christmas was the first day of the year in the calendar *a Nativitate* (in effect in Rome until 1750), and the cycle of moveable feasts that depended on the changing date of Easter gave the year its particular character. The feast day spread out across the city, since it was movement: procession, cavalcade, and the parade of carriages. If the feast day was anchored to a specific location such as a city square, a palace, or a church, the crowds converged on the location, which had been transformed by temporary decorations. Feast days meant music, songs, and concerts, but more than anything, they meant light: *fiaccole* that highlighted architecture, and fireworks that punctuated night skies. There was no clear boundary between the sacred and the profane; feast days took identical paths to impress both senses and imagination.

Churches celebrated their patron saint as well as the order of the religious community that served the church or the "nation" to which they belonged. The French gathered at St. Louis on 25 August, but those from Lorraine met at St. Nicholas, while the French from the Comtat would gather at St. Claude, and the Bretons at St. Yves. The Spanish had St. James of Compostela, while the Catalans had the Madonna of Monserrat. A not-yet-unified Italy was represented by a number of peoples who came to Rome to venerate their patron saints: the Lombards, Charles Borromeo; the Venetians, Mark; the Sicilians, Our Lady of Constantinople. Brotherhoods copied the nationalities; thus, painters celebrated St. Luke on 18 October in their church in the Forum.

The feast day took shape within these extraordinary gatherings; it was prayer, but especially conviviality, with no disdain whatsoever for the less ethereal pleasures like banquets or refreshments. The fireworks that topped off the feast brought together neighborhoods that were otherwise separate, and the "machine" (the structure from which the rockets were set off), was to be a work of art in itself, to be admired before it was ignited. The Romans had no fear of syncretism: for the feast day of St. Felix in 1707, the Capuchins portrayed Venus weeping for Adonis and the Madonna of the Mountains, and, the same year, the struggle between Hercules and the Nemean lion. These festivities were seen as rivalries in which the great orders attempted to affirm their preeminence and universality through the richness and the number of their saints. The JESUITS celebrated Ignatius, Aloysius Gonzaga, and Stanislaus with splendor; the DOMINICANS did likewise with Dominic, Thomas Aquinas, and CATHERINE OF SIENA, who had brought the papacy back to Rome from Avignon. St. Philip Neri, the most popular of Rome's saints, was venerated by members of the Oratory and the music they brought in.

There were three magnificent feast days in the liturgical CALENDAR that involved the entire city. The feast of Sts. PETER and PAUL commemorated the origin of the Church on the predestined spot in Rome; adding the temporal to the spiritual, it also celebrated the return of tribute to Naples. Corpus Christi, also called *Corpus Domini*, was the occasion for a procession around the *borghi*, made all the more splendid because the pope was one of the actors; he was carried, on his knees, before the Blessed Sacrament on the *faldistorio*, a kind of litter invented by Bernini. Stendahl was in awe at the shimmering ecclesiastical vestments, and enjoyed watching the people crowded into richly decorated grandstands—seating for which they had paid. One of the most beautiful feasts was the Assumption on 15 August. In 1727, the di-

rector of the Académie de France, described it with these words: "They do magnificent illuminations here and, in some parts of Rome, there are entire streets carpeted both day and night, where there are over two hundred chandeliers, and that does not include the candles in the windows. At night there is music and during the day there are people everywhere because paintings are on display."

The exhibitions, cultural distractions of which the people were extremely fond, were always associated with some religious feast: on 19 March one of them was organized by the *Virtuosi al Pantheon*, who included all artists, be they academicians or not, under the invocation of St. Joseph. On 16 August, another took place in St. Roch, on the 24th in San Bartolomeo dei Bergamaschi, on the 29th in the cloister of San Giovanni Decollato. Starting in 1776, the pensioners at the Académie de France exhibited their works on 25 August, for the feast day of St. Louis. HOLY YEARS increased the magnitude of the celebration. Every twenty-five years waves of pilgrims descended upon Rome. New events were superimposed over the habitual celebrations. The opening of the holy door was key among these. Each nation had a reception for its compatriots. A warm breeze of reunion whispered over the pious exercises.

There was little distinction between feast days and politics for the people. The CEREMONIAL that surrounded the pope was a perpetual attraction for the streets of Rome where he went out every day to pray in one of his churches; despite his grandeur, he was a sovereign close, and familiar, to his people. His election was a long period of waiting punctuated by spectacles: the arrival of CARDINALS from elsewhere, crossing the city with their parade of carriages; the CONCLAVE's ballots, which could be seen in the famous trail of smoke that rose from the Sistine Chapel during the midday ANGELUS; the coronation came to a climax at St. Peter's in an enchanting display of light, with the *girandole* enveloping a CASTEL SANT'ANGELO reflected in the Tiber, while the basilica and its colonnade covered with *fiaccole*, glowed incandescently. Then there was the pope's taking possession of ST. JOHN LATERAN, his cathedral. The work of the cardinals was reflected in the city through the illumination of palaces: those of the winning groups or victorious "nations," each of which counted points in concern for the game its clientele was playing. The parade of horses that subsequently led the new prince of the Church to the QUIRINAL so that he could receive his hat was also a spectacle of great interest, comparable to the official entrance of the ambassadors; curiosity mixed with admiration as hundreds of new liveries and carved and painted carriages rolled by, even if they were but pale reflections of what legend recounted of yesteryear's entrances of sovereigns: of Charlemagne or Charles V, or the more recent arrival of Christina of Sweden, not to mention Marcantonio Colonna's old-fashioned triumph, with two hundred Turkish prisoners from the battle of LEPANTO.

Of both political and religious interest, canonizations were also important events, and all the more prestigious because they happened only rarely and involved a number of both congregations and countries. Processions, each exalting a new saint, left from different churches to converge in St. Peter's Square, which was decorated with paintings recalling the heroic virtues of those chosen: paintings and the banners with the portrait of the new saint that accompanied the procession were the works of the best artists of the day.

In its celebrations, Rome wrote the history of Catholic countries: accessions to the throne and victories, marriages and births—all the more important in that they assured the continuity of a dynasty. Ambassadors were ordered to capture the hearts of the Roman people through celebrations where sumptuousness was the sign of power. Illumination of palaces, houses, and churches within the province of the "nation" in celebration (an example of which was Louis XIV's healing in 1687, marked by an extraordinary *girandole* on SS. Trinita dei Monti); dressing up monuments, which might go as far as building a "speaking" facade with both symbolic and historical meaning. There were two levels of feasts: first were the great ones with singers or operas in important locations. In 1748, in honor of the birth of the dauphin in France, the great hall of the Farnese palace was transformed into a theater by the painter-architect Giovanni Paolo Panini. But the people were not totally excluded, since they were authorized to visit it: for three days in 1737 they paraded through the appartments of the French ambassador decorated with paintings and wall hangings. And the open-air festival was available to everyone. In 1729, the cardinal of Polignac transformed Piazza Navona into a circus, a brilliant and artistic play conceived by Pier-Leone Ghezzi. Fountains of wine flowed freely, and there were horse races reminiscent of those during carnival. The spell was always cast with the fireworks and their "machine," a thought-provoking masterpiece of virtuosity. The spontaneity of the popular feast was not urban, but rather rural, and peripheral. Following ancient traditions, the nobility opened their villas a few rare days of the year, organizing games of skill and strength, horse races and bull races, for which everyone paid via participation. But the most famous was the wine harvest feast, the *ottobrate*, in which the city people mingled as neighbors with the *paesani* to help with the chores and, after a full day of work, they drank and danced to improvised music. This taste of freedom is seen in the paintings of the *bamboccianti*, painters of a world eclipsed by the splendor of papal Rome.

Olivier Michel

Bibliography

Dell'Arco, F., and Carandini, S. *L'effimero barocco*, Rome, 1977–78, 2 vols.

Dell'Arco, F., and Carandini, S. *Roma sancta. La città delle basiliche*, Rome, 1985.

Riti, cerimonie, feste e vita di popolo nella Roma dei papi, Bologna, 1970.

Thomas, A. *Un an à Rome*, Paris, 1823.

FELIX I. *(d. late 274). Saint.*

Felix followed DIONYSIUS (who died on 26 December 268) a few days after his death. He took the throne in early January 269, probably on 3 January (according to the *Liberian Catalogue*, *MGH*, *AA*, 9/1, 75), shortly after the beginning of Claude the Goth's reign as prince. He was Roman by birth, according to the *Liber Pontificalis* (*LP*, 1, 159, *MGH, GPR*, I, 37). His papacy stretched through the reigns of Claude the Goth, Quintillus, and Aurelian (*MGH, AA*, 9/1, 75).

A letter on the nature of Christ as a member of the Trinity has been attributed to him and is believed to have been addressed to Maximus, Dionysius's successor in the diocese of ALEXANDRIA since 264. But the letter was a forgery composed in preceding years because of the conflict between the "two Dionysiuses" on the subject. The theological dispute was actually quickly calmed, thanks to the conciliatory will of the bishop of Alexandria.

The problems of doctrine had actually moved from Egypt to Syria, where the new bishop of Antioch, Paul, had developed a heretical teaching—which was quickly a matter of concern to his Eastern colleagues—on the nature of Christ. In 264, a COUNCIL, held in Antioch, attempted to reestablish orthodoxy. But Paul, initially evasively but then rather provocatively opposed his adversaries. Thus, in 268 a second council met in Antioch and condemned his teaching (Eusebius, *Ecclesiastical History*, VII, 30) and excommunicated him. The decisions made by the council, which had taken an air of certain importance because of the number of individuals participating in it, were communicated to Dionysius in Rome shortly before his death in late 268. The authority of the Roman SEE in matters of doctrine was undisputed.

However, the weakening of imperial power in the East under Claude the Goth, and then during the brief reign of Quintillus, gave free rein to inclinations toward independence in Palmyra, located between Rome and Persia. This movement found support from populations in the provinces throughout Syria. Paul profited from the situation to resist the partisans of orthodoxy: he formed an alliance with queen Zenobia and the rhetor Longin, her principal adviser. He refused to leave the buildings the Christian community of Antioch had been using. But when Palmyra's independence was destroyed by Aurelian (who reigned from 270 to 275), the adversaries of the heretical bishop, now without support and compromised with the opponents of Rome, sought out the emperor when he passed through Antioch. Aurelian looked into the affair, prepared the case and judged it, ordering "that the house of the Church be awarded to those to whom the bishops of Italy and the city of Rome would have it awarded" (Eusebius, *HE*, VII, 30). One more time, the holder of the Roman See was given preeminence in matters of doctrine, the effects of which were of paramount importance for the devolution of the patrimony of the Church. Legitimacy was based on communion with the Roman Church. But it was not a bishop who assserted this, it was the prince in his counsel who was passing judgment. Nothing shows better how, at the end of the 3d century, a quarter century after the beginning of the great persecutions by Decius, and later, Valerian, the Church was a reality that the imperial state could not ignore, and how in this Church the primacy of Rome seemed natural.

Michel Christol

Bibliography

Lebreton, J., and Zeiller, J. *De la fin du IIe siècle à la paix constantinienne* (Fliche-Martin, 2), Paris, 1943, 158, 345–50.

Munier, C. *L'Église dans l'Empire romain. Église et cité (Histoire du droit et des institutions de l'Église en Occident)*, under the dir. of G. Le Bras and J. Gaudemet, II, 3, Paris, 1979, 264–74.

Turner, C. H. "The Papal Chronology of the Third Century," *JThS*, 17 (1916), 348–51.

[FELIX II]. *(d. 25 November 365). Antipope from late 355 / early 356 to 358.*

Felix's rise to episcopacy in the See of Rome was brought about by Emperor Constantius, who had banned Pope LIBERIUS. This unusual situation caused a schism in the Roman clergy, which lasted until after the deaths of both bishops.

Felix was archdeacon for Liberius when the latter was sent into exile to Beroea in Thrace, because he refused to condemn Athanasius of Alexandria (late 355 or early 356). Prior to Liberius's departure, Felix, with the deacon Damasus, pledged an oath of fidelity to Liberius, standing before the clergy who had gathered in the presence of the Roman people, according to the anonymous writer of the time who authored the *Gesta inter Liberium et Felicem*. Then Felix went to Milan at the emperor's request to accept being the exiled pontiff's successor; he was ordained bishop, in the presence of eunuchs, by three Arian bishops, one of whom may have been Epictetus of Centumellae (Civitavecchia), according to Athanasius. When he returned to Rome he was welcomed by some of the clergy and the people who had remained faithful to him. After two years of banishment, Liberius agreed to condemn Athanasius; Constantius, on a trip to Rome in April

357, then took it upon himself to have him returned to the Roman people, "better than when he left." But it was still to "Bishop Felix" and to the prefect of the city that, on 6 December 357, he addressed a law included in the Theodosian Code exempting from taxes clerics, artisans, businessmen, and their families as well. Constantius agreed, probably in 358, to recall Liberius under certain conditions: Felix would continue to occupy the throne, Liberius and Felix would exercise authority together.

The Eastern bishops met in Sirmium (358) after Liberius had signed, in their presence, a profession of faith prepared by Basil of Ancyre; they wrote to Felix and the Roman clergy informing them that, henceforth, "the two bishops would occupy the Apostolic See together." According to Theodoret, the Romans received the decision with anger; they demanded "one God, one Christ, and one bishop." Liberius's return, according to Sozomenius, was a cause of violent riots, which Felix did nothing to curtail, forcing him to leave the city. Some time later, with the help of part of the clergy, Felix attempted to take over the basilica of Jules in the Trastevere but failed and withdrew outside the city with his partisans. He died on 22 November 365, a little before Liberius, who had recovered some of his authority as head of the Church. Considered "perjurers" by the author of the *Gesta* favorable to Liberius, the clerics of Felix's party who had exercised their ministry in Rome in establishments that belonged to them were, nevertheless, integrated into Liberius's clergy. When Liberius died, on 24 September 366, his adversaries gathered in the basilica Giulia and pronounced the deacon Ursinius bishop, while, simultaneously, another assembly was electing the deacon Damasus.

Curiously, although Felix does not figure on the list of bishops of Rome drawn up by Optatus of Mileve and redone by Augustine, he is mentioned on the episcopal lists from the 5th to the 7th centuries, and the *LIBER PONTIFICALIS* makes note of him between Liberius and DAMASUS (355–8). But the role it ascribes him as defender and martyr of the Nicaean faith can only be explained in contrast to the memory of Liberius, which was marred by his compromises with the Arians. If, as Duchesne has suggested, the roles of Liberius and Felix are clearly reversed in the *Liber Pontificalis*, we should also be careful in accepting the information it provides regarding Felix's acquisition of property on Via Aurelia to construct a church where he might be buried. To add to the confusion, he has been wrongly identified with one of the Felixes who was a Roman martyr and was buried on the Via Portuense and mentioned in the *Martyrologie Hieronymien*. An illegitimate competitor for the episcopacy of Rome, Felix is most often ranked among the antipopes, even though his contemporaries called him "bishop in the place of Liberius."

Elisabeth Paoli

Bibliography

LP, I, CXX–CXXV and 207–11.

Ammien Marcellin, *Hist.*, 15, 7, 10.

Amore, A. "Felice II," *EC*, 5 (1950), 1134–35.

Athanasius, *Hist. Arian.*, 75, ed. Opitz, II–1, 225, 3–12.

Bardy, G. "Felix II," *Catholicisme*, 4 (1956), 1148–49.

Batiffol, J. *Le Siège apostolique (359–451)*, Paris, 1924, 7 ff.

Caspar, E. *Geschichte des Papsttums*, I, Tübingen, 1930, 188–89, 590.

Jerome, *Chron. a. 356*, ed. Helm, 240; *De viris*, II, 98, 14, 1.

Jerome, *Quae gesta sunt inter Liberium et Felicem episcopos*, CSEL, 35, 1, 1–4.

Kirsch, J. P. "Die Grabstätte der Felices duo pontifices et martyres an der Via Aurelia," *Römische Quartalschrift*, 33 (1925), 1–20.

Mommsen, T. "Die römischen Bischöfe Liberius und Felix II.," *Zeitschrift für Geschichtswissenschaft*, n.s., 1 (1896–97), 167–79.

Nautin, P. *DHGE*, 16 (1967), 887–9.

Pietri, C. *Roma christiana*, Rome, 1976, I, 248–51, 259–60 and II, 1692.

Saltet, L. "La formation de la légende des papes Libère et Félix," *Bulletin de littérature ecclésiastique*, 26 (1905), 222–36.

Schwaiger, G. "Felix II.," *LTK*, 4 (1960), 67–8.

Seppelt, F. X. *Papstgeschichte von den Anfängen bis zur Gegenwart*, Munich, 1933, I, 2, 18ff.

Socrates, *HE*, II, 37, *PG*, 67, 33–841.

Sozomenes, *HE*, IV, 11, *GCS*, 50, 154 and IV, 15, 158.

Theodoret, *HE*, II, 14K, *GCS*, 44, 136 and II, 17.

Theodosian Code, XVI, 2, 14, ed. Mommsen, I, 839.

FELIX III. (*b. Rome, ?, d. Rome, 1 March 492). Elected pope on 13 March 483. Saint.*

Felix governed the Church of Rome during the final years of the reign of Odoacer, and he was a contemporary of Theodoric, whose entry into Italy and victory he witnessed. But his papacy is known less for this political background than for the beginnings of the schism that split the Eastern Churches from the Roman community for over thirty years.

Felix's family is known by an inscription, which we no longer have, found in the pavement of ST. PAUL'S OUTSIDE THE WALLS. His father must have been the priest Felix, to whom Pope LEO had entrusted the responsibility of restoring the basilica. While he was still a deacon, Felix buried his wife, Petronia, there, and later, during his papacy, he also buried his children, Paula, Gordianus, and the consecrated virgin, Aemiliana. Gordianus, the father of GREGORY I the Great, was pope Felix's great-grandson.

When SIMPLICIUS died, the prefect of Odoacer's praetorium took the election of the new pope into his hands.

Affirming that he was following the will of the deceased pope in order to avoid conflicts, he gathered an assembly of senators in the mausoleum next to ST. PETER'S BASILICA. Before Felix's election, he proposed a set of rules regarding the use of ecclesiastical goods: the property of the Church was absolutely inalienable; personal property that cannot be used in the liturgy should be sold and used for alms. Any infraction of these rules would be invalidated and punishable by ANATHEMA. How the clergy voted on this *scriptura* is unknown. Felix's election took place the same day.

He had scarcely begun his papacy when he was confronted with problems with which his predecessor Simplicius had not had time to become familiarized: Emperor Zeno had published an edict of union, the *Henoticon*, aimed at appeasing Monophysite opposition to the Christology of two natures proclaimed at Chalcedon. The edict, which annulled what had been accepted at the COUNCIL and did not even mention the writings of Leo I, was not acceptable to Felix. In the meantime, John Talaia, who had been elected patriarch of Alexandria by the Chalcedonian contingent of the city's clergy, fled to Rome. The emperor deposed him, recognizing instead Peter Mongos, Monophysite. Felix immediately sent an embassy to Constantinople. He sent the emperor a legation composed of the bishops Vitalis and Misenus, soon to be joined by the deacon Tutus. The pope, who no longer had an emperor in the West to whom to announce his election, informed Zeno. He asked for assistance for African Catholics who were being persecuted by Arian Vandals, and encouraged him to depose Peter Mongos and defend the faith of Chalcedonia. The legation was also entrusted with two letters for Acacius, the partriarch of Constantinople. The first reproached him for putting up with Peter Mongos and the *Henoticon*, and the second called him to Rome to respond to the accusations brought against him by John Talaia. But the legates allowed themselves to be convinced, and concelebrated a mass with Acacius during which the patriarch of Constantinople cited Peter Mongos's name in the diptychs, leading people to believe that Rome accepted the situation in the East. When he was informed of their defection, Felix assembled a synod in Rome (28 July 484), excommunicating the legates and Acacius of Constantinople. The sentence was not carried via official channels, but by some Chalcedonian monks who managed to attach it to Acacius's vestments during a solemn celebration. Acacius had the monks punished, and, in turn, excommunicated Felix. Since these reciprocal excommunications also affected the recipient's respective followers, all the Churches of the East and the West were separated. In Rome, a SYNOD, on 5 October 585, confirmed the sentence against Acacius, and included Peter Mongos along with it. Felix thus took a stance from which neither he nor his successors would depart: a reconciliation was possible only at the price of deposing Acacius and Peter Mongos and, after their deaths (28 November 489 and 29 October 490, respectively), if their names and those of their successors were stricken from the diptychs.

Little is known of Felix's activity in the West because the canonical collections have preserved only the texts concerning the quarrel with the East. In March 487, Felix convened another synod to look into the case of Catholics who, giving in to the Vandal persecution, accepted Arian baptism. The synod decreed that clerics were excommunicated up to the hour of their deaths, while lay people would need to spend a number of years among the ranks of the penitents.

An erudite tradition maintains that Felix's successor, GELASIUS, who was a deacon at the time and Felix's secretary, was the real inspiration behind his politics. A second tradition, on the other hand, credits Felix with the composition of the manuscripts that bear the name of Gelasius (the letter against Pelagianism and the treatise on the festival of the Lupercalia). These hypotheses are based on stylistic arguments; given that the style of papal writings is characterized essentially by the rules of the CHANCERY, it is impossible to have complete confidence in such analyses.

Felix was buried in the basilica of St. Paul's Outside the Walls, with his family.

Claire Sotinel

Bibliography

LP, I, 252–54.

Felix II (III), *Epistulae XVIII*, Thiel, 222–77; *Fragm. apud Nicolaum I, MGH*, Ep. VI, 491 and 518.

Schwartz, E. "Publizistische Sammlungen zum Acacianischen Schisma," *Abhandlung der Bayerischen Akademie der Wissenschaften*, 10 (1934), 202–19.

FELIX IV. (*b. Samnium, ?, d. Rome, 22 September 530). Elected pope 12 July 526. Saint.*

During the four years of his papacy, Felix IV maintained good relations with the Ostrogothic government of Ravenna and increased the prestige of the papacy. A native of Samnium, he was the son of Castorius, according to the *LIBER PONTIFICALIS*. He has sometimes been identified, albeit without conclusive proof, as the Roman deacon Felix who took part with Dioscorus in the legation sent by pope Hormisdas to the East in 519, to put an end to Acacius's SCHISM.

He succeeded Pope JOHN I, who died on 18 May 526, after two months of vacancy in the episcopal see. He was imposed by King Theodoric, whose aim it was to protect himself against the hostile feelings of the clergy and the SENATE "by naming a pontiff who was likely to displease no one." He had to eliminate one candidate whose name is unknown, although it may have been the deacon Dioscorus from the legation in 519. The rescript addressed to the Senate by Athalaric, the successor to Theodoric, who had died on 30 August 526, provoked a conflict. The Senate sent the LEGATE Publianus to Ravenna to confirm its agreement with the royal choice. The pope obtained other favors from the king: an edict by Athalaric reestablished the custom of having any complaint against an ecclesiastic that expanded the privileges of clerics in the pope's inner circle brought before the court instituted by the pope.

The *Liber Pontificalis* credits Felix with construction of the basilica of Sts. Cosmas and Damian. He remodeled a large room in the basilica of Maxentius and Constantine so that it could be used for Christian worship, by replacing the back wall with a semicircular apse. The Temple of Romulus served as an atrium for the new basilica. Felix's portrait on the apse's mosaic (completely redone in the 17th century) bears witness to the eminent role played by the pope. He also reconstructed a basilica on the Via Salaria, which had been destroyed by a fire. In addition, he made changes in the day-to-day workings of the Church. On 3 February 528, he wrote to Caesarius, bishop of Arles, to approve the acts of the COUNCIL of Carpentras (November 527) concerning the *praemissa missio*, the lay person's obligation to make a one-year retreat in preparation for ministry. He supported Caesarius in his wish to condemn the errors of the semi-Pelagians regarding grace and free will. Having received from Caesarius a plan for council decisions in nineteen *capitula* undoubtedly drawn from John Maxence's work, he accepted only eight, which became the first eight canons of the council of Orange. To them he added an additional sixteen sentences, from Prosper of Aquitaine. The pope also arbitrated the conflict that opposed Ecclesius, the bishop of Ravenna, and part of his clergy, over the subject of the distribution of Church revenue. The opposing parties came to Rome to present their differences before the pope. Felix settled the conflict by blaming the revolters and reaffirmed the rules for management that Ecclesius had been using, especially the allocation of a quarter of the revenue for the clergy.

Before his death, he resolved to name his own successor, in order to avoid electoral abuses that were costly to the Church and to ensure understanding between the new pope and the court in Ravenna. A collection by Novarus has preserved Felix's precepts, which he wrote after 31 August 530, in which the pope, sensing that his end was near, announced to the Roman clerics, the Senate, and the people that he had conferred the *pallium* to the archdeacon Boniface. A *contestatio* by the Senate, posted in all titular churches, stipulated that those who participated in the election prior to the pope's death would lose half their property, and the premature candidates would be exiled. Felix died on 22 September 530, at the latest, after four years, two months, and thirteen days of papacy, according to the *Liber Pontificalis*. His epitaph recalls his humility, his generosity toward the poor, and his good management of finances. He was buried in St. Peter's Basilica.

Janine Desmulliez

Bibliography

ICUR, 2, n.s., 4152.

LP, I 56, 279.

PL, 65, 11, Agnellus, A. *Lib. Pont. Raven.*, 23, *MGH, SRL*, 318–21.

Cassiodorus, *Variae*, 8, 15 and 8, 24, *C, C*, 96, 319, 330–1.

Duchesne, L. *La Succession du pape Félix IV*, *MEFR*, 1883, 239–66.

Felix, *Ep. ad Caes.*

"Felix IV," *LTK*, 4, 68–9 and *DHGE*, 16, 895–6.

Pietri, C. *Aristocratie et société cléricale*, *MEFRA*, 93, 1981, 461–7.

Pontal, O. *Histoire des conciles mérovingiens*, Paris, 1989, 75–9.

Schwartz, E. *ACO*, IV, 2, 96–7.

Wilpert, J. *Die römischen Mosaiken und Malereien*, Freiburg, 1917, 102.

[FELIX V]. *Amadeus VIII of Savoy (b. Chambéry, 4 September 1383, d. Geneva, 7 January 1451). Buried in Ripaille.*

The CONCLAVE that met at the Council of Basel after EUGENE IV was deposed presented its own candidate for pope, Prince Amadeus VIII of Savoy. The son of Amadeus VII, he became count of Savoy in 1391 following the death of his father. In February 1416, Emperor Sigismund raised Savoy to a duchy. Then in 1434, at the apogee of his power, Amadeus decided to leave the world. He created the chivalrous order of St. Maurice and, with six colleagues, retired to the Chateau de Ripaille on Lake Leman, to live as a hermit. He left the general care of his states in the hands of his brother, Louis.

It was at Ripaille that the council of Basel sought Amadeus out to make him pope or, better said, antipope. On 17 December 1439, Amadeus accepted the TIARA that the council delegation, led by the cardinal from Bresse, Louis Aleman, had come to offer him in his hermitage. On Christmas day he received minor orders, and on 6 January he abdicated in favor of his son, Louis. It was not until May 1440 that he left Savoy and, on 24 June, he made his solemn entrance into Basel where, on 21 July, he was ordained a priest. A few days later he was crowned as Pope Felix V.

In November 1442, Felix left the council to go live with his antipope court, sometimes in Lausanne, and sometimes in Geneva. The conflicts that had opposed the members of the council from the beginning were the real reason behind the antipope's departure. But if Felix left his Basel electors, he did not leave empty handed. On 29 January 1442, after long quarrels, he obtained the right to reserve for himself the commend of a bishopric, of an abbey, or of a priory that had come to the States of the House of Savoy through the death of its title holder. The concession, which was aimed at assuring Felix of civil holdings for the upkeep of his papal court, was openly contrary to the reforms introduced by the council regarding papal reserves of ecclesiastical benefices. The decree was nevertheless approved by the council assembly, claiming juridical reasons for it. The States of Savoy were accorded the same treatment as were territories that were directly dependent on the Roman Church, for which any papal reserves were authorized. In effect, however, the council's pope was reduced to his former States.

Since Eugene IV's deposition took place despite the opposition of the governments represented in Basel, obedience to Felix V was imposed only with difficulty. The council's pope had partisans in a number of dioceses in Germany, Poland, and France. The universities of Vienne, Leipzig, Cologne, Erfurt, and Cracow had announced their support of him. Among the religious orders, the Carthusians and the Teutonic order recognized Felix V, while the Dominicans and the Friars Minor split into two enemy camps. But there were always cases of isolated affiliation. The princes, whose support would have permitted some exercise of immediate control over dioceses and their revenues, preferred to align themselves with Rome, or to be neutral. The antipope's departure from Basel struck "a fatal blow" to the council. In 1447, Eugene IV's death helped to resolve the schism. Nicholas V, who succeeded him, authorized the king of France, Charles VII, to play the role of mediator. In 1449, an agreement was finally reached. On 7 April, at the convent of the Friars Minor in Lausanne, Felix gave up the papacy. On 25 April the council, which had moved to Lausanne in July 1448, announced its own dissolution. After his abdication, Amadeus received the title of cardinal-bishop of Sabine and perpetual vicar of the Holy See in the lands under his dominion. His legation lasted only twenty-one months.

Elisa Mongiano

Bibliography

Andenmatten, B., and Paravicini Bagliani, A. *Amédée VIII-Félix V*, Lausanne, 1992.

Cognasso, F. "Amedeo VIII," *DBI*, II, 749–53.

De Savoie, M. *Amédée VIII: le duc qui devint pape*, I–II, 1962.

Mongiano, E. *La Cancelleria di un antipapa. Il Bollario di Felice V (Amedeo VIII di Savoia)*, 1988.

FERULA. A ferula is a command baton symbolizing the spiritual and temporal power of the pope, similar to the scepter of kings and emperors. From the 12th to the end of the 16th century, each new pope received the ferula at the time of his taking solemn possession of the basilica of ST. JOHN LATERAN, the cathedral of Rome and the mother of all the churches in the world. It was brought by the prior of the basilica of St. Lawrence, who passed it, along with the keys, to the pope seated upon his porphyry throne, and it was returned to the same dignitary by the pope after he took another seat. Consequently, the ceremony should have been limited only to the handing over of the keys, indicative of the papal jurisdiction over the Lateran Palace.

The ferula was a long stick of wood or precious metal richly decorated with sculptures, jewels, or ivory, with a golden knob at the end. It was not originally a liturgical insignia, but rather a temporal one. But in 963 LEO VIII deposed BENEDICT V, breaking his ferula and throwing its pieces to the people. A liturgical ferula, however, was later to make its appearance in the form of a golden shaft topped by a cross with arms of equal lengths, but without the crucified Christ. The pope used it whenever liturgical protocol called for a bishop to use his crozier, thus, primarily at times like the ordination of priests, the consecration of a bishop, or the dedication of a church. Actually, because of his sovereignty, the Roman pontiff cannot use a crozier with a curved volute, since it signifies the submission of episcopal jurisdiction to pontifical jurisdiction.

Use of the ferula has become obsolete for the pope. There were traces of it in the cross that PAUL VI decided to hold in his hand during papal chapels, a custom that his successors, JOHN PAUL I and JOHN PAUL II kept. In contrast to the ferula, however, it bears a reproduction of the tormented body of the crucified Christ.

The papal ferula has coexisted with two cardinal ferulas consisting of staffs approximately a meter in length, sheathed in red velvet and decorated with a red cord, topped with two similar acorns; its ends were in vermillion, although the extremities varied depending on the status of its owner.

The ferula (which is also called a *baculum*, "a small wand") of the cardinal CAMERLENGO of the Holy Roman Church is given to him by the pope at the time of his nomination, as a symbol of his charge as interim governor of the Apostolic SEE during time of vacancy; it is carried only during the conclave, and specifically during solemn processions where the cardinals are dressed in liturgical VESTMENTS. It is thus used only rarely, if ever. Nevertheless, in the CONCLAVE of October 1958, Cardinal Benedetto Aloisi Masella, elected CAMERLENGO by the Holy College (since Pius XII had not named a successor to the last CAMERLENGO named, Cardinal Lorenzo Lauri, who died in 1941), never let the ferula out of his hand, taking it with him everywhere, even to meals.

On the other hand, the ferula of the first deacon cardinal was often used, since it was carried in liturgical processions over which the pope presided, accompanied by the cardinals in full regalia. The protodeacon cardinal, dressed in his dalmatic and with a white damask miter on his head, held the ferula in his right hand to order the start of the papal procession, especially at the time of the sovereign pontiff's coronation, at masses of beatification and canonization, and during processions for Candlemas and Palm Sunday. This ferula has disappeared.

Joël-Benoît D'Onorio

Bibliography

Battandier, A. "La ferula," *Annuaire pontifical catholique*, 1921.
Noirot, M. "Férule," *Catholicisme*, IV.

FINANCES, PAPAL.
6th to 12th Centuries. The frequent changes in the papacy's political situation—it was first made subject to an Ostrogoth king, and then to the Byzantine emperor, and later given autonomy, before finding itself at the head of an independent state "protected" by a number of Western emperors in a more or less imposed manner—are reflected in the origins of the revenues it had at its disposition. Nevertheless, sources never make the slightest reference to a radical change in papal finances; cartularies carefully kept proof of old rights, and individuals kept their titles and their allocations. The general organization of the budget was modified in its details, but never in its essence. The contradiction is only clearer when this study is placed back into the framework of traditional public finances.

In 493, Theodoric established himself as the emperor's representative in Italy. He kept the general organization of the budget; nevertheless, the Ostrogoths, who were Arians, allocated a portion of the funds for their churches. Since the time of Constantine, moreover, the Vandals had been depriving the papacy of revenues it had coming from the islands in the Tyrrhenian Sea and from Africa. Justinian's slow reconquest, from 534 to 552, nearly restored the situation to what it had been previously and, in order to gain a clear view of all his rights, GREGORY I the Great was satisfied with bringing Gelasius's polyptych up to date, as proof that it had been in use during the 6th century. The polyptych was a complicated register of funds, which were public by nature, at the disposition of the Roman SEE or any other institution that had one. Actually, according to the laws, which were identical in all Papal States, the Church's assets, or "assets of the poor," became public at the moment they became the property of the Church, regardless of their nature (goods of which it was sole owner, or bases for taxation) or their origin (donations from individuals or public endowments); they fed into an autonomous budget under the supervision of agents of the Papal States. Private generosity did exist, but for the most part resources came from state holdings, as is shown by a number of examples, and particularly by the situation under GREGORY II's papacy, as we shall see.

In about 600, the greater part of the resources came from the "patrimonies," grouped together according to geographic location: the patrimonies of Sicily, Africa, Campagna, and even Gaul, since the FRANKS left the pope's lands that they managed when the Ostrogoths gave them Provence. Each was managed by a rector, named directly by the pope. The patrimony of each rector was divided into units of smaller sizes, called *massae*, and placed under the authority of a *conductor* who took the tax lease in exchange for emoluments. Their accounts were checked regularly, especially when one of them died, and inheritors asked for what he left. Some of these holdings were lands that the Church of Rome considered especially useful, and which she rented to farmers when this solution seemed to be the most financially advantageous. But the majority were composed of pure tax bases. The pope only had eminent ownership over *coloni*, small landowners who were completely free to manage and to sell their inherited lands, provided they fulfilled the one condition of paying taxes. The vocabulary is often deceptive since, for example, *mancipium*, which in earlier times referred to a slave, was later applied to a small landowner whose tax was paid via the intermediary of a *dominus*, which in this case was the rector or his agents. Moreover, this tax could be paid by land, by mines, or by artisans or merchants who were subject to rights on traffic.

An analysis of expenditures reveals a situation that is at least as complicated, since in these patrimonies there were districts over which the Church retained only the advantage of management in the name of the State. In these cases, the tax paid had to be turned over to the agents of the civil or military administration, which gave rise to disputes of all sorts. Elsewhere, all the profit was allocated to the civil budget of the Church of Rome, since the pope, like all other bishops, was the individual who was ultimately responsible for the municipal administration. This is how the public ANNONA, which was increased by Theodoric, was still managed by the Church up to the time of the papacy of SABINIAN (604–6). Gregory the Great admonished his agents who did not collect the necessary sums on time and argued with municipal functionaries over allocations of products that were stocked in the Church's granaries and that should have been given, in his opinion, for the needs of Rome and not those of the Sicilian administration. Likewise, the pope paid soldiers' wages, he paid for the upkeep of the city walls, and he eventually paid for the Lombard tributes, without seeing in this the slightest confusion between ecclesiastical resources and civil needs.

Of more direct interest, however, are allocations for the specific budget of the Church. Management of sums was assured by an *acarius* for money coming in, and by a *sacellarius* for outgoing sums. As was the case in all dioceses, there were four parts to the post of *sacellarius*: that of the central services of the bishopric (*episcopium*), that of the clergy, that of the FABRIC, managed by the *mansionarii*, and that of the charity, of the diacony. Monasteries enjoyed an autonomy of management under papal control, since it was necessary to ensure that abbots fulfilled the commitments they had made, in conformity with the rule in force in their monastery and with the will of those who had given revenue allocated for a specific expense.

There are a number of examples to show that the same methods were in effect as everywhere else. A scale was used for the fiscal value of a piece of land, to determine how much each *colonus* owed; the situation was similar for *conductores* and rectors, by adding up all the individual contributions. For each district an extract (*brevis*) of the great polyptych was drawn up, in which all the receipts and expenses of the Church were kept. Thus, the concentration of accounts was complete. But not enough personnel was available to collect, concentrate, and pay out all the proceeds, money, or services that were due as taxes. This is why allocation of resources was extremely decentralized. Such and such important individual to whom one wished to grant a favor or subsidy was to receive the revenues from such and such district, but he was in charge of all fiscal management. Such and such elderly person was to receive a small sum listed in a particular *massa*'s budget, and he thus went directly to the *massa* to collect his due. A central bookkeeping system kept track of the budget with methods that were remarkably efficient. All these accounts were calculated in gold *soldi*, converted into a public tarif (*pretia publica*) that varied depending on the time and location. All payments were written on the spot in the debit book of the *conductor* who paid it. In Rome, it was his credit, since an account was opened in the name of each of the pope's agents; in the central bookkeeping office, it was again debited from the papal budget.

These methods did not really change during the entire 7th century, as is shown by a few extracts preserved in the *LIBER CENSUUM*, the oldest of which go back to the papacy of HONORIUS (625–38). They conform to the prescriptions of the *Liber Diurnus*, composed late in the 7th century, and are part of a long chain of documents that are uninterrupted up to the time of the period in question here. The *LIBER PONTIFICALIS* confirms the durability of the Gelasian system in a number of places; the system was brought up to date by Gregory the Great. Allocation of revenues from the papal treasury or from patrimonies raised questions that were all the more poignant since there was a severe dearth of money in an empire threatened by the Arabs. When the popes, profiting from their marginal situation, became autonomous, they allowed gifts for their services that were greatly in excess of what the laws authorized, and their biographers never failed to mention the sum. Finally, under GREGORY II, the iconoclastic crisis led to a split when Emperor Leo III divulged his real intentions: to draw from the ecclesiastical budget in order to provide additional revenue for the military portion of the empire's general budget. Although Leo was perfectly within his rights when he took 25,200 *soldi* that the Church had collected from her patrimonies in Sicily, the pope took advantage of the situation to break with him.

The alliance with the Carolingians earned Gregory II recognition for the false Donation of Constantine and status as head of state. The *arcarius* and the *sacellarius* were still responsible for finances. Management remained the same and the effect on the people was nonexistent, since those who lived off the land were paying identical sums, the totality of which fed the papal budgets instead of being shared between Rome and Constantinople. The heads of the great Roman families got contracts for revenues as rector-counts: they were neither private individuals nor public entities, but rather nobles placed at the head of administrative districts still referred to as "patrimonies." Thus, the Theophylacts received the management of a *castrum*—a synonym for *castellum*, which since antiquity referred to a town, sometimes fortified— "that is said to be old" and "that is on a road," since the monastery that was supposed to receive the profits wanted to, and was supposed to, confer this administration upon them. In the 11th century, these concessions gradually became permanent and hereditary. Like the emperor in Lombardy, the papal power was incapable of maintaining its authority over all those who drew on its budget. The *Liber Censuum* shows the fate of public revenues, which were held by private citizens whose obligations to the pope varied considerably and were often quite weak. Basically, their situation was the same as that of the nearly hereditary *conductores* from the time of Gregory the Great. All that changed was the pope's authority, which was noticeably diminished. Quarrels increased between dependents and benefice holders, and among benefice holders. The almost independent hereditary lordships remained in place in the small region they controlled, as is shown by the reports drawn up by the pope's representatives: the *dominus* was master in his own domain, as long as he fulfilled his obligations.

The Roman Empire had granted the pope revenues to manage, the profit from which was to be used for goals that were clearly defined by the court. The Western patriarch, who had become independent, pursued the same management over the lands where the Carolingians recognized his authority. The country folk remained small landowners, obliged only to pay taxes that were held as public. Quarrels between lords and the "plunderers" about which religious institutions complained were of no concern to them, since they preserved all their rights for use of their lands. They put up with constant responsibilities in exchange for services that, though certainly meager, were relatively constant and stable, and pertained primarily to issues of justice, defense, or local administration as much as they did to the religious establishment or charity.

Jean Durliat

Bibliography

LP, 1, 285–521; 2, 1–264.

Diacre, J. *Vie de Grégoire le Grand, PL*, 75, 63–242.

Durliat, J. *Les Finances publiques de Dioclétien aux Carolingiens*, Sigmaringen, 1990, 95–290; *De la ville antique à la ville byzantine. Le problème des subsistances*, Rome, 1990, 126–84.

Fabre, P. *Étude sur le* Liber censuum *de l'Église romaine*, Paris, 1892.

Förster, H. *Liber Diurnus Romanorum Pontificium*, Berne, 1958.

Gregorii Papae Registrum Epistularum, ed. E. Ewald and L. M. Hartmann, 2 vols., Berlin, 1887–89 (*MGH, Ep.* 1–2).

Jenal, G. "Gregor der Grosse und die Stadt Rom (590–604)," 145.

Le Liber censuum de l'Église romaine, ed. P. Fabre and L. Duchesne, Paris, 1910.

Toubert, P. *Les Structures du Latium médiéval. Le Latium méridional et la Sabine du IXe à la fin du XIIe siècle*, 2 vols., Rome, 1973.

13th to 15th Centuries. Beginning in the 13th century, and particularly after the LATERAN IV COUNCIL (1215), the papacy had revenues available that exceeded those of the territorial state inherited from Pepin the Short and Charlemagne. In addition to these, at a time when proceeds from the State's provinces were relatively weak, once expenses for management and defense were paid, we see the appearance of "extraterritorial" revenues into which no liabilities had to dip other than diplomacy, which kept them coming in, and tax collection, which was paid, as was the case for all the papal apparatus, by ecclesiastical benefices granted to papal agents more often than it was by the modest wages allocated for administrative and financial functions. First of all, there were census taxes or "Peter's pence" owed by the kingdoms that were vassals of the Holy See or subject to it under some title: England, Poland, and the kingdoms of Scandinavia and Aragon. To these were added the sums due either for collations made in the Roman court or for the conferment of benefices that were vacant in the

CURIA, and the taxes due by prelates upon their arrival for their *ad limina* visits to the pope.

Thus, under the heading of papal fiscality are grouped a whole series of deductions by the papacy from the Church's temporal holdings, deductions for its own profit, and in some cases for the profit of princes. Excluded were taxes that were normally—albeit with difficulty—collected by the king and princes on patrimonial lands and the clerics' personal revenues. Just as was the case for lay princes, the system of taxation appeared and remained a source of extraordinary revenue, justified by the circumstances and either real or invented purposes. It thus differed from ordinary revenue, called domain revenue by temporal princes, and which, for the papacy, came primarily from the Papal State created in the 8th century; to it were added certain "seigniorial" revenues like the taxes owed to the Holy See by vassal kingdoms and the proceeds from domains in the Comtat Venaissin (since 1274) and Avignon (starting in 1348). In the 13th century, ordinary revenues began to be insufficient to finance politics on a European scale. The Papal State's political situation led to military expenses (for companies and garrisons) that absorbed, and would continue to absorb up to the beginning of the 15th century, the greater part of the income. Even the Italian politics of the AVIGNON popes were financed in large part by proceeds from the papal tax system. Things would not be otherwise until the middle of the 15th century, when the discovery of Tolfa's ALUM would make the papacy the main producer of the caustic, so indispensable to the clothing industry, just at the time when the TURK advance into Asia Minor ruined the Genoan exploitation of Phocaea's alum.

Papal taxation came into being in the 13th century, when the last of the CRUSADES were being financed, and took advantage of old rights, like that of the annate—a year of revenue—levied beginning in the 11th century on a number of those who had recently received benefices, either for the benefit of the patron or the ordinary conferrer of the benefice, or for needs of the Church herself. It also included a practice that was initially alien to papal finances, that of tithing, but it originated primarily from the need for increased financing for the institutions that the Holy See developed in the 14th century, as well as for the defense of its political and state-owned interests in Italy. Thus it was under JOHN XXII and BENEDICT XII, and under the immediate authority of the CHAMBERLAIN Gasbert de Laval (head of the APOSTOLIC CAMERA from 1319 to 1347) that the papacy's financial demands increased and weighty institutions like the Apostolic Camera and the papal Treasury were put into place, with their centralized services and their network of provincial collectors and diocesan subcollectors.

Fiscal deductions were in effect for both the collation of benefices and their exploitation; they even included the pure and simple confiscation of benefices and revenues.

All the benefices of Christianity were "taxed" for this purpose, that is, they were appraised for revenue, on the base of which taxes were calculated. The system of taxation, which was fixed, theoretically, once and for all, was nevertheless revised on a number of different occasions, especially after the demographic and economic crises of the middle of the 14th century. Such revisions, always presented as irregular occasional and exceptional gestures of benevolence, gave rise to a number of letters and PETITIONS through which those who held benefices estimated decreases in revenue they were experiencing either because of wars and epidemics or because of the effect of a more general economic crisis like income from lands. Use of this abundant, but necessarily skewed, documentation has led some historians to dramatize the situation of the Church's temporal assets in the 14th century. The level at which something was taxed, which was reached through bargaining, only imperfectly reflected the real value of benefices, which was corrected through the influence of the holder of the benefice or one of his protectors. In short, a rate was arrived at upon which taxes were based, as were those for royal and municipal tax bases, appraisals, and land registries, or the lists of households, which were the object of hard negotiations.

There was one deduction affecting collations called the annate, in the case of minor benefices, and "common and minor services" in the case of bishoprics and abbeys: the recently endowed cleric owed one year of net revenue, after expenses were deducted. In reality, it sometimes took clerics several decades to pay their due, as partial payments and delays granted in order to escape excommunication accumulated. The cleric or prelate who was transferred remained in debt for payments not made on his previous benefices. A number of collations were made on the condition that the annates or services of predecessors who had died without leaving solvent successors be paid. Annates and the common services were due to the pope alone. Lesser services were shared by the cardinals present in the consistory at the time of the prelate's nomination, and by the members of the Curia fulfilling certain functions at that time. The share for cardinals who died in the meantime constituted the revenue of their "hat" and became part of their estate. Annates and services were due only once for a collation; that is, one year of net income spread out over a number of years represented a relatively light obligation. Long delays that took place in the case of some prelates, particularly those who entrusted their interests to a skillful prosecutor in the Curia, resulted more often from ill will than from inability to pay. This was particularly significant at the time of the GREAT SCHISM in the West, when "wait and see" attitudes were plentiful: some important archbishops took twenty to thirty years to pay off the most miniscule of balances. The accumulation of annates and services was nevertheless heavy for clerics highly placed in the Curia, who piled up minor benefices, with exemptions for residence, and who often changed benefices to go off to prestigious and financially rewarding bishoprics or abbeys. Unable to denounce a system of which they were beneficiaries, they got around it by buying time.

Heavier still was the 10 percent tax. We must be clear here, even though there is but one Latin word (*decima*) for the two terms, and even though the vocabulary in daily language was not set until the 13th century: the *decima* was a tax due by benefice holders; and the tithe was due by lay feudal tenants to their bishop and to their parish priest. Since the time of the Third Crusade, when the "Saladin tithe" was levied, provoking serious unrest, especially in England, the purpose of the 10 percent tax was to finance crusades. It thus ended up in the coffers of temporal princes who as early as the second half of the 13th century entered into agreements with one another to get the pope and the clergy to admit the juridical myth that princes could not leave for the crusade until they put an end to the quarrels that were splitting the West. This allowed them to levy the *decima* for the crusade while using it for affairs of the state. Since by the 1300s the crusade was no longer anything more than a pretext for getting clerics to contribute for the expenses of the lay world, the pope only allowed it to princes and to sovereigns of high rank, through a political *quid pro quo* for the Holy See, and often a share in the profits. To the extent that it ended up in the hands of temporal princes, the *decima*s caused the income from the Church's temporal assets to leave the Church. Its imposition thus called for the Church's consent, either by the benefice holders or their representatives, or by the pope. St. Louis IX alternately employed both procedures, cleverly using the hostility of the bishops for each extension of papal authority. He more or less negotiated *en force* with provincial councils incapable of putting up any real resistance and easily obtained *decima*s from the French popes. In 1296, when Philip the Fair was attempting to raise a *decima* that was increased by a fiftieth with no other approval than that of an assembly of nobles and prelates, the clergy showed reluctance and Pope BONIFACE VIII seized the opportunity to remind everyone of the canonical arrangements governing clergy contributions to the responsibilities of lay princes (bull *Clericis Laicos*, 24 February 1296). Borrowing his arguments from most of the canonists of the time, Boniface VIII compared nonconsensual taxes to a form of servitude and declared that he alone could give the Church's consent. The stern reply of the Capetian jurists ("Render unto Caesar . . ."), and especially the royal order forbidding exportation of cash and thus drying up the papal tax system that included the French Church (especially annates), led to a veritable canonical war. In the bull *Ineffabilis Amor* (20 September 1296), the pope set himself up as judge, even of the king, in temporal matters, subject to the pontifical magisterium *ratione peccati*. Troubled by the situation in Rome and central Italy, Boniface VIII came to a compromise. In case of emergency, the king could levy a *decima* without waiting for the pope's agreement, and judgment of urgency was left up to the king (bulls *Romana Mater Ecclesia* and *Etsi de Statu*, 7 February and 31 July 1297). During the time of the papacy in Avignon, Western sovereigns got a *decima* practically every year, which was usually shared with the pope. The *decima* was occasionally imposed in advance for a number of consecutive years. It amounted to only one-tenth of the tax, thus 10 percent of the net revenue, which made it a relatively light tax, but, thus renewed at will by an agreement between the pope and territorial princes, it doubled the annate in ten years. It thus weighed heavily on the modest receivers of benefices who did not change their benefices and could spread the payment of their annate over a number of years. Collectors, however, could not avoid the spread of fractionalized payments, and each had in his books long lists of unpaid arrears.

Proxies were the rights owed to the bishop or the archdeacon by a parish priest and other minor benefice holders on the occasion of a pastoral visit. By reserving proxies for themselves, which they did occasionally and as the concession to bishops starting in 1319, and regularly after 1369, the Avignon popes diminished frequency in visits, and commensurately reduced hierarchical control over the spiritual life of dioceses. Reformers at the end of the 14th century had no trouble demonstrating that this practice was scandalous because it was prejudicial to the faithful.

Confiscations took place in two ways and were less systematic than might first appear on reading the bulls on reserves. The bulls stipulated general reserves which then allowed administrators to judge opportunities. They nevertheless fed a whole polemical literature that seemed more interested in recounting spectacular cases than in analyzing numbers.

On the one hand, there were "vacancy revenues": the reserving of vacant benefices; in such cases the pope kept the revenue for a period of time, waiting for a new benefice holder to be named. The vacancy revenues of any benefice whose collation was reserved for the pope were reserved for the Holy See in the 14th century. Actually, the measure was not truly applied by apostolic collectors except in the case of major benefices, bishoprics and abbeys, or minor benefices chosen for their proximity or their revenue. In reality, vacancies were a source of illusions, since the collector needed to assume responsibility for the economical management of the revenue thus confiscated and leave the new holder a part of the annual revenue proportional to the time between his collation and the coming harvest of grain, grapes, or other crops or terms of payment for annuities and debts. The popes in Avignon made it a systematic practice to keep a few benefices vacant, taken especially from the bishoprics and abbeys in the south of France. The practice, which was loudly deplored by clerics and university figures, allowed the Apostolic Camera to collect the net revenue from such benefices for a number of months, and in some cases even years. But during this time it deprived the Apostolic Camera of what a collation might have procured, especially in *servitia communia*. It was no less detrimental in the short term, since the individual who received his benefice in this way, and thus found his revenue amputated, had all the more trouble paying what he owed for his collation, and in particular his *servitia communia*. Since the spiritual charge could not be left vacant indefinitely, the pope was often forced to name an "administrator," normally a prelate already endowed, who collected the net revenue of the vacant benefice as complementary remuneration. Weak resources for the Treasury, vacancies were thus also an excellent way to remunerate services without having recourse to the Treasury. Costly for the fiscal administration and scandalous for the Church, keeping vacancies only hit hard at a few bishoprics and abbeys from whom the popes made a considerable temporary profit. In most cases, the collector reached a compromise with the new holder of the benefice and gave up all direct collections. Competition between the reserve of vacancies for the pope and REGALIA, which left the king the revenue from churches called "royal" during their vacancy, made the pope extremely prudent in matters concerning some of the principal churches of France. It should be noted that the king also had spiritual *regalia* in these churches, which allowed him, during the vacancy of an episcopal see or abbacy, to make nominations that were normally reserved for the bishop or the abbot. Reserving collations for the pope, and the willingness to oblige on the part of the Avignon popes, who satisfied all the king of France's requests for benefices in favor of clerics in the royal entourage, took all reality out of this competition. In practice, all parties worked to keep from upsetting others.

The right to SPOILS was a very different matter, as it allowed the goods of clerics to be seized upon their death. In fact, and for the same reason of material impossibility, estates were not seized except to assure the payment of rights (annates, *servitia communia*, or *decimas*) that had not been paid for some time. Stories of clerics being left naked on their death beds belonged to the realm of legend, or at least they were limited to a few individual cases. In most cases, the collector appropriated nothing, or limited his seizure to a piece of furniture, an article of clothing, or a dish.

Other deductions were the result of negotiations between princes and the clergy: they were primarily charitable subsidies the rate and distribution of which varied from one case to another, but which in fact were demanded only at times when it was evident that it would be easier to levy a one-time tax than to deal with improbable arrears of *decimas* and ANNATES. A number of charitable subsidies were negotiated on the spot by NUNCIOS and LEGATES who used them to finance their missions more often than they sent money to the Treasury. The multiplication of these subsidies was due more to their limitation in time and space, and sometimes to the impossibility of actually levying them, than to an actual increase in taxes.

It would be impossible to construct a tally sheet, as we have no access to the accounts of all the collectors, and only they would render an accurate picture of the total of receipts and expenses. The sums transferred to Rome or Avignon by commercial or banking companies in the service of the Apostolic Camera, or brought to the Treasury by collectors and nuncios, were only surpluses, after payments were made on location and expenses deducted from what was collected. The records of the Treasury, called *Introitus et Exitus*, offer but a partial view of the financial sums available to the pope. It might be added that no one can calculate what the pope paid for services expected and rendered through the right of collation. Other than in a few rare exceptions, diplomacy, administration, and pontifical justice cost only a few bishoprics, prebends, and parishes, which showed up neither in budgets nor on balance sheets, since their number could be extended, and their real revenue was never declared. On the other hand, we are able to know precisely the share of different revenues that made up this impossible register, because of the collector records left to us. For the Avignon papacy in the time of the Great Schism, and thus at the time when fiscal pressures were greatest due to the fact that contributions were, basically, half of what they had been prior to 1378 in an undivided Church and needs were far from diminished, the *decima* represented approximately 20 percent, annates 20 percent, *servitia communia* from 10 percent to 20 percent, and proxies 25 percent. Despite the scandal, it is understandable why the papacy did not give up proxies. The totality of this tax system furnishes historians with sources that are as irreplaceable on the state of churches (annate books, ledgers) as they are on the economic situation (petitions, correspondence, accounting). The archives of the Apostolic Camera, with their lists of benefices and their levying records, comprise the most complete body of information available on ecclesiastical geography, the topography of the habitat, and the toponymy of the West.

The papal tax system was ruined by the reformational actions of the great councils of the 15th century, Constance and especially Basel, the way for which was prepared by withdrawals of obedience that had, especially in France, freed churches from collation by the Holy See and the tax system tied to it. The council of Constance never came to any agreement, and it was MARTIN V who, through a number of concordats, reduced deductions, most notably by arranging things such that tax debts would not be transferred to successors. The council of Basel abolished annates and, in general, the entire papal tax system (1435), but the measure, taken up for France by the Pragmatic Sanction of Bourges (1438), was poorly applied. For the most part, Martin V's decisions remained in effect until the time of the concordats of the 16th century and were unequally applied because of arbitrary taxations. The discovery of Tolfa's alum near Civitavecchia arrived propitiously in 1462 to raise the level of resources in the pope's lands. From the outset, the alum industry was leased out, including both mining and commercialization, even in localities—the most notable of which was Bruges—where the wool industry got its supplies. Rents paid by the miners, among which were the largest of Tuscany and Genoa's banking establishments, provided on the average a net revenue of 10,000 ducats per year. This clearly meant that the pope, at the time of the papal court's greatest splendor, would survive essentially from the ordinary revenue of the Papal State: a revenue that reflected the new political conditions of central Italy. The time of the great papal tax system was past.

Jean Favier

Bibliography

Archivio di Stato di Roma, *Mandati della Reverenda Camera apostolica (1418–1802)*, a cura di P. Cherubini, Rome, 1988 (*Quaderni della Rassegna degli Archivi di Stato*, 55).

Baethgen, F. "Quellen und Untersuchungen zur Geschichte der päpstlichen Hof- und Finanzverwaltung unter Bonifaz VIII.," *QFIAB*, 20 (1928–29), 114–237.

Berliere, U. *Les Collectories pontificales dans les anciens diocèses de Cambrai, Thérouanne et Tournai au XIVe siècle*, Rome-Brussels, 1929 (*Analecta vaticano-belgica*, 10).

Desportes, P. "Le clergé des campagnes rémoises à la fin du XIVe siècle d'après les registres de la fiscalité pontificale," *RHEF*, 72 (1986), 1–36.

Favier, G. *Les Finances pontificales à l'époque du Grand Schisme d'Occident (1378–1409)*, Paris, 1966 (*BEFAR*, 211).

Goñi Gaztambide, J. "El fiscalismo pontificio en España en tiempo de Juan XXII," *Anthologica annua*, 14 (1966), 65–9.

Gottlob, A. *Aus der Camera apostolica des 15. Jahrhunderts: ein Beitrag zur Geschichte des päpstlichen Finanzwesens und des endenden Mittelalters*, Innsbruck, 1889.

Guillemain, B. *Les Recettes et dépenses de la Chambre apostolique pour la quatrième année du pontificat de Clément V (1308–1309)*, Rome, 1978 (*CEFR*, 39).

Kirsch, J. P. *Die päpstlichen Kollectorien in Deutschland während des XIV. Jahrhunderts*, Paderborn, 1894.

Lunt, W. E. *Accounts rendered by Papal Collectors in England, 1317–1378*, Philadelphia, 1968.

Lunt, W. E. *Papal Revenues in the Middle Ages*, 2 vols., New York, 1934 (2d. ed., 1965). This work contains an appendix with a classification of the financial administration's documents, among which are a number of specimens in English translation.

Lunt, W. E. *Financial Relations of the Papacy with England to 1327*, Cambridge, Massachusetts, 1939.

Lunt, W. E. *Financial Relations of the Papacy with England, 1327–1534*, ibid., 1962.

Pfaff, V. "Die Einnahmender römischen Kurie am Ende des 12. Jahrhunderts," *Vierteljahrschrift für Sozial- und Wirtschaftsgeschichte*, 40 (1953), 97–118.

Repertorium Germanicum, alias Verzeichnis der in den päpstlichen Registern und Kameralakten vorkommenden Personen, Kirchen und Orte des deutschen Reiches, Berlin, 1916 (period from 1378 to 1455 in preparation).

Samaran, C., and Mollat, G. *La Fiscalité pontificale en France au XIVe siècle*, Paris, 1905 (*BEFAR*, 96).

Schmidt, T. *Libri rationum camerae Bonifatii papae VIII*, Vatican, 1984.

Vatikanische Quellen zur Geschichte der päpstlichen Hof- und Finanzverwaltung, 1316–1378. Kirsch, J. P. et al., *Die Einnahmen der apostolischen Kammer . . .*, Paderborn, 1898–1955 [from Benedict XII to Gregory XI]. Schafer, K. H. et al., *Die Ausgaben der apostolischen Kammer . . .*, Paderborn, 1911–37 [from John XXII to Gregory XI].

Weakland, J. E. "Administration and Fiscal Centralization under Pope John XXII, 1316–1334," *Catholic Historical Review*, 54 (1968), 39–54, 285–310.

Modern Era. As long as temporal power lasted, the pope was able to count on the public revenue that possession of a state and the government of subjects guaranteed. This situation, which did not end until 1870, was the result of the progressive creation of the PAPAL STATE and its financial institutions. In the Middle Ages, as the central government of the Church was taking shape, the pope needed to find resources outside the territories under his control. Thus, a complex system of taxation of ecclesiastical benefices was developed, with its apogee coming while the popes were residing in Avignon, even though at the time they did have trouble assuring revenue from their Italian possessions. This system of taxation, which touched all of Christendom, was slowly eroded by wars, SCHISMS, HERESIES, and national identities, such that in modern times the strictly ecclesiastic revenues of the papacy represent but a small portion of the papal budget. Even up to the 19th century, the pope never lived off the charity of the faithful, but off sums set aside from revenues that he controlled.

When the Italians entered Rome (20 September 1870), papal finances ceased to be the finances of a state and the Holy See's budget became confidential, at least until quite recently. In making up for the loss of the Papal States, the Italian government proposed to PIUS IX an annual payment from a civil list the sum of which was to be the equivalent of the sums listed in the earlier papal budget for the needs of the Apostolic PALACE (which included the services of the CURIA, among other expenses) as well as for maintaining a diplomatic presence and an official armed staff to ensure the sovereign pontiff's safety. The pope refused to deal with the usurper government and vigorously affirmed his willingness to depend solely on the charity of the faithful.

In reality, he had been living from charity for a few years thanks to Peter's Pence, a voluntary offering the name of which was borrowed from the annual tribute paid to the pope by the kingdom of England, from the 11th century until 1534, as a sign of vassalage. In 1860, after the loss of Romagna, Umbria, and the Marches, a few English Catholics, who were soon imitated by the faithful from Belgium, France, and Austria, got the idea of collecting funds, which they sent to Rome, either directly or via NUNCIOS. Placed in one of the finance minister's accounts, these funds were used both by the pope, personally, and by the papal administration. From 1860 to 1870, these contributions of additional cash staved off the State's bankruptcy by serving as a guarantee for loans it had taken out in foreign marketplaces. The 5 million lire that remained in the account when Rome was invaded were left to the Holy See by the Italian government. With this capital and the annual income from Peter's Pence, Pius IX was able to build a new financial base for the Holy See's needs.

The individual behind this operation was Cardinal Giacomo Antonelli (1806–76), who, since 1848, had been in charge of the prefecture of the Apostolic Palace, that is, of the administrative and fiscal management of the papal residences and the Roman Curia. Upon his death, Pius IX officially allowed a savings account to be set up, since the new secretary of state, Cardinal Giovanni Simeoni, was named administrator of the Holy See's assets. At the time, they were evaluated at the sum of about 30 million lire, with annual expenses of 6 million for the needs of what was from that time on called the Vatican. Later administrators faced the problem of holding on to the permanent, albeit fluctuating, source represented by Peter's Pence, and of gradually letting the principal grow via excess receipts. Since 1870, papal finances have not departed from this framework.

Up to 1929, that is, before Italy recognized the Vatican as an official territorial entity in the LATERAN PACTS, the popes proceeded rather empirically. Under Pius IX, the secretary of state centralized the management of all finances. Beginning in 1880, LEO XIII had him assisted by

a commission of cardinals whose secretary, Msgr. Folchi, was in complete control until his risky actions and a crisis in financial markets forced him to retire in 1891. The commission's powers were then strengthened, but to the exclusive profit of one of its members, Cardinal lmario Mocenni, who took the title of "special deputy" (*incaricatio speciale*). Leo XIII nevertheless kept a tight hand on Peter's Pence and on personal gifts, only part of which did he place back into the PATRIMONY's administration: at the time of his death, nearly 9 million lire were passed on to his successor. PIUS X was a scrupulous administrator. He relieved the Patrimony's administration of management of the Apostolic Palace and placed it in the hands of the secretary of state, Cardinal Merry del Vall, who at the same time was named president of the Patrimony's administrative committee, and prefect of the Apostolic Palace. For the pope, this was a means of personally controlling the management of all finances, something in which he had great interest. At the same time, with the assistance of the members of his antechamber, the NOBLE GUARD, or discreet advisers, he acquired a few buildings in the immediate vicinity of the Vatican. At the time of the reform of the Curia, he generalized the use of a fixed monthly salary, thus ending the custom—although it would not completely disappear until the time of PIUS XII—of obligatory bonuses and even a share in the revenues of some dicasteries between the Holy See and those who were in charge of them. On top of all this, Pius X carefully staved off the kind of risky moves that had taken their toll on papal finances in the time of Leo XIII. But he also put a stop to any risk of compromising the Holy See in political and financial matters, as might have been the case at the time of the war between Italy and Turkey that was ecouraged behind the scenes by the Banco di Roma, a bank in which the Holy See had a partial interest and whose president, Ernesto Pacelli, had been adviser to Leo XIII and Pius X for a number of investments. At the time of his death, Pius X left 6 million lire to his successor, BENEDICT XV, who did not like savings, and dipped deeply into the papacy's funds to help relieve some of the misery caused by World War I. At the end of the war, the economic situation was not good. Peter's Pence continued to accrue (although we do not know its amount, since papal largesse was distributed widely), but monetary fluctuations and changes in financial markets left the Holy See's situation more precarious than it had been previously. This was so much the case that at the beginning of his papacy PIUS XI probably had to seek loans from banks in America.

The Lateran Pacts put an end to the so-called Roman question. One of the thorny issues in preliminary discussions was an understanding of how to settle the financial losses incurred by the Holy See following the annexation of the Papal States to the kingdom of Italy. From the outset, the possibility of collecting sixty years of arrears from the civil list was dismissed; they were provided for in 1871 by what was called the Law of Guarantees but were never paid nor placed in a reserve account. Finally, at the end of a financial convention appended to the treaty, a much more modest sum was agreed upon: 750 million lire and coupons corresponding to an Italian consolidated annuity of 5 percent on the face value of one billion lire. This capital allowed Pius XI to organize the Vatican City, to redevelop the palace of Castel Gandolfo and Villa Barberini, which the Italian State had offered him, and to construct new locations for the papal congregations and the Gregorian University in Rome: in short, to give the Church's central government the architectural face by which it is known in the 21st century.

To manage the funds paid by the Italian government, Pius X created a special body called the *Amministrazione Speciale*. It worked not only with the administration of the Patrimony, which continued to manage the assets acquired by the Holy See since 1870, but also with a more recently created institution, the governing body of the Vatican City. The latter was involved in its own economic interests as a result of the sale of postage stamps and benefices made possible because of the *Annona*, a store selling food and other staples to an authorized public of employees, lay diplomats, and individuals from the Church. This increase in economic bodies must not have appeared cumbersome during the time of Pius XI, who oversaw the general workings of the papal administration with great authority. Over the years, however, it became more cumbersome as different administrative entities claimed autonomy. This was especially true, since in the meantime a modest foundation created by Leo XIII had risen out of its ashes: the institute for religious works (*Istituto per le opere di religione*, abbreviated IOR).

The IOR was created in 1887, when Italian legislation made gifts and bequests for religious works or charitable organizations aleatory. It did exist earlier, however, in the form of a commission of cardinals *ad pias causas*. It was primarily concerned with transforming donations of cash and property into bearer securities; from the very beginning, therefore, it played the role of a real estate agent and stock portfolio manager helping works both in Italy and abroad. In 1904, a good part of what fell under its purview was passed to the Congregation of the Council, the traditional guardian of ecclesiastical assets; the Congregation transferred the disposition of devises to diocesan bishops in 1906. The Congregation, whose activities were then quite limited, involved only Church dignitaries, and was barely known. It came back into view in 1941, undoubtedly due to difficulties created by the war for a number of European religious organizations. Pius XII endowed what he called the *Amministrazione per le opere di religione* with a new status and, on 27 June 1942, all its benefits were transferred to the *Istituto per le opere di re-*

ligione, recognized as an organ of the Holy See, thus exempt from taxes on dividends it earned, in a notice from the Italian finance minister (31 December 1942). In addition to managing the funds for its own activites, the IOR was entrusted with management of Peter's Pence. It thus quite naturally metamorphosed into a veritable bank, with checking accounts open not only to religious organizations and congregations and their representatives, but also to some of the Vatican's employees and dignitaries, and to the staffs of diplomatic missions.

The financial sums available to the IOR, under the direction of its president Archbishop Paul Marcinkus, dragged it into a whirlwind of dealings that ended in 1984 with a net loss of $240,900,000 after the Institute's involvement in the bankruptcy of the Banco Ambrosiano in Milan. Because of the unrest stirred up by the financial scandal, but with the slowness characteristic of the decisions of recent papacies, the IOR's administrative structure was not modified until March 1989. A commission of cardinals composed of five members named by the pope for a period of five years oversees IOR. The office of president was abolished and replaced by a prelate secretary who is not a bishop. The commission of cardinals names a commission of superintendents composed of five lay members chosen from among the great Catholic experts in the world of finance. These individuals name a director, an adjunct director, and account auditors. These changes at the top, aimed at avoiding a return to risky ventures, have not changed, however, the role of the IOR; it remains a fiduciary administration for the needs of the Roman Curia and Catholic bodies throughout the world. These receive from the IOR only the interest on sums they have entrusted to it.

The reforms desired and brought into effect by PAUL VI in his goal of simplification (constitution *Regimini Ecclesiae Universae*, 15 August 1967) brought few substantial modifications to the Holy See's financial institutions. The pope combined the old administration of the Patrimony, henceforth called an ordinary section, and the *Amministrazione Speciale*, called an extraordinary section, into a single body called Administration for the Patrimony of the Apostolic See (abbreviated APSA); each of the sections retained its autonomy under the high authority of a cardinal president and a prelate secretary. The governance of the Vatican City and the IOR have remained independent. The Congregation for Evangelization of the People (the former Propagation of the Faith), on the other hand, with its considerable budget (some $80 million in 1992), and particular goals, has allowed it to enjoy greater financial autonomy. Above all these bodies, Paul VI created a prefecture of Economic Affairs for the Holy See, presided over by a cardinal, to function both as an accounting office and a budget commission. It has thus been possible, at least on paper, to centralize control over all the apostolic administrations. The IOR however, is excluded from this, as is Peter's Pence—and all extraneous (often considerable) revenue—since they are not related to these administrations. With the constitution *Pastor Bonus* (28 June 1988), JOHN PAUL II created a council of resident cardinal bishops (the list does not appear in the *Annuario Pontificio*) that meets twice yearly, when convoked by the secretary of state, to approve the budget and outline its general focus. It was at the recommendation of this council that financing for the Roman vicariate was gradually separated from APSA and put under the auspices of the Italian episcopacy. The constitution *Pastor Bonus*, moreover, specifies explicitly (article 25, section 2) that the council is to be kept informed of activities in the IOR, whose restructuring it dictated in March 1989.

Since John Paul II's papacy, it has been customary to publish regularly the basics of the Holy See's budget. Since the practice began, it has been possible to estimate APSA's income from the patrimony at about 40 billion lire. The revenue corresponds to APSA's receipts (30 percent of the total is furnished by the extraordinary section), to the receipts from certain congregations, and to benefices eventually taken over by administrations attached to the Holy See (old Palatine administrations, among others). The total receipts came to about 70 billion lire in 1981, and 117 billion lire in 1992. Expenses went from 92 billion lire in 1981 to 219 billion lire. The deficit was made up by the net benefits from governorship (approximately 10 billion lire) in 1992 and by Peter's Pence, the total of which surpassed 30 billion lire in 1981 and 60 billion lire in 1992. The rest was absorbed either by deductions from the capital (although it is unknown whether this was ever done) or by individual gifts made to the pope, either through contributions from dioceses (600 billion lire for the first ten months of 1992) that became the canonical norm, or through gifts to the Church—to the Holy See in this case—to which all religious institutions are bound according to canon law (canon 640). The deficit, which has been chronic since the papacy of Paul VI, has increased by salary expenses and the payment of pensions (one-third of the budget), by the creation of new bodies within the Roman Curia, and by certain administrative costs related to the Holy See, like VATICAN RADIO and *L'OSSERVATORE ROMANO* (a little less than a quarter of the budget), the deficit for which is considerable. Nevertheless, the Holy See prefers to find supplementary sources of finance rather than give up activities it judges to be indispensable for its mission. As of the mid-1990s, an American initiative, the Papal Foundation, had collected some $40 million to finance papal activities.

During the vacancy of the Holy See, since all the cardinals who are heads of dicasteries cease to exercise their mandates, the responsibility for apostolic finances passes into the hands of the *camerlengo* and the Apostolic Cam-

era. The latter is responsible for answering the specifics of the cardinals' questions, as was the case after Paul VI's death, when members of the Sacred College asked for explanations—which were ultimately refused—regarding the activities of the IOR.

François-Charles Uginet

Bibliography

Due to a paucity of sources, the history of the Holy See's finances since 1870 has been little studied by historians. The archives of the prefecture of the Apostolic Palace, of the Administration of the Patrimony, and of Peter's Pence since 1870, are not available to researchers. Two works that do have the advantage of access to firsthand parallel sources are nevertheless available: Lai, B. *Finanze e finanzieri vaticani tra l'Ottocento e il Novecento, da Pio IX a Benedetto XV*, 2 vols., Milan, 1979; and Crocella, C. *"Augusta miseria." Aspetti della finanza vaticana nell'età del capitalismo*, Rome, 1970. Questions concerning the IOR have been studied by Levillain, P., and Uginet, F. C. *Le Vatican ou les frontières de la grâce*, Paris, 1984 (Italian translation in Milan, 1984, revised and updated).

The institutional aspects of the financial administration are well known in official texts, of which there are not many, a good overview of which has been offered by Ceretti, G. "Les ressources et les activités financières du Saint-Siège," *Concilium*, 14 (1978), 421–30.

Budgetary figures are available in press releases. The pope's thoughts on the economic contingencies of the Roman Curia and matters related to it are nicely outlined in a letter from John Paul II to his secretary of state (20 November 1982) regarding the meaning of the work in which the Holy See is involved, the text of which was inserted into Appendix II of the constitution *Pastor Bonus* (28 June 1988). In the early 1990s, Cardinal Rosalio José Castillo Lara, president of the Administration for the Patrimony of the Apostolic See, gave interviews to Italian newspapers, clearly outlining the Holy See's budgetary difficulties and its intentions (*Il sole 24 ore*, 26 April 1992; *Il corriere della sera*, 17 June 1992).

FIRST FRENCH EMPIRE AND THE PAPACY. The beginning of the 19th century saw a revival of the old CHURCH-STATE CONFLICT. The conflict was all the more surprising in that when PIUS VII became pope, in 1799, the Church was just emerging from a serious crisis that had all but destroyed it, and the French Empire had only just been proclaimed, in 1804.

Cardinal Chiaramonti was elected on 14 March 1800, taking the name Pius VII. Bonaparte had been First Consul since November 1799. After the violent confrontation pitting the papacy against the FRENCH REVOLUTION, the two men were fated to come to an understanding. At stake were, on the one hand, the future of the Holy See, which was at the mercy of a new Italian campaign and had nearly been annihilated by the war with revolutionary France. Also at issue was the question of the credibility of the First Consul, who in order to ensure his power needed to bring the pacification of France to a successful conclusion. The way to this pacification was through the Church.

The pope came to Rome on 3 July 1800, where a few days later, on 18 June, he received the first overtures of Bonaparte, flush with his victory at Marengo. The chosen intermediary was Cardinal Martiniana, the bishop of Vercelli. Bonaparte outlined to him his plan for an agreement on the reorganization of the Church: fewer dioceses, salaries for a new clergy, in return for which the Church would give up its properties, which would be sold as national possessions. The proposals were sent to Rome by the cardinal's nephew, Count Alciati.

Pius VII's reaction was one of surprise. He feared a fresh offensive against the PAPAL STATES, and he was being offered a concordat. The surprise was a pleasant one, but he requested details and dispatched Archbishop Spina of Corinth to find out more. News of the negotiations quickly spread, and was met with resistance. Many in Rome were hostile to a government born of the Revolution. Louis XVIII, for his part, tried to impose the indefatigable Cardinal Maury on the pope as "cardinal protector of the Churches of France," a convenient way of preventing any agreement with Bonaparte, but Pius VII rejected Maury.

In France, the royalists were not the only ones opposed to any agreement between the pope and the "usurper": the army had also to be reckoned with, together with the majority assemblies, which were anti-Catholic, not to mention die-hard Gallicans like Grégoire.

Yet Bonaparte was determined to have an accord with Pius VII. He knew that his first appeasement measures in favor of the Catholics had been well received and had enabled him to pacify the Vendée. Realist that he was, he intended to work the religious revival to his advantage. On 16 August 1800, he declared to the Council of State: "My policy is to govern men as most of them want to be governed. By becoming Catholic I won the war in the Vendée, by becoming a Muslim I came to rule Egypt, by becoming an Ultramontanist I won over the people of Italy; if I were to govern a Jewish people, I would rebuild the temple of Solomon." The concordat was designed to allow Bonaparte to use the Church as a basis for his regime. He understood full well that he could not create that Church by himself: for that, he needed the pope. He would not commit the mistake of the Constituents when they drew up the Civil Constitution of the Clergy without consulting Rome. The Roman negotiators, Archbishop Spina and Fr. Caselli, reached Paris on 15 November 1800. Talleyrand introduced their interlocutor, Abbé Bernier, whose role had been decisive in the pacification of the Vendée.

From the outset, the negotiations came up against three problems: the division of the clergy into oath-swearers and rebels, which was a division inherited from the Revolution; the sale of Church properties; and the place of Catholicism in the new regime. The divergences illustrated the incompatibility of the Roman idea of religion with the Napoleonic system, which proclaimed the supremacy of the civil over the ecclesiastical.

For the moment, the two "theologies" had no choice but to come to an understanding; failure would finish them both. Agreement was reached on the resignation of all bishops, whether rebels or constitutionals, with each one giving up what was his. Only a few rebels put up any resistance, those who made up the Little Church, a new but not widespread SCHISM.

The pope had to acknowledge the sale of Church properties by the Revolution, an acknowledgment that was only *de facto* but sufficient to appease the other side.

The battle was tougher over the place of Catholicism, which Rome wished to see recognized as the state religion; it would in fact be the religion of the consuls.

Everything—the bitterness of the negotiations, the succession of plans and counterplans, Rome's dispatch to Paris of Cardinal Consalvi, Bonaparte's threats—presaged storms to come, even if in fact the concordat was finally signed at midnight on 15 July 1801.

Pius VII had made many concessions; he had renounced his claim to the properties confiscated from the Church by the Revolution; he had sacrificed the bishops who had remained faithful to him; he had given the First Consul the right of episcopal nominations; and Catholicism would no longer be the state religion of France. But in return he settled the quarrel that pitted him against the Revolution, he ended a formidable schism, he saw a restoration of Catholic worship in France, and, above all, he once more had the right of investiture of bishops. In Rome, there was rejoicing: "A severe blow has been dealt to Gallican liberties."

But if there was great satisfaction in Rome, in Paris Bonaparte was encountering strong resistance on the part of the assemblies. His opponents were eliminated in a purge. At length, the legislature ratified the accord.

What had happened was that a new element had been added, unilaterally, by the French government: the Organic Articles. An analysis of this text shows that Bonaparte was strengthening his hold on the French Church. Title I stipulated that all bulls, briefs, and decrees emanating from the Holy See should be submitted for government approval before publication. The same held for the convening of synods, and the nuncio was forbidden to carry out on French soil "functions relating to the affairs of the Gallican Church." Title II went further: bishops were not allowed to leave their dioceses, and the declaration of 1682 had to be taught in the seminaries. Title III called for the adoption of one catechism throughout France, and the primacy of civil over religious marriage. These were blows aimed at the authority of Rome, and they were not well received.

Still, the organization of the concordatory Church was headed by the papal legate, Caprara, who was old and accommodating, and by the French minister of worship, Portalis, who, owing to his origins, was "steeped in Gallicanism." The map of the new dioceses was drawn up, and their titulars, appointed by the First Consul, received their investiture from the pope.

This religious pacification worked mainly to Bonaparte's advantage. At the Tribunate, after the resumption of the war and the failure of the Cadoudal-Pichegru plot, Curée, in 1804, proposed a motion "that Napoleon Bonaparte, at present First Consul, be declared emperor of the French and, by this right, that the imperial title be declared hereditary in his family." The proposal was accepted by the Senate and changed to a decree of the Senate of 18 May 1804. By a referendum, the First Consul became Emperor of the French.

Napoleon was not content with this popular approval. On 10 May, in Caprara's presence, he expressed the desire to be consecrated by the pope. He wanted to have his dynasty take root by giving it a mystical aura that would confer legitimacy on it; hence, the recourse to consecration. Pepin the Short and, first and foremost, Charlemagne offered marvelous precedents. Appealing to the pope and summoning him to Paris could not help but make an impression where it counted—in this regard, the reactions of Louis XVIII and Joseph de Maistre, for example, showed that Napoleon had judged well. Despite the Roman cardinals' objections, Pius VII set out for Paris on 2 November 1804.

They discussed the ceremonial. The pope had wanted the Roman ceremonial, but Talleyrand was against it; those rites recalled "a time when ecclesiastical authority still wanted to give the impression that the Church invested the civil power." Nor was there a question of following the ceremonial of Reims for the crowning of the kings of France. Bernier, now bishop of Orléans, devised a new ceremonial that was a sort of compromise between the other two.

The coronation took place on 2 December 1804 in Paris. Pius VII did the anointing that performed the actual consecration, said the prayers, and blessed the insignia, but Napoleon placed the crown on his own head. With that gesture, he signaled his independence with regard to the religious power. Then, the emperor took the constitutional oath while the pope withdrew to a chapel to remove his papal vestments. This symbolized his wish not to sanction Napoleon's pledges by his presence. Each of them, therefore, as he saw fit, could consider either the consecration or the oath as the essential.

In so readily agreeing to come to Paris, Pius VII hoped to gain a revision of the Organic Articles, which he did not obtain. Nevertheless, the success of his French visit enhanced his prestige. Everywhere, both en route to Paris and on the homeward journey, he was acclaimed with an enthusiasm that pushed Gallican ideas into the shadows. Napoleon, for his part, derived an important political benefit from the consecration; he believed that the pope, henceforth associated with his fortunes, would be a docile servant. It was this error of judgment that provoked the battle between Church and Empire.

The war between France and England, which had resumed in 1803, caused Napoleon to close off the Continent to English goods. This was the Continental Blockade, which prohibited all forms of neutrality. The Papal States had ports that the emperor wanted to see closed. After all, the war was being waged against a schismatic sovereign, whereas Napoleon had been consecrated by Pius VII. The latter should therefore join the Napoleonic system. The pope refused, "taking up the pen of GREGORY VII," as the emperor put it. This frail old man, seemingly obliged to bend to the imperial will, showed an unexpected resistance. This was especially surprising in that Napoleon had set his brother Joseph on the throne of Naples in place of the Bourbons and that, now that he himself was king of Italy in Milan, he held the pope in a pincer-like grasp. He fumed: "Your Holiness is sovereign of Rome, but I am its emperor. All my enemies must be yours." Pius VII replied that, because of its calling, the Church could not take part in a temporal conflict.

A rupture seemed imminent: Fresch, the emperor's uncle, who had been dispatched to Rome as ambassador, left the city. He was replaced by a former Conventional regicide, Alquier. Meanwhile, Consalvi sent in his resignation as secretary of state. Casoni, who succeeded him, was ineffective.

On 21 January 1808, Napoleon gave General Miollis the order to occupy Rome, which the French troops entered on 2 February. Although the papal forces put up no resistance, Pius VII did not yield. "My predecessor had the impetuosity of a lion," he asserted. "I have lived like a lamb, but I could defend myself and die like a lion." Alquier warned him: "You do not know this man."

On 16 May 1809, Napoleon annexed Rome to his empire. Pius VII flung back a bull of excommunication. During the night of 5 to 6 July, General Radet—not on his orders, Napoleon would affirm—arrested the pope. The old man was moved to Savona in inhumane conditions.

With this imprisonment, the emperor intended to break Pius VII and force him to come to Paris to take up residence there. Already the Roman archives, like the cardinals, were on their way to the capital of the Grand Empire. Yet Pius VII refused to be "the pope of the French": he was head of a universal Church.

The excommunication of the emperor had had no repercussions. True, it became known only by being clandestinely broadcast by the young members of a secret association, the Knights of the Faith. The effectiveness of such an excommunication had weakened considerably since medieval times, in any case.

Yet Pius VII had a formidable weapon up his sleeve: the refusal of canonical investiture. At one stroke, Napoleon was rendered quite powerless to provide for vacant dioceses, in particular that of Paris, whose bishop, Cardinal de Belloy, had died. The newly appointed bishops, without spiritual investiture, were no better than simple administrators. It was a return, in the early 1800s, to the conflict between Gregory VII and Henry IV.

In order to intimidate the pope, "that old fool," Napoleon tried to unite the French clergy around himself by means of two ecclesiastical committees, from 1809 to 1811, and then by means of a council that opened in Notre-Dame on 17 June 1811. These failed; he even had three opposing bishops arrested. He decided to negotiate with Pius VII face to face and ordered him transferred to Fontainebleau, where the pope arrived on 19 June 1812.

But when Napoleon returned from Russia, he was in a less advantageous position. The negotiations began in January 1813, and issued in the "concordat" of Fontainebleau. Physically exhausted, Pius VII agreed to grant the bishops the right of canonical investiture for a period of six months, after which time investiture would be conferred by the metropolitan. This agreement, which the pope regarded as no more than a plan, was to remain secret. Napoleon hastened to publish it and to have a *Te Deum* sung in celebration. Betrayed, Pius VII retracted. Napoleon hoped to settle everything on his return from the German campaign, but he was vanquished at Leipzig. On 21 January 1814, he gave orders for the pope to be moved back to Savona, and then on 19 March, to be taken back to Rome.

The spiritual force had triumphed over the force of arms; the pope had conquered the emperor. But what would have happened if Napoleon had returned from Russia victorious remains a question.

Jean Tulard

Bibliography

Bindel, V. *Le Vatican à Paris*, Paris, 1942.
Latreille, A. *L'Église catholique et la Révolution française*, II, Paris, 1950.
Leflon, J. *La Crise révolutionnaire*, Paris, 1951.
Welschinger, H. *Le Pape et l'Empereur*, Paris, 1905.

FISHERMAN'S RING (ANULUS PISCATORIS). The fisherman's ring is so named because it represents, in its most usual form, Saint Peter fishing with a net in his boat. This was the origin of the private papal seal, as opposed to the lead bull, the official and solemn seal of the pope. Its existence has been known since the 13th century. CLEMENT IV mentioned it in the following terms in a letter dated 1 March 1265 addressed to his nephew: "*Scribimus tibi et familiaribus nostris non sub bulla sed sub piscatoris anulo quo romani pontifices in suis secretis utuntur*" ("We write to you as to all our intimates not under the bull but under the fisherman's annular which is used by Roman pontiffs for their secret matters.")

The oldest known example of its use is a seal by NICHOLAS III (pope from 1277–80), attached not to an act, but to a reliquary. From the end of the 14th century on, the fisherman's annular was used to authenticate a new category of papal acts, the BRIEFS, expedited by the pope's secretaries. This red wax oval seal, approximately 2 centimeters high, bears the name of the pope and his number above Saint Peter's effigy. Announced in the date with the words *sub an(n)ulo piscatoris*, it was affixed on the act, which had been prefolded both lengthwise and width-wise in order to form a rather narrow package. When used to seal the act, as was generally the case, the wax covered and affixed the ends of the parchment flaps, which were inserted into slits through the document made for this purpose.

In the beginning, the use of the brief was limited to matters of a political and administrative nature. As of the middle of the 15th century, graces begin to be bestowed in this way. In such cases, and when it contained dispositions of a general nature, the brief was sent open, not closed. The wax seal was applied either on the back of the act, or on the front under the text. During the modern period, the seal thus applied was surrounded by a twist of parchment or covered with a sheet of paper, or even protected by a metal capsule in the form of a heart. Very few of these imprints have been preserved.

Before being established under NICHOLAS V (1447–55), the rules and uses described above varied under different pontificates. Thus, the secret seal of Nicholas III represented a beardless young man, line fishing, while that of CLEMENT VII (pope of Avignon) had a blazon topped by a TIARA and KEYS. EUGENE IV's seal had the heads of the apostles Peter and Paul (like the obverse of the lead bull). The motto on the seal changed also. In BONIFACE IX's acts, we find the expression *sub an(n)ulo fluctuantis navicule*, but in Eugene IV's, we see *sub an(n)ulo capitum principum apostolorum*. In a few rare cases, under INNOCENT VII, GREGORY XII, and EUGENE IV, we also encounter the phrase *sub an(n)ulo nostro secreto*.

From 1842 on, the wax seal was replaced by a round, red stamp with an analogous representation. It was applied under the text on the left. However, the mention in the date of the fisherman's annular remains to this day. Today, the *anulus piscatoris* no longer serves as a seal, but remains one of the symbols of pontifical power. After the death of each pope, it is broken in the presence of the cardinals.

Bernard Barbiche

Bibliography

Battelli, G. "Anello del pescatore," *EC*, 1 (1948), 1219–1220.

Frenz, T. *Papsturkunden des Mittelalters und der Neuzeit*, Stuttgart, 1986 (*Historische Grundwissenschaften in Einzeldarstellungen*, 2) 44 [Ital. trans. Vatican City, 1989, 50–51] (with bibliography).

FISTULA. See Mass, Papal: Liturgical Objects.

FLABELLUM. The *flabellum* is a giant fan made of large ostrich and peacock feathers that is attached to a red velvet pole decorated with gold embroidery. Always used in pairs and reserved for liturgical use, *flabelli* were carried by the two chamberlains who escorted the pope when he was carried, in the shelter of the dais, on the SEDIA GESTATORIA, or during the procession of Corpus Christi (in Rome, called *Corpus Domini*), on the *talamo* (a large kneeler carried by the *sediari* and upon which the pope, wrapped in an immense cope, knelt before the exposed holy sacrament). During papal masses or consistories, the *flabelli* were set on either side of the papal throne.

First used in the East by Assyrian, Babylonian, and Egyptian sovereigns, *flabelli* were introduced into the Catholic liturgy in the East in the 4th century, when they were waved on the altar by deacons between the offertory and the consecration of the eucharist. In all probability, it was Pope AGAPITUS I who brought them to the West in the 6th century; by the 10th century they were used everywhere. Up until the 17th century, before they were reserved for the exclusive use of the pope, they were called *cherubini* because of their resemblance to the wings of cherubim. Their use was abandoned by PAUL VI in 1968. Since that time, a *flabellum* has been on exhibit in the museum in the Lateran Palace.

Joël-Benoît D'Onorio

Bibliography

Noirot, M. "Flabelli," *Catholicisme*, IV.

FLORERIA. The floreria is the warehouse where objects necessary for the papal apartments and papal ceremonies are stored, with the exception of liturgical ornaments, which are left in the care of the sacristan. It has been in existence since at least the time of the papacy in AVIGNON. Derived from the Latin name *folreria*, the Italian word *floreria* specifically refers to the place where the warehouse is located. The QUIRINAL Palace had its own *floreria* (the entry to which was in the great Courtyard of the Clock). In the Vatican Palace, the *floreria* is still entered through the Saint Damasus courtyard.

In 1800, PIUS VII established the floreria's role, which has not changed up to the present day. The 19th century abounded in regulations regarding the floreria, which had become a permanent fixture in the Apostolic Palace's administration. The individual in charge was the *floriere*; he acted primarily under the authority of the major quartermaster, who supervised all the Apostolic Palace's materials. The *floriere* was in charge of preparing the chapels and churches where the pope would be celebrating mass or attending a religious function.

Since the breakup of the Papal States, the role of the *floreria* has been limited to the Vatican, where it is particularly active during the time of a conclave. The changes introduced into papal ceremonies since the time of PAUL VI have transformed the *floreria*'s storage rooms into a museum. When they are not on display in the museum in the Lateran Palace, it is in these storerooms that unusual articles are now kept, including *FLABELLI* (large fans decorated with ostrich feathers that were formerly carried on either side of the pope during solemn occasions) and the SEDIA GESTATORIA (sedan chairs). Several gifts made to the pope have found their way to the *floreria*, and their numbers have multiplied since the popes began to travel throughout the world. Cardinals and certain dignitaries who reside in the Vatican's buildings are allowed to borrow objects from the *floreria* in order to decorate or furnish their apartments. The practice, which is quite common, lends an unmistakable unity of decor to Vatican residences.

François-Charles Uginet

See also HOUSEHOLD, PAPAL.

Bibliography

Moroni, G. *Dizionario di erudizione storico-ecclesiastica*, XXV, Venice, 1844, 104–10.

FORGERIES. Since the 12th century, CANON LAW has defined forgery as an "alteration of the truth" (novelle 73: *Falsum est vertiatis immutatio*), a broad definition derived from Roman law. Through the centuries, popes have been faced with the problem of counterfeit money (since they once held monetary authority) or, in the capacity of judge, with false witness. Even more widespread, however, were false documents and false canonicals.

The high Middle Ages saw the beginnings of forgeries of papal acts and punishments such as excommunication, and there was a "golden age" of forgery during the 11th and 12th centuries. False documents were numerous because the written word was taken as proof in legal matters, and judges were often incapable of proving a document false. The pope's was a good name to put on a document because the papacy had grown in prestige, and the name of an earlier pope lent additional authority. If the creator of a false document was an ecclesiastic, he was generally not working for his own personal gain, but for his establishment (if he was reputable). Toward the end of the 12th century, however, falsification became more a matter of individual interest, and the help of professional forgers became more common. There was no dearth of forgers at this time, sometimes even within the CHANCERY itself. The great majority of forgers produced documents granting benefices, and they sometimes produced marriage dispensations or the legalization of a bastard. Others took up fraudulent collections by using false indulgences or false relics. These proliferated, always using the name of the reigning pope or that of a recent predecessor. In 1198, INNOCENT III discovered a location where false BULLS were being made in Rome, and he sent an alert to all of Christendom. From 8 May 1334 to 23 February 1356, entrance records from the papal prison in Avignon listed more than ninety forgers out of some six-hundred prisoners. In the first half of the 14th century, more lay people began to enter the profession, including notaries and nobles. The work of these forgers was easier to detect, compared with the quite rigid norms of the chancery forgers.

In 1198, Innocent III set down rules for evaluating forgeries. These fell under the heading *De Crimini Falsi* in GREGORY IX's *Decrees* (book 5, title 20); and the rules spread rapidly through ecclesiastical courts, where they were used to examine the composition of bulls, including handwriting and style. A number of forgeries were discovered because they did not pay attention to correct abbreviation, or because of a *falsa latinitas* or a *peccatum in constructione*. But a lack of elements to use for comparison left the inspector of an older document helpless. In 1205, Innocent III failed when faced with two forged privileges from Constantine I (709 and 713), as did BENEDICT XIII's experts when faced with a bull supposedly written by CLEMENT IV in 1266. It would not be until 1886 that Julien Havet demonstrated the falseness of a letter from ANASTASIUS II congratulating Clovis for his conversion, the hoax of an erudite 17th century member of the Oratory.

Canonical forgeries posed the same problems as the forgeries of earlier times, although with more formidable consequences: the counterfeiter lent support to an ecclesiological program by padding recent texts, or invented ones, with the moral weight of an *auctoritas* (authority), such as an early synod or pope. From the Carolingian reorganization in the 9th century to the Gregorian reform, falsifications abounded. Their success was assured by the channel of canonical collections into which they were incorporated. The greatest success was seen by the pseudodecretals known as pseudo-Isidorians, a group of compilations drawn up in Gaul toward the middle of the 9th century in order to promote the power of the bishop and, as a result, that of the pope. By 858 they were being sought out in Rome, and by the time of HADRIAN II, papal letters were citing them.

The first systematic critique of the pseudo-Isidorians was not done until 1628, and they were still the source for three hundred citations in the annotations from the 1917 Code of Canon Law. When a forgery belongs to the domain of what is useful, as in this case, technical and intellectual methodology to critique authenticity and to facilitate the precise dating of a text's composition or the burial of a saint's body has long been lacking. For this to happen, clearer feelings about the split between the past and the present, a new hierarchy of "authorities," and attacks by humanists and non-Catholic Christians are needed. Not that the examination of the DONATION OF CONSTANTINE by Lorenzo Valla or the all-out polemic of the Protestants against papal acts are models of a method; but in the context of Catholic REFORM and the birth of historical knowledge, the great enterprises of Catholic erudition such as Baronius' *Annals* and the Bollandist' endeavor in the area of hagiography, demonstrate the importance of a change in thinking.

The critique of pious Medieval legends and the forged documents that support them has, at times, stirred up a certain unrest: for denying the antiquity of the foundation of the Carmelites, Papebroch drew the wrath of the Spanish Inquisition, and for being overly critical of Merovingian royal acts, he gave rise to the composition of the first great treatise on diplomacy, in which, Mabillon, in 1681, laid the foundations for a science for critiquing medieval forgeries. Having up to that time given the benefit of the doubt in matters of the authenticity of relics, the papacy was to become more circumspect in the 18th century. This transformation was completed on 10 October 1987, when the Holy See authorized carbon-14 dating of the Shroud of Turin, which had become one of its possessions.

Olivier Guyotjeannin

Bibliography

Constable, G. "Forgery and Plagiarism in the Middle Ages," *Archiv für Diplomatik*, 29 (1983), 1–41.

Fälschungen im Mittelalter (Congrès Munich, 1986), Hanover, 1988, 5 vol. (*MGH, Schriften*, 33; with bibliography).

Guénée, B. *Histoire et culture historique dans l'occident médiéval*, Paris, 1981 (*Collection historique*), 129–47.

Herde, P. *Beiträge zum päpstlichen Kanzlei- und Urkundewesen im 13. Jahrhundert*, Kallmünz, 1967, 86–124.

Hermann-Mascard, N. *Les Reliques des saints: formation coutumière d'un droit*, Paris, 1975, 113–42.

Naz, R. "Faux," *DDC*, 5 (1953), 816–21.

Polman, B. *L'Elément historique dans la controverse religieuse du XVIe siècle*, Gembloux, 1932.

Saxer, V. "Le suaire de Turin aux prises avec l'histoire," *RHEF*, 76 (1990), 21–55.

FORMOSUS. (*b. ca. 816, d. 4 April 896*). *Elected pope on 3 October 891.*

Nothing specific is known about Formosus's family, except the name of his father, Leo. Successor to the bishop of Porto, who was deposed in 863, Formosus began his ecclesiastical and political career in service to the papal government, where he was a talented, competent, and ambitious assistant. In 866 he was sent on a mission to Bulgaria by Pope NICHOLAS I (858–67), but the canonical prohibition involving the translation of bishops from one see to another did not allow his becoming archbishop of Bulgaria, as he and Prince Boris I would have wished. Formosus also fulfilled missions for Pope HADRIAN II (867–72). The most noteworthy of these was perhaps his role as legate to Constantinople, and, during the talks in Trent in 872, between King Louis the German and Empress Engelberge.

Pope JOHN VIII (872–82), who might have been in competition with Formosus at the time of his accession to the papacy, would still have taken him into his confidence at the beginning of his papacy. On 19 April 896, however, he excommunicated Formosus and some of his supposed accomplices following the accusation of a plot against the emperor and the pope. The sentence, which Formosus dodged by fleeing into the kingdom of Western France, was renewed at the time of the synods of Ponthion (July 876) and Troy (August 878). In Troy, Formosus ended up submitting, although he reentered the Church only with lay status. He was restored as archbishop of Porto by Pope MARINUS I in 883/884. Formosus consecrated Pope STEPHEN V, elected in 885, and became pope himself on 3 October 891, counter to the prohibition against translation, which was paid little heed at the time. The fact that Formosus was bishop even before being elected pope allowed a new form of consecration to be identified, which would later be referred to as *inthronizatio*.

Through the concession of privileges, and via correspondence, Formosus entered into contact with the most important centers of the *orbis christianus*. He corresponded with England regarding noncanonical procedures in the naming of bishops and the primate of Canterbury; with Catalonia for the concession of privileges to Gerona; and with the German Church at the time of the dispute raised by the question of whether Bremen belonged to the ecclesiastical province of Cologne or of Hamburg. The contacts the pope had with archbishop Foulques of Reims are known with more specificity, through an account made later by Flodoard of Reims.

In the quarrel between Eudes and Charles the Simple over the succession to the throne of Western Francia, Formosus undoubtedly gave his early support to Charles. To settle the dispute with Byzantium that had already broken out under Stephen V's papacy, Formosus proposed to annul the sacraments conferred by Patriarch Photios at the time of his first mandate, and to declare those of the second valid, but this solution did not succeed in establishing a definitive peace. In Italy, Formosus had decisive dealings with the dukes of Spoleto, which deteriorated after the coronation of Emperor Guido II and his son Lambert (pact concluded on 30 April 892). The recent discovery in Remirement's "book of fraternization" of an inscription that identifies the political factions toward the end of the Formosus papacy makes clear that Arnoul, Eudes, Berenger, and Formosus were opposed by Lambert and Charles the Simple. To defend himself against the threat of the Spoletos, Formosus turned on two different occasions to the king of Germany, Arnoul, whom he crowned emperor in February 896, shortly before his own death.

Formosus's papacy has a macabre epilogue. In 897, Pope STEPHEN VI had Formosus's body exhumed and posthumously condemned because, out of ambition, he had violated the prohibition against translation and had not paid attention to the excommunication pronounced by John VIII. In addition, he had not respected the oath he made in Troy in 878 to no longer solicit ecclesiastical charges. The sacraments conferred by Formosus were declared null. Formosus's body, which had been buried in a Roman cemetery for pilgrims, was then thrown into the Tiber. It was recovered a few months later, however, and the remains were buried in Saint Peter's by Pope THEODORE II, who, following the example of JOHN IX (Council of Ravenna, 898), revoked the judgment of Stephen VI's "Cadaver Synod."

Formosus's apologists, Auxilius of Naples and Eugenius Vulgarius, as well as the anonymous *Invectiva in Romam*, praise the pope's piety and erudition. These virtues were clearly connected, however, to his ambition.

Klaus Herbers

Bibliography

JL, I 435–49 II, 705, 746.

LP, 2, 227.

MGH; Epist., 7, 366–70.

Arnaldi, G. "Papa Formoso e gli imperatori della casa di Spoleto," *Annali Fac. di lettere Univ. Napoli*, 1 (1951), 85–104.

Auxilius of Naples, ed. E. Dummler, *Auxilius und Vulgarius*, Leipzig, 1866.

Domenici, G. "Il papa Formoso," *La Civiltà cattolica*, 75 (1924), I, 106–20, 518–36; II, 121–35.

Droulers, P. "À propos de pape Formose du P. A. Lapôtre," *AHP*, 19 (1981), 327–32.

Ducev, I. "Uno studio inedito di Mons. G. C. Campini sul papa Formoso," *ASR*, 59 (1936), 137–77 (*Medioevo Bizantino-Slavo*, 1, Rome, 1965, 149–81, 548–51).

"Formosus," *DHGE*, 17 (1971), 1093–4, complément à F. Vernet, *DTC*, 6–1 (1924), 594–9.

Gussone, N. *Thron und Inthronisation des Papstes*, Bonn, 1978 (*Bonner Historische Forschung*, 41), 200–13.

Invectiva in Romam, ed. E. Dummler, *Gesta Berengarii imperatoris*, 1871, 137–54.

Lapôtre, A. "Le pape Formose. Étude critique sur les rapports du Saint-Siège avec Photios," *Études sur la Papauté au IXe siècle*. ed. A. Vauchez, Turin, 1978, 1, 1–120.

Peri, V. "Le ricerche di P. Arthur Lapôtre sulla politica dei Papi alla fine del IX secolo," *RSCI*, 36 (1982), 125–45.

Pop, D. *La Défense du pape Formose*, Paris, 1933.

Zimmermann, H. *Papstabsetzungen des Mittelalters*, Graz-Vienna-Cologne, 1968, 49–73.

FRANCISCANS.

In October 1209 (or Spring 1210), a group of lay penitents from Assisi, led by Francesco di Bernardone, traveled to Rome to obtain papal approval of a *propositum vitae* defining the specific contours of their evangelical life in the Umbrian Valley. Believing this new way of life had universal value for all of God's creatures, they desired to share their charism beyond the borders of the diocese of Assisi. For this, the nascent fraternity required the approval of the Holy See. With the help of the bishop of Assisi, Guido II, and his friend in the Curia, Cardinal John of St. Paul, the minorite fraternity obtained not only the desired audience before INNOCENT III but an oral approval of their *forma vitae*—enshrined in the earliest layers of the *Regula non bullata* (or Rule of 1221)—as well as permission to preach penitential sermons to all whom they might meet. The historic encounter at the Lateran began the long and sometimes problematic relationship between the Franciscan order and the papacy.

During the Lifetime of Francis of Assisi.

The relationship of the Friars Minor with the papacy prior to 1226 pivots on the person of Hugolino dei Segni, cardinal-bishop of Ostia. As legate of HONORIUS III in north and central Italy, responsible for monitoring the development of religious life in the region, Hugolino played a major role in giving shape to the three branches of the Franciscan family between 1218 and 1223. Not only did he firmly channel the religious inspiration of Clare of Assisi into a more traditional form of religious life for women (i.e., the cloister) and help draft the first known rule of the Third Order (the *memoriale* of 1221), he was also active in the affairs of the Friars Minor. Concerned about the potential abuses inherent in the fabled freedom of these itinerant preaching friars, Hugolino attempted to provide structure, organization, and stability to the new movement—even at the risk of sacrificing some of its more original characteristics (e.g., the attenuation of the poverty of the Clares and the lay eremitical orientation of the friars). This concern explains why he discouraged Francis from journeying to France in 1217, lest his fraternity be left unattended. Unable to stop the Poverello from voyaging to the Levant in 1219 at the time of the Fifth Crusade, the cardinal did summon Francis to Bologna upon his return in 1220, informing him of the criticisms being lodged against the friars by certain ecclesiastics and of the dissatisfaction of clerics within his own order over the direction of the community. Chastened, the founder resigned his charge as minister of the friars. He then sought (or agreed to accept) the more direct guidance of Hugolino as cardinal protector of the order. One of the immediate results of this relationship was the drafting of a new, more juridically precise rule for the community—the *Regula bullata* of 1223—to replace the earlier, more ample foundational document. Another was the growing engagement of the friars in the clerical apostolate of the Church. By the time of his death in 1226, however, Francis had grown wary of the role that the Holy See was coming to play in the fraternity. In his *Testament*, he explicitly forbade his friars from running to the Curia to obtain privileges that would ease the privations of their way of life or circumvent the obstacles to their ministry.

After the death of the founder, the order would enter upon a significantly different path, thanks largely to the convergence of ideals between the papacy (personified by the same Hugolino, elected GREGORY IX in 1227) and the clerical party in the order. This coherence of vision occurred mainly in two areas: the interpretation and observance of the Rule (particularly in reference to the manner of living poverty) and the increasing involvement of the friars in the clerical apostolate (e.g., preaching, confession of sins, and burial of the dead) and in direct service to the Church as bishops, legates, or even popes.

The Interpretation and Observance of the Rule.

The tumultuous General Chapter of 1230 reached an impasse over three major questions: whether the admonitions in the *Testament* of Francis were binding on all the friars; whether the profession of obedience to follow the Gospel meant that the evangelical precepts as well as the counsels had to be obeyed; and how various prescriptions of the Rule—especially regarding poverty—were to be interpreted. Unable to resolve the matters among themselves, the chapter sent a delegation of five representative friars to Rome to lay their quandary before

Gregory IX. Claiming to know the mind and intentions of Francis, Gregory issued a series of rulings in his historic bull *Quo elongati* of 28 September. On the *Testament*: however inspiring a document it might be, the last wishes of Francis could have no juridical validity in the life of the friars "*quod omnes tangit ab omnibus tractari et approbari debet*"—which it had not. On the profession of the Gospel: only the precepts were binding unto mortal sin, whereas the counsels—though encouraged for true followers of evangelical perfection—were not. And on poverty: while maintaining absolute lack of ownership of all goods which they might use and avoiding all direct contact with money, the friars could, however, have recourse to a *nuntius* who, as the legal representative of the donor, was to manage the provisioning of the needs of the friars. *Quo elongati* is thus significant for two reasons: it initiated a process whereby the friars became dependent upon the papacy to interpret the specific manner in which they were to live their rule; and it set the Minors on a path of defining their life, especially their poverty, not as a *forma vitae* but increasingly in terms of juridical categories—a development that would divide the order into opposing camps and ultimately lead to the poverty controversies of the early 14th century.

The next instance of this process occurred on 14 November 1245 when the friars received a second bull interpreting the poverty of the Rule: *Ordinem vestrum* of Innocent IV. *Quo elongati* had not resolved all the juridical problems associated with providing for the needs of an order claiming total lack of ownership of the things of the earth. This bull is notable for several innovations. First, it preserved the friars' juridical claim to be living in total poverty by asserting that, whereas the ownership of their movable goods was retained by the donor, that of their immovable goods was now assumed by the papacy. Second, it asserted that the *nuntius* was to act as the representative of the donor as well as the local guardian and gave him the discretion to provide not just for their necessities but also their conveniences. The bull proved controversial, as the Chapter of Metz (1254) voted not to take advantage of the liberties available to them.

The papacy, in the person of NICHOLAS III, issued a third critical bull regarding the observance of poverty on 14 August 1279: *Exiit qui seminat*. This bull explicitly asserted that Christ and his apostles, like the friars themselves, had lived in evangelical poverty (with all the legal distinctions this assertion now implied). Further, Nicholas entered into the juridical dispute on how the friars could use things without actually possessing them by adding a further distinction: between *usus iuris* (which an owner exercises) and *usus facti* (which a friar exercises). But to ensure that such use would not evolve into unrestrained use (and thus luxury), the pope declared that the Rule restricted the friars to *usus moderatus* or *usus simplex*. The latter term came to be associated with yet an-

other, *usus pauper*, whose precise meaning and connection to the vow would be debated by the friars in the next decades.

The "juridicization" of the meaning of evangelical poverty culminated in the controversy between the Franciscan Spirituals and the representatives of the Community from 1309 to 1312. With the growing division in the order between exponents of a more rigorous form of poverty consistent with the life of the real poor and the leaders of the order who defended both the moderate form of poverty set forth in the three major papal interpretations of the Rule as well as the current practice of the community, CLEMENT V gathered representatives of both tendencies in Avignon in October 1309 to attempt a resolution of these conflicting visions. The debates continued up to the opening of the 1311 Council of Vienne which, at its conclusion, issued the bull *Exivi de paradiso*, specifically addressing the issue of Franciscan poverty. While acknowledging the rectitude of the Spirituals' criticisms of the Community and agreeing that *usus pauper* (that is, use impelled only by necessity) was central to the friar's vow of poverty, Clement nonetheless left the interpretation of what constituted legitimate use to local guardians—a decision that would ultimately undermine the call to genuine reform.

Indeed, it led to rebellion within the order by rigorist friars in southern France and central Italy. The election of JOHN XXII as pontiff in 1316 signaled a toughening of the papal attitude with respect to these friars, and to the Franciscan order as a whole. John radicalized events in two ways. First, he shifted the issue from poverty to obedience: obedience of the friars to their superiors and ultimately to the pope himself. In this way, he began to force the fractious Spirituals to heel, symbolized in the burning at the stake of four friars in Marseilles on 7 May 1318. Second, in a series of devastating bulls between 1322 and 1323, he challenged the Franciscan equivalence of the evangelical perfection of Christ and the apostles with their own claim of absolute poverty (understood as total legal dispossession). His bull of 8 December 1322, *Ad conditorem*, denounced the distinctions made by Nicholas III and his predecessors in *Exiit* as so much legal nonsense and rejected any notion of the papal ownership of the friars' goods. Then on 12 November 1323, in *Cum inter nonnullos*, he denied that Christ and his apostles were ever poor in this legalistic Franciscan sense. Thus, with a few strokes of the pen, John had vitiated what had become the very core of Franciscan self-understanding. Such actions provoked a schism within the order as the minister general, Michael of Cesena, attempted to contest the papal rulings. Called by John to Avignon in 1328, he eventually fled with three other friars to the court of Louis of Bavaria, first in Italy then to Munich. With the election in 1328 at the Chapter of Paris of a close associate of the pope, Gerald Odonis, as minister general, the order, called to obedience, entered a new phase in its history.

The Friars in the Ministry of the Church. Although originating as a lay penitential movement with a spirituality particularly responsive to the challenges posed by the new urban environment of the High Middle Ages, the Friars Minor soon attracted men who had been trained in the revived cathedral schools or the new universities: in short, clerics. The papacy, aware of the inadequacies of its clergy and eager to regain a foothold in the cities of northern and central Italy, saw in the Minors—as well as the Friars Preachers of Dominic Guzman—an apt instrument for effecting an authentic reform of Christian life here, throughout Europe, and in lands where the Gospel had not yet been preached.

Whereas the Dominicans, composed primarily of canons regular, had received the full complement of privileges from the Holy See to preach, confess, and bury the dead by 1227, the insertion of the Franciscans into the clerical apostolate developed more slowly. On 12 June 1235, Gregory IX issued *Cum qui recipit* granting the Minors full authorization to preach without episcopal interference. Permission to confess the faithful followed on 6 April 1237 with *Quoniam abundavit iniquitas*. With the granting of the right to bury the dead accorded on 25 February 1250 in *Cum a nobis*, the Franciscans had gained ministerial parity with the Dominicans. The papacy had come to view the two mendicant orders as virtual twins (*foeti*) in the work of the renewal of the Church. Indeed, much to the consternation of the eremitical wing of the community, Gregory's bull of 19 June 1241, *Gloriantibus vobis*, urged the friars to be careful to accept into their ranks especially those who could contribute to the *salus animarum*, i.e., priests. The papacy's vision of the order had thus become decidedly clerical.

This clerical orientation had already received a major boost forward at the Chapter of Rome in 1239. Here Gregory IX, pressed particularly hard by the friar-clerics (but for reasons far more complex), deposed the lay minister general Elias of Cortona, replacing him with Albert of Pisa, the first friar-priest to head the order. Dead six months later, he was replaced by Haymo of Faversham who, more than any other general thus far, placed the Franciscan order at the disposition of the papacy. During his generalate, the friars began to be named more regularly as bishops, especially but not exclusively in mission territories; served as papal penitentiaries and in other positions at the Curia; and were pressed into service in the campaign of INNOCENT IV against Emperor Frederick II.

But full insertion into the clerical ministry of the Church required learning. Indeed, by the late 1220s, the Minors were already present in Paris and Oxford, having set up their own *studia* (like the Dominicans) to teach their own. Both orders began attracting some of the brightest minds of the age—some of whom were already masters at the University. This auspicious development, however, created an acrimonious relationship with the consortium of masters at the University of Paris whose long struggle for autonomy was being threatened by the growing number of religious holding chairs of theology. Once the candidacy of the Dominican Aquinas and the Franciscan Bonaventure as masters assured the loss of their majority in the consortium, they reacted. As tensions mounted, on 4 February 1254 they issued a manifesto, addressed to the churchmen of France, attempting to rally their support against the friars who were depicted—at the university as well as in the dioceses of Christendom—as intruding themselves unwanted but by papal fiat into the traditional structures of society, perverting the divine order of things.

But once again, the mendicant orders found the papacy to be its most steadfast ally. Innocent IV consistently supported the friars until November 1254. With the revelation that a Friar Minor had been the author of a suspect treatise strongly critical of the papacy—the *Introduction to the Eternal Gospel* by Gerard of Borgo San Donnino—Innocent issued the bull *Etsi animarum*, sharply curtailing their apostolic freedoms vis-à-vis the bishops. But Innocent died one week later, and in the bull *Nec insolitum* his successor Alexander IV, former cardinal protector of the Minors, immediately overturned the ruling and even extended the mendicants' pastoral privileges. With the status of Aquinas and Bonaventure approved, the position of the mendicants in Paris—with the exception of a second round of controversy between 1268 and 1272—was secure thanks to the cogency of their self-defense and unstinting papal support against their detractors. Indeed, it was the personal rapport of Bonaventure and the Dominican Peter of Tarantaise with GREGORY X (who had personally chosen them to serve as his cardinals) that enabled the pontiff to resist efforts of the episcopacy at the Second Council of Lyons in 1274 to suppress the two mendicant orders whose "manifest usefulness to the Church" was deemed essential for mounting the pope's new crusade and furthering the ecclesial mission.

Meanwhile, the work of the friars in the pastoral ministry continued unabated, in spite of persistent episcopal objections. On 13 December 1281, MARTIN IV issued the most sweeping bull to date on these matters—*Ad fructus uberes*—which granted the mendicant orders virtually unfettered permission to preach and hear confessions anywhere as well as to bury the dead (with the legacies associated with them). It is not surprising that these concessions remained protected under the pontificate of the first Franciscan pope, Jerome of Ascoli, who became NICHOLAS IV (1288–92). But the *carte blanche* pastoral exemptions would be curtailed with the judicious bull of

BONIFACE VIII, *Super cathedram*, of 18 February 1300. Dissatisfied with these restrictions, the friars had his successor, the Dominican pope BENEDICT XI annul them with his own bull *Inter cunctas* of 17 February 1304. CLEMENT V, however, would restore the more equitable provisions of Boniface—and these became the *modus operandi* between the friars and the secular clergy thereafter.

The Papacy and the Observant Reform. The debacle of the conflict between JOHN XXII and the Franciscan order never resolved the question of the faithful observance of the Rule raised by the Spirituals. Quite the contrary, during the generalate of Gerald Odonis, the order began to take on a more monastic orientation thanks to the imposition of new constitutions by the Cistercian pope, BENEDICT XII, in 1336. Nevertheless, the ideal of a poor life, lived out in simple hermitages far from the bustling urban convents of the friars engaged in active ministry, continued to live on. The Observant Reform movement began in the general area where the Spirituals of Angelo Clareno still continued to exert a certain influence: the Marches of Ancona. Yet the call for a more literal observance of the Rule in central Italy remained primarily a local issue—a struggle to be worked out between ardent friars and their provincial superiors. It was in those areas of Europe where the resistance of Franciscan authorities to the call for a more eremitical existence was strongest (with its concomitant component, simplicity of life) that the papacy would enter once again to mediate the controversy.

The papacy, however, was in the throes of the Great Schism at the turn of the 15th century, divided between Roman and Avignon claimants. BONIFACE IX, the pontiff of the Roman line, in 1392 authorized the first group of Spanish friars, led by a certain Gonzalo, to live a reformed life apart from the community in the Santiago province. He likewise gave authorization in 1397 for Peter of Villacreces to withdraw with a companion in the province of Castile to the cave of San Pedro de Arlanza—the beginning of the Recollectio Villacreciana. However, it was a pope of the Avignon line, Benedict XIII, who, between 1409 and 1415, confirmed and supported the creation of numerous other eremitical settings in both provinces.

Indeed, this same pontiff, a Frenchman, would emerge as the champion of the French Observants in the early 15th century. Here the reformers were refusing to comply with their superiors' orders to use money, a practice becoming more common among the friars in this area. In order to protect the reformers from their leaders, Benedict ordered the creation of a parallel system of authority within the three French provinces whereby the Observants would be placed under their own vicars provincial, subject only to a French Vicar General and the Minister General of the order. Benedict's creation would become the normative manner of resolving these tensions throughout the order.

But with the repudiation of Benedict XIII in 1407 by the French bishops preparing for the Council of Pisa of 1409, the French Observants lost their primary champion. The council fathers proceeded to depose both popes (who refused to resign) and to elect another—a Franciscan, Peter Philargus of Candia, who took the name of ALEXANDER V. This friar from Crete, however, was unsympathetic to the reformers in the order. His first bull, *Ordinem fratrum minorum*, suppressed the parallel structure of reformed friaries that Benedict had previously erected. With three rival popes, a new council was called at Constance in 1414. Here, the reformers placed before the council fathers a document, the *Quaerimonae*, which laid out their case for a parallel structure of reformed friars under their own authorities. The council responded positively on 23 September 1415 with the bull *Supplicationibus personarum*, authorizing this structure under their own Vicar General. Only the Coletans remained under their original superiors.

In the wake of events at Constance, the leaders of the Franciscan order were determined to prevent a further splintering of the fraternity in reform-minded Italy. Thus all attempts to inspire reform by a second generation of Italian Observants were blocked at the level of the General Chapters. However, the momentum for renewal was with the Observants. To accommodate their way of life, in 1421 MARTIN V authorized the use of reformed provincial vicars in Italy. In an attempt to maintain unity within the order, John Capistran designed a plan for unity that would be presented at the Chapter of Assisi in 1430 by Martin V in the guise of a new set of constitutions for the order. The main feature of these Martinian Constitutions was that all friars were to agree to live according to a minimum standard of poverty based on the papal declarations on the Rule in exchange for the Observants giving up their separate system of vicars: hence, moderate poverty (including total lack of ownership and use of money) in exchange for unity. The Chapter ended with all the friars taking solemn oaths to abide by these constitutions. However, certain friars, including the new minister general, Anthony of Massa, inveighed upon Martin V to grant them an exemption from these obligations. Indeed, on 23 August 1430, upon the request of these same friars, Martin V issued the bull *Ad statum* that effectively legitimated the right of such friars to possess property and have regular sources of income. This ratification of a Conventual party distinct from the Observants doomed the plan of unity to failure. On 11 January 1446, Martin's successor, EUGENE IV, frustrated by the efforts of the Conventuals to prevent further reform in the Order, issued the bull *Ut sacra*, announcing the virtual separation of the Franciscan order into two branches—Conventuals and Observants (with cismontane and ultramontane Vicars General)—though both still juridically subject to the minister general of the whole order.

The situation in the order remained essentially the same for the next fifty years. The papacy tried several times after 1500 to effect reform and reunification in the order. In 1501 the minister general, Giles Delfini, issued a new set of compromise statutes promulgated by Alexander VI, called the *Statuta alexandrina*; they were ignored. In 1503, Julius II convoked a *capitulum generalissimum*, gathering representatives of all sectors of the order to accept his efforts, the *Statuta juliana*; they also came to naught.

Finally, in the spring of 1517, LEO X moved to definitively resolve the Franciscan problem at another *capitulum generalissimum* in Rome. On 29 May, after a day of fruitless bickering and mutual recrimination, followed by the exit of the Observant delegates who refused to consider unity with the Conventuals unless they pledged to undertake genuine reform, Leo decided to confide the election of the next general, for the first time, to the Observants and the various smaller *reformati* parties in the order that had proliferated in Spain and Italy during the previous century. Calling the friars back together on the 30th, he had it announced that henceforth only this united reform element would be considered the Order of Friars Minor and only its members legitimate candidates for authority within the order. The specifics of the pope's decision were contained in his bull *Ite vos in vineam*, the so-called "Bull of Union" (sealed the previous day on 29 May), in which reform groups throughout the order were ordered to give up their separate authority arrangements and to unite under the one banner of the Order of Friars Minor. The Conventuals, however, were in a quandary. Unwilling to subscribe to the observance of poverty as defined in the papal declarations on the Rule (requiring their surrender of ownership and regular sources of income), they withdrew to the Church of the Twelve Apostles and proceeded to elect their own general. Only on 10 June did Leo, in his bull *Omnipotens Deus*, recognize this election and thereby establish the Conventual Franciscans as a separate religious order within the Franciscan family, with their own minister general and officials and with the right to possess property intact.

Leo's actions had gone a considerable way to resolving the longstanding conflict over observance and obedience within the Franciscan order. However, by 1517 the Observant party in Italy (and elsewhere) had become the majority party of Franciscans, living near or in the cities, fully involved in the ministry of the Church, and engaged in the studies that such work required. This evolution had negative repercussions upon the eremitical tenor of their friaries and the level of poverty that could be observed in such large houses. It was, therefore, not surprising that smaller reform groups continued to attempt to survive

apart from the Observant family; nor that new groups would emerge as a reaction against the moderate form of life ultimately adopted by them.

One such group of the latter was the Capuchins. Originating in 1525 as a reaction to the tepid observance of the Friars Minor in the Marches of Ancona, this small group of friars survived its earliest years only through the intervention and protection offered by CLEMENT VII and his niece, Caterina Cibo, who held its founders Ludovico and Raffaele da Fossombrone in great esteem. Indeed, on 3 July 1528 she was able to persuade her uncle to issue the first approval of this new group, *Religionis zelus*—a bull that protected the fledgling group from suppression by their Observant superiors. PAUL III renewed this bull in 1536 but placed them under the jurisdiction of the Conventuals rather than the antagonistic Observants. It was also Paul III who in the 1540s navigated them through the difficult circumstances created by the apostasy to Calvinism of their vicar, Bernardino d'Ochino. In exchange for their survival, he prohibited them from expanding beyond the Alps, lest their proximity to Protestantism result in renewed problems. Thanks to an excellent generation of leadership and continued papal support, the Capuchins gained legitimacy in 1563 at the Council of Trent (canon 3 of the 25th session) as being representatives, along with the Observants, of that tradition which continued to uphold the total poverty of St. Francis.

A new phase in Capuchin development opened in 1574 when Gregory XIII lifted the ban against ultramontane expansion imposed by Paul III. As a result, the Capuchins would contribute greatly to the efforts of the Counter-Reformation to educate the faithful (particularly in rural areas) in Catholic doctrine and practice. It was through PAUL V, in his bull of 23 July 1619 *Alias felicis recordationis*, that the Capuchin Franciscans were finally recognized as a self-standing independent branch of the First Order Franciscan family.

Although *Ite vos* had ordered the smaller reformed groups (whether sprung from the Observant or Conventual tree) to unite in 1517 under the one banner of the Order of Friars Minor, several nevertheless continued to perdure. One such group was the Spanish Discalced friars. Originating in the hills of the Sierra Morena in the last decades of the 15th century, these single-minded friars had already been able to survive the initial opposition of their superiors, largely through the support of INNOCENT VIII and PIUS III. Outlasting all calls to surrender their eremitical identity to join the Spanish Observants after 1517, GREGORY XIII finally recognized the sincerity of their tenacity, exempting this movement of strictest observance in 1578 from the obligation to unite. Given their own Vicar General by GREGORY XV in 1621, their continued existence into the 20th century was assured.

Two other groups—both with a similarly eremitical orientation, each representing a further reform of the Observant family—would likewise endure into the modern era. The first group, the Reformati, arose in Italy out of a dissatisfaction with the loss of an environment of prayerfulness in their increasingly active convents. Their repeated calls for the creation of houses of recollection (*retiros*) in the provinces was finally addressed, thanks to the 1532 bull of CLEMENT VII, *In suprema militantis ecclesiae*, which not only mandated their creation but authorized a special lifestyle consistent with their eremitical desires and ideals of stricter poverty. In 1579, similar to what he had already ordered for the Discalced, Gregory XIII exempted the Reformati from their Observant provincial superiors. This autonomy, definitely confirmed by CLEMENT VIII in 1596, allowed the reform to grow and become both the seed of the wholesale reform of Observant provinces in central Europe and the creation of totally new "reformed" provinces in Italy. A second group of like-minded friars, the Recollects, emerged in France with origins far more obscure. The house of recollection begun at Nièvre in 1586 represents the heart of the movement. Although the reform of this Observant house was initiated by the Duke of Nièvre, Louis Gonzaga, it might not have survived without the support of Sixtus V, the first Conventual pope who, as Felice Peretti da Montalto, had been a voice for reform within his own branch of the order. In 1599 Clement VIII granted the Recollects an autonomy similar to what he had accorded the Reformati just a few years earlier. Once again, it was the ability to control their lifestyle that fostered the growth and extension of the Recollect reform well beyond its original borders.

The Leonine Union of 1897. By 1650, the Order of Friars Minor comprised four different families, each with different statutes defining the specifics of their life: the Observants, the Reformati, the Recollects, and the Discalced. The centuries that followed—which witnessed the splintering of the Church in Europe into national churches, the challenges of the Enlightenment, and the advent of secular humanism—were difficult ones for the Church in general and religious life in particular. During these troubled times, the pontificate of the Franciscan Conventual, CLEMENT XIV, whose primary notoriety comes from his suppression of the Jesuits in his brief *Dominus ac Redemptor* (1773), was emblematic of the strains with the Church and on the papacy itself. These same tensions had a negative effect within the Franciscan Order. Between 1768 and 1862, a span of ninety-four years, only three General Chapters were held by the Minors. But toward the end of the 19th century, calls for reform began to be heard. The pontificate of LEO XIII, a member of the Franciscan Third Order himself, marked a watershed in these attempts to revitalize the Friars Minor. Due to the peculiar composition of the Observant family

and the resulting diversity of observance, neither the Capuchins nor the Conventuals would receive the same intense attention by the papacy in this period.

Without regularly scheduled chapters and the remarkable minister general Bernardino da Portogruaro ailing, he and Leo XIII decided to convoke a General Chapter in Rome in October 1889 with the express purpose of electing a new general. The pope, however, also had another reason in mind: to call for the unification of the four families based on an entirely new set of constitutions. The General Definitorium (ruling council) of the Order demurred, however, with resistance coming especially from Reformati members fearful of losing their identity. It was therefore decided to remain silent on the question of union at chapter and to set up, instead, a special commission, representative of the four families, to develop a proposal for new constitutions. Luigi da Parma was elected general.

The Chapter of 1895 in Assisi was to be a chapter of reunification. Leo delegated the Dominican, Giles Mauri, to serve as his representative and to conduct the difficult negotiations that would be required to achieve reunion. His approach was to surmount the opposition to the plan by presenting unification as the desire of the Pope himself. Faced with open opposition on the chapter floor (mainly from the Reformati and Discalced), Giles met privately with each of the three smaller groups to gauge support for the plan. The primary issue remained the proposed constitutions, in which the particular customs and emphases of each family would either be honored, tempered, or excised altogether. Thus, when the public sessions turned acrimonious, it was decided to again postpone the plan and to revisit the constitutions one more time. In December 1895, the revised constitutions were sent to every province for discussion and comment. Luigi da Parma wrote an accompanying letter, presenting reunification as the fervent desire of Leo XIII and explaining that the constitutions would allow individual provinces to adopt measures of greater austerity through the vehicle of particular statutes. The responses from the provinces were unenthusiastic.

To achieve reunification, Leo XIII now took the initiative. In spite of their lukewarm reception by the Reformati and Recollects, he submitted the constitutions to the Congregation for Bishops and Regulars, which approved the document (with certain changes). Then, to give the reunification plan legal weight, he issued an apostolic constitution proclaiming the union on the basis of this new set of constitutions. Finally, on 4 October 1897, he officially proclaimed the reunion of the Order of Friars Minor in the bull *Felicitate quadam*. Due to complex national issues, only the Spanish friars remained outside the unifying efforts of this great pontiff, but they abandoned their insistence on having a separate Vicar General and joined the reunified Observant family in 1932.

The primary task of the new Minister General, Aloys Lauer (from the Thuringian province of Recollects), and his successor, Dionysius Schuler, was to craft a uniform observance among the newly amalgamated groups and to work toward a thorough reorganization of the provinces. A reduction in the number of provinces was finally agreed to in 1908 and new constitutions for this branch of the family were drafted and approved by PIUS X in 1913.

The papacy, however, recognized the anomaly of having officially named only one branch of the First Order (the reunified Observants) as *the* Order of Friars Minor. What of the Conventuals and the Capuchins who were also First Order Franciscans? Pius X addressed this situation in his 1909 encyclical *Septimo jam pleno*, asserting that the title "Order of Friars Minor" would indeed remain the official designation only of the reunified Observant family. Nevertheless, he declared that all three families were to be considered true Franciscans, all three Ministers General legitimate sons of St. Francis and that the title "Minister General of the whole Order," though reserved for the leader of the Observant family, would henceforth carry only an honorary, not a juridical, significance. In this manner, he brought greater cohesion to the three branches of the First Order, thus setting the stage for the cooperative efforts of all three families in the last decades of the twentieth century.

Michael F. Cusato

Bibliography

Carmody, M. *The Leonine Union of the Order of Friars Minor 1897*, Franciscan Institute Publications. History Series, 8. St. Bonaventure, N.Y., 1994.

Lawrence, C. H. *The Friars*, London, 1994.

Moorman, J. *A History of the Franciscan Order from its Origins to the Year 1517*. Oxford, 1968.

Nimmo, D. *Reform and Division in the Franciscan Order from Saint Francis to the Foundation of the Capuchins*, Bibliotheca Seraphico-Capuccina, 33. Rome, 1987.

FRANKS. Toward the end of the 5th century, the Frankish kings became the first barbarian sovereigns to be baptized in the Catholic rite. Because of this, their relations with the popes were somewhat privileged, though the real alliance between popes and Franks dates only from the middle of the 8th century.

The Franks and the Papacy Before Gregory the Great. When Clovis (ca. 461–511), the king of the Franks, was baptized as a Catholic in 446 under the influence of Queen Clothilde and Remi, the archbishop of Reims, he gave up worship of the pagan gods and became a faithful believer in the Catholic Church. In emulation of the Byzantine emperors, he had a church built in Paris dedicated to the apostles Peter and Paul, but it appears he considered himself to be the head of the Church in Gaul, and he seems to have had no relationship with the popes. According to the *Liber Pontificalis*, however, his son Clodomir sent a golden crown to Pope HORMISDAS (514–23).

When the Franks occupied Provence (538), Caesar of Arles, who was considered the pope's vicar, was the intermediary between the papacy and the Frankish kings. The "Three Chapters" affair and the 5th council of Constantinople had repercussions in Gaul. The bishops who gathered in Orleans with Childebert I in 549 joined the pope in condemning the heretics. VIGILIUS (537–55) brought King Childebert up to date on the situation in the Roman Church. His successor, PELAGIUS I (556–61), sent four letters to the king, to whom Provence belonged, and he asked his representative, Sapaude, bishop of Arles, to see to the orthodoxy of the faith in Gaul. Under JOHN III (561–74), Bishops Salonius of Embrun and Sagittarius of Gap, who were deposed by the SYNOD of Lyon, appealed to Rome. King Gontran agreed with their reasoning and the pope asked that they be reinstated. This was the only known appeal sent to Rome during this period.

The LOMBARD invasion of Northern and Central Italy put the papacy in a difficult situation. PELAGIUS II (579–90) wrote to Aunaire, bishop of Auxerre, on 5 October 580, asking him to intervene with the king of the Franks to provide assistance against the Lombards. He wrote: "We believe that it is not without reason and not without a special design of Providence that your kings profess the same orthodox faith as the Roman Empire. It wanted to give to the city of Rome, the cradle of this faith, and to all of Italy, neighbors who might be protectors," echoing the phrase that had announced the alliance between Pepin III and the pope one-and-a-half centuries earlier.

Gregory the Great and the Merovingian Kings. During his papacy (590–604), GREGORY I sent some thirty letters to the bishops of Gaul, and about twenty letters to Frankish kings. In his first letters to the kings, which date from 595, he asked Childbert II to reestablish the vicarate for the metropolitan of Arles, and he congratulated Brunhild on the fine education she was giving her son. Gregory was already thinking about a MISSION of Roman monks to England, and he needed the kings to help the missionaries in their travels. A number of letters dating from 596 referred to this mission. Even though he declared to the Byzantines that "barbarian kings are reigning over slaves," Gregory recognized the importance of royal dignity. "Being a king is not a marvel," he wrote to Childbert II, "but being a Catholic when others do not have the merit to be one, that is what is greatest. The splendor of your faith radiates out from the center of the faithless darkness of other peoples" (letter VI, 6). Gregory went so far as to write that princes are kings "by the grace of God" (letter XIII, 9), and that if they do what God wills, their kingdoms will prosper.

Besides the conversion of the Anglo-Saxons, which Gregory spoke to the kings about, questions of concern at this time related to the vicarate of Arles (the Roman Church had a patrimony in Provence); to sending the *pallium* to Syagrius of Autun, who was a simple bishop but was a friend of Brunhild; and to the relationship between kings and emperors. Gregory wanted Brunhild and her sons to get rid of the pagan practices in their kingdom, and he hoped to avoid the elections of bishops being corrupted by simony. He also wanted Jews to have no Christian slaves.

The pope also intervened in administrative questions in his letters to the bishops of Autun and Lyon, and he agreed to take into his protection certain monasteries. Gregory the Great also wished to hold a national council to look into all the points of reform. He wrote to Brunhild, queen of Austrasia, about this, and to Clotaire, king of Neustria. Unfortunately, Gregory would not live to see the council, which was convened by Clotaire II in 614.

Gregory's politics vis-à-vis the Merovingian kings cannot be separated from his politics relative to other barbarian nations. Roman that he was, he realized that he needed to look west, and this was all the more important since he knew that the East was becoming increasingly distant—for political and cultural, as well as religious, reasons.

The Papacy and the Franks up to the 8th Century. Relations between the popes and 7th century Gaul were less frequent, if we are to judge by the number of letters exchanged—at least if we judge by the number of authentic letters, for there were a plethora of forgeries. BONIFACE IV (608–615) wrote to King Thierry about the *pallium* sent to Florian, bishop of Arles. MARTIN I (649–653) replied to Saint Amand of Elnone, who was requesting manuscripts from the Lateran library. He congratulated him on his missionary work, and aroused his interest in the theological questions of the moment. Martin I had actually convoked a council in 649 to defend Catholic orthodoxy against Byzantine deviants. He had the council's acts brought to the West, hoping that King Sigebert III of Austrasia would send bishops from Gaul to Constantinople to accompany the Italian bishops. The council's acts, it appears, were also known in Neustria, as is evidenced by the *Life of Saint Eloi*. Although PILGRIMAGES to Rome by subjects of the Merovingian kings increased, relations between the popes and the Church in Gaul, which was fairly disorganized at the end of the 7th century, remained limited. It would not be until the time of SERGIUS I (687–701) and GREGORY II (715–31) that popes would be able to again interest the Franks in their religious politics. In 692, Sergius I received Willibrord, an Anglo-Saxon who, with the support of the mayor of Pepin II's palace, began to evangelize Frisia.

Willibrord obtained relics for the churches he founded. In 695, Pepin sent Willibrord back to Rome. The pope consecrated him bishop of the Frisians, and placed the *pallium* upon him. He chose Utrecht as his cathedral.

Gregory II, in conflict with Leo the Isaurian, emperor of Constantinople, about the worship of images, counted on the West for assistance. In a letter to the emperor, he contrasted the barbarianism of an East that called itself civilized with the Christian civilization that was being organized in the West. In 718, he received the Anglo-Saxon Wynfrith, who at the time was pursuing a mission in Frisia, and gave him the name Boniface, confirming him in his mission. In 722, Gregory II consecrated Boniface bishop for the regions of Thuringia and Hesse. He asked Charles Martel, the palace mayor, to assist him. GREGORY III (731–41) sent the *pallium* to Boniface, and entrusted him with the reorganization of the Bavarian Church. In 739, the pope, worried about the advance of the Lombards and the threats hanging over Rome, made an appeal to Charles Martel, whose prestige was high after his victory over the Arabs. In three letters preserved in the Carolingian archives, he petitioned the "viceroy" (*subregulus*) to intervene in his favor; he sent him the "KEYS" and chains of Saint Peter—a reliquary containing some filings from the chains incorporated into a key. He perhaps meant it to symbolize for Charles that Saint Peter was the doorkeeper to heaven, the one who opens paradise to those who assist him. These letters and presents were without effect, however, since Charles needed Lombard assistance to fight the Muslims in Provence, and he merely sent an embassy to Rome with kind words and gifts for the Church of Saint Peter in the Vatican. Though Gregory III's appeal was not acted on, it did prepare the way for the future.

The Alliance Between the Papacy and the Franks. The alliance between the Franks and the papacy was initially the work of Gregory III's successors and of the palace mayors Pepin and Carloman (the sons of Charles Martel). The Church in Gaul needed reform, and Pepin (mayor of the palace of Neustria) and Carloman (mayor of the palace of Austrasia), assisted by Boniface, who represented the pope, convened councils. Boniface kept Pope ZACHARIAS abreast of events, and also sought advice from Rome, writing: "Thus, if I am to undertake and to direct this affair at the request of the duke [Carloman], and at your command, I wish to have in hand a precept and a decision from the Apostolic See with the ecclesiastical canons." At Boniface's request, the pope sent the *pallium* to the metropolitans—who were beginning to be called "archbishops"—of Rouen, Sens, and Reims. Carloman, attracted to the religious life, abdicated in 747, left for Rome, and retired at Mount Soracte, and Pepin, now the only palace mayor, henceforth reigned over the kingdom in the name of the Merovingian king, Childeric, who had neither power nor prestige. Therefore, in 751, Pepin decided to replace him and sent Fulrad, abbot of Saint-Denis, to Rome, along with Burchard of Würzburg, one of Boniface's disciples, to ask the advice of Pope Zacharias. The pope replied that it was "better to call him who has power king than him who does not have power," and ordered "by his apostolic authority" that Pepin become king. Pepin then had himself consecrated, undoubtedly by Boniface, in order to reinforce his royal power.

Meanwhile, the Lombards were becoming increasingly threatening, especially after taking RAVENNA in 751, and were preparing to take Rome to complete the unification of Italy. The pope, who could not count on the Byzantines because of the continuing conflict over images, turned to King Pepin. STEPHEN II, Zacharias's successor, decided to go to Gaul to discuss possible interventions with the king. This was the first time that a pope had gone to the West, the land of the "barbarians." On 6 January 754, after a difficult crossing of the Alps, Stephen met Pepin. He moved into Saint-Denis to spend the winter of 754–5, and again blessed Pepin and his children, calling them "Roman patricians," meaning that they were protectors of the city and of the patrimonies of the Roman Church. During the course of these meetings, the pope convinced Pepin to intervene in Italy, and, in 755, with Pepin's help, the Lombard king Astolf was defeated and promised to return some lands taken from the Byzantines to the pope. When Astolf failed to fulfill this promise, Pepin returned in the spring of 756. He decided to give "to Saint Peter" the cities located in the EXARCHATES OF RAVENNA, Emilia, and Pentapolis. This territory was joined to the duchy of Rome to form the PAPAL STATE, and the pope became the "sovereign pontiff," the master of a large territory in Italy. He would remain so until 1870. In order to win over the Franks, it is possible that it was at this time that the Lateran clerics fabricated the "DONATION OF CONSTANTINE." Pepin, the blessed king, remained on good terms with the papacy and introduced the Roman liturgy into Gaul. The head of the *Schola cantorum* went to instruct clerics in Rouen, at the request of Bishop Remi, Pepin's brother. Chrodegand, the bishop of Metz, organized a seasonal liturgy, in imitation of the one in Rome, and imposed the *cantilena romana* on clerics and canons.

The Papacy and Charlemagne. Pepin's son Charles (Charlemagne) shared power with his brother at first, but after the latter's death in 771 he ruled alone. His mother, Bertrade, who wished for a rapprochement between the Franks and the Lombards, had him betrothed to Desiree, King Didier's daughter. This displeased the papacy, for the pope feared that the Lombards might seek revenge and retake the territories they abandoned in 756. Stephen III's successor, HADRIAN I, a man of strong personality,

informed Charles and asked him to intervene. The king broke his engagement to Desiree and intervened in Italy, triumphing over King Didier, after which he assumed the Lombard iron crown (774). He took advantage of his presence in Italy to go to Rome to celebrate Easter, and he renewed his father's donation, clarifying the boundaries between the Papal State from the Lombard kingdom.

Charles returned to Rome again in 781 with his sons. He had his four-year-old son, Pepin, blessed as the king of Italy, installed in Pavia with Frankish administrators. In principle, the Papal State was independent, but the Franks had no qualms about intervening. The pope complained, but he could not prevent action on the part of the invading protector king. Moreover, Charles intervened in the duchy of Benevento, which had been given to the pope in 774. He finally submitted to duke Arichis while sojourning in Rome in 787.

Despite these political problems, relations between Hadrian and Charles were good. The king was very fond of the pope, and the two men were of one mind on theological questions. In Byzantium, Empress Irene wanted to restore image veneration, thereby increasing relations with Rome. She called a council in Nicaea (787), which put an end to iconoclasm. The council's acts were sent to Rome, and to the Frankish court. Charlemagne, who misunderstood the decisions, reproached the Byzantines for worshiping images; that is, for being idolaters. He convened a counter-council in Frankfurt in 794, and sent Angilbert, abbot of Saint Riquier, on a mission to the pope. Hadrian, who had approved the Nicaea decisions, found himself in a difficult situation and reminded Charlemagne in a report of all the images his predecessors had had painted in Roman churches.

The council in Frankfurt also looked into the question of the adoptionist HERESY that was then rampant in Spain. The pope intervened with Elipand of Toledo to condemn the definition of Christ as the adopted son of the Father. He sent two representatives to the council of Frankfurt and accepted the decisions of the bishops and the king. Hadrian I died in 795. His successor, LEO III, carried on his politics and convened a council in Rome to condemn Felix, bishop of Urgel, one of the propagators of the adoptionist heresy. But Leo had neither the aristocratic origins nor the stature of his predecessor. Charlemagne was aware of this and made himself the pope's protector. He asked Angilbert, his ambassador to the Lateran, to remind the pope of his duties. While the king was defending the Church against heretics, infidels, and pagans, the pope, like Moses, was to raise his hands to God and pray for the success of the royal arms.

In 798, the city of Rome was troubled by various factions. On 25 April 799, Leo III was attacked and taken prisoner, although he managed to escape and take refuge in Saint Peter's before making his way to Paderborn, the king's residence. The subsequent interview between Charles and Leo III was set to music by an anonymous poet who emphasized the king's role. Charles had Leo taken back to Rome under strong guard, and went to the city himself in 800 to preside over an inquiry into the complaints made against the pope. Leo confounded his accusers, however, and freed himself with a purgative oath. Two days later, on Christmas day, he crowned Charlemagne emperor in Saint Peter's in the Vatican. Historians have wondered if the idea did not come from the pope, who was happy to again have primacy in Rome, or if the coronation ceremony was perhaps prepared several months in advance by Charlemagne. The latter hypothesis is the more likely one. When Charles visited Alcuin before his trip to Rome, he was already contemplating taking over the Empire. But for Romans, the pope was not destined to wear the imperial crown of the West, as the patriarch of Constantinople wore that of the East. For the Franks, the restored Empire was more Christian and Frank than it was Roman. When, in 813, a now quite aged Charles wished to make his son Louis emperor, he crowned him himself, in Aix-la-Chapelle, without asking for the pope's participation. This was the beginning of a number of difficulties between the papacy and the Empire. Leo III attempted to regain a certain autonomy when, in 809, Charlemagne decided to introduce the word *Filioque* into the Nicene creed. The cause of this innovation was the new emperor's desire to distinguish himself from his Eastern colleague, with whom he had been in conflict since the time of his coronaton in 800. The theologians sent to Rome after the council of Aix in 809 did not win the pope over to this wording. Leo III extricated himself from the matter by proposing that the Creed not be sung, and the papacy refused the *Filioque* until the beginning of the 9th century.

The Popes and Louis the Pious (814–40). Charles's son was much more submissive to the Church than his father. In 816 he welcomed Leo III's successor in Reims, and from him Louis received the imperial crown. STEPHEN IV died shortly thereafter, and his successor, PASCHAL I, asked Louis to confirm the donation of 774. This was called the *Ludovicianum*, "the privilege of Emperor Louis." But the Carolingian officials needed to intervene continually to arbitrate between the many factions in Rome. Lothair, Louis's eldest son, who was crowned emperor by his father and then by the pope on Easter in 823, decided to intervene and went to Rome. By the *Constitutum* of 824, the papal administration was placed under Carolingian control, and the elected pope was to take an oath of loyalty to the emperor.

Paschal's successor, Eugene II, took a different stance vis-à-vis Louis, even when the question of images was again raised. After the reign of Leo the Armenian, who had reestablished iconoclasm, the Eastern Roman Emperor Michael II had wanted a rapprochement with both the Carolingian emperor and the pope. The Frankish theologians, still reticent about the worship of images, had accepted the Byzantine propositions, but EUGENE I had demurred, wanting to hold the council of Nicaea of 787.

The council of Paris in 825 felt that the Roman Church was mistaken in exaggerating the religious value of images. Jeremia, archbishop of Sens, and Jonas, archbishop of Orleans, were sent to Rome with the acts of the council. The pope remained faithful to the tradition of the Roman Church, which since the time of Gregory the Great felt that images could be important in the transmission of faith. When Empress Theodora officially reestablished image worship in 843, the pope could not help feeling satisfaction. The year 843 was also that of the Treaty of Verdun, which put an end to the unity of the Empire. This new situation would be to the popes' advantage.

The Emancipation of the Popes. Starting in 833, Pope GREGORY IV (827–44) wanted to arbitrate the quarrel between Lothair and his father, Louis, over the plans for division that the emperor was making, which favored his other sons, particularly the young Charles, who was born of a second marriage. Lothair invited Gregory to go to France. The pope reminded Louis that "the government of souls that belongs to the pontiff is more important than the temporal government that belongs to the emperor." Gregory was doing nothing more here than repeating the words of GELASIUS I's letter to Anastasius. He accompanied the rebellious sons to see Louis, and then had an interview with him. Louis gave in, and his wife Judith was taken to Italy by the pope. After the death of Louis, his sons quarreled over the empire, and they agreed in Verdun to split it up. It appears that the pope did not intervene this time. Gregory's successor, Sergius II (844–7), agreed to name Drogon, bishop of Metz and bastard son of Charlemagne, vicar to the Holy See.

The pope had more serious problems to solve with the Saracens. LEO IV, the successor to Sergius, held out against them. He refused the *pallium* that Emperor Lothair was requesting for the bishop of Autun, and he intervened in a conflict between Hincmar of Reims and a vassal who was appealing to Rome, and then in favor of the clerics who had been ordained by Ebbon, Hincmar's predecessor. Louis II, eldest son of Lothair I (who had the imperial title and resided in Italy), began to fear the new politics of the papacy. The priest Anastasius schemed against the pope on his behalf, but Leo IV had Anastasius deposed. When Leo IV died, Roman aristocrats and clerics chose the priest Benedict to succeed him, but Anastasius, with the support of his father, Arsenius, and some imperial officials, attempted to replace BENEDICT III. He failed, however, and retired to Pavia. Benedict III's papacy (855–8) was short, but it continued the work of Leo IV, preparing the way for the "reign" of NICHOLAS I. Until the end of the 9th century, Nicholas, and then HADRIAN II and JOHN VIII, took advantage of internal divisions in the empire to carry on their own independent politics, which were occasionally hostile to the Franks. Unfortunately, the fragmentation, and then the disappearance, of the Carolingian Empire had negative repercussions even in Rome, and at the end of the 9th and during the first half of the 10th century the popes fell under the power of the Roman aristocracy. The papacy would need to await the restoration of the empire by Otto I in 963 to regain some of its prestige.

Pierre Riché

Bibliography

Engels, O. "Zum päpstlich-frankischen Bündnis in VIII. Jahrhundert," *Ecclesia et regnum . . . Festschrift F. J. Schmale*, Bochum, 1989, 21–38.

Fliche-Martin, IV–VI.

Fritze, W. H. *Papst und Frankenkönig: Studien zu den päpstlich-frankischen Rechstgeziehungen von 754 bis 824*, Sigmaringen, 1973.

Halphen, L. *Charlemagne et l'Empire carolingien*, Paris, 1947; 2nd ed. 1968.

Piétri, L. *La Ville de Tours du IVe siècle au VIe siècle: naissance d'une cité chrétienne*, Rome, 1983 (*Collection de l'École française de Rome*, 69).

Riché, P. *Les Carolingiens, une famille qui fit l'Europe*, Paris, 1983.

Werner, K. F. "Le rôle de l'aristocratie dans la christianisation du nord-est de la Gaule," *RHEF*, 62 (1976), 45–73 (reprinted as *La Christianisation des pays entre Loire et Rhin*, under the dir. of P. Riché, Paris, 1993).

FREEMASONRY. The history of the Holy See's relations with the instition of Freemasonry was, for over two centuries (from the 1730s to the 1960s), marked by confrontations that were sometimes brutal. The court of Rome, and then the Holy See, were often on the brink of war against the Freemasons with national episcopacies playing a secondary role. The list of anti-Masonic interventions is long: Father G. Caprile, an informed "Masonologist" and active correspondent for the authoritative *Civiltà cattolica*, the Roman Jesuit magazine, has pointed out some two hundred papal interventions, some quite solemn and others quite modest (as in the cases of the addresses by PIUS IX and LEO XIII against the "sect"). The battle against Freemasonry is inextricably tied to the more general, and vehement, struggle that the Roman Church waged against LIBERALISM.

A number of interventions are of particular importance. Some of these texts—the encyclicals of GREGORY XVI and Pius IX, in particular—were far from being concerned exclusively with the Masons, while others were devoted exclusively to them. All, however, accentuate the Roman Church's battle against Freemasonry:

Constitution *In Eminenti* (28 April 1738), Clement XII

Constitution *Providas Romanorum Pontificum* (18 May 1751), Benedict XIV

Constitution *Ecclesiam a Iesu Christo* (13 September 1821), Pius VII

Constitution *Quo Graviora Mala* (13 March 1825), Leo XII

Encyclical *Traditi Humilitati* (24 May 1829), Pius VIII

Encyclical *Mirari Vos* (15 August 1832), Gregory XVI

Encyclical *Qui Pluribus* (9 November 1846), Pius IX

Encyclical *Quanta Cura* (8 December 1864), Pius IX

Address *Multiplices Inter* (25 September 1865), Pius IX

Constitution *Apostolicae Sedis* (12 October 1869), Pius IX

Encyclical *Humanum Genus* (20 April 1884), Leo XIII

The study of the Roman MAGISTERIUM's anti-Masonism involves no particular difficulty other than that of the abundance of sources—yesteryear's passions abated in the 1960s, and modern historians are not greatly taxed in attempting to reach equanimity. Nevertheless, certain aspects of Catholic anti-Masonism are not well known. For example, the specific circumstances that precipitated the great 19th-century encyclicals againt the Freemasons are unknown, and there is no way to gauge the influence that "specialists" in the anti-Masonic battle might have had on the Roman magisterium. Likewise, very little is known at least as far as the 19th century is concerned, about how the main pontifical condemnations were received. The abundant anti-Masonic literature has yet to be systematically examined, with the exception of certain specific periods in time: the birth of anti-Masonic sentiment in France in the second half of the 18th century has been well studied, as has, in the following century, the anti-Mason phobia that Léo Taxil mocked and ridiculed. There is no doubt that a better understanding of anti-Mason sentiment would enrich our understanding of Catholic thought during this period.

Freemasonry in the Enlightenment. At the end of the 17th and the beginning of the 18th centuries, there was a slow transformation of practical Freemasonry (that of the cathedral builders, for example) into a speculative Freemasonry—trowels, squares, and compasses became merely symbols, and, in the lodges, artisans were replaced by the bourgeoisie and aristocrats. The founding of the Great Lodge in London (1717), which was quickly followed by the first lodges on the continent, marks the birth of "modern" Freemasonry (although some authors posit an earlier Jacobite Freemasonry, that of the partisans of the Catholic Stuart dynasty). By 1723, English Freemasonry was armed with James Anderson's famous constitutions, which remain the essential reference text for "regular" Freemasonry. Anderson, a Presbyterian pastor, composed them at the encouragement of Jean-Théophile Désaguliers, an Anglican priest who was the son of a French Huguenot pastor. One article of the constitutions that is as famous as it is controversial deals with the religious duties of the Freemason. "A Mason," Anderson wrote, "by virtue of his state, is obliged to obey moral law, and if he has a good understanding of the Art [of Freemasonry], he will never be a stupid atheist or an irreligious libertine. Just as Masons, in early times, were obliged to profess the religion of whatever country in which they lived, regardless the religion, it is today considered appropriate to subject them only to that Religion upon which all men are in agreement, and to leave to each his own opinions. This consists in being good, sincere men of honor and probity, in whatever denomination or specific belief they might distinguish themselves."

This text is deceptive. According to the interpretation it is most often given, Masonic tolerance concerns only the followers of the revealed religions and excludes all atheists, not just "stupid atheists." Whatever the case, it is clear that Freemasonry regardless where it erected its columns—in the British Isles, on the continent, or across the Atlantic—remained fundamentally deistic during the Enlightenment, despite the agnostic tendencies that were characteristic of the rationalism of the Age of Enlightenment.

The Constitution *In Eminenti* (1738). Anderson's constitutions were but fifteen years old when *In Eminenti* was made public, showing that the papacy was amazingly quick and so resolute in condemning Freemasonry. After denouncing the illegality and the secrecy of "societies, assemblies, meetings, gatherings, or conventicles called Freemason," the pope concluded by saying: "We absolutely command them [the faithful of Jesus Christ] to eschew completely these societies, assemblies, meetings, gatherings, or conventicles, at the risk of excommunication for all . . . offenders . . . , for which no one, even at the moment of death, will receive the benefit of absolution from anyone other than Ourselves or the Roman pontiff of the day.

"We further wish and command that all bishops and superior prelates, and other ordinaries in their regions, and all inquisitors of heresy, inform and proceed against transgressors, regardless their state, grade, condition, rank, dignity, or preeminence, reprimanding and punishing them with the sanctions deserved for someone highly suspect of heresy."

A Spanish historian and expert in Freemasonry, the Jesuit José A. Ferrer-Benimeli, has specialized in the history of the first papal condemnations. His main conclusions, supported by rich archival documentation, are shared by the majority of experts. Ferrer-Benimeli believes that Clement XII was acting out of essentially political concerns. He points out that the earliest pontifical condemnations were links in a long chain of prohibitions against Freemasonry formulated between 1735 and 1800 by a wide variety of European governments—both Protestant and Catholic, as well as the Great Sultan of Constantinople. Thus, CLEMENT XII was preceded on the path of rigor by the États Généraux in Holland (1735), by the Council of the Republic and of the Canton of Geneva (1736), and by the Very Christian King (1737). Even before the turn of the century, the pope's condemnation was followed by that of some twenty governments.

Ferrer-Benimeli cogently asserts that Clement XII's primary and essential motivations (and later, those of BENEDICT XIV) were identical to those of the civil governments, and, as such, of a political nature. Freemasonry was condemned because of the rigorous secrecy in which it enshrouded its activities, including its use of a solemn oath of secrecy, and because of the terrible sanctions that loomed over the brother who transgressed. European public law, which was for the most part derived from Roman law (to which Benedict XIV would refer explicitly), was ignorant of freedom of association, and any unauthorized association was perceived to be potentially subversive to the public order and the tranquillity of the state, particularly a secret association. In short, the court of Rome reacted like any other government, adding spiritual reasons—the only ones that could justify excommunication—to these political reasons.

The very text of *In Eminenti* makes it difficult to take sides between Ferrer-Benimeli and those, although they are few in number, who see spiritual reasons as being uppermost in Clement's condemnation. It is true that the religious grounds for excommunication are mentioned prior to the political motives. But on a number of occasions the sovereign pontiff takes a stand behind the opinion of civil authorities. Moreover, the theological poverty of the text is not really in question: the spiritual motives of excommunication are announced in a quite vague manner, and the accusation of latitudinarianism is only implicit. Clement XII even goes so far as to mention secret reasons, which are undoubtedly political, in order to condemn . . . Masonic secrecy. What is surprising about this dispute is that there is no specific allusion to Anderson's constitutions, nor is the "Protestant" origin of the institution of Freemasonry denounced.

On the whole, Ferrer-Benimeli's theses are sound. Far from limiting himself to a study of the text of the papal condemnation, he explains its origin through an exhaustive examination of the correspondence between the Roman court and the main courts of Europe, as well as that between Roman congregations and the Inquisition in Lisbon, Seville, Madrid, Florence, Venice, and Foligno. In this abundant documentation, it appears as though the primary causes of the condemnation were indeed political—for the general causes (the pope-king's concern for preserving the tranquillity of his states) as well as for the specific and "immediate" causes (the wish to arrest the rising popularity of a Florentine lodge whose members were non-Catholic, anti-Jacobite Englishmen).

Ferrer-Benimeli is likewise compelling when he underscores how unaware the Roman offices were about the realities of Masonic life, pointing out that the canonists of the CURIA used excommunication as a sanction for what was, to use their own words, a "suspicion of heresy." He believes that Freemasonry in the age of the Enlightenment did not "deserve" rigorous papal condemnation, and that the hybrid nature of papal power was at the base of an immense misunderstanding. This perhaps minimizes the spiritual reasons invoked by Clement XII, however, specifically that latitudinarianism was not a purely illusory danger, even if the Masonic institution remained impregnated with Christianity.

In 1739, Cardinal Firrao, Clement XII's secretary of state (and as such, responsible for carrying out the bull *In Eminenti* in the PAPAL STATES) published, at the request of the Congregation of the Sacred Office, a decree that showed how strictness had increased. Under this decree, becoming a Freemason, or even getting information about Freemasonry or helping its members, would be punishable by death (and with confiscation of the property of the condemned). Ferrer-Benimeli sees in such strictness the confirmation of his general thesis, for the cardinal referred to "the suspicion of heresy and sedition," implying that sedition was a more immediate danger than was heresy. Otherwise, why impose the death penalty upon the brothers, when the Inquisition itself used this greatest of punishments only in the case of heretics who were impenitent?

Benedict XIV's Actions and the Reception of Papal Condemnations. Provoked by a desire to break the popularity of Neapolitan Freemasonry, Benedict XIV's constitution *Providas* followed in the same line as *In Eminenti*, which it cited extensively. The reasons it invoked were the same: illegality, secrecy, immorality, suspicion of heresy. This new condemnation explicitly revealed Benedict XIV's political motivations, however, when he called for the assistance of secular powers, supporting his call with decisions by Catholic powers.

The effects of papal interventions were quite variable. They were quite real in the countries (Spain, Portugal, and part of Italy) where the Inquisition was still in a position to require strict application of the Roman condemnations. But some Catholic States were not even aware of them. In the kingdom of France, for example, the two encyclicals were neither presented to the Gallic parliament in Paris, nor were they noted by the parliament. Although it is true that examples of Freemason bishops were extraordinary, and that some prelates condemned Freemasonry, the clergy itself showed indifference, even rebelliousness, to the Roman injunctions, and they provided a number of initiates to the movement. Ferrer-Benimeli has counted some 2,000 ecclesiastics who attended lodges on the continent.

How did Freemasonry evolve in the second half of the 18th century? Even in Latin countries the institution's infiltration by Christianity was strong. In France, the Masonic statutes of 1755 and 1777 required that brothers be baptized and that masses be celebrated for deceased brothers. The feast of Saint John was also to be celebrated with appropriate solemnity. The Masonic rituals show less incipient secularization (e.g., the disappearance of the Masonic prayers) than borrowings from hermeticism (e.g., the candidate's entrance into the reflection room and the purification ceremonies to which the initiate was subjected). It is more difficult to make a statement about the brothers' inner feelings, even though the Anderson constitutions authorized a real diversity of confessions and ideologies. On the eve of the FRENCH REVOLUTION, lodges still had a majority of Catholics (although it is not known how many of these were devout). Rationalists and mystics were minorities. Masonic rationalism, which borrowed heavily, although perhaps not consciously, from Locke, Hume, and Kant, could be tainted with anti-Catholicism, although it was rarely anti-Christian. It was later given a pounding by occultism and the mysticism of the Theosophists and the Martinists. Nevertheless, rationalists and mystics were often in agreement in reducing God to an architectonic principle. Such evolution was one discreet sign, among others, of secularization within lodges.

Nothing, however, in the Masonic order's activities could justify the criticism it would soon receive. Abbot Augustin de Barruel, in his famous *Mémoires pour servir à l'histoire du jacobinisme* (1797), asserted that the Revolution was the result of a triple plot perpetrated by philosophers, the Freemasons, and the Jacobins. The inanity of this thesis no longer needs to be shown, for the brothers hatched no plot for the overthrow of either society or the Catholic religion, and the lodges were in no way laboratories of subversion. During the Revolution, the brothers' commitments took a number of different directions. In a book published posthumously in 1921, Augustin Cochin undoubtedly saw things correctly when he described the lodges—and, more generally, societies for thought—as vectors for democratic ideals in the 1760s, the 1770s, and the 1780s. But the "democratic sociability" to which the lodges were accused of playing host should not be overly emphasized; recruitment for lodges remained homogenous, for the most part, comprising mostly aristocrats and the bourgeoisie, with only the slightest of room remaining for brothers from the lower classes of society.

From the French Revolution to Vatican I. Although the Roman magisterium paid but modest attention to the deep split that gradually took place within the Freemason family, the main currents of evolution that Freemasonry underwent in the nineteenth century should be remembered from the outset.

Around the turn of the century, the Masonic family's unity was shattered. Since that time there have been two quite different ways to be a Freemason, exemplified by the English lodges ("regular" Freemasonry) and the French lodges ("liberal" Freemasonry).

Regular Freemasonry, exemplified by the Great Unified Lodge in England, was largely majoritarian, and it was particularly well-established in Anglo-Saxon countries. It was characterized by an unfailing fidelity to the original principles, called landmarks, of speculative Freemasonry, including the belief in the existence of a revealed God. This did not keep it from being antipapist. Composed largely of noteworthy individuals, often members of the "establishment," regular Freemasonry avoided any political or social action in the secular world. Its activities were essentially philanthropic. Far from seeing this as a limitation, English Freemasonry soon came to consider as irregular any religious persuasion that did not follow the same principles.

The Grand Orient of France played an essential role in the constitution of liberal Freemasonry. It progressively affirmed that the brothers should fear neither theoretical discussions of a political, social, or religious nature, nor involvement in civic affairs. Its evolution was slow because, after the difficult experience of the Revolution, French Freemasonry took the better part of three quarters of a century to commit itself to a path of action, a path often turned into militantism and activism. But Freemasonry was first and foremost "the missionary of liberalism" (under the July Monarchy, the Second Republic, and the Second Empire), and only secondly "the Church of the Republic."

Similarly, Masonic spirituality underwent considerable evolution. Lodges at the beginning of the 19th century were populated by a large number of professed Catholics, while by the end of the century Catholics had totally disappeared from the lodges attached to the Grand Orient. The famous convention of 1877 did away with the obligation to believe in the immortality of the soul and the existence of God.

This was certainly not a proclamation of atheism. But the famous vote favored the entrance into the lodge of Jews and Protestants, as well as deists, theists, agnostics, and atheists. All these newcomers were to some extent motivated by anti-Catholicism, and many of them failed to hide their hostility to all revealed religions.

The convention of 1877 had tremendous international repercussions: given that regular Freemasonry was so solidly implanted in Anglo-Saxon countries, it favored the emergence of liberal Freemasonry—a progressive lay movement that no longer had any qualms about involvement in political or social action. Always anticlerical, often anti-Catholic, and sometimes anti-Christian (at least toward the end of the century), it entered into a merciless battle against the Church of Rome, in which it saw the incarnation of blind dogmatism, criminal intolerance, and brazen sectarianism. This liberal Freemasonry, which entailed a minority of Freemasons worldwide, became the major form of Freemasonry in Latin countries such as Brazil, Mexico, Spain, and Portugal, and it was particularly strong in France, Belgium, and Italy.

Under the Third Republic, Freemasonry was, in the words of P. Chevallier, "the school of the Republic," even if Catholics did considerably exaggerate its influence, which was rarely omnipotent. Its political role was, and continues to be, widely appreciated. Its social role, which owed more to reflection than to militant action, was undoubtedly and largely positive. The lodges worked indefatigably for the laicization of French society.

Belgian Freemasonry underwent a similar evolution. At times it preceded French Freemasonry, an example of which is the foundation, as early as 1834, of the free university in Brussels, a center of "free-examinist" culture.

The case of Italian Freemasonry was quite different. Regardless of the fears of Catholics and the claims of the brothers, Freemasonry's influence was considerably less in Italy. It had a later, albeit more radical, entry into the political arena, though it was often no more than a parapolitical institution. Its greatly impoverished anticlericalism frequently limited it to an agressive and stale activism, which was mainly sectarian. For example, in July, 1881, the Grand Orient of Italy had a medal coined in commemoration of the demonstrators who, in the center of Rome, tried to throw the dead body of Pius IX into the Tiber as it was being transported to its permanent gravesite.

It is important to bear in mind how heavily Italian affairs weighed upon the Curia during both the 18th and 19th centuries. From the 1820s through the 1850s, the court of Rome had been directly concerned with the birth of a number of secret sectarian societies, which all seemed to have a predilection for papal Romagna. Consequently, when the Carbonari *vendite* made way for lodges of brotherhoods, the pope-king tended to blame the brotherhoods for all his woes. This tendency culminated, in 1870, with the definitive disappearance of his temporal power: Porta Pia was to Pius IX the result of a conspiracy and revolutionary action on the part of the lodges. In the 1880s and the 1890s, the papacy did not remain indifferent to the ambitions of Grand Master Lemmi, who occasionally behaved, if not as an antipope, at least as the head of a "counter-church." As if to challenge the universality of the Church of Rome, he went so far as to proclaim: "We are the catholics of liberty and reason."

Without exception, all the popes of the 19th century dedicated at least one encyclical to denouncing secret societies, particularly Freemasonry. Eight of the ten constitutions or encyclicals listed above are from the 19th century, with six of them being composed within a fifty year period. The fact that four pontiffs followed one another closely in the 1820s and 1830s only partially explains the intensification of the anti-Masonic struggle. As has been said, it fits into the wider framework of the battle against liberalism. Some texts, not necessarily the most interesting ones, are dedicated specifically to secret societies, which since the time of Pius VII had been branded as "sects." Others, beginning with *Mirari Vos* and *Quanta Cura*, are of greater value, since they extend condemnation to liberal heresy in the broader sense. The denunciations pronounced by Gregory XVI and Pius IX, for example, concern socialism and communism as much as they do liberalism itself; pantheism and naturalism as much as rationalism and latitudinarianism; and Bible societies as much as secret societies. Contemporaries often interpreted the crude battle waged by Catholicism and liberalism as the clash of two *Weltanschauungen*.

Nevertheless, none of the pontifical condemnations, at least up to Vatican I, were really innovative, compared to Clement XII's *In Eminenti* and Benedict XIV's *Providas*. As in the 18th century, both religious motives and political motives (secrecy, illegality, the danger of subversion) are alleged by the different popes in order to justify their condemnation. The 18th century had not only forged a veritable tradition in this regard (the references to *In Eminenti* are countless), but the pope remained the "pope-king," adding his functions as temporal sovereign to his duties as the head of Catholicism.

More original, and even essential, is a second constant in the papal interventions: the spiritual reasons appear to count as much as the political motives. Historians have shown, in the case of Pius IX, a passionate attachment to temporal power and a lively concern for obedience to spiritual motivations—without too much compromise with the temporal powers, even those that were Catholic.

A third point in common, and one that was already perceptible in the 18th century, is the difficulty the canonists and theologians in the Roman Curia had in defining specifically the shape of Freemasonry. The Carbonari and Freemasonry had long been seen as the two most dangerous avatars of the nefarious "secret societies," and it was the lot of Pius IX to concentrate his attacks on Freema-

sonry, for the Carbonari was on the decline by the time of his papacy.

A few differences can also be seen among these texts. Some arguments show up almost incidentally. For example, when Pius VII refers to Baal, he seems to be inveighing against the ritual debauchery in which the brothers indulged. The accusation was taken up again toward the end of the century by those who led the anti-Masonic battle. Leo XII, Pius IX, and Leo XIII explicitly accused the devil of inspiring the sect's actions. It should be pointed out, however, that historians never again touched on the bizarre accusations of the celebration of black masses in the presence of Satan or the profanation of the eucharist. At the turn of the century, Léo Taxil must not have had these scruples. Pius IX was the only one to entertain the rumor that Freemasonry was in fact led, behind the scenes, by "unknown superiors." Taxil must have remembered such charges when he invented the existence of a high Palladian Freemasonry.

There was also some diversity in sanctions, which for the most part were severe. Pius VII condemned not only the partisans of the Carbonari, but also everyone who showed any sympathy for it. In *Apostolicae Sedis*, which deeply reworked censorship legislation, Pius IX imposed excommunication *latae sententiae* upon the brothers; it was thus in effect the moment a crime was consummated, with no need to proceed to a canonical judgment. Leo XII and Gregory XVI pronounced no excommunication, but their meekness should not be exaggerated: the legate Cardinal Rivarili brutally reprimanded the Carbonari in Romagna in the name of Leo XII.

The effectiveness of these condemnations seems to have been relative, as their composers sometimes recognized. However, in those times of growing, and then triumphant, Ultramontanism, there was much more assurance of an encyclical being well received than had been the case in the preceding century, especially in France.

The pontifical condemnations naturally had a universal value. However, the response given to bishops who sought to find out if they should take local considerations into account when applying condemnations was invariably that they were valid *in quacumque orbis regione*. In fact, they seemed to have been provoked by the activities of liberal Freemasonry in Latin countries alone; the Curia, and particularly the Congregations of the Holy Office and of the penitentiary office seem to have been obsessed by Italian and French vicissitudes. Their prohibitions were nevertheless applied to all the different "types" of Freemasonry. It is easy to imagine that in the first half of the 19th century, Rome made no distinction between "regular" Freemasonries and those that were "liberal," since the difference between the two existed only latently. But it is harder to explain holding on to these univocal positions in the following decades. This is undoubtedly evidence of a limited understanding, on the part of both canonists and Roman theologians, of the increasing diversity taking place in Freemasonry.

Leo XIII's *Humanum Genus* and Its Outcomes. *Humanum Genus* deserves a discussion all by itself. It was unquestionably the most important of the 19th century's anti-Masonic encyclicals, and it remained an essential point of reference for decades, almost up to the time of Vatican II.

Humanum Genus offers nothing original relative to Leo XIII's other encyclicals, however, including the more famous *Aeterni Patris*, *Libertas*, and *Rerum Novarum*. Not only was the pope in line with the anti-Masonic thinking and politics of his predecessors, but not one of the arguments he proffered to justify condemnation of the "sect" was really innovative. If there is an area where it is impossible to distinguish between the "liberal" Leo XIII and the "conservative" Pius IX, it is in the struggle against Freemasonry. Like that of his predecessor, the great pontiff's thought might occasionally look Manichean; such as when he writes, in the beginning of the encyclical: "Two enemy camps . . . are in continuous battle, one of which is for truth and virtue, and the other for everything that is contrary to truth and virtue. The first is the kingdom of God on earth, that is, the true Church of Jesus Christ. The second is the kingdom of Satan." (It is true that the Freemasons themselves held military terminology in high esteem.)

Humanum Genus was no less impressive for the tightness of its construction and the breadth of its words. Leo XIII's aim was to attack Freemasonry at its very foundations—he was more interested in Masonic ideology than he was in its actions. He also showed a certain interest in Freemasonry's internal debates.

The beginning of *Humanum Genus* is not the most original part of the encyclical. If Leo XIII was careful to recall the condemnations pronounced by his predecessors, it was, he tells us, because they were completely exempt of injustice or even of exaggeration. At every possible opportunity, he emphasizes the "unbelieveable progress" of a sect that has "invaded all levels of the social hierarchy, and has begun to gain power within modern States that almost rivals sovereignty." The pope dedicated some space to denouncing the misdeeds of Masonic secrecy, the scope of which he perhaps exaggerated when he wrote that new members "must take a solemn oath never, at any time or in any manner, to reveal the names of members, or the society's characteristic notes or teachings." The sovereign pontiff added that the organization of Freemasonry made this secrecy particularly dreadful: "This law of secrecy is marvellously supported by the division among members in duties, offices, and responsibilities; by the wisely organized hier-

archical distinction of orders and degrees, and by the severe discipline to which all are subject." Leo XIII even alluded briefly to the occult role of "intimate and superior counsel." In dealing with Masonic discipline, the encyclical did not show great discernment: "It is not rare that the death penalty be administered to those who are convicted either of having betrayed the secrecy of the society, or of having been insubordinate to the commands of the leaders . . . . These are monstrous practices condemned by nature itself."

The pope was amazed that government authorities did not remain faithful to the prohibition measures their predecessors had taken in the 18th century. Freemasonry was hostile to all power that did not submit to its own demands. Its very nature was revolutionary, and Leo XIII went so far as to attribute to it hidden sympathies for communism and socialism. This was an idea that was dear to the heart of 19th-century mainstream Catholicism, which saw in communism and socialism only degenerate avatars of liberalism. Thus, Leo XIII made Freemasonry out to be both a revolutionary association and an oligarchical association that, despite all its beautiful words, had no real concern for public interests.

Under the name of naturalism, Leo XIII then denounced the principles that inspired Freemasonry, writing that their aim was "the complete destruction of any religious and social discipline that is born out of Christianity, and replacing it with a new one . . . the fundamental principles and laws of which are borrowed from naturalism." Under this term, Leo XIII meant to brand freedom of thought. Later, he wrote: "The first principle of naturalists is that nature or human reason should be mistress and sovereign in all matters. Given this, when it comes to a question of duties to God, either they pay little heed or they change the essence of the matter with vague opinions and erroneous feelings. They affirm that God has revealed nothing to men. For them, outside that which can be understood by reason, there is no religious dogma, no truth, nor any teacher in whose words, given his official authority as teacher, one might have faith."

Leo XIII referred in fairly nuanced language to the attitude of French Freemasons regarding the "Great Architect of the Universe," with a clear reference to the battle that ended, at the time of the 1877 convention, with the victory of the French "abolitionists": "Even though, in effect, and when taken as a whole, the sect professes to believe in the existence of God, the testimony of its own members establishes that this belief, for each of them individually, is not a matter of firm assent or unshakable certainty. They do not hide the fact that the question of God is a cause for considerable dissent among them. It has even been confirmed that a short time ago a serious controversy arose among them on the subject. In fact, the sect leaves initiates complete freedom to speak in one direction or another, either to affirm the existence of God or to deny it." The attitude of the brothers toward the Church of Rome was, therefore, evidence of Masonic skill and duplicity, as it avoided proclaiming that its ultimate goal resided in the pure and simple destruction of the Catholic religion.

Leo's denunciation of the "works" of Freemasonry was of rare force, and he criticized Freemasonry's goals of secularizing the State and society in general. He denounced the frequent prohibition of public worship, the confiscation of Church property, the banishment of religious congregations. The pope was also indignant over the secularization of society through divorce and schooling, two domains into which Freemasons were extending their efforts. Nor did Leo XIII fail to deplore the brothers' supreme insult against Peter's successor: that his temporal sovereignty, "the necessary guarantee of the liberty and rights of the pope," should disappear by force.

The last part of the encyclical was devoted to outlining an anti-Masonic pastoral message, urging the clergy to inform the faithful of the sect's perverse intentions. The pope also advocated defensive actions, claiming a solution to the problem of Freemasonry resided in solid Christian instruction. Leo XIII suggested that the clergy seek help among the lay members of the Third Order of Saint Francis. He also expressed his wish for the resurrection of workers' corporations and guilds, with the aim of "coming to the aid of the honorable class of the proletariat."

This part of the encyclical dedicated to the pastoral message makes current ignorance of how the papal teaching was received by local churches all the more regrettable. Similarly, we do not know to what kinds of influences the encyclical's composers might have been subject. Anti-Masonism was much less known than anti-Protestantism or anti-Judaism, with which it was sometimes confused (more so with the former than with the latter during the 19th century, even though Pius IX did lash out against the "synagogue of Satan"). The list of those who made anti-Masonism their specialty is long. In France, between 1860 and 1895, the following can be cited: among the prelates: Msgr. de Ségur, Msgr. Meurin, and the quite active Msgr. Fava—and Fathers Benoît, Deschamps, and Turinaz; among the laity: Alexandre de Saint-Albin, Paul Rosen, Émile Avense, Paul Nourrisson, and Copin-Albancelli. In Italy, the influence of the Jesuit Father Bresciani was immense. In Germany, as early as the middle of the century, it was a Protestant, Eckart, who was the most vehement in his denunciations of the sect's occult role in the "springtime of peoples" and in all the revolutionary episodes that had followed.

Reading these authors would undoubtedly highlight Leo XIII's relative moderation, since he never completely believed in the most fanciful of the accusations against the brothers that were current in Catholic circles. Despite everything, it would be interesting to have a greater understanding of the relationships that existed between certain champions of the battle against Freemasonry and the Vatican. Léo Taxil, for example, was received personally by Leo XIII in 1894. And the Universal Anti-Masonic Union, whose first congress was held in Trent in 1896, had its own ecclesiastical assistants and the benefit of the Holy See's strong encouragement.

From the 1890s to the 1960s. This is the period that is least well known in the history of Catholic anti-Masonism, since the Holy See did not feel the need to reiterate its earlier condemnations. But it was in this period that the constitution of the two great "blocs" was completed, distinguishing regular Freemasonry from liberal, or progressive, Freemasonry. Regular Freemasons, in the great majority, were organized as early as 1929 around the Great Unified Lodge of England, which gave itself the right to measure the authenticity of persuasions throughout the world, and which defined, also in 1929, the "fundamental Principles for the recognition of the Great Lodges." The second of these eight principles was worded as follows: "Belief in the Great Architect of the Universe and in his revealed will is an essential condition for the admission of every member." The seventh reminded members of the absolute prohibition of political or religious discussions, which was not always respected in countries like Italy and the United States, where anticlericalism or antipapism were most alive. The third obedience in France is attached to regular Freemasonry: the Grande Loge Nationale Française was founded in 1913. The role played by regular French Freemasons (A. Mellor, J. Baylot) in efforts of rapprochement with the Catholic Church will be discussed below.

Progressive Freemasonry is found primarily in Latin countries. Spearheaded by the laity, it demands the total secularization of society; it rises up against any danger, or even any simple manifestation, of clericalism; it advocates the adoption of lay morality; and it confuses its cause with that of democracy. The word "bloc" is perhaps too strong in reference to this second form of Freemasonry, which is completely irregular in the eyes of the first. It was only in 1961 that, at the instigation of the Grand Orient of France and the Grand Orient of Belgium, a simple liaison center was formed. This was not, however, an international Masonic organization with authority over the branches connected to it.

There may also be reason to mention a third Masonic family, which is sometimes called "spiritualist." In Europe, it is represented by the Grande Loge de France, the second largest group in the country after the Grand-Orient, and the Grande Loge de Belgique, created in 1959. It is greatly in the minority, and is characterized by a certain originality. For example, on the question of religion it stands halfway between regular Freemasonry and progressive Freemasonry. Though it denounces the latter's frequent lack of religion and continues to refer to the Great Architect, it does not force its belief in a revealed God, as is the case in regular Freemasonry. The "Great Architect of the Universe" may refer simply to a spiritual or moral principle. This third branch is of value for the importance it assigns to the esoteric, initiatory, and symbolic traditions of Freemasonry.

The Catholic teaching on Freemasonry has been so constant through the years that sometimes it appeared useless to bring up the subject again. *Humanum Genus* was followed by no other encyclical dedicated to Freemasonry. Even Pius X, an avowed adversary (e.g., in his polemics with Grand Master Nathan), made no solemn pronouncements on the subject. The Church was content to codify its previous positions: four articles from the Code of Canon Law (completed in 1917, to remain in effect until 1983) dealt with Freemasonry. The most important was canon 2335, which stated: "Those who give their name to a Masonic sect or to any other association of the same kind that plots against the Church or legitimate civil powers will incur by their very actions an excommunication reserved solely by the Apostolic See." It is noteworthy that the only reason mentioned is that of plotting—neither secrecy nor the oath was explicitly mentioned. Canon 2336, dealing with clerics and members of religious orders who are suspected of belonging to Freemasonry, specified that their cases would be referred to the Holy Office.

Some of these arrangements might be interpreted as an encouragement to informers. There was thus still considerable strictness, and the Vatican reserved an icy welcome for the first attempts at rapprochement extended by a few fearless Masons and Catholics. As late as 1959, Father Caprile was quick to describe Freemasonry as a "school for treason."

Even less is known about Catholic anti-Masonism in the first half of the 20th century than about that of the preceding half century. It was visible only in its most extreme factions, those who propagated an obsessive anti-Masonism and denounced the Judeo-Masonic plot. On the eve of the First World War, and in the period between the wars, the *Revue Internationale des Sociétés Secrètes* was perhaps the main voice for these views. Although its editor, Msgr. Jouin, enjoyed the confidence of BENEDICT XV and PIUS XI, only very specific camps appear to have been influenced by such positions, particularly the fundamentalists and/or those who tended toward fascism. These groups applauded the proscription measures adopted in Mussolini's Italy, Nazi Germany, Franco's Spain, Salazar's Portugal, and in France during the time of the Vichy government.

Since Vatican II: Toward Rapprochement. Since Vatican II, the Church has judged Freemasonry with much more understanding. Based on the evidence, the time of anathema has passed. Even though the sealing of reconciliation between Catholics and the "Sons of Light" is still far off, and rapprochement is only in embryonic stages, there is tremendous contrast with the vehement condemnations of the two previous centuries.

Nevertheless, reciprocal warnings have been such that pioneers of this rapprochement were not heard for almost fifty years. As Father Riquet declared in 1961, "three centuries of history need to be digested on both sides." It was Vatican II that allowed the Church to comprehend Masonic realities in a more nuanced and positive manner. Little by little, it realized the diversity (philosophical, persuasional, and national) in Freemasonry.

Pioneers of rapprochement began to make themselves known, albeit quite timidly, in the aftermath of the Second World War. Certainly the Bolshevik revolution had a role to play in the convictions that took hold of some; namely, that the Catholic Church and Freemasonry had everything to lose in continuing their fratricidal battles. A short time later, Catholics and Freemasons discovered that the totalitarian regimes were persecuting both of them because of their humanistic ideals. It was a sign of the times that the Society of Jesus, which for years had provided anti-Masonism with champions, began to look more closely at the matter.

Such was the case for Herman Gruber, a Jesuit, historian, and expert in Freemasonry. In contrast to a number of Catholic propagandists, Gruber showed a remarkable knowledge of Masonic sources in his combat against Italian and German Freemasonry. When he noticed the positive attitudes of a large portion of regular Freemasons, Father Gruber was willing to meet with three high Masonic dignitaries in 1928; two of which were historians, the Austrian Eugen Lennhoff, and the American Ossian Lang. But the meeting was never followed up, and another Jesuit (also a historian), Father Pietro Pirri, in the columns of *La Civiltà Cattolica*, pointed out the Vatican's strong reservations about such an initiative.

Ten years later, Albert Lantoine did not get a more favorable welcome when, in 1937, he had the audacity to publish a "Letter to the Sovereign Pontiff." Lantoine, who belonged to the Grande Loge de France and was a man with a rare independence of mind, had already established friendly relations with another Jesuit, Father Berteloot. Lantoine, who was an atheist, had no illusions about denying the tremendous differences that continued to set Catholics against Freemasons. But he did recognize, in both of them, the same desire for truth, especially in the face of totalitarianism. However, on both sides, spirits were not sufficiently willing, and Lantoine's call fell on deaf ears. Father Berteloot had to wait until after WORLD WAR II to publish his best known words on the relationship between the Church of Rome and Freemasonry. Though he was interested only in regular Freemasonry, he called for concessions.

In 1948, a meeting took place in Bad Hofgastein between Cardinal Innitzer and the Grand Master Scheichelbauer. The meeting was not followed up, however, and, in 1950, Father Mario Cordovani, Master of the Sacred Palace, reasserted the validity of canon 2335 in a column in *L'Osservatore Romano*.

Then, in the spring of 1961, in the French department of Mayenne in Laval, Marius Lepage, a venerable from the *Volney* Lodge, under the Laval Orient (a lodge under the dependence of the Grand Orient), received the Jesuit Michel Riquet, who had come into the hall of closed white costumes to give a lecture on atheism. The publicity related to this meeting was in large part due to the personality of the speaker, who preached at Notre Dame. Some were scandalized to hear him address his Freemason audience members as "brothers." But the importance of this event should not be exaggerated. Lepage was chastised by the Grand Orient and transferred to the Grande Lodge Nationale Française, where he met J. Baylot, and, later, A. Mellor (who in 1961 published *Nos frères séparés, les francs-masons* [Our separated brethren, the Freemasons], although he was not initiated until 1969). It should be remembered that the writings of Baylot, Mellor, and Riquet stood simultaneously for the condemnation of irregular Freemasonry and for raising sanctions against those brothers who, though enrolled in a "regular" lodge, were not motivated by hostility to the Church.

Eight years later, a meeting in Savona between Don Rosario Esposito, the esteemed historian of Italian Freemasonry, and Giordano Gamberini, a former grand master from the Grand Orient of Italy, did not have the same resonances, and Esposito did not have the same reputation as the French Jesuit; what had been considered truly original had lost some of its flavor after Vatican II. The meetings between the two sides that followed (e.g., Msgr. Pézeril, the auxiliary bishop of Paris, visiting the headquarters of the Grande Loge de France) looked almost banal in the period after the council.

When these pioneer attempts are looked at as a whole, three observations stand out: (1) their initiators were Freemasons more often than they were Catholics; (2) those on both sides met with (sometimes discreet, and sometimes brutal) rejection; and (3) neither Gruber, Berteloot, nor Riquet ever foresaw the slightest chance of an alliance. They knew that reconciliation would be for later, and were merely calling for a cease-fire. In this sense, their struggle was not in vain.

Vatican II spent little time on Freemasonry. While a Mexican bishop, Msgr. Mendez Arceo, invited the Vatican to reflect on the soundness of excommunication for Freemasons who were not adversarial to the Church, the council's assembly saw no utility in working out a special declaration regarding Freemasonry.

However, it was a council decision and the great encyclicals of Paul VI that offered the conditions necessary for rapprochement to begin. The council's declaration on religious freedom, *Dignitatis Humanae*, emphasized the dignity and the freedom of every man in search of truth, and the dialogue hoped for in the encyclical *Ecclesiam Suam* implied knowledge of one's companion in dialogue, confidence in him or her, and rejection of offending polemics. In addition, the encyclical *Gaudium et Spes* admitted that the Church held some responsibility for the development of atheism.

The effects of some two hundred fifty years of mistrust and hostility do not, however, dissipate over the course of a few years. Some late-20th-century decisions reveal the Church's difficulty in understanding Freemasonry's diversity. For example, relegating relations with Freemasonry to the Secretariat for Nonbelievers suggests that all Freemasons are nonbelievers, which is clearly not true. And, as *Ecclesiam Suam* did not fail to mention, dialogue was to be based on the greatest frankness and could not be based on difference or doctrinal relativism. Rome changed its earlier positions only very slowly, and it did not always adopt a clear line of thought.

The approach adopted makes this clear. The Roman offices, which were legitimately worried about the diversity of local situations, accepted that, as a first step, national conferences of bishops should make pronouncements on relations with Freemasonry. The 1966 conferences did so in considerably different ways. The conference of bishops in the Scandinavian countries nearly came to the point of recognizing the possibility of "dual affiliation," at least in the case of a Mason who converted to Catholicism. In 1974, the English and Welsh bishops, albeit more prudently, made a very similar pronouncement. The 1980 episcopal conference in West Germany, however, announced a staunch rejection of the idea of dual affiliation. If the German bishops were willing to recognize the Christian inspiration that motivated the Great Unified Lodge of Germany, with which they had been engaged in a real dialogue for six years, they nevertheless concluded that Freemasonry's indifference and relativism forbade satisfaction being given to those who claimed the possibility of dual affiliation. Rome acknowledged these differences, but never opposed either formal or informal dialogue, which was bringing Catholics and Masons together in a number of countries, including, in addition to those cited, the Netherlands, Belgium, Switzerland, Austria, Italy, the United States, and the Philippines.

In 1971 and 1972, two consultants from the Congregation for the Propagation of the Faith, Father Jean Beyer, S.J., and Don Miano, allowed that excommunication was no longer incurred automatically, and that it did not apply to brothers who were not motivated by hostility toward the Church. In 1974, Cardinal Seper himself asserted something similar, though the prefect of the Congregation for the Propagation of the Faith recognized at the same time that the positions of national councils of bishops were too diverse to allow the Church to revise canon 2335 at that time. The Code of Canon Law was, however, in the process of revision.

The new Code of Canon Law was finally released ten years later, in 1983. Freemasonry, the object of so many anathemas in the past, was not specifically mentioned, however. Certainly the Church's new discipline remained prudent, and canon 1374 of the new code affirmed "That he who affiliates himself with an association that acts against the Church should be meted just punishment; that he who promotes or leads such an association be punished with an interdict." Such a reminder was not formal, and Cardinal Ratzinger, prefect of the Congregation for the Doctrine of the Faith, added the final touches when he published, on the eve of the new code taking effect, a declaration affirming that, in principal, the negative stance of the Church remained unchanged. But the manner in which some Catholics reacted suggested the possibility of further evolution. Some, particularly in France, judged the positions defended by Ratzinger to be too restrictive. In 1987, leaders of both SIF (Service Incroyance-Foi) and IDERM (the Institute for Masonic Study and Research, a branch of the Grand Orient) organized a historical colloquium on relations between the Catholic Church and Freemasonry. Alluding to the Roman declaration of 1983, the SIF representative stated: "We cannot believe that that is a definitive decision," and French public opinion still held on to the many "gestures" attesting to a common effort of Christian humanism and lay humanism for a more fraternal world. The permanent conference of bishops and the representative authorities of the other spiritual families of the country cosigned a call for brotherhood concerning the fate of immigrants that had been composed in common by the different branches of Freemasonry. In the spring of 1988, the rector of the Institut Catholique in Paris, the president of the Fédération Protestante de France, and the former grand master of the Grand Orient participated (at the request of the prime minister) in a mission of reconciliation in New Caledonia. Moreover, in 1985 and 1987, the funerals of two former grand masters of the Grande Loge, and also of the Grand Orient, were celebrated religiously.

Nevertheless, it would be somewhat ridiculous to judge relationships between the Catholic Church and Freemasonry solely on the situation in France. On the one hand, it is without a doubt that anathemas have given way to study, to listening, to esteem, and sometimes even to friendship and common action. Only the latest admirers of Barruel, or the most worn-out proponents of laicism could complain. On the other hand, there are serious differences in the area of doctrine. If it is true that Christian humanism and lay humanism share a number of common values, the anthropocentrism of Christians and of the brothers are not the same. And Masonic immanentism, antidogmatism, and a certain latitudinarianism will always present problems for the Church.

Jean-Pierre Viallet

Bibliography

The Latin text of the encyclicals can be consulted in the *Enchiridion* published by H. Denzinger, or in the *Fontes Juris Canonici*, edited under the direction of Cardinal Gasparri, which include a number of the Holy Office's decisions in respect to Freemasonry. Translations of the main encyclicals are also available. It may be expedient to consult anti-Masonic works, which often quote the entire text and a translation of the encyclicals (e.g., De Saint-Albin, A. *La Maçonnerie et les sociétés secrètes*, Paris, 2nd ed., 1867, 479–506, or Benoît, Dom P. *La Cité antichrétienne du XIXe siècle, II, La maçonnerie*, 2, Paris, 1895, 498–584).

Most of the authors cited below are Catholics. The selection, which is not the personal preference of the author, is explained by the fact that: (1) the article is devoted essentially to the way in which the Vatican understood Freemasonry, and only incidentally to the inverse phenomenon; and (2) Masonic authors are more interested in the evoluton of intellectual and spiritual orientations within Freemasonry than in relationships with the Holy See. It was therefore not possible to consider their studies here.

Armogathe, J. R. "Église catholique," *Dictionnaire de la franc-maçonnerie*, 1987, 398–400.

Caprile, G. "I documenti pontifici intorno alla Massoneria," *Civiltà cattolica*, 29 July 1958, 167–76, and 6 September 1958, 504–17.

Église, maçonnerie, condamnations ou malentendu? Deux siècles de conflits, Toulouse, 1987.

Dolhagaray, B. "Franc-maçonnerie," *DTC*, 6, 1913, 722–31.

Esposito, R. *Le buone opere dei laicisti, degli anticlericali e dei framassoni*, Rome, 1970.

Ferrer-Benimeli, J. A. *Massoneria e Chiesa cattolica, ieri, oggi e domani*, Rome, 1979, 1982.

Ferrer-Benimeli, J. A. *Los Archivos Secretos Vaticanos y la Masoneria. Motivos políticos de una condena pontifica*, Caracas, 1979 (French translation, *Les Archives secrètes du Vatican et de la maçonnerie*); *Masonería, Iglesia e Ilustración. Un conflicto ideológico-político-religioso*, Madrid, 1976–7, 4 vols.; *La Masonería después del Concilio*, Barcelona, 1968; "Franc-maçonnerie et Église catholique? Motivations politiques des premières condamnations papales." *XVIIIe siècle*, 1987, 19, 7–19.

Jacquemet, G. "Franc-maçonnerie," *Catholicisme*, 4, 1956, 1501–10.

Lemaire, J. *Les Origines françaises de l'antimaçonnisme (1744–1797)*, Brussels, 1985.

Naz, R. "Franc-maçonnerie," *DDC*, 4, 1949, 896–9.

Nefontaine, L. *Église et franc-maçonnerie*, Paris, 1990 (the most useful of works available in French).

Roberts, J. *The Mythology of the Secret Societies*, London, 1972.

FRENCH REVOLUTION AND THE PAPACY. In its earliest stages, the French Revolution of 1789 bore no grudge against the papacy. In the period of triumphant GALLICANISM, the records of grievances drawn up at the time of the Estates General elections contained few allusions to the pope. They criticized the wealth of the Church, the religious orders, and the ecclesiastical territorial divisions, but Christian faith was still deep-seated and sincere. "A people without religion will soon be a people without morality" was written in one notebook.

In Rome, a worried Church followed with incomprehension a development that no one at the time could predict would end in the capture and death of PIUS VI in Valence. The attention of the Curia, never abreast of current events, was more absorbed in the rise of regalism in Spain and the JOSEPHIST crisis in Austria.

To be sure, events unfolded at a rapid pace, and information reached Rome only after the fact and in muddled form. Furthermore, the French representative, Cardinal de Bernis, was perhaps not the best qualified person to help the pope grasp the changes that were taking place.

The abolition of the tithe together with ecclesiastical privileges on the night of 4 August 1798 caused astonishment. But astonishment turned to anxiety when it was learned that a priest of Lorraine had asked that "while remaining united in spirit and heart to the head of the Church, they should stipulate the suppression of the annates (taxes to be paid on receiving a benefice)."

As viewed from Rome, events took a tragic turn when Parisian rioters abducted the king to Paris on 6 October. It was unknown whether Louis XVI was still a free man. Passions took on an antireligious color against a background of famine and the miserable state of the public finances. By this point, de Juign was giving the signal for ecclesiastical emigration.

Another blow came in October when Talleyrand, the bishop of Autun, proposed the nationalization of clerical possessions as a solution to the crisis of the royal finances. He argued that the clergy merely administered these possessions, and that the state could take over provided it gave the clergy "an honorable subsistence." His arguments won the day. On 2 November 1789, the Constituent Assembly placed the possessions of the Church at the nation's disposal. In return, the government would ensure the maintenance of clerics, who would become public officials. This nationalization had two consequences:

the suppression of the religious on 13 February 1790, chiefly the contemplatives, who were deemed "idle," and the establishment of a new statute, the Civil Constitution of the Clergy.

This constitution was voted in on 12 July 1790. Chapterhouses and collegiate churches were abolished. Henceforward, France was divided into eighty-three dioceses corresponding to the new administrative division into departments. At the head of the diocese was the bishop, and at the head of the parishes, the distribution of which was also simplified, was the priest. Bishops and priests would receive a salary. That meant they were considered civil servants and, therefore, were elected, the bishop by the electoral body of the department, the parish priest by that of the district. The parish priest received his canonical institution from the bishop, and the bishop received his from the metropolitan archbishop (there were ten metropolitan sees). The bishop notified the pope of his appointment "in witness of the unity of faith and communion which he must keep with him," but was forbidden to ask the pope to confirm the nomination.

Not only was the reform put through without consultation with the Holy See, but the break with Rome was complete. The bishop was no longer dependent upon the pope for canonical installation as provided for in the concordat of 1516. Abbé Grégoire justified this decision as follows: "The Assembly's intention is to reduce the authority of the supreme pontiff to just limits. But it is also its intention not to create a schism." Moreover, the Constitutent National Assembly was careful not to touch dogma. It was interested in the priest only as a citizen, whence the importance of the word "civil" used to qualify the constitution of the clergy.

A reaction from the Holy See was awaited. Steps were taken by Msgr. de La Tour du Pin to prevent an overnegative reaction that would compromise the reform. For several months, Pius VI officially kept silent. Whether he was wisely biding his time or, prompted by the émigrés and Cardinal de Bernis, was intending to try for a test of force is not known. On 10 July, the pope had written to Louis XVI asking him not to approve the Civil Constitution of the Clergy, but the letter arrived a day too late.

Two difficulties poisoned relations between the Revolution and the papacy. On 27 November 1790, the Constitutent Assembly held bishops and curates to the oath "to be loyal to the nation and the king and to uphold with everything in their power the constitution decreed by the Assembly." This oath had as its purpose the creation of a national Church. It provoked deep distress among the clergy, and gave rise to the division between "juring" and "non-juring" priests.

The other difficulty was Avignon, which had been a possession of the popes in France since the 14th century. Here, papal finances had been ill supported by a bourgeoisie that was well on the rise. Pius VI's refusal to grant rights comparable to those obtaining in the rest of France caused an insurrection and, despite some resistance in the countryside, a plea to be incorporated into France, which was granted after consultation with the people. Pius VI's exasperation is understandable.

The pope finally made a pronouncement on the Civil Constitution of the Clergy on 10 March 1791, in the brief *Quod aliquantum*, in which he replied to the deputy bishops. He condemned the text of the constitution as seeking the destruction of the Catholic faith. Beyond the dispositions regarding the election of priests and canonical installation, he rejected the very principles of the Revolution, in particular "this abolute liberty, which not only ensures the right never to be troubled concerning one's religious opinions, but which also arrogates to itself the license to think, write, and even print with impunity, in matters of religion, everything that the wildest imagination may suggest."

In a second brief, on 13 April, the pope rejected the first canonical institutions of the metropolitans as sacrilegious. This brought matters to the brink of a schism. Some metropolitans chose to accept the reform and subsequently, when they were already committed to the new organization, retracted. Others, like the bishop of Haute-Loire, Delcher, challenged Pius VI to intervene, all the while affirming that they were "united in communion with the Holy See."

In May 1791, the diplomatic rupture between France and the Holy See was complete. Pius VI had refused to welcome Cardinal de Bernis's replacement in Rome. In response, "the ogre of the Tiber" was burnt in effigy at the Palais-Royal. Having failed to obtain apologies, the nuncio Dugnani made the decision to leave Paris. A simple chargé d'affaires, Abbot de Salomon, handled day-to-day problems.

In France, there was religious war. Juring and nonjuring priests came to blows and fought over each other's congregations. On 29 November 1791, the Legislature, which had replaced the Constituent Assembly, responded by punishing those members of the clergy who had not taken the oath, forcing them to leave the communes where the disturbances had broken out.

This trend toward persecution had been accentuated by the Assembly's decision of 20 April 1792 to declare war on the "king of Bohemia and Hungary." The deputies thought they could limit the conflict to the Austrian Empire, but before long all Europe would be ignited.

Whether or not the Holy See could preserve its traditional neutrality became a question. All the evidence points to the disgust and horror in which Pius VI held the French Revolution. He fulminated against the threat it represented for each of the thrones of Europe. After the Comtat Venaissin and Avignon were annexed by France, Cardinal Zelada, the secretary of state, wrote: "Must not the principle whereby the confiscation of Avignon was decreed strike terror in all the cabinets of Europe? What sovereign can now count on the preservation of his states if all it takes to legitimize similar conquests is to incite an insurrection and extort from the people a promise of union with a foreign domination?" The diplomats posted to Rome, in particular the aristocrat Azara, the Spanish minister, agreed with this thinking, and the French émigrés who had found refuge in the Papal States urged the formation of a Holy League. In the spirit of a crusade, Pius VI sent briefs to the sovereigns, even schismatic rulers such as Catherine II of Russia and George III of England. Maury, the former deputy who had been promoted to the cardinalate, was despatched to the German lands to mobilize them against France.

The execution of Louis XVI on 21 January 1793 encouraged the creation of the first external coalition, while the policy of de-Christianization under the Terror confirmed Pius VI's worst fears.

It was not long before the distinction between jurors and non-jurors grew dim. Catholicism appeared as the driving counterrevolutionary force, and this was confirmed, in the view of many, by the great revolt in the Vendée. The nationalization of the civil state and the massacres of September 1792 had prepared the way. Marat blamed the Constitutionals as much as the rebels: "Jacobins, I must tell you the truth. You do not know who are your most deadly enemies. They are the Constitutional priests, who would set up their priestly throne on the ruins of liberty. Cut the roots of superstition!"

Next came the replacement of the Gregorian calendar, the prohibition of saints' names, and the expulsion of priests, not to mention a host of antireligious spectacles. But this de-Christianizing movement had never enjoyed the support of the Convention, and once Hébert and his followers had been arrested and executed it ran out of steam. Robespierre was no longer tolerant of worship of the Supreme Being. His enemies, the Thermidorians, opted for the separation of Church and State. The Convention voted in favor of a decree presented by Boissy d'Anglas that established religious liberty, yet a liberty without the right of association, and without bell-ringing or processions, and which its authors intended should foster the impoverishment of a clergy deprived of subsidies and salaries.

Still, the war went on. It was now being waged in Italy, where the young General Bonaparte, having crossed the Alps at the Cadibone Pass on 11 April 1796, separated the Austrian and Piedmontese armies and forced Piedmont to sign a peace treaty. 15 May found him in Milan.

Since 1795, France had been headed by a Directory of five members, at least three of whom—Barras, Reubell, and especially La Revellière-Lépeaux, the father of theophilanthropy—were hostile to Catholicism. The instructions received by Bonaparte after his victories were unequivocal: he should leave Kellermann to maneuver in northern Italy and march down on Rome to snuff out "the torch of fanaticism." The papacy was now in the forefront of opposition to the Revolution.

Negotiations got under way. General Bonaparte paid little heed to the instructions from Paris and blew hot and cold. To Cacault, who represented the French government in Rome, he declared, "I aspire to the title of savior more than of destroyer of the Holy See," but at the same time he denounced "the pope's unparalleled folly" and pronounced himself ready to "chastise the proud city."

Even the Directory, behind its threats, sought to be conciliatory. Faced with a strong royalist upsurge, it hoped for a gesture of appeasement from the Holy See, counseling Catholics to submit to the republican government. This was the sense of the brief, *Pastoralis*, that was drawn up in Rome, but the Directory was disappointed. Finally, peace was signed without Bonaparte's having to intervene militarily. The treaty of Tolentino, of 19 February 1797, whereby the pope abandoned Ancona and gave up Avignon and Venaissin, poured thirty-one million livres as well as many works of art into the French Republic.

This pact, owed to Bonaparte (who declared, "For us, thirty millions are worth ten Romes; that old machine would depreciate on its own"), was shattered after the army's coup d'état of 18 Fructidor, which deflected all royalist threats from the Directory. As a result, religious persecution resumed in France: eleven thousand French and Belgian priests (Belgium having been overrun) were hit with deportation orders. The Directory's policy toward the Holy See was equally bellicose.

Counseled by his secretary of state, Doria, Pius VI seemed resigned to the conditions of the treaty of Tolentino. But the Roman people, and especially the *zelanti*, found it difficult to tolerate the French pillage, signified by the many convoys headed north for Paris. For their part, the so-called patriots, who collaborated with the envoys of the Directory, were hoping that papal authority would fail. Confrontations ensued. On 28 December 1797, some insurgents were pursued by the papal forces and found refuge in the Corsini Palace, where the new French ambassador, Joseph Bonaparte, the general's elder brother, had taken up residence. Joseph left, accompanied by General Duphot. Duphot was killed. The secretary of state at once presented his apologies, but Joseph left Rome. This diplomatic rupture resulted in the intervention of the troops of General Berthier, who entered Rome at the beginning of the year 1798. On 15 February 1798, a Roman Republic was proclaimed. Pius VI was arrested and moved to Tuscany, then to France, where he died on 29 August 1799.

The papacy was destroyed. The French Revolution had triumphed in Belgium, in Italy, and on the left bank of the Rhine. Spain had become its ally, and Poland had been erased from the map by the powers of central and eastern Europe. The German historian Spittler announced that Catholicism had ceased to exist.

Jean Tulard

Bibliography

Latreille, A. *L'Église catholique et la Révolution française*, I, Paris, 1946.

Leflon, J. *La Crise révolutionnaire*, Paris, 1951.

FUNCTIONARIES. See **Administration, Papal.**

FUNERALS, PAPAL. See **Death of the Pope, Middle Ages.**

FURNISHINGS. See **Floreria.**